GOVERNMENT CONTRACT LAW

The Deskbook for Procurement Professionals

FOURTH EDITION

Based on the Contract Attorney's Course of the
Judge Advocate General's Legal Center and School, U.S. Army

AMERICAN BAR ASSOCIATION
Section of
Public Contract Law

24 23 22 21 20   6 5 4 3 2

ISBN: 978-1-63425-822-7

Discounts are available for books ordered in bulk. Special consideration is given to state bars, CLE programs, and other bar-related organizations. Inquire at Book Publishing, ABA Publishing, American Bar Association, 321 N. Clark Street, Chicago, Illinois 60654-7598.

www.shopABA.org

CONTRIBUTORS

**Contract and Fiscal Law Department
The Judge Advocate General's Legal
Center and School, U.S. Army
2014 Contract Law Deskbook**

Lieutenant Colonel Dana Chase

Major Marlin Paschal

Major Janet Eberle (USAF)

Major Travis Elms

Major Jessica Farrell

Major Ryan Howard

Major Ryan Leary

Major Dale McFeatters

and their predecessors on the faculty of
the Contract and Fiscal Law Department.

**American Bar Association
Section of Public Contract Law**

John T. Jones, Jr.
LK Global

Robert Wu
Government Accountability Office

Michael Barnicle
Duane Morris LLP

S. Mark Boroski
Department of the Air Force

Louis Chiarella
Government Accountability Office

Martin Chu
Baltimore District, USACE

Eric Crusius
Miles & Stockbridge P.C.

Stanley Dees
Retired

Tamara Droubi
Law Counsel

Stacy Hadeka
Hogan Lovells

Paul Haseman
Raytheon Corp.

Kristen Kiel
Georgetown Law School

Elizabeth Lindquist
King & Spaulding

Kevin Misener
George Mason University

Thomas C. Papson
George Washington University

George Petel
Wiley Rein LLP

Anthony Scalice
Baker Botts LLP

Robert J. Sneckenberg
Crowell & Moring LLP

Oliya Zamaray
Rogers Joseph O'Donnell P.C.

The substantive contents of this publication, which are unchanged from the *2014 Contract Attorneys Deskbook*, The Judge Advocate General's Legal Center and School, U.S. Army, are a work of the United States. It is available at: http://www.loc.gov/rr/frd/Military_Law/Contract-Fiscal-Law-Department.html

PREFACE

This fourth edition of the ABA's revisions to the Judge Advocate General's Legal Center and School's *Contract Law Deskbook*, is long overdue. When I returned from an expatriate assignment in 2015, I undertook the task of revising the previous edition, this time with the assistance of Robert Wu at the GAO and his fellow members of the Public Contract Law Section's Young Lawyers Committee. With their assistance, we were able to update references, add new chapters (which do not appear in the JAG School's version), and revise many other chapters to include material useful to contractor attorneys and the private bar. We have also deleted some material that is of interest solely to military attorneys. The American Bar Association is solely responsible for these changes, and the reader should not attribute these changes to the United States Army, or to any member of the JAG School faculty. We based this revision on the 2014 edition of the JAG School Deskbook, and the contributors from the Contract and Fiscal Law Department are those active duty faculty members listed in that work.

Since the last edition, there have been many changes in government contract law. The executive branch has implemented several policy initiatives through the power of federal contracting, including revised labor policies. Similarly, Congress has implemented changes, including regulation of contractor business systems, trafficking in persons, and provisions addressing problems that have been identified in the past decade, such as perceived misuse of previous changes such as commercial items. What has not changed is the basic system of acquiring goods and services for the federal government. We still have a FAR and DFARS; competitive negotiations and truth in negotiations; changes and differing site conditions; a Court of Federal Claims and Boards of Contract Appeals. While the system is constantly evolving, we haven't seen dramatic changes such as occurred in the 1980s and early 1990s.

Over the past several decades, these materials have become one of the principal references for government contracts attorneys, along with Nash and Cibinic's landmark textbooks. The Deskbook has been cited by the U.S. Supreme Court, served as the foundation for numerous continuing legal education materials, and is used daily by hundreds of attorneys. Each and every faculty member in the Contract and Fiscal Law Department at The Judge Advocate General's School, U.S. Army, and the members of the Public Contract Law Section's Young Lawyers Committee can be proud of their contributions to this work.

John T. Jones, Jr.
LK Global
Scottsdale, Arizona

Table of Contents

CHAPTER 17: INTELLECTUAL PROPERTY

CHAPTER 18: ETHICS IN GOVERNMENT CONTRACTING

INTRODUCTION TO GOVERNMENT CONTRACT LAW

I. INTRODUCTION.

This Desk Book has its origins in the instructional materials for the Contract Law Course offered by the Judge Advocate General's School, U.S. Army, located on the campus of the University of Virginia. For decades, the JAG School has taught thousands of military lawyers the arcane rules and regulations that govern the military procurement process. Originally, the Contract Law Division of the JAG School prepared a Department of Army Pamphlet 27-153, Procurement Law, but the format proved unsuitable for introducing lawyers to a complex area of the law. To help their students, the JAG School instructors prepared teaching outlines, suitable for student note taking, which evolved over time to the detailed outlines that are used today.

As the JAG School's graduates have migrated to other agencies, entered civil life, and the student base expanded to include civilian attorneys, students from other services, and the federal government as a whole, the teaching outlines became an important set of reference materials for federal procurement attorneys, as well as the private sector. There was an unsatisfied demand for the updated outlines from the JAG School, which was difficult to meet in the days preceding the internet. Recognizing the need, the American Bar Association published the first edition of the Government Contract Law Desk Book in the mid-1990s, having modified the original materials to meet the needs of a wider audience. Since then, it has had two subsequent editions, and this 2015 version is the fourth edition.

One of the reasons that this Desk Book has proven so useful is that it focuses on procurement by the Department of Defense. While the numbers change from year to year, the Department of Defense procures approximately 70% of all the goods and services

acquired by the United States. Consequently, most government contract law issues are governed by the laws, regulations, and decisions applicable to the Department of Defense.

II. ORGANIZATION.

The TJAGSA Contract Law Desk Book is organized into two volumes. Volume I is primarily focused on the law and regulations governing the formation of a procurement contract with the United States Government. Volume II is primarily focused on issues that arise during the performance of a U.S. Government procurement contract and on special topics.

This version of the Desk Book is a single volume. Chapters 1 through 15 primarily address public policies and contract formation. Many important public policies are involved in deciding who should receive a procurement contract from the United States Government, and what its terms should be. Most of the rules are oriented at fairly selecting a contractor on the basis of the best offer to the government, assuming the contractor is an ethical person who can compliantly perform the contract as written. Fairness is generally perceived as maximizing competition, following the rules, selecting the offeror offering the best deal, and rejecting offers from unscrupulous businesses.

Major legal topics include:

- Authority of government employees,
- Funding of government procurements,
- Competition,
- Methods of acquisition (e.g., simplified acquisition, sealed bidding, contracting by negotiation),
- Contract types,
- Social and economic policies implemented in contract,
- Protests, and

Introduction

- Pricing of contracts.

Chapters 16 through 33 of this Desk Book address contract performance and special topics. Contract performance involves two related legal issues. The first issue is the substantive contract provisions included in the most significant standard terms and conditions incorporated by reference into a typical government procurement contract. These terms and conditions describe many of the obligations of both the government and the contractor. The second issue is allocation of risk: the terms and conditions identify how risks are allocated between the government and the contractor(s). The later chapters also address a number of special topics regarding contract formation as well as contract performance issues, or that are otherwise important in the practice of government contract law.

Major topics include:
- Contract changes,
- Inspection and acceptance,
- Payments to contractors and contract financing terms,
- Terminations for the default of the contractor and for the convenience of the government,
- Litigation of contract claims and disputes,
- Ethics,
- Intellectual property,
- Construction contracting, and
- Contracting in military deployments.

III. ADDITIONAL RESOURCES.

Government contracting, as a separate legal discipline, owes a great deal to Professors Ralph Nash and the late John Cibinic of the National Law Center at the George Washington University. Nash and Cibinic created the Government Contracts Program at GW, introduced many practitioners to government contracting, and authored numerous books on government contracting. They also authored numerous other publications for their CLE courses, which are now available from a commercial publisher at http://www.wklawbusiness.com/store.

1. John Cibinic, Jr., and Ralph C. Nash, Formation of Government Contracts, published by Government Contracts Program, George Washington University, 3d edition, 1998.

2. Cibinic and Nash, Administration of Government Contracts, published by The George Washington University, 3d edition, 1995.

3. Related CLE Materials available from http://www.wklawbusiness.com/store include:

- Formation of Government Contracts
- Administration of Government Contracts
- The Government Contracts Reference Book
- Competitive Negotiation: The Source Selection Process
- Cost-Reimbursement Contracting
- Intellectual Property in Government Contracts and
- History of Government Contracting.

CONTINUED ON NEXT PAGE

IV. OVERVIEW OF THE GOVERNMENT CONTRACTING PROCESS.

Government contracting follows a process in both the selection and award of contracts and in the performance of the contract by the contractor.

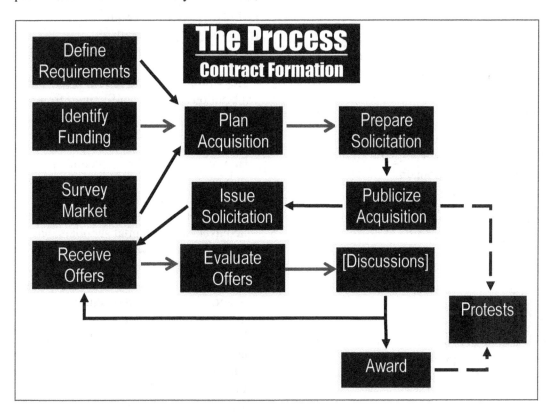

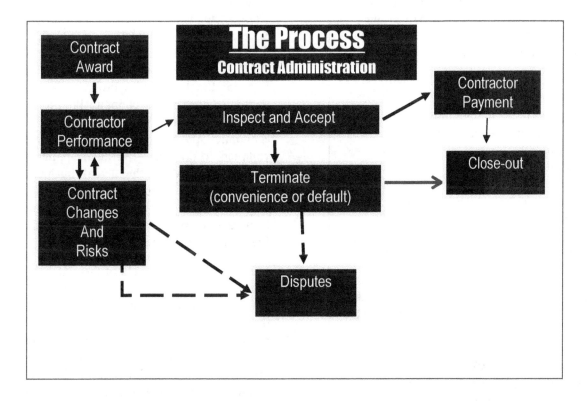

Introduction

V. COMMERCIAL/GOVERNMENT CONTRACT COMPARISON.

A. **Interrelationship of Commercial and Government Contract Law**. The government, when acting in its proprietary capacity, is bound by ordinary commercial law unless otherwise provided by statute or regulation.

> "If [the government] comes down from its position of sovereignty, and enters the domain of commerce, it submits itself to the same laws that govern individuals there." Cooke v. United States, 91 U.S. 389, 398 (1875).

Thus, many of the legal rules that govern public contracting are familiar to commercial contractors. What is different, however, is the enormous regulatory structure and the many additional public policies that overlay ordinary commercial contract law.

B. **Federal Statutes and Regulations Preempt Commercial Law**. Government statutes and regulations predominate over commercial law in nearly every aspect.

> Our statute books are filled with acts authorizing the making of contracts with the government through its various officers and departments, but, in every instance, the person entering into such a contract must look to the statute under which it is made, and see for himself that his contract comes within the terms of the law. The Floyd Acceptances, 74 U.S. 666, 680 (1868).

VI. ROLE OF PUBLIC POLICY IN GOVERNMENT CONTRACT LAW.

A. **Objectives of Government Contracting** (See Steven L. Schooner, *Desiderata: Objectives for a System of*

Government Contract Law, 11 PUBLIC PROCUREMENT LAW REVIEW 103 (2002), available at (http://papers.ssrn.com/ sol3/papers.cfm?abstract_id=304620).

1. Core Principles. The public has many expectations, some conflicting, from its system for awarding public contracts. Among the more important are:

   - Competition – the government will maximize its use of competitive procedures to set prices.
   - Transparency – the public, both taxpayers and potential suppliers, have a right to know how contracts will be, or were, awarded.
   - Integrity – public officials will not benefit now, or in the future, from the award of public contracts.
   - Fairness – all bidders for a public contract will be treated fairly, and similarly.
   - Prudence – public funds for a contract are the taxes paid by the public and the public expects that the government will not waste them.

2. Socioeconomic Policies: i.e., Labor Standards, Federal Acquisition Regulation (FAR) Part 22; Foreign Acquisition, FAR Part 25; Small Business Programs, FAR Part 19; Other Socioeconomic Programs, FAR Part 26. The government uses the economic power inherent in public contracts to promote government policies remotely related to the actual business transaction the contract documents. This includes both policies enacted by Congress and policies implemented by the President on his or her own authority.

3. Meeting the requirements of the end user: While in commercial contracting, meeting the requirements of the person acquiring the goods and services is usually the only objective of the buyer, in public contracting it is only one of many objectives, albeit an important objective. Not all contracts, however, are intended to benefit an end user. In grant agreements,

there is no government end user of the goods and/or services; there is only an often vaguely defined public benefit.

B.   The Procurement Environment: The Acquisition Workforce.

1.   Government contracting is executed by a widely diverse group of public employees and their supporting contractors. These individuals work for different agencies, and often have different objectives. Employees of individual agencies are advocates for their agency objectives, which may be quite narrow and wholly separate from obtaining the goods and services needed by the end users.

2.   Procuring Contracting Officers (PCO). The individual who actually possesses legal authority to bind the United States Government is a Contracting Officer. The PCO is the individual that solicits and awards a contract, and during contract performance, represents the interests of the end user. PCOs are assisted by contract specialists, subordinates who lack authority to contract, but who do much of the work.

3.   Administrative   Contracting   Officer (ACO). This is a Contracting Officer typically located at the work site that administers performance of contracts from multiple agencies. They often work for the   Defense   Contract   Management Command. Within the Defense Contract Management Command, the ACO is supported by specialists, such as cost analysts, industrial engineers, quality assurance specialists, etc., to assist in managing the contractor.

4.   Comptrollers.   Funding   is   of   key importance in contracting. The Finance Officers of the contracting agency play a key role in certifying the availability of funds to support a contract.

5.   Technical   Personnel.   Government contracts often involved state-of-the-art technologies. The technical personnel who advise the government used to be government employees. Today, they are often employees of other government contractors, or of contractor-operated government laboratories. They typically draft the specifications and statements of work included in the contract.

6.   Auditors. Congress, the public, and senior managers use auditors to monitor and provide critical analysis of government contracts. Not only do they verify the accounting, ensuring that the correct price is paid for the goods or services acquired, but auditors are tasked to provide analysis on subjects far outside the field of accounting. Key auditors include the Government Accountability Office, the Defense Contract Audit Agency, Agency Inspectors   General,   and   commercial accounting firms under contract with the government.

7.   Small Business Advocates. One popular socioeconomic policy is the promotion of contract awards to small businesses. These individuals counter the natural tendency of risk-averse government employees to prefer large, established, successful businesses with good track records as contractors.

8.   Test and Evaluation Agencies. When acquiring military equipment, independent defense agencies test the equipment under development for both compliance with the contract requirements and for its suitability for its intended purpose. Meeting requirements does not guarantee suitability, and sometimes guarantees the item purchased is not suitable for its intended purpose.

9.   Headquarters Staff. At each management level in a government organization, there will be individuals, both line managers and staff, who can impact a government contract, often through a power to say "No."

10.   Program   Managers.   To   marshal   the diverse   government   organizations involved   in   government   contracting,

internal executive authority is often placed in a program manager who is ultimately responsible for the success or failure of a government contract.

11. End Users. End Users can be anyone in the government whom the goods and/or services acquired are intended to benefit. For example, the end users for an armored vehicle contract are the soldiers who operate the vehicle, their commanders, and the personnel who train, maintain, and repair the vehicle. End Users often lack any formal role in a government contract, but satisfying their needs is one objective of the procurement process.

C. Contractor Workforce.

1. Many contractors have a workforce that mirrors their government customer's organization because contractors know that the best way to get paid is to have satisfied customers. Thus, contractors have contract administrators, program managers, engineering staff, finance personnel, etc.

2. What is different about contractors is that a prime contractor rarely does the majority of the work contracted. Instead, the prime contractor subdivides the work and contracts with other suppliers for individual components that the prime is responsible for assembling and delivering. This supply chain, which can involve thousands of suppliers and many tiers, is a key aspect of compliant and profitable contract performance.

3. Where government agencies are responsive to taxpayers and elected officials, contractors are ultimately responsible to their owners or shareholders, and to the financial markets which underwrite their investments. Additionally, the contractor is responsible to its employees, who are free to seek other employment at any time. These other stakeholders, especially the financial industry, have a powerful role in government contracting.

D. Public Policy and Contract Clauses.
Public policy and compliance with laws and regulations have such an important role in government contracting, Some policies and regulations are so important that regardless of what the contracting officer and the contractor actually agreed to, the actual agreement between the parties may be altered to implement these important policies.

1. Clauses required by statute or regulation will be incorporated into a contract by operation of law. Voices R Us, ASBCA Nos. 51026, 51070, 98-1 BCA ¶ 29,660; G. L. Christian & Assoc. v. United States, 160 Ct. Cl. 1, 312 F.2d 418, cert. denied, 375 U.S. 954 (1963) (regulations published in the Federal Register and issued under statutory authority have the force and effect of law).

2. Clauses included in a contract in violation of statutory or regulatory criteria will be read out of a contract. Empresa de Viacao Terceirense, ASBCA No. 49827, 00-1 BCA ¶ 30,796; Charles Beseler Co., ASBCA No. 22669, 78-2 BCA ¶ 13,483 (where contracting officer acts beyond scope of actual authority, the government is not bound by his acts).

3. A clause incorporated erroneously will be replaced with the correct one. S.J. Amoroso Constr. Co. v. United States, 12 F.3d 1072 (Fed. Cir. 1993).

4. Contracts tainted by fraud in the inducement may be void ab initio, cannot be ratified, and contractors may not recover costs incurred during performance. Schuepferling GmbH & Co., KG, ASBCA No. 45564, 98-1 BCA ¶ 29,659; Godley v. United States, 5 F.3d 1473 (Fed. Cir. 1993).

5. Consequently, both the government and the contractor should strive to have a contractual document that mirrors the actual contractual requirements as closely as possible.

VII. ATTORNEY ROLES IN GOVERNMENT CONTRACTING.

A. Government Attorneys.

1. Counseling and legal advice on contract law and regulations.

2. Counseling and advice on fiscal law issues.

3. Litigator of protests in the formation stage, disputes in the performance phase, and on collateral matters, such as bankruptcy filings.

4. Advice on ethics, compliance, and fraud prevention.

5. Business Counselor, providing advice on actions that, while legally permissible, are poor business practices, or which detract from accomplishment of the agency's mission. While a law degree does not automatically confer sound business judgment, many government contract attorneys develop good business judgment that can be valued by clients.

B. Contractor Attorneys.

1. Industry attorneys resemble their government counterparts in many ways. They provide advice and counseling on contract formation and contract performance.

2. Generally, litigation is conducted using outside counsel, often those who are specialists in government contracting.

3. Industry attorneys have a key role in compliance matters, guiding their companies to comply with the contract's requirements and to avoid even the appearance of improper conduct.

4. Often contractor attorneys take on business functions, such as contract management and program management.

VIII. CONCLUSION.

Government contract law is a very specialized area. Because of the numerous differences from commercial contracting, inexperienced practitioners are at a distinct disadvantage. Government contracting combines contract law, business management, accounting, and science and technology into an integrated field. Successful practitioners are often knowledgeable in multiple fields. Government contracting is, however, a very rewarding area of practice. The standards of ethics are high, and the work is both interesting and rewarding for both government and private-sector attorneys. For those attorneys who devote the time and effort to learning the law in this area, there are many opportunities.

CONTRACT FORMAT

AND

THE FAR SYSTEM

I. INTRODUCTION TO CONTRACT REVIEW.

A. Contract attorneys, whether supporting the government buyer or a prospective supplier, are often tasked with reviewing draft contracts. The objective of this chapter is to provide some tools that will assist the attorney in performing this task quickly and effectively.

B. The key to successful contract review is to start early. Clients and attorneys who first begin a review immediately prior to signature will find their efforts wasted. Final reviews are typically performed under extreme time pressures, and at a point where it may be impossible to correct problems. Attorneys will find that it is much better to involve yourself in the acquisition from the very beginning. Then, you can provide advice in time for clients to act on it, rather than making a choice between signing a bad contract or walking away from the deal.

C. For government attorneys, every acquisition starts with budgeting for future years' requirements, and with *Acquisition Planning.* See Federal Acquisition Regulation (FAR) Part 7; Defense Federal Acquisition Regulation Supplement (DFARS) Part 207. When possible, a contract attorney should be a part of the *Acquisition Planning Team.* Establish a rapport with the supported contracting office/resource management office.

D. For industry attorneys, contract reviews should start with your business development process. Industry uses their interactions with the government's resource management and acquisition planning processes to determine their company's strategy for winning a program or contract. At these very early stages, industry attorneys can influence the information provided to the government with a view toward avoiding bad contracts.

E. **Checklists.**

1. New attorneys will find contract review checklists to be very helpful when they first start reviewing contracts. If your office does not already have one, borrow one from another office. A basic contract review checklist is at Attachment A.

2. For industry attorneys, checklists are less important. What is important is knowing what contract obligations are embodied in various contract provisions, especially where a contract incorporates standard clauses, specifications and standards, and other publications by reference. The key question for an industry contract review is whether a contractor is able to comply with a specific requirement, whether it is willing to comply given the cost of compliance, and what are the risks inherent in contractual provisions. Answers to these questions are less susceptible to checklists, and more a function of pattern recognition.

II. CONTRACT FORMAT

A. **Overview.**

1. Contract reviews of prime contracts are greatly helped by the government's use of a Uniform Contract Format for many acquisitions, and of software programs that implement rules and regulations into

the drafting process. Consequently, the quality of solicitations and contracts issued by buying agencies have improved significantly over what was common many years ago.

B.   Uniform Contract Format.

1.   A typical prime contract is divided into four parts and into fourteen sections. They are:

   a.   Part I – The Schedule: Sections A-H.

   b.   Part II – Contract Clauses: Section I.

   c.   Part III – List of Documents, Exhibits and Other Attachments: Section J.

   d.   Part IV – Representations and Instructions: Sections K-M.

The advantage of this standard organization is that clauses addressing common topics are usually located together in a single section. They are not distributed somewhat randomly throughout a document, as is common with commercial contracts. This makes it easier to note omissions, and to quickly locate relevant terms and conditions. The 13 sections are set forth below.

2.   Section A: Solicitation/Contract Form (SF 33).

   Typically, a contract begins with a cover sheet, normally Standard Form 33, which contains administrative information pertinent to the solicitation (i.e., solicitation number, proposal due date, government points of contact, table of contents, etc.)

3.   Section B: Supplies or Services and Prices/Cost.

   Section B is the Schedule of Supplies and Services acquired. It contains a brief description of the supplies and services (often a reference to Section C), the quantities required, the unit prices, and total prices. This description of supplies, services, quantities, and associated pricing is

organized by Contract Line Item Number (CLIN or CLINs). Typically, CLINs are used when it important to the government to separate different requirements: for example, where the services are to be performed in different years, or at different locations.

4.   Section C: Description/Specifications/Statement of Work.

   Section C contains the technical requirements and, where extensive, may simply refer to one or more Attachments listed in Attachment J. Contains a more elaborate description of the items contained in Section B, and describes what the government's technical requirements are and what the contractor is to accomplish/deliver. Where the government has separate CLINS with different technical requirements, the specifications and statements of work should be similarly organized to easily determine what requirements apply and which do not apply.

5.   Section D: Packaging and Marking (Only for Supplies, including Data Item Deliverables).

   Section D contains specific requirements for packaging and marking of deliverables.

6.   Section E: Inspection and Acceptance (IAW).

   Section E contains several types of requirements. First, it will generally contain requirements for the type of quality assurance system a contractor must maintain during the course of the contract. Typically, a contractor is expected to maintain a system meeting the current International Standards Organization (ISO) 9001. Section E also contains information on where the government will inspect the contractor's performance, when it will inspect, and when it will accept or reject tendered performance. Lastly, Section E will often contain the terms of the warranty that a contractor must provide for its goods and services.

7. Section F: Deliveries or Performance.

    Section F specifies the requirements for time, place, and method of delivery or performance for items and services the contractor is obligated to deliver under the contract.

8. Section G: Contract Administration Data.

    Section G contains accounting and appropriations data the government uses to charge the underlying appropriation, as well as other accounting requirements, and information related to contract administration.

9. Section H: Special Contract Requirements.

    Section H contains contractual requirements that are not included in other parts of the contract, including special clauses that only pertain to that particular acquisition.

10. Section I: Contract Clauses.

    Section I contains the "Boiler Plate." It incorporates by reference the standard clauses required by law, regulation, or deemed necessary by the contracting officer. In federal government contracting, these clauses, if printed in full text at readable font size, would be quite extensive.

11. Section J: List of Attachments.

    Section J lists documents, attachments, or exhibits that are a material part of the contract. Some examples of these documents are specifications that are referenced elsewhere in the Contract. Typical attachments also include the contract data requirements list (CDRL) and/or checklists of mandatory minimum requirements.

12. Section K: Representations, Certifications and other Statements of Offerors.

    Section K contains representations, certifications, and other information required from each contractor. Some examples are: Procurement Integrity Certification, Small Business Certification, Place of Performance, and Ownership. With the introduction of a System for Acquisition Management, Section K has been materially reduced because an offeror may make blanket certifications and representation.

13. Section L: Instructions, Conditions and Notices to Offerors.

    Section L tells the offerors what information the government wants them to include in their proposals and how that information should be formatted. Section L guides offerors in preparing their proposals, and should support the government's evaluation of proposals.

14. Section M: Evaluation Factors for Award.

    Section M states how the government will evaluate each offeror's proposal. It informs offerors of the relative order of importance of assigned criteria so that an integrated assessment can be made of each offeror's proposal.

III. FEDERAL ACQUISITION REGULATION (FAR) SYSTEM.

A. Federal Acquisition Regulation (FAR).

1. The FAR became effective on 1 April 1984. The FAR replaced two pre-existing regulatory systems: the Defense Acquisition Regulation (DAR) for DOD and a similar regulation for NASA; and the Federal Procurement Regulation (FPR) for civilian agencies.

2. The General Services Administration (GSA) has been tasked with the responsibility for publishing the FAR and any updates to it. FAR 1.201-2.

3. Locating the FAR.

    a. The Government Printing Office (GPO) previously printed periodic updates to the FAR in the form of Federal Acquisition Circulars (FAC). Effective 31 December 2000, the GPO no longer produces printed copies of the FACs or updated versions of the FAR. See 65 Fed. Reg. 56,452 (18 September 2000).

    b. Currently only electronic versions of the FAR and the FACs are available. The FAR is found at Chapter 1 of Title 48 of the Code of Federal Regulations (C.F.R.). Proposed and final changes to the FAR are published electronically in the Federal Register.

    c. The official electronic version of the FAR (maintained by GSA) is available at http://www.arnet.gov/far/ [Note: this site also permits you to sign up for an electronic notification of proposed and final changes to the FAR]. The Air Force FAR Site contains a very user-friendly version of the FAR as well as several supplements. It is found at: http://farsite.hill.af.mil/.

B. Departmental and Agency Supplemental Regulations. FAR Subpart 1.3.

1. Agencies are permitted to issue regulations that implement or supplement the FAR.

2. Most agencies have some form of supplemental regulation. The Department of Defense has issued the Defense Federal Acquisition Regulation Supplement (DFARS). The FAR requires these supplements to be published in Title 48 of the C.F.R. FAR 1.303. The chart on the following page shows the location within Title 48 of the Code of Federal Regulations for each of the respective agency supplements.

3. The Air Force operates a web site that contains most of the acquisition regulations for the various federal agencies. http://farsite.hill.af.mil

Chapter	Agency/Department
2	Defense FAR Supplement (DFARS). The DFARS was completely revised in 1991. Available at each of the following sites: http://www.acq.osd.mil/dp/dars/dfars.html and http://farsite.hill.af.mil/vfdfara.htm.
3	Health and Human Services.
4	Agriculture.
5	General Services Administration.
6	State.
7	Agency for International Development.
8	Veterans Affairs.
9	Energy. Available at http://farsite.hill.af.mil/vfdoea.htm/
10	Treasury.
12	Transportation.
13	Commerce.
14	Interior.
15	Environmental Protection Agency.
16	Office of Personnel Management (Federal Employees Health Benefits).
17	Office of Personnel Management.
18	National Aeronautics and Space Administration (NASA). Available at: http://farsite.hill.af.mil/vfnasaa.htm.

Chapter	Agency/Department
19	Broadcasting Board of Governors.
20	Nuclear Regulatory Commission.
21	Office of Personnel Management (Federal Employees Group Life Insurance).
23	Social Security Administration.
24	Housing and Urban Development.
25	National Science Foundation.
28	Justice.
29	Labor.
30	Homeland Security.
34	Education.
51	Army FAR Supplement (AFARS). Also available at: http://farsite.hill.af.mil/vfafara.htm.
52	Navy Acquisition Procedures Supplement (NAPS). Also available at: http://farsite.hill.af.mil/vfnapsa.htm.
53	Air Force FAR Supplement (AFFARS). Also available at: http://farsite.hill.af.mil/vfaffara.htm.
54	Defense Logistics Acquisition Regulation Supplement (DLAR).

Contract Format & FAR System

C. Organization of the FAR.

    1. The FAR is divided into eight subchapters and fifty-three parts. Parts are further divided into subparts, sections, and subsections.

    2. The FAR organizational system applies to the FAR and all agency supplements to the FAR. See FAR 1.303.

Subchapter A: General	
Part 1:	Federal Acquisition Regulation System
Part 2:	Definitions of Words and Terms
Part 3:	Improper Business Practices and Personal Conflicts of Interest
Part 4:	Administrative Matters
Subchapter B: **Acquisition Planning**	
Part 5:	Publicizing Contract Actions
Part 6:	Competition Requirements
Part 7:	Acquisition Planning
Part 8:	Required Sources of Supplies and Services
Part 9:	Contractor Qualifications
Part 10:	Market Research
Part 11:	Describing Agency Needs
Part 12:	Acquisition of Commercial Items
Subchapter C: Contracting Methods **and Contract Types**	
Part 13:	Simplified Acquisition Procedures
Part 14:	Sealed Bidding
Part 15:	Contracting by Negotiation
Part 16:	Types of Contracts
Part 17:	Special Contracting Methods
Part 18:	[Reserved]
Subchapter D: **Socioeconomic Programs**	
Part 19:	Small Business Programs
Part 20:	[Reserved]
Part 21:	[Reserved]
Part 22:	Application of Labor Law to Government Acquisitions

Part 23:	Environment, Conservation, Occupational Safety, and Drug-Free Workplace
Part 24:	Protection of Privacy and Freedom of Information
Part 25:	Foreign Acquisition
Part 26:	Other Socioeconomic Programs
Subchapter E: General Contracting **Requirements**	
Part 27:	Patents, Data, and Copyrights
Part 28:	Bonds and Insurance
Part 29:	Taxes
Part 30:	Cost Accounting Standards Administration
Part 31:	Contract Cost Principles and Procedures
Part 32:	Contract Financing
Part 33:	Protests, Disputes, and Appeals
Subchapter F: Special Categories of **Contracting**	
Part 34:	Major System Acquisition
Part 35:	Research and Development Contracting
Part 36:	Construction and Architect-Engineer Contracts
Part 37:	Service Contracting
Part 38:	Federal Supply Schedule Contracting
Part 39:	Acquisition of Information Technology
Part 40:	[Reserved]
Part 41:	Acquisition of Utility Services
Subchapter G: Contract Management	
Part 42:	Contract Administration and Audit Services
Part 43:	Contract Modifications

Part 44:	Subcontracting Policies and Procedures
Part 45:	Government Property
Part 46:	Quality Assurance
Part 47:	Transportation
Part 48:	Value Engineering
Part 49:	Termination of Contracts

Part 50:	Extraordinary Contractual Actions
Part 51:	Use of Government Sources by Contractors
Subchapter H: Clauses and Forms	
Part 52:	Solicitation Provisions and Contract Clauses
Part 53:	Forms

3. Arrangement. The digits to the left of the decimal point represent the part number. The digits to the right of the decimal point AND to the left of the dash represent the subpart and section. The digits to the right of the dash represent the subsection. See FAR 1.105-2.

> a. **Example:** FAR 45.303-2. We are dealing with FAR Part 45. The Subpart is 45.3. The Section is 45.303 and the subsection is 45.303-2.

4. Correlation Between FAR Parts and Clauses/Provisions. All clauses and provisions are found in FAR Subpart 52.2. As a result, they each begin with "52.2." The next two digits in each clause or provision correspond to the FAR Part in which that particular clause or provision is discussed and prescribed. The number following the hyphen is assigned sequentially and relates to the number of clauses and provisions related to that FAR Part. See FAR 52.101(b).

5. **Example:** FAR 52.245-2 (prescribed by FAR 45.303-2). This was the second clause developed dealing with government owned property (the subject of FAR Part 45).

6. How to Determine if a Clause or Provision Should Be Included in the Contract. Each clause or provision listed in the FAR cross-references a FAR Section that prescribes when it should or may be included into a contract. The "FAR Matrix" summarizes these prescriptions. It is found at: http://www.arnet.gov/far/current/matrix/Matrix.pdf

7. Correlation Between FAR and Agency Supplements. Agency FAR Supplements that further implement something that is also addressed in the FAR must be numbered to correspond to the appropriate FAR number. Agency FAR Supplements that supplement the FAR (discuss something not addressed in the FAR) must utilize the numbers 70 and up. See FAR 1.303(a).

8. **Example:** FAR 45.407 discusses contractor use of government equipment. The portion of the DFARS addressing this same topic is found at DFARS 245.407. The portion of the AFARS further implementing this topic is found at AFARS 5145.407. FAR 6.303-2 addresses what needs to be included in a justification and approval document (for other than full & open competition). It does not prescribe the actual format, however. The Army has developed a standardized format for its justification and approval documents. AFARS 5106.303-2-90 provides the supplemental requirement to use this format which is contained in the supplemental form AFARS 5153.9005.

II. CONCLUSION.

Due to the substantial uniformity practiced across agencies in formatting their contracts and in the collection of most acquisition regulations in a single, government-wide regulation, review of government contracts is greatly simplified over what one might otherwise expect. Indeed, a

contract for medical research issued by the
National Institutes of Health has much in
common with a construction contract issued by
the US Army Corps of Engineers in
Afghanistan.

Attachment A

Sample CONTRACT REVIEW Checklist

NOTE: The following checklist is a "broad brush" tool designed to GENERALLY assist a government attorney in conducting solicitation and contract award reviews. DO NOT use this checklist as a substitute for examining the relevant statutes and regulations.

Section I--Solicitation Documentation

1. **_Purchase Request._**

_____ a. Is it in the file?

_____ b. Is the desired delivery or start date consistent with the date stated in the IFB/RFP?

_____ c. Does the description of the desired supplies or services correspond to that of the IFB/RFP?

_____ d. Does the purchase request contain a proper fund citation?

_____ e. Are funds properly certified as available for obligation?

_____ f. Are the funds cited proper as to purpose? 31 U.S.C § 1301.

_____ g. Are the funds cited current and within their period of availability? 31 U.S.C. § 1552.

_____ h. Are the funds cited of sufficient amount to avoid Anti-Deficiency Act issues? 31 U.S.C. §§ 1341, 1511-1517.

_____ i. Is the procurement a severable services contract to which the provisions of 10 U.S.C. § 2410a apply?

_____ j. If appropriate, does the solicitation contain either the Availability of Funds clause at FAR 52.232-18 or the Availability of Funds for the Next Fiscal Year at FAR 52.232-19 (one-year indefinite quantity contracts)?

2. **_Method of Acquisition._**

_____ a. What is the proposed method of acquisition?

_____ b. Is the "sealed bidding" method required? FAR 6.401(a).

_____ c. Has the activity excluded sources? If so, have applicable competition requirements been met? FAR Subpart 6.2.

_____ d. Has the activity proposed meeting its requirements without obtaining full and open competition? FAR Subpart 6.3.

_____ e. Does a statutory exception permit other than full and open competition? FAR 6.302.

_____ f. If other than full and open competition is proposed, has the contracting officer prepared the required justification and included all required information? FAR 6.303. Does it make sense?

_____ g. Have the appropriate officials reviewed and approved the justification? FAR 6.304.

_____ h. Is this a contract for supplies, services, or construction amounting to $100,000 or less ($1,000,000 in a contingency), triggering the simplified acquisition procedures? FAR 2.101; FAR Part 13.

_____ i. May the activity meet its needs via the required source priorities listed in FAR Part 8?

3. **_Publicizing the Solicitation._**

_____ a. Has the contracting officer published the solicitation as required by FAR 5.101 and FAR Subpart 5.2?

_____ b. Has the activity allowed adequate time for publication? FAR 5.203.

Contract Format & FAR System

    c.   If acquiring commercial items, does the combined synopsis/solicitation procedure apply? FAR 12.603.

4. Solicitation Instructions.
    a.   Does the solicitation state the date, time, and place for submitting offers? Is the notation on the cover sheet consistent with the SF 33?
    b.   Is the time for submitting offers adequate? FAR 14.202-1.
    c.   Are the required clauses that are listed in FAR 14.201 (for IFBs) or FAR 15.209 and FAR 15.408 (for RFPs) and the matrix at FAR 52 included in the solicitation?
    d.   If a construction contract, have the special requirements and procedures of FAR Part 36 been followed?

5. Evaluation Factors.
    a.   Does the solicitation state the evaluation factors that will be used to determine award? FAR 14.101(e) and FAR 14.201-8 (for IFBs); FAR 15.304 (for RFPs).
    b.   Are the evaluation factors clear, reasonable, and not unduly restrictive?
    c.   In competitive proposals or negotiations, are all evaluation factors identified, including cost or price and any significant subfactors that will be considered? Is the relative importance of each disclosed? FAR 15.304 and FAR 15.305.
    d.   If past performance is required as an evaluation factor, has it been included? FAR 15.304(c)(3); FAR 15.305(a)(2).

6. Pricing.
    a.   Is the method of pricing clear?
    b.   Are appropriate audit clauses included in the solicitation? FAR 14.201-7; FAR 15.408.
    c.   Does the Truth in Negotiations Act apply to this solicitation or request? FAR Subpart 15.4; FAR 15.403.
    d.   If the Truth in Negotiations Act applies, does the solicitation contain the required clauses? FAR 15.408.

7. Contract Type.
    a.   Is the proposed type of contract appropriate? FAR 14.104; FAR 16.102.
    b.   If the proposed contract is for personal services, has the determination concerning personal services been executed? FAR 37.103. Does a statutory exception permit the use of a personal services contract? FAR 37.104; 5 U.S.C. § 3109 and 10 U.S.C. § 129b.
    c.   If the proposed contract is a requirements contract, is the estimated total quantity stated? Is the estimate reasonable? If feasible, does the solicitation also state the maximum quantity? FAR 16.503. Is appropriate ordering and delivery information set out? FAR 16.506. Are required clauses included in the solicitation? FAR 16.506.
    d.   If the proposed contract is an indefinite quantity-type contract, are the minimum and maximum quantities stated and reasonable? FAR 16.504. Is appropriate ordering and delivery information set out? FAR 16.505. Are required clauses included in the solicitation? FAR 16.506.
    e.   Does the preference for multiple awards apply? FAR 16.504(c).

8. Purchase Description or Specifications.
    a.   Are the purchase descriptions or specifications adequate and unambiguous? FAR 11.002; FAR 14.201-2(b) and (c); FAR 15.203.
    b.   If a brand name or equal specification is used, is it properly used? FAR 11.104?
    c.   Are the provisions required by FAR 11.204 included in the solicitation?

9. ___Descriptive Data and Samples.___
    _____ a.   Will bidders be required to submit descriptive data or bid samples with their bids?
    _____ b.   If so, have the requirements of FAR 14.202-4 and FAR 14.202-5 been met?

10. ___Packing, Inspection, and Delivery.___
    _____ a.   Is there an F.O.B. point? FAR 46.505.
    _____ b.   Are appropriate quality control requirements identified? FAR 46.202.
    _____ c.   Is there a point of preliminary inspection and acceptance? FAR 46.402.
    _____ d.   Is there a point of final inspection? FAR 46.403.
    _____ e.   Have the place of acceptance and the activity or individual to make acceptance been specified? FAR 46.502; FAR 46.503.
    _____ f.   Is the delivery schedule reasonable? FAR 11.402.

11. ___Bonds and Liquidated Damages.___
    _____ a.   Are bonds required? FAR Part 28.
    _____ b.   If so, are the requirements clearly stated in the specification?
    _____ c.   Is there a liquidated damages clause? Does it conform to the requirements of FAR 11.502? Is the amount reasonable? Are required clauses incorporated? FAR 11.503.

12. ___Government-Furnished Property.___
    _____ a.   Will the government furnish any type of property, real or personal, in the performance of the contract?
    _____ b.   If so, is the property clearly identified in the schedule or specifications? Is the date of delivery clearly specified?
    _____ c.   Has the contractor's property accountability system been reviewed and found adequate? FAR 45.104.
    _____ d.   Are the contractor's and the government's responsibilities and liabilities stated clearly? FAR 52.245-2; FAR 52.245-5.
    _____ e.   Have applicable requirements of FAR Part 45 been met? Are required clauses present?

13. ___Small Business Issues.___
    _____ a.   Is the procurement one that has been set aside for small businesses? FAR Subpart 19.5. If so, is the procurement a total set-aside pursuant to FAR 19.502-2 or a partial set-aside pursuant to FAR 19.502-3?
    _____ b.   Is the procurement appropriate for a "small disadvantaged business" participating as part of the Small Business Administration's "8(a) Program"? FAR Subpart 19.8. If so, does the entity meet the eligibility criteria for 8(a) participation?
    _____ c.   If the solicitation contains bundled requirements, has the activity satisfied the requirements of FAR 7.107, FAR 10.001, FAR 15.305, and FAR 19.101, 19.202-1?
    _____ d.   Does the solicitation contain the small business certification? FAR 19.301.
    _____ e.   Does the solicitation contain the proper Standard Industrial Classification code or North American Industry Classification System code? FAR 19.102.

14. ___Environmental Issues.___
    _____ a.   Has the government considered energy efficiency and conservation in drafting its specifications and statement of work? FAR 23.203.
    _____ b.   Has the government considered procuring items containing recycled or recovered materials? FAR 23.401.
    _____ c.   Has the government considered procuring environmentally preferable and energy-efficient products and services? FAR 23.700.

_____ d.   Do the contract specifications require the use of an ozone-depleting substance? FAR 23.803; DFARS 207.105.

_____ e.   Do the Toxic Chemical Reporting requirements apply to the solicitation (for contracts exceeding $100,000)? FAR 23.906.

15.   *Labor Standards*.

_____ a.   Does the Davis-Bacon Act or the Service Contract Act apply to this acquisition? FAR Subparts 22.4 and 22.10.

_____ b.   If so, have the proper clauses and wage rate determinations been incorporated into the solicitation?

16.   *Clarity and Completeness*.

_____ a.   Have you read the entire solicitation?

_____ b.   Do you understand it?

_____ c.   Are there any ambiguities?

_____ d.   Is it complete?

_____ e.   Are the provisions, requirements, clauses, etc., consistent?

_____ f.   Are there any unusual provisions or clauses in the solicitation? Do you understand them? Do they apply?

Section II--Contract Award Checklist

1.   *Sealed Bid Contracts*.

_____ a.   Review the previous legal review of the solicitation. Has the contracting activity made all required or recommended corrections?

_____ b.   Did the contracting officer amend the solicitation? If so, did the contracting officer distribute amendments properly? FAR 14.208.

_____ c.   Has a bid abstract been prepared? FAR 14.403. Is it complete? Does it disclose any problems?

_____ d.   Is the lowest bid responsive? FAR 14.301; FAR 14.404-1; FAR 14.103-2(d). Are there any apparent irregularities?

_____ e.   Is there reason to believe that the low bidder made a mistake? FAR 14.407. Has the contracting officer verified the bid?

_____ f.   Has the contracting officer properly determined the low bidder? FAR 14.408-1.

_____ g.   Is the price fair and reasonable? FAR 14.408-2.

_____ h.   Has the contracting officer properly determined the low bidder to be responsible? FAR 14.408-2; FAR Subpart 9.1.

_____ i.   If the low bidder is a small business that the contracting officer has found non-responsible, has the contracting officer referred the matter to the SBA? FAR 19.601. If so, has the SBA issued or denied a Certificate of Competency to the offeror? FAR 19.602-2.

_____ j.   Did the contracting officer address any late or improperly submitted bids? FAR Subpart 14.4.

_____ k.   Are sufficient and proper funds cited?

_____ l.   Has the activity incorporated all required clauses and any applicable special clauses?

_____ m.   Is the proposed contract clear and unambiguous? Does it accurately reflect the requiring activity's needs?

_____ n.   If a construction contract, have FAR Part 36 requirements been satisfied?

_____ o.   If the acquisition required a synopsis in the fedbizopps.gov, is there evidence of that synopsis in the file? Was the synopsis proper?

2.   *Negotiated Contracts*.

_____ a. Review the previous legal review of the RFP. Have all required or recommended corrections been made?

_____ b. Were any amendments made to the RFP? If so, were they prepared and distributed properly? FAR 15.206.

_____ c. Was any pre-proposal conference conducted properly? FAR 15.201.

_____ d. Did the contracting officer address any late or improperly submitted proposals? FAR 15.208.

_____ e. Has an abstract of proposals been prepared? Is it complete? Does it reveal any problems?

_____ f. Is a pre-negotiation Business Clearance Memorandum (BCM) required? Is it complete? Does it reveal any problems?

_____ g. Were discussions conducted? FAR 15.209; FAR 15.306. If not, did the solicitation contain a clause notifying offerors that the government intended to award without discussions? FAR 15.209(a). If so, were discussions held with all offerors in the properly determined competitive range? FAR 15.209(a); FAR 15.306(c).

_____ h. Were proposals evaluated in accordance with the factors set forth in the request for proposals? FAR 15.305; FAR 15.303.

_____ i. Did the contracting officer properly address any changes to the government's requirements? FAR 15.206.

_____ j. Were applicable source selection procedures followed and documented? FAR 15.308; FAR 15.305.

_____ k. If applicable, did the contracting officer address make-or-buy proposals? FAR 15.407-2.

_____ l. If the Truth in Negotiations Act applies, has the contractor submitted a proper certification? Is it complete and signed? FAR 15.406-2.

_____ m. Is a post-negotiation Business Clearance Memorandum (BCM) required? Is it complete? Does it reveal any problems?

_____ n. Are all negotiated prices set forth in the contract?

_____ o. Has the contracting officer incorporated required and special clauses in the proposed contract?

_____ p. Is the proposed price fair and reasonable?

_____ q. Are sufficient and proper funds cited?

_____ r. Is the proposed contract clear and unambiguous? Does it make sense? Does it reflect the requiring activity's needs?

_____ s. If a construction contract, has the contracting officer satisfied the requirements of FAR Part 36 (and supplements)?

AUTHORITY TO CONTRACT

I. INTRODUCTION.

A. "The United States employs over 3 million civilian employees. Clearly, federal expenditures would be wholly uncontrollable if government employees could, of their own volition, enter into contracts obligating the United States." City of El Centro v. U.S., 922 F.2d 816 (Fed. Cir. 1990).

B. The Federal Government is a government of limited powers. Each action of the government must derive from the Constitution of the United States. Unlike an officer of a private company, federal employees have no inherent authority or apparent authority. Federal employees can only bind the United States if they have been delegated authority to act.

C. Consequently, private entities who contract with the Federal Government must ensure that the agency has the authority to act, and the employee representing the agency has authority to contract. Many companies have learned to their financial detriment, as will be further explained below, that relying on the actions of unauthorized federal employees is financially hazardous.

D. Contract attorneys should understand the constitutional, statutory, and regulatory bases that permit federal executive agencies to contract, obligating the either appropriated funds or non-appropriated funds.

E. Additionally, contract attorneys should understand how, under limited circumstances, the law can overcome barriers posed by the limited authority of agencies and their employees.

II. AUTHORITY OF AGENCIES.

A. **Constitutional.** The US Constitution does not explicitly grant the power to contract to either the executive branch or to the Congress. However, for as long as the United States has been a sovereign nation, it has contracted with private citizens. The US Supreme Court ruled long ago that as a sovereign entity, the United States has inherent authority to contract to discharge governmental duties. United States v. Tingey, 30 U.S. (5 Pet.) 115 (1831). This authority to contract, however, is limited. Specifically, a government contract must:

1. not be prohibited by law; and

2. be an appropriate exercise of the federal government's powers and duties.

B. **Statutory.** Congress has enacted, and continues to enact, numerous statutes regulating the acquisition of goods and services by the federal government. Through the exercise of their express legislative powers and their power of the purse, the Congress has in large part created the current federal procurement system. At the present time, the most important legislation includes the:

1. Armed Services Procurement Act of 1947 (ASPA), codified at 10 U.S.C. §§ 2301-2337. The ASPA applies to the procurement of all property (except land) and services purchased with appropriated funds by the Department of Defense (DOD), Coast Guard, and National Aeronautics and Space Administration (NASA).

2. Federal Property and Administrative Services Act of 1949 (FPASA), 41 U.S.C. Subtitle I, Division C. The FPASA governs the acquisition of all property and services by all executive agencies except

Authority

DOD, Coast Guard, NASA. 41 U.S.C. § 3101(c)(1).

3. Office of Federal Procurement Policy Act (OFPPA), 41 U.S.C. §§ 1101-2313. This legislation applies to all executive branch agencies, and created the Office of Federal Procurement Policy (OFPP) within the Office of Management and Budget. The Administrator of the OFPP is given responsibility to "provide overall direction of procurement policy and leadership in the development of procurement systems of the executive agencies." 41 U.S.C. § 1121(a).

4. Competition in Contracting Act of 1984 (CICA), 10 U.S.C. Chapter 137; 41 U.S.C. Subtitle I, Division C.

   a. CICA amended the ASPA and the FPASA to make them identical. Because of subsequent legislative action, they are now different in some significant respects.

   b. CICA mandates full and open competition for many, but not all, purchases of goods and services.

5. The Federal Acquisition Streamlining Act of 1994 (FASA), Pub. L. No. 103-355, 108 Stat. 3243. FASA amended various sections of the statutes described above, and eliminated some of the differences between the ASPA and the FPASA.

6. Clinger-Cohen Act, Pub. L. No. 104-106, Division E, § 5101, 110 Stat. 680 (1996) (previously known as the Information Technology Management Reform Act (ITMRA)). This statute governs the acquisition of information technology by federal agencies. It repealed the Brooks Automatic Data Processing Act, 40 U.S.C. § 759.

7. Annual DOD Authorization and Appropriation Acts. Most years, as part of the appropriation and authorization process, the Congress enacts various changes to the acquisition laws. Some changes only apply to acquisitions made using specific appropriations; other changes are general in nature.

C. **Regulatory.**

1. The authority granted agencies by statute is typically subject to further regulation, most prominently the Federal Acquisition Regulation (FAR), codified at 48 C.F.R. chapter 1.

   a. As discussed in Chapter 2, the FAR is the principal regulation governing federal executive agencies in the use of appropriated funds to acquire supplies and services.

   b. The DOD, NASA, and the General Services Administration (GSA) issue the FAR jointly, acting through a FAR Council.

   c. These agencies publish proposed, interim, and final changes to the FAR in the <u>Federal Register</u>. They issue changes to the FAR in Federal Acquisition Circulars (FACs).

2. Agency regulations. The FAR system consists of the FAR and the agency regulations that implement or supplement it. The following regulations supplement the FAR. (The FAR and its supplements are available at <u>http://farsite.hill.af.mil</u>.)

   a. Defense Federal Acquisition Regulation Supplement (DFARS), codified at 48 C.F.R. chapter 2. The Defense Acquisition Regulation (DAR) Council publishes DFARS changes/proposed changes in the <u>Federal Register</u> and issues them as Defense Acquisition Circulars (DACs).

   b. Army Federal Acquisition Regulation Supplement (AFARS).

   c. Air Force Federal Acquisition Regulation Supplement (AFFARS).

   d. Navy Marine Corps Acquisition Regulation Supplement (NMCARS).

e. The AFARS, AFFARS, and NMCARS are not codified in the C.F.R. The military departments do not publish changes to these regulations in the <u>Federal Register</u> but, instead, issue them pursuant to departmental procedures.

3. Major command and local command regulations.

III. CREATING A BINDING CONTRACT.

A. **Commercial Contracts**. Between private parties, the law of contract formation is a matter of state law and, for the sale of goods, is set forth in UCC Article 2, Chapter 2. A contract for sale of goods may be made in any manner sufficient to show agreement, including conduct by both parties which recognizes the existence of such a contract. UCC § 2-204(1). In the private sector, a buyer may insert a coin into a machine and purchase a soft drink. This creates a binding contract, even though no words are spoken nor is the agreement reduced to writing. These simple transactions occur many times a second.

B. **FAR Definition of a Contract**. The FAR defines a "Contract" differently: "A contract is a mutually binding legal relationship obligating the seller to furnish supplies and services (including construction) and the buyer to pay for them. It includes all types of commitments obligating the government to expend appropriated funds and, except as otherwise authorized, must be in writing. Contracts include bilateral agreements; job orders or task letters issued under a Basic Ordering Agreement; letter contracts; and orders, such as purchase orders, under which the contract becomes effective by written acceptance or performance." FAR 2.101.

C. Comparing the UCC and the FAR, one immediately notices that under the FAR, there is greater formality and definition.

D. **Express Contract.**

1. Unlike the private sector, the overwhelming majority of government contracts are express and reduced to writing.

2. An express contract is a contract whose terms the parties have explicitly set out. BLACK'S LAW DICTIONARY 321 (7th ed. 1999).

3. The required elements to form a government contract are:

a. mutual intent to contract;

b. offer and acceptance; and

c. conduct by an officer having the actual authority to bind the government in contract. <u>Allen Orchards v. United States</u>, 749 F.2d 1571, 1575 (Fed. Cir. 1984); <u>OAO Corp. v. United States</u>, 17 Cl. Ct. 91 (1989).

4. Requirement for contract to be in writing. <u>See</u> FAR 2.101 definition of contract, supra.

a. Oral contracts are generally not enforceable against the government unless supported by documentary evidence. <u>See</u> 31 U.S.C. § 1501(a)(1) (an amount shall be recorded as an obligation of the United States Government only when supported by documentary evidence of a binding agreement between an agency and another person that is in writing, in a way and form, and for a purpose authorized by law).

b. The predecessor provision to 31 U.S.C. § 1501(a)(1) was construed as requiring a written contract to obtain court enforcement of an agreement. <u>United States v. American Renaissance Lines, Inc.</u>, 494 F.2d 1059 (D.C. Cir. 1974), <u>cert. denied</u>, 419 U.S. 1020 (1974). (Government unable to obtain damages for an unperformed oral contract for carriage.)

c. The Court of Claims held that failure to reduce a contract to writing under 31 U.S.C. § 1501(a)(1) should not preclude recovery. Rather, a party can prevail if it introduces additional facts from which a court can infer a meeting of the minds. <u>Narva Harris Construction Corp. v. United States</u>, 574 F.2d 508 (1978).

d. The Ninth Circuit has held that FAR 2.101 does not prevent a court from finding an implied-in-fact contract. <u>PACORD, Inc. v. United States</u>, 139 F.3d 1320 (9th Cir. 1998).

e. The Armed Services Board of Contract Appeals has followed the <u>Narva Harris</u> position. Various correspondence between parties can be sufficient "additional facts" and "totality of circumstances" to avoid the statutory prohibition in 31 U.S.C. § 1501(a)(1) against purely oral contracts. <u>Essex Electro Engineers, Inc.</u>, ASBCA Nos. 30118, 30119, 88-1 BCA ¶ 20,440; <u>Vec-Tor, Inc.</u>, ASBCA Nos. 25807 and 26128, 84-1 BCA ¶ 17,145.

f. The ASBCA has found a binding oral contract existed where the Army placed an order against a GSA requirements contract. <u>C-MOR Co.</u>, ASBCA Nos. 30479, 31789, 87-2 BCA ¶ 19,682 (however, the Army placed a written delivery order following a telephone conversation between the contract specialist and C-MOR). <u>Cf.</u> <u>RMTC Sys.</u>, AGBCA No. 88-198-1, 91-2 BCA ¶ 23,873 (shipment in response to phone order by employee without contract authority did not create a contract).

5. A contractor is well advised to not assume that it has a contract with the government unless and until it has received a written contract executed by both parties, and has reason to believe the government official has authority to contract.

E. **Implied Contracts.**

1. Written contracts are not the only type of contracts that the United States enters into. The Courts and Boards of Contract Appeals recognize contracts that are "implied-in-fact."

2. Implied-in-Fact Contract.

   a. Consider a situation where a flood breaches a levy, threatening a town. An Army Corps of Engineers official arrives on the scene and asks a nearby construction contractor to fill the breach. The contractor agrees to the official's request. The next day, having saved the town, the contractor bills the Army Corp of Engineers for the services rendered. This is an example of an "implied in fact" contract. Rather than pay the bill with the thanks of a grateful nation, the disbursing officer questions the obligation for lack of a writing.

   b. An implied-in-fact contract is "founded upon a meeting of the minds, which, although not embodied in an express contract, is inferred, as a fact, from conduct of the parties showing, in the light of the surrounding circumstances, their tacit understanding." <u>Baltimore & Ohio R.R. Co. v. United States</u>, 261 U.S. 592, 597 (1923).

   c. The requirements for an implied-in-fact contract are the same as for an express contract; only the nature of the evidence differs. <u>OAO Corp. v. United States</u>, 17 Cl. Ct. 91 (1989) (finding implied-in-fact contract for start-up costs for AF early warning system). <u>See, generally,</u> Willard L. Boyd III, <u>Implied-in-Fact Contract: Contractual Recovery against the Government without an Express Agreement</u>, 21 Pub. Cont. L. J. 84-128 (Fall 1991).

3. Implied-in-Law Contracts Distinguished.

   a. Return to the breached levy. Instead of asking a contractor to repair the damaged levy, assume the Army Corps of Engineers official hot-wired some construction equipment parked near the breach and repaired the dike herself using the "borrowed" equipment. Those actions could create an "implied-in-law" contract to pay the owner for the value of using the equipment.

   b. An implied-in-law contract is not a true agreement to contract. It is a "fiction of law" where "a promise is imputed to perform a legal duty, as to repay money obtained by fraud or duress." <u>Baltimore & Ohio R.R. Co. v. United States</u>, 261 U.S. 592, 597 (1923).

4. Contractor Recovery for Implied-in-Fact and Implied-in-Law Contracts.

   a. The first challenge in implied-in-fact and implied-in-law contracts is factual; what really happened? Unlike the contractor who has a written contract signed by a contracting officer, there no such incontrovertible evidence of an agreement. Sometimes the facts are clear, sometimes they are murky, and sometimes they are clear but for the contractor's efforts to make them murky. Both contractors and government officials should marshal all the evidence and avoid premature conclusions.

   b. The second challenge in implied-in-fact contracts is that neither the Contract Disputes Act (CDA) nor the Tucker Act grants jurisdiction to courts and boards to hear cases involving implied-in-law contracts. 41 U.S.C. §§ 601-613; 28 U.S.C. §§ 1346 and 1491. <u>See</u> <u>Hercules, Inc. v. United States</u>, 516 U.S. 417 (1996); <u>Amplitronics, Inc</u>., ASBCA No. 44119, 94-1 BCA ¶ 26,520. Thus, an implied-in-fact contract between a company and an authorized federal employee provides a contractual remedy. The "borrowing" of property by a government official does not. If an inexperienced counsel representing a company pleads the claim as seeking "Quantum Meruit," a classic remedy for an implied-in-law contract, this creates a jurisdictional bar to recovery. If not remedied prior to the expiration of the statute of limitations for taking's claims, it may bar recovery.

   c. It is in the long-term interest of the Agency to treat citizens and suppliers fairly. Where the claim is doubtful, the law provides ample protection for the government. Where an authorized government official impliedly agreed to pay for goods and services, then the government should honor its implied in fact contracts, as further discussed in Section VI, below.

IV. AUTHORITY OF PERSONNEL.

A. **Contracting Authority.**

1. Agency Head.

   a. The FAR vests contracting authority in the head of the agency. FAR 1.601(a). Within DOD, the heads of the agencies are the Secretaries of Defense, the Army, the Navy, and the Air Force. DFARS 202.101.

   b. In turn, the head of the agency may establish subordinate contracting activities and delegate broad contracting authority to the heads of the subordinate activities. FAR 1.601(a).

2. Heads of Contracting Activities (HCAs).

    a. HCAs have overall responsibility for managing all contracting actions within their activities.

    b. There are over 60 DOD contracting activities, plus others that possess contracting authority delegated by the heads of the various defense agencies. Examples of DOD contracting activities include Army Forces Command, Naval Air Systems Command, and Air Force Materiel Command. DFARS 202.101.

    c. HCAs are contracting officers by virtue of their position. See FAR 1.601; FAR 2.101.

    d. HCAs may delegate some of their contracting authority to deputies.

        (1) In the Army, HCAs appoint a Principal Assistant Responsible for Contracting (PARC) as the senior staff official of the contracting function within the contracting activity. The PARC has direct access to the HCA and should be one organizational level above the contracting office(s) within the HCA's command. AFARS 5101.601(4).

        (2) The Air Force and the Navy also permit delegation of contracting authority to certain deputies. AFFARS 5301.601-92; NMCARS 5201.603-1.

3. Contracting officers.

    a. Agency heads or their designees select and appoint contracting officers. Appointments are made in writing using the SF 1402, Certificate of Appointment. Delegation of micropurchase authority shall be in writing, but need not be on a SF 1402. FAR 1.603-3.

    b. Contracting officers may bind the government only to the extent of the authority delegated to them on the SF 1402. Information on a contracting officer's authority shall be readily available to the public and agency personnel. FAR 1.602-1(a).

4. Contracting Officer Representatives (COR).

    a. Contracting officers may authorize selected individuals to perform specific technical or administrative functions relating to the contract. A COR may also be referred to as a Contracting Officer's Technical Officer (COTR) or Quality Assurance Representative (QAR).

    b. Typical COR designations do not authorize CORs to take any action, such as modification of the contract, that obligates the payment of money. See AFARS 53.9001, Sample COR designation.

B. Actual Authority.

1. The government is bound only by government agents acting within the actual scope of their authority to contract. Federal Crop Ins. Corp. v. Merrill, 332 U.S. 380 (1947) (government agent lacked authority to bind government to wheat insurance contract not authorized under Wheat Crop Insurance Regulations); Hawkins & Powers Aviation, Inc. v. United States, 46 Fed. Cl. 238 (2000) (assistant director of Forest Service lacked authority to modify aircraft contract); Schism v. United States, 316 F.3d 1259 (Fed. Cir. 2002) (military recruiters lacked the authority to bind the government to promises of free lifetime medical care).

2. Actual authority can usually be determined by viewing a contracting officer's warrant or a COR's letter of appointment. See Farr Bros., Inc., ASBCA No. 42658, 92-2 BCA ¶ 24,991 (COR's authority to order suspension of work not specifically prohibited by appointment letter).

3. The acts of government agents which exceed their contracting authority do not bind the government. See HTC Indus., Inc., ASBCA No. 40562, 93-1 BCA ¶ 25,560 (contractor denied recovery although contracting officer's technical representative encouraged continued performance despite cost overrun on the cost plus fixed-fee contract); Johnson Management Group CFC v. Martinez, 308 F.3d. 1245 (Fed. Cir. 2002) (contracting officer was without authority to waive a government lien on equipment purchased with government funds).

C. **Apparent Authority.**

1. Definition. Apparent authority is authority that a third party reasonably believes an agent has, based on the third party's dealings with the principal. BLACK'S LAW DICTIONARY 128 (7th ed. 1999). Thus, in commercial contracting, a principal can, through its actions, create the appearance that an agent is authorized and will be bound by the agent's actions.

2. No Apparent Authority. The federal government is not bound by actions of one who has apparent authority to act for the government. Federal Crop Ins. Corp. v. Merrill, 332 U.S. 380 (1947); Sam Gray Enterprises, Inc. v. United States, 43 Fed. Cl. 596 (1999) (embassy chargé d'affaires lacked authority to bind government); Mark L. McAfee v. United States, 46 Fed. Cl. 428 (2000) (Assistant U.S. Attorney lacked authority to forgive plaintiff's farm loan in exchange for cooperation in foreclosure action); Austin v. United States, 51 Fed. Cl. 718 (2002) (employees of the US Marshal Service possessed no authority to bind the government beyond the scope of the Witness Security Program).

3. In contrast, contractors are bound by apparent authority in their dealings with the federal government. American Anchor & Chain Corp. v. United States, 331 F.2d 860 (Ct. Cl. 1964) (government justified in assuming that contractor's plant manager acted with authority).

V. **DOCTRINES THAT BIND THE GOVERNMENT.**

Because the number of federal employees with formal delegations of authority to contract are few compared to the number of employees who interact with the public, questions often arise about whether an alleged agreement was authorized. A number of legal principles have been used alone or in combination to justify the conclusion that an agreement was authorized.

A. **Implied Authority.**

1. Implied authority is the powers granted, though not stated, to a federal employee in addition to his or her actual authority. While an employee with no actual authority will also have no implied authority, a federal employee is assumed to receive the authority necessary to carry out his or her express responsibilities.

2. Courts and boards will find implied authority to contract if the questionable acts, orders, or commitments of a government employee are an integral or inherent part of that person's assigned duties. See H. Landau & Co. v. United States, 886 F.2d 322, 324 (Fed. Cir. 1989); Confidential Informant v. United States, 46 Fed. Cl. 1 (2000) (even though FBI agents lacked actual authority to contract for rewards, government may be liable under theory of "implied actual authority"); Jess Howard Elec. Co., ASBCA No. 44437, 96-2 BCA ¶ 28,345 (contract administrator had implied actual authority to grant contract extension

despite written delegation to the contrary); Sigma Constr. Co., ASBCA No. 37040, 91-2 BCA ¶ 23,926 (contract administrator at work site had implied authority to issue change orders issued under exigent circumstance [drying cement]); Switlik Parachute Co., ASBCA No. 17920, 74-2 BCA ¶ 10,970 (quality assurance representative [QAR] had implied authority to order 100% testing of inflatable rafts).

3. The authority of officials subordinate to the contracting officer is derived from the facts of each case, based on the words of the contract and the conduct of the parties during contract administration. See Jordan & Nobles Constr. Co., GSBCA No. 8349, 91-1 BCA ¶ 23,659 (on-site representative had authority to inspect supplies and direct work according to his contract interpretation, making the government liable for direction to contractor to stop rejecting defective brick).

4. A common fact pattern is one where a federal employee is granted authority to make a decision, such as to accept conforming goods. An agency may contest the employee's authority to accept non-conforming goods. As a general principle, however, authority to make a decision includes the authority to make an incorrect decision.

B. Ratification.

1. Where an unauthorized federal employee makes a contractual commitment, an authorized federal employee may ratify the unauthorized action after the fact, and bind the government.

2. Formal or Express. FAR 1.602-3 grants the Head of a Contracting Activity with authority to ratify certain unauthorized commitments, and may delegate that authority to the head of a contracting office. See section VI, infra. Henke v. United States, 43 Fed. Cl. 15 (1999); Khairallah v. United States, 43 Fed. Cl. 57 (1999) (no ratification of unauthorized

commitments by DEA agents). Agency acquisition regulations provide procedures for exercising this.

3. Implied. Ratification need not be explicit. Ratification may be found where an authorized individual has actual or constructive knowledge of the unauthorized commitment and adopts the act as his own. The contracting officer's failure to process a claim under the procedures of FAR 1.602-3 does not preclude ratification by implication. Reliable Disposal Co., ASBCA No. 40100, 91-2 BCA ¶ 23,895 (KO ratified unauthorized commitment by requesting payment of the contractor's invoice); Tripod, Inc., ASBCA No. 25104, 89-1 BCA ¶ 21,305 (KO's knowledge of contractor's complaints and review of inspection reports evidenced implicit ratification); Digicon Corp. v. United States, 56 Fed. Cl. 425 (2003) (COFC found "institutional ratification" where Air Force issued task orders and accepted products and services from appellant over a sixteen-month period).

C. Imputed Knowledge.

1. In some instances, liability may depend on whether an authorized person knew of the event alleged to create a contractual liability. Where no direct evidence of an individual's knowledge is forthcoming, the facts and circumstances may be such that knowledge will be imputed to the authorized person. An example of this doctrine is Williams v. United States, 127 F. Supp. 617 (Ct. Cl. 1955), where the contracting officer was imputed with knowledge of a road-paving agreement on Air Force base because the contracting officer drove on those very roads every day as the work progressed. By his inaction, the contracting officer ratified the unauthorized commitment.

2. When the relationship between two persons creates a presumption that one would have informed the contracting officer of certain events, the boards may

impute the knowledge of the person making the unauthorized commitment to the contracting officer. Sociometrics, Inc., ASBCA No. 51620, 00-1 BCA ¶ 30,620 ("While the [contract] option was not formally exercised, the parties conducted themselves as if it was."); Leiden Corp., ASBCA No. 26136, 83-2 BCA ¶ 16,612, mot. for recon. denied, 84-1 BCA ¶ 16,947 ("It would be inane indeed to suppose that [the government inspector] was at the site for no purpose.").

3. Contractors can avoid questions of imputed knowledge by routinely copying the contracting officer on all correspondence.

D. Equitable Estoppel.

1. A contractor's reasonable, detrimental reliance on statements, actions, or inactions by a government employee may estop the government from denying liability for the actions of that employee. Lockheed Shipbldg. & Constr. Co., ASBCA No. 18460, 75-1 BCA ¶ 11,246, aff'd on recon., 75-2 BCA ¶ 11,566 (government estopped by Deputy Secretary of Defense's consent to settlement agreement).

2. Traditionally, to prove estoppel in a government contract case, the party must establish:

    a. knowledge of the facts by the party to be estopped;

    b. intent, by the estopped party, that his conduct shall be acted upon, or actions such that the party asserting estoppel has a right to believe it is so intended;

    c. ignorance of the true facts by the party asserting estoppel; and

    d. detrimental reliance. Emeco Industries, Inc. v. United States, 485 F.2d 652, at 657 (Ct. Cl. 1973).

3. If asserted against the government, a contractor must demonstrate the government's affirmative misconduct as a prerequisite for invoking equitable estoppel. Zacharin v. United States, (213 F.3d 1366) (Fed. Cir. 2001); Rumsfeld v. United Technologies Corp., 315 F.3d 1361 (Fed. Cir. 2003); Appeal of F Splashnote Systems, Inc., 12-1 BCA ¶ 34899, Nov. 29, 2011; and Appeal of F Unitech Services Group, Inc., 16 ASBCA No. 56482, May 22, 2012.

4. However, in Mabus v. General Dynamics C4 Systems, Inc., 633 F.3d 1356 (Fed. Cir. Feb. 4, 2011), the Federal Circuit cited A.C. Aukerman Co. v. R.L. Chaides Construction Co., 960 F.2d 1020 (Fed. Cir. 1992) and rejected the four-part estoppel test. Over a strong dissent, the Federal Circuit applied a three-part test requiring:

    a. Misleading conduct, which may include not only statements and actions but silence and inaction, leading another to reasonably infer that rights will not be asserted against it;

    b. Reliance upon this conduct; and

    c. Due to this reliance, material prejudice.

VI. UNAUTHORIZED COMMITMENTS.

A. Definition. An unauthorized commitment is an agreement that is nonbinding solely because the government representative who made it lacked the authority to enter into that agreement. FAR 1.602-3.

B. Ratification.

1. Ratification is the act of approving an unauthorized commitment, by an official who has the authority to do so, for the purpose of paying for supplies or services

provided to the government as a result of an unauthorized commitment. FAR 1.602-3(a).

2. The government may ratify unauthorized commitments if:

    a. The government has received and accepted supplies or services, or the government has obtained or will obtain a benefit from the contractor's performance of an unauthorized commitment.

    b. At the time the unauthorized commitment occurred, the ratifying official could have entered into, or could have granted authority to another to enter into, a contractual commitment which the official still has authority to exercise.

    c. The resulting contract otherwise would have been proper if made by an appropriate contracting officer.

    d. The price is fair and reasonable.

    e. The contracting officer recommends payment and legal counsel concurs, unless agency procedures expressly do not require such concurrence.

    f. Funds are available and were available when the unauthorized commitment occurred.

    g. Ratification is within limitations prescribed by the agency.

3. Army HCAs may delegate the authority to approve ratification actions, without the authority to redelegate, to the following individuals.

    a. PARC (for amounts of $100,000 or less) (AFARS 5101.602-3(b)(3)(A)); and

    b. Chiefs of Contracting Offices (for amounts of $10,000 or less) (AFARS 5101.602-3(b)(3)(B)).

4. The Air Force and the Navy also permit ratification of unauthorized commitments, but their limitations are different than those of the Army. See AFFARS 5301.602-3; NMCARS 5201.602-3.

C. **Alternatives to Ratification.** If the agency refuses to ratify an unauthorized commitment, a binding contract does not arise. A contractor can pursue one of the following options:

1. Requests for extraordinary contractual relief.

    a. Contractors may request extraordinary contractual relief in the interest of national defense. Pub. L. No. 85-804 (50 U.S.C. §§ 1431-1435); FAR Part 50.

    b. FAR 50.302-3 authorizes, under certain circumstances, informal commitments to be formalized for payment where, for example, the contractor, in good faith reliance on a government employee's apparent authority, furnishes supplies or services to the agency. Radio Corporation of America, ACAB No. 1224, 4 ECR ¶ 28 (1982) (contractor granted $648,747 in relief for providing, under an informal commitment with the Army, maintenance, repair, and support services for electronic weapon system test stations).

    c. Operational urgency may be grounds for formalization of informal commitments under P.L. 85-804. Vec-Tor, Inc., ASBCA Nos. 25807, 26128, 85-1 BCA ¶ 17,755.

2. Doubtful Claims.

    a. Prior to 1995-1996, the Comptroller General had authority under 31 U.S.C. § 3702 to authorize reimbursement on a quantum meruit or quantum valebant basis to a firm that performed work for the government without a valid written contract.

b. Under quantum meruit, the government pays the reasonable value of services it actually received on an implied, quasi-contractual basis. <u>Maintenance Svc. & Sales Corp.</u>, 70 Comp. Gen. 664 (1991).

c. The GAO used the following criteria to determine justification for payment:

(1) The goods or services for which the payment is sought would have been a permissible procurement had proper procedures been followed;

(2) The government received and accepted a benefit;

(3) The firm acted in good faith; and

(4) The amount to be paid did not exceed the reasonable value of the benefit received. <u>Maintenance Svc. & Sales Corp.</u>, 70 Comp. Gen. 664 (1991).

d. Congress transferred the claims settlement functions of the Government Accountability Office to the Office of Management and Budget (OMB), which then further delegated settlement authority. <u>See</u> The Legislative Branch Appropriations Act, 1996, Pub. L. 104-53, 109 Stat. 514, 535 (1995); 31 U.S.C. 3702.

e. The Claims Division at the Defense Office of Hearings and Appeals (DOHA) settles these types of claims for the Department of Defense. DOHA decisions can be found at <u>www.defenselink.mil/dodgc/doha</u>.

3. Contract Disputes Act (CDA) claims. If the contractor believes it can meet its burden in proving an implied-in-fact contract, it can appeal a contracting officer's final decision to the United States Court of Federal Claims or the cognizant board of contract appeals. 41 U.S.C. §§ 601-613; FAR Subpart 33.2.

VII. CONCLUSION.

Federal agencies have the authority to contract, and to exercise that authority through specifically designated officials known as contracting officers. Federal agencies are protected from unauthorized contractual actions by a number of legal principles, such as the "no apparent authority" rule.

These principles, however, are intended to protect the government from unjustified claims. There are other legal principles, such as implied authority and ratification, that permit the federal government to pay contractual claims, where justified.

To avoid unnecessary disputes, federal employees and contractors are both well served by focusing their communications and commitments through the appropriate empowered officials, the designated Contracting Officer.

FUNDING
AND
FUND LIMITATIONS

I.   REFERENCES.

This chapter is a summary of relevant Fiscal Law concepts that affect government contracting. For a more thorough discussion of Fiscal Law topics, you should refer to:

- Principles of Federal Appropriations Law, GAO-04-261SP (2004-2015), available at: http://www.gao.gov/legal/red-book/current-edition

- 2014 Fiscal Law Deskbook, The Judge Advocate General's Legal Center and School, United States Army, available at: http://www.loc.gov/rr/frd/Military_Law/pdf/fiscal-law-deskbook_2014.pdf

II.   INTRODUCTION.

A.   **Funding and Government Contracts.** Fiscal Law, also known as the Law of Federal Appropriations, is an important part of government contracting. The reason it is so important is that the Congress uses its power of the purse as a tool to promote its policy choices. For executive branch agencies, this means that the Congress, by choosing what to fund, how much to fund, and what conditions to attach to the funding it appropriates, exercises considerable control over when and what the agencies buy.

Before entering into a contract, an agency must verify that Congress has provided the funding needed to pay the contractor for the goods or services. If the funding is available, the government proceeds consistent with conditions attached to that funding.

Because funding is usually provided by a federal law, known as an appropriation, that results from the political processes established by the U.S. Constitution, federal funding is subject to the vagaries of the political process; various individuals and groups jockey to influence the outcome, policy compromises are reflected in ambiguous language, and the processes can appear illogical. What is clear, however, is that agencies and contractors who understand Fiscal Law can navigate the many obstacles and fulfill the intent of the voters.

In commercial contracting, a key concern is whether the buyer will have the financial ability to pay the seller at the times specified in the contract. Knowing your buyer and negotiating terms to mitigate the risk of non-payment are key issues. In government contracting, the Federal Government's ability to pay is rarely questioned because of the size of federal tax revenues and a nearly unblemished payment history. The key concern is demonstrating that Congress has made funding available for the contract. Available funding is a pre-condition to the government accepting the legal obligation to pay. Once a government contract is concluded, thus obligating the government; payment (eventually) for completing the required contract performance is assured. Checks drawn on the U.S. Treasury are honored.

B.   **Source of Funding and Fund Limitations.** The U.S. Constitution gives Congress the authority to raise revenue,

Funding

borrow funds, and appropriate the proceeds for federal agencies. This Constitutional "power of the purse" includes the power to establish restrictions and conditions on the use of funds appropriated. To curb fiscal abuses by the executive departments, Congress has enacted additional fiscal controls through statute.

1. U.S. Constitution, Art. I, § 8, grants to Congress the power to "lay and collect Taxes, Duties, Imports, and Excises, to pay the Debts and provide for the common Defense and general Welfare of the United States . . ."

2. U.S. Constitution, Art. I, § 9, provides that "[N]o Money shall be drawn from the Treasury but in Consequence of an Appropriation made by Law. . . ."

3. The "Purpose Statute," 31 U.S.C. § 1301, provides that agencies shall apply appropriations only to the objects for which the appropriations were made, except as otherwise provided by law.

4. The Anti-Deficiency Act (ADA), 31 U.S.C. §§ 1341, 1342, 1350, 1351, and 1511-1519 (2000), consists of several statutes that authorize administrative and criminal sanctions for the unlawful obligation and expenditure of appropriated funds.

5. Congress and the Department of Defense (DOD) have agreed informally to additional restrictions. The DOD refrains from taking certain actions without first giving prior notice to, and receiving consent from, Congress. These restraints are embodied in regulation.

C. The Basic Fiscal Limitations.

1. An agency may obligate and expend appropriations only for a proper purpose;

2. An agency may obligate only within the time limits applicable to the appropriation (e.g., O&M funds are available for obligation for one fiscal year); and

3. An agency may not obligate more than the amount appropriated by the Congress.

D. **Congress Has the Power:** "The established rule is that the expenditure of public funds is proper only when authorized by Congress, not that public funds may be expended unless prohibited by Congress." United States v. MacCollom, 426 U.S. 317 (1976).

E. **Fiscal Law Affects Contract Terms.** Many contract terms are a direct result of Fiscal Law constraints. For example, because of limitations discussed below about contracting in advance of an appropriation, the government often uses options and ordering agreements to limit its obligations. Additionally, since Congress limits the purposes for which agencies may expend funds, contract terms prohibiting specific conduct are common.

III. KEY TERMINOLOGY.

Understanding Fiscal Law requires understanding the precise definitions of many terms. These terms have a technical meaning that defines the processes for obtaining funding, and the restrictions on using the funding Congress does provide. Some of the more important terms are:

A. **Fiscal Year (FY).** The Federal Government's fiscal year begins on 1 October and ends on 30 September.

B. **Period of Availability.** Most appropriations are available for obligation for a limited period of time. If the government does not obligate the funds during the period of availability, the funds expire and are generally unavailable for subsequent obligation.

C. **Obligation.** An obligation is any act that legally binds the government to make payment. Obligations represent the amount of orders placed, contracts awarded, options exercised, and similar transactions during an accounting period

36

that will require payment during the same or a future period. DOD Financial Management Regulation 7000.14, Glossary, p. G-22.

D. **Budget Authority.** Agencies do not receive cash to fund their programs and activities. Instead, Congress grants "budget authority," also called obligational authority. Budget authority means "the authority provided by Federal law to incur financial obligations. . . ." 2 U.S.C. § 622(2).

E. **Contract Authority.** Contract authority is a limited form of "budget authority." Contract authority permits agencies to enter into obligations in advance of appropriations, but not to disburse those from the treasury funds absent appropriations authority. See, e.g., 41 U.S.C. § 6301 (Feed and Forage Act).

F. **Authorization Act.** An authorization act is a statute, usually passed annually by Congress, that authorizes the appropriation of funds for programs and activities. An authorization act does not provide budget authority. That authority stems from the appropriations act. Authorization acts frequently contain restrictions or limitations on the obligation of appropriated funds.

G. **Appropriations Act.** An appropriation is a statutory authorization to "incur obligations and make payments out of the U.S. Treasury for specified purposes." An appropriations act is the most common form of budget authority.

1. The Army receives the bulk of its funds from two annual Appropriations Acts: (1) the Department of Defense Appropriations Act; and (2) the Military Construction Appropriations Act.

2. The making of an appropriation must be stated expressly. An appropriation may not be inferred or made by implication. Principles of Fed. Appropriations Law, Vol. I (4th ed.), p. 2-23, GAO-16-464SP (2016).

H. **Treasury.** The Department of Treasury is an agency in the executive branch that collects the taxes and other revenue authorized by Congress, and borrows money as authorized by Congress. The Department of Treasury also expends funds that the Congress appropriates to meet obligations incurred.

I. **Comptroller General and Government Accountability Office (GAO).**

1. Investigative arm of Congress charged with examining all matters relating to the receipt and disbursement of public funds.

2. The GAO was established by the Budget and Accounting Act of 1921 (31 U.S.C. § 702) to audit government agencies.

3. The Comptroller General issues opinions and reports to federal agencies concerning the propriety of appropriated fund obligations or expenditures.

J. **Accounting Classifications.** Accounting classifications are codes used to manage appropriations. They are used to implement the administrative fund control system and to ensure that funds are used correctly. An accounting classification is commonly referred to as a "fund cite." DFAS-IN 37-100-XX, The Army Mgmt. Structure, provides a detailed breakdown of Army accounting classifications. By reviewing the fund cite, you can learn the many things about the appropriation that the buying agency has concluded are appropriate to use in making the acquisition. A sample fund cite appears on the following page.

37

Funding

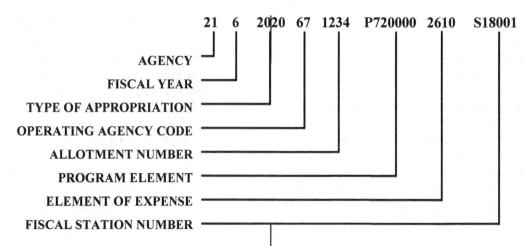

21 6 2020 67 1234 P720000 2610 S18001

AGENCY ┘
FISCAL YEAR ─────────
TYPE OF APPROPRIATION ─────────
OPERATING AGENCY CODE ─────────
ALLOTMENT NUMBER ─────────
PROGRAM ELEMENT ─────────
ELEMENT OF EXPENSE ─────────
FISCAL STATION NUMBER ─────────

1. The first two digits represent the military department. In the example above, the "**21**" denotes the Department of the Army. For the Air Force, these two digits will be **57**; for the Navy, **17**; and for the Department of Defense, **97**.

2. The third digit shows the fiscal year/period of availability of the appropriation. The "6" in the example shown indicates FY 2006 funds. Installation contracting typically uses annual appropriations. Other fiscal year designators encountered less frequently include:

   a. Third Digit = X = No year appropriation. This appropriation is available for obligation indefinitely.

   b. Third Digit = 6/9 = Multi-year appropriation. In this example, funds were appropriated in FY 2006 and remain available through FY 2009.

3. The next four digits reveal the type of the appropriation. The following Table contains the designators used within DOD fund citations to designate the commonly recurring appropriations the Congress makes for the Department of Defense:

Appropriation Type	Army	Navy	Marine Corps	Air Force	OSD
Military Personnel	21*2010	17*1453	17*1105	57*3500	N/A
Reserve Personnel	21*2070	17*1405	17*1108	57*3700	N/A
National Guard Personnel	21*2060	N/A	N/A	57*3850	N/A
Operations & Maintenance	21*2020	17*1804	17*1106	57*3400	97*0100
Operations & Maintenance, Reserve	21*2080	17*1806	17*1107	57*3740	N/A
Operations & Maintenance, National Guard	21*2065	N/A	N/A	57*3840	N/A

Appropriation Type	Army	Navy	Marine Corps	Air Force	OSD
Procurement, Aircraft	21*2031	17*1506		57*3010	N/A
Procurement, Missiles	21*2032	17*1507 (not separate – the combined appropriation is entitled Weapons Procurement)	17*1109	57*3020	N/A
Procurement, Weapons & Tracked Vehicles	21*2033			N/A	N/A
Procurement, Other	21*2035	17*1810		57*3080	97*0300
Procurement, Ammunition	21*2034	17*1508		57*3011	N/A
Shipbuilding & Conversion	N/A	17*1611		N/A	N/A
Res., Develop., Test, & Eval.7	21*2040	17*1319		57*3600	97*0400
Military Construction	21*2050	17*1205		57*3300	97*0500
Family Housing Construction	21*0702	17*0703		57*0704	97*0706
Reserve Construction	21*2086	17*1235		57*3730	N/A
National Guard Construction	21*2085	N/A	N/A	57*3830	N/A

* The asterisk in the third digit is replaced with the last number in the relevant fiscal year. For example, Operations & Maintenance, Army funds for FY2016 would be depicted as 2162020.

** Source for the codes found in Federal Account Symbols and Titles (FAST) Book I, Supplement 1 to Volume I, Treasury Financial Manual, beginning at page A-23. The FAST Book is available at: https://www.fiscal.treasury.gov/fsreports/ref/fastBook/fastbook_december2015.pdf

IV. OVERVIEW OF FUNDING CONTRACTS.

Prior to signing a binding contract, a buying agency must identify the appropriation(s) it will use to pay the contractor. The agency determines the appropriation that is available considering the purpose of the contract, when the contract is awarded and performed, and verifies that Congress has provided adequate funding. Upon award, the buying agency sets aside the funding to pay the contractor. As the contractor invoices per the contract, the buying agency writes checks on the U.S. Treasury. The agency contract attorney has an important

quality assurance function over the accounting personnel who make these determinations.

V. AVAILABILITY AS TO PURPOSE.

A. Prior to entering into a contract, the buying agency must determine that an appropriation exists whose purpose encompasses the contract.

B. The "Purpose Statute" provides that agencies shall apply appropriations only to the objects for which the appropriations were made, except as otherwise provided by law. 31 U.S.C. § 1301(a).

Funding

1. The Purpose Statute does not require Congress to specify every item of expenditure in an appropriation act, although it does specify the purpose of many expenditures. Rather, agencies have reasonable discretion to determine how to accomplish the purpose of an appropriation. Internal Revenue Serv. Fed. Credit Union—Provision of Automatic Teller Mach., B-226065, 66 Comp. Gen. 356 (1987).

2. An appropriation for a specific purpose is available to pay expenses necessarily incident to accomplishing that purpose. Secretary of State, B-150074, 42 Comp. Gen. 226, 228 (1962); Major General Anton Stephan, A-17673, 6 Comp. Gen. 619 (1927).

C. **Three-Part Test for a Proper Purpose.**

1. The expenditure must be for a specified purpose of the appropriation, or be reasonably related to the purposes that Congress intended the appropriation to fulfill (the "necessary expense doctrine").

   a. In other words, it must make a direct contribution to carrying out either a specific appropriation or an authorized agency function for which more general appropriations are available. Department of Def-- Transfer and Use of Def. Emergency Response Funds, B-303145, 2005 U.S. Comp. Gen. LEXIS 221 (Dec. 7, 2005).

   b. Another way this prong has been articulated is that an expenditure is permissible if it reasonably necessary in carrying out an authorized function or will contribute materially to the effective accomplishment of that function. Internal Revenue Serv. Fed. Credit Union—Provision of Automatic Teller Machine, B-226065, 66 Comp. Gen. 356 (1987).

   c. A necessary expense does not have to be the only way, or even the best way, to accomplish the object of an appropriation. A necessary expense, however, must be more than merely desirable. Utility Costs under Work-at-Home Programs, B-225159, 68 Comp. Gen. 505 (1989).

2. The expenditure must not be prohibited by law.

3. The expenditure must not be otherwise provided for, i.e., it must not be an item that falls within the scope of some other appropriation or statutory funding scheme.

D. **Determining the Purpose of a Specific Appropriation.**

1. Appropriations Acts. (http://thomas.loc.gov/home/approp)

   a. An appropriation is a statutory authorization to incur obligations and make payments out of the Treasury for specified purposes. Aside from any emergency supplemental appropriations, Congress generally enacts thirteen (13) appropriations acts annually, two of which are devoted specifically to DOD: The Department of Defense Appropriation Act and the Military Construction Appropriations Act. Within these two appropriations acts, the DOD receives hundreds of separate appropriations available to it for different purposes.

   b. Appropriations are differentiated by service (Army, Navy, etc.), component (Active, Reserve, etc.), and purpose (Procurement, Research and Development, etc.). The major DOD appropriations provided in the annual Appropriations Act are:

      (1) Operation & Maintenance (O&M) – used for the day-to-day expenses of training exercises, deployments, operating and maintaining installations, etc.;

(2) Personnel – used for pay and allowances, permanent change of station travel, etc.;

(3) Research, Development, Test and Evaluation (RDT&E) – used for expenses necessary for basic and applied scientific research, development, test, and evaluation, including maintenance and operation of facilities and equipment; and

(4) Procurement – used for production and modification of aircraft, missiles, weapons, tracked vehicles, ammunition, shipbuilding and conversion, and "other procurement."

c. By regulation, the DOD has assigned most types of expenditures to a specific appropriation. See DFAS-IN Manual 37-100-XXXX, The Army Management Structure (August XXXX). The manual is reissued every FY. XXXX= appropriate FY.

2. Authorization Act. (http://thomas.loc.gov)

a. Theoretically, Congress enacts an authorization act prior to enacting DOD's two appropriations acts. There is no constitutional requirement to have an authorization in order for an appropriation to occur. However, Congress has by statute stated it must both authorize and appropriate funds. For example, 10 U.S.C. § 114(a) states that "No funds may be appropriated for any fiscal year" for certain purposes, including procurement, military construction, and RDT&E "unless funds therefore have been specifically authorized by law."

b. Authorization acts are a result of the political process. For DOD, the Defense Committees of the House and Senate primarily draft authorization acts, which may clarify the intended purpose of a specific appropriation or contain restrictions on the use of appropriated funds.

3. Organic Legislation. Organic legislation is legislation that creates a new agency or establishes a program or function within an existing agency that a subsequent appropriation act will fund. This organic legislation provides the agency with authority to conduct the program, function, or mission and to utilize appropriated funds to do so. However, organic legislation rarely provides any money for the agency, program, or activity it establishes.

4. Miscellaneous Statutory Provisions. Congress often enacts statutes that expressly allow, prohibit, or place restrictions upon the usage of appropriated funds. For example, 10 U.S.C. § 2246 prohibits DOD from using its appropriated funds to operate or maintain a golf course except in foreign countries or isolated installations within the United States.

5. Legislative History. Legislative history is any Congressionally-generated document related to a bill from the time the bill is introduced to the time it is passed. This includes the text of the bill itself, conference and committee reports, floor debates, and hearings.

a. Legislative history can be useful for resolving ambiguities or confirming the intent of Congress where the statute fails to clearly convey Congress's intent, but may not be used to justify an otherwise improper expenditure. When confronted with a statute plain and unambiguous on its face, courts ordinarily do not look to the legislative history as a guide to its meaning. Tennessee Valley Authority v. Hill, 437 U.S. 153, 191 (1978); see also Lincoln v. Vigil, 508 U.S. 182, 192 (1993); Thompson v. Cherokee Nation of Oklahoma, 334 F.3d 1075 (Fed. Cir. 2003).

Funding

b. The legislative history is not necessarily binding upon the executive branch. If Congress provides a lump-sum appropriation without restricting what may be done with the funds, a clear inference is that it did not intend to impose legally binding restrictions. <u>SeaBeam Instruments, Inc.</u>, B-247853.2, July 20, 1992, 92-2 CPD ¶ 30; <u>LTV Aerospace Corp.</u>, B-183851, Oct. 1, 1975, 75-2 CPD ¶ 203.

6. Budget Request Documentation.

   a. Agencies are required to justify their budget requests. Within DOD, Volumes 2A and 2B of the DOD FMR provide guidance on the documentation that must be generated to support defense budget requests. These documents are typically referred to as Justification Books, with a book generated for each appropriation. As with legislative histories, the Budget Request Documentation may aid in interpretation of ambiguous statutory language, but cannot change it.

   b. These justification documents contain a description of the proposed purpose for the requested appropriations. An agency may reasonably assume that appropriations are available for the specific purposes requested, unless otherwise prohibited.

7. Agency Regulations.

   a. When Congress enacts organic legislation, it rarely prescribes exactly how the agency is to carry out that new mission. Instead, Congress leaves it up to the agency to implement the authority in agency-level regulations.

   b. The President controls the executive branch through regulations. If the agency, in drafting a regulation, interprets a statute, that interpretation is granted a great deal of deference. Thus, if an agency regulation

determines that appropriated funds may be used for a particular purpose, that agency-level determination will normally not be overturned unless it is clearly erroneous.

   c. Agency-level regulations may also place restrictions on the use of appropriated funds not present in the statute—for example, to control expenditures.

8. Case Law. Comptroller General opinions are a valuable source of guidance as to the permitted uses of appropriated funds. While not technically binding on the executive branch, GAO opinions are nonetheless deemed authoritative, especially where they approve specific expenditures.

9. Impact on Contractors. If Congress has prohibited expending appropriations on a supply or service offered by a Contractor, the Contractor will not receive a contract until Congress changes the law. The reverse is rarely true. As a result of internal rule changes in Congress, it does not often appropriate funds for a specific purchase from a specific contractor (a practice previously known as "earmarks"). Consequently, a contractor typically must convince the buying agency to allocate scarce appropriations to purchase goods and services that the contractor supplies, rather than for goods and services that are available from other sources.

VI. AVAILABILITY AS TO TIME.

The buying agency must conclude that a contract fits within the "window" the agency has to obligate the appropriation. It must execute the contract and create the obligation within an appropriations period of availability, and the object of the contract must represent, with exceptions, a bona fide need of that period of availability. These are the "Time Rule" and the "Bona Fide Needs Rule."

A. **The Time Rule.** 31 U.S.C. §§ 1502(a), 1552. An appropriation is available for obligation for a definite period of time. An agency must obligate appropriations within their period of availability. If an agency fails to obligate appropriations before they expire, those unobligated appropriations are no longer available for new obligations − a consequence of the Time Rule that agencies devote significant efforts to ensuring that all available appropriations are obligated before the period of availability expires.

1. Expired funds retain their "fiscal year identity" for five years after the end of the period of availability. During this time, the funds are available to adjust existing obligations, or to liquidate prior valid obligations, but not to incur new obligations.

2. There are several important exceptions to the general prohibition against obligating funds after the period of availability.

   a. Protests. Upon a protest, the appropriation that would have funded the contract remains available for obligation for 100 days after a final ruling on the protest. 31 U.S.C. § 1558(a). This statutory provision is incorporated at FAR 33.102(c).

   b. Terminations for default. See Lawrence W. Rosine Co., B-185405, 55 Comp. Gen. 1351 (1976).

   c. Terminations for convenience, pursuant to a court order or agency determination of erroneous award. Navy, Replacement Contract, B-238548, Feb. 5, 1991, 91-1 CPD ¶ 117; Matter of Replacement Contracts, B-232616, 68 Comp. Gen. 158 (1988).

B. **The "Bona Fide Needs" Rule.** Agencies may obligate appropriated funds only for requirements that represent bona fide needs during an appropriation's period of availability. 31 U.S.C. § 1502(a). See U.S. Dep't of Education's Use of Fiscal Year Appropriations to Award Multiple Year Grants, B-289801, 2002 U.S. Comp. Gen. LEXIS 258 (Dec. 30, 2002); National Park Serv. Soil Surveys, B-282601, 1999 U.S. Comp. Gen. LEXIS 254 (Sept. 27, 1999).

C. **Bona Fide Needs Rule Applied to Supply Contracts.**

1. Supplies are generally the bona fide need of the period in which they are needed or consumed. Orders for supplies are proper only when the supplies are actually required. Thus, supplies needed for operations during a given fiscal year are bona fide needs of that year. Maintenance Serv. and Sales Corp., B-242019, 70 Comp. Gen. 664 (1991); 64 Comp. Gen. 359 (1985).

2. Exceptions. Supply needs of a future fiscal year are the bona fide needs of the subsequent fiscal year, unless an exception applies. Two recognized exceptions are the lead-time exception and the stock-level exception. DOD Reg. 7000.14-R, vol. 3, para. 080303.

   a. Stock-Level Exception. Supplies ordered to meet authorized stock levels are the bona fide need of the year of purchase, even if the agency does not use them until a subsequent fiscal year. A bona fide need for stock exists when there is a present requirement for items to meet authorized stock levels (replenishment of operating stock levels, safety levels, mobilization requirements, authorized backup stocks, etc.). To Betty F. Leatherman, Dep't of Commerce, B-156161, 44 Comp. Gen. 695 (1965); DOD Financial Management Regulation 7000.14-R, vol. 3, chapter 8, para. 080303A.

   b. Lead-Time Exception. This exception recognizes that agencies may need and contract for an item in a current FY, but cannot physically obtain the item in the current FY due to the lead time necessary to produce and/or deliver it. There are two variants that comprise the lead-time exception.

(1) Delivery Time. If an agency cannot obtain materials in the same FY in which they are needed and contracted for, delivery in the next FY does not violate the Bona Fide Needs Rule as long as the time between contracting and delivery is not excessive, and the procurement is not for standard, commercial items readily available from other sources. <u>Administrator, General Services Agency</u>, B-138574, 38 Comp. Gen. 628, 630 (1959).

(2) Production Lead Time. An agency may contract in one FY for delivery and use in the subsequent FY if the item cannot be obtained on the open market at the time needed for use, so long as the intervening period is necessary for the production. <u>Chairman, United States Atomic Energy Commission</u>, B-130815, 37 Comp. Gen. 155 (1957).

D. **Bona Fide Needs Rule Applied to Service Contracts.**

1. General Rule. Services are generally the bona fide need of the fiscal year in which they are performed. <u>Theodor Arndt GmbH & Co.</u>, B-237180, Jan. 17, 1990, 90-1 CPD ¶ 64; <u>EPA Level of Effort Contracts</u>, B-214597, 65 Comp. Gen. 154 (1985). This general rule applies where the services are "severable." A service is severable if it can be separated into components that independently meet a separate need of the government. Examples include grounds and facilities maintenance, dining facility services, and transportation services. Most service contracts are severable. Therefore, as a general rule, use current funds to obtain current services.

2. Statutory Exception for Severable Services. 10 U.S.C. § 2410a permits DOD agencies to award severable service contracts for a period not to exceed 12 months at any time during the fiscal year, funded completely with current appropriations. This statutory exception essentially swallows the general rule. Non-DOD agencies have similar authority. <u>See</u> 41 U.S.C. § 2531. For the Coast Guard, the authority is found in 10 U.S.C. § 2410a(b).

3. Non-severable Services. If the services are non-severable (i.e., a contract that seeks a single or unified outcome, product, or report), agencies must obligate funds for the entire undertaking at contract award, even if performance will cross fiscal years. <u>See</u> <u>Incremental Funding of U.S. Fish & Wildlife Serv. Research Work Orders</u>, B-240264, 73 Comp. Gen. 77 (1994) (work on an environmental impact statement properly crossed fiscal years); <u>Proper Fiscal Year Appropriation to Charge for Contract and Contract Increase</u>, B-219829, 65 Comp. Gen. 741 (1986) (contract for study and report on psychological problems among Vietnam veterans was non-severable).

VII. AVAILABILITY BASED UPON AMOUNT.

Agencies are prohibited from incurring obligations in advance of, or in excess of, available appropriations. The accounting procedures that agencies follow to avoid violations of this rule are complex. Agencies are allotted funds; unobligated funds can be withdrawn for other uses; once obligated, the obligation is recorded against the appropriation. When paid, the obligation is converted to a reduction in the appropriation. The statute that underlies this system is the Anti-Deficiency Act.

A. **The Anti-Deficiency Act (ADA).** 31 U.S.C. §§ 1341-1344, 1511-1517, prohibits:

1. Making or authorizing an expenditure or obligation in excess of the amount

available in an appropriation. 31 U.S.C. § 1341(a)(1)(A).

2. Making or authorizing expenditures or incurring obligations in excess of an apportionment or a formal subdivision of funds. 31 U.S.C. § 1517(a).

    a. Apportionment. The Office of Management and Budget (OMB) apportions funds over their period of availability to agencies for obligation. 31 U.S.C. § 1512. This means that OMB divides the funds into quarterly installments to prevent agencies from obligating the entire fiscal year's appropriations too quickly and needing supplemental appropriations.

    b. Formal Administrative Subdivisions. The ADA also requires agencies to establish certain administrative controls of apportioned funds. 31 U.S.C. § 1514. These formal limits are referred to as allocations and allotments. In the Army, the Operating Agency/Major Command (MACOM) generally is the lowest command level at which the formal administrative subdivisions of funds are maintained for O&M appropriations.

    c. Informal Administrative Subdivisions. DFAS-IN 37-1, ch. 3, para. 031402. Agencies may further subdivide funds at lower levels, e.g., within an installation. These subdivisions are generally informal targets or allowances. These are not formal subdivisions of funds, and obligating in excess of these limits does not, in itself, violate the ADA.

3. Incurring an obligation in advance of an appropriation, unless authorized by law. 31 U.S.C. § 1341(a)(1)(B).

4. Accepting voluntary services, unless otherwise authorized by law. 31 U.S.C. § 1342.

B. **Investigating Violations.** If an Anti-Deficiency Act violation occurs, the agency must investigate to identify the responsible individual. The agency must report the violation to Congress through the Secretary of the Army. Violations could result in administrative and/or criminal sanctions. See DOD 7000.14-R, vol. 14.

1. The head of the agency must report to the President and Congress whenever a violation of 31 U.S.C. §§ 11(a), 1342 or 1517 is discovered. OMB Cir. A-34, para. 32.2; DOD 7000.14-R, Vol. 14, ch. 7, para. A. The head of the agency must also now report the violation to GAO, per 31 U.S.C. § 1351 (as amended by Consolidated Appropriations Act, 2005).

2. Individuals responsible for an Anti-Deficiency Act violation shall be sanctioned commensurate with the circumstances and the severity of the violation. See DOD 7000.14-R, Vol. 14, ch. 9; see also 31 U.S.C.§§ 1349(a).

VIII. LEGAL REVIEW OF FUNDING ISSUES.

A. **Government Attorneys.**

1. As previously mentioned, government attorneys have an important quality assurance function over funding decisions. They act as an independent reviewer of funding decisions made by accounting and program personnel. While the final decision may ultimately reside elsewhere, government attorneys often protect accounting and program personnel from themselves.

2. When reviewing a draft request for proposals, the government attorney should determine whether the appropriate finance official has certified the availability of funds and which appropriation and fiscal year is identified. If there is an apparent mismatch between the appropriation and the acquisition, request clarification.

Funding

3. When a draft RFP is issued in advance of appropriations (a common practice for goods and services funded by annual appropriations), the government attorney should ensure that the RFP includes FAR 52.232-18, Availability of Funds.

4. When reviewing a proposed award, the government attorney should verify that the appropriate finance official has certified the availability of funds for the award, and that the appropriation supporting the obligation is appropriate considering the purpose, time and amount rules discussed previously.

5. In acquisition planning, an attorney can assist the contracting and program personnel in structuring the acquisition such that it conforms to the fiscal realities. Continuing Resolutions and delayed appropriations are common. Technical requirements may be severable in a way that solves fiscal issues.

6. Government attorneys often confront questions about whether the purchase of a particular supply or service is an appropriate use of agency appropriations. Commercial companies such as Google, Inc. may provide their employees with free soft drinks, food, recreational activities, motivational items such as shirts, etc., but the federal government does not. For a detailed discussion of the various laws, regulations and opinions on these types of questions, see the references cited in paragraph I., above.

B. Contractor Attorney.

1. Contractor attorneys provide their clients with advice about the extent of the contractual commitment made by the government, and about the compliance commitments that accompany the contract.

2. One common technique the government uses to avoid Fiscal Law issues is unilateral options and various ordering agreements that have no commitment. Contractor attorneys should highlight the risks associated with the government's lack of commitment, such as making investments and long-term agreements, when the government is only committed to purchase a small quantity.

3. A second area where a contractor attorney can assist his clients is in compliance. While a contractor need not accept changes in terms and conditions post-award, often such changes are precipitated by funding restrictions. Agreement to revised terms, with price adjustments where warranted, may be the price for receiving an order for additional goods and services.

IX. AUGMENTATION OF APPROPRIATIONS & MISCELLANEOUS RECEIPTS.

A. Contractor Payments and Repayments. As discussed below, a collection of rules commonly referred to as "Augmentation of Funds" can affect how the government may wish to structure a payment received from a contractor or other source. For example, an agency that receives a repayment from a contractor by cash or check may have to deposit the sum in the Treasury as a miscellaneous receipt, but could retain in-kind consideration (i.e., additional products or services) of an equivalent amount.

B. General Rule. Augmentation of appropriations is prohibited.

1. Augmentation is action by an agency that increases the effective amount of funds available in an agency's appropriation. This generally results in expenditures by the agency in excess of the amount originally appropriated by Congress.

2. Basis for the Augmentation Rule. An augmentation normally violates one or more of the following provisions:

   a. U.S. Constitution, Article I, section 9, clause 7: "No Money shall be drawn from the Treasury, but in

Consequence of Appropriations made by Law."

b. 31 U.S.C. § 1301(a) (Purpose Statute): "Appropriations shall be applied only to the objects for which the appropriations were made except as otherwise provided by law."

c. 31 U.S.C. § 3302(b) (Miscellaneous Receipts Statute): "Except as [otherwise provided], an official or agent of the government receiving money for the government from any source shall deposit the money in the Treasury as soon as practicable without any deduction for any charge or claim."

3. Types of Augmentation.

a. Augmenting by using one appropriation to pay costs associated with the purposes of another appropriation. This violates the Purpose Statute, 31 U.S.C. § 1301(a). U.S. Equal Employment Opportunity Comm'n – Reimbursement of Registration Fees for Fed. Executive Board Training Seminar, B-245330, 71 Comp. Gen. 120 (1991); Nonreimbursable Transfer of Admin. Law Judges, B-221585, 65 Comp. Gen. 635 (1986); Department of Health and Human Servs. – Detail of Office of Cmty. Servs. Employees, B-211373, 64 Comp. Gen. 370 (1985).

Example: If the Air Force were to buy air-to-air missiles using its "Procurement, Ammunition, Air Force" appropriation instead of its more specific "Procurement, Missiles, Air Force" appropriation, this would enable it to purchase a greater quantity of missiles (some using the missile appropriation and some using the ammunition appropriation) than Congress desired.

b. Augmenting an appropriation by retaining government funds received from another source.

(1) This violates the Miscellaneous Receipts Statute, 31 U.S.C. § 3302(b). See Scheduled Airlines Traffic Offices, Inc. v. Dep't of Def., 87 F.3d 1356 (D.C. Cir. 1996) (indicating that a contract for official and unofficial travel, which provided for concession fees to be paid to the local morale, welfare, and recreation account, violates Miscellaneous Receipts Statute; note, however, that Congress has subsequently enacted statutory language – found at 10 U.S.C. § 2646 – that permits commissions or fees in travel contracts to be paid to morale, welfare, and recreation accounts); Interest Earned on Unauthorized Loans of Fed. Grant Funds, B-246502, 71 Comp. Gen. 387 (1992); but see Bureau of Alcohol, Tobacco, and Firearms – Augmentation of Appropriations – Replacement of Autos by Negligent Third Parties, B-226004, 67 Comp. Gen. 510 (1988) (noting that 31 U.S.C. § 3302 only applies to monies received, not to other property or services).

(2) Expending the retained funds generally violates the constitutional requirement for an appropriation. See Use of Appropriated Funds by Air Force to Provide Support for Child Care Ctrs. for Children of Civilian Employees, B-222989, 67 Comp. Gen. 443 (1988).

C. **Statutory Exceptions to the Miscellaneous Receipts Statute.** Some examples of the statutes Congress has enacted which expressly authorize agencies to retain funds received from a non-Congressional source include:

1. Economy Act. 31 U.S.C. § 1535 authorizes interagency orders. The

ordering agency must reimburse the performing agency for the costs of supplying the goods or services. 31 U.S.C. § 1536 specifically indicates that the servicing agency should credit monies received from the ordering agency to the "appropriation or fund against which charges were made to fill the order." See also 41 U.S.C. § 23 (providing similar intra-DOD project order authority).

2. Foreign Assistance Act. 22 U.S.C. § 2392 authorizes the President to transfer State Department funds to other agencies, including DOD, to carry out the purpose of the Foreign Assistance Act.

3. Revolving Funds. Revolving funds are management tools that provide working capital for the operation of certain activities. The receiving activity must reimburse the funds for the costs of goods or services when provided. See 10 U.S.C. § 2208; National Technical Info. Serv., B-243710, 71 Comp. Gen. 224 (1992); Administrator, Veterans Admin., B-116651, 40 Comp. Gen. 356 (1960).

4. Proceeds received from bond forfeitures, but only to the extent necessary to cover the costs of the United States. 16 U.S.C. § 579c; USDA Forest Serv. – Auth. to Reimburse Gen. Appropriations with the Proceeds of Forfeited Performance Bond Guarantees, B-226132, 67 Comp. Gen. 276 (1988); National Park Serv. – Disposition of Performance Bond Forfeited to Gov't by Defaulting Contractor, B-216688, 64 Comp. Gen. 625 (1985) (forfeited bond proceeds to fund replacement contract).

5. Defense Gifts. 10 U.S.C. § 2608. The Secretary of Defense may accept monetary gifts and intangible personal property for defense purposes. However, these defense gifts may not be expended until appropriated by Congress.

6. Health Care Recoveries. 10 U.S.C. § 1095(g). Amounts collected from third-party payers for health care services provided by a military medical facility may be credited to the appropriation supporting the maintenance and operation of the facility.

7. Recovery of Military Pay and Allowances. Statutory authority allows the government to collect damages from third parties to compensate for the pay and allowances of soldiers who are unable to perform military duties as a result of injury or illness resulting from a tort. These amounts "shall be credited to the appropriation that supports the operation of the command, activity, or other unit to which the member was assigned." 42 U.S.C. § 2651. The U.S. Army Claims Service has taken the position that such recoveries should be credited to the installation's operation and maintenance account. See Affirmative Claims Note, *Lost Wages under the Federal Medical Care Recovery Act*, ARMY LAW., Dec, 1996, at 38.

8. Military Leases of Real or Personal Property. 10 U.S.C. § 2667(d)(1). Rentals received pursuant to leases entered into by a military department may be deposited in special accounts for the military department and used for facility maintenance, repair, or environmental restoration.

9. Damage to Real Property. 10 U.S.C. § 2782. Amounts recovered for damage to real property may be credited to the account available for repair or replacement of the real property at the time of recovery.

10. Proceeds from the sale of lost, abandoned, or unclaimed personal property found on an installation. 10 U.S.C. § 2575. Proceeds are credited to the operation and maintenance account and used to pay for collecting, storing, and disposing of the property. Remaining funds may be used for morale, welfare, and recreation activities.

11. Host nation contributions to relocate armed forces within a host country. 10 U.S.C. § 2350k.

D. GAO Sanctioned Exceptions to the Miscellaneous Receipts Statute. In addition to the statutory authorities detailed above, the Comptroller General recognizes other exceptions to the Miscellaneous Receipts Statute, including:

1. Replacement Contracts. An agency may retain recovered excess reprocurement costs to fund replacement contracts. Bureau of Prisons – Disposition of Funds Paid in Settlement of Breach of Contract Action, B-210160, 62 Comp. Gen. 678 (1983).

   a. This rule applies regardless of whether the government terminates for default or simply claims for damages due to defective workmanship.

   b. The replacement contract must be coextensive with the original contract, i.e., the agency may reprocure only those goods and services that would have been provided under the original contract.

   c. Amounts recovered that exceed the actual costs of the replacement contract must be deposited as miscellaneous receipts.

2. Refunds.

   a. Refunds for erroneous payments, overpayments, or advance payments may be credited to agency appropriations. Department of Justice – Deposit of Amounts Received from Third Parties, B-205508, 61 Comp. Gen. 537 (1982) (agency may retain funds received from carriers/insurers for damage to employee's property for which agency has paid employee's claim); International Natural Rubber Org. – Return of United States Contribution, B-207994, 62 Comp. Gen. 70 (1982).

   b. Amounts that exceed the actual refund must be deposited as miscellaneous receipts. Federal Emergency Mgmt. Agency – Disposition of Monetary Award Under False Claims Act, B-230250, 69 Comp. Gen. 260 (1990) (agency may retain reimbursement for false claims, interest, and administrative expenses in revolving fund; treble damages and penalties must be deposited as miscellaneous receipts).

   c. Funds recovered by an agency for damage to government property, unrelated to performance required by the contract, must be deposited as miscellaneous receipts. Defense Logistics Agency – Disposition of Funds Paid in Settlement of Contract Action, B-226553, 67 Comp. Gen. 129 (1987) (negligent installation of power supply system caused damage to computer software and equipment; insurance company payment to settle government's claim for damages must be deposited as miscellaneous receipts).

   d. Refunds must be credited to the appropriation charged initially with the related expenditure, whether current or expired. Accounting for Rebates from Travel Mgmt. Ctr. Contractors, B-217913.3, 73 Comp. Gen. 210 (1994); To The Sec'y of War, B-40355, 23 Comp. Gen. 648 (1944). This rule applies to refunds in the form of a credit. See Principles of Fed. Appropriations Law, vol. II, ch. 6, 6-111, GAO/OGC 92-13 (2d ed. 1992), Appropriation Accounting— Refunds and Uncollectibles, B-257905, Dec. 26, 1995, 96-1 CPD ¶ 130 (recoveries under fraudulent contracts are refunds, which should be credited to the original appropriation, unless the account is closed).

Funding

3. Receipt of property other than cash. When the government receives a replacement for property damaged by a third party in lieu of cash, the agency may retain the property. Bureau of Alcohol, Tobacco, and Firearms – Augmentation of Appropriations – Replacement of Autos by Negligent Third Parties, B-226004, 67 Comp. Gen. 510 (1988) (replacement by repair of damaged vehicles).

4. Funds held in trust for third parties. When the government receives custody of cash or negotiable instruments that it intends to deliver to the rightful owner, it need not deposit the funds into the treasury as a miscellaneous receipt. The Honorable John D. Dingell, B-200170, 60 Comp. Gen. 15 (1980) (money received by Department of Energy for oil company overcharges to customers may be held in trust for specific victims).

5. Nonreimbursable Details. The Comptroller General has held that nonreimbursable agency details of personnel to other agencies are generally unallowable. Department of Health and Human Servs. – Detail of Office of Cmty. Servs. Employees, B-211373, 64 Comp. Gen. 370 (1985). However, as exceptions to this rule, nonreimbursable details are permitted under the following circumstances:

    a. A law authorizes nonreimbursable details. See, e.g., 3 U.S.C. § 112 (nonreimbursable details to White House); The Honorable William D. Ford, Chairman, Comm. on Post Office and Civil Serv., House of Representatives, B-224033, 1988 U.S. Comp. Gen. LEXIS 1695 (Jan. 30, 1987).

    b. The detail involves a matter similar or related to matters ordinarily handled by the detailing agency and will aid the detailing agency's mission. Details to Congressional Comm'ns, B-230960, 1988 U.S. Comp. Gen. LEXIS 334 (Apr. 11, 1988).

    c. The detail is for a brief period, entails minimal cost, and the agency cannot obtain the service by other means. Department of Health and Human Servs. Detail of Office of Cmty. Servs. Employees, B-211373, 64 Comp. Gen. 370 (1985).

X. EXPENSE/INVESTMENT THRESHOLD.

A. Procurement or Operations and Maintenance?

A recurring Fiscal Law issue faced by government attorneys is determining whether acquisition of a particular product should be funded by a procurement-type appropriation or by an operation and maintenance (O&M)-type appropriation. This arises because costly items with long useful lives (i.e., airplanes and ships) are generally procured with procurement appropriations. Supplies with low cost and short lives (i.e., pencils or fuel) are bought with O&M. DOD has now provided its entities with relatively clear guidance on making this decision. Contractors should be aware of this guidance so they can structure their offerings to not create unintended obstacles to concluding contracts.

B. Expenses are costs of resources consumed in operating and maintaining DOD, and are normally financed with O&M appropriations. See DOD Reg. 7000.14-R, vol. 2A, ch 1, para. 010201. Expenses generally include:

1. Civilian employee labor;

2. Rental charges for equipment and facilities;

3. Food, clothing, and fuel;

4. Maintenance, repair, overhaul, and rework of equipment; and

5. Utilities.

C. Investments are items purchased with procurement appropriations when the term is used in federal budgeting. As an accounting term, investments represent the value of securities and other assets held for the production of revenues in the form of interest, dividends, rentals or lease payments, net of premiums or discounts. DOD FMR, Glossary, page G-20.

D.   **Exception Permitting Purchase of Investments with O&M Funds.** In each year's Defense Appropriation Act, Congress has permitted DOD to utilize its Operation and Maintenance appropriations to purchase investment items having a unit cost that is less than a certain threshold. See, e.g., Department of Defense Appropriation Act, 2006, Pub. L. No. 109-148, § 8036, 119 Stat. 2680 (Dec. 30, 2005) (current threshold is $250,000). Previous appropriation acts established that threshold at $100,000 or less. See, e.g., The Department of Defense Appropriations Act, 2003, Pub. L. No. 107-248, § 8040 (Oct. 23, 2002) (establishing the threshold at $100,000); see also DOD FMR, vol. 2A, ch. 1, para. 010201. (implementing the $250,000 threshold), as well as DFAS-IN Manual 37-100-03, Appendix A, Expense/Investment Criteria (indicating that all Army purchases made prior to 20 February 2003 should utilize the old $100,000 threshold and all purchases after 20 February 2003 should use the new $250,000 threshold to determine the proper source of funding).

E.   **Systems.** Various audits have revealed that local activities use O&M appropriations to acquire computer systems, security systems, video telecommunication systems, and other systems costing more than the investment/expense threshold. This constitutes a violation of the Purpose Statute, and may result in a violation of the Anti-Deficiency Act.

1.   Agencies must consider the "system" concept when evaluating the procurement of items. The determination of what constitutes a "system" must be based on the primary function of the items to be acquired, as stated in the approved requirements document.

2.   A system exists if a number of components are designed primarily to function within the context of a whole and will be interconnected to satisfy an approved requirement.

3.   Agencies may purchase multiple end items of equipment (e.g., computers), and treat each end item as a separate "system" for funding purposes, only if the primary function of the end item is to operate independently.

4.   Do not fragment or piecemeal the acquisition of an interrelated system of equipment merely to avoid exceeding the O&M threshold.

5.   Example: An agency is acquiring 200 stand-alone computers and software at $2,000 each (for a total of $400,000). The computers are being purchased primarily to operate as independent workstations. The agency should use O&M funds for this acquisition. If one of the primary reasons for purchasing the computers is so that their users could tie into a network and communicate with one another via email, the computers should be purchased with Procurement funds.

XI. MILITARY CONSTRUCTION.

A.   **Congressional oversight of the Military Construction Program** is extensive and pervasive. For example, no public contract relating to erection, repair, or improvements to public buildings shall bind the government for funds in excess of the amount specifically appropriated for that purpose. 41 U.S.C. § 6303. There are different categories of construction work with distinct funding requirements.

B.   **Specified Military Construction (MILCON) Program** -- projects costing over $1.5 million.

Funding

1. Congress authorizes these projects by location and funds them in a lump sum by service. The Army's principal appropriations are the "Military Construction, Army" (MCA) appropriation, and the "Family Housing, Army" (FHA) appropriation.

2. The conference report that accompanies the Military Construction Appropriations Act breaks down the lump-sum appropriations by specific individual projects.

C. **Unspecified Minor Military Construction (MMC) Program** -- military construction projects costing between $750,000 and $1.5 million. 10 U.S.C. § 2805(a).

1. Congress provides annual funding and approval to each military department for minor construction projects that are not specifically identified in a Military Construction Appropriations Act.

2. The Service Secretary concerned uses these funds for minor projects not specifically approved by Congress.

3. Statute and regulations require approval by the Secretary of the Department and notice to Congress before a minor military construction project exceeding $750,000 is commenced.

4. If a military construction project is intended solely to correct a deficiency that is life-threatening, health-threatening, or safety-threatening, an unspecified minor military construction project may have an approved cost equal to or less than $1.5 million.

D. **O&M Construction.** Minor Military Construction projects costing less than $750,000. 10 U.S.C. § 2805(c); DOD Dir. 4270.36; AR 415-15, para. 1-6.c(1).

1. The secretary of a military department may use O&M funds to finance Unspecified Minor Military Construction projects costing less than:

a. $1.5 million if the project is intended solely to correct a deficiency that threatens life, health, or safety. 10 U.S.C. § 2801(b).

b. $750,000 if the project is intended for any other purpose.

2. Construction includes alteration, conversion, addition, expansion, and replacement of existing facilities, plus site preparation and installed equipment.

3. Project splitting is prohibited. The Honorable Michael B. Donley, B-234326.15, 1991 U.S. Comp. Gen. LEXIS 1564 (Dec. 24, 1991) (Air Force improperly split into multiple projects a project involving a group of twelve related buildings).

4. Using O&M funds for construction in excess of the $750,000 project limit violates the Purpose Statute and may result in a violation of the Anti-Deficiency Act. See DOD Accounting Manual 7220.9-M, Ch. 21, para. E.4.e; AFR 177-16, para. 23c; The Honorable Bill Alexander, B-213137, 63 Comp. Gen. 422 (1984).

E. **Maintenance and Repair Projects.**

1. DOD funds these projects with O&M appropriations.

2. "Maintenance" is work required to preserve and maintain a real property facility in such condition that it may be used effectively for its designated functional purpose. Maintenance includes work done to prevent damage which would be costlier to restore than to prevent. Maintenance includes work to sustain components. Examples include renewal of disposable filters, painting, caulking, refastening loose siding, and sealing bituminous pavements. "Preventive maintenance" (PM) is routine, recurring work performed on all real property facilities. PM is systematic inspection, care, and servicing of equipment, utility plants and systems,

buildings, structures, and grounds facilities for detecting and correcting incipient failures and accomplishing minor maintenance. See AR 420-10, Glossary.

3. DOD guidance. Memorandum, Office of the Secretary of Defense, Comptroller, 2 July 97, subject: Definition for Repair and Maintenance.

   a. Repair means to restore a real property facility, system, or component to such a condition that it may be used effectively for its designated purpose.

   b. When repairing a facility, the components of the facility may be repaired by replacement, and the replacement may be up to current standards or codes. For example, Heating, Ventilation, and Air Conditioning (HVAC) equipment may be repaired by replacement, be state-of-the-art, and provide for more capacity than the original unit due to increased demand/standards. Interior rearrangements (except for load-bearing walls) and restoration of an existing facility to allow for effective use of existing space or to meet current building code requirements (e.g., accessibility, health, safety, or environmental) may be included as repair.

   c. Additions, new facilities, and functional conversions must be done as construction. Construction projects may be done concurrently with repair projects as long as the work is separate and segregable.

4. Army guidance. See AR 420-10, Management of Installation Directorates of Public Works; see also DA Pamphlet 420-11, Project Definition and Work Classification.

   a. A facility must be in a failed or failing condition to be considered for a repair project.

   b. When repairing a facility, you may bring it (or a component of a facility) up to applicable codes or standards as repair. An example would be adding a sprinkler system as part of a barracks repair project. Another example would be adding air conditioning to meet a current standard when repairing a facility. Moving load-bearing walls, additions, new facilities, and functional conversions must be done as construction.

   c. Bringing a facility (or component thereof) up to applicable codes or standards for compliance purposes only, when a component or facility is not in need of repair, is construction.

5. When construction and maintenance or repair are performed together as an integrated project, each type of work is funded separately unless the work is so integrated that separation of construction from maintenance and repair is not possible. In the latter case, fund all work as construction.

6. Improperly classifying work as maintenance or repair, rather than construction, may lead to exceeding the $750,000 project limit.

F. **Exercise-Related Construction**. See The Honorable Bill Alexander, B-213137, Jan. 30, 1986 (unpub.); The Honorable Bill Alexander, B-213137, 63 Comp. Gen. 422 (1984).

1. Congress has prohibited the use of O&M for minor construction outside the U.S. on Joint Chiefs of Staff (JCS) directed exercises.

2. All exercise-related construction projects coordinated or directed by the JCS outside the U.S. are limited to unspecified minor construction accounts of the Military Departments. Furthermore, Congress has limited the authority for exercise-related construction to no more than $5 million per Department per fiscal year. 10 U.S.C. § 2805(c)(2). Currently,

Funding

Congress funds exercise-related construction as part of the Military Construction, Defense Agencies, appropriation.

3. DOD's interpretation excludes from the definition of exercise-related construction only truly temporary structures, such as tent platforms, field latrines, shelters, and range targets that are removed completely once the exercise is completed. DOD funds the construction of these temporary structures with O&M appropriations.

G. **Combat and Contingency-Related O&M-Funded Construction.** Within the last decade, significant interaction between the executive branch and the Congress has occurred regarding construction in support of combat operations. The executive branch believes it may use O&M funding for construction in support of combat operations of military forces. See Under Secretary of Defense (Comptroller)'s 27 February 2003 policy memorandum and the 22 February 2000 Deputy General Counsel (Ethics & Fiscal), Department of the Army Memorandum. The Congress, in a Conference Report for the Emergency Wartime Supplemental Appropriation for the Fiscal Year 2003, Pub. L. No. 108-11, 117 Stat. 587 (2003) took a different tack. The conference report stated, in rather harsh language, the conferees' legal objections to the position of DOD. While there are some open questions about the powers of Congress vs. the powers of the President as Commander in Chief of the Armed Forces, government attorneys should refer to current guidance from the Department of Defense.

XII. CONCLUSION.

The law of federal appropriations is another very specialized area of the law, primarily of interest to the executive and legislative branches of government. Its importance to federal contracting is obvious; if the agency does not have an appropriation available, it cannot award a contract or easily pay the contractor should it perform work. Many of the terms and conditions in a federal contract are driven by requirements in the law of federal appropriations, or to ease the government's compliance with those requirements.

Fortunately, the GAO has a comprehensive publication to reference, and The Judge Advocate General's School – U.S. Army has a useful work targeted at agency lawyers and excellent CLE courses for agency lawyers. Industry attorneys who have not had the benefit of government training should seek to attend similar training from commercial vendors to better acquaint themselves with the concepts, and download the latest versions of the GAO and TJAGSA publications.

COMPETITION

I. INTRODUCTION.

A. Competition Promotes the Public Interest.

"As every individual, therefore, endeavors as much he can both to employ his capital in the support of domestic industry, and so to direct that industry that its produce may be of the greatest value; every individual necessarily labors to render the annual revenue of the society as great as he can. He generally, indeed, neither intends to promote the public interest, nor knows how much he is promoting it. By preferring the support of domestic to that of foreign industry, he intends only his own security; and by directing that industry in such a manner as its produce may be of the greatest value, he intends only his own gain, and he is in this, as in many other cases, led by an invisible hand to promote an end which was no part of his intention." Adam Smith, *The Wealth of Nations* (ed. Edwin Canaan, University of Chicago Press, 1976), p. 477.

B. Competition Yields Value.

A competitive procurement process produces the best value for the government – it enables agencies to acquire high-quality goods and services with the most favorable contract terms for the best possible price. See generally Professor Steven L. Schooner, *Desiderata: Objectives for a System of Government Contract Law*, 11 PUBLIC PROCUREMENT LAW REVIEW 103 (2002) (found at: http://scholarship.law.gwu.edu/cgi/viewcontent.cgi?article=1101&context=faculty_publications) (discussing competition as an overarching principle of government procurement).

C. Federal Policies.

Competition is the tool used in federal contracting to achieve several policy goals. First, of course, is statutory compliance, since Congress has in several places mandated that agencies obtain the maximum practical competition when acquiring goods and services by following competitive procedures. Second, economic competition usually results in the best value to the government when the government acquires goods and services. Third, transparent competitive procedures discourage corrupt practices on the part of contractors and government officials. Fourth, competitive procedures give bidders the confidence necessary to justify the large investments in competing for some projects. Finally, competition provides the taxpayer with confidence that its tax dollars have been wisely used.

Competition is encouraged through compliance with procedures designed to favor competitive acquisitions. These procedures include pre-solicitation contacts with industry, publication of pending solicitations, requiring documentation and publication of justifications for restricting competition, publicizing contract awards, and providing independent review of complaints by disappointed bidders. Additionally, competition is encouraged by the broad acceptance by the acquisition workforce that competition is the best way to obtain quality goods and services at fair and reasonable prices.

The benefits of competition, however, come at a cost. Competitive acquisitions can take more time and resources, provide increased opportunities for errors and time-consuming reviews, and may not result in award to a preferred source.

This chapter focuses on the procedural requirements for maximizing competition. Compliance with the procedural requirements, along with taking practical measures to encourage competition, will provide an agency the full benefits from competitive acquisitions.

Competition

II. COMPETITION REQUIREMENTS.

A. **The Competition in Contracting Act of 1984.** Pub. L. No. 98-369, Title VII, § 2701, 98 Stat. 1175 (July 18, 1984) [hereinafter CICA].

1. Statutory Objectives. In 1984, the Congress enacted the Competition in Contracting Act to increase the percentage of acquisitions that were conducted competitively. Congress believed that agencies were conducting too many non-competitive acquisitions with poor results. The Congress decided to promote economy, efficiency, and effectiveness in the procurement of supplies and services by requiring agencies to conduct acquisitions on the basis of full and open competition to the maximum extent practicable. CICA defined the procedures that Congress thought would encourage competition, and harmonized the procedures applicable to defense and civilian agencies. CICA implemented measures to discourage non-competitive acquisitions.

2. While the Senate originally proposed a marketplace standard of "effective competition" (whereby two or more contractors acting independent of each other, and the government, submit bids or proposals), Congress ultimately adopted the "full and open competition" requirement. H.R. Rep. No. 98-369, at 1421, reprinted in 1984 U.S.C.C.A.N. (98 Stat.) 2109-2110. The standard chosen emphasizes following procedures rather than trying to judge whether the government obtained two or more proposals from independent offerors.

3. The Competition Pendulum. Following competitive procedures comes at a cost in time and resources. Congress has periodically revisited the statutory requirements in an effort to strike a balance between efficient, commercial-like contracting procedures and without losing the benefits of full and open competition. In the 1990s, Congress reduced the procedures required for certain acquisition methods and contract types, to include raising the threshold for using simplified acquisition procedures, reduced requirements when acquiring commercial items, and easing the resources required when obtaining competition through indefinite delivery contracts. These adjustments were implemented through the Federal Acquisition Streamlining Act of 1994, Pub. L. No. 103355, 108 Stat. 3243 (1994) [hereinafter FASA]; and the Federal Acquisition Reform (Clinger-Cohen) Act of 1996, Pub. L. No. 104106, §§ 4001-4402, 110 Stat. 186,642-79 (1996) [hereinafter FARA]. More recently, Congress has retreated from the loosening particularly for indefinite delivery contracting. See, e.g., National Defense Authorization Act for Fiscal Year 2008, Pub. L. No. 110-181, § 843, 122 Stat. 3,236-39 (2008). Notwithstanding these pendulum swings, the policy favoring full and open competition to the maximum extent practicable remains unchanged.

4. Summary of Changes.

   • CICA eliminated the statutory preference for use of sealed bidding procedures, recognizing that competitive negotiation procedures are equally capable of achieving economic competition. It also recognized other procedures, such as Broad Agency Announcements, as full and open competition.

- CICA required agencies to publicize procurement actions by publishing or posting procurement notices.
- CICA required agencies to appoint competition advocates to promote competition and challenge barriers to competition.
- CICA required agencies to draft justifications and obtain management approval to use other than full and open competition. Later amendments required publication of these Justifications and Approvals (J&As).

B.   Levels of Competition.

1.   CICA pursues competition by requiring use of competitive procedures to the maximum extent practicable.

2.   Congress categorized competitive procedures in three levels.

   a.   Full and Open Competition. Procedures affording responsible contractors the opportunity to submit responsive bids. This includes acquisitions conducted using: 1) sealed bidding procedures in FAR Part 14; competitive negotiation procedures in FAR Part 15; Broad Agency Announcement procedures for basic and applied research per FAR 35.016; and architect-engineer contract procedures under 40 U.S.C. § 1102 and FAR Subpart 36.6.

   b.   Full and Open Competition After Exclusion of Sources. Procedures affording most, but not all, responsible contractors the opportunity to submit proposals. Specific contractors are excluded, for example, when contracting to develop additional competitive sources.

   c.   Other Than Full and Open Competition. These include both sole source and limited source acquisitions.

3.   By focusing on the procedures used, Congress created a system by which an acquisition could be considered "Full and Open Competition" even though only one bid was received for the goods and services. Similarly, an acquisition with multiple, vigorous competitors could be classified as "Other than Full and Open Competition" and indistinguishable from a sole source award.

4.   Regardless of which type of procedures are used, agencies must achieve competition to the maximum extent practicable.

C.   FAR Competition Requirements.

1.   FAR Part 5 sets forth the requirements for publicizing contract actions to seek competition. FAR Part 6 sets forth many of the procedural requirements intended to achieve competition, principally those procedures required to justify not obtaining full and open competition. FAR Parts 13, 14, 15, 35., etc. describe specific procedures to conduct competitions.

2.   Summary of Requirements.

   a.   Publication. FAR Part 5 regulates the statutory requirements for publicizing solicitations, awards, sources sought, and other contract actions.

   b.   Waiting Periods. FAR Part 5 also regulates minimum time periods between publication and dates for receiving proposals, etc.

   c.   J&As. FAR Part 6 requires justifying sole source awards and limited source competitions, and approvals of sole source awards and limited source competitions.

   d.   Non-competitive Practices. Limitations on non-competitive requirements.

Competition

D. **Full and Open Competition Defined.** 10 U.S.C. § 2304(a)(1); 41 U.S.C. § 3301(a)(1); FAR Subpart 6.1.

1. Definition. 41 U.S.C. § 107 and FAR 2.101.

   a. "Full and open competition" refers to a contract action in which all responsible sources are permitted to compete.

   b. Full and open competition may not actually achieve competition. The standard is that interested parties are afforded the opportunity to submit bids or proposals – agencies are not required to receive more than one bid or proposal.

2. Policy. FAR 6.101.

   a. Contracting officers must promote full and open competition by using competitive procedures to solicit offers and award contracts <u>unless</u> they can justify using full and open competition after exclusion of sources (FAR Subpart 6.2), or other than full and open competition (FAR Subpart 6.3).

   b. Contracting officers must use the competitive procedure that is best suited to the particular contract action.

3. Examples of competitive procedures that promote full and open competition include:

   a. Sealed bidding. FAR Part 14.

   b. Contracting by negotiation. FAR Part 15.

   c. Combinations (e.g., two-step sealed bidding). FAR Part 14.5.

4. Eliminating Unfair Competitive Advantages. Competition must be conducted on an equal basis. <u>The Eloret Corp.</u>, B-402696.2, Jul. 16, 2010, 2010 CPD ¶ 182 (stating a fundamental principle of government procurement is that competitions are held on an equal basis. Offerors are treated equally and are provided a common basis to prepare proposals.). An "unfair competitive advantage" including those arising from organizational conflicts of interest are addressed in Chapter 10, Section II.

E. **Full and Open Competition After Exclusion of Sources Defined.** 10 U.S.C. § 2304(b); 41 U.S.C. § 3303; FAR Subpart 6.2; DFARS Subpart 206.2.

1. Policy. FAR 6.201.

   a. Under <u>limited</u> circumstances, a contracting officer may exclude one or more sources from a particular contract action.

   b. After excluding these sources, a contracting officer must use competitive procedures that promote full and open competition.

2. A contracting officer may generally exclude one or more sources under two circumstances.

   a. Establishing or maintaining alternative sources for supplies or services. FAR 6.202; DFARS 206.202. Restricting sources on this basis is relatively uncommon.

      (1) The agency head must determine that the exclusion of one or more sources will serve one of six purposes.

      (a) Increase or maintain competition <u>and</u> probably result in reduced overall costs.

      (b) Enhance national defense by ensuring that facilities, producers, manufacturers, or suppliers are available to furnish necessary supplies and services in the event of a national emergency or industrial mobilization. <u>Hawker Eternacell, Inc.</u>, B-283586, 1999

U.S. Comp. Gen. LEXIS 202 (Nov. 23, 1999); <u>Right Away Foods Corp.</u>, B-219676.2, B-219676.3, Feb. 25, 1986, 86-1 CPD ¶ 192; <u>Martin Elecs. Inc.</u>, B-219803, Nov. 1, 1985, 85-2 CPD ¶ 504.

(c) Enhance national defense by ensuring that educational institutions, nonprofit institutions, or federally funded research and development centers will establish and maintain essential engineering, research, and development capabilities.

(d) Ensure the continuous availability of a reliable source of supply.

(e) Satisfy projected needs based on historical demand.

(f) Satisfy a critical need for medical, safety, or emergency supplies.

(2) The agency head must support the decision to exclude one or more sources with written determinations and findings (D&F). <u>See generally</u> FAR Subpart 1.7; <u>see also</u> DFARS 206.202 (providing sample format and listing required contents).

(a) The agency head or his designee must sign the D&F.

(b) The agency head <u>cannot</u> create a blanket D&F for similar classes of procurements.

b. Set-asides for small businesses. FAR 6.203; DFARS 206.203. These acquisitions exclude large businesses, and in some instances, many small businesses for the purpose of giving the favored group a better opportunity to compete.

(1) A contracting officer may limit competition to small business concerns to satisfy statutory or regulatory requirements. <u>See</u> FAR Subpart 19.5.

(2) The contracting officer is <u>not</u> required to support the determination to set aside a contract action with a separate written justification or D&F.

(3) Competition under FAR 6.203 cannot be restricted to only certain small businesses. <u>Department of the Army Request for Modification of Recommendation</u>, Comp. Gen. B-290682.2, Jan. 9, 2003, 2003 CPD ¶ 23 (CICA allows for the exclusion of non-small business concerns to further the Small Business Act, but it still requires "competitive procedures" for small business set-asides. Such procedures must allow all responsible eligible business concerns [i.e., small business concerns] to submit offers.).

(4) Set-asides include:

- FAR 6.204—Set-asides for Section 8(a) competitions;
- FAR 6.205—Set-asides for HUBZone small business concerns;
- FAR 6.206—Set-asides for service-disabled veteran-owned small business concerns;
- FAR 6.207—Set-asides for Economically Disadvantaged Women-owned Small Business (EDWOSB) Concerns or Women-owned Small Business (WOSB) Concerns Eligible under the WOSB Program.
- FAR 6.208—Set-asides for local firms during a major disaster or emergency.

F. **Other Than Full and Open Competition Defined.** 10 U.S.C. § 2304(c); 41 U.S.C. § 3304; FAR Subpart 6.3; DFARS Subpart 206.3; AFARS Subpart 6.3.

1. Acquisitions not addressed in Sections D and E, above, are "Other Than Full and Open Competition." This classification includes both sole source awards, awards following vigorous competition between a limited number of sources, and everything in between.

2. Policy. FAR 6.301.

   a. Executive agencies <u>cannot</u> contract without providing for full and open competition <u>unless</u> one of the statutory exceptions listed in FAR 6.302 applies. Agencies may not restrict their competition to just a few sources without following J&A procedures citing an applicable statutory exception.

   b. Lack of Planning. Agencies <u>cannot</u> justify contracting without providing for full and open competition based on a lack of advance planning. 10 U.S.C. § 2304(f)(5)(A); FAR 6.301(c)(1); <u>RBC Bearings, Inc.</u>, Comp. Gen. B401661, Oct. 27, 2009, 2009 CPD ¶ 207 (finding Army's failure to qualify a source for 10 years amply established a failure to conduct adequate and reasonable advance planning); <u>VSE Corp.</u>, Comp. Gen. B-290452.3, May 23, 2005, 2005 CPD ¶ 103 (disapproving award of sole source bridge contract in part due to agency's failure to conduct advance planning); <u>Worldwide Language Resources, Inc.</u>, Comp. Gen. B-296984, Nov. 14, 2005, 2005 CPD ¶ 206 (determining that a justification and approval for sole source award of bilingual/bicultural advisors contract revealed lack of advance planning and not unusual and compelling circumstances).

   c. Advance planning must be reasonable, not completely error-free. <u>Pegasus</u>

<u>Global Strategic Solutions, LLC</u>, Comp. Gen. B 400422.3, Mar. 24, 2009, 2009 CPD ¶ 73 (upholding sole source based on unusual and compelling urgency notwithstanding errors in agency planning); <u>Bannum, Inc.</u>, Comp. Gen. B289707, Mar. 14, 2002, 2002 CPD ¶ 61 (finding that while the agency's planning ultimately was unsuccessful, this was due to unanticipated events, not a lack of planning); <u>Diversified Tech. & Servs. of Virginia, Inc.</u>, B-282497, July 19, 1999, 99-2 CPD ¶ 16 (refusing to fault the Department of Agriculture where the procurement was delayed by the agency's efforts to implement a long range acquisition plan).

   d. To avoid a finding of "lack of advance planning," agencies must make reasonable efforts to obtain competition. <u>Heros, Inc.</u>, Comp. Gen. B-292043, June 9, 2003, 2003 CPD ¶ 111 (Agencies "must act affirmatively to obtain and safeguard competition; they cannot take a passive approach and remain in a sole source situation when they could reasonably take steps to enhance competition."). See also <u>Raytheon Co. - Integrated Defense Sys.</u>, Comp. Gen. B-400610, Dec. 22, 2008, 2009 CPD ¶ 8 (finding Navy's follow-on, sole source award of three contracts to modernize automated portions of the Aegis Combat System and make the software commercial-off-the-shelf (COTS) compatible promoted competition and did not constitute a lack of advance planning).

3. Agencies cannot justify contracting using other than full and open competitive procedures due to concerns regarding the availability of funds. 10 U.S.C. § 2304(f)(5)(A); FAR 6.301(c)(2). Cf. <u>AAI ACL Tech., Inc.</u>, B-258679.4, Nov. 28, 1995, 95-2 CPD ¶ 243 (distinguishing the expiration of funds from the unavailability of funds).

4. The contracting officer must solicit offers from as many potential sources as is practicable under the circumstances. See Kahn Indus., Inc., B-251777, May 3, 1993, 93-1 CPD ¶ 356 (holding that it was unreasonable to deliberately exclude a known source simply because other agency personnel failed to provide the source's telephone number).

5. Justifying Use of Other Than Full and Open Competitive Procedures. There are seven statutory exceptions to the requirement to provide for full and open competition.

   a. Only One Responsible Source and No Other Supplies or Services Will Satisfy Agency Requirements. 10 U.S.C. § 2304(c)(1); 41 U.S.C. § 3304(a)(1); FAR 6.302-1; DFARS 206.302-1; AFARS 6.302-1. This is (usually) a sole source or a limited number of sources that do not provide adequate competition. The two factual elements are:

      (1) There is only one or a limited number of responsible sources; and

      (2) No other supplies or services will satisfy the agency's requirements.

   b. Unusual or Compelling Urgency. 10 U.S.C. § 2304(c)(2); 41 U.S.C. § 3304(a)(2); FAR 6.302-2; DFARS 206.302-2; AFARS 6.302-2. These are classic emergency situations, such as disaster response, or urgent military needs. An agency is not required to provide for full and open competition if:

      (1) Its needs are of unusual and compelling urgency; and

      (2) The government will be seriously injured unless the agency can limit the number of sources from which it solicits offers.

      (a) Examples include:

      - Supplies, services, or construction needed at once because of fire, flood, explosion, or other disaster.
      - Essential equipment or repair needed at once to— (A) Comply with orders for a ship; (B) Perform the operational mission of an aircraft; or (C) Preclude impairment of launch capabilities or mission performance of missiles or missile support equipment.
      - Construction needed at once to preserve a structure or its contents from damage.

Smith and Wesson, Inc., B-400479, Nov., 20, 2008, 2008 CPD ¶ 215 (upholding the rationality of the agency's decision to purchase Glock firearms for the Pakistani military as the Pakistanis already had a logistics system to support the weapons and supporting a new firearm would be overly burdensome); Cubic Defense Sys., Inc. v. United States, 45 Fed. Cl. 239 (1999); Metric Sys. Corp. v. United States, 42 Fed. Cl. 306 (1998); Datacom, Inc., Comp. Gen. B-274175., Nov. 25, 1996, 96-2 CPD ¶ 199; but see Lockheed Martin Sys. Integration—Owego, Comp. Gen. B-287190.2, May 25, 2001, 2001 CPD ¶ 110 (when an agency relies on this exception, the agency must give other sources "notice of its intentions, and an opportunity to respond to the agency's requirements." The agency must "adequately apprise" prospective sources of its needs so that those sources have a "meaningful opportunity to demonstrate their ability" to satisfy the agency's needs. When the agency gave "misleading guidance" which prejudiced the protestor, GAO invalidated the sole source award); National Aerospace Group, Inc., Comp. Gen. B-282843, Aug. 30, 1999, 99-2 CPD ¶ 43 (sustaining protest where the Defense

Competition

Logistics Agency's documentation failed to show that only the specific product would satisfy the agency's need).

    c.   Industrial Mobilization, Engineering, Developmental, or Research Capability, Expert Services. 10 U.S.C. § 2304(c)(3); 41 U.S.C. § 3304(a)(3)(A); FAR 6.302-3; AFARS 6.302-3. An agency may justify limited competitions and sole source awards to preserve critical industrial and scientific capabilities. An agency is not required to provide for full and open competition if it must limit competition to:

        (1)   Maintain facilities, producers, manufacturers, or suppliers to furnish supplies or services in the event of a national emergency or industrial mobilization. Greenbrier Indus., B-248177, Aug. 5, 1992, 92-2 CPD ¶ 74. Cf. Outdoor Venture Corp., B-279777, July 17, 1998, 98-2 CPD ¶ 2 (permitting the DLA to exercise an option for tents at a lower price because it awarded the initial contract on a sole-source basis to an industrial mobilization base producer).

        (2)   Ensure that educational institutions, nonprofit institutions, or federally funded research and development centers will establish and maintain essential engineering, research, and development capabilities.

        (3)   Acquire the services of an expert for litigation. See SEMCOR, Inc.; HJ Ford Assocs. Inc., B-279794, B-279794.2, B-279794.3, July 23, 1998, 98-2 CPD ¶ 43 (defining "expert").

    d.   International Agreement. 10 U.S.C. § 2304(c)(4); 41 U.S.C. § 3304(a)(4); FAR 6.302-4. An agency is not required to provide for full and open competition if it is precluded by:

        (1)   An international agreement or treaty (e.g., a status of forces agreement (SOFA)); or

        (2)   The written direction of a foreign government that will reimburse the agency for its acquisition costs (e.g., pursuant to a foreign military sales agreement). See Electro Design Mfg., Inc., B-280953, Dec. 11, 1998, 98-2 CPD ¶ 142 (upholding agency's decision to combine system requirements into single procurement at foreign customer's request); Goddard Indus., Inc., B-275643, Mar. 11, 1997, 97-1 CPD ¶ 104; Pilkington Aerospace, Inc., B-260397, June 19, 1995, 95-2 CPD ¶ 122.

    e.   Authorized or required by statute. 10 U.S.C. § 2304(c)(5); 41 U.S.C. § 3304(a)(5); FAR 6.302-5; DFARS 206.302-5. An agency is not required to provide for full and open competition if:

        (1)   A statute authorizes or requires the agency to procure the supplies or services from a specified source.[1] See, e.g., 18 U.S.C. §§ 4121-4128; 41 U.S.C. §§ 8501-8506; FAR Subpart 8.6 (acquisitions from Federal Prison Industries, Inc.); FAR Subpart 8.7 (acquisitions from

---

[1] DFARS 206.302-5 generally permits agencies to use this authority to acquire: (1) supplies and services from military exchange stores outside the United States for use by armed forces stationed outside the United States pursuant to 10 U.S.C. § 2424(a); and (2) police, fire protection, airfield operation, or other community services from local governments at certain military installations that are being closed. However, DFARS 206.302-5 also limits the ability of agencies to use this authority to award certain research and development contracts to colleges and universities. See 10 U.S.C. § 2424(b) (limiting the authority granted by 10 U.S.C. § 2424(a)).

nonprofit agencies employing people who are blind or severely disabled); see also JAFIT Enter., Inc., B-266326, Feb. 5, 1996, 96-1 CPD ¶ 39.

(2)   The agency needs a brand name commercial item for authorized resale. Defense Commissary Agency – Request for Advance Decision, B-262047, Feb. 26, 1996, 96-1 CPD ¶ 115.

f.   National Security. 10 U.S.C. § 2304(c)(6); 41 U.S.C. § 3304(a)(6); FAR 6.302-6. An agency is not required to provide for full and open competition if disclosure of the government's needs would compromise national security. However, the mere fact that an acquisition is classified, or requires contractors to access classified data to submit offers or perform the contract, does not justify limiting competition.

g.   Public Interest. 10 U.S.C. § 2304(c)(7); 41 U.S.C. § 3304(a)(7); FAR 6.302-7; DFARS 206.302-7. An agency is not required to provide for full and open competition if the agency head determines that full and open competition is not in the public interest.

(1)   The agency head (i.e., the Secretary of Defense for all defense agencies) must support the determination to use this authority with a written D&F.

(2)   The agency must notify Congress at least 30 days before contract award. Northrop Grumman Corp. v. United States, 46 Fed. Cl. 622 (2000) (holding that NASA's use of the public interest exception required Congressional notice, and not Congressional consent). See also Spherix, Inc. v. United States, 58 Fed. Cl. 351 (2003).

6.   Justifications and Approvals (J&As) for Other Than Full and Open Competition. FAR 6.303; FAR 6.304; DFARS 206.303; DFARS 206.304; AFARS 5106.303; AFARS 5106.304. Two helpful J&A Guides are: Air Force Guide to Developing and Processing Justification and Approval (J&A) Documents, *available at* http://www.safaq.hq.af.mil/contracting /toolkit/part06/word/5306-j-and-a.doc and Air Force Materiel Command Justification and Approval Preparation Guide and Template), *available at* https://www.afmc-mil.wpafb.af.mil/HQ-AFMC/PK/pkp/polvault/guides/jaguid e.doc.

a.   Basic Requirements. FAR 6.303-1(a); AFARS 6.303-1(a). The contracting officer must prepare a written justification, certify its accuracy and completeness, and obtain all required approvals before negotiating or awarding a contract using other than full and open competitive procedures.

(1)   Individual v. Class Justification. FAR 6.303-1(c); DFARS 206.303-1; AFARS 6.303-1(c). The contracting officer must prepare the justification on an individual basis for contracts awarded pursuant to the "public interest" exception (FAR 6.302-7). Otherwise, the contracting officer may prepare the justification on either an individual or class basis.

(2)   Ex Post Facto Justification. FAR 6.303-1(e); AFARS 6.303-1(e). The contracting officer may prepare the written

justification within a reasonable time <u>after</u> contract award <u>if</u>:[2]

(a) The contract is awarded pursuant to the "unusual and compelling urgency" exception (FAR 6.302-2); <u>and</u>

(b) Preparing the written justification before award would unreasonably delay the acquisition.

(3) Requirement to Amend the Justification. AFARS 6.303-1-90. The contracting officer must prepare an amended J&A if:

(a) An increase in the estimated dollar value of the contract causes the agency to exceed the approval authority of the previous approval official;

(b) A change in the agency's competitive strategy reduces competition; or

(c) A change in the agency's requirements affects the basis for the justification.

b. Contents. FAR 6.303-2; DFARS 206.303-2; AFARS 6.303-2.

(1) Format. AFARS 53.9005.[3]

(2) The J&A should be a stand-alone document. DFARS 206.303-2. <u>Sabreliner Corp.</u>, B-288030, Sep. 13, 2001, 2001 Comp. Gen. LEXIS 154 (inaccuracies and inconsistencies in the J & A and between the J & A and other documentation invalidated the sole source award).

(a) Each justification must contain sufficient information to justify the use of the cited exception. FAR 6.303-2(a).

(b) The J&A must document and adequately address all relevant issues.

(3) At a minimum, the justification must:

(a) Identify the agency, contracting activity, and document;

(b) Describe the action being approved;[4]

(c) Describe the required supplies or services and state their estimated value;

(d) Identify the applicable statutory exception;

(e) Demonstrate why the proposed contractor's unique qualifications and/or the nature of the acquisition requires the use of the cited exception;

(f) Describe the efforts made to solicit offers from as many potential sources as practicable;[5]

(g) Include a contracting officer's determination that the anticipated cost to the government will be fair and reasonable;

(h) Describe any market research conducted, or state why no market research was conducted;

(i) Include any other facts that justify the use of other than full

---

[2] If the contract exceeds $50,000,000, the agency must forward the justification to the approval authority within 30 working days of contract award. AFARS 5106.303-1(d).

[3] The format specified in AFARS 53.9005 is mandatory for contract actions greater than $50,000,000.

[4] The justification should identify the type of contract, type of funding, and estimated share/ceiling arrangements, if any. AFARS 53.9005.

[5] The justification should indicate: (1) whether the COMMERCE BUSINESS DAILY (CBD) notice was (will be) published; and, if not, (2) which exception under FAR 5.202 applies. FAR 6.303-2; AFARS 53.9005.

and open competitive procedures, such as:

(i) An explanation of why the government has not developed or made available technical data packages, specifications, engineering descriptions, statements of work, or purchase descriptions suitable for full and open competition, and a description of any planned remedial actions;

(ii) An estimate of any duplicative cost to the government and how the estimate was derived if the cited exception is the "sole source" exception (FAR 6.302-1);

(iii) Data, estimated costs, or other rationale to explain the nature and extent of the potential injury to the government if the cited exception is the "unusual and compelling urgency" exception (FAR 6.302-2).[6]

(j) List any sources that expressed an interest in the acquisition in writing;[7]

(k) State any actions the agency may take to remove or overcome barriers to competition for future acquisitions; and

(l) Include a certification that the justification is accurate and complete to the best of the contracting officer's knowledge and belief.

(4) Each justification must also include a certificate that any supporting data provided by technical or requirements personnel is accurate and complete to the best of their knowledge and belief. FAR 6.303-2(b).

c. Approval. FAR 6.304(a); DFARS 206.304; AFARS 6.304.

(1) The appropriate official must approve the justification in writing.

(2) Approving officials.

(a) The approval official for proposed contract actions not exceeding $500,000 is the contracting officer.

(b) The approval official for proposed contract actions greater than $500,000, but not exceeding $10,000,000, is normally the competition advocate.[8]

(c) The approval official for proposed contract actions greater than $10,000,000, but not exceeding $50,000,000 (most agencies) or $75,000,000 (DOD, NASA, Coast Guard) is the head of the contracting activity or his designee.[9]

---

[6] The justification should include a description of the procurement history and the government's plan to ensure that the prime contractor obtains as much competition as possible at the subcontractor level if the cited exception is the "sole source" section (FAR 6.302-1). AFARS 53.9005.

[7] If applicable, state: "To date, no other sources have written to express an interest." AFARS 53.9005. See Centre Mfg. Co., Inc., B-255347.2, Mar. 2, 1994, 94-1 CPD ¶ 162 (denying protest where agency's failure to list interested sources did not prejudice protester).

[8] A higher-level official can withhold approval authority. See FAR 6.304(a)(2).

[9] The designee must be a general officer, a flag officer, or a GS-16 or above. FAR 6.304(a)(3).

(d) The approval official for proposed contract actions greater than $50,000,000 (most agencies) or $75,000,000 (DOD, NASA, Coast Guard) is the agency's senior procurement executive.[10]

(3) The justification for a contract awarded pursuant to the "public interest" exception (FAR 6.302-7) is considered approved when the D&F is signed. FAR 6.304(b).

(4) The agency must determine the appropriate approval official for a class justification based on the total estimated value of the class. FAR 6.304(c).

(5) The agency must include the estimated dollar value of all options in determining the appropriate approval level. FAR 6.304(d).

III. IMPLEMENTATION OF COMPETITION REQUIREMENTS.

A. **Competition Advocates.** 41 U.S.C. § 1705; FAR Subpart 6.5; AFARS Subpart 6.5; AR 715-31, Army Competition Advocacy Program; AFI 63-301, Air Force Competition Advocacy.

1. Requirement. FAR 6.501; AFARS 6.501. The head of each agency must designate a competition advocate for the agency itself, and for each procuring activity within the agency.[11] The designated officer or employee must:

   a. Not be the agency's senior procurement executive;

   b. Not be assigned duties or responsibilities that are inconsistent with the duties and responsibilities of a competition advocate; and

   c. Be provided with whatever staff or assistance is necessary to carry out the duties and responsibilities of a competition advocate (e.g., specialists in engineering, technical operations, contract administration, financial management, supply management, and utilization of small and small disadvantaged business concerns).

2. Duties and Responsibilities. FAR 6.502. Competition advocates must generally challenge barriers to and promote the acquisition of commercial items and the use of full and open competitive procedures. For example, competition advocates must challenge unnecessarily restrictive statements of work, unnecessarily detailed specifications, and unnecessarily burdensome contract clauses.

   a. Agency Competition Advocates. FAR 6.502(b). Agency competition advocates must:

      (1) Review the agency's contracting operations and identify conditions or actions that unnecessarily restrict the acquisition of commercial items and the use of full and open competitive procedures;

---

[10] The approval authority within DOD is the Under Secretary of Defense (Acquisition & Technology); however, the Under Secretary may delegate this authority to: (1) an Assistant Secretary of Defense; or (2) a general officer, flag officer, or civilian employee at least equivalent to a major general. DFARS 206.304.

[11] The ASA (ALT) appoints the Army Competition Advocate General. The Deputy Assistant Secretary of the Army for Procurement (SAAL-ZP) is the Army Competition Advocate General (ACAG). AFARS 6.501.

(2)   Prepare and submit an annual report to the agency senior procurement executive; and

(3)   Recommend goals and plans for increasing competition.

b.   Special Competition Advocates. AFARS 6.502; AR 715-31, para. 1.13. Special competition advocates oversee Major Army Command/Major Subordinate Command (MACOM/MSC) Competition Advocacy Programs. Their duties include, but are not necessarily limited to, the duties set forth in FAR 6.502 and AFARS 6.502.

c.   Local Competition Advocates. AR 715-31, para. 1.14. Local competition advocates oversee Competition Advocacy Programs below the MACOM/MSC level for contracts less than $100,000.

3.   A competition advocate's "review" of an agency's procurement is not a substitute for normal bid protest procedures. See Allied-Signal, Inc., B-243555, May 14, 1991, 91-1 CPD ¶ 468 (holding that a contractor's decision to pursue its protest with the agency's competition advocate did not toll the bid protest timeliness requirements). But see Liebert Corp., B-232234.5, Apr. 29, 1991, 91-1 CPD ¶ 413 (holding that a contractor's reasonable reliance on the competition advocate's representations may extend the time for filing a bid protest).

B.   **Acquisition Planning.** 10 U.S.C. § 2305; 10 U.S.C. § 2377; 41 U.S.C. § 3306; FAR Part 7; DFARS Subpart 207.

1.   Definition. FAR 2.101. "Acquisition planning" is the process of coordinating and integrating the efforts of the agency's acquisition personnel through a comprehensive plan that provides an overall strategy for managing the acquisition and fulfilling the agency's need in a timely and cost-effective manner.

2.   Policy. FAR 7.102(a). Agencies must perform acquisition planning and conduct market research for all acquisitions to promote:

a.   The acquisition of commercial or nondevelopmental items to the maximum extent practicable (10 U.S.C. § 2377; 41 U.S.C. § 3307); and

b.   Full and open competition (or competition to the maximum extent practicable) (10 U.S.C. § 2305(a)(1)(A); 41 U.S.C. § 3301.

3.   Timing. FAR 7.104.

a.   Acquisition planning should begin as soon as the agency identifies its needs.

b.   Agency personnel should avoid issuing requirements on an urgent basis, or with unrealistic delivery or performance schedules.

4.   Written Acquisition Plans. FAR 7.105.

a.   Written acquisition plans are not required for every acquisition.

b.   DFARS 207.103(d)(i) requires a written acquisition plan for:

(1)   Development acquisitions with a total estimated cost of $5,000,000 or more;

(2)   Production and service acquisitions with a total estimated cost of $15,000,000 or more for any fiscal year, or $30,000,000 or more for the entire contract period (including options); and

(3)   Other acquisitions that the agency considers appropriate.

c.   Contents. FAR 7.105. The specific contents of a written acquisition plan will vary; however, it must identify decision milestones and address all the technical, business, management, and other significant considerations that will control the acquisition.

C. **Market Research.** 10 U.S.C. § 2305; 10 U.S.C. § 2377; 41 U.S.C. § 3307(d); FAR Part 10.

1. Definition. FAR 2.101. "Market research" refers to the process of collecting and analyzing information about the ability of the market to satisfy the agency's needs.

2. Policy. FAR 10.001.

   a. Agencies must conduct market research "appropriate to the circumstances" before:

      (1) Developing new requirements documents;

      (2) Soliciting offers for acquisitions with an estimated value that exceeds the simplified acquisition threshold ($100,000); and

      (3) Soliciting offers for acquisitions with an estimated value of less than the simplified acquisition threshold if:

         (a) Adequate information is not available; and

         (b) The circumstances justify the cost; and

         (c) Before soliciting offers for acquisitions that could lead to a bundled contract (15 U.S.C. 644(e)(2)(A)).

   b. Agencies must use the results of market research to determine:

      (1) If sources exist to satisfy the agency's needs;

      (2) If commercial (or nondevelopmental) items are available that meet (or could be modified to meet) the agency's needs;

      (3) The extent to which commercial (or nondevelopmental) items can be incorporated at the component level; and

      (4) The practice(s) of firms engaged in producing, distributing, and supporting commercial items.

3. Procedures. FAR 10.002.

   a. The extent of market research will vary.

   b. Acceptable market research techniques include:

      (1) Contacting knowledgeable government and/or industry personnel;

      (2) Reviewing the results of market research for the same or similar supplies or services;

      (3) Publishing formal requests for information;

      (4) Querying government data bases;

      (5) Participating in interactive, on-line communications with government and/or industry personnel;

      (6) Obtaining source lists from other sources (e.g., contracting activities, trade associations, etc.);

      (7) Reviewing catalogs and other product literature;

      (8) Conducting interchange meetings; and/or

      (9) Holding pre-solicitation conferences with potential offerors.

D. Developing Specifications. 10 U.S.C. § 2305; 41 U.S.C. § 3306; FAR Part 11; DFARS Part 211.

1. Types of Specifications.

    a. Design specifications. Specifications that set forth precise measurements, tolerances, materials, in-process and finished product tests, quality control measures, inspection requirements, and other specific information. The Government Contracts Reference Book 185-86 (2d Ed. 1998).

    b. Performance specifications. Specifications that indicate what the final product must be capable of accomplishing rather than how the product is to be built. The Government Contracts Reference Book 394 (2d Ed. 1998)

    c. Purchase descriptions. A description of the essential physical characteristics and functions required to meet the government's requirements. The Government Contracts Reference Book 426 (2d Ed. 1998).

    d. Brand Name or Equal Purchase Description. Identifies a product by its brand name and model or part number . . . and permits offers on products essentially equal to the specified brand name. The Government Contracts Reference Book 67 (2d Ed. 1998).

    e. Mixed specifications.

2. Policy. Agencies are required to develop specifications that:

    a. Permit full and open competition;

    b. State the agency's minimum needs; and

    c. Include restrictive provisions or conditions only to the extent they satisfy the agency's needs or are required by law.

See Systems Management, Inc., Qualimetrics, Inc., Comp. Gen. B-287032.4; B-287032.4, Apr. 16, 2001, 2001 CPD ¶ 85 (the Air Force violated CICA when it "overstated its minimum needs in requiring" an FAA-certified weather observation system and then "either waived or relaxed this requirement" by awarding to a vendor whose system was not FAA-certified); CHE Consulting, Inc., B-284110 et al., Feb. 18, 2000, 2000 CPD ¶ 51 (holding that requiring offerors to obtain support agreements from 65% of the original equipment manufacturers satisfied a legitimate agency need and did not unduly restrict competition); American Eurocopter Corp., B-283700, Dec. 16, 1999, 99-2 CPD ¶ 110 (holding that requiring a certain model Bell helicopter was a reasonable agency restriction); Instrument Specialists, Inc., B-279714, July 14, 1998, 98-2 CPD ¶ 106 (holding that a mere disagreement with an agency requirement did not make it an unreasonable restriction); APTUS, Co., B-281289, Jan. 20. 1999, 99-1 CPD ¶ 40 (holding that so long as the specification was not unduly restrictive, the agency had the discretion to define its own requirements).

    d. Hot Issue. In FY 2002 alone, the Comptroller General heard nine protests alleging government specifications were "unduly restrictive" and thereby violated CICA. Recent GAO decisions include: C. Lawrence Constr. Co., Inc., B-290709, 2002 U.S. Comp. Gen. LEXIS 140 (Sept. 20, 2002); Vantex Serv. Corp., Comp. Gen. B-290415, Aug. 15, 2002, 2002 CPD ¶ 131; Military Agency Servs. Pty., Ltd, Comp. Gen. B-290414, B-290441, B-290468, B-290496, Aug. 1, 2002, 2002 CPD ¶ 130; Instrument Control Serv., Inc., Comp. Gen. B-289660, B-

289660.2, Apr. 15, 2002, 2002 CPD ¶ 66; Mark Dunning Industries, Inc., Comp. Gen. B-289378, Feb. 27, 2002, 2002 CPD ¶ 46; Flowlogic, Comp. Gen. B-289173, Jan. 22, 2002, 2002 CPD ¶ 22; Keystone Ship Berthing, Inc., Comp. Gen. B-289233, Jan. 10, 2002, 2002 CPD 19; C. Lawrence Constr. Co., Inc., Comp. Gen. B-289341, Jan. 8, 2002, 2002 CPD ¶ 17; Apex Support Servs., Inc., Comp. Gen. B-288936, B-288936.2, Dec. 12, 2001, 2001 CPD ¶ 202.

e. The trend continued in FY 2003. Again, the GAO heard nine protests alleging unduly restrictive specifications: Amer. Artisan Productions, Inc., Comp. Gen. B-292380, July 30, 2003, 2003 CPD ¶132; AirTrak Travel, Comp. Gen. B-292101, June 30, 2003, 2003 CPD ¶ 117; Prisoner Transport. Servs., LLC, Comp. Gen. B-292179, et al., June 27, 2003, 2003 CPD ¶ 121; EDP Enter., Inc., Comp. Gen. B-284533.6, May 19, 2003, 2003 CPD ¶ 93; Atl. Coast Contracting, Inc., Comp. Gen. B-291893, Apr. 24, 2003, 2003 CPD ¶ 87; MCI Worldcom Deutschland GmbH, Comp. Gen. B-291418, et. al., Jan. 2, 2003, 2003 CPD ¶ 1; USA Info. Sys., Inc., Comp. Gen. B-291417, Dec. 30, 2002, 2002 CPD ¶ 224; ABF Freight Sys., Inc., Comp. Gen. B-291185, Nov. 8, 2002, 2002 CPD ¶ 201; Dynamic Instruments, Inc., Comp. Gen. B-291071, Oct. 10, 2002, 2002 CPD ¶ 183.

f. In FY 2004 the Comptroller General considered only four protests alleging unduly restrictive government specifications in violation of the CICA. The GAO denied all four. See Teximara, Inc., Comp. Gen. B-293221.2, July 9, 2004, 2004 CPD ¶ 151; Reedsport Machine & Fabrication, Comp. Gen. B-293110.2, Apr. 13, 2004, 2004 CPD ¶ 91; Ocean Svs., LLC, Comp. Gen. B-2922511.2, Nov. 6, 2003, 2003 CPD ¶ 206; and NVT Technologies, Inc., Comp. Gen.

B-292302.3, Oct. 20, 2003, 2003 CPD ¶ 174.

3. Compliance with statutory and regulatory competition policy.

a. Specifications must provide a common basis for competition.

b. Competitors must be able to price the same requirement. See Deknatel Div., Pfizer Hosp. Prod. Grp., Inc., B-243408, July 29, 1991, 91-2 CPD ¶ 97 (finding that the agency violated the FAR by failing to provide the same specification to all offerors); see also Valenzuela Eng'g, Inc., B-277979, Jan. 26, 1998, 98-1 CPD ¶ 51 (chastising the Army because its "impermissibly broad" statement of work failed to give potential offerors reasonable notice of the scope of the proposed contract).

4. Common Pre-award Problems Relating to Specifications.

a. Brand Name or Equal Purchase Descriptions.

(1) While the use of performance specifications is preferred to encourage offerors to propose innovative solutions, the use of brand name or equal purchase descriptions may be advantageous under certain circumstances. FAR 11.104(a).

(2) Brand name or equal purchase descriptions must include, in addition to the brand name, a general description of those salient physical, functional, or performance characteristics of the brand name item that an "equal" item must meet to be acceptable for award. Use brand name or equal descriptions when the salient characteristics are firm requirements. FAR 11.104(b).

(3) Failure of a solicitation to list an item's salient characteristics improperly restricts competition by precluding potential offerors of equal products from determining what characteristics are considered essential for its item to be accepted, and cancellation of the solicitation is required. T-L-C Sys, B-227470, Sept. 21, 1987, 87-2 CPD ¶ 283. But see Micro Star Co., Inc., GSBCA No. 9649-P, 89-1 BCA ¶ 21,214 (holding that failing to list salient characteristics merely meant that the protester's bid could not be deemed nonresponsive for failure to meet that particular characteristic).

b. Items Peculiar to One Manufacturer. Agency requirements shall not be written so as to require a particular brand-name product, or a feature of a product, peculiar to one manufacturer, thereby precluding consideration of a product manufactured by another company, unless --

(1) The particular brand name, product, or feature is essential to the government's requirements, and market research indicates other companies' similar products, or products lacking the particular feature, do not meet, or cannot be modified to meet, the agency's needs;

(2) The authority to contract without providing for full and open competition is supported by the required justifications and approvals (see 6.302-1); and

(3) The basis for not providing for maximum practicable competition is documented in the file when the acquisition is awarded using simplified acquisition procedures. FAR 11.105.

c. Ambiguous Specifications.

(1) Specifications or purchase descriptions that are subject to two or more reasonable interpretations are ambiguous and require the amendment or cancellation of the solicitation. Arora Group, Inc., B-288127, Sep. 14, 2001, 2001 CPD ¶ 154; Flow Tech., Inc., B-228281, Dec. 29, 1987, 67 Comp. Gen. 161, 87-2 CPD ¶ 633. As a general rule, the contracting agency must give offerors sufficient detail in a solicitation to enable them to compete intelligently and on a relatively equal basis. There is no requirement that a competition be based on specifications drafted in such detail as to eliminate completely any risk or remove every uncertainty from the mind of every prospective offeror. RMS Indus., B-248678, Aug. 14, 1992, 92-2 CPD 109.

(2) Issues raised by ambiguous (defective) specifications:

(a) Adequacy of competition.

(b) Contract interpretation.

(c) Constructive change.

d. Unduly Restrictive Specifications.

(1) Specifications must promote full and open competition. Agencies may only include restrictive provisions to meet their minimum needs. 10 U.S.C § 2305(a)(1)(B); 41 U.S.C. § 3306(a)(2)(B). See Apex Support Services, Inc., B-288936, B-288936.2, Dec. 12, 2001, 2001 CPD 202 (unnecessary bonding

requirements); <u>CHE Consulting, Inc.</u>, B-284110 et al., Feb. 18, 2000, 2000 CPD ¶ 51; <u>Hoechst Marion Roussel, Inc.</u>, B-279073, May 4, 1998, 98-1 CPD ¶ 127 (holding that the VA's decision to restrict solicitation for Diltiazem to lower dosage strengths lacked any basis in the agency's needs); <u>Chadwick-Helmuth Co., Inc.</u>, B-279621.2, Aug. 17, 1998, 98-2 CPD ¶ 44 (holding that a requirement for a test instrument capable of operating existing program-specific software was unduly restrictive, where the requirement did not accurately reflect the agency's actual needs); <u>cf.</u> <u>Instrument Specialists, Inc.</u>, B-279714, 98-2 CPD ¶ 1 (holding that requirements for monthly service calls and a 15 working day turn-around time for off-site repairs of surgical instruments were not unduly restrictive); <u>Caswell Int'l Corp.</u>, B-278103, Dec. 29, 1997, 98-1 CPD ¶ 6 (holding that a requirement to obtain interoperable equipment to ensure operational safety and military readiness was reasonably related to the agency's needs); <u>Laidlaw Envtl</u>, B-272139, Sept. 6, 1996, 96-2 CPD ¶ 109 (holding that a prohibition against using open burn/open detonation technologies to demilitarize conventional munitions was unobjectionable where it reflected Congress's legitimate environmental concerns).

(2) Common examples of restrictive specifications:

(a) Specifications written around a specific product. <u>Ressler Assoc.</u>, B-244110, Sept. 9, 1991, 91-2 CPD ¶ 230.

(b) Geographical restrictions that limit competition to a single source and do not further a federal policy. <u>But see</u>, e.g., <u>Marlen C. Robb & Son Boatyard & Marina, Inc.</u>, B-256316, June 6, 1994, 94-1 CPD ¶ 351 (denying the protest and providing "an agency properly may restrict a procurement to offerors within a specified area if the restriction is reasonably necessary for the agency to meet its needs. The determination of the proper scope of a geographic restriction is a matter of the agency's judgment which we will review in order to assure that it has a reasonable basis."); <u>H & F Enters.</u>, B-251581.2, July 13, 1993, 93-2 CPD ¶ 16.

(c) Specifications that exceed the agency's minimum needs. <u>But see</u> <u>Trilectron Indus.</u>, B-248475, Aug. 27, 1992, 92-2 CPD ¶ 130 (denying protest and providing "determinations of the agency's minimum needs and the best method of accommodating those needs are primarily matters within the agency's discretion. Where, as here, a specification is challenged as unduly restrictive of competition, we will review the record to determine whether the restriction imposed is reasonably related to the agency's minimum needs."); <u>CardioMetrix</u>, B-248295, Aug. 14, 1992, 92-2 CPD ¶ 107.

(d) Requiring approval by a testing laboratory (e.g., Underwriters Laboratory (UL)) without recognizing equivalents. <u>HazStor Co.</u>, B-251248, Mar. 18, 1993, 93-1 CPD ¶ 242. <u>But see</u> <u>G.H. Harlow Co.</u>, B-254839, Jan 21, 1994, 94-1 CPD ¶ 29 (upholding requirement for approval by testing laboratory for fire alarm and computer-aided dispatch system).

   (e)   Improperly bundled specifications. <u>Vantex Serv. Corp.</u>, Comp. Gen. B-290415, Aug. 15, 2002, 2002 CPD ¶ 131; <u>EDP Enterprises, Inc.</u>, Comp. Gen. B-284533.6, May 19, 2003, 2003 CPD ¶ 93 (bundling food services, with the "unrelated base, vehicle and aircraft maintenance services," restricted competition; because the agency bundled the requirements for administrative convenience, the specification violated the CICA); <u>but see AirTrak Travel</u>, Comp. Gen. B-292101, June 30, 2003, 2003 CPD ¶ 117, and <u>USA Info. Sys., Inc.</u>, Comp. Gen. B-291417, Dec. 30, 2002, 2002 CPD ¶ 224 (in both decisions GAO denied allegations that bundled specifications violated CICA, because the agencies convinced GAO that mission-related reasons justified bundling requirements).

E.   Publicizing Contract Actions. 41 U.S.C. § 6101; FAR Part 5; DFARS Subpart 205.

1.   Policy. FAR 5.002. Publicizing contract actions increases competition. FAR 5.002(a). <u>But see Interproperty Investments, Inc.</u>, B-281600, Mar. 8, 1999, 99-1 CPD ¶ 55 (holding that an agency's diligent good-faith effort to comply with publicizing requirements was sufficient); <u>Aluminum Specialties, Inc. t/a Hercules Fence Co.</u>, B-281024, Nov. 20, 1998, 98-2 CPD ¶ 116 (holding that there was no requirement for the agency to exceed publicizing requirements, even if it had done so in the past).

2.   Methods of Disseminating Information. FAR 5.101.

   a.   FedBizOpps.gov. FAR 5.101(a)(1).

   (1)   Commerce Business Daily phased out in favor of FedBizOpps.gov.

In the past, synopses were posted in the Commerce Business Daily. Effective 1 October 2001, all agencies had to use one single electronic portal to publicize government-wide procurements greater than $25,000. Designated "FedBizOpps.gov," the web site is "the single point where government business opportunities greater than $25,000, including synopses of proposed contract actions, solicitations, and associated information, can be accessed electronically by the public." From 1 October 2001 till 1 January 2002, agencies posted their solicitations on FedBizOpps.gov and in the Commerce Business Daily (CBD). Beginning 1 January 2002, agencies no longer needed to post solicitations in the CBD, and now agencies may rely solely on the web site. Electronic Commerce in Federal Procurement, 66 Fed. Reg. 27,407 (May 16, 2001) (to be codified at 48 C.F.R. pts. 2, 4-7, 9, 12-14, 19, 22, 34-36).

   (2)   Contracting officers must synopsize proposed contract actions expected to exceed $25,000 in FedBizOpps.gov. <u>unless</u>:

   (a)   The contracting officer determines that one or more of the fourteen exceptions set forth in FAR 5.202 applies (e.g., national security, urgency, etc.).

   (b)   The head of the agency determines that advance notice is inappropriate or unreasonable.

(3)   Contracting officers must wait at least:

(a)   15 days after synopsizing the proposed contract action to issue the solicitation; and

(b)   if the proposed action is expected to exceed the simplified acquisition threshold, 30 days after issuing the solicitation to open bids or receive initial proposals. FAR 5.203.

(4)   Commercial Item Acquisitions

(a)   CO may establish a shorter period for issuance of the solicitation or use the combined synopsis and solicitation procedure. 5.203(a).

(b)   CO must establish a reasonable opportunity to respond (rather than the 30 days required for non-commercial items above the simplified acquisition threshold). FAR 5.203(b).

(5)   The decision not to synopsize a contract action must be proper when the solicitation is issued. American Kleaner Mfg. Co., B-243901.2, Sept. 10, 1991, 91-2 CPD ¶ 235.

(6)   If the agency fails to synopsize (or improperly synopsizes) a contract action, the agency may be required to cancel the solicitation. Sunrise Int'l Grp., B-252892.3, Sept. 14, 1993, 93-2 CPD ¶ 160; RII, B-251436, Mar. 10, 1993, 93-1 CPD ¶ 223. But see Kendall Healthcare Products Co., B-289381, February 19, 2002, 2002 Comp. Gen. LEXIS 23 (misclassifying procurement in CBD did not deny protestor opportunity to compete).

b.   Posting. FAR 5.101(a)(2).

(1)   Contracting officers must display proposed contract actions expected to fall between $10,000 and $25,000 in a public place.

(2)   The term "public place" includes electronic means of posting information, such as electronic bulletin boards.

(3)   Contracting officers must display proposed contract actions for 10 days or until bids/offers are opened, whichever is later, beginning no later than the date the agency issues the solicitation.

(4)   Contracting officers are not required to display proposed contract actions in a public place if the exceptions set forth in FAR 5.102(a)(1), (a)(4) through (a)(9), or (a)(11) apply, or the agency uses an oral or FACNET solicitation.

c.   Handouts, announcements, and paid advertising. FAR 5.101(b).

3.   Pre-solicitation Notices. FAR 14.205. A contracting officer may send pre-solicitation notices to concerns on the solicitation mailing list. The notice shall (a) specify the final date for receipt of requests for a complete bid set, (b) briefly describe the requirement and furnish other essential information to enable concerns to determine whether they have an interest in the invitation, and normally not include drawings, plans, and specifications.

4.   Solicitation Mailing Lists (Bidders Lists). Prior to 25 August 2003, the FAR required contracting officers to establish solicitation mailing lists to ensure access to adequate sources of supplies and services. The Civilian Agency Acquisition Council and

Defense Acquisition Regulations Council eliminated the Standard Form 129 (SF 129), Solicitation Mailing List effective 25 August 2003. The Central Contract Registry, "a centrally located, searchable database, accessible via the Internet," is a contracting officer's "tool of choice for developing, maintaining, and providing sources for future procurements." FedBizOpps.gov, "through its interested vendors list, has the capability to generate a list of vendors who are interested in a specific solicitation." Federal Acquisition Regulation; Elimination of the Standard Form 129, Solicitation Mailing List Application, 68 Fed. Reg. 43,855 (July 24, 2003). For solicitations that used Solicitation Mailing Lists (i.e., before 25 August 2003), the following rules apply:

a. Contracting officers may use different portions of large lists for separate acquisitions. However, contracting officers must generally solicit bids from:

    (1)   The incumbent. Kimber Guard & Patrol, Inc., B-248920, Oct. 1, 1992, 92-2 BCA ¶ 220. See Qualimetrics, Inc., B-262057, Nov. 16, 1995, 95-2 CPD ¶ 228 (concluding that GSA should have verified mailing list to ensure that incumbent's successor was on it). But see Cutter Lumber Products, B-262223.2, Feb. 9, 1996, 96-1 CPD ¶ 57 (holding that agency's inadvertent failure to solicit incumbent does not warrant sustaining protest where agency otherwise obtained full and open competition).

    (2)   Any contractor added to the list since the last solicitation.

Holiday Inn, Inc., B-249673-2, Dec. 22, 1992, 92-2 CPD ¶ 428.

    (3)   All contractors on the segment of the list designated by the contracting officer.

IV. EXCEPTIONS.

The provisions of FAR Part 6 do not apply to all procurement actions. FAR 6.001. Competition requirements for these types of procurements are set forth in the acquisition regulations which address them:

A. **Simplified Acquisitions**. FAR Part 13; American Eurocopter Corp., B-283700, Dec. 16, 1999, 99-2 CPD ¶ 110 (holding that the simplified acquisition of a Bell helicopter was exempt from the statutory requirement for full and open competition). But see L.A. Sys. v. Dep't of the Army, GSBCA No. 13472-P, 96-1 BCA ¶ 28,220 (holding that the Army improperly fragmented its requirements in order to use simplified acquisition procedures and avoid the requirement for full and open competition).

B. **Contracts Awarded Using Other Statutory Procedures**. See, e.g.:

1. 18 U.S.C. §§ 4121-4128 and FAR Subpart 8.6 (acquisitions from Federal Prison Industries, Inc.); and

2. 41 U.S.C. § 8504 and FAR Subpart 8.7 (acquisitions from nonprofit agencies employing people who are blind or severely disabled, such as NISH).

C. **In Scope Contract Modifications**. AT&T Communications, Inc. v. Wiltel, Inc., 1 F.3d 1201 (Fed. Cir. 1993) (holding that a modification adding T3 circuits was within the scope of a comprehensive contract for telecommunication services; reversing G.S.A. Board of Contract Appeals decision granting the protest); VMC Behavioral Healthcare Services v. U.S., 50 Fed. Cl. 328 (2001) (a modification which increased the number of employees on a services contract did not exceed the scope of the original contract when the original solicitation put potential bidders on notice that the number of employees to be covered could have been increased); Northrop Grumman Corp. v. U.S., 50 Fed. Cl. 443 (2001); Phoenix Air Group, Inc. v. U.S., 46 Fed. Cl. 90 (2000) (holding that a modification for flight training services was within the scope of the original contract despite different geographical area); Paragon Systems, Inc., B-284694.2, July 5, 2000, 2000 CPD ¶ 114. But see Makro Janitorial Svcs, Inc., B-282690, Aug. 18, 1999, 99-2 CPD ¶ 39 (holding that a task order for housekeeping services improperly exceeded the scope of a contract for preventive maintenance and inventory); Ervin and Assocs., Inc., B-278850, Mar. 23, 1998, 98-1 CPD ¶ 89 (holding that a task order to support HUD's Portfolio Reengineering/Mark-to-Market Demonstration Program was outside the scope of an accounting support services contract). Recent cases include: CESC Plaza LP v. United States, 52 Fed. Cl. 91 (2002); Northrop Grumman Corp. v. United States, 50 Fed. Cl. 443 (2001); HG Properties A, LP, Comp. Gen. B-290416, B-290416.2, July 25, 2002, 2002 CPD 128; Atlantic Coast Contracting, Inc., Comp. Gen. B-288969.4, June 21, 2002, 2002 CPD 104; Symetrics Industries, Inc., Comp. Gen. B-289606, Apr. 8, 2002, 2002 CPD 65; Engineering and Professional Servs., Inc., Comp. Gen. B-289331, Jan. 28, 2002, 2002 CPD 24; Specialty Marine, Comp. Gen. B-293871, B-293871.2, June 17, 2004, 2004 CPD 130; Information Ventures, Comp. Gen. B-293743, May 20, 2004, 2004 CPD 97; Firearms Training, Comp. Gen. B-292819.2, et al., Apr. 26, 2004, 2004 CPD 107; Computers Universal, Comp. Gen. B-293548, Apr. 9, 2004, 2004 CPD 78; Anteon Corp, Comp. Gen. B-293523, Mar. 29, 2004, 2004 CPD 51; CourtSmart Digital, Comp. Gen. B-292995.2, B-292995.3, Feb. 13, 2004, 2004 CPD 79.

D. Contract Orders Under Indefinite Delivery Contracts.

1. Orders placed under requirements contracts and indefinite delivery contracts. FAR 16.505(a)(1).

2. Orders placed under indefinite-quantity contracts entered into pursuant to FAR Part 6. Corel Corp., B-283862, Nov. 18, 1999, 99-2, CPD ¶ 90; Corel Corp. v. United States, Civil Action No. 99-3348, (D.D.C., Mem. Op. & Order filed Sept. 17, 2001), at http://www.dcd.uscourts.gov/99-3348.pdf. But see Electro-Voice, Inc., B-278319, B-278319.2, Jan. 15, 1998, 98-1 CPD ¶ 23 (holding that orders which implement a "downselect" that result in the elimination of a vendor to which a delivery order contract has been issued from consideration for future orders are not exempt from competition requirements).

3. Reprocurement Contracts. FAR 49.402-6.

   a. If the repurchase quantity is less than or equal to the terminated quantity, the contracting officer can use any acquisition method the contracting officer deems appropriate; however, the contracting officer must obtain competition to the maximum extent practicable.

   b. The GAO will review the reasonableness of an agency's acquisition method against the standard specified in FAR 49.402-6(b). See International Tech. Corp., B-250377.5, Aug. 18, 1993, 93-2 CPD ¶ 102 (recognizing that "the statutes and regulations governing regular procurements are not strictly applicable to reprocurements after a default").

   c. If there is a relatively short time between the original competition and the default, it is reasonable to award to the second or third lowest offeror of the original solicitation at its original price. Vereinigte Geb

Udereinigungsgesellschaft, B-280805, Nov. 23, 1998, 98-2 CPD ¶ 117 (holding that an agency could modify the contract requirements in its reprocurement without resolicitation); Performance Textiles, Inc., B-256895, Aug. 8, 1994, 94-2 CPD ¶ 65; DCX, Inc., B-232672, Jan. 23, 1989, 89-1 CPD ¶ 55.

d. If the repurchase quantity is greater than the terminated quantity, the contracting officer must treat the entire quantity as a new acquisition subject to the normal competition requirements.

e. Contracting officers have wide latitude to decide whether to solicit the defaulted contractor. Montage, Inc., B-277923.2, Dec. 29, 1997, 97-2 CPD ¶ 176; ATA Defense Indus., Inc., B-275303, Feb. 6, 1997, 97-1 CPD ¶ 61.

E. Exempt Agencies.

CICA and FAR Part 6 does not apply to all federal agencies. CICA does not apply to the U.S. Postal Service, United States v. Elec. Data Sys. Fed. Corp., 857 F.2d 1444, 1446 (Fed. Cir. 1988), or to the Federal Aviation Administration, 49 U.S.C. § 40110(d).

V. CONCLUSION.

Economic competition is the most effective tool for obtaining goods and services of high quality and at a low price. Federal statutes and regulations seek to achieve economic competition by requiring compliance with procedures, including: planning, publicizing, drafting fair specifications justifying use of non-competitive procedures, and obtaining higher-level approval.

Unfortunately, following required procedures can still result in little or no competition. Consequently, agency attorneys should learn the markets in which their agencies acquire goods and services, and encourage contracting officers to take discretionary actions that promote real competition. Only through a combination of compliance with procedures and removing barriers to competition will an agency obtain the full benefits of competition.

TYPES OF CONTRACTS

I. INTRODUCTION.

Contracts are categorized into various types, which are not mutually exclusive. A contract may be categorized by the pricing term, the goods or services acquired, the ordering mechanism, etc. The various types of contracts each have a set of standard terms and conditions that are (usually) included in the contract by reference. Thus, determining the contract type will lead you to the applicable terms and conditions. Terms and conditions allocate risk between the parties. See Figure 1.

In determining which type of contract was entered into by the parties, the court is not bound by the name or label given to a contract. Rather, it must look beyond the first page of the contract to determine what were the legal rights for which the parties bargained, and only then characterize the contract. Crown Laundry & Dry Cleaners, Inc. v. United States, 29 Fed. Cl. 506, 515 (1993).

Determining the type of contract is made more difficult by the common practice of combining contract types in a single procurement. For example, a contract may include cost reimbursement work and separate work that is firm fixed price. In theory, the separately priced work should be separated into different Contract Line Items ("CLINs" for Contract Line Item Numbers). However, the nature of some procurements makes separation difficult.

Contract lawyers must thoroughly understand the types of contracts for many reasons:

- Contract type(s) determine which standard clauses should be included in the contract, and which clauses apply to which CLIN. Many standard clauses have different provisions for different contract types. Additionally, attorneys must draft unique clauses consistent with the contract type selected.

- Selection of contract type is a key part of the government's acquisition strategy. Experience has taught that some contract types are not suitable for certain types of acquisitions. Selection of an appropriate contract type will contribute to a good outcome for an acquisition. Inappropriate contract types can motivate undesirable conduct by the parties. For government attorneys, statutes and regulations may limit the available types.

- Contract type impacts each party's contractual obligations. Knowing what the obligations are under all contract types allows attorneys to properly counsel their clients to comply with the contract. Misunderstanding of contract type leads to needless disputes.

II. CONTRACT TYPES - CATEGORIZED BY PRICE.

A. Fixed-Price Contracts. FAR Subpart 16.2.

A Fixed-Price contract is familiar to all because it is the type of contract most individuals agree to when acquiring goods and services. In a Fixed-Price contract, the contractor promises to deliver a product or perform a service at a fixed price, and bears the responsibility for increased costs of performance. ITT Arctic Servs., Inc. v. United States, 207 Ct. Cl. 743 (1975); Chevron U.S.A., Inc., ASBCA No. 32323, 90-1 BCA ¶ 22,602 (the risk of increased performance costs in a fixed-price contract is on the contractor absent a clause stating otherwise). Conversely, when a contractor has performed the specified task or delivered a conforming product, the government is obligated to pay the price, even if the work is not what the government realizes it now wants.

There are several Fixed-Price contract types. The principal distinction between the Fixed-Price contracts is the potential for price variation.

Contract Types

1. Fixed-Price Development Contracts.

Use of a Fixed-Price contract is normally inappropriate for research and development work. See FAR 35.006(c) (the use of cost-reimbursement contracts is usually appropriate); But see American Tel. and Tel. Co. v. United States, 48 Fed. Cl. 156 (2000) (upholding completed FP contract for developmental contract despite stated prohibition contained in FY 1987 Appropriations Act).

The reasons are that in development contracts, the specifications are often insufficiently detailed and the risks are insufficiently understood to be accurately reflected in the price.

Over the past decades, Fixed-Price contracts have repeatedly been suggested as the solution to control costs on development programs. When these suggestions have been implemented on specific programs, the results are unsuccessful programs and prolonged litigation. See General Dynamics Corp. v. United States, 563 U.S. 478 (2011).

2. Firm-Fixed-Price Contracts (FFP). FAR 16.202.

A FFP contract is not subject to any adjustment on the basis of the contractor's cost experience on the contract. It provides maximum incentive for the contractor to control costs and perform effectively, and imposes a minimum administrative burden on the contracting parties. FAR 16.202-1. When the contractor performs the contract requirements, the government is obligated to pay a fixed price that does not vary, regardless of the contractor's costs of performing the contract.

FAR 16.202-2 states an FFP contract is appropriate when acquiring:

- Commercial Items, and

- Supplies and Services where detailed specifications or reasonably definite functional specifications are available.

FAR 16.202-2 also requires pricing certainty when using an FFP contract. Pricing certainty results from adequate price competition, or price comparisons for similar items, or available cost or price information. Additionally, the parties must understand the performance risks and be able to price those risks.

For the government, using an FFP contract creates a risk is that it pays too much for the goods or services. Therefore, the FAR 16.202-2 recommends an FFP contract when there is price certainty, such as from price competition, competitively determined comparable prices, or available cost or pricing information.

For a contractor, accepting an FFP contract creates a risk that the costs of performance will exceed the price paid. Therefore, the contractor must ensure that the contract requirements are achievable, sufficiently defined, and are not subject to subjective judgment of the customer. An FFP contract must state when a contractor is done and entitled to payment. The contractor must also ensure that performance risks are well understood and capable of realistic cost estimates. Advancing the state of the art, inflation, exchange rates, and commodity prices are major risks that can be difficult to foresee, estimate, or mitigate.

3. Fixed-Price Contracts with Economic Price Adjustment (FP EPA). FAR 16.203; FAR 52.216-2; FAR 52.216-3; and FAR 52.216-4.

A Fixed-Price Contract with Economic Price Adjustment is a type of Fixed-Price contract that shifts some risks from the contractor to the government. An FP EPA contract provides for upward and downward revisions of the stated contract price upon the occurrence of specified contingencies. See Transportes Especiales de Automoviles, S.A. (T.E.A.S.A.), ASBCA No. 43851, 93-2 B.C.A. ¶ 25,745 (stating that "EPA provisions in government contracts serve an important purpose, protecting both parties from certain specified contingencies"); MAPCO Alaska Petroleum v. United States, 27 Fed. Cl. 405 (1992) (indicating the potential price revision serves the further salutary purpose of minimizing the need for contingencies in offers and, therefore, reducing offer prices).

Fixed-Price with Economic Price Adjustment contracts may be used when the contracting officer believes:

- Prices of labor or materials may vary over an extended period of contract performance, and
- Variations in prices of labor and/or materials can be measured and used to adjust the contract price.
- The contract price and contract term are sufficiently great to justify the administrative costs of adjusting the contract price.

Where appropriate, use of an EPA clause should result in lower prices for the government on longer-term contracts by eliminating a contingency from the contract price. There are several methods for adjusting the contract price for variations in economic factors. FAR 16.203-1.

- Using cost indexes of labor, material, or other economic conditions. For example, the Producer Price Index is a broad measure of inflation for manufacturers. The parties should specifically identify the applicable indexes in the contract. There is no standard FAR clause prescribed when using this method. The DFARS provides extensive guidelines for use of indexes. See DFARS 216.203-4(d).
- Using variations in published or similar established prices of labor, material, or end items. For example, a published market price for fuel would be an appropriate index where fuel was a major cost of performance. See FAR 52.216-2 (standard supplies) and FAR 52.216-3 (semi-standard supplies); DFARS 216.203-4 (indicating one should ordinarily only use EPA clauses when contract exceeds simplified acquisition threshold and delivery will not be completed within six months of contract award). The CAFC recently held that market-based EPA clauses are

permitted under the FAR. Tesoro Hawaii Corp., et al v. United States, 405 F.3d 1339 (2005).

- Actual costs of labor or material. However, price adjustments should be limited to costs beyond the contractor's reasonable control. For example, an aircraft production contract may adjust based on the price of aluminum. See FAR 52.216-4.

In practice, many EPA clauses are tailored to specific acquisitions. In drafting a contract with specific EPA clauses, the government should ensure the clause provides the contractor with the protection envisioned by regulation. Courts and boards may reform EPA clauses to conform to regulations. See Beta Sys., Inc. v. United States, 838 F.2d 1179 (Fed. Cir. 1988) (reformation appropriate where chosen index failed to achieve purpose of EPA clause); Craft Mach. Works, Inc., ASBCA No. 35167, 90-3 BCA ¶ 23,095 (EPA clause did not provide contractor with inflationary adjustment from a base period paralleling the beginning of the contract, as contemplated by regulations). Alternatively, a party may be entitled to fair market value, or *quantum valebant* recovery. Gold Line Ref., Ltd. v. United States, 54 Fed. Cl. 285 (2002) (*quantum valebant* relief OR reformation of clause to further parties' intent to adjust prices in accordance with the FAR); Barrett Ref. Corp. v. United States, 242 F.3d 1055 (Fed. Cir. 2001).

A contractor may waive its entitlement to an adjustment by not submitting its request within the time specified in the contract. Bataco Indus., 29 Fed. Cl. 318 (1993) (contractor filed requests more than one year after EPA clause deadlines).

B. Incentive Contracts. FAR 16.4.

In an incentive-type contract, the government agrees to vary the contract price based on the contractor's cost and technical performance.

1. Fixed-Price Incentive (FPI) Contracts. FAR 16.204; FAR 16.403; FAR 52.216-16; and FAR 52.216-17.

In an FPI contract, the government gives the contractor protection against increases in the costs of performance by sharing in cost overruns, up to a stated ceiling price. Conversely, the government shares cost underruns with the contractor by reducing the contract price, if the costs of performance are less than expected, by a stated percentage of the cost underrun. This sharing of over-runs and underruns is subject to a fixed ceiling price beyond which the contractor bears all the cost of performing the contract. Because the contractor must complete the specified scope of work for the fixed ceiling price, the contract is a Fixed-Price contract.

During negotiations, the government and the contractor agree to an estimated target cost, a target profit, a profit adjustment formula, and a ceiling price. For example, the parties may agree on a target cost of $90, a target profit of $10, and a ceiling price of $150. As sharing, the government and the contractor may agree that the government will receive 50% of any under-run in target cost, and will assume 75% of overruns in target cost up to the ceiling price.

The government will use an FPI contract when the scope of work is insufficiently defined, and/or the risks of performance are such that an FFP contract is not suitable, but the performance risks are sufficiently understood so that a contractor can agree on a fixed ceiling price. Usually, the ceiling price is significantly higher than the estimated cost of performance. A typical application is in a contract that combines development and production tasks. The government and the contractor might agree to a cost reimbursement development task and an FPI production task.

There are two variations on FPI contracts. The more common variation is FPI (firm target). FAR 52.216-16. The less common variation is FPI (successive targets). FAR 16.403(a), FAR 52.216-17. In FPI (successive targets), the government and the contractor agree on an initial target cost, target profit, ceiling price, and sharing formulas. They also agree to renegotiate a final target cost, target profit, ceiling price, and sharing formula at a specific point in the production cycle, normally once the major uncertainties have been reduced or eliminated.

2. Fixed-Price Contracts with Award Fees. FAR 16.404.

Fixed Price contracts with award fees are a contract type that allows the government to increase the contract price after performance is complete. Basically, the government determines whether to increase the price based on a subjective evaluation of performance.

The contractor receives a fixed price for satisfactory contract performance. The government may award an additional fee (if any) in addition to that fixed price if the contractor's actual performance exceeds the minimum satisfactory performance. Typically, the government performs a subjective evaluation of subjective factors.

The contract must provide for periodic evaluations of the contractor's performance against an award fee plan. Examples of award fee plans are found in the Air Force Award Fee Guide, http://www.safaq.hq. af.mil/contracting/toolkit/part16/acrobat/award-feeguide.pdf, and the National Aeronautics and Space Administration Award Fee Contracting Guide, available at http://www.hq.nasa.gov/office/procurement/regs/afguidee.html. Both documents contain helpful guidance on setting up award fee evaluation plans.

Fixed-Price Award Fee contracts should be used when the government wants to motivate a contractor, but other incentives cannot be used because the contractor's performance is not measurable objectively. Because the process for determining award fees is administratively costly, the government must conclude that the benefits of superior performance outweigh the administrative costs.

An individual above the level of the contracting officer must approve use of the fixed-price-award-fee contract. FAR 16.401(e).

3. Award Term Contracts.

Award Term contracts are a recent innovation in incentive-type contracts. In this type, the contractor is awarded additional performance periods upon a determination of exceptional performance. There has been no guidance from the FAR on this type of contract. Some agency FAR Supplements address this type. See EPAAR 1516.401-70. The Air Force Material Command issued an Award Fee & Award Term Guide, dated December 2002, which contains guidance.

For a contractor, the "incentive" is similar to an option for an additional period of performance at the same price as the base period. The "incentive" of an additional term without a price increase appears to favor the government, which avoids the administrative burden of a new competition. The contractor avoids the costs of competing for a further contract period, but loses the right to reprice its work in that competition. The government's right to terminate a contract for convenience further limits the "incentive" provided by an award term contract.

4.   There are incentive mechanisms that are combined with cost-reimbursement contracts. These are discussed in paragraph II.C.10 and C.11, below.

C. Cost-Reimbursement Contracts. FAR Subpart 16.3.

1.   Cost-Reimbursement-type contracts are common in US Government contracting and uncommon elsewhere. In a Cost-Reimbursement-type contract, the contractor promises to deliver a product or perform a service. Instead of paying a fixed price upon completion, the government promises to pay the contractor's allowable[1] incurred costs (to the extent prescribed in the contract). In most Cost-Reimbursement-type contracts, the government also promises to pay the contractor a fee for completion of the specified work. In exchange, the contractor promises to use its best efforts to perform the work within the estimated cost.

2.   Allowable Costs. FAR 52.216-7, Allowable Cost and Payment, is the contract provision on when and how the government pays the contractor's allowable costs. FAR Part 31 regulates contract costs. A detailed discussion of costs and cost accounting is beyond the scope of this Desk Book.

3.   Fee. For completion of the specified work in the contract, the government usually pays a fee to the contractor. Fee is different from profit, because the contractor inevitably has actual costs that are not allowable (such as income taxes and alcohol) that it must pay. While a Cost-Reimbursement contract may provide for payment of the specified fee only after completion of the specified work, the more common practice is to provide for provisional payments of fee as the work progresses, as measured by the costs incurred.

4.   Application. The government should consider a cost-reimbursement contract when uncertainties involved in contract performance do not permit costs to be estimated with sufficient accuracy to use any type of fixed-price contract. FAR 16.301-2. Uncertainty may result from unknown risks, such as development of complex systems; lack of detailed specifications and firm requirements; lack of time; etc.

5.   The decision to use a cost-type contract is within the contracting officer's discretion. Crimson Enters., B-243193, June 10, 1991, 91-1 CPD ¶ 557 (decision to use cost-type contract reasonable considering uncertainty over requirements causing multiple changes).

6.   The government bears the majority of cost or performance risk. In a cost-reimbursement-type contract, a contractor is only required to use its "best efforts" to perform. A contractor will be reimbursed its allowable costs, regardless of how well it performs the contract. General Dynamics Corp. v. United States, 671 F.2d 474, 480-81 (Ct. Cl. 1982),

---

[1] To be allowable, a cost must be reasonable, allocable, properly accounted for, and not specifically disallowed. FAR 31.201-2.

McDonnell Douglas Corp. v. United States, 27 Fed. Cl. 295, 299 (1997) (noting that ". . . the focus of a cost-reimbursement contract is contractor input, not output.")

7. Limitations on Cost-Type Contracts. FAR 16.301-3.

The contractor must have an adequate cost accounting system. See CrystaComm, Inc., ASBCA No. 37177, 90-2 BCA ¶ 22,692 (contractor failed to establish required cost accounting system).

The government must exercise appropriate surveillance to provide reasonable assurance that efficient methods and effective cost controls are used.

The government may not use a Cost Reimbursement contract for the acquisition of commercial items. FAR 16.301-3(b).

The Department of Defense may not use a cost reimbursement contract to acquire the production of a major system. Pub. L. 112-239, §811 (Jan. 2, 2013); see DFARS Class Deviation 2013-O0009.

8. Cost ceilings are imposed through the Limitation of Cost clause, FAR 52.232-20 (if the contract is fully funded); or the Limitation of Funds clause, FAR 52.232-22 (if the contract is incrementally funded).

When awarding a Cost-Reimbursement-type contract, the government limits its obligation by including an estimated total cost or other funding ceiling for completing the work. (See paragraph II.B.7, below.) If the government does not increase its obligation by raising the ceiling, the contractor has no obligation to continue work beyond the ceiling amount.

When the contractor has reason to believe it is approaching the estimated cost of the contract or the limit of funds allotted, it must give the contracting officer written notice.

FAR 32.704 provides that a contracting officer must, upon receipt of notice, promptly obtain funding and programming information pertinent to the contract and inform the contractor in writing that:

*   Additional funds have been allotted, or the estimated cost has been increased, in a specified amount; or
*   The contract is not to be further funded and the contractor should submit a proposal for the adjustment of fee, if any, based on the percentage of work completed in relation to the total work called for under the contract; or
*   The contract is to be terminated; or
*   The government is considering whether to allot additional funds or increase the estimated cost, the contractor is entitled to stop work when the funding or cost limit is reached, and any work beyond the funding or cost limit will be at the contractor's risk.

The contractor may not recover costs above the ceiling unless the contracting officer authorizes the contractor to exceed the ceiling. JJM Sys., Inc., ASBCA No. 51152, 03-1 BCA ¶ 32,192; Titan Corp. v. West, 129 F.3d 1479 (Fed. Cir. 1997); Advanced Materials, Inc., 108 F.3d 307 (Fed. Cir. 1997). Exceptions to this rule include:

*   The overrun was unforeseeable. Johnson Controls World Servs. Inc. v. United States, 48 Fed. Cl. 479 (2001); RMI, Inc. v. United States, 800 F.2d 246 (Fed. Cir. 1986) (burden is on contractor to show overrun was not reasonably foreseeable during time of contract performance); F2 Assoc., Inc., ASBCA No. 52397, 01-2 BCA ¶ 31,530. To establish unforeseeability, the contractor must establish that it maintained an adequate accounting system. SMS Agoura Sys., Inc., ASBCA No. 50451, 97-2 BCA ¶ 29,203 (contractor foreclosed from arguing unforeseeability by prior decision).
*   Estoppel. Am. Elec. Labs., Inc. v. United States, 774 F.2d 1110 (Fed. Cir. 1985) (partial estoppel where government induced continued performance through representations of additional availability of funds); Advanced Materials, Inc., 108 F.3d 307 (Fed. Cir. 1997) (unsuccessfully asserted); F2 Assoc., Inc., ASBCA No. 52397, 01-2 BCA ¶ 31,530 (unsuccessfully asserted).

- Cost-Plus-Fixed-Fee (CPFF) Contracts. FAR 16.306; FAR 52.216-8.
- In a CPFF contract, government pays a contract price for completion of the work, consisting of the contractor's allowable costs plus a fixed fee that is negotiated and set prior to award. Regardless of the actual costs of performance, the contractor earns its fixed fee only upon completion of the specified work.
- CPFF contracts are typically used instead of another Cost-Reimbursement-type contract when the total contract value is low, and the government will benefit from the lower administrative costs of a fixed fee, as compared to an incentive or award fee-type Cost-Reimbursement contract.
- Limitation on Maximum Fee for CPFF contracts. 10 U.S.C. § 2306(d); 41 U.S.C. § 3905(b); FAR 15.404-4(c)(4).
- Maximum fee limitations are based on the estimated cost at the time of award, not on the actual costs incurred.
- For research and development contracts, the maximum fee is a specific amount no greater than 15% of estimated costs at the time of award.
- For contracts other than R&D contracts, the maximum fee is a specific amount no greater than 10% of estimated costs at the time of award.
- DOD agencies may not use CPFF contracts on construction contracts estimated to exceed $25,000 that are funded by a military construction appropriations act, and are to be performed in the United States (except Alaska). DFARS 216.306. Exceptions exist for environmental work with written approval of the secretaries of the military departments (non-construction) or the Secretary of Defense (construction).

9. Cost-Plus-Incentive-Fee (CPIF) Contracts. FAR 16.304; FAR 16.405-1; and FAR 52.216-10.

A CPIF contract is a Cost-Reimbursement contract where the contractor is incentivized to minimize the actual costs by sharing with the government cost underruns (rare) and cost over-runs (common).

A CPIF contract specifies a target cost, a target fee, minimum and maximum fees, and a fee adjustment formula. After contract performance, the contractor's fee is determined in accordance with the formula. See Bechtel Hanford, Inc., B-292288, et al., 2003 CPD ¶ 199.

A CPIF is appropriate for services or development and test programs. FAR 16.405-1. See Northrop Grumman Corp. v. United States, 41 Fed. Cl. 645 (1998) (Joint STARS contract).

The government may combine technical incentives and schedule incentives with cost incentives. FAR 16.405-1(b)(2). However, every CPIF contract must have cost incentives. Absent cost incentives, the contractor might incur costs earning the maximum incentives which outweigh their value to the government. FAR 16.402-4 (b).

If a contractor meets the contract criteria for achieving the maximum fee, the government must pay that fee despite minor problems with the contract. North American Rockwell Corp., ASBCA No. 14329, 72-1 BCA ¶ 9207 (1971) (government could not award a zero fee due to minor discrepancies when contractor met the target weight for a fuel-tank, which was the sole incentive criteria).

A contractor is not entitled to a portion of the incentive fee upon termination of a CPIF contract for convenience. FAR 49.115 (b)(2).

10. Cost-Plus-Award-Fee (CPAF) Contracts. FAR 16.305 and FAR 16.405-2.

In a CPAF contract, the contractor receives its allowable costs plus a fee consisting of a base amount (which may be zero) and an award amount based upon a judgmental evaluation by the government. The objective of award fees is to provide motivation to the contractor for excellent contract performance.

Award Fee determinations may be made periodically (for example, as services are performed) or at the completion of specific tasks.

Limitations on CPAF base fee. DOD contracts limit base fees to 3% of the estimated cost of the contract exclusive of fee. DFARS 216.405-2(c)(ii).

Award fee. The DFARS lists sample performance evaluation criteria in a table that includes time of delivery, quality of work, and effectiveness in controlling and/or reducing costs. See DFARS Part 216, Table 16-1. The Air Force Award Fee Guide (Mar. 02) and the National Aeronautics and Space Administration Award Fee Contracting Guide (Jun. 27, 01) both contain helpful guidance on setting up award fee evaluation plans.

The FAR requires that an appropriate award-fee clause be inserted in solicitations and contracts when an award-fee contract is contemplated, and that the clause '[e]xpressly provide[s] that the award amount and the award-fee determination methodology are unilateral decisions made solely at the discretion of the government.' FAR 16.406 (e)(3). There is no standard award fee clause in the FAR. Therefore, award fee clauses are tailored for each acquisition. The solicitation may include an award fee plan, which describes the structure, evaluation methods, and timing of evaluations.

Since the available award fee during the evaluation period must be earned, the contractor begins each evaluation period with 0% of the available award fee and works up to the evaluated fee for each evaluation period. AFARS 5116.4052(b)(2). If performance is deemed either unsatisfactory or marginal, no award fee is earned. DFARS 216.405-2(a)(i).

A CPAF contract shall provide for evaluations at stated intervals during performance, so the government informs the contractor periodically of the quality of its performance and the areas in which improvement is desired. FAR 16.405-2(b)(3).

Generally, award fee plans provide for a fee-determining official, an award-fee board (typical members include the KO and knowledgeable technical staff). See NASA and Air Force Award Fee Guides.

Where award fee plans are included in the contract, unilateral changes are generally limited to before the start of an evaluation period with written notification by the KO. Changes to an evaluation plan incorporated into the contract can only be done through bilateral modifications. See Air Force Award Fee Guide. When an award fee plan is not included in the contract, the contracting officer should still communication changes to the non-binding plan in advance of their implementation.

A contractor is entitled to unpaid award fee attributable to completed performance when the government terminates a cost-plus-award fee contract for convenience. Northrop Grumman Corp. v. Goldin, 136 F.3d 1479 (Fed. Cir. 1998).

The award fee schedule determines when the award fee payments are made. The fee schedule does not need to be proportional to the work completed. Textron Defense Sys. v. Widnall, 143 F.3d 1465 (Fed. Cir. 1998) (end-loading award fee to later periods)

11. Cost Contracts. FAR 16.302; FAR 52.216-11.

In a Cost contract, the contractor receives its allowable costs but no fee.

Cost contracts may be appropriate for research and development work, particularly with nonprofit educational institutions or other nonprofit organizations, and for facilities contracts (where a contractor manages government property under a separate contract). Similarly, a Cost contract may be appropriate where the contractor receives some other benefit from successful performance of a contract.

12. Cost-Sharing Contracts. FAR 16.303; FAR 52.216-12.

In a Cost-Sharing contract, the contractor is reimbursed only for an agreed-upon portion of its allowable cost.

Normally a cost-sharing contract is used where the contractor will receive substantial benefit from the effort. For example, an aircraft engine manufacturer may accept a cost-sharing contract to develop a more fuel-efficient engine for a military aircraft when successful completion will provide the manufacturer an engine that it can sell commercially.

III. CONTRACT TYPES – SERVICES MEASURED BY TIME WORKED. FAR 16.207, 16.601, AND 16.602.

When contracting for services where the work product is uncertain, the work conditions are uncertain, the skills required are uncertain, or the effort required is uncertain, a buyer can employ a contract type where the price is measured by the time spent performing the work. This mechanism is effective when the factors affecting price are truly unknowable at the time of contracting. However, this type of contract is susceptible to overuse, since it can compensate for poor requirements definition and lack of planning.

A. Time-and-Materials (T&M) and Labor Hour Contracts. FAR Subpart 16.601.

1. Fixed Price, Cost-Reimbursement, and Incentive contracts all are based on the contractor's completion of a defined scope of work. A separate category of contracts bases payment of the contract price on completion of labor hours, regardless of whether or not the effort has accomplished the intended task. In the private sector, similar pricing arrangements are common for auto mechanics, plumbers, and lawyers.

2. Application. Use these contracts when it is not possible at contract award to estimate accurately or to anticipate with any reasonable degree of confidence the extent or duration of the work. FAR 16.601(b); FAR 16.602. Where the amount of work needed is so uncertain, the government avoids the risk of paying too much if the labor needed is small; and the contract avoids the risk that the labor required is far more than anticipated. For small tasks, T&M contracts may save administrative costs of negotiating firm fixed-price contracts.

3. Government Surveillance. Because the contractor is paid for labor, not results, the government should exercise appropriate surveillance to ensure that the contractor is using efficient methods to perform these contracts. In fact, the incentive in such contracts is to work less efficiently, since taking longer means greater profits. FAR 16.601(b)(1); FAR 16.602. <u>CACI, Inc. v. General Services Administration</u>, GSBCA No. 15588, 03-1 BCA ¶ 32,106.

4. Limitation on use. The contracting officer must execute a Determination & Finding (D&F) that no other contract type is suitable, and include a contract price ceiling. FAR 16.601(c); FAR 16.602.

5. Types. The difference between a Time & Material and a Labor Contract is the inclusion of material.

Time-and-materials (T&M) contracts provide for acquiring supplies or services on the basis of:

- Direct labor hours at specified fixed hourly rates that include wages, overhead, general and administrative expenses, and profit; and
- Materials at cost, including, if appropriate, material handling costs as part of material costs. An optional pricing method described at FAR 16.601(b)(3) may be used when the contractor is providing material it sells regularly to the general public in the ordinary course of business, and several other requirements are met.
- A recurring issue in T&M contracts involves services provided by subcontractors and affiliates. The current versions of the FAR Clauses for T&M contracts (FAR 52.216-29, 52.216-30, and 52.216-31) state that effort provided by subcontractors and affiliates may be priced separately or identically to the prime contractor, depending on the services and availability of competition.

Labor-hour contracts differ from T&M contracts only in that the contractor does not supply the materials. FAR 16.602.

B. Level of Effort Contracts.

1. Firm-fixed-price, level-of-effort term contract. FAR 16.207. Government buys a level of effort for a certain period of time,

i.e., a specific number of hours to be performed in a specific period. Suitable for investigation or study in a specific R&D area, typically where the contract price is $100,000 or less.

2. Cost-plus-fixed-fee-term form contract. FAR 16.306(d)(2). Similar to the firm-fixed-price level-of-effort contract except that the contract price equals the cost incurred plus a fee. The contractor is required to provide a specific level of effort over a specific period of time. It is paid the costs of providing the services plus a fixed fee.

IV. CONTRACT TYPES - INDEFINITE DELIVERY CONTRACTS.

A. Indefinite Delivery Contracts. FAR Subpart 16.5.

Indefinite Delivery-type contracts provide the government with the flexibility to change or specify key business terms during the contract term. FAR 16.501-2(a) recognizes three types of indefinite delivery contracts: definite-quantity contracts, requirements contracts, and indefinite-quantity contracts. These types of contracts give the government the flexibility to alter the quantity purchased to reflect actual requirements (Requirements contracts and Indefinite Delivery-Indefinite Quantity contracts) or to alter the time and place of delivery (Indefinite Delivery-Definite Quantity contracts).

In some contracts, this additional flexibility comes at a price. Where the contract does not give the contractor a firm quantity, the contractor may not offer prices that reflect economies of continuous production and quantity discounts on materials. Where the quantity is fixed but the time and place of delivery is uncertain, a contractor may include in its prices the cost of carrying inventory or worldwide delivery.

The advantages of the three types are minimizing government inventories and direct shipment to users.

B. Definite-Quantity/Indefinite-Delivery Contracts. FAR 16.502; FAR 52.216-20.

In a Definite-Quantity/Indefinite-Delivery-type contract, the quantity and price are specified for a fixed period. The government issues delivery orders that specify the delivery date and location. The contractor ships in response to delivery orders.

The contractor must maintain an inventory sufficient to meet the government's actual demands, but is able to take advantage of supplier quantity discounts and efficiencies of continuous production.

C. Indefinite-Quantity Contracts. FAR 16.504.

Indefinite- or variable-quantity contracts permit flexibility in both quantities and delivery schedules. They come in two variants: a Requirements contract and a Minimum Quantity contract. These contracts permit ordering of supplies or services as requirements and/or funding materializes.

An indefinite quantity contract must be either a requirements or an ID/IQ contract. See Satellite Servs., Inc., B-280945, B-280945.2, B-280945.3, Dec. 4, 1998, 98-2 CPD ¶ 125 (solicitation flawed where it neither guaranteed a minimum quantity nor operated as a requirements contract).

Where the government desires an arrangement where it need not commit to ordering any supplies or services, the contracting officer may consider a Basic Ordering Agreement or similar arrangement. See FAR Subpart 16.7; DFARS 216.7.

D. Requirements Contracts. FAR 16.503; FAR 52.216-21.

In a Requirements contract, the government promises to order all of its requirements, if any, from the contractor, and the contractor promises to fill all requirements. See Sea-Land Serv., Inc., B-266238, Feb. 8, 1996, 96-1 CPD ¶ 49 (solicitation for requirements contract which contained a "Limitation of Government

Liability" clause purporting to allow the government to order services elsewhere rendered contract illusory for lack of consideration). Requirements contracts are a common commercial transaction. See UCC § 2.306(1).

1.   The government must order all its requirements from the contractor. FAR 52.216-21.

Disputes arise when the government fails to do so. The government breaches the contract when it purchases its requirements from another source. Datalect Computer Servs. Inc. v. United States, 56 Fed. Cl. 178 (2003) (finding agency breached its requirements contract covering computer maintenance services where agency later obtained extended warranty from equipment manufacturer covering same items); Torncello v. United States, 681 F.2d 756 (Ct. Cl. 1982) (Navy diverted rodent pest control services); T&M Distributors, Inc., ASBCA No. 51279, 01-2 BCA ¶ 31,442 (finding that Ft. Carson breached its requirements contract covering the operation of an auto parts store when certain tenant units elected to order their parts from cheaper suppliers). Therefore, the government and the contractor should clearly define the scope of the requirements the government is contracting for.

The government also may breach the contract if it performs the contracted-for work in-house. C&S Park Serv., Inc., ENGBCA Nos. 3624, 3625, 78-1 BCA ¶ 13,134 (failure to order mowing services in a timely fashion combined with use of government employees to perform mowing services entitled contractor to equitable adjustment under changes clause). The government deferral or backlogging of its orders such that it does not order its actual requirements from a contractor is also a breach of a requirements contract. R&W Flammann GmbH, ASBCA Nos. 53204, 53205, 02-2 BCA ¶ 32,044.

Contractors may receive lost profits as a measure of damages when the government purchases supplies or services from an outside source. See T&M Distributors, Inc., ASBCA No. 51279, 01-2 BCA ¶ 31,442; Carroll Auto., ASBCA No. 50993, 98-2 BCA ¶ 29,864.

The government cannot escape liability for the breach of a requirements contract by retroactively asserting constructive termination for convenience. T&M Distributors, Inc., ASBCA No. 51279, 01-2 BCA ¶ 31,442; Carroll Auto., ASBCA No. 50993, 98 2 BCA ¶ 29,864 (government invoked constructive T4C theory two years after contract performance); Torncello v. United States, 231 Ct. Cl. 20, 681 F.2d 756 (Ct. Cl. 1982).

If the government inadvertently or intentionally omits FAR 52.216-21, a court or board will examine other intrinsic/extrinsic evidence to determine whether the contract is a requirements contract. See, e.g., Centurion Elecs. Serv., ASBCA No. 51956, 03-1 BCA ¶ 32,097 (holding that a contract to do all repairs on automated data-processing equipment and associated network equipment at Fort Leavenworth was a requirements contract despite omission of requisite clause).

2.   Estimates of Requirements. FAR 16.503(a)(1).

The Contracting Officer shall state a realistic estimated total quantity in the solicitation and resulting contract. The estimate is not a representation to an offeror or contractor that the estimated quantity will be required or ordered, or that conditions affecting requirements will be stable or normal. The estimate may be obtained from records of previous requirements and consumption, or by other means, and should be based on the most current information available. FAR 16.503(a)(1).

The estimate is not a guarantee or a warranty of a specific quantity. Shader Contractors, Inc. v. United States, 149 Ct. Cl. 535, 276 F.2d 1, 7 (Ct. Cl. 1960).
There is no need to create or search for additional information. Medart v. Austin, 967 F.2d 579 (Fed. Cir. 1992) (court refused to impose a higher standard than imposed by regulations in finding reasonable the use of prior year's requirements as estimate). The standard is for the government to base its estimates on "all relevant information that is reasonably available to it." Womack v. United States, 182 Ct. Cl. 399, 401, 389 F.2d 793, 801 (1968). Of course,

Contract Types

the government should not misrepresent its estimated requirements.

The estimates can be based on personal experience as long as it is reasonable. National Salvage & Service Corp., ASBCA No. 53750 (Jun. 18, 2004).

The GAO will sustain a protest if a solicitation contains flawed estimates. Beldon Roofing & Remodeling Co., B-277651, Nov. 7, 1997, CPD 97-2 ¶ 131 (recommending cancellation of IFB where solicitation failed to provide realistic quantity estimates).

Failure to use available data or calculate the estimates with due care may also entitle the contractor to additional compensation. See Hi-Shear Tech. Corp. v. United States, 53 Fed. Cl. 420 (2002) (noting the government "is not free to carelessly guess at its needs" and that it must calculate its estimates based upon "all relevant information that is reasonably available to it."); S.P.L. Spare Parts Logistics, Inc., ASBCA Nos. 51118, 51384, 02-2 BCA ¶ 31,982; Crown Laundry & Dry Cleaners v. United States, 29 Fed. Cl. 506 (1993) (finding the government was negligent where estimates were exaggerated and not based on historical data); and Contract Mgmt., Inc., ASBCA No. 44885, 95-2 BCA ¶ 27,886 (granting relief under the Changes clause where the government failed to revise estimates between solicitation and award to reflect funding shortfalls).

Contractors are generally not entitled to lost profits for negligent estimates. Recovery is generally limited to reliance damages and a price adjustment. See Rumsfeld v. Applied Companies, Inc., 325 F.3d 1329 (Fed. Cir. 2003), and Everett Plywood v. United States, 190 Ct. Cl. 80, 419 F.2d 425 (Ct. Cl. 1969) (contractor entitled to adjustment of the contract price applied to the volume of timber actually cut).

A negligent estimate that was too low may result in a constructive change to the contract. Chemical Technology v. United States, 227 Ct. Cl. 120, 645 F.2d 934 (1981).

3. Actual requirements may differ from pre-award estimates if done in good faith.

The government acts in good faith if it has a valid business reason for varying its requirements other than dissatisfaction with the contract. Technical Assistance Int'l, Inc. v. United States, 150 F.3d 1369 (Fed. Cir. 1998) (no breach or constructive change where government diminished need for vehicle maintenance and repair work by increasing rate at which it added new vehicles into the installation fleet); Shear Tech. Corp. v. United States, 53 Fed. Cl. 420 (2002); Maggie's Landscaping, Inc., ASBCA Nos. 52462, 52463 (June 2, 2004) (government had valid reasons to reduce orders to include dry and wet conditions).

"Bad faith" includes actions "motivated solely by a reassessment of the balance of the advantages and disadvantages under the contract" such that the buyer decreases its requirements to avoid its obligations under the contract. Technical Assistance Int'l, Inc. v. United States, 150 F.3d 1369, 1372 (Fed. Cir. 1998) (citing Empire Gas Corp. v. Am. Bakeries Co., 840 F. 2d 1333, 1341 (7th Cir. 1988)).

The government is not liable for acts of God that cause a reduction in requirements. Sentinel Protective Servs., Inc., ASBCA No. 23560, 81-2 BCA ¶ 15,194 (drought reduced need for grass cutting).

4. Limits on use of requirements Contracts for Advisory and Assistance Services[2] (CAAS). 10 U.S.C. § 2304b(e)(2); FAR 16.503(d).

---

[2] "Advisory and assistance services" means those services provided under contract by nongovernmental sources to support or improve organizational policy development; decision making; management and administration; program and/or program management and administration; or R&D activities. It can also mean the furnishing of professional advice or assistance rendered to improve the effectiveness of federal management processes or procedures (including those of an engineering or technical nature). All advisory and assistance services are classified as Management and professional support services; Studies, analyses and evaluations; or Engineering and technical services. FAR 2.101. See also DOD Directive 4205.2, Acquiring and Managing Contracted Advisory and Assistance Services (CAAS) (10 Feb. 92); as well AR 5-14, Management of Contracted Advisory and Assistance Services (15 Jan. 93).

Activities may not issue solicitations for requirements contracts for advisory and assistance services in excess of three years and $10 million, including all options, unless the contracting officer determines in writing that the use of the multiple award procedures is impracticable. See paragraph IV.F.4, below.

E. Indefinite-Quantity/Indefinite-Delivery Contracts (ID/IQ or Minimum-Quantity Contracts). FAR 16.504.

1. In an ID/IQ contract, the government shall order and the contractor shall furnish at least a stated minimum quantity of supplies or services. In addition, if ordered, the contractor shall furnish any additional quantities, not to exceed the stated maximum. FAR 16.504(a).

2. Application.

Contracting officers may use an ID/IQ contract when the government cannot predetermine, above a specified minimum, the precise quantities of supplies or services that the government will require during the contract period, and it is inadvisable for the government to commit itself for more than a minimum quantity. The contracting officer should use an indefinite-quantity contract only when a recurring need is anticipated. FAR 16.504(b).

When selecting an ID/IQ contract type, the government should expect that the unit price will be higher than if it committed to buying a larger quantity. Consequently, if the government can commit to larger minimum quantities, then it may be able to achieve lower prices through either competition or negotiation based on cost or pricing data.

3. Nominal Minimum Quantities.

In order for the contract to be binding, the minimum quantity in the contract must be more than a nominal quantity. FAR 16.504(a)(2). See CW Government Travel, Inc., B-295530 ($2500 minimum adequate when it represented several hundred transactions in travel services); Wade Howell, d.b.a. Howell Constr, v. United States, 51 Fed. Cl. 516 (2002); Aalco Forwarding, Inc., et al., B-277241.15, Mar. 11, 1998, 98-1 CPD

¶ 87 ($25,000 minimum for moving and storage services); Sea-Land Serv. Inc., B-278404.2 Feb. 9, 1998, 98-1 CPD ¶ 47 (after considering the acquisition as a whole, found guarantee of one "FEU"[3] per contract carrier was adequate consideration to bind the parties).

If the contract contains option year(s), only the base period of performance must contain a non-nominal minimum to constitute adequate consideration. Varilease Technology Group, Inc. v. United States, 289 F.3d 795 (Fed. Cir. 2002).

4. Guaranteed Minimum.

The contractor is entitled to receive only the guaranteed minimum. Travel Centre v. Barram, 236 F.3d 1316 (Fed. Cir. 2001) (holding that agency met contract minimum, so "its less than ideal contracting tactics fail to constitute a breach"); Crown Laundry & Dry Cleaners, Inc., ASBCA No. 39982, 90-3 BCA ¶ 22,993; but see Community Consulting Int'l., ASBCA No. 53489, 02-2 BCA ¶ 31,940 (granting summary judgment on a breach of contract claim despite the government satisfying the minimum requirement).

In practice, the government obligates funding sufficient to cover the guaranteed minimum at the time of contract award, and issues an order for the minimum quantity at or shortly after contract award.

5. Terminations for Convenience.

The government may not retroactively use the Termination for Convenience clause to avoid damages for its failure to order the minimum quantity. Compare Maxima Corp. v. United States, 847 F.2d 1549 (Fed. Cir. 1988) (termination many months after contract completion where minimum not ordered was invalid), and PHP Healthcare Corp., ASBCA No. 39207, 91-1 BCA ¶ 23,647 (contracting officer may not terminate an indefinite-quantity contract for convenience after end of contract term), with Hermes Consolidated, Inc. d/b/a Wyoming Refining Co., ASBCA Nos. 52308,

---

[3] Meaning Forty-Foot Equivalent Unit, an FEU is an industry term for cargo volumes measuring 8 feet high, 8 feet wide, and 40 feet deep.

91

Contract Types

52309, 2002 ASBCA LEXIS 11 (partial T4C with eight days left in ordering period proper) and Montana Ref. Co., ASBCA No. 50515, 00-1 BCA ¶ 30,694 (partial T4C proper when government reduced quantity estimate for jet fuel eight months into a twelve-month contract).

6.   Breach Damages.

The contractor must prove the damages suffered when the government fails to order the minimum quantity. The standard rule of damages is to place the contractor in as good a position as it would have been had it performed the contract. White v. Delta Contr. Int'l., Inc., 285 F.3d 1040, 43 (Fed. Cir. 2002) (noting that "the general rule is that damages for breach of contract shall place the wronged party in as good a position as it would have been in, had the breaching party fully performed its obligation"); PHP Healthcare Corp., ASBCA No. 39207, 91-1 BCA ¶ 23,647 (holding the contractor was not entitled to receive the difference between the guaranteed minimum and requiring the parties to determine an appropriate quantum); AJT Assocs., Inc., ASBCA No. 50240, 97-1 BCA ¶ 28,823 (holding the contractor was only entitled to lost profits on unordered minimum quantity).

7.   ID/IQ Statements of Work for Services.

An ID/IQ contract is not a mechanism for avoiding competition. The contract statement of work cannot be so broad as to be inconsistent with statutory authority for task order contracts and the requirements of the Competition in Contracting Act. See Valenzuela Eng'g, Inc., B-277979, Jan. 26, 1998, 98-1 CPD ¶ 51 (statement of work for operation and maintenance services at any government facility in the world deemed impermissibly broad).

8.   Ordering.

FAR 16.505(a) sets out the general requirements for orders under delivery or task order contracts. A separate synopsis under FAR 5.201 is not required for task or delivery orders.

F. Multiple Award Indefinite-Quantity/Indefinite-Delivery Contracts. FAR 16.504(c), DFARS .

1.   ID/IQ contracts can be either a single award or multiple awards. Use of multiple awards, however, have expanded over the past few years. In theory, several competitively awarded multiple award ID/IQ contracts provide a mechanism for quickly obtaining competition on task orders and avoiding bid protests by disappointed bidders.

2.   FAR 16.504(c) establishes a preference for making multiple awards of indefinite-quantity contracts under a single solicitation for similar supplies or services. See Nations, Inc., B-272455, Nov. 5, 1996, 96-2 CPD ¶ 170 (GAO ruled that the government must make multiple awards in CAAS indefinite delivery/indefinite quantity type of contracts). The contracting officer must document the decision whether or not to make multiple awards in the acquisition plan or contract file.

3.   During acquisition planning, the contracting officer determines whether or not to make multiple awards. FAR 16.504(c)(1)(ii) provides guidance on when multiple awards are appropriate.

4.   Multiple awards for CAAS are the norm where the contract exceeds three years and $10 million (including all options). FAR 16.504(c)(2) provides procedures for documenting and approving decisions not to use multiple awards.

5.   Placing Orders Under Multiple Award Contracts. FAR 16.505 (b).

- Fair Opportunity. Each multiple awardee must be given a "fair opportunity to be considered for each order in excess of $2,500." See Nations, Inc., B-272455, Nov. 5, 1996, 96-2 CPD ¶ 170.

- Exceptions. Awardees need not be given an opportunity to be considered for an order if: there is an urgent need; there is only one capable source; the order is a logical follow-on to a previously placed order; or the order is necessary to satisfy a minimum guarantee. FAR 16.505(b)(2).

- DFARS 216.505-70 requires any task order in excess of $100,000 placed under a non-FSS multiple award contract (MAC) to also be made on a competitive basis. All awardees that offer the required work must be provided a copy of the description of work, the basis upon which the contracting officer will make the selection, and given the opportunity to submit a proposal.

- DFARS 208.404-70 requires that any order off of a Federal Supply Schedule (FSS) in excess of $100,000 be made on a competitive basis. The Contracting Officer must either: issue the notice to as many schedule holders as practicable, consistent with market research appropriate to the circumstances, to reasonably ensure that proposals will be received from at least three sources that offer the required work; or contact all schedule holders that offer the required work by informing them of the opportunity for award.

- The contract may specify maximum or minimum quantities that may be ordered under each task or delivery order. FAR 16.504(a)(3). However, individual orders need not be of some minimum amount to be binding. See C.W. Over and Sons, Inc., B-274365, Dec. 6, 1996, 96-2 CPD ¶ 223 (individual delivery orders need not exceed some minimum amount to be binding).

- Any sole source order under the FSS or MAC requires approval consistent with the approval levels in FAR 6.304. See Memorandum, Director, Defense Procurement and Acquisition Policy, to Senior Procurement Executives & Directors of Defense Agencies, subject: Approval Levels for Sole Source Orders Under FSS and MACs (13 Sep. 04). See also Chapter 5.

6. Protesting Task and Delivery Orders. The GAO may not hear protests associated with the placement of a task or delivery order under a multiple-award ID/IQ contract except when the order "increases the scope, period, or maximum value" of the underlying contract, or is an order valued in excess of $10,000,000. 10 U.S.C. § 2304(c); 41 U.S.C. § 4106. See, e.g., EA Eng'g, Science, and Tech., Inc.,

B-411967.2, Apr. 5, 2016, 2016 CPD ¶ __; Goldbelt Glacier Health Servs, LLC--Reconsideration, B-410378.3, Feb. 6, 2015, 2015 CPD ¶ 75; Military Agency Services Pty., Ltd., B-290414, Aug. 1, 2003, 2002 CPD ¶ 130. The GAO, however, has held that it has protest jurisdiction over task and delivery orders placed under Federal Supply Schedule (FSS) contracts. Severn Co., Inc., B-275717.2, Apr. 28, 1997, 97-1 CPD ¶ 181 at 2-3, n.1. Additionally, the GAO will hear cases involving the "downselect" of multiple awardees, if that determination is implemented by the issuance of task and delivery orders. See Electro-Voice, Inc., B-278319; Jan. 15, 1998, 98-1 CPD ¶ 23. See also Teledyne-Commodore, LLC --Reconsideration, B-278408.4, Nov. 23, 1998, 98-2 CPD ¶ 121.

7. The FAR requires the head of an agency to designate a Task and Delivery Order Ombudsman to review complaints from contractors and ensure they are afforded a fair opportunity to be considered for orders. The ombudsman must be a senior agency official independent of the contracting officer and may be the agency's competition advocate. FAR 16.505(b)(5).

V.   LETTER CONTRACTS. FAR 16.603, DFARS SUBPART 217.74.

A. General.

Letter contracts are an interim contractual agreement that are intended to document some of the terms agreed by the parties, pending negotiation of a final and definitive agreement. Letter contracts are binding on the parties, unlike similar commercial documents. Letter contracts can range from a few sentences scribbled on a blackboard[4] to a fairly complete

---

[4] In awarding a letter contract for what later became the Wild Weasel program for suppression of enemy air defenses during the Vietnam war, supposedly the Assistant Secretary of the Air Force and the contractor's president signed a blackboard outlining the scope of work for the effort so the contractor could start work that day.

contract, albeit with a few open terms. Upon award of a Letter contract, the government obligates funding, and the contractor can start work in the expectation that it will be paid. Typically, a letter contract includes a preliminary scope of work, a ceiling price, a limitation on the government's obligation pending definitization, and whatever other terms and conditions are agreed to at the time of award. When the contractor was selected in a price competition, the Letter contract should contain a ceiling price. FAR 16.603-2(b).

B. Use.

Letter contracts are used when the government must give the contractor a binding commitment so that the contractor can start work immediately. The government and the contractor then negotiate the final contract while the contractor starts work. Letter contracts are a type of Undefinitized Contract Actions (UCA).

C. Approval.

The head of the contracting activity (HCA) or designee must determine in writing that no other contract is suitable. FAR 16.603-3; DFARS 217.7404-1. Approved Letter contracts must include a not-to-exceed (NTE) price.

D. Definitization.

The parties must definitize the contract (negotiate agreement on all contractual terms, specifications, and price) by the earlier of the end of the 180-day period after the date of the Letter contract or the date on which the amount of funds obligated under the contractual action is equal to more than 50 percent of the negotiated overall ceiling price for the contractual action.[5] 10 U.S.C. § 2326; DFARS 217.7404-3.

E. Ceiling.

The maximum liability of the government shall be the estimated amount necessary to cover the contractor's requirements for funds before definitization, but shall not exceed 50 percent of

---

[5] FAR 16.603-2(c) provides for definitization within 180 days after date of the letter contract or before completion of 40 percent of the work to be performed, whichever occurs first.

the estimated cost of the definitive contract unless approved in advance by the official who authorized the Letter contract. 10 U.S.C. § 2326(b)(2); FAR 16.603-2(d); DFARS 217.7404-4.

F. Restrictions. Letter contracts shall not:

1. Commit the government to a definitive contract in excess of funds available at the time of contract.

2. Be entered into without competition when required.

3. Be amended to satisfy a new requirement unless that requirement is inseparable from the existing Letter contract. FAR 16.603-3.

G. Government Liability for Failure to Definitize?

Letter contracts are binding agreements. The government and the contractor must negotiate in good faith to reach a definitive agreement. See Sys. Mgmt. Am. Corp., ASBCA Nos. 45704, 49607, 52644, 00-2 BCA ¶ 31,112 (finding the Assistant Secretary of the Navy unreasonably refused to approve a proposed definitization of option prices for a small disadvantaged business's supply contract).

H. Delays in Definitizing.

A very common problem is the time it takes contracting activities to definitize a Letter contract. Because the contractor is working, the pressure to finish is less. As work progresses, the government customers often identify changed requirements, the inclusion of which further delays completion. The Air Force has added a Mandatory Procedure tracking UCAs and definitization schedules. Any failure to definitize within one year must be report to the Deputy Assistant Secretary of the Air Force for Contracting. AFFARS MP5317.7404-3.

VI. OPTIONS. FAR SUBPART 17.2.

A. Definition.

Options in government contract law are similar to options in commercial contracts. An option is a unilateral right in a contract by which, for a specified time, the government may elect to purchase additional supplies or services called for by the contract, or may elect to extend the term of a services contract.

B. Use of Options. FAR 17.202.

Options are very common for several reasons:

- Options allow contractual agreements in advance of the availability of appropriations which must fund the agreement.
- Options allow the government flexibility to meet changed requirements.
- Options allow the government to establish prices for future work at the time of initial award when greater competition may exist.

The government can use options in contracts awarded under sealed bidding and negotiated procedures when in the government's interest.

Inclusion of an option is normally not in the government's interest when:

- The foreseeable requirements involve minimum economic quantities and
- Delivery requirements are far enough into the future to permit competitive acquisition, production, and delivery.

An indefinite quantity or requirements contract could be more appropriate than a contract with options. However, this does not preclude the use of an ID/IQ or requirements contract with options.

The contracting officer shall not employ options if:
- The contractor will incur undue risks; e.g., the price or availability of necessary materials or labor is not reasonably foreseeable;
- Market prices for the supplies or services involved are likely to change substantially; or
- The option represents known firm requirements for which funds are available.

C. Proposing Options.

When preparing a proposal that contains an option, the contractor faces several considerations. First, the contractor must estimate the costs of performing the option with due consideration of the risks involved, such as inflation, availability of materials, breaks in production, etc. Second, the contractor must determine whether the option price will be included in the evaluated contract price. Third, the contractor must determine whether to recover its non-recurring costs over the option quantities. Additionally, the contractor must consider the likelihood of option exercise and the worst-case timing of option exercise.

D. Evaluation of Options.

Normally, offers for option quantities or periods are evaluated when awarding the basic contract. FAR 17.206(a). This means that a contractor's option prices are included in the contract price considered when selecting the contractor.

Occasionally, the government may solicit options for less common contingencies (i.e., mobilization) which it does not wish to evaluate at the time of source selection. FAR 17.206(b). When an option is not evaluated at the time of competitive award, then the Contracting Officer may need to justify the option exercise as a non-competitive award under FAR Part 6.

E. Drafting Option Provisions.

FAR 52.217-6 thru 52.217-9 are the suggested option clauses. It is common, however, to draft more detailed option clauses when using options. In drafting a clause:

1. The option clause should require written exercise, and may require preliminary notice of intent to exercise.

2. The contract shall state the period within which the government may exercise the option. Options cannot be indefinite, but need not be a specific date if an objectively determinable event is used.

3. Where multiple options are included, consider whether the government must

exercise one option in order to exercise a second option. For example, the government should not demand the right to purchase a second production lot if it has not exercised an earlier option for a first production lot.

4. The option should state the quantity of the goods or services that may be acquired.

F. Limitations on Total Contract Period.

1. Generally, a contract, including all options, may not exceed five years. See FAR 17.204(e).

2. The "Five Year Rule" has numerous exceptions and alternate limitations for specific contracts. See 10 U.S.C. 2306b and FAR Subpart 17.1 (limiting multi-year contracts); 10 U.S.C. 2306c and FAR 17.204(e) (limiting certain service contracts); 41 U.S.C. § 6707(d) and FAR 22.1002-1 (limiting contracts falling under the SCA to five years in length); see also Delco Elec. Corp., B-244559, Oct. 29, 1991, 91-2 CPD ¶ 391 (use of options with delivery dates seven and half years later does not violate FAR 17.204(e), because the five-year limit applies to five years' requirements in a supply contract); Freightliner, ASBCA No. 42982, 94-1 BCA ¶ 26,538 (option valid if exercised within five years of award).

3. Variable option periods do not restrict competition. Madison Servs., Inc., B-278962, Apr. 17, 1998, 98-1 CPD ¶ 113 (Navy's option clause that allowed the Navy to vary the length of the option period from one to twelve months did not unduly restrict competition).

G. Exercising Options.

1. FAR 17.207 provides guidance on when the Contracting Officer may exercise options. The requirements may be summarized as:

- The option was properly considered in competitively selecting the contractor, or in justifying the lack of competition;

- Exercising the option now is still advantageous to the government; and
- The option has not expired.

2. The government must comply with applicable statutes and regulations before exercising an option. Golden West Ref. Co., EBCA No. C 9208134, 94-3 BCA ¶ 27,184 (option exercise invalid because statute required award to bidder under a new procurement); New England Tank Indus. of N.H., Inc., ASBCA No. 26474, 90-2 BCA ¶ 22,892 (option exercise invalid because of agency's failure to follow DOD regulation by improperly obligating stock funds).

3. The government must exercise the option according to its terms.

The government may not include new terms in the option. See 4737 Connor Co., L.L.C. v. United States, 2003 U.S. App. LEXIS 3289 (Fed. Cir. 2003) (option exercise was invalid where the government added a termination provision not present in the base period of the contract at the time of exercise of the option); VARO, Inc., ASBCA No. 47945, 47946, 96-1 BCA ¶ 28,161 (inclusion of eight additional contract clauses in option exercise invalidated the option).

The government must follow the contract requirements for exercising the option to include timing of notice. See Lockheed Martin Corp. v. Walker, 149 F.3d 1377 (Fed. Cir. 1998) (government wrongfully exercised options out of sequence); The Boeing Co., ASBCA No. 37579, 90-3 BCA ¶ 23,202 (Navy failed to exercise the option within the 60 days allowed in the contract and the board invalidated the option); and White Sands Construction, Inc., ASBCA Nos. 51875, 54029 (Apr. 16, 2004) (exercise improper when preliminary notice of intent to exercise was mailed on last day available and contractor received it after the deadline). Compare The Cessna Aircraft Co. v. Dalton, 126 F.3d 1442 (Fed. Cir. 1997) (exercise of option on 1 Oct. proper).

4. If a contractor contends that an option was exercised improperly, and performs, it may be entitled to an equitable

adjustment. See Lockheed Martin IR Imaging Sys., Inc. v. West, 108 F.3d 319 (1997) (partial exercise of an option was held to be a constructive change to the contract).

5.   Decisions to Exercise Options.

The government has the discretion to decide whether or not to exercise an option. Among the reasons an agency may decide not to exercise an option are:

- The option quantity is not needed.
- There is a possibility of obtaining a better price by competing the requirement.
- The incumbent has had performance issues and the agency may wish to conduct a new competition.
- The decision not to exercise an option is generally not a protestable issue since it involves a matter of contract administration. See Young-Robinson Assoc., Inc., B 242229, Mar. 22, 1991, 91-1 CPD ¶ 319 (contractor cannot protest agency's failure to exercise an option because it is a matter of contract administration); but see Mine Safety Appliances Co., B-238597.2, July 5, 1990, 69 Comp. Gen. 562, 90-2 CPD ¶ 11 (GAO reviewed option exercise which was, in effect, a source selection between parallel development contracts).
- A contractor may file a claim under the Disputes clause, but must establish that the government abused its discretion or acted in bad faith. See Kirk/Marsland Adver., Inc., ASBCA No. 51075, 99-2 ¶ 30,439 (summary judgment to government); Pennyrile Plumbing, Inc., ASBCA Nos. 44555, 47086, 96-1 BCA ¶ 28,044 (no bad faith or abuse of discretion).

A potential competitor may protest a decision to exercise an option. See Alice Roofing & Sheet Metal Works, Inc., B-283153, Oct. 13, 1999, 99 2 CPD ¶ 70 (protest denied where agency reasonably determined that option exercise was most advantageous means of satisfying needs).

VII. CONTRACT TYPES CLASSIFIED BY SUPPLIES OR SERVICES ACQUIRED.

A. Types of Requirements.

Agencies fulfill many types of requirements through contracting. Because differences in requirements require different contract terms, contracts are usually differentiated by the primary type of requirement fulfilled. The principal categories of requirements are:

- Supplies - all property except land or interest in land (See FAR 2.101)
- Services (See FAR Part 37)
- Construction, alteration, or repair of buildings (See FAR Part 36)
- Research and Development (See FAR Part 35)

A Firm Fixed Price for construction will contain many different clauses than a Firm Fixed Price contract for supplies and will be subject to different statutes and regulations.

B. Performance-Based Contracting. FAR Subpart 37.6.

1.   Performance-Based Contracts are a type of Service contract that focuses on results rather than methods. For example, a maintenance contractor may be required to maintain a specified fleet availability, rather than being required to perform defined maintenance tasks.

2.   The difference between an ordinary service contract and a performance-based contract is the latter uses a clearly defined concise statement of objectives (SOO) derived from a Performance Work Statement (PWS) which is individually tailored to consider the period of performance, deliverable items, and the desired degree of performance flexibility. FAR 37.602-1(a).

C. Government-wide Acquisition Contracts (GWACs). FAR 2.101

Contract Types

1. Government-wide Acquistion Contracts are task order or delivery order contracts for Information Technology where the IT supplies or services are acquired for government-wide use.

2. In a GWAC, the contracting agency is an executive agent designated by the Office of Management and Budget pursuant to 40 U.S.C. 11302(e), or under a delegation of procurement authority issued by the General Services Administration (GSA) prior to August 7, 1996, under authority granted GSA by former section 40 U.S.C. 759, repealed by Pub. L. 104-106.

3. The Economy Act does not apply to orders under a government-wide acquisition contract.

4. There are different types of GWACs. See the GSA website for more info: http://www.gsa.gov/portal/content/104874

VIII. SELECTION OF CONTRACT TYPE.

A. Regulatory Limitations.

1. Sealed Bid Procedures (FAR Part 14) are limited to soliciting firm-fixed-price contracts or fixed-price contracts with economic price adjustments. FAR 16.102(a) and FAR 14.104.

2. Contracting by Negotiation (FAR Part 15). Any contract type or combination of types described in the FAR may be selected for contracts negotiated under FAR Part 15. FAR 16.102(b).

3. Commercial items. Agencies must use firm-fixed-price contracts or fixed-price contracts with economic price adjustment to acquire commercial items. As long as the contract utilized is either a firm-fixed-price contract or fixed-price contract with economic price adjustment, however, it may also contain terms permitting indefinite delivery. FAR 12.207. Agencies may also utilize award fee or performance or delivery incentives when the award fee or incentive is based solely on factors other than cost. FAR 12.207; FAR 16.202-1; FAR 16.203-1.

B. Factors to Consider.

1. Selecting the contract type is generally a matter for negotiation and requires the exercise of sound judgment. The objective is to negotiate a contract type and price (or estimated cost and fee) that will result in reasonable contractor risk and provide the contractor with the greatest incentive for efficient and economical performance. FAR 16.103(a). (See Figure 1, below).

2. Selection of a contract type is ultimately left to the reasonable discretion of the contracting officer. Diversified Tech. & Servs. of Virginia, Inc., B 282497, July 19, 1999, 99-2 CPD ¶ 16 (change from cost-reimbursement to fixed-price found reasonable).

3. There are numerous factors that the contracting officer should consider in selecting the contract type. FAR 16.104.

   - Availability of price competition.
   - The accuracy of price or cost analysis.
   - The type and complexity of the requirement.
   - Urgency of the requirement.
   - Period of performance or length of production run.
   - Contractor's technical capability and financial responsibility.
   - Adequacy of the contractor's accounting system.
   - Concurrent contracts.
   - Extent and nature of proposed subcontracting.
   - Acquisition history.

4. In the course of an acquisition, changing circumstances may make a different type appropriate. Contracting Officers should avoid protracted use of cost-reimbursement or time-and-materials contracts after experience provides a basis for firmer pricing. FAR 16.103(c).

C. Statutory Prohibition Against Cost-Plus-Percentage-of-Cost (CPPC) Contracts.

1. The cost-plus-percentage-of-cost system of contracting is prohibited. 10 U.S.C. § 2306(a); 41 U.S.C. § 3905(a); FAR 16.102(c).

2. Cost-plus-percentage of cost contracts were used in the First World War to construct military encampments at a time of highly volatile prices due to the rapid mobilization. The contractor earned a specific profit rate based on the actual costs incurred, which decreased as costs grew.

3. Identifying cost-plus-percentage-of-cost. In general, any contractual provision is prohibited that assures the Contractor of greater profits if it incurs greater costs. The criteria used to identify a proscribed CPPC system, as enumerated by the court in Urban Data Sys., Inc. v. United States, 699 F.2d 1147 (Fed. Cir. 1983) (adopting criteria developed by the Comptroller General at 55 Comp. Gen. 554, 562 (1975)), are:

   • Payment is on a predetermined percentage rate;
   • The percentage rate is applied to actual performance costs;
   • The Contractor's entitlement is uncertain at the time of award; and
   • The Contractor's entitlement increases commensurately with increased performance costs. See also Alisa Corp., AGBCA No. 84-193-1, 94-2 BCA ¶ 26,952 (finding contractor was entitled to *quantum valebant* basis of recovery where contract was determined to be an illegal CPPC contract).

4. Compare The Dep't of Labor-Request for Advance Decision, B-211213, Apr. 21, 1983, 62 Comp. Gen. 337, 83-1 CPD ¶ 429 (finding the contract was a prohibited CPPC) with Tero Tek Int'l, Inc., B-228548, Feb. 10, 1988, 88-1 CPD ¶ 132 (determining the travel entitlement was not uncertain; therefore, CPPC was not present).

5. Equitable adjustments are not CPPC contracts because the fee earned is not predetermined. If the government directs the contractor to perform additional work not covered within the scope of the original contract, the contractor is entitled to additional fee. Digicon Corp., GSBCA No. 14257-COM, 98-2 BCA ¶ 29,988.

IX. CONCLUSION.

Federal government contracting has an array of contract types that are tailored to specific types of acquisitions. While there is some flexibility within specific types of contracts, there is much more consistency, so both the government and the contractor know the basic terms and conditions when a contract is described as a "Cost Plus Fixed Fee R&D Contract." This consistency reflects the government's need to manage its huge procurement workload. The consistent terms and conditions are frequently adopted in large measure when prime contractors award subcontracts to their suppliers. Consequently, what might be a complex area of the law is actually well understood by almost every contractor and contracting officer. Most importantly, the selection of type allocates the risk of cost growth.

FIGURE 1

ALLOCATION OF COST RISK

GOVERNMENT RISK	↑	CPFF-LOE T & M CPFF CPFF CPAF CPIF COST – NO FEE COST SHARING FPAF FPI
CONTRACTOR RISK	↓	FFP W/ EPA FFP

SIMPLIFIED ACQUISITION PROCEDURES

I. INTRODUCTION. While all government contracting is heavily regulated, there is a general acknowledgment that in smaller purchases many requirements are unnecessary, or the added cost far outweighs the added value. Furthermore, smaller purchases are often made by government employees with less training and experience, or whose purchasing duties are secondary to their primary job. Consequently, statutes and regulations implement simplified procedures for smaller acquisitions. These procedures are the subject of FAR Part 13 and DFARS Part 213.

This chapter describes the simplified procedures available and the conditions under which they may be used. Simplified acquisition procedures include use of imprest funds, purchase orders, credit cards, and blanket purchase agreements.

II. WHEN TO USE SIMPLIFIED ACQUISITION PROCEDURES.

A. Simplified Acquisition Threshold.

1. The dividing line that separates smaller acquisitions permitted to use simplified procedures from larger purchases that must comply with the full range of procedures is known as the "Simplified Acqusition Threshold." Many statutory and regulatory requirements do not apply to purchases below this threshold. The threshold is defined in FAR 2.101.

2. As of August, 2015, FAR 2.101 states: "Simplified acquisition threshold" means $150,000, except for acquisitions of supplies or services that, as determined by the head of the agency, are to be used to support a contingency operation or to facilitate defense against or recovery from nuclear, biological, chemical, or radiological attack (41 U.S.C. 1903), the term means--

(1) $300,000 for any contract to be awarded and performed, or purchase to be made, inside the United States; and

(2) $1 million for any contract to be awarded and performed, or purchase to be made, outside the United States.

3. The Simplified Acquisition Threshold is set by statute. See 41 U.S.C. § 134; 41 U.S.C. § 153; 10 U.S.C. § 2302a. The threshold is adjusted every five years using the Consumer Price Index (CPI) for all urban consumers. 41 U.S.C. § 1908.

B. Micro-Purchase Threshold.

1. For very small purchases, acquisition regulations are further relaxed. Very small purchases are defined by a "Micro-Purchase Threshold."

2. As of August 2015, the "Micro-Purchase Threshold" means acquisitions under $3,000. FAR 2.101.

3. For acquisitions of construction subject to the Davis Bacon Act, 40 U.S.C. chapter 31, subchapter IV, Wage Rate Requirements (Construction), the threshold is $2,000.

4. For acquisitions subject to the Service Contract Act, 41 U.S.C. chapter 67, Service Contract Labor Standards, the threshold is $2,500.

5. For acquisitions of supplies or services that, as determined by the head of the agency, are to be used to support a contingency operation or to facilitate defense against or recovery from nuclear, biological, chemical or radiological attack (except for construction), the threshold is $15,000 in the case of any contract to be awarded and performed, or purchase to

be made, inside the United States; and $30,000 in the case of any contract to be awarded and performed, or purchase to be made, outside the United States.

C. Application of the Thresholds.

1. Do not use simplified acquisition procedures to acquire supplies and services:

   - initially estimated to exceed a threshold, or
   - that will, in fact, exceed a threshold. FAR 13.003(c).

2. Dividing requirements to keep purchases under a threshold is prohibited. 10 U.S.C. § 2304(g)(2); FAR 13.003(c). See L.A. Systems v. Department of the Army, GSBCA 13472-P, 96-1 BCA ¶ 28,220 (government improperly fragmented purchase of computer upgrades into four parts because agency knew that all four upgrades were necessary and were therefore one requirement). But see Petchem, Inc. v. United States, 99 F. Supp. 2d 50 (D.D.C. 2000) (Navy did not violate CICA by purchasing tugboat services on a piecemeal basis even though total value of the services exceeded [the Simplified Acquisition Threshold]).

3. Agencies shall use simplified acquisition procedures to the maximum extent practicable for all below threshold purchases of supplies or services. FAR 13.003(a).

4. Agencies need not use simplified acquisition procedures if it can meet its requirement using:

   - Required sources of supply under FAR part 8 (e.g., Federal Prison Industries, Committee for Purchase from People who are Blind or Severely Disabled, and Federal Supply Schedule contracts);

   - Existing indefinite delivery/indefinite quantity contracts; or
   - Other established contracts.

D. Simplified Acquisitions of Commercial Items.

1. Commercial Items are defined in FAR 2.101.

2. When a contracting officer reasonably expects, based on the nature of the supplies or services sought, and on market research, that offers will include only Commercial Items, he or she may use simplified acquisition procedures up to a much higher threshold. FAR 13.500(a). As of August 2015, the higher thresholds for Commercial Items were:

   - $6.5 million, including options; and
   - $12 million for acquisitions of supplies or services that the head of the agency determines are to be used to support a contingency operation or to facilitate defense against or recovery from nuclear, biological, chemical or radiological attack.

3. These thresholds permit the acquisition of large and sophisticated items. See American Eurocopter Corporation, B-283700, Dec. 16, 1999, 1999 U.S. Comp. Gen. LEXIS 222 (agency used authority of FAR 13.5 to purchase Bell Helicopter).

4. Special Documentation Requirements. FAR 13.501. Contracting officers must document sole source acquisitions of commercial items using simplified acquisition procedures. While such acquisitions are exempt from the requirements in FAR Part 6 (Competition), the contracting officer must justify his or her actions in writing and obtain approval at higher levels as specified in FAR 13.501(a).

FAR 13.501(b) requires the contract file to include:

- A brief written description of the procedures used in awarding the contract,
- The number of offers received;
- An explanation, tailored to the size and complexity of the acquisition, of the basis for the contract award decision; and
- Any approved justification to conduct a sole-source acquisition.

III. SIMPLIFIED ACQUISITION PROCEDURES.

A. **Small Business Set-Aside Requirement.** FAR 13.003(b).

1. Simplified acquisition procedures are used to set aside work for small businesses. Any acquisition for supplies or services that has an anticipated dollar value exceeding the Micro-Purchase Threshold (usually $3,000 at the time of this writing), but not over the Simplified Acquisition Threshold (usually $150,000 at the time of this writing), is automatically reserved for small business concerns.[1] FAR 13.003(b)(1); FAR 19.502-2.

2. Contracting officers should take steps to maximize competition among small businesses as provided in FAR 13.003(h); 13.104.

3. Exceptions. The set-aside requirement does not apply when:

- There is no reasonable expectation of obtaining quotations from two or more responsible small business concerns that are competitive in terms of market prices, quality, or delivery. FAR 19.502-

2(a). See Hughes & Sons Sanitation, B-270391, Feb. 29, 1996, 96-1 CPD ¶ 119 (finding reasonable the agency's use of unrestricted procurement based on unreasonably high quotes received from small businesses for recently cancelled RFQ); But see American Imaging Servs., Inc., B-246124.2, Feb. 13, 1992, 92-1 CPD ¶ 188 (limited small business response to unrestricted solicitation for maintenance services did not justify issuance of unrestricted solicitation for significantly smaller acquisition of similar services);

- Purchases occur outside the United States, its territories and possessions, Puerto Rico, and the District of Columbia. FAR 19.000(b).

4. Canceling a small business set-aside. FAR 19.502-2(a); 19.506.

If the government does not receive an acceptable (e.g., fair market price) quote from a responsible small business concern, the contracting officer shall withdraw the set-aside and compete the purchase on an unrestricted basis. In establishing that an offered price is unreasonable, the contracting officer may consider such factors as the government estimate, the procurement history for the supplies or services in question, current market conditions, and the "courtesy bid" of an otherwise ineligible large business. Vitronics, Inc., B-237249, Jan. 16, 1990, 69 Comp. Gen. 170, 90-1 CPD ¶ 57.

The GAO will review the contracting officer's decision to withdraw a set-aside, using a standard of no rational basis, or was based on fraud or bad faith. See Omni Elevator, B-233450.2, Mar. 7, 1989, 89-1 CPD ¶ 248 (quote 95% higher than government estimate was unreasonable); Vitronics, Inc., B-237249, Jan. 16, 1990, 69 Comp. Gen. 170, 90-1 CPD ¶ 57 (protester's quote that was 6% higher than large business courtesy quote was not per se unreasonable and required explanation from contracting officer).

B. **Synopsis and Posting Requirements.** FAR 13.105.

---

[1] Contracting offices should maintain source lists of small business concerns to ensure that small business concerns are given the maximum practicable opportunity to respond to simplified acquisition solicitations. FAR 13.102.

Simplified Acquisition

1. Activities must meet the posting and synopsis requirements of FAR 5.101 and 5.203 ($15,000-$25,000, post in public place; >$25,000, synopsize in FedBizOpps.gov).

2. When acquiring commercial items, the contracting officer can use the combined synopsis/solicitation procedure detailed at FAR 12.603.

C. Competition Requirements. FAR 13.104; FAR 13.106-1.

1. Competition standard.

   a. The Competition in Contracting Act of 1984 (CICA) exempts simplified acquisition procedures from the requirement that agencies obtain full and open competition.10 U.S.C.§ 2304(g)(1); 41 U.S.C. § 3901(b)(3).

   b. For simplified acquisitions, CICA requires only that agencies obtain competition to the "maximum extent practicable." 10 U.S.C. § 2304(g)(3); 41 U.S.C. 1901(c); FAR 13.104.

2. Defining "maximum extent practicable."

   a. The contracting officer must make reasonable efforts, consistent with efficiency and economy, to give responsible sources the opportunity to compete. Gateway Cable Co., B-223157, Sep. 22, 1986, 65 Comp. Gen. 854, 86-2 CPD ¶ 333.

   b. Generally, the contracting officer should solicit at least three sources. FAR 13.104. Additionally, the Agency should try to include at least sources that were not included in previous solicitations.

   c. Ordinarily, adequate competition can be obtained by soliciting quotes from sources within the local trade area. FAR 13.104(b).

   d. Vendors who ask should be afforded a reasonable opportunity to compete. An agency does not obtain maximum practicable competition where it fails to solicit other responsible sources who request the opportunity to compete. Gateway Cable Co., B-223157, Sep. 22, 1986, 65 Comp. Gen. 854, 86-2 CPD ¶ 333 (agency failed to solicit protester who had called contracting officer 19 times).

   e. An agency's failure to solicit an incumbent is not in itself a violation of the requirement to promote competition. Rather, the determinative question where an agency has deliberately excluded a firm which expressed an interest in competing is whether the agency acted reasonably. See SF & Wellness, B-272313, Sep. 23, 1996, 96-2 CPD ¶ 122 (protest denied where contract specialist left message on incumbent's answering machine); Bosco Contracting, Inc., B-270366, Mar. 4, 1996, 96-1 CPD ¶ 140 (protest sustained where decision not to solicit incumbent was based on alleged past performance problems that were not factually supported).

   f. The contracting officer should avoid restrictive provisions, such as specifying a particular manufacturer's product, only to the extent necessary to satisfy the agency's needs. See American Eurocopter Corporation, B-283700, Dec. 16, 1999, 1999 U.S. Comp. Gen. LEXIS 222 (finding reasonable the solicitation for a Bell Helicopter model 407); Delta International, Inc., B-284364.2, May 11, 2000, 00-1 CPD ¶ 78 (agency could not justify how only one type of x-ray system would meet its needs).

   g. Sole source and brand name acquisitions. An agency may limit an RFQ to a single source if only one source is reasonably available (e.g., urgency, exclusive licensing agreements, or industrial mobilization). FAR 13.106-1(b). However, the contracting officer must furnish potential offerors a reasonable opportunity to respond to the agency's notice of intent to award on a sole source basis. See Jack Faucett Associates, Inc., B-279347, June 3, 1998, 1998 U.S. Comp. Gen. LEXIS 215 (unreasonable to issue purchase order one day after providing FACNET notice of intent to sole-source award). Where a proposed sole source or brand name acquisition exceeds $150,000, the contracting officer must use the procedures in FAR 15.501 to document the decision.

h. Competition for Micro-Purchases. FAR 13.202. While common sense supports obtaining prices from multiple sources, micro-purchase procedures do not require formal solicitation of multiple sources where the contracting officer finds the price is reasonable. FAR 13.203(a)(2). To the extent practicable, micro-purchases shall be distributed equitably among qualified suppliers. FAR 13.202(a)(1). See Grimm's Orthopedic Supply & Repair, B-231578, Sept. 19, 1988, 88-2 CPD ¶ 258 (agency properly distributed orthopedic business based on a rotation list).

IV. SIMPLIFIED ACQUISITION METHODS.

There are several types of simplified acquisition methods. The more common include the Government Purchase Card (credit card), imprest funds, priced and unpriced purchase orders, blanket ordering agreements, etc.

No specific method is preferred. "Authorized individuals"[2] shall use the simplified acquisition method that is most suitable, efficient, and economical. FAR 13.003(g).

A. **Purchase Orders.** FAR 13.302.

1. Definition. A purchase order is a government offer to buy certain supplies, services, or construction, from commercial sources, upon specified terms and conditions. FAR 13.004. A purchase order is different than a delivery order, which is placed against an established contract. Unlike a delivery order, a contractor is free to accept or reject a purchase order.

2. In summary, simplified acquisition procedures using purchase orders consists of:

- Soliciting quotes from 3 or more small business sources;
- Synopsize the solicitation, if required;
- Issuing a written purchase order to the selected source submitting a quotation;
- The selected source accepting the purchase order in writing, by starting performance, or by delivering the goods and services.

3. The first step in acquiring goods or services by purchase order is obtaining maximum practicable competition as discussed in III.B and III.C, above. Competition is good. Contracting officers shall promote competition to the maximum extent practicable to obtain supplies and services from the source whose offer is most advantageous to the government considering the administrative cost of the purchase. FAR 13.104. Do not:

---

[2] An "authorized individual" is someone who has been granted authority under agency procedures to acquire supplies and services under simplified acquisition procedures. FAR 13.001.

- solicit quotations based on personal preference; or
- restrict solicitation to suppliers of well-known and widely distributed makes or brands.

4. In evaluating whether the contracting officer has achieved maximum practicable competition, the attorney should consider:

- The goods or services acquired;
- Recent purchases;
- Urgency of the proposed purchase;
- The dollar value of the proposed purchase; and
- Price history.

5. As a minimum, solicitations should communicate the requirements and the basis of award. Regardless of the method used to solicit quotes, the contracting officer shall notify potential quoters of the basis on which award will be made (price alone or price and other factors, e.g., past performance and quality). Contracting officers are encouraged to use best value. FAR 13.106-1(a)(2).

6. Methods of soliciting quotes. Solicitations are typically referred to as Requests for Quotations ("RFQ"). An RFQ may be:

a. Oral. Oral solicitations of quotations are permitted, and encouraged where written synopses are not required. FAR 13.106-1(c)

Oral solicitations may not be practicable for actions exceeding $15,000 unless covered by an exception in FAR 5.202.

b. Electronic. Many agencies use online tools to solicit quotes for purchase orders. See https://contracting.tacom.army.mil/cfdata/sol/sol01.cfm?. The FAR

encourages use of such tools. FAR 13.003(f); FAR Subpart 4.5.

c. Written. FAR 13.106-1(d); Standard Form 18.

(1) Contracting officers shall issue a written solicitation for construction requirements exceeding $2,000.

(2) Contracting officers should issue written solicitations for non-construction contract actions likely to exceed $30,000.

7. Quotations. Potential sources respond to RFQs with quotations. A quotation is a non-binding price for performing the solicited work. A quotation is not an offer, and can't be accepted by the government to form a binding contract. FAR 13.004(a); Eastman Kodak Co., B-271009, May 8, 1976, 96-1 CPD 215.

8. Receipt of Quotes. The contracting officer reviews the quotes received and selects a supplier based on the considerations communicated in the solicitation.

a. Contracting officers shall establish deadlines for the submission of responses to solicitations that afford suppliers a reasonable period of time to respond. FAR 13.003(h)(2). See American Artisan Productions, Inc., B-281409, Dec. 21, 1998, 98-2 CPD ¶ 155 (finding fifteen-day response period reasonable). But see KPMG Consulting, B-290716, B-290716.2, Sept. 23, 2002, 2002 CPD ¶ 196 (agency may, if not prohibited by solicitation, consider a late quote).

Contracting officers shall consider all quotations that are timely received. FAR 13.003(h)(3). The government can solicit and receive new quotations any time before contract formation, unless a request for quotations establishes a firm closing date. Technology Advancement Group, B-238273, May 1, 1990, 90-1 CPD ¶ 439; ATF Constr. Co., Inc., B-260829, July 18, 1995, 95-2 CPD ¶ 29. When a purchase order has been issued prior to receipt of a quote, the agency's decision not to consider the quote is unobjectionable. Comspace Corp. B-274037, Nov. 14, 1996, 96-2 CPD ¶ 186.

9.   Evaluation of Quotations.

Contracting officers must evaluate quotations fairly and in accordance with the terms of the solicitation. FAR 13.106-2(a)(2); Kathryn Huddleston & Assocs., Ltd., B-289453, Mar. 11, 2002, 2002 CPD ¶ 167; Finlen Complex Inc., B-288280, Oct. 10, 2001, 2001 CPD ¶ 167.

The contracting officer has broad discretion in fashioning suitable evaluation criteria. At the contracting officer's discretion, one or more, but not necessarily all, of the evaluation procedures in FAR Parts 14 or 15 may be used. FAR 13.106-2(b). See Cromartie and Breakfield, B-279859, Jul. 27, 1998, 1998 U.S. Comp. Gen. LEXIS 266 (upholding rejection of quote using Part 14 procedures for suspected mistake).

If a solicitation contains no evaluation factors other than price, price is the sole evaluation criterion. United Marine International, Inc., B-281512, Feb. 22, 1999, 99-1 CPD ¶ 44.

If using price and other factors, ensure quotes can be evaluated in an efficient and minimally burdensome fashion. Formal evaluation plans, discussions, and scoring of quotes are not required. Contracting officers may conduct comparative evaluations of offers. FAR 13.106-2(b)(2); See United Marine International LLC, B-281512, Feb. 22, 1999, 99-1 CPD ¶ 44 (discussions not required).

The contracting officer may use factors such as past performance in selecting a supplier. The contracting officer need not create a formal data base (although use of existing data bases is a good practice). The contracting officer may consider personal knowledge of and previous experience with the supply or service being acquired, customer surveys, or other reasonable basis. FAR 13.106-2(b)(2); See MAC's General Contractor, B-276755, July 24, 1997, 97-2 CPD ¶ 29 (reasonable to use protester's default termination under a prior contract as basis for selecting a higher quote for award); Environmental Tectonics Corp., B-280573.2, Dec. 1, 1998, 98-2 CPD ¶ 140 (Navy properly considered evidence of past performance from sources not listed in vendor's quotation).

The contracting officer must always determine that the proposed price is fair and reasonable. FAR 13.106-3(a).

10.   Issuing a Purchase Order.

A purchase order is a government offer to buy supplies or services under specified terms and conditions. A supplier creates a contract when it accepts the government's order. C&M Mach. Prods., Inc., ASBCA No. 39635, 90-2 BCA ¶ 22,787 (bidder's response to a purchase order proposing a new price was a counteroffer that the government could accept or reject).

Contractor acceptance of the purchase order. FAR 13.004(b). A contractor may accept a government order by:

- notifying the government, preferably in writing; or
- furnishing supplies or services; or
- proceeding with work to the point where substantial performance has occurred.

The contracting officer may require the contractor to accept the purchase order in writing. See DD Form 1155, Block 16.

For contractors, the benefits of immediately accepting a purchase order in writing are many. Most notably, a contractor's written acceptance means the government may not withdraw or cancel the order.

11.   Documentation. FAR 13.106-3.

Typically, a purchase order is issued using standard forms, such as the DD Form 1155 for the Department of Defense, or the Standard Form 44.

The contracting officer must include a statement in the contract file supporting the award decision if other than price-related factors were considered in selecting the supplier. FAR 13.106-3(b)(3)(ii); see Universal Building Maintenance, Inc, B-282456, Jul. 15, 1999, 1999 U.S. Comp. Gen. LEXIS 132 (protest sustained because contracting officer failed to document award selection, and FAR Parts 12 and 13 required some explanation of the award decision).

The contracting officer should provide a notice to unsuccessful vendors if requested. FAR 13.106-3(c) and (d).

12. Termination of Purchase Orders. FAR 13.302-4.

Before acceptance, the government may withdraw, amend, or cancel an order, unless the contractor has begun performance. See Alsace Industrial, Inc., ASBCA No. 51708, 99-1 BCA ¶ 30,220 (holding that the government's offer under the unilateral purchase order lapsed by its own terms when Alsace failed to deliver on time); Master Research & Mfg., Inc., ASBCA No. 46341, 94-2 BCA ¶ 26,747. Consequently, contractors have a strong motivation to accept in writing immediately.

The government's ability to cancel a purchase order is limited when the Contractor has begun performance. In Comptech Corp., ASBCA No. 55526, 08-2 BCA ¶ 33,982, the ASBCA discusses the common law applicable to situations where a contractor begins performance in reliance on an offer. It concluded that beginning performance makes the purchase order irrevocable before the delivery date, or for a reasonable time.

Where a contractor has not accepted the purchase order in writing, the government has a dilemma. If the contractor has not begun performance, then the contracting officer may notify the contractor in writing and cancel the purchase order. If the contractor does not accept the cancellation, or claims that it incurred costs

as a result of beginning performance, then the contracting officer may terminate the purchase order as provided in the contract. See Rex Sys., Inc., ASBCA No. 45301, 93-3 BCA ¶ 26,065 (contractor's substantial performance only required the government to keep its unilateral purchase order offer open until the delivery date, after which the government could cancel when goods were not timely delivered).

Once the contractor accepts a purchase order in writing, the government cannot cancel it; the contracting officer must terminate the contract in accordance with:

- Commercial Items - FAR 12.403(d) and 52.212-4(l); or
- Non-Commercial Items - FAR Part 49 and FAR 52.213-4.

13. Documentation should be kept to a minimum. FAR 13.106-3(b) provides examples of the types of information that should be recorded. Typically, agency procedures will specify the documentation that must accompany the invoice for payment.

14. For delivery and payment of contractor's invoices, see Chapter 21.

B. **Blanket Purchase Agreements.** FAR 13.303.

1. In summary, a Blanket Purchase Agreement (BPA) is an ordering arrangement between the government and a contractor. For example, the government may set up a BPA with a local bakery. The dining facility will place orders with the bakery daily for bread, and each order is a contract, incorporating the BPA terms.

2. Definition. A Blanket Purchase Agreement (BPA) is a simplified method of filling anticipated repetitive needs for supplies or services by establishing "charge accounts" with qualified sources of supply. FAR 13.303-1(a). A BPA is not a contract.

The actual contract is not formed until an order is issued or the basic agreement is incorporated into a new contract by reference. Modern Technology Corp. v. United States, 24 Cl. Ct. 360 (1991) (Judge Bruggink provides comprehensive analysis of legal effect of a BPA in granting summary judgment to Postal Service in breach claim).

3. BPAs do not necessarily obligate public funds. BPAs may be issued without a commitment of funds; however, a commitment and an obligation of funds must separately support each order placed under a BPA. Nor does a BPA necessarily obligate the contractor to specific prices for its products.

4. Competition on BPA Orders.

The use of a BPA does not justify purchasing from only one source or avoiding small business set-asides. FAR 13.303-5(c). Ideally, the contracting officer should negotiate a sufficient number of BPAs to ensure maximum practicable competition. For example, the contracting officer should enter into BPAs with several bakeries serving its dining facility. FAR 13.303-5(d).

A BPA is an efficient acquisition method when:
- There is a wide variety of items in a broad class of supplies and services that are generally purchased, but the exact items, quantities, and delivery requirements are not known in advance and may vary considerably.
- There is a need to provide commercial sources of supply for one or more offices or projects that do not have or need authority to purchase otherwise.
- Use of BPAs would avoid the writing of numerous purchase orders.
- There is no existing requirements contract for the same supply or service that the contracting activity is legally obligated to use.

5. Establishment of BPAs. FAR 13.303-2(b-c). BPAs are very flexible.

    a. BPAs may be established with a single supplier or many suppliers.

    b. A BPA may be created under the Federal Supply Schedule (FSS) "if not inconsistent with the terms of the applicable schedule contract." FAR 13.303-2(c)(3).[3] FAR 8.404(b)(4) provides guidance for creating a BPA under the FSS. GSA provides a sample BPA format for agencies to use.

    c. Pricing is a key issue in BPAs, and there are various approaches to establishing pricing. One approach is to have a price list attached, which the vendor may update. A second approach is to reference a published price, with or without a discount.

6. Ordering under BPAs.

Typically, orders under BPAs are placed by designated persons, with specified limits of authority. For example, in our hypothetical BPA with a local bakery, the dining facility manager may be designated as the ordering official.

7. Review of BPAs. The contracting officer who entered into the BPA shall (FAR 13.303-6):

    a. ensure it is reviewed at least annually and updated if necessary;

    b. maintain awareness in market conditions, sources of supply, and other pertinent factors that warrant new arrangements or modifications of existing arrangements; and

    c. review a sufficient random sample of orders at least annually to make sure authorized procedures are being followed.

___

[3] All schedule contracts contain BPA provisions. FAR 8.404(b)(4).

C. Imprest Funds. FAR Part 13.305; DFARS 213.305.

1. In summary, imprest funds are the federal equivalent of a "petty cash" fund that commercial businesses maintain to make immediate payments of cash for small purchases. With the advent of credit cards, debit cards, and mobile payment systems in first-world countries, the need for imprest funds has greatly diminished. In less-developed countries, cash transactions are still an important economic tool, necessitating the need for imprest funds.

2. Definition. An imprest fund is a "cash fund of a fixed amount established by an advance of funds, without charge to an appropriation, from an agency finance or disbursing officer to a duly appointed cashier, for disbursement as needed from time to time in making payment in cash for relatively small amounts." FAR 13.001.

3. DOD Policy. DOD discourages cash payments from imprest funds. This policy is based, in part, on the mandatory electronic funds transfer requirements of the Debt Collection Improvement Act of 1996 (Pub. L. 104-134). DFARS 213.305-1(1).

Use of imprest funds must comply with the conditions stated in the DOD Financial Management Regulation[4] and the Treasury Financial Manual.[5] Imprest funds can be used without further approval for:
- Overseas transactions at or below the micro-purchase threshold in support of a contingency operation as defined in 10 U.S.C. § 101(a)(13) or a humanitarian or peacekeeping operation as defined in 10 U.S.C. § 2302(7); and
- Classified transactions. 213.305-3(d)(ii).

Otherwise, use of imprest funds requires high-level approval. DFARS 213.305-1(2) restricts the authority to the Director for Financial Commerce, Office of the Deputy Chief Financial Officer, Office of the Under Secretary of Defense (Comptroller). DFARS 213.305-3(d)(I)(B).

D. Government-wide Commercial Purchase Card. FAR 13.301.

1. The Government-wide Commercial Purchase Card is similar to a private credit card in the sense that it can be used for over-the-counter purchases, up to the credit limit of the card holder. It is different from a private credit card in the sense that the government is not borrowing the money that the vendor receives. Instead, the government pays the card issuer for charges to the card, which the issuer pays to the merchant, less a service fee.

2. Purpose. The government-wide commercial purchase card is authorized for use in making and/or paying for purchases of supplies, services, or construction.[6] Generally the card is used for Micro-Purchases. DOD contracting officers must use the card for all acquisitions at or below $2,500. DOD FMR Vol. 5, ¶ 0210. Warranted DOD contracting officers may use the card for purchases up to $25,000. DFARS 213.301(2). The purchase card is funded with appropriated funds.

3. Implementation.

In the past, some card holders have abused their authority to make purchases with a purchase card. Government Purchase Cards: Control Weaknesses Expose Agencies to Fraud and Abuse, GAO-02-676T, May 1, 2002. For that

---

[4] DOD 7000.14-R, Volume 5, Disbursing Policy and Procedures.

[5] Part 4, Chapter 3000, section 3020.

[6] DOD's purchase card limit is the simplified acquisition threshold for contingency, humanitarian, or peacekeeping operations. DFARS 213.301(2); 66 Fed. Reg. 55,123 (Nov. 1, 2001). However, the AFARS currently retains a $2,500 limit for most purchases. AFARS 5113.270.

reason, agencies using government-wide commercial purchase cards shall establish procedures for use and control of the card. FAR 13.301(b). Procedures and purchasing authority differ among agencies. Agencies must have effective training programs in place to avoid card abuses. For example, cardholders may be bypassing required sources of supply. See Memorandum, Administrator of the Office of Federal Procurement Policy, to Agency Senior Procurement executives, subject: Applicability of the Javits-Wagner-O'Day Program for Micropurchases (Feb. 16, 1999) (clarifies that JWOD's status as a priority source under FAR 8.7 applies to micropurchases). See http://www.acq.osd.mil/dpap/pdi/pc/docs/DoD_Charge_Card_Guidebook_5-30-14_Release_10-5-15.doc

4.   Consequences to the Contractor from Government Purchase Card.

There are two primary impacts to contractors stemming from accepting Government Purchase Cards, one good and one bad. The good impact is that use of credit cards is easy for the agency, facilitating sales to contractors who accept credit cards. The bad impact is that by accepting credit cards, the contractor will actually receive less than the contract price when paid because of the service fee charged the merchant by the card issuer. For commercial products with consumer sales, this service fee is ordinarily accounted for in the price. For traditional government contractors, prices may not have accounted for this service fee when previous sales were typically by check or electronic funds transfer. Today, however, most contractors should have adjusted their prices to account for the costs of accepting purchase cards.

E.   Electronic Commerce.

Electronic commerce has the potential for greatly reducing the transactional costs of federal procurement. It has not, however, met early hopes. Some of the more widely implemented initiatives are:

1.   Electronic Signatures are acceptable in federal procurement. FAR 4.502(d).

2.   Publicizing Opportunities. There is a mandatory single point of electronic access to government-wide procurement opportunities. See www.fedbizopps.gov.

3.   Electronic Funds Transfers. FAR 52.232-34 requires use of electronic fund transfers, with limited exceptions. See FAR Subpart 32.11.

4.   System for Award Management ("SAM"). SAM is the single point for registering contractors and potential contractors, and for making annual certifications and representations. See FAR Subpart 4.11.

5.   GSA has undertaken a number of initiatives in electronic commerce.

V.   CONCLUSION.

Small purchases do not have to conform to the same procedures as larger purchases. The procedures applicable depend on the amount of the purchase. Fewer procedures, however, does not mean no procedures. Even small purchases have much more process than a consumer's purchase of a like item. Small purchases must still seek competition, a fair and reasonable price, support small businesses, and other socio-economic policies. Manipulating the acquisition to take advantage of the streamlined process and ignoring applicable procedures has consequences. Abusing the simplified acquisitions for personal gain can put perpetrators in jail.

SEALED BIDDING

I. INTRODUCTION.

"The purpose of these statutes and regulations is to give all persons equal right to compete for government contracts; to prevent unjust favoritism, or collusion or fraud in the letting of contracts for the purchase of supplies; and thus to secure for the government the benefits which arise from competition. In furtherance of such purpose, invitations and specifications must be such as to permit competitors to compete on a common basis." United States v. Brookridge Farm, Inc., 111 F.2d 461, 463 (10th Cir. 1940).

There are three principal methods for awarding federal contracts: 1) Simplified Acquisition Procedures under FAR Part 13; 2) Sealed Bidding under FAR Part 14; and 3) Negotiations under FAR Part 15. Prior to World War II, the federal government used sealed bidding-type procedures for the overwhelming majority of its acquisitions, and sealed bidding was the preferred method of competitive acquisition until 1984. The reason was that sealed bidding uses a fixed process, conducted in the open, to minimize the possibility of fraud or favoritism determining the award of contracts. Today, sealed bidding is much less common, but still in use.

II. FRAMEWORK OF THE SEALED BIDDING PROCESS.

A. Current Statutes.

1. DOD, Coast Guard, and NASA – Armed Services Procurement Act of 1947, 10 U.S.C. §§ 2301-2331.

2. Other federal agencies – Federal Property and Administrative Services Act of 1949, 41 U.S.C. §§ 3701-3708.

3. These parallel statutory structures provide that:

   a. The head of an agency shall solicit sealed bids if—

      (1) time permits the solicitation, submission, and evaluation of sealed bids;

      (2) the award will be made on the basis of price and other price-related factors [see FAR 14.201-8];

      (3) it is not necessary to conduct discussions with the responding sources about their bids; and

      (4) there is a reasonable expectation of receiving more than one sealed bid.

   b. The head of an agency shall request competitive proposals if sealed bids are not required. See Racal Filter Technologies, Inc., B-240579, Dec. 4, 1990, 70 Comp. Gen. 127, 90-2 CPD ¶ 453 (sealed bidding required when all elements enumerated in the Competition in Contracting Act (CICA) are present—agencies may not use negotiated procedures); see also UBX Int'l, Inc., B-241028, Jan. 16, 1991, 91-1 CPD ¶ 45 (use of sealed bidding procedures for ordnance site survey was proper).

B. Regulations.

1. FAR Part 14--Sealed Bidding.

2. DOD and agency regulations:

   a. Defense FAR Supplement (DFARS), Part 214--Sealed Bidding.

   b. Air Force FAR Supplement (AFFARS), Part 314--Sealed Bidding.

c.   Army FAR Supplement (AFARS), Part 14--Sealed Bidding.

d.   Navy Marine Corps Acquisition Regulation Supplement (NMCARS), Part 14--Sealed Bidding.

e.   Defense Logistics Acquisition Regulation (DLAR), Part 5214--Sealed Bidding.

C.   Overview of Sealed Bidding Process: The Five Phases. FAR 14.101.

1.   Preparation of the Invitation for Bids (IFB). The contracting officer prepares a solicitation that includes a complete description of the government's needs.

2.   Publicizing the Invitation for Bids. The contracting officer publicizes the government's requirements to obtain maximum competition.

3.   Submission of Bids. Contractors submit their firm fixed prices for the work solicited in the Invitation for Bids by delivering a signed offer sealed in an envelope to the specified location by the specified time.

4.   Evaluation of Bids. The contracting officer publicly opens each bid received and announces and records the prices quoted on a bid worksheet. The contracting officer evaluates the lowest bid to determine whether the bid is responsive to the IFB, the bidder is responsible, and whether the bidder was mistaken.

5.   Contract Award. The contracting officer awards the contract to the responsible bidder submitting lowest responsive bid. There is no discretion and no opportunity to select a better value proposal.

III.   PREPARATION OF INVITATION FOR BIDS.

A.   Format of the IFB.

1.   Uniform Contract Format. FAR 14.201-1.

2.   Standard Form 33 - Solicitation, Offer and Award. FAR 53.301-33.

3.   Standard Form 30 - Amendment of Solicitation; Modification of Contract.

B.   Specifications.

1.   Clear, complete, and definite.

2.   Minimum needs of the government.

3.   Preference for Commercial Items. FAR 12.000 and FAR 12.101(b).

C.   Definition. "Offer" means "bid" in sealed bidding. FAR 2.101.

D.   Contract Type: Contracting officers may use only firm fixed-price and fixed-price with economic price adjustment contracts in sealed bidding acquisitions. FAR 14.104.

IV.   PUBLICIZING THE INVITATION FOR BIDS.

A.   Policy on Publicizing Contract Actions. FAR 5.002. Contracting officers must publicize contract actions to increase competition, broaden industry participation, and assist small business concerns in obtaining contracts and subcontracts. With limited exceptions, contracting officers shall promote full and open competition. This means that all responsible sources are permitted to compete. FAR 2.101. See generally FAR Subpart 6.1.

B.   Methods of Soliciting Potential Bidders. FAR 5.101; FAR 5.102. DOD uses three primary methods to promote competition: the Government Point of Entry, Solicitation or Bidders Mailing Lists, and copies of the solicitations posted in public places.

1.   Government Point of Entry (GPE) http://www.fedbizopps.gov. FAR Subpart 5.2. The contracting officer may not issue a solicitation until at least 15 days after publication in the GPE. Further, when synopsis in the GPE is required, the

contracting officer must give bidders a minimum of 30 days after issuance of the IFB to prepare and submit their bids. These time limits may be shortened when procuring commercial items.

2. Solicitation Mailing Lists (Bidders Mailing Lists). FAR 14.205.

    a. Prior to 25 August 2003. Contracting activities previously developed sources through the use of the SML. Such lists consisted of firms known to supply particular goods or services. When a requirement existed for an item for which an SML exists, the contracting agency would send copies of the IFB to firms on the list. Failure to solicit a contractor that requested to be included on the list could require resolicitation. Applied Constr. Technology, B-251762, May 4, 1993, 93-1 CPD ¶ 365. If the SML was excessively long, the contracting officer could rotate portions of the list for separate acquisitions. The rules required the contracting officers to use a different portion of large lists for separate acquisitions, solicit any contractor added to the list since the last solicitation (Holiday Inn, Inc., B-249673-2, Dec. 22, 1992, 92-2 CPD ¶ 428), and solicit the incumbent. Kimber Guard & Patrol, Inc., B-248920, Oct. 1, 1992, 92-2 BCA ¶ 220. See Qualimetrics, Inc., B-262057, Nov. 16, 1995, 95-2 CPD ¶ 228 (concluding that GSA should have verified mailing list to ensure that incumbent's successor was on it). But see Cutter Lumber Products, B-262223.2, Feb. 9, 1996, 96-1 CPD ¶ 57 (holding that agency's inadvertent failure to solicit incumbent does not warrant sustaining protest where agency otherwise obtained full and open competition).

    b. Effective 25 August 2003, the Civilian Agency Acquisition Council and Defense Acquisition Regulations Council eliminated the SML and the applicable form, the Standard Form 129 (SF 129). The Central Contract Registry, "a centrally located, searchable database, accessible via the Internet," is a contracting officer's "tool of choice for developing, maintaining, and providing sources for future procurements." FedBizOpps.gov, "through its interested vendors list, has the capability to generate a list of vendors who are interested in a specific solicitation." Federal Acquisition Regulation; Elimination of the Standard Form 129, Solicitation Mailing List Application, 68 Fed. Reg. 43,855 (July 24, 2003).

3. Posting in a Public Place. FAR 5.101. Every proposed contract action expected to exceed $10,000 but not expected to exceed $25,000 must be posted in a public place at the contracting office issuing the solicitation not later than the date the solicitation is issued and for at least ten days. Electronic posting may be used to satisfy this requirement.

C. **Late Receipt of Solicitations.** Failure of a potential bidder to receive an IFB in time to submit a bid, or to receive a requested solicitation at all, does not require postponement of bid opening unless adequate competition is not obtained. See Family Carpet Serv. Inc., B-243942.3, Mar. 3, 1992, 92-1 CPD ¶ 255. See also Educational Planning & Advice, B-274513, Nov. 5, 1996, 96-2 CPD ¶ 173 (refusal to postpone bid opening during a hurricane was not an abuse of discretion where adequate competition was achieved and agency remained open for business); Lewis Jamison Inc. & Assocs., B-252198, June 4, 1993, 93-1 CPD ¶ 433 (GAO denies protest where contractor had "last clear opportunity" to avoid being precluded from competing). But see Applied Constr. Technology, B-251762, May 4, 1993, 93-1 CPD ¶ 365 (although agency received 10 bids in response to IFB, GAO sustained protest where agency failed to solicit contractor it had advised would be included on its bidder's mailing list).

D. **Failure to Solicit the Incumbent Contractor.** Failure to give notice of a solicitation for supplies or services to a contractor currently providing such supplies or services may be fatal to the solicitation, unless the agency:

1. Made a diligent, good-faith effort to comply with statutory and regulatory requirements regarding notice of the acquisition and distribution of solicitation materials; and

2. Obtained reasonable prices (competition). Transwestern Helicopters, Inc., B-235187, July 28, 1989, 89-2 CPD ¶ 95 (although the agency failed inadvertently to solicit incumbent contractor, the agency made reasonable efforts to publicize the solicitation, which resulted in 25 bids). But see Professional Ambulance, Inc., B-248474, Sep. 1, 1992, 92-2 CPD ¶ 145 (agency failed to solicit the incumbent and received only three proposals; GAO recommended resolicitation).

V. SUBMISSION OF BIDS.

A. **Safeguarding Bids.** FAR 14.401.

1. Bids (including bid modifications) received before the time set for bid opening generally must remain unopened in a locked box or safe. FAR 14.401.

2. A bidder generally is not entitled to relief if the agency negligently loses its bid. Vereinigte Gebudereinigungsgesellschaft, B-252546, June 11, 1993, 93-1 CPD ¶ 454.

B. **Method of Submission.** FAR 14.301.

1. To be considered for award, a bid must comply in all material respects with the invitation for bids, including the method of submission, i.e., the bid must be responsive to the solicitation. FAR 14.301(a); LORS Medical Corp., B-259829.2, Apr. 25, 1995,

95-1 CPD ¶ 222 (bidder's failure to return two pages of IFB does not render bid nonresponsive; submission of signed SF 33 incorporates all pertinent provisions).

a. General Rule - Offerors may submit their bids by any written means permitted by the solicitation.

b. Unless the solicitation specifically allows it, the contracting officer may not consider telegraphic bids. FAR 14.301(b); MIMCO, Inc., B-210647.2, Dec. 27, 1983, 84-1 CPD ¶ 22 (telegraphic bid, which contrary to solicitation requirement makes no mention of bidder's intent to be bound by all terms and conditions, is nonresponsive).

c. The government will not consider facsimile bids unless permitted by the solicitation. FAR 14.301(c); FAR 14.202-7; Recreonics Corp., B-246339, Mar. 2, 1992, 92-1 CPD ¶ 249 (bid properly rejected for bidder's use of fax machine to transmit acknowledgment of solicitation amendment); but see Brazos Roofing, Inc., B-275113, Jan. 23, 1997, 97-1 CPD ¶ 43 (bidder not penalized for agency's inoperable FAX machine); PBM Constr. Inc., B-271344, May 8, 1996, 96-1 CPD ¶ 216 (ineffective faxed modification had no effect on the original bid, which remained available for acceptance); International Shelter Sys., B-245466, Jan. 8, 1992, 92-1 CPD ¶ 38 (hand-delivered facsimile of bid modification is not a facsimile transmission).

C. **Time and Place of Submission.** FAR 14.301.

1. Reasons for specific requirements.

a. Equality of treatment of bidders.

b. Preserve integrity of system.

c. Convenience of the government.

2. Place of submission—as specified in the IFB. FAR 14.302(a); CSLA, Inc., B-255177, Jan. 10, 1994, 94-1 CPD ¶ 63; Carolina Archaeological Serv., B-224818, Dec. 9, 1986, 86-2 CPD ¶ 662.

3. Time of submission—as specified in the IFB. FAR 14.302(a).

   a. The official designated as the bid opening officer shall decide when the time set for bid opening has arrived and shall so declare to those present. FAR 14.402-1; J. C. Kimberly Co., B-255018.2, Feb. 8, 1994, 94-1 CPD ¶ 79; Chattanooga Office Supply Co., B-228062, Sept. 3, 1987, 87-2 CPD ¶ 221 (bid delivered 30 seconds after bid opening officer declared the arrival of the bid opening time is late).

   b. The bid opening officer's declaration of the bid opening time is determinative unless it is shown to be unreasonable. Action Serv. Corp., B-254861, Jan. 24, 1994, 94-1 CPD ¶ 33. The bid opening officer may reasonably rely on the bid opening room clock when declaring bid opening time. General Eng'g Corp., B-245476, Jan. 9, 1992, 92-1 CPD ¶ 45.

   c. Where the government has control of a sealed bid at or before the time set for bid opening, the bid is not late, even if the government subsequently time stamps the bid after the time set for bid opening. Amfel Constr., Inc., B-233493.2, May 18, 1989, 89-1 CPD ¶ 477 (bid was within government control before the time stamp clock advanced to 2:01 pm and was not late); Reliable Builders, Inc., B-249908.2, Feb. 9, 1993, 93-1 CPD ¶ 116 (bid which was time/date stamped one minute past time set for bid opening was timely since bidder relinquished control of bid at the exact time set for bid opening).

   d. Arbitrary early or late bid opening is improper. William F. Wilke, Inc., B-185544, Mar. 18, 1977, 77-1 CPD ¶ 197.

4. Amendment of IFB.

   a. The government must display amendments in the bid room and must send, before the time for bid opening, a copy of the amendment to everyone that received a copy of the original IFB. FAR 14.208(a).

   b. If the government furnishes information to one prospective bidder concerning an invitation for bids, it must furnish that same information to all other bidders as an amendment if (1) such information is necessary for bidders to submit bids or (2) the lack of such information would be prejudicial to uninformed bidders. FAR 12.208(c). See Phillip Sitz Constr., B-245941, Jan. 22, 1992, 92-1 CPD ¶ 101; see also Republic Flooring, B-242962, June 18, 1991, 91-1 CPD ¶ 579 (bidder excluded from BML erroneously).

5. Postponement of bid opening. FAR 14.208; FAR 14.402-3.

   a. The government may postpone bid opening before the scheduled bid opening time by issuing an amendment to the IFB. FAR 14.208(a).

   b. The government may postpone bid opening even after the time scheduled for bid opening if:

      (1) The contracting officer has reason to believe that the bids of an important segment of bidders have been delayed in the mails for causes beyond their control and without their fault or negligence, Ling Dynamic Sys., Inc., B-252091, May 24, 1993, 93-1 CPD ¶ 407; or

(2) Emergency or unanticipated events interrupt normal governmental processes so that the conduct of bid opening as scheduled is impractical. If urgent requirements preclude amendment of the solicitation:

(a) the time for bid opening is deemed extended until the same time of day on the first normal workday; and

(b) the time of actual bid opening is the cutoff time for determining late bids. FAR 14.402-3 (c). See ALM, Inc., B-225679, Feb. 13, 1987, 87-1 CPD ¶ 165, but note that this case pre-dates the applicable FAR provision.

c. For postponement due to the delay of an important segment of bids in the mails, the contracting officer publicly must announce postponement of bid opening and issue an amendment.

D. The Firm Bid Rule.

1. Distinguish common law rule, which allows an offeror to withdraw an offer any time prior to acceptance. See Restatement (Second) of Contracts § 42 (1981).

2. Firm Bid Rule:

a. After bid opening, bidders may not withdraw their bids during the period specified in the IFB, but must hold their bids open for government acceptance during the stated period. FAR 14.201-6(j) & 52.214-16.

b. If the solicitation requires a minimum bid acceptance period, a bid that offers a shorter acceptance period than the minimum is nonresponsive. See Banknote Corp. of America, Inc., B-278514, 1998 U.S. Comp. Gen. LEXIS 33 (Feb. 4, 1998) (bidder offered 60-day bid acceptance period when solicitation required 180 days and advised bidders to disregard 60-

day bid acceptance period provision); see also Hyman Brickle & Son, Inc., B-245646, Sept. 20, 1991, 91-2 CPD ¶ 264 (30-day acceptance period offered instead of the required 120 days).

c. The bid acceptance period is a material solicitation requirement. The government may not waive the bid acceptance period because it affects the bidder's price. Valley Constr. Co., B-243811, Aug. 7, 1991, 91-2 CPD ¶ 138 (60-day period required, 30-day period offered).

d. A bid that fails to offer an unequivocal minimum bid acceptance period is ambiguous and nonresponsive. See John P. Ingram Jr. & Assoc., B-250548, Feb. 9, 1993, 93-1 CPD ¶ 117 (bid ambiguous even where bidder acknowledged amendment which changed minimum bid acceptance period). But see Connecticut Laminating Company, Inc., B-274949.2, Dec. 13, 1999, 99-2 CPD ¶ 108 (bid without bid acceptance period is acceptable where solicitation did not require any minimum bid acceptance period).

e. Exception - the government may accept a solitary bid that offers less than the minimum acceptance period. Professional Materials Handling Co., -- Reconsideration, 61 Comp. Gen. 423 (1982).

f. After the bid acceptance period expires, the bidder may extend the acceptance period only where the bidder would not obtain an advantage over other bidders. FAR 14-404-1(d). See Capital Hill Reporting, Inc., B-254011.4, Mar. 17, 1994, 94-1 CPD ¶ 232. See also NECCO, Inc., B-258131, Nov. 30, 1994, 94-2 CPD ¶ 218 (bidder ineligible for award where bid expired due to bidder's offering a shorter extension period than requested by the agency).

E. Late Bids.

1. In the solicitation, the contracting officer states the date, time, and place for submission of bids and proposals. See SF 33, Block 9. Bidders must submit their bid by the time and at the place designated in the solicitation. The reason is one of fundamental fairness. In a sealed-bid procurement, the bids are opened in public and the bidders' prices are disclosed. To permit late bids invites fraud by allowing a late bidder to modify its bid based on the disclosed prices. Therefore, late bids are rejected, with very narrow exceptions. In competitively negotiated procurements, a nearly identical rule applies, as is discussed in Chapter 9.

2. Definition of "late." A "late" bid/proposal, modification, or withdrawal is one that is received in the office designated in the IFB or RFP after the exact time set in the solicitation for bid opening. FAR 14.304(b)(1); FAR 15.208. If the IFB or RFP does not specify a time, the time for receipt is 5:00 P.M., local time, at the designated government office. FAR 14.304(b)(1); FAR 15.208.

3. **LATE IS LATE**; FAR 14.304(b)(1); FAR 15.208; FAR 52.214-7; FAR 52.215-1. As discussed above, in almost every instance that a bid is late, the contracting officer must reject the late bid or proposal.

   a. The bidder or offeror is responsible for the timely submission of its bid or proposal to the proper location. Lani Eko & Company, CPAs, PLLC, B-404863, June 6, 2011 (it is an offeror's responsibility to deliver its proposal to the place designated in the solicitation by the time specified, and late receipt generally requires rejection of the proposal); O.S. Sys., Inc., B-292827, Nov. 17, 2003, 2003 CPD ¶ 211; Integrated Support Sys.,

Inc., B-283137.2, Sept. 10, 1999, 99-2 CPD ¶51; The Staubach Co., B-276486, May 19, 1997, 97-1 CPD ¶ 190, citing Carter Mach. Co., B-245008, Aug. 7, 1991, 91-2 CPD ¶ 143.

   b. While there are exceptions to the late bid rule, they only apply if the contracting officer receives the late bid or proposal before contract award. FAR 14.304(b)(1), FAR 15.208. There are no exceptions for bids that are so late that they arrive after contract award.

4. **Exceptions to the Late Bid/Proposal Rule**. There are exceptions to the late bid rule in the FAR, and there are additional exceptions based on case law. All these exceptions have several characteristics in common: 1) the bid or proposal must get to agency before contract award; 2) the bid or proposal must be out of offeror's control; and 3) accepting the late bid or proposal must not unduly delay the acquisition.

   a. **Late electronically submitted bids.** The contracting officer may consider a bid or proposal if: 1) it was transmitted through an electronic commerce method authorized by the solicitation; and 2) the bid or was received at the initial point of entry to the government infrastructure (i.e., into the government network) not later than 4:30 P.M. one working day prior to the date specified for the receipt of bids or proposals. FAR 14.304(b)(1)(i); but see Watterson Constr. Co. v United States, 98 Fed. Cl. 84; see also Insight Systems Corp. and Centerscope Technologies, Inc., 110 Fed. Cl. 564, 2013 WL 1875987 (Fed. Cl.). Under this FAR rule, the contractor is responsible for network delays of less than one day. However, see the next exception.

   b. **Government control.** A contracting officer may consider a bid or proposal if there is acceptable evidence to establish that it was received at the government installation designated for receipt of bids or proposals and was under the government's control prior to the time set for receipt of bids or proposals. FAR 14.304(b)(1)(ii).

(1) Government control includes receipt by contractors working for the contracting officer. J. L. Malone & Associates, B-290282, July 2, 2002 (receipt of a bid by a contractor, at the direction of the contracting officer, satisfied receipt and control by the government).

(2) Watterson Constr. Co. v. U.S., 98 Fed. Cl. 84 (recognizing that the express terms of this exception do not apply to proposals submitted by e-mail, court finds, nevertheless, that once the proposal reaches the government server it is within the government's control; actual receipt by contracting officer is not necessary).

(3) Insight Systems Corp., and Centerscope Technologies, Inc., 110 Fed. Cl. 564, 2013 WL 1875987 (Fed. Cl.) (wherein the court found that a proposal transmitted and received by the government email server prior to the deadline, but not forwarded to the next server in the government email system was covered under the "Government Control" exception).

5. **"Government Frustration" Exception.** GAO case law recognizes an additional exception where the government has frustrated the offeror's efforts to timely submit its bid. If: 1) timely delivery of a bid or proposal, modification thereto, or withdrawal that is hand-carried by the offeror (or commercial carrier) is frustrated by the government; 2) the government's action is the paramount cause of the late delivery; and 3) consideration of the bid would not compromise the integrity of the competitive procurement system, then the bid is timely. U.S. Aerospace, Inc., B403464, B-403464.2, Oct. 6, 2010, 2010 CPD ¶ 225 (a late hand-carrier offer may be considered for award if the government's misdirection or improper action was the paramount cause of the late delivery and consideration would not compromise the integrity of the competitive process). Examples include:

a. Lani Eko & Co., CPAs, PLLC, B-404863, June 6, 2011 (citing Caddell Constr. Co., Inc., B-280405, Aug. 24, 1998, 98-2 CPD ¶ 50) (improper government action is "affirmative action that makes it impossible for the offeror to deliver the proposal on time");

b. Computer Literacy World, Inc., GSBCA 11767-P, May 22, 1992, 92-3 BCA ¶ 25,112 (government employee gave unwise instructions, which caused the delay); Kelton Contracting, Inc., B-262255, Dec. 12, 1995, 95-2 CPD ¶ 254 (Federal Express package misdirected by agency); Aable Tank Services, Inc., B-273010, Nov. 12, 1996, 96-2 CPD ¶ 180 (bid should be considered when its arrival at erroneous location was due to agency's affirmative misdirection).

c. Richards Painting Co., B-232678, Jan. 25, 1989, 89-1 CPD ¶ 76 (late proposal should be considered when bid opening room was in a different location than bid receipt room; protestor arrived at bid receipt location before the time set for bid opening, the room was locked, there was no sign directing bidder to the bid opening room and protestor arrived at bid opening room 3 minutes late).

d. <u>Palomar Grading & Paving, Inc.</u>, B-274885, Jan. 10, 1997, 97-1 CPD ¶ 16 (late proposal should be considered where lateness was due to government misdirection and bid had been relinquished to UPS); <u>Select, Inc.</u>, B-245820.2, Jan. 3, 1992, 92-1 CPD ¶ 22 (bidder relinquished control of bid by giving it to UPS).

e. The government may consider commercial carrier records to establish time of delivery to the agency, if corroborated by relevant government evidence. <u>Power Connector, Inc.</u>, B-256362, June 15, 1994, 94-1 CPD ¶ 369 (agency properly considered Federal Express tracking sheet, agency mail log, and statements of agency personnel in determining time of receipt of bid).

f. Paramount cause not found. If government action is not the paramount cause of the late delivery of the hand-carried bid/proposal, then "late is late" applies. <u>U.S. Aerospace, Inc.</u>, B-403464, B-403464.2, Oct. 6, 2010, 2010 CPD ¶ 225 (even in cases where the late receipt may have been caused, in part, by erroneous government action, a later proposal should not be considered if the offeror significantly contributed to the late receipt by not doing all it could or should have done to fulfill its responsibility); <u>Lani Eko & Co., CPAs, PLLC</u>, B-404863, June 6, 2011 (paramount cause of late delivery was the courier's late arrival at the designated building with one minute to spare; contractor assumed risk that any number of events might intervene to prevent the timely submission of the proposals); <u>Pat Mathis Constr. Co., Inc.</u>, B248979, Oct. 9, 1992, 92-2 CPD ¶ 236; <u>B&S Transport, Inc.</u>, B-404648.3, Apr. 8, 2011, 2011 CPD ¶ 84 (despite government misdirection

to the wrong bid opening room, protester's actions were paramount cause for the late delivery; record shows courier was not entered in the visitor system prior to arrival, did not have appropriate contact information to obtain a sponsor for entry, arrived less than 10 min before proposal receipt deadline); <u>ALJUCAR, LLC</u>, B-401148, June 8, 2009, 2009 CPD ¶ 124 (a protester contributed significantly to a delay where it failed to provide sufficient time for delivery at a secure government facility); <u>Selrico Services, Inc.</u>, B-259709.2, May 1, 1995, 95-1 CPD ¶ 224 (erroneous confirmation by agency of receipt of bid); <u>O.S. Sys., Inc.</u>, B-292827, Nov. 17, 2003, 2003 CPD ¶ 211 (while agency may have complicated delivery by not including more explicit instructions in the RFP and by designating a location with restricted access, the main reason that the proposal was late was because the delivery driver was unfamiliar with the exact address, decided to make another delivery first, and attempted to find the filing location and the contracting officer unaided, rather than seeking advice concerning the address and location of the contracting officer immediately upon entering the facility).

g. The bidder must not have contributed substantially to the late receipt of the bid; it must act reasonably to fulfill its responsibility to deliver the bid to the proper place by the proper time. <u>Bergen Expo Sys., Inc.</u>, B-236970, Dec. 11, 1989, 89-2 CPD ¶ 540 (Federal Express courier refused access by guards, but courier departed); <u>Monthei Mechanical, Inc.</u>, B-216624, Dec. 17, 1984, 84-2 CPD ¶ 675 (bid box moved, but bidder arrived only 30 seconds before bid opening).

F. Extension of Bid Opening to Prevent "Late" Bids.

1. Historically, even if the deadline for proposals had passed, GAO allowed contracting officers to extend the closing time for receipt of proposals if they did so to enhance competition. The contracting officer simply issued an amendment to the solicitation extending the deadline. The GAO has permitted a contracting officer to extend the deadline as late as five days after the original bid due date. GAO permitted this as a way to enhance competition under the Competition In Contracting Act (CICA). Geo-Seis Helicopters, Inc., B-299175, B-299175.2, Mar. 5, 1997 (holding an agency may amend a solicitation to extend closing after the expiration of the original closing time in order to enhance competition); but see Chestnut Hill Constr. Inc., B-216891, Apr. 18, 1985, 85-1 CPD ¶ 443 (importance of maintaining the integrity of the competitive bidding system outweighs any monetary savings that would be obtained by considering a late bid); Varicon Int'l, Inc.; MVM, Inc., B-255808, B-255808.2, Apr. 6, 1994, 94-1 CPD ¶ 240 (it was not improper for agency to amend a solicitation to extend the closing time for receipt of proposals five days after the initial proposal due date passed because the agency extended the date to enhance competition and allow two other offerors to submit proposals); Institute for Advanced Safety Studies--Recon., B-21330.2, July 25, 1986, 86-2 CPD ¶ 110 at 2 (it was not improper for agency to issue an amendment extending the closing time three days after expiration of the original closing time); Fort Biscuit Co., B-247319, May 12, 1992, 92-1 CPD ¶ 440 at 4 (it was not improper for agency to extend closing time to permit one of four offerors more time to submit its best and final offer).

2. The U.S. Court of Federal Claims (COFC) does not recognize GAO's exception as valid. There is no CAFC decision reconciling GAO and COFC. COFC's rationale is that the GAO exception is not permitted by the FAR. In 1997, the FAR Council considered an amendment identical to the GAO exception but rejected it after public comment. In Geo-Seis Helicopters v. United States, 77 Fed. Cl. 633 (2007), the COFC rejected the agency's reliance on the GAO exception. Thereafter, it awarded the protestor fees under the Equal Access to Justice Act (EAJA). Geo-Seis Helicopters v. United States, 79 Fed. Cl. 74 (2007) finding the government's position was "not substantially justified." 79 Fed. Cl. at 70 (quoting Filtration Dev. Co. v. U.S., 63 Fed. Cl. 612, 621 (2005).

G. Modifications and Withdrawals of Bids.

1. When may offerors modify their bids?

   a. Before bid opening: Bidders may modify their bids at any time before bid opening. FAR 14.303; FAR 52.214-7.

   b. After bid opening: Bidders may modify their bids only if one of the exceptions to the Late Bid Rule applies to the modification. FAR 14.304(b)(1); FAR 52.214-7(b).

      (1) See FAR exceptions to Late Bid Rule in paragraph F. above.

      (2) Government Frustration Rule. I & E Constr. Co., B-186766, Aug. 9, 1976, 76-2 CPD ¶ 139.

      (3) The government may also accept a late modification to an otherwise successful bid if it is more favorable to the government. FAR 14.304(b)(2); FAR 52.214-7(b)(2);

Environmental Tectonics Corp., B-225474, Feb. 17, 1987, 87-1 CPD ¶ 175.

2. When may offerors withdraw their bids?

   a. Before bid opening: Bidders may withdraw their bids at any time before bid opening. FAR 14.303 and 14.304(e); FAR 52.214-7.

   b. After bid opening. Because of the Firm Bid Rule, bidders generally may withdraw their bids only if one of the exceptions to the Late Bid Rule applies. FAR 14.304(b)(1); FAR 52.214-7(b)(1). See Para. VII.G, infra.

3. Transmission of modifications or withdrawals of bids. FAR 14.303 and FAR 52.214-7(e).

   a. Offerors may modify or withdraw their bids by written or telegraphic notice, which must be received in the office designated in the invitation for bids before the exact time set for bid opening. FAR 14.303(a). See R.F. Lusa & Sons Sheetmetal, Inc., B-281180.2, Dec. 29, 1998, 98-2 CPD ¶ 157 (unsigned/uninitialed inscription on outside envelope of bid not an effective bid modification).

   b. The exceptions to the late bid rule apply to bid modifications and bid withdrawals only if the modification or withdrawal is received prior to contract award, unless it is a modification of the successful offeror's bid. FAR 14.304(b)(1); FAR 14.304(b)(2).

VI. EVALUATION OF BIDS.

A. Evaluation of Price.

1. Contracting officer evaluates price and price-related factors. FAR 14.201-8.

2. Award made on basis of lowest price offered.

3. Evaluating Bids with Options. Evaluate bid prices by adding the total price of the options to the price of the basic requirement, unless such an evaluation is not in "the government's best interests." FAR 17.206. Kruger Construction Inc., Comp. Gen. B-286960, Mar. 15, 2001, 2001 CPD ¶ 43 (not in the government's best interests to add two option prices when options were alternative). See also TNT Industrial Contractors, Inc., B-288331, Sep. 25, 2001, 2001 CPD ¶ 155.

4. The government may reject a materially unbalanced bid. A materially unbalanced bid contains inflated prices for some contract line items and below-cost prices for other line items, and gives rise to a reasonable doubt that award will result in the lowest overall cost to the government. FAR 14.404-2(g); LBCO, Inc., B-254995, Feb. 1, 1994, 94-1 CPD ¶ 57 (inflated first article prices).

B. Evaluation of Responsiveness of Bids. 10 U.S.C. § 2305; 41 U.S.C. § 3702.

1. The government may accept only a responsive bid. The government must reject any bid that fails to conform to the essential requirements of the IFB. FAR 14.301(a); FAR 14.404-2.

2. A bid is responsive if it unequivocally offers to provide the requested supplies or services at a firm, fixed price. Unless something on the face of the bid either limits, reduces, or modifies the obligation to perform in accordance with the terms of the invitation, the bid is responsive. Tel-Instrument Electronics Corp. 56 Fed. Cl. 174, Apr. 8, 2003 (a bid conditioned on the use of equipment not included in the solicitation, requiring special payment terms, or limiting its warranty obligation modifies a material requirement and is nonresponsive); New Shawmut Timber Co., Comp. Gen. B-286881, Feb. 26, 2001, 2001 CPD ¶ 42 (blank line item "rendered the bid equivocal regarding whether [protestor] intended to obligate itself to perform that element of the

requirement." Bid was nonresponsive.) New Dimension Masonry, Inc., B-258876, Feb. 21, 1995, 95-1 CPD ¶ 102 (statements in cover letter conditioned the bid); Metric Sys. Corp., B-256343, June 10, 1994, 94-1 CPD ¶ 360 (bidder's exception to IFB indemnification requirements changed legal relationship between parties). All Seasons Construction, Inc. v. United States, 55 Fed. Cl. 175 (2003) (All documents accompanying a bid bond, including the power of attorney appointing the attorney-in-fact, must unequivocally establish, at bid opening, that the bond is enforceable against the surety).

3. The government may not accept a nonresponsive bid even though it would result in monetary savings to the government, since acceptance would compromise the integrity of the bidding system. MIBO Constr. Co., B-224744, Dec. 17, 1986, 86-2 CPD ¶ 678.

4. When is responsiveness determined? The contracting officer determines the responsiveness of each bid at the time of bid opening by ascertaining whether the bid meets all of the IFB's essential requirements. See Gelco Payment Sys., Inc., B-234957, July 10, 1989, 89-2 CPD ¶ 27. See also Stanger Indus. Inc., B-279380, June 4, 1998, 98-1 CPD ¶ 157 (agency improperly rejected low bid that used unamended bid schedule that had been corrected by amendment where bidder acknowledged amendments and bid itself committed bidder to perform in accordance with IFB requirements).

5. Essential requirements of responsiveness. FAR 14.301; FAR 14.404-2; FAR 14.405; Tektronix, Inc.; Hewlett Packard Co., B-227800, Sep. 29, 1987, 87-2 CPD ¶ 315.

   a. Price. The bidder must offer a firm, fixed price. FAR 14.404-2(d); United States Coast Guard—Advance Decision, B-252396, Mar. 31, 1993, 93-1 CPD ¶ 286 (bid nonresponsive where price included fee of $1,000 per hour for "additional unscheduled testing" by government); J & W Welding & Fabrication, B-209430, Jan. 25, 1983, 83-1 CPD ¶ 92 ("plus 5% sales tax if applicable"—nonresponsive).

   b. Quantity. The bidder must offer the quantity required in the IFB. FAR 14.404-2(b). Inscom Elec. Corp., B-225221, Feb. 4, 1987, 87-1 CPD ¶ 116 (bid limited government's right to reduce quantity under the IFB); Pluribus Prod., Inc., B-224435, Nov. 7, 1986, 86-2 CPD ¶ 536.

   c. Quality. The bidder must agree to meet the quality requirements of the IFB. FAR 14.404-2(b); Reliable Mechanical, Inc; Way Eng'g Co., B-258231, Dec. 29, 1994, 94-2 CPD ¶ 263 (bidder offered chiller system which did not meet specifications); Wyoming Weavers, Inc., B-229669.3, June 2, 1988, 88-1 CPD ¶ 519.

   d. Delivery. The bidder must agree to the delivery schedule. FAR 14.404-2(c); Valley Forge Flag Company, Inc., B-283130, Sept. 22, 1999, 99-2 CPD ¶ 54 (bid nonresponsive where bidder inserts delivery schedule in bid that differs from that requested in the IFB); Viereck Co., B-256175, May 16, 1994, 94-1 CPD ¶ 310 (bid nonresponsive where bidder agreed to 60-day delivery date only if the cover page of the contract were faxed on the day of contract award). But see Image Contracting, B-253038, Aug. 11, 1993, 93-2 CPD ¶ 95 (bidder's failure to designate which of two locations it intended to deliver did not render bid nonresponsive where IFB permitted delivery to either location).

6. Other bases for rejection of bids for being nonresponsive.

   a. Ambiguous, indefinite, or uncertain bids. FAR 14.404-2(d); Trade-Winds Envtl. Restoration, Inc., B-259091,

Mar. 3, 1995, 95-1 CPD ¶ 127 (bid contained inconsistent prices); Caldwell & Santmyer, Inc., B-260628, July 3, 1995, 95-2 CPD ¶ 1 (uncertainty as to identity of bidder); Reid & Gary Strickland Co., B-239700, Sept. 17, 1990, 90-2 CPD ¶ 222 (notation in bid ambiguous).

b. Variation of acceptance period. John's Janitorial Serv., B-219194, July 2, 1985, 85-2 CPD ¶ 20.

c. Placing a "confidential" stamp on bid. Concept Automation, Inc. v. General Accounting Office, GSBCA No. 11688-P, Mar. 31, 1992, 92-2 BCA ¶ 24,937. But see North Am. Resource Recovery Corp., B-254485, Dec. 17, 1993, 93-2 CPD ¶ 327 ("proprietary data" notation on cover of bid did not restrict public disclosure of the bid where no pages of the bid were marked as proprietary).

d. Bid conditioned on receipt of local license. National Ambulance Co., B-184439, Dec. 29, 1975, 55 Comp. Gen. 597, 75-2 CPD ¶ 413.

e. Requiring government to make progress payments. Vertiflite, Inc., B-256366, May 12, 1994, 94-1 CPD ¶ 304.

f. Failure to furnish required or adequate bid guarantee. Interstate Rock Products, Inc. v. United States, 50 Fed. Cl. 349 (2001) (COFC seconded a long line of GAO decisions holding that "the penal sum [of a bid bond] is a material term of the contract (the bid bond) and therefore its omission is a material defect rendering the bid nonresponsive"); Schrepfer Industries, Inc., B-286825, Feb. 12, 2001, 01 CPD ¶ 23 (photocopied power of attorney unacceptable); Quantum Constr., Inc., B-255049, Dec. 1, 1993, 93-2 CPD ¶ 304 (defective power of attorney submitted with bid bond);

Kinetic Builders, Inc., B-223594, Sept. 24, 1986, 86-2 CPD ¶ 342 (bond referenced another solicitation number); Clyde McHenry, Inc., B-224169, Sept. 25, 1986, 86-2 CPD ¶ 352 (surety's obligation under bond unclear). But see FAR 28.101-4(c) (setting forth nine exceptions to the FAR's general requirement to reject bids with noncompliant bid guarantees) and South Atlantic Construction Company, LLC., Comp. Gen. B-286592.2, Apr. 13, 2001, 2001 CPD ¶ 63.

g. Exception to liquidated damages. Dubie-Clark Co., B-186918, Aug. 26, 1976, 76-2 CPD ¶ 194.

h. Solicitation requires F.O.B. destination; bid states F.O.B. origin. Taylor-Forge Eng'd Sys., Inc., B-236408, Nov. 3, 1989, 89-2 CPD ¶ 421.

i. Failure to include sufficient descriptive literature (when required by IFB) to demonstrate offered product's compliance with specifications. FAR 52.214-21; Adrian Supply Co., B-250767, Feb. 12, 1993, 93-1 CPD ¶ 131. NOTE: The contracting officer generally should disregard unsolicited descriptive literature. However, if the unsolicited literature raises questions reasonably as to whether the offered product complies with a material requirement of the IFB, the bid should be rejected as nonresponsive. FAR 14.202-5(f); FAR 14.202-4(g); Delta Chem. Corp., B-255543, Mar. 4, 1994, 94-1 CPD ¶ 175; Amjay Chems., B-252502, May 28, 1993, 93-1 CPD ¶ 426.

C. **Responsiveness Distinguished from Responsibility.** Data Express, Inc., B-234685, July 11, 1989, 89-2 CPD ¶ 28.

1. Bid responsiveness concerns whether a bidder has offered unequivocally in its bid

documents to provide supplies in conformity with all material terms and conditions of a solicitation for sealed bids, and it is determined as of the time of bid opening.

2. Responsibility refers to a bidder's apparent ability and capacity to perform, and it is determined any time prior to award. <u>Triton Marine Constr. Corp.</u>, B-255373, Oct. 20, 1993, 93-2 CPD ¶ 255 (bidder's failure to submit with its bid pre-award information to determine the bidder's ability to perform the work solicited does not render bid nonresponsive). <u>Great Lakes Dredge & Dock Company</u>, B-290158, June 17, 2002, 2002 CPD ¶ 100 (the terms of the solicitation cannot convert a matter of responsibility into one of responsiveness).

3. The issue of responsiveness is relevant only to the sealed-bidding method of contracting.

D. Informalities or Irregularities in Bids. FAR 14.405.

1. Minor irregularities.

    a. Definition: A minor informality or irregularity is merely a matter of form, not of substance. The defect or variation is immaterial when the effect on price, quantity, quality, or delivery is negligible when contrasted with the total cost or scope of supplies or services acquired. FAR 14.405.

    b. To determine whether a defect or variation is immaterial, review the facts of the case with the following considerations:

       (1) whether item is divisible from solicitation requirements;

       (2) whether cost of item is de minimis as to contractor's total cost; and

       (3) whether waiver or correction clearly would not affect competitive standing of bidders.

<u>Red John's Stone Inc.</u>, B-280974, Dec. 14, 1998, 98-2 CPD ¶ 135.

c. Examples of minor irregularities.

   (1) Failure to return the number of copies of signed bids required by the IFB. FAR 14.405(a).

   (2) Failure to submit employer identification number. <u>Dyneteria, Inc.</u>, B-186823, Oct. 18, 1976, 76-2 CPD ¶ 338.

   (3) Use of abbreviated corporate name if the bid otherwise establishes the identity of the party to be bound by contract award. <u>Americorp</u>, B-232688, Nov. 23, 1988, 88-2 CPD ¶ 515 (bid also gave Federal Employee Identification Number).

   (4) Failure to certify as a small business on a small business set-aside. <u>See</u> <u>J. Morris & Assocs.</u>, B-259767, 95-1 CPD ¶ 213 (bidder may correct erroneous certification after bid opening).

   (5) Failure to initial bid correction. <u>Durden & Fulton, Inc.</u>, B-192203, Sept. 5, 1978, 78-2 CPD ¶ 172.

   (6) Failure to price individually each line item on a contract to be awarded on an "all or none" basis. <u>See</u> <u>Seaward Corp.</u>, B-237107.2, June 13, 1990, 90-1 CPD ¶ 552; <u>see also</u> <u>Vista Contracting, Inc.</u>, B-255267, Jan. 7, 1994, 94-1 CPD ¶ 61 (failure to indicate cumulative bid price).

   (7) Failure to furnish information with bid, if the information is not necessary to evaluate bid and bidder is bound to perform in accordance with the IFB. <u>W.M. Schlosser Co.</u>, B-258284, Dec. 12, 1994, 94-2 CPD ¶ 234 (equipment history); but <u>see</u> <u>Booth & Assocs., Inc. -- Advisory</u>

Opinion, B-277477.2, Mar. 27, 1998, 98-1 CPD ¶ 104 (agency properly reinstated bid where bidder failed to include completed supplemental schedule of hourly rates but schedule was not used in the bid price evaluation).

(8) Negligible variation in quantity. Alco Envtl. Servs., Inc., ASBCA No. 43183, 94-1 BCA ¶ 26,261 (variation in IFB quantity of .27 percent).

(9) Failure to acknowledge amendment of the solicitation if the bid is clearly based on the IFB as amended, or the amendment is a matter of form or has a negligible impact on the cost of contract performance. See FAR 14.405(d).

d. Discretionary decision—the contracting officer shall give the bidder an opportunity to cure any deficiency resulting from a minor informality or irregularity in a bid or waive the deficiency, whichever is to the government's advantage. FAR 14.405; Excavation Constr. Inc. v. United States, 494 F.2d 1289 (Ct. Cl. 1974).

2. Signature on bid.

a. Normally, a bidder's failure to sign the bid is not a minor irregularity, and the government must reject the unsigned bid. See Firth Constr. Co. v. United States, 36 Fed. Cl. 268 (1996) (no signature on SF 1442); Power Master Elec. Co., B-223995, Nov. 26, 1986, 86-2 CPD ¶ 615 (typewritten name); Valencia Technical Serv., Inc., B-223288, July 7, 1986, 86-2 CPD ¶ 40 ("Blank" signature block); but see PCI/RCI v. United States, 36 Fed. Cl. 761 (1996) (one partner may bind a joint venture).

b. Exception. If the bidder has manifested an intent to be bound by the bid, the failure to sign is a minor irregularity. FAR 14.405(c).

(1) Adopted alternative. A & E Indus., B-239846, May 31, 1990, 90-1 CPD ¶ 527 (bid signed with a rubber stamp signature must be accompanied by evidence authorizing use of the rubber stamp signature).

(2) Other signed materials included in bid. Johnny F. Smith Truck & Dragline Serv., Inc., B-252136, June 3, 1993, 93-1 CPD ¶ 427 (signed certificate of procurement integrity); Tilley Constructors & Eng'rs, Inc., B-251335.2, Apr. 2, 1993, 93-1 CPD ¶ 289; Cable Consultants, Inc., B-215138, 63 Comp. Gen. 521 (1984).

E. Failure to Acknowledge Amendment of Solicitations.

1. General rule: Failure to acknowledge a material amendment renders the bid nonresponsive. See Christolow Fire Protection Sys., B-286585, Jan. 12, 2001, 01 CPD ¶ 13 (amendments "clarifying matters that could otherwise engender disputes during contract performance are generally material and must be acknowledged." Amendment revising inaccurate information in bid schedule regarding number, types of, and response times applicable to service calls was material;); Environmediation Svcs., LLC, B-280643, Nov. 2, 1998, 98-2 CPD ¶ 103. See also Logistics & Computer Consultants Inc., B-253949, Oct. 26, 1993, 93-2 CPD ¶ 250 (amendment placing additional obligations on contractor under a management contract); Safe-T-Play, Inc., B-250682.2, Apr. 5, 1993, 93-1 CPD ¶ 292 (amendment classifying workers under Davis-Bacon Act).

2. Even if an amendment has no clear effect on the contract price, it is material if it changes the legal relationship of the parties. Specialty Contractors, Inc., B-258451, Jan. 24, 1995, 95-1 CPD ¶ 38 (amendment changing color of roofing panels); Anacomp, Inc., B-256788, July 27, 1994, 94-2 CPD ¶ 44 (amendment requiring contractor to pick up computer tapes on "next business day" when regular pickup day was a federal holiday); Favino Mechanical Constr., Ltd., B-237511, Feb. 9, 1990, 90-1 CPD ¶ 174 (amendment incorporating Order of Precedence clause).

3. An amendment that is nonessential or trivial need not be acknowledged. FAR 14.405(d)(2); Lumus Construction, Inc., B-287480, June 25, 2001, 2001 CPD ¶ 108 (Where an "amendment does not impose any legal obligations on the bidder different from those imposed by the original solicitation," the amendment is not material); Jackson Enterprises, Comp. Gen. B-286688, Feb. 5, 2001, 2001 CPD ¶ 25; L&R Rail Serv., B-256341, June 10, 1994, 94-1 CPD ¶ 356 (amendment decreasing cost of performance not material); Day & Night Janitorial & Maid Serv., Inc., B-240881, Jan. 2, 1991, 91-1 CPD ¶ 1 (negligible effect on price, quantity, quality, or delivery).

4. How does a bidder acknowledge an amendment?

    a. In writing only. Oral acknowledgment of an amendment is insufficient. Alcon, Inc., B-228409, Feb. 5, 1988, 88-1 CPD ¶ 114.

    b. Formal acknowledgment.

        (1) Sign and return a copy of the amendment to the contracting officer.

        (2) Standard Form 33, Block 14.

        (3) Notify the government by letter or by telegram of receipt of the amendment.

    c. Constructive acknowledgment. The contracting officer may accept a bid that clearly indicates that the bidder received the amendment. C Constr. Co., B-228038, Dec. 2, 1987, 67 Comp. Gen. 107, 87-2 CPD ¶ 534.

F. **Rejection of All Bids—Cancellation of the IFB.**

1. Prior to bid opening, almost any reason will justify cancellation of an invitation for bids if the cancellation is "in the public interest." FAR 14.209.

2. After bid opening, the government may not cancel an IFB unless there is a compelling reason to reject all bids and cancel the invitation. FAR 14.404-1(a)(1). See Grot, Inc., B-276979.2, Aug. 14, 1997, 97-2 CPD ¶ 50 (cancellation proper where all bids exceeded the "awardable range" and agency concluded that specifications were unclear); Site Support Services, Inc., B-270229, Feb. 13, 1996, 96-1 CPD ¶ 74 (cancellation proper where IFB contained incorrect government estimate); Canadian Commercial Corp./ Ballard Battery Sys. Corp., B-255642, Mar. 18, 1994, 94-1 CPD ¶ 202 (no compelling reason to cancel simply because some terms of IFB are somehow deficient); US Rentals, B-238090, Apr. 5, 1990, 90-1 CPD ¶ 367 (contracting officer cannot deliberately let bid acceptance period expire as a vehicle for cancellation); C-Cubed Corporation, B-289867, Apr. 26, 2002, 2002 CPD ¶ 72 (agency may cancel a solicitation after bid opening if the IFB fails to reflect the agency's needs).

3. Examples of compelling reasons to cancel.

    a. Violation of statute. Sunrise International Group, B-252892.3, Sep. 14, 1993, 93-2 CPD ¶ 160 (agency's failure to allow 30 days in IFB for submission of bids in violation of CICA was compelling reason to cancel IFB).

b. Insufficient funds. Michelle F. Evans, B-259165, Mar. 6, 1995, 95-1 CPD ¶ 139 (management of funds is a matter of agency judgment); Armed Forces Sports Officials, Inc., B-251409, Mar. 23, 1993, 93-1 CPD ¶ 261 (no requirement for agency to seek increase in funds).

c. Requirement disappeared. Zwick Energy Research Org., Inc., B-237520.3, Jan. 25, 1991, 91-1 CPD ¶ 72 (specification required engines driven by gasoline; agency directive required diesel).

d. Specifications are defective and fail to state the government's minimum needs, or unreasonably exclude potential bidders. McGhee Constr., Inc., B-250073.3, May 13, 1993, 93-1 CPD ¶ 379; Control Corp.; Control Data Sys., Inc.—Protest and Entitlement to Costs, B-251224.2, May 3, 1993, 93-1 CPD ¶ 353; Digitize, Inc., B-235206.3, Oct. 5, 1989, 90-1 CPD ¶ 403; Chenga Management, B-290598, Aug. 8, 2002, 02-1 CPD ¶ 143 (specifications that are impossible to perform provide a basis to cancel the IFB after bid opening).

e. Agency decides to perform the services in-house. Mastery Learning Sys., B-258277.2, Jan. 27, 1995, 95-1 CPD ¶ 54.

f. Time delay of litigation. P. Francini & Co. v. United States, 2 Cl. Ct. 7 (1983).

g. All bids unreasonable in price. California Shorthand Reporting, B-250302.2, Mar. 4, 1993, 93-1 CPD ¶ 202.

h. Eliminate appearance of unfair competitive advantage. P&C Constr., B-251793, Apr. 30, 1993, 93-1 CPD ¶ 361.

i. Failure to incorporate wage rate determination. JC&N Maint., Inc., B-253876, Nov. 1, 1993, 93-2 CPD ¶ 253.

j. Failure to set aside a procurement for small businesses or small disadvantaged businesses when required. Baker Support Servs., Inc.; Mgmt. Technical Servs., Inc., B-256192.3, Sept. 2, 1994, 95-1 CPD ¶ 75; Ryon, Inc., B-256752.2, Oct. 27, 1994, 94-2 CPD ¶ 163.

4. Before canceling the IFB, the contracting officer must consider any prejudice to bidders. If cancellation will affect bidders' competitive standing, such prejudicial effect on competition may offset the compelling reason for cancellation. Canadian Commercial Corp., supra.

5. If an agency relies on an improper basis to cancel a solicitation, the cancellation may be upheld if another proper basis for the cancellation exists. Shields Enters. v. United States, 28 Fed. Cl. 615 (1993).

6. Cancellation of the IFB may be post-award. Control Corp., B-251224.2, May 3, 1993, 93-1 CPD ¶ 353.

G. **Mistakes in Bids Asserted Before Award.** FAR 14.407-1.

1. General rule. A bidder bears the consequences of a mistake in its bid unless the contracting officer has actual or constructive notice of the mistake prior to award. Advanced Images, Inc., B-209438.2, May 10, 1983, 83-1 CPD ¶ 495.

2. After bid opening, the government may permit the bidder to remedy certain substantive mistakes affecting price and price-related factors by correction or withdrawal of the bid. For example, a clerical or arithmetical error normally is correctable or may be a basis for withdrawal. United Digital Networks, Inc., B-222422, July 17, 1986, 86-2 CPD ¶ 79 (multiplication error); but see

Virginia Beach Air Conditioning Corp., B-237172, Jan. 19, 1990, 90-1 CPD ¶ 78 (bid susceptible to two interpretations—correction improper).

3. Mistakes in bid that are NOT correctable.

   a. Errors in judgment. R.P. Richards Constr. Co., B-274859.2, Jan. 22, 1997, 97-1 CPD ¶ 39 (bidder's misreading of a subcontractor quote and reliance on its own extremely low estimate for certain work were mistakes in judgment).

   b. Omission of items from the bid. McGhee Constr., Inc., B-255863, Apr. 13, 1994, 94-1 CPD ¶ 254. But see Pacific Components, Inc., B-252585, June 21, 1993, 93-1 CPD ¶ 478 (bid correction permitted for mistake due to omissions from subcontractor quotation).

   c. Nonresponsive bid. Temp Air Co., Inc., B-279837, Jul. 2, 1998, 98-2 CPD ¶ 1 (bid could not be made responsive by post-bid opening explanation or correction).

4. Only the government and the bidder responsible for the alleged mistake have standing to raise the issue of a mistake. Huber, Hunt & Nichols, Inc., B-271112, May 21, 1996, 96-1 CPD 246 (contractor's negligence in bid preparation does not preclude correction); Reliable Trash Serv., Inc., B-258208, Dec. 20, 1994, 94-2 CPD ¶ 252.

5. Contracting Officer's responsibilities.

   a. The contracting officer must examine each bid for mistakes. FAR 14.407-1; Andy Elec. Co.—Recon., B-194610.2, Aug. 10, 1981, 81-2 CPD ¶ 111.

      (1) Actual notice of mistake in a bid.

      (2) Constructive notice of mistake in a bid, e.g., price disparity among bids or comparison with government estimate. R.J. Sanders, Inc. v. United States, 24

Cl. Ct. 288 (1991) (bid 32% below government estimate insufficient to place contracting officer on notice of mistake in bid); Central Mechanical, Inc., B-206250, Dec. 20, 1982, 82-2 CPD ¶ 547 (allocation of price out of proportion to other bidders).

   b. Bid verification. The contracting officer must seek verification of each bid that he has reason to believe contains a mistake. FAR 14.407-1 and 14.407-3(g).

      (1) To ensure that the bidder is put on notice of the suspected mistake, the contracting officer must advise the bidder of all disclosable information that leads the contracting officer to believe that there is a mistake in the bid. Liebherr Crane Corp., ASBCA No. 24707, 85-3 BCA ¶ 18,353, aff'd, 810 F.2d 1153 (Fed. Cir. 1987) (procedure inadequate); but see Foley Co., B-258659, Feb. 8, 1995, 95-1 CPD ¶ 58 (bidder should be allowed an opportunity to explain its bid); DWS, Inc., ASBCA No. 29743, 93-1 BCA ¶ 25,404 (particular price need not be mentioned in bid verification notice).

      (2) Effect of bidder verification. Verification generally binds the contractor unless the discrepancy is so great that acceptance of the bid would be unfair to the submitter or to other bidders. Trataros Constr., Inc., B-254600, Jan. 4, 1994, 94-1 CPD ¶ 1 (contracting officer properly rejected verified bid that was far out of line with other bids and the government estimate). But see Foley Co., B-258659, Feb. 8, 1995, 95-1 CPD ¶ 58 (government improperly rejected low bid where there was no evidence of mistake); Aztech Elec., Inc. and

Rod's Elec., Inc., B-223630, Sept. 30, 1986, 86-2 CPD ¶ 368 (below-cost bid is a matter of business judgment, not an obvious error requiring rejection).

(3) Effect of inadequate verification. If the contracting officer fails to obtain adequate verification of a bid for which the government has actual or constructive notice of a mistake, the contractor may seek additional compensation or rescission of the contract. See, e.g., Solar Foam Insulation, ASBCA No. 46921, 94-2 BCA ¶ 26,901.

c. The contracting officer may not award a contract to a bidder when the contracting officer has actual or constructive notice of a mistake in the bid, unless the mistake is waived or the bid is properly corrected in accordance with agency procedures. Sealtite Corp., ASBCA No. 25805, 83-1 BCA ¶ 16,243.

6. Correction of mistakes prior to award—standard of proof and allowable evidence. FAR 14.407-3.

a. The bidder alleging the mistake has the burden of proof. VA—Advance Decision, B-225815.2, Oct. 15, 1987, 87-2 CPD ¶ 362.

b. Apparent clerical mistakes. FAR 14.407-2; Brazos Roofing, Inc., B-275319, Feb. 7, 1997, 97-1 CPD ¶ 66 (incorrect entry of base price used in calculation of option year prices was an obvious transcription error); Action Serv. Corp., B-254861, Jan. 24, 1994, 94-1 CPD ¶ 33 (additional zero); Sovran Constr. Co., B-242104, Mar. 18, 1991, 91-1 CPD ¶ 295 (cumulative pricing); Engle Acoustic & Tile, Inc., B-190467, Jan. 27, 1978, 78-1 CPD ¶ 72 (misplaced decimal point); Dependable Janitorial Serv. & Supply

Co., B-188812, July 13, 1977, 77-2 CPD ¶ 20 (discrepancy between unit and total prices); B&P Printing, Inc., B-188511, June 2, 1977, 77-1 CPD ¶ 387 (comma rather than period—correct bid not approved).

(1) Contracting officer may correct, before award, any clerical mistake apparent on the face of the bid.

(2) The contracting officer must first obtain verification of the bid from the bidder.

c. Other mistakes disclosed before award. FAR 14.407-3.

(1) Correction by low bidder. Circle, Inc., B-279896, July 29, 1998, 98-2 CPD ¶ 67. Shoemaker & Alexander, Inc., B-241066, Jan. 15, 1991, 91-1 CPD ¶ 41.

(a) The low bidder must show by clear and convincing evidence: (i) the existence of a mistake in its bid; and (ii) the bid it actually intended or that the intended bid would fall within a narrow range of uncertainty and remain low. FAR 14.407-3. See Three O Constr., S.E., B-255749, Mar. 28, 1994, 94-1 CPD ¶ 216 (no clear and convincing evidence where bidder gave conflicting explanations for mistake). Will H. Hall and Son, Inc. v. United States, 54 Fed. Cl. 436 (2002) (a contractor's 'careless' reliance on a subcontractor's quote that excluded a price for a portion of the work solicited is a correctable mistake).

(b) Bidder can refer to such things as: (i) bidder's file copy of the bid; (ii) original work papers; (iii) a subcontractor's or supplier's quotes; or (iv) published price lists.

(2) Correction of a bid that displaces a lower bidder. J & J Maint., Inc., B-251355, Mar. 1, 1993, 93-1 CPD ¶ 187; Virginia Beach Air Conditioning Corp., B-237172, Jan. 19, 1990, 90-1 CPD ¶ 78; Eagle Elec., B-228500, Feb. 5, 1988, 88-1 CPD ¶ 116.

(a) Bidder must show by clear and convincing evidence: (a) the existence of a mistake; and (b) the bid actually intended. FAR 14.407-3.

(b) Limitation on proof - the bidder can prove a mistake only from the solicitation (IFB) and the bid submitted, not from any other sources. Bay Pacific Pipelines, Inc., B-265659, Dec. 18, 1995, 95-2 CPD ¶ 272.

d. Action permitted when a bidder presents clear and convincing evidence of a mistake, but not as to the bid intended; or evidence that reasonably supports the existence of a mistake, but is not clear and convincing. Advanced Images, Inc., B-209438.2, May 10, 1983, 83-1 CPD ¶ 495.

(1) The bidder may withdraw the bid. FAR 14.407-3(c).

(2) The bidder may correct the bid where it is clear the intended bid would fall within a narrow range of uncertainty and remain the low bid. Conner Bros. Constr. Co., B-228232.2, Feb. 3, 1988, 88-1 CPD ¶ 103; Department of the Interior—Mistake in Bid Claim, B-222681, July 23, 1986, 86-2 CPD ¶ 98.

(3) The bidder may waive the bid mistake if it is clear that the intended bid would remain low. William G. Tadlock Constr., B-251996, May 13, 1993, 93-1 CPD ¶ 382 (waiver not permitted);

Hercules Demolition Corp. of Virginia, B-223583, Sep. 12, 1986, 86-2 CPD ¶ 292; LABCO Constr., Inc., B-219437, Aug. 28, 1985, 85-2 CPD ¶ 240.

e. Once a bidder asserts a mistake, the agency head or designee may disallow withdrawal or correction of the bid if the bidder fails to prove the mistake. FAR 14.407-3(d); Duro Paper Bag Mfg. Co., B-217227, Jan. 3, 1986, 65 Comp. Gen. 186, 86-1 CPD ¶ 6.

f. Approval levels for corrections or withdrawals of bids.

(1) Apparent clerical errors: The contracting officer. FAR 14.407-2.

(2) Withdrawal of a bid on clear and convincing evidence of a mistake, but not of the intended bid: An official above the contracting officer. FAR 14.407-3(c).

(3) Correction of a bid on clear and convincing evidence both of the mistake and of the bid intended: The agency head or delegee. FAR 14.407-3(a). Caveat: If correction would displace a lower bid, the government shall not permit the correction unless the mistake and the intended bid are both ascertainable substantially from the IFB and the bid submitted.

(4) Withdrawal rather than correction of a low bidder's bid: If (a) a bidder requests permission to withdraw a bid rather than correct it, (b) the evidence is clear and convincing both as to the mistake in the bid and the bid intended, and (c) the bid, both as uncorrected and as corrected, is the lowest received, the agency head or designee may determine to correct the bid and not permit its withdrawal. FAR 14.407-3(b).

(5) Neither correction nor withdrawal. If the evidence does not warrant correction or withdrawal, the agency head may refuse to permit either withdrawal or correction. FAR 14.407-3(d).

(6) Heads of agencies may delegate their authority to correct or permit withdrawal of bids without power of redelegation. FAR 14.407-3(e). This authority has been delegated to specified authorities within Defense Departments and Agencies.

VII. AWARD OF THE CONTRACT.

A. **Evaluation of the Responsibility of the Successful Bidder.** 10 U.S.C. § 2305; 41 U.S.C. § 3702.

1. Government acquisition policy requires that the contracting officer make an affirmative determination of responsibility prior to award. FAR 9.103.

2. General rule. The contracting officer may award only to a responsible bidder. FAR 9.103(a); Theodor Arndt GmbH & Co., B-237180, Jan. 17, 1990, 90-1 CPD ¶ 64 (responsibility requirement implied); Atlantic Maint., Inc., B-239621.2, June 1, 1990, 90-1 CPD ¶ 523 (an unreasonably low price may render bidder nonresponsible); but see The Galveston Aviation Weather Partnership, B-252014.2, May 5, 1993, 93-1 CPD ¶ 370 (below-cost bid not legally objectionable, even when offering labor rates lower than those required by the Service Contract Act).

3. Responsibility defined. Responsibility refers to an offeror's apparent ability and capacity to perform. To be responsible, a prospective contractor must meet the standards of responsibility set forth at FAR 9.104. FAR 9.101; Kings Point Indus., B-223824, Oct. 29, 1986, 86-2 CPD ¶ 488.

4. Responsibility is determined at any time prior to award. Therefore, the bidder may provide responsibility information to the contracting officer at any time before award. FAR 9.103; FAR 9.105-1; ADC Ltd., B-254495, Dec. 23, 1993, 93-2 CPD ¶ 337 (bidder's failure to submit security clearance documentation with its bid is not a basis for rejection of bid); Cam Indus., B-230597, May 6, 1988, 88-1 CPD ¶ 443.

B. **Minimum Standards of Responsibility—Contractor Qualification Standards.**

1. General standards of responsibility. FAR 9.104-1.

   a. Financial resources. The contractor must demonstrate that it has adequate financial resources to perform the contract or that it has the ability to obtain such resources. FAR 9.104-1(a); Excavators, Inc., B-232066, Nov. 1, 1988, 88-2 CPD ¶ 421 (a contractor is nonresponsible if it cannot or does not provide acceptable individual sureties).

      (1) Bankruptcy. Nonresponsibility determinations based solely on a bankruptcy petition violate 11 U.S.C. § 525. This statute prohibits a governmental unit from denying, revoking, suspending, or refusing to renew a license, permit, charter, franchise, or other similar grant to, or deny employment to, terminate employment of, or discriminate with respect to employment against, a person that is or has been a debtor under 11 U.S.C. § 525, solely because such person has been a debtor under that title. Bender Shipbuilding & Repair Company v. United States, 297 F.3d 1358 (Fed. Cir. 2002), (upholding contracting officer's determination that awardee was responsible even though awardee

Sealed Bidding

filed for Chapter 11 Bankruptcy reorganization); Global Crossing telecommunications, Inc., B-288413.6, B-288413.10, June 17, 2002, 2002 CPD ¶ 102 (upholding contracting officer's determination that a prospective contractor who filed for Chapter 11 was not responsible).

(2) The courts have applied the bankruptcy anti-discrimination provisions to government determinations of eligibility for award. In re Son-Shine Grading, 27 Bankr. 693 (Bankr. E.D.N.C. 1983); In re Coleman Am. Moving Serv., Inc., 8 Bankr. 379 (Bankr. D. Kan. 1980).

(3) A determination of responsibility should not be negative solely because of a prospective contractor's bankruptcy. The contracting officer should focus on the contractor's ability to perform the contract, and justify a nonresponsibility determination of a bankrupt contractor accordingly. Harvard Interiors Mfg. Co., B-247400, May 1, 1992, 92-1 CPD ¶ 413 (Chapter 11 firm found nonresponsible based on lack of financial ability); Sam Gonzales, Inc.—Recon., B-225542.2, Mar. 18, 1987, 87-1 CPD ¶ 306.

b. Delivery or performance schedule: The contractor must establish its ability to comply with the delivery or performance schedule. FAR 9.104-1(b); System Dev. Corp., B-212624, Dec. 5, 1983, 83-2 CPD ¶ 644.

c. Performance record: The contractor must have a satisfactory performance record. FAR 9.104-1(c). Information Resources, Inc., B-271767, July 24, 1996, 96-2 CPD ¶ 38; Saft America, B-270111, Feb. 7, 1996, 96-1 CPD ¶

134; North American Constr. Corp., B-270085, Feb. 6, 1996, 96-1 CPD ¶ 44; Mine Safety Appliances, Co., B-266025, Jan. 17, 1996, 96-1 CPD ¶ 86. The contracting officer shall presume that a contractor seriously deficient in recent contract performance is nonresponsible. FAR 9.104-3(b). See Schenker Panamericana (Panama) S.A., B-253029, Aug. 2, 1993, 93-2 CPD ¶ 67 (agency justified in nonresponsiblity determination where moving contractor had previously failed to conduct pre-move surveys, failed to provide adequate packing materials, failed to keep appointments or complete work on time, dumped household goods into large containers, stacked unprotected furniture onto trucks, dragged unprotected furniture through hallways, and wrapped fragile goods in a single sheet of paper; termination for default on prior contract not required). See also Pacific Photocopy & Research Servs., B-281127, Dec. 29, 1998, 98-2 CPD ¶ 164 (contracting officer properly determined that bidder had inadequate performance record on similar work based upon consistently high volume of unresolved customer complaints).

d. Management/technical capability: The contractor must display adequate management and technical capability to perform the contract satisfactorily. FAR 9.104-1(e); TAAS-Israel Indus., B-251789.3, Jan. 14, 1994, 94-1 CPD ¶ 197 (contractor lacked design skills and knowledge to produce advanced missile launcher power supply).

e. Equipment/facilities/production capacity: The contractor must maintain or have access to sufficient equipment, facilities, and production capacity to accomplish the work required by the contract. FAR 9.104-1(f); IPI Graphics, B-286830, B-286838, Jan. 9, 2001, 01 CPD ¶ 12 (contractor lacked adequate production controls and quality assurance methods).

f. Business ethics: The contractor must have a satisfactory record of business ethics. FAR 9.104-1(d); FAR 9.407-2; FAR 14.404-2(h); Interstate Equip. Sales, B-225701, Apr. 20, 1987, 87-1 CPD ¶ 427.

2. Special or definitive standards of responsibility: Definitive responsibility criteria are specific, objective standards established by an agency to measure an offeror's ability to perform a given contract. FAR 9.104-2(a); D.H. Kim Enters., B-255124, Feb. 8, 1994, 94-1 CPD ¶ 86.

a. An example is to require that a prospective contractor have a specified number of years of experience performing the same or similar work. Hardie-Tynes Mfg. Co., B-237938, Apr. 2, 1990, 90-1 CPD ¶ 587 (agency properly considered manufacturing experience of parent corporation in finding bidder met the definitive responsibility criterion of five years' manufacturing experience); BBC Brown Boveri, Inc., B-227903, Sept. 28, 1987, 87-2 CPD ¶ 309 (IFB required five years of experience in transformer design, manufacture, and service; GAO held that this definitive responsibility criterion was satisfied by a subcontractor).

b. Although the GAO will not readily review affirmative responsibility determinations based on general responsibility criteria, it will review affirmative responsibility determinations where the solicitation contains definitive responsibility requirements. 4 C.F.R. § 21.5(c) (1995).

c. Evaluations using definitive responsibility criteria are subject to

review by the Small Business Administration (SBA) through its Certificate of Competency process. FAR 19.602-4.

d. Statutory/Regulatory Compliance.

(1) Licenses and permits.

(a) When a solicitation contains a general condition that the contractor comply with state and local licensing requirements, the contracting officer need not inquire into what those requirements may be or whether the bidder will comply. James C. Bateman Petroleum Serv., Inc., B-232325, Aug. 22, 1988, 88-2 CPD ¶ 170; but see International Serv. Assocs., B-253050, Aug. 4, 1993, 93-2 CPD ¶ 82 (where agency determines that small business will not meet licensing requirement, referral to SBA required).

(b) On the other hand, when a solicitation requires specific compliance with regulations and licensing requirements, the contracting officer may inquire into the offeror's ability to comply with the regulations in determining the offeror's responsibility. Intera Technologies, Inc., B-228467, Feb. 3, 1988, 88-1 CPD ¶ 104.

(2) Statutory certification requirements.

(a) Small business concerns. The contractor must certify its status as a small business to be eligible for award as a small business. FAR 19.301.

(b) Equal opportunity compliance. Contractors must certify that they will comply with "equal opportunity" statutory requirements. In addition, contracting officers must obtain pre-award clearances from the Department of Labor for equal opportunity compliance before awarding any contract (excluding construction) exceeding $10 million. FAR Subpart 22.8. Solicitations may require the contractor to develop and file an affirmative action plan. FAR 52.222-22 and FAR 52.222-25; Westinghouse Elec. Corp., B-228140, Jan. 6, 1988, 88-1 CPD ¶ 6.

    (c) Submission of lobby certification. Tennier Indus., B-239025, July 16, 1990, 90-2 CPD ¶ 25.

    (3) Organizational conflicts of interest. FAR Subpart 9.5. Government policy precludes award of a contract without some restriction on future activities if the contractor would have an actual or potential unfair competitive advantage, or if the contractor would be biased in making judgments in performance of the work. Necessary restrictions on future activities of a contractor are incorporated in the contract in one or more organizational conflict of interest clauses. FAR 9.502(c); The Analytic Sciences Corp., B-218074, Apr. 23, 1985, 85-1 CPD ¶ 464.

C. Responsibility Determination Procedures.

1.   Sources of information. The contracting officer must obtain sufficient information to determine responsibility. FAR 9.105.

    a. Contracting officers may use pre-award surveys. FAR 9.105-1(b); FAR 9.106; DFARS 209.106; Accurate Indus., B-232962, Jan. 23, 1989, 89-1 CPD ¶ 56.

    b. Contracting officer must check the list titled Parties Excluded from Procurement Programs. FAR 9.105-1(c)(1); see also AFARS 9.4 and FAR Subpart 9.4. But see R.J. Crowley, Inc., B-253783, Oct. 22, 1993, 93-2 CPD ¶ 257 (agency improperly relied on non-current list of ineligible contractors as basis for rejecting bid; agency should have consulted electronic update).

    c. Contracting and audit agency records and data pertaining to a contractor's prior contracts are valuable sources of information. FAR 9.105-1(c)(2).

    d. Contracting officers also may use contractor-furnished information. FAR 9.105-1(c)(3). International Shipbuilding, Inc., B-257071.2, Dec. 16, 1994, 94-2 CPD ¶ 245 (agency need not delay award indefinitely until the offeror cures the causes of its nonresponsibility).

2.   Standards of review of contracting officer determinations of responsibility.

    a. Prior to 1 January 2003, GAO would not review affirmative responsibility determinations absent a showing of bad faith or fraud. 4 C.F.R. § 21.5(c) (1995); see Hard Bottom Inflatables, Inc., B-245961.2, Jan. 22, 1992, 92-1 CPD ¶ 103. The GAO amended its Bid Protest Regulations and now will consider a protest challenging that the definitive responsibility criteria in the solicitation were not met and those that identify evidence raising serious concerns that, in reaching a particular responsibility determination, the contracting officer unreasonably failed to consider available relevant information or otherwise violated statute or regulation. 67 Fed. Reg. 79,833 (Dec. 31, 2002). See Impresa Construzioni Geom. Domenico Garufi, 52 Fed. Cl. 421 (2002) (finding the contracting officer failed to conduct an independent and informed responsibility determination).

   b. The GAO will review nonresponsibility determinations for reasonableness. <u>Schwender/Riteway Joint Venture</u>, B-250865.2, Mar. 4, 1993, 93-1 CPD ¶ 203 (determination of nonresponsibility unreasonable when based on inaccurate or incomplete information).

3. Subcontractor responsibility issues.

   a. The agency may review subcontractor responsibility. FAR 9.104-4(a).

   b. Subcontractor responsibility is determined in the same fashion as is the responsibility of the prime contractor. FAR 9.104-4(b).

D. Award of the Contract.

1. Statutory standard. The contracting officer shall award with reasonable promptness to the responsible bidder whose bid conforms to the solicitation and is most advantageous, considering price and other price-related factors. 10 U.S.C. § 2305(b)(4)(B); 41 U.S.C. § 3702(b); FAR 14.408-1(a).

2. Multiple awards. If the IFB does not prohibit partial bids, the government must make multiple awards when they will result in the lowest cost to the government. FAR 52.214-22; <u>WeatherExperts, Inc.</u>, B-255103, Feb. 9, 1994, 94-1 CPD ¶ 93.

3. An agency may not award a contract to an entity other than that which submitted a bid. <u>Gravely & Rodriguez</u>, B-256506, Mar. 28, 1994, 94-1 CPD ¶ 234 (sole proprietorship submitted bid, partnership sought award).

4. Communication of acceptance of the offer and award of the contract. The contracting officer makes award by giving written notice within the specified time for acceptance. FAR 14.408-1(a).

5. The "mailbox" rule applies to award of federal contracts. Award is effective upon mailing (or otherwise furnishing the award document) to the successful offeror. FAR 14.408-1(c)(1). <u>Singleton Contracting Corp.</u>, IBCA 1770-1-84, 86-2 BCA ¶ 18,800 (notice of award and request to withdraw bid mailed on same day); <u>Kleen-Rite Corp.</u>, B-190160, July 3, 1978, 78-2 CPD ¶ 2.

E. Mistakes in Bids Asserted After Award. FAR 14.407-4; FAR Subpart 33.2 (Disputes and Appeals).

1. The contracting officer may correct a mistake by contract modification if correction would be favorable to the government and would not change the essential requirements of the specifications.

2. The government may:

   a. Rescind the contract;

   b. Reform the contract

      (1) to delete items involved in the mistake; or

      (2) to increase the contract price if the price as increased does not exceed that of the next lowest acceptable bid; or

   c. Make no change in the contract, if the evidence does not warrant rescission or reformation.

3. Rescission or reformation may be made only on the basis of clear and convincing evidence that a mistake in bid was made, and only if the mistake was (i) mutual or (ii) if unilaterally made by the contractor, was so apparent that the contracting officer should be charged with having had notice of the mistake. <u>Government Micro Resources, Inc. v. Department of Treasury</u>, GSBCA No. 12364-TD, 94-2 BCA ¶ 26,680 (government on constructive notice of mistake where contractor's price exceeded government

estimate by 62% and comparison quote by 33%); Kitco, Inc., ASBCA No. 45347, 93-3 BCA ¶ 26,153 (mistake must be clear cut clerical or arithmetical error, or misreading of specifications, not mistake of judgment); Liebherr Crane Corp., 810 F.2d 1153 (Fed. Cir. 1987) (no relief for unilateral errors in business judgment).

4. Reformation is not available for contract formation mistakes. Gould, Inc. v. United States, 19 Cl. Ct. 257 (1990).

    a. Reformation is a form of equitable relief that applies to mistakes made in reducing the parties' intentions to writing, but not to mistakes that the parties made in forming the agreement. To show entitlement to reformation, the contractor must prove (i) a clear agreement between the parties and (ii) an error in reducing the agreement to writing.

    b. The contractor must prove four elements in a claim for reformation based on mutual mistake. Management & Training Corp. v. General Servs. Admin., GSBCA No. 11182, 93-2 BCA ¶ 25,814. These elements are:

        (1) The parties to the contract were mistaken in their belief regarding a fact. See Dairyland Power Co-op v. United States, 16 F.3d 1197 (1994) (mistake must relate to an existing fact, not future events);

        (2) The mistake involved a basic assumption of the contract;

        (3) The mistake affected contract performance materially; and

        (4) The party seeking reformation did not agree to bear the risk of a mistake.

5. Proof requirements. Mistakes alleged or disclosed after award are processed in accordance with FAR 14.407-4(e) and FAR Subpart 33.2. The contracting officer shall request the contractor to support the alleged mistake by submission of written statements and pertinent evidence. See Government Micro Resources, Inc. v. Department of Treasury, supra (board awards contractor recovery on *quantum valebant* basis).

6. Mistakes alleged after award are subject to the Contract Disputes Act of 1978 and the Disputes and Appeals provisions of the FAR. FAR Subpart 33.2; ABJ Servs., B-254155, July 23, 1993, 93-2 CPD ¶ 53 (the GAO will not review a mistake in bid claim alleged by the contractor after award).

7. Extraordinary contractual relief under Public Law No. 85-804. National Defense Contracts Act, 72 Stat. 972, 50 U.S.C. § 1431-1435; DFARS Subpart 250.

VIII. CONCLUSION.

Sealed bidding is a rigid procedure. A contracting officer must award a contract to the lowest bidder, even if a slightly higher-priced bidder is offering a much better product or service. Conversely, a contracting officer must award to a higher-priced bidder where a lower bidder submits a technically non-responsive bid that could easily be corrected through discussions. Its rigidity gives the process transparency at the expense of common-sense decisions. The reduction in its use reflects a belief that the greater flexibility of negotiated procurement procedures will more often result in a better outcome for the government.

NEGOTIATIONS

I. INTRODUCTION.

A. Background.

1. Throughout much of the history of the United States, the only authorized method for acquiring goods and services in peacetime was sealed bidding. Negotiated procurements were known as "open market purchases," and these procurements were authorized only in emergencies, such as war.

2. The Army Air Corps began using negotiated procurements in the 1930s to develop and acquire aircraft. Negotiated procurements were widely used with great success during World War II. Subsequently, Congress enacted the Armed Services Procurement Act of 1947 and authorized negotiated procurements for peacetime use, providing one of seventeen exceptions to formal advertising (now sealed bidding) applied.

3. In 1962, Congress codified agency regulations that required contractors to submit cost/pricing data for certain procurements to aid in the negotiation process. Pricing of negotiated procurements is discussed in Chapter 14.

4. The Competition in Contracting Act (CICA) of 1984 expanded the use of negotiated procurements by eliminating the statutory preference for formal advertising (now sealed bidding).

5. In the early 1990s, Congress: (a) modified the procedures for awarding contracts on initial proposals; (b) expanded debriefings; and (c) made other minor procedural changes in the negotiated procurement process.

6. In 1997, the FAR Part 15 rewrite effort resulted in significant changes to the rules regarding: (a) exchanges with industry; (b) the permissible scope of discussions; and (c) the competitive range determination.

7. Today, the majority of federal procurements use negotiated procurement procedures, both for sole and limited source acquisitions, and for competitive procurements. Consequently, thoroughly understanding the process of negotiated procurements is key to being able to successfully solicit and compete for federal contracts.

B. References.

1. Statutory

   - 10 U.S.C. § 2305;
   - 41 U.S.C. § 3306.

2. Regulatory.

   - FAR Part 15.
   - DFARS Part 215.

3. Agency Guidance.

   - DOD Source Selection Procedures (March 2011)
   - Army Source Selection Supplement (AS3) to the Department of Defense Source Selection Procedures, December 21, 2012

II. CHOOSING NEGOTIATIONS.

A. **Sealed Bidding or Competitive Negotiations.** The CICA eliminated the historical preference for formal advertising (now sealed bidding). Statutory criteria now determine which procedures to use.

B. **Criteria for Selecting Competitive Negotiations.** 10 U.S.C. § 2304(a)(2)(A) and 41 U.S.C.

Negotiations

§ 3301(b)(1). The Act provides that, in determining the appropriate competitive procedure, agencies:

1. Shall solicit sealed bids <u>if</u>:

    a. Time permits the solicitation, submission, and evaluation of sealed bids;

    b. The award will be made solely on the basis of price and other price-related factors;

    c. It is unnecessary to conduct discussions with responding sources; and

    d. There is a reasonable expectation of receiving more than one sealed bid.

2. Shall request competitive proposals <u>if</u> sealed bids are not appropriate under B.1, above.

3. Competitive proposals are the default for contracts awarded and performed outside the United States. <u>See</u> FAR 6.401(b)(2). The reasons for preferring negotiations include the nearly universal need for discussions because of differences in language, law, culture, etc.

C. Contracting Officer's Discretion.

1. The decision to negotiate involves a contracting officer's business judgment, which will not be upset unless it is unreasonable. The contracting officer, however, must demonstrate that one or more of the sealed bidding criteria is not present. <u>Specialized Contract Serv., Inc.</u>, B-257321, Sept. 2, 1994, 94-2 CPD ¶ 90 (finding that the Army reasonably concluded that it needed to evaluate more than price in procuring lodging services). <u>Compare</u> <u>Racal Corp.</u>, B-240579, Dec. 4, 1990, 70 Comp. Gen. 127, 90-2 CPD ¶ 453 (finding that the possible need to hold discussions to assess offerors' understanding did not justify the use of negotiated procedures where the Army did not require offerors to submit technical proposal) <u>with</u> <u>Enviroclean Sys.</u>, B-278261, Dec. 24, 1997, 97-2 CPD ¶ 172 (finding that the Army reasonably concluded that discussions might be required before award).

2. A Request for Proposals (RFP) by any other name is still an RFP. <u>Balimoy Mfg. Co. of Venice, Inc.</u>, B-253287.2, Oct. 5, 1993, 93-2 CPD ¶ 207 (finding that an IFB that calls for the evaluation of factors other than price is not an IFB).

D. Comparing the Two Methods.

	Sealed Bidding	*Negotiations*
Evaluation Criteria	Price and Price-Related Factors	Price and Non-Price Factors
Responsiveness	Determined at Bid Opening	N/A
Responsibility	Based on Pre-Award Survey; SBA May Issue COC	May be Evaluated Comparatively Based on Disclosed Factors
Contract Type	FFP or FP w/EPA	Any Type
Discussions	Prohibited	Required (Unless Properly Awarding w/o Discussions)

	Sealed Bidding	*Negotiations*
Right to Withdraw	Firm Bid Rule	No Firm Bid Rule
Public Bid Opening	Yes	No
Flexibility to Use Judgment	None	Much
Late Offer/Modifications	Narrow Exceptions	Narrow Exceptions
Past Performance	Evaluated on a Pass/Fail Basis as Part of the Responsibility Determination	Included as an Evaluation Factor; Comparatively Assessed; Separate from the Responsibility Determination

III. CONDUCTING COMPETITIVE NEGOTIATIONS.

A. DOD Source Selection Procedures.

1. The FAR provides agencies a great deal of flexibility in how they conduct competitive negotiations, especially in the evaluation of competitive offers. Consequently, the armed services had evolved different approaches to competitive source selection.

2. In 2011, the Department of Defense (DOD) issued uniform procedures for conducting competitively negotiated source selections, outlining a common set of principles and procedures. The goal of uniform procedures is to ensure that DOD's source selection process delivers quality, timely products and services at the best value for the taxpayer. The uniform procedures followed a series of challenged source selections that did not reflect well on DOD. Subsequent GAO reviews have not found fault with DOD's uniform procedures. See GAO 14-584, Defense Contracting: Factors DOD Considers When Choosing Best Value Processes Are Consistent with Guidance for Selected Acquisitions (July 2014). DOD updated their Source Selection Procedures in April 2016, and the 2016 procedures are available at:

http://www.acq.osd.mil/dpap/policy/policyvault/USA004370-14-DPAP.pdf.

Source selections in process under an approved source selection plan as of 1 April 2016 may continue to follow the 2011 DOD procedures. USD, AT&L Letter dated 1 April 2016, Subject: Department of Defense Source Selection Procedures.

B. Developing a Request for Proposals (RFP). The three major sections of an RFP are: Specifications (Section C), Instructions to Offerors (Section L), and Evaluation Criteria (Section M). Contracting activities should develop these three sections simultaneously so that they are tightly integrated.

1. Section C describes the required work. Accurately describing the work sought is the single most important task in developing a request for proposals.

    a. Attorneys should review the requirements documents for inconsistencies, conflicts with standard FAR and DFARS clauses, completeness, etc. The contract attorney should also use the review to educate themselves on what the agency is acquiring, prior to reviewing the rest of the RFP.

b.　Contractors should take maximum advantage of exchanges with industry to ensure that they fully understand the technical requirements, advise the government of draft requirements that are impossible or expensive to meet, and alternative methods of performance the government should not inadvertently prohibit. Waiting until proposals are submitted to point out problem requirements is less successful.

2.　Section L describes what information offerors should provide in their proposals and prescribes the format for the proposals.

- Instructions reduce the need for discussions merely to understand the offerors' proposals.
- Instructions also make the evaluation process more efficient by dictating page limits, paper size, organization, and content. [NOTE: An offeror ignores these instructions and limitations at its peril. See Coffman Specialists, Inc., B-284546; B-284546.2, May 10, 2000, 2000 U.S. Comp. Gen. LEXIS 58 (agency reasonably downgraded a proposal that failed to comply with solicitation's formatting requirement). See also U.S. Envtl. & Indus., Inc., B-257349, July 28, 1994, 94-2 CPD ¶ 51 (concluding that the agency properly excluded the protester from the competitive range after adjusting its proposal length for type size smaller than the minimum allowed and refusing to consider the "excess" pages)].

3.　Section M describes how the government will evaluate proposals.

a.　Within DOD, the evaluation is either a Best Value Trade-Off, or a Low Price Technically Acceptable (LPTA) evaluation.

b.　The criteria must be detailed enough to address all aspects of the required

work, yet not so detailed as to mask differences in proposals.

c.　Solicitations must provide offerors enough information to compete equally and intelligently, but they need not give precise details of the government's evaluation plan. See QualMed, Inc., B-254397.13, July 20, 1994, 94-2 CPD ¶ 33.

d.　Evaluation scheme must include an adequate basis to determine cost to the government. S.J. Thomas Co., Inc., B-283192, Oct. 20, 1999, 99-2 CPD ¶ 73.

C.　Drafting Evaluation Criteria.

1.　Statutory Requirements.

a.　10 U.S.C. § 2305(a)(2) and 41 U.S.C. § 3306(c)(1) require each solicitation to include a statement regarding:

(1)　All the significant factors and subfactors the agency reasonably expects to consider in evaluating the proposals; and

(2)　The relative importance of each factor and subfactor. See FAR 15.304(d).

b.　10 U.S.C. § 2305(a)(3)(A) and 41 U.S.C. § 3306(b)(1) further require agency heads to:

(1)　State the relative importance of the quality factors;

(2)　Include cost/price as an evaluation factor; and

(3)　Disclose whether all of the non-cost and non-price factors, when combined, are:

(a)　Significantly more important than cost/price;

(b)　Approximately equal in importance to cost/price; or

(c)   Significantly less important than cost/price. <u>See</u> FAR 15.304(e).

c.   Agencies occasionally omit either: (1) significant evaluation factors and subfactors; (2) their relative importance; or (3) both. <u>See</u> <u>Stone & Webster Eng'g Corp.</u>, B-255286.2, Apr. 12, 1994, 94-1 CPD ¶ 306 (finding no prejudice even though the evaluation committee applied different weights to the evaluation factors without disclosing them); <u>cf</u>. <u>Danville-Findorff, Ltd</u>, B-241748, Mar. 1, 1991, 91-1 CPD ¶ 232 (finding no prejudice even though the agency listed the relative importance of an evaluation factor as 60 in the RFP, used 40 as the weight during evaluation, and used the "extra" 20 points for an unannounced evaluation factor).

d.   While procuring agencies are required to identify the significant evaluation factors and subfactors, they are not required to identify the various aspects of each factor which might be taken into account, provided that such aspects are reasonably related to or encompassed by the RFP's stated evaluation criteria. <u>NCLN20, Inc.</u>, B-287692, July 25, 2001, 2001 CPD ¶ 136.

e.   The GAO will generally excuse an agency's failure to specifically identify subfactors <u>if</u> the subfactors are: (1) reasonably related to the stated criteria, and (2) of relatively equal importance. <u>See</u> <u>Johnson Controls World Servs., Inc.</u>, B-257431, Oct. 5, 1994, 94-2 CPD ¶ 222 (finding that "efficiency" was reasonably encompassed within the disclosed factors); <u>AWD Tech., Inc.</u>, B-250081.2, Feb. 1, 1993, 93-1 CPD ¶ 83 (finding that the agency properly considered work on similar superfund sites even though the agency did not list it as a subfactor). The GAO, however, has held that an agency must disclose reasonably related subfactors if the agency gives them significant weight. <u>See</u> <u>Devres, Inc.</u>, B-224017, 66 Comp. Gen. 121, 86-2 CPD ¶ 652 (1986) (concluding that an agency must disclose subfactors that have a greater weight than the disclosed factors).

2.   Mandatory Evaluation Factors.

a.   Cost or Price. 10 U.S.C. § 2305(a)(3)(A)(ii); 41 U.S.C. § 3306(c)(1); FAR 15.304(c)(1). Agencies must evaluate cost/price in every source selection. <u>See also</u> <u>Spectron, Inc.</u>, B-172261, 51 Comp. Gen. 153 (1971); <u>but see</u> <u>RTF/TCI/EAI Joint Venture</u>, B-280422.3, Dec. 29, 1998, 98-2 CPD ¶ 162 (GAO denied protest alleging failure to consider price because protestor unable to show prejudice from Army's error).

b.   Technical and Management (i.e., Quality) Factors. The government must also consider quality in every source selection. <u>See</u> FAR 15.304(c)(2).

(1)   The term "quality" refers to evaluation factors other than cost/price (e.g., technical capability, management capability, prior performance, and past performance). <u>See</u> 10 U.S.C. § 2305(a)(3)(A)(i); 41 U.S.C. § 3306(c)(1)(A); FAR 15.304(c)(2).

(2)   FAR 15.304(a) recommends tailoring the evaluation factors and subfactors to the acquisition, and FAR 15.304(b) recommends including only evaluation factors and subfactors that:

(a) Represent key areas that the agency plans to consider in making the award decision; and

(b) Permit the agency to compare competing proposals meaningfully.

c. Past Performance.

(1) Statutory Requirements.

(a) The Federal Acquisition Streamlining Act of 1994, Pub. L. No. 103-355, § 1091, 108 Stat. 3243, 3272 [hereinafter FASA], added a note to 41 U.S.C. § 1126 expressing Congress's belief that agencies should use past performance as an evaluation factor because it is an indicator of an offeror's ability to perform successfully on future contracts.

(b) The FASA also directed the Administrator of the Office of Federal Procurement Policy (OFPP) to provide guidance to executive agencies regarding the use of past performance information in awarding contracts. 41 U.S.C. § 1126.

(c) The OFFP publishes A Guide to Best Practices for Past Performance, May 2000 (available at http://www.acqnet.gov/Library/OFPP/BestPractices/pastpeformguide.htm). The Office of the Under Secretary of Defense for Acquisition, Technology and Logistics issues A Guide to Collection and Use of Past Performance Information (available at https://apps.altess.army.mil/ppims/prod/common/DISAPPIDeskbookJul03.pdf. The Air Force also has a very good Past Performance Evaluation Guide (available at https://www.safaq.hq.af.mil/contracting/affars/5315/informational/IG5315.305(a)(2).doc

(2) FAR Requirements. FAR 15.304(c)(3); FAR 15.305(a)(2).

(a) Agencies must include past performance as an evaluation factor in all RFPs over the simplified acquisition threshold.

(b) DOD has a class deviation to this requirement. DAR Tracking Number: 2013-O0018. For the Department of Defense, past performance is mandatory only for the following contracts:

(i) Systems & operation support > $5 million.

(ii) Services, information technology, or science & technology > $1 million.

(iii) Ship repair or overhaul > $500,000.

(c) The contracting officer may make a determination that past performance is not an appropriate evaluation factor even if the contract falls in either category (a) or (b).

(d) The RFP must:

(i) Describe how the agency plans to evaluate past performance;

(ii) Provide offerors with an opportunity to identify

past or current contracts for similar work; and

    (iii) Provide offerors an opportunity to provide information regarding any problems they encountered on the identified contracts and their corrective actions.

d.   Small Business Participation.

    (1) FAR 15.304(c)(3)(ii) requires past performance in meeting small business subcontracting goals to be an evaluation factor where there are substantial subcontracting opportunities.

    (2) FAR 15.304(c)(4) requires evaluation of proposed small business subcontracting participation goals when there are substantial subcontracting opportunities.

    (3) DFARS 215.304 requires DOD to evaluate the extent to which small businesses and historically black colleges will participate in the performance of the contract in best value source selections requiring a subcontracting plan.

3.   Requirement to Disclose Relative Importance. FAR 15.304(d).

a.   Agencies must disclose the relative importance of all significant evaluation factors and subfactors.

b.   Agencies may disclose the relative order of importance by:

    (1) Providing percentages or numerical weights[1] in the RFP;

    (2) Providing an algebraic paragraph;

    (3) Listing the factors or subfactors in descending order of importance; or

    (4) Using a narrative statement. But see Health Servs. Int'l, Inc., B-247433, June 5, 1992, 92-1 CPD ¶ 493 (finding that the agency misled offerors by listing equal factors in "descending order of importance").

c.   The GAO states that where an RFP omits the relative importance, the weights are approximately equal. For example, in Fintrac, Inc., B-311462.3, Oct. 14, 2008, 2008 CPD ¶ 191, the RFP listed the major evaluation factors in "descending order of importance" but was silent as to the weight of the subfactors. GAO stated that where a solicitation does not disclose the relative weight of evaluation factors or subfactors in the solicitation, they are presumed approximately equal in importance or weight. See also Bio-Rad Labs., Inc., B-297553, Feb. 15, 2006, 2007 CPD ¶ 58 (finding that where an agency failed to inform offerors it was conducting the procurement as a simplified acquisition and conducted the

---

[1] On 5 March 2001, Mr. Elgart, Acting Deputy Assistant Secretary of the Army (Procurement), issued a memorandum prohibiting the use of numerical weighting to evaluate proposals in the Army. Numerical weighting is no longer an authorized method of expressing the relative importance of factors and subfactors. Evaluation factors and subfactors must be definable in readily understood qualitative terms (i.e., adjectival, colors, or other indicators, but not numbers). See AFARS 5115.304(b)(2)(iv).

acquisition in a manner indistinguishable from a negotiated procurement, offerors could reasonably presume listed subfactors were approximately equal in importance). The GAO presumes that all of the listed factors are equal if the RFP does not state their relative order of importance. See North-East Imaging, Inc., B-256281, June 1, 1994, 94-1 CPD ¶ 332; cf. Isratex, Inc. v. United States, 25 Cl. Ct. 223 (1992).

    (1)   The better practice is to state the relative order of importance expressly.

    (2)   Agencies should rely on the "presumed equal" line of cases only when an RFP inadvertently fails to state the relative order of importance. See High-Point Schaer, B-242616, May 28, 1991, 70 Comp. Gen. 525, 91-1 CPD ¶ 509 (applying the "equal" presumption).

d.   Agencies need not disclose their specific rating methodology. FAR 15.304(d). See ABB Power Generation, Inc., B-272681, Oct. 25, 1996, 96-2 CPD ¶ 183.

e.   Contract attorneys should pay careful attention when they review the evaluation factors and the relative importance of those factors. A common source of error in competitive negotiations is failure to follow the disclosed evaluation factors and the relative importance of the factors. While the factors and weights selected are mostly a matter of business judgment once the statutory factors are included, the agency must apply the factors as disclosed.

4.   Requirement to Disclose Basis of Award. FAR 15.101-1; FAR 15.101-2.

a.   Agencies must disclose how they intend to make the award decision.

b.   Agencies generally choose:

    (1)   The Best Value tradeoff process; or

    (2)   The lowest-priced technically acceptable process.

c.   A "Best Value" tradeoff typically takes the lowest-priced, technically acceptable offer as the baseline, then evaluates higher-priced, more highly rated proposals to determine whether the advantages of the more highly rated proposals merit the higher price. This process allows the government to award to higher-priced offers where the perceived benefits of the higher-priced proposal merit the additional cost. The evaluation must consider the disclosed non-price factors and relative importance of the factors.

d.   A "Low-Priced, Technically Acceptable" evaluation is used where price is the determinative factor.

    (a)   The requirements must be clearly defined and the risks of unsuccessful performance are minimal.

    (b)   Technical factors are "Go"/"No Go."

    (c)   A cost/technical tradeoff is not permitted; award will go to the lowest-priced offer which meets the minimum technical standards. FAR 15.101-2.

5.   Problem Evaluation Factors.

a.   Options.

(1) The evaluation factors should address all evaluated options clearly. A solicitation that fails to state whether the agency will evaluate options is defective. See generally FAR Subpart 17.2; see also Occu-Health, Inc., B-270228.3, Apr. 3, 1996, 96-1 CPD ¶ 196 (sustaining a protest where the agency failed to inform offerors that it would not evaluate options due to a change in its requirements).

(2) Agencies must evaluate options at the time of award; otherwise, they cannot exercise options unless the agency prepares a Justification and Approval (J&A). FAR 17.207(f).

b. Key Personnel.

(1) The skills of a contractor's personnel are very important in evaluating a proposal for a service contract. The contract should require identification of any critical employees and limit the contractor's freedom to replace the key personnel with less-skilled employees.

(2) Evaluation criteria for staffing should address:

(a) The education, training, and experience of the proposed employee(s);

(b) The percentage of time the highly skilled employee(s) are expected to devote to contract performance (highly skilled experts may be stretched between several contracts);

(c) The likelihood that proposed new hires will agree to work for the contractor; and

(d) The impact of diverting the proposed employee(s) from the contractor's other contracts. See Biospherics, Inc., B-253891.2, Nov. 24, 1993, 93-2 CPD ¶ 333; cf. ManTech Advanced Sys. Int'l, Inc., B-255719.2, May 11, 1994, 94-1 CPD ¶ 326 (finding that the awardee's misrepresentation of the availability of key personnel justified overturning the award). But see SRS Tech., B-258170.3, Feb. 21, 1995, 95-1 CPD ¶ 95 (concluding that it was not improper for an offeror to provide a substitute where it did not propose the key employee knowing that he would be unavailable).

(3) Agencies should request resumés, hiring or employment agreements, and proposed responsibilities in the RFP.

D. Notice of Intent to Hold Discussions.

1. 10 U.S.C. § 2305(a)(2)(B)(ii)(I) and 41 U.S.C. § 3306(b)(2)(B)(i) require RFPs to contain either:

a. "[A] statement that the proposals are intended to be evaluated with, and award made after, discussions with the offerors," (FAR 52.215-1 Alt. 1, (f)(4)) or

b. "[A] statement that the proposals are intended to be evaluated, and award made, without discussions with the offerors (other than discussion conducted for the purpose of minor clarification[s]), unless discussions are determined to be necessary." (FAR 52.215-1(f)(4).

2. Statutes and regulations provide no guidance on whether an agency should award with or without discussions. Contracting officers should consider

factors indicating that discussions may be necessary (e.g., procurement history, competition, contract type, specification clarity, etc.). Discussions may be as short or as long as required, but offerors must be given an opportunity to revise proposals after discussions end.

3. A protest challenging the failure to include the correct notice in the solicitation is untimely if filed after the date for receipt of initial proposals. See Warren Pumps, Inc., B-248145.2, Sept. 18, 1992, 92-2 CPD ¶ 187.

E. Exchanges with Industry before Receipt of Proposals.

1. The FAR encourages the early exchange of information among all interested parties to improve the understanding of the government's requirements and industry capabilities, provided the exchanges are consistent with procurement integrity requirements. See FAR 15.201. There are many ways an agency may promote the early exchange of information, including:

- Industry/small business conferences;
- Draft RFPs;
- Requests for Information (RFIs);
- Site visits.

2. Because the agency will receive better proposals and more competition when industry understands the agency's requirements and has time to assemble the resources to bid, contract attorneys should encourage frequent and fair contacts with industry. Additionally, industry is an excellent resource for identifying unrealistic requirements, requirements that eliminate competition, and unaffordable requirements.

F. Issuing the Request for Proposals.

1. Absent an emergency, the contracting officer will issue the Request for Proposals in the Uniform Contract Format

discussed in Chapter 2, with a Standard Form 30 as the cover sheet.

2. The availability of the RFP is publicized as provided in Chapter 5.

3. When the contents of the RFP are not available to the general public for reasons of export control or classification, the agency should have procedures for disseminating the contents to eligible offerors.

4. RFP Amendments.

a. An agency must amend the RFP if it changes its requirements (or terms and conditions) significantly. FAR 15.206(b). See United Tel. Co. of the Northwest, B-246977, Apr. 20, 1992, 92-1 CPD ¶ 374; see also MVM, Inc. v. United States, 46 Fed. Cl. 126 (2000).

b. After amending the RFP, the agency must give prospective offerors a reasonable time to modify their proposals, considering the complexity of the acquisition, the agency's needs, etc. See FAR 15.206(g).

c. Timing:

(1) Before established time and date for receipt of proposals, amendment goes to all parties receiving the solicitation. FAR 15.206 (b).

(2) After established time and date for receipt of proposals, amendment goes to all offerors that have not been eliminated from the competition. FAR 15.206 (c).

(3) If the change is so substantial as to exceed what prospective offerors reasonable could have anticipated, the contracting officer shall cancel the original solicitation and issue a new one,

regardless of the stage of the acquisition. FAR 15.206 (e).

G.   Preparation and Submission of Initial Proposals.

1.   Proposal Preparation Time.

a.   Agencies must give potential offerors at least 30 days after they issue the solicitation to submit initial proposals for contracts over the simplified acquisition threshold. 15 U.S.C. § 637(d)(3); FAR 5.203. But see FAR 12.603 and FAR 5.203 for streamlined requirements for commercial items.

b.   In solicitations of any size or complexity, the contracting officer should consider giving offerors additional time to prepare and submit proposals because 30 days is very little time to prepare a proposal that conforms to Section L.

2.   Offerors should prepare their proposals to meet or exceed the government's requirements at a price that is both competitive and profitable.

3.   "Early" Proposals.

a.   FAR 2.101 defines "offer" as a "response to a solicitation that, if accepted, would bind the offeror to perform the resultant contract."

b.   Agencies must evaluate offers that respond to the solicitation, even if the offer pre-dates the solicitation. STG Inc., B-285910, 2000 U.S. Comp. Gen. LEXIS 133 (Sept. 20, 2000).

c.   If agency wants to preclude evaluation of proposals received prior to RFP issue date, it must notify offerors and allow sufficient time to submit new proposals by closing date. Id. at *5 n.3.

4.   Late Proposals. FAR 15.208; FAR 52.215-1.

a.   Offerors should deliver timely proposals in compliance with the instructions in the RFP.

b.   A proposal is late if the agency does not receive it by the time and date specified in the RFP. Haskell Company, B-292756, Nov. 19, 2003, 2003 CPD ¶ 202 (key is whether the government could verify that a timely proposal was submitted).

(1)   If no time is stated, 4:30 p.m. local time is presumed.

(2)   FAR 52.215-1 sets forth the circumstances under which an agency may consider a late proposal.

(3)   The late proposal rules mirror the late bid rules in Chapter 8. See FAR 14.304.

c.   Both technical and price proposals are due before the closing time. See Inland Serv. Corp., B-252947.4, Nov. 4, 1993, 93-2 CPD ¶ 266.

d.   Agencies must retain late proposals unopened in the contracting office.

5.   No "Firm Bid Rule." An offeror's proposal is an offer the government may accept, but an offeror may withdraw its proposal at any time before award. FAR 52.215-1(c)(8).

a.   Generally, offers may be accepted at any time during the period of proposal validity stated in Block 12 on the SF 30. The agency, however, only has a reasonable time in which to accept a proposal. See Western Roofing Serv., B-232666.4, Mar. 5, 1991, 70 Comp. Gen. 324, 91-1 CPD ¶ 242 (holding that 13 months was too long).

b.   The offeror should extend the validity period of its proposal in writing if it desires to remain in the competition and the contracting officer has not yet accepted its proposal.

c.   An offeror may submit modifications in response to an RFP amendment or to correct a mistake at any time before award. FAR 52.215-1(c)(6)

6.   Oral Presentations. FAR 15.102.

a.   While competitive negotiations are often conducted entirely in writing, oral presentations are also common and can be quite helpful for summarizing and explaining the initial proposal for evaluators.

b.   The RFP may request oral presentations as part of the initial proposal. See NW Ayer, Inc., B-248654, 92-2 CPD ¶ 154. When oral presentations are required, the solicitation shall provide offerors with sufficient information to prepare them. FAR 15.102(d). The following are examples of information that may be put into the solicitation:

(1)   The types of information to be presented orally and the associated evaluation factors that will be used;

(2)   The qualifications for personnel required to provide the presentation;

(3)   Requirements, limitations and/or prohibitions on supplemental written material or other media;

(4)   The location, date, and time;

(5)   Time restrictions; or

(6)   Scope and content of exchanges between the government and the offeror, to include whether or not discussions will be permitted. *Id.*

c.   The FAR does not require a particular method of recording what occurred during oral presentations, but agencies must maintain a record adequate to permit meaningful review. See Checchi & Co. Consulting, Inc., B-285777, Oct. 10, 2000, 2001 CPD ¶ 132. A common practice is to give a PowerPoint® presentation and to use the visual materials as the record of the oral discussions.

d.   Agency questions during oral presentations could be interpreted as discussions if an offeror is allowed to modify its proposal. In Global Analytic Info. Tech. Servs., Inc., B-298840.2, Feb. 6, 2007, 2007 CPD ¶ 57, GAO held if agency personnel comment on or raise substantive questions about a proposal during an oral presentation, and afford an opportunity to revise a proposal in light of the agency's comments, then discussions have occurred. Therefore, the contracting officer should limit questions to those appropriate to understand the information presented.

7.   Confidentiality.

a.   Prospective offerors may restrict the use and disclosure of information contained in their proposals by marking the proposal with an authorized restrictive legend. FAR 52.215-1(e).

b.   Agencies must safeguard proposals from unauthorized disclosure. FAR 15.207(b).

c.   When use of non-government advisors is anticipated, the agency should notify the offerors, obtain the offerors' consent, and eliminate or mitigate the non-government advisors' personal or organizational conflicts of interest.

H.   Timeliness of Initial Proposals.

The general rule that "Late is Late" and the exceptions to the general rule discussed in Chapter 8, Section V.E. apply to competitive proposals. FAR 52.215-1.

I. Evaluation of Initial Proposals.

1. General Considerations.

   a. The composition of an evaluation team is left to the agency's discretion and the GAO will not review it absent a showing of conflict of interest or bias. See University Research Corp., B-253725.4, Oct. 26, 1993, 93-2 CPD ¶ 259.

   b. Evaluators must read the entire proposal. Intown Properties, Inc., B-262362.2, Jan. 18, 1996, 96-1 CPD ¶ 89 (record failed to demonstrate whether agency had considered information contained in offeror's best and final offer).

   c. Evaluators must be reasonable and follow the evaluation criteria in the RFP. See Marquette Med. Sys. Inc., B-277827.5; B-277827.7, Apr. 29, 1999, 99-1 CPD ¶ 90; Foundation Health Fed. Servs., Inc., B-254397.4, Dec. 20, 1993, 94-1 CPD ¶ 3. Evaluators have no discretion to deviate from the solicitation's stated evaluation criteria. See, e.g., Y & K Maintenance, Inc., B-405310.6, Feb 2, 2012, 2012 CPD ¶ 93 (sustaining a protest because the agency failed to evaluate the experience of the awardee's key personnel consistent with the RFP's stated evaluation criteria).

   d. Evaluators must be consistent. If evaluators downgrade an offeror for a deficiency, they must downgrade other offerors for the same deficiency. See Park Sys. Maint. Co., B-252453, June 16, 1993, 93-1 CPD ¶ 466.

   e. Evaluators must avoid double-scoring or exaggerating the importance of a factor beyond its disclosed weight. See J.A. Jones Mgmt. Servs., B-254941.2, Mar. 16, 1994, 94-1 CPD ¶ 244.

   f. Evaluators must evaluate compliance with the stated requirements. If an offeror proposes a better—but noncompliant—solution, the agency should amend the RFP and solicit new proposals, provided the agency can do so without disclosing proprietary data. FAR 15.206(d). See Beta Analytics, Int'l, Inc. v. U.S., 44 Fed. Cl. 131 (1999); GTS Duratek, Inc., B-280511.2, B-285011.3, Oct. 19, 1998, 98-2 CPD ¶ 130; Labat-Anderson Inc., B-246071, Feb. 18, 1992, 92-1 CPD ¶ 193; cf. United Tel. Co. of the Northwest, B-246977, Apr. 20, 1992, 92-1 CPD ¶ 374 (holding that substantial changes required the agency to cancel and reissue the RFP).

   g. Evaluators may consider matters outside the offerors' proposals if their consideration of such matters is not unreasonable or contrary to the stated evaluation criteria. See Intermagnetics Gen. Corp.—Recon., B-255741.4, Sept. 27, 1994, 94-2 CPD ¶ 119.

   h. Agencies may not downgrade past performance rating based on offeror's history of filing claims. See AmClyde Engineered Prods. Co., Inc., B-282271, June 21, 1999, 99-2 CPD ¶ 5. On 1 April 2002, the Office of Federal Procurement Policy instructed all federal agencies that the "filing of protests, the filing of claims, or the use of Alternative Dispute Resolution must not be considered by an agency in either past performance or source selection decisions."[2]

i. A "cost/technical trade-off" evaluation requires evaluation of differences in technical merit beyond RFP's minimum requirements. See Johnson Controls World Servs., Inc.; Meridian Mgmt., B-281287.5; B-281287.6; B-281287.7, June 21, 1999, 2001 CPD ¶ 3.

j. In reviewing protests against allegedly improper evaluations, the GAO will examine the record to determine whether the agency's evaluation was reasonable and in accordance with the solicitation's stated evaluation criteria. MCR Fed., Inc., B-280969, Dec. 14, 1998, 99-1 CPD ¶ 8.

2. Evaluating Cost/Price.

a. Contracting activities should score cost/price in dollars and avoid schemes that: (1) mathematically relate cost to technical point scores; or (2) assign point scores to cost.

b. Evaluation scheme must be reasonable and provide an objective basis for comparing cost to government. SmithKline Beecham Corp., B-283939, Jan. 27, 2000, 2000 CPD ¶ 19.

c. Firm Fixed-Price Contracts. FAR 15.305(a)(1).

(1) Price Reasonableness. A price reasonableness analysis determines whether an offeror's price is fair and reasonable to the government, and focuses primarily on

whether the offered price is too high (not too low). CSE Constr., B-291268.2, Dec. 16, 2002, 2002 CPD ¶ 207; SDV Solutions, Inc., B-402309, Feb. 1, 2010, 2010 CPD ¶ 48. The concern that an offeror submitted a price that is "too low" is not a valid part of a price reasonableness evaluation; similarly, the allegation that an awardee submitted an unreasonably low price does not provide a basis upon which to sustain a protest because there is no prohibition against an agency accepting a below-cost proposal for a fixed-price contract. See First Enter., B-292967, Jan. 7, 2004, 2004 CPD ¶ 11.

(2) However, unreasonably low prices may evidence a lack of understanding of the technical requirements, or a mistake in bid. Therefore, contracting officers may investigate these areas in discussions. Comparing proposed prices usually satisfies the requirement to perform a price analysis because an offeror's proposed price is also its probable price. See Ball Technical Prods. Group, B-224394, Oct. 17, 1986, 86-2 CPD ¶ 465. But see Triple P Servs., Inc., B-271629.3, July 22, 1996, 96-2 CPD ¶ 30 (indicating that an agency may evaluate the reasonableness of the offeror's low price to assess its understanding of the solicitation requirements if the RFP permits the agency to evaluate offerors' understanding of

[2] Memorandum, Angela B. Styles, Administrator, Office of Federal Procurement Policy, to Senior Procurement Executives, subject: Protests, Claims, and Alternative Dispute Resolution (ADR) as Factors in Past Performance and Source Selection Decisions (Apr. 1, 2002).

requirements as part of technical evaluation).

(3) To the extent an agency elects to perform a realism analysis as part of the award of a fixed-price contract, its purpose is not to evaluate an offeror's price, but to measure an offeror's understanding of the solicitation's requirements; further, the offered prices may not be adjusted as a result of the analysis. FAR § 15.404-1(d)(3); IBM Corp., B299504, B-299504.2, June 4, 2007, 2008 CPD ¶ 64 (sustaining protest challenging the agency's evaluation of offerors' price and cost proposals where the agency improperly adjusted upward portions of the protester's fixed-price proposals); ITT Elec. Sys. Radar Recon. & Acoustic Sys., B-405608, Dec. 5, 2011, 2012 CPD ¶ 7 ("Where, as here, an RFP provides for the award of a fixed price contract, the contracting agency may not adjust offerors' prices for purposes of evaluation.").

(4) Where the agency has not disclosed price realism as an evaluation factor, a below-cost price is a matter of the offeror's responsibility, i.e., the offeror's ability to absorb the loss and perform the contract. Flight Safety Servs. Corp., B–403831, B–403831.2, Dec. 9, 2010, 2010 CPD ¶ 294 at 5.

d. Cost Reimbursement Contracts. FAR 15.305(a)(1).

(1) Agencies should perform a cost realism analysis and

evaluate an offeror's probable cost of accomplishing the solicited work, rather than its proposed cost.[3] See FAR 15.404-1(d); see also Kinton, Inc., B-228260.2, Feb. 5, 1988, 67 Comp. Gen. 226, 88-1 CPD ¶ 112 (indicating that it is improper for an agency to award based on probable costs without a detailed cost analysis or discussions with the offeror).

(2) Agencies should evaluate cost realism consistently from one proposal to the next.

(a) Agencies should consider all cost/price elements. It is unreasonable to ignore unpriced "other cost items," even if the exact cost of the items is not known. See Trandes Corp., B-256975.3, Oct. 25, 1994, 94-2 CPD ¶ 221; cf. Stapp Towing Co., ASBCA No. 41584, 94-1 BCA ¶ 26,465.

(b) Agencies may not apply estimated adjustment factors mechanically. A proper cost realism analysis requires the agency to analyze each offeror's proposal independently based on its particular circumstances, approach, personnel, and other unique factors. See The Jonathan Corp., B-251698.3, May 17, 1993, 93-2 CPD ¶ 174; Bendix Field Eng'g Corp., B-246236, Feb. 25, 1992, 92-1 CPD ¶ 227.

(3) Agencies must document their cost realism analysis. See KPMG LLP, B-406409, et

---

[3] Probable cost is the proposed cost adjusted for cost realism.

seq., May 21, 2012, 2012 WL 2020396 (explaining that GAO "will sustain a protest where the cost realism analysis [is] not adequately documented").

3. Scoring Technical and Management Factors. See FAR 15.305(a).

   a. Agencies possess considerable discretion in evaluating proposals, and particularly in making scoring decisions. See Billy G. Bassett, B-237331, Feb. 20, 1990, 90-1 CPD ¶ 195 (indicating that the GAO will not rescore proposals; it will only review them to ensure that the agency's evaluation is reasonable and consistent with the stated evaluation criteria). See also Antarctic Support Associates v. United States, 46 Fed. Cl. 145 (2000) (court cited precedent of requiring "great deference" in judicial review of technical matters).

   b. Rating Methods. An agency may adopt any method it desires, provided the method is not arbitrary and does not violate any statutes or regulations. See BMY, A Div. of Harsco Corp. v. United States, 693 F. Supp. 1232 (D.D.C. 1988). At a minimum, an agency must give better proposals higher scores. See Trijicon, Inc., B-244546, Oct. 25, 1991, 71 Comp. Gen. 41, 91-2 CPD ¶ 375 (concluding that the agency failed to rate proposals that exceeded the minimum requirements higher than those offering the minimum). An agency may give higher scores to proposals that exceed the minimum requirements, even if the RFP does not disclose how much extra credit will be given under each subfactor. See PCB Piezotronics, Inc., B-254046, Nov. 17, 1993, 93-2 CPD ¶ 286.

   (1) Numerical.[4] An agency may use point scores to rate individual evaluation factors. But see Modern Tech. Corp., B-236961.4, Mar. 19, 1990, 90-1 CPD ¶ 301 (questioning the use of arithmetic scores to determine proposal acceptability). The agency, however, should only use point scores as guides in making the award decision. See Telos Field Eng'g B-253492.6, Dec. 15, 1994, 94-2 CPD ¶ 240 (concluding that it was unreasonable for the agency to rely on points alone, particularly when the agency calculated the points incorrectly).

   (2) Adjectives. An agency may use adjectives (e.g., excellent, good, satisfactory, marginal, and unsatisfactory)—either alone or in conjunction with other rating methods—to indicate the degree to which an offeror's proposal meets the requisite standards for each evaluation factor. See Hunt Bldg. Corp., B-276370, June 6, 1997, 98-1 CPD ¶ 101 (denying a challenge to the assigned adjectival ratings where the evaluators adequately documented the different features offered by each firm and conveyed the comparative merits of the proposals to the selection official); see also FAR 15.305(a); Biospherics Incorp., B-278508.4; B-278508.5; B-278508.6, Oct 6, 1998, 98-2 CPD ¶ 96 (holding that while adjectival ratings and point scores are useful

---

[4] See supra note 1 for Army policy regarding use of numerical scoring.

guides to decision making, they must be supported by documentation of the relative differences between proposals).

(3) Colors. An agency may use colors in lieu of adjectives to indicate the degree to which an offeror's proposal meets the requisite standards for each evaluation factor.

(4) Narrative. An agency must provide a narrative to rate the strengths, weaknesses, and risks of each proposal. The narrative provides the basis for the source selection decision; therefore, the narrative should reflect the relative importance of the evaluation factors accurately.

(5) GO/NO GO. The FAR does not prohibit a pure pass/fail method, but the GAO disfavors it. See CompuChem Lab., Inc., B-242889, June 19, 1991, 91-1 CPD ¶ 572. Because pass/fail criteria imply a minimum acceptable level, these levels should appear in the RFP. See National Test Pilot School, B-237503, Feb. 27, 1990, 90-1 CPD ¶ 238 (holding that award to the low-cost, technically acceptable proposal was inconsistent with the statement that the technical factors were more important than cost).

(6) Dollars. This system translates the technical evaluation factors into dollars that are added or subtracted from the evaluated price to get a final dollar price adjusted for technical quality.

See DynCorp, B-245289.3, July 30, 1992, 93-1 CPD ¶ 69.

c. In DOD, current guidance recommends use of qualitative evaluations (Color/Adjectives) for non-price factors. Department of Defense Source Selection Procedures, Chapter 3.

d. Agencies must reconcile adverse information when performing technical evaluation. See Maritime Berthing, Inc., B-284123.3, Apr. 27, 2000, 2000 CPD ¶ 89.

e. A responsibility determination is not strictly part of the technical evaluation, but the evaluation process may include consideration of responsibility matters. See Applied Eng'g Servs., Inc., B-256268.5, Feb. 22, 1995, 95-1 CPD ¶ 108. If responsibility matters are considered without a comparative evaluation of offers, however, a small business found technically unacceptable may appeal to the SBA for a COC. See Docusort, Inc., B-254852, Jan. 25, 1994, 94-1 CPD ¶ 38.

f. Ratings are merely guides for intelligent decision making in the procurement process. See Citywide Managing Servs. of Port Washington, Inc., B-281287.12, B-281281.13, Nov. 15, 2000, 2001 CPD ¶ 6 at 11. The focus in the source selection decision should be the underlying bases for the ratings, considered in a fair and equitable manner consistent with the terms of the RFP. See Mechanical Equipment Company, Inc., et al., B-292789.2, et al., Dec. 15, 2003.

4. Evaluating Past Performance or Experience. See John Brown U.S. Servs., Inc., B-258158, Dec. 21, 1994, 95-1 CPD ¶ 35 (comparing the evaluation of past performance and past experience); OFPP

Negotiations

Memo, dated July 10, 2014, Subject: Making Better Use of Contractor Performance Information; and DOD Source Selection Procedures, discussed in Section III.A, above.

a.   The RFP may ask offerors to identify previous contracts that are similar to the work being solicited.

b.   The agency may use its own experience with an offeror's past performance. See Birdwell Bros. Painting and Refinishing, B-285035, July 5, 2000, 2000 CPD ¶ 129.

c.   Agencies have business systems to accumulate past performance data.

- Contractor Performance Assessment Reporting System (CPARS) (http://www.cpars.csd.disa.mil/cparsmain.htm); and
- Past Performance Information Retrieval System (PPIRS) (www.ppirs.gov/).

d.   Using the Experience of Others. Agencies may attribute the past performance or experience of parents, affiliates, subsidiaries, officers, and team members, although doing so can be difficult. See U.S. Textiles, Inc., B-289685.3, Dec. 19, 2002, Oklahoma County Newspapers, Inc., B-270849, May 6, 1996, 96-1 CPD ¶ 213; Tucson Mobilephone, Inc., B-258408.3, June 5, 1995, 95-1 CPD ¶ 267; Aid Maint. Co., B-255552, Mar. 9, 1994, 94-1 CPD ¶ 188; FMC Corp., B-252941, July 29, 1993, 93-2 CPD ¶ 71; Pathology Assocs., Inc., B-237208.2, Feb. 20, 1990, 90-1 CPD ¶ 292.

e.   Comparative Evaluations of Small Businesses' Past Performance.

(1)   If an agency comparatively evaluates offerors' past performance, small businesses may not use the SBA's

Certificate of Competency (COC) procedures to review the evaluation. See Nomura Enter., Inc., B-277768, Nov. 19, 1997, 97-2 CPD ¶ 148; Smith of Galeton Gloves, Inc., B-271686, July 24, 1996, 96-2 CPD ¶ 36.

(2)   If an agency fails to state that it will consider responsibility-type factors, small businesses may seek a COC. See Envirosol, Inc., B-254223, Dec. 2, 1993, 93-2 CPD ¶ 295; Flight Int'l Group, Inc., B-238953.4, Sept. 28, 1990, 90-2 CPD ¶ 257.

(3)   If an agency uses pass/fail scoring for a responsibility-type factor, small businesses may seek a COC. See Clegg Indus., Inc., B-242204, Aug. 14, 1991, 70 Comp. Gen. 680, 91-2 CPD ¶ 145.

f.   Evidence of Past Performance.

(1)   Agencies may consider their own past experience with an offeror rather than relying solely on the furnished references. See Birdwell Bros. Painting and Refinishing, B-285035, July 5, 2000, 2000 CPD ¶ 129.

(2)   In KMS Fusion, Inc., B-242529, May 8, 1991, 91-1 CPD ¶ 447, an agency properly considered extrinsic past performance evidence when past performance was a disclosed evaluation factor. In fact, ignoring extrinsic evidence may be improper. See SCIENTECH, Inc., B-277805.2, Jan. 20, 1998, 98-1 CPD ¶ 33; cf. Aviation Constructors, Inc., B-244794,

Nov. 12, 1991, 91-2 CPD ¶ 448.

(3)   Past Performance Evaluation System. FAR Subpart 42.15.

(a)   Agencies must establish procedures for collecting and maintaining performance information on contractors. These procedures should provide for input from technical offices, contracting offices, and end users. FAR 42.1503.

(b)   Agencies must prepare performance evaluation reports for each contract in excess of The Simplified Acquisition Threshold. FAR 42.1502. DOD has a deviation that significantly raises the threshold for certain contracts. DAR Tracking Number: 2013-O0018.

g.   Agencies must make rational— rather than mechanical— comparative past performance evaluations. In Green Valley Transportation, Inc., B-285283, Aug. 9, 2000, 2000 CPD ¶ 133, GAO found unreasonable an agency's use of absolute numbers of performance problems, without considering the "size of the universe of performance" where problems occurred.

h.   Agencies cannot ignore information that is personally known by agency evaluators. Evaluators may consider and rely upon their personal knowledge in the course of evaluating an offeror's past performance. Del-Jen Int'l Corp., B-297960, May 5, 2006, 2006 CPD ¶ 81; NVT Techs., Inc., B-297524, B-297524.2, Feb. 2, 2006, 2006 CPD ¶ 36; see TPL, Inc., B-297136.10, B-297136.11, May 2005, 2005 CPD ¶

(finding that a conflict of interest does not exist where the same contracting agency or contracting agency employees prepare both an offeror's past performance reference and perform the evaluation of offerors' proposals). In fact, in some circumstances, agency evaluators cannot ignore past performance information of which they are personally aware. The MIL Corp., B-297508, B-297508.2, Jan. 26, 2006, 2006 CPD ¶ 34; Northeast Military Sales., Inc., B404153, Jan. 2011, 2011 CPD ¶ 2 (sustaining a protest challenging an agency's assessment of the awardee's past performance as exceptional where the agency failed to consider adverse past performance information of which it was aware).

i.   Lack of past performance history should not bar new firms from competing for government contracts. See Espey Mfg. & Elecs. Corp., B-254738, Mar. 8, 1994, 94-1 CPD ¶ 180; cf. Laidlaw Envtl. Servs., Inc., B-256346, June 14, 1994, 94-1 CPD ¶ 365 (permitting the agency to give credit for commercial past performance if it is equivalent to comparable prior government experience). Agencies must give a neutral rating to firms "without a record of relevant past performance." FAR 15.305(a)(2)(iv). See Excalibur Sys., Inc., B-272017, July 12, 1996, 96-2 CPD ¶ 13 (holding that a neutral rating does not preclude award to a higher-priced, higher technically-rated offeror in a best value procurement).

j.   Agencies must clarify adverse past performance information when there is a clear basis to question the past performance information. See A.G. Cullen Construction, Inc., B-

284049.2, Feb. 22, 2000, 2000 CPD ¶ 145.

k.   The Air Force has issued a guide on Performance Price Tradeoffs dated May 2005 which can be found at https://www.safaq.hq. af.mil/contracting/affars/5315/infor mational/archive/ppt-guide-may05.doc.

5.   Scoring disparities are not objectionable or unusual. See Resource Applications, Inc., B-274943.3, Mar. 5, 1997, 97-1 CPD ¶ 137 (finding that the consensus score accurately reflected the proposal's merit, even though it was higher than any of the individual evaluator's scores); Executive Security & Eng'g Tech., Inc., B-270518, Mar. 15, 1996, 96-1 CPD ¶ 156 (holding that the mere presence of apparent inconsistencies is not a basis for disturbing the award); Dragon Servs., Inc., B-255354, Feb. 25, 1994, 94-1 CPD ¶ 151 (noting that the individual evaluators' ratings may differ from the consensus evaluation). Consistency from one proposal to the next, however, is essential. See Myers Investigative and Security Services, Inc., B-288468, Nov. 8, 2001, 2001 CPD ¶ 189 (finding unreasonable an award based on the agency's unequal treatment in assessing the past performance of the protestor and awardee).

6.   Products of the Evaluation Process.

a.   Evaluation Report.

(1)   The evaluators must prepare a report of their evaluation. See Son's Quality Food Co., B-244528.2, Nov. 4, 1991, 91-2 CPD ¶ 424; Amtec Corp., B-240647, Dec. 12, 1990, 90-2 CPD ¶ 482.

(2)   The contracting officer should retain all evaluation records. See FAR 4.801; FAR 4.802; FAR 4.803; see also United Int'l Eng'g, Inc., B-245448.3,

Jan. 29, 1992, 71 Comp. Gen. 177, 92-1 CPD ¶ 122; Southwest Marine, Inc., B-265865.3, Jan. 23, 1996, 96-1 CPD ¶ 56.

(3)   If evaluators use numerical scoring, they should explain the scores. See J.A. Jones Mgmt Servs, Inc., B-276864, Jul. 24, 1997, 97-2 CPD ¶ 47; TFA, Inc., B-243875, Sept. 11, 1991, 91-2 CPD ¶ 239; S-Cubed, B-242871, June 17, 1991, 91-1 CPD ¶ 571.

(4)   Evaluators should ensure that their evaluations are reasonable. See DNL Properties, Inc., B-253614.2, Oct. 12, 1993, 93-2 CPD ¶ 301.

b.   Deficiencies. The initial evaluation must identify all parts of the proposals that fail to meet the government's minimum requirements.

c.   Advantages and Disadvantages. The initial evaluation should identify the positive and negative aspects of acceptable proposals.

d.   Questions and Items for Negotiation. The initial evaluation should identify areas where discussions are necessary/desirable.

e.   Competitive Range Recommendation. The evaluation report should recommend the proposals to include in a competitive range.

J.   Award Without Discussions.

1.   Notice Required.

a.   An agency may not award on initial proposals if it:

(1)   States its intent to hold dis-cussion in the solicitation; or

(2) Fails to state its intent to award without discussions in the solicitation (omits FAR 52.215-1 from the solicitation).

b. A proper award on initial proposals need not result in the lowest overall cost to the government.

2. To award without discussions, an agency must:

a. Give notice in the solicitation that it intends to award without discussions;

b. Select a proposal for award which complies with all of the material requirements of the solicitation;

c. Properly evaluate the selected proposal in accordance with the evaluation factors and subfactors set forth in the solicitation;

d. <u>Not</u> have a contracting officer determination that discussions are necessary; and

e. <u>Not</u> conduct discussions with any offeror, other than for the purpose of minor clarifications. <u>See</u> <u>TRI-COR Indus.</u>, B-252366.3, Aug. 25, 1993, 93-2 CPD ¶ 137.

3. Discussions v. Clarifications. FAR 15.306(a), (d).

a. Award without discussions means **NO DISCUSSIONS**.

(1) "Discussions" are "negotiations that occur <u>after</u> establishment of the competitive range that may, at the Contracting Officer's discretion, result in the offeror being allowed to revise its proposal." FAR 52.215-1(a). However, communications that constitute discussions can occur at any time.

(a) The COFC has found "mutual exchange" a key element in defining discussions. <u>See</u> <u>Cubic Defense Systems, Inc. v. United States</u>, 45 Fed. Cl. 450 (2000).

(b) The GAO has focused on "opportunity to revise" as the key element. <u>See</u> <u>MG Industries</u>, B-283010.3, Jan. 24, 2000, 2000 CPD ¶ 17.

(2) An agency may <u>not</u> award on initial proposals if it conducts discussions with <u>any</u> offeror. <u>See</u> <u>To the Sec'y of the Navy</u>, B-170751, 50 Comp. Gen. 202 (1970); <u>see also</u> <u>Strategic Analysis, Inc.</u>, 939 F. Supp. 18 (D.D.C. 1996) (concluding that communications with one offeror concerning the employment status of its proposed key personnel were discussions). <u>But see</u> <u>Data General Corp. v. Johnson</u>, 78 F.3d 1556 (Fed. Cir. 1996) (refusing to sustain a protest because the protester could not show that there was a "reasonable likelihood" that it would have been awarded the contract in the absence of the improper discussions).

b. An agency, however, may "clarify" offerors' proposals.

(1) "Clarifications" are "limited exchanges, between the government and offerors, that may occur when award without discussions is contemplated." FAR 15.306(a).

(2) Clarifications include:

(a) The opportunity to clarify— rather than revise—certain aspects of an offeror's proposal (e.g., the relevance of past performance information to which the offeror has not previously had an opportunity to respond); and

(b) The opportunity to resolve minor irregularities, informalities, or clerical errors.

(c) The parties' actions control the determination of whether "discussions" have been held and not the characterization by the agency. See Priority One Services, Inc., B-288836, B-288836.2, Dec. 17, 2001, 2002 CPD ¶ 79 (finding "discussions" occurred where awardee was allowed to revise its technical proposal, even though the source selection document characterized the communication as a "clarification").

c. Examples.

(1) The following are "discussions":

(a) The substitution of resumés for key personnel. See University of S.C., B-240208, Sept. 21, 1990, 90-2 CPD ¶ 249; Allied Mgmt. of Texas, Inc., B-232736.2, May 22, 1989, 89-1 CPD ¶ 485. But see SRS Tech., B-258170.3, Feb. 21, 1995, 95-1 CPD ¶ 95.

(b) Allowing an offeror to explain a warranty provision. See Cylink Corp., B-242304, Apr. 18, 1991, 91-1 CPD ¶ 384.

(2) The following are not "discussions.".

(a) Audits. See Data Mgmt. Servs., Inc., B-237009, Jan. 12, 1990, 69 Comp. Gen. 112, 90-1 CPD ¶ 51.

(b) Allowing an offeror to correct a minor math error, correct a certification, or acknowledge a nonmaterial amendment. See E. Frye Enters., Inc., B-258699, Feb. 13, 1995, 95-1 CPD ¶ 64; cf. Telos Field Eng'g, B-253492.2, Nov. 16, 1993, 93-2 CPD ¶ 275.

(c) A request to extend the proposal acceptance period. See GPSI-Tidewater, Inc., B-247342, May 6, 1992, 92-1 CDP ¶ 425.

d. Minor clerical errors should be readily apparent to both parties.

(1) If the agency needs an answer before award, the question probably rises to the level of discussions.

(2) The only significant exception to this rule involves past performance data.

K. Determination to Conduct Discussions.

1. To conduct discussions with one or more offerors after stating an intent to award without discussions, the contracting officer must find that discussions are necessary and document this conclusion in writing. FAR 15.306(a)(3).

2. Statutes and implementing regulations provide little guidance for making this determination. A contracting officer should consider factors such as favorable but noncompliant proposals, unclear proposals, incomplete proposals, unreasonable costs/prices, suspected mistakes, and changes/clarifications to specifications See Milcom Sys. Corp., B-255448.2, May 3, 1994, 94-1 CPD ¶ 339.

L. Communications. FAR 15.306(b).

1. The contracting officer may need to hold "communications" with some offerors before establishing the competitive range.

2. "Communications" are "exchanges of information, between the government and offerors, after receipt of proposals, leading to establishment of the competitive range." FAR 15.306(b).

3. The purpose of communications is to help the contracting officer and/or the evaluators:

   a. Understand and evaluate proposals; and

   b. Determine whether to include a proposal in the competitive range. FAR 15.306(b)(2) and (3).

4. The parties, however, cannot use communications to permit an offeror to revise its proposal. FAR 15.306(b)(2).

5. The contracting officer <u>must</u> communicate with offerors who will be excluded from the competitive range because of adverse past performance information. Such communications must give an offeror an opportunity to respond to adverse past performance information to which it has not previously had an opportunity to respond. FAR 15.306(1)(i).

6. The contracting officer may also communicate with offerors who are neither clearly in nor clearly out of the competitive range. FAR 15.306(b)(1)(ii). The contracting officer may address "gray areas" in an offeror's proposal (e.g., perceived deficiencies, weaknesses, errors, omissions, or mistakes). FAR 15.306(b)(3).

7. As a practical matter, the contracting officer may wish to set a competitive range and conduct discussions if the subject matter of the "communications" is not clearly permitted.

M. Establishing the Competitive Range. FAR 15.306(c).

1. The competitive range is the group of offerors with whom the contracting officer will conduct discussions, and from whom the agency will seek revised proposals.

2. The contracting officer (or SSA) may establish the competitive range any time after the initial evaluation of proposals. See <u>SMB, Inc.</u>, B-252575.2, July 30, 1993, 93-2 CPD ¶ 72.

3. The contracting officer must consider all of the evaluation factors (including cost/price) in making the determination. See <u>Kathpal Technologies, Inc.</u>, B-283137.3, Dec. 30, 1999, 2000 CPD ¶ 6.

   a. The contracting officer may exclude a proposal from the competitive range despite its lower cost or the weight accorded cost in the RFP if the proposal is technically unacceptable. <u>See</u> <u>Crown Logistics Servs.</u>, B-253740, Oct. 19, 1993, 93-2 CPD ¶ 228.

   b. The contracting officer may exclude an unacceptable proposal that requires major revisions to become acceptable if including the proposal in the competitive range would be tantamount to allowing the offeror to submit a new proposal. <u>See</u> <u>Harris Data Communications v. United States</u>, 2 Cl. Ct. 229 (1983), aff'd, 723 F.2d 69 (Fed. Cir. 1983); <u>see also</u> <u>Strategic Sciences and Tech., Inc.</u>, B-257980, 94-2 CPD ¶ 194 (holding that it was reasonable for the agency to exclude an offeror who proposed inexperienced key personnel—which was the most important criterion—from the competitive range); <u>InterAmerica Research Assocs., Inc.</u>, B-253698.2, Nov. 19, 1993, 93-2 CPD ¶ 288 (holding that it was proper for the agency to exclude an offeror that merely repeated back language from solicitation and failed to provide required information).

4. The contracting officer must include all of the "most highly rated proposals" in the competitive range <u>unless</u> the contracting officer decides to reduce the competitive range for purposes of efficiency. <u>See</u> FAR 15.306(c)(2).

    a. The GAO ordinarily gives great deference to the agency. To prevail, a protester must show that the decision to exclude it was: (1) clearly unreasonable; or (2) inconsistent with the stated evaluation factors. <u>See</u> <u>Mainstream Eng'g Corp.</u>, B-251444, Apr. 8, 1993, 93-1 CPD ¶ 307; <u>cf</u>. <u>Intertec Aviation</u>, B-239672, Sept. 19, 1990, 69 Comp. Gen. 717, 90-2 CPD ¶ 232 (holding that the agency improperly excluded an offeror from the competitive range where its alleged technical deficiencies were minor, its cost was competitive, and the agency's action seriously reduced available competition).

    b. Previously, the FAR had a more expansive definition and included any proposal in the competitive range that had a reasonable chance of receiving award. The FAR was changed in 1997 to permit a competitive range more limited than under the "reasonable chance of receiving award" standard. <u>See</u> <u>SDS Petroleum Prods.</u>, B-280430, Sept. 1, 1998, 98-2 CPD ¶ 59.

5. The contracting officer may limit the number of proposals in the competitive range to "the greatest number that will permit an efficient competition among the most highly rated offerors" <u>if</u>:

    a. The agency notified offerors in the solicitation that the contracting officer may limit the competitive range for purposes of efficiency; and

    b. The contracting officer determines that the number of proposals the contracting officer would normally include in the competitive range is too high to permit efficient competition.

6. The contracting officer must continually reassess the competitive range. If, after discussions have begun, an offeror is no longer considered to be among the most highly rated, the contracting officer may eliminate that offeror from the competitive range despite not discussing all material aspects in the proposal. The excluded offeror will not receive an opportunity to submit a proposal revision. FAR 15.306(d)(5).

7. Common Errors.

    a. Reducing competitive range to one proposal. A competitive range of one is not "per se" illegal or improper. See <u>Clean Svs. Co., Inc.</u>, B-281141.3, Feb. 16, 1999, 99-1 CPD ¶ 36; <u>SDS Petroleum Prods.</u>, B-280430 Sept. 1, 1998, 98-2 CPD ¶ 59 (concluding that the new standard for establishing the competitive range does not preclude a range of one per se). However, a contracting officer's decision to reduce a competitive range to one offeror will receive "close scrutiny." <u>See</u> <u>Rockwell Int'l Corp. v. United States</u>, 4 Cl. Ct. 1 (1983); <u>Aerospace Design, Inc.</u>, B-247793, July 9, 1992, 92-2 CPD ¶ 11.

    b. Excluding an offeror from the competitive range for omissions that the offeror could easily correct during discussions. <u>See</u> <u>Dynalantic Corp.</u>, B-274944.2, Feb. 25, 1997, 97-1 CPD ¶ 101.

    c. Using predetermined cutoff scores. <u>See</u> <u>DOT Sys., Inc.</u>, B-186192, July 1, 1976, 76-2 CPD ¶ 3.

d. Excluding an offeror from the competitive range for "nonresponsiveness."

    (1) An offeror may cure a material defect in its initial offer during negotiations; therefore, material defects do not necessarily require exclusion from the competitive range. See <u>ManTech Telecomm & Info. Sys. Corp.</u>, 49 Fed. Cl. 57 (2001).

    (2) The concept of "responsiveness" is incompatible with the concept of a competitive range. See <u>Consolidated Controls Corp.</u>, B-185979, Sept. 21, 1976, 76-2 CPD ¶ 261.

N. Conducting Discussions. FAR 15.306(d).

1. The contracting officer must conduct oral or written discussions with each offeror in the competitive range. FAR 15.306(d)(1).

    a. The contracting officer may <u>not</u> hold discussions with only one offeror. See <u>Raytheon Co.</u>, B-261959.3, Jan. 23, 1996, 96-1 CPD ¶ 37 (stating that the "acid test" of whether discussions have been held is whether an offeror was provided the opportunity to modify/revise its proposal).

    b. The contracting officer may hold face-to-face discussions with some—but not all—offerors, provided the offerors with whom the contracting officer did not hold face-to-face discussions are not prejudiced. See <u>Data Sys. Analysts, Inc.</u>, B-255684, Mar. 22, 1994, 94-1 CPD ¶ 209.

2. The contracting officer determines the scope and extent of the discussions;

however, the discussion must be fair and meaningful.

    a. The contracting officer must discuss any matter that the RFP states the agency will discuss. See <u>Daun-Ray Casuals, Inc.</u>, B-255217.3, 94-2 CPD ¶ 42 (holding that the agency's failure to provide an offeror with an opportunity to discuss adverse past performance information was improper—even though the offeror received a satisfactory rating—because the RFP indicated that offerors would be allowed to address unfavorable reports).

    b. The contracting officer must tailor discussions to the offeror's proposal. FAR 15.306(d)(1). See <u>Cherokee Info. Svs.</u>, B-287270, April 12, 2001, 2001 CPD ¶ 61 (citing <u>The Pragma Group</u>, B-255236, et al., Feb. 18, 1994, 94-1 CPD ¶ 124).

    c. At a minimum, the contracting officer must notify each offeror in the competitive range of deficiencies, significant weaknesses, and adverse past performance information to which the offeror has not yet had the opportunity to respond. FAR 15.306(d)(3). <u>But see</u> FAR 15.306(d)(5) (indicating that the contracting officer may eliminate an offeror's proposal from the competitive range after discussions have begun, even if the contracting officer has not discussed all material aspects of the offeror's proposal or given the offeror an opportunity to revise it).

        (1) Deficiencies.

        (a) A "deficiency" is "a material failure . . . to meet a government requirement or a combination of significant weaknesses . . . that increases the risk of unsuccessful contract performance to an unacceptable level." FAR 15.001. See CitiWest Properties, Inc., B-274689, Nov. 26, 1997, 98-1 CPD ¶ 3; Price Waterhouse, B-254492.2, Feb. 16, 1994, 94-1 CPD ¶ 168; Columbia Research Corp., B-247631, June 22, 1992, 92-1 CPD ¶ 536.

(b) The contracting officer does not have to specifically identify each deficiency. Instead, the contracting officer merely has to lead the contractor into areas requiring improvement. See Du & Assocs., Inc., B-280283.3, Dec. 22, 1998, 98-2 CPD ¶ 156; Arctic Slope World Services, Inc., B-284481, B-284481.2, Apr. 27, 2000, 2000 CPD ¶ 75.

(c) The contracting officer does not have to point out a deficiency if discussions cannot improve it. See Encon Mgmt., Inc., B-234679, June 23, 1989, 89-1 CPD ¶ 595 (business experience).

(d) The contracting officer does not have to inquire into omissions or business decisions on matters clearly addressed in the solicitation. See Wade Perrow Constr., B-255332.2, Apr. 19, 1994, 94-1 CPD ¶ 266; National Projects, Inc., B-283887, Jan. 19, 2000, 2000 CPD ¶ 16.

(e) The contracting officer does not have to actually "bargain" with an offeror. See Northwest Regional Educ. Lab., B-222591.3, Jan. 21, 1987, 87-1 CPD ¶ 74. But cf.

FAR 15.306(d) (indicating that negotiations may include bargaining).

(2) Significant Weaknesses.

(a) A "significant weakness" is "a flaw that appreciably increases the risk of unsuccessful contract performance." FAR 15.001. Examples include:

(i) Flaws that cause the agency to rate a factor as marginal or poor;

(ii) Flaws that cause the agency to rate the risk of unsuccessful contract performance as moderate to high; and

(iii) Relatively minor flaws that have a significant cumulative impact (e.g., minor flaws in several areas that impact the overall rating).

(b) The contracting officer does not have to identify every aspect of an offeror's technically acceptable proposal that received less than a maximum score. See Robbins-Gioia, Inc., B-274318, Dec. 4, 1996, 96-2 CPD ¶ 222; SeaSpace Corp., B-252476.2, June 14, 1993, 93-1 CPD ¶ 462, recon. denied, B-252476.3, Oct. 27, 1993, 93-2 CPD ¶ 251.

(c) In addition, the contracting officer does not have to advise an offeror of a minor weakness that the agency does not consider significant, even if it subsequently becomes a determinative factor between two closely ranked proposals. See Brown & Root, Inc. and

Perini Corp., A Joint Venture, B-270505.2, Sept. 12, 1996, 96-2 CPD ¶ 143; cf. Professional Servs. Group, B-274289.2, Dec. 19, 1996, 97-1 CPD ¶ 54 (holding that the discussions were inadequate where "deficient" staffing was not revealed because the agency perceived it to be a mere "weakness").

(d)   The contracting officer does not have to inform offeror that its cost/price is too high where the agency does not consider the price unreasonable or a significant weakness or deficiency. See JWK Int'l Corp. v. United States, 279 F.3d 985 (Fed. Cir. 2002); SOS Interpreting, Ltd., B-287477.2, May 16, 2001, 2001 CPD ¶ 84.

(3)   Other Aspects of an Offeror's Proposal. Although the FAR used to require contracting officers to discuss other material aspects, the rule now is that contracting officers are "encouraged to discuss other aspects of the offeror's proposal that could, in the opinion of the contracting officer, be altered or explained to enhance materially the proposal's potential for award (emphasis added). FAR 15.306(d)(3)

d.   Since the purpose of discussions is to maximize the agency's ability to obtain the best value, the contracting officer should do more than the minimum necessary to satisfy the requirement for meaningful discussions. See FAR 15.306(d)(2).

e.   An agency is not obligated to spoon-feed an offeror. ITT Fed. Sys.

Int'l Corp., B-285176.4, B-285176.5, Jan. 9, 2001, 2001 CPD ¶ 45 at 7.

f.   An agency is not obligated to conduct successive rounds of discussions until all proposal defects have been corrected. OMV Med., Inc., B-266299, Feb. 9, 1996, 96-1 CPD ¶ 61 at 4.

3.   Limitations on Exchanges.

a.   FAR Limitations. FAR 15.306(e).

(1)   The agency may not favor one offeror over another.

(2)   The agency may not disclose an offeror's technical solution to another offeror.[5]

(3)   The agency may not reveal an offeror's prices without the offeror's permission.

(4)   The agency may not reveal the names of individuals who provided past performance information.

(5)   The agency may not furnish source selection information in violation of the Procurement Integrity Act (41 U.S.C. Chapter 21).

b.   Other Prohibitions. The FAR no longer includes specific prohibitions on technical leveling, technical transfusion, and auctioning; however, the Procurement Integrity Act and the Trade Secrets Act still apply.

(1)   Technical leveling involves helping an offeror bring its proposal up to the level of

[5] This prohibition includes any information that would compromise an offeror's intellectual property (e.g., an offeror's unique technology or an offeror's innovative or unique use of a commercial item). FAR 15.306(e)(2).

other proposals through successive rounds of discussion. See Creative Mgmt. Tech., Inc., B-266299, Feb. 9, 1996, 96-1 CPD ¶ 61.

(2)   Technical Transfusion. Technical transfusion involves the government disclosure of one offeror's proposal to another to help that offeror improve its proposal.

(3)   Auctioning.

(a)   Auctioning involves the practice of promoting price bidding between offerors by indicating the price offerors must beat, obtaining multiple proposal revisions, disclosing other offerors' prices, etc.

(b)   Auctioning is not inherently illegal. See Nick Chorak Mowing, B-280011.2, Oct. 1, 1998, 98-2 CPD ¶ 82. Moreover, the GAO usually finds that preserving the integrity of the competitive process outweighs the risks posed by an auction. See Navcom Defense Electronics, Inc., B-276163.3, Oct. 31, 1997, 97-2 CPD ¶ 126; Baytex Marine Communication, Inc., B-237183, Feb. 8, 1990, 90-1 CPD ¶ 164.

(c)   The government's estimated price will not be disclosed in the RFP.[6] FAR 15.306(e)(3) allows discussion of price. See National Projects, Inc., B-

283887, Jan. 19, 2000, 2000 CPD ¶ 16.

(i)   The contracting officer may advise an offeror that its price is too high or too low and reveal the results of the agency's analysis supporting that conclusion. FAR 15.306(e)(3)

(ii)   In addition, the contracting officer may advise all of the offerors of the price that the agency considers reasonable based on its price analysis, market research, and other reviews. FAR 15.306(e)(3)

c.   Fairness Considerations.

(1)   Discussions, when conducted, must be meaningful and must not prejudicially mislead offerors. See Metro Machine Corp., B-281872.2, Apr. 22, 1999, 99-1 CPD ¶ 101 (finding that a question about a proposal that did not reasonably put the offeror on notice of agency's actual concern was not adequate discussions); see also SRS Tech., B-254425.2, Sept. 14, 1994, 94-2 CPD ¶ 125 (concluding that the Navy misled the offeror by telling it that its prices were too low when all it needed was better support for its offered prices); Ranor, Inc., B-255904, Apr. 14, 1994, 94-1 CPD ¶ 258 (concluding that the agency misled the offeror and caused it to raise its price by telling it that its price was below the government estimate); DTH

---

[6] In the area of construction contracting, the FAR requires disclosure of the magnitude of the project in terms of physical characteristics and estimated price range, but not a precise dollar amount (i.e., a range of $100,000 to $250,000). See FAR 36.204.

Mgmt. Group, B-252879.2, Oct. 15, 1993, 93-2 CPD ¶ 227 (concluding that the agency misled an offeror by telling it that its price was below the government estimate when it knew that the government estimate was faulty); Creative Information Technologies, B-293073.10, Mar. 16, 2005, 2005 CPD ¶ 110 (holding that discussions must deal with the underlying cause and that notifying an offeror that its price was overstated was insufficient).

(2)　The contracting officer must provide similar information to all of the offerors. See Securiguard, Inc., B-249939, Dec. 21, 1992, 93-1 CPD ¶ 362; Grumman Data Sys. Corp. v. Sec'y of the Army, No. 91-1379, slip op. (D.D.C. June 28, 1991) (agency gave out answers, but not questions, misleading other offerors); SeaSpace Corp., B-241564, Feb. 15, 1991, 70 Comp. Gen. 268, 91-1 CPD ¶ 179.

O.　Final Proposal Revisions (Formerly Called "Best and Final Offers" or "BAFOs"). FAR 15.307.

1.　Upon the completion of discussions, the contracting officer must request final proposal revisions. The request must notify offerors that:

a.　Discussions are over;

b.　They may submit final proposal revisions to clarify and document any understandings reached during negotiations;

c.　They must submit their final proposal revisions in writing;

d.　They must submit their final proposal revisions by the common cutoff date/time; and

e.　The government intends to award the contract without requesting further revisions.

2.　Agencies do not have to reopen discussions to address deficiencies introduced in the final proposal revision. See Ouachita Mowing, Inc., B-276075, May 8, 1997, 97-1 CPD ¶ 167; Logicon RDA, B-261714.2, Dec. 22, 1995, 95-2 CPD ¶ 286; Compliance Corp., B-254429, Dec. 15, 1993, 94-1 CPD ¶ 166.

a.　Agencies, however, must reopen discussions in appropriate cases. See TRW, Inc., B-254045.2, Jan. 10, 1994, 94-1 CPD ¶ 18 (holding that the agency erred in not conducting additional discussions where there were significant inconsistencies between technical and cost proposals that required resolution); cf. Dairy Maid Dairy, Inc., B-251758.3, May 24, 1993, 93-1 CPD ¶ 404 (holding that a post-BAFO amendment that changed the contract type from a requirements contract to a definite quantity contract was a material change that required a second round of BAFOs); Harris Corp., B-237320, Feb. 14, 1990, 90-1 CPD ¶ 276 (holding that the contracting officer properly requested additional BAFOs after amending the RFP).

b.　Agencies may request additional FPRs even if the offerors' prices were disclosed through an earlier protest if additional FPRs are necessary to protect the integrity of the competitive process. BNF Tech., Inc., B-254953.4, Dec. 22, 1994, 94-2 CPD ¶ 258.

3.　If the agency reopens discussions with one offeror, the agency must reopen discussions with all of the remaining offerors. See International Resources Group, B-286663, Jan. 31, 2001, 2001 CPD ¶ 35 (citing Patriot Contract Servs., LLC et al., B-278276 et al., Sept. 22, 1998, 98-2 CPD ¶ 77).

4. An agency is not obligated to reopen negotiations to give an offeror the opportunity to remedy a defect that first appears in a revised proposal. American Sys. Corp., B-292755, B-292755.2, Dec. 3, 2003.

P. Selection for Award.

1. Agencies must evaluate final proposals using the evaluation factors set forth in the solicitation.

    a. Bias in the selection decision is improper. See Latecoere Int'l v. United States, 19 F.3d 1342 (11th Cir. 1994) (stating that bias against a French firm "infected the decision not to award it the contract . . .").

    b. There is no requirement that the same evaluators who evaluated the initial proposals also evaluate the final proposals. See Medical Serv. Corp. Int'l, B-255205.2, April 4, 1994, 94-1 CPD ¶ 305.

2. A proposal that fails to conform to a material solicitation requirement is technically unacceptable and cannot receive award. Farmland National Beef, B-286607, B-286607.2, Jan. 24, 2001, 2001 CPD ¶ 31. If the agency wants to accept an offer that does not comply with the material solicitation requirements, the agency must issue a written amendment and give all of the remaining offerors an opportunity to submit revised proposals. FAR 15.206(d). See Beta Analytics Int'l, Inc. v. U.S., 44 Fed. Cl. 131 (U.S. Ct. Fed. Cl. 1999); 4th Dimension Software, Inc., B-251936, May 13, 1993, 93-1 CPD ¶ 420.

3. The evaluation process is inherently subjective.

    a. The fact that an agency reasonably might have made another selection does not mean that the selection made was unreasonable. See Red R. Serv. Corp., B-253671.4, Apr. 22, 1994, 94-1 CPD ¶ 385. However, the decision must be based on accurate information. See CRA Associated, Inc., B-282075.2, B-282075.3, Mar. 15, 2000, 2000 CPD ¶ 63.

    b. Point-scoring techniques do not make the evaluation process objective. See VSE Corp., B-224397, Oct. 3, 1986, 86-2 CPD ¶ 392. Therefore, the RFP should not state that award will be made based on the proposal receiving the most points. See Harrison Sys. Ltd., B-212675, May 25, 1984, 84-1 CPD ¶ 572.

4. A cost/technical trade-off analysis is essential to any source selection decision using a trade-off (rather than a lowest-priced, technically acceptable) basis of award. See Special Operations Group, Inc., B-287013; B-287013.2, Mar. 30, 2001, 2001 CPD ¶ 73. More than a mere conclusion, however, is required to support the analysis. See Shumaker Trucking and Excavating Contractors, B-290732, 2002 U.S. Comp. Gen. LEXIS 151 (Sept. 25, 2002) (finding the award decision unreasonable where the "agency mechanically applied the solicitation's evaluation method" and provided no analysis of the advantages to the awardee's proposal); Beacon Auto Parts, B-287483, June 13, 2001, 2001 CPD ¶ 116 (finding that a determination that a price is "fair and reasonable" doesn't equal a best-value determination); ITT Fed. Svs. Int'l Corp., B-283307, B-283307.2, Nov. 3, 1999, 99-2 CPD ¶ 76 (quoting Opti-Lite Optical, B-281693, Mar. 22, 1999, 99-1 CPD ¶ 61 at 5); Redstone Technical Servs., B-259222, Mar. 17, 1995, 95-1 CPD ¶ 181.

a. Agencies have broad discretion in making cost/technical trade-offs, and the extent to which one is sacrificed for the other is tested for rationality and consistency with the stated evaluation factors. See MCR Fed. Inc., B-280969, Dec. 4, 1999, 99-1 CPD ¶ 8; see also Widnall v. B3H Corp., 75 F. 3d 1577 (Fed. Cir. 1996) (stating that "review of a best value agency procurement is limited to independently determining if the agency's decision was grounded in reason").

b. Beware of tradeoff techniques that distort the relative importance of the various evaluation criteria (e.g., "Dollars per Point"). See Billy G. Bassett; Lynch Dev., Inc., B-237331, Feb. 20, 1990, 90-1 CPD ¶ 195; T. H. Taylor, Inc., B-227143, Sept. 15, 1987, 87-2 CPD ¶ 252.

c. Comparative consideration of features in competing proposals is permissible—even if those features were not given quantifiable evaluation credit under disclosed evaluation criteria—if the basis for award stated in the RFP provides for an integrated assessment of proposals. See Grumman Data Sys. Corp. v. Dep't of the Air Force, GSBCA No. 11939-P, 93-2 BCA ¶ 25,776, aff'd sub nom. Grumman Data Sys. Corp. v. Widnall, 15 F.3d 1044 (Fed. Cir. 1994) (concluding that the SSA's head-to-head comparison of proposals may permissibly look at features not directly evaluated).

d. A cost/technical trade-off analysis may consider relevant matters not disclosed in the RFP as tools to assist in making the trade-off. See Advanced Mgmt., Inc., B-251273.2, Apr. 2, 1993, 93-1 CPD ¶ 288 (holding that it is permissible to consider that loss of efficiency in awarding to a new contractor would reduce effective price difference between the contractor and the incumbent).

e. Agencies should make the cost/technical trade-off decision after receiving final proposals if final proposals were requested. See Halter Marine, Inc., B-255429, Mar. 1, 1994, 94-1 CPD ¶ 161.

5. The selection decision documentation must include the rationale for any trade-off made, "including benefits associated with additional costs." FAR 15.308; Opti-Lite Optical, B-281693, Mar. 22, 1999, 99-1 CPD ¶ 61 (finding it improper to rely on a purely mathematical price/technical trade-off methodology).

6. A well-written source selection memorandum should contain:

    a. A summary of the evaluation criteria and their relative importance;

    b. A statement of the decision maker's own evaluation of each of the proposals: (1) adopting recommendations of others or stating a personal evaluation; and (2) identifying major advantages and disadvantages of each proposal (see J&J Maintenance Inc., B-284708.2, B-284708.3, June 5, 2000, 2000 CPD ¶106); and

    c. A description of the reasons for choosing the successful offeror, comparing differences in cost with differences in technical factors.

7. The source selection authority (SSA) need not personally write the decision memorandum. See Latecoere Int'l Ltd., B-239113.3, Jan. 15, 1992, 92-1 CPD ¶ 70. However, the source selection decision must represent the SSA's independent judgment. FAR 15.308.[7]

8. The GAO reviews source selection decisions for reasonableness, consistency with the RFP's evaluation criteria, and adequacy of supporting documentation. See AIU North America, Inc., B-283743.2, Feb. 16, 2000, 2000 CPD ¶ 39; Cortland Memorial Hospital, B-286890, Mar. 5, 2001, 2001 CPD ¶ 48 and Wackenhut Servs, Inc., B-286037; B-286037.2, Nov. 14, 2000, 2001 CPD ¶ 114 (emphasizing the importance of contemporaneous documentation). The SSA has considerable discretion. See Calspan Corp., B-258441, Jan. 19, 1995, 95-1 CPD ¶ 28.

   a. The SSA may consider slightly different scores a tie and award to the lower-cost offeror. See Tecom, Inc., B-257947, Nov. 29, 1994, 94-2 CPD ¶ 212; Duke/Jones Hanford, Inc., B-249637.10, July 13, 1993, 93-2 CPD ¶ 26.

   b. Conversely, the SSA may consider slightly different scores to represent a significant difference justifying the greater price. See Macon Apparel Corp., B-253008, Aug. 11, 1993, 93-2 CPD ¶ 93; Suncoast Assoc., Inc., B-265920, Dec. 7, 1995, 95-2 CPD ¶ 268.

   c. In one case, an SSA's decision to award to a substantially lower-scored offeror, whose cost was only slightly lower, was not adequately justified. TRW, Inc., B-234558, June 21, 1989, 68 Comp. Gen. 512, 89-1 CPD ¶ 584. However, after the SSA's reconsideration, the same outcome was adequately supported. TRW, Inc., B-234558.2, Dec. 18, 1989, 89-2 CPD ¶ 560.

   d. Reliance on the scores of evaluators alone, without looking at strengths and weaknesses of each proposal, may be unreasonable. See SDA, Inc., B-248528.2, Apr. 14, 1993, 93-1 CPD ¶ 320.

   e. SSAs may disagree with the analyses of and conclusions reached by evaluators; however, they must be reasonable when doing so and adequately support their source selection decision. DynCorp Int'l LLC, B-289863.2, May 13, 2002, 2002 CPD ¶ 83 (finding no support in the record for the SSA to question the weaknesses in the awardee's proposal as identified by the evaluation teams).

9. The standard of review for the Court of Federal Claims is whether the agency's decision is "arbitrary, capricious, an abuse of discretion, or otherwise not in accordance with law." 5 U.S.C. § 706(A)(2); Cubic Applications, Inc. v. U.S., 37 Fed. Cl. 339, 342 (1997).

10. The contracting officer awards a contract to the successful offeror by signing Block 27 on the SF 33, which the contractor should have previously signed and included in its initial proposal or its final proposal revision.

Q. **Debriefings.** 10 U.S.C. § 2305(b)(5); 41 U.S.C. §§ 3704-3705; FAR 15.505-506.

1. Notices to Unsuccessful Offerors. FAR 15.503.

   a. Pre-award Notices of Exclusion from the Competitive Range.

      (1) The contracting officer must provide prompt, written notice to offerors excluded or eliminated from the competitive range, stating the basis for the determination and that revisions will not be considered. FAR 15.503(a)(1).

      (2) Small Business Set-Asides. FAR 15.503(a)(2).

         (a) The contracting officer must provide written notice to the unsuccessful offerors before award.

(b) The notice must include the name and address of the apparently successful offeror and state that:

   (i) The government will not consider additional proposal revisions; and

   (ii) No response is required unless the offeror intends to challenge the small business size status of the apparently successful offeror.

b. Post-award Notices. FAR 15.503(b).

(1) Within 3 days after the contract award date, the contracting officer must notify in writing unsuccessful offerors.

(2) The notice must include the number of offerors solicited, the number of proposals received, the names and addresses of the awardee(s), the awarded items, total price, and a general description of why the unsuccessful offeror's proposal was not accepted.

(3) FAR 15.503(b)(1)(iv) requires disclosure of quantities and unit prices if requested. However, in Essex Electro Eng'rs, Inc. v. U.S. Sec'y of the Army, No. 09-372 (D.D.C. Feb. 26, 2010), the U.S. District Court for the District of Columbia upheld withholding unit prices. See Chapter 29, Section II.H.5.

2. Debriefings.

a. Pre-award Debriefings. FAR 15.505.

(1) An offeror excluded from the competitive range (or otherwise eliminated from consideration for award) may request a pre-award debriefing.

(a) An offeror must submit a written request for a debriefing within 3 days of the date it receives its notice of exclusion.

(b) If the offeror does not meet this deadline, the offeror is not entitled to either a pre-award or post-award debriefing.

(2) The contracting officer must "make every effort" to conduct the pre-award debriefing as soon as practicable.

(a) The offeror may request the contracting officer to delay the debriefing until after contract award.

(b) The contracting officer may delay the debriefing until after contract award if the contracting officer concludes that delaying the debriefing is in the best interests of the government. See Global Eng'g & Const. Joint Venture, B-275999, Feb. 19, 1997, 97-1 CPD ¶ 77 (declining to review the contracting officer's determination).

(3) At a minimum, pre-award debriefings must include:

(a) The agency's evaluation of significant elements of the offeror's proposal;

(b) A summary of the agency's rationale for excluding the offeror; and

(c) Reasonable responses to relevant questions.

(4) Pre-award debriefings must <u>not</u> include:

(a) The number of offerors;

(b) The identity of other offerors;

(c) The content of other offerors' proposals;

(d) The ranking of other offerors;

(e) The evaluation of other offerors; or

(f) Any of the information prohibited in FAR 15.506(e).

(5) A summary of the debriefing is to be included in the contract file.

b. Post-award Debriefings. FAR 15.506.

(1) An unsuccessful offeror may request a post-award debriefing.

(a) An offeror must submit a written request for a debriefing within 3 days of the date it receives its post-award notice.

(b) The agency may accommodate untimely requests; however, the agency decision to do so does not automatically extend the deadlines for filing protests.

(2) The contracting officer must conduct the post-award debriefing within 5 days of the date the agency receives a timely request "to the maximum extent practicable."

(3) At a minimum, post-award debriefings must include:

(a) The agency's evaluation of the significant weak or deficient factors in the offeror's proposal;

(b) The overall evaluated cost or price, and technical rating, if applicable, of the awardee and the debriefed offeror, and past performance information on the debriefed offeror;

(c) The overall rankings of all of the offerors;

(d) A summary of the rationale for the award decision;

(e) The make and model number of any commercial item(s) the successful offeror will deliver; and

(f) Reasonable responses to relevant questions.

(4) Post-award debriefings must <u>not</u> include:

(a) A point-by-point comparison of the debriefed offeror's proposal with any other offeror's proposal; and

(b) Any information prohibited from disclosure under FAR 24.202 or exempt from release under the Freedom of Information Act, including the names of individuals providing past performance information.

(5) A summary of the debriefing must be included in the contract file.

(6) General Considerations. The contracting officer should:

172

(a) Tailor debriefings to emphasize the fairness of the source selection procedures;

(b) Point out deficiencies that the contracting officer discussed but the offeror failed to correct;

(c) Point out areas for improvement of future proposals.

IV. NEGOTIATING SOLE SOURCE AWARDS.

A. General.

1. Many negotiated procurements are awarded without competition. Where there is limited competition, but not full and open competition, the agency should follow competitive negotiated procedures discussed above. FAR 15.002(b). However, when negotiating a sole source award, the contracting officer has substantial leeway to tailor the procedures followed to minimize the administrative burden and to expedite award. FAR 15.002(a).

2. Negotiating a sole source contract award requires approval of the justification, as provided in FAR Subpart 6.3. The contracting officer should obtain the approval of the justification prior to beginning negotiations for a sole source award. FAR 6.303-1(a).

3. To avoid violations of procurement integrity should the contracting officer not obtain approval of his justification to use other than full and open competitive procedures, the agency should carefully conduct pre-solicitation exchanges with industry following FAR 15.201.

B. Sole Source Negotiations. Prior to beginning negotiations with a sole source, the contracting officer must accomplish three important tasks: 1) issue a sources sought notice; 2)

identify the requirement; and 3) draft and obtain approval of the J&A.

1. Requirements. The agency must first describe its requirements as a prerequisite to preparing other documentation. A sources sought notice must contain a summary of the requirements, the J&A must contain a summary of the requirements, and the contractor must receive at least a summary of the requirements to enable it to prepare a proposal. The requirements, however, need not be as detailed as those for a competitive procurement. The sources sought notice and the J&A only require a summary; and the contractor and the government can prepare a detailed SOW and specification during negotiation of the sole source contract.

2. Sources Sought. An agency desiring to negotiate a sole source award normally issues a pre-solicitation notice known as a "Sources Sought" through www.fedbizopps.gov. See FAR Subpart 5.2. The sources sought contains a synopsis of the requirements and invites interested sources to express their interest in competing, along with information demonstrating the sources' ability to timely meet the government's requirements. If the sources sought notice reveals more than one potential source, then the contracting officer proceeds with competitive procedures. The results of the sources sought notice are included in the sole source justification submitted for approval. FAR 6.303-2(b)(6). Within DOD, there are provisions to waive the requirement for issuing a sources sought notice. See PGI 206.302-1 (d).

3. Justification and Approval. The contracting officer must prepare a justification for approval of a non-competitive award, discussed in Chapter 5.

4. Request for Proposal. While most negotiations for a sole source award are initiated by sending the proposed source a

request for proposal, this is not an absolute prerequisite. For example, the contractor may submit an "unsolicited proposal" without having received a request for proposal. Prior to award or definitization, however, the contracting officer must prepare a draft contract containing the required clauses, plus the requirements documents.

C.   Contractor Proposal.

1.   In a sole source negotiation, the contractor prepares a proposal for submission to the government. Where the proposal exceeds the Truth in Negotiations Act threshold, the proposal must include cost or pricing data, as discussed in Chapter 14, unless an exception applies.

2.   The contractor and the government then negotiate the draft contract, based on the solicitation, the model contract, and the contractor's proposal.

D.   Contract Award.

1.   To expedite beginning performance, the contractor and the government may agree to a letter contract, as discussed in Chapter 6, Section V. Negotiations then continue after award of the letter contract until the parties reach agreement on all contract terms and execute a definitive agreement.

2.   Alternatively, the government may withhold award until the parties reach agreement on all the terms and conditions, and the contract provides its final proposal accompanied by its certificate of current cost or pricing data. See Chapter 14.

E.   Post-award Actions. Following award of a sole source contract, the contracting officer must publish a notice of award, and make the J&A authorizing the sole source publicly available, as provided in Chapter 6.

V.   CONCLUSION.

The principal objective of negotiating competitive proposals is to obtain goods and services at a fair and reasonable price. This is accomplished by awarding the contract to the offeror providing either the best value or the low-priced, technically acceptable offer. The procedures in FAR Part 15 are intended to achieve that goal in a process that is transparent and fair to the participants.

An agency attorney can materially assist his clients by thoroughly understanding both the required statutory and regulatory procedures and the policies that underlie those requirements. Achieving the principal objective requires the attorney to counsel his or her client to follow the process, since shortcuts can lead to long delays.

Industry attorneys should thoroughly understand the procedures of competitive negotiation as well. Knowing the process and the constraints it imposes on the government permits the industry attorney to counsel on available alternatives. Furthermore, knowing the process allows an industry attorney to spot procedural errors, and discuss with the client whether to raise the error or waive/ignore it.

ELIGIBLE CONTRACTORS

I.   INTRODUCTION

Even when following procedures designated as full and open competition, not all prospective offerors are eligible to submit bids or proposals in response to agency solicitations. Some prospective offerors are excluded to promote social policies, such as promoting small businesses by excluding large and foreign-owned businesses, as discussed in Chapter 15.

Even in non-set-aside procurements, the government excludes some prospective offerors for various reasons. The first category of excluded contractors consists of those the contracting officer has determined are not responsible. The government does not wish to award to offerors that lack skills, resources, or business integrity. To be eligible for award, a contractor must be considered responsible. Contractors who do not have a satisfactory record of complying with their contract's requirements may be excluded from competing through a process known as Suspension and Debarment. A debarred contractor is not responsible during the period of its debarment.

A second category of contractors who are excluded from award is composed of those who, through their performance of government service contracts, have obtained an unfair competitive advantage, or who could provide biased advice, were they awarded the contract. These issues are called "organizational conflicts of interest," and with the government's greatly increased use of contractor services, this has grown in importance over the past twenty years. Contractors possessing an organizational conflict of interest are excluded from specific contracts, but are free to compete on others.

II.   RESPONSIBILITY

A.   Overview:

1. The government, as a matter of policy, only does business with responsible contractors. Government acquisition policy requires that the contracting officer make an affirmative determination of responsibility prior to award. FAR 9.103.

2. Who is a responsible contractor? The prospective contractor must possess the financial resources to perform the contract, such as the working capital to finance purchase of materials and payment of labor and subcontractors, between starting work and getting paid for work performed. A prospective contractor must also have the technical resources, the production capacity, etc., to timely perform the contract. The prospective contractor should have a satisfactory record of successful past performance of similar contracts and a satisfactory record of business integrity. FAR 9.104-1. Additionally, the prospective contractor must not be suspended or debarred from government contracting.

3. Companies are NOT presumed responsible. FAR 9.103(b). The contracting officer must make an affirmative determination that the offeror is responsible. If the offeror is a small business, the contracting officer makes responsibility determinations in conjunction with the Small Business Administration.

4. General rule. The contracting officer may award only to a responsible bidder. FAR 9.103(a); Theodor Arndt GmbH & Co., B-237180, Jan. 17, 1990, 90-1 CPD ¶ 64 (responsibility requirement implied); Atlantic Maint., Inc., B-239621.2, June 1, 1990, 90-1 CPD ¶ 523 (an unreasonably low price may render bidder nonresponsible); but see The Galveston Aviation Weather Partnership, B-252014.2, May 5, 1993, 93-1 CPD ¶ 370 (below-cost bid not legally objectionable, even when offering labor rates lower than those required by the Service Contract Act).

B.   Responsibility Defined.

1. Responsibility refers to an offeror's apparent **ability** and **capacity** to perform. To be responsible, a prospective contractor must meet the standards of responsibility set forth at FAR 9.104. Kings Point Indus., B-223824, Oct. 29, 1986, 86-2 CPD ¶ 488.

Eligible Contractors

2. Responsibility is determined at any time prior to award. Therefore, the bidder may provide responsibility information to the contracting officer at any time before award. FAR 9.103; FAR 9.105-1; ADC Ltd., B-254495, Dec. 23, 1993, 93-2 CPD ¶ 337 (bidder's failure to submit security clearance documentation with bid is not a basis for rejection of bid); Cam Indus., B-230597, May 6, 1988, 88-1 CPD ¶ 443.

C. Types of Responsibility.

1. General standards of responsibility. FAR 9.104-1. The general standards of responsibility apply to all bidders and all contracts. These standards include:

    a. Financial resources. The contractor must demonstrate that it has adequate financial resources to perform the contract or that it has the ability to obtain such resources. FAR 9.104-1(a); Excavators, Inc., B-232066, Nov. 1, 1988, 88-2 CPD ¶ 421 (a contractor is nonresponsible if it cannot or does not provide acceptable individual sureties).

        Bankruptcy does not necessarily disqualify a bidder. Non-responsibility determinations based solely on filing a bankruptcy petition violate 11 U.S.C. § 525. This statute prohibits a governmental unit from denying, revoking, suspending, or refusing to renew a license, permit, charter, franchise, or other similar grant to, or deny employment to, terminate employment of, or discriminate with respect to employment against, a person that is or has been a debtor under 11 U.S.C. § 525, solely because such person has been a debtor under that title. Bender Shipbuilding & Repair Company v. United States, 297 F.3d 1358 (Fed. Cir. 2002) (upholding contracting officer's determination that awardee was responsible even though awardee filed for Chapter 11 Bankruptcy reorganization); Global Crossing Telecommunications, Inc.,

    B-288413.6, B288413.10, June 17, 2002, 2002 CPD ¶ 102 (upholding contracting officer's determination that a prospective contractor who filed for Chapter 11 was not responsible where the pre-award survey included a detailed financial analysis and the contracting officer reasonably concluded that the firm's poor financial condition made the firm a high financial risk).

    The courts have applied the bankruptcy anti-discrimination provisions to government determinations of eligibility for award. In re Son-Shine Grading, 27 Bankr. 693 (Bankr. E.D.N.C. 1983); In re Coleman Am. Moving Serv., Inc., 8 Bankr. 379 (Bankr. D. Kan. 1980).

    A determination of responsibility should not be negative solely because of a prospective contractor's bankruptcy. The contracting officer should focus on the contractor's ability to perform the contract, and justify a nonresponsibility determination of a bankrupt contractor accordingly. Harvard Interiors Mfg. Co., B247400, May 1, 1992, 92-1 CPD ¶ 413 (Chapter 11 firm found nonresponsible based on lack of financial ability); Sam Gonzales, Inc.—Recon., B-225542.2, Mar. 18, 1987, 87-1 CPD ¶ 306.

    b. Resources for Timely Performance. The contractor must possess or be able to obtain the personnel, plant, and equipment necessary to comply with the delivery or performance schedule. FAR 9.104-1(b); System Dev. Corp., B-212624, Dec. 5, 1983, 83-2 CPD ¶ 644. Where the contractor does not have the production resources or people to perform, it must demonstrate that it can obtain them in time to meet the performance schedule. Even if it has the resources, the prospective contractor must demonstrate that considering its existing workload, the resources are adequate for an additional contract.

c. Satisfactory Record of Performance. The contractor must have a satisfactory performance record. FAR 9.104-1(c). Information Resources, Inc., B-271767, July 24, 1996, 96-2 CPD ¶ 38; Saft America, B-270111, Feb. 7, 1996, 96-1 CPD ¶ 134; North American Constr. Corp., B-270085, Feb. 6, 1996, 96-1 CPD ¶ 44; Mine Safety Appliances, Co., B-266025, Jan. 17, 1996, 96-1 CPD ¶ 86.

The contracting officer shall presume that a contractor seriously deficient in recent contract performance is nonresponsible. FAR 9.104-3(b). See Schenker Panamericana (Panama) S.A., B-253029, Aug. 2, 1993, 93-2 CPD ¶ 67 (agency justified in nonresponsiblity determination where moving contractor had previously failed to conduct pre-move surveys, failed to provide adequate packing materials, failed to keep appointments or complete work on time, dumped household goods into large containers, stacked unprotected furniture onto trucks, dragged unprotected furniture through hallways, and wrapped fragile goods in a single sheet of paper; termination for default on prior contract not required). See also Pacific Photocopy & Research Servs., B-281127, Dec. 29, 1998, 98-2 CPD ¶ 164 (contracting officer properly determined that bidder had inadequate performance record on similar work based upon consistently high volume of unresolved customer complaints). See Ettefaq-Meliat-Hai-Afghan Consulting, Inc. v. United States, 106 Fed. Cl. 429 (2012) (Contracting Officer's decision to find contractor nonresponsible based upon an intelligence report that stated contractor submitted fraudulent statements and credentials and failed to meet delivery requirements on a previous contract was reasonable).

A prospective contractor shall not be determined responsible or nonresponsible solely on the basis of a lack of relevant performance history, except as provided in 9.104-2.

d. Integrity and Business Ethics. The contractor must have a satisfactory record of business ethics. FAR 9.104-1(d); FAR 9.407-2; FAR 14.404-2(h); Interstate Equip. Sales, B-225701, Apr. 20, 1987, 87-1 CPD ¶ 427. See Ettefaq-Meliat-Hai-Afghan Consulting, Inc. v. United States, 106 Fed. Cl. 429 (2012). (Contracting Officer decision to find a contractor nonresponsible must be rational and reasonable; given issues with contractor's performance in previous contract and submission of fraudulent statements, credentialing, and noncompliance, a Contracting Officer does not need to look at each instance to determine if the instance supports nonresponsibility, but at the totality of circumstances to find nonresponsibility.)

e. Have the Necessary Business Processes and Systems. Government contracting often requires the contractor to implement business systems, such as those discussed in Chapter 20. Such processes and systems are not implemented overnight. They may consist of accounting, quality assurance, systems engineering, property control, safety, and production engineering applicable to work to be performed by the prospective contractor and subcontractors). (See 9.104-3 (a).)

The contractor must display adequate management and technical capability to perform the contract satisfactorily. FAR 9.104-1(e); TAAS-Israel Indus., B-251789.3, Jan. 14, 1994, 94-1 CPD ¶ 197 (contractor lacked design skills and knowledge to produce advanced missile launcher power supply).

Eligible Contractors

f. Adequate production, construction, and technical equipment and facilities or the ability to obtain them. FAR 9.104-1(f)

g. Be otherwise qualified and eligible to receive an award under applicable laws and regulations. Active Deployment Sys., Inc., B-404875, May 25, 2011; Bilfinger Berger AG Sede Secondaria Italiana, B-402496, May 13, 2010, 2010 CPD ¶ 125.

Unpaid taxes disqualify a prospective bidder on DOD contracts. DFARS 252. 209-7999. Appropriated funds cannot be used to enter into a contract with a corporation that has unpaid federal tax liability (after exhaustion of remedies) or that was convicted of a felony criminal violation in the preceding 24 months, unless the agency considered suspension or debarment and decided this action was not necessary to protect the interests of the government.

Many inverted domestic corporations are prohibited from receiving awards. FAR 9.108. These are entities that, after the applicable date, have, through a merger or other corporate transaction, changed their tax status to foreign owned without a significant change in ownership. See 6 U.S.C. § 395 (DHS contractors); FAR 52.209-10 (all contractors). Agency counsel are encouraged to carefully review the date of applicability to their agency and the complete circumstances of the corporate transaction that created the inverted domestic corporation.

2. Special or definitive standards of responsibility. FAR 9.104-2(a). In addition to the general standards of responsibility discussed above, the contracting officer may establish specific responsibility-type requirements for a specific acquisition. These solicitation-specific criteria measure an offeror's ability to perform a given contract. The special criteria may be qualitative or

quantitative. D.H. Kim Enters., B-255124, Feb. 8, 1994, 94-1 CPD ¶ 86.

The solicitation provision must reasonably inform that offerors must demonstrate compliance with the standard as a precondition to receiving the award. Public Facility Consortium I, LLC; JDL Castle Corp., B-295911, B-295911.2, May 4, 2005, 2005 CPD ¶ 170 at 3. Examples include:

a. Requiring that a prospective contractor have a specified number of years of experience performing the same or similar work is a definitive responsibility standard. J2A2JV, LLC, B-401663.4, Apr. 19, 2010, 2010 CPD ¶ 102 (did not meet definitive responsibility criterion requiring at least 5 years' experience, and solicitation language may not reasonably be interpreted as permitting use of a subcontractor's experience); M & M Welding & Fabricators, Inc., B-271750, July 24, 1996, 96-2 CPD ¶ 37 (IFB requirement to show documentation of at least three previous projects of similar scope); D.H. Kim Enters., B-255124, Feb. 8, 1994, 94-1 CPD ¶ 86 (IFB requirements for 10 years of general contracting experience in projects of similar size and nature and successful completion of a minimum of two contracts of the same or similar scope within the past two years, on systems of a similar size, quantity and type as present project); Roth Brothers, Inc., B-235539, 89-2 CPD ¶ 100 (IFB requirement to provide documentation of at least three previously completed projects of similar scope); J.A. Jones Constr. Co., B-219632, 85-2 CPD ¶ 637 (IFB requirement that bidder have performed similar construction services within the United States for three prior years); Hardie-Tynes Mfg. Co., B-237938, Apr. 2, 1990, 90-1 CPD ¶ 587 (agency properly considered manufacturing experience of parent corporation in finding bidder met the definitive responsibility criterion of five years manufacturing experience); <u>BBC Brown Boveri, Inc.</u>, B-227903, Sept. 28, 1987, 87-2 CPD ¶ 309 (IFB required five years of experience in transformer design, manufacture, and service; GAO held that this definitive responsibility criterion was satisfied by a subcontractor).

b. A requirement for an offeror to demonstrate in its proposal the capability to pass an audit by completing and submitting prescreening audit forms is not a definitive responsibility standard because it did not contain a specific and objective standard. It related only to the general responsibility of the awardee to perform the contract specific with all legal requirements. <u>T.F. Boyle Transportation, Inc.</u>, B310708; B-310708.2, Jan. 29, 2008.

c. Requirement for an offeror to "specify up to three contracts of comparable magnitude and similar in nature to the work required and performed within the last three years" was not a definitive responsibility criterion, but an informational requirement. <u>Nilson Van & Storage, Inc.</u>, B-310485, Dec. 10, 2007. <u>Compare Charter Envtl., Inc.</u>, B-207219, Dec. 5, 2005, 2005 CPD ¶ 213 at 2-3 (standard was definitive responsibility criterion where it required that offeror success-fully completed at least three projects that included certain described work, and at least three projects of comparable size and scope).

D. Procedures.

1. For many contracts, the prospective awardees regularly do business with the contracting activity, so responsibility determinations are relatively pro-forma. Where the prospective awardee is unknown to the contracting activity, or where there are specific responsibility criteria, the contracting officer's

responsibility determination will require a more detailed examination. The determination of responsibility is made after the apparently successful bidder is identified, but before the actual award of a contract.

2. The primary source of information for the contracting officer making affirmative determinations of responsibility is the prospective contractor itself. The prospective contractor may provide information directly to the contracting officer either as part of its proposal or in response to contracting officer inquiries; by completing its contractor registration at SAM.gov; or indirectly through the administrative contracting officer or contract auditor.

3. Contracting officers may perform a pre-award survey. FAR 9.105-1(b); FAR 9.106; DFARS 209.106; <u>Accurate Indus.</u>, B-232962, Jan. 23, 1989, 89-1 CPD ¶ 56.

4. Finally, a competitor may make the contracting officer aware of matters he or she should consider in assessing the responsibility of the prospective awardee.

5. Contracting officers must review information in government databases, such as SAM.gov, PPIRS.gov, and other past performance databases. FAR 9.105-1(c); <u>see also</u> AFARS 9.4 and FAR Subpart 9.4. The principal review is the list of excluded parties, where the contracting officer ascertains whether the prospective contractor has been suspended or debarred.

6. Where the contracting officer determines that a successful bidder is responsible, he or she documents the determination by signing the award document.

7. Where the contracting officer determines that a prospective awardee is not responsible, he or she shall prepare a written determination and include that determination in the contract files.

8. If the prospective awardee that is considered not responsible is a small business, the contracting officer shall

Eligible Contractors

follow the procedures in FAR Subpart 19.6, and forward the determination to the Small Business Administration. See Chapter 15.

E. GAO Review of Responsibility Determinations.

1. Affirmative Determinations of Responsibility. Historically, the GAO would not review any affirmative responsibility determinations absent a showing of bad faith or fraud. 4 CFR § 21.5(c) (1995); see Hard Bottom Inflatables, Inc., B-245961.2, Jan. 22, 1992, 92-1 CPD ¶ 103; Active Development Sys., Inc., B-404875, May 25, 2011; Navistar Defense, LLC; BAE Sys., Tactical Vehicle Sys. LP, B-401865 et al., Dec. 14, 2009, 2009 CPD ¶ 258. However, there are two exceptions:

   a. The GAO will review definitive responsibility criteria and protests that the awardee does not meet the criteria. 4 C.F.R. § 21.5(c); Active Development Sys., Inc., B-404875, May 25, 2011; T.F. Boyle Transp., Inc., B-310708, B-310708.2, Jan. 29, 2008, 2008 CPD ¶ 52.

   b. GAO will review allegations that, in reaching a particular responsibility determination, the contracting officer unreasonably failed to consider available relevant information or otherwise violated statute or regulation. 4 C.F.R. § 21.5(c); 67 Fed. Reg. 79,833 (Dec. 31, 2002); Active Development Sys., Inc., B-404875, May 25, 2011; T.F. Boyle Transp., Inc., B-310708, B-310708.2, Jan. 29, 2008, 2008 CPD ¶ 52. American Printing House for the Blind, Inc., B-298011, May 15, 2006, 2006 CPD ¶ 83 at 5-6; Government Contracts Consultants, B-294335, Sept. 22, 2004, 2004 CPD ¶ 202 at 2. See Impresa Construzioni Geom. Domenico Garufi, 52 Fed. Cl. 421 (2002) (finding the contracting officer failed to conduct an independent and informed responsibility determination); Southwestern Bell Tel. Co., B-

292476, Oct. 1, 2003, 2003 CPD ¶ 177 at 7-11 (GAO reviewed allegation where evidence was presented that the contracting officer failed to consider serious, credible information regarding awardee's record of integrity and business ethics).

2. Nonresponsibility Determinations. GAO will review a contracting officer's determination that a prospective awardee is not responsible for reasonableness of the determination. Schwender/Riteway Joint Venture, B250865.2, Mar. 4, 1993, 93-1 CPD ¶ 203 (determination of nonresponsibility unreasonable when based on inaccurate or incomplete information).

F. Subcontractor Responsibility.

1. Prime contractors make responsibility-type determinations about their subcontractors as a matter of course when acquiring materials or subcontracting work.

2. FAR 52.209-6 requires prime contractors to review the list of excluded parties at SAM.gov to verify that a subcontractor receiving an award over $35,000 is not proposed for debarment, suspended or debarred. This requirement does not apply to subcontracts for commercially available off-the-shelf (COTS) items as defined in the clause. If the prime contractor believes that there is a compelling reason to award the subcontract, the prime contractor must notify the contracting officer in writing.

3. FAR 52.209-6 is a mandatory flow-down in all subcontracts over $35,000, other than for COTS items. Consequently, subcontractors at all levels must notify the contracting officer before awarding to a subcontractor that is proposed for debarment, suspended, or debarred.

4. The procuring agency may review a subcontractor's responsibility. FAR 9.104-4(a). This ordinarily only occurs when the subcontract effort is especially critical or significant in size.

5. Subcontractor responsibility is determined in the same way as is the responsibility of the prime contractor. FAR 9.104-4(b)

6. Subcontractor Statutory and Regulatory Compliance.

    a. Licenses and permits. Contractors and their subcontractors are often required to comply with state and local licensing requirements by contract, as well as by state or local law. See FAR 52.236-7.

    b. When a solicitation contains a general condition that the contractor comply with state and local licensing requirements, the contracting officer need not inquire into what those requirements may be or whether the bidder will comply. James C. Bateman Petroleum Serv., Inc., B-232325, Aug. 22, 1988, 88-2 CPD ¶ 170; but see International Serv. Assocs., B-253050, Aug. 4, 1993, 93-2 CPD ¶ 82 (where agency determines that small business will not meet licensing requirement, referral to SBA required).

    c. On the other hand, when a solicitation requires specific compliance with regulations and licensing requirements, the contracting officer may inquire into the offeror's ability to comply with the regulations in determining the offeror's responsibility. Intera Technologies, Inc., B-228467, Feb. 3, 1988, 88-1 CPD ¶ 104.

III. ORGANIZATIONAL CONFLICTS OF INTEREST (OCI)

A. Overview.

1. One category of prospective bidders is routinely excluded from competing on specific acquisitions: individuals and companies with an organizational conflict of interest. This topic has grown in importance with the growth of reliance on service contractors. An organizational conflict of interest is one where the bidder, by virtue of prior or concurrent work for the government, has either: 1) an "Unfair Competitive Advantage" or 2) may provide "biased advice" to the government, were the bidder allowed to compete on or perform the contract at issue. Where the bidder with the organizational conflict of interest has an unfair competitive advantage, allowing it to compete may affect the integrity of the procurement process, potentially harming both the other bidders and the government. Where the organizational conflict of interest may give rise to biased advice, the government is the one harmed because it will not receive the services it expected on the existing contract. However, as the affected party, the government has greater discretion to waive the conflict.

2. Organizational conflicts of interest are governed by statute, regulations including FAR 9.5, and numerous bid protest decisions.

3. The contracting officer is responsible for determining whether an actual or apparent conflict of interest will arise, and whether and to what extent the firm should be excluded from the competition. FAR 9.504 - 9.505.

4. In analyzing a potential OCI, the contracting officer must compare the contractor's duties on the existing contract with the scope of the new procurement.

B. Types of OCIs

1. Unequal Access to Information. A contractor may have an unfair competitive advantage when it has access to information not available to other competitors ("Unfair access to non-public information."). The OCI is created when, as part of its performance of a government services contract, a firm has access to non-public information such as proprietary information of its competitors, non-public source selection information, etc., that may provide a competitive advantage in a new procurement. Similarly, the OCI may be created when the contractor hires an

Eligible Contractors

employee who had access through his or her previous job. FAR 9.505-4. Aetna Gov't Health Plans, Inc., B-254397.15, July 27, 1995, 95-2 CPD ¶ 129. Access to the information creates an OCI; the government does not need to show the contractor actually used it.

a. In Health Net Fed. Servs., LLC, B-401652.3,.5, Nov. 4, 2009, 2009 CPD ¶ 220, the GAO sustained a finding of an OCI where awardee employed a former high-ranking official of the procuring agency in its proposal preparation who had participated in planning procurement and had access to nonpublic competitor and source selection information.

b. In Johnson Controls World Serv., B-286714.2, Feb. 13, 2001, 2001 CPD ¶ 20, GAO found an OCI where the awardee's subcontractor, under separate contract, had access to a competitively beneficial but nonpublic data base of maintenance activities that was beyond what would be available to a typical incumbent installation logistics support contractor.

c. Kellogg, Brown, & Root Serv., Inc., Comp. Gen. B-400787.2, Feb. 23, 2009 CPD ¶ 692647 (upholding the contracting officer's decision to disqualify KBR from competing for two task orders under the LOGCAP IV contract because the KBR program manager improperly accessed rival propriety information erroneously forwarded to the program manager by the contracting officer. The GAO stated, "[W]herever an offeror has improperly obtained proprietary proposal information during the course of a procurement, the integrity of the procurement is at risk, and an agency's decision to disqualify the firm is generally reasonable, absent unusual circumstances.").

d. For there to be an unequal access OCI, the information received must be real, substantial, competitively useful, and nonpublic. (1) When a government employee participates in the drafting of an SOW, this does not necessarily demonstrate that the employee's post-government work for an offeror created an OCI where the employee's work was later released to the public as part of the solicitation. Further, the contracting officer could neither "conclusively establish, nor rule out the possibility" that former government employee had access to competitively useful source selection information, determination that appearance of impropriety had been created by the protester's hiring of a former government employee was unreasonable, because determination was based on assumptions rather than hard facts. VSE Corp., B-404833.4, Nov. 21, 2011, 2011 CPD ¶ 268; Raytheon Technical Servs. Co. LLC, B-404655, Oct. 11, 2011, 2011 CPD ¶ 236 ("unequal access to information" protest denied where allegations were based upon suspicion rather than "hard facts," and contracting officer conducted reasonable investigation and concluded that awardee did not have access to competitively useful non-public information); (3) CACI Inc., Federal, B-4030642, Jan. 28, 2011, 2011 CPD ¶ 31 (holding no unequal access to information OCI resulted from access to protester's information, where information had been furnished to the government without restriction as to its use); (4) ITT Corp. – Electronic Sys., B-402808, Aug. 6, 2010, 2010 CPD ¶178 (no OCI where the awardee had access to information that the protestor had provided to the government under a Government Purpose Rights license, since the protester had access to same information and government had the legal right to provide it to the awardee); and (5) Dayton T. Brown, Inc., B402256, Feb. 24, 2010, 2010 CPD ¶ 72 (finding where protocols were provided to all offerors, awardee with access to protocols did not have unfair access to information OCI).

e. Contractors are well advised to identify potential OCIs well in advance of bidding and to put in place mitigation measures to keep the nonpublic information from the business unit competing for the new work.

f. The access must be "unfair." Usually, the existing contractor will know much about its work that may not be publicly known. The "natural advantage of incumbency" however, will not create an OCI by itself. See Qineti North America, Inc., B-405008, July 27, 2011, 2011 CPD ¶ 154 (holding that an offeror may possess unique information, advantages and capabilities due to its prior experience under a government contract – either as an incumbent contractor or otherwise; the government is not necessarily required to equalize competition to compensate for such an advantage, unless there is evidence of preferential treatment or other improper action); PAI Corp. vs. United States, 2009 WL 3049213 (Ct. of Fed. Cl. Sept. 14, 2009 (stating that any competitive advantage was result of natural advantage of incumbency rather than access to nonpublic information which had no competitive value; since contracting officer found that no significant OCI existed, she was not required to prepare written analysis), affirmed, 614 F.3d 1347 (Fed. Cir. 2010); ARINC Eng'g Servs., LLC, 77 Fed. Cl. 196 (2007) (prejudice is presumed when offeror has nonpublic information that is competitively useful and unavailable to protester, but in order to prevail the protestor must show that contractor had more than just the normal advantages of incumbency – e.g., that awardee was "so embedded in the agency as to provide it with insight into the agency's operations beyond

that which would be expected of a typical government contractor"); and Systems Plus Inc. v. United States, 69 Fed. Cl. 1 (2003) (the natural advantage of incumbency, by itself, does not create an OCI).

g. The actions or knowledge of a subcontractor or other team member can create an OCI. In B.L. Harbert-Brasfield & Gorie, Comp. Gen. B-402229, Feb. 16, 2010, 2010 CPD ¶ 69, the awardee had unequal access to information when subcontractor that it ultimately acquired following contract award had access to competitively useful, nonpublic information. In Maden Techs., B-298543.2, Oct. 30, 2006, 2006 CPD ¶ 167 the potential OCI from awardee's use of subcontractor that had served as evaluator for agency in previous procurement was mitigated where subcontractor had signed nondisclosure agreement and did not aid awardee in preparing proposal. In Mech. Equip. Co., Inc., et al, B-292789, Dec. 15, 2003, 2004 CPD ¶ 192 (no unequal access OCI where awardee's subcontractor was long time incumbent services provider but there was no evidence it had advance access to procurement information).

h. Some contractors know more than others, and an unequal access to information OCI will not result from information that is obtained other than by a government contract. CapRock Govt. Solutions, Inc., B-402490, May 11, 2010, 2010 CPD ¶ 124 (no unequal access to information OCI where information in dispute was not obtained as part of performance of government contract).

i. Information from a former government employee. Where nonpublic information is obtained from a former government employee, the issue will be treated as if the information had been obtained under a government contract. GAO generally will not presume access to non-public, competitively sensitive information, but will presume prejudicial use of such information once access is shown. TeleCommunication Sys. Inc., B-404496.3, Oct. 26, 2011, 2011 CPD ¶ 229; Unisys Corp., B-403054.2, Feb. 8, 2011, 2011 CPD ¶ 61; Chenega Fed. Sys., B-299310.2, Sept. 28, 2007, 2007 CPD ¶ 70

2. Impaired Objectivity OCIs. A second type of OCI is created when the nature of a contractor's work under one contract could give it the opportunity to benefit on other contracts, were it allowed to compete. For example, a contractor that is providing advice about the best product on the market, might be affected if it was allowed to compete to supply the recommended product. Other examples include evaluating its own performance, or that of a direct competitor. The issue is not whether biased advice was actually given but whether a reasonable person would find that the contractor's objectivity could have been impaired. FAR § 9.505-3. Aetna Gov't Health Plans, Inc., B-254397.15, July 27, 1995, 95-2 CPD ¶ 129. See Cahaba Safeguard Adm'r, LLC, Comp. Gen. B-401842.2, Jan. 25, 2010, 2010 CPD ¶ 39 (discussing agency's handling of an impaired objectivity conflict of interest); L-3 Serv., Inc., Comp. Gen. B-400134.11, Sept. 3, 2009, 2009 CPD ¶ 171.

   a. A protest was sustained where the awardee of a contract for advisory and assistance services and technical analysis sold related products and services and could provide information that might influence acquisition decisions concerning those products. The Analysis Group, LLC, B-401726.2, Nov. 13, 2009, 2009 CPD ¶ 237; The Analysis Group, LLC, B401726.3, Apr. 18, 2011, 2011 CPD ¶ 166 (protest denied where agency conducted its own investigation and thoroughly analyzed potential OCI, concluding that risk of potential OCI remained but was outweighed by benefit to the government, and properly executed a waiver).

   b. Nortel Govt. Solutions, B-299522.5, B-299522.6, Dec. 30, 2008, 2009 CPD ¶ 10 (protest sustained where agency did not give meaningful consideration to a potential impaired objectivity OCI, also noted: firewall is "virtually irrelevant to an OCI involving potentially impaired objectivity," because the OCI involves the entire organization, not just certain individuals).

   c. Remote relationships. Some relationships are too "remote" to create an impaired objectivity OCI risk, and some activities are too "ministerial" to give the contractor an opportunity to act in other than the government's interest. In Valdez Int'l Corp., B402256.3, Dec. 29, 2010, 2011 CPD ¶ 13, the GAO, after comprehensive and well-documented review, affirmed a contracting officer decision that impaired objectivity OCI was minimal because standardized protocols and processes limited the amount of independent judgment required. In Marinette Marine Corp., B-400697 et al., Jan. 12, 2009, 2009 CPD ¶ 16, the GAO held there was no impaired objectivity OCI where entity that helped agency in proposal evaluation provided advice to both awardee and protester without any contractual or financial arrangement. In Leader Comm'ns, Inc, B-298734, Dec. 7, 2006, 2006 CPD ¶ 192 (finding that awardee did not have impaired objectivity OCI as a result of its performance of separate contract because any services that overlapped would be administrative only).

3. Biased Ground Rules OCI. The third type of OCI is created when, as part of its performance on a government contract, a firm has helped (or is in a position to help)

set the ground rules for procurement of another government contract. Examples include writing the statement of work or the specifications, establishing source selection criteria, or otherwise drafting the solicitation documents. The primary concern is that the company drafting the solicitation documents could skew the competition in its own favor, either intentionally or not. FAR 9.505-1 and 9.505-2. <u>Aetna Gov't Health Plans, Inc.</u>, B254397.15, July 27, 1995, 95-2 CPD ¶ 129.

a. The FAR standard is whether the information supplied led "directly, predictably, and without delay" to the statement of work. FAR 9.505-2(b).

b. Examples include: (1) <u>Energy Sys. Group</u>, B402324, Feb. 26, 2010, 2010 CPD ¶ 73, where the GAO upheld a protestor's exclusion on the basis of "biased ground rules" OCI. The protestor prepared a report that the agency used to draft the statement of work. Despite the fact that the awardee expected the report to be used only as part of a sole source procurement, rather than competitive procurement, the protestor was properly excluded. There is no "foreseeability" required; (2) <u>L3 Servs., Inc.</u>, B-400134.11, Sept. 3, 2009, 2009 CPD ¶ 171, where the GAO held that the relevant concern is not whether a firm drafted specifications that were adopted into the solicitation, but whether the firm was in a position to affect the competition, intentionally or not, in favor of itself. Also, it was unreasonable for the agency to rely on a mitigation plan that was undisclosed to, unevaluated by, and unmonitored by the agency; (3) <u>Celadon Labs., Inc.</u>, B-298533, Nov., 1 2006, 2006 CPD ¶ 158 (sustaining a protest where outside evaluators, retained to review proposals involving two different, competing technologies, were all employed by firms that promoted the

technology challenged by protestor's proposal); (4) <u>Filtration Dev. Co. LLC</u>, 60 Fed. Cl. 371 (2004), where a Systems Engineering and Technical Assistance (SETA) contractor was in a position to favor its own products, so it was precluded from supplying components even though the agency claimed the contractor had not provided services in connection with those products. The court held that the OCI had to be evaluated when the contractor became contractually obligated to perform SETA services, regardless of whether it actually performed them.

c. No OCI is created where the contractor has overall systems responsibility, or where input is provided by a developmental contractor or industry representative. <u>Lockheed Martin Sys. Integration – Owego</u>, B-287190.2, May 25, 2001, 2001 CPD ¶ 110; <u>Vantage Assoc., Inc. v. United States</u>, 59 Fed. Cl. 1, 10 (2003).

C. **Common OCI Situations. FAR Subpart 9.5.**

1. SETA Contracts. FAR 9.505-1. Systems Engineering and Technical Assistance contracts provide systems engineering and technical direction for a system but without having overall contractual responsibility for its development or for its integration, assembly and checkout, or its production. Thus, a systems integrator/prime contractor who has total system responsibility is not a SETA contractor. The SETA contractor "occupies a highly influential and responsible position in determining a system's basic concepts and supervising their execution by other contractors," and should <u>not be in a position to make decisions favoring its own products or capabilities.</u>

2. Preparing and Furnishing Complete Specifications Covering Non-Developmental Items. FAR 9.505-2.

Eligible Contractors

a. Where a contractor drafts the SOW, or specification, it generally cannot compete. The government's concern is that the contractor "could draft specifications favoring its own products or capabilities," which might not provide the government with unbiased advice.

b. This rule is not absolute. For example, a contractor who furnishes specifications regarding a product it provides (e.g., where the government purchases a data package from the original manufacturer, to use for future competitions) is generally considered not to have an organizational conflict of interest. Likewise, contractors acting as industry representatives that are supervised and controlled by government representatives when drafting specifications (e.g., when the government issues a Request For Information ("RFI")) are not considered to have an OCI based on their input.

c. Systems development contractors generally are not considered to have an OCI. Systems developers often draft the specifications as part of their development activities that the government may use in subsequent acquisitions. Naturally, the developer contractor will draft a specification or SOW that is tailored to its own products and practices.

d. Where a contractor prepares a work statement to be used in a competitive acquisition – "or provides material leading directly, predictably, and without delay to such a work statement" – the government's concern is that the contractor might favor its own products or capabilities. (FAR 9.505-2(b)) Accordingly, the contractor may not supply the system or services unless: 1) it is a sole source; 2) it participated in the development and design work; or 3) more than one contractor helped prepare the work statement.

3. Evaluation Services. A contractor should not be awarded a contract to evaluate its own (or a competitor's) products or services without "proper safeguards to ensure objectivity." FAR 9.505-3.

4. Third-Party Proprietary Information. If a contractor requires proprietary information from third parties to perform a contract, it creates an organizational conflict of interest. The contractor receiving the proprietary information must agree with the information owner to protect the information from unauthorized use or disclosure and to refrain from using the information for any other purpose. FAR 9.505-4.

a. The contracting officer must obtain copies of the required confidentiality agreements.

b. These restrictions also apply to proprietary and source selection information obtained from "marketing consultants," who are defined (in FAR 9.501) as independent contractors who provide advice, information, direction or assistance in connection with an offer, not including legal, accounting, training, routine technical services, or "advisory and assistance services" (as defined in Subpart 37.2).

D. **Contractor Responsibilities.** While FAR Subpart 9.5 is directed principally at the government, contractors should actively manage potential conflicts to safeguard both the government's interests and their own. Specifically, contractors should:

1. Identify actual and potential OCIs. They should act proactively and when requested by the contracting officer.

2. Actively communicate with the contracting officer early and often to agree upon measures to avoid or mitigate potential OCIs. This includes both the contracting officer for the existing work, and the contracting officer for the new acquisition. Many OCIs can be effectively mitigated if identified early.

3. Execute appropriate confidentiality agreements when proprietary information

from third parties will be needed to perform a contract.

4. Make necessary inquiries of marketing consultants to ensure that they do not provide information that creates an unfair competitive advantage.

E. Government Responsibilities for OCIs.

1. Oversight.

    a. OCIs are principally a government responsibility. Contracting officers (and other contracting officials) must identify and evaluate potential OCIs as early in the contracting process as possible. FAR 9.504(a)(1). Each individual contracting situation should be examined on the basis of its facts and the nature of the proposed contract. QinetiQ North America, Inc., Comp. Gen. B-405008, B405008.2, July 27. 2011, 2011 CPD ¶ 154. Because conflicts of interest may arise in situations not specifically addressed in FAR Subpart 9.5, individuals need to use common sense, good judgment, and sound discretion when determining whether a potential conflict exists. FAR 9.505. See L-3 Serv., Inc., Comp. Gen. B-400134.11, Sept. 3, 2009, 2009 CPD ¶ 171.

    b. Contracting Officers must act when an OCI is identified to avoid, neutralize, or mitigate potential significant conflicts of interest. Mitigation is effective when it prevents unfair competitive advantage or the likelihood that conflicting roles might impair a contractor's objectivity. FAR 9.504(a)(2); Energy Sys. Group, Comp. Gen. B-402324, Feb. 26, 2010, 2010 CPD ¶ 73.

    c. The GAO review found the contracting officer failed to adequately analyze whether a biased ground rules OCI existed, and that there were no hard facts to show that awardees' work had put it in a position to materially affect the competition. To succeed, the protester

must also demonstrate that contracting officer's failure could have materially affected the outcome of the competetion. QinetiQ North America, Inc., B-405008, July 27, 2011, 2011 CPD ¶ 154.

    d. Responsibility for determining whether an actual or apparent conflict of interest will arise, and to what extent the firm should be excluded from competition, rests with the contracting agency. The GAO will not overturn an agency's determination unless a protestor can show, based upon "hard facts," the agency's OCI determination is arbitrary and capricious. QinetiQ North America, Inc., Comp. Gen. B405008, B405008.2, July 27, 2011, 2011 CPD ¶ 154.

2. Reasonable consideration of an offeror's mitigation plan. When a contractor identifies a potential OCI, it may prepare a plan to eliminate or mitigate the conflict, or to avoid harm. The contracting officer must reasonably consider an offeror's OCI mitigation plan prior to excluding it from the competition.

    a. The GAO sustained a protest where the agency excluded the protestor from a competition because of a possible impaired objectivity OCI, but the agency failed to give the contractor the opportunity to avoid or mitigate the OCI, and had not given the protestor an opportunity to respond to agency concerns. AT&T Gov't Solutions, Inc., B-400216, Aug. 28, 2008, 2008 CPD ¶ 170.

    b. Evaluating proposals evenly (agency improperly downgraded score of protester, based on OCI risk, while failing to evaluate potential OCI of awardees on equal basis). Research Analysis & Maintenance, Inc., Westar Aerospace & Def. Group, Inc., B292587.4 et al., Nov. 17, 2003, 2004 CPD ¶ 100.

Eligible Contractors

3. Apparent OCI. The contracting officer may exclude an offeror based on an "apparent" OCI, even if there is no evidence of an actual impact.

   a. An appearance of an unfair competitive advantage based upon hiring of a government employee, without proof of an actual impropriety, is enough to exclude an offeror if the determination of unfair competitive advantage is based upon facts and not on mere innuendo. Health Net Fed. Servs., LLC, B-401652.3, B-401652.5, Nov. 4, 2009, 2009 CPD ¶ 220 at 28; see NKF Eng'g, Inc., v. US, 805 F.2d 372 (Fed. Cir 1986) (overturning lower court's holding that appearance of impropriety alone is not a sufficient basis to disqualify an offeror, and finding that the agency reasonably disqualified the offeror based upon the appearance of impropriety).

   b. In VRC, Inc., B-310100, Nov. 2, 2007, 2007 CPD ¶ 202, the contracting officer properly excluded offeror because there was an appearance of a conflict where an employee of a company with ownership ties to the offeror worked in the agency's contracting division and had direct access to source selection information.

   c. In Lucent Tech. World Servs. Inc., B-295462, Mar. 2, 2005, 2005 CPD ¶ 55, a protest challenging exclusion from the procurement was denied where the contracting officer reasonably determined that the protester had an OCI arising from its preparation of technical specification used by agency in solicitation. The agency was kept appraised of Lucent's progress in drafting specifications, it did not exercise supervision and control, the Army's modification was not a major revision, and vast majority of technical specifications remained unchanged.

F. Waiver.

The government has the right to waive an OCI requirement. FAR 9.503.

1. The Analysis Group, LLC, B-401726.3, Apr. 18, 2011, 2011 CPD ¶ 166 (protest denied where agency conducted its own investigation, thoroughly analyzed potential OCI, concluded that risk of potential OCI remained but was outweighed by benefit to the government, and properly executed waiver).

2. Cigna Govt. Servs., LLC, B-401068, Sept. 9, 2010, 2010 CPD ¶ 230 (denying protest challenging agency's waiver of OCI where, in compliance with FAR requirements, waiver request detailed extent of conflict, and authorized agency official determined that waiver was in government's interest).

3. MCR Federal, LLC, B-401854.2, Aug. 17, 2010, 2010 CPD ¶ 196 (where, in compliance with FAR 9.504, the agency made a written request for a waiver that described OCI concerns, the potential effect if not avoided, neutralized, or mitigated, and the government's interest in allowing the offerors to compete for the award notwithstanding the OCI concerns; the designated official approved the waiver, the agency met waiver requirements).

G. Mitigating OCIs.

In most cases it is not possible to mitigate an OCI after the fact, so an effective mitigation plan must address prospective OCIs. In general, GAO will give substantial deference to a mitigation plan, as long as the agency has investigated and dealt with the conflict issues and the plan is tailored to the specific situation.

1. Unequal access OCIs

   a. Firewalls. Firewalls are written procedures that block the flow of information between a support contractor with access to non-public information and another business unit that desires to compete for work without the benefit of the non-public information. The firewall is a combination of procedures and security measures that block the flow of information between contractor personnel who have access to non-public competitive information and other contractor employees who are preparing the proposal. The potential competitive advantage resulting from the unequal access will be nullified if the information cannot cross the firewall to be used in a competitive procurement. Enterprise Information Servs., B405152, Sept. 2, 2011, 2011 CPD ¶ 174; LEADS Corp., B292465, Sept. 26, 2003, 2003 CPD ¶ 197. Typically, the procedures should be documented in a written plan and audited to verify they are implemented as written.

b.   Disclosure. If preferential access to information creates the OCI, disclosure to all competitors removes the preference. Johnson Controls World Servs., Inc., B-286714.3, Aug. 20, 2001, 2001 CPD ¶ 145; Sierra Military Health Servs., Inc. vs. United States, 58 Fed. Cl. 573 (2003) (sharing information with competing offerors could adequately mitigate the OCI).

2.   Impaired objectivity OCIs

a.   A common type of OCI is where a government support contractor wants to act as a subcontractor on the contract about which it is providing advice.

b.   Where a subcontractor creates the biased advice OCI, the prime contractor can mitigate the OCI by excluding from work, or even removing, a conflicted subcontractor. Karrar Sys. Corp., B-310661, Jan. 3, 2008, 2008 CPD ¶ 51; Business Consulting Assocs., LLC, B-299758.2, Aug. 1, 2007, 2007 CPD ¶ 134.

c.   An impaired objectivity OCI can be mitigated by the agency assigning a support contractor to other work, and replacing it with a non-conflicted

support contractor, or even doing the work itself. Cahaba Safeguard Administrators, LLC, B-401842.2; C2C Solution, Inc., B-401106.5,6, Jan. 25, 2010, June 21, 2010, 2010 CPD ¶ 38 and 39; Alion Sci. & Tech. Corp., B-297022.4, Sept. 26, 2006, 2006 CPD ¶ 146. (Alion II) (GAO upheld the agency's analysis and approval of ITT's firewalled subcontractor plan even though one-third of the work would be done by a subcontractor, because the conflicted work could easily be segregated and assigned to the subcontractor).

d.   Increased oversight of work. Potentially biased advice can be mitigated by increased government oversight of the work. Valdez Int'l Corp., B402256.3, Dec. 29, 2010, 2011 CPD ¶ 13, affirmed the contracting officer's decision, after comprehensive and well-documented review that impaired objectivity OCI was minimal because standardized protocols and processes limited the amount of independent judgment required, and analysis would be done by subcontractors. In Wyle Labs., Inc., B-288892.2, Dec. 19, 2001, 2002 CPD ¶ 12, GAO held that where government personnel, rather than contractor personnel, would be measuring contractor performance, no OCI was created by the award of multiple contracts to the contractor. In Deutsche Bank, B-289111, Dec. 12, 2001, 2001 CPD ¶ 210, the GAO found dispositive that the firewalled subcontractor reported directly to the agency.

3.   Biased ground rules OCIs.

OCIs created by a potential competitor drafting key acquisition documents, such as the SOW, specification, evaluation criteria, etc., are difficult to mitigate. This is for several reasons, including the difficulty of correcting the harm and the need to preserve the integrity of the system. The best mitigation strategy is avoidance. A support contractor and the government might agree that the contractor can opt out of drafting procurement documents where a potential OCI exists, assign the work to a non-conflicted subcontractor, or otherwise not working on procurement documents. Once the support contractor drafts key procurement documents, it should not compete as either a prime contractor or a subcontractor.

H.   Weapon System Acquisitions.

1.   Congress directed the Department of Defense to develop uniform guidance on organizational conflicts of interest in Section 207 of the Weapons System Acquisition Reform Act of 2009 (WSARA), Pub. L. 111-23, 123 Stat. 1704, 10 U.S.C. § 2304. Congress was primarily concerned with the use of lead systems integrators on major defense acquisition programs[1] (MDAPs). DOD has issued uniform guidance in DFARS Subpart 209.5, which takes precedence to the extent that the rules are inconsistent. DFARS 209.571-2(b).

2.   Mitigating OCIs on MDAPs. DFARS 209.571-4.

   a.   Where the contracting officer and contractor have agreed to mitigate an OCI, a government-approved OCI Mitigation Plan should be incorporated into the contract. This has several benefits. It facilitates enforcement and predictability. Both the contractor and the government (as well as subsequent contracting officers) will be bound by the plan.

   b.   Where the contracting officer (after consulting with legal counsel) determines that an otherwise successful offeror is unable to effectively mitigate an OCI, the contracting officer shall use another approach to resolve the OCI, select

another offeror, or request a waiver (in accordance with the procedure set forth in the FAR).

3.   Restrictions on SETA (systems engineering and technical assistance) contractors.

   a.   DFARS 209.571-7(a) requires that if a DOD agency obtains advice from SETA contractors about MDAPs, it do so from sources that are objective and unbiased, such as Federally Funded Research and Development Centers[2] (FFRDCs) or other sources independent of major defense contractors.

   b.   SETA work is defined in DFARS 209.571-1.

   c.   Contracts for SETA services for MDAPs or Pre-MDAPs shall prohibit the contractor (or any affiliate) from participating as contractor or major subcontractor in the development or construction of a weapons system under such program. DFARS 209.571-7(b)(1).

IV. CONCLUSION

Not all prospective bidders are eligible to compete or receive award under full and open competition. The government awards contracts to responsible contractors and excludes other potential competitors to protect against receipt of biased advice or creation of an unfair competitive advantage.

These ineligible competitors are excluded, regardless of the types of procedures used, whether simplified acquisitions, sealed bids, competitive negotiations, broad agency announcements, or architect-engineer procedures.

---

[1] MDAPs are defined in 10 U.S.C. § 2430 as DOD acquisition programs (excluding highly classified programs) that are so designated by the Secretary of Defense or that are estimated to require an eventual total expenditure for R&D, test and evaluation of more than $300 million or total expenditure for procurement of more than $1.8 billion, based on FY 1990 dollars.

---

[2] Federally Funded Research and Development Centers are defined in FAR 2.101 and include entities such as the National Laboratories (i.e., Los Alamos or Oak Ridge) and think tanks (i.e., Rand Corp. or Institute for Defense Analyses).

COMPETITIVE SOURCING

AND

PRIVATIZATION

I.   COMPETITIVE SOURCING.[1]

A.   Introduction.

Competitive sourcing and privatization refer to the policies that govern replacing work performed by government employees with contractor supplied services. Throughout its history, the policies have been very controversial.

Since the beginnings of our nation, the military departments have grappled with maintaining capabilities in peacetime that were essential when mobilizing for war. Consequently, the nation had developed a network of depots, arsenals, shipyards, and air logistics centers where blue-collar government employees manufactured, maintained and overhauled weapons systems. Similarly, on government installations, until relatively recently, government employees performed many of the services for operating the facilities, from janitorial services through construction and skilled trades.

Some officials have observed that many of the services and industrial operations were identical to those services performed in the private sector at a much lower cost. Consequently, converting services performed by government employees into services performed by the private sector appeared to be a cost-saving strategy with considerable potential. Unfortunately, the conversion process was fraught with political pitfalls. The loss of jobs in a government work force, often unionized; the relocation of work from government facilities to commercial facilities in different states or congressional districts; the loss of in-house expertise that might prove essential in national emergencies; and disputes between competing contractors all contributed to a process that has been less than smooth. Additionally, it appears that some agencies have contracted out functions, such as contracting, that might better be performed by government employees.

B.   Origins and Development.

1.   1955: The Bureau of the Budget (predecessor of the Office of Management and Budget (OMB)) issued a series of bulletins establishing the federal policy to obtain goods and services from the private sector. See Federal Office of Management and Budget Circular A-76, Performance of Commercial Activities, ¶ 4.a (Aug. 4, 1983, Revised 1999) [hereinafter Circular A-76 (1999)].

2.   1966: The OMB first issued Circular A-76, which restated the federal policy and the principle that "[i]n the process of governing, the government should not compete with its citizens." The OMB revised the Circular in 1967, 1979, 1983, and again in 1999. See Circular A-76 (1999), ¶ 4.a.

3.   1996: The OMB issued a Revised Supplemental Handbook setting forth procedures for determining whether commercial activities should be performed under contract by a commercial source or in-house using government employees. In June 1999, OMB updated the Revised

---

[1] While referred to in the past as "contracting out" or "outsourcing," the current and preferred term-of-art is "competitive sourcing."

Supplemental Handbook. See Circular A-76 (1999), ¶ 1.[2]

4.   2009: By the spring of 2009 public-private competitions which would convert federal employee jobs into contractor jobs under Circular A-76 had been suspended, and in most cases remain so.[3] Competitive sourcing is currently only permitted in DOD, where the result is to determine how to best source work that is not currently performed by federal employees (i.e., new work, or work currently done by contractors). In March 2009, President Obama reiterated the importance of Congress's taskings and further directed the OMB to "clarify when governmental outsourcing of services is, and is not, appropriate, consistent with section 321 of the 2009 NDAA."[4]

5.   2010: In the National Defense Authorization Act for Fiscal Year 2010 (NDAA 2010), Congress imposed a temporary moratorium on new competitions involving functions currently performed by DOD civilian employees until, among other things, DOD reviewed and reported to Congress on various aspects of its public-private competition policies.[5] DOD complied with the statutory requirements in conducting its review of public-private competitions and in submitting its June 2011 report to Congress.

6.   2011: In response to the directive of 2009, OMB (OFPP) issued Policy Letter 11-01.[6] Policy Letter 11-01 is the most recent attempt to define inherently governmental functions and, subsequently, what functions may and may not be outsourced. In essence, Policy Letter 11-01 prohibits outsourcing "inherently governmental functions" and cautions against outsourcing "closely associated with inherently governmental functions" and "critical functions." Policy Letter 11-01 is composed of six parts, but for purposes of this primer, only three of the relevant parts are discussed below.

7.   2011: In addition to the important Policy Letter 11-01 issued by OFPP referenced above, the GAO published in 2011, DOD MET STATUTORY REPORTING REQUIREMENTS ON PUBLIC-PRIVATE COMPETITIONS, which was a review of the 2010 competitive sourcing review conducted by DOD.

8.   As of February 2016, the process of competitive sourcing is halted with little likelihood that it will resume absent a change in policy. This appears to be the result of policy differences between the parties and partially because after nearly 50 years of contracting out, all the low-hanging fruit has been picked. The

---

[2] The Circular A-76 (1999), Revised Supplemental Handbook, and associated updates issued through OMB Transmittal Memoranda are available at http://www.whitehouse.gov/omb/circulars_indexproc ure [hereinafter Circular A-76 (Revised)].

[3] Omnibus Appropriations Act, 2009, Pub. L. No. 111-8, § 737 (2009); Department of Defense Appropriations Act, 2010, Pub. L. No. 111-118, § 325 (2009).

[4] Memorandum of the President to the Heads of Exec. Dep'ts and Agencies, subject: Government Contracting (Mar. 4, 2009), available at http://www.whitehouse.gov/the_press_office/Memor andum-for-the-Heads-ofExecutive-Departments-and-Agencies-Subject-Government.

[5] Pub. L. No. 111-84 § 325 (2009).

[6] Office of Fed. Procurement Pol., Office of Mgmt. & Budget, Exec. Office of the President, OFPP Pol. Letter 11-01, Performance of Inherently Governmental and Critical Functions (2011) [hereinafter Policy Letter 11-01]. On February 13, 2012, OFPP published a correction to Policy Letter 11-01. Policy Letter 11-01 was originally addressed only to the Civil Executive Branch Departments and Agencies. See 77 Fed. Reg. 29, 7609 (Feb. 13, 2012) (extending the application of Policy Letter 11-01 to Defense Executive Branch Departments and Agencies). (Sec. C, Public Comments to the Notice of Final Policy Letter). The OFPP published its proposed policy letter on March 31, 2010, for public comments. More than 30,000 public and private organizations and/or citizens submitted comments and recommendations. Some recommendations were adopted by OFPP and incorporated into Policy Letter 11-01. A review of Section C, Public Comments, is instructive and may be used as a resource when dealing with Closely Associated and Critical Functions.

remaining opportunities for privatization present difficult choices to agencies.

9. Between Fiscal Year (FY) 1997 and FY 2001, DOD had completed approximately 780 sourcing decisions involving more than 46,000 government positions (approximately 34,000 civilian positions and 12,000 military provisions). See GEN. ACCT. OFF., COMMERCIAL ACTIVITIES PANEL, IMPROVING THE SOURCING DECISIONS OF THE GOVERNMENT (2002), *available at* www.gao.gov. However, during 2004, DOD completed 70 sourcing decisions affecting over 8,200 jobs; ninety percent of these sourcing decisions resulted in a decision not to contract out the function. See OMB, REPORT ON COMPETITIVE SOURCING RESULTS: FISCAL YEAR 2004 (May 2005), *available at* www.whitehouse.gov/omb. During 2005, DOD completed 35 sourcing decisions affecting 2,500 jobs; seventy-one percent of these sourcing decisions resulted in not contracting out the function. See OMB, REPORT ON COMPETITIVE SOURCING RESULTS: FISCAL YEAR 2005 (April 2006), *available at* www.whitehouse.gov/omb.

C. **The Future.**

1. In 2003, OMB issued the "new" Circular A-76, effective 29 May 2003, and a Revised Supplemental Handbook, OMB Circular A-76 Transmittal Memoranda Nos. 1-25, and Office of Federal Procurement Policy (OFPP) Policy Letter 92-1, *Inherently Governmental Functions*, Sept. 23, 1992. See Federal Office of Management and Budget Circular A-76 (Revised), Performance of Commercial Activities, ¶ 2 (May 23, 2003) [hereinafter Circular A-76 (Revised)].[7]

2. Should the political leadership elect to continue the competitive sourcing process, it is likely to follow the processes outlined

in OMB Cir. A-76, as further discussed below. In general, the process consists of identifying activities currently performed by government employees which are commercial- or industrial-type activities and not inherently governmental in nature. Then, the agency conducts a competition between the in-house work force and contractors to determine whether contracting out the function will yield cost savings.

II. **AGENCY ACTIVITY INVENTORY.**

A. **Introduction**. The first step in the contracting process is determining those activities suitable for contracting out.

B. **Key Terms.** The heart and soul of competitive sourcing rests on whether a governmental activity/function is categorized as commercial or inherently governmental in nature.

1. Commercial Activity. A recurring service that could be performed by the private sector. Circular A-76 (Revised), Attachment A, ¶ B.2.

2. Inherently Governmental Activities. An activity so intimately related to the public interest as to mandate performance by government personnel. Such "activities require the exercise of substantial discretion in applying government authority and/or making decisions for the government."[8] Circular A-76 (Revised), Attachment A, ¶ B.1.a. Inherently governmental activities fall into two broad categories:

a. The exercise of sovereign government authority.

b. The establishment of procedures and processes related to the oversight of

---

[7] The full text of Circular A-76 (2003) is available on-line at http://www.whitehouse.gov/omb/circulars/index.html .

[8] Cf. Federal Activities Inventory Reform Act (FAIR Act) of 1998, Pub. L. No. 105-270, 112 Stat. 2382 (1998) (codified at 31 U.S.C. § 501 (note)), which states the term "inherently governmental function" includes activities that merely require the "exercise of discretion."

monetary transactions or entitlements.

C. **Inventory Requirement.** Federal executive agencies are required to prepare annual inventories categorizing all activities performed by government personnel as either commercial or inherently governmental. The requirement is based on statute and the Circular A-76 (Revised).

1. Statutory Requirement - Federal Activities Inventory Reform Act (FAIR Act) of 1998, Pub. L. No. 105-270, 112 Stat. 2382 (1998) (codified at 31 U.S.C. § 501 (note)).

    a. Codifies the definition of "inherently governmental" activity.

    b. Requires each executive agency to submit to OMB an annual list (by 30 June) of non-inherently governmental (commercial) activities. After mutual consultation, both OMB and the agency must make the list of commercial activities public. The agency must also forward the list to Congress.

    c. Provides "interested parties" the chance to challenge the list within 30 days after its publication. The "interested party" list includes a broad range of potential challengers to include the private sector, representatives of business/professional groups that include private-sector sources, government employees, and the head of any labor organization referred to in 5 U.S.C. § 7103(a)(4).

2. Circular A-76 (Revised) Inventory Requirements.

    a. Requires agencies to submit to OMB by 30 June each year an inventory of commercial activities, an inventory of inherently governmental activities, as well as an inventory summary report.

Circular A-76 (Revised), Attachment A, ¶ A.2.

    b. After OMB review and consultation, agencies will make both the inventory of commercial activities and the inventory of inherently governmental functions available to Congress and the public unless the information is classified or protected for national security reasons. Circular A-76 (Revised), Attachment A, ¶ A.4.

    c. Categorization of Activities.

        (1) The agency competitive sourcing official (CSO)[9] must justify in writing any designation of an activity as inherently governmental. The justification will be provided to OMB and to the public upon request. Circular A-76 (Revised), Attachment A, ¶ B.1.

        (2) Agencies must use one of six reason codes to identify the reason for government performance of a commercial activity.[10] When using reason

_____

[9] The CSO is an assistant secretary or equivalent-level official within an agency responsible for implementing the policies and procedures of the circular. Circular A-76 (Revised) ¶ 4.f. For the DOD, the designated CSO is the Deputy Under Secretary of Defense (Installations and Environment). Memorandum, Deputy Secretary of Defense, to Secretaries of the Military Departments et al., subject: Designation of the Department of Defense Competitive Sourcing Official (12 Sept. 2003). The DOD CSO has in turn appointed DOD Component CSOs and charged them with providing Circular A-76 (Revised) implementation guidance within their respective Components. Memorandum, Deputy Under Secretary of Defense (Installations and Environment), to Assistant Secretary of the Army (Installations and Environment) et al., subject: Responsibilities of the DOD CSO and Component CSOs (29 Mar. 2004).

[10] The six reason codes include the following:

Reason code A – "commercial activity is not appropriate for private sector performance";

code A, the CSO must provide sufficient written justification, which will be made available to OMB and the public upon request. Circular A-76 (Revised), Attachment A, ¶ C.2.

d.   Challenge Process.

(1)   The head of the agency must designate an inventory challenge authority and an inventory appeal authority.

(a)   Inventory Challenge Authorities. Must be "agency officials at the same level as, or a higher level than, the individual who prepared the inventory." Circular A-76 (Revised), Attachment A, ¶ D.1.a.

(b)   Inventory Appeal Authorities. Must be "agency officials who are independent and at a higher level in the agency than inventory challenge authorities." Circular A-76 (Revised), Attachment A, ¶ D.1.b.

(2)   Inventory challenges are limited to "classification of an

---

Reason code B – "commercial activity is suitable for a streamlined or standard competition";

Reason code C – "commercial activity is subject of an in-progress streamlined or standard competition";

Reason code D – "commercial activity is performed by government personnel as the result of a streamlined or standard competition . . . within the past five years";

Reason code E – "commercial activity is pending an agency approved restructuring decision" (e.g., base closure, realignment);

Reason code F – "commercial activity is performed by government personnel due to a statutory prohibition against private sector performance."

Circular A-76 (Revised), Attachment A, ¶ C.1, Figure A2.

activity as inherently governmental or commercial" or to the "application of reason codes." Circular A-76 (Revised), Attachment A, ¶ D.2.[11]

III.   CIRCULAR A-76 COMPETITION PROCEDURES (REVISED).

A.   Overview.

The objectives of OMB Cir. A-76 procedures are to:

1.   Improve the efficiency of the existing government work force;

2.   Assist the existing government work force in competing against commercial sources; and

3.   Fairly and transparently select the source (government or commercial) that will perform the function going forward.

B.   Resources.

1.   OMB Guidance. OMB Circular A-76 (2003).

2.   DOD Guidance.[12]

a.   U.S. Dep't of Defense, Dir. 4100.15, Commercial Activities Program (10 Mar. 1989).

---

[11] Originally the Circular A-76 (Revised) stated interested parties could only challenge "reclassifications" of activities. The OMB issued a technical correction, however, revising Attachment A, paragraph D.2 by deleting the word "reclassification" and inserting "classification." Office of Mgmt. & Budget, Technical Correction to Office of Management and Budget Circular No. A-76, "Performance of Commercial Activities," 68 Fed. Reg. 48,961, 48,962 (Aug. 15, 2003).

[12] The DOD Directive, Instruction, Interim Guidance, as well as the applicable regulations, instructions, and guidance of the various Armed Services are available at DOD's SHARE A-76 website located at http://sharea76.fedworx.org/inst/sharea76.nsf/CONTDEFLOOK/HOME-INDEX.

b.   U.S. Dep't of Defense, Instr. 4100.33, <u>Commercial Activities Program Procedures</u> (9 Sept. 1985 through Change 3 dated 6 Oct. 1995).

c.   U.S. Dep't of Defense, Department of Defense Strategic and Competitive Sourcing Programs Interim Guidance (Apr. 3, 2000).

3.   Military Department Guidance.

a.   U.S. Dep't of Army, Reg. 5-20, <u>Competitive Sourcing Program</u> (23 May 2005).

b.   U.S. Dep't of Army, Pam. 5-20, <u>Commercial Activities Study Guide</u> (31 Jul. 1998).

c.   U.S. Dep't of Air Force, Instr. 38-203, <u>Commercial Activities Program</u> (19 Jul. 2001).

d.   U.S. Dep't of Navy, Instr. 4860.7D, <u>Navy Commercial Activities Program</u> (28 Sept. 2005).

C.   Key Players/Terms.

1.   <u>Agency Tender</u>. The agency management plan submitted in response to and in accordance with the requirements in a solicitation. The agency tender includes an MEO, agency cost estimate, MEO quality control and phase-in plans, and any subcontracts. Circular A-76 (Revised), Attachment D.

2.   <u>Agency Tender Official (ATO)</u>. An inherently governmental official with decision-making authority who is responsible for developing, certifying, and representing the agency tender. The ATO also designates members of the **MEO Team** and is considered a "directly interested party" for contest purposes. The ATO must be independent of the contracting officer, SSA/SSEB, and the PWS team. Circular A-76 (Revised), Attachment B, ¶ A.8.a.

a.   <u>Conflict of Interest Avoidance</u>. *Directly affected government personnel* (i.e., employees whose positions are being competed) may participate on the MEO Team. However, to avoid any appearance of a conflict of interest, members of the MEO Team <u>shall not</u> be members of the PWS Team.

3.   <u>Contracting Officer (CO)</u>. An inherently governmental official who is a member of the PWS team and is responsible for issuing the solicitation and the source selection methodology. The CO must be independent of the ATO, MEO team, and the human resource advisor (HRA). Circular A-76 (Revised), Attachment B, ¶ a.8.b and Attachment D.

4.   <u>PWS Team Leader.</u> An inherently governmental official, independent of the ATO, HRO, and MEO team, who develops the PWS and QASP, determines government-furnished property and assists the CO in developing the solicitation. Responsible for appointing members of the PWS Team. Circular A-76 (Revised), Attachment B, ¶ a.8.c.

a.   <u>Conflict of Interest Avoidance</u>. *Directly affected government personnel* (i.e., employees whose positions are being competed) may participate on the PWS Team. However, to avoid any appearance of a conflict of interest, members of the MEO Team <u>shall not</u> be members of the PWS Team.

5.   <u>Human Resource Advisor (HRA)</u>. An inherently governmental official and human resource expert. The HRA must be independent of the CO, SSA, PWS team, and SSEB. As a member of the MEO team, the HRA assists the ATO and MEO team in developing the agency tender. The HRA is also responsible for employee and labor-relations requirements. Circular A-76 (Revised), Attachment B, ¶ a.8.d.

6.   <u>Source Selection Authority (SSA)</u>. An inherently governmental official appointed IAW FAR 15.303. The SSA must be independent of the ATO, HRA, and MEO team. Responsible for appointing

members of the Source Selection Evaluation Board Team (SSEB Team).

7.   Conflict of Interest Avoidance. *Directly affected personnel* (i.e. employees whose positions are being competed) and other personnel (including but not limited to the ATO, HRA, MEO team members, advisors, and consultants) *with knowledge of the agency tender* shall not participate in any manner on the SSEB Team (as member or as advisors).

D.   Competition Procedures.

1.   Previously, agencies could "directly convert" to contractor performance functions performed by 10 or fewer full-time equivalents (FTEs). The Revised Circular A-76 eliminates the use of "direct conversions." Office of Management and Budget; Performance of Commercial Activities, 68 Fed. Reg. 32,134; 32,136 (May 29, 2003).[13]

2.   Streamlined Competitions. The new "streamlined competition" process must be used for activities performed by 65 or fewer FTEs "and/or any number of military personnel," unless the agency elects to use the standard competition. Circular A-76 (Revised), Attachment B, ¶¶ A.5.b and C. The streamlined competition process includes:

      a.   Determining the Cost of Agency Performance. An agency may determine the agency cost estimate on the incumbent activity; "however, an agency is encouraged to develop a more efficient organization, which may be an

MEO." Circular A-76 (Revised), Attachment B, ¶ C.1.a.[14]

      b.   Determining the Cost of Private-Sector/Public Reimbursable Performance. An agency may use documented market research or solicit proposals IAW the FAR, to include using simplified acquisition tools. Circular A-76 (Revised), Attachment B, ¶ C.1.b; Office of Management and Budget; Performance of Commercial Activities, 68 Fed. Reg. 32,134; 32,137 (May 29, 2003).

      c.   Establishing Cost Estimate Firewalls. The individual(s) preparing the in-house cost estimate and the individual(s) soliciting private-sector/public reimbursable cost estimates must be different and may not share information. Circular A-76 (Revised), Attachment B, ¶ C.1.d.

      d.   Implementing the Decision. For private-sector performance decisions, the CO awards a contract IAW the FAR. For agency performance decisions, the CO

---

[13] While Circular A-76 (Revised) eliminates "direct conversions," recall that Congress permits the DOD to directly convert performance of functions to: 1) Javits-Wagner-O'Day (JWOD) Act firms that employ blind or severely handicapped employees; or 2) firms that are at least fifty-one percent owned by an American Indian tribe or Native Hawaiian organization. See Department of Defense Appropriations Act for FY 2006, Pub. L. No. 109-148, § 8014(b), 119 Stat. 2680 (2005).

[14] Though civilian agencies have historically been able to determine the estimated cost of in-house performance without creating an MEO, the DOD's ability to do so is limited. Recall that the DOD generally must complete a "most efficient and cost-effective organization analysis" prior to converting any function that involves *more than 10 civilian employees*. See Department of Defense Appropriations Act for FY 2006, Pub. L. No. 109-148, § 8014(a), 119 Stat. 2680 (2005). Note, however, that the Department of Defense Authorization Act for FY 2006, Pub. L. 109-163, § 341, 119 Stat. 3136 (2005) and 10 U.S.C. § 2461(a), Pub. L. No. 109-163 (2006), conflict with the FY 2006 DOD Appropriations Act on the minimum number of civilian employees that must be affected to make the creation of an MEO mandatory. These provisions state that DOD must complete an "MEO" prior to converting any function that involves *10 or more civilian employees*. Thus, DOD should rely on the language (of "10 or more"—vice "more than 10") contained in the FY 2006 DOD Authorization Act and in 10 U.S.C. 2461(a).

executes a "letter of obligation" with an agency official responsible for the commercial activity. Circular A-76 (Revised), Attachment B, ¶ C.3.a.

3. Standard Competitions. The new "standard competition" procedures must be used for commercial activities performed by more than 65 FTEs. Circular A-76 (Revised), Attachment B, ¶ A.5.

    a. Solicitation. When issuing a solicitation, the agency must comply with the FAR and clearly identify all the evaluation factors.

        (1) The solicitation must state the agency tender is not required to include certain information, such as a subcontracting plan goals, licensing or other certifications, or past performance information (unless the agency tender is based on an MEO implemented IAW the circular). Circular A-76 (Revised), Attachment B, ¶ D.3.a(4).

        (2) The solicitation closing date will be the same for private-sector offers and agency tenders. Circular A-76 (Revised), Attachment B, ¶ D.3.a(5). If the ATO anticipates the agency tender will be submitted late, the ATO must notify the CO. The CO must then consult with the CSO to determine if amending the closing date is in the best interest of the government. Circular A-76 (Revised), Attachment B, ¶ D.4.a(2).

    b. Source Selection.

        (1) In addition to sealed bidding and negotiated procurements based on a lowest-priced technically acceptable source

selections IAW the FAR, the Circular A-76 (Revised) also permits:

(a) Phased Evaluation Source Selections.

    (i) Phase One – only technical factors are considered and all prospective providers (private sector, public reimbursable sources, and the agency tender) may propose alternative performance standards. If the SSA accepts an alternate performance standard, the solicitation is amended and revised proposals are requested. Circular A-76 (Revised), Attachment B, ¶ D.5.b.2.

    (ii) Phase Two – the SSA makes the performance decision after price/cost realism analyses on all offers/tenders determined technically acceptable. Circular A-76 (Revised), Attachment B, ¶ D.5.b.2.

(b) Cost-Technical Tradeoff Source Selections. May only be used in standard competitions for (1) information technology activities, (2) commercial activities performed by the private sector, (3) new requirements, and (4) segregable expansions. Circular A-76 (Revised), Attachment B, ¶ D.5.b.3.

(2) The agency tender is evaluated concurrently with the private-sector proposals and may be excluded from a standard competition if

198

materially deficient. Circular A-76 (Revised), Attachment B, ¶ D.5.c.1.

(a) If the CO conducts exchanges with the private-sector offerors and the ATO, such exchanges must be IAW FAR 15.306, except that exchanges with the ATO must be in writing and the CO must maintain records of all such correspondence. Circular A-76 (Revised), Attachment B, ¶ D.5.c.2.

(b) If an ATO is unable to correct a material deficiency, "the CSO may advise the SSA to exclude the agency tender from the standard competition." Circular A-76 (Revised), Attachment B, ¶ D.5.c.3.

(3) All standard competitions will include the cost conversion differential (i.e., 10% of personnel costs or $10 million, whichever is less). Circular A-76 (Revised), Attachment B, ¶ D.5.c.4.[15]

c. Implementing a Performance Decision. For private-sector performance decisions, the CO awards a contract IAW the FAR. For agency performance decisions, the CO executes a "letter of obligation" with an agency official responsible for the commercial activity. Circular A-76 (Revised), Attachment B, ¶ D.6.f.

d. Contests.[16]

(1) A "directly interested party" (i.e., the agency tender official, a single individual appointed by a majority of directly affected employees, a private-sector offeror, or the certifying official of a public reimbursable tender) may contest certain actions in a standard competition. Circular A-76 (Revised), Attachment B, ¶ F.1.

(2) All such challenges will now be governed by the agency appeal procedures found at FAR 33.103. Circular A-76 (Revised), Attachment B, ¶ F.1.

(3) No party may contest any aspect of a streamlined competition. Circular A-76 (Revised), Attachment B, ¶ F.2.

e. Protests.

(1) Shortly after OMB issued the Circular A-76 (Revised), GAO published a notice in the Federal Register requesting comments on whether the GAO should accept jurisdiction over bid protests submitted by the Agency Tender Official and/or an

---

[15] As stated above, the "10% or $10 million" conversion differential requires the DOD to apply the differential in all competitions (streamlined or standard) involving 10 or more civilian employees. See Department of Defense Authorization Act for FY 2006, Pub. L. 109-163, § 341, 119 Stat. 3136 (2005) and 10 U.S.C. § 2461(a), Pub. L. No. 109-163 (2006). Additionally, the Department of Defense Appropriations Act for FY 2006, Pub. L. No. 109-148, § 8014(a), 119 Stat. 2680 (2005), contains a limitation that states the contractor cannot receive an advantage for a proposal that reduces DOD costs by "not making an employer-sponsored health insurance plan available" to the workers who will perform the work under the proposal, or by "offering to such workers an employer-sponsored health benefits plan that requires the employer to contribute less towards the premiums" than the amount paid by the DOD under chapter 89, title 5 of the United States Code. Id.

[16] A "contest" is the term the OMB Circular A-76 (Revised) uses to describe what is referred to in FAR Part 33 as an agency-level protest.

"agent" for affected employees. Government Accountability Office; Administrative Practices and Procedures; Bid Protest Regulations, Government Contracts, 68 Fed. Reg. 35,411 (June 13, 2003).

(2) In April 2004, the GAO ruled that notwithstanding the changes in the Circular A-76 (Revised), the in-house competitors in public/private competitions are not offerors and, therefore, under the current language of the Competition in Contracting Act of 1984, 31 U.S.C. §§ 3551-56 (2000), no representative of an in-house competitor is an "interested party" eligible to maintain a protest before the GAO. Dan Dufrene et al., B-293590.2 et al. (April 19, 2004).[17]

(3) In response, Congress included section 326 in the Ronald W. Reagan National Defense Authorization Act, 2005 (2005 NDAA), and granted ATOs limited, yet significant bid protest rights.

Pub. L. No. 108-375, § 326, 118 Stat. 1811, 1848 (2004).

(a) Amends the CICA's definition of "interested party" by specifying that term includes ATOs in public-private competitions involving more than sixty-five FTEs. *See* 31 U.S.C. § 3551(2).

(b) States that ATOs "shall file a protest" in a public-private competition at the request of a majority of the affected federal civilian employees "unless the [ATO] determines that there is no reasonable basis for the protest." The ATO's determination whether to file a protest "is not subject to administrative or judicial review"; however, if the ATO determines there is no reasonable basis for a protest, the ATO must notify Congress.

(c) Additionally, in any protest filed by an interested party in competitions involving more than sixty-five FTEs, a representative selected by a majority of the affected employees may "intervene" in the protest.

(4) On 14 April 2005, the GAO amended its Bid Protest Regulations by revising the definition of "interested party" and "intervenor" IAW with the 2005 NDAA. 70 Fed. Reg. 19,679 (Apr. 14, 2005).

4. Time frames.

a. Streamlined Competitions. Must be completed within 90 calendar days from "public announcement" to "performance decision," unless the agency CSO grants an extension not

---

[17] Recognizing the concerns of fairness that weigh in favor of correcting the current situation, where an unsuccessful private-sector offeror has the right to protest to the GAO, while an unsuccessful public-sector competitor does not, the Comptroller General sent a letter to Congress suggesting that Congress may wish to consider amending the CICA to provide for MEO standing. Dan Dufrene et al., B-293590.2 (April 19, 2004). The letter also suggested that any amendment to the CICA specify who would be authorized to protest on the MEO's behalf: the ATO, affected employees (either individually or in a representative capacity), and/or employees' union representatives. Id. On 18 May 2004, a bipartisan group of senators introduced legislation that would amend the CICA's definition of "interested party" to include the ATO and any one person selected as a representative by a majority of the affected federal employees. S. 2438, 108th Cong. (2004).

to exceed 45 days. Circular A-76 (Revised), Attachment B, ¶ C.2.

b. Standard Competitions. Must not exceed 12 months from "public announcement" to "performance decision," unless the CSO grants a time limit waiver not to exceed six months. Circular A-76 (Revised), Attachment B, ¶ D.1.

c. Preliminary Planning. Because time frames for completing competitions have been reduced, preliminary planning takes on increased importance. The new rules state that prior to public announcement (start date)[18] of a streamlined or standard competition, the agency must complete several preliminary planning steps to include: scoping the activities and FTEs to be competed, grouping business activities, assessing the availability of workload data, determining the incumbent activities' baseline costs, establishing schedules, and appointing the various competition officials. Circular A-76 (Revised), Attachment B, ¶ A.

E. Post-competition Accountability.

1. Monitoring. After implementing a performance decision, the agency must monitor performance IAW with the performance periods stated in the solicitation. The CO will make option year exercise determinations IAW FAR 17.207. Circular A-76 (Revised), Attachment B, ¶¶ E.4 and 5.

2. Terminations for Failure to Perform. The CO must follow the cure notice and show cause notification procedures consistent with FAR Part 49 prior to issuing a notice

---

[18] DOD has a statutory requirement to notify Congress "before commencing a public-private competition" of the function to be competed, the location of the proposed competition, the number of civilian employees potentially affected, and the anticipated length of the competition. 10 U.S.C. § 2461(b).

of termination. Circular A-76 (Revised), Attachment B, ¶ E.6.

IV. CIVILIAN PERSONNEL ISSUES.

A. Employee Consultation. By statute, the DOD must consult with affected employees. In the case of affected employees represented by a union, consultation with union representatives satisfies this requirement. 10 U.S.C. § 2467(b).

B. Right of First Refusal of Employment.

1. The CO must include the Right of First Refusal of Employment clause in the solicitation. See Circular A-76 (Revised), Attachment B, ¶ D.6.f.1.b; Revised Supplemental Handbook, Part I, Chapter 3, ¶ G.4; and FAR 7.305.

2. The clause, at FAR 52.207-3, requires:

a. The contractor to give the government employees, who have been or will be adversely affected or separated due to the resulting contract award, the right of first refusal for employment openings under the contract in positions for which they are qualified, if that employment is consistent with post-government employment conflict of interest standards.

b. Within 10 days after contract award, the contracting officer must provide the contractor a list of government employees who have been or will be adversely affected or separated as a result of contract award.

c. Within 120 days after contract performance begins, the contractor must report to the contracting officer the names of displaced employees who are hired within 90 days after contract performance begins.

C. Right of First Refusal and the Financial Conflict of Interest Laws.

Competitive Sourcing

1. Employees will participate in preparing the PWS and the MEO. Certain conflict of interest statutes may impact their participation, as well as when and if they may exercise their Right of First Refusal.

2. Procurement Integrity Act, 41 U.S.C. § 2102; FAR 3.104.

   a. Disclosing or Obtaining Procurement Information (41 U.S.C. § 2102(a)-(b)). These provisions apply to all federal employees, regardless of their role during a Circular A-76 competition.

   b. Reporting Employment Contacts (41 U.S.C. § 2103).

      (1) FAR 3.104-1(iv) generally excludes from the scope of "personally and substantially" the following employee duties during an OMB Cir. A-76 study:

         (a) Management studies;

         (b) Preparation of in-house cost-estimates;

         (c) Preparation of the MEO; or

         (d) Furnishing data or technical support others use to develop performance standards, statements of work, or specifications.

      (2) PWS role. Consider the employee's role. If strictly limited to furnishing data or technical support to others developing the PWS, then they are not "personally and substantially" participating. See FAR 3.104-1(iv). If the PWS role exceeds that of data and technical support, then the restriction would apply.

   c. Post-Employment Restrictions (41 U.S.C. § 2104). Bans certain employees for one year from accepting compensation.

      (1) Applies to contracts exceeding $10 million, and

         (a) Employees in any of these positions:

            (i) Procuring contracting officer;

            (ii) Administrative Contracting Officer;

            (iii) Source Selection Authority;

            (iv) Source Selection Evaluation Board member;

            (v) Chief of Financial or Technical team;

            (vi) Program Manager; or

            (vii) Deputy Program Manager.

         (b) Employees making these decisions:

            (i) Award contract or subcontract exceeding $10 million;

            (ii) Award modification of contract or subcontract exceeding $10 million;

            (iii) Award task or delivery order exceeding $10 million;

            (iv) Establish overhead rates on contract exceeding $10 million;

            (v) Approve contract payments exceeding $10 million; or

            (vi) Pay or settle a contract claim exceeding $10 million.

      (2) No exception exists to the one-year ban for offers of employment pursuant to the

Right of First Refusal. Thus, employees performing any of the listed duties or making the listed decisions on a cost comparison resulting in a contract exceeding $10 million are barred for one year after performing such duties from accepting compensation/employment opportunities from the contractor via the Right of First Refusal.

3. Financial Conflicts of Interest, 18 U.S.C. § 208. Prohibits officers and civilian employees from participating personally and substantially in a "particular matter" affecting the officer's or employee's personal or imputed financial interests.

    a. Cost comparisons conducted under OMB Cir. A-76 are "particular matters" under 18 U.S.C. § 208.

    b. Whether 18 U.S.C. § 208 applies to officers and civilian employees preparing a PWS or MEO depends on whether the participation will have a "direct and predictable" effect on their financial interests. This determination is very fact-specific.

4. Representational Ban, 18 U.S.C. § 207. Prohibits individuals who personally and substantially participated in, or were responsible for, a particular matter involving specific parties while employed by the government from switching sides and representing any party back to the government on the same matter. The restrictions in 18 U.S.C. § 207 do not prohibit employment; they only prohibit communications and appearances with the "intent to influence."

    a. The ban may be lifetime, for two years, or for one year, depending on the employee's involvement in the matter.

    b. Whether 18 U.S.C. § 207 applies to employees preparing a PWS or

MEO depends on whether the cost comparison has progressed to the point where it involves "specific parties."

    c. Even if 18 U.S.C. § 207 does apply to these employees, it would not operate as a bar to the Right of First Refusal. The statute only prohibits representational activity; it does not bar behind-the-scenes advice.

V. HOUSING PRIVATIZATION.

A. **General.** Housing privatization is a DOD initiative to replace a small inventory of government owned and maintained housing on military bases with a larger, commercially run inventory of rental properties, which military personnel were free to choose in competition with the private sector. Housing privatization addressed an ongoing problem that DOD was unable to build or rehabilitate sufficient housing for its personnel. It turned to the private sector to finance and rehabilitate existing housing, construct new housing, and operate and maintain the resulting inventory.

B. Privatization is different from contracting out in that ownership of the existing inventory of family housing is transferred to the private entity, not just the work force maintaining the housing. The private entity runs the housing operations, finances and constructs additional housing, and rents the housing to military personnel. This program has dramatically increased the quantity and quality of housing available at military installations where implemented.

C. **Authority.** 10 U.S.C. §§ 2871-2885 provides permanent authority for military housing privatization.[19]

1. This authority applies to family housing units on or near military installations

_____

[19] Originally granted in 1996 as "temporary" legislation, this authority was made permanent by the FY 2005 National Defense Authorization Act. Pub. L. No. 108-375, § 2805, 115 Stat. 1012 (2005).

within the United States and military unaccompanied housing units on or near installations within the United States.

2. Service Secretaries may use any authority or combination of authorities to provide for acquisition or construction by private persons. Authorities include:

   a. Direct loans and loan guarantees to private entities.

   b. Build/lease authority.

   c. Equity and creditor investments in private entities undertaking projects for the acquisition or construction of housing units (up to a specified percentage of capital cost). Such investments require a collateral agreement to ensure that a suitable preference will be given to military members.

   d. Rental guarantees.

   e. Differential lease payments.

   f. Conveyance or lease of existing properties and facilities to private entities.

3. Establishment of Department of Defense housing funds.

   a. The Department of Defense Family Housing Improvement Fund.

   b. The Department of Defense Military Unaccompanied Housing Improvement Fund.

D. Implementation.

1. The service conveys ownership of existing housing units and leases the land upon which the units reside for up to 50 years.

2. The consideration received for the sale is the contractual agreement to renovate, manage, and maintain existing family housing units, as well as construct, manage, and maintain new units.

3. The contractual agreement may include provisions regarding:

   a. The amount of rent the contractor may charge military occupants (rent control).

   b. The manner in which soldiers will make payment (allotment).

   c. Rental deposits.

   d. Loan guarantees to the contractor in the event of a base closure or realignment.

   e. Whether soldiers are required to live there.

   f. The circumstances under which the contractor may lease units to nonmilitary occupants.

E. Issues and Concerns.[20]

1. Making the transition positive for occupants, including keeping residents informed during the process.

2. Loss of control over family housing.

3. The effect of long-term agreements.

   a. Future of installation as a potential candidate for housing privatization.

      (1) DOD must determine if base is a candidate for closure.

      (2) If not, then DOD must predict its future mission, military population, future housing availability and prices in the local community, and housing needs.

   b. Potential for poor performance or nonperformance by contractors.

---

[20] *See* Government Accountability Office, Military Housing: Management Improvements Needed as Privatization Pace Quickens, Report No. GAO-02-624 (June 2002); Government Accountability Office, Military Housing: Continued Concerns in Implementing the Privatization Initiative, NSIAD-00-71 (March 30, 2000); Government Accountability Office, Military Housing: Privatization Off to a Slow Start and Continued Management Attention Needed, Report No. GAO/NSIAD-98-178 (July 17, 1998).

(1)   Concerns about whether contractors will perform repairs, maintenance, and improvements in accordance with agreements. Despite safeguards in agreements, enforcing the agreements might be difficult, time-consuming, and costly.

(2)   Potential for a decline in the value of property toward the end of the lease might equal decline in service and thus quality of life for military member.

4.   Effect on federal employees.

a.   The privatization of housing will result in the elimination of those government employee positions that support family housing.

b.   Privatization is not subject to Circular A-76.

5.   Prospect of civilians living on base.

a.   Civilians allowed to rent units not rented by military families.

b.   This prospect raises some issues, such as security concerns and law enforcement roles.

VI. UTILITIES PRIVATIZATION.

A.   **Background**. Military installations have had a wide range of arrangements with local utilities for the provision of electricity, gas, sewer, and water to the installation. These range from total government ownership to complete ownership and operation by local utilities. Turning over utility services to local providers has been seen as a potential source of significant savings.

B.   **Authority.** 10 U.S.C. § 2688 (originally enacted as part of the FY 1998 National Defense Authorization Act) permits the service secretaries to convey all or part of a utility system to a municipal, private, regional, district, or cooperative utility company. This permanent legislation supplements several specific land conveyances involving utilities authorized in previous National Defense Authorization Acts.

C.   **Implementation.**

1.   In 1998, DOD set a goal of privatizing all utility systems (water, wastewater, electric, and natural gas) by 30 September 2003, except those needed for unique mission/security reasons or when privatization is uneconomical. Memorandum, Deputy Secretary of Defense, to Secretaries of the Military Departments, et al., subject: Defense Reform Initiative Directive (DRID) #49—Privatizing Utility Systems (23 Dec. 1998).

2.   In October 2002, DOD revised its goal and replaced DRID #49 with updated guidance. Memorandum, Deputy Secretary of Defense, to Secretaries of the Military Departments, et al., subject: Revised Guidance for the Utilities Privatization Program (9 Oct. 2002) [hereinafter Revised Guidance Memo]. The Revised Guidance Memo establishes 30 September 2005 as the date by which "Defense Components shall complete a privatization evaluation of each system at every Active, Reserve, and National Guard installation, within the United States and overseas, that is not designated for closure under a base closure law." In addition to revising the milestones for utilities privatization, the Revised Guidance Memo addresses:

a.   updated guidance concerning the issuance of solicitations and the source selection considerations in utilities privatization;

b.   DOD's position concerning the applicability of state utility laws and regulations to the acquisition and conveyance of the government's utility systems;

c.   new instruction on conducting the economic analysis, including a class deviation from the cost principle at FAR 31.205-20 authorized by DOD for "utilities privatization contracts under which previously government-owned utility systems are <u>conveyed</u> by a Military Department or Defense Agency to a contractor"; and

    d.   the authority granted the Service Secretaries to include "reversionary clauses" in transaction documents to provide for ownership to revert to the government in the event of default or abandonment by the contractor.

3.   Requests for exemption from utility systems privatization, based on unique mission or safety reasons or where privatization is determined to be uneconomical, must be approved by the Service Secretary.

4.   Agencies must use competitive procedures to sell (privatize) utility systems and to contract for receipt of utility services. 10 U.S.C. § 2688(b). DOD may enter into 50-year contracts for utility service when conveyance of the utility system is included. 10 U.S.C. § 2688(c)(3).

5.   Any consideration received for the conveyance of the utility system may be accepted as a lump-sum payment, or a reduction in charges for future utility services. If the consideration is taken as a lump sum, then payment shall be credited at the election of the Secretary concerned for utility services, energy savings projects, or utility system improvements. If the consideration is taken as a credit against future utility services, then the time period for reduction in charges for services shall not be longer than the base contract period. 10 U.S.C. § 2688(c).

6.   Installations may, with Secretary approval, transfer land with a utility system privatization. 10 U.S.C. § 2688(i)(2); U.S. Dep't of Army, Privatization of Army Utility Systems—Update 1 Brochure (March 2000). In some instances (environmental reasons)

installations may want to transfer the land under wastewater treatment plants.

7.   Installations must notify Congress of any utility system privatization. The notice must include an analysis demonstrating that the long-term economic benefit of privatization exceeds the long-term economic cost, and that the conveyance will reduce the long-term costs to the DOD concerned for utility services provided by the subject utility system. The installation must also wait 21 days after providing such congressional notice. 10 U.S.C. § 2688(e).

D.   Issues and Concerns.

1.   Effect of State Law and Regulation. State utility laws and regulations, the application of which would result in sole-source contracting with the company holding the local utility franchise at each installation, do not apply in federal utility privatization cases. <u>See</u> <u>Virginia Electric and Power Company; Baltimore Gas & Electric</u>, B-285209, B-285209.2 (Aug. 2, 2000), 2000 U.S. Comp. Gen. LEXIS 125 (holding 10 U.S.C. § 2688 does not contain an express and unequivocal waiver of federal sovereign immunity); <u>see also</u> <u>Baltimore Gas & Electric v. United States</u>, US District Court, District of Maryland, No AMD 00-2599 Mar. 12, 2001 (following the earlier GAO decision and finding no requirement for the Army to use sole-source procedures for the conveyance of utilities distribution systems and procurement of utilities distribution services). The DOD General Counsel has issued an opinion that reached the same conclusion. <u>Dep't of Def. General Counsel</u>, The Role of State Laws and Regulations in Utility Privatization (Feb. 24, 2000).

2.   Utility Bundling. An agency may employ restrictive provisions or conditions only to the extent necessary to satisfy the agency's needs. Bundled utility contracts, which not only achieve significant cost savings, but also ensure the actual privatization of all utility systems, are

proper. <u>Virginia Electric and Power Company; Baltimore Gas & Electric</u>, B-285209, B-285209.2 (Aug. 2, 2000), 2000 U.S. Comp. Gen. LEXIS 125.

3.   Reversionary Clauses. The contractual agreement must protect the government's interests in the event of a default termination. The use of reversionary clauses, which revoke the conveyance of the utility system, are an option. Revised Guidance Memo, <u>supra</u>.

VII. CONCLUSION.

For nearly 50 years, the Department of Defense has pursued contracting out and privatization to obtain significant cost savings and improved levels of service in the operation and maintenance of military facilities. Given the sums involved, the impact on the existing government work force and potential impact on agency missions, these activities have significant statutory and regulatory procedures. The result of this 50-year effort has been a significant shift to private-sector performance of services within DOD, and progressively few opportunities. At present, this process has paused, while policy makers consider whether additional opportunities for savings are available, desirable, and achievable in the current environment.

Privatization

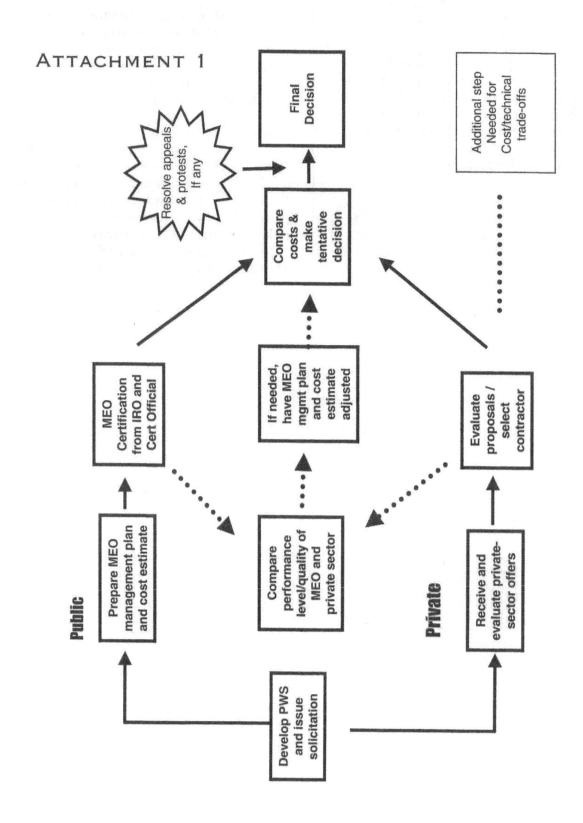

Process under "Old" Circular A-76 (1999 version)

ATTACHMENT 2

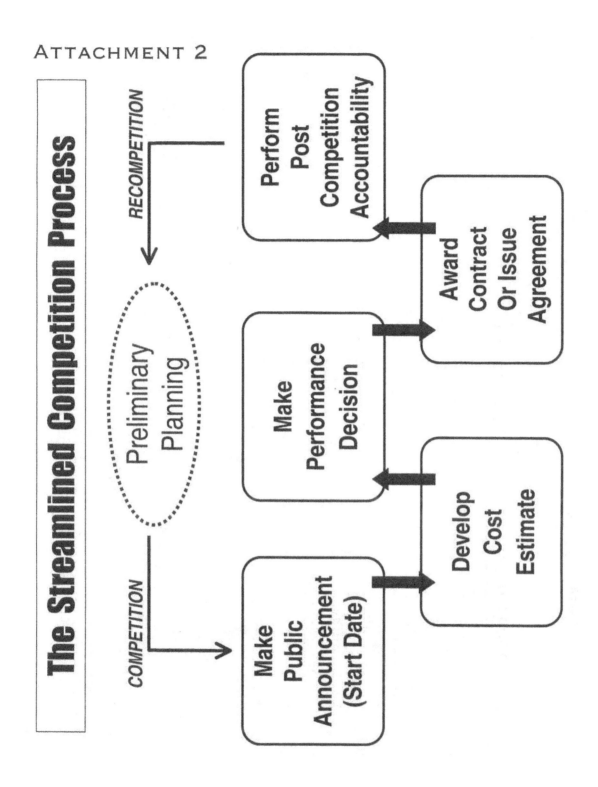

The Streamlined Competition Process

RECOMPETITION

Perform Post Competition Accountability

Preliminary Planning

COMPETITION

Make Public Announcement (Start Date)

Develop Cost Estimate

Make Performance Decision

Award Contract Or Issue Agreement

Process under "New" Circular A-76 (2003 version)

ATTACHMENT 3

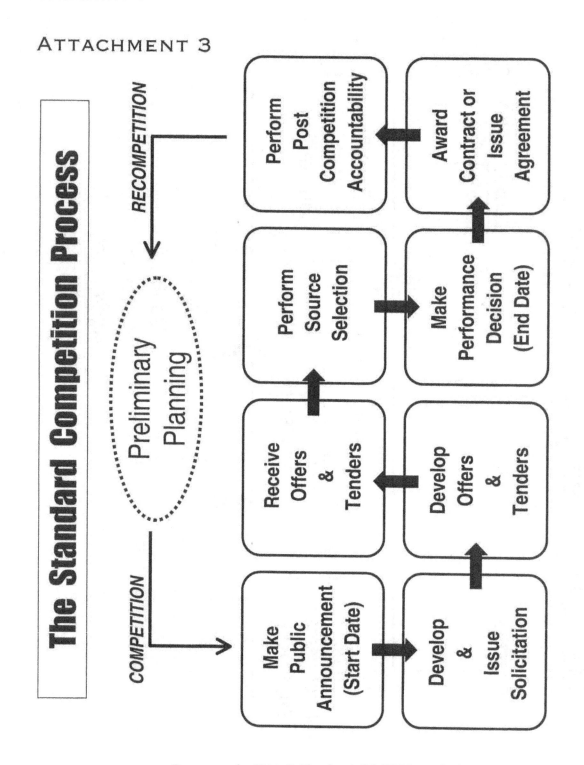

The Standard Competition Process

Process under "New" Circular A-76 (2003 version)

COMMERCIAL ITEM ACQUISITIONS

I. INTRODUCTION. Commercial item acquisitions reflect several competing policy goals. One of these goals is to encourage commercial companies to sell their products to the government because commercial products are usually cheaper to acquire and maintain. A second goal is to reduce the time it takes to acquire commercial items. The procedures for commercial item acquisitions attempt to achieve those objectives by minimizing the procedural hurdles and eliminating or modifying terms and conditions. This conflicts directly with the myriad of government policies that have resulted in the many FAR and DFARS standard terms and conditions, including labor standards, socio-economic policies, domestic preferences, audit, information disclosure, intellectual property, etc. Each of these policies has a stakeholder that is concerned when their clause is removed from a contract. Lastly, some stakeholders are concerned that traditional government contractors use commercial item acquisitions as a mechanism to avoid those policies when the government does not receive the benefits of buying a product that is widely sold in the broad commercial marketplace.

Contractors often sell their products and services in the commercial marketplace at profit levels that exceed the norms the government expects to pay. Where commercial sales are significant, a contractor may be unwilling to risk commercial profit levels for relatively modest government sales. Consequently, protecting commercial profit levels is a key determinant in entering the government market. Equally important, compliantly selling to the government requires contractors to adopt internal policies and procedures that purely commercial companies are free to ignore. The costs of compliance and the risks of non-compliance are significant. The smaller the compliance burden, the more likely a company is to enter the government marketplace.

The current procedures represent compromises to reconcile these conflicting policies and goals.

II. REFERENCES.

A. Federal Acquisition Streamlining Act of 1994, Pub. L. No. 103-355, 108 Stat. 3243 (1994) [hereinafter FASA].

B. Federal Acquisition Reform (Clinger-Cohen) Act of 1996, Pub. L. No. 104-106, §§ 4001-4402, 110 Stat. 186,642-79 (1996) [hereinafter FARA].

C. FAR Parts 8 and 12.

D. Assistant Secretary of Defense (Command, Control, Communications & Intelligence) and Under Secretary of Defense (Acquisition, Technology & Logistics), COMMERCIAL ITEM ACQUISITIONS: CONSIDERATIONS AND LESSONS LEARNED (June 26, 2000).

E. DOD's Commercial Item Handbook, www.acq.osd.mil/ar/docs/commitemhndbk-031601.doc.; and www.acq.osd.mil/dpap/cpic/draftcihandbook08012011.docx.

III. POLICY.

A. **Title VIII of the Federal Acquisition Streamlining Act of 1994** (Public Law 103-355) states a preference for government acquisition of commercial items. The purchase of proven products such as commercial and non-developmental items can eliminate the need for research and development, minimize acquisition lead time, and reduce the need for detailed design specifications or expensive product testing. S. Rep. No. 103-258, at 5 (1994), reprinted in 1994 U.S.C.C.A.N. 2561, 2566.

B. **FAR Part 12** implements the statutory preference for purchase of commercial items by prescribing policies and

Commercial Items

procedures unique to the acquisition of commercial items.

C. Identifying Suitable Commercial Items.

The key to acquiring commercial items is the government's requirements. For example, when acquiring food staples, fuel, office supplies, and other commodities, the government's needs are identical to those of a consumer or commercial company: that the commercial item will satisfy the requirement. For other products, such as military weapons systems, there is no consumer/commercial equivalent; or the government has unique safety, reliability, and performance requirements. Between the extremes, there are products that, with modifications, are capable of satisfying the requirement.

In the commercial marketplace, vendors market their products to potential customers. Agencies shall conduct market research to determine whether commercial items or non-developmental items are available that can meet the agency's requirements. FAR 12.101(a). Often, market research consists of gathering this widely available commercial marketing material, and reviewing the materials and evaluating the products to see whether they can satisfy realistic agency requirements.

D. Commercial Item Acquisition Procedures.

1. The government may use the procedures in FAR Parts 12 through 15, where appropriate, to acquire commercial items. FAR 12.102(b).

2. Regardless of the procedures used, however, the government must acquire commercial items using Fixed-Price-type contracts. This policy is intended to mirror the commercial practice of using Fixed-Price-type contracts. FAR 12.207(a) requires agencies to use firm-fixed-price (FFP) contracts or fixed-price contracts with economic price adjustments (FP/EPA). Award fees and performance or delivery incentives in FFP and FP/EPA contracts are permitted if the fee is based

solely on factors other than cost. FAR 12.207(d).

3. The government may use a time and materials (T&M) contract to acquire commercial services under limited circumstances. FAR 12.207(b). In summary, T&M-type contracts are permitted when the award is competitive and the contracting officer prepares a written justification (D&F) that the use of a T&M type is in the best interest of the government. FAR 12.207(b)(1). Within the Department of Defense, the use of T&C contracts is further restricted. DFARS 212.207(b).

IV. WHAT IS A COMMERCIAL

ITEM?The term "Commercial Item" has a specific definition in government contracting that has a statutory basis. 41 U.S.C. § 103; FAR Part 2.101. The definition has evolved over the past two decades as the government has gained experience in acquiring commercial items and identified unintended consequences of the original statutory definition. Even today, however, the definition of a "Commercial Item" allows for the exercise of considerable discretion by the contracting officer.

A. Commercial Item. FAR 2.101.

1. Any item, other than real property, that is of a type customarily used for non-governmental purposes and that:

    a. Has been sold, leased, or licensed to the general public; or

    b. Has been offered for sale, lease, or license to the general public. Matter of Coherent, Inc., B-270998, May 7, 1996, 96-1 CPD ¶ 214 (actual sale or license to general public not required for commercial item classification; determination of commercial item status is discretionary agency decision).

This definition is quite broad in several respects. First, the item must be customarily used for non-governmental purposes, but the item need not be exclusively or primarily used for governmental purposes. Second, the item must be "of a type" that is customarily used for non-governmental purposes. The item itself need not be used for non-governmental purposes if other items of the same type are. Third, the item acquired need not be sold in the commercial sector, it only needs to be offered for sale to the general public.

Clearly a nuclear weapon is not a commercial item. Other major weapons systems may be treated as a commercial item under limited circumstances. See DFARS 212.270 and 234.70. However, many items predominantly used for government purposes are also customarily used for non-government purposes. For example, many "MIL-SPEC" components are routinely used in industrial and commercial applications where greater reliability is desired. Where such customary non-government uses exist, an item may be determined commercial. Contractors should be prepared to document such customary non-governmental uses.

Second, the specific product need not be sold or offered for sale to the public if it is of a type sold or offered for sale. An item can be "of a type" without being identical. This affords the contracting officer a great deal of discretion. Contractors should be prepared to document the type of item being acquired.

Commercial sales and offers for sale are not restricted to substantial sales. Any quantity of sales, including an offer for sale to the general public, is sufficient.

2. Product Updates. A commercial item also includes any item that evolved from an item described in paragraph (a) of this definition through advances in technology or performance and is not yet available in the commercial marketplace, but will be available in time to satisfy the delivery requirements specified in the government solicitation. This definition allows the government to acquire updated products prior to the contractor offering the updated product for commercial sales.

3. Any item that would satisfy a criterion expressed in paragraphs IV.A.1 or 2 of this definition but for:

- Modifications of a type customarily available in the commercial marketplace. See Crescent Helicopters, B-284706 et al., May 30, 2000, 2000 CPD ¶ 90 (helicopter wildfire suppression was "commercial").

- Minor modifications of a type not customarily available in the commercial marketplace made to meet federal government requirements.

Items with commercially available modifications are commercial items. Therefore, if the commercial market provides a wide range of modifications, then commercial items will be similarly broad.

Government unique modifications are acceptable if "minor." "Minor" modifications do not significantly alter the non-governmental function or essential physical characteristics of an item or component, or change the purpose of a process. Matter of Canberra Indus., Inc., B-271016, June 5, 1996, 96-1 CPD ¶ 269 (combining commercial hardware with commercial software in new configuration, never before offered, did not alter "non-governmental function or essential physical characteristics"). Among the factors to be considered in determining whether a modification is minor include the value and size of the modification, and the comparative value and size of the final product. There are no firm boundaries. Thus, a commercial aircraft (including modifications) may be a commercial item if the government unique modifications are determined to be minor.

4. Commercial items include a non-developmental item[1], if the agency

---

[1] Defined in FAR 2.101 as (1) [a]ny previously developed item of supply used exclusively for governmental purposes by a Federal agency, a State or local government, or a foreign government with which the United States has a mutual defense cooperation agreement; (2) any item described in paragraph (1) of this definition that requires only minor modification or modifications of a type customarily available in the commercial marketplace in order to meet the requirements of the procuring department or agency; or (3) any item of supply

determines it was developed exclusively at private expense and sold in substantial quantities, on a competitive basis, to multiple state and local governments. An item that does not exist, or that requires major redesign, is not a non-developmental item. Trimble Navigation, Ltd., B-271882, August 26, 1996, 96-2 CPD ¶ 102 (award improper where awardee offered a GPS receiver that required major design and development work to meet a material requirement of the solicitation that the receiver be an NDI).

5.   Commercial items also include any combination of items meeting the requirements of paragraphs IV.A.1-4 that are of a type customarily combined and sold in combination to the general public. Therefore, a computer that is a commercial item with installed software with minor modifications to meet government requirements could be considered a commercial item, even if the combined products are not offered for sale commercially.

B.   Commercial Services (defined as commercial items).

Commercial items are not limited to tangible products; they include services meeting one of three tests.

1.   Installation services, maintenance services, repair services, training services, and other services for commercial items, if the contractor provides similar services contemporaneously to the general public under terms and conditions similar to those offered to the federal government. For example, the federal government can acquire maintenance for its copiers as a commercial item under the same or similar terms as a commercial customer could purchase the service. FAR 2.101.

2.   Services of a type offered and sold competitively in substantial quantities in the commercial marketplace based on established catalog or market prices for

being produced that does not meet the requirements of . . . (1) or (2) solely because the item is not yet in use.

specific tasks performed under standard commercial terms and conditions. This does not include services that are sold based on hourly rates without an established catalog or market price for a specific service performed. See Envirocare of Utah, Inc. v. United States, 44 Fed. Cl. 474 (1999) (holding there was no market price for radioactive waste disposal services). For example, the government could acquire transportation services as a commercial item based on the rates established in the transportation market.

3.   The scope of commercial services is not nearly as expansive as the definition for commercial items. Many services the government acquires are not sold to the general public, in either substantial quantities or at all. Therefore, contracting officers have difficulty in employing commercial item procedures when acquiring many services.

4.   Construction may be considered a service; however, a construction contract typically involves different types of standard clauses allocating risk between the government and the contractor. For that reason, the Administrator of the Office of Federal Procurement Policy issued a July 3, 2003 memorandum indicating that commercial item acquisition policies in FAR Part 12 "should rarely, if ever, be used for new construction acquisitions or non-routine alteration and repair services." Instead, agencies are encouraged to use the procedures are FAR Part 36. The memorandum is available at https://www.whitehouse.gov/sites/default/files/omb/assets/omb/procurement/far/far_part12.pdf

C.   Commercially Available Off-the-Shelf Item.

1.   What is a Commercially Available Off-the-Shelf Item (COTS)? COTS items are defined in FAR 2.101 as:

•   Commercial Items,

- Sold in substantial quantities in the commercial marketplace, and
- Offered to the government, without modification, in the same form in which it is sold in the commercial marketplace.

Thus, COTS items are not new, and not modified. COTS items exist and have substantial sales. See Chant Engineering Co., Inc., B-281521, Feb. 22, 1999, 99-1 CPD ¶ 45 ([n]ew equipment like Chant's proposed test station, which may only become commercially available as a result of the instant procurement, clearly does not satisfy the RFP requirement for commercial-off-the-shelf (existing) equipment.").

2. COTS items are a subset of commercial items. COTS items are exempt from more mandatory clauses than commercial items, specifically the Buy America Act clauses (FAR 52.225-1, 2, 9, and 11) and the Trafficking in Persons clauses (FAR 52.222-50 and 56).

D. Exercising Discretion.

1. As discussed in paragraph IV.A. above, a contracting officer has considerable discretion to determine whether a specific item is commercial as defined in the FAR. To guide that discretion, a draft checklist is attached.

2. In the exercise of business judgment, the contracting officer should consider whether the particular item provides the government with the benefits of a commercial item. For example, are there competitive items allowing competition? Are there sufficient sales of the same or similar items to the general public so as to support price reasonableness? Is there sufficient commercial demand such that the government is likely to benefit from continuing product availability? Where sales to the public are few, and there are no comparable products, the government may not benefit from buying an item using commercial procedures.

V. GSA SCHEDULES.

Commercial items are sourced, in the end, from their manufacturer, a regular dealer, or another distribution chain. Agencies, however, do not always have to contract directly with the source. Some preferred sources (Unicor and AbilityOne) are discussed in Chapter 13. Also, agencies may have the opportunity to acquire commercial items through the General Services Administration using Federal Supply Schedules and Multiple Award Schedules, collectively known as GSA Schedules.[2]

A. Background.

1. The General Services Administration ("GSA") offers the GSA Schedule program pursuant to 41 U.S.C. § 152(3) and FAR Subpart 38.1. The GSA Schedules program provides federal agencies with a simplified process for obtaining commonly used commercial supplies and services at prices associated with volume buying. The GSA Schedules program provides over four million commercial off-the-shelf products and services, at stated prices, for given periods of time.

2. The GSA Schedules program can qualify as a full and open competition procedure if:

- participation in the program has been open to all responsible sources, and
- orders and contracts placed under the program will result in the lowest overall cost alternative to the United States. 41 U.S.C. § 152(3); 10 U.S.C. § 2302(2)(C). See Reep, Inc., B-290665, Sep. 17, 2002, 2002 CPD ¶ 158 (to satisfy the statutory obligation of competitive acquisitions . . . "an agency is required to consider reasonably available information . . . typically by reviewing the prices of at

---

[2] GSA Schedules are referred to as Federal Supply Schedules and/or Multiple Award Schedules in acquisition regulations and were separate programs in the past. GSA currently operates GSA Schedules for agencies as a single program.

least three schedule vendors." The agency failed to meets its obligation by not awarding to a vendor providing the best value to the government at the lowest overall cost.).

Therefore, when an agency properly follows applicable regulations, it need not seek further competition or synopsize the requirement. FAR 8.404(a). But see Draeger Safety, Inc., B-285366, B-285366.2, Aug. 23, 2000, 2000 CPD ¶ 139 (though the government need not seek further competition when buying from the FSS, if it asks for competition among FSS vendors, it must give those vendors sufficient details about the solicitation to allow them to compete intelligently and fairly).

3. Pricing. While GSA believes the prices are fair and reasonable, agency contracting officers must continue to make their own determination of fair and reasonable pricing. FAR 8.404(d).

4. Small Business Set-Asides. Agencies can set aside GSA Schedule purchases for Small Businesses. Note that in accordance with FAR 19.502-1(b), a GSA Schedule award is exempt from the mandatory small business set-aside requirements.

B. Ordering Under GSA Schedules.[3]

1. Agencies place orders to obtain supplies or services from a GSA Schedule contractor. When placing the order, the agency must conclude that the order represents the best value and results in the lowest overall cost alternative (considering price, special features, administrative costs, etc.) to meet the government's needs. FAR 8.404(b)(2).

2. An agency must reasonably ensure that the selection meets its needs by considering reasonably available information about products offered under GSA Schedule contracts. Pyxis Corp., B-

282469, B-282469.2, July 15, 1999, 99-2 CPD ¶ 18.

3. If an agency places an order against an expired GSA Schedule contract, it may result in an improper sole-source award. DRS Precision Echo, Inc., B-284080; B-284080.2, Feb. 14, 2000, 2000 CPD ¶ 26.

4. If an agency places an order against a GSA Schedule contract, it may also add additional items, not on the Schedule GSA Schedule contract, under limited circumstances, for administrative convenience. See FAR 8.402(f). In ATA Defense Industries, Inc., 38 Fed. Cl. 489 (1997), the Court of Federal Claims ruled that "bundling" non-schedule products with schedule products violated the Competition in Contracting Act. The contract in question involved the upgrade of two target ranges at Fort Stewart, Georgia. The non-schedule items amounted to thirty-five percent of the contract value. Consequently, open order items must be clearly identified, and the contracting officer must comply with applicable competition regulations. Otherwise, all items or supplies ordered must be covered by the vendor's GSA Schedule contact (no "off the schedule buys"). Symplicity Corp., B-291902, Apr. 29, 2003, 2003 CPD ¶ 89; Omniplex World Servs. Corp., B-291105, Nov. 6, 2002, 2002 CPD ¶ 199.

5. Thresholds.

a. At or under the Micro-Purchase Threshold (currently $3500), agencies can place an order with any FSS contractor. FAR 8.405-1(b)(1).

b. Above the Micro Purchase Threshold, but below the Simplified Acquisition Threshold (currently $150,000 with exceptions), the agency should evaluate "at least three GSA Schedule contractors." FAR 8.405-1(c). Use the GSA Advantage! on-line shopping service to identify potential schedule contractors and review the catalogs/pricelists of at least three

---

[3] Unfortunately, many contracting officers do not follow GSA's established procedures when using the FSS. GOVERNMENT ACCOUNTABILITY OFFICE, GAO-01-125, NOT FOLLOWING PROCEDURES UNDERMINES BEST PRICING UNDER GSA'S SCHEDULE (Nov. 2000).

schedule contractors. Select the best-value or lowest-price vendor.

c. Acquisitions above the Simplified Acquisition Threshold. For over threshold acquisitions, the agency may issue a synopsis, an RFQ, and consider all responsive schedule contractors in compliance with FAR 8.405-1(d).

C. Decision to Use GSA Schedules.

1. An agency's decision to use a GSA Schedule contract or an open market purchase from commercial sources is a matter of business judgment that the GAO will not question unless there is a clear abuse of discretion. AMRAY, Inc., B-210490, Feb. 7, 1983, 83-1 CPD ¶ 135.

2. In exercising the business judgment, a contracting officer weighs the administrative cost savings from using a GSA Schedule against the likelihood of receiving a lower quoted price through the use of an RFQ process. An agency may consider administrative costs in deciding whether to proceed with a GSA Schedule order, even though it knows it can satisfy requirements at a lower cost through a competitive procurement. Precise Copier Services, B-232660, Jan. 10, 1989, 89-1 CPD ¶ 25. The GAO will review orders to ensure the choice of a vendor is reasonable. Commercial Drapery Contractors, Inc., B-271222, June 27, 1996, 96-1 CPD ¶ 290 (protest sustained where agency's initial failure to follow proper order procedures resulted in "need" to issue order to higher-priced vendor, on the basis it was now the only vendor that could meet delivery schedule).

3. A 2015 GAO Report, GAO-15-590, FEDERAL SUPPLY SCHEDULES: More Attention Needed to Competition and Prices, July 2015, studied actual practices using GSA Schedules. It discovered that agencies considered three or more sources in only about 40% of their purchases. GAO also expressed concerns about prices, including obtaining discounts for larger orders.

D. Contract Administration of Schedule Orders.

GSA awards and administers the contract (not the order). Problems with orders should be resolved directly with the contractor. Failing that, complaints concerning deficiencies can be lodged with GSA telephonically (1-800-488-3111) or electronically (through "GSA Advantage!").

Allowing the contractor to deliver material of lower cost and quality does not afford vendors fair and equal treatment. See Marvin J. Perry & Associates, B-277684, Nov. 4, 1997, 97-2 CPD ¶ 128 (protest sustained where contractor substituted ash wood rather than red oak in FSS furniture buy resulted in an unfair competition).

VI. COMMERCIAL ITEM ACQUISITION PROCEDURES. FAR SUBPART 12.2.

A. Streamlined Solicitation of Commercial Items. Commercial item acquisitions can benefit from expedited procedures whether using simplified acquisition, sealed bid, or negotiation procedures.

1. Publication. FAR 5.203(a). A contracting officer shortens the 15-day public notice period when purchasing commercial items. A contracting officer may issue a solicitation less than 15 days after publishing notice (FAR 5.203(a)(1)), or may combine the synopsis with the solicitation procedure. FAR 5.203(a)(2), FAR 12.603.

2. Combined Synopsis and Solicitations are common. They are suitable where the requirements are relatively simple, allowing the entire synopsis/solicitation to fit within the size constraints applicable to the notice procedure. Amendments to the solicitation are published in the same manner as the initial synopsis/solicitation. FAR 12.603(c)(4).

3. Response time. FAR 5.203(b). The contracting officer shall establish a solicitation response time that affords

potential offerors a <u>reasonable opportunity to respond</u> to commercial item acquisitions. <u>See</u> <u>American Artisan Productions, Inc.</u>, B-281409, Dec. 21, 1998, 98-2 CPD ¶ 155 (finding fifteen-day response period reasonable).

    a.   The contracting officer should consider the circumstances of the individual acquisition, such as its complexity, commerciality, availability, and urgency, when establishing the solicitation response time.

4.   Offers. FAR 12.205.

    a.   Contracting officers should allow offerors to propose more than one product that will meet the agency's needs.

    b.   If adequate, request only existing product literature from offerors in lieu of unique technical proposals.

B.   Streamlined Evaluation of Offers.

1.   FAR 52.212-2, Evaluation-Commercial Items. Paragraph (a) of the provision shall be tailored to the specific acquisition to describe the evaluation factors and relative importance of those factors. The sample factors of technical (capability of the item offered to meet the agency need), price and past performance are sufficient for most acquisitions.

C.   Award. Select the offer that is most advantageous to the government based on the factors contained in the synopsis/solicitation. Fully document the rationale for selection of the successful offeror, including discussion of any trade-offs considered. FAR 12.602(c); <u>Universal Building Maintenance, Inc.</u>, B-282456, July 15, 1999, 99-2 CPD § 32.

D.   Reverse Auctions. Reverse auctions are a commercial technique that uses the Internet to allow suppliers to compete in real time for contracts by lowering their prices until the lowest bidder prevails. Reverse auctions can further streamline

the already abbreviated simplified acquisition procedures. Award is based on technically acceptable, low price.

1.   Commercial item acquisitions lend themselves to reverse auctions because many commercial items are commodities that are acquired to a standard government or industry specification.

2.   GSA can facilitate reverse auctions through its online systems. <u>See</u> .

VII. CLAUSES FOR COMMERCIAL ITEM CONTRACTS.

A.   One of the major benefits of using FAR Part 12 procedures is the reduction in the mandatory clauses included in the contract. When first enacted over 20 years ago, the objective was to minimize the number of mandatory clauses. Over the years, the list of mandatory clauses has grown, as the executive and legislative branches have used government contracts as a mechanism to implement socio-economic policies.

B.   The first group of clauses included in commercial item contracts are those listed in FAR 52.212-4, Contract Terms and Conditions. These clauses are the terms relating to the actual acquisition, such as warranty, indemnity for infringement of intellectual property rights, etc. These terms were intended to be consistent with customary commercial practices. FAR 12.301(a)(2). FAR 52.212-4 tends to resemble commercial terms of purchase, not terms of sale. FAR 52.212-4 are negotiable in theory, but seldom in practice.

C.   The second group of clauses are FAR 52.212-5, Contract Terms and Conditions Required to Implement Statutes or Executive Orders-Commercial Items. This group of clauses incorporates by reference clauses required to implement provisions of law or executive orders applicable to commercial items. The contracting officer must determine whether many of the clauses are applicable and "check the box" to incorporate them into the contract. Generally, these clauses are not negotiable, unless the contracting officer has erred in selecting mandatory clauses.

D. Tailoring of Provisions and Clauses.

1. Contracting officers may, after conducting <u>appropriate market research</u>, tailor FAR 52.212-4 to adapt to the market conditions for a particular acquisition. FAR 12.302(a). <u>See</u> <u>Smelkinson Sysco Food Services</u>, B-281631, Mar. 15, 1999, 99-1 CPD ¶ 57 (protest sustained where agency failed to conduct market research before incorporating an "interorganizational transfers clause"). What is difficult to resolve is the common practice in industry of having different terms and conditions, depending on whether a party is a buyer or a seller. Often a commercial company will adopt very different risk allocation provisions.

2. Certain clauses of FAR 52.212-4 implement statutory requirements and shall not be tailored. FAR 12.302(b). These include:

   - Assignments.
   - Disputes.
   - Payment.
   - Invoice.
   - Other compliances.
   - Compliance with laws unique to government contracts.
   - Unauthorized obligations.

3. Contracting officers are prohibited from adding a term or condition that is inconsistent with customary commercial practice for the acquisition, unless they obtain a waiver under agency procedures. FAR 12.302(c). However, the contracting officer determines consistency with commercial practices in the first instance, and may tailor clauses in a manner consistent with commercial practices.

VIII. UNIQUE TERMS AND CONDITIONS FOR COMMERCIAL ITEMS.

A. Termination.

1. FAR Clause 52.212-4, Contract Terms and Conditions - Commercial Items permits government termination of a commercial items contract either for convenience of the government or for cause. <u>See</u> FAR 12.403(c)-(d).

2. This clause is much more simply worded than the equivalent non-commercial FAR clauses. Termination for convenience is very concise. Terminations for default do not specify the procedural formalities in the equivalent clauses.

3. Contracting officers may use FAR Part 49 as guidance to the extent Part 49 does not conflict with FAR Part 12 and the termination language in FAR 52.212-4.

B. Warranties. The government's post-award rights contained in 52.212-4 include the implied warranty of merchantability and the implied warranty of fitness. FAR 12.404. Such warranties are nearly universally disclaimed by sellers in commercial sales.

1. Merchantability. Provides that an item is reasonably fit for the ordinary purposes for which such items are used.

2. Fitness. Provides that an item is fit for use for the particular purpose for which the government will use the item. The seller must know the purpose for which the government will use the item, and the government must have relied upon the contractor's skill and judgment that the item would be appropriate for that purpose. Legal counsel must be consulted prior to the government asserting a claim of breach of this warranty.

3. Express warranties. Warranties are a standard commercial practice in many product sales. As a standard practice, the government should require offerors to offer at least the same warranty terms,

Commercial Items

including offers of extended warranties, offered to the general public. Where required, the government may specify minimum warranty terms.

IX. CONCLUSION.

Hardware, software and services that are sold competitively in the commercial marketplace offer the government many advantages: 1) it doesn't have to pay for development, 2) it may receive a lower cost due to a much larger commercial sales volume, 3) delivery schedules may be shorter due to current production, 4) the private sector offers logistics support, and 5) commercial items often offer state-of-the-art technology. These benefits accrue when the item is, in fact, "commercial."

The government does not always receive these benefits, however. It may require performance, modifications, or features not offered in versions sold commercially; the commercial product may be free of competitors and priced accordingly; and commercial markets may change, orphaning the product the government bought. Furthermore, since commercial item contracts were initially introduced, there has been a steady growth in the number of government-unique clauses, limiting the interest of commercial firms in serving government customers.

Where the government's legitimate needs can be met by a commercial item available from several competitors, the advantages to the government are real and significant. Agencies are well served by not allowing perceived problems to stop pursuing the real benefits of commercial items.

Draft DOD Commercial Item Handbook
Appendix B
Sample Commercial Item Checklist

Commercial Item Checklist
(Part 1: Items, Part 2: Services)

Item: _____

Part 1: Acquisition of Items

Can the government's requirements (which should be performance based) be satisfied by—

1. An item that is *of a type* customarily used by the general public or by nongovernmental entities for purposes other than government purposes and that has been sold, leased, or licensed to the general public or that has been offered for sale, lease, or license to the general public?

   A. If Yes, designate the item as commercial and annotate evidence of actual sale, lease, or license to the general public (or offer for the same), as appropriate:

   _____

   _____

   B. If No, proceed.

2. An item that has evolved from an item described in 1 above through advances in technology or performance and that is not yet available in the commercial marketplace but will be available in time to satisfy the government's delivery requirements?

   A. If Yes, designate the item as commercial and annotate evidence that the item will be available in time to satisfy the government's requirements.

   _____

   _____

   B. If No, proceed.

3. An item that would meet 1 or 2 above but requires modifications of a type customarily available in the commercial marketplace or minor modifications of a type not customarily available in the commercial marketplace, made to meet Federal Government requirements?

   A. If Yes, designate the item as commercial and annotate either evidence of the customary availability of modification in the commercial marketplace or the technical relationship between the modified item and the item that meets 1 or 2. (For the latter, attach drawings or comparison of the characteristics of the commercial item and the modified item, as appropriate).

   _____

   _____

   B. If No, proceed.

Commercial Items

4. Any combination of items meeting 1, 2, or 3 above that are of a type customarily combined and sold in combination to the general public?

    A. If Yes, designate the combination as commercial and annotate evidence of the customary combination being sold to the general public.

        _____

        _____

    B. If No, proceed.

5. Any item or combination of items that would meet 1, 2, 3, or 4 above and is transferred between or among separate divisions, subsidiaries, or affiliates of a contractor?

    A. If Yes, designate the item as commercial and annotate how the item would meet 1, 2, 3, or 4.

        _____

        _____

    B. If No, proceed.

6. A nondevelopmental item that the procuring agency determines was developed exclusively at private expense and sold in substantial quantities, on a competitive basis, to multiple State and local governments?

    A. If Yes, designate the nondevelopmental item as commercial and annotate evidence that it was 1) developed exclusively at private expense, and 2) sold competitively in substantial quantities to multiple state and local governments.

        _____

        _____

    B. If No, recommend that the agency's requirements be revised to permit commercial solutions. If they cannot, recommend that noncommercial acquisition be considered (include an appropriate notice in the synopsis).

Part 2: Acquisition of Services
Can the government's requirements be satisfied by—

    1. Installation services, maintenance services, repair services, training services, and other services?

    A. If Yes, proceed to 2 below.

    B. If No, proceed to 4 below.

    2. Services in 1 above in support of an item that has been, or could be, designated a commercial item in Part 1 above, regardless of whether such services are provided by the same source or at the same time as the item?

    A. If Yes, proceed to 3 below.

B. If No, proceed to 4 below.

3. Services in 2 above from a source that provides similar services contemporaneously to the general public and the government under similar terms and conditions, similar to those offered to the Federal Government?

A. If Yes, designate the services as commercial and annotate information concerning their source, as appropriate.

_____

_____

B. If No, proceed to 4 below.
4. Services of a type offered and sold competitively in substantial quantities in the commercial marketplace based on established catalog or market prices for specific tasks performed or specific outcomes to be achieved?

A. If Yes, proceed to 5 below.

B. If No, proceed to 6 below.

5. Services in 4 above that are offered under standard commercial terms and conditions?

A. If Yes, designate the services as commercial and annotate pricing information, as appropriate.

_____

_____

B. If No, proceed to 6 below.

6. Any combination of services that would meet 3 or 5 above, is transferred between or among separate divisions, subsidiaries, or affiliates of a contractor?

A. If Yes, designate the combination as commercial and annotate how the services would meet 3 or 5 above.

_____

_____

B. If No, recommend that the agency's requirements be revised to permit commercial solutions. If they cannot, recommend that noncommercial acquisition be considered (include an appropriate notice in the synopsis).

INTERAGENCY ACQUISITIONS

AND

REIMBURSABLE WORK

I.   INTRODUCTION.

Contracts are not the only way that a federal agency may acquire goods and services; they also may be able to make their acquisition through another federal agency. These interagency acquisitions can take many forms, including placing orders on another agency's existing ID/IQ type contract, and having the other agency act as the procuring agent. An agency can also request the other agency to perform the services or manufacture the supplies itself on a reimbursable basis.

There are many advantages to using interagency acquisitions, but the two major benefits are: (a) potential cost and schedule savings from combined purchases and avoiding a second, lengthy procurement; and (b) taking advantage of the other agency's technical expertise in the subject matter. There are some disadvantages, primarily: (a) the potential lessening of competition, and losing the benefits which flow from competitive procurements; and (b) omission of agency-specific statutory and regulatory requirements.

Unfortunately, some government agencies took advantage of interagency acquisitions, which resulted in Congress and DOD implementing additional controls on the use of such methods. In 2005, GAO identified interagency contracting as a high-risk area. GAO, High-Risk Series: An Update, GAO-05-207 (Washington, D.C.: January 2005).

In 2008, the Administrator, Office of Federal Procurement Policy, issued guidance to address the problems with interagency contracting, and this policy guidance has been incorporated into acquisition regulations implementing tighter controls.

II.   REFERENCES.

A.   Statutes.

1.   The Economy Act, 31 U.S.C. §§ 1535-1536.

2.   Project Orders, 41 U.S.C. § 6307.

B.   Regulations.

1.   FAR Subpart 17.5, 17.7.

2.   Department of Defense Financial Management Regulation (DOD FMR), DOD 7000.14-R (June 2011), Volume 11A, chapters 1-4. Available at: http://comptroller.defense.gov/FMR/fmrv olumes.aspx.

3.   Department of Defense Instruction (DODI) 4000.19, Support Agreements (April 25, 2013).

C.   Guidance.

1.   OMB Memorandum, Improving the Management and Use of Interagency Acquisitions, June 6, 2008.

2.   OMB Memorandum, Development, Review and Approval of Business Cases for Certain Interagency and Agency-Specific Acquisitions, Sept. 29, 2011.

Interagency Acquisitions

III. TYPES OF INTERAGENCY ACQUISITIONS.

A. General.

1. There are several types of Interagency Acquisitions, as further discussed below. In each such acquisition, there is a requesting or ordering agency that desires the goods or services acquired. The ordering agency's request is sent to the servicing agency.

2. Intra-agency acquisitions distinguished. from interagency acquisitions. Executive agencies are defined in FAR 2.101, which references 5 U.S.C. §§ 101-102, 104(1); and 31 U.S.C. § 9101. Within DOD, the services are each an agency, as is the Department of Defense. Where one Army organization uses another Army organization, the procurement is not an interagency acquisition.

3. Other reimbursable work. Interagency acquisitions do not include other reimbursable work pursuant to statutory authority. Reimbursable work includes Economy Act Orders, Project Orders, and similar actions where the employees of the servicing agency perform the work.

B. Direct Acquisitions.
In direct acquisitions, the ordering agency places an order under the servicing agencies contract, such as when a contracting officer places an order against a GSA Schedule contract.

C. Assisted Acquisitions.
In assisted acquisitions, the requesting agency agrees with the servicing agency that the servicing agency will perform acquisition activities, such as issuing a delivery order on an existing contract or awarding a new contract, to fulfill the requesting agencies' needs.

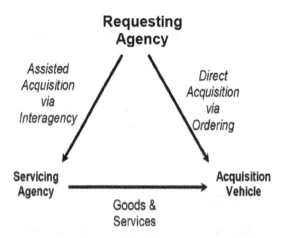

IV. PROCEDURES FOR INTERAGENCY ACQUISITIONS.

A. Determination of Best Procurement Approach.

For all direct acquisitions and assisted acquisitions subject to FAR Subpart 17.5,[1] the requesting agency must determine that an interagency acquisition is the best procurement approach. For assisted acquisitions, a contracting officer of the requesting agency must approve this determination, considering the requesting agency's schedule, performance, and delivery requirements; its cost-effectiveness (taking into account the reasonableness of the servicing agency's fees); and whether the acquisition will comply with fiscal, statutory, and regulatory requirements. FAR 17.502-1(a)(1). For direct acquisitions, the requesting agency's contracting officer must approve a determination that the other agency's contract vehicle is suitable for use, and the benefits such as administrative cost savings, lower prices, greater number of vendors, fees, and the requesting agency's expertise make placing orders the best procurement approach. FAR 17.502-1(a)(2). The requirement for a written approval

---

[1] FAR 17.500(c) excludes interagency reimbursable work (other than acquisition assistance), interagency activities where contracting is incidental to the purpose of the transaction, and orders of $550,000 or less issued against Federal Supply Schedules, from the application of FAR 17.5.

prevents circumvention of the local contracting office.

B.   Interagency Agreements.

1.   Assisted Acquisitions. Prior to the issuance of a solicitation under an assisted acquisition, the servicing and requesting agencies shall sign a written interagency agreement that establishes the general terms and conditions governing the relationship between the parties. The agreement should cover roles and responsibilities for acquisition planning, contract execution, and contract administration. It should also include any unique terms and conditions[2] of the requesting agency that must be incorporated into the order or contract awarded by the assisting agency. If there are no unique terms or conditions, the agreement should so state. A copy of the interagency agreement, prepared in accordance with current OFPP guidance, must be included in the files of both the servicing and requesting agencies. FAR 17.502-1(b).

2.   Direct Acquisitions. Since the requesting agency administers its own order under a direct acquisition, an interagency agreement is not required under the FAR. FAR 17.502-1(b)(2).

C.   Contract Vehicles.

1.   Interagency acquisitions are often implemented using indefinite delivery/indefinite quantity contracts, under FAR Subpart 16.5. The General Services Administration's Schedules (the Federal Supply Schedules), and similar government-wide acquisition contracts (or GWACs) and multi-agency contracts (or MACs), are the most frequently used types.

2.   Before soliciting a new multi-agency or government-wide acquisition contract, the buying activity must prepare a business-

case analysis and obtain approval in accordance with current Office of Federal Procurement Policy (OFPP) guidance. FAR 17.502-1(c).

V.   THE ECONOMY ACT (31 U.S.C. §§ 1535-1536).

A.   Purpose.

The Economy Act provides authority for federal agencies to order goods and services from other federal agencies, or with a major organizational unit within the same agency.

B.   Criteria for Use. See Dictaphone Corp., B-244691.2, 92-2 Comp. Gen. Proc. Dec. ¶ 380 (Nov. 25, 1992). See also DOD FMR, Vol. 11a, Chpt. 3, Para. 030104.A.

1.   Funds are available;

2.   The head of the ordering agency or unit decides the order is in the best interests of the government;

3.   The agency or unit filling the order can provide or get by contract the goods or services; and

4.   The head of the agency decides that the ordered goods or services cannot be provided as conveniently or cheaply by a commercial enterprise.

C.   Determinations and Findings (D&F) Requirements. FAR Subpart 17.502-2(c); DOD FMR, Vol. 11A, Chapt. 3, Para. 030302.

1.   Justifying Use of Economy Act. All Economy Act orders must be supported with a written determination and finding by the requesting agency as provided in FAR 17.502-2(c)(1).

2.   DOD-specific Determinations.

a.   Interservice Support. DOD activities shall render requested support to other DOD activities when the requesting activity head determines (1) it would be in the government's best interest and (2) the servicing activity head determines that capabilities exist to render support without jeopardizing assignment missions. DOD FMR, Vol. 11A, Chapt. 3, Para. 030203. If DOD agencies use a DD Form 1144 to document the request, then no further D&F is required.

b. Requesting Support from Non-DOD Agencies. DOD may obtain support from civilian agencies after preparing a detailed D&F and obtaining approval by an designated official of SES or flag officer levels. DOD FMR, Vol. 11A, Chapt. 3, Para. 030204.

3. D&F Approval Authority. FAR 17.502-2(c)(2). The D&F must be approved by a contracting officer of the requesting agency with the authority to contract for the supplies or services ordered (or by another official designated by the agency head). Additional approvals may be required when issuing an economy act order to a non-DOD agency (see below), or as required by service regulations.

D. Economy Act Orders Exceeding the Simplified Acquisition Threshold to Non-DOD Agencies.

1. One of the main problems with prior practices was that non-DOD agencies failed to include DOD-specific provisions in contracts when conducting an assisted acquisition under the Economy Act.

2. To address this concern, a DOD agency must make additional determinations and findings when issuing an Economy Act order to a non-DOD agency. See DFARS 217.770.

3. Additionally, the non-DOD servicing agency must certify to the requesting DOD agency that it will comply with applicable DOD-specific regulations. FAR 17.703(a).

E. Reimbursement of Costs.

1. Economy Act orders are funded either on a reimbursable basis or by a direct fund citation basis. The ordering agency must pay the actual costs of the goods or services provided by the servicing agency. 31 U.S.C. § 1535(b); DOD FMR, Vol. 11A, Chapt. 3, Para. 030501 and 030601.

VI. THE PROJECT ORDERS STATUTE (41 U.S.C. § 6307).

A. **Purpose.** A "project order" is a specific, definite and certain order issued under the authority of 41 U.S.C. § 6307 (DOD) or 14 U.S.C § 151 (Coast Guard) for the performance of work by the servicing organization.

B. **Government-Owned Facilities.**

1. DOD and the Coast Guard place project orders with government-owned establishments, such as shipyards, depots, arsenals, etc.

2. The facility must perform at least 51% of the work in-house, but may contract for incidental goods and services. DOD FMR, Vol. 11A, Chapt. 2, Para. 020515

3. Ordering agencies may use project orders for non-severable contracts. DOD FMR, Vol. 11A, Chapt. 2, Para. 020509. Non-severable projects obtain a single or unified outcome or product. Examples include the manufacture, overhaul, or modification of military equipment, construction or conversion of buildings and other structures, utility and communication systems, and development of software programs.

C. **Form of Agreement.**

1. Project orders are issued using a Military Interdepartmental Purchase Request (MIPR) or DD Form 448.

2. Project orders are place on a reimbursable basis, with the reimbursement being either a fixed amount or cost reimbursement.

VII. OTHER COMMON AUTHORITIES.

A. Government Employees Training Act (GETA). 5 U.S.C. § 4104.

1. Purpose. To permit agencies to provide training to employees of other federal agencies on a <u>reimbursable</u> basis.

2. The servicing agency is authorized to collect and to retain a fee to offset the costs associated with training the employees of other agencies, except when the agencies' appropriation provides for interagency training.

3. Federal agencies must provide for training, insofar as practicable, by, in, and through government facilities under the jurisdiction or control of the particular agency.

B. Federal Supply Schedules (FSS). 41 U.S.C. § 152(3). The Federal Property and Administrative Services Act of 1949; 40 U.S.C. § 501; FAR Subpart 8.4. <u>See</u> Chapter 12, Section V.

C. Federal Prison Industries, Inc. (FPI or UNICOR). 18 U.S.C. §§ 4121-4128; FAR Subpart 8.6.

1. Historically, federal departments and agencies were required to purchase products of FPI that met requirements and were available at market price or less, unless FPI granted a waiver for purchase of the supplies from another source. 10 U.S.C. § 2410n.

2. Current Policy. FPI is no longer considered a mandatory source. <u>See</u> <u>National Defense Authorization Act for FY2002</u>, Pub. L. No. 107-107; <u>Bob Stump National Defense Authorization Act for FY2003</u>, Pub. L. No. 107-314; Consolidated Appropriations Act of 2004, Pub. L. No. 108-199.

a. When acquiring an item for which FPI has a significant market share, DOD must use competitive procedures or fair opportunity procedures under the FAR to procure the product. DFARS 208.602-70.

b. If FPI does not have a significant market share, comply with procedures under FAR 8.602. Significant market share is defined as "FPI share of the Department of Defense market is greater than five percent." <u>See</u> <u>Appendix E</u>, Office of the Under Secretary of Defense (AT&L) Policy Memorandum, Subject: Competition Requirements for Purchases from Federal Prison Industries, dated 28 March 2008.

3. Before purchasing products from FPI, agencies must conduct market research to determine whether the FPI item is comparable to supplies available from the private sector in terms of price, quality, and time of delivery. This is a unilateral determination of the contracting officer that is not subject to review by FPI. FAR 8.602. If the FPI item is determined not to be comparable, then agencies should acquire the items using normal contracting (i.e., competitive) procedures, and no waiver from FPI is required. If the FPI item is comparable, then the agency must obtain a waiver to purchase the item from other sources. Exceptions include: (i) public exigency requires immediate delivery or performance; (ii) used or excess supplies are available; (iii) the supplies are acquired and used outside the United States; (iv) acquiring supplies totaling $2,500 or less; or (v) acquiring services.

VIII. CONCLUSION.

As a result of agency abuses, interagency acquisitions and orders are subject to many more procedural requirements than previously. Consequently, agency attorneys should carefully

Interagency Acquisitions

review proposed interagency acquisitions to promote compliance.

CONTRACT PRICING

I. INTRODUCTION.

A. Why Contract Pricing?

One aspect of government contracting that is quite different from commercial contracting is the government's use of analysis of a contractor's prices and historical costs to help negotiate the contract price. A consumer buying a car generally has no idea what it costs the automobile company to make the car and deliver it to the dealership. Nor does the consumer generally know the price for which the dealership sold identical or similar cars to previous buyers. Instead, the consumer relies on the competitive forces in the market to help the consumer pay a fair and reasonable price. If the price asked for a car seems high, the consumer can always go to one of several nearby dealerships offering the same or equivalent cars.

For many products and services the government acquires, there are no alternative sources, or only limited alternative sources. This lack of downward competitive pressure on prices has prompted the government to adopt alternative measures to ensure that it pays a fair and reasonable price. The alternative measures adopted when competition is absent are: 1) calculating the cost of the product or service and adding a reasonable profit; or 2) analyzing what commercial businesses operating in a competitive market pay for the product or service, and adjusting for differences unique to the government. The government requires the prospective contractor to disclose its cost data and its pricing offered to other customers, so the contracting officer can analyze if the price offered is fair and reasonable. This extraordinary right has no equivalent, except in regulated utility pricing.

Additionally, even when competition exists, the contracting officer must determine that the prices offered are fair and reasonable.

B. Scope.

This chapter covers the different types of contractor pricing information available for determining price reasonableness, and when the government can and should require their submission. This chapter focuses on the requirements of the Truth in Negotiations Act, what contractor actions constitute defective pricing, and what remedies are available to the government.

This chapter does not cover the methodologies for determining cost-based pricing, as those require a basic understanding of production engineering, accounting, and specific industry practices.

C. References.

1. Federal Acquisition Regulation 15.4, Contract Pricing.

2. DOD Contract Pricing Reference Guide, available from the Defense Acquisition University at its Acquisition Community Connection.

3. The Truth in Negotiations Act (TINA), 10 U.S.C. § 2306a and 41 U.S.C. § 3502.

4. DCAA Contract Audit Manual (DCAM), Chapter 9, available at: http://www.dcaa.mil/cam.html.

II. DETERMINING PRICE REASONABLENESS.

A. **Requirement.** Contracting officers are required to determine the contract price is fair and reasonable before making a contract award. FAR 15.402(a).

1. The FAR, however, does not define what is meant by a fair and reasonable price. The FAR does define "price" as: "cost plus any fee or profit applicable to the contract type."

2. The Defense Acquisition University suggests that a fair and reasonable price is "… the price that a prudent businessperson would pay for an item or service under competitive market conditions, given a reasonable knowledge of the marketplace." DAU Definition

3. The DOD Contract Pricing Reference Guides suggest that a fair and reasonable price is fair to the buyer, fair to the seller, and what a reasonable, competent, and knowledgeable buyer would be willing to pay. DOD Contract Pricing Reference Guides, Volume 1, Chapter 0 [sic], paragraph 1.2.1. The guides warn of the disadvantages of below-cost prices.

4. If a contracting officer cannot conclude that a price is fair and reasonable, the contracting officer is required to obtain more data. FAR 15.402(a)(3).

5. A contracting officer may not award a contract unless he or she can determine price reasonableness, or the Head of Contracting Activity (HCA) determines that it is in the best interest of the government to make the award to that offeror, based on consideration of the following: (i) the effort made to obtain the data, (ii) the need for the item or service, or (iii) increased cost or significant harm to the government if award is not made. FAR 15.403-3(a)(4).

B. How Contracting Officers Determine Price Reasonableness.

1. Where adequate price competition exists (see FAR 15.403-1(c)(1)), generally no additional data are necessary to determine the reasonableness of price. In unusual circumstances the contracting officer may resort to additional data from other sources to support price reasonableness.

2. In sealed bid procurements, generally adequate price competition exists. Where there is only one bidder, the contracting officer may use the price analysis techniques in FAR 15.404-1(b) as a guideline. FAR 14.408-2(a).

3. Where certified cost or pricing data is not required, but the contracting officer needs additional information to support price reasonableness not available elsewhere, the contracting officer may resort to data other than cost or pricing data. (See paragraph III, below.)

4. Where certified cost or pricing data is required, the contracting officer may rely on the certified data and his or her analysis of that data, as further described in Section IX, below.

5. Typically, in the absence of adequate price competition, the contracting officer will use price analysis, cost analysis, or a combination of the two techniques to analyze price reasonableness.

   - Price analysis looks at historical price data, and the offeror's disclosed current and historical pricing, to determine whether the offered price is fair and reasonable. For example, a price that is significantly higher than historical prices, and the increase is not justified by inflation, changes in commodity prices, differences in quantity, or other objective factors, may not be reasonable. See FAR 15.404-1(b).
   - Cost analysis is typically used when certified cost or pricing data is required. Cost analysis looks at the contractor's disclosed breakdown of estimated costs of performance, plus a reasonable profit. See FAR 15.404-1(c). The more complex the system acquired, the more detailed the analysis.

6. Generally, contractors are reluctant to share pricing data and cost data because they fear that their competitors and their customers would use such data to the contractor's disadvantage. However, sophisticated contractors generally understand the legal requirements and will provide the minimum required cost or pricing data to support the contracting officer's finding of price reasonableness.

C. Performance Risk. A fair and reasonable price is fair and reasonable to both the government and the contractor. While much of a contracting officer's analysis should be focused on avoiding overpaying for the goods or services, the contracting officer should also focus on not placing the contractor in a position of incurring a loss. This is because contractors who are not covering their costs and earning a profit may take measures to stem losses that result in a minimally compliant though unsatisfactory product, or may default. Large losses can threaten the continued existence of contractors, especially small businesses, and threaten the government's supplier base. Loss contracts are undesirable for both the contractor and the government.

III. REQUIRING DATA OTHER THAN COST OR PRICING DATA.

A. **Purpose**. The objective in acquiring data other than cost or pricing data is to support a determination that the price is fair and reasonable. Once the contracting officer determines that the prices offered are fair and reasonable, then the contracting officer has no reason to seek additional data.

B. **Government Data and Secondary Source Data.** The contracting officer first looks to the information available within the government and secondary sources. FAR 15.403-3(a)(1)(i). This may include prices previously paid by the government, market prices, or the prices paid for similar items.

C. **Contractor-Furnished Pricing Data.** Only when available data from the government and secondary sources is insufficient to support a determination may the contracting officer require the contractor to furnish data other than certified cost or pricing data to support a finding of price reasonableness. FAR 15.403-3(a)(1)(ii). As a minimum, such information includes "appropriate information on the prices at which the

same item or similar items have previously been sold that is adequate for evaluating the reasonableness of the price for the procurement." 10 U.S.C. § 2306a(d); 41 U.S.C. § 3505; FAR 15.403-3(a)(1)(iv).

D. **Contractor-Furnished Cost Data.** Typically, "data other than cost or pricing data" is pricing-type data. However, when the lack of adequate price competition suggests that cost data is necessary for a determination of price reasonableness, the contracting officer may consider requesting cost-type data. FAR 15.403-3(a)(1)(iii).

E. **Commercial Items.** 10 U.S.C. § 2306a(d)(2); 41 U.S.C. § 3505(b)(1); FAR 15.403-3(c).

1. FAR 15.403-3(c)(1) advises contracting officers that existence of a price in a price list, catalog, or advertisement does not, in and of itself, establish a price to be fair and reasonable.

2. In requesting data other than cost or pricing data on commercial items, the contracting officer shall:

   - limit requests for sales data relating to commercial items to data for the same or similar items during a relevant time period.
   - to the maximum extent practicable, limit the scope of the request for data relating to commercial items to include only data that are in the form regularly maintained by the offeror as part of its commercial operations.
   - not disclose outside the government data obtained relating to commercial items that is exempt from disclosure under FAR 24.202(a) or the Freedom of Information Act (5 U.S.C. 552(b)).

F. **Submission of Other Than Cost or Pricing Data.** FAR 15.403-3(a)(2); FAR 15.403-5(a)(3) and (b)(2).

1. The contracting officer includes the requirement to submit information other

Contract Pricing

than cost or pricing data in the solicitation. See FAR 52.215-20, Requirements for Cost or Pricing Data or Information Other Than Cost or Pricing Data; and FAR 52.215-21, Requirements for Cost or Pricing Data or Information Other Than Cost or Pricing Data – Modifications.

2. If the contracting officer requires the submission of information other than cost or pricing data, the contractor may submit the information in its own format unless the contracting officer concludes that the use of a specific format is essential and describes the required format in the solicitation.

3. The offeror is not required to certify information other than cost or pricing data. However, the contractor is well advised to ensure that the information it does submit is accurate and not misleading. Inaccurate or misleading data may support a finding of a false claim.

IV. CERTIFIED COST OR PRICING DATA – THE TRUTH IN NEGOTIATIONS ACT.

A. Historical Development.

1. Historically, the military services required prospective contractors to furnish them with historical cost data to support negotiations of estimated costs for large non-competitive contracts, both new contracts and modifications to existing contracts. GAO and the services also had a right to audit incurred costs.

2. In May 1959, the General Accounting Office (GAO) reported problems with overpricing negotiated contracts.

3. In October 1959 the DOD revised the Armed Services Procurement Regulation (ASPR, predecessor to the FAR and DFARS) to require contractors to certify that their cost or pricing data provided during contract negotiations was current, accurate and complete. In 1961, DOD added a standard clause permitting the government to reduce the price if the

contractor failed to provide current, accurate or complete data.

4. In 1962, Congress provided a statutory basis for DOD's regulations when it passed the Truth in Negotiations Act, Pub. L. No. 87-653, 76 Stat. 528 (1962) (codified at 10 U.S.C. § 2306f; commonly referred to as "TINA"). TINA applied to DOD, the Coast Guard, and NASA. Thereafter, Public Law 89-369 extended TINA's reach to all executive branch departments and agencies. Congress has amended TINA several times since it was first enacted.

5. TINA is currently codified at 10 U.S.C. § 2306a and 41 U.S.C. Chapter 35 (Truthful Cost or Pricing Data), and it is covered in FAR 15.403.

B. Why have the TINA?

1. The government's objective in negotiating a non-competitive contract is to obtain a fair and reasonable price for the goods and services it is acquiring. The government has concluded that this is only possible if the government and the contractor have equal access to the factual data supporting the estimated costs of performing the new work. TINA, and the clauses that implement it, require the contractor to disclose the data related to the estimated costs, to make the disclosure current, accurate, and complete as of the date of price agreement, and to certify that it has done so. If the contractor fails to disclose available data, the government may reduce the contract price. See S. REP. NO. 1884, at 3 (1962), reprinted in 1962 U.S.C.C.A.N. 2476, 2478. More simply, TINA's purpose is to "level the playing field" during negotiations. The certification emphasizes the seriousness of the requirement, and the price adjustment provides an administrative remedy for failures to comply.

2. TINA does not apply to all non-competitive negotiated contract awards. Congress has exempted some contracts, such as smaller purchases (currently under $750,000) and purchases where alternative

factors assure the government is paying a fair and reasonable price.

V. WHEN MUST CONTRACTORS SUBMIT CERTIFIED COST OR PRICING DATA?

A. **Disclosure Requirements.** Contractors submit cost or pricing data only for large-dollar, negotiated contract actions. Disclosure can be mandatory or non-mandatory.

1. Mandatory Disclosures. 10 U.S.C. § 2306a(a)(1); 41 U.S.C. § 3502(a); FAR 15.403-4(a)(1). Submission of cost or pricing data is mandatory when: a) negotiating a contract, subcontract, or modification, b) over the current threshold, and c) where no exemption applies. This includes:

   a. Award of a negotiated contract expected to exceed $750,000[1] (except an undefinitized action such as a letter contract). New awards following sealed bidding are exempt. FAR 52.215-10

   b. Award of a subcontract at any tier expected to exceed $750,000 if the government required the prime contractor and each higher-tier subcontractor to furnish cost or pricing data, and no exemption applies.[2] FAR 52.215-12.

   c. Prime contract modifications (both negotiated prime contracts and sealed bid prime contracts) where the price adjustment[3] exceeds $750,000; and

   d. Subcontract modifications at any tier where the price adjustment exceeds $750,000, if the government required the prime contractor and each higher-tier subcontractor to furnish cost or pricing data under the original contract or subcontract. FAR 52.215-13.

2. Non-mandatory. 10 U.S.C. § 2306a(c); 41 U.S.C. § 3504(a); FAR 15.403-4(a)(2).

   a. The government may obtain certified cost or pricing data below the current threshold. The Head of the Contracting Activity (HCA) can authorize a contracting officer to obtain cost or pricing data for pricing actions expected to cost between the simplified acquisition threshold (currently $150,000) and the TINA threshold (currently $750,000) if the HCA finds that the submission of such data is necessary to determine price reasonableness. The HCA must justify the decision in writing, and cannot delegate this authority to another agency official.

   b. Below threshold requirements for certified cost or pricing data are not common.

B. **Prohibition on Requiring Submission of Cost or Pricing Data.**

1. Simplified Acquisitions. FAR 15.403-1(a). A contracting officer cannot require a contractor to submit cost or pricing data for an acquisition that is at or below the simplified acquisition threshold (currently $150,000).

2. Adequate Price Competition. 10 U.S.C. § 2306a(b)(1)(A)(i); 41 U.S.C. § 3503(a)(1)(A); FAR 15.403-1(b)(1) and (c)(1).

---

[1] The threshold periodically adjusts for inflation. See 65 Fed. Reg. 60,553. See also 10 U.S.C. § 2306a(a)(7) and 41 U.S.C. § 3502(g).

[2] At each tier in the subcontract chain, the Buyer must obtain certified cost or pricing data from a subcontractor expected to exceed the $750,000 threshold, unless an exception. FAR 15.403-1(c)(4).

[3] Price adjustment amounts shall consider both increases and decreases. For example, a $100,000

---

modification, resulting from a decrease of $400,000 for work deleted and an increase of $500,000 for work added, is an adjustment of $900,000, and exceeds the current threshold. FAR 15.403-4(a)(1)(iii).

Contract Pricing

a. A contracting officer cannot require a contractor to submit cost or pricing data if the agreed-upon price is based on adequate price competition.

b. "Adequate Price Competition" is defined in FAR 15.403-1(c)(1) as:

   (1) Two or more responsive offers are received from responsible offerors, competing independently;

     (a) The government awarded the contract to the offeror whose proposal represented the best value;

     (b) Price was a substantial factor in the source selection; and

     (c) The contracting officer did not find the successful offeror's price unreasonable.[4] See Serv-Air, Inc., B-189884, Sept. 25, 1978, 78-2 CPD ¶ 223, aff'd on recons., Mar. 29, 1979, 79-1 CPD ¶ 212 (holding that cost or pricing data was not required because there was adequate price competition); cf. Litton Sys., Inc., Amecom Div., ASBCA No. 35914, 96-1 BCA ¶ 28,201 (denying the contractor's motion for summary judgment because a dispute of fact existed regarding whether there was adequate price competition).

c. "Adequate Price Competition" with only one offer received. FAR 15.403-1(c)(1)(ii).

     (a) Adequate price competition exists if the government reasonably expected that two or more responsible offerors, competing independently, would submit offers;

     (b) The contracting officer reasonably concluded that the offeror submitted its offer with the expectation of competition.[5]

d. "Adequate Price Competition" based on current or recent prices. FAR 15.403-1(c)(1)(iii). Adequate price competition exists if price analysis clearly demonstrates that the proposed price is reasonable in comparison with current or recent prices for the same or similar items, adjusted to reflect changes in market conditions, economic conditions, quantities, or terms and conditions under contracts that resulted from adequate price competition. See Norris Industries, Inc., ASBCA No. 15442, 74-1 BCA ¶ 10,482 (concluding that there was not adequate price competition where only one recent previous contract was for a quantity comparable to current contract).

3. Prices set by law or regulation. FAR 15.403-1(c)(2).

a. A contracting officer is prohibited from obtaining certified cost or pricing data when the prices are set by law or regulation.

b. The best example of prices set by law or regulation are purchases of

---

[4] To support any finding that the successful offeror's price was unreasonable, the contracting officer must: (1) submit a statement of facts; and (2) obtain approval at a level above the contracting officer. FAR 15.403-1(c)(1)(i)(B).

[5] The contracting officer can reasonably conclude that the offeror submitted its offer with the expectation of competition if (1) circumstances indicate that the offeror believed that at least one other offeror was capable of submitting a meaningful offer, and had no reason to believe that other potential offerors did not intend to submit offers; and (2) the determination that the proposed price is based on adequate competition is reasonable and is approved at a level above the contracting officer. FAR 15.403-1(c)(1)(ii)(A)(B).

utility services at prices determined by a regulatory body, such as a state utility commission. The reason for this exception is the assumption that the legal or regulatory process that established the price determined the price was fair and reasonable.

   c. A contractor asserting this exemption applies must submit information about the action establishing the prices, including a copy of the action setting the prices. FAR 52.215-20(a)(1)(i).

4. Commercial items. Contracting officers are prohibited from obtaining certified cost or pricing data when acquiring commercial items or services as defined in FAR 2.101. FAR 15.403-1(c)(3).

   a. The rationale for this exemption is that the prices of commercial items are set by the competition in the commercial marketplace. Commercial Items are discussed in Chapter 12.

   b. A contractor asserting this exemption applies must submit information on prices at which the same item or similar items have previously been sold in the commercial market that is adequate for evaluating the reasonableness of the price for this acquisition. FAR 52.215-20(a)(1)(ii).

5. HCA Waivers. FAR 15.403-1(c)(4). An HCA, without power of delegation, may waive in writing the requirement for cost or pricing data in exceptional cases if the price can be determined to be fair and reasonable without submission of cost or pricing data. HCA waivers are not common.

6. Requiring a contractor to submit cost or pricing data when there is adequate competition may be an abuse of the contracting officer's discretion. See United Technologies Corp., Pratt & Whitney, ASBCA No. 51410, 99-2 BCA ¶ 30,444 (rejecting Air Force's contention that the contracting officer had absolute discretion both to require certified cost or pricing data and to include a price adjustment clause where the price was negotiated based on adequate price competition).

VI. WHAT DATA IS COST OR PRICING DATA?

A. **Cost or Pricing Data.** 10 U.S.C. 2306a(h)(1), 41 U.S.C. chapter 35, and FAR 2.101 define cost or pricing data to mean all facts that, as of the date of price agreement, or, if applicable, an earlier date agreed upon between the parties that is as close as practicable to the date of agreement on price, prudent buyers and sellers would reasonably expect to affect price negotiations significantly. Cost or pricing data are factual, not judgmental, and are verifiable. While they do not indicate the accuracy of the prospective contractor's judgment about estimated future costs or projections, they do include the data forming the basis for that judgment. Cost or pricing data are more than historical accounting data; they are all the facts that can be reasonably expected to contribute to the soundness of estimates of future costs and to the validity of determinations of costs already incurred.

B. Cost or pricing data generally includes historical cost data that permits the estimate of future costs, incurred costs for the work being negotiated (if any), and prices charged to other customers for same or similar work. Cost or pricing data includes:

1. Vendor quotations;

2. Nonrecurring costs;

3. Information on changes in production methods and production or purchasing volume;

4. Data supporting projections of business prospects, objectives, and related operational costs;

5. Unit-cost trends, such as those associated with labor efficiency;

6. Make-or-buy decisions;

7. Estimated resources to attain business goals;

8. Information on management decisions that could have a significant bearing on costs;

9. Prices charged other customers;

10. Prices offered other customers; and

11. Quantity discounts, rebates, and similar incentives.

C. Board Guidance.

1. According to the Armed Services Board of Contract Appeals (ASBCA), whether a particular item is cost or pricing data is a factual question. Appeal of PAE International, ASBCA 20595, 76-2 BCA 12044 (1976).

2. Contractors do not define what is cost or pricing data. The statutory and regulatory definitions "plainly denote" a more expansive interpretation of cost or pricing data than routine corporate policy, practice, and procedures. United Techs. Corp./Pratt & Whitney, ASBCA No. 43645, 94-3 BCA ¶ 27,241 (applying objective reasonable person test); see Plessey Indus., ASBCA No. 16720, 74-1 BCA ¶ 10,603 (applying the "traditional 'reasonable man' test" to determine whether data constitutes cost or pricing information).

D. Fact vs. Judgment.

1. Factual information is data and must be disclosed. Judgments are not data, although the existence of a judgment is factual. For example, the historical labor cost per unit is factual and must be disclosed. A projection of lower future labor costs (learning curve) is judgment and need not be certified, although the

contractor must disclose the existence of such an estimate, if it makes one.

2. Factual information is discrete, quantifiable information that can be verified and audited. Litton Sys., Inc., Amecom Div., ASBCA No. 36509, 92-2 BCA ¶ 24,842. Information that mixes fact and judgment may require disclosure because of the underlying factual information. See, e.g., Texas Instruments, Inc., ASBCA No. 23678, 87-3 BCA ¶ 20,195; cf. Litton Sys., Inc., Amecom Div., ASBCA No. 36509, 92-2 BCA ¶ 24,842 (holding that reports regarding estimated labor hours were not required to be disclosed because they were "pure judgment").

3. Management decisions are generally a conglomeration of facts and judgment. See, e.g., Lockheed Corp., ASBCA No. 36420, 95-2 BCA ¶ 27,722. To determine whether management decisions can be classified as cost or pricing data, one should consider the following factors:

a. Did management actually make a "decision?" Kasco Co., ASBCA No. 18432, 76-2 BCA ¶ 12,147.

b. Was the management decision made by a person or group with the authority to approve or disapprove actions affecting costs?

c. Did the management decision require some sort of "action" affecting the relevant cost element, or was the "decision" more along the lines of preliminary planning for possible future action?

d. Is there a substantial relationship between the management decision and the relevant cost element?

e. Is the management decision the type of decision that prudent buyers and sellers would reasonably expect to affect price negotiations significantly?

E. Cost or Pricing Data Must Be Significant.

1. The contractor must disclose the data if a reasonable person, i.e., a prudent buyer or seller, would expect it to have a significant effect on price negotiations. Plessey Indus., Inc., ASBCA No. 16720, 74-1 BCA ¶ 10,603. As interpreted by many court and Board of Contract Appeals decisions, this requires contractors to disclose a large amount of data.

2. The duty to disclose extends not only to data that the contractor knows it will use, but also to data that the contractor thinks it might use. If a reasonable person would consider the data in determining cost or price, the data is significant and the contractor must disclose it. Hardie-Tynes Mfg., Co., ASBCA No. 20717, 76-2 BCA ¶ 12,121; P.A.L. Sys. Co., GSBCA No. 10858, 91-3 BCA ¶ 24,259 (holding that a contractor should have disclosed vendor discounts even though the government was not entitled to them).

3. Prior purchases of similar items may be "significant data." Kisco Co., ASBCA No. 18432, 76-2 ¶ 12,147; Hardie-Tynes Mfg., Co., ASBCA No. 20717, 76-2 BCA ¶ 12,121.

4. The amount of the overpricing is not determinative of whether the information is significant. See Conrac Corp. v. United States, 558 F.2d 994 (1977) (holding that the government was entitled to a refund totaling one-tenth of one percent of the total contract price); Kaiser Aerospace & Elecs. Corp., ASBCA No. 32098, 90-1 BCA ¶ 22,489 (holding that the government was entitled to a refund totaling two-tenths of one percent of the total contract price). But see Boeing Co., ASBCA No. 33881, 92-1 BCA ¶ 24,414 (holding that a $268 overstatement on a $1.7 billion contract was "de minimis").

5. Note: The DCAA Contract Audit Manual (DCAA Manual 7640.1) states that auditors should consider potential price adjustments of less than 5% of the contract value or less than $50,000 immaterial. DCAA CAM Para. 14-120.1.

This materiality criterion does not apply when:

a. A contractor's deficient estimating practices results in recurring defective pricing; or

b. The potential price adjustment is due to a systemic deficiency which affects all contracts priced during the period. DCAA CAM ¶ 14-120.1.

VII. SUBMITTING CERTIFIED COST OR PRICING DATA.

A. Procedural Requirements.

1. Format. FAR 15.403-5.

    a. DOD contractors must submit proposals that are adequate, as determined by DFARS Table 215.403-1.

    b. Contracting officer can:

    (1) Require contractors to submit cost or pricing data in the format specified in FAR 15.408, Table 15-2;

    (2) Specify an alternate format; or

    (3) Allow contractors to use their own format.

    c. Contractors may either physically submit the data, or may specifically identify the data in writing.

    d. Contractors are required to have an approved estimating system prepare their proposals and supporting data using the procedures in the approved estimating system.

    e. Typically, contractors, their contract auditors, and their customers have developed agreed practices for the submission of cost or pricing data, and experienced contractors carefully follow their procedures for disclosure.

2. Submittal to Proper Government Official.

    a. Contractors must generally submit cost or pricing data to the contracting officer or the contracting officer's authorized representative. 10 U.S.C. § 2306a(a)(3); 41 U.S.C. § 3502(c).

    b. The boards often look at whether the person to whom the disclosure was made participated in the negotiation of the contract. See Singer Co., Librascope Div. v. United States, 576 F.2d 905 (1978) (holding that disclosure to the auditor was not sufficient where the auditor was not involved in the negotiations); Sylvania Elec. Prods., Inc. v. United States, 479 F.2d 1342 (1973) (holding that disclosure to the ACO was not sufficient where the ACO had no connection with the proposal and the contractor did not ask the ACO to forward the data to the PCO); cf. Texas Instruments, Inc., ASBCA No. 30836, 89-1 BCA ¶ 21,489 (holding that disclosure to the ACO was sufficient where the ACO was involved in the negotiation of the disputed rates and knew that the subject contract was being negotiated); Litton Sys., Inc., Amecom Div., ASBCA Nos. 34435, et al., 93-2 BCA ¶ 25,707 (holding that disclosure of indirect cost actuals to resident auditor based on established practice was sufficient disclosure though auditor did not participate in negotiations).

3. Adequate Disclosure. A contractor can meet its obligation if it provides the data physically to the government and discloses the significance of the data to the negotiation process. M-R-S Manufacturing Co. v. United States, 492 F.2d 835 (1974).

    a. The contractor must advise government representatives of the kind and content of the data and their bearing on the prospective contractor's proposal. Texas Instruments, Inc., ASBCA No. 23678, 87-3 BCA ¶ 20,195.

    b. Making records available to the government may constitute adequate disclosure. Appeals of McDonnell Douglas Helicopter Sys., ASBCA Nos. 50447, 50448, 50449, 2000 BCA ¶ 31,082 (furnishing or making available historical reports to DCAA resident auditor and DLA in-plant personnel in connection to Apache procurement make-buy decisions held adequate).

    c. Knowledge by the other party of the data's existence is no defense to a failure to provide data. Grumman Aerospace Corp., ASBCA No. 35188, 90-2 BCA ¶ 22,842 (prime contractor's alleged knowledge of subcontractor reports not sufficient because subcontractor was obligated to physically deliver the data or specifically identify it in writing).

B.   Obligation to Update Data.

1. The contractor certifies its data as current, accurate and complete as of the date of price agreement or contract award. Consequently, the contractor must update its disclosed data after submitting its initial proposal through the date of price agreement or contract award. Facts occurring before price agreement and coming to the negotiator's attention after that date must be disclosed before award if they were "reasonably available" before the price agreement date.

2. The contractor's duty to provide updated data is not limited to the personal knowledge of its negotiators. Data within the contractor's (or subcontractor's) organization are considered readily available.

3. In practice, the contracting officer will request the contractor to update its proposal from time to time during

negotiations and upon reaching price agreement. The contractor will update its proposal as requested and will make a final update, disclosing any data not included in previous updates, after price agreement and prior to executing its certificate.

C. Certification of Data.

1. Contractors must certify that their cost or pricing data physically delivered, or specifically identified in writing, is current accurate and complete as of the date of price agreement. The language of the certificate appears in FAR 15.406-2(a). See 10 U.S.C. § 2306a(a)(2) and 41 U.S.C. § 3502(b) (requiring any person who submits cost or pricing data to certify that the data is accurate, complete, and current).

2. Due Date for Certificate. FAR 15.406-2(a). The certificate is due as soon as practicable after the date the parties conclude negotiations and agree to a contract price. Typically, a contractor will not submit the certificate until it has completed a "sweep" to ensure all available data has been disclosed.

3. Failure to Submit Certificate. 10 U.S.C. § 2306a(f)(2); 41 U.S.C. § 3507(b). A contractor's failure to certify its cost or pricing data does not relieve it of liability for defective pricing. See S.T. Research Corp., ASBCA No. 29070, 84-3 BCA ¶ 17,568.

VIII. ESTIMATING SYSTEM REQUIREMENTS.

A. Estimating Systems.

1. Contractors preparing proposals for larger contracts have developed internal estimating systems or have adopted commercial estimating systems to price their proposals to customers. Estimating systems are an internal computer application that permits a large organization to prepare an integrated cost proposal in a systematic way, thereby reducing the chance of errors and omissions.

2. A typical estimating system includes:

    - Standard procedures for developing a logical decomposition of the contract's requirements into a Work Breakdown Structure (WBS).
    - Preparing a Basis of Estimate (BOE) for the individual tasks in the WBS, identifying the capital equipment, labor hours, material, and schedule needed to complete the tasks.
    - The Basis of Estimates are compiled into a total estimate, applying projected indirect costs rates, proposals from projected subcontractors, and estimated Other Direct Costs (ODC), such as travel and consultants, etc.

B. Estimating Systems Requirements.

1. DFARS 215.408(2) requires the contracting officer awarding a prime contract based on certified cost to include DFARS 252.215-7002, Cost Estimating Systems Requirements. The DFARS clause requires the prime contractor to develop and maintain an acceptable estimating system. When the prime contractor has more than $50 million in TINA awards in the contractor's preceding fiscal year, the prime contractor's estimating system must conform to a detailed set of requirements in subparagraphs (d) and (e) of the clause.

2. Thus, large DOD contractors must prepare their cost estimates for their TINA proposals using an approved estimating system. Failure to maintain an acceptable estimating system can result in the adverse actions described in Chapter 19 and DFARS 252.242-7005.

3. As the term is used in DFARS 252.215-7002, a contractor's estimating system is quite expansive. It includes all the contractor's policies, procedures, and practices for budgeting and planning controls, and generating estimates of costs and other data included in proposals.

4. Since the prime contractor must use its estimating system consistently, it must follow its procedures when pricing subcontracts.

C. Contractors effectively implementing approved estimating systems tend to experience fewer problems with defective pricing.

IX. COST OR PRICE ANALYSIS.

A. References.

DOD Contract Pricing Reference Guides, available at: https://acc.dau.mil/CommunityBrowser.aspx?id=406579&lang=en-US.

B. Price Analysis.

1. Price analysis is addressed in DOD Contract Pricing Reference Guide, Volume 1. Price analysis is the process of determining a fair and reasonable price without evaluating individual cost elements. It is used in negotiating the prices of commercial-type items, where cost data may be unavailable or not useful in determining the contract price, or to validate the results of cost analysis. Essentially, price analysis looks at historical prices agreed to by the contractor and by suppliers of similar products, plus other factors, to determine a fair and reasonable price.

2. Price data is available from many sources, including: 1) prior purchases, 2) catalogs and price lists, 3) prices paid by other customers, and 4) published market prices. Economic data is also useful, such as market trends, inflation data, inventory levels, etc. Furthermore, data regarding a specific acquisition is useful, such as the quantity purchased, schedule requirements, delivery requirements, warranty requirements, and other contract risks.

3. Price analysis takes all the available price data and estimates a fair and reasonable price for a future purchase. For example, a contracting officer may take a price paid a year ago for 10 units, increase the price by 2% for inflation, and estimate the price reduction for a 100-unit purchase.

C. Cost Analysis.

1. Cost analysis is addressed in DOD Pricing Reference Guides, Volume 3. Cost analysis is used where competitively determined prices are not available to support a determination of a fair and reasonable price. It is primarily used when negotiating non-competitive awards.

2. Cost data is principally obtained from the contractor, but will also include external data, such as current market prices for materials, economic projections, and profit rates.

3. The techniques of cost analysis are discussed in Chapter 25, Pricing of Adjustments.

X. DEFECTIVE PRICING AND GOVERNMENT REMEDIES.

A. Definition. Defective cost or pricing data is data that is subsequently discovered to not have been current, accurate, or complete as certified by the contractor. 10 U.S.C. § 2306a(e)(1)(B); 41 U.S.C. § 3506(a)(2). Under TINA and contract price reduction clauses, the government is entitled to an adjustment in the contract price, to include profit or fee, when it relied on defective cost or pricing data.

B. Example. An example of defective pricing is a contractor submitting a proposal and reaching price agreement based on disclosed data that includes a price quotation from a prospective subcontractor. If, at the time of price agreement, the contractor had an available but undisclosed updated subcontractor quotation with a lower price or a quotation at a lower price from another supplier, then the contractor's certified cost or pricing data was not current, accurate and complete. There is no intent required, no negligence required, etc. All that is required for defective pricing is available data that is not current, accurate, or complete, as certified.

C. **Undisclosed Data.** While the above example is relatively straightforward, not all examples of defective pricing are so simple. Information about actions and events that have no direct connection with a contract may require disclosure if the actions and events will affect a contractor's indirect cost rates used in preparing the cost estimate. For example, contractors may have information about new orders that would expand the allocation base for indirect costs, or about management actions to reduce the pool of indirect costs.

D. **Contractual Remedies.**

1. Price Adjustment. 10 U.S.C. § 2306a(e)(1)(A); 41 U.S.C. § 3506(a)(1); FAR 15.407-1(b)(1); FAR 52.215-10 (Price Reduction for Defective Cost or Pricing Data); FAR 52.215-11 (Price Reduction for Defective Cost or Pricing Data – Modification). The government can reduce the contract price if the government discovers that a contractor, prospective subcontractor, or actual subcontractor submitted defective cost or pricing data.

    a. Amount. 10 U.S.C. § 2306a(e)(1)(A); 41 U.S.C. § 3506(a)(1); FAR 15.407-1(b)(1); FAR 52.215-10 (Price Reduction for Defective Cost or Pricing Data); FAR 52.215-11 (Price Reduction for Defective Cost or Pricing Data – Modification).

        (1) The government can reduce the contract price by any significant amount by which the contract price was increased because of the defective cost or pricing data. Unisys Corp. v. United States, 888 F.2d 841 (Fed. Cir. 1989); Kaiser Aerospace & Elec. Corp., ASBCA No. 32098, 90-1 BCA ¶ 22,489; Etowah Mfg. Co., ASBCA No. 27267, 88-3 BCA ¶ 21,054.

        (2) The amount of the reduction is assumed to be dollar for dollar based on the difference between the disclosed and undisclosed data, including applicable indirect costs. For example, if the defective data is a $10,000 higher supplier quotation than the undisclosed data, then the price adjustment would be $10,000, plus applicable material overhead, applicable general and administrative expenses, and applicable indirect costs by higher-tier subcontractors and the prime contractor.

        (3) The price adjustment will include a reduction for the impact on profit or fee.

        (4) Interest. The government can recover interest on any overpayments it made because of the defective cost or pricing data. 10 U.S.C. § 2306a(f)(1)(A); 41 U.S.C. § 3507(a)(1); FAR 15.407-1(b)(7); FAR 52.215-10 (Price Reduction for Defective Cost or Pricing Data); FAR 52.215-11 (Price Reduction for Defective Cost or Pricing Data – Modification). The contracting officer must:

        (a) Determine the amount of the overpayment;

        (b) Determine the date the overpayment was made;[6] and

        (c) Apply the appropriate interest rate.[7]

---

[6] For prime contracts, the date of overpayment is the date the government paid for a completed and accepted contract item. For subcontracts, the date of overpayment is the date the government paid the prime contractor for progress billings or deliveries that included a completed and accepted subcontract item. FAR 15.407-1(b)(7).

[7] The Secretary of the Treasury sets interest rates on a quarterly basis. 26 U.S.C. § 6621(a)(2).

b. Defective Subcontractor Data. FAR 15.407-1(e)-(f).

   (1) Adjustments for defective subcontractor cost or pricing data can be very complicated, since the timing of price agreement often differs.

   (2) The government can reduce the prime contract price based on subcontractor defective pricing regardless of whether the defective subcontractor data supported subcontract cost estimates, or firm agreements between the subcontractor and the prime.

   (3) If the prime contractor uses defective subcontractor data but subcontracts with a lower-priced subcontractor (or fails to subcontract at all), the government can only reduce the prime contract price by the difference between the subcontract price the prime contractor used to price the contract and:

   (a) The actual subcontract price if the contractor subcontracted with a lower-priced subcontractor; or

   (b) The contractor's actual cost if the contractor failed to subcontract the work.

   (4) The government can disallow payments to subcontractors that are higher than they would have been absent the defective cost or pricing data under:

   (a) Cost-reimbursement contracts; and

   (b) All fixed-price contracts except firm fixed-price contracts and fixed-price contracts with economic price adjustments (e.g., fixed-price incentive contracts and fixed-price award fee contracts).

2. If the government fails to include a price reduction clause in the contract, courts and boards will read them in pursuant to the Christian Doctrine. University of California, San Francisco, VABCA No. 4661, 97-1 BCA ¶ 28,642; Palmetto Enterprises, Inc., ASBCA No. 22839, 79-1 BCA ¶ 13,736.

3. A defective pricing claim cannot be asserted as an affirmative defense by the government to a contractor's money claim. Computer Network Sys., Inc., GSBCA No. 11368, 93-1 BCA ¶ 25,260. Defective pricing is a government claim.

4. Penalties. 10 U.S.C. § 2306a(f)(1)(B); 41 U.S.C. § 3507(a)(2); FAR 15.407-1(b)(7); FAR 52.215-10 (Price Reduction for Defective Cost or Pricing Data); FAR 52.215-11 (Price Reduction for Defective Cost or Pricing Data – Modification).

   a. The government can collect penalty amounts where the contractor (or subcontractor) knowingly submitted defective cost or pricing data.

   b. The contracting officer can obtain a penalty amount equal to the amount of the overpayment.

   c. The contracting officer must consult an attorney before assessing any penalty.

5. Government's Burden of Proof. The government bears the burden of proof in a defective pricing case. General Dynamics Corp., ASBCA No. 32660, 93-1 BCA ¶ 25,378. To meet its burden, the government must prove that:

   a. The information meets the definition of cost or pricing data;

   b. The information existed before the date of agreement on price;

   c. The data was reasonably available before the date of agreement on price;

   d. The data the contractor (or subcontractor) submitted was not accurate, complete, or current;

e. The undisclosed data was the type that prudent buyers or sellers would have reasonably expected to have a significant effect upon price negotiations;

f. The government relied on the defective data; and

g. The government's reliance on the defective data caused an increase in the contract price.

6. Once the government establishes nondisclosure of cost and pricing data, there is a rebuttable presumption of prejudice.

   a. The contractor must then demonstrate that the government would not have relied on this information.

   b. Once demonstrated, the burden of showing detrimental reliance shifts back to the government.

   c. Hence, the ultimate burden of showing prejudice rests with the government.

7. The ASBCA often views defective pricing cases as "too complicated" to resolve by summary judgment. Grumman Aerospace Corp., ASBCA No. 35185, 92-3 BCA ¶ 25,059; McDonnell Douglas Helicopter Co., ASBCA No. 41378, 92-1 BCA ¶ 24,655. But see Rosemount, Inc., ASBCA No. 37520, 95-2 BCA ¶ 27,770 (granting the contractor's motion for summary judgment because the government failed to meet its burden of proof).

8. Successful Defenses to Price Reductions.

   a. The information at issue was not cost or pricing data. For example, the information was judgmental.

   b. The government did not rely on the defective data. 10 U.S.C. § 2306a(e)(2); 41 U.S.C. § 3506(b). For example, the government used a different estimating technique which did not require the undisclosed data.

c. The price offered by the contractor was a "floor" below which the contractor would not have gone.

9. Unsuccessful Defenses to Price Reductions. 10 U.S.C. § 2306a(e)(3); 41 U.S.C. § 3506(c); FAR 15.407-1(b)(3).

   a. The contractor (or subcontractor) was a sole source supplier or otherwise was in a superior bargaining position.

   b. The contracting officer should have known that the cost or pricing data the contractor (or subcontractor) submitted was defective. FMC Corp., ASBCA No. 30069, 87-1 BCA ¶ 19,544.

   c. The contract price was based on total cost and there was no agreement about the cost of each item procured under the contract.

   d. The contractor (or subcontractor) did not submit a Certificate of Current Cost or Pricing Data.

10. Offsets. 10 U.S.C. § 2306a(e)(4)(A)-(B); 41 U.S.C. § 3506(d); FAR 15.407-1(b)(4)-(6); FAR 52.215-10 (Price Reduction for Defective Cost or Pricing Data); FAR 52.215-11 (Price Reduction for Defective Cost or Pricing Data – Modification).

    a. The contracting officer must allow an offset for any understated cost or pricing data the contractor (or subcontractor) submitted.

    b. The amount of the offset may equal, but not exceed, the amount of the government's claim for overstated cost or pricing data arising out of the same pricing action.

    c. The offset does not have to be in the same cost grouping as the overstated cost or pricing data (e.g., material, direct labor, or indirect costs).

    d. The contractor must prove that the higher cost or pricing data:

(1) Was available before the "as of" date specified on the Certificate of Current Cost or Pricing Data; and

(2) Was not submitted.

e. The contractor is not entitled to an offset under two circumstances:

(1) The contractor knew that its cost or pricing data was understated before the "as of" date specified on the Certificate of Current Cost or Pricing Data. See United Tech. Corp., Pratt & Whitney v. Peters, No. 98-1400, 1999 U.S. App. LEXIS 15490 (Fed. Cir. July 12, 1999) (affirming in part ASBCA's denial of offsets for "sweep" data intentionally withheld from government).

(a) Prior to the 1986 TINA amendments, contractors could obtain offsets for intentional understatements. See United States v. Rogerson Aircraft Controls, 785 F.2d 296 (Fed. Cir. 1986) (holding that a contractor, under pre-1986 TINA, could offset intentional understatements that were "completely known to the government at the time of the negotiations and in no way hindered or deceived the government").

(b) Even under the pre-1986 TINA, the offset must be based on cost or pricing data. Errors in judgment cannot serve as a basis for an offset. See AM General Corp., ASBCA No. 48476, 99-1 BCA ¶ 30,130 (characterizing contractor's decision to amortize nonrecurring costs of HMMWV production as "at most, errors of judgment" that failed to support an offset).

(2) The government proves that submission of the data before the "as of" date specified on the Certificate of Current Cost or Pricing Data would not have increased the contract price in the amount of the proposed offset.

E. **Administrative Remedies.**

1. Termination of the Contract. Defective pricing is a breach of contract, which can justify termination for default. FAR Part 49; Joseph Morton Co. v. United States, 3 Cl. Ct. 120 (1983), aff'd, 757 F.2d 1273 (Fed. Cir. 1985).

2. Suspension and Debarment. Knowing or reckless defective pricing can support a finding of lack of business integrity. FAR Subpart 9.4; DFARS Subpart 209.4.

3. Cancellation of the Contract. Criminal defective pricing can support a cancellation for fraud in the inducement. 18 U.S.C. § 218; FAR Subpart 3.7.

F. **Judicial Remedies.**

1. Criminal.

   a. False Claims Act. 18 U.S.C. § 287. See Communication Equip. and Contracting Co., Inc. v. United States, 37 CCF ¶ 76,195 (Cl. Ct. 1991) (unpub.) (holding that TINA does not preempt the False Claims Act so as to limit the government's remedies).

   b. False Statement Act. 18 U.S.C. § 1001. See, e.g., United States v. Shah, 44 F.3d 285 (5th Cir. 1995).

   c. The Major Fraud Act. 18 U.S.C. § 1031.

2. Civil.

   a. False Claims Act. 10 U.S.C. §§ 3729-33. Civil penalty between $5,000 and $10,000, plus treble damages. 10 U.S.C. §§ 3729(a).

   b. The Program Fraud Civil Remedies Act of 1986. 31 U.S.C. §§ 3801-3812; DOD Dir. 5505.5 (Aug. 30, 1988).

G. **Defective Pricing or Fraud.** While not all instances of defective pricing are the result of fraud, some are. The DOD

Inspector General's Handbook on Indicators of Fraud contains factors that may support a finding that an incident of defective pricing is the result of fraud. The Handbook is available at http://www.dodig.mil/resources/fraud/scenarios.html.

1. High incidence of persistent defective pricing.

2. Continued failure to correct known system deficiencies.

3. Consistent failure to update cost or pricing data with knowledge that past activity showed that prices have decreased.

4. Failure to make complete disclosure of data known to responsible personnel.

5. Protracted delay in updating cost or pricing data to preclude possible price reduction.

6. Repeated denial by responsible contractor employees of the existence of historical records that are later found to exist.

7. Repeated utilization of unqualified personnel to develop cost or pricing data used in estimating process.

XI. GOVERNMENT AUDIT RIGHTS.

A. **Historical Basis.** Historically, the Comptroller General has had the right to audit all government contracts over a stated amount. The contracting officer has also had the right to audit certain types of contracts, such as negotiated contracts, cost reimbursement contracts, etc. These rights were based on statutes, and the government's audit rights are quite different from commercial contracting, where audit rights are much less common. Audits are used to validate cost estimates, incurred costs, cost and schedule reporting, management activities, etc.

B. **Current Requirements.**

1. All negotiated contracts contain FAR 52.215-2, Audit and Records –

Negotiation, which grants the government audit rights.

2. Statutory Basis. 10 U.S.C. § 2306a(g); 10 U.S.C § 2313(a)(2); 41 U.S.C. § 3508; 41 U.S.C. § 4706(b)(2). The contracting officer and the contracting activity has the right to examine contractor (or subcontractor) records to:

    - determine the costs incurred in cost-type contracts;
    - determine the accuracy, completeness, and currency of the cost or pricing data disclosed to the contracting officer or the subcontract buyer, to determine the cost incurred on cost-type contracts.

    Additionally, the Comptroller General may audit costs that are directly related to the contract.

3. Definition of auditable records. 10 U.S.C. § 2313(i); 41 U.S.C. § 4706(a). The term "records" includes "books, documents, accounting procedures and practices, and any other data, regardless of type and regardless of whether such items are in written form, in the form of computer data, or in any other form."

4. Pre-Award Audit Rights. The government has the right to audit cost or pricing data submitted with the contractor's proposal. Currently, DCAA limits pre-award contract audits to larger proposals.

5. Post-Award Audit Rights. The government has the right to audit contracts and subcontracts awarded based on submission of certified cost or pricing data.

    a. In DOD, routine defective pricing audits are typically performed by DCAA after the contractor has begun performance of the contract. By examining incurred costs, the auditor can determine where the contractor has experienced cost savings over the proposed costs, and determine whether those cost savings are related to undisclosed data existing at the time of price negotiation.

b. The government's audit right expires 3 years after final payment on the contract.

c. Subpoena Power. 10 U.S.C. § 2313(b); 41 U.S.C. § 4706(c)(1).

   (1) The Director of the Defense Contract Audit Agency (DCAA)[8] can subpoena any of the records that 10 U.S.C. § 2313(a) gives the agency the right to examine.

   (2) The Director of the DCAA can enforce this subpoena power by seeking an order from an appropriate U.S. district court.

6. Comptroller General's Right.

   a. Statutory Basis. 10 U.S.C. § 2313(c), (e)-(f); 41 U.S.C. § 4706(d), (f)-(g). The Comptroller General (or the Comptroller General's authorized representative) has the right "to examine any records of the contractor, or any of its subcontractors, that directly pertain to, and involve transactions relating to, the contract or subcontract."

   b. The Comptroller General's examination right only applies to contracts awarded using other than sealed bid procedures. The Comptroller General's examination right expires 3 years after final payment on the contract.

   c. The Comptroller General's examination right does not apply to contracts (or subcontracts) that do not exceed the simplified acquisition threshold.

   d. Subpoena Power. 31 U.S.C. § 716.

   (1) The Comptroller General has the power to subpoena the records of a person to whom the Comptroller General has access by law or agreement.

   (2) The Comptroller General can enforce this subpoena power by seeking an order from an appropriate U.S. district court. United States v. McDonnell-Douglas Corp., 751 F.2d 220 (8th Cir. 1984).

   e. Scope of the Comptroller General's Examination Right.

   (1) The term "contract," as used in the statute, embraces not only the specific terms and conditions of a contract, but also the general subject matter of the contract. Hewlett-Packard Co. v. United States, 385 F.2d 1013 (9th Cir. 1967), cert. denied, 390 U.S. 988 (1968).

   (2) For cost-based contracts, the Comptroller General's examination right is extremely broad; however, for fixed-price contracts, the books or records must bear directly on the question of whether the government paid a fair price for the goods or services. Bowsher v. Merck & Co., 460 U.S. 824 (1983).

7. Inspector General's Right. 5 U.S.C. App. 3 § 6.

   a. Statutory Basis. 5 U.S.C. App. 3 § 6(a)(1).

   (1) The Inspector General of an agency has the right "to have access to all records, reports, audits, reviews, documents, papers, recommendations, or other material . . . which relate to programs and operations with respect to which that Inspector General has responsibilities. . . ."

   (2) This statutory right has no contractual implementation.

---

[8] For civilian agencies, this right extends to the Inspector General of the agency and, upon the request of the HCA, the Director of the DCAA or the Inspector General of the General Services Administration. § 4706(c)(1).

b. Subpoena Power. 5 U.S.C. 3 § 6(a)(4).

(1) The Inspector General has the power to subpoena all data and documentary evidence necessary to perform the Inspector General's duties.

(2) The Inspector General can enforce this subpoena power by seeking an order from an appropriate U.S. district court.

c. Scope of the Inspector General's Right. The scope of the Inspector General's right is extremely broad and includes internal audit reports. <u>United States v. Westinghouse Elec. Corp.</u>, 788 F.2d 164 (3d Cir. 1986).

8. Obstruction of a Federal Audit. 18 U.S.C. § 1516.

a. This statute does not increase or enhance the government's audit rights.

b. The statute makes it a crime for anyone to influence, obstruct, or impede a government auditor (full or part-time government/ contractual employee) with the intent to deceive or defraud the government.

XII. CONCLUSION.

The Truth in Negotiations Act and its implementing regulations substitute for competition as a tool to ensure that the government pays a fair and reasonable price. As such, TINA is imperfect, as is the system of negotiating prices based on cost estimates. The system, however, does regulate many government contracts, and both contractors and the government should devote the time to learning the details of the system far beyond the brief introduction provided by this chapter.

SOCIOECONOMIC POLICIES

I. INTRODUCTION.

A. Goals of the Acquisition Process.

Most citizens understand the goals of the acquisition process in terms of the results: 1) obtaining quality goods and services; 2) at a fair and reasonable price; and 3) in a timely manner. Additionally, important goals are the integrity and transparency of the decision-making process and treating the competitors fairly. All of these goals are focused on the principal reason for the agency's acquisition: the accomplishment of the agency's mission.

B. Collateral Policies.

Government contracting, however, has effects far beyond the specific agency and its mission. The government's purchasing activities are enormous in scope, and involve a broad swath of the American economy. Because of the size and breadth of government contracting, purchasing provides a powerful tool for implementing policies only tangentially related to the principal missions of individual agencies.

The President has used, and continues to use, the economic power of government contracting to induce industry to follow regulations implementing desirable social and economic policies that the Congress might not pass as legislation. The Congress has used the economic power of government contracting to induce "voluntary" compliance with laws and regulations that voters might not accept as laws of general applicability.

This chapter describes the principal social and economic policies implemented through the economic power of government contracting, and the requirements placed on the government and on the contractor.

II. POLICY AND PROCEDURE IN SUPPORT OF SMALL BUSINESS.

A. Background.

There is an understandable tendency for acquisition officials to prefer large contractors over small contractors. Large contractors are often financially more stable, they tend to have a longer record of performance, and they tend to have employees, plant, and equipment to apply to a program. Small business, however, comprises a significant portion of America's industrial might, but they have suffered when competing with larger businesses. Congress has enacted preference programs for small businesses to overcome the natural biases and to fully use American industry.

B. Policy. 15 U.S.C. §§ 631-650; FAR 19.201.

1. Place a fair proportion of acquisitions with small business concerns.

2. Promote maximum subcontracting opportunities for small businesses.

C. Small Business Defined.

1. A small business is defined by 15 U.S.C. § 632(a) and FAR 19.001 as a business that is:

    a. Independently owned and operated;

    b. Not dominant in its field; and

    c. Meets applicable size standards.

2. In 13 C.F.R. § 121.105, the Small Business Administration defines a "business" as "… a business entity organized for profit, with a place of business located in the United States, and which operates primarily within the United States or which makes a significant contribution to the U.S. economy through

payment of taxes or use of American products, materials or labor." This means that foreign firms are generally ineligible for small business preferences.

3. Consequently, the focus in identifying qualified small businesses is on affiliations between the entity in question and other entities, and on whether the business, including affiliates, meets the applicable size standard.

D. Size Determination Procedures.

1. The Small Business Administration (SBA) establishes small business size standards, which are based either on the number of employees or annual receipts. The SBA matches a size standard with a supply, service or construction classification that best describes the principal nature of the work.

2. The contracting officer adopts an appropriate product or service classification from the North American Industry Classification System (NAICS) code and includes it in the solicitation. FAR 19.102.

   a. This classification establishes the applicable size standard for businesses competing for the acquisition.

   b. Contractors may appeal the contracting officer's NAICS code selection as a matter of right to the SBA's Office of Hearings and Appeals (OHA) no later than 10 calendar days after issuance of the initial solicitation. The appellant must exhaust the OHA appeal process before seeking judicial review in court. See FAR 19.303(c).

   c. The contracting officer need not delay bid opening or contract award pending a NAICS code appeal. See Aleman Food Serv., Inc., B-216803, Mar. 6, 1985, 85-1 CPD ¶ 277. If the SBA finds the original NAICS code improper, the contracting

officer must amend the solicitation only if he receives the SBA determination before the date offers are due. See FAR 19.303(c)(5).

   d. The GAO does not review NAICS code appeals. 4 C.F.R. § 21.5(b)(1); A-P-T Research, Inc.—Costs, B-298352.3, Sept. 28, 2006, 2007 CPD ¶ 60; Tri-Way Sec. & Escort Serv., Inc., B-238115.2, Apr. 10, 1990, 90-1 CPD ¶ 380; JC Computer Servs., Inc. v. Nuclear Regulatory Comm'n, GSBCA No. 12731-P, 94-2 BCA ¶ 26,712; Cleveland Telecommunications Corporation, B-247964, July 23, 1992, 92-2 CPD ¶ 47.

3. Small business certification. FAR 19.301.

   a. Self-certification. To be eligible for award as a small business, an offeror must represent, in good faith, that it is a small business at the time of the certification/representation. Randolph Eng'g Sunglasses, B-280270, Aug. 10, 1998, 98-2 CPD ¶ 39; United Power Corp., B-239330, May 22, 1990, 90-1 CPD ¶ 494. Contracting officer may accept the self-certification unless contracting officer has information prior to award that reasonably impeaches the certification. AMI Constr., B-286351, Dec. 27, 2000, 2000 CPD ¶ 211; Fiber-Lam, Inc., B-237716.2, Apr. 3, 1990, 90-1 CPD ¶ 351.

   b. SBA certification. MTB Investments, Inc., B-275696, March 17, 1997, 97-1 CPD ¶ 112; Olympus Corp., B-225875, Apr. 14, 1987, 87-1 CPD ¶ 407.

   c. If an acquisition is set aside for small business, failure to certify status does not render the bid nonresponsive. Last Camp Timber, B-238250, May 10, 1990, 90-1 CPD ¶ 461; Concorde Battery Corp., B-235119, June 30, 1989, 89-2 CPD ¶ 17.

d. Re-representations of Size Status. FAR 52.219-28, Post-Award Small Business Program Re-representation (July 2013) requires a small business awarded a small business set-aside to re-represent its size status after award. First, a business must re-represent its size status 60-120 days prior to the end of the fifth year of contract performance, and within 60-120 days prior to the award of any subsequent option. Second, a business must re-represent its size status within 30 days following a novation agreement, a merger or acquisition not requiring a novation agreement, or inclusion of the clause in the contract.

e. For set-aside contracts awarded prior to the effective date of FAR 52.219-28 and which have not been modified to incorporate the clause, a firm need not re-certify size status before an agency exercises an option. See Vantex Serv. Corp., B-251102, Mar. 10, 1993, 93-1 CPD ¶ 221. But see CMS Info. Servs., Inc., B-290541, Aug. 7, 2002, 2002 CPD ¶ 132 (holding that agency may properly require firms to certify their size status as of the time they submit their quotes for an indefinite delivery/indefinite quantity (IDIQ) task order).

f. If a contractor intentionally misrepresents its status as a small business, the contract is void or voidable. C&D Constr., Inc., ASBCA No. 38661, 90-3 BCA ¶ 23,256; J.E.T.S., Inc., ASBCA No. 28642, 87-1 BCA ¶ 19,569, aff'd, J.E.T.S., Inc. v. United States, 838 F.2d 1196 (Fed. Cir. 1988). Cf. Danac, Inc., ASBCA No. 30227, 92-1 BCA ¶ 24,519. Additionally, such a misrepresentation may be a false statement under 18 U.S.C. § 1001 and 15 U.S.C. § 645.

4. Size status protests. FAR 19.302.

a. An offeror, the SBA, or another interested party (including the contracting officer) may challenge a small business certification. A protest is "timely" if received by the contracting officer within 5 business days after bid opening or after the protester receives notice of the proposed awardee's identity in negotiated actions. A contracting officer's challenge is always timely. 13 C.F.R. § 121.1603. Alliance Detective & Sec. Serv., Inc., B-299342, Apr. 13, 2007, 2007 CPD ¶ 56; Eagle Design and Mgmt., Inc., B-239833, Sept. 28, 1990, 90-2 CPD ¶ 259.

(1) The contracting officer must forward the protest to the SBA Government Contracting Area Office and withhold award absent a finding of urgency. FAR 19.302(h)(1); Alliance Detective & Sec. Serv., Inc., supra; Aquasis Servs., Inc., B-240841.2, June 24, 1991, 91-1 CPD ¶ 592.

(2) The SBA Government Contracting Area Office must rule within 10 business days or the contracting officer may proceed with award. Systems Research and Application Corp., B-270708, Apr. 15, 1996, 96-1 CPD ¶ 186; International Ordnance, Inc., B-240224, July 17, 1990, 90-2 CPD ¶ 32.

(3) Area Office decisions are appealable to the Office of Hearings and Appeals (OHA). Agencies need not suspend contract action pending appeals to OHA. If an activity awards to a firm that the Area Office initially finds is "small," the activity need not terminate the contract if the SBA OHA later reverses the

Area Office's determination. FAR 19.302(i); McCaffery & Whitener, Inc., B-250843, Feb. 23, 1993, 93-1 CPD ¶ 168; Verify, Inc., B-244401.2, Jan. 24, 1992, 92-1 CPD ¶ 107.

b. In negotiated small business set-asides, the agency must inform each unsuccessful offeror prior to award of the name and location of the apparent successful offeror. FAR 15.503(a)(2) and FAR 19.302(d)(1); Resource Applications, Inc., B-271079, August 12, 1996, 96-2 CPD ¶ 61; Phillips Nat'l, Inc., B-253875, Nov. 1, 1993, 93-2 CPD ¶ 252.

c. Late protests (and timely protests filed after contract award) generally do not apply to the current contract. FAR 19.302(j). See Chapman Law Firm v. United States, 63 Fed. Cl. 25 (2004). But see Adams Indus. Servs., Inc., B-280186, Aug. 28, 1998, 98-2 CPD ¶ 56 (protester filed protest after award; however, under the circumstances of this procurement, simplified acquisition procedures did not require the agency to issue a pre-award notice to unsuccessful vendors. Since the protest was filed within 5 days after the protester received notice of the issuance of a purchase order to the awardee, the protest was considered timely).

d. The GAO does not review size protests. Hughes Grp. Sol., B-408781.2, Mar. 5, 2014, 2014 CPD ¶ 91;DynaLantic Corp., B-402326, 2010 CPD ¶ 103; McCaffery & Whitener, Inc., supra.

e. Courts will not overrule an SBA determination unless it is arbitrary, capricious, an abuse of discretion, or not in accordance with law or regulation. STELLACOM, Inc, v. United States, 24 Cl. Ct. 213 (1991).

E. **Competition Issues:** Contract Bundling. FAR 7.107; DFARS 202.170; 15 U.S.C. § 657q; 13 C.F.R. § 125.2.

1. Contract bundling is the practice of combining two or more procurement requirements, provided for previously under separate contracts, into a solicitation for a single contract. 15 U.S.C. § 632(o)(2); USA Info. Sys., Inc., B-291417, Dec. 30, 2002, 2002 CPD ¶ 224. Bundling may create barriers to some small businesses competing because the small businesses may be unable to meet all the combined requirements.

2. Bundling rules apply to multiple awards of IDIQ contracts and all orders placed under Federal Supply Schedule orders.

3. Congress and the SBA have taken steps to rein in bundled contracts through the Small Business Jobs Act of 2010 and its implementing regulations. Pub. L. No. 111-240, §§ 1312-13; 13 C.F.R. § 125.2; FAR 7.107, FAR 2.101.

   a. "Teaming" among two or more small firms is permitted, which may then submit an offer on a bundled contract.

   b. Agencies must submit to the SBA for review any statement of work containing bundled requirements. If the SBA concludes that the bundled requirements are too large, it may appeal to the agency. See, e.g., Phoenix Scientific Corp., B-286817, Feb. 24, 2001, 2001 CPD ¶ 24.

   c. When the solicitation requirements are "substantial," the agency must show that the bundling is "necessary and justified" and that it will obtain "measurably substantial benefits."

      (1) "Substantial bundling" means a contract consolidation resulting in an award with an annual average value of $10 million or more.

(2) An agency may find a bundled requirement "necessary and justified" if it will derive more benefit from bundling than from not bundling. See TRS Research, B-290644, Sept. 13, 2002, 2002 CPD ¶ 159.

(3) The agency must show that the benefits are "measurably substantial," defined as cost savings, price reduction, quality improvements, and other benefits that will lead to the following:

(a) Benefits equivalent to 10% if the contract value (including options) is $94 million or less; or

(b) Benefits equivalent to 5% or $9.4 million, whichever is greater, if the contract value (including options) is over $94 million.

(c) Reducing only administrative or personnel costs does not justify bundling unless those costs are expected to be at least 10% of the estimated bundled requirements (including options).

(4) Bundling rules do not apply to cost comparison studies conducted under OMB Circular A-76 or contracts awarded and performed entirely outside the United States.

4. Notice. When a proposed acquisition is funded entirely using DOD funds and potentially involves bundling, the contracting officer shall, at least 30 days prior to the release of a solicitation or 30 days prior to placing an order without a solicitation, publish in FedBizOpps.gov a notification of the intent to bundle the requirement and the substantial benefits expected. DFARS 205.205-70. A

proposed FAR rule would expand this DFARS provision to all agencies when requirements in excess of $2 million are bundled. 80 Fed. Reg. 31,561 (June 3, 2015).

F. **Responsibility Determinations and Certificates of Competency (COCs).** Federal Acquisition Streamlining Act of 1994, Pub. L. No. 103-355, § 7101, 108 Stat. 3243, 3367 [hereinafter FASA] (repealing § 804, National Defense Authorization Act, 1993, Pub. L. No. 102-484), 106 Stat. 2315, 2447 (1992); FAR Subpart 19.6.

1. The contracting officer must determine an offeror's responsibility. FAR 9.103(b).

2. If the contracting officer finds a small business nonresponsible, he must forward the matter to the SBA Contracting Area Office immediately. FAR 19.602-1(a)(2).

3. The SBA issues a COC if it finds that the offeror is responsible.

a. The burden is on the offeror to apply for a COC. Thomas & Sons Bldg. Contr., Inc., B-252970.2, June 22, 1993, 93-1 CPD ¶ 482.

b. The contracting officer may appeal a decision to issue a COC to the SBA Central Office. FAR 19.602-3; Department of the Army - Recon., B-270860, July 18, 1996, 96-2 CPD ¶ 23.

4. The contracting officer "shall" award to another offeror if the SBA does not issue a COC within 15 business days of receiving a referral. FAR 19.602-4(c); Mid-America Eng'g and Mfg., B-247146, Apr. 30, 1992, 92-1 CPD ¶ 414. Cf. Saco Defense, Inc., B-240603, Dec. 6, 1990, 90-2 CPD ¶ 462.

5. If the SBA refuses to issue a COC, the contracting officer need not refer the case back to the SBA upon presentation of new evidence by the contractor. Discount Mailers, Inc., B-259117, Mar. 7, 1995, 95-1 CPD ¶ 140.

6. Once issued, a COC is conclusive as to all elements of responsibility. GAO review of the COC process is limited to determining whether government officials acted in bad faith or failed to consider vital information. The Gerard Co., B-274051, Nov. 8, 1996, 96-2 CPD ¶ 177; UAV Sys., Inc., B-255281, Feb. 17, 1994, 94-1 CPD ¶ 121; J&J Maint., Inc., B-251355.2, May 7, 1993, 93-1 CPD ¶ 373; Accord Accurate Info. Sys., Inc. v. Dep't of the Treasury, GSBCA No. 12978-P, Sept. 30, 1994, 1994 BPD ¶ 203, mot. for recon. denied, 1994 BPD ¶ 236. But see Pittman Mech. Contractors, Inc.-Recon., B-242242.2, May 31, 1991, 91-1 CPD ¶ 525.

7. The COC procedure does not apply when an agency declines to exercise an option due to responsibility-type concerns. E. Huttenbauer & Son, Inc., B-258018.3, Mar. 20, 1995, 95-1 CPD ¶ 148.

8. The COC procedure generally does not apply when the contracting officer rejects a technically unacceptable offer. See Paragon Dynamics, Inc., B-251280, Mar. 19, 1993, 93-1 CPD ¶ 248; Pais Janitorial Serv. & Supplies, Inc., B-244157, June 18, 1991, 91-1 CPD ¶ 581.

9. The COC procedure applies when an agency determines that a small business contractor is nonresponsible based solely on a pass/fail evaluation of the firm's past performance. See Phil Howry Co., B-291402.3, B-291402.4, Feb. 6, 2003, 2003 CPD ¶ 33.

G. Regular Small Business Set-Asides. FAR Subpart 19.5.

1. The decision to set aside a procurement is within the "discretion" of the agency. FAR 19.501; Information Ventures, B-27994, Aug. 7, 1998, 98-2 CPD ¶ 37; Espey Mfg. & Elecs. Corp., B-254738.3, Mar. 8, 1994, 94-1 CPD ¶ 180; State Mgmt. Serv., Inc., B-251715, May 3, 1993, 93-1 CPD ¶ 355; but see Safety Storage, Inc., B2510851, Oct. 29, 1998, 98-2 BCA ¶ 102.

2. The agency must exercise its discretion reasonably and in accordance with statutory and regulatory requirements. DCT Inc., B-252479, July 1, 1993, 93-2 CPD ¶ 1; Neal R. Gross & Co., B-240924.2, Jan. 17, 1991, 91-1 CPD ¶ 53; Quality Hotel Offshore, B-290046, May 31, 2002, 2002 CPD ¶ 91.

3. DFARS 219.201(d) requires small business specialist review of all acquisitions over $10,000, except those restricted for exclusive small business participation.

4. Types of set-asides.

   a. Total Set-Asides.

      (1) Acquisitions over $150,000. FAR 19.502-2(b). The contracting officer shall setaside any acquisition over $150,000 for small business participation when:

      (a) The contracting officer reasonably expects to receive offers from two or more responsible small businesses, and

      (b) Award will be made at a fair market price.

      (2) Acquisitions between $3,000 and $150,000. FAR 19.502-2(a):

      (a) Each acquisition that has an anticipated dollar value exceeding $3,000, but not over $150,000, is automatically reserved for small business concerns.

      (b) Exceptions. There is no requirement to set aside if there is no reasonable expectation of receiving offers from two or more responsible small businesses that will be competitive in terms of price, quality, and delivery schedule.

b. Partial. FAR 19.502-3; <u>Aalco Forwarding, Inc., et. al.</u>, B-277241.16, Mar. 11, 1998, 98-1 CPD ¶ 75. The contracting officer must set aside a <u>portion</u> of an acquisition, except for construction, for exclusive small business participation when:

(1) A total set-aside is not appropriate;

(2) The requirement is severable into two or more economic production runs or reasonable lots;

(3) One or more small business concerns are expected to have the technical competence and capacity to satisfy the requirement at a fair market price; and

(4) The acquisition is not subject to simplified acquisition procedures.

5. Subcontractor Limitations. If the agency sets aside an acquisition, certain subcontracting and domestic end item limitations apply. FAR 52.219-14, Limitation on Subcontracting; <u>Innovative Refrigeration Concepts</u>, B-258655, Feb. 10, 1995, 95-1 CPD ¶ 61; <u>Adrian Supply Co.</u>, B-257261, Sept. 15, 1994, 95-1 CPD ¶ 21; <u>Kaysam Worldwide, Inc.</u>, B-247743, June 8, 1992, 92-1 CPD ¶ 500; <u>Vanderbilt Shirt Co.</u>, B-237632, Feb. 16, 1990, 90-1 CPD ¶ 290.

a. Services. The contractor must spend at least 50% of contract costs on its own employees.

b. Supplies.

(1) A small business manufacturer must perform at least 50% of the cost of manufacturing.

(2) A small business non-manufacturer (i.e., a dealer) must provide a small business

product unless the SBA determines that no small business in the federal market produces the item. <u>See</u> <u>Fluid Power Int'l, Inc.</u>, B-278479, Dec. 10, 1997, 97-2 CPD ¶ 162.

(3) Both manufacturers and non-manufacturers must provide domestically produced or manufactured items.

c. Construction. The contractor's employees must perform at least 15% of the cost of the contract. If special trade contractors perform construction, the threshold is 25%.

d. On 2014, the SBA issued a proposed rule that would amend these requirements. The so called "50% rule," which currently requires the calculation of the limitation on subcontracting thresholds based on the contractor's costs, would change to a simplified calculation based on total revenues received under the contract. 79 Fed. Reg. 77,967 (Dec. 29, 2014).

e. The SBA also issued a proposed rule in 2015 that would exempt "similar situated" subcontractors (i.e., those subcontractors who would be eligible for the same set-aside program) from the calculation of the limitation on subcontracting. Any revenues expended on those subcontractors would be treated as if the prime contractor was performing the work. <u>Id.</u>

6. Rejecting SBA set-aside recommendations and withdrawal of set-asides. FAR 19.505, 19.506.

a. The contracting officer may reject an SBA recommendation or withdraw a set-aside before award. <u>Aerostructures, Inc.</u>, B-280284, September 15, 1998, 98-2 CPD ¶ 71.

The contracting officer must notify the SBA of the rejection.

b. The FAR sets forth notice and appeal procedures for resolving disagreements between the agency and the SBA. If the contracting agency and the SBA disagree, the contracting agency has the final word on set-aside or withdrawal decisions.

c. Potential offerors also may challenge the contracting officer's decision to issue unrestricted solicitations or withdraw set-asides. DMS Pharmaceutical Group, Inc., B-406305, Apr. 6, 2012, 2012 CPD ¶ 140; American Imaging Servs., B-238969, July 19, 1990, 90-2 CPD ¶ 51.

d. If the activity receives no small business offers, the contracting officer may not award to a large business but must withdraw the solicitation and resolicit on an unrestricted basis. Western Filter Corp., B-247212, May 11, 1992, 92-1 CPD ¶ 436; CompuMed, B-242118, Jan. 8, 1991, 91-1 CPD ¶ 19; Ideal Serv., Inc., B-238927.2, Oct. 26, 1990, 90-2 CPD ¶ 335.

7. An agency is not required to set aside the reprocurement of a defaulted contract. Premier Petro-Chemical, Inc., B-244324, Aug. 27, 1991, 91-2 CPD ¶ 205.

8. Small business set-asides also apply to multiple-award IDIQ contracts. Regardless of whether the overall contract was restricted, a contracting officer may set aside a specific task/delivery order for small business concerns. FAR 19.504-4.

III. PROGRAMS FOR SMALL DISADVANTAGED BUSINESSES.

A. **Contracting Officers' Discretion**: Contracting Officers may freely choose among available socioeconomic programs when determining whether to set aside an acquisition, provided the relevant criteria are met – there is no longer any order of precedence. See FAR 19.203

B. **Contracting with the SBA's "8(a)" Business Development Program.** 15 U.S.C. § 637(a); 13 C.F.R. Part 124; FAR Subpart 19.8.

1. The primary program in the federal government designed to assist small disadvantaged businesses is commonly referred to as the 8(a) program. The program derives its name from Section 8(a) of the Small Business Act. Section 8(a) authorizes the SBA to enter into contracts with other federal agencies. The SBA then subcontracts with eligible small disadvantaged businesses (SDBs). 15 U.S.C. § 637(a).

a. By partnership agreement between DOD and the SBA, DOD can bypass SBA and contract directly with 8(a) SDBs on behalf of the SBA. The agreement delegates only the authority to sign contracts on behalf of the SBA. The SBA remains the prime contractor on all 8(a) contracts, continues to determine eligibility of concerns for contract award, and retains appeal rights under FAR 19.810. See DFARS 219.800(a) and FAR 19.8.

b. Either the SBA or the contracting activity may initiate selection of a requirement or a specific contractor for an 8(a) acquisition. FAR 19.803.

c. Businesses must meet the criteria set forth in 13 C.F.R. §§ 124.102-124.109 to be eligible under the 8(a) program. Autek Sys. Corp., 835 F. Supp. 13 (D.D.C. 1993), aff'd, 43 F.3d 712 (D.C. Cir. 1994).

(1) The firm must be owned and controlled by socially and economically disadvantaged persons. The regulations require 51% ownership and

control by one or more individuals who are <u>both</u> socially and economically disadvantaged. <u>See Software Sys. Assoc. v. Saiki</u>, No. 92-1776 (D.D.C. June 24, 1993); <u>SRS Technologies v. United States</u>, No. 95-0801 (D.D.C. July 18, 1995).

(a) Socially disadvantaged individuals are those who have been subjected to racial or ethnic prejudice or cultural bias within American society because of their identities as members of groups and without regard to their individual qualities. The social disadvantage must stem from circumstances beyond their control. 13 C.F.R. § 124.103(a).

    (i) There is a rebuttable presumption that members of certain designated groups are socially disadvantaged. 13 C.F.R. § 124.103(b)(1).

    (ii) Individuals who are not members of designated socially disadvantaged groups must establish individual social disadvantage by a "preponderance of the evidence." 13 C.F.R § 124.103(c)(1). Previously, individuals not members of designated groups needed to prove social disadvantage by "clear and convincing evidence."

(b) Economically disadvantaged individuals are socially disadvantaged individuals whose ability to compete in the free enterprise system has been impaired due to diminished credit capital and credit opportunities as compared to others in the same or similar line of business who are not socially disadvantaged. 13 C.F.R. § 124.104(a).

    (i) In considering diminished capital and credit opportunities, the SBA will consider such factors as:

        (a) Personal income for the last two years;

        (b) Personal net worth and the fair market value of all assets; and

        (c) Financial condition of the applicant compared to the financial profiles of small businesses in the same primary industry classification.

    (ii) Net Worth. 13 C.F.R. § 124.104(c). For initial 8(a) eligibility, the net worth of an individual claiming disadvantage must be less than $250,000. For continued 8(a) eligibility, net worth must be less than $750,000.

(2) The firm must have been in business for two full years in the industry for which it seeks certification.

(3) The firm must possess the potential for success. 15 U.S.C. § 637(a)(7).

(4) The SBA is responsible for determining which firms are eligible for the 8(a) program. The SBA has reasonable

discretion to deny participation in the 8(a) program to clearly unqualified firms as long as applications receive careful and thorough review. See Neuma Corp. v. Abdnor, 713 F. Supp. 1 (D.D.C. 1989).

d.   The firm must have an approved business plan. 15 U.S.C. § 636(j)(10)(1).

e.   Generally, the SBA will not accept an 8(a) reservation if:

   (1)   An activity already has issued a solicitation as a small business or SDB set-aside;

   (2)   The SBA determines that inclusion of a requirement in the 8(a) program will affect a small business or SDB adversely. 13 C.F.R. § 124.504(c)(1)-(3)(2004). See Designer Assocs., B-293226, Feb. 12, 2004, 2004 CPD ¶ 114; C. Martin Co., Inc., B-292662, Nov. 6, 2003, CPD ¶ 2007; John Blood, B-280318-19, Aug. 31, 1998, 98-2 CPD ¶ 58; McNeil Technologies, Inc., B-254909, Jan. 25, 1994, 94-1 CPD ¶ 40.

2.   Procedures.

   a.   If the activity decides that an 8(a) contract is feasible, it offers SBA an opportunity to participate.

   b.   If the SBA accepts, the agency or the SBA chooses a contractor, or eligible firms compete for award. See FAR 19.800(b); Defense Logistics Agency and Small Bus. Admin. Contract No. DLA100-78-C-5201, B-225175, Feb. 4, 1987, 87-1 CPD ¶ 115.

   c.   Activities must generally compete for acquisitions if:

   (1)   The activity expects offers from two eligible, responsible 8(a) firms at a fair market price, see Horioka Enters., B-259483, Dec. 20, 1994, 94-2 CPD ¶ 255; and

   (2)   The value of the contract is expected to exceed $6.5 million for actions assigned manufacturing NAICS codes or $4 million for all other codes. See 13 C.F.R. § 124.506(a); FAR § 19.805-1(a)(2). The threshold applies to the agency's estimate of the total value of the contract, including all options. Id.

   (3)   If neither of these apply, the contracting officer must prepare a written Justification & Approval (J&A) to sole source to an 8(a) if an acquisition exceeds $20 million. FAR 19.808-1; FAR 6.303. Any sole source to an 8(a) with a value over $20 million must be approved by an appropriate agency official (as currently defined by FAR 6.304) and made public after award. FAR 6.303.

   d.   The COC procedures do not apply to sole source 8(a) acquisitions. DAE Corp. v. SBA, 958 F.2d 436 (1992); Action Serv. Corp. v. Garrett, 797 F. Supp. 82 (D.P.R. 1992); Universal Automation Leasing Corp., GSBCA No. 11268-P, 91-3 BCA ¶ 24,255; Joa Quin Mfg. Corp., B-255298, Feb. 23, 1994, 94-1 CPD ¶ 140; Aviation Sys. & Mfg., Inc., B-250625.3, Feb. 18, 1993, 93-1 CPD ¶ 155; Alamo Contracting Enters., B-249265.2, Nov. 20, 1992, 92-2 CPD ¶ 358.

   e.   Subcontracting limitations apply to competitive 8(a) acquisitions. See

FAR 52.219-14; <u>Data Equip., Inc. v. Dep't of the Air Force</u>, GSBCA No. 12506-P, 94-1 BCA ¶ 26,446; <u>see also</u> <u>Tonya, Inc. v. United States</u>, 28 Fed. Cl. 727 (1993); <u>Jasper Painting Serv., Inc.</u>, B-251092, Mar. 4, 1993, 93-1 CPD ¶ 204.

f. Partnership between General Services Administration (GSA) and SBA.

(1) SBA agreed to accept all 8(a) firms in GSA's Multiple Award Schedule Program.

(2) Agencies that buy from a Federal Supply Schedule 8(a) contractor may count the purchase toward the agency's small business goals.

g. Graduation from 8(a) program. Firms graduate from the 8(a) program when they successfully achieve the targets, objectives, and goals set forth in their business plan prior to expiration of the program term. 13 C.F.R. § 124.302. <u>See</u> <u>Gutierrez-Palmenberg, Inc.</u>, B-255797.3, Aug. 11, 1994, 94-2 CPD ¶ 158.

(1) 8(a) time period upheld. <u>Minority Bus. Legal Defense & Educ. Funds, Inc. v. Small Bus. Admin.</u>, 557 F. Supp. 37 (D.D.C. 1982). No abuse of discretion by refusing to keep a contractor in 8(a) program beyond nine years. <u>Woerner v. United States</u>, 934 F.2d 1277 (App. D.C. 1991).

h. The GAO will not consider challenges to an award of an 8(a) contract by contractors that are not eligible for the program or particular acquisition. <u>CW Constr. Servs. & Materials, Inc.</u>, B-279724, July 15, 1998, 98-2 CPD ¶ 20; <u>AVW Elec. Sys., Inc.</u>, B-252399, May 17, 1993, 93-1 CPD ¶ 386. Likewise, the GAO

will not consider challenges to an SBA decision that an 8(a) contractor is not competent to perform a contract. <u>L. Washington & Assocs.</u>, B-255162, Oct. 19, 1993, 93-2 CPD ¶ 254.

i. The SBA has broad discretion in selecting procurements for the 8(a) program; the GAO will not consider a protest challenging a decision to procure under the 8(a) program absent a showing of possible bad faith on the part of the government officials or that regulations may have been violated. 4 C.F.R. § 21.5(b)(3)(2004). <u>See</u> <u>American Consulting Servs., Inc.</u>, B-276149.2, B-276537.2, July 31, 1997, 97-2 CPD ¶ 37; <u>Comint Sys. Corp.</u>, B-274853, B-274853.2, Jan. 8, 1997, 97-2, CPD ¶ 14.

3. Mentor/Protégé Program. 13 C.F.R. § 124.520.

a. The Mentor/Protégé Program is designed to encourage approved mentors to provide various forms of assistance to eligible 8(a) contractors. The purpose of mentor/protégé relationship is to enhance the capabilities of the protégé and to improve its ability to successfully compete for contracts. This assistance may include:

(1) Technical and/or management assistance;

(2) Financial assistance in the form of equity investments and/or loans;

(3) Subcontracts; and

(4) Joint venture arrangements.

b. Mentors. Any concern that demonstrates a commitment and the ability to assist an 8(a) contractor may act as a mentor.

261

c. A mentor benefits from the relationship in that it may:

(1) Joint venture as a small business for any government procurement;

(2) Own an equity interest in the protégé firm up to 40%; and

(3) Qualify for other assistance by the SBA.

d. In late 2014, the SBA issued a proposed rule that would expand the mentor/protégé program beyond the 8(a) program to all other programs for disadvantaged small businesses. 79 Fed. Reg. 77,959 (Dec. 29, 2014).

C. Challenges to the 8(a) Program.

1. Adarand Constructors, Inc. v. Pena, 115 S. Ct. 2097 (1995). In a five to four holding, the Supreme Court declared that all racial classifications, whether benign or pernicious, must be analyzed by a reviewing court using a "**strict scrutiny**" standard. Thus, only those affirmative action programs that are narrowly tailored to achieve a compelling government interest will pass constitutional muster. Cf. American Federation of Government Employees (AFL-CIO) v. United States, 195 F. Supp. 2d 4 (D.D.C. 2002) (holding that the rational basis standard is still applicable to "political" (Native-American) rather than racial classifications).

2. Post-Adarand Reactions and Initiatives. *See* 49 C.F.R. § 26 (current DOT regulations implementing DBE program).

3. Post-Adarand Cases. Sherbrooke Turf Inc. v. Minn. Dep't of Transp., 2001 U.S. Dist. LEXIS 19565 (Nov. 14, 2001); Cache Valley Elec. Co. v. State of Utah, 149 F.3d 1119 (10th Cir. 1998); Cortez III Serv. Corp. v. National Aeronautics & Space Admin., 950 F. Supp. 357 (D.D.C. 1996); Ellsworth Assoc. v. United States, 937 F. Supp. 1 (D.D.C. 1996); SRS Technologies v. Department of Defense, 917 F. Supp. 841 (D.D.C. 1996); Dynalantic Corp. v. Department of Defense, 894 F. Supp. 995 (D.D.C. 1995); C.S. McCrossan Constr. Co., Inc. v. Cook, 1996 U.S. Dist. LEXIS 14721 40 Cont. Cas. Fed. ¶ 76,917 (D.N.M. 1996).

4. Adarand on Remand. Adarand Constructors, Inc. v. Pena, 965 F. Supp. 1556 (D. Colo. 1997). But see Adarand Constructors, Inc. v. Slater, 169 F.3d 1292 (10th Cir. 1999); Adarand Constructors, Inc. v. Slater, 120 S. Ct. 722 (2000). Adarand Constructors, Inc. v. Slater, 228 F.3d 1147 (10th Cir. 2000); Adarand Constructors, Inc. v. Mineta, 122 S. Ct. 511 (2001) (cert. dismissed).

5. Rothe Development Corporation v. Department of Defense, 545 F.3d 1023 (Fed. Cir. 2008). The United States Court of Appeals for the Federal Circuit held that 10 U.S.C. § 2323, granting evaluation preferences to SDBs, failed to withstand strict scrutiny analysis and violated the Equal Protection Clause. The court found that there was not sufficient evidence to show a national pattern of discrimination in either private or public contracting. This was a fact-specific case and does not unequivocally rule out any future SDB-like programs. Accordingly, the FAR Council and DOD removed the FAR and DFARS provisions that were based upon 10 U.S.C. § 2323. Those provisions based on the Small Business Act were retained.

D. HUBZone. HUBZone Act of 1997, Title VI of Public Law 105-135, enacted on December 2, 1997 (111 Stat. 2592). Incorporated at FAR Subpart 19.13.

1. The purpose of the HUBZone program is to provide federal contracting assistance for qualified small business concerns located in historically underutilized business zones in an effort to increase employment opportunities. 13 C.F.R. § 126.100, FAR 19.1301, *et seq.*

2. Benefits to HUBZone Small Business Concerns:

a. Price preference of 10% generally applied to other than small-business concerns in acquisitions expected to exceed the simplified acquisition threshold. FAR 19.1307.

b. Set-aside authority similar to all other small business programs: where acquisition is above micro-purchase threshold, and the contracting officer has a reasonable expectation that: (1) he/she will receive offers from two or more HUBZone SBCs and (2) award will be made at fair market price. FAR 19.1305.

c. Sole source awards. A contracting officer may award a contract to a HUBZone SBC on a sole source basis if: (1) only one HUBZone SBC can satisfy the requirement, (2) the anticipated price of the contract (including options) will not exceed $6.5M for NAICS codes for manufacturing or $4M for any other NAICS codes, (3) the requirement is not being performed by another HUBZone SBC, (4) the acquisition is greater than the simplified acquisition threshold, (5) the HUBZone SBC has been determined to be a responsible contractor, and (6) award can be made at a fair and reasonable price. FAR 19.1306.

3. The program applies to all federal departments and agencies that employ contracting officers. 13 C.F.R. § 126.101.

4. Requirements to be a Qualified HUBZone Small Business Concern (SBC). 13 C.F.R. § 126.103; FAR 19.1303.

a. The concern must be a HUBZone SBC as defined by 13 C.F.R. § 126.103;

b. Principal office must be in a HUBZone (see Mark Dunning Industries, Inc. v. U.S., 64 Fed. Cl. 374 (2005) (holding that a "principal office" under HUBZone regulations can be very different than the typical company headquarters. "Principal office" is where the greatest number of employees at any one location perform their work.); and

c. At least 35% of the SBC's employees working on the contract must reside in the HUBZone and the concern must certify that it will attempt to maintain this percentage during the performance of any HUBZone contract.

5. An owner of a HUBZone SBC is a person who owns any legal or equitable interest in the concern. More specifically, SBCs include: corporations, partnerships, sole proprietorships and limited liability companies. 13 C.F.R. § 126.201. See also § 126.6161 (Joint Ventures).

6. Size standards. 13 C.F.R. § 126.203. At time of application for certification, a HUBZone SBC must meet SBA's size standards for its primary industry classification.

7. Certification. 13 C.F.R. § 126.300. An SBC must apply to the SBA for certification.

8. Methods of Acquisition. 13 C.F.R. § 126.600. HUBZone contracts can be awarded through any of the following procurement methods:

a. Sole source awards;

b. Set-aside awards based on competition restricted to qualified HUBZone SBCs; or

c. Awards to qualified HUBZone SBCs through full and open competition after a price evaluation preference in favor of qualified HUBZone SBCs.

9. Simplified Acquisition Procedures. 13 C.F.R. § 126.608. If the requirement is below the simplified acquisition threshold, the contracting officer should set aside the requirement for consideration among

qualified HUBZone SBCs using simplified acquisition procedures.

10. A concern that is both a qualified HUBZone SBC and an SDB must receive the benefit of both the HUBZone price evaluation preference and the SDB price evaluation preference described in 10 U.S.C. § 2323, in full and open competition.

11. Subcontracting Limitations. 13 C.F.R. § 126.700. A qualified HUBZone SBC prime contractor can subcontract part of its HUBZone contract provided:

   a. Service Contract (except Construction) – the SBC must spend at least 50% of the cost of the contract performance incurred for personnel on the concern's employees or on the employees of other qualified HUBZone SBCs;

   b. General Construction – the SBC must spend at least 15% of the cost of the contract performance incurred for personnel on the concern's employees or on the employees of other qualified HUBZone SBCs;

   c. Special Trade Construction – the SBC must spend at least 25% of the cost of the contract performance incurred for personnel on the concern's employees or on the employees of other qualified HUBZone SBCs; and

   d. Supplies – the SBC must spend at least 50% of the cost of the contract performance incurred for personnel on the concern's employees or on the employees of other qualified HUBZone SBCs.

   e. As noted in paragraph II.G.5.d above, the SBA has issued a new proposed rule with a new method of calculating these limitations on subcontracting.

12. Protest Procedures. HUBZone status challenges have similar procedures to size

status protests. FAR 19.306; 13 C.F.R. § 126.801.

E. **Service-Disabled, Veteran-Owned Small Businesses (SDVOSB)**. FAR 19.14; 13 C.F.R.§ 125.8 to 125.29.

1. Status as a SDVOSB is determined in accordance with 13 C.F.R. parts 125.8-125.13 and FAR 19.14. SDVOSBs may self-certify.

2. SDVOSB status protests are handled similar to HUBZone status protests. FAR 19.307.

3. Set-aside authority. A contracting officer may set aside acquisitions exceeding the micro-purchase threshold for competition restricted to SDVOSB concerns if the contracting officer has a reasonable expectation that: (1) offers will be received from two or more SDVOSBs and (2) award will be made at a fair market price.

F. **Sole Source Award Authority**. A contracting officer may award contracts to SDVOSBs on a sole source basis if: (1) only one such business can satisfy the requirement; (2) the anticipated award price of the contract (including options) will not exceed $6.5M for a requirement with a NAICS code for manufacturing or $4M for all other NAICS codes; (3) the SDVOSB has been determined to be responsible; and (4) award can be made at a fair and reasonable price. 13 C.F.R.§ 125.20.

G. **The Women-Owned Small Business (WOSB) Program**. 15 U.S.C. § 637(m); FAR 19.15.

1. This program includes economically disadvantaged women-owned small businesses (EDWOSB).

2. Status as an economically disadvantaged women-owned small business (EDWOSB) or WOSB concern is determined in accordance with 13 C.F.R. part 127. FAR 19.1503(a).

3. EDWOSB and WOSB concerns may self-certify, but the self-certification program was eliminated in the 2015 National Defense Authorization Act. SBA has suggested that self-certification can continue until SBA establishes a regulatory framework for formal certification.

4. EDWOSB and WOSB status protests are handled similar to HUBZone status protests. FAR 19.308.

5. Set-Asides for EDWOSBs and WOSBs. The contracting officer may set aside acquisitions exceeding the micro-purchase threshold for competition restricted to EDWOSB or WOSB concerns eligible under the WOSB Program in those NAICS codes in which SBA has determined that women-owned small business concerns are underrepresented or substantially underrepresented in Federal procurement, as specified on SBA's website at http://www.sba.gov/WOSB. FAR 19.1505; 13 C.F.R. Part 127a.

    a. For requirements in NAICS codes designated by SBA as underrepresented, a contracting officer may restrict competition to EDWOSB concerns or qualified WOSBs if the contracting officer has a reasonable expectation that (1) two or more WOSB or EDWOSB concerns will submit offers; and (2) the award will be made at a fair and reasonable price.

    b. The contracting officer may make an award if only one acceptable offer is received from a qualified EDWOSB or WOSB concern, but if no acceptable offers are received from an EDWOSB or WOSB concern, the set-aside shall be withdrawn and the requirement, if still valid, must be considered for set-aside in accordance with 19.203 and subpart 19.5. FAR 19.1505(d), (f).

6. Sole source award authority. A contracting officer may award contracts to a WOSB or EDWOSB on a sole source basis if: (1) only one such business can satisfy the requirement, (2) the anticipated award price of the contract (including options) will not exceed $6.5M for a requirement with an NAICS code for manufacturing or $4M for all other NAICS codes, (3) the WOSB or EDWOSB has been determined to be responsible, and (4) award can be made at a fair and reasonable price.

H. Contractor Obligations to Support Small Businesses.

1. The overwhelming majority of contract awards are made to large businesses. Large businesses receiving a government contract have several obligations to support small businesses. FAR 52.219-8, Utilization of Small Business Concerns (Oct. 2014).

2. Prior to award of a contract, offerors are typically requested to submit and negotiate a subcontracting plan containing percentage goals for placing subcontracts with the various categories of small businesses.

3. After award, the prime contractor must make a good faith effort to comply with its plan, and must flow down its small business obligations in subcontracts awarded to large businesses. FAR 52.219-8(d)(9) and (k).

IV. THE RANDOLPH-SHEPPARD ACT.

A. References.

1. The Randolph-Sheppard Act for the Blind 20 U.S.C. §§ 107-107f.

2. U.S. Dept. of Defense, Directive 1125.3, Vending Facility Program for the Blind on Federal Property (7 Apr. 1978) [hereinafter DOD Dir. 1125.3]

3. 34 C.F.R. Part 395, Vending Facility Program for the Blind on Federal Property (Department of Education).

4. 32 C.F.R. Part 260, Vending Facility Program for the Blind on Federal Property (Department of Defense).

5. Gaydos, The Randolph-Sheppard Act: A Trap for the Unwary Judge Advocate, ARMY LAW. Feb. 1984, at 21.

B. History of the RSA.

1. Purpose. The purpose of the Randolph-Sheppard Act was to provide blind persons with remunerative employment, enlarge the economic opportunities of the blind, and stimulate the blind to greater efforts in making themselves self-supporting. 20 U.S.C. § 107a.

2. Original Act. Act of June 20, 1936, Pub. L. No. 732, 49 Stat. 1559.

    a. The purpose of the Act was for federal agencies to give blind vendors the authorization to operate in federal buildings.

    b. The Act gave agency heads the discretion to exclude blind vendors from their building if the vending stands could not be properly and satisfactorily operated by blind persons.

    c. Location of the stand, type of stand and issuing the license were all subject to approval of the federal agency in charge of the building.

    d. Office of Education, Department of Interior, was designated to administer the program, and could designate state commissions or agencies to perform licensing functions. Department of Education Regulations appear to take precedence over other agency regulations in the event of a conflict. 61 Fed. Reg. 4,629, February 7, 1996.

3. The 1954 Amendments. Act of Aug. 3, 1954, Pub. L. No. 565m, 68 Stat. 663 (1954).

    a. The invention of vending machines served as an impetus to re-examine the Act. The amendments also showed concern for expanding the opportunities of the blind.

    b. The amendments made three main changes to the act:

        (1) The vending program was changed from federal *buildings* to federal *properties*. Federal property was defined as "any building, land, or other real property owned, leased, or occupied by any department or agency of the United States." The Act applies to all federal activities—whether appropriated or non-appropriated activities.

        (2) Agencies were required to give blind persons a preference, so far as feasible, when deciding who could operate vending stands on federal property.

        (3) This preference was protected by requiring agencies to write regulations ensuring the preference.

    c. The "so far as feasible" language still gave agencies wide discretion in administering the Act, and reality fell far short of Congressional intent to expand the blind vending program.

4. The 1974 Amendments. Act of Dec 7, 1974, Pub. L. No. 516, 88 Stat. 1623 (1974).

    a. Impetus—the proliferation of automatic vending machines and lack of enthusiasm for the Act by federal agencies.

    b. Comptroller General study showcased the abuses and ineffectiveness of the Act. Review of

<u>Vending Operations on Federally Controlled Property</u>, Comp. Gen. Rpt. No. B-176886 (Sept. 27, 1973).

C.   Current Act.

1.   The current RSA imposes several substantive and procedural controls. The Act mandated three main substantive provisions:

 a.   Give blind vendors priority on federal property;

 b.   New buildings to include satisfactory sites for blind vendors; and

 c.   Require paying some vending machine income to the blind.

2.   Priority to Blind Vendors.

 a.   In authorizing the operation of vending facilities on federal property, priority <u>shall</u> be given to blind persons licensed by a state agency. 20 U.S.C. § 107(b).

 b.   The Secretary of Education, the Commissioner of Rehabilitative Services Administration, and the federal agencies shall prescribe regulations that ensure priority.

 c.   Vending facilities are defined as "automatic vending machines, cafeterias, snack bars, cart services, shelters, counters, and such other appropriate auxiliary equipment … [which is] … necessary for the sale of articles or services … and which may be operated by blind licensees." 20 U.S.C. § 107e(7).

  (1)   Vending facilities typically sell newspapers, periodicals, confections, tobacco products, foods, beverages, and other articles or services dispensed automatically or manually and prepared on or off the premises, and include the vending or exchange of

chances for any state lottery. 20 U.S.C. § 107a(a)(5). <u>See, e.g.,</u> Conduct on the Pentagon Reservation, 32 C.F.R. Parts 40b and 234, para. 234.16, exempting sale of lottery tickets by RSA vending facilities from the general prohibition of gambling.

  (2)   Vending machines are defined as coin- or-currency operated machines that dispense articles or services, except for items of a recreational nature, such as jukeboxes, pinball machines, electronic game machines, pool tables, and telephones. 32 C.F.R. § 260.6(q).

  (3)   The Act's definition of vending facilities lumps vending machines, vending stands, and cafeterias into the same definition. Despite this single definition, DOD once treated vending machines and vending stands much differently from cafeteria operations.

  (4)   Opportunities regarding vending machines and stands are the burden of the State Licensing Agency (SLA). The SLA must seek out and apply for a permit. The installation has no affirmative obligation until the permit request is received. Once received, the blind vendor has priority unless the interests of the U.S. are adversely affected.[1]

---

[1] The DOD regulation, 32 C.F.R. § 260.3(i), requires notification to the SLA at least 60 days prior to the intended acquisition, alteration, or renovation of agency buildings. Opportunities regarding cafeterias must be solicited by sending the SLA a copy of each solicitation. If the proposal is not within the competitive range, the award may be made to another offeror. If the submitted proposal is within the

Socioeconomic Policies

D.   Arbitration Procedures.

1.   Two roads to arbitration:

a.   Grievances of blind vendors. A dissatisfied blind vendor may submit a request to the SLA for a full evidentiary hearing on any action arising from the operation or administration of the vending facility program. 20 U.S.C. § 107d-1. If the blind vendor is dissatisfied with the decision made by the SLA, the vendor may file a complaint with the Secretary of Education, who shall convene a panel to arbitrate the dispute.

b.   Complaints by the SLA. SLA may file a complaint with the Secretary of Education if it determines that the agency is failing to comply with the Randolph-Sheppard Act or its implementing regulations. Upon filing of such a complaint, the Secretary convenes a panel to arbitrate. The panel's decision is final and binding on the parties, except that appeal may be made under the Administrative Procedure Act. 20 U.S.C. § 107d-1(b) and 20 U.S.C. § 107d-2(a). NOTE: The arbitration procedures do not provide the blind vendors with a cause of action against any agency. The blind vendors have an avenue to complain of wrongs by the SLA. The SLA has a forum to complain against a federal agency, which it believes is in violation of the act.

E.   Protests to GAO.

1.   Relationship to the Small Business Act's 8(a) Provisions. The requirements of the RSA take precedence over the 8(a)

program. Triple P. Services, Inc., Recon., B-250465.8, December 30, 1993, 93-2 CPD ¶ 347 (denying challenge to agency's decision to withdraw an 8(a) set-aside and to proceed under the Randolph-Sheppard Act). But see Intermark, B-290925, Oct. 23, 2002 (holding that the Army improperly withdrew a small-business set-aside solicitation for food services at Fort Rucker and reissued a solicitation for RSA businesses. GAO recommended a "cascading" set of priorities whereby competition is limited to small business concerns, with the SLA receiving award if its proposal is found to be within the competitive range).

2.   Protest by SLA. The GAO will not consider a protest lodged by an SLA, because binding arbitration is the appropriate statutory remedy for the SLA. Washington State Department of Services for the Blind, B-293698.2, Apr. 27, 2004, 2004 CPD ¶ 84 (dismissing a protest filed by the SLA, stating that the RSA "vests exclusive authority with the Secretary [of Education] regarding complaints by SLAs concerning a federal agency's compliance with the Act, including challenges to agency decisions to reject proposals in response to a solicitation"); Mississippi State Department of Rehabilitation Services, B-250783.8, Sept. 7, 1994, 94-2 CPD ¶ 99 (unpub).

F.   Controversial Issues.

1.   Burger King and McDonald's restaurants on military installations. Army and Air Force Exchange Services ("AAFES") Burger King and McDonald's franchise agreements violated two provisions of the Randolph-Sheppard Act:

a.   DOD failed to notify state licensing agencies of its intention to solicit bids for vending facilities, and

b.   DOD's solicitation for nationally franchised fast-food restaurants constituted a limitation on the placement or operation of a vending facility. DOD violated the RSA by

---

competitive range, the blind vendor receives the contract unless the award adversely affects the interests of the U.S., or if the vendor does not have the capacity to operate a cafeteria in such a manner as to provide food service at a comparable cost and quality as other providers.

failing to seek the Secretary of Education's approval for such limitation.

c. Arbitration Panel's remedy:

(1) AAFES must contact the SLA in each state with a Burger King facility to establish a procedure acceptable to the SLA for identifying, training, and installing blind vendors as managers of all current and future Burger King operations. Additionally, DOD should give the SLA 120 days' written notice of any new Burger King operations.

(2) AAFES will provide the appropriate SAL with 120 days' notice of any new McDonald's facility. The SLA must determine whether it wishes to exercise its priority and to provide funds to build and operate a new McDonald's facility. 60 Fed. Reg. 4406, January 23, 1995.

d. Randolph-Sheppard Vendors of America v. Weinberger, 795 F.2d 90 (Fed. Cir. 1986). SLA protested contracts between AAFES and Burger King, and the Navy Exchange Service and McDonald's. The court remanded to the District Court with an order to dismiss, because the SLA had failed to exhaust administrative remedies.

G. Applicability to Military Mess Hall Contracts.

GAO has determined that the RSA applies to military dining facilities. In doing so, the GAO focused on the regulatory definition of "cafeteria." In addition, the GAO gave significant weight to the regulatory interpretation of the Department of Education and to interpretations by certain high-level officials within DOD. Department of the Air Force—

Reconsideration, B-250465.6, June 4, 1993, 93-1 CPD ¶ 431. The applicability of the RSA to mess halls remains a topic of considerable debate.

1. In NISH v. Cohen, 247 F.3d 197 (4th Cir. 2001), the Fourth Circuit affirmed a District Court holding that the Act applied to military "mess hall services." Court relied heavily on the DOD position that RSA applies.

2. In Automated Comm'n Sys., Inc. v. United States, 49 Fed. Cl. 570 (2001), the Court of Federal Claims (COFC) refused to hear a challenge to the validity of DOD Directive 1125.3, which mandated the RSA preference for dining facility contracts. COFC concluded that only federal district courts may hear a challenge to the validity of procurement statutes and regulations under their federal question and declaratory judgment authorities. COFC also held that the more specific RSA preference takes precedence over less-specific statutes, specifically the HUBZone preference.

V. THE BUY AMERICAN ACT (BAA).

A. Origin and Purpose. 41 U.S.C. Chapter 83; Executive Order 10582 (1954), as amended, Executive Order 11051 (1962). The Act was passed during the Depression of the 1930s and was designed to save and create jobs for American workers.

B. Preference for Domestic Products/Services.

1. As a general rule, under the BAA, agencies may acquire only domestic end items. Unless another law or regulation prohibits the purchase of foreign end items, however, the contracting officer may not reject as nonresponsive an offer of such items.

2. The prohibition against the purchase of foreign goods does not apply if: the product is not available in sufficient commercial quantities; domestic

preference would be inconsistent with the public interest; the product is for use outside the United States; the cost of the domestic product would be unreasonable; the product is for commissary resale; or the purchase is under the micro-purchase threshold. The Trade Agreements Act and the North American Free Trade Agreement may also provide exceptions to the BAA for many countries.

C. **Definitions and Applicability.** FAR 25.003.

1. Manufactured domestic end products are those articles, materials, and supplies acquired for public use under the contract that are:

    a. Manufactured in the United States. Valentec Wells, Inc., ASBCA No. 41659, 91-3 BCA ¶ 24,168; General Kinetics, Inc., Cryptek Div., 242052.2, May 7, 1991, 70 Comp. Gen. 473, 91-1 CPD ¶ 445 ("manufacture" means completion of the article in the form required for use by the government); A. Hirsh, Inc., B-237466, Feb. 28, 1990, 69 Comp. Gen. 307, 90-1 CPD ¶ 247 (manufacturing occurs when material undergoes a substantial change); Ballantine Labs., Inc., ASBCA No. 35138, 88-2 BCA ¶ 20,660; and

    b. Comprised of "substantially all" domestic components (over 50% test by cost). For DOD, the components may be domestic or qualifying country components. See DFARS 252.225-7001.

2. An unmanufactured domestic end product must be mined or produced in the United States. Geography determines the origin of an unmanufactured end product. 41 U.S.C. § 8302(a)(1).

3. The nationality of the company that manufactures an end item is irrelevant. Military Optic, Inc., B-245010.3, Jan. 16, 1992, 92-1 CPD ¶ 78.

4. Components are materials and supplies incorporated directly into the end product. Orlite Eng'g Co., B-229615, Mar. 23, 1988, 88-1 CPD ¶ 300; Yohar Supply Co., B-225480, Feb. 11, 1987, 66 Comp. Gen. 251, 87-1 CPD ¶ 152.

    a. Parts are not components, and their origin is not considered in this evaluation. Hamilton Watch Co., B-179939, June 6, 1974, 74-1 CPD ¶ 306.

    b. A component is either entirely foreign or entirely domestic. A component is domestic only if it is manufactured in the United States. Computer Hut Int'l, Inc., B-249421, Nov. 23, 1992, 92-2 CPD ¶ 364.

    c. A foreign-made component may become domestic if it undergoes substantial remanufacturing in the United States. General Kinetics, Inc, Cryptek Div., B-242052.2, May 7, 1991, 70 Comp. Gen. 473, 91-1 CPD ¶ 445.

    d. Material that undergoes manufacturing is not a "component" if the material is so transformed that it loses its original identity. See Orlite Eng'g and Yohar Supply Co., supra.

    e. The cost of components includes transportation costs to the place of incorporation into the end product, and any applicable duty. FAR 25.101; DFARS 252.225-7001(a)(5)(ii). Component costs do NOT include:

        (1) Packaging costs, S.F. Durst & Co., B-160627, 46 Comp. Gen. 784 (1967);

        (2) The cost of testing after manufacture, Patterson Pump Co., B-200165, Dec. 31, 1980, 80-2 CPD ¶ 453; Bell Helicopter Textron,

B-195268, 59 Comp. Gen. 158 (1979); or

(3) The cost of combining components into an end product, To the Secretary of the Interior, B-123891, 35 Comp. Gen. 7 (1955).

5. Qualifying country end products/components. See DFARS 225.872.

   a. DOD does not apply the restrictions of the BAA when acquiring equipment or supplies that are mined, produced, or manufactured in "qualifying countries." Qualifying countries are countries with which we have reciprocal defense agreements, listed at DFARS 225.872-1(a).

   b. A manufactured, qualifying country end product must contain over 50% (by cost) components mined, produced, or manufactured in the qualifying country or the United States. DFARS 252.225-7001(a)(7).

   c. Qualifying country items thus receive a "double benefit" under the BAA. First, qualifying country components may be incorporated into a product manufactured in the United States to become a domestic end product. Second, products manufactured by a qualifying country are exempt from the BAA.

D. Certification Requirement.

1. A contractor certifies by its offer that each end product is domestic and/or indicates which end products are foreign. FAR 52.225-1; DFARS 252.225-7006.

2. The contracting officer may rely on the offeror's certification that its product is domestic, unless, prior to award, the contracting officer has reason to question the certification. New York Elevator Co., B-250992, Mar. 3, 1993, 93-1 CPD ¶ 196 (construction materials); Barcode Indus.,

B-240173. Oct. 16, 1990, 90-2 CPD ¶ 299; American Instr. Corp., B-239997, Oct. 12, 1990, 90-2 CPD ¶ 287.

E. Exceptions. As a general rule, the BAA does not apply in the following situations:

1. The required products are not available in sufficient commercial quantities. FAR 25.103(b); Midwest Dynamometer & Eng'g Co., B-252168, May 24, 1993, 93-1 CPD ¶ 408.

2. The agency head (or designee) determines that domestic preference is inconsistent with the public interest. FAR 25.103(a). DOD has determined that it is inconsistent with the public interest to apply the BAA to qualifying countries. Technical Sys. Inc., B-225143, Mar. 3, 1987, 87-1 CPD ¶ 240.

3. The Trade Agreements Act (TAA) authorizes the purchase. 19 U.S.C. §§ 2501-82; FAR 25.4; Olympic Container Corp., B-250403, Jan. 29, 1993, 93-1 CPD ¶ 89; Becton Dickinson Acute Care, B-238942, July 20, 1990, 90-2 CPD ¶ 55; IBM Corp., GSBCA No. 10532-P, 90-2 BCA ¶ 22,824.

   a. If the TAA applies to the purchase, only domestic products, products from designated foreign countries, qualifying country products, and products which, though comprised of over 50% foreign components, are "substantially transformed" in the United States or a designated country, are eligible for award. See Compuadd Corp. v. Dep't of the Air Force, GSBCA No. 12021-P, 93-2 BCA ¶ 25,811 ("manufacturing" standard of the BAA is less stringent than "substantial transformation" required under TAA); Hung Myung (USA) Ltd., B-244686, Nov. 7, 1991, 71 Comp. Gen. 64, 91-2 CPD ¶ 434; TLT-Babcock, Inc., B-244423, Sept. 13, 1991, 91-2 CPD ¶ 242.

b. The TAA applies only if the estimated cost of an acquisition equals or exceeds a threshold (currently $191,000 for supplies) set by the U.S. Trade Representative. 80 Fed. Reg. 77,695 (Dec. 15, 2015).

c. The TAA does **not** apply to DOD unless the DFARS lists the product, even if the threshold is met. See DFARS 225.401-70. If the TAA does not apply, the acquisition is subject to the BAA. See, e.g., Hung Myung (USA) Ltd., B-244686, Nov. 7, 1991, 91-2 CPD ¶ 434; General Kinetics, Inc, Cryptek Div., 242052.2, May 7, 1991, 91-1 CPD ¶ 445.

d. Because of the component test, the definition of "domestic end product" under the BAA is more restrictive than the definition of "U.S.-made end product" under the TAA. Thus, for DOD, if an offeror submits a U.S.-made end product, the BAA evaluation factor still may apply.

4. The North American Free Trade Agreement (NAFTA) Implementation Act authorizes the purchase. Pub. L. No. 103-182, 107 Stat. 2057 (1993); FAR 25.402. Note, however, that NAFTA does not apply to DOD procurements unless the DFARS lists the product. See DFARS 225.401-70.

5. The Caribbean Basin Economic Recovery Act authorizes the purchase. 19 U.S.C. §§ 2701-05; FAR 25.400.

6. Other Trade Agreements. The United States has entered into numerous other trade agreements on a bilateral basis, including agreements with Australia, Bahrain, Chile, Colombia, Jordan, Korea, Panama, and Singapore. Attorneys should review FAR Part 25 and DFARS Part 225 periodically for the implementation of bilateral agreements.

7. The product is for use outside the United States. Note: under the Balance of Payments Program, an agency must buy domestic even if the end item is to be used overseas. A number of exceptions allow purchase of foreign products under this program. If both domestic and foreign products are offered, and if the low domestic price exceeds the low foreign price by more than 50%, the contracting officer must buy the foreign item. FAR Subpart 25.3; DFARS Subpart 225.3.

8. The cost of the domestic product is unreasonable. FAR 25.105; DFARS 225.103(c); FAR 225.5. Although cost reasonableness normally is a pre-award determination, an agency may also make this determination after award. John C. Grimberg Co. v. United States, 869 F.2d 1475 (Fed. Cir. 1989).

a. Civilian agencies.

(1) If an offer of a non-domestic product is low and a large business offers the lowest-priced domestic product, increase the non-domestic product by 6%.

(2) If an offer of a non-domestic product is low and a small business offers the lowest-priced domestic product, increase the non-domestic product by 12%.

b. DOD agencies increase offers of non-domestic, non-qualifying country products by 50%, regardless of the size of the business that offers the lowest-priced domestic end product. Under the DFARS, if application of the differential does not result in award on a domestic product, disregard the differential and evaluate offers at face value. DFARS 225.502.

c. Do not apply the evaluation factor to post-delivery services such as installation, testing, and training. Dynatest Consulting, Inc., B-

272

257822.4, Mar. 1, 1995, 95-1 CPD ¶ 167.

d. In a negotiated procurement, agencies may award to a firm offering a technically superior but higher priced non-domestic, non-qualifying country product. STD Research Corp., B-252073.2, May 24, 1993, 93-1 CPD ¶ 406.

F. **Construction Materials.** 41 U.S.C. § 8302; FAR Subpart 25.2.

1. The BAA requires contractors to use only domestic materials in performing contracts for the construction, alteration, or repair of any public building or public work in the United States.

2. Exceptions. See FAR 25.202.

    a. The cost would be unreasonable, as determined by the head of agency;

    b. The agency head (or delegee) determines that use of a particular domestic construction material would be impracticable; or,

    c. The material is not available in sufficient commercial quantities.

3. Application of the restriction. The restriction applies to the material in the form that the contractor brings it to the construction site. See S.J. Amoroso Constr. Co. v. United States, 26 Cl. Ct. 759 (1992), aff'd, 12 F.3d 1072 (Fed. Cir. 1993); Mauldin-Dorfmeier Constr., Inc., ASBCA No. 43633, 93-2 BCA ¶ 25,790 (board distinguishes "components" from "construction materials"); Mid-American Elevator Co., B-237282, Jan. 29, 1990, 90-1 CPD ¶ 125.

4. Post-award exceptions.

    a. Contractors must formally request waiver of the BAA. C. Sanchez & Son v. United States, 6 F.3d 1539 (Fed. Cir. 1993) (contractor failed to formally request waiver of BAA;

claim for equitable adjustment for supplying domestic wire denied).

    b. Failure to grant a request for waiver may be an abuse of discretion. John C. Grimberg Co. v. United States, 869 F.2d 1475 (Fed. Cir. 1989) (contracting officer abused discretion by denying post-award request for waiver of BAA, where price of domestic materials exceeded price of foreign materials plus differential).

5. The DOD qualifying country source provisions do not apply to construction materials. DFARS 225.872-2(b).

G. **Remedies for Buy American Act Violations.**

1. If the agency head finds a violation of the BAA—Construction Materials, the findings and the name of the contractor are made public. The contractor will be debarred for three years. FAR 25.206.

2. Termination for default is proper if the contractor's product does not contain over 50% (by cost) domestic or qualifying country components. H&R Machinists Co., ASBCA No. 38440, 91-1 BCA ¶ 23,373.

3. A contractor is not entitled to an equitable adjustment for providing domestic end items if required by the BAA. Valentec Wells, Inc., ASBCA No. 41659, 91-3 BCA ¶ 24,168; LaCoste Builders, Inc., ASBCA No. 29884, 88-1 BCA ¶ 20,360; C. Sanchez & Son v. United States, supra.

H. **The Berry Amendment.** 10 U.S.C. §§ 2533a and 2533b; DFARS Subpart 225.70.

1. Since 1941, Congress has enacted domestic preferences for various commodities and components that apply to many purchases by the Department of Defense. The preferences favor specific industries, such as textile manufacturing and suppliers of metal alloys.

Socioeconomic Policies

2. 10 U.S.C. § 2355a requires DODs to purchase items "grown, reprocessed, reused, or produced" in the U.S. from domestic firms, including food, clothing, tents, fabric components, and hand tools. The statute contains numerous exceptions, and the highly technical nature of those exceptions requires careful analysis when applied to specific acquisitions.

3. The Beret Saga. See 43 THE GOV'T CONTRACTOR 18 at ¶ 191 (Associate Professor Stephen L. Schooner, George Washington University Law School, and Judge Advocate (USAR), discussing the purchase of black berets from foreign-owned contractors and Congress's response).

4. Specialty Metals. 10 U.S.C. § 2533B.

   a. The statute requires that DOD-acquired aircraft, missile and space systems, ships, tank and automotive items, weapons systems, and ammunition be manufactured using specialty metals melted or produced in the United States.

   b. Specialty metals are defined by their chemical content. 10 U.S.C. § 2533b(l). Contractors should consult technical experts to determine whether the specific metals used in manufacture meet the definition.

   c. There are several exceptions available for specialty metals. The most commonly applicable exception relates to agreements with foreign governments that provide for removal of competitive barriers in the sales of defense products. DOD has negotiated many such agreements with (mostly) European countries. DFARS 7003-3(b)(4). Contractors should carefully review the requirements for an applicable exception.

I. **Appropriation Act Restrictions.**

1. Department of Defense Annual Appropriations Acts, from time to time, enact domestic preference restrictions applicable to specific goods and services acquired with funds provided by the act. Many restrictions are reenacted year after year, but change as new restrictions are added, and occasionally are dropped.

2. Typically, such restrictions are included in DFARS Subpart 225.70 and are incorporated into contracts by general provisions. See DFARS Subpart 252.225. Contract attorneys should consult the restrictions to see if any apply to a contractor's goods and services.

VI. EQUAL OPPORTUNITY AND AFFIRMATIVE ACTION

A. **Introduction.**

In 1941, President Roosevelt issued a series of Executive Orders beginning with E.O. 8802, 6 Fed. Reg. 3109 (1941), which prohibited discrimination in defense industries and in the federal government. With this exercise of executive power, President Roosevelt launched the federal government on a path of implementing social policies through the economic power of government contracting. Today, there are contractual clauses promoting elimination of discrimination, favoring veterans and the disabled, prohibiting child labor, and eliminating human trafficking. Contractors assume an obligation to comply with the implementing regulations as part of accepting award of almost every government contract or subcontract.

B. **Equal Employment Opportunity. E.O. 11246; FAR Subpart 22.8.**

1. Every government contract and subcontract and their solicitations contain a number of equal opportunity clauses, including:

   a. FAR 52.222-26, Equal Opportunity;

   b. FAR 52.222-21, Prohibition of Segregated Facilities;

c. FAR 52.222-22, Previous Contracts and Compliance Reports;

d. FAR 52.222-25, Affirmative Action Compliance

e. FAR 52.222-29, Notification of Visa Denial, if the contractor is required to perform in or on behalf of a foreign country.

2. Pre-award Clearance.

a. Contracting officers must obtain pre-award clearance from the Department of Labor on contract awards over $10M. FAR 22.805(a).

b. Prime contractors must obtain pre-award clearance on first-tier subcontract awards over $10M. FAR 52.222-24.

3. Contractor EEO Obligations.

a. Generally, the EEO clauses apply to a contractor if the value of all government contracts and subcontracts awarded over the course of a year exceeds $10,000.

b. The EEO clauses generally require compliance with Executive Order 11246 and the Department of Labor's implementing regulations at 40 C.F.R. Part 60.

c. Obligations include, but are not limited to, non-discrimination based on many identified criteria and reporting requirements.

d. The Department of Labor has compliance guides for contractors.

4. Contractor Affirmative Action Plans.

a. When a contractor or subcontractor has more than 50 employees and a contract or subcontract over $50,000, then the contractor must develop a written affirmative action plan. Contractors should consult knowledgeable counsel in the preparation of such plans.

b. The contractor must complete its affirmative action plan within 120 days of the first contract/subcontract award.

5. The Office of Federal Contract Compliance audits contractors for compliance with its regulations.

C. **Veterans.**

1. All government contracts and subcontracts over $150K must contain clauses giving preferences to certain veterans in hiring and promotion. FAR 22.1310. Covered contractors/subcontractors are required to comply with DOL regulations at 40 C.F.R. Part 60-300.

2. Contractors and subcontractors must report annually veteran-related employment information. FAR 52.222-37. They must also represent that they have filed their reports when submitting a bid or proposal on a new contract.

D. **Disabled Persons**.

1. All government contracts and subcontracts over $15K must contain a clause requiring equal opportunity and affirmative action for qualified disabled employees. FAR 22.1408(a).

2. Covered contractors must comply with the regulations at 41 C.F.R. § 60.741.5(a).

VII. HUMAN TRAFFICKING.

A. What is Human Trafficking?

Human trafficking consists of two types of activities. The first group is using fraud, coercion, or involuntary servitude in the employment process, such as withholding passports from employees to prevent them from quitting. The second group is activities related to commercial sex acts, whether procuring or supplying.

B. Prohibitions.

FAR 52.222-50 prohibits human trafficking in all forms, and is included in all solicitations, contracts, and subcontracts. Specific employment practices that are common in many countries are prohibited in the performance of government contracts and subcontracts.

C.   Subcontracts.

The contractors and subcontractors must include FAR 52.222-50 in all subcontracts. Contractors should take specific care that their subcontractors understand and follow the clause, since violations by subcontractors affect the prime contractor.

VIII. CONCLUSION.

The socioeconomic policies reflected in the mandatory clauses are broadly viewed as desirable practices, and contractors who avoid government contracts to avoid compliance with the clauses have experienced significant adverse publicity. The clauses sweep in many businesses because of the low thresholds for applicability and the lack of exemptions. Consequently, the practices required by the clauses are (or should be) followed by most employers of any size.

SELECTED LABOR STANDARDS

I. INTRODUCTION.

Some of the most significant policies implemented in government contracts are the policies regulating a contractor's treatment of its employees. Acquisition regulations implement policies in various federal statutes and executive orders. Labor policies have always been controversial, and because of the differing views of the two major political parties, labor policies have changed over time depending on which party controls the executive and legislative branches of government. Both the Congress and the executive branch have used government contracts as a mechanism for regulating labor/management relations in U.S. industry for many years. Early prohibitions on contractors using convict labor, child labor, etc., have been expanded to include regulatory regimes controlling wages, working hours, hiring and firing decisions, and many other topics.

Today, labor/management relations are the subject of heated political discourse, with many differing opinions on the best policies. Government and contractor attorneys, however, need only focus on the current requirements to ensure that their respective organizations diligently comply with the applicable laws and regulations. The government maintains a policy of impartiality in labor disputes. FAR 22.101-1(b).

The sections of this chapter will cover a number of labor/management relations topics, some statutorily based and longstanding, and some based on Executive Orders and/or relatively recent. Together, they give government contractors and their employees rights and responsibilities in the workplace, and government agencies oversight responsibilities.

The U.S. Department of Labor, Wage and Hour Division, provides extensive guidance on compliance with applicable laws and regulations. See https://www.dol.gov/compliance/guide/index.htm.

Each military service has a designated labor advisor to support contracting officers on contract labor matters. See FAR 22.1001 and 22.1003-7; DFARS 222.001; and http://www.wdol.gov/ala.aspx for names and phone numbers. The Defense Procurement and Acquisition Policy (DPAP) office has a helpful website to assist government officials. See http://www.acq.osd.mil/dpap/cpic/cp/labor_information.html.

II. MINIMUM WAGES: THE FAIR LABOR STANDARDS ACT OF 1938 (FLSA) AND EXECUTIVE ORDER 13658.

A. **Legal Authority.**

1. FLSA. 29 U.S.C. §§ 201-219; FAR Subpart 22.10.

2. Executive Order (E.O.) 13658, Establishing a Minimum Wage for Contractors, dated February 12, 2014. Implemented at 29 C.F.R. Part 10; FAR Subpart 22.19.

B. **Fair Labor Standards Act.**

1. General. The FLSA was the first federal wage-hour law having general applicability; its application is not limited to government contracts.

2. Coverage. The FLSA covers employees engaged in interstate commerce and the production of goods for interstate commerce. Various categories of employees are exempt from the FLSA requirements. See 29 C.F.R. Part 541.

3. Purpose. The FLSA specifies a federal minimum wage, currently $7.25 per hour, and payment of overtime wages at time and one half of their regular rate of pay

for all hours in excess of 40 hours in a work week.

4. The FLSA also restricts the use of child labor.

C. **E.O. 13658**.

1. General. In 2014, the President issued E.O. 13658, to establish minimum wages for employees performing work on a federal contract, including prime contractors and all tiers of subcontractors.

2. Coverage. The minimum wage under E.O. 13658 is implemented in contracts by FAR 52.222-55. The clause applies to work performed in the United States on all contracts performed in whole or in part in the United States that include either FAR 52.222-6 (Davis Bacon Act) or FAR 52.222-41 (Service Contract Act). The regulations do not apply to contracts for the manufacturing or furnishing of materials, supplies, articles, or equipment to the Federal Government that are subject to the Walsh-Healey Public Contracts Act. See 79 Fed. Reg. 34,577 June 17, 2014.

3. Minimum Wage. The minimum wage was originally set at $10.10 per hour, with annual adjustments. Currently, the minimum hourly wage is $10.15 for 2016. The contractor may not meet its obligations by the payment of benefits.

4. Flow Down. The prime contractor or higher-tier subcontractor must flow down the clause to lower-tier subcontractors. FAR 52.222-55(k).

5. Adjustment. The contractor may be entitled to an adjustment in the contract price should the government increase the amount of the minimum wage payable under the Executive Order. FAR 52.222-55(b)(3)(i).

D. **Other Minimum Wage Laws.**

1. Various state and local government have established minimum wage laws within their jurisdictions providing for the payment of higher wages than those under the FLSA or the E.O.

2. The FLSA and E.O. 13658 <u>do not</u> preempt those state and local minimum wage laws, and a contractor must pay higher minimum wages, if applicable. FAR 52.222-55(b)(8).

III. SICK LEAVE.

A. **Legal Authority.** The President issued E.O. 13706 on 7 September 2015; 81 Fed. Reg. 9591. The Department of Labor has issued a notice of proposed rulemaking, and the department is expected to issue regulations by 30 September 2016. The expected effective date of those regulations is January 1, 2017.

B. **Coverage.** The coverage of the proposed regulations is expected to be identical to that for the Executive Order on minimum wages for contractor employees. https://www.dol.gov/whd/flsa/eo13706/faq.htm. The regulations will apply to all contracts awarded based on solicitations issued after 1 January 2017 that are subject to the Davis Bacon Act or the Service Contract Act, plus various concession- and service-type contracts.

C. **Requirements.** The E.O. requires covered contractors to:

1. Provide one hour of sick leave for every 30 hours worked.

2. Allow employees to carry over no less than 56 hours of time.

3. Reinstate sick leave if the employee returns within 12 months.

4. Honor sick leave accrued by employees if the contractor is a successor contractor on a federal contract when the work is at the same location doing the same or similar work.

5. Comply with state and local requirements in effect that impact an employer.

IV. CONTRACT WORK HOURS AND SAFETY STANDARDS ACT (CWHSSA).

A. **Legal Authority.** 40 U.S.C. Chapter 37; FAR Subpart 22.3; FAR 22.403-3; DFARS Subpart 222.3.Application.

1. Types of employees covered--laborers and mechanics.

2. The CWHSSA applies to construction and service contracts in excess of $100,000.

3. The CWHSSA usually does not apply to supply contracts. FAR 22.305(b).

B. **Purposes.**

1. CWHSSA establishes a forty-hour work week and requires the payment of overtime wages for public works and other covered contracts. See Maitland Bros. Inc., ENG BCA No. 5782, 94-1 BCA ¶ 26,473.

2. CWHSSA specifies health and safety requirements.

C. **Government Overtime Policy.** It is government policy that contractors perform without using overtime. FAR 22.103-2. The government will not reimburse the contractor for overtime payments unless the contracting officer determines that overtime is in the government's interest. FAR 52.222-2. Consult agency regulations for guidance on disposition of withheld funds. See, e.g., Defense Finance and Accounting Service-Indianapolis Regulation 37-1, ch. 9, para. 092028.B.2 [hereinafter DFAS-IN 37-1].

V. COPELAND (ANTI-KICKBACK) ACT.

A. **Legal Authority.** 18 U.S.C. § 874; 40 U.S.C. § 3145; 29 C.F.R. Part 3; FAR 22.403-2.Application.

1. The Anti-Kickback Act protects the wages of any person engaged in the construction or repair of a public building or public

work (including projects that are financed at least in part by federal loans or grants).

2. The Act requires prime contractors and subcontractors to submit a weekly statement of compliance pertaining to the wages paid to each employee during the preceding week. FAR 22.403-2; FAR 52.222-10.

B. **Purpose.** The Act prohibits employers from exacting "kickbacks" from employees as a condition of employment.

C. **Recordkeeping Requirements.** The Anti-Kickback Act requires contractors and subcontractors to submit weekly payroll reports and statements of compliance. Both the contractors and the agency must keep these records for three years after completion of the contract. FAR 22.406-6.

VI. DAVIS-BACON ACT (DBA).

A. **Legal Authority.** 40 U.S.C. §§ 3141-3144; 29 C.F.R. Part 5; FAR Subpart 22.4; DFARS Subpart 222.4.

B. **Statutory Requirements.** 40 U.S.C. § 3142; FAR 22.403-1.

1. Contractors must pay mechanics and laborers a "prevailing wage rate" on federal construction projects performed in the United States that exceed $2,000. The underlying policy is to prevent contractors in low-wage areas from importing workers into higher-wage areas and undercutting local contractors. It does so by requiring all contractors to pay the prevailing wages in the geographic area.

2. The prevailing wage rate is the key to the Davis-Bacon labor standards. The Department of Labor determines the minimum wage, which normally is based on the wage paid to the majority of a class of employees in an area. 29 C.F.R. § 1.2 (1999).

a. A wage determination is not subject to review by the Government Accountability Office or boards of contract appeals. See

Labor Standards

American Fed'n of Labor - Congress of Indus. Org., Bldg., and Constr. Trades Dep't, B-211189, Apr. 12, 1983, 83-1 CPD ¶ 386; Woodington Corp., ASBCA No. 34053, 87-3 BCA ¶ 19,957; but see Inter-Con Sec. Sys., Inc., ASBCA No. 46251, 95-1 BCA ¶ 27,424 (finding board has jurisdiction to consider effect of wage rate determination on contractual rights of a party).

b. "Wages" under the terms of the DBA include the basic hourly pay rates plus fringe benefits.

C. Application. FAR 22.402.

1. The DBA applies to federal contracts involving construction of public buildings or public works.

a. "Public building" or "public work" means a construction or repair project that is carried on by the authority, or with the funds, of a federal agency to serve the interests of the general public.

b. The DBA applies only to construction activity performed at the worksite.

c. The "site of the work" is limited to the geographical confines of the construction jobsite, but this is a fluid concept. See L.P. Cavett Co. v. Dep't of Labor, 101 F.3d 1111 (6th Cir. 1996); Ball, Ball, and Brossamer, Inc. v. Reich, 24 F.3d 1447 (D.C. Cir 1994), rev'g Ball, Ball, and Brossamer, Inc. v. Martin, Sec'y of Labor, 800 F. Supp. 967 (D.D.C. 1992); see also Bechtel Constructors Corp., DOL ARB No. 95-045A, July 15, 1996. DOL finally changed its regulations in response to these decisions in late 2000. See 65 Fed. Reg. 80,268 (Dec. 20, 2000) (amending 5 C.F.R. §§ 5.2j and 5.2l).

d. Transportation of materials to and from the site is not considered "construction" covered by the DBA. See 65 Fed. Reg. 80,268 (Dec. 20, 2000) (amending 29 C.F.R. § 5.2(j) (1)(iv) and 5.2(j)(2)); Building & Constr. Trades Dep't, AFL-CIO v. Department of Labor Wage Appeals Board, 932 F.2d 985 (D.C. Cir.

1991), rev'g 747 F. Supp. 26 (D.D.C. 1990) (holding invalid C.F.R. provision that included as "construction" transportation of materials and supplies to and from the site); but see 29 C.F.R. § 3.2(b) (1999); FAR 22.401.

2. Dual Coverage. See FAR 22.402(b); DFARS 222.402-70.

a. The DBA also may apply to construction work performed under a non-construction contract, e.g., installation support contracts. Apply DBA standards if the contract requires a substantial and segregable amount of construction, repair, painting, alteration, or renovation.

b. The DBA applies to repairs but not to maintenance. The DFARS provides a bright-line test to determine whether work is maintenance (Service Contract Act work) or repair (Davis-Bacon Act work). If a service order requires 32 or more work hours, the work is "repair." Otherwise, consider the work to be "maintenance." For painting, the work is subject to the DBA if the service order requires painting of 200 square feet or more, regardless of work hours.

3. Non-Dual Coverage. The DBA does not apply to construction work to be performed as part of non-construction contracts if:

a. The construction work is incidental to other contract requirements; or

b. The construction work is so merged with non-construction work, or so fragmented in terms of the locations or time spans in which it is to be performed, that it cannot be segregated as a separate contractual requirement.

D. Employees Covered and Exempted. 29 C.F.R. § 5.2(m) (1999); FAR 22.401.

1. "Laborers or mechanics" are covered, including:

a. Manual laborers employed by a contractor or subcontractor at any tier. Cf. Ken's Carpets Unlimited v. Interstate

Landscaping, Inc., 37 F.3d 1500 (6th Cir. 1994) (non-precedential) (holding prime contractor alone responsible for DBA wages where prime failed to include proper clauses in subcontract); and

b. Working foremen who devote more than 20 percent of their time during a workweek to performing duties as a laborer or mechanic.

2. Office workers, superintendents, technical engineers, scientific workers, and other professionals, executives, and administrative personnel are <u>exempt</u>. 29 C.F.R. Part 541.

E. Types of Wage Determinations. 29 C.F.R. § 1.6 (1999); FAR 22.404-1.

1. General Wage Determinations. 29 C.F.R. §§ 1.5(b) and 1.6(a)(2) (1999); FAR 22.404-1(a). A general wage determination contains prevailing wage rates for the types of construction specified in the determination, and is used in contracts performed within a specified geographical area. General wage determinations remain valid until modified or canceled by the Department of Labor.

2. Project Wage Determinations. 29 C.F.R. § 1.6(a)(1) (1999); FAR 22.404-1(b).

a. The contracting officer uses a project wage determination when no general wage determination applies to the work. The determination is effective for 180 calendar days from the date of its issuance. Once incorporated into a contract, the project wage determination is effective for the duration of that contract.

b. If the project wage determination expires, the contracting officer must follow special procedures; these vary depending on whether the activity was contracted by sealed bidding or negotiation. FAR 22.404-5.

F. Procedures for Obtaining Wage Determinations. FAR 22.404-3.

1. General requirements.

a. If a general wage determination is applicable to the project, the agency may use it without notifying DOL. These wage determinations are available on the Internet. Go to the Wage Determinations OnLine.gov website (http://www.wdol.gov) or your respective civilian agency website.

b. If necessary, a contracting officer may request that DOL establish a recurring general wage determination.

c. A contracting officer may request a project wage determination from DOL by specifying the location of the project and including a detailed description of the types of construction involved and the estimated cost of the project.

d. Processing time for wage rate determinations is at least 30 days.

e. DOL (Wage and Hour Division) defines types of construction for use in selecting proper wage rate schedules. FAR 22.404-2(c).

2. If possible, the contracting officer must include the proper wage rate determination in each solicitation covered by the DBA.

a. Solicitations issued without a wage rate determination must advise that the contracting officer will issue a schedule of minimum wage rates as an amendment to the solicitation. FAR 22.404-4(a). If an offeror fails to acknowledge an amendment to an IFB that adds or modifies a wage rate, the offer <u>may</u> be nonresponsive. <u>ABC Project Mgmt., Inc.</u>, B-274796.2, Feb. 14, 1997, 97-1 CPD ¶ 74.

b. If the activity uses sealed bidding, it may not open bids until a reasonable time after furnishing the wage determination to all bidders.

c. In negotiated acquisitions, the contracting officer may open the proposals and conduct negotiations before obtaining the wage determination, but must include the wage determination in the solicitation before calling for final proposal revisions. FAR 22.404-4(c).

G. **Failure to Incorporate a Wage Determination.** If the contracting officer fails to incorporate a wage determination in a contract upon award, the contracting officer must:

1. Modify the contract to incorporate the required wage rate determination retroactive to the date of award, and equitably adjust the contract price, if appropriate. FAR 22.404-9(b)(1). See BellSouth Comm. Sys., Inc., ASBCA No. 45955, 94-3 BCA ¶ 27,231; or

2. Terminate the contract. FAR 22.404-9(b)(2). Sunspot Garden Ctr. & Country Craft Gift Shop, B-237065.2, Feb. 26, 1990, 90-1 CPD ¶ 224.

H. **Modifications of Wage Determinations.** FAR 22.404-6.

1. DOL may modify a general or project wage determination. The requirement to include a modification in a solicitation or contract depends upon when the agency receives notice of the modification and the method of acquisition.

a. General determinations. Actual receipt or constructive notice.

b. Project determinations. Actual receipt by the agency.

2. Sealed Bidding. FAR 22.404-6(b).

a. Before bid opening, a modification is effective if:

(1) The agency actually receives it, or DOL publishes notice of the modification in the Federal Register, 10 or more calendar days before the bid opening date; or

(2) The agency actually receives it, or DOL publishes notice, less than 10 calendar days before the date of bid opening, unless the contracting officer finds there

is insufficient time before bid opening to notify prospective bidders.

b. If the contracting officer receives an effective modification before bid opening, the contracting officer must extend the opening and permit bidders to revise their offers. FAR 22.404-6(b)(3).

c. If notice of a modification to a general wage determination is published in the Federal Register or posted on the Internet after bid opening, but before award, the modification is effective only if award is not made within 90 days of opening. FAR 22.404-6(b) (6). See Twigg Corp. v. General Servs. Admin., GSBCA No. 14639, 99-1 BCA ¶ 30,217 (holding contractor entitled to an equitable adjustment where agency failed to incorporate revised wage determination).

d. The contracting officer receives an effective rate modification after bid opening, but before award. The contracting officer must:

(1) Award the contract and incorporate the new determination to be effective on the date of contract award; or

(2) Cancel the solicitation.

e. The contracting officer receives an effective rate modification after award. The contracting officer shall change the contract to incorporate the wage modification retroactive to the date of award. FAR 22.404-6(b)(5).

3. Contracting by Negotiation. FAR 22.404-6(c).

a. Any modification received by the contracting agency or published in the Federal Register before award is effective. FAR 22.404-6(c)(1).

b. The contracting officer receives an effective rate modification before award. The contracting officer must amend the solicitation to include the modification and must allow prospective offerors to revise their proposals if the closing date for receipt of proposals has not yet passed. If the closing date has passed, the contracting officer must notify offerors who submitted proposals. FAR 22.404-6(c)(2).

c. The <u>contracting officer</u> receives an effective modification <u>after award.</u> The contracting officer must change the contract to incorporate the rate modification. FAR 22.404-6(c)(3).

I. Contract Administration--Compliance Checks and Investigations.

1. The contracting officer must make checks and conduct investigations to ensure compliance with the DBA requirements. FAR 22.406-7; DFARS 222.406-1.

2. Regular compliance checks include:

a. Employee interviews;

b. On-site inspections;

c. Payroll reviews; and

d. Comparison of information gathered during checks with available data, e.g., inspector reports and construction activity logs.

3. The contracting officer must conduct special compliance checks when inconsistencies, errors, or omissions are discovered during regular checks or if complaints are filed.

4. Labor Standards Investigations. FAR 22.406-8; DFARS 222.406-8.

a. The contracting agency investigates when compliance checks indicate that violations are substantial in amount, willful, or uncorrected. The DOL also may perform or request an investigation.

b. The contracting officer notifies the contractor of preliminary findings, proposed corrective actions, and certain contractor rights. FAR 22.406-8(c).

c. The contracting officer forwards a report to the agency head who, in certain cases, must forward it to DOL. If the contracting officer finds substantial evidence of criminal activity, the agency head must forward the report to the U.S. Attorney General.

J. Withholding and Suspending Contract Payments. FAR 22.406-9.

1. The contracting officer shall <u>withhold</u> contract payments if the contracting officer believes a violation of the DBA has occurred, or upon request by the DOL. 29 C.F.R. § 5.5(a)(2)(1999); FAR 22.406-9(a)(1) (allowing cross-withholding). See <u>M.E. McGeary Co.</u>, ASBCA No. 36788, 90-1 BCA ¶ 22,512; <u>see also</u> DFAS-IN 37-1, ch. 9, para. 092028.B.1 (prescribing procedures for disposition of withheld funds). <u>See</u> <u>Westchester Fire Insurance Co. v. United States</u>, 52 Fed. Cl. 57 (2002) (although contract terminated five months before, contracting officer was required to withhold funds pursuant to DOL request).

2. The contracting officer shall <u>suspend</u> any further payment, advance, or guarantee of funds otherwise due to a contractor if a contractor or subcontractor fails or refuses to comply with the DBA.

K. Disputes Relating to DBA Enforcement. FAR 22.406-10; FAR 52.222-14.

1. The DOL settles labor disputes that are not resolved at the local level. Labor disputes are not reviewable under the Disputes clause. <u>Emerald Maint., Inc. v. United States</u>, 925 F.2d 1425 (Fed. Cir. 1991); <u>Page Constr. Co.</u>, ASBCA No. 39685, 90-3 BCA ¶ 23,012; <u>M.E. McGeary Co.</u>, <u>supra</u>.

2. Boards of contract appeals and courts review claims relating to labor disputes if the dispute is based on the contractual rights and obligations of the parties. See, e.g., <u>MMC Constr., Inc.</u>, ASBCA No. 50,863, 99-1 BCA ¶ 30,322 (assuming jurisdiction over claim for excessive DBA wage withholding); <u>Commissary Servs. Corp.</u>, ASBCA No. 48613, 97-1 BCA ¶ 28,749 (assuming jurisdiction over dispute regarding DBA offset when ultimate issue was whether same prime

contractor was involved in both contracts); <u>American Maint. Co.</u>, ASBCA No. 42011, 92-2 BCA ¶ 24,806 (assuming jurisdiction over contractor's claim for reimbursement of fringe benefits); <u>Central Paving, Inc.</u>, ASBCA No. 38658, 90-1 BCA ¶ 22,305 (assuming jurisdiction over claim that original wage rate information in contract was incorrect). <u>Cf.</u> <u>Page Constr. Co.</u>, ASBCA No. 39685, 90-3 BCA ¶ 23,012 (declining jurisdiction over claim that government breached statutory obligation).

3. Federal district courts have jurisdiction to review DOL's implementation of the DBA, i.e., district courts entertain appeals from DOL decisions. <u>See</u>, <u>e.g.</u>, <u>Building and Constr. Trades Dep't, AFL-CIO v. Secretary of Labor</u>, 747 F. Supp. 26 (D.D.C. 1990).

L. Subcontracting. Prime contractors must flow down the DBA requirements and the applicable wage determination to their subcontractors. Prime contractors have a strong incentive to monitor the performance of their subcontractors in complying with the Davis-Bacon Act. Prime contractors are ultimately liable for failures by their subcontractors to pay the correct prevailing wages. Where a subcontractor underpays its workers and is unavailable to remedy the error, the Department of Labor will look to the prime contractor. Consequently, prime contractors typically monitor their subcontractors for violations and train their subcontractors and subcontractor employees on the applicable requirements.

VII. MCNAMARA-O'HARA SERVICE CONTRACT ACT OF 1965 (SCA).

A. Legal Authority. 41 U.S.C. Chapter 67; 29 C.F.R. Part 4; FAR Subpart 22.10; DFARS Subpart 222.10.Statutory Requirements.

1. Contractors performing any service contract shall pay their employees not less than the FLSA minimum wage.

2. Service contracts over $2,500 shall contain mandatory provisions regarding minimum wages and fringe benefits, safe and sanitary working conditions, notification to employees of the minimum allowable compensation, and equivalent federal employee classifications and wage rates. However, even if omitted from the solicitation, the SCA and applicable wage determinations are binding on contractors. <u>Kleenco, Inc.</u>, ASBCA No. 44348, 93-2 BCA ¶ 25,619; <u>Miller's Moving Co.</u>, ASBCA No. 43114, 92-1 BCA ¶ 24,707.

3. For contracts over $2,500, the minimum wage and fringe benefits are based on either:

a. Wage and fringe benefit determinations issued by DOL (FAR 22.1002-2), or

b. Wages and fringe benefits established by a predecessor contractor's collective bargaining agreement (CBA). 29 C.F.R. §§ 4.5 and 4.152 (1999); FAR 22.1002-3.

B. Application. FAR 22.1002; FAR 22.1003. The SCA applies to:

1. Service contracts.

a. "Service contract" means any federal contract, except as exempted by the SCA, the principal purpose of which is to furnish services through the use of service employees. 29 C.F.R. § 4.111 (1999); FAR 22.1001. <u>See</u> <u>Ober United Travel Agency, Inc. v. United States Department of Labor</u>, 135 F.3d 822 (D.C. Cir. 1998) (holding that SCA applies to concession contracts for travel services).

b. The SCA applies only to service contracts performed in the United States. 29 C.F.R. § 4.112(a) (1999); FAR 22.1003-2. "United States" includes any state, the District of Columbia, Puerto Rico, and certain possessions and territories.

c. The SCA does <u>not</u> apply if the <u>principal purpose</u> of a contract is to provide something other than services of the character contemplated by the SCA. Further, the SCA is not applicable to services performed <u>incidentally</u> to a non-service contract. <u>J.L. Assocs.</u>, B-236698.2, Jan. 17, 1990, 90-1 CPD ¶ 60. <u>See</u> <u>Westbrook Indus., Inc.</u>, B-248854, Sept. 28, 1992, 92-2 CPD ¶ 213 (finding reasonable an agency determination that rental of washers and dryers was not subject to SCA). Typically, construction contracts (Davis-Bacon Act) and contracts to supply goods (Walsh-Healey Act) are not service contracts.

2.   Performed by service employees.

a.   The SCA applies only to service employees. "Service employee" means any person engaged in the performance of a service contract or subcontract, other than persons employed in bona fide executive, administrative, or professional capacities. 29 C.F.R. § 4.113 (1999); FAR 22.1001. <u>See</u> 29 C.F.R. Part 541 (defines executives, professionals, and others).

b.   The term "service employee" includes all nonexempt persons engaged in the performance of a service contract regardless of any contractual relationship alleged to exist between a contractor or subcontractor and such persons. 29 C.F.R. §§ 4.113 and 4.155 (1999); FAR 22.1001.

C.   **Statutory Exemptions and Dual Coverage Under the Service Contract Act.** 41 U.S.C. § 6702(b); 29 C.F.R. §§ 4.115 to 4.122 (1999); FAR 22.1003-3.

1.   Davis-Bacon Act (DBA) coverage.

a.   The SCA does not apply if the principal purpose of a contract is to obtain construction work. In such a situation, the DBA covers all work done under the contract, including any incidental service-type work.

b.   Dual Coverage. The DBA requires contracting officers to incorporate DBA provisions and clauses into a service contract if there is a substantial amount of segregable construction work.

2.   Walsh-Healey Public Contracts Act of 1938 (WHA) coverage.

a.   The SCA does not apply if the principal purpose of the contract is the manufacture or delivery of supplies, materials, or equipment.

b.   Dual Coverage. Some work under a service contract may be exempt from the SCA because it entails the manufacture or delivery of supplies, materials, or equipment, or construction of public works.

3.   Miscellaneous statutory exemptions. <u>See</u> FAR 22.1003-3.

D.   **Administrative Variances and Exemptions.**

1.   The DOL may establish reasonable variations, tolerances, and exemptions from SCA provisions. 41 U.S.C. § 6707(b).

2.   Requirements exempted from SCA coverage by the DOL are found at 29 C.F.R. § 4.123 (1999) and FAR 22.1003-4.

3.   Rules for Commercial Items Contracts.

a.   Under very limited circumstances, contracts and subcontracts for certain types of commercial services may be exempted from SCA coverage. <u>See</u> 66 Fed. Reg. 5,327 (Jan. 19, 2001) (amending 29 C.F.R. § 4.123(e)).

b.   Eight categories of services are potentially exempt under the new rule. 29 C.F.R. §§ 4.123(e)(1) and (e)(2)(i) (2001).

c.   The exemption applies only when <u>all</u> of seven criteria are satisfied. 29 C.F.R. § 4.123(e)(2)(ii) (2001).

E.   **Compensation Standards Under the SCA.**

1.   Regardless of the amount of a contract or subcontract, a contractor or subcontractor on a contract covered by the SCA must pay service employees <u>at least</u> the minimum wage specified by the FLSA. 29

Labor Standards

C.F.R. §§ 4.159 and 4.160 (1999); FAR 22.1002-4.

2. Service contracts over $2,500. 29 C.F.R. §§ 4.161 through 4.163 (1999); FAR 22.1002-2.

a. A contractor must pay service employees not less than the wage rate issued by DOL for the contract. See General Sec. Servs. Corp., B-280959, Dec. 11, 1998, 98-2 CPD ¶ 143 (holding that agencies may require offerors to propose rates greater than the DOL wage determination). Cf. Ashford v. United States, 43 Fed. Cl. 1 (1997) (holding contractor bound by CBA rates incorporated in contract, even though the CBA was void).

b. If there is no wage determination or effective CBA, the FLSA minimum wage applies.

F. Obtaining Wage Determinations. FAR 22.1007 and 22.1008; DFARS 222.1008; 29 C.F.R. § 4.143 (1999); http://www.wdol.gov.

1. The contracting officer must obtain wage determinations for:

a. Each new solicitation and contract exceeding $2,500;

b. A contract modification that increases the contract to over $2,500;

c. An extension of the contract pursuant to an option clause or otherwise; or

d. Changes to the scope of a contract that affect labor requirements significantly.

2. On multiple-year contracts in excess of $2,500, the contracting officer must request a wage determination annually if funding is annual, or biennially if funding is not subject to annual appropriations.

3. Wage determinations (WD) are now obtained on-line from the Wage Determinations OnLine.gov website, at: http://www.wdol.gov.

a. Contracting officers should include the Internet WD in the solicitation or

modification. These WDs should be obtained no earlier than 15 days before issuance of a solicitation.

b. The contracting officer must provide DOL a copy of the WD so DOL can confirm its propriety. The contracting officer may proceed with the acquisition, however, unless DOL advises otherwise.

4. Likewise, if a WD is not available on the Internet or the "successor contract" rule applies (see para. G., infra), the contracting officer must request a WD from DOL by submitting an electronic SF 98 ("e98") from DOL (http://www.dol.gov/esa/whd/contracts/sca/sf98/index.asp). This DOL website can also be conveniently accessed from the Wage Determinations OnLine.gov website, at: http://www.wdol.gov.

a. DOL then issues a WD, and the contracting officer must include it in the solicitation and contract. FAR 22.1012-1. Information Handling Servs., Inc., B-240011, Oct. 19, 1990, 90-2 CPD ¶ 306. Cf. Allen-Norris-Vance Enter., B-243115, July 5, 1991, 91-2 CPD ¶ 23 (contractor that quotes rates below those set forth in the WD is eligible for award).

b. The contracting officer must request a WD not less than 60 days before initiation or renewal of an acquisition action. If an action is for a nonrecurring or unknown requirement and advance planning was not possible, only 30 days' advance notice is required. FAR 22.1008-7.

G. "Successor Contract" Rule.

1. If an agency competes a new contract for substantially the same services and the contract is to be performed in the same locality, the successor contractor must pay wages and fringe benefits at least equal to those contained in a CBA effective under the previous contract. 29 C.F.R. § 4.163 (1999); FAR 22.1008-3(b). See Klate Holt Co. v. International Bhd. of Elec. Workers, 868 F.2d 671 (4th Cir. 1989); Professional Servs. Unified, Inc., ASBCA No. 45799, 94-1 BCA ¶ 26,580.

2. A new CBA will not apply to the follow-on contract if:

a. The incumbent enters into a CBA that will not be effective until after the incumbent's contract expires;

b. The agency has timely notified the incumbent contractor and bargaining agent of the applicable acquisition dates, but the agency has <u>not</u> received timely notice of the terms of a new CBA. FAR 22.1008-3(c); <u>see</u> <u>Tecom, Inc.</u>, ASBCA No. 51591, 2001-1 BCA ¶ 31,156; or

c. DOL determines that the CBA was not negotiated in good faith or that the rates set by the CBA vary substantially from the prevailing rates. <u>Vigilantes, Inc. v. United States</u>, 968 F.2d 1412 (1st Cir. 1992).

3. The "Successor Contract" rule applies only to the base period of the follow-on contract. After the base period, the contractor and the employee bargaining unit may renegotiate the CBA. Per the regulations, each option period, for example, is considered a new contract. 29 C.F.R. §§ 4.143; 4.145 (1999). <u>See</u> <u>Fort Hood Barbers Assn. v. Herman</u>, 137 F.3d 302 (5th Cir. 1998) (holding contractor required to pay wages no less than those in the preceding contract's CBA only for the first two years of a follow-on multi-year contract); <u>but</u> <u>see</u> <u>American Maritime Officers v. Hart</u>, No. 99-1054 (D.D.C. Oct. 14, 1999) (unpub.) (holding that a predecessor contractor's CBA applied to the entire term of a follow-on multiyear contract).

H. **Right of First Refusal.** <u>See</u> Executive Order 12,933; 59 Fed. Reg. 53,559 (1994).

1. Until 17 February 2001, a successor contractor on a contract for maintenance of public buildings was required by Executive Order 12,933 to offer the predecessor contractor's employees a right of first refusal for positions the employees are qualified for. This right applied only to "public buildings," and

did not include buildings on military installations.

2. The requirements of Executive Order 12,933 were revoked by Executive Order 13,204, 66 Fed. Reg. 11,228 (2001). <u>See</u> 66 Fed. Reg. 11,228 for DOL implementation of the revocation (removes 29 C.F.R. Part 9). The FAR Council has issued a final rule amending FAR Parts 22 and 52 to reflect these changes. <u>See</u> 67 Fed. Reg. 6111 (2002).

I. **Price Adjustments for Wage Rate Increases.** FAR 52.222-43; 52.222-44.

1. If the FLSA minimum wage rate is amended or a wage rate incorporated upon exercise of an option increases labor costs, the contractor is entitled to a price adjustment. Adjustments are allowed only for increases due to congressional or DOL action. <u>See</u> <u>United States v. Serv. Ventures, Inc.</u>, 899 F.2d 1 (Fed. Cir. 1990); <u>Williams Servs., Inc.</u>, ASBCA No. 41121, 91-1 BCA ¶ 23,486; <u>see</u> <u>also</u> <u>Gricoski Detective Agency</u>, GSBCA No. 8901, 90-3 BCA ¶ 23,131 (disallowing adjustment because contract included priced option years and contractor failed to factor vacation pay costs into option year prices). <u>Cf.</u> <u>Sterling Servs., Inc.</u>, ASBCA No. 40475, 91-2 BCA ¶ 23,714 (allowing partial relief on claim arising from corrected wage determination).

a. Adjustments for increased wages arising out of a CBA negotiated during contract performance are not retroactive to date of CBA execution. Adjustments in these cases are required only upon option exercise. <u>See</u> <u>Ameriko, Inc., d/b/a Ameriko Maint. Co.</u>, ASBCA No. 50356, 98-1 BCA ¶ 29,505 (holding contractor was not entitled to price adjustment for increase in base year wages where increase was due to CBA executed after contract award); <u>Classico Cleaning Contractors, Inc.</u>, DOTBCA No. 2786, 98-1 BCA ¶ 29,648 (holding contractor could not recover during first option year for increases under CBA executed during

Labor Standards

same year). <u>Phoenix Management, Inc.</u>, ASBCA No. 53409, 02-1 BCA¶ 31,704 (agency required to comply with DOL wage determination because contracting officer failed to seek clarification regarding employees included in the CBA).

b. A contractor is not entitled to a price adjustment for the increased costs of complying with a wage determination that existed at the time of contract award. <u>Holmes & Narver Servs.</u>, ASBCA No. 40111, 93-3 BCA ¶ 26,246 (holding contractor could not recover cost of complying with wage determination that had not changed). <u>See Johnson Controls World Servs., Inc.</u>, ASBCA No. 40233, 96-2 BCA ¶ 28,548 (agency not liable for failing to inform contractor of previously disapproved conformance request).

2. Recovery under the price adjustment clauses is limited to the types of costs set forth expressly therein. <u>See</u> FAR 52.222-43; FAR 52.222-44 (limiting recovery to wages, fringe benefits, social security and unemployment taxes, and workers' compensation insurance); <u>see also All Star/SAB Pacific, J.V.</u>, ASBCA No. 50,856, 98-2 BCA ¶ 29,958 (holding state excise taxes occasioned by a wage rate increase were not compensable).

3. Not all adjustments for increased wage rates, however, are made under the FAR "price adjustment" clauses. If a contractor shows that recovery is based on a clause other than a price adjustment clause, e.g., changes clause, the price adjustment clause limitations are inapplicable.

a. The parties may agree to wage revisions outside the terms of the price adjustment clauses. <u>Security Servs. Inc. v. General Servs. Admin.</u>, GSBCA No. 11052, 93-2 BCA ¶ 25,667.

b. The price adjustment clauses may not apply where the adjustment occurred during base year of contract and was not due to an FLSA minimum wage increase. <u>See, e.g., Lockheed Support Sys., Inc. v.</u>

<u>United States</u>, 36 Fed. Cl. 424 (1996) (holding that price adjustment clause did not apply to a wage rate price adjustment made four months after the start of a contract); <u>Professional Servs. Unified, Inc.</u>, ASBCA No. 45799, 94-1 BCA ¶ 26,580 (price adjustment clause inapplicable where adjustment occurred after contract award).

4. Mutual mistake concerning employee classification or the propriety of a wage determination may shift the cost burden to the government. <u>See, e.g., Richlin Sec. Serv. Co.</u>, DOTBCA Nos. 3034, 3035, 98-1 BCA ¶ 29,651 (mutual mistake as to employee classification).

VIII. WALSH-HEALEY PUBLIC CONTRACTS ACT OF 1936 (WHA).

A. **Legal Authority.** 41 U.S.C. Chapter 65; 41 C.F.R. Parts 50-201 to 50-210; FAR Subpart 22.6; DFARS Subpart 222.6.

B. **Section 7201 of the Federal Acquisition Streamlining Act of 1994**, Pub. L. No. 103-355, 108 Stat. 3243 (1994), eliminated the requirement that contractor must be a regular dealer or manufacturer of the items to be furnished under a contract. <u>See</u> Federal Acquisition Circular 97-1, 62 Fed. Reg. 44,802 (1997).

C. **What Is Left?**

1. Wage Rate Determinations. 41 U.S.C. § 6502(1).

a. Under the WHA, DOL determines the prevailing minimum wages based on similar wages in the applicable industry and locale in which the supplies are to be manufactured or furnished under a contract. 41 U.S.C. § 6502(1). Presently, however, there is no wage rate determination activity under the Act.

b. The FLSA minimum wage is the Walsh-Healey Act wage rate.

2. Overtime Provisions. Employees are subject to the FLSA overtime provisions as discussed in Section II.A.1.

3. Child and Convict Labor is prohibited. 41 U.S.C. § 6502(3).

4. Health and Safety Requirements. 41 U.S.C. § 6502(4). Contractors must furnish a safe and healthy workplace through compliance with applicable health and safety laws.

IX. REMEDIES FOR LABOR STANDARDS VIOLATIONS.

A. Termination for Default.

1. Walsh-Healey Act. 41 U.S.C. § 6503(c).

2. Davis-Bacon Act. 40 U.S.C. § 3143. See Kelso v. Kirk Bros. Mech. Contractors, Inc., 16 F.3d 1173 (Fed. Cir. 1994); Quality Granite Constr. Co., ASBCA No. 43846, 93-3 BCA ¶ 26,073, aff'd sub nom. Quality Granite Constr. Co. v. Aspin, 26 F.3d 138 (Fed. Cir. 1994) (non-precedential); Glazer Constr. Co., Inc., v. U.S., COFC No. 98-400C May 7, 2002.

3. Service Contract Act. 41 U.S.C. § 6705(c).

4. CWHSSA. 40 U.S.C. § 3704(b) (after DOL makes a determination of noncompliance).

B. Debarment.

1. Walsh-Healey Act. 41 U.S.C. § 6504; 41 C.F.R. § 50-203.1 (1999) (violation of stipulations or representations of the Act).

2. Davis-Bacon Act. 40 U.S.C. § 3144(b); 29 C.F.R. § 5.12 (1999) (for disregard of its obligations to employees or subcontractors under the Act).

3. Service Contract Act. 41 U.S.C. § 6706 (providing that absent unusual circumstances, no contract shall be awarded to contractors who violate the SCA). See 29 C.F.R. § 4.188(b)(3) (i)-(ii); Dantran Inc. v. Department of Labor, 171 F.3d 58 (1st Cir. 1999) (holding

debarment unwarranted for SCA violation where mitigating circumstances and no aggravating factors were present).

4. CWHSSA - 40 U.S.C. § 3704(c); 29 C.F.R. § 5.12 (1999) (for aggravated or willful violation).

C. Withholding Contract Funds.

1. Walsh-Healey Act. 41 U.S.C. § 6403(d) (held in account and paid directly to employees on order of DOL).

2. Davis Bacon Act. 40 U.S.C. § 3142(c)(3) (turned over to GAO, which may pay employees directly). For a discussion of the constitutionality of such withholding, see Lujan v. G&G Fire Sprinklers, Inc., 121 S. Ct. 1446 (2001) (withholding of contract funds pursuant to State "Little Davis-Bacon Act" statute, without providing the right to a hearing, does not violate 14th Amendment right to due process).

3. Service Contract Act. 41 U.S.C. § 6705(b); 29 C.F.R. § 4.187 (1999) (turned over to DOL on order); Castle Bldg. Maint., Inc., GSBCA No. 10003, 90-3 BCA ¶ 23,271; National Sec. Serv. Co., DOT CAB No. 1033, 80-1 BCA ¶ 14,268. See Jeanette M. Bailey v. Dep't of Labor, 810 F. Supp. 261 (Alaska D.C., 1993) (contracting officer's withholding of underpaid SCA wages arising under another contract was unconstitutional denial of contractor's due process).

4. CWHSSA - 40 U.S.C. § 3703(b) (held in account and paid directly to employees).

D. Liquidated Damages.

1. Prior to August 1, 2016, the contractor was subject to liquidated damages of $10.00 per day for each employee.

2. Beginning August 1, 2016, liquidated damages are increased to $25 per day for each employee paid improperly.

3. Walsh-Healey Act. 41 U.S.C. § 6503(b).

4.   CWHSSA provides for withholding of liquidated damages for contracts subject to the Davis Bacon Act and the Service Contract Act. 40 U.S.C. § 3703(b)(2); United States v. Munsey Trust Co., 332 U.S. 234 (1947); To the Secretary of the Air Force, B-123227, 48 Comp. Gen. 387 1968).

E.   Reporting Labor Standard Violations.

1.   E.O. 13673, Fair Pay Safe Workplaces, dated July 31, 2014, 80 Fed. Reg. 30,547.

2.   To enhance compliance with labor standards, contractors are now required to disclose certain labor violations going back three years when submitting proposals over $500,000 to the government, or to certify that there are no such violations. The contracting officer must then assess the contractor's responsibility based on its disclosed violations.

3.   Violations are defined as encompassing "administrative merits determinations," "arbitral awards or decisions," or "civil judgments" of violations of 14 federal labor laws and their state equivalents, if any.

4.   If the contracting officer desires to award a contract to a contractor with violations, the contracting officer, after coordination with the agency's Labor Compliance Advisor, will determine whether a contractor has the requisite responsibility to obtain a federal contract.

5.   After award, the contractor must notify the contracting officer of new violations every six months.

6.   Prime contractors are required to make similar assessments of their subcontractors on non-commercial item subcontracts over $500,000.

7.   Other Provisions. The Executive Order requires covered contractors and subcontractors to provide "paycheck transparency." The employer must provide wage statements to covered workers giving them information concerning their hours worked, overtime hours, pay, and any additions to or deductions made from their pay. The Executive Order also requires covered contractors and subcontractors to provide to workers whom they treat as independent contractors a document informing them of their independent contractor status.

X.   CONCLUSION.

Federal contracts require labor/management policies, such as minimum wages, prevailing wages, work hours, overtime premiums, sick leave, etc., for contractor and subcontractor employees. Such policies make contracting officers and prime contractors responsible for monitoring and enforcing the labor practices of contractors and subcontractors.

Contracting officers must consider a contractor's compliance record when making responsibility determinations. Contractors and subcontractors must concern themselves with the compliance of their supply chain because, in the end, the prime contractor is financially responsible for the errors and omissions of its supply chain in this area. Consequently, both must understand the details to properly perform their responsibilities.

INTELLECTUAL PROPERTY

I. REFERENCES.

A. Department of Defense, Intellectual Property: Navigating Through Commercial Waters (Version 1.1, Oct. 15, 2001) (a.k.a. "The DOD IP Guide"), located at: http://www.acq.osd.mil/dpap/Docs/intelprop.pdf.

B. RALPH C. NASH, JR. & LEONARD RAWICZ, INTELLECTUAL PROPERTY IN GOVERNMENT CONTRACTS (George Washington University, 5th ed. 2001). A three-volume treatise.

C. MATTHEW S. SIMCHAK & DAVID A. VOGEL, LICENSING SOFTWARE AND TECHNOLOGY TO THE U.S. GOVERNMENT: THE COMPLETE GUIDE TO RIGHTS TO INTELLECTUAL PROPERTY IN PRIME CONTRACTS AND SUBCONTRACTS (2000). A one-volume treatise.

D. Major Gregg Sharp, *A Layman's Guide to Intellectual Property in Defense Contracts*, 33 PUB. CONTRACT. L.J. (2003).

II. OVERVIEW.

A. Intellectual property (IP) law protects the product of authors, inventors, and businesses that is of an intangible nature. Generally, intellectual property law includes patent law, copyright law, trademark law and trade secret law. The product of the efforts of authors and inventors is intangible; it is inventions, designs, writings, audiovisual works, performances, marks identifying products, and secrets. These products are fundamentally different from other types of property, such as real estate or movable physical objects, because they lack a physical embodiment.

B. Intellectual property law protects these intangible products, usually as a form of property. Thus intellectual property law protects the value of the resources invested in its creation and improvements thereto. Some intellectual property laws create property rights granting the owner of the property the right to exclude others from making use of the intellectual property. Trade secret law protects confidential relationships, but does not prevent independent discovery by lawful means.

C. The policies underlying intellectual property law are myriad, and several are embodied in the U.S. Constitution. These policies include, but are not limited to: 1) encouraging inventors, authors, and other creators to advance science, technology, the arts, and creativity; 2) protecting investments in creative activities; 3) protecting buyers and sellers of goods and services; and promoting fair business practices.

D. Intellectual property law is important in government contracting because the U.S. government is a major funder of research and development. Thus it has interests in advancing scientific knowledge, while not overpaying for the service. However, the government is rarely the only source of funding for research and development; therefore, the public interest of promoting progress by protecting the investment of the researchers is equally important. This creates an inherent conflict which government and industry attorneys should recognize and strive to fairly balance the interests of all concerned.

E. Unfortunately, intellectual property law and the acquisition regulations governing it are commonly misunderstood by contracting personnel in government and industry. This chapter provides a brief introduction to types of intellectual property and how intellectual property rights are regulated in government contracting. It does not, however, attempt to provide a thorough presentation of either intellectual property law and the applicable contract laws, regulations and clauses, nor the technology, technical data, or computer software which the clauses regulate.

III. TYPES OF INTELLECTUAL PROPERTY.

A. Patents.

1. Patents protect inventions, and granting patents is an express power of the federal government. Art. I, § 8, cl. 8 of the U.S. Constitution (in order "[t]o promote the progress of science and useful arts, by securing for limited times to authors and inventors the exclusive right to their respective writings and discoveries") authorizes the patent system. Based upon this authority, Congress enacted the Patent Act of 1952 (Ch. 950, 66 Stat. 792, codified as amended at 35 U.S.C. §§ 1-376).

2. A patent is a written instrument issued by the U.S. Patent and Trademark Office (PTO), an agency of the Department of Commerce granting the owner the right to exclude others from making, using, offering for sale, or selling the invention throughout the United States or importing the invention into the United States for a period of 20 years from the date of filing of the patent application. 35 U.S.C. § 154 (a)(2).

3. Thus, a patent owner may exclude others from using his or her invention, although a patent does not grant a right to actually use the claimed inventions. This is because most patents are granted for improvements of previous inventions, and the right to use an invention may be restricted by patents granted on the original invention.

4. Types of patents:

    a. Plant (e.g., a new variety of rosebush). Governed by 35 U.S.C. §§ 161-164;

    b. Design (e.g., a new design for a piece of furniture). Governed by 35 U.S.C. §§ 171-173;

    c. Utility. Governed by 35 U.S.C. §§ 100-157. Can be a "new and useful process, machine, manufacture or composition of matter, or any new and useful improvement thereof." 35 U.S.C. § 101. Examples would be: instant film processing (process); the steam engine (machine); and nylon (product).

5. The inventor must apply for a patent, and as part of that application process, must describe the invention in such a manner that another person skilled in the technology can make and use the invention. 35 U.S.C. §§ 111 and 112.

6. The invention may not merely represent an obvious improvement to an existing invention within the public domain. 35 U.S.C. § 103.

7. Generally, if an inventor places her/his invention into the public domain prior to applying for a patent (publicly using it, writing a trade article about it, or selling it), s/he cannot obtain a patent on that invention. The exception to this general proposition is if a valid patent application is filed within one year of the invention's introduction into the public domain. 35 U.S.C. § 102(b) and (d).

8. Multiple inventors.

    a. When multiple inventors make the same invention, the inventor(s) that is/are "first to file" their application with the Patent Office have priority for patent protection. The first to file's patent application destroys the novelty of inventions in subsequent applications. 35 U.S.C. § 102(a).

    b.   Previously, the United States, virtually alone in the world, had a "first to invent" system that accorded priority to an inventor who could demonstrate that he or she conceived an invention prior to another.

9.   In government contracting, patent applications and patents may result from work done under contract. Additionally, the government may assume the financial responsibility for infringing uses of third-party patents.

B.   Trade Secrets.

1.   A trade secret is a type of intellectual property that is secret, has value, and has its secrecy protected by its owner. Its protection lies in its secrecy, and the law's protection against discovery by improper means. The recipe for Coca-Cola® is a frequently cited example of a trade secret. See https://en.wikipedia.org/wiki/Coca-Cola_formula.

2.   The U.S. Constitution does not grant the federal government the express power to protect trade secrets. This lack of express authority does not, however, prevent the federal government from promising to protect trade secrets, or from regulating trade secrets in furtherance of protecting interstate commerce, or in foreign affairs.

    a.   It is a crime for a Federal Government employee to release confidential or proprietary information gained during the course of her employment. 18 U.S.C. § 1905.

    b.   There are several federal statutes that criminalize acts to misappropriate trade secrets. See 18 U.S.C. §§ 1831-1839.

    c.   Congress has granted U.S. District Courts broad jurisdiction over civil

suits for theft of trade secrets in The Defend Trade Secrets Act of 2016, Pub. L. 114–153 (May 11, 2016).

3.   State Law. State common law has protected trade secrets from misappropriation, and many states had codified their trade secret law. Today, most states (New York is a notable and increasingly lonely exception) have adopted a version of a uniform act.

    a.   The Restatement (First) of Torts §§ 757-759.

    b.   The Uniform Trade Secrets Act. See UTSA with 1985 Amend. PREFATORY NOTE, 14 U.L.A. 433, 434-35 (2000), available at http://www.uniformlaws.org/Act.aspx?title=Trade+Secrets+Act.

    c.   The Restatement (Third) of Unfair Competition §§ 39-45.

4.   Uniform Trade Secrets Act (UTSA). Published in 1979 and amended in 1985. The USTA has been adopted in some form by 47 states and the District of Columbia.

5.   The definition of trade secret is any information that has "economic value . . . from not being generally known . . . and is the subject of efforts that are reasonable under the circumstances to maintain secrecy." UTSA § 1(4).

    a.   Majority of trade secret litigation centers on whether the company seeking protection took reasonable measures to keep the information a secret.

    b.   Owners of trade secrets economically benefit by being able to use the secret, while others, who don't know it, cannot. Owners can also disclose a trade secret to another in confidence, in exchange for economic benefits.

    c.   As long as the disclosure is made to a recipient who agrees to keep the information confidential, the trade secret retains its protection.

6. The information can be of virtually any type, including but not limited to: "a formula, pattern, compilation, program, device, method, technique, or process." UTSA § 1(4).

7. There is no limit to how long a trade secret may last; duration depends only upon how long it remains secret and retains value.

8. In government contracting, examples of trade secrets are detailed manufacturing data, software source code, parts lists, etc. The issues are what are the rights of the contractor and the government.

C. Copyrights.

1. Copyrights protect an author's creative work in the form of expression.

2. Granting copyrights is an express power of the federal government authorized by Art. I, § 8, cl. 8 of the U.S. Constitution.

3. Congress extensively amended Copyright Laws in 1976. See Pub. L. No. 94-553, 90 Stat. 2599 (1976) (codified at 17 U.S.C. §§ 101-702).

4. The Register of Copyrights within the Library of Congress (LOC) is the government agency that has oversight responsibility for the copyright system. 17 U.S.C. § 701.

5. Copyright laws give the author of an original work the exclusive right to:

    a. Reproduce the copyrighted work;

    b. Prepare derivative works based upon the original work;

    c. Distribute copies of the work to others;

    d. Perform the work in public; and

    e. Display the work in public. 17 U.S.C. § 106.

6. Typical examples of works protected by copyright include, but are not limited to:

    a. Literary works;

    b. Musical works, including any accompanying words;

    c. Dramatic works, including any accompanying music;

    d. Pantomimes and choreographic works;

    e. Pictorial, graphic, and sculptural works;

    f. Motion pictures and other audiovisual works;

    g. Sound recordings; and

    h. Architectural works. 17 U.S.C. § 102(a).

7. In government contracting, copyright law protects technical data, computer software, and all other data delivered to the government or generated by the contractor.

8. The term of copyright protection varies. For a sole author who created a work after 1998, the term is for the life of the author plus 70 years. Alternate terms depend upon when the work was created, whether there was more than one author, whether the work was done anonymously, and whether the work qualifies as a "work made for hire." 17 U.S.C. §§ 301-305.

9. Although the work has to be "original," the statute does not define the term. The courts have interpreted the term to merely require that the work be independently created and possess some degree of creativity (unlike patents, the work need not entail more than an obvious revision to existing art). Feist Publications, Inc. v. Rural Telephone Service Co., Inc., 499 U.S. 340 (1991).

10. Authors may (but are not required to) register for a copyright in a work by depositing a copy of the work at the LOC

for review. 17 U.S.C. § 407(a). Additionally, an author may place the world on notice that s/he is claiming a copyright in the work by placing a notice on all distributed copies of the work. This notice commonly consists of the symbol "©" followed by the year the work was first published and the name of the author. 17 U.S.C. § 401.

11. Distribution of material without this notice may invalidate the copyright under certain circumstances. 17 U.S.C. § 405(a). Even where the copyright is not invalidated, the author will not be able to recover royalties from an innocent infringer, one who was unaware of the copyright. 17 U.S.C. § 405(b).

12. In government contracting, contractors author reports, technical documentation and software, and create audiovisual works for presentation and delivery to the government. Each work is protected by copyright from the point it was created, and contract clauses regulate the rights of the government and the contractor.

D. Trademarks.

1. Trademarks are the words and markings used to identify the source of goods and services, and to represent the quality of the goods and services. Coca-Cola® is a trademark for a popular drink sold around the world. Trademarks were protected by common law, but unlike patents and copyrights, the U.S. Constitution does not expressly grant Congress the authority to enact trademark laws. Many states enacted trademark laws.

2. In 1870, Congress, relying upon its inherent authority under the Constitution's Interstate Commerce Clause, enacted the first federal trademark statute, but opted not to preempt state law.

3. The Lanham Act of 1946, Ch. 540, 60 Stat. 427 (1946) (codified as amended at 15 U.S.C. §§ 1051-1129) established the current federal trademark law.

4. Trademark law allows manufacturers and service providers to use (and restrict others from using) marks that distinguish their goods or services from the goods and services of others. 15 U.S.C. § 1127.

5. Types of marks:

   a. Trademarks (Coke);

   b. Service marks (McDonald's or Golden Arches symbol);

   c. Collective marks. Used by members of an organization or group to distinguish their products or services from non-group members (PGA);

   d. Certification marks. Used to show the product or service meets certain characteristics or function levels (Underwriters Laboratories).

6. The first user of a mark that is "distinctive" or "descriptive but having acquired secondary meaning" has the right to continue to make use of that mark so long as the mark is used in commerce in association with goods or services. The first user can exclude others from using the mark in a confusingly similar manner.

7. The user of a trademark may register its mark with the federal government (USPTO) and with state governments. Registration of the mark with the USPTO is not required to gain trademark rights, but doing so conveys many benefits, including establishing prima facie evidence of the registrant's exclusive right to use the mark. 15 U.S.C. §§ 1051(a) and 1057(b). If the user registers the mark and makes continuous use of the mark for five years, the user's right to continued use of the mark becomes uncontestable. 15 U.S.C. § 1058.

E. Multiple Avenues of Protection.

1. The various types of intellectual property protection (patent, copyright, trademark, and trade secret) are not exclusive. Many such innovations/creative concepts are

susceptible to protection under more than one of the above legal regimes. For example, a piece of software may implement a patented process, the source and object code expressions of the software are protected by copyright, and the source code may be protected as a trade secret. One software supplier protects its open source software by embedding the company's trademarks in what is otherwise open source software, presumably to prevent copying without removing the embedded trademarks.

2.   Opting to protect technology under one regime often will not prevent the owner from obtaining protection under an alternate regime. In fact, multiple forms of protection are common.

3.   Sometimes inventors will have to choose among alternate regimes. Example: software source code - you cannot protect as a trade secret subject matter you must disclose to obtain a utility patent.

IV. PATENT RIGHTS IN INVENTIONS MADE UNDER GOVERNMENT CONTRACTS.

A.   **No Single Uniform Policy.** The federal government does not have a single, uniform government-wide patent policy, for several reasons. First, some agencies must comply with specific statutes that address patent rights, such as the Department of Energy on nuclear technology and NASA on space technology. Second, different agencies have different policy concerns. For example, intelligence agencies may require the contractor to assign title to inventions to the United States to protect the secrecy of the contractor's activities. The President, however, has taken actions to promote uniformity, as discussed below.

B.   **Title or License?** Historically, there has been a debate between policy makers as to whether the public is better served by the government taking title to patents on

inventions funded by the government, or is a license sufficient. Today, the debate is generally settled; a government license for government purposes best serves the public's interests. When the government retains title to a patent, its title impedes the commercialization of the technology described in the patent, depriving the public of the benefits of the research.

C.   **Contractor Title to Patents on Inventions.**

1.   FAR 52.227-11, Patent Rights-Ownership by the Contractor, is the most commonly used clause to allocate patent rights on inventions made under contract. The basic terms are that the government obtains a license to inventions made or first actually reduced to practice during the performance of the contract. The contractor receives title to such inventions, provided it complies with the notice and other obligations in the clause.

2.   FAR 52.227-11 implements the policies in the Bayh-Dole Act (Pub. L. No. 96-517, 94 Stat. 3019 and codified at 35 U.S.C. §§ 200-212), which allowed small businesses and educational institutions to obtain title to patents. FAR 52.227-11, however, applies to all contractors, not just small businesses, educational institutions, and nonprofits. This policy originated in a 1983 Presidential Memorandum that extended coverage of the Bayh-Dole Act to large, for-profit firms. Presidential Memorandum on Governmental Patent Policy to the Heads of Executive Departments and Agencies, Feb. 18, 1983 (reprinted in 1983 Public Papers 248). This memo may be waived under certain circumstances.

D.   **What Is a "Subject Invention?"** FAR 52.227-11 applies to "Subject Inventions"; inventions that are conceived or first actually reduced to practice during performance of the contract. Determining what is the invention, when it was conceived, and when the invention was first actually reduced to practice (the invention exists, is tested in a suitable environment, and is shown to work) is a difficult question, and often only possible in hindsight. For contractors, the best approach is to treat an invention as a "Subject Invention" if there is any doubt, because the consequences for not reporting subject inventions are many, and the benefits that are lost by misclassifying a non-subject invention are few. However, where an invention is neither conceived nor first actually reduced to practice in performance of a government contract, the government does not receive a license, other than the implied licenses that accompany the sale of products. See Jacobs v. Nintendo of Am., Inc., 370 F.3d 1097-1100 (Fed. Cir. 2004) ("The implied license defense is typically presented "when a patentee or its licensee sells an article and the question is whether the sale carries with it a license to engage in conduct that would infringe the patent owner's rights"); UCC § 2-313(3).

E.   Notice of Invention.

1.   To obtain title, the contractor must timely notify the government when it becomes aware of an invention it has either conceived or first actually reduced to practice in the performance of work under a government contract and which the contractor believes may be patentable. 35 U.S.C. § 202(c)(1); FAR 52.227-11(c).

2.   This notice informs the government about its rights under FAR 52.227-11.

3.   While the Bayh-Dole Act requires notification within a reasonable time, FAR 52.227-11(c)(1) sets a time limit of two months after the inventor notifies the contractor's patent personnel about the invention. FAR 52.227-12(c)(1). The time may be extended upon request.

4.   The contractor must also completely disclose how the invention works to the government and also tell the government if it has taken any action that would statutorily bar issuance of a patent. FAR

52.227-11(c)(1); FAR 52.227-12(c)(1). For DOD contracts, this disclosure is made on a DD Form 882. DFARS 227.304-1.

5.   In practice, many contractors have internal policies on reporting potentially patentable inventions to their management. This internal reporting triggers the obligation to notify the government, and the internal forms often provide the same information sought by the government.

F.   Election of Title.

1.   After notifying the government, the contractor must decide if it wants to retain title to the subject invention. FAR 27.302(b). The contractor has two years to make its election. FAR 52.227-11(c)(2).

2.   If the contractor elects to retain title, it is required to file a patent application within one year, and prior to a statutory bar based on the contractor's publication, sale, or public use. 35 U.S.C. § 202(c)(3); FAR 52.227-11(c)(3).

3.   If the contractor does not elect to retain title (for example, because it does not desire to go to the expense of patenting the invention), then the contractor retains a broad, nonexclusive, royalty-free license throughout the world in each subject invention to which the government obtains title. The contractor can forfeit this license if it fails to disclose the invention within the times specified in paragraph (c) of this clause. FAR 52.227-11(b)(2)(i).

4.   Where the government takes title to a subject, it may attempt to obtain a patent. FAR 52.227-11(d).

G.   Government License. Where the contractor retains title, the government is granted a "nonexclusive, nontransferable, irrevocable, paid-up license" to use the invention or to have someone else use the invention on behalf of the government. 35

Intellectual Property

U.S.C. § 202(c)(4); FAR 27.302(c); FAR 52.227-11(b).

H. March-in Rights. If the contractor elects to retain title, the government may, in rare cases, direct the contractor to license the invention to another firm. 35 U.S.C. § 203; FAR 27.302(f); FAR 52.227-11(j). These "March-in" rights are rarely, if ever, exercised. They are only used where the contractor has failed to commercialize the invention, or where the contractor is not meeting the health or safety needs of the public. The contractor is given procedural due process before exercise of "March in" rights, and only the head of the agency can exercise these rights. 35 U.S.C. § 203 (2); FAR 27.302(f); and FAR 27.304-1(g).

I. Domestic Licensing. The contractor is prohibited from <u>exclusively</u> licensing its patented invention to U.S. firms unwilling to "substantially manufacture" its product within the U.S. 35 U.S.C. § 204; FAR 27.302(g); FAR 52.227-11(i); FAR 52.227-12(i); FAR 52.227-13(i). There are exceptions if the contractor can demonstrate it was unable to find a domestic licensee or that domestic manufacturing is infeasible. 35 U.S.C. § 204; FAR 27.302(g); FAR 52.227-11(i); FAR 52.227-12(i); FAR 52.227-13(i).

J. Compulsory Foreign Licensing. If the contract contains Alternate Clauses I or II of the Patent Rights Clauses, the government is able to sublicense its rights to a foreign government. FAR 52.227-11, Alternate I and II.

1. Alternate I under each of the above clauses is used if the government knows of any foreign governments to which it desires to sublicense.

2. Alternate II under each of the above clauses is used if the government has reason to believe that post-award it will enter into a treaty or agreement with a foreign government to which it will want to sublicense.

K. Subcontractor Inventions.

1. Prime contractors and higher-tier subcontractors must flow down FAR 52.227-11 to their subcontractors. FAR 52.227-11(k). Subcontractors have the same rights and obligations as the prime for notifying the contracting officer, electing title, etc.

2. The Bayh-Dole Act and FAR 52.227-11 prevent prime contractors from obtaining rights in subcontractor subject inventions within the subcontract itself. 35 U.S.C. § 202(a); FAR 27.304-4; FAR 52.227-11(g).

   a. The contractor may obtain rights in subcontractor subject inventions but must do so outside of the subcontract and must pay some additional compensation to the subcontractor. FAR 27.304-4; FAR 52.227-11(g).

   b. These same protections are also given to lower-tier subcontractors. FAR 52.227-11(g); DFARS 227.304-4; DFARS 252.227-7034.

L. Government Title Clauses.

1. FAR 52.227-13, Patent Rights -- Ownership by the government is one of the clauses used in those contracts where the government desires, at least as an initial position, to obtain title to subject inventions. A government title clause is used where statute requires the government to obtain title and in those rare contracts, usually benefitting intelligence agencies, where the government needs to obtain title in subject inventions and their patents.

2. The procedures are similar to FAR 52.227-11, except that where the contractor has the right to elect to obtain title under FAR 52.227-11, the contractor may only request title under FAR 52.227-13. Granting the request is discretionary, but title is routinely granted by most agencies.

V. AUTHORIZATION AND CONSENT; INFRINGEMENT OF THIRD-PARTY PATENTS.

A. **Background.** Government contractors may infringe third-party patents in the performance of a government contract. In the commercial marketplace, a seller impliedly warrants non-infringement. See UCC § 2-312(3). In government contracting, the government often directs the contractor to perform, and assumes the risk of most or all patent infringement. This policy is intended to prevent patent disputes between the contractor and a third party from delaying performance of public contracts.

B. **Authorization, Consent, and Notice.**

1. 28 U.S.C. § 1498 provides that a patent owner's exclusive remedy for infringement of a valid patent by the United States and those acting with its authorization and consent is a suit for damages in the U.S. Court of Federal Claims. Injunctive relief is not available. Government contractors are the persons most commonly granted authorization and consent. Within the Department of Defense, 10 U.S.C. § 2386 authorizes the agency to acquire licenses and releases for past infringement.

2. There are four types of contracts for the purposes of authorization and consent and/or indemnity: 1) research and development contracts, 2) non-R&D contracts, 3) commercial item contracts, and 4) other contracts.

   a. Non-commercial Item Contracts. FAR 27.201-2 requires inclusion of FAR 52.227-1 in all contracts over the simplified acquisition threshold that are performed in whole or in part in the United States. This clause authorizes a contractor to use a U.S. patent that is necessary to perform the contract. Use is optional in smaller contracts.

   b. R&D Contracts. In research and development contracts, FAR 27.201-2 requires inclusion of Alternate 1 of FAR 52.227-1. This version authorizes the use of patented inventions whether necessary or not. The purpose is to permit a contractor to develop the best solution to the government's requirements without regard to any patents that may exist.

   c. In those contracts below the Simplified Acquisition Threshold, authorization and consent is optional, but the policies underlying the clause are equally applicable.

3. As discussed above, the third-party patent owner's only remedy is to file a claim or lawsuit against the government in the U.S. Court of Federal Claims to be reasonably compensated for the infringement. Because injunctive relief is not available, and the United States vigorously defends patent infringement suits, this remedy is not pursued as often as might be warranted.

4. Contractors should urge inclusion of FAR 52.227-1 wherever warranted, and Alternate 1, whenever warranted.

C. **Third-Party Infringement Claims.**

1. Each contract granting authorization and consent also must include FAR 52.227-2, Notice and Assistance Regarding Patent and Copyright Infringement. FAR 27.201-2(b). Under this clause, the contractor must provide notice of an infringement suit to the government so the government can obtain a dismissal. FAR 52.227-2.

2. FAR 52.227-2 also obligates the contractor to cooperate with the government's defense of the claim, at the government's expense.

3. Sophisticated plaintiffs are aware of FAR 52.227-1 and generally avoid pursuing claims where it applies.

Intellectual Property

4. For DOD contracts, there is an administrative remedy for patent infringement claims that a plaintiff must exhaust before pursuing its claim in the U.S. Court of Federal Claims. See DFARS Subpart 227.70.

D. Indemnification and Waiver. Granting a contractor "Authorization and Consent," does not necessarily absolve a contractor from all financial responsibility for third-party patent infringement. Indemnification for patent infringement is a separate issue.

1. The government may require a contractor to offer an indemnity for patent infringement. FAR 27.203. Government policy is to obtain patent indemnity for commercial items because the cost of the indemnity is assumed to be included in the commercial price.

2. The contractor's indemnity may cover all deliverables on a commercial item contract (FAR 52.227-3) and commercial components of non-commercial items. FAR 52.227-3 Alt. 1; FAR 52.227-4.

3. The government generally does not request patent indemnity for research and development contracts, or for contracts for non-commercial items. The reason is that the government has significant involvement in the design and that involvement excuses the contractor from indemnification. See FAR 52.227-2(b).

4. The government may tailor the indemnity clause where it desires to include or exclude specified patents or technology from the indemnity.

5. Note that the government, by furnishing specifications to a contractor, must hold the contractor harmless against any third-party infringement claim which arises out of compliance with the specifications. See UCC § 2-312(3).

E. Notification of Royalties.

1. The government will include FAR 52.227-6, Royalty Information, in solicitations for negotiated contracts subject to the Truth in Negotiations Act. FAR 227.202-5(a). The purpose of the clause is to highlight licensing costs for patents.

2. Where there is a significant cost, the government may negotiate with the contractor to remove the royalty costs in consideration of granting "Authorization and Consent" and excluding the licensed patent from any indemnity obligation.

F. Invention Secrecy.

1. Patent applications are subject to review by federal agencies, and interested agencies may request a secrecy order under the authority of 37 U.S.C. §§ 181-188.

2. The process is relatively straightforward. Patent applications are reviewed by the Department of Defense and other agencies, and, where detrimental to the national security, the agency will request the U.S. Patent Office to order the patent application to remain secret. Applications subject to a secrecy order are not published. The inventor may prosecute the application to the point of allowance, but the patent is not granted while under secrecy order. Secrecy orders are reviewed periodically to determine whether they are still justified.

3. There are procedures for challenging the imposition of a secrecy order, and for obtaining compensation for use of an invention under a secrecy order by others, where the government does not have a license. 37 U.S.C. § 183.

VI. TECHNICAL DATA RIGHTS.

A. References.

1. 10 U.S.C. §§ 2302(4), 2305(d)(4), 2320, 2321, and 2325.

2. FAR Subpart 27.4.

3. DFARS Subpart 227.71.

B. **Purpose.** FAR 27.402; DFARS 227.7102-1; DFARS 227.7103-1.

1. Rights in technical data is to many the most important intellectual property issue in government contracting, and one where it has been difficult to satisfy both the interests of the government and the interests of industry.

2. Government buyers want to:

   a. Maintain and repair systems using sources other than the original manufacturer, such as by going directly to subcontractors, using an in-house depot workforce, or by contracting out to lower-cost service providers.

   b. Acquire systems and services through competitive reprocurement, thereby obtaining lower prices.

   c. Promote contractor independent development of new products and services for government needs.

3. Industry sellers want to:

   a. Protect their investments in developing the technology described in their technical data from disclosure to competitors for government requirements.

   b. Protect their investments in technology described in their technical data from commercial competitors.

   c. Maximize shareholder return by selling goods and services free from competitive pressures.

4. The current DOD system for allocating rights in technical data between government and industry fully satisfies neither party. DOD's current regulations do represent a rough approximation of a fair allocation of rights that has been begrudgingly accepted by both sides to the issue.

C. **Background.**

1. Technical Data Rights are not a separate area of intellectual property law. They are basically a combination of trade secret law and copyright law.

2. There are two separate technical data regimes: one for DOD and one for all other agencies. DFARS Part 227 and FAR 27.400.

3. When military forces and budgets were small and weapons development was centered in government arsenals and depots, rights in technical data were less important. Since the lead up to WWII, weapons development has shifted dramatically to the private sector, albeit with substantial government support. Early technical data regulations provided the government with complete access to contractor technical data. This was unacceptable to many contractors, so they refused to do work for the government.

4. The current systems have evolved in an atmosphere of competing policies. Competition is good! Protecting investments in new technology is good! High prices are bad! Consequently, the regulations governing technical data have evolved.

5. The current DOD system has several characteristics:

   a. Contractors own the data describing the technologies they develop. The government receives a license.

   b. Some data, such as maintenance manuals, is always provided to the government with an unlimited license.

   c. Most data describing technology developed entirely at government expense is delivered with an unlimited license.

   d. Most data describing technology developed entirely at private expense is delivered with a limited license for internal government use.

e. Data describing technology developed with mixed government and private funding is delivered with a license for use for government purposes, including competitive reprocurement.

D. Definition of Technical Data.

1. The term "technical data" means recorded information (regardless of the form or method of the recording) of a scientific or technical nature (including computer software documentation) relating to supplies procured by an agency.

2. "Technical Data" does not include computer software or financial, administrative, cost or pricing, or management data or other information incidental to contract administration. 10 U.S.C. § 2302(4); FAR 27.401; DFARS 252.227-7013(a)(14); DFARS 252.227-7015(a)(4). Government personnel frequently attempt to misapply technical data rights rules to administrative, financial, and management data.

3. It is important to understand the distinction between the data and the technology the data describes. Technology encompasses the items, components, and processes protected, such as the aircraft, the aluminum structure, the engines, and the welding procedures for manufacturing the aircraft. The data that describes the technology is different: it is the engineering drawings, parts lists, assembly instructions, etc., that describe how to build, maintain and repair the technology. The reason the distinction is important is that rights often depend on the source of funding for developing the technology, not the actual data.

E. Government Rights in Technical Data.

1. Unlimited Rights.

a. The government obtains "Unlimited Rights" if the data pertains to an item or process developed <u>exclusively</u> with government funding. 10 U.S.C. § 2320(a)(2)(A); DFARS 227.7103-5(a); DFARS 252.227-7013(b)(1).

b. Unlimited Rights are not limited. They mean the government may "use, modify, reproduce, perform, display, release, or disclose" the data to anyone and for any purpose. 10 U.S.C. § 2320(a)(2)(A); DFARS 252.227-7013(a)(15).

c. Granting Unlimited Rights destroys the contractor's ability to protect the data as a trade secret. <u>See</u> III.B.5, above in this outline.

2. Limited Rights.

a. The government obtains "Limited Rights" to technical data that pertains to an item or process developed <u>exclusively</u> with <u>private</u> funding. 10 U.S.C. § 2320(a)(2)(B); DFARS 227.7103-5(c); DFARS 252.227-7013(b)(3).

b. Limited Rights means the government may "use, modify, reproduce, perform, display, release, or disclose" the data only <u>within the government</u> except that the government may release to another if "necessary for emergency repair and overhaul." 10 U.S.C. § 2320(a)(2)(B) and (D); DFARS 252.227-7013(a)(13).

c. Limited Rights technical data remains a trade secret. The government (and anyone the government subsequently furnishes the information to) has an obligation to keep the data confidential. See DFARS 252.227-7013(b)(2)(iii) and DFARS 252.227-7013(b)(3)(ii).

3. Government Purpose Rights.

    a. The government obtains "Government Purpose Rights" if the data pertains to an item or process developed with both government and private funding. 10 U.S.C. § 2320(a)(2)(E); DFARS 227.7103-5(b); DFARS 252.227-7013(b)(2).

    b. Government Purpose Rights means the government may "use, modify, reproduce, perform, display, release, or disclose" the data within the government or may release or disclose such data to someone outside the government so long as the recipient uses the data for government purposes. DFARS 252.227-7013(a)(11).

    c. After the passage of a set period of time (the default term in the DFARS is five years, but this is negotiable), the government's rights become unlimited. 10 U.S.C. § 2320(c); DFARS 227.7103-5(b); DFARS 252.227-7013(b)(2). Agencies will often agree to extend the term for an indefinite period.

4. Negotiated Rights. The government and the contractor may modify these pre-determined levels of rights so long as the government receives no less than limited rights in the data. 10 U.S.C. § 2320(a)(2) and (c); DFARS 227.7103-5(d); DFARS 252.227-7013(b)(4).

5. The government never receives ownership of the rights in the data – just a license to use the data. DFARS 227.7103-4(a). The government does receive title to the copy of the data.

F. **Funding Source Determination.** Defining whether development is privately funded, government funded, or mixed funded is often not a simple task.

1. Independent research and development costs, bid & proposal costs, and manufacturing and production engineering costs are not considered government funds, even though they may be reimbursable by the government. 10 U.S.C. § 2320(a)(3); DFARS 252.227-7013(a)(7) and (9). Of course, contractor profits are also private funds.

2. As previously mentioned, it is the funding of the technology (the item, component, or process) which the data describes, not the funding of the particular data item, that is important. A contractor may completely develop an item on its own funding, then take government funding to document the design. The latter government funding is irrelevant.

3. The funding determination is made at the lowest level possible. A contractor can assert Limited Rights in a "segregable sub-item, subcomponent, or portion of a process." DFARS 227.7103-4(b); DFARS 252.227-7013(a)(7)(i). Thus, a contractor may be entitled to assert Limited Rights in key components, while the government may gain rights in other parts of the system.

4. What constitutes "developed"? DFARS basically adopts a definition similar to "actual reduction to practice" in patent law. DFARS 252.227-7013(a)(7). Essentially, the technology must: a) exist, b) have been tested, and c) have been shown to work to the satisfaction of knowledgeable individuals. Unresolved is how the definition of "developed" is affected by modern modeling and simulation techniques. Is testing always necessary? Was it necessary for a particular technology?

5. Thus, to determine the rights the government receives, the government must identify the technology, identify when it was developed, and identify the source of funding for that development.

G. **How Is Protection Obtained?**

1. The government receives Unlimited Rights in data unless the contractor takes affirmative steps to limit such rights.

Intellectual Property

DFARS 227.7103-5(a)(7); DFARS 227.7103-10(c)(1); DFARS 252.227-7013(b)(1)(vii).

2. Data List.

    a. In its offer, a contractor must develop a listing of all technical data and computer software that it will submit to the government and in which the government will not receive Unlimited Rights. DFARS 227.7103-3(b); DFARS 227.7103-10(a)(1); DFARS 227.7104(e)(2); DFARS 227.7203-3(a); DFARS 252.227-7017(c).

    b. This listing should be included in the awardee's contract. DFARS 227.7103-10(a)(3).

    c. The contractor must deliver any technical data not included on this listing with Unlimited Rights unless it obtains the government's permission to add the data to this listing. DFARS 227.7103-3(c); DFARS 252.227-7013(e)(2) and (3).

    d. Problem area: modifications to contracts. Often, in the course of development, a contractor will identify a design alternative that uses technology entitled to Limited Rights. The contractor should request that the government modify the attached list prior to adopting that design alternative. See General Atronics, Corp., ASBCA No. 49196, 02-1 BCA ¶ 31,798.

3. Data Marking.

    a. When the contractor delivers data to the government, it must mark each piece of data on which it asserts restrictions with a marking or legend indicating the level of rights it believes the government should have in the data. DFARS 252.227-7013(f).

    b. This marking is placed on the transmittal sheet and each page of the printed material containing the technical data for which the contractor is asserting restrictions. DFARS 252.227-7013(f)(1).

    c. The DFARS prescribes the "legends" or markings that must be used. DFARS 252.227-7013(f)(2) – (4).

    d. Unmarked data.

        (1) If the contractor mistakenly delivers unmarked data, it can request to have the data subsequently marked so long as the request is made within six months after the data was submitted or any extension of time granted by the contracting officer. DFARS 227.7103-10(c)(2).

        (2) While such request is pending, the government may not release the data until the matter is resolved. DFARS 227.7103-10(c)(1).

        (3) If the request is made after the data has already been released, nothing can be done to correct the omission if the recipient had no restrictions on usage of the data. DFARS 227.7103-10(c)(3).

    e. If the contractor delivers data with a marking not corresponding to those specified in the DFARS, the government must notify the contractor of this non-conformity. DFARS 252.227-7013(h)(2). If the contractor fails to correct this non-conformity within 60 days, the DFARS permits the government to remove or ignore the marking. DFARS 227.7103-12. NOTE: consult with competent legal counsel prior to release.

4. Government Challenge of Asserted Restrictions. 10 U.S.C. § 2321. Any contract that entails delivery of technical data will include the "Validation of Restricted Marking on Technical Data" clause. DFARS 227.7103-13; DFARS 252.227-7037.

   a. The contractor is required to set up and maintain a system of records that can validate and justify the restrictive markings it places on its data. 10 U.S.C. § 2321(b); DFARS 227.7103-11; DFARS 252.227-7037(c).

   b. If the Contracting Officer disagrees with the asserted restrictions, she sends a written notice to the contractor providing the basis for challenging the restriction and notifies the contractor that it has 60 days to respond. 10 U.S.C. § 2321(d)(3); DFARS 227.7103-13(c); DFARS 252.227-7037(e)(1).

   c. The challenge may occur as late as three years after contract completion. 10 U.S.C. § 2321(d)(2)(B); DFARS 227.7103-13(c)(1); DFARS 252.227-7037(i).

   d. The contractor's response to the challenge is considered a claim under the Contract Disputes Act and must be certified regardless of the amount at issue. 10 U.S.C. § 2321(h); DFARS 252.227-7037(e)(3).

   e. If the contractor fails to respond, or responds but does not justify the asserted restrictions, the KO issues a final decision indicating his determination that the government has unlimited rights in the data. However, the government must abide by the asserted restrictions for 90 days after issuance of the final decision (giving the contractor time to file suit). DFARS 252.227-7037(g)(2).

H. **Subcontractor Technical Data.** As with patents, the government does not want the contractor to be able to use its leverage to obtain subcontractor technical data. The subcontractor is therefore able to submit its technical data directly to the government. 10 U.S.C. § 2320(a)(1); DFARS 227.7103-15; DFARS 252.227-7013(k)(3) and (4). This can present practical problems, since the prime contractor is responsible for the entire system, and for contract performance.

I. **Deferred Delivery and Ordering of Data.**

1. Deferred Delivery. Several versions of an item or process may be developed before the government ultimately finalizes the item for production and fielding. It does not want or need data related to each iteration (logistical nightmare). Under these circumstances, the government may defer delivery of data for up to two years after contract termination if it includes a special clause in the contract. DFARS 227.7103-8(a); DFARS 252.227-7026.

2. Deferred Ordering. Alternatively, the government may not know at contract award whether it will need data. Again, the government may include a special clause in the contract to permit it to order data, this time up to three years after contract termination. DFARS 227.7103-8(b); DFARS 252.227-7027. The contractor may deliver the ordered data with the rights applicable.

J. **Non-conforming Data and Data Warranty.**

1. If the contractor does not deliver the contractually required technical data, the government may withhold payment. 10 U.S.C. § 2320(b)(8) and (9); DFARS 227.7103-14(b); DFARS 252.227-7030. The amount withheld is set at 10% but may be adjusted based upon the relative value and importance of the data. DFARS 227.7103-14(b)(2).

2. When the contractor submits data to the government, the data must be complete and accurate and satisfy the contractual requirements. 10 U.S.C. § 2320(b)(7); DFARS 227.7103-14(a)(1); DFARS 227.7103-6(e); DFARS 227.7104(e)(5); DFARS 252.227-7036. The DFARS no longer requires written assurance of completeness/accuracy. See DFARS subpt. 227.71.

3. If the contractor submits defective data to the government which is accepted by the government, the government would only have a remedy if it obtained a warranty on the data from the contractor. 10 U.S.C. § 2320(b)(8); DFARS 227.7103-14(c); DFARS 246.710; DFARS 252.246-7001.

K. Release of Data.

1. If the government has unlimited rights in the data, the government may release the data to anyone without restriction. 10 U.S.C. § 2320(a)(2)(A); DFARS 252.227-7013(a)(15). See Part VI.E.1 above in this outline. However, this does not excuse the government from complying with the Arms Export Control Act, or other restrictions on dissemination of technical data. Furthermore, the fact that the government may provide a third party with a copy of Unlimited Rights data does not mean the third party can copy or modify the data for non-government purposes.

2. If the government has government purpose or specially negotiated rights in the data, it may be able to release the data to others in the government and possibly to non-governmental personnel for limited purposes (See Part VI.E above in this outline).

   a. Unless the recipient is being provided the data under another contract with the government, it will have to sign a "Use and Non-Disclosure Agreement." 10 U.S.C. § 2320(a)(2)(D)(ii); DFARS 227.7103-7(a).

   b. If the recipient is being provided the data under another contract with the government, that contract should have DFARS 252.227-7025 in it, which requires the contractor to have its employees sign a "Use and Non-Disclosure Agreement" prior to giving them restricted data. DFARS 227.7103(b).

   c. In either case, the government will also have to notify the data owner of the release. 10 U.S.C. § 2320(a)(2)(D)(iii); DFARS 252.227-7013(a)(13)(iv).

L. Foreign Contracts. If the contract is with a Canadian firm, use the same technical data clauses as is required for American firms. DFARS 227.7103-17(c). If the contract is with a firm from any other country, the government may use a special clause giving the government unlimited rights regardless of the funding source. DFARS 227.7103-17(a).

M. Commercial Item Technical Data.

1. Commercial companies are not used to supplying technical data about their products, except for operating and installation manuals, or disclosures under a non-disclosure agreement. Commercial companies are very concerned that the government will disclose valuable trade secrets to competitors, damaging competitive advantages. Such concerns are not unjustified.

2. The government has much the same need for Unlimited Rights in technical data, such as Form/Fit/Function Data, Users Manuals, Installation Manuals, etc., for commercial items as it does for non-commercial items.

3. DFARS 252.227-7015, Technical Data – Commercial Items, describes the rights the government receives in technical data for commercial items. Basically, it requires unlimited rights for three categories of technical data, regardless of who funded it, and a much more limited

set of rights to all other technical data. The limited rights the government receives allows internal use, including use by government support contractors.

4. There is a presumption that commercial items are developed exclusively at private expense. 10 U.S.C. § 2320(b)(1); 10 U.S.C. § 2321(f); DFARS 252.227-7037(b). The government should not challenge the contractor's asserted markings unless the government can demonstrate it contributed financially toward the development of the item. DFARS 252.227-7037(b)(1). However, there is no presumption, except for commercially available off-the-shelf items, that a component of a major system or a subsystem was developed exclusively at private expense. The contractor or subcontractor must demonstrate that the item was developed exclusively at private expense if challenged. DFARS 252.227-7037(b)(2).

5. Deferred Delivery and Ordering of Data. There are no clauses permitting deferred ordering/delivery of data related to commercial items, so the government must identify its needs up-front.

6. Non-conforming Data and Data Warranty. There is no provision requiring the contractor to furnish written assurance that the data is accurate and complete, authorizing the government to obtain a data warranty, or permitting withholding of payment if the contractor submits non-conforming data. But see 10 U.S.C. § 2320(b)(7)–(9).

7. Subcontractor Data. There is no requirement to permit subcontractors to deliver their data directly to the government.

8. Release of Data. Under certain circumstances, the government may release data to third parties. DFARS 227.7102-2(a) and DFARS 252.227-7015(b). There is no specified agreement that the third party must sign, however. Consult competent legal authority!

N. Bid and Proposal Data.

1. Offerors/Bidders may want to or may be required to furnish technical data to demonstrate their expertise.

2. Bidders and their subcontractors and suppliers should provide any required notices describing technical data and computer software that is offered with less than Unlimited Rights. See FAR 52.227-15, DFARS 252.227-7017. Failure to do so may prevent the assertion of such rights. DFARS 252.227-7013(e).

3. Pre-award Protections. Prior to award of a contract, Section 27 of the Office of Federal Procurement Policy Act protects bid and proposal data. 41 U.S.C. Chapter 21. The solicitation for negotiated contracts typically includes an express contractual promise of confidentiality. See FAR 52.215-1(e) and DFARS 252.227-7016.

4. Post-award Protection. The government receives the rights in the contractor's technical data stated in the prime contract, normally those specified in the standard FAR and DFARS clauses. See FAR 52.215-1(e); DFARS 252.227-7016(c).

5. Unsolicited Proposals. Data submitted as part of an unsolicited proposal is protected by FAR 15.609.

VII. ACQUISITION OF COMPUTER SOFTWARE.

A. A thorough treatment of the acquisition of computer software is beyond the scope of this basic work because of the complexity of the subject matter, the wide variety of licenses offered by industry, the wide differences in needs between different federal agencies, the greater role of commercial software, and the lack of subject matter expertise by some federal agencies. The standard agency clauses have different definitions. All this complexity often results in contract and software-specific language, rather than reliance on standard clauses.

B. Civilian Agencies.

1. For Civilian Agencies, FAR 52.227-19, Commercial Computer Software License, provides a basic set of rights based on the concept that software is one copy running on one computer, at one time. The clause grants a right to archive a backup copy and to transfer the software to a replacement computer. Its use is permissive, not prescribed. See FAR 27.409(g). More typically, an agency would incorporate a modified commercial software license.

2. DOD both licenses existing computer software, commercial and non-commercial, and develops considerable software.

   a. Non-commercial Computer Software. DFARS 252.227-7014, Rights in Noncommercial Computer Software and Noncommercial Computer Software Documentation, follows the same statutory policies that apply to non-commercial technical data. When the contractor develops software entirely at private expense, DOD receives "Restricted Rights" which limit its use of the software to internal use, one computer at one time, with a right to backup and modify the software. Disclosure to IT support contractors is allowed. See DFARS 252.227-7014(a)(15). When developed entirely at government expense, DOD receives Unlimited Rights. See DFARS 252.227-7014(a)(16). Since software is inherently capable of being subdivided into modules, different rights may apply to different parts of an entire program. Where mixed funding was used to develop an indivisible part of a computer program, DOD receives Government Purpose Rights.

   b. DOD agencies acquire commercial computer software under commercial licenses, unless the agency negotiates a broader license. DFARS 227.7202-3.

   c. In practice, DOD agencies are required to negotiate multiple individual licenses for deliverable software because the deliverable software includes both commercial and non-commercial software, and the software owners are both the prime contractor and its suppliers. The software was or will be developed using multiple funding sources, and the agency will have its own unique requirements. Commercial software delivered under commercial licenses is often much less expensive to license than non-commercial software, giving commercial vendors negotiating leverage.

3. In practice, licenses to computer software can be subject to considerable negotiation between the parties.

VIII. COPYRIGHT LICENSES TO SPECIAL AND EXISTING WORKS.

A. Typically, the applicable data rights clause will include language granting licenses for both copyright and for the trade secrets embodied in the data. For example, DFARS 252.227-7014 requires technical data submitters to grant the government the right to "reproduce data, distribute copies of the data, publicly perform or display the data, or . . . modify the data to prepare derivative works." See DFARS 252.227-7103(a)(16). The DFARS also requires any data submitter who has incorporated a third party's work into its own technical data to obtain a copyright license from that third party prior to submitting the data to the government. DFARS 227.7103-9(a)(2).

B. Occasionally the government acquires existing works, or commissions the preparation of a special work and desires ownership of the work product. Examples include the purchase of an existing video, or the creation of a commercial. In such circumstances, the government needs to acquire ownership to prevent misuse of the work by the contractor. To acquire ownership of existing works, see FAR 27.405-2; FAR 52.227-18; DFARS 227.7105-1; and DFARS 252.227-7021. To acquire ownership of works created under contract, known as "Special Works," see FAR 27.405-1; FAR 52.227-17; DFARS 227.7106; and DFARS 252.227-7020.

C. Acquisition of the greater rights in Special Works and Existing Works is intended for specific circumstances which require greater rights. See FAR 227.405-1(a); DFARS 227.7106(d). Such procedures should not be used in typical contracts for research and development or to acquire items.

D. Construction contracts. DFARS 227.7107-1.

1. If the government hires an architect-engineer who develops a unique design that the government does not want to be duplicated, the government will have to acquire ownership of the drawings and related data. DFARS 227.7107-1(b); DFARS 252.227-7023.

2. If the government hires an architect-engineer and it does not care whether the design gets replicated, the government obtains unlimited rights in the drawings. DFARS 227.7107-1(a); DFARS 252.227-7022.

3. Similarly, if the construction contractor develops shop drawings, the government obtains unlimited rights in those drawings permitting it to freely reproduce and distribute them. DFARS 227.7107-1(c); DFARS 252.227-7033.

IX. CONCLUSION.

Intellectual property rights are a very complex area of government contract law. Because of the various requirements of the government and its suppliers, IPR is one area where negotiations occur in fact, rather than in theory. The assistance of specialists is essential to reaching an agreement that complies with law, regulation, and the needs of the parties.

ETHICS IN GOVERNMENT CONTRACTING

"Always do right. This will gratify some people and astonish the rest."
Mark Twain

I. REFERENCES.

A. Statutes.

1. 18 U.S.C. § 208, Acts Affecting a Personal Financial Interest.

2. 41 U.S.C. § 2101 <u>et seq</u>., The Procurement Integrity Act.

3. 18 U.S.C. § 207, Restrictions on Former Officers, Employers, and Elected Officials of the Executive and Legislative Branches.

B. Regulations.

1. 5 C.F.R. Part 2635, Standards of Ethical Conduct for Employees of the Executive Branch.

2. 5 C.F.R. Part 2640, Interpretations, Exemptions and Waiver Guidance Concerning 18 U.S.C. § 208.

3. 5 C.F.R. Part 2641, Post-Employment Conflict of Interest Restrictions.

4. OGE Memorandum, Summary of Post-Employment Restriction of 18 U.S.C. § 207 (July 29, 2004).

5. Federal Acquisition Regulation (FAR) Part 3, Improper Business Practices and Personal Conflicts of Interest (Dec. 4, 2015).

6. Department of Defense (DOD) Defense Federal Acquisition Reg. Supp. (DFARS) Part 203, Improper Business Practices and Personal Conflicts of Interest (Feb. 28, 2014).

C. Directives: DOD Directive 5500.7-R, Joint Ethics Regulation (JER), including changes 1-7 (Nov. 17, 2011).

II. INTRODUCTION.

This chapter focuses on the following topics:

A. The conflict of interest prohibitions of 18 U.S.C. § 208.

B. The scope of the Procurement Integrity Act.

C. The procurement-related restrictions on seeking and accepting employment when leaving government service.

D. The Contractor Code of Business Ethics and Conduct (FAR 52.203-13)

III. FINANCIAL CONFLICTS OF INTEREST.

An executive branch employee ("employee") is prohibited from participating personally and substantially in his or her official capacity in any particular matter in which he or she has a financial interest, if the particular matter will have a direct and predictable effect on that interest. 18 U.S.C. § 208; 5 C.F.R. § 2635.402(a).

A. The financial conflict of interest prohibitions apply in three key situations.

1. An employee may not work on an assignment that will affect the employee's financial interests, or the financial interests of the employee's spouse or minor child.

2. An employee may not work on an assignment that will affect the financial interests of a partner or organization where the employee serves as an officer, director, employee, general partner, or trustee.

3. An employee may not work on an assignment that will affect the financial interest of someone with whom the employee either has an arrangement for employment or is negotiating for employment.

B. Definition of Key Terms.

1. **Financial Interests.** The term includes any current or contingent ownership, equity, or security interest in real property or a business and may include an indebtedness or compensated employment relationship. Financial interest includes stocks, bonds, partnership interests, leasehold interests, mineral and property rights, deeds of trust, liens, options, or commodity futures. 5 C.F.R. § 2635.403(c)(1). The statute specifically defines negotiating for employment as a financial interest. Thus, negotiating for employment is the equivalent of owning stock in a company.

2. **Personally.** Defined as direct participation, or direct and active supervision of a subordinate. 5 C.F.R. § 2635.402(b)(4).

3. **Substantially.** Defined as an employee's involvement that is significant to the matter. Examples include a decision, approval, disapproval, recommendation, investigation, or the rendering of advice in a particular matter. 5 C.F.R. § 2635.402(b)(4).

4. **Particular Matter.** Defined as a matter involving deliberation, decision, or action focused on the interests of specific persons or an identifiable class of persons. However, matters of broad agency policy are not particular matters. 5 C.F.R. § 2635.402(b)(3). It is properly understood to apply to those matters in which a federal employee's representational assistance could potentially distort the government's process for making a decision to confer a benefit, impose a sanction, or otherwise to directly affect the interests of discrete and identifiable persons or parties. VanEe v. EPA, 202 F. 3d 296, 340 (D.C. Cir. 2000).

5. **Direct and Predictable Effect.** Defined as a close, causal link between the official decision or action and its expected effect on the financial interest. The predictable effect must be real, as opposed to a speculative possibility that the matter will affect a financial interest. 5 C.F.R. § 2635.402(b)(1).

C. The financial interests of the following persons are imputed to the employee:

1. The employee's spouse;

2. The employee's minor child;

3. The employee's general partner;

4. An organization or entity which the employee serves as an officer, director, trustee, general partner, or employee; and

5. A person with whom the employee is negotiating for employment or has an arrangement concerning prospective employment. 5 C.F.R. § 2635.402(b)(2).

D. This statute does not apply to enlisted members, but the Joint Ethics Regulation (JER) subjects enlisted and National Guard members to similar regulatory prohibitions. See JER, para. 5-301. Regulatory implementation of 18 U.S.C. § 208 is found in the JER, Chapters 2 and 5, and in 5 C.F.R § 2640.

E. Options for Employees with Conflicting Financial Interests.

1. **Disqualification.** With the approval of his or her supervisor, the employee must change duties so the employee is not participating in the particular matter from which he or she is disqualified. 5 C.F.R. § 2635.402(c); 5 C.F.R. § 2640.103(d).

2. **Waiver.** An employee otherwise disqualified by 18 U.S.C. § 208(a) may be permitted to participate personally and substantially in a particular matter if the disqualifying interest is the subject of an

individual waiver or regulatory exemption. 5 C.F.R. § 2635.402(d).

a. Individual Waivers. The rules for individual waivers are at 5 C.F.R. § 2635.402(d)(2) and 5 C.F.R. § 2640.301. An employee may seek an individual waiver in advance of his or her participation in a particular matter. The employee must make a full disclosure regarding the nature and extent of the disqualifying financial interest to the government official responsible for his or her appointment. The official must determine, in writing, that the employee's financial interest in the particular matter is not so substantial as to be deemed likely to affect the integrity of the services the employee provides. 5 C.F.R. § 2635.402(d)(2)(ii); 5 C.F.R. § 2640.301(a).

b. Regulatory Exemptions. The rules for blanket waivers are at 5 C.F.R. § 2640 Subpart B - Exemptions Pursuant to 18 U.S.C. 208(b)(2). Blanket waivers include the following:

   (1) Diversified Mutual Funds. Diversified funds do not concentrate in any industry, business, or single country other than the United States. In the case of an employee benefit plan, this means that the plan's trustee has a written policy of varying plan investments. 5 C.F.R. § 2640.102(a). Owning a diversified mutual fund does not create a conflict of interest. 5 C.F.R. § 2640.201(a).

   (2) Sector Funds. Sector funds are those funds that concentrate investments in an industry, business, or single country other than the United States. 5 C.F.R. § 2640.102(q).

      (a) Owning a sector fund may create a conflict of interest, but there is a regulatory exemption if the holding that creates the conflict is not invested in the sector where the fund or funds are concentrated. 5 C.F.R. § 2640.201(b)(1).

      (b) An employee may participate in a particular matter affecting one or more holdings of a sector mutual fund where the disqualifying financial interest in the matter arises because of ownership of an interest in the fund and the aggregate market value of interests in any sector fund or funds does not exceed $50,000. 5 C.F.R. § 2640.201(b)(2).

   (3) De Minimis. Regulations create a *de minimis* exception for ownership by the employee, spouse, or minor child in:

      (a) Publicly traded securities; if

      (b) The aggregate value of the holdings of the employee, spouse, or minor child does not exceed $15,000. 5 C.F.R. § 2640.202(a).

3. Divestiture. Upon the sale or divestiture of the asset or interest that causes the disqualification, the prohibition from acting in the particular matter is eliminated. The divesture may either be voluntary or directed. 5 C.F.R. § 2640.103(e).

F. **Negotiating for Employment.** The term "negotiating" is interpreted broadly.

United States v. Schaltenbrand, 930 F.2d 1554 (11th Cir. 1991).

1. Any discussion regarding employment opportunities, however tentative, may be considered negotiating for employment. Something as simple as going to lunch to discuss future prospects could be the basis of a conflict of interest.

2. Negotiating for employment can be considered the equivalent to buying stock in a company. If an employee could own stock in a company without creating a conflict of interest with his official duties (e.g., the company does not do business with the government), then that person may negotiate for employment with that company.

3. Conflicts of interest are always analyzed in the present tense. If an employee interviews for a position and decides not to work for that company, then he or she is free to later work on matters affecting that company.

4. Seeking Employment. The Office of Government Ethics (OGE) regulations contain additional requirements for disqualification of employees who are "seeking employment." 5 C.F.R. §§ 2635.601-2635.606. "Seeking employment" is a term broader than "negotiating for employment" found in 18 U.S.C. § 208.

    a. An employee begins "seeking employment" if he or she has directly or indirectly:

        (1) Engaged in employment negotiations with any person. "Negotiations" means discussing or communicating with another person, or that person's agent, with a view toward reaching an agreement for employment. This term is not limited to discussing specific terms and conditions of employment. 5 C.F.R. § 2635.603(b)(1)(i).

        (2) Made an unsolicited communication to any person or that person's agent about possible employment. 5 C.F.R. § 2635.603(b)(1)(ii).

        (3) Made a response other than rejection to an unsolicited communication from any person or that person's agent about possible employment. 5 C.F.R. § 2635.603(b)(1)(iii).

    b. An employee has not begun "seeking employment" if he or she makes an unsolicited communication for the following reasons:

        (1) For the sole purpose of requesting a job application. 5 C.F.R. § 2635.603(b)(1)(ii)(A).

        (2) For the sole purpose of submitting a résumé or employment proposal only as part of an industry or other discrete class. 5 C.F.R. § 2635.603(b)(1)(ii)(B).

    c. An employee is no longer "seeking employment" under the following circumstances:

        (1) The employee rejects the possibility of employment and all discussions have terminated. 5 C.F.R. § 2635.603(b)(2)(i). However, a statement by the employee that merely defers discussions until the foreseeable future does not reject or close employment discussions. 5 C.F.R. § 2635.603(b)(3).

        (2) Two months have transpired after the employee has submitted an unsolicited résumé or employment proposal with no response

from the prospective employer. 5 C.F.R. § 2635.603(b)(2)(ii).

5. The Stop Trading on Congressional Knowledge Act.

    a. During 2011, Congress faced increased scrutiny regarding the lack of restrictions imposed on legislators' trading activity. As a result, Congress passed the Stop Trading on Congressional Knowledge Act of 2012 (STOCK Act), Pub. L. No. 112-105, 126 Stat. 291 (2012)

    b. The STOCK Act includes a provision that applies to OGE 278 filers who are negotiating, or have secured, future employment or compensation.

    c. OGE 278 filers may not directly negotiate, or have any agreement of future employment or compensation, unless such individual, within 3 business days after the commencement of such negotiation or agreement of future employment or compensation, files with the individual's supervising ethics office a statement, signed by such individual, regarding such negotiations or agreement, including the name of the private entity or entities involved in such negotiations or agreement, and the date such negotiations or agreement commenced.

    d. OGE 278 filers shall recuse themselves whenever there is a conflict of interest, or appearance of a conflict of interest, for such individual with respect to the subject matter of the required statement, and shall notify the individual's supervising ethics office of such recusal.

G. **Penalties.** Violating 18 U.S.C. § 208 may result in imprisonment up to one year or,

if willful, five years. In addition, a fine of $50,000 to $250,000 is possible. See 18 U.S.C. § 3571.

1. Government contractors are required to report conflicts of interest that violate 18 U.S.C. § 208.

    a. FAR 52.203-13, Contractor Code of Business Ethics and Conduct, requires contractors to disclose credible evidence of violations of federal criminal law involving conflicts of interest. This is also known as the Mandatory Disclosure Rule. FAR 52.203-13(b)(3)(i).

IV. THE PROCUREMENT INTEGRITY ACT (PIA).

A. **Background Information** about the Procurement Integrity Act (PIA), 41 U.S.C. §§ 2101-2107.

1. Generally, the PIA prohibits:

    a. Disclosing and obtaining bid, proposal, and source-selection-sensitive procurement information. 41 U.S.C. § 2102(a)(1).

    b. Former government officials serving in key procurement positions from accepting compensation from a contractor within one year from the date of certain actions by that official. 41 U.S.C. § 2104.

2. The basic provisions of the PIA are set forth in FAR 3.104-2.

B. **Restrictions on Disclosing and Obtaining Procurement Information.**

1. The following persons are forbidden from knowingly disclosing contractor bid or proposal information or source selection information before the award of a contract to which the information relates:

    a. Present or former federal officials; or

Ethics

b. Persons who are advising or have advised the federal government with respect to a procurement (i.e., contractor employees);

c. Persons who have access to such information by virtue of their office, employment, or relationship. 41 U.S.C. § 2102(a)(3).

2. Restrictions on Obtaining Information. 41 U.S.C. § 2102(b). Persons (other than as provided by law) are forbidden from obtaining contractor bid or proposal information or source selection information before the award of a federal agency procurement contract to which the information relates.

3. Contractor Bid or Proposal Information. 41 U.S.C. § 2101(2). Contractor bid or proposal information means any of the following information submitted to a federal agency as part of, or in connection with, a bid or proposal to enter into a federal agency procurement contract, if that information was not previously disclosed publicly:

a. Cost or pricing data;

b. Indirect costs or labor rates;

c. Proprietary information marked in accordance with applicable law or regulation; and

d. Information marked by the contractor as "contractor bid or proposal information" in accordance with applicable law or regulation. If the contracting officer disagrees, he or she must give the contractor notice and an opportunity to respond prior to release of marked information. FAR 3.104-4. See Chrysler Corp. v. Brown, 441 U.S. 281 (1979); CNA Finance Corp. v. Donovan, 830 F.2d 1132 (D.C. Cir. 1987), cert. den., 485 U.S. 917 (1988).

4. Source Selection Information. 41 U.S.C. § 2101(7). Defined as any of the following:

a. Bid prices before bid opening;

b. Proposed costs or prices, or lists of those proposed costs or prices;

c. Source selection plans;

d. Technical evaluation plans;

e. Technical evaluations of proposals;

f. Cost or price evaluations of proposals;

g. Competitive range determinations that have a reasonable chance of being selected for award of a contract;

h. Rankings of bids, proposals, or competitors;

i. Reports and evaluations of source selection panels, boards, or advisory councils; and

j. Other information marked as "source selection information" if release would jeopardize the integrity of the competition.

C. **Reporting Non-federal Employment Contacts.**

1. Mandatory Reporting Requirement. 41 U.S.C. § 2103(a). An agency official who is participating personally and substantially in an acquisition over the simplified acquisition threshold must report employment contacts with bidders or offerors. Reporting may be required even if the contact is through an agent or intermediary. FAR 3.104-5.

a. Report must be in writing.

b. Report must be made to supervisor and designated agency ethics official. This may include:

(1)   Designated agency ethics official in accordance with 5 C.F.R. § 2638.201.

(2)   Deputy agency ethics officials in accordance with 5 C.F.R. § 2638.204 if authorized to give ethics advisory opinions.

(3)   Alternate designated agency ethics officials in accordance with 5 C.F.R. § 2638.202(b). See FAR 3.104-3.

c.   Additional Requirements. The agency official must:

(1)   Promptly reject employment; or

(2)   Disqualify him/herself from the procurement until authorized to resume participation in accordance with 18 U.S.C. § 208.

(a)   Disqualification notice. Employees who disqualify themselves must submit a disqualification notice to the Head of the Contracting Activity (HCA) or designee, with copies to the contracting officer, source selection authority, and immediate supervisor. FAR 3.104-5(b).

(b)   Note: 18 U.S.C. § 208 requires employee disqualification from participation in a particular matter if the employee has certain financial interests in addition to those which arise from employment contacts.

2.   Both officials and bidders who engage in prohibited employment contacts are subject to criminal penalties and administrative actions.

3.   Participating personally and substantially means active and significant involvement in:

a.   Drafting, reviewing, or approving a statement of work;

b.   Preparing or developing the solicitation;

c.   Evaluating bids or proposals, or selecting a source;

d.   Negotiating price or terms and conditions of the contract; or

e.   Reviewing and approving the award of the contract. FAR 3.104-1.

4.   The following activities are generally considered **not** to constitute personal and substantial participation:

a.   Certain agency-level boards, panels, or advisory committees that review program milestones or evaluate and make recommendations for approaches to satisfying broad agency-level missions or objectives;

b.   General, technical, engineering, or scientific effort of broad applicability and not directly associated with a particular procurement;

c.   Clerical functions in support of a particular procurement; and

d.   For OMB Circular A-76 cost comparisons:

(1)   Participating in management studies;

(2)   Preparing in-house cost estimates;

(3)   Preparing "most efficient organization" (MEO) analyses; and

(4)   Furnishing data or technical support **to be used by others** in the development of performance standards, statements of work, or specifications. FAR 3.104-1.

Ethics

D. Post-Government Employment Restrictions.

1. **One-Year Ban**. 41 U.S.C. § 2104(a). A former official of a federal agency may not accept compensation from a contractor that was awarded a contract in excess of $10 million, as an employee, officer, director, or consultant of the contractor within 1 year after the official served with respect to that contract as:

   a. Procuring Contracting Officer (PCO);

   b. Source Selection Authority (SSA);

   c. Members of the Source Selection Evaluation Board (SSEB);

   d. Chief of a financial or technical evaluation team;

   e. Program Manager;

   f. Deputy Program Manager; and

   g. Administrative Contracting Officer (ACO).

   h. The one-year ban applies to a government official that personally made a decision to:

      (1) Award a contract, subcontract, or a task or delivery order in excess of $10 million to that contractor;

      (2) Establish overhead or other rates valued in excess of $10 million to that contractor;

      (3) Approve issuing one or more contract payments in excess of $10 million to that contractor; or

      (4) Pay or settle a claim in excess of $10 million with that contractor.

2. The Ban Period.

   a. If the former official was in a specified position (source selection type) on the date of contractor selection, but not on the date of award, the ban begins on the date of selection.

   b. If the former official was in a specified position (source selection type) on the date of award, the ban begins on the date of award.

   c. If the former official was in specified position (program manager, deputy program manager, administrative contracting officer), the ban begins on the last date of service in that position.

   d. If the former official personally made certain decisions (award, establish overhead rates, approve payment, settle claim), the ban begins on date of decision. FAR 3.104-3(d)(2).

3. In "excess of $10 million" means:

   a. The value or estimated value of the contract including options;

   b. The total estimated value of all orders under an indefinite-delivery, indefinite-quantity contract or a requirements contract;

   c. Any multiple award schedule contract, unless the contracting officer documents a lower estimate;

   d. The value of a delivery order, task order, or order under a Basic Ordering Agreement;

   e. The amount paid, or to be paid, in a settlement of a claim; or

   f. The estimated monetary value of negotiated overhead or other rates when applied to the government portion of the applicable allocation base. FAR 3.104-1.

318

4. The one-year ban does not prohibit a former official of a federal agency accepting compensation from a division or affiliate of a contractor that does not produce the same or similar products or services. 41 U.S.C. § 2104(b).

5. Ethics Advisory Opinion. Current and former agency officials may request an advisory opinion from the appropriate agency ethics official as to whether he or she would be precluded from accepting compensation from a particular contractor. FAR 3.104-6.

E. **Penalties and Sanctions.**

1. Criminal Penalties. Violating the prohibition on disclosing or obtaining procurement information in exchange for something of value, or to obtain or give a competitive advantage, may result in confinement for up to five years and a fine. 41 U.S.C. 2105(a).

2. Civil Penalties.

   a. The Attorney General may take civil action for wrongfully disclosing or obtaining procurement information, failing to report employment contacts, or accepting prohibited employment.

   b. Civil penalty is up to $50,000 (individuals) and up to $500,000 (organizations) for each violation plus twice the amount of compensation received or offered. 41 U.S.C. 2105(b).

3. Administrative actions. If violations occur, the agency shall consider cancellation of the procurement, rescission of the contract, suspension or debarment, adverse personnel action, and recovery of amounts expended by the agency under the contract. 41 U.S.C. § 2105(c).

   a. For purposes of a suspension or debarment proceeding, engaging in conduct constituting a PIA offense

affects the present responsibility of a Federal Government contractor or subcontractor. 41 U.S.C. § 2105(c)(3).

   b. FAR 52.203-8 advises contractors of the potential for cancellation or rescission of a contract, recovery of any penalty prescribed by law, and recovery of any amount expended under the contract. FAR 52.203-10 advises the contractor that the government may reduce contract payments by the amount of profit or fee for violations.

4. A contracting officer may disqualify a bidder from competition whose actions fall short of a statutory violation, but call into question the integrity of the contracting process. See Compliance Corp., B-239252, Aug. 15, 1990, 90-2 CPD ¶ 126, aff'd on recon., B-239252.3, Nov. 28, 1990, 90-2 CPD ¶ 435; Compliance Corp. v. United States, 22 Cl. Ct. 193 (1990), aff'd, 960 F.2d 157 (Fed. Cir. 1992) (contracting officer has discretion to disqualify from competition a bidder who obtained proprietary information through industrial espionage not amounting to a violation of the Procurement Integrity Act); see also NKF Eng'g, Inc. v. United States, 805 F.2d 372 (Fed. Cir. 1986) (contracting officer has authority to disqualify a bidder based solely on appearance of impropriety when done to protect the integrity of the contracting process).

5. Limitation on Protests. 41 U.S.C. § 2106. No person may file a protest, and GAO may not consider a protest, alleging a PIA violation unless the protester first reported the alleged violation to the agency within 14 days of its discovery of the possible violation. FAR 33.102(f).

6. Contracting Officer's Duty to Take Action on Possible Violations.

   a. The Contracting Officer must determine the impact of the

violation on award or source selection.

b. If the Contracting Officer determines that there is no impact, the Contracting Officer must forward information concerning the violation or potential violation to the individual designated by agency. Proceed with procurement, subject to contrary instructions.

c. If there is an impact on procurement, the Contracting Officer must forward the information to the Head of the Contracting Activity (HCA) or designee, and take further action in accordance with HCA's instructions. FAR 3.104-7.

V. REPRESENTATIONAL PROHIBITIONS.

A. Basic Prohibition.

1. 18 U.S.C. § 207 and its implementing regulations bar certain acts by former employees which may reasonably give the appearance of making unfair use of their prior employment and affiliations. 5 C.F.R. § 2641.101. 18 U.S.C. § 207 prohibits former employees from knowingly, with the intent to influence, making any communication to or appearance before an employee of the U.S. on behalf of any other person in connection with a particular matter involving a specific party or parties, in which he or she participated personally and substantially as an employee, and in which the U.S. is a party or has a direct and substantial interest. 5 C.F.R. § 2641.201

2. A former employee involved in a particular matter while working for the government must not "switch sides" after leaving government service to represent another person on that matter.

B. Scope.

1. Employee means, for purposes of determining individuals subject to 18 U.S.C. § 207, any officer or employee of the executive branch or any independent agency that is not a part of the legislative or judicial branches. 5 C.F.R. § 2641.104.

2. 18 U.S.C. § 207 applies to <u>all</u> former officers and civilian employees whether or not retired, but does not apply to enlisted personnel because they are not included in the definition of "officer or employee" in 18 U.S.C. § 202.

3. "Participated" means an action taken as an officer or employee through decision, approval, disapproval, recommendation, the rendering of advice, investigation or other such action. 18 U.S.C. § 207(i)(2).

4. "Particular matter" includes any investigation, application, request for a ruling or determination, rulemaking, contract, controversy, claim, charge, accusation, arrest, judicial, or other proceeding. 18 U.S.C. § 207(i)(3).

5. Communication includes only those communications to which the former employee intends that the information conveyed will be attributed to him- or herself. 5 C.F.R. § 2641.201(d)(1).

6. A former employee makes an appearance when he or she is physically present before an employee of the U.S., in either a formal or an informal setting. An appearance need not involve any communication by the former employee. 5 C.F.R. § 2641.201(d)(2).

7. 18 U.S.C. § 207 does not prohibit an employee from working for any entity, but it does restrict how a former employee may work for the entity.

a. The statute does not bar behind the scenes involvement.

b. A former employee may ask questions about the status of a particular matter, request publicly available documents, or communicate factual information unrelated to an adversarial proceeding. 5 C.F.R. § 2641.201 (d).

C. Permanent Restriction.

1. 18 U.S.C. § 207 imposes a lifetime prohibition on the former employee against communicating or appearing, with the intent to influence a particular matter, on behalf of anyone other than the government, when:

   a. The government is a party, or has a direct and substantial interest in the matter;

   b. The former officer or employee participated personally and substantially in the matter while in his or her official capacity; and

2. At the time of the participation, specific parties other than the government were involved.

3. The restriction lasts for the life of the particular matter involving specific parties in which the employee participated personal and substantially. 5 C.F.R. 2641.201(d). To the extent the particular matter is of limited duration, so is the coverage of the statute. Further, it is important to distinguish among particular matters. The statute does not apply to a broad category of programs when the specific elements may be treated as severable.

D. Two-Year Restriction.

1. 18 U.S.C. § 207 prohibits, for two years after leaving federal service, a former employee from communicating or appearing, with the intent to influence a particular matter, on behalf of anyone other than the government, when:

   a. The government is a party, or has a direct and substantial interest in the matter;

   b. The former employee knew or should have known that the matter was pending under his or her official responsibility during the one-year period prior to leaving federal service; and

   c. At the time of the participation, specific parties other than the government were involved.

E. One-Year Restriction.

1. 18 U.S.C. § 207(c) prohibits, for one year after leaving federal service, "senior employees" (determined by specified pay thresholds, typically general or flag officers and SES Level V and VI) from communicating or appearing, with the intent to influence a particular matter, on behalf of anyone other than the government, when:

   a. The matter involves the department or agency the officer or employee served during his last year of federal service as a senior employee; and

   b. The person represented by the former officer or employee seeks official action by the department or agency concerning the matter.

F. Penalties.

1. Criminal. Imprisonment for up to one year and a fine. 18 U.S.C. § 216 (a).

2. Civil. $50,000 for each violation or the amount of compensation which the person received or offered for the prohibited conduct, whichever amount is greater. 18 U.S.C. § 216 (b).

3. Injunctive relief. The Attorney General may petition an appropriate U.S. district court for an order prohibiting a person from engaging in the conduct that constitutes the representation ban offense. 18 U.S.C. § 216 (c).

VI. SENIOR DOD OFFICIAL SEEKING EMPLOYMENT WITH DEFENSE CONTRACTORS.

A. **Section 847 of Pub. L. 110-181.** Covered DOD Employees, implemented by Defense Federal Acquisition Regulations (DFARS) 203.171.

1. A "covered DOD official" who, within 2 years after leaving DOD service, expects to receive compensation from a DOD contractor, shall, prior to accepting such compensation, request a written opinion from the appropriate DOD ethics counselor regarding the applicability of post-employment restrictions to activities that the official may undertake on behalf of a contractor. DFARS 203.171-3.

2. The DFARS defines "covered DOD official" as an individual that -

    a.   Leaves or left DOD service on or after January 28, 2008; and

    b.   Participated personally and substantially in an acquisition as defined in 41 U.S.C. 131 with a value in excess of $10 million, and serves or served—

        (1)   in an Executive Schedule position under subchapter II of chapter 53 of Title 5, United States Code;

        (2)   in a position in the Senior Executive Service under subchapter VIII of chapter 53 of Title 5, United States Code; or

        (3)   in a general or flag officer position compensated at a rate of pay for grade O-7 or above under section 201 of Title 37, United States Code; or

    c.   Serves or served in DOD in one of the following positions:

        (1)   Program manager,

        (2)   Deputy program manager,

        (3)   Procuring contracting officer,

        (4)   Administrative contracting officer,

        (5)   Source selection authority, member of the source selection evaluation board, or chief of a financial or technical evaluation team for a contract in an amount in excess of $10 million. DFARS 252.203-7000(a).

3. A DOD contractor shall not knowingly provide compensation to a covered DOD official within 2 years after the official leaves DOD service without first determining that the official has sought and received, or has not received after 30 days of seeking, a written opinion from the appropriate DOD ethics counselor regarding the applicability of post-employment restrictions to the activities that the official is expected to undertake on behalf of the contractor. DFARS 252.203-7000(b).

    a.   Failure by the contractor to comply with this DFARS clause may subject the contractor to rescission of this contract, suspension, or debarment in accordance with 41 U.S.C. 2105(c). DFARS 252.203-7000(c).

VII. GOVERNMENT DEALINGS WITH CONTRACTORS.

A. **General Rule.** Government business shall be conducted in a manner that is above reproach, with complete impartiality, and with preferential treatment for none. FAR 3.101-1.

B. **Some pre-contract contacts with industry are permissible**, and in fact are encouraged where the information exchange is beneficial (e.g., necessary to learn of industry's capabilities or to keep them informed of our future needs). FAR Part 5. Some examples are:

1. Research and development (R&D) advance notices. Contracting officers may transmit to the government-wide point of entry (GPE), advance notices of their interest in potential R&D programs whenever market research does not produce a sufficient number of concerns to obtain adequate competition. Advance notices will enable potential sources to learn of R&D programs and provide these sources with an opportunity to submit information, which will permit evaluation of their capabilities. FAR 5.205.

2. Unsolicited proposals. Companies are encouraged to make contacts with agencies before submitting proprietary data or spending extensive effort or money on these efforts. FAR 15.604.

VIII. RELEASE OF ACQUISITION INFORMATION.

A. **The integrity of the acquisition process** requires a high level of business security. When it is necessary to obtain information from potential contractors and others outside the government for use in preparing government estimates, contracting officers shall ensure that the information is not publicized or discussed with potential contractors. FAR 5.401(a).

B. **Contracting officers may make available the maximum amount of information** to the public except information (FAR 5.401(b)):

1. On plans that would provide undue discriminatory advantage to private or personal interests;

2. Received in confidence from offerors; 18 U.S.C. § 1905; FAR 15.506(e).

3. Otherwise requiring protection under the Freedom of Information Act or Privacy Act; or

4. Pertaining to internal agency communications (e.g., technical reviews).

C. **Information regarding unclassified long-range acquisition estimates** is releasable as far in advance as practicable to assist industry planning and to locate additional sources of supply. FAR 5.404.

D. **General limitations on release of acquisition information.** FAR 14.203-2; FAR 15.201. Exchanges of information among all interested parties, from the earliest identification of a requirement through receipt of proposals, are encouraged. However, any exchange of information must be consistent with procurement integrity requirements (see FAR 3.104).

1. Agencies should furnish identical information to all prospective contractors.

    a. When specific information about a proposed acquisition that would be necessary for the preparation of proposals is disclosed to one or more potential offerors, that information must be made available to the public as soon as practicable, but no later than the next general release of information, in order to avoid creating an unfair competitive advantage. Information provided to a potential offeror in response to its request must not be disclosed if doing so would reveal the potential offeror's confidential business strategy, and is protected under FAR 3.104 or FAR Subpart 24.2.

2. Agencies should release information as nearly simultaneously as possible, and only through designated officials (i.e., the contracting officer).

IX. CONTRACTOR PERSONAL CONFLICTS OF INTEREST.

A. **Background.** In November 2011, DOD, GSA and NASA issued a final rule amending the FAR to include a new subpart (FAR 3.11) and new contract clause (52.203-16) addressing personal conflicts of interest of federal contractor and subcontractor employees performing "acquisition functions closely associated with inherently governmental functions." This subpart and clause implements the policy on personal conflicts of interest by employees of government contractors required by the Duncan Hunter National Defense Authorization Act, 41 U.S.C. § 2303.

B.   **Policy**. The government's policy is to require contractors to:

1.   Identify and prevent personal conflicts of interest of their covered employees; and

2.   Prohibit covered employees who have access to non-public information by reason of performance on a government contract from using such information for personal gain. FAR 3.1102.

C.   **Rule.** The new rule requires federal government contractors and qualifying subcontractors to:

1.   Have procedures in place to screen covered employees for personal conflicts of interest through the use of disclosure forms;

2.   Assign only employees without personal conflicts to perform certain tasks under government contracts;

3.   Ensure that employees do not use non-public information for personal gain;

4.   Report violations to the applicable contracting officer.

5.   To avoid even the appearance of personal conflicts of interest

6.   Take appropriate disciplinary actions in the case of covered employees who fail to comply with policies established pursuant to FAR 3.11

D.   **Mitigation or Waiver**. if the contractor cannot satisfactorily prevent a personal conflict of interest, the contractor may

submit a request, through the contracting officer, for the head of the contracting activity to:

1.   Agree to a plan to mitigate the personal conflict of interest; or

2.   Waive the requirement to prevent personal conflicts of interest.

E.   **Applicability.** FAR 52.203-16, Preventing Personal Conflicts of Interest, must be included in Federal contracts and task or delivery orders that:

1.   Exceed the simplified acquisition threshold; and

2.   Include a requirement for services by contractor employees that involve performance of acquisition functions closely associated with inherently government functions for, or on behalf of, a Federal agency or department. FAR 3.1106.

X.   **POLITICAL CONTRIBUTIONS.**

A.   **Prohibition for Government Contractors.** Government contractors are prohibited from making political contributions.

1.   It is unlawful for any person who enters into any contract with the U.S. or any department or agency thereof either for the rendition of personal services or furnishing any material, supplies, or equipment or real property to the United States or any department or agency with funds appropriated by Congress to make or promise to make contributions to any political party, committee, or candidate for public office or to any person for any political purpose. 52 U.S.C. § 30119(a)

2.   The knowing solicitation of such a contribution from any such person is also prohibited. 52 U.S.C.§ 30119(a)

3.   Prohibitions last from the commencement of negotiations with the United States or its agencies or departments until either the

completion of the performance under the contract, or the termination of the negotiations. 52 U.S.C. § 30119(a)

XI. CONTRACTOR CODES OF BUSINESS ETHICS AND CONDUCT.

A. **Contracts and subcontracts expected to exceed $5.5 million** and last 120 days or more are required to include contract provisions mandating a code of business ethics and compliance, requiring:

1. Within 30 days, the contractor must have a written code of business ethics and conduct, unless the Contracting Officer establishes a longer time period.

    a. A copy of the code must be available to each employee engaged in performance of the contract.

2. The contractor must exercise due diligence to prevent and detect criminal conduct.

3. The contractor must promote an organizational culture that encourages ethical conduct and a commitment to compliance with the law.

4. The contractor must disclose, in writing, to the agency Office of the Inspector General and Contracting Officer, whenever, in connection with the award, performance, or closeout of the contract or any subcontract thereunder, the contractor has credible evidence that a principal, employee, agent or subcontractor has committed:

    a. A violation of federal law involving fraud, conflict of interest, bribery, or gratuity violations found in Title 18 of the United States Code; or

    b. A violation of the civil False Claims Act.

5. Qualifying contractors except those representing themselves as Small Business Concerns pursuant to the award

of the contract, or if the contract is for a commercial item as defined under FAR 2.101, are required to establish, within 90 days:

a. Ongoing business ethics awareness and compliance programs.

b. Internal control systems involving:

    (1) Assignment of responsibility at a sufficiently high level with adequate resources to ensure effectiveness of the business ethics awareness and compliance program and internal control system.

    (2) Reasonable efforts not to include principals whom due diligence would have exposed as having engaged in conduct contrary to the contractor's code of conduct.

    (3) Periodic reviews of business practices, procedures, policies and internal controls for compliance with the code of conduct.

    (4) Internal reporting mechanisms, such as a hotline, which allows for anonymity or confidentiality, by which employees may report suspected instances of improper conduct, and instructions that encourage employees to make such reports.

    (5) Disciplinary action for improper conduct or for failing to take reasonable steps to prevent or detect improper conduct.

    (6) Timely disclosure to the agency OIG, with a copy to the contracting officer, of credible evidence of a violation of federal criminal

law involving fraud, conflict of interest, bribery, gratuity, or a violation of the civil False Claims Act.

(7) Full cooperation with government agencies responsible for audits, investigations, or corrective actions.

6. FAR 3.1004(a); FAR 52.203-13.

B. Hotline Posters.

1. Contracts exceeding $5.5 million, or a lesser amount established by the agency, must include a provision requiring Display of Hotline Posters, unless:

a. The agency does not have a fraud poster and is not funded with disaster assistance funds;

b. The contract is for a commercial item; or

c. The contract will be performed entirely outside of the United States. FAR 3.1004(a); FAR 52.203-14.

2. Contracts with a Display of Hotline Posters must:

a. Display hotline posters prominently in common work areas within the business performing the work as well as contract worksites.

b. Display an electronic copy of the poster on the contractor's website, if the contractor maintains a

company website, as a method of providing information to employees

XII. CONCLUSION.

A. The ethical rules governing procurement officials are stricter than the general rules governing federal employees. The ethical rules for all federal employees prohibit employees from accepting many business gratuities, or providing unequal treatment.

B. Government procurement officials and government contractors should be familiar with the various ethical statutes and regulations addressed in this chapter, especially 18 U.S.C. § 208, Acts Affecting a Personal Financial Interest, 18 U.S.C. § 207, Restrictions on Former Officers, Employers, and Elected Officials of the Executive and Legislative Branches, and the Procurement Integrity Act, 41 U.S.C. §§ 2101-2107.

C. Government contractors should be aware of the prohibitions on former government employees when evaluating former officials for employment opportunities.

D. Government contractors should have conflict of interest policies in place as required by FAR 52.203-16, in addition to establishing and maintaining a Code of Ethics and Business Conduct as required by FAR 52.203-13.

E. The key to a successful ethics program is training that continuously reinforces what constitutes acceptable conduct, unacceptable conduct, and the consequences of unacceptable conduct.

BID PROTESTS

"The laws and regulations that govern contracting with the federal government are designed to ensure that federal procurements are conducted fairly. On occasion, bidders or others interested in government procurements may have reason to believe that a contract has been, or is about to be, awarded improperly or illegally, or that they have been unfairly denied a contract or an opportunity to compete for a contract."

OFFICE OF GENERAL COUNSEL, UNITED STATES GOVERNMENT ACCOUNTABILITY OFFICE, BID PROTESTS AT GAO: A DESCRIPTIVE GUIDE (9TH ED. 2009)

I. INTRODUCTION.

A. **Background.** The General Accounting Office had heard bid protests for many years under its general statutory authority. Congress granted explicit statutory authority to the existing protest system when it enacted the Competition in Contracting Act of 1984 (CICA). The Government Accountability Office, as it is currently titled, or "GAO," implemented CICA in its Bid Protest Regulations. The current system is intended to provide for the expeditious and fair resolution of protests with only minimal disruption to the procurement process. DataVault Corp., B-249054, Aug. 27, 1992, 92-2 CPD ¶ 133. See FAR Subpart 33.1.

B. **Jurisdiction.** There are currently three fora for filing a protest against a procurement action. An unsuccessful offeror may protest to: 1) the agency, 2) the GAO, or 3) the United States Court of Federal Claims (COFC). See Appendix.

C. **Remedies.**

1. Generally, protest fora do not direct the award of a contract and may not award lost profits. Instead, typical remedies for prejudicial errors include directing or recommending that the agency correct the error and reconsider its decision; or awarding the successful protestor bid and proposal costs.

2. Whether the filing of a protest to challenge a contract solicitation or an award creates an automatic stay or suspension of any work on the procurement is of critical importance and varies from forum to forum.

II. AGENCY PROTESTS.

A. **Authority.**

1. Agency protests are filed[1] directly with the contracting officer or other cognizant government official within the agency. These protests are governed by FAR 33.103, AFARS 33.103, NAPS 5233.103, AFFARS 5333.102 and 5333.103.

2. Contracting officers must seek and consider legal advice regarding all protests filed with the agency. FAR 33.102(a).

B. **Procedures.** FAR 33.103. In late 1995, President Clinton issued an Executive Order directing all executive agencies to establish alternative disputes resolution (ADR) procedures for bid protests. The order directs agency heads to create a system that, "to the maximum extent possible," will allow for the "inexpensive, informal, procedurally simple, and expeditious resolution of protests." FAR 33.103 implements this Order. Exec. Order No. 12,979, 60 Fed. Reg. 55,171 (1995).

1. Open and frank discussions. Prior to the submission of a protest, all parties shall use "their best efforts" to resolve issues and concerns raised by an "interested party" at the contracting officer level.

---

[1] FAR 33.101 defines "filed" to mean:

[t]he complete receipt of any document by an agency before its close of business. Documents received after close of business are considered filed as of the next day. Unless otherwise stated, the agency close of business is presumed to be 4:30 p.m., local time.

"Best efforts" include conducting "open and frank discussions" among the parties.

2. Objectives. FAR 33.103(d). The goal of an effective agency protest system is to:

   a. resolve agency protests effectively;

   b. help build confidence in the federal acquisition system; and

   c. reduce protests to the GAO and other judicial protest fora.

3. Protesters are not required to exhaust agency administrative remedies.

4. Procedures tend to be informal and flexible.

   a. Protests must be clear and concise. Failure to submit a coherent protest may be grounds for dismissal. FAR 33.103(d)(1).

   b. "Interested parties" may request review at a "level above the contracting officer" of any decision by the contracting officer that allegedly violated an applicable statute or regulation and, thus, prejudiced the offeror. FAR 33.103(d)(4).

5. Timing of Protests.

   a. Pre-award protests, to include protests challenging the propriety of a solicitation, must be filed prior to bid opening or the date for receipt of proposals.

   b. In all other cases, the contractor must file its protest to the agency within 10 days of when the protester knew or should have known of the bases for the protest. For "significant issues" raised by the protester, however, the agency has the discretion to consider the merits of a protest that is otherwise untimely. FAR 33.103(e).

6. Suspension of Procurement.

   a. Pre-award Stay. The contracting officer shall not make award if an agency protest is filed before award. FAR 33.103(f)(1) imposes an administrative stay of the contract award.

      (1) The agency may override the stay if one of the following applies:

      (a) contract award is justified in light of "urgent and compelling" reasons; or

      (b) determined award is in "the best interests of the government."

      (2) The override decision must be made in writing and then approved by an agency official "at a level above the contracting officer" or another official pursuant to agency procedures. FAR 33.103(f)(1).

      (3) If the contracting officer elects to withhold award, he must inform all interested parties of that decision. If appropriate, the contracting officer should obtain extensions of bid/proposal acceptance times from the offerors. If the contracting officer cannot obtain extensions, he should consider an override of the stay and proceed with making contract award. FAR 33.103(f)(2).

   b. Post-award Stay. If the agency receives a protest within 10 days of contract award or 5 days of a "required" debriefing date offered by the agency,[2] the contracting officer shall suspend contract performance immediately. FAR 33.103(f)(3).

---

[2] See FAR 15.505 and FAR 15.506.

(1) The agency may override the stay if one of the following applies:

(a) contract performance is justified in light of "urgent and compelling" reasons; or

(b) determined contract performance is in "the best interests of the government."

(2) The override determination must be made in writing and then approved by an agency official "at a level above the contracting officer" or another official pursuant to agency procedures. FAR 33.103(f)(3).

C. Processing Protests.

1. Contractors generally present protests to the contracting officer; but they may also request an independent review of their protest at a level above the contracting officer, in accordance with agency procedures. Solicitations should advise offerors of this option. FAR 33.103(d)(4).

   a. Agency procedures shall inform the protester whether this independent review is an alternative to consideration by the contracting officer or as an "appeal" to a contracting officer's protest decision.

   b. Agencies shall designate the official who will conduct this independent review. The official need not be in the supervisory chain of the contracting officer. However, "when practicable," the official designated to conduct the independent review "should" not have previous "personal involvement" in the procurement.

   c. NOTE: This "independent review" of the contracting officer's initial protest decision, if offered by the agency, does NOT extend GAO's timeliness requirements.

2. Agencies "shall make their best efforts" to resolve agency protests within 35 days of filing. FAR 33.103(g).

3. Discovery. To the extent permitted by law and regulation, the agency and the protester may exchange information relevant to the protest. FAR 33.103(g).

4. The agency decision shall be "well reasoned" and "provide sufficient factual detail explaining the agency position." The agency must provide the protester a written copy of the decision via a method that provides evidence of receipt. FAR 33.103(h).

D. Remedies. FAR 33.102.

1. Failure to Comply with Applicable Law or Regulation. FAR 33.102(b). If the agency head determines that, as a result of a protest, a solicitation, proposed award, or award is improper, he may:

   a. take any action that the GAO could have "recommended," had the contractor filed the protest with the GAO; and

   b. award costs to the protester for prosecution of the protest.

2. Misrepresentation by Awardee. If, as a result of awardee's intentional or negligent misstatement, misrepresentation, or miscertification, a post-award protest is sustained, the agency head may require the awardee to reimburse the government's costs associated with the protest. The government may recover this debt by offsetting the amount against any payment due the awardee under any contract between the awardee and the government.[3] This provision also applies to GAO protests. FAR 33.102(b)(3).

3. Follow-On Protest. If unhappy with the agency decision, the protester may file its protest with either the GAO or COFC (see

---

[3] In determining the liability of the awardee, the contracting officer shall take into consideration "the amount of the debt, the degree of fault, and the costs of collection." FAR 33.102(b)(3)(ii).

Appendix). If the vendor elects to proceed to the GAO, it must file its protest within 10 days of receiving notice of the agency's initial adverse action.[4] 4 C.F.R. § 21.2(a)(3).

III. GOVERNMENT ACCOUNTABILITY OFFICE (GAO).

A. **Statutory Authority.** The Competition in Contracting Act of 1984, 31 U.S.C. §§ 3551-3556, is the current statutory authority for GAO bid protests of federal agency procurements. 31 U.S.C. § 3533 authorizes GAO to issue implementing regulations.

B. **Regulatory Authority.** The GAO's bid protest regulations are set forth at 4 C.F.R. Part 21. FAR provisions governing GAO bid protests are at FAR 33.104. Agency FAR supplements contain regulatory procedures for managing GAO protests. See generally DFARS 233.1; AFARS 5133.104; AFFARS 5333.104; NAPS 5233.104; DLAAR 33.104.

C. **Who May Protest?**

1. 31 U.S.C. § 3551(1) and 4 C.F.R. § 21.1(a) (2000) provide that an "interested party" may protest to the GAO.

2. An "interested party" is "an actual or prospective bidder or offeror whose direct economic interest would be affected by the award of a contract or by the failure to award a contract." 31 U.S.C § 3551(2)(A); 4 C.F.R. § 21.0(a)(1).

a. Before bid opening or proposal submission due date, a protester must be a prospective bidder or offeror with a direct economic interest. A prospective bidder or offeror is one who has expressed an interest in competing. Total Procurement Servs., Inc., B-272343, Aug. 29, 1996, 96-2 CPD ¶ 92; D.J. Findley, Inc., B-221096, Feb. 3, 1986, 86-1 CPD ¶ 121.

b. After bid opening or the submission of proposals, a protester must be an actual bidder or offeror with a direct economic interest.

(1) A bidder or offeror must be "next-in-line" for award. If a protester cannot receive award if it prevails on the merits, it is not an interested party. International Data Prods., Corp., B-274654, Dec. 26, 1996, 97-1 CPD ¶ 34 (protesters rated eighth and ninth in overall technical merit were interested parties); Comspace Corp., B-274037, Nov. 14, 1996, 96-2 CPD ¶ 186 (contractor not in line for award where electronic quote not properly transmitted); Ogden Support Servs., Inc., B-270354.2, Oct. 29, 1996, 97-1 CPD ¶ 135 (protester not an interested party where an intervening offeror has a higher technical score and a lower cost); Recon Optical, Inc., B-272239, July 17, 1996, 96-2 CPD ¶ 21 (recipients of multiple award contracts may not protest the others' award); Watkins Sec. Agency, Inc., B-248309, Aug. 14, 1992, 92-2 CPD ¶ 108 (highest priced of three technically equal bidders was not in line for award).

(2) A high-priced bidder may be able to demonstrate that all

---

[4] In its "White Book," the GAO advises that it applies a "straightforward" interpretation of what constitutes notice of adverse agency action. Specific examples include: bid opening; receipt of proposals; rejection of a bid or proposal; or contract award. OFFICE OF GENERAL COUNSEL, UNITED STATES GOVERNMENT ACCOUNTABILITY OFFICE, BID PROTESTS AT GAO: A DESCRIPTIVE GUIDE 7 (9th ed. 2009). **The reader can obtain a free copy of this booklet by accessing the GAO Internet Homepage at:** http://www.gao.gov **(direct PDF link:** http://www.gao.gov/products/GAO-09-471SP).

lower-priced bidders would be ineligible for award. Professional Medical Prods., Inc., B-231743, July 1, 1988, 88-2 CPD ¶ 2.

(3) In a "best value" or negotiated procurement, the GAO determines whether a protester is an interested party by examining the probable result if the protest is successful. Government Tech. Servs., Inc., B-258082, Sept. 2, 1994, 94-2 BCA ¶ 93 (protester not an interested party where it failed to challenge higher-ranked intervening offers); Rome Research Corp., B-245797, Sept. 22, 1992, 92-2 CPD ¶ 194.

(4) An actual bidder, not in line for award, is an interested party if it would regain the opportunity to compete if the GAO sustains its protest. This occurs if the GAO could recommend resolicitation. Teltara, Inc., B-245806, Jan. 30, 1992, 92-1 CPD ¶ 128 (11th low bidder protested the adequacy of the solicitation's provisions concerning a prior collective bargaining agreement; remedy might be resolicitation); Remtech, Inc., B-240402, Jan. 4, 1991, 91-1 CPD ¶ 35 (protest by nonresponsive second low bidder challenged IFB as unduly restrictive; interested party because remedy is resolicitation).

3. Intervenors. Immediately after receipt of the protest notice, the agency must notify awardee (post-award protest) or all offerors who have a "substantial prospect" of receiving award if the protest is denied (pre-award protest). 4 C.F.R. § 21.0(b), § 21.3(a).

D. What May Be Protested?

1. The protester must allege a violation of a procurement statute or regulation. 31 U.S.C. § 3552. The GAO will also review allegations of unreasonable agency actions. S.D.M. Supply, Inc., B-271492, June 26, 1996, 96-1 CPD ¶ 288 (simplified acquisition using defective FACNET system failed to promote competition "to the maximum extent practicable" in violation of CICA). This includes the termination of a contract where the protest alleges the government's termination was based upon improprieties associated with contract award (sometimes referred to as a "reverse protest"). 4 C.F.R. § 21.1(a); Severn Cos., B-275717.2, Apr. 28, 1997, 97-1 CPD ¶ 181.

2. The GAO generally will NOT consider protests on the following matters:

a. Contract Administration. 4 C.F.R. § 21.5(a). Health Care Waste Servs., B-266302, Jan. 19, 1996, 96-1 CPD ¶ 13 (registration or licensing requirement a performance obligation and not one of responsibility); JA & Assocs., B-256280, Aug. 19, 1994, 95-1 CPD ¶ 136 (decision to novate contract to another firm rather than recompete); Caltech Serv. Corp., B-240726, Jan. 22, 1992, 92-1 CPD ¶ 94 (modification of contract unless it is a cardinal change); Casecraft, Inc., B-226796, June 30, 1987, 87-1 CPD ¶ 647 (decision to terminate a contract for default); but see Marvin J. Perry & Assocs., B-277684, Nov. 4, 1997, 97-2 CPD ¶ 128 (GAO asserts jurisdiction over agency acceptance of different quality office furniture that was shipped by mistake); Sippican, Inc., B-257047, Nov. 13, 1995, 95-2 CPD ¶ 220 (GAO will review agency exercise of contract option).

b. Small Business Size and Industrial Classification Determinations. 4

Bid Protests

C.F.R. § 21.5(b)(1). Challenges to size or status of small businesses are left to exclusive review by the Small Business Administration. <u>Lawyers Advantage Title Group, Inc.</u>, B-275946, Apr. 17, 1997, 97-1 CPD ¶ 143; <u>Columbia Research Corp.</u>, B-247073, June 4, 1992, 92-1 CPD ¶ 492.

c. Small Business Certificate of Competency (COC) Determinations. 4 C.F.R. § 21.5(b)(2). Referrals made to the Small Business Administration (SBA) pursuant to sec. 8(b)(7) of the Small Business Act, or the issuance of, or refusal to issue, a certificate of competency under that section will generally not be reviewed by GAO. Narrow exception to consider protests that show possible bad faith on the part of government officials, or that present allegations that the SBA failed to follow its own published regulations or failed to consider vital information bearing on the firm's responsibility.

d. Procurements Under Section 8(a) of the Small Business Act (i.e., small disadvantaged business contracts). The GAO will review a decision to place a procurement under the 8(a) program only for possible bad faith by agency officials or a violation of applicable law or regulation. 4 C.F.R. § 21.5(b)(3). See <u>Grace Indus., Inc.</u>, B-274378, Nov. 8, 1996, 96-2 CPD ¶ 178. See also <u>Security Consultants Group, Inc.</u>, B-276405.2, June. 9, 1997, 97-1 CPD ¶ 207 (protest sustained where agency failed to provide complete and accurate information of all vendors eligible for an 8(a) award).

e. Affirmative Responsibility Determinations. 4 C.F.R. § 21.5(c)(2000); <u>Imaging Equip. Servs., Inc.</u>, B-247197, Jan. 13, 1992, 92-1 CPD ¶ 62.

(1) Exception: Where solicitation includes definitive responsibility criteria. <u>King-Fisher Co.</u>, B-236687, Feb. 12, 1990, 90-1 CPD ¶ 177.

(2) Exception: Where protester alleges fraud or bad faith. <u>HLJ Management Group, Inc.</u>, B-225843, Mar. 24, 1989, 89-1 CPD ¶ 299.

(3) Exception: the contracting officer unreasonably failed to consider available relevant information or otherwise violated statute or regulation. <u>SumCo Eco-Contracting LLC</u>, B-409434, B-409434.2, Apr. 15, 2014, 2014 CPD ¶ 129.

f. Procurement Integrity Act Violations. The protester must first report information supporting allegations involving violations of the Procurement Integrity Act to the agency within 14 days after the protester first discovered the possible violation. 4 C.F.R. § 21.5(d); 41 U.S.C. Chapter 21. See, e.g., <u>SRS Techs.</u>, B-277366, July 30, 1997, 97-2 CPD ¶ 42.

g. Subcontractor Protests. The GAO will not consider subcontractor protests unless requested to do so by the procuring agency. 4 C.F.R. § 21.5(h). See <u>RGB Display Corporation</u>, B-284699, May 17, 2000, 2000 CPD ¶ 80. See also <u>Compugen, Ltd.</u>, B-261769, Sept. 5, 1995, 95-2 CPD ¶ 103. However, the GAO will review subcontract procurements where the subcontract is "by" the government. See, supra, <u>RGB Display Corp.</u> (subcontract procurement is "by" the government where agency handles substantially all the substantive aspects of the procurement and the prime contractor acts merely as a conduit for the government).

h. Procurements by Non-federal Agencies (e.g., United States Postal Service, Federal Deposit Insurance Corporation (FDIC), non-appropriated fund activities [NAFIs]). 4 C.F.R. § 21.5(g). The GAO will consider a protest involving a non-federal agency if the agency involved has agreed in writing to have the protest decided by the GAO. 4 C.F.R. § 21.13.

i. Judicial Proceedings. 4 C.F.R. § 21.11. The GAO will not hear protests that are the subject of pending federal court litigation unless requested by the court for an advisory opinion. SRS Techs., B-254425, May 11, 1995, 95-1 CPD ¶ 239; Snowblast-Sicard, Inc., B-230983, Aug. 30, 1989, 89-2 CPD ¶ 190. The GAO also will not hear a protest that has been finally adjudicated, e.g., dismissed with prejudice. Cecile Indus., Inc., B-211475, Sept. 23, 1983, 83-2 CPD ¶ 367.

j. Task and Delivery Orders. The GAO may not hear protests associated with the placement of a task or delivery order except when the order "increases the scope, period, or maximum value" of the underlying contract, or is an order valued in excess of $10 million. 10 U.S.C. § 2304(c); 41 U.S.C. § 4106. See, e.g., EA Eng'g, Science, and Tech., Inc., B-411967.2, Apr. 5, 2016, 2016 CPD ¶ __; Goldbelt Glacier Health Servs, LLC--Reconsideration, B-410378.3, Feb. 6, 2015, 2015 CPD ¶ 75; Military Agency Services Pty., Ltd., B-290414, Aug. 1, 2003, 2002 CPD ¶ 130. The GAO, however, has held that it has protest jurisdiction over task and delivery orders placed under Federal Supply Schedule (FSS) contracts. Severn Co., Inc., B-275717.2, Apr. 28, 1997, 97-1 CPD ¶ 181 at 2-3, n.1. Additionally, the GAO will hear cases involving the "downselect" of multiple awardees, if that determination is implemented by the issuance of task and delivery orders. See Electro-Voice, Inc., B-278319; Jan. 15, 1998, 98-1 CPD ¶ 23. See also Teledyne-Commodore, LLC - - Reconsideration, B-278408.4, Nov. 23, 1998, 98-2 CPD ¶ 121.

k. Debarment & Suspension Issues. The GAO will not review protests that an agency improperly suspended or debarred a contractor. 4 C.F.R. § 21.5(i); see Shinwha Electronics, B-290603, Sept. 3, 2002, 2002 CPD ¶ 154.

3. What Is a Procurement?

a. A procurement of property or services by a federal agency. 31 U.S.C. § 3551. New York Tel. Co., B-236023, Nov. 7, 1989, 89-2 CPD ¶ 435 (solicitation to install pay phones is an acquisition of a service). The transaction, however, must relate to the agency's mission or result in a benefit to the government. Maritime Global Bank Group, B-272552, Aug. 13, 1996, 96-2 CPD ¶ 62 (Navy agreement with a bank to provide on-base banking services not a procurement). See also Starfleet Marine Transportation, Inc., B-290181, July 5, 2002, 2002 CPD ¶ 113 (GAO holding that it had jurisdiction of a mixed transaction involving both the "sale" of a business opportunity and the procurement of services); Government of Harford County, Md., B-283259, B-283259.3, Oct. 28, 1999, 99-2 CPD ¶ 81.

b. Sales of government property are excluded. Fifeco, B-246925, Dec. 11, 1991, 91-2 CPD ¶ 534 (sale of property by FHA not a procurement of property or services); Columbia Communications Corp., B-236904, Sept. 18, 1989, 89-2 CPD ¶ 242

(GAO declined to review a sale of satellite communications services). The GAO will consider protests involving such sales, however, if the agency involved has agreed in writing to allow GAO to decide the dispute. 4 C.F.R. § 21.13(a); Assets Recovery Sys., Inc., B-275332, Feb. 10, 1997, 97-1 CPD ¶ 67. See also Catholic University of America v. United States, 49 Fed. Cl. 795 (2001) (COFC holding that the Administrative Dispute Resolution Act's (ADRA) amendment to the Tucker Act broadened its scope of post-award protests to include solicitation of government assets).

c.   The GAO has also considered a protest despite the lack of a solicitation or a contract when the agency held "extensive discussions" with a firm and then decided not to issue a solicitation. Health Servs. Mktg. & Dev. Co., B-241830, Mar. 5, 1991, 91-1 CPD ¶ 247. Accord, RJP Ltd., B-246678, Mar. 27, 1992, 92-1 CPD ¶ 310.

d.   A "Federal Agency" includes executive, legislative, or judicial branch agencies. 31 U.S.C. § 3551(3) (specifically refers to the definition in the Federal Property and Administrative Services Act of 1949 at 40 U.S.C. § 472); 4 C.F.R. § 21.0(c). However, it excludes:

(1)   The Senate, House of Representatives, the Architect of the Capitol, and activities under his direction. 40 U.S.C. § 472(b); 4 C.F.R. § 21.0(c) (2000). Court Reporting Servs., Inc., B-259492, Dec. 12, 1994, 94-2 CPD ¶ 236.

(2)   Government corporations identified in 31 U.S.C. § 9101 that are only partially owned by the United States, e.g., FDIC. 31 U.S.C. § 3501;

Cablelink, B-250066, Aug. 28, 1992, 92-2 CPD ¶ 135. This exclusion does not apply to wholly government-owned corporations, e.g., TVA. See Kennan Auction Co., B-248965, June 9, 1992, 92-1 CPD ¶ 503 (Resolution Trust Corporation); Monarch Water Sys., Inc., B-218441, Aug. 8, 1985, 85-2 CPD ¶ 146. See also 4 C.F.R. § 21.5(g).

(3)   The United States Postal Service (USPS). 4 C.F.R. § 21.5(g). The USPS is not a federal agency under procurement law; therefore, the GAO does not hear USPS protests. But see Emery WorldWide Airlines, Inc. v. Federal Express Corp., 264 F.3d 1071 (2001) (the Court of Appeals for the Federal Circuit held that the USPS was a federal agency as specified by the Administrative Dispute Resolution Act of 1996, not federal procurement law; therefore, the Postal Service is not exempt from the court's bid protest jurisdiction as it is from GAO's).

e.   Generally, the GAO does not view procurements by non-appropriated fund instrumentalities (NAFIs) as "agency procurements." 4 C.F.R. § 21.5(g). The Brunswick Bowling & Billiards Corp., B-224280, Sept. 12, 1986, 86-2 CPD ¶ 295.

f.   The GAO will consider procurements conducted by federal agencies (i.e., processed by an agency contracting officer) on behalf of a NAFI, even if no appropriated funds are to be obligated. Premier Vending, Inc., B-256560, July 5, 1994, 94-2 CPD ¶ 8; Americable Int'l, Inc., B-251614, Apr. 20, 1993, 93-1 CPD ¶ 336.

334

g. The GAO will consider a protest involving a NAFI-conducted procurement if there is evidence of pervasive involvement of federal agency personnel in the procurement and the NAFI is acting merely as a conduit for the federal agency. See Asiel Enters., Inc., B-408315.2, Sept. 5, 2013, 2013 CPD ¶ 205.

h. The GAO will consider protest challenging terms of solicitation for the award of a lease of federal property where the record shows that the agency will receive benefits in connection with the award of the lease, such that the agency is, in effect, conducting a procurement for goods and services. See Blue Origin, LLC, B-408823, Dec 12, 2013, 2013 CPD ¶ 289.

i. While the GAO does not have jurisdiction to review protests of the award, or protests of solicitations for award, of non-procurement instruments, it does have jurisdiction over a protest challenging whether an agency is improperly using a non-procurement instrument in lieu of a required procurement contract. Assisted Housing Servs. Corp. et al., B-406738 et al., Aug. 15, 2012, 2012 CPD ¶ 236.

E. When Must a Protest Be Filed?

1. Time limits on protests are set forth in 4 C.F.R. § 21.2.[5]

    a. Defective Solicitation. GAO must receive protests based on alleged improprieties or errors in a

solicitation that are apparent on the face of the solicitation, i.e., patent ambiguities or defects, prior to bid opening or the closing date for receipt of initial proposals. 4 C.F.R. § 21.2(a)(1); Carter Indus., Inc., B-270702, Feb. 15, 1996, 96-1 CPD ¶ 99 (untimely challenge of agency failure to include mandatory clause indicating whether agency will conduct discussions prior to making award).

b. Protesters challenging a government-wide point of entry (GPE) notice of intent to make a sole source award must first respond to the notice in a timely manner. See Norden Sys., Inc., B-245684, Jan. 7, 1992, 92-1 CPD ¶ 32 (unless the specification is so restrictive as to preclude a response, the protester must first express interest to the agency); see also PPG Indus., Inc., B-272126, June 24, 1996, 96-1 CPD ¶ 285, fn. 1 (timeliness of protests challenging CBD notices discussed).

c. When an amendment to a solicitation provides the basis for the protest, then the protest must be filed by the next due date for revised proposals. 4 C.F.R. § 21.2(a)(1).

d. Required Debriefing. Procurements involving competitive proposals carry with them the obligation to debrief the losing offerors, if the debriefing is timely requested. See FAR 15.505 and 15.506. In such cases, protesters may not file a protest prior to the debriefing date offered by the agency. The protester, however, must file its protest no later than 10 days "after the date on which the debriefing is held." 4 C.F.R. § 21.2(2); Fumigadora Popular, S.A., B-276676, Apr. 21, 1997, 97-1 CPD ¶ 151 (protest filed four days after debriefing of sealed bid procurement not timely); The Real

---

[5] Under the GAO bid protest rules, "days" are calendar days. In computing a period of time for timeliness purposes, do not count the day on which the period begins. When the last day falls on a weekend day, federal holiday, or day GAO or agency where submission is due is closed for all or part of the last day, the period extends to the next working day. 4 C.F.R. § 21.0(d).

Estate Center, B-274081, Aug. 20, 1996, 96-2 CPD ¶ 74.

e. Government Delay of Pre-award Debriefings. The agency may delay pre-award debriefings until after award when it is in the best interests of the government. FAR 15.505(b). If the agency decides to delay a pre-award debriefing that is otherwise timely requested and required, the protester is entitled to a post-award debriefing and the extended protest time frame. Note that if a protester files its protest within five days of the offered debrief, protester will also be entitled to stay contract performance. 31 U.S.C. § 3553(d)(4)(B); FAR 33.104(c). Global Eng'g & Constr. Joint Venture, B-275999, Feb. 19, 1997, 97-1 CPD ¶ 77 (protest of exclusion from competitive range).

f. Protests based on any other matter must be submitted within 10 days after receiving actual or constructive knowledge of the basis for protest. 4 C.F.R. § 21.2(a)(2). Learjet, Inc., B-274385, Dec. 6, 1996, 96-2 CPD ¶ 215 (interpretation of solicitation untimely); L. Washington & Assocs., Inc., B-274749, Nov. 18, 1996, 96-2 CPD ¶ 191 (untimely protest of elimination from competitive range).

g. Protests initially filed with the agency:

(1) The agency protest must generally be filed within the same time restrictions applicable to GAO protests, unless the agency has established more restrictive time frames. 4 C.F.R. § 21.2(a)(3). Orbit Advanced Techs., Inc., B-275046, Dec. 10, 1996, 96-2 CPD ¶ 228 (protest dismissed where protester's agency-level protest untimely even though

it would have been timely under GAO rules); IBP, Inc., B-275259, Nov. 4, 1996, 96-2 CPD ¶ 169.

(2) If the contractor previously filed a timely agency protest, a subsequent GAO protest must be filed within 10 days of formal notice, actual knowledge, or constructive knowledge of the initial adverse agency decision. 4 C.F.R. § 21.2(a)(3). Consolidated Mgt. Servs., Inc.--Recon., B-270696, Feb. 13, 1996, 96-1 CPD ¶ 76 (oral notice of adverse agency action starts protest time period. Continuing to pursue agency protest after initial adverse decision does not toll the GAO time limitations. Telestar Int'l Corp.--Recon., B-247029, Jan. 14, 1992, 92-1 CPD ¶ 69.

2. Protesters must use due diligence to obtain the information necessary to pursue the protest. See Automated Medical Prods. Corp., B-275835, Feb. 3, 1997, 97-1 CPD ¶ 52 (protest based on FOIA-disclosed information not timely where protester failed to request debriefing); Products for Industry, B-257463, Oct. 6, 1994, 94-2 CPD ¶ 128 (protest challenging contract award untimely where protester failed to attend bid opening and did not make any post-bid attempt to examine awardee's bid); Adrian Supply Co.--Recon., B-242819, Oct. 9, 1991, 91-2 CPD ¶ 321 (use of FOIA request rather than the more expeditious document production rules of the GAO may result in the dismissal of a protest for lack of due diligence and untimeliness). But see Geo-Centers, Inc., B-276033, May 5, 1997, 97-1 CPD ¶ 182 (protest filed three months after contract award and two months after debriefing is timely where the information was obtained via a FOIA request that was filed immediately after the debriefing).

3. Exceptions for otherwise untimely protests. 4 C.F.R. § 21.2(c).

   a. Significant Issue Exception: The GAO may consider a late protest if it involves an issue significant to the procurement system. See Pyxis Corp., B-282469, B-282469.2, Jul. 15, 1999, 99-2 CPD ¶ 18; Premier Vending, Inc., B-256560, Jul. 5, 1994, 94-2 CPD ¶ 8.

   b. Significant issues generally: 1) have not been previously considered; and 2) are of widespread interest to the procurement community. Pyxis Corp., B-282469, B-282469.2, Jul. 15, 1999, 99-2 CPD ¶ 18. DynCorp, Inc., B-240980, Oct. 17, 1990, 90-2 CPD ¶ 310.

   c. The GAO may consider a protest if there is good cause, beyond the protester's control, for the lateness. A.R.E. Mfg. Co., B-246161, Feb. 21, 1992, 92-1 CPD ¶ 210; Surface Combustion, Inc.--Recon., B-230112, Mar. 3, 1988, 88-1 CPD ¶ 230.

F. **"The CICA Stay"—Automatic Stay.** 31 U.S.C. § 3553(c) and (d).

1. Pre-award Protests: An agency may <u>not</u> award a contract after receiving notice of a timely protest from the GAO. 31 U.S.C. § 3553(c); 4 C.F.R. § 21.6; FAR 33.104(b); AFARS 5133.104(b); AFFARS 5333.104(b).

2. Post-award Protests: The contracting officer shall suspend contract performance immediately when the agency receives notice of protest from the GAO within 10 days of the date of contract award or within five days <u>after the date offered</u> for the required post-award debriefing. The CICA stay applies under either deadline, whichever is the later. 31 U.S.C. § 3553(d); 4 C.F.R. § 21.6; FAR 33.104(c); AFARS 5133.104(c); AFFARS 5333.104(c).

3. The automatic stay is triggered only by notice from GAO. 31 U.S.C. § 3553, <u>Florida Professional Review Org.</u>, B-253908.2, Jan. 10, 1994, 94-1 CPD ¶ 17 (no duty to suspend performance where protest filed on eighth day after award [Friday] but GAO notified agency of protest on eleventh day after award [Monday]).

4. "Proposed Award" Protests: An agency's decision to cancel a solicitation based upon the determination that the costs associated with contract performance would be cheaper if performed in-house (i.e., by federal employees) may be subject to the CICA stay. See <u>Inter-Con Sec. Sys., Inc. v. Widnall</u>, No. C 94-20442 RMW, 1994 U.S. Dist. LEXIS 10995 (D.C. Cal. July 11, 1994); <u>Aspen Sys. Corp.</u>, B-228590, Feb. 18, 1988, 88-1 CPD ¶ 166. In reviewing a protest of an in-house cost comparison, the GAO will look to whether the agency complied with applicable procedures in selecting in-house performance over contracting. DynCorp, B-233727.2, June 9, 1989, 89-1 CPD ¶ 543.

5. "The CICA Override"—Relief from the CICA Stay. 31 U.S.C. § 3553(c) and (d); FAR 33.104(b) and (c); AFARS 5133.104; AFFARS 5333.104.

   a. Pre-award Protest Stay: The head of the contracting activity may, on a non-delegable basis, authorize the award of a contract:

      (1) Upon a written finding that urgent and compelling circumstances which significantly affect the interest of the United States will not permit waiting for the decision of the Comptroller General; AND

      (2) The agency is likely to award the contract within 30 days of the written override determination.

b. Post-award Protest Stay: The head of the contracting activity may, on a non-delegable basis, authorize continued performance under a previously awarded contract upon a written finding that:

(1) Continued performance of the contract is in the best interests of the United States; or

(2) Urgent and compelling circumstances that significantly affect the interest of the United States will not permit waiting for the decision of the Comptroller General.

c. In either instance, if the agency is going to override the automatic stay, it must notify the GAO. Banknote Corp. of America, Inc., B-245528, Jan. 13, 1992, 92-1 CPD ¶ 53 (GAO will not review the decision).

6. Override decisions, however, are subject to judicial review. See Ramcor Servs. Group, Inc. v. United States, 185 F.3d 1286 (Fed. Cir. 1999).

G. Availability of Funds. The "end-of-fiscal-year spending spree" results in a large volume of protest action during the August-November time frame. To allay worries about the loss of funds pending protest resolution, 31 U.S.C. § 1558 provides that funds will not expire for 100 days following resolution of the bid protest.[6] FAR 33.102(c).

H. Scope of GAO Review.

1. The scope of GAO's review of protests is similar to that of the Administrative Procedures Act. 5 U.S.C. § 706. GAO does not conduct a de novo review. Instead, it reviews the agency's actions for reasonableness, and to ensure, consistent with the solicitation, procurement statutes and regulations. Philips Med. Sys. N. Am. Co., B-293945.2, June 17, 2004, 2004 CPD ¶ 129.

2. The protester generally has the burden of demonstrating that the agency action is clearly unreasonable. The Saxon Corp., B-232694, Jan. 9, 1989, 89-1 CPD ¶ 17.

3. When conducting its review, the GAO will consider the entire record surrounding agency conduct, including statements and arguments made in response to the protest, so long as those statements are credible and consistent with the contemporaneous record. Management Sys. Int'l, Inc., B-409415, B-409415.2, Apr. 2, 2014, 2014 CPD ¶ 117; AT&T Corp., B-260447, Mar. 4, 1996, 96-1 CPD ¶ 200. The agency may not, however, for the first time in a protest, provide its rationale for the decision in a request for reconsideration. Department of the Army—Recon., B-240647, Feb. 26, 1991, 91-1 CPD ¶ 211.

4. As part of its review, the GAO has demonstrated a willingness to probe factual allegations and assumptions underlying agency determinations or award decisions. See, e.g., Redstone Tech. Servs., B-259222, Mar. 17, 1995, 95-1 CPD ¶ 181; Secure Servs. Tech., Inc., B-238059, Apr. 25, 1990, 90-1 CPD ¶ 421 (GAO conducted a comparative analysis of competitors' proposals and the alleged deficiencies in them and sustained the protest when it determined that the agency had not evaluated the proposals in a consistent manner); Frank E. Basil, Inc., B-238354, May 22, 1990, 90-1 CPD ¶ 492 (GAO reviewed source selection plan).

5. If the protester alleges bad faith, the GAO will presume the agency acted in good faith. The protester must present convincing evidence clearly demonstrating bad faith. Advanced Sciences, Inc., B-259569.3, July 3, 1995, 95-2 CPD ¶ 52.

---

[6] This authority applies to protests filed with the agency, at the GAO, or in a federal court. 31 U.S.C. § 1558. See also OFFICE OF THE GENERAL COUNSEL, U.S. GOV'T ACCOUNTABILITY OFFICE, Principles of Federal Appropriations Law 5-76 (3d ed. 2004).

6. Timeliness Exceptions. Protester has the burden of showing its protest is timely. However, the GAO will generally draw inferences in favor of protester with respect to whether protester is timely. Packaging Corp. of America, B-225823, July 20, 1987, 87-2 CPD ¶ 65; CAD Language Sys., Inc., B-233709, Apr. 3, 1989, 89-1 CPD ¶ 405. If untimely on its face, the protester is required to include "all the information needed to demonstrate . . . timeliness." 4 C.F.R.§ 21.2(b); Foerster Instruments, Inc., B-241685, Nov. 18, 1991, 91-2 CPD ¶ 464.

7. If a protester alleges that a requirement is unduly restrictive, the government must make a prima facie case that the restriction is necessary to meet agency needs. Mossberg Corp., B-274059, Nov. 18, 1996, 96-2 CPD ¶ 189 (solicitation requirements for procurement of shotguns overly restrictive). The burden then shifts to the protester to show that the agency justification is clearly unreasonable. See Morse Boulger, Inc., B-224305, Dec. 24, 1986, 86-2 CPD ¶ 715. See also Saturn Indus., B-261954, Jan. 5, 1996, 96-1 CPD ¶ 9 (Army requirement for qualification testing of transmission component for Bradley Fighting Vehicle was reasonable).

8. To prevail, a protester must demonstrate prejudice. To meet this requirement, a protester must show that but for the agency error, there existed "a substantial chance" that the offeror would have been awarded the contract. Bath Iron Works Corp., B-290470, Aug. 19, 2002, 2002 CPD ¶ 133 (denying protester's use of a decommissioned destroyer for at-sea testing while at the same time accepting awardee's proposed use constituted unequal treatment, but did not result in competitive prejudice); Northrop Worldwide Aircraft Servs., Inc.—Recon., B-262181, June 4, 1996, 96-1 CPD ¶ 263 (agency failure to hold discussions); ABB Envtl. Servs., Inc., B-258258.2, Mar. 3, 1995, 95-1 CPD ¶ 126 (agency used evaluation criteria not provided for in solicitation).

I. **Bid Protest Procedures.**

1. The Protest. 4 C.F.R. § 21.1.

   a. Protests must be written.

   b. Although the GAO does not require formal pleadings submitted in a specific technical format, a protest, at a minimum, shall:

      (1) include the name, address, electronic mail address, telephone and facsimile (fax) numbers of the protester (or its representative);

      (2) be signed by the protester or its representative;

      (3) identify the contracting agency and the solicitation and/or contract number;

      (4) provide a detailed legal and factual statement of the bases of the protest, including copies of relevant documents;

      (5) provide all information demonstrating that the protester is an interested party and that the protest is timely;

      (6) specifically request a decision by the Comptroller General; and

      (7) state the form of relief requested.

   c. If appropriate, the protest may also include:

      (1) a request for a protective order;

      (2) a request for specific documents relevant to the protest; and

      (3) a request for a hearing.

   d. The GAO may dismiss a protest which is frivolous, or which does not state a valid ground for a protest. 31 U.S.C. ¶ 3554(a)(4); Federal

Computer Int'l Corp.--Recon., B-257618, July 14, 1994, 94-2 CPD ¶ 24 (mere allegation of improper agency evaluation made "on information and belief" not adequate); see also Siebe Envtl. Controls, B-275999, Feb. 12, 1997, 97-1 CPD ¶ 70 ("information and belief" allegations not adequate even though government delayed debriefing regarding competitive range exclusion); Abhe & Svoboda, Inc.--Costs, B-412504.2, Apr. 1, 2016, 2016 U.S. Comp. Gen. LEXIS 85 (defining frivolous in the context of a protest).

(1) At a minimum, a protester must make a prima facie case asserting improper agency action. Brackett Aircraft Radio, B-244831, Dec. 27, 1991, 91-2 CPD ¶ 585.

(2) Generalized allegations of impropriety are not sufficient to sustain the protester's burden under the GAO's Bid Protest Rules. See 4 C.F.R. § 21.5(f); Bridgeview Mfg., B-246351, Oct. 25, 1991, 91-2 CPD ¶ 378; Palmetto Container Corp., B-237534, Nov. 5, 1989, 89-2 CPD ¶ 447.

(3) The protester must show prejudice. Bannum, Inc., B-408838, Dec. 11, 2013, 2013 CPD ¶ 288 (prejudice is an element of every viable protest); Tek Contracting, Inc., B-245590, Jan. 17, 1992, 92-1 CPD ¶ 90 (protest that certification requirement was unduly restrictive is denied where protester's product was not certified by any entity); IDG Architects, B-235487, Sept. 18, 1989, 89-2 CPD ¶ 236.

e. The protest must include sufficient information to demonstrate that it is timely. The GAO will not permit protesters to introduce for the first time, in a motion for reconsideration, evidence to demonstrate timeliness. 4 C.F.R. § 21.2(b). Management Eng'g Assoc.--Recon., B-245284, Oct. 1, 1991, 91-2 CPD ¶ 276.

2. The protester must provide the contracting activity timely notice of the protest. This notification allows the agency to prepare its administrative report for the protest.

a. The agency must receive a complete copy of the protest and all attachments no later than one day after the protest is filed with the GAO. 4 C.F.R. § 21.1(e); Rocky Mountain Ventures, B-241870.4, Feb. 13, 1991, 91-1 CPD ¶ 169 (failure to give timely notice may result in dismissal of the protest).

b. The GAO will not dismiss a protest, absent prejudice, if the protester fails to timely provide the agency a copy of the protest document. Arlington Pub. Schs., B-228518, Jan. 11, 1988, 88-1 CPD ¶ 16 (although protester was late in providing agency protest documents, agency already knew of protest and its underlying bases).

3. The GAO generally provides immediate telephonic notice of a protest to the agency. It is this notice by the GAO that triggers the CICA stay, discussed above. 4 C.F.R. § 21.3(a).

4. Agency List of Documents. In response to a protester's request for production of documents, the agency must provide to all interested parties and the GAO, at least five days prior to submission of the administrative report, a list of:

a. documents or portions of documents which the agency has released to the protester or intends to produce in its report; and

b. documents which the agency intends to withhold from the protester and the reasons underlying this decision.

c. Parties to the protest must then file any objections to the agency list within two days of receipt of the list.

5. Agency's Administrative Report. The agency must file an administrative report within 30 days of telephonic notice by the GAO. 4 C.F.R. § 21.3(c); FAR 33.104(a)(3)(i). Subject to any protective order, discussed below, the agency will provide copies of the administrative report simultaneously to the GAO, protester(s), and any intervenors. 4 C.F.R. § 21.3(e).

a. Contents of an agency report. 4 C.F.R. § 21.3(c).

(1) Contracting officer's statement of the relevant facts;

(2) Memorandum of Law;

(3) An index of all relevant documents provided under the protest; and

(4) All relevant documents not previously produced.

b. Agencies must include all relevant documents in the administrative report. See Federal Bureau of Investigation—Recon., B-245551, June 11, 1992, 92-1 CPD ¶ 507 (incomplete report misled GAO about procurement's status).

c. Late agency reports. Given the relatively tight time constraints associated with the protest process, the GAO will consider agency requests for extensions of time on a case-by-case basis. 4 C.F.R. § 21.3(f).

6. Document Production.[7] Except as otherwise authorized by GAO, all requests

for documents must be filed with GAO and the contracting agency no later than two days after their existence or relevance is known or should have been known, whichever is earlier. The agency then must either provide the documents or explain why production is not appropriate. 4 C.F.R. § 21.3(g).

7. Protective Orders. Either on its own initiative or at the request of a party to the protest, the GAO may issue a protective order controlling the treatment of protected information. 4 C.F.R. § 21.4.

a. The protective order is designed to limit access to trade secrets, confidential business information, and information that would result in an unfair competitive advantage.

b. The request for a protective order should be filed as soon as possible. It is the responsibility of protester's counsel to request issuance of a protective order and submit timely applications for admission under the order. 4 C.F.R. § 21.4(a).

c. The GAO shall determine the terms of the protective order prior to the due date for the agency administrative report. 4 C.F.R. § 21.4(a).

d. Individuals seeking access to protected information may not be involved in the competitive decision-making process of the protester or interested party. 4 C.F.R. § 21.4(c).

(1) Protesters may retain outside counsel or use in-house counsel, so long as counsel is not involved in the competitive decision-making process. Robbins-Gioia, Inc., B-274318, Dec. 4, 1996, 96-2 CPD ¶ 222 (access to

---

[7] **PRACTICE TIP:** Keep in mind that the government has every right to request relevant documents from the protester. See 4 C.F.R. 21.3(d).

See also "GAO Orders Protester to Comply with Agency's Document Request," 61 FED. CONT. REP. 409 (1994).

protected material appropriate even though in-house counsel has regular contact with corporate officials involved in competitive decision-making); Mine Safety Appliance Co., B-242379.2, Nov. 27, 1991, 91-2 CPD ¶ 506 (retained counsel).

(2) The GAO grants access to protected information upon application by an individual. The individual must submit a certification of the lack of involvement in the competitive decision-making process and a detailed statement in support of the certification. Atlantic Research Corp., B-247650, June 26, 1992, 92-1 CPD ¶ 543.

(3) The GAO may report violations of the protective order to the appropriate bar association of the attorney who violated the order, and may ban the attorney from GAO practice. Additionally, a party whose protected information is disclosed improperly retains all of its remedies at law or equity, including breach of contract. 4 C.F.R. § 21.4(d). See also "GAO Sanctions 2 Attorneys for Violating Terms of Protective Order by Releasing Pricing Info," 65 FED. CONT. REP. 17 (1996).

(4) If the GAO does not issue a protective order, the government has somewhat more latitude in determining the contents of the administrative report. If the government chooses to withhold any documents from the report, it must include in the report a list of the

documents withheld and the reasons therefor. The agency must furnish all relevant documents. Absent a protective order, the agency may withhold protected information and submit such information to the GAO for in camera review. 4 C.F.R. § 21.4(b).

e. If the agency fails to produce all relevant or requested documents, the GAO may impose sanctions. Among the possible sanctions are:

(1) Providing the document to the protester or to other interested parties.

(2) Drawing adverse inferences against the agency. Textron Marine Sys., B-243693, Aug. 19, 1991, 91-2 CPD ¶ 162 (GAO refused to draw an adverse inference when an agency searched for and was unable to find a document that protester speculated should be in the files).

(3) Prohibiting the government from using facts or arguments related to the unreleased documents.

8. Protester must comment on the agency report within 10 days of receipt. Failure to comment or request a decision on the record will result in dismissal. 4 C.F.R. § 21.3(i). Keymiaee Aero-Tech, Inc., B-274803.2, Dec. 20, 1996, 97-1 CPD ¶ 153; Piedmont Sys., Inc., B-249801, Oct. 28, 1992, 92-2 CPD ¶ 305 (agency's office sign-in log used to establish date when protester's attorney received agency report); Aeroflex Int'l, Inc., B-243603, Oct. 7, 1991, 91-1 CPD ¶ 311 (protester held to deadline even though the agency was late in submitting its report); Kinross Mfg. Co., B-232182, Sept. 30, 1988, 88-2 CPD ¶ 309.

9. Hearings. On its own initiative or upon the request of the protester, the government, or any interested party, the GAO may conduct a hearing in connection with a protest. The request shall set forth the reasons why the requester believes a hearing is necessary and why the matter cannot be resolved without oral testimony. 4 C.F.R. § 21.7(a).

   a. The GAO officer has the discretion to determine whether or not to hold a hearing and the scope of the hearing.[8] Jack Faucett Assocs.--Recon., B-254421, Aug. 11, 1994, 94-2 CPD ¶ 72.

      (1) As a general rule, the GAO conducts hearings where there is a factual dispute between the parties which cannot be resolved without oral examination or without assessing witness credibility, or where an issue is so complex that developing the protest record through a hearing is more efficient and less burdensome than proceeding with written pleadings only. Southwest Marine, Inc., B-265865, Jan. 23, 1996, 96-1 CPD ¶ 56 (as a result of improper destruction of evaluation documentation by agency, GAO requested hearing to determine adequacy of agency award decision); see also Allied Signal, Inc., B-275032, Jan. 17, 1997, 97-1 CPD ¶ 136 (protest involving tactical intelligence system required hearing and technical assistance from GAO staff).

      (2) Absent evidence that a protest record is questionable or incomplete, the GAO will not hold a hearing "merely to permit the protester to reiterate its protest allegations orally or otherwise embark on a fishing expedition for additional grounds of protest" since such action would undermine GAO's ability to resolve protests expeditiously and without undue disruption of the procurement process. Town Dev., Inc., B-257585, Oct. 21, 1994, 94-2 CPD ¶ 155.

   b. The GAO may hold pre-hearing conferences to resolve procedural matters, including the scope of discovery, the issues to be considered, and the need for or conduct of a hearing. 4 C.F.R. § 21.7(b).

   c. Note that the GAO may draw an adverse inference if a witness fails to appear at a hearing or fails to answer a relevant question. This rule applies to the protester, interested parties and the agency. 4 C.F.R. § 21.7(f).

   d. Alternative Dispute Resolution. The GAO has three available forms of alternative dispute resolution (ADR): Negotiation Assistance, Litigation Risk Assessment and Outcome Prediction.

   e. Negotiation Assistance. The GAO attorney will assist the parties with reaching a "win/win" situation. This type of ADR occurs usually with protests challenging a solicitation term or a cost claim.

   f. Litigation Risk Assessment. The GAO attorney will provide a discussion of the risks in protest.

   g. Outcome Prediction. The GAO attorney will inform the parties of

---

[8] According to the GAO's procedural rules, hearings are ordinarily conducted in Washington, D.C. The rule further notes that hearings may also be conducted at other locations, by telephone or other electronic means. 4 C.F.R. § 21.7(c).

what he or she believes will be the protest decision. The losing party can then decide whether to withdraw or continue with the protest. Outcome prediction may involve an entire protest or certain issues of a multi-issue protest. The single most important criterion in outcome prediction is the GAO attorney's confidence in the likely outcome of the protest.

h. For more information on GAO's use of ADR techniques, see GAO's Use of *"Negotiation Assistance" and "Outcome Prediction" as ADR Techniques*, FEDERAL CONTRACTS REPORT, vol. 71, page 72.

10. The GAO will issue a decision within 100 days after the filing of the protest. 31 U.S.C. § 3554(a)(1); 4 C.F.R. § 21.9.

11. Express Option. 31 U.S.C. § 3554(a)(2); 4 C.F.R. § 21.10.

a. Decision in 65 days.

b. The protester, agency, or other interested party may request the express option in writing within five days after the protest is filed. The GAO has discretion to decide whether to grant the request. Generally, the GAO reserves use of this expedited procedure for protests involving relatively straightforward facts and issues.

c. The GAO has considerable flexibility in how a protest under the express option is conducted, to include accelerating the protest schedule and issuing a summary decision. 4 C.F.R. § 21.10(e) (2000).

J. Remedies.

1. GAO decisions are "recommendations." 31 U.S.C. § 3554; Rice Servs., Ltd. v. United States, 25 Cl. Ct. 366 (1992); Wheelabrator Corp. v. Chafee, 455 F.2d 1306 (D.C. Cir. 1971).

2. Agencies that choose not to implement GAO's recommendations fully within 60 days of a decision must report this fact to the GAO. FAR 33.104(g). The GAO, in turn, must report all instances of agency refusal to accept its recommendations to Congress. 31 U.S.C. § 3554(e).

3. The GAO may recommend that an agency grant the following remedies (4 C.F.R. § 21.8):

a. Refrain from exercising options under an existing contract;

b. Termination of an existing contract;

c. Recompete the contract;

d. Issue a new solicitation;

e. Award of the contract consistent with statute and regulation; or

f. Such other recommendation(s) as the GAO determines necessary to promote compliance with CICA.

4. Impact of a Recommended Remedy. In crafting its recommendation, the GAO will consider all circumstances surrounding the procurement, including: the seriousness of the deficiency; the degree of prejudice to other parties or the integrity of the procurement process; the good faith of the parties; the extent of contract performance; the cost to the government; the urgency of the procurement; and the impact on the agency's mission. 4 C.F.R. § 21.8(b).

5. CICA Override. However, where the head of the contracting activity decides to continue contract performance because it represents the best interests of the government, the GAO "shall" make its recommendation "without regard to any cost or disruption from terminating, recompeting, or re-awarding the contract." 4 C.F.R. § 21.8(c). Department of the Navy – Modification of Remedy, B-274944.4, July 15, 1997, 97-2 CPD ¶ 16 (Navy contends that "it may not be able to afford" costs associated with GAO recommendation).

K. Protest Costs, Attorneys' Fees, and Bid Preparation Costs.

1. The GAO will issue a declaration on the entitlement to costs of pursuing the protest, to include attorneys' fees, in each case after agencies take corrective action. 4 C.F.R. § 21.8(d). The recovery of protest costs is neither an "award" to protester nor is it a "penalty" imposed upon the agency, but is "intended to relieve protesters of the financial burden of vindicating the public interest." Defense Logistics Agency—Recon., B-270228, Aug. 21, 1996, 96-2 CPD ¶ 80.

   a. In practice, if the agency takes remedial action promptly, GAO generally will not award fees. See J.A. Jones Management Servs., Inc., -- Costs B-284909.4, Jul. 31, 2000, 2000 CPD ¶ 123 (GAO declined to recommend reimbursement of costs where agency took corrective action promptly to supplemental protest allegation); Tidewater Marine, Inc.—Request for Costs, B-270602, Aug. 21, 1996, 96-2 CPD ¶ 81 (the determination of when the agency was on notice of error is "critical"); see also LORS Medical Corp., B-270269, Apr. 2, 1996, 96-1 CPD ¶ 171 (timely agency action measured from filing of initial protest, not time of alleged improper action by agency). The GAO has stated that, in general, if the agency takes corrective action by the due date of the agency report, such remedial action is timely. Kertzman Contracting, Inc., B-259461, May 3, 1995, 95-1 CPD ¶ 226 (agency's decision to take corrective action one day before agency report was due was "precisely the kind of prompt reaction" GAO regulations encourage); Holiday Inn - Laurel— Entitlement to Costs, B-265646, Nov. 20, 1995, 95-2 CPD ¶ 233 (agency took corrective action five days after comments filed by protester).

   b. If the agency delays taking corrective action unreasonably and the protest is otherwise clearly meritorious, the GAO may award fees. Griner's-A-One Pipeline Servs., B-255078, July 22, 1994, 94-2 CPD ¶ 41 (corrective action taken two weeks following filing of agency administrative report found untimely). The GAO will consider the complexity of the protested procurement in determining what is timely agency action. Lynch Machiner Co., Inc., B-256279, July 11, 1994, 94-2 CPD ¶ 15 (protester's request for costs denied where agency corrective action was taken three months following filing of protest complaint).

   c. Agency corrective action must result in some competitive benefit to the protester. Tri-Ex Tower Corp., B-245877, Jan. 22, 1992, 92-1 CPD ¶ 100 (protester not entitled to fees and costs where the agency cancels a competitive solicitation and proposes to replace it with a sole source acquisition; no corrective action taken in response to the protest).

   d. Protester must file its request for declaration of entitlement to costs with the GAO within 15 days after learning (or should have learned) that GAO has closed the protest based on the agency's decision to take corrective action. 4 C.F.R. § 21.8(e). Dev Tech Sys., Inc., B-284860.4, Aug. 23, 2002, CPD ¶ 150.

2. If the GAO determines that the protester is entitled to recover its costs:

   a. The protester must submit a claim for costs within 60 days of the receipt of the GAO decision. Failure to file within 60 days may result in forfeiture of the right to costs. 4 C.F.R. § 21.8(f). See Aalco Forwarding, Inc., B-277241.30, July

30, 1999, 99-2 CPD ¶ 36 (protesters' failure to file an adequately supported initial claim within the 60-day period resulted in forfeiture of right to recover costs). See also Dual Inc. -- Costs, B-280719.3, Apr. 28, 2000 (rejecting claim for costs where claim was filed with contracting agency more than 60 days after protester's counsel received a protected copy of protest decision under a protective order).

b.   Recovery of costs is limited to those costs incurred in pursuing the claim before the GAO. 4 C.F.R. § 21.8(f)(2); DIVERCO, Inc.— Claim for Costs, B-240639, May 21, 1992, 92-1 CPD ¶ 460.

3.   Interest on costs is not recoverable. Techniarts Eng'g—Claim for Costs, B-234434, Aug. 24, 1990, 90-2 CPD ¶ 152.

4.   Amount of attorney's fees and protest costs is determined by reasonableness. See, e.g., JAFIT Enters., Inc. – Claim for Costs, B-266326.2, Mar. 31, 1997, 97-1 CPD ¶ 125 (GAO allowed only 15% of protest costs and fees). Equal Access to Justice Act (EAJA) standards do not apply. Attorneys' fees (for other than small business concerns) are limited to not more than $150 per hour, "unless the agency determines, based on the recommendation of the Comptroller General on a case-by-case basis, that an increase in the cost of living or a special factor, such as the limited availability of qualified attorneys for the proceedings involved, justifies a higher fee." 31 U.S.C. § 3554(c)(2)(B). See also Sodexho Mgmt., Inc. -- Costs, B-289605.3, Aug. 6, 2003, 2003 CPD ¶ 136. Similarly, fees for experts and consultants are capped at "the highest rate of compensation for expert

witness paid by the Federal Government." 31 U.S.C. § 3554(c)(2); FAR 33.104(h).[9]

5.   Unlike the EAJA, a protestor need not be a "prevailing party" where a "judicial imprimatur" is necessary to cause a change in the legal relationship between the parties. Georgia Power Company, B-289211.5, May 2, 2002, 2002 CPD ¶ 81 (rejecting the agency's argument that the Supreme Court's holding in Buckhannon Bd. and Care Home, Inc., v. W. Va. Dep't of HHR, 532 U.S. 598 (2001), rejecting the "catalyst theory" to fee-shifting statutes applied to the Competition in Contracting Act).

6.   As a general rule, a protester is reimbursed costs incurred with respect to all protest issues pursued, not merely those upon which it prevails. AAR Aircraft Servs.--Costs, B-291670.6, May 12, 2003, 2003 CPD ¶ 100. Department of the Army -- Modification of the Remedy, B-292768.5, Mar. 25, 2004, 2004 CPD ¶ 74. The GAO has limited award of costs to successful protesters where part of their costs is allocable to a protest issue that is so clearly severable as to essentially constitute a separate protest. TRESP Associates, Inc. -- Costs, B-258322.8, Nov. 3, 1998, 98-2 CPD ¶ 108 (no need to allocate attorneys' fees between sustained protest and those issues not addressed where all issues related to same core allegation that was sustained); Interface Flooring Sys., Inc. -- Claim for Attorneys' Fees, B-225439.5, July 29, 1987, 87-2 CPD ¶ 106.

7.   A protester may recover costs on a sustained protest despite the fact that the protester did not raise the issue that the GAO found to be dispositive. The GAO may award costs even though the protest is sustained on a theory raised by the GAO sua sponte. Department of Commerce—Recon., B-238452, Oct. 22, 1990, 90-2 CPD ¶ 322.

---

[9] The FAR refers to 5 U.S.C. § 3109 and Expert and Consultant Appointments, 60 Fed. Reg. 45,649, Sept. 1, 1995, citing 5 C.F.R. § 304.105.

8. The protester must document its claim for attorneys' fees. Consolidated Bell, Inc., B-220425, Mar. 25, 1991, 91-1 CPD ¶ 325 (claim for $376,110 reduced to $490 because no reliable supporting documentation). See also Galen Medical Associates, Inc., B-288661.6, July 22, 2002, 2002 CPD ¶ 56 (GAO recommending that the agency reimburse the protestor $110.65 out of the $159,195.32 claim due to a lack of documentation).

9. Bid Preparation Costs. 4 C.F.R. § 21.8(d)(2).

   a. Anticipatory profits are not recoverable. Keco Indus., Inc. v. United States, 192 Ct. Cl. 773, 784 (1970); DaNeal Constr., Inc., B-208469, Dec. 14, 1983, 83-2 CPD ¶ 682.

   b. GAO has awarded bid preparation costs when no other practical relief was feasible. See, e.g., Tri Tool, Inc.—Modification of Remedy, B-265649.3, Oct. 9, 1996, 96-2 CPD ¶ 139.

   c. As with claims for legal fees, the protester must document its claim for bid preparation and protest costs. A protester may not recover profit on the labor costs associated with prosecuting a protest or preparing a bid. Innovative Refrigeration Concepts — Claim for Costs, B-258655.2, July 16, 1997, 97-2 CPD ¶ 19 (protester failed to show that claimed rates for employees reflected actual rates of compensation).

L. "Appeal" of the GAO Decision.

1. Reconsideration of GAO Decisions. The request for reconsideration must be submitted to the GAO within 10 days of learning of the basis for the request or when such grounds should have been known, whichever is earlier. Speedy Food Serv., Inc.—Recon., B-274406, Jan. 3, 1997, 97-1 CPD ¶ 5 (request for reconsideration untimely where it was filed more than 10 days after protester noted the initial decision on GAO's Internet site). The requester must state the factual and legal grounds upon which it seeks reconsideration. Rehashing previous arguments is not fruitful. 4 C.F.R. § 21.14; Banks Firefighters Catering, B-257547, Mar. 6, 1995, 95-1 CPD ¶ 129; Windward Moving & Storage Co.—Recon., B-247558, Mar. 31, 1992, 92-1 CPD ¶ 326.

2. Requests for reconsideration must be based upon new facts, unavailable at the time of the initial protest. The GAO does not allow piecemeal development of protest issues. Consultants on Family Addiction —Recon., B-274924.3, June 12, 1997, 97-1 CPD ¶ 213; Department of the Army — Recon., B-254979, Sept. 26, 1994, 94-2 CPD ¶ 114.

3. The GAO will not act on a motion for reconsideration if the underlying procurement is the subject of federal court litigation, unless the court has indicated interest in the GAO's opinion. Department of the Navy, B-253129, Sept. 30, 1993, 96-2 CPD ¶ 175.

4. A protester always may seek judicial review of an agency action under the Administrative Procedures Act. Courts may, however, give great deference to the GAO in light of its considerable procurement expertise. Shoals American Indus., Inc. v. United States, 877 F.2d 883 (11th Cir. 1989). But see California Marine Cleaning, Inc. v. United States, 42 Fed. Cl. 281 (1998) (COFC overturned GAO decision finding that decision was irrational, that GAO misapplied the late bid rule, and that it failed to consider all relevant evidence).

5. This deference is not absolute. A court may still find an agency decision to lack a rational basis, even if the agency complies with the GAO's recommendations in a bid protest. Firth Constr. Co. v. United States, 36 Fed. Cl. 268, 271-72 (1996); Advanced Distribution Sys., Inc. v. United States, 34 Fed. Cl. 598, 604 n.7 (1995); see also

Mark Dunning Indus. v. Perry, 890 F. Supp. 1504 (M.D. Ala. 1995) (court holds that "uncritical deference" to GAO decisions is inappropriate). But see Honeywell, Inc. v. United States, 870 F.2d 644, 648 (Fed. Cir. 1989) (Federal Circuit notes that "[i]t is the usual policy, if not the obligation, of procuring departments to accommodate themselves to positions formally taken by the Government Accountability Office.").

IV. UNITED STATES COURT OF FEDERAL CLAIMS.

A. Statutory Authority. 28 U.S.C. § 1491.

1. Historically, the COFC exercised bid protest jurisdiction under the Tucker Act, 28 U.S.C. § 1491(a)(1), which provides the COFC jurisdiction "to render judgment upon any claim against the United States founded either upon the Constitution, or any Act of Congress or any regulation of an executive department, or upon any express or implied contract with the United States . . . ." The COFC exercised jurisdiction over bid protests under the theory that an implied-in-fact contract to treat bids honestly and fairly existed whenever the government received bids in response to a solicitation. See Keco Indus., Inc. v. United States, 428 F.3d 1233 (Ct. Cl. 1970).

2. In the Administrative Dispute Resolution Act of 1996, Pub. L. No. 104-320, § 12, 110 Stat. 3870, 3874 (1996) [hereinafter "ADRA"], Congress amended and made more explicit the COFC's jurisdiction over protests involving procurement contracts, i.e., situations where the government is acquiring property or services. Specifically, ADRA provides the COFC jurisdiction over "an action by an interested party objecting to a solicitation by a Federal agency for bids or proposals for a proposed contract [i.e., a pre-award protest] or to a proposed award or the award of a contract [i.e., a post-award protest] or any alleged violation of statute or regulation in connection with a procurement or a proposed procurement."

28 U.S.C. § 1491(b)(1); see also Res. Conservation Grp., LLC v. United States, 597 F.3d 1238, 1244-46 (Fed. Cir. 2010) (explaining that § 1491(b)(1) "is exclusively concerned with procurement solicitations and contracts").

3. Today, the vast majority of bid protests before the COFC involve procurement contracts and are brought pursuant to 28 U.S.C. § 1491(b)(1). However, the Federal Circuit has stated that the COFC's "implied-in-fact contract jurisdiction [i.e., pre-ADRA § 1491(a)(1) jurisdiction] does survive as to claims where [ADRA] does not provide a remedy." Res. Conservation, 597 F.3d at 1245.

B. COFC Rules.

1. The Rules of the United States Court of Federal Claims (the "RCFC") govern all suits before the Court and are available at http://www.uscfc.uscourts.gov/rcfc. The RCFC are modeled after the Federal Rules of Civil Procedure.

2. Appendix C to the RCFC describes standard practices in protest cases filed pursuant to 28 U.S.C. § 1491(b), and is cited throughout the remainder of this Chapter.

C. Who May Protest?

1. ADRA provides the COFC jurisdiction over a bid protest filed by an "interested party." 28 U.S.C. § 1491(b)(1). To be an interested party, a protester must be "'[1] an actual or prospective bidder or offeror [2] whose direct economic interest would be affected by the award of the contract or by failure to award the contract.'" Am. Fed'n Gov't Employees, AFL-CIO v. United States, 258 F.3d 1294, 1299, 1302 (Fed. Cir. 2001) (applying "interested party" definition from CICA, 31 U.S.C. § 3551(2)).

2. To be an "actual or prospective bidder or offeror," a protester must generally participate in the procurement or be eligible to receive the contract at issue in the protest. Compare Rex Serv. Corp. v.

United States, 448 F.3d 1305 (Fed. Cir. 2006) (protester that did not submit a bid was not an interested party), with CGI Fed. Inc. v. United States, 779 F.3d 1346 (Fed. Cir. 2015) (protester that filed GAO protest prior to deadline for receipt of proposals and thereafter diligently pursued COFC protest, even though submission deadline had run, was an interested party); see also, e.g., CCL Inc. v. United States, 39 Fed. Cl. 780, 790 (1997) (protester was an interested party where "it likely would have competed for the contract had the government publicly invited bids or requested proposals").

3.   To demonstrate a "direct economic interest" in a post-award protest, the protester "must establish not only some significant error in the procurement process, but also that there was a substantial chance it would have received the contract award but for that error." Statistica, Inc. v. Christopher, 102 F.3d 1577, 1582 (Fed. Cir. 1996). By contrast, in the pre-award context, the protester need only demonstrate "a non-trivial competitive injury which can be redressed by judicial relief." Weeks Marine, Inc. v. United States, 575 F.3d 1352, 1362 (Fed. Cir. 2009). But see Orion Tech., Inc. v. United States, 704 F.3d 1344, 1348–49 (Fed. Cir. 2013) (explaining that, even in the pre-award context, where a protester challenges the agency's application of solicitation criteria rather than the criteria itself, the protester must demonstrate that it stood a "substantial chance" of receiving the award but for the alleged errors).

D.   Who May Intervene?

1.   RCFC 24 provides for both intervention as a matter of right and permissive intervention.

2.   As a practical matter, provided it timely moves to intervene, a contract awardee is virtually always admitted as a party-defendant in response to a post-award protest. See, e.g., RCFC App'x C ¶ 8(b) (listing the "admission of any successful offeror as an intervenor" among the topics to be addressed during the initial status conference). Additionally, "[t]he apparently successful bidder/offeror may enter a notice of appearance at any hearing on the application for a temporary restraining order/preliminary injunction if it advises the court of its intention to move to intervene pursuant to RCFC 24(a)(2) or has moved to intervene before the hearing." RCFC App'x C ¶ 12.

3.   Whether intervention is permitted in other situations (e.g., pre-award protests) will depend on the specific facts of the case and the justification cited by the party seeking to intervene.

E.   What May Be Protested?

1.   28 U.S.C. § 1491(b)(1), as amended by ADRA, provides the COFC jurisdiction "to render judgment on an action by an interested party objecting to a solicitation by a Federal agency for bids or proposals for a proposed contract or to a proposed award or the award of a contract or any alleged violation of statute or regulation in connection with a procurement or a proposed procurement."

2.   "Federal Agency." The term "agency" includes "any department, independent establishment, commission, administration, authority, board or bureau of the United States or any corporation in which the United States has a proprietary interest, unless the context shows that such term was intended to be used in a more limited sense." 28 U.S.C. § 451. This definition of "agency" has been construed in certain circumstances as broader than the definition employed in GAO's bid protest regulations (4 C.F.R. § 21.0). E.g., Emery Worldwide Airlines, Inc. v. United States, 264 F.3d 1071, 1080 (Fed. Cir. 2001).

3.   Pre- and Post-award Protests. The COFC has jurisdiction over both pre- and post-award protests. See 28 U.S.C. § 1491(b)(1) ("[T]he United States Court of Federal Claims . . . shall have jurisdiction to entertain such an action

without regard to whether suit is instituted before or after the contract is awarded."). However, as noted above, to fall within the ambit of § 1491(b)(1) jurisdiction, any pre- or post-award protest must concern a "procurement" contract whereby the government is acquiring property or services. See Res. Conservation, 597 F.3d at 1244-46.

4.   Alleged Violations of Statute or Regulation. The COFC also has jurisdiction over a catch-all category of protests alleging a "violation of statute or regulation in connection with a procurement or a proposed procurement." 28 U.S.C. § 1491(b)(1). The Federal Circuit has interpreted this language broadly as encompassing "'all stages of the process of acquiring property or services, *beginning with the process for determining a need* for property or services and ending with contract completion and closeout.'" Distributed Solutions , Inc. v. United States, 539 F.3d 1340, 1344 (Fed. Cir. 2008) (emphasis in original; quoting 41 U.S.C. § 403(2), now codified at 41 U.S.C. § 111). Some of the more notable examples of this "third prong" of the COFC's bid protest jurisdiction involve agency uses of less than full and open competition and CICA stay overrides.

   a.   Less Than Full and Open Competition. The COFC has heard protests alleging that federal agencies acquired property or services through a variety of processes that circumvented CICA's competition requirements. For example, the COFC has taken jurisdiction over protests alleging that:

      (1)   a modification to an existing contract was beyond the scope of that contract and should have been competed, CCL, Inc. v. United States, 39 Fed. Cl. 780, 789 (1997) (taking jurisdiction over allegation that agency was "*procuring*

goods and services through a process that should have been the subject of competition; and that the failure to compete the procurement [wa]s *in violation of law*" (emphasis in original));

      (2)   an agency improperly delegated to a prime contractor the task of selecting subcontractors to provide software for a government program, rather than competing the requirements (as the government had originally planned), Distributed Solutions, Inc. v. United States, 539 F.3d 1340 (Fed. Cir. 2008); and

      (3)   an agency could not insource certain work previously performed by contractors, Dellew Corp. v. United States, 108 Fed. Cl. 357 (2012).

   b.   CICA Stay Overrides.

      (1)   As discussed above, when a protester files a GAO protest within the time frames established in 31 U.S.C. § 3553, the procuring agency may not either award a contract or order performance thereunder unless the agency determines that "urgent and compelling circumstances" will not permit waiting for GAO's decision or that performance of the contract is in the "best interests" of the United States. See 31 U.S.C. § 3553(c)(2), (d)(3)(C).

      (2)   Where an agency makes such a determination to "override" the CICA stay, or otherwise fails to implement an applicable CICA stay, the protester may challenge that

determination in the COFC. See, e.g., RAMCOR Servs. Grp., Inc. v. United States, 185 F.3d 1286, 1288-90 (Fed. Cir. 1999).

(3)   Many judges have analyzed the following factors, and an agency's consideration thereof, to determine whether the agency's decision to override the CICA stay was arbitrary and capricious: (i) "whether significant adverse consequences will necessarily occur if the stay is not overridden"; (ii) "whether reasonable alternatives to the override exist"; (iii) "how the potential cost of proceeding with the override, including the costs associated with the potential that the GAO might sustain the protest, compare to the benefits associated with the approach being considered for addressing the agency's needs"; and (iv) "the impact of the override on competition and the integrity of the procurement system." Reilly's Wholesale Produce v. United States, 73 Fed. Cl. 705, 711 (2006).

(4)   Similarly, the COFC will often reject agency override defenses that "the new contract would be better than the old one" or that "the override and continuation of the contract is otherwise simply preferable to the agency." Id.

(5)   Where a protester succeeds on the merits in challenging an override as arbitrary and capricious, the COFC may issue declaratory relief ordering that the agency's action was arbitrary and capricious, and thus that the

automatic CICA stay remains in effect. See Supreme Foodservice GmbH v. United States, 109 Fed. Cl. 369, 396-97 (2013).

5.   Other Considerations.

a.   The FASA Bar. The Federal Acquisition Streamlining Act of 1994, Pub L. No. 103-355, 108 Stat. 3243, codified in Titles 10 and 41 of the United States Code) [hereinafter "FASA"], precludes COFC jurisdiction over protests "in connection with the issuance or proposed issuance of a task or delivery order," except for those alleging that the order "increases the scope, period, or maximum value of the contract under which the order is issued." 41 U.S.C. § 4106(f); 10 U.S.C. § 2304c(e); see also SRA Int'l, Inc. v. United States, 766 F.3d 1409, 1413 (Fed. Cir. 2014) (holding COFC lacked jurisdiction to hear protester challenge to agency waiver of organizational conflict of interest for task order award because "Congress's intent to ban protests on the issuance of task orders is clear from FASA's unambiguous language"). However, the FASA bar does not apply to protests involving task and delivery orders placed under GSA Federal Supply Schedule contracts. See, e.g., Idea Int'l, Inc. v. United States, 74 Fed. Cl. 129, 135 (2006).

b.   Contract Administration. The COFC does not have jurisdiction over protests challenging the administration of existing contracts. See, e.g., Kellogg Brown & Root Servs., Inc. v. United States, 117 Fed. Cl. 764, 768-70 (2014) (no COFC jurisdiction over agency request that contractor submit proposal for closeout activities under existing contract); Gov't Tech. Servs. LLC v. United States, 90 Fed. Cl. 522, 527, 529-31 (2009) (no COFC bid protest jurisdiction over challenge to agency exercising option under existing contract). But see Magic Brite Janitorial v. United States, 72 Fed. Cl. 719, 721-22 (2006) (finding jurisdiction over protest of agency decision not to exercise option under protester's existing contract and instead to award new contract to another contractor).

F.   When Must a Protest Be Filed?

1.   28 U.S.C. § 1491(b) does not impose any specific statute of limitations for the filing of a bid protest.

2.   However, for pre-award protests, the Federal Circuit has held that a party seeking to object to the terms of a solicitation that contains a patent error must file its protest "prior to the close of the bidding process." Blue & Gold Fleet, L.P. v. United States, 492 F.3d 1308, 1313 (Fed. Cir. 2007).

   a.   If a defect is incorporated into the solicitation only after the submission of initial proposals, then the protester must file its protest prior to the deadline for receipt of revised proposals or prior to contract award, whichever comes first. See COMINT Sys. Corp. v. United States, 700 F.3d 1377, 1382 (Fed. Cir. 2012); Ne. Constr., Inc. v. United States, 119 Fed. Cl. 596, 611 (2015).

   b.   Likewise, where a protester wishes to challenge a defect in the ground rules of a corrective action, it must file its protest during the corrective action, and may not wait until after the corrective action and new award are completed. See NVE, Inc. v. United States, 121 Fed. Cl. 169, 179 (2015).

3.   For post-award protests, although there are no strict time limitations, serious delay in filing may harm a protester's case or even result in dismissal under the equitable doctrine of laches. See Wit Assocs., Inc. v. United States, 62 Fed. Cl. 657, 662 n.5 (2004) ("[I]n some cases, serious delay in raising a claim may impact the equities in determining whether an injunction should issue or lead to the imposition of laches."); see also, e.g., Nat'l Telecommuting Inst., Inc. v. United States, 123 Fed. Cl. 595, 602-03 (2015) (holding protest barred under the doctrine of laches where protester filed suit six months after the official notice of award).

G.   Filing Procedures and Scheduling.

1.   Pre-filing Notification. Except in exceptional circumstances, a protester must provide at least 24-hours' advance notice of filing a protest case to the COFC; the Department of Justice ("DOJ"), which will defend the protest on behalf of the government; the procuring agency's contracting officer; and the awardee, if known. RCFC, App'x C ¶ 2. Pursuant to RCFC, App'x C ¶ 3, the pre-filing notice must include:

   a.   a corporate disclosure statement;

   b.   the name of the procuring agency and the number of the solicitation in the contested procurement;

   c.   the name and telephone number of the contracting officer responsible for the procurement;

   d.   the name and telephone number of the principal agency attorney, if known, who represented the agency in any prior protest of the same procurement;

   e.   whether the protester contemplates requesting temporary or preliminary injunctive relief pursuant to RCFC 65;

      (1)   Unlike at GAO, there is no automatic CICA stay for bid protests at the COFC. Thus, a protester seeking to forestall an award or contract performance must seek either

a voluntary stay from the agency or preliminary injunctive relief from the Court.

(2) RCFC 65 provides for Temporary Restraining Orders and Preliminary Injunctions. However, because the COFC expedites bid protest matters as much as possible, a protester often need not seek a temporary restraining order. See RCFC, App'x C ¶ 9. Additionally, to obviate disputes over the propriety of injunctive relief, the COFC will often encourage an agency to voluntarily stay an award or performance pending the outcome of the protest. And, regardless of whether or not performance is voluntarily stayed, the COFC often consolidates briefing on the preliminary injunction with briefing and argument on the merits to further expedite the proceedings.

f. whether the protester has discussed the need for temporary or preliminary injunctive relief with DOJ counsel and the response, if any;

g. whether the action was preceded by the filing of a protest before the GAO and, if so, the "B-" number of the protest and whether a decision was issued; and

h. whether the protester contemplates the need for the court to enter a protective order.

2. Initial Filings.

a. The protester must file an original and 2 copies of the protest complaint, attaching a completed cover sheet (RCFC Form 2) to the original. RCFC 5.5(d)(1). If the complaint exceeds 20 pages, the protester must also submit one copy of the complaint in CD-ROM format. Id.

b. Additionally, if the protester seeks to keep the material in its complaint confidential, or if it must do so to preserve protected material gleaned during a prior GAO protest, the protester must file the complaint under seal along with a motion to seal, a motion for protective order, and a redacted copy of the sealed filing (prepared subject to any pre-existing GAO protective order, if applicable). See RCFC, App'x C ¶¶ 4-7; GAO Protective Order. The COFC's standard Protective Order in Procurement Protest Cases is included as an Appendix to the RCFC. See RCFC Form 8.

c. The protester may also file an application for preliminary injunctive relief along with or after filing its protest complaint. See RCFC 65. Any such application must be accompanied by affidavits, supporting memoranda, and any other documents upon which the protester intends to rely, and must certify that the application and accompanying documents have been provided to DOJ and the awardee, if known. Id.; RCFC, App'x C ¶¶ 10-11.

3. Initial Status Conference. "[A]s soon as practicable after the filing of the complaint," and generally within one week, the COFC will schedule an initial status conference to address, *inter alia*:

a. identification of all interested parties;

b. admission of any successful offeror as an intervenor;

c. any request for temporary or preliminary injunctive relief;

d. the content of a protective order, if requested by one or more of the parties, and the requirement for redacted copies;

e. the content of and time for filing the administrative record;

f. whether it may be appropriate to supplement the administrative record; and

g. the nature of and schedule for further proceedings. RCFC, App'x C ¶ 8.

4. Where a protester has requested preliminary injunctive relief, it must also be prepared to address the following issues during the initial status conference:

a. whether and to what extent, absent temporary or preliminary injunctive relief, the court's ability to afford effective final relief is likely to be prejudiced;

b. whether plaintiff has discussed any request it has made for a temporary restraining order in advance with DOJ counsel and, if so, defendant's response;

c. whether the government will agree to withhold award or suspend performance pending a hearing on any motion for preliminary injunction;

d. whether the government will agree to withhold award or suspend performance pending a final decision on the merits;

e. an appropriate schedule for completion of the briefing on any motion for a preliminary injunction;

f. the security requirements of RCFC 65(c); and

g. whether the hearing on the preliminary injunction should be consolidated with a final hearing on the merits. RCFC, App'x C ¶ 15.

5. Given the wide range of issues addressed at the initial status conference, it can have a significant impact on the prosecution of the protest going forward.

H.   Standard of Review.

1. Pursuant to 28 U.S.C. § 1491(b)(4), the COFC reviews agency procurement decisions against the standards set forth in the Administrative Procedure Act, 5 U.S.C. § 706. Thus, the COFC will hold unlawful and set aside agency action, findings, and conclusions found to be "arbitrary, capricious, an abuse of discretion, or otherwise not in accordance with law."

2. Preliminary Injunctive Relief.

a. Where a protester requests preliminary injunctive relief, the COFC applies the traditional four-part test, evaluating (1) the protester's likelihood of success on the merits, (2) whether the protester will suffer irreparable harm absent preliminary injunctive relief, and whether (3) the balance of harms and (4) the public interest favor the granting of preliminary injunctive relief. See Winter v. Nat. Res. Def. Council, Inc., 555 U.S. 7, 20 (2008).

b. Additionally, for the COFC to grant preliminary injunctive relief, the RCFC require the movant to "give[] security in an amount that the court considers proper to pay the costs and damages sustained by any party found to have been wrongfully enjoined or restrained." RCFC 65(c).

3. Judgment on the Administrative Record.

a. The "focal point" for the COFC's review in a bid protest is the administrative record that was before the agency when it made its procurement decision. Axiom Res. Mgmt., Inc. v. United States, 564 F.3d 1374, 1379 (Fed. Cir. 2009).

b.   Thus, RCFC 52.1 requires an agency to certify and file with the court the administrative record supporting the agency's action. RCFC 52.1(a); see also RCFC, App'x C ¶ 21 (identifying 21 categories of "core documents" to be included in the administrative record).

   (1)   The parties may move to supplement the administrative record with materials that are "necessary in order not to frustrate effective judicial review." Axiom, 564 F.3d at 1381 (quotation omitted).

   (2)   Additionally, in circumstances where the existing record is insufficient for the court to assess the basis for or the propriety of the agency's action, the court may order supplementation of the administrative record including limited discovery, such as the taking of the deposition of the contracting officer. E.g., Impresa Construzioni Geom. Domenico Garufi v. United States, 238 F.3d 1324 (Fed. Cir. 2001).

c.   Most bid protests are resolved via cross-motions for judgment on the administrative record. See RCFC 52.1(c). The briefing schedule for such cross-motions will ordinarily be established during the initial status conference. RCFC, App'x C ¶ 8. The COFC may or may not hear oral argument from the parties following the conclusion of briefing in the case.

I.   Remedies.

1.   Declaratory and Injunctive Relief. The COFC may award both declaratory and injunctive relief, as it considers proper. See 28 U.S.C. § 1491(b)(2).

2.   However, unlike in certain other APA review regimes, permanent injunctive relief is not automatic where a protester succeeds on the merits of its case; rather, the court must assess each of the four traditional injunctive relief factors. See PGBA, LLC v. United States, 389 F.3d 1219, 1225-26 (Fed. Cir. 2004). Additionally, 28 U.S.C. § 1491(b)(3) specifically requires the court to "give due regard to the interests of national defense and national security and the need for expeditious resolution of the action."

3.   The COFC may also award monetary relief in the form of bid preparation and proposal costs. 28 U.S.C. § 1491(b)(2). However, such costs are only available where the following three conditions are met: "(i) the agency has committed a prejudicial error in conducting the procurement; (ii) that error caused the protester to incur unnecessarily bid preparation and proposal costs; and (iii) the costs to be recovered are both reasonable and allocable, *i.e.*, incurred specifically for the contract in question." Insight Sys. Corp. v. United States, 115 Fed. Cl. 734, 738-39 (2014). Moreover, under the second prong of this analysis, a protester may not recover compensation if the costs wasted on an initial procurement become necessary in a second procurement in which the protester has the opportunity to compete. Id. at 739.

4.   Regardless of any other relief awarded, the COFC will generally not direct an agency to make an award to any specific party, not even a successful protester.

5.   Attorney Fees. The COFC may award attorney fees in bid protest cases pursuant to the Equal Access to Justice Act. See 28 U.S.C. § 2412.

J.   **Appeals.** Appeals from decisions of the COFC are taken to the United States Court of Appeals for the Federal Circuit. See 28 U.S.C. § 1295(a)(3). The Notice of Appeal must be filed within 60 days after the COFC's entry of judgment. See Fed. R. App. P. 4(a)(1)(B).

Bid Protests

V.   FEDERAL DISTRICT COURTS.

A.   Prior to ADRA, federal district courts reviewed challenges to agency procurement decisions pursuant to the Administrative Procedure Act. 5 U.S.C. § 702. Such authority was popularly known as the "Scanwell Doctrine." Scanwell Lab., Inc. v. Shaffer, 424 F.2d 859 (D.C. Cir. 1970).

B.   ADRA granted the COFC and federal district courts concurrent jurisdiction to hear pre- and post-award bid protests. However, ADRA provided for the "sunset" of the district courts' bid protest jurisdiction on January 1, 2001, unless Congress acted affirmatively to extend the jurisdiction, which it did not. Thus, federal district courts have generally not exercised bid protest jurisdiction since 2001.

C.   Note, though, that in 2010 the Federal Circuit held that ADRA did not displace existing jurisdiction over protests not involving procurement contracts. See Res. Conservation Grp., LLC v. United States, 597 F.3d 1238, 1246 (Fed. Cir. 2010). Thus, the district courts may still retain a subset of their prior bid protest jurisdiction.

VI.   CHOICE OF FORUM.

A.   Alternatives.

1.   A disappointed bidder has several alternatives when it is informed that another contractor has received the award of work that it seeks.

2.   First, a disappointed bidder can do nothing. It accepts the award decision and looks forward to competing on other requirements.

3.   Second, a disappointed bidder can protest to the agency.

4.   Third, the disappointed bidder can file a protest before the Government Accountability Office.

5.   Fourth, a disappointed bidder can file a protest before the U.S. Court of Federal Claims.

B.   Factors to Consider.

1.   Ongoing Customer Relationships. The most significant factor affecting a decision on whether to file a protest is the disappointed bidder's perception of the impact its decision to protest may have on the relationship with their customer. Contractors are constantly seeking discretionary decisions from their customers; they typically are pursuing multiple proposals with the agency; and they are performing numerous current contracts. Naturally, disappointed bidders are very concerned about the impact of their decision to protest on existing customer relationships. Even though protests are not uncommon, and most agencies consider protesting a right of the contractor, contractors do not enjoy suing a customer.

2.   Merits. The second most significant factor affecting a decision to protest is the underlying decision. Where a disappointed bidder has been evaluated as low technical and high price, it is difficult to justify protesting, even when there appears to be a demonstrable error by the agency. Contractors understand when they have lost. Additionally, disappointed bidders typically understand that relief is granted only in a minority of protests, so regardless of their belief that an agency erred, they are unlikely to prevail in a typical case.

3.   Costs. When filing a protest at the GAO or the COFC, a disappointed bidder generally retains outside counsel. Counsel come at a cost, which may be partially reimbursed if the protest is successful. However, the costs of filing a protest tend to filter out protests of smaller awards and less profitable work.

4.   Continuing Work for an Incumbent. Protests take time to resolve. Where an incumbent contractor has a profitable

356

contract, the earnings on continued performance while resolving a protest may outweigh the costs of pursuing an ultimately unsuccessful protest.

5.   Type of Error. A protestor must raise an error that is apparent on the face of the solicitation prior to the date for submission of proposals. Doing so, however, creates a fear that the decision to protest may somehow prejudice the evaluation. Protesting an error after you know the agency has selected another bidder is a much easier decision to make. Additionally, some private-sector counsel believe that certain types of arguments are better received by the COFC than at GAO.

C.   Practice Notes.

1.   Generally, an agency protest is considered to have less impact on customer relationships and be less costly; however, it is generally considered less effective a forum. GAO protests are less costly than COFC litigation, more effective than agency protests, and impact customer relations less than litigation before the COFC. COFC protests have the added benefit of an opportunity to appeal to the Federal Circuit, albeit at a cost.

2.   The numbers of protest actions reveal the collective wisdom of industry that the GAO provides a cost-effective and independent review of award decisions.

VII. CONCLUSION.

The right to seek independent review of award decisions is something which distinguishes federal contracting from the commercial sector. It provides an important quality assurance function for award decisions. Notwithstanding the availability of this remedy, the overwhelming majority of federal contract awards are not protested, reflecting the fairness and professionalism of the acquisition workforce.

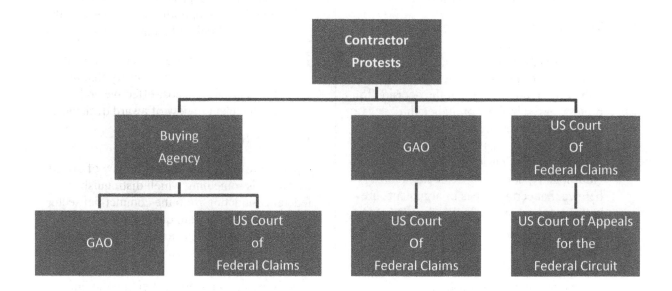

CONTRACTOR BUSINESS SYSTEMS

I. REFERENCES.

A. DFARS Subpart 242.70.

B. DCMA-INST 131, Contractor Business Systems.

II. OVERVIEW.

A. The government has, over the past century, slowly, but steadily, introduced requirements for government contractors to adopt specific business practices as a condition for receiving a government contract. The first two areas where the government required contractors adopt specific business practices were accounting and quality and inspections. Over time, the scope of these required practices have expanded, and the government has introduced additional practices affecting the contractor's supply chain, property management, IT systems, ethics and compliance, etc.

B. These required business practices, now referred to collectively as "Contractor Business Systems," are intended to require best practices for the government's supply chain, while allowing flexibility in the actual implementation. In that sense, they are similar to the practices in many industries where the buyer requires its suppliers to implement specific practices, such as Quality Systems conforming to ISO 9001, if the supplier wishes to sell to the buyer.

C. Generally, government contractors are not required to implement all business systems. Each specific business system is only applicable to contracts and/or contractors that meet specific criteria. Furthermore, a contractor often has the option to implement the system post award. While the government may review a contractor's system pre-award as a matter of responsibility, the clauses requiring specific systems generally allow a contractor to implement the system post award, and only for applicable contract.

D. Defense Contracts. For larger defense contracts, which represent a majority of federal contracts in terms of dollars, the government requires the contractor to possess approved systems as a condition of payment. Uncorrected significant deficiencies can have a serious impact on the cash flow of the contractor. This is further discussed in Section X, below.

E. This chapter will briefly review the requirements for the following business systems.

- Purchasing Systems
- Accounting Systems
- Inventory Management Systems
- Earned Value Management Systems
- Government Property Systems
- Information Technology Systems

The following contractor business systems are addressed elsewhere in this Deskbook.

- Estimating Systems – Chapter 14, Section VIII.
- Quality Systems – Chapter 22, Section II.
- Business Ethics – Chapter 33, Section X.

III. CONTRACTOR PURCHASING SYSTEMS.

A. Introduction.

In many government contracts, there is little competition at the prime contract level, or where competition exists, the government bears substantial cost risks because the contract is a flexibly priced type, such as a cost

Business Systems

reimbursement contract. To control costs, it is considered critical that the prime contractor and higher-tier subcontractors try to maximize competition in the selection of lower-tier suppliers. Furthermore, the government has an interest in insuring that the prime contractor and higher-tier subcontractors properly flow down requirements from the prime contract to subcontractors. The government, generally, prohibits a contractor from awarding many subcontracts without the review and approval of the government. These procedures are quite burdensome. If, however, the contractor has an approved purchasing system, then the contractor can often act without prior government approval. The benefits resulting from avoiding prior review are such that contractors eagerly pursue approval of their purchasing systems. The requirements for purchasing systems are generally stated in FAR Part 44, DFARS Part 244, and in guidance issued by the Defense Contract Management Agency.

B. Covered Contracts and Contractors.

1. A contractor or subcontractor is required to obtain prior approval of its subcontracts when its contract contains FAR 52.244-2, Subcontracts. Generally, FAR 52.244-2 is included in all contracts that are:

   * Cost-reimbursement contracts;
   * Letter contracts that exceeds the simplified acquisition threshold;
   * Fixed-price contracts that exceeds the simplified acquisition threshold under which unpriced contract actions (including unpriced modifications or unpriced delivery orders) are anticipated;
   * Time-and-materials contracts that exceeds the simplified acquisition threshold; or
   * Labor-hour contracts that exceeds the simplified acquisition threshold.

   Essentially, this means most contracts over the Simplified Acquisition Threshold will include FAR 52.244-2.

2. Within DOD, where FAR 52.244-2 is required, the contracting officer must include DFARS 252.244-7001, which requires an approved purchasing system.

3. As a general practice, most prime contractors flow down FAR 52.244-2 to their subcontractors on the same types of subcontracts that trigger flow down at the prime level.

4. FAR 52.244-2 does not require that a contractor have an approved purchasing system. However, the requirements for prior notification and approval are so burdensome that most contractors seek approval of their purchasing systems.

C. Overview of the Requirements for an Approved Purchasing System.

1. FAR Subpart 44.3 and DFARS 252.244-7001(c) address Contractor Purchasing System Reviews.

2. Generally, a contractor must have written policies and procedures governing its purchasing activities. FAR 44.303, DFARS 252.244-7001(c). While such policies need not mirror those the government follows in the FAR and DFARS, the closer the contractor's policies follow the government's policies, the better.

3. Additionally, the government expects a contractor to:

   * Conduct market research;
   * Obtain price competition;
   * Obtain certified cost or pricing data, when required, and follow pricing policies and techniques;
   * Evaluate subcontractor responsibility, including review of the System for Award Management, and Exclusion Lists;
   * Avoid favorable treatment of affiliates;
   * Support small business programs;
   * Manage major subcontracts;
   * Comply with CAS;
   * Use appropriate contract types;
   * Implement internal controls;
   * Implement higher-level quality standards; and

- Properly flow down clauses to subcontractors.

4. Most important, the contractor must document that it has followed its policies and procedures, so it may demonstrate its system when reviewed for approval.

D.   Government Review and Approval.

1. The government reviews a contractor's Purchasing System every two years (three years in DOD), when the contractor is expected to award more than $25 million in subcontracts (excluding competitively awarded FFP subcontracts) in the following 12 months. See FAR 44.302. In practice, the government is often delinquent in performing its reviews, and adjusts the thresholds upward for low risk contractors.

2. Most Contractor Purchasing System Reviews (CPSRs) are performed by the Defense Contract Management Agency. See DCMA-INST 109, using a multi-disciplinary team.

3. A typical CPSR follows a defined audit plan, looks at the contractor's written policies, and reviews selected subcontracts for evidence that the contractor complies with its policies. Where shortcomings exist, the government will require corrective action. Where satisfactory, the government grants a systems approval. See FAR 44.303

4. The government conducts surveillance between systems reviews, and may revoke prior approvals where significant issues are discovered. FAR 44.304.

IV.   COUNTERFEIT PARTS.

A.   Introduction.

1. Technically, counterfeit part systems are not a system specifically called out in DFARS 52.242-7005, Contractor Business Systems, but it is a part of a Contractors Purchasing System and are evaluated as such.

2. Many government contracts contain detailed specifications that specify the materials and components that a contractor must use to meet the requirements. These specified materials and components may be called out directly, or may be called out by government or industry specifications and standards incorporated by reference into the prime contract. In other contracts, the contractor may be required to comply with its own internal specifications for an item, and the contractor's specification may require use of specific materials or components. Because the government has exacting requirements and often demands state of the art performance from its contractors, this can result in the government specifying more expensive parts and materials than might be required by other customers.

3. Where a contract requires an expensive material and the selection of the contractor is based in whole or in part on price, contractors and their supply chain are tempted to substitute less expensive materials than required. Similarly, a contractor who fails to carefully review the technical requirements may miss requirements, and carelessly use the more common, less expensive materials. In the past, some agencies included traceability requirements in their technical specifications and statements of work. These requirements meant that contractors must document the source of parts used in manufacturing an item back to the original manufacturer.

4. A number of recent, egregious examples of bad parts, especially in the electronics industry, have resulted in the Congress requiring business practices to prevent the use of counterfeit electronic parts, and to correct end items that are delivered with such parts. See Pub. L. 112-81, §818(c), Dec. 31, 2011; 79 Fed. Reg. 26092, May 6, 2014.

B.   Covered Contractors and Contracts.

1. Currently, DOD and NASA have contractual requirements for a system to detect and prevent counterfeit electronic parts. 42 U.S.C. §18444; DFARS 252.246-

Business Systems

7007. A draft FAR rule published on 10 June 2014 proposes broadening the scope to cover all non-conforming parts and all federal agencies.

2. At present, in DOD contracts which may involve the supply of electronic parts, end items containing electronic parts, or services including electronic parts, the contracting officer must include DFARS 252.246-7007. See DFARS 246.870-3. The requirements in the rule apply to all contractors who are CAS covered. DFARS 252.246-7007.

3. Exemptions.

- Small Businesses are exempt. DFARS 246-870-3(b)

- Non-CAS covered contractors and subcontractors. DFARS 252.246-7007.

4. Subcontracts.

- Prime contractors and higher-tier subcontractors must flow down DFARS 252.246-7007 to subcontractors who supply electronic parts, or items containing electronic parts.

- Subcontractors should expect that prime contractors will routinely include DFARS 252.246-7007 in the subcontract in order to allow the prime contractor to meet its contractual obligations.

- Because counterfeit electronic parts are such a major issue, industry is adopting standard requirements for counterfeit parts detection. See SAE STD AS6174.

C. Requirements. DFARS 252.246-7007(c).

1. Generally, a contractor's system for preventing use of counterfeit electronic parts focuses on knowing the supplier of the parts used to perform the contract and excluding the parts from the supply chain.

2. A contractor must train its personnel and document its training.

3. A contractor should, preferably, buy from the part's original equipment manufacturer (OEM), or a franchised dealer appointed by the OEM.

4. Where a contractor purchases from other than an OEM, the contractor should: require traceability through written records to the OEM, and perform incoming inspection to minimize the risk to the government.

5. When counterfeit parts are suspected, a contractor must: a) report the suspected parts to the contracting officer and to the Government-Industry Data Exchange Program (GIDEP); b) segregate the suspected counterfeits to prevent their use; and c) cooperate with government investigations.

6. Flow down system requirements to suppliers.

D. Government Review and Approval. A contractor's systems for counterfeit parts is reviewed as part of a CPSR.

V. ACCOUNTING SYSTEMS

A. Introduction.

1. Probably the most burdensome business system that a contractor must implement when it undertakes to contract with the federal government is its accounting system. The reasons that implementing an approved accounting system is so difficult is because a business must satisfy requirements from multiple regulators, with differing concerns, and differing requirements. A contractor must implement an accounting system acceptable to: a) the Security and Exchange Commission, the exchanges where its stock is traded, and its banks; b) an accounting system acceptable to the federal, state, local and foreign tax authorities; and c) an accounting system acceptable to its federal government customer, typically meaning the

362

Defense Contract Audit Agency and the Cost Accounting Standards Board. Satisfying all these stakeholders, plus a company's management that needs accounting data to manage the business is challenging, to say the least, especially when various stakeholders appear insensitive to the requirements of other stakeholders.

2. Federal government customers insist on contractors implementing accounting systems for a very simple reason: the government often pays a contractor based on incurred costs, and expects the contractor to be able to accurately report what those costs are. Without an approved accounting system, a contractor may be unable to bill the government, significantly affecting its cash flow. Even where an approved accounting system is not required, contractors find that having an approved system materially assists them in pricing contracts and equitable adjustments.

B. Covered Contracts and Contractors.

1. For DOD contractors, if a contract includes DFARS 252.242-7005, Contractor Business Systems, and DFARS 252.242-7006, Accounting Systems Administration, then the contractor must establish an acceptable accounting system. These clauses are included in contracts that either are flexibly priced, or that provide for progress payments based on costs. DFARS 242.7001 and 242.7503.

2. Progress Payments. A key business concern of contractors is cash flow—that is having the customer make payments as work progresses so that the contractor can pay its employees and suppliers. Of the many types of contract financing discussed in FAR Part 32, Progress Payments Based on Costs are probably the most common method utilized. A contractor who has an accounting system judged adequate can expect to receive progress payments in a timely fashion. In DOD, a contractor receiving progress payments must have an acceptable accounting system.

3. Flexibly priced contracts. In order for a contractor to receive award of a contract that is flexibly priced, such as a cost-reimbursement contract; the contractor must have an approved accounting system. As discussed in Chapter 6, Section II.C, an acceptable accounting system is a matter of contractor responsibility, and a contractor is must have an adequate accounting system to receive a cost type contract. FAR 16.301-3(a)(3).

4. The requirements for an acceptable accounting system apply at both the prime contract, and to subcontracts. A prime will not award a cost type subcontract to a supplier whose accounting system in not assessed as adequate.

C. Requirements.

1. The detailed requirements for an acceptable accounting system are set forth in DFARS 252.242-7006(c). To further explain these requirements to contractors, the Defense Contract Audit Agency has published DCAA Manual No. 7641.90 Information for Contractors, and review checklists: http://www.dcaa.mil/Preaward_Survey_of_Prospective_Contractor_Accounting_System_Check list.pdf.

2. As a general matter, an adequate accounting system must be acceptable for accumulating costs under a government contract and have the ability to generate the specific cost information required under the anticipated contract. Typically, this means that the contractor will have a "job cost" type accounting system, which allows the allocation and accumulation of costs by final cost objective (normally a contract), consistent treatment of direct and indirect costs, labor charging procedures, etc.

3. For larger contracts and contractors, the accounting system must also comply with applicable Cost Accounting Standards, 48 C.F.R. Chapter 99. A discussion of these standards is beyond the scope of this deskbook.

D. Government Review and Approval.

Business Systems

1. A contract auditor typically reviews and recommends approval or disapproval of a contractor's accounting system as part of a pre-award survey supporting a responsibility determination. See DCAA Manual No. 7641.90, p. 12.

2. Thereafter, the contract auditor will periodically conduct system audits as part of it normal audit oversight of the contractor's accounting system.

3. Where a contract auditor reports system deficiencies, the government will typically exercise its rights to withhold payments pending correction. See DFARS 252.242-7006(f). This remedy has such an adverse impact on the typical contractor that corrective action usually follows relatively promptly.

VI. CONTRACTOR MATERIAL MANAGEMENT ACCOUNTING SYSTEMS.

A. Introduction.

1. In addition to the basic accounting system requirements discussed in Section V.C, some contractors are required to maintain a system for managing the costs of materials transferred from inventory for use on a particular contract, and for transferring inventory between different contracts. Such transfers are routine within industry.

2. The reason that DOD requires contractors to implement business practices for controlling inventory costs are directly related to the government's unique practices of acquiring hardware using flexibly priced contracts and by providing contract financing based on incurred costs. Some contractors have used inventory transfers to favor their fixed-priced and commercial work, to the detriment of government work. Consequently, the Department of Defense requires that a contractor's financial and inventory management systems meet specified standards to ensure that the government is treated fairly on inventory transfers.

B. Covered Contractors and Contracts.

1. DFARS 252.242-7004, Material Management Accounting Systems, is included in all DOD contracts over the Simplified Acquisition Threshold that are either cost-reimbursement or fixed-price with progress payments based on costs.

2. Exclusions:

    • Contracts with small businesses, educational institutions, and non-profits;

    • Contracts that are fixed-price, but use another method of contract financing, such as performance based payments.

3. When a contractor has one contract that includes DFARS 252.242-7004, then all contracts are potentially affected. The reason is that when the contractor's inventory systems must meet DOD's MMAS standards, this usually means that all contracts requiring an inventory transfer must comply with the procedures. A contractor cannot cannibalize a part from another unit without properly documenting the transfer.

C. Requirements.

1. The detailed requirements for an acceptable Material Management Accounting System are stated in DFARS 252.242-7004(b)-(d).

2. Generally, the requirements include:

    • Written policies;

    • Transfer materials and costs based on valid time-phased requirements;

    • Maintain accurate bills of material and production schedules;

    • Provide audit trails and maintain accurate records;

    • Control transfers of parts;

- Maintain a consistent, equitable, and unbiased logic for costing of material transactions;

- Control allocations from common inventory accounts

- Have adequate controls for physically commingled inventories

- Conduct periodic internal reviews to ensure compliance with established policies and procedures.

D.   Government Review and Approval.

1.   Where a contractor: a) has $40 million of qualifying sales to the government during the contractor's preceding fiscal year and b) the administrative contracting officer (ACO), with advice from the auditor, determines an MMAS review is needed based on a risk assessment of the contractor's past experience and current vulnerability, then the government will review a contractor's MMAS.

2.   Qualifying sales are sales for which certified cost or pricing data were required under 10 U.S.C. 2306a, as implemented in FAR 15.403, or that are contracts priced on other than a firm-fixed-price or fixed-price with economic price adjustment basis. Sales include prime contracts, subcontracts, and modifications to such contracts and subcontracts.

3.   Where a contractor has significant deficiencies in its MMAS, the ACO may withhold up to 5% of contract payments, until the contractor corrects the deficiencies.

VII. EARNED VALUE MANAGEMENT SYSTEMS. FAR SUBPART 34.2.

A.   Introduction.

1.   Earned Value Management Systems (EVMS) are a management tool designed to give managers early visibility of cost growth and schedule delays in performing contracts and other projects. These systems work by breaking down the entire effort into many discrete work packages using a structured process, developing a budget and schedule for each work package, and monthly reporting costs and work accomplished against the planned costs and schedule. Where costs incurred and work accomplished deviate from the plan, the managers can project how those deviations will affect final costs and schedule, and react accordingly.

2.   Earned value management systems are expensive to implement, and their value is reduced when the government changes the baseline schedule, technical requirements, or contract funding.

3.   Earned value management systems have been used on large defense contracts for decades, and they are used in managing programs outside of government contracting.

B.   Covered Contractors and Contracts.

1.   The FAR does not specify when EVMS is required. EVMS is not required on all contracts; it is only required by agency management when the costs of implementing the system are outweighed by the expected benefits.

2.   In DOD, DFARS 234.201(1) requires EVMS on a contract by contract basis:

- On cost-type and incentive-type contracts and subcontracts over $50M, the contractor must have an approved system;

- On cost-type and incentive-type contracts and subcontracts from $20M to $50M, the contractor must agree to implement a system;

- On cost-type and incentive-type contracts and subcontracts under $20M, the contracting officer may implement EVMS where a cost-benefit analysis validates the benefit to the government.

Business Systems

- Use of EVMS on fixed-price type contracts is discouraged.

- Within DOD, use of EVMS on short term contracts (less than 12 months) is discouraged.

C. Requirements.

1. Earned Value Management Systems must conform to industry standard ANSI/EIA Standard 748. FAR 52.234-2; DFARS 252.234-7002;

2. ANSI/EIA Standard 748 has 32 general standards. The Defense Contract Management Agency has issued Department of Defense Earned Value Management Implementation Guide, October 2006, containing DOD's interpretation of the ANSI standards.

3. Generally, a compliant system will breakdown the work into work packages using a Contract Work Break Down Structure; develop a critical path project schedule for the work packages; develop detailed cost estimates for the work packages; project the incurrence of costs during the period of performance for individual work packages; track the incurrence of costs and work accomplished by the work package during contract performance; analyze variances of actual costs and schedule performance against planned costs and schedule; and report periodically the performance and variances to management and the customer.

4. Implementing EVMS adds costs, and there are diverse views on the impact. DCMA believes that EVMS is a normal management cost. Some industry participants believe that a DCMA-approved system can add 20% to the cost of performance, a considerable sum in an era of billion dollar programs.

D. Government Review and Approval.

1. DOD requires a contractor to have an approved EVMS system to receive a cost- or incentive-type contract over $50M.

2. In DOD, contractor EVMS systems are evaluated by a specialized office within the Defense Contract Management Agency, under the overall supervision of the Deputy Director, Earned Value Management Performance Assessments and Root Cause Analyses (PARC), Office of the Assistant Secretary of Defense for Acquisition.

3. A contractor's system is reviewed periodically to ascertain that it remains in compliance with the ANSI Standard.

4. In DOD, where a contractor has significant deficiencies in its EVMS, the contracting officer may withhold payments up to 5% of the contract price as provided in DFARS 252.242-7005, Contractor Business Systems.

VIII. GOVERNMENT PROPERTY MANAGEMENT SYSTEMS.

A. Introduction.

1. Contractors often receive significant amounts of property from the government for use in performing a contract. Furthermore, as contractors incur costs on cost-type contracts, and receive contract financing payments on other contracts, the contractor work in process on those contracts becomes government property. Because a contractor is often unable to perform a contract without government property, an approved system can be a prerequisite to receiving many government contracts.

2. The detailed requirements for government property are set forth in FAR Part 45, and FAR 52.245-1, Government Property.

B. Covered Contractors and Contracts.

1. Fixed-Price Contracts. Where a contractor under a fixed-price type contract is furnished government property for the performance of the contract, the government will include FAR 252.245-1 in the contract.

2. Additionally, the government will include FAR 52.245-1 in any contract that is: a) cost-reimbursement type; b) time-and-material type; and c) other labor-hour type when property is expected to be furnished.

3. FAR 25.245-1 is also included in subcontracts, where the supplier will receive or acquire government property. Prime contractors may supplement the FAR requirements with additional requirements, usually reflecting the prime contractor's internal processes.

C. Requirements.

1. The requirements for a government property system are relatively straight forward when compared to other business systems.

2. As a general matter, the contractor must have written procedures, incoming inspection, marking ownership, maintain accountability, use only for permitted purposes, protection from damage, and use, delivery, or return at the end of the contract.

3. The contractor shall include the requirements of this clause in all subcontracts under which government property is acquired or furnished for subcontract performance.

4. The key issue with government property systems is compliance; a contractor must perform periodic internal reviews to ensure that the system is working and is being followed.

D. Government Review and Approval.

Government property administrators in the Defense Contract Management Agency perform routine surveillance of government property systems, as required.

IX. INFORMATION TECHNOLOGY SYSTEMS.

A. Introduction.

1. Historically, the government has included requirements for contractor Information Technology (IT) systems as part of government security requirements. See NISPOM, Chapter 8. Such requirements typically applied to contractors who received classified information, and to those IT systems that processed classified information.

2. As has been widely reported, foreign powers have penetrated the unclassified networks of government contractors and stolen huge amounts of sensitive, but unclassified, data such as technical data controlled under the International Traffic in Arms Regulations. See The Department Of Defense Cyber Strategy (April 2015).

3. In response, the Department of Defense initiated a voluntary program to harden the networks of key contractors, and later expanded this program to implement contractual requirements addressing the security of a DOD contractor's unclassified information. DFARS 252.204-7012, Safeguarding of Unclassified Controlled Technical Information.

4. Most recently, the government has added a standard FAR clause: FAR 52.204-21, Basic Safeguarding of Covered Contractor Information Systems, to virtually all government contracts. Additionally, other civilian agencies have developed their own requirements for IT systems security. See HSAR 3052.204-70, Security Requirements For Unclassified Information Technology Resources.

B. Covered Contractors and Contracts.

1. FAR Subpart 4.19, and its implementing clause FAR 52.204-21, Basic Safeguarding of Covered Contractor Information Systems is the uniform government-wide standard stating the minimum federal cybersecurity standards a contractor's IT system must comply with.

2. Generally, a contractor who is expected to have access to unclassified, but sensitive, information, such as technical data about military and intelligence systems, private personal information, financial information, healthcare information, etc., should expect

Business Systems

that the buying agency will include additional requirements for the contractor's IT systems in the contract.

3. For DOD contractors, the applicable clause is DFARS 252.204-7012, Safeguarding of Unclassified Controlled Technical Information. It is included in all prime contracts, and must be flowed down to all subcontractors. DFARS 204.7004

C. Requirements.

1. FAR 52.204-21. The basic FAR requirements for contractor IT systems apply to all contracts where the contractor will store non-public information related to a federal contract on the contractor's or a subcontractor's computer system. This information is defined as "Federal Contract Information" in FAR 4.1901. While not all contracts are included, many are and contractors should expect to see the clause widely included in both prime contracts and lower tier subcontracts.

2. There are 15 requirements in FAR 52.204-21, which generally are those recommended for any networked computer system. The FAR requirements include:

   - Limit access and use of the system to authorized users, authorized devices, and processes acting on behalf of authorized users. In other words, the users, hardware, and processes should have to authenticate they are authorized.
   - Limit the system to the types of transactions and functions that authorized users are permitted to execute. In other words, your system should prohibit unapproved software and actions.
   - Verify and control/limit connections to and use of external information systems. In other words, authenticate and restrict connections outside the network.
   - If you have a publicly accessible website, or terminal, have a system to control the information available on the site, and the software that may run on the site.

   - Identify network users, hardware, and the programs they run.
   - Authenticate (or verify) the identities of all users, software, and hardware before allowing access to the network.
   - Sanitize or destroy hardware and storage media containing Federal Contract Information before disposal or release for reuse.
   - Limit physical access to computers, network equipment, and the operating systems to authorized individuals.
   - Escort visitors and monitor visitor activity; maintain audit logs of physical access; and control locks, keys, access cards, etc.
   - Monitor, control, and protect organizational communications (i.e., use hardware or software firewall to control data transmitted or received) outside the network, and between key internal boundaries of the network.
   - Create a protected subnetwork (DMZ) for publicly accessible parts of your network. This separation may be physical or logical.
   - Identify, report, and correct information and information system flaws in a timely manner. In other words, keep up with bug fixes, and eliminate hardware and software with uncorrected flaws.
   - Use anti-virus software and other malicious code protections, internally as well as at external boundaries.
   - Keep your anti-virus protection up to date.
   - Periodically scan all your network, and real-time scan all files from external sources as the files are downloaded, opened, or executed.

3. As one might expect, the cybersecurity requirements for DOD contracts are more rigorous. DOD has a very broad definition of "Covered Defense Information." DFARS 204.7301. DOD requires that every contractor and subcontractor that stores or processes Covered Defense Information on a computer system must comply with DOD cybersecurity requirements. DFARS 204.7302(a). The technical requirements are

set forth in NIST Special Publication 800-171, which is a more comprehensive and detailed exposition of requirements for protecting unclassified systems. By bidding, a contractor represents its computer systems completely comply with the NIST requirements, unless it informs DOD where its computer networks do not meet requirements in NIST SP 800.171. DFARS 252.204-7008. Contracting officers must assess such disclosures and approve systems prior to award of a contract.

4. During performance, the contractor and its subcontractors must comply with the NIST SP 800-171, which includes more detailed requirements regarding use of passwords, intrusion detection, control of hardware and software on a network, updating software, etc., than that stated in the FAR clause. Additionally, the prime contractor and its subcontractors must rapidly report cyber incidents, and cooperate in the investigation of the incidents. DFARS 252.204-12.

5. Generally, the government intends that the NIST requirements are implemented in a risk-based manner. A contractor may elect not to implement a requirement, or to implement a requirement differently, where the specific network and the information it contains justifies acceptance of the risk involved in not implementing the requirement. This risk-based approach is combined with strong incident reporting requirements. However, the contractor must disclose how its systems deviate from NIST 800-171, and the contracting officer must approve the deviations. DFARS 252.204-7008.

6. Subcontracts. The FAR and DFARS clauses on cybersecurity must be included in subcontracts where Federal Contract Information, or Covered Defense Information is involved. FAR 52.204-21(c); DFARS 252.204-7012(m).

7. Commercial Items. Commercial Item subcontracts are not exempt from either the FAR or DFARS requirements.

D. Government Review and Approval.

1. Contractors, in their own self interest, should perform self assessments using both internal and external assessors. Knowledgeable personnel assume that all network systems are penetrated at some point.

2. The government often performs its assessment of a contractor's IT systems in the course of conducting an assessment of a data breach the contractor reports, or the government detects through other means.

3. Where a DOD contractor's system deviates from NIST SP 899-171, the DOD Chief Information Officer will review and must approve of the deviation prior to award, and the deviation included into the contract document. The contracting officer will withhold the award of new contracts with unapproved deviations, or where a contractor fails to maintain an acceptable system. The contracting officer can terminate a contract for breach if the applicable NIST Standard is not maintained.

X. DEFENSE CONTRACTOR BUSINESS SYSTEMS.

A. Requirements.

1. DFARS 252.242-7005, Contractor Business Systems (FEB 2012), is included in all defense contracts that contain one or more requirements for:

   - Compliance with Cost Accounting Standards,
   - Cost Estimating Systems,
   - Earned Value Management System,
   - Material Management and Accounting Systems,
   - Accounting Systems,
   - Contractor Purchasing Systems, or
   - Contractor Property Management Systems

2. Essentially, DFARS 252.242-7005, provides an additional contractual remedy for a contractor's failure to maintain approval of

seven required business systems. If a system is not approved because it contains one or more significant deficiencies, the government may withhold up to 5 percent of contract payments due a contractor (10 percent in the event two or more systems are not approved). The withholding affects both the instant contract, and all other contracts that are cost-reimbursement, labor-hour, and time-and-materials type. Therefore, the clause provides a powerful incentive for contractors to correct business systems with significant deficiencies.

3. The contractor is required to report its proposed corrective action to the contracting officer within 45 days, and to implement that corrective action. The contracting officer, along with the appropriate specialists, will review the corrective action, and may modify or cancel the withholding of payments pending completion of the corrective action and reassessment of the system.

4. Withholding payments has a significant and immediate impact on the contractor's cash flow.

5. Not all business systems are covered by DFARS 252.242-7005. For example, significant deficiencies in cyber security, quality, counterfeit parts, and other systems not identified in the DFARS clause do not result in the broad withholding.

XI. CONCLUSION.

Submitting an offer for a government contract or subcontract often includes a commitment that the contractor's business systems will conform to government requirements. Achieving this conformance may require a substantial initial investment, and failure to achieve or maintain conformance is likely to create substantial financial and legal problems.

CONTRACT FINANCING

AND

PAYMENT

I. INTRODUCTION.

The government, as the buyer in the typical government contract, has one overriding contractual obligation. The government is required to the contract price for timely delivery of conforming goods and services. Additionally, the government often undertakes to provide a form of financing to a contractor by paying the contractor progress payments, performance-based payments, or reimbursing its costs of performance prior to completion of performance. Contractors are well advised to thoroughly understand the financing and payment process.

Failure to timely pay for delivery of conforming goods and services has consequences. The Prompt Payment Act requires the contracting officer to automatically pay interest on delayed payments, other than contract financing payments.

An important qualification on the government's obligation to pay is its right to recover debts owed to it on a contract. This tool for recovering sums owed the government is both practical, and potentially damaging to a contractor who may not be able to stop work when the contractor is not paid. Similarly, the government's right to suspend some contract financing payments can materially impact a contractor's ability to perform its contract.

Although not a legal issue, the various payment systems are heavily focused more on tracking payments to individual fund citations. Timely paying suppliers for delivery of conforming goods is less important, and the complexity introduced by these concerns results in multiple opportunities to cause breakdowns in the process.

II. REFERENCES.

A. Statutes.

1. 10 U.S.C. § 2307, Contract Financing.

2. 31 U.S.C. § 3901, Prompt Payment.

3. 31 U.S.C. § 3701, Claims.

4. 31 U.S.C. § 3727 and 41 U.S.C. § 6305, Assignment of Claims Act of 1940.

5. 41 U.S.C. § 4503, Advance or other payments.

B. Regulations.

1. FAR Part 32, Contract Financing.

2. DFARS Part 232, Contract Financing.

3. DOD Financial Management Regulation (FMR), (DOD 7000.14-R), vol. 10, Contract Payment Policy and Procedures.

4. 5 CFR Part 1315, "Prompt Payment."

C. Guides.

1. Defense Finance and Accounting Service Contractor and Vendor Payment Information Guidebook available at http://www.dfas.mil/dam/jcr:b22e2f82-835c-4b49-a18b-e7d5d1dcda43/ContractPayInformation-011110.pdf

III. TYPES OF CONTRACT PAYMENTS.

A. **General.** There are two general types of payments made under government contracts: 1) contract payments for delivery/performance of contract requirements and 2) contract financing payments.

B.   Payments on Completion. Contract payments for delivery/performance, either partial or final, are the government's principal contract obligation. The process consists of contractor delivery, government acceptance, contractor submission of a proper invoice, and government payment. It is further described in paragraph IV, below.

C.   Contract Financing. Contract financing payments are payments by the government prior to completion of contract performance, or a severable portion thereof. Financing payments are intended to finance the contractor's performance of work. Without contract financing, many small and medium-sized businesses would be excluded from bidding on government contracts, and even large businesses might have difficulty financing large, multi-year contracts. Additionally, the U.S. government has much lower borrowing costs, and when it provides contract financing, it permits contractors to offer lower prices.

While FAR Part 32 includes many types of contract financing, the three most common are: a) progress payments on fixed-price contracts; b) performance-based payments; and c) interim payments on cost-type contracts. These common forms of contract financing are further described in paragraph V, below.

IV. CONTRACT PAYMENTS – DELIVERY/PERFORMANCE.

A.   Invoice Payments. FAR Subpart 32.9.

1.   Invoice payments are payments made upon delivery and acceptance of goods or performance of services by the government. Deliveries can be partial or final. Delivery and performance schedules are discussed at FAR 11.401. Acceptance is discussed at FAR 32.905.

2.   All payments require a proper invoice. FAR 32.905 (a); FMR Para 070203 B,). Further, "[a]ll invoice payments, with the exception of interim payments on cost-reimbursement contract for services, must be supported by a receiving report or other government documentation authorizing payment." FAR 32.905(c).

3.   Receipt of goods or services is insufficient to trigger a government obligation to pay. Payment must be based on acceptance of the goods or services as authenticated by the signature of a government official. FMR Para 070203 C.2.

4.   Invoice payments include:

a.   Final payments of the contract price, costs, or fees in accordance with the contract or as settled by the government and the contractor.

b.   Payments for partial deliveries or partial performance under fixed-price contracts.

c.   Progress payments under: 1) construction contracts and 2) architect/engineer contracts. These progress payments are not financing because the government receives the benefit of construction work performed on government property.

5.   Invoice Format.

a.   Typically, the contract will contain detailed instructions regarding the contents of a contractor's invoice; however, the FAR does not require use of a specific form and, unless otherwise stated in the contract, a contractor may use its standard commercial invoice, as long as it contains the contractually required information. FAR 32.905(b).

b.   Within DOD, the contractor is required to submit electronic invoices and other payment requests. DFARS 252.232-7003 Electronic Submission of Payment Requests and Receiving Reports.

c. Contractors are well advised to exactly follow the instructions on invoices and payments to obtain prompt payment. Fortunately, federal contractors have much less concern with the credit risk of their customer, unlike commercial and international contracts.

B. **Payments for Commercial Items.** The process for payment for commercial items is described in FAR 52.212-4, Contract Terms and Conditions.

1. The contractor's invoice must contain the information listed in FAR 52.212-4(g), unless modified elsewhere in the contract.

2. The government will generally pay for accepted items by electronic payment. FAR 52.212-5(b)(50).

C. **Payments for Non-commercial Items.** FAR 52.232-1.

1. The Payments clause provides:

FAR 52.232-1 – Payments (Apr. 1984)

The government shall pay the contractor, upon the submission of proper invoices or vouchers, the prices stipulated in this contract for supplies delivered and accepted or services rendered and accepted, less any deductions provided in this contract. Unless otherwise specified in this contract, payment shall be made on partial deliveries accepted by the government if —

(a) The amount due on the deliveries warrants it or
(b) The contractor requests it and the amount due on the deliveries is at least $1,000 or 50 percent of the total contract price.

2. Typically, Section G. of the contract will contain the agency's requirements for submission of contractor invoices and for payments.

3. Payments by DOD are typically made using the Wide-Area Work Flow (WAWF) system. Contractors must submit invoices electronically, and payments are made electronically. DFARS 252.232-7003, Electronic Submission of Payment Requests and Receiving Reports.

D. **Partial Payments.**

1. Partial payments are payments made under fixed-price contracts for supplies or services that are accepted by the government but are only part of the contract requirements. FAR 32.102(d).

2. Although partial payments are a method of payment and not a method of contract financing, using partial payments can help contractors participate in government contracts with minimal contract financing. This is because the contractor is paid as it performs, rather than waiting for contract completion.

E. **Payments on Construction Contracts.** FAR 52.232-5, Payments Under Fixed-Price Construction Contracts.

1. As the contractor performs construction work at the job site, it invoices periodically for payment based on the work completed.

2. Final payment, including retainages, is made upon final acceptance of the work, invoicing, and a release of claims. FAR 52.232-5(h).

3. Because construction contractors typically receive progress payments based on the percentage of completion, as measured by costs incurred/paid, the final payment represents the profit the contractor has earned on the contract, plus any retainages and/or withholdings.

V. **CONTRACT FINANCING PAYMENTS – PROGRESS PAYMENTS.**

A. **General.**

1. Financing payments are made to a contractor before acceptance of goods or

Financing and Payment

services by the government. See ¶ 100401, Ch. 10, Vol. 10 of DOD FMR.

2. FAR Part 32 describes various types of contract financing, including: 1) advance payments, 2) loan guarantees, 3) progress payments based on a percentage of completion, 4) progress payments based on costs, and 5) performance-based payments,. Of these types of contract financing, only the latter three are commonly used in defense contracting.

3. FAR 32.106 states the government's preference for contract financing: a) no financing; b) customary contract financing as defined in FAR 32.113; and c) loan guarantees, advance payments, and other unusual forms contract financing[1] that are rarely used. Contractors prefer the type of contract financing that best meets their cash flow requirements and has the fewest administrative requirements.

4. The government will typically provide contract financing payments for larger contracts with longer estimated performance periods where the contractors can demonstrate a need for financing.

   a. Small businesses may generally expect contract financing when the performance period is greater than four months and the contract price is greater than the simplified acquisition threshold. FAR 32.104(d).

   b. Large business may expect contract financing when the contract price exceeds $2.5 million and the performance period exceeds six months. FAR 32.104(d).

B.   Progress Payments on Construction Contracts. FAR 52.232-5.

1. Prime contractors are paid progress payments, as the construction progresses, based on the contractor's submission of the costs of work performed, less a retainage if progress is not satisfactory. The costs of construction are used as a

measure of percent of completion, and typically have a large subcontractor content.

2. The prime contractor submits vouchers of costs incurred in performance of the contract, for review and approval by the contracting officer or its onsite representative.

3. Security. Payments under fixed-price construction contracts are typically secured by a performance bond. See FAR 28.102. Furthermore, since the government typically owns the worksite and takes title to materials as they are acquired, the government has security for its payments.

C.   Progress Payments Based on Costs. FAR 52.232-16.

1. On fixed-price type supply and services contracts over $25,000, the contractor may request progress payments based on costs. Typically, the contractor will not do so for contracts where the goods will be delivered quickly (i.e., within six months) because the costs incurred in seeking progress payments and in complying with the requirements in FAR 52.232-16, outweigh the benefits of contract financing.

2. To obtain progress payments based on costs, the contractor must have an accounting system acceptable to the government. FAR 52.232-16(f).

3. The contractor may submit requests for progress payments monthly, for costs incurred as described in FAR 52.232-16(a). The amount of progress payments may vary, but currently are limited to 80% of total incurred costs for large businesses and 90% for small businesses.

4. Progress payments are secured by the government taking title to work in process, the costs of which have been paid by the government. FAR 32.503-14, FAR 52.232-16(d). The contractor must protect the work in progress to which the government takes title. The government

---

1 See FAR 32.114.

374

may also require additional protection, such as performance bonds, but bonds are not common.

5. The contractor liquidates (repays) its progress payments by delivering conforming goods and invoicing for the contract price. For example, when a contractor has been paid progress payments at the rate of 80% of incurred costs, it invoices for deliveries. The government will apply 80% of the invoiced amount to reduce the balance of the contractor's outstanding progress payments, and will pay the contractor the remaining 20% of the invoiced amount.

6. The government may suspend paying progress payments for reasons such as failure to make progress, or failure to maintain an acceptable accounting system.

D. **Progress Payments Based on Percent Completed.** Progress payments can also be based on a percentage or stage of contract completion, if authorized by agency procedures.

1. Progress payments based on percent completed are authorized for construction contracts, shipbuilding, and ship conversion, alteration, or repair. DFARS 232.102.

2. The agency must ensure that payments are commensurate with the work accomplished. Greenhut Constr. Co., ASBCA No. 41777, 93-1 BCA ¶ 25,374 (after hurricane damaged previously completed construction work, Navy was entitled to review the work and pay only the amount representing satisfactorily completed work).

VI. CONTRACT FINANCING — PERFORMANCE-BASED PAYMENTS. FAR 52.232-32.

A. Performance-based payments are a form of contract financing where the financing payment is made based on accomplishment of specified milestones or tasks, rather than incurred costs, up to

90% of the contract price. For example, the contractor may propose several key events (ordering parts, receipt of inventory, commencement of production, etc.) that are measurable, and reflect a proportional amount of completion. The performance-based payment may be either a stated amount or a percentage of the contract price.

B. Performance-based payments can be simpler to administer, and permit a contractor to finance a greater percentage of the contract price than typically allowed for progress payments.

C. As with progress payments, performance-based payments are secured by the government taking title to the work in process. FAR 52.232-32(f).

D. Performance-based payments are liquidated at a negotiated rate from payments invoiced at delivery and acceptance.

E. A 2014 Performance-Based Payments Guide, is available at http://www.acq.osd.mil/dpap/cpic/cp/docs/Performance_Based_Payment_(PBP)_Guide.pdf. The Defense Contract Management Agency website at http://guidebook.dcma.mil/7/index.cfm also provides guidance on the use and administration of performance-based payments (PBPs).

F. Performance-based payments are not partial payments for completed performance. FAR 32.1001(c).

VII. CONTRACT FINANCING – PAYMENTS ON COST-TYPE CONTRACTS.

A. References.

1. FAR 52.216-7, Allowable Cost and Payment.

2. FAR Part 31.

3. FAR Part 42.7.

B.   **General.** Federal contracting is unique in its use of reimbursement of costs incurred as the price paid for work performed. The payments take two forms: interim payments and final payment. As the contractor performs the contract, it submits interim payment requests for reimbursement of its incurred costs, and, if authorized in the contract, its fee. Each accounting year, the contractor submits an accounting of its indirect costs incurred to set the final rates for that year, which the government audits and negotiates. At the completion of performance of a cost-reimbursement contract, and settlement of the final indirect cost rates for the final year of performance, the contractor and the government close out the contract by calculating the final contract price. Upon agreement or determination, the contractor invoices or pays back the amount owed, normally insignificant compared to the total contract price. The process for accomplishing these tasks is detailed, but is generally described below.

C.   **Interim Payments of Incurred Costs.** FAR 52.216-7, Allowable Cost and Payment.

The contractor may submit vouchers for incurred costs not more frequently than once every two weeks, for their reasonable, allowable, properly accounted for, and not specifically disallowed costs of performance, as provided in FAR 52.216-7(b). Generally, this includes all incurred direct and indirect costs as determined using the cost principles in FAR Part 31.

1.   The government will typically pay the vouchers within 30 days of receipt, subject to audit, as a form of contract financing. FAR 52.216-7(a)(3).

2.   Indirect costs are reimbursed at billing rates either mutually agreed by the government and the contractor, or established by the administrative contracting officer. FAR 52.216-7(e).

3.   Within six months following the end of an accounting year, the contractor must submit a final indirect rate cost proposal to the government for audit and negotiation. FAR 52.216-7(d).

4.   Within 120 days after the contractor and the government agree on final rates (or the contracting officer unilaterally determines the final rates) for all accounting years for the contract, the contractor must submit its final voucher to close out the contract. Payment of that final voucher is final payment on the cost-type contract, and may occur years after the actual work has been completed.

VIII. CONTRACT FINANCING OF SUBCONTRACTS.

A.   Prime contractors and higher-tier subcontractors may provide contract financing to lower-tier subcontractors, on terms substantially similar to those applicable to the prime contractor. FAR 52.232-22(j); FAR 52.216-7(b)(1)(iii).

B.   Prime contractors may include contract financing payments to subcontractors in their costs used to determine progress payments under FAR 52.232-22 and interim payments under FAR 52.216-7.

IX. THE GOVERNMENT PAYMENT SYSTEM.

A.   **Disbursing Authority.**

1.   The Department of Treasury, Bureau of the Fiscal Service (formerly the Financial Management Service), is the principal disbursing agent of the federal government, accounting for approximately 85% of all federal payments (contract payments, civil servant salaries and pensions, Social Security, Medicare, veterans, etc.). The Bureau of the Fiscal Service website is at: http://www.fiscal.treasury.gov/.

2.   A few agencies, including the Department of Defense, the United States Marshal's Office, and the Department of Homeland Security (with respect to public money

available for the Coast Guard's expenditure when it is not operating as a service in the Navy) also have statutory authority to disburse public money. 31 U.S.C. § 3321. For DOD, the Defense Finance and Accounting Service (DFAS) make payments. Its website is: http://www.dfas.mil/.

B.   When Payments Are Made.

1.   The government generally pays its contractual invoices within 30 days. FAR 32.904(b). The 30 days begins to run from the later of: a) submission of a proper invoice or b) acceptance of the goods or services.

2.   Contractors are well served to negotiate, if possible, a clear description of the contents of an invoice and a fixed period for the government to inspect and accept the goods or services.

C.   When Financing Payments Are Made.

1.   Generally, the due date for contract financing payments is 30 days from date of receipt by the designated payment office of a proper payment request. FAR 32.007.

2.   Late payment of a financing payment can be a defense to a default termination, the contractor will succeed in appealing a default termination of a contract only if the late payment rendered appellant financially incapable of continuing performance, was the primary or controlling cause of the default, or was a material rather than insubstantial or immaterial breach. Jones Oil Company, ASBCA No. 42651, 98-1 BCA ¶ 29,691.

D.   Prompt Payment Act and Late Payments. 31 U.S.C. §§ 3901-3907, FAR Subpart 32.9; FAR 52.232-25; and 5 C.F.R. Part 1315.

1.   Congress and the GAO have recognized that delays in payment have serious adverse effects on the government and its contractors. GAO-06-358, DOD Payments

To Small Businesses: Implementation and Effective Utilization of Electronic Invoicing Could Further Reduce Late Payments, May 2006. Consequently, the Prompt Payment Act was passed in 1983 to partially remedy these impacts by requiring agencies to pay interest on late contract payments. Entitlement is automatic for delays between 45 days and one year.

2.   Coverage.

   a.   The Prompt Payment Act applies to all government contracts except for contracts where payment terms and late payment penalties have been established by other governmental authority (e.g., tariffs). FAR 32.901. See Prompt Payment Act Interest on Utility Bills, B-214479, Sept. 22, 1986, 1986 U.S. Comp. Gen. LEXIS 497. See also National Park Service— Late Payment Charges for Utility Services, B-222944, Oct. 23, 1987, 1987 U.S. Comp. Gen. LEXIS 316 (holding that elements of implied contract governed payment terms with private, unregulated utility company).

   b.   The Prompt Payment Act applies to all government agencies.

   c.   The Prompt Payment Act applies overseas. FAR 32.901. Ingenieurgesellschaft Fuer Technische Dienste, ASBCA No. 42029, 42030, 94-1 BCA ¶ 26,569.

3.   Contract payments are covered by the Prompt Payment Act; some contract financing payments are excluded. The interest penalty at 31 U.S.C. § 3902 only applies to late payments for each complete delivered item of property or service. Payments covered by the Prompt Payment Act include:

   •   Payment for supplies or services accepted by the government;
   •   Payment for partial deliveries accepted by the government under fixed-price contracts;

Financing and Payment

- Final cost or fee payments where the government and the contractor have settled the amounts owed;
- Progress payments under fixed-price architect-engineer contracts (FAR 52.232-26);
- Progress payments under fixed-price construction contracts (FAR 52.232-27); and
- Interim payments on cost reimbursement service contracts (FAR 52.232-25, Alt. 1).

4. Other contract financing payments and interim payments on cost-type contracts for goods are <u>not</u> considered payments for completed items or services. 5 CFR § 1315.2(h).

5. Interest Penalty on Delayed Payments.

   a. When the Prompt Payment Act applies, the government must pay an interest penalty on late payments.

   b. The interest rate is set by the Secretary of the Treasury. <u>See</u> https://www.fiscal.treasury.gov/fsservices/gov/pmt/promptPayment/rates.htm

   c. Generally, a payment is late if it is not paid within 30 days of submission of a proper invoice (seven days for certain perishable food products). If the agency does not believe the invoice is proper, it must notify the contractor within seven days.

   d. When the payment is late, the government must calculate the interest penalty and automatically pay the contract interest on the delayed payment. FAR 52.232-25(a)(4).

6. No interest is due when the reason for nonpayment is a dispute regarding entitlement to payment. FAR 52.232-25(a)(4)(ii); <u>Active Fire Sprinkler Corp. v. General Servs. Admin.</u>, 2001 GSBCA LEXIS 172 (July 11, 2001), WL 782915. GSBCA No. 15318.

7. The interest penalty is not excused by temporary unavailability of funds. FAR 32.907(f).

8. The Prompt Payment Act interest penalty does not accrue after one year. 31 U.S.C. § 3901(d)(3)(A). After one year, the contractor must file a Contract Disputes Act claim for payment with the contracting officer, triggering the application of the interest provisions in that Act. If a contractor files a claim earlier than one year, it will only receive interest under the Contract Disputes Act once the claim is received. <u>Technocratica</u>, ASBCA No. 44444, 94-1 BCA ¶ 26,584.

X. PROMPT PAYMENT DISCOUNTS.

A. **General**. To encourage the government to promptly pay its bills, some vendors offer a small reduction in the contract price under FAR 52.232-8, Discounts for Prompt Payment. The amounts offered are stated in Block 13 of the SF 33.

B. **Entitlement to a Discount.**

1. The government may take prompt payment discounts offered by a contractor only when it makes payment within the specified discount period.

2. Calculating the discount period. The discount period is calculated from the date of the contractor's invoice. If the contractor has not placed a date on the invoice, the due date is calculated from the date the designated billing office receives a proper invoice, provided the agency annotates such invoice with the date of receipt at the time of receipt. When the end of the discount period falls on a Saturday, Sunday, or legal holiday when federal government offices are closed and government business is not expected to be conducted, payment may be made on the following business day and a discount may be taken. FAR 32.906(e).

3.   The Prompt Payment Act imposes an interest penalty on improperly taken discounts. The agency must pay the penalty without request by the contractor. FAR 32.907(b).

XI. CONCLUSION.

Early payment of the contract price is the most important objective of contractors. For that reason, payment terms are an area where the government can bargain with the contractor. The United States government can borrow money much more cheaply than its contractors. Therefore, by providing contract financing, the government can potentially induce contractors to submit lower bids. Conversely, where no financing is provided, the contractor must consider its costs of financing in establishing its price (usually as a higher fee where the cost principles apply). Additionally, different contractors have different costs of financing. Larger profitable contractors present less risk and borrow at lower rates than smaller contractors, or contractors that are less profitable. Thus, contract financing permits small businesses to compete against larger businesses with better access to capital.

Conversely, failing to pay a contractor when promised can cause considerable harm to the contractor's business and its ability to complete the work on schedule. Therefore, where warranted by a contractor's performance deficiencies and where the government accepts the risk of impacting the contractor's continued performance, withholding payment provides great leverage for prompt corrective action.

The regulations addressing contract payments and financing protect the government's interest. Understanding the process, and following it, are key to getting contractors paid for conforming work. Timely paying for conforming work is the right thing to do, it expands the number of competitors, and lowers the overall cost to the government.

INSPECTION, ACCEPTANCE, AND WARRANTY

I. INTRODUCTION.

A fundamental goal of the acquisition process is to obtain quality goods and services. In furtherance of this goal, the government inspects tendered supplies or services to insure that they conform with contract requirements. While the right to inspect and test is very broad, it is not without limits. Occasionally, government inspectors perform unreasonable inspections, rendering the government liable to the contractor for additional costs. Proper inspections are critical, because, once the government accepts a product or service, it cannot revoke its acceptance except in narrowly defined circumstances.

Contractors are very interested in inspections and acceptance because they want to get paid. The quicker the government completes its inspections and accepts the tendered goods and services, the earlier the contractor may invoice for payment.

Attorneys can contribute to the success of the government procurement process by working with government inspectors and contracting officers to insure that each of these individuals understands the government's rights and obligations regarding inspection, acceptance, and warranty under government contracts. Attorneys can assist in drafting provisions that are consistent with established practices, clear, and efficient using the fundamental principle of KISS (Keep It Simple Stupid).

Inspection and testing, however, do not assure a quality product. As successful companies have learned over the past 50 years, product quality is assured by implementing a quality system that identifies and eliminates the causes of defects from the manufacturing process. Quality systems and quality assurance are a separate technical disciplines and various quality systems are described in government and industry specifications and standards. Contractors adopt a suitable quality system, implement tailored practices that meet the requirements of the applicable standard or specification, and may undergo independent assessments to validate that their quality system conforms to the standard or specification. Contractors with such quality systems typically require less government oversight because they control themselves.

II. THE GOVERNMENT'S RIGHT TO INSPECT AND TEST.

A. General.

1. The standard terms and conditions incorporated into Section E in the Uniform Contract Format give the government significant rights and remedies. FAR Part 46 and DFARS Part 246 specify the standard terms and conditions that the government should incorporate into its contracts.

2. The standard clauses contain the minimum requirements that a contractor's quality system must meet for the contract, the government's rights to inspect the work in progress and upon delivery, and the government's available remedies in the event of a delivery of nonconforming goods and services. In a dispute regarding nonconforming supplies and services, the parties should refer, in the first instance, to applicable contractual provisions. See Morton-Thiokol, Inc., ASBCA No. 32629, 90-3 BCA ¶ 23,207 (government denial of cost reimbursement rejected, board noted government's failure to cite Inspection clause).

Inspection, Acceptance & Warranty

B. Inspection Clauses.

1. Unless otherwise provided in the contract, a buyer has the right to inspect tendered supplies and services prior to payment to ensure that it receives conforming supplies. UCC § 2-513(1). FAR Part 46 directs the Contracting Officer to include an appropriate Inspection clause in a contract, further detailing the government's inspection rights for different contract types, and the government's remedies for a contractor's tender of nonconforming goods and services. The clauses are quite detailed.

2. Contract inspections fall into three general categories, depending on the extent of quality assurance needed by the government for the acquisition involved. These include:

   a. Government reliance on inspection by the contractor (FAR 46.202-2);

   b. Standard inspection requirements (FAR 46.202-3); and

   c. Higher-level contract quality requirements (FAR 46.202-4). The latter implement requirements for specific contractor quality systems.

3. The FAR contains several different inspection clauses. In determining which clause to use, consider:

   a. The contract type (e.g., fixed-price, cost-reimbursement, time-and-materials, and labor-hour); and

   b. The nature of the item procured (e.g., supply, service, construction, transportation, or research and development).

   4. Depending upon the specific clauses in the contract, the government has the right to inspect and test supplies, services, materials furnished, work required by the contract, facilities, and equipment at all places and times, and, in any event, before acceptance. See, e.g., FAR 52.246-2 (supplies-

fixed-price), -4 (services-fixed-price), -5 (services-cost-reimbursement), -6 (time-and-materials and labor-hour), -8 (R&D-cost-reimbursement), -9 (R&D), -10 (facilities), and -12 (construction).

C. Quality Systems.

Many contractors have implemented higher-level quality assurance systems for their own benefit. As one shrewd observer has noted, it costs a lot to make defective products. Defective products result in scrapped work, causing losses of material and the labor invested in the defective product. Defective products also cause recall costs, legal liability for personal injury and property damage caused by product failures, and loss of business to competitors.

The most common higher-level quality system requirement is a quality system that complies with International Standards Organization (ISO) Standard 9001. ISO 9001:2008 (the most recent standard) sets out the criteria for a quality management system. It can be used by any organization, large or small, regardless of its field of activity. ISO 9001:2008 is implemented by over one million companies and organizations in over 170 countries. Various third-party organizations can assess and certify an organization's compliance with ISO 9001, although assessment and certification are not required to meet the standard. See ISO Quality Management Principles.

Many government contracts will require contractors to comply with ISO 9001 or equivalent in performing the contract, and to provide evidence that their existing quality system complies with ISO 9001 as part of the contractor's bid or proposal. Many prime contractors include similar requirements in most or all subcontracts, even when not required by the prime contract.

Consequently, maintaining QA system compliant to ISO 9001 is a prerequisite to award of many subcontracts and prime contracts.

Other quality-type systems that may be required for specific prime contracts or subcontracts are: 1) AS 9100C, Quality Management Systems for aviation, space, and defense systems and 2) Software Engineering Institute Capability Maturity Model Integration (SE-CMMI) for systems engineering and software development.

III. RIGHTS UNDER INSPECTION CLAUSES

As previously discussed, there are many different, though similar, inspection clauses in government contracts. For the following discussion, this chapter will refer to the clause applicable to fixed-price contracts for supplies, FAR 52.246-2, Inspection of Supplies — Fixed-Price. Other FAR clauses will contain similar requirements, where appropriate. Attorneys should review the appropriate clause and applicable provision in the contract in question.

A. Typical Inspection and Test Requirements.

1. Definitions.

   a. "Government contract quality assurance" is "the various functions, including inspection, performed by the government to determine whether a contractor has fulfilled the contract obligations pertaining to quality and quantity." FAR 46.101

   b. "Testing" is "that element of inspection that determines the properties or elements of products, including the functional operation of supplies or their components, by the application of established scientific principles and procedures." FAR 46.101

2. Minimum Requirements for a Contractor Quality System.

The government may require a contractor to maintain an inspection system that is adequate to ensure delivery of supplies and services that conform to the requirements of the contract. David B. Lilly Co., ASBCA No. 34678, 92-2

BCA ¶ 24,973 (government ordered contractor to submit new inspection plan to eliminate systemic shortcomings in the inspection process). This requirement appears in FAR 52.246-2(b). A minimally conforming systems must:

- Be acceptable to the government.
- The contractor must keep records evidencing all inspections made under the system, including the results of the inspection.
- The records shall be complete.
- The records must be made available to the government during contract performance and for as long afterwards as the contract requires (see FAR Subpart 4.7).
- Only tender for delivery those supplies that have been inspected in accordance with the contractor's system.

In many contracts, the contractor performs all the inspections and testing under the contract, and provides the government with a "Certificate of Conformance," along with the results of the contractor's inspection and testing. The government's role is merely reviewing the results of the contractors inspection system.

3. Government Inspection and Testing.

The standard inspection clauses (see FAR 52.246-2(c)) give the government the right to inspect and test:

- all supplies called for by the contract, to the extent practicable,
- at all places and times, including the during manufacture, and in any event before acceptance.
- The government assumes no contractual obligation to perform any inspection and test for the benefit of the contractor unless specifically set forth in the contract.
- The government shall perform inspections and tests in a manner that will not unduly delay the contractor's work.

Inspection, Acceptance & Warranty

4. While the government's rights to inspect and test are broad, they are not wholly unconstrained. Government inspection and testing must reasonably relate to the determination of whether performance is in compliance with contractual requirements.

a. Contractually specified inspections or tests are presumed reasonable unless they conflict with other contract requirements. General Time Corp., ASBCA No. 22306, 80-1 BCA ¶ 14,393.

b. If the contract specifies a test, the government may not require a higher level of performance than measured by the method specified. United Technologies Corp., Sikorsky Aircraft Div. v. United States, 27 Fed. Cl. 393 (1992).

c. The government may use tests other than those specified in the contract provided the tests do not impose a more stringent standard of performance. Donald C. Hubbs, Inc., DOT BCA No. 2012, 90-1 BCA ¶ 22,379 (use of rolling straight-edge permitted after initial inspection determined that road was substantially nonconforming); Puroflow Corp., ASBCA No. 36058, 93-3 BCA ¶ 26,191 (board upholds government's rejection of First Article Test Report for contractor's failure to perform an unspecified test).

d. Absent contractually specified tests, the government may use any tests that do not impose different or more stringent standards than those required by the contract. Space Craft, Inc., ASBCA No. 47997, 98-1 BCA ¶ 29,341 (government reasonably measured welds on clamp assemblies); Davey Compressor Co., ASBCA No. 38671, 94-1 BCA ¶ 26,433; Al Johnson Constr. Co., ENG BCA No. 4170, 87-2 BCA ¶ 19,952.

e. If the contract specifies no particular tests, consider the following factors in selecting a test or inspection technique:

(1) Consider the intended use of the product or service. A-Nam Cong Ty, ASBCA No. 14200, 70-1 BCA ¶ 8,106 (unreasonable to test coastal water barges on the high seas while fully loaded).

(2) Measure compliance with contractual requirements, and inform the contractor of the standards it must meet. Service Eng'g Co., ASBCA No. 40275, 94-1 BCA ¶ 26,382 (board refused to impose a military standard on contract for ship repair, where contract simply required workmanship in accordance with "best commercial marine practice"); Tester Corp., ASBCA No. 21312, 78-2 BCA ¶ 13,373, mot. for recon. denied, 79-1 BCA ¶ 13,725.

(3) Use standard industry tests, if available. DiCecco, Inc., ASBCA No. 11944, 69-2 BCA ¶ 7,821 (use of USDA mushroom standards upheld). But see Chelan Packing Co., ASBCA No. 14419, 72-1 BCA ¶ 9,290 (government inspector failed to apply industry standard properly).

(4) The government must inspect and test correctly. Baifield Indus., Div. of A-T-O, Inc., ASBCA No. 13418, 77-1 BCA ¶ 12,308 (cartridge cases/ rounds fired at excessive pressure).

(5) Generally, the government is not required to perform inspections. Cannon Structures, Inc., AGBCA No. 90-207-1, 93-3 BCA ¶ 26,059. See FAR 52.246-2(c).

(a) The government's failure to discover defects during inspection does not relieve the contractor of the requirement to tender conforming supplies. FAR 52.246-2(c); George Ledford Constr., Inc., ENGBCA No. 6218, 97-2 BCA ¶ 29,172.

(b) However, the government may not unreasonably deny a contractor's request to perform preliminary or additional testing. Alonso & Carus Iron Works, Inc., ASBCA No. 38312, 90-3 BCA ¶ 23,148 (no liability for defective fuel tank because government refused to allow a preliminary water test not prohibited by the contract); Praoil, S.R.L., ASBCA No. 41499, 94-2 BCA ¶ 26,840 (government unreasonably refused contractor's request, per industry practice, to perform retest of fuel; termination for default overturned).

(6) Requiring a contractor to perform tests not specified in the contract may entitle the contractor to an equitable adjustment of the contract price. CBI NA-CON, Inc., ASBCA No. 42268, 93-3 BCA ¶ 26,187.

5. Costs of Inspection and Testing.

a. In a firm fixed-price contract, the contractor bears the costs of contractor inspection and testing similar to any other cost of performance.

b. The burden of paying for government inspection and testing depends on the clause used in the contract. For supplies, generally the contractor pays for all reasonable facilities and assistance for the safe and convenient performance of government inspectors. FAR 52.246-2 (d). The government pays for all expenses for inspections or tests at other than the contractor or subcontractor's premises. FAR 52.246-2 (d).

c. Re-inspections. If supplies are not ready for tests or inspections, the contractor may be charged for the additional costs of re-inspection or tests. FAR 52.246-2 (e)(1). The contractor may also be charged for additional costs of inspection following a prior rejection. FAR 52.246-2 (e)(2).

d. The government is required to perform tests and inspections in a manner that will not unnecessarily delay the work. FAR 52.246-2(b). The government may engage in destructive testing, i.e. examining already completed work by removing it or tearing it out, or by performing tests that result in the destruction of the supplies. Generally, the government bears the costs of destructive testing, unless the work is defective.

e. If a test is found to be unreasonable, courts and boards may find that the government assumed the risk of loss resulting from an unreasonable test. See Alonso & Carus Iron Works, Inc., ASBCA No. 38312, 90-3 BCA ¶ 23,148.

IV. GOVERNMENT REMEDIES UNDER THE INSPECTION CLAUSE.

A. Introduction.

1. The inspection clauses give the government significant remedies for nonconforming work. FAR 46.407; FAR 52.246-2(f)-(i) ; DFARS 246.407

2. The government's remedies under the inspection clauses operate in two phases. Initially, the government may demand correction of deficiencies. If this proves to be unsuccessful, the government may

obtain corrective action from other sources.

3.   Under the inspection clauses, the government's remedies depend upon when the contractor delivers nonconforming goods or services.

B.   Defective Performance <u>BEFORE</u> the Required Delivery Date.

1.   If the contractor delivers defective goods or services before the required delivery date, the government may:

a.   Reject the tendered product or performance. FAR 52.246-2(f); <u>Andrews, Large & Whidden, Inc. and Farmville Mfg. Corp.</u>, ASBCA No. 30060, 88-2 BCA ¶ 20,542 (government demand for replacement of nonconforming windows sustained); <u>But see</u> <u>Centric/Jones Constr.</u>, IBCA No. 3139, 94-1 BCA ¶ 26,404 (government failed to prove that rejected work was noncompliant with specifications; contractor entitled to equitable adjustment for performing additional tests to secure government acceptance);

b.   Require the contractor to correct the nonconforming goods or service, giving the contractor a reasonable opportunity to do so. FAR 52.246-2(g); <u>Premiere Bldg. Servs., Inc.</u>, B-255858, Apr. 12, 1994, 94-1 CPD ¶ 252 (government may charge re-inspection costs to contractor); or,

c.   Accept the non-conforming goods or services at a reduced price. FAR 52.246-2(h)(1); <u>Federal Boiler Co.</u>, ASBCA No. 40314, 94-1 BCA ¶ 26,381 (change in cost of performance to the contractor, not the damages to the government, is the basis for adjustment); <u>Blount Bros. Corp.</u>, ASBCA No. 29862, 88-2 BCA ¶ 20,644 (government entitled to a credit totaling the amount saved by contractor for using nonconforming concrete). <u>See also</u> <u>Valley Asphalt</u>

<u>Corp.</u>, ASBCA No. 17595, 74-2 BCA ¶ 10,680 (although runway built to wrong elevation, only nominal price reduction allowed because no loss in value to the government).

2.   The government may not terminate the contract for default based on the tender of nonconforming goods or services before the required delivery date.

C.   Defective Performance <u>ON</u> the Required Delivery Date.

1.   If the contractor delivers nonconforming goods or services on the required delivery date, the government may:

a.   Reject or require correction of the nonconforming goods or services;

b.   Reduce the contract price and accept the nonconforming product; or

c.   Terminate for default if performance is not in substantial compliance with the contract requirements. <u>See</u> FAR 52.249-6 to 52.249-10. When the government terminates a contract for default, it acquires rights and remedies under the Termination clause, including the right to reprocure supplies or services similar to those terminated and charge the contractor the additional costs. <u>See</u> FAR 52.249-8(b).

2.   If the contractor has complied substantially with the requirements of the contract, the government must give the contractor notice and the opportunity to correct minor defects before terminating the contract for default. <u>Radiation Tech., Inc. v. United States</u>, 366 F.2d 1003 (Ct. Cl. 1966).

D.   Defective Performance <u>AFTER</u> the Required Delivery Date.

1.   Generally, the government may terminate the contract for default.

2. If the contractor has complied substantially with the requirements of the contract, albeit after the required delivery date, the government should give the contractor notice of the defects and an opportunity to correct them. See Franklin E. Penny Co. v. United States, 524 F.2d 668 (Ct. Cl. 1975) (late nonconforming goods may substantially comply with contract requirements).

3. The government may accept nonconforming goods or services at a reduced price.

E. Remedies if the Contractor Fails to Correct Defective Performance.

If the contractor fails to correct defective performance after receiving notice and a reasonable opportunity to correct the work, the government may:

1. Contract with a commercial source to correct or replace the defective goods or services (obtaining funding is often difficult and may make this remedy impracticable), George Bernadot Co., ASBCA No. 42943, 94-3 BCA ¶ 27,242; Zimcon Professionals, ASBCA Nos. 49346, 51123, 00-1 BCA ¶ 30,839 (government may contract with a commercial source to correct or replace the defective goods or services and may charge cost of correction to original contractor);

2. Correct or replace the defective goods or services itself;

3. Accept the nonconforming goods or services at a reduced price, or;

4. Terminate the contract for default. FAR 52.246-4(f); Firma Tiefbau Meier, ASBCA No. 46951, 95-1 BCA ¶ 27,593.

F. Special Rules for Service Contracts.

1. The inspection clause for fixed-price service contracts, FAR 52.246-4, is different than FAR 52.246-2, which pertains to fixed-price supply contracts.

2. The government's remedies depend on whether it is possible for the contractor to perform the services correctly.

a. Normally, the government should permit the contractor to re-perform the services and correct the deficiencies, if possible. Pearl Properties, HUD BCA No. 95-C-118-C4, 96-1 BCA ¶ 28,219 (government's failure to give contractor notice and an opportunity to correct deficient performance waived right to reduce payment).

b. Otherwise, the government may:

(1) Require the contractor to take adequate steps to ensure future compliance with the contract requirements; and

(2) Reduce the contract price to reflect the reduced value of services received. Teltara, Inc., ASBCA No. 42256, 94-1 BCA ¶ 26,485 (government properly used random sampling inspections to calculate contract price reductions); Orlando Williams, ASBCA No. 26099, 84-1 BCA ¶ 16,983 (although termination for default (T4D) of janitorial contract was sustained, the government acted unreasonably by withholding maximum payments when some work had been performed satisfactorily). Even if it reduces the contract price, the government may also recover consequential damages. Hamilton Securities Advisory Servs., Inc. v. United States, 46 Fed. Cl. 164 (2000).

c. Authorities disagree about whether the same failure in contract performance can support both a reduction in contract price and a termination for default. Compare W.M. Grace, Inc., ASBCA No. 23076, 80-1 BCA ¶ 14,256 (monthly deductions due to poor performance waived right to T4D during those months) and <u>Wainwright Transfer Co.</u>, ASBCA No. 23311, 80-1 BCA ¶ 14,313 (deduction for HHG shipments precluded termination) <u>with Cervetto Bldg. Maint. Co. v. United States</u>, 2 Cl. Ct. 299 (1983) (reduction in contract price and termination cumulative remedies).

V. STRICT COMPLIANCE VS. SUBSTANTIAL COMPLIANCE.

A. **Common Law.** The common law doctrine of substantial performance does not apply to government contracts. The doctrine of substantial performance is a legal principle that says that if a good faith attempt is made to perform the requirements of the agreement, even if it does not precisely meet the terms of the agreement or statutory requirements, the performance will still be considered complete if the essential purpose is accomplished. However, this is subject to claim of damages for shortfall. A seller when sued for nonperformance cannot avoid paying damages by showing it substantially performed or came near to performing the requirements of the contract.

B. **Strict Compliance.**

1. As a general rule, the government is entitled to strict compliance with its specifications. <u>Blake Constr. Co. v. United States</u>, 28 Fed. Cl. 672 (1993); <u>De Narde Construction Co.</u>, ASBCA No. 50288, 00-2 BCA ¶ 30,929 (government entitled to type of rebar it ordered, even if contrary to trade practice). <u>See also Cascade Pac. Int'l v. United States</u>, 773 F.2d 287 (Fed. Cir. 1985); <u>Ace Precision Indus.</u>, ASBCA No. 40307, 93-2 BCA ¶ 25,629 (government rejection of line block final assemblies that failed to meet contract specifications was proper). <u>But see Zeller Zentralheizungsbau GmbH</u>, ASBCA No. 43109, 94-2 BCA ¶ 26,657 (government improperly rejected

contractor's use of "equal" equipment where contract failed to list salient characteristics of brand name equipment).

2. Contractors must comply with specifications even if they vary from standard commercial practice. <u>R.B. Wright Constr. Co. v. United States</u>, 919 F.2d 1569 (Fed. Cir. 1990) (contract required three coats over painted surface although commercial practice was to apply only two); <u>Graham Constr., Inc.</u>, ASBCA No. 37641, 91-2 BCA ¶ 23,721 (specification requiring redundant performance sustained).

3. Slight defects are still defects. <u>Mech-Con Corp.</u>, GSBCA No. 8415, 88-3 BCA ¶ 20,889 (installation of 2-inch pipe insulation did not satisfy 1½-inch requirement).

C. **Substantial Compliance.**

1. "Substantial compliance" is a judicially created concept to avoid the harsh result of termination for default based upon a minor breach, and to avoid economic waste. The concept originated in construction contracts and has been extended to other types of contracts. <u>See Radiation Tech., Inc. v. United States</u>, 366 F.2d 1003 (Ct. Cl. 1966).

2. Substantial Performance Distinguished. Under the doctrine of substantial performance, a contractor is potentially liable for damages, but need not correct the defective work. The doctrine of "substantial compliance" gives the contractor the right to cure defective performance.

3. The elements of substantial compliance are:

    a. Timely delivery;

    b. Contractor's good faith belief that it has complied with the contract's requirements, <u>see Louisiana Lamps & Shades</u>, ASBCA No. 45294, 95-1 BCA ¶ 27,577 (no substantial compliance because contractor had attempted unsuccessfully to persuade government to permit substitution of American-made sockets for specified German-made sockets);

   c. Minor defects;

   d. Defects that can be corrected within a reasonable time; and

   e. Time is <u>not</u> of the essence, i.e., the government does not require strict compliance with the delivery schedule.

4. Generally, the doctrine of substantial compliance does not require the government to accept defective performance by the contractor. <u>Cosmos Eng'rs, Inc.</u>, ASBCA No. 19780, 77-2 BCA ¶ 12,713. Except in those rare situations involving economic waste, the doctrine of substantial compliance still requires the contractor to correct its nonconforming work.

5. Substantial compliance does not preclude termination for default if the contractor fails to correct defective performance. The government:

   a. Must give the contractor a reasonable amount of time to correct its work, including, if necessary, an extension beyond the original required delivery date.

   b. May terminate for default if the contractor fails to correct defects within a reasonable period of time. <u>Firma Tiefbau Meier</u>, ASBCA No. 46951, 95-1 BCA ¶ 27,593 (termination for default justified by contractor's repeated refusal to correct defective roof panels).

D. Substantial Compliance and Late Delivery?

1. <u>Radiation Technology</u>, <u>supra</u>, established the concept of substantial compliance for the timely delivery of nonconforming goods. <u>Franklin E. Penny Co. v. United States</u>, <u>supra</u>, arguably expanded the concept to include late delivery of nonconforming goods.

2. The courts and boards have not widely followed <u>Penny</u>; however, they have not overruled it.

E. Economic Waste.

1. Common Law. The doctrine of "economic waste" is a limitation on remedies where the cost of correcting noncompliant work is grossly disproportionate to the benefits of correction, and the nonconforming work is suitable for its intended purpose. Economic waste applies to government contracts.

2. The doctrine of economic waste requires the government to accept noncompliant construction if the work, as completed, is suitable for its intended purpose and the cost of correction would far exceed the gain that would be realized. <u>Granite Constr. Co. v. United States</u>, 962 F.2d 998 (Fed. Cir. 1992), <u>cert. denied</u>, 113 S. Ct. 965 (1993); <u>A.D. Roe Co., Inc.</u>, ASBCA No. 48782, 99-2 BCA ¶ 30,398 (economic waste is exception to general rule that government can insist on strict compliance with contract terms).

3. To be "suitable for its intended purpose," the work must substantially comply with the contract. <u>Amtech Reliable Elevator Co. v. General Servs. Admin.</u>, GSBCA No. 13184, 95-2 BCA ¶ 27,821 (no economic waste where contractor used conduits for fire alarm wiring that were not as sturdy as required by specifications and lacked sufficient structural integrity); <u>Triple M Contractors</u>, ASBCA No. 42945, 94-3 BCA ¶ 27,003 (no economic waste where initial placement of reinforcing materials in drainage gutters reduced useful life from 25 to 20 years); <u>Shirley Constr. Corp.</u>, ASBCA No. 41908, 93-3 BCA ¶ 26,245 (concrete slab not in substantial compliance even though it could support the design load; without

substantial compliance, doctrine of economic waste inapplicable); Valenzuela Engineering, Inc., ASBCA No. 53608, 53936, 04-1 BCA ¶ 32,517 (absent expert testimony, government can demand strict performance for structure designed to contain explosions).

4. Unlike substantial completion, where the contractor is given time to correct the nonconforming work, economic waste excuses further performance. The government's remedy is the reduction in value for the nonconforming performance (normally the contractor's cost savings).

VI. PROBLEM AREAS IN TESTING AND INSPECTION.

A. Contractor Claims for Unreasonable Inspections.

1. Government inspections may give rise to equitable adjustment claims if they delay the contractor's performance or cause additional work. The government:

    a. Must perform reasonable inspections. FAR 52.246-2. Donald C. Hubbs, Inc., DOT BCA No. 2012, 90-1 BCA ¶ 22,379 (more sophisticated test than specified, rolling straight-edge, was reasonable).

    b. Must avoid overzealous inspections. The government may not inspect to a level beyond that authorized by the contract. Overzealous inspection may impact adversely upon the government's ability to reject the contractor's performance, to assess liquidated damages, or to otherwise assert its rights under the contract. See The Libertatia Associates, Inc., 46 Fed. Cl. 702 (2000) (COR told contractor's employees that he was Jesus Christ and that CO was God); Gary Aircraft Corp., ASBCA No. 21731, 91-3 BCA ¶ 24,122 ("overnight change" in inspection standards was unreasonable); Donohoe Constr. Co., ASBCA No.

47310, 98-2 BCA ¶ 30,076, motion for reconsideration granted in part on other grounds, ASBCA No. 47310, 99-1 BCA ¶ 30,387 (government quality control manager unreasonably rejected proposed schedules, ignored contractor submissions for weeks, and told contractor he would "get even" with him).

c. Must resolve ambiguities involving inspection requirements in a timely manner. P & M Indus., ASBCA No. 38759, 93-1 BCA ¶ 25,471.

d. Must exercise reasonable care when performing tests and inspections prior to acceptance of products or services, and may not rely solely on destructive testing of products after acceptance to discover a deficiency it could have discovered before acceptance. Ahern Painting Contractors, Inc., GSBCA No. 7912, 90-1 BCA ¶ 22,291.

2. Improper inspections:

    a. May excuse a contractor's delay, thereby delaying or preventing termination for default. Puma Chem. Co., GSBCA No. 5254, 81-1 BCA ¶ 14,844 (contractor justified in refusing to proceed when government test procedures subjected contractor to unreasonable risk of rejection).

    b. May justify claims for increased costs of performance under the delay of work or changes clauses in the contract. See, e.g., Hull-Hazard, Inc., ASBCA No. 34645, 90-3 BCA ¶ 23,173 (contract specified joint inspection, however, government conducted multiple inspections and bombarded contractor with "punch lists"); H.G. Reynolds Co., ASBCA No. 42351, 93-2 BCA ¶ 25,797; Harris Sys. Int'l, Inc., ASBCA No. 33280, 88-2 BCA ¶ 20,641 (10% "spot mopping" specified, government demanded 100% for "uniform appearance"). But see Trans

Western Polymers, Inc. v. Gen. Servs. Admin., GSBCA No. 12440, 95-1 BCA ¶ 27,381 (government properly performed lot-by-lot inspection after contractor failed to maintain quality control system); Space Dynamics Corp., ASBCA No. 19118, 78-1 BCA ¶ 12,885 (defects in aircraft carrier catapult assemblies justified increased government inspection).

c. May give rise to a claim of government breach of contract. Adams v. United States, 358 F.2d 986 (Ct. Cl. 1966) (government breached contract when inspector disregarded inspection plan, doubled inspection points, complicated construction, delayed work, increased standards, and demanded a higher-quality tent pin than specified); Electro-Chem Etch Metal Markings, Inc., GSBCA No. 11785, 93-3 BCA ¶ 26,148. But see Southland Constr. Co., VABCA No. 2217, 89-1 BCA ¶ 21,548 (government engineer's "harsh and vulgar" language, when appellant contributed to the tense atmosphere, did not justify refusal to continue work); Olympia Reinigung GmbH, ASBCA Nos. 50913, 51225, 51258, 02-2 BCA ¶ 32,050 (allegation of aggressive government inspections did not render contract termination for default arbitrary or capricious).

3. It is a constructive change to test a standard commercial item to a higher level of performance than is required in commercial practice. Max Blau & Sons, Inc., GSBCA No. 9827, 91-1 BCA ¶ 23,626 (insistence on extensive deburring and additional paint on a commercial cabinet was a constructive change).

4. Government breach of its duty to cooperate with the contractor may shift the cost of damages caused by testing to the government. See Alonso & Carus Iron Works, Inc., ASBCA No. 38312, 90-3 BCA ¶ 23,148 (government refusal to

permit reasonable, preliminary test proposed by contractor shifted the risk of loss to the government).

B. **Waiver, Prior Course of Dealing, and Other Acts Affecting Testing and Inspection.**

1. By his actions, an authorized government official may waive contractual requirements if the contractor reasonably believes that a required specification has been suspended or waived. Gresham & Co. v. United States, 470 F.2d 542, 554 (Ct. Cl. 1972), Perkin-Elmer's Corp. v. United States, 47 Fed. Cl. 672 (2000).

2. The government may also be estopped from enforcing a contract requirement. The elements of equitable estoppel are:

   a. Authorized government official;

   b. Knowledge by government official of true facts;

   c. Ignorance by contractor of true facts; and

   d. Detrimental reliance by the contractor. Longmire Coal Corp., ASBCA No. 31569, 86-3 BCA ¶ 19,110.

3. Normally, previous government acceptance of similar nonconforming performance is insufficient to demonstrate waiver of specifications.

   a. Government acceptance of nonconforming performance by other contractors normally does not waive contractual requirements. Moore Elec. Co., ASBCA No. 33828, 87-3 BCA ¶ 20,039 (government's allowing deviation to another contractor on prior contract for light pole installation did not constitute waiver, even where both contractors used the same subcontractor).

   b. Government acceptance of nonconforming performance by the same contractor normally does not waive contractual requirements. <u>Basic Marine, Inc.</u>, ENG BCA No. 5299, 87-1 BCA ¶ 19,426.

4. Numerous government acceptances of similar nonconforming performance by the same contractor may waive the requirements of that particular specification. <u>Gresham & Co. v. United States</u>, 470 F.2d 542 (Ct. Cl. 1972) (acceptance of dishwashers without detergent dispensers eventually waived requirement to equip with dispensers); <u>Astro Dynamics, Inc.</u>, ASBCA No. 28381, 88-3 BCA ¶ 20,832 (acceptance of seven shipments of rocket tubes with improper dimensions precluded termination for default for same reason on the eighth shipment). <u>But see</u> <u>Kvass Constr. Co.</u>, ASBCA No. 45965, 94-1 BCA ¶ 26,513 (Navy's acceptance on four prior construction contracts of "expansion compensation devices" for a heat distribution system did not waive contract requirement for "expansion loops").

5. Generally, an inspector's failure to require correction of defects is insufficient to waive the right to demand correction. <u>Hoboken Shipyards, Inc.</u>, DOT BCA No. 1920, 90-2 BCA ¶ 22,752 (government not bound by an inspector's unauthorized agreement to accept improper type of paint if a second coat was applied).

VII. ACCEPTANCE.

A. Definition.

Acceptance is the "act of an authorized representative of the government that asserts ownership of identified supplies tendered or approves specific services rendered as partial or complete performance of the contract." FAR 46.101.

B. General Principles of Acceptance.

1. Acceptance is <u>conclusive</u> except for latent defects, fraud, gross mistakes amounting to fraud, or as otherwise provided for in the contract, e.g., warranties. FAR 52.246-

2(k); <u>Hogan Constr., Inc.</u>, ASBCA No. 39014, 95-1 BCA ¶ 27,398 (government improperly terminated contract for default after acceptance). Unlike commercial law, conclusive acceptance means the government may no longer claim damages for breach by delivery of nonconforming supplies or services. This doctrine, however, is substantially limited by the common practices of including warranty clauses and requiring certificates of conformance. Where delivery of nonconforming supplies or services was the result of knowing or reckless conduct, the government has other remedies. <u>See</u> Chapter 33.

2. Acceptance entitles the contractor to payment.

3. Acceptance means that title passes from the contractor to the government. FAR 52.246-16.

4. The government generally uses a DD Form 250 to expressly accept tendered goods or services.

5. Implied Acceptance. The government may impliedly accept goods or services by:

    a. Making final payment. <u>Norwood Precision Prods.</u>, ASBCA No. 24083, 80-1 BCA ¶ 14,405. <u>See also</u> <u>Farruggio Constr. Co.</u>, DOT CAB No. 75-2-75-2E, 77-2 BCA ¶ 12,760 (progress payments on wharf sheeting contract did not shift ownership and risk of loss to the government). Note, however, that payment, even if no more monies are due under a contract, does not necessarily constitute final acceptance. <u>Spectrum Leasing Corp.</u>, GSBCA No. 7347, 90-3 BCA ¶ 22,984 (no acceptance because contract provided that final testing and acceptance would occur after the last payment). <u>See also</u> <u>Ortech, Inc.</u>, ASBCA No. 52228, 00-1 BCA ¶ 30,764 (a contractor's acceptance of final payment from the government may preclude a later claim by the contractor).

b. Unreasonably delaying acceptance. See, e.g., Cudahy Packing Co. v. United States, 75 F. Supp. 239 (Ct. Cl. 1948) (government took two months to reject eggs); Mann Chem. Labs, Inc. v. United States, 182 F. Supp. 40 (D. Mass. 1960).

c. Using or changing a product. Ateron Corp., ASBCA No. 46,867, 96-1 BCA ¶ 28,165 (government use of products inconsistent with contractor's ownership); The Interlake Cos. v. General Servs. Admin., GSBCA No. 11876, 93-2 BCA ¶ 25,813 (government improperly rejected material handling system after government changes rendered computer's preprogrammed logic useless).

6. Unconditional acceptance of partial deliveries may waive the right to demand that the final product perform satisfactorily. See Infotec Dev., Inc., ASBCA No. 31809, 91-2 BCA ¶ 23,909 (multi-year contract for Minuteman Missile software).

7. As a general rule, contractors bear the risk of loss or damage to the contract work prior to acceptance. See FAR 52.246-16, Responsibility for Supplies (supply); FAR 52.236-7, Permits and Responsibilities (construction). See also Meisel Rohrbau GmbH, ASBCA No. 40012, 92-1 BCA ¶ 24,716 (damage caused by children); DeRalco Corp., ASBCA No. 41306, 91-1 BCA ¶ 23,576 (structure destroyed by 180 MPH hurricane winds although construction was 97% complete and only required to withstand 100 MPH winds); G&C Enterprises, Inc. v. United States, 55 Fed. Cl. 424 (2003) (no formal acceptance where structure destroyed by windstorm after project 99% complete and Army had begun partial occupation) .

a. If the contract specifies f.o.b. destination, the contractor bears the risk of loss during shipment even if the government accepted the supplies prior to shipment. FAR 52.246-16; KAL M.E.I. Mfg. & Trade Ltd., ASBCA No. 44367, 94-1 BCA ¶ 26,582 (contractor liable for full purchase price of cover assemblies lost in transit, even though cover assemblies had only scrap value).

b. In construction contracts, the government may use and possess the building prior to completion. FAR 52.236-11, Use and Possession Prior to Completion. The contractor is relieved of responsibility for loss of or damage to work resulting from the government's possession or use. See Fraser Eng'g Co., VABCA No. 3265, 91-3 BCA ¶ 24,223 (government responsible for damaged cooling tower when damage occurred while tower was in its sole possession and control).

C. **Exceptions to the Finality of Acceptance.**

1. Latent defects may enable the government to avoid the finality of acceptance. To be latent, a defect must have been:

a. Unknown to the government. See Gavco Corp., ASBCA No. 29763, 88-3 BCA ¶ 21,095;

b. In existence at the time of acceptance. See Santa Barbara Research Ctr., ASBCA No. 27831, 88-3 BCA ¶ 21,098; mot. for recon. denied, 89-3 BCA ¶ 22,020 (failure to prove crystalline growths were in laser diodes at the time of acceptance and not reasonably discoverable); and

c. Not discoverable by a reasonable inspection. Munson Hammerhead Boats, ASBCA No. 51377, 00-2 BCA ¶ 31,143 (defects in boat surface, under paint and deck covering, not

Inspection, Acceptance & Warranty

reasonably discoverable by government till four months later); <u>Stewart & Stevenson Services, Inc.</u>, ASBCA No. 52140, 00-2 BCA ¶ 31,041 (government could revoke acceptance even though products passed all tests specified in contract); <u>Wickham Contracting Co.</u>, ASBCA No. 32392, 88-2 BCA ¶ 20,559 (failed spliced telephone and power cables were latent defects and not discoverable); <u>Dale Ingram, Inc.</u>, ASBCA No. 12152, 74-1 BCA ¶ 10,436 (mahogany plywood was not a latent defect because a visual examination would have disclosed); <u>but see</u> <u>Perkin-Elmer Corp. v. United States.</u>, 47 Fed. Cl. 672 (2000) (six years was too long to wait before revoking acceptance based on latent defect).

2. Contractor fraud allows the government to avoid the finality of acceptance. <u>See</u> <u>D&H Constr. Co.</u>, ASBCA No. 37482, 89-3 BCA ¶ 22,070 (contractors' use of counterfeited National Sanitation Foundation and Underwriters' Laboratories labels constituted fraud). To establish fraud, the government must prove that:

a. The contractor intended to deceive the government;

b. The contractor misrepresented a material fact; and

c. The government relied on the misrepresentation to its detriment. <u>BMY – Combat Sys. Div. Of Harsco Corp.</u>, 38 Fed. Cl. 109 (1997) (contractor's knowing misrepresentation of adequate testing was fraud); <u>United States v. Aerodex, Inc.</u>, 469 F.2d 1003 (5th Cir. 1972).

3. A gross mistake amounting to fraud may avoid the finality of acceptance. The elements of a gross mistake amounting to fraud are—

a. A major error causing the government to accept nonconforming performance;

b. The contractor's misrepresentation of a fact, <u>Bender GmbH,</u> ASBCA No. 52266, 2004-1 B.C.A. (CCH) ¶ 32,474 (repeated false invoices in "wanton disregard of the facts" allowed government to revoke final acceptance); and

c. Detrimental government reliance on the misrepresentation. <u>Z.A.N. Co.</u>, ASBCA No. 25488, 86-1 BCA ¶ 18,612 (gross mistake amounting to fraud established where the government relied on Z.A.N. to verify watch caliber and Z.A.N. accepted watches from subcontractor without proof that the caliber was correct);

4. Warranties. Warranties operate to revoke acceptance if the nonconformity is covered by the warranty.

5. Revocation of Acceptance.

a. Once the government revokes acceptance, its normal rights under the inspection, disputes, and default clauses of the contract are revived. FAR 52.246-2(l) (Inspection-Supply clause expressly revives rights); <u>Spandome Corp. v. United States</u>, 32 Fed. Cl. 626 (1995) (government revoked acceptance, requested contractor to repair structure, and demanded return of purchase price when contractor refused); <u>Jo-Bar Mfg. Corp.</u>, ASBCA No. 17774, 73-2 BCA ¶ 10,311 (contractor's failure to heat treat aircraft bolts entitled government to recover purchase price paid). <u>Cf.</u> FAR 52.246-12 (Inspection-Construction clause is silent on reviving rights).

b. Failure to timely exercise revocation rights may waive the government's contractual right to revoke acceptance. <u>Perkin-Elmer's Corp. v. United States</u>, 47 Fed. Cl. 672 (2000)

(Air Force attempted to revoke acceptance of "portable wear metal analyzer" six years after acceptance; Court of Federal Claims held the six-year delay in revoking acceptance was unreasonable, thus prohibiting government recovery on the claim).

VIII. WARRANTY.

A.   General Principles.

1.   Warranties may extend the period for conclusive government acceptance. FAR 46.7; DFARS 246.7; AR 700-139, ARMY WARRANTY PROGRAM (9 Feb 04).

2.   Warranties may be express or implied. Fru-Con Constr. Corp., 42 Fed. Cl. 94 (1998) (design specifications result in an implied warranty; no implied warranty with performance specifications because of the broader discretion afforded the contractor in their implementation).

3.   Normally, warranties are defined by the time and scope of coverage.

4.   The use of warranties is not mandatory. FAR 46.703. In determining whether a warranty is appropriate for a specific acquisition, consider:

a.   Nature and use of the supplies or services;

b.   Cost;

c.   Administration and enforcement;

d.   Trade practice; and

e.   Reduced quality assurance requirements, if any.

f.   GSA schedule contracts may no longer routinely provide commercial warranties.

B.   Asserting Warranty Claims.

1.   When asserting a warranty claim, the government must prove:

a.   That there was a defect when the contractor completed performance. Vistacon Inc. v. General Servs. Admin., GSBCA No. 12580, 94-2 BCA ¶ 26,887;

b.   That the warranted defect was the most probable cause of the failure. Hogan Constr., Inc., ASBCA No. 38801, 95-1 BCA ¶ 27,396, A.S. McGaughan Co., PSBCA No. 2750, 90-3 BCA ¶ 23,229; R.B. Hazard, Inc., ASBCA No. 41061, 91-2 BCA ¶ 23,709 (government denied recovery under warranty theory because it failed to prove that pump failure was not the result of government misuse and that defective material or workmanship was the most probable cause of the damage);

c.   That the defect was within the scope of the warranty;

d.   That the defect arose during the warranty period;

e.   That the contractor received notice of the defect and its breach of the warranty, Land O'Frost, ASBCA Nos. 55012, 55241, 2003 B.C.A. (CCH) ¶ 32,395 (Army's warranty claim failed to provide specific notice of a defect covered by the warranty); and

f.   The cost to repair the defect, if not corrected by the contractor. Hoboken Shipyards, Inc., DOT BCA No. 1920, 90-2 BCA ¶ 22,752. See Globe Corp., ASBCA No. 45131, 93-3 BCA ¶ 25,968 (board reduced government's claim against the contractor because the government inconsistently allocated the cost of repairing the defects).

2.   The government may invalidate a warranty through improper maintenance, operation, or alteration.

3.   A difficult problem in administering warranties on government contracts is

identifying and reporting defects covered by the warranty.

4.   Warranty clauses survive acceptance. <u>Shelby's Gourmet Foods</u>, ASBCA No. 49883, 01-1 BCA ¶ 31,200 (government entitled to reject defective "quick-cooking rolled oats" under warranty even after initial acceptance).

C.   Remedies for Breach of Warranty.

The FAR provides the basic outline for governmental remedies. <u>See</u> FAR 52.246-17 and 52.246-18. If the contractor breaches a warranty clause, the government may—

1.   Order the contractor to repair or replace the defective product;

2.   Retain the defective product at a reduced price;

3.   Correct the defect in-house or by contract if the contractor refuses to honor the warranty; or

4.   Permit an equitable adjustment in the contract price. However, the adjustment cannot reduce the price below the scrap value of the product.

D.   Mitigation of Damages.

1.   The government must attempt to mitigate its damages.

2.   The government may recover consequential damages. <u>Norfolk Shipbldg. and Drydock Corp.</u>, ASBCA No. 21560, 80-2 BCA ¶ 14,613 (government entitled to cost of repairs caused by ruptured fuel tank).

IX. CONCLUSION.

During the past forty years, a revolution has occurred in the government's approach to managing a contractor's quality system. In the middle of the 20th century, the government had large teams of inspectors at contractors facilities to inspect items tendered for delivery, and large teams of inspectors at receiving locations to inspect goods as they were delivered, depending on the point of acceptance. Today, the government uses government inspection much less frequently, and inspects the contractor's quality system for consistent implementation of procedures that prevents delivery of non-conforming goods and services. This follows best practices in quality assurance. It is complemented by the government's purchasing of warranties to provide an effective remedy for delivery of non-conforming goods.

The inspection clauses, however, were written in a different time. While they have been modified to include the requirements of modern quality assurance practices, the major thrust assumes inspection by the government at the source. The government's rights to inspect, and accept or reject goods are significant, comprehensive, and the result of many lessons learned from the prior era.

CONTRACT CHANGES

I.   INTRODUCTION.

The government has an extraordinary right to unilaterally change the terms of its contracts. In similar contracts between private parties, the right to unilaterally change the terms is either narrowly prescribed or nonexistent. In consideration of this right, the contract gives the contractor an equitable adjustment in the contract price and schedule.

This chapter addresses the procedures for changing a contract and the scope of the Changes clause.

Generally, government contracts are not perfect when awarded. During performance, many changes may be required in order to fix inaccurate or defective specifications, react to newly encountered circumstances, or modify the work to ensure the contract meets changing government requirements. Any changes made to a government contract may force a contractor to perform more work, or to perform in an often more costly fashion, and may require additional funding. Unfortunately, the parties do not always agree on the scope, value, or even the existence of a contract change. Contract changes account for a significant portion of contract litigation. All of this makes understanding contract changes a key skill for a government contract attorney.

A.   References.

1.   Federal Acquisition Regulation (FAR) part 43, 50.1, 52.243-1 to 7, 52.233-1.

2.   John Cibinic, Ralph Nash and James Nagle, Administration of Government Contracts, Ch. 4, Changes (4th ed., 2006).

3.   Ralph C. Nash, Jr. & Steven W. Feldman, Government Contract Changes (3d ed. 2007).

II.   FORMAL CONTRACT CHANGES.

A.   What Are "Formal" Changes?

The Changes clause assumes that the government drafts a flawless contract and administers that contract without error. Where subsequent events reveal the need to change some of the terms, such as the specification, place of delivery, packaging for shipment, etc., then the Changes clause presumes that the contracting officer will promptly issue a change order directing the contractor to perform the contract, as changed, and to submit a request for an equitable adjustment. This contracting officer order and the process related to this action are "formal" changes.

B.   Types of Formal Changes.

1.   Administrative changes. A unilateral written change that does not affect the substantive rights of the parties. FAR 43.101. Examples of administrative changes are a change in paying office or a change in telephone number for an agency point of contact. Contracting officers routinely issue unilateral administrative changes communicating such minor revisions that have no cost impact.

2.   Change order. A unilateral, written order, signed by the contracting officer, directing the contractor to make a change that a Changes clause authorizes, with or without the contractor's consent. FAR 2.101 and 43.201. A change order is substantive in nature, altering the terms and conditions of the contract as permitted by the Changes clause by adding, deleting, or changing the work required. By issuing a change order, the contracting officer grants the contractor a right to an equitable adjustment for the impact of the change on the price and schedule. For example, the contracting officer might unilaterally order the contractor to paint

the goods a different color than that stated in the specification.

3. Bilateral modification. A contract modification signed by the contractor and the contracting officer, i.e., a supplemental agreement. FAR 43.103(a). Bilateral modifications are used for:

   a. Changes authorized by the Changes clause where the price and schedule adjustment is negotiated in advance.

   b. The amount of the equitable adjustment to the contract price and schedule negotiated after issuance of a unilateral change order;

   c. Definitizing a letter contract; and

   d. Incorporating other agreements of the parties affecting the terms of a contract, including changes outside the scope of the Changes clause.

C. Modifying a Contract.

1. Authority. As discussed in chapter 3, only contracting officers acting within the scope of their authority may execute contract modifications. FAR 43.102(a); Hensel Phelps Constr. Co., GSBCA Nos. 14744, 14877, 01-1 BCA ¶ 31,249; Daly Constr., Inc., ASBCA No. 34322, 92-1 BCA ¶ 24,469; Commercial Contractors, Inc., ASBCA No. 30675, 88-3 BCA ¶ 20,877.

2. Format. Contracting officers typically issue contract modifications, either unilateral or bilateral, on a SF 30, "Amendment of Solicitation/Modification of Contract." FAR 43.301; Staff, Inc., AGBCA Nos. 96-112-1, 96-159-1, 97-2 BCA ¶ 29,285 (oral modifications are unenforceable); Texas Instr., Inc. v. United States, 922 F.2d 810 (Fed. Cir. 1990); Daly Constr., Inc., ASBCA No. 34322, 92-1 BCA ¶ 24,469; but see Robinson Contracting Co. v. United States, 16 Cl. Ct. 676 (1989) (SF 30 not required). A copy of an SF30 is provided at Appendix D.

3. Definitization. Definitization is the process of reaching bilateral agreement on the price and schedule adjustment due to a unilateral change. Preferably, the contracting officer will price modifications before executing them, if this can be done without adversely affecting the interests of the government. If the parties cannot reach price prior to execution, the contracting officer should attempt to negotiate a maximum price unless impractical. FAR 43.102(b).

4. Timing. The contracting officer may order a change at any time prior to final payment on the contract. Final payment means payment in the full amount of the contract balance owed, received, and accepted by the contractor after delivery of supplies or the performance of services, with the understanding that no further payments are due. See Design & Prod., Inc. v. United States, 18 Cl. Ct. 168 (1989); Gulf & Western Indus., Inc. v. United States, 6 Cl. Ct. 742 (1984).

D. Prerequisites for Formal Changes.

1. The government must receive a benefit. G. Issaias & Co. (Kenya), ASBCA No. 30359, 88-1 BCA ¶ 20,441; Northrop Grumman Computing Sys. Inc., GSBCA No. 16367, 2006-2 BCA ¶ 33,324.

2. The contracting officer must confirm the availability of the sufficient funds of the proper type. Otherwise, the contracting officer must try to condition the government's obligation based on availability of funds or include a ceiling. FAR 43.105; DOD 7000.14-R, vol. 3, ch. 8, para. 080304.C–E; DFAS-IN Reg. 37-1, tbl. 8-7; AFI 65-601, vol. I, para. 6.3.7 and Figure 6.1.

III. SCOPE OF CHANGES CLAUSE.

A. Purpose of the Clause.

The purpose of the Changes clause is give the contracting officer the right to direct specific types of changes in the contract terms without breaching the contract. The contractor is obligated to proceed with the work, as changed, and is entitled to receive an equitable adjustment in the contract price and schedule.

B.   Limitations.

1.   Contracting officers do not have the right to unilaterally change every term and condition in the contract. The power to issue unilateral changes is limited to those provisions specified in the Changes clause. BMY Div. of Harsco Corp., ASBCA No. 36926, 91-1 BCA ¶ 23,565 (contracting officer could not unilaterally change the warranty terms). For example, in a fixed-price supply contracts, the contracting officer has the unilateral right to change: (a) drawings, designs, or specifications when the supplies to be furnished are to be specially manufactured for the government; (b) the method of shipment or packing; and (c) the place of delivery. The contracting officer cannot unilaterally change the specification when buying a brand name product, the delivery schedule, or the quantity of goods purchased.

2.   A change, either unilateral or bilateral, must be within the general scope of the contract. See FAR 52.243-1(a) (make changes within the general scope of this contract). For example, the government cannot direct a submarine contractor to build an aircraft or a tank.

C.   Scope Determinations.

1.   Most decisions on whether a particular change is within the general scope of the contract are made by contracting officers and their legal advisors. When the agency desires to change the contract, the contracting officer (usually with legal advice) determines whether the change is within the contract's general scope. If so, then the contracting officer may issue the change order. If not, the contracting officer must decide between various alternatives, such as: (a) terminating the contract and recompeting, (b) preparing a J&A justifying a sole source acquisition from the incumbent, (c) acquiring the out-of-general-scope work as a separate

requirement, or (d) proceeding no further with the change.

2.   Bid protests alleging out-of-general-scope changes.

a.   When an agency modifies a contract to acquire a change outside the general scope of the original contract, other prospective competitors may have a basis to file a bid protest. An out-of-general-scope modification essentially constitutes an improper sole-source contract award, unless a J&A has been prepared and approved. See Engineering & Prof'l Servs., Inc., B-289331, Jan. 28, 2002, 2002 CPD ¶ 24 (if the protestor alleges that a contract modification is out-of-scope of the original contract, an exception exists to the GAO's restriction on reviewing contract administration matters because, absent a valid sole-source determination, the work covered by the modification would be subject to the statutory requirements for competition).

b.   GAO and the COFC review the allegedly improper change to determine whether the change so materially altered the contract that the field of competition for the contract as modified would be significantly different from that obtained for the original contract as awarded, i.e., the scope of competition. AT&T Communications, Inc. v. Wiltel, Inc., 1 F.3d 1201, 1205 (Fed. Cir. 1993) (holding a modification falls within the scope of the original procurement if potential offerors would have reasonably anticipated such a change prior to initial award); Phoenix Air Group, Inc. v. United States, 46 Fed. Cl. 90 (2000); DOR Biodefense, Inc., B-296358.3 et al., 2006 CPD ¶ 35 (a modification is in-scope if the solicitation for the original contract adequately advised offerors of the potential for the type of change found in the modification); Engineering & Professional Svcs., Inc., B-289331, 2002 U.S. Comp. Gen. LEXIS 11; Hughes Space and Communications Co., B276040, 97-1 CPD ¶ 158.

c. In Hughes Space and Communications Co., B-276040, 97-1 CPD ¶ 158, the GAO considered the following factors in determining whether the modification was in-scope:

- The extent of any changes in the contract as awarded and as modified in the type of work, the performance period, and the difference in costs;
- Whether the agency had historically procured the services under a separate contract; and
- Whether potential offerors would have anticipated the modification.

3. Contractor Challenges Under the CDA. The contractor receiving a change may allege the change was out of the general scope of the original contract in a contract dispute. The contractor's motivation for doing so may include a desire to recover breach damages, or to defend against a termination for non-performance. Courts and boards review allegations of out-of-general-scope changes by examining whether the modification, "should be regarded as having been fairly and reasonably within the contemplation of the parties when the contract was entered into." Freund v. United States, 260 U.S. 60 (1922); Shank-Artukovich v. United States, 13 Cl. Ct. 346 (1986); Air-A-Plane Corp. v. United States, 408 F.2d 1030 (Ct. Cl. 1969); GAP Instrument Corp., ASBCA No. 51658, 01-1 BCA ¶ 31,358; Gassman Corp., ASBCA Nos. 44975, 44976, 00-1 BCA ¶ 30,720.

Of course, a contractor receiving an out-of-general-scope change that it can perform successfully and profitably has little motivation to complain.

D. **Significant Factors When Determining the General Scope.**

1. Changes in the Function of the Item or the Type of Work.

a. In determining the materiality of a change, the most important factor to consider is the extent to which a product or service, as changed, differs from the requirements of the original contract. See E. L. Hamm & Assocs., Inc., ASBCA No. 43792, 94-2 BCA ¶ 26,724 (change from lease to lease/purchase was out-of-scope); Matter of: Makro Janitorial Servs., Inc., B-282690, Aug. 18, 1999, 99-2 CPD ¶ 39 (task order for housekeeping outside scope of an IDIQ contract for preventive maintenance); Hughes Space and Communications Co., B-276040, May 2, 1997, 97-1 CBD ¶ 158; Aragona Constr. Co. v. United States, 165 Ct. Cl. 382 (1964).

b. Substantial changes in the work may be in-scope if the parties entered into a broadly conceived contract. AT&T Communications, Inc. v. Wiltel, Inc., 1 F.3d 1201 (Fed. Cir. 1993) (more latitude allowed where the activity requires a state-of-the-art product); Engineering & Professional Svcs., Inc., B-289331, 2002 U.S. Comp. Gen. LEXIS 11 (provision of technologically advanced, ruggedized, handheld computers was not beyond the scope of the original contract that called for a wide array of hardware and software and RFP indicated the engineering change proposal process would be utilized to implement technological advances); Paragon Sys., Inc., B-284694.2, 2000 CPD ¶ 114 (contract awarded for broad range of services given wide latitude when issuing a task order); Gen. Dynamics Corp. v. United States, 585 F.2d 457 (Ct. Cl. 1978).

c. An agency's pre-award statements that certain work was outside the scope of the contract can bind the agency if it later attempts to modify the contract to include the work. Octel Communications Corp. v. Gen. Servs. Admin., GSBCA No. 12975-P, 95-1 BCA ¶ 27,315.

2. Changes in Quantity.

   a. Generally, increases in quantities of goods and services procured are out or general scope. The contracting officer must justify a change adding quantity as a sole-source procurement. Decreases in quantity are generally partial terminations for convenience. Cf. Lucas Aul, Inc., ASBCA No. 37803, 91-1 BCA ¶ 23,609 (order was deductive change, not partial termination).

   b. Major increases and decreases in the quantity of items or portions of the work on indefinite quantity type contracts may not be "within the scope" of the contract. See, e.g., Valley Forge Flag Co., Inc., VABCA Nos. 4667, 5103, 97-2 BCA ¶ 29,246 (a major increase (over 109,000) in a requirements contract was outside the scope of the contract); Liebert Corp., B-232234.5, Apr. 29, 1991, 91-1 CPD ¶ 413 (order in excess of maximum quantity was a material change). But see Master Security, Inc., B-274990, Jan. 14, 1997, 97-1 CPD ¶21 (tripling the number of worksites not out-of-scope change); Caltech Serv. Corp., B-240726.6, Jan. 22, 1992, 92-1 CPD ¶ 94 (increase in cargo tonnage on containerization requirements contract was within scope).

   c. Generally, the Changes clause permits increases and decreases in the quantity of minor items or portions of the work unless the variation alters the entire bargain. See Connor Bros. Const. Co. v.

United States, 65 Fed. Cl. 657 (2005) (modification of ductwork in Army hospital was not an out-of-scope change). Cf. Lucas Aul, Inc., ASBCA No. 37803, 91-1 BCA ¶ 23,609. See also Kentucky Bldg. Maint., Inc., ASBCA No. 50535, 98-2 BCA ¶ 29,846 (holding that agency clause that supplements the standard Changes clause was not illegal).

3. Number and Cost of Changes.

   a. Neither the number nor the cost of changes alone dictates whether modifications are beyond the scope of a contract. PCL Constr. Serv., Inc. v. United States, 47 Fed. Cl. 745 (2000) (series of contract modifications did not constitute cardinal change); Triax Co. v. United States, 28 Fed. Cl. 733 (1993); Reliance Ins. Co. v. United States, 20 Cl. Ct. 715 (1990), aff'd, 931 F.2d 863 (Fed. Cir. 1991) (over 200 changes still held to be within scope); Coates Indus. Piping, Inc., VABCA No. 5412, 99-2 BCA ¶ 30,479; Combined Arms Training Sys., Inc., ASBCA Nos. 44822, 47454, 96-2 BCA ¶ 28,617; Bruce-Andersen Co., ASBCA No. 35791, 89-2 BCA ¶ 21,871.

   b. However, the cumulative effect of a large number of changes is controlling. Air-A-Plane Corp. v. United States, 408 F.2d 1030 (Ct. Cl. 1969) (dispute involving over 1,000 changes sent back for trial on merits). See Caltech Serv. Corp., B-240726-6, Jan. 22, 1992, 92-1 CPD ¶ 94 at 5 (a 30% increase in workload volume was not beyond the scope of the original contract).

4. Changes in Time of Performance.

   a. The supply contract Changes clause does not authorize unilateral acceleration of performance. FAR 52.243-1(a).

b. Under the service contract Changes clause, the contracting officer may unilaterally change "when" a contractor is to perform but not the overall performance period. FAR 52.243-1, Alternate I.

c. The construction contract Changes clause authorizes the government to order unilateral acceleration of performance. FAR 52.243-4(a)(4).

d. The business reason for the differences between supply and construction contracts is that supply contract schedules are often fixed by production capacity and component lead times. Construction schedules have greater flexibility.

e. Granting a contractor additional time to perform will normally be considered within scope. Saratoga Indus., Inc., B-247141, 92-1 CPD ¶ 397.

5. Acceptance of a Change.

a. If a contractor performs under a change order, the contractor may not subsequently argue that the change was out of general scope and a breach of contract. Amertex Enter., Ltd. v. United States, 1997 U.S. App. LEXIS 3301 (Fed. Cir. 1997), cert. denied, 522 U.S. 1075 (1998); Silberblatt & Lasker, Inc. v. United States, 101 Ct. Cl. 54 (1944); C.E. Lowther & Son, ASBCA No. 26760, 85-2 BCA ¶ 18,149. Similarly, once the contractor waives the breach and performs, the government is obligated to pay for the out-of-scope work. Mac-Well Co., ASBCA No. 23097, 79-2 BCA ¶ 13,895.

b. Agreeing to a change does not convert an out-of-scope change into one that is within the scope of the contract for competition purposes. It simply means that the parties have agreed to process the change under the Changes clause. The contracting officer may not use modifications to avoid the statutory mandate for competition. Corbin Superior Composites, Inc., B-235019, July 20, 1989, 89-2 CPD ¶ 67.

c. A bilateral modification including a price for a change operates as an accord and satisfaction to further adjustment claims arising from the modification. Corners and Edges, Inc., CBCA nos. 693, 762, Sept. 23, 2008; Trataros Constr., Inc. v. Gen. Servs. Admin., GSBCA No. 15344, 03-1 BCA ¶ 32,251; Cygnus Corp. v. United States, 63 Fed. Cl. 150 (2004) aff'd, 177 Fed. Appx. 186 (Fed. Cir. 2006) (finding no government liability arising from bilateral modification eliminating database from option year of contract and repricing option year work).

E. **The Duty to Continue Performance.**

1. The standard Changes and Disputes clauses require the contractor to continue performance pending the resolution of a dispute over an in-scope change. See FAR 52.233-1(i), Disputes; FAR 52.243-1(e),Changes—Fixed-Price; see also FAR 33.213, Obligation to continue performance.

2. Conversely, a contractor has no duty to proceed diligently with performance pending resolution of any dispute concerning a change outside-the-general scope of the contract. See FAR 52.233-1(i). Alliant Techsys., Inc. v United States, 178 F.3d 1260 (Fed. Cir. 1999); CTA Inc., ASBCA No. 47062, 00-2 BCA ¶ 30,947; Airprep Tech., Inc. v. United States, 30 Fed. Cl. 488 (1994). An out-of-scope change is also called a "cardinal change"—a change to the contract that is so material that it cannot be redressed under the contract, thus rendering the government in breach. Thomson and Pratt Ins. Assoc., Inc., GSBCA No. 15979-ST, 2005-1 BCA ¶ 32,944.

3. Exceptions to the contractor's duty to proceed.

   a. The government withholds progress payments improperly. See Sterling Millwrights v. United States, 26 Cl. Ct. 49 (1992). But see D.W. Sandau Dredging, ENG BCA No. 5812, 96-1 BCA ¶ 28,064 (holding two late payments of 12 days and 19 days did not discharge the contractor from its duty to continue performance where contractor did not demonstrate the late payments had impacted its ability to perform).

   b. Continued performance is impractical. See United States v. Spearin, 248 U.S. 132 (1918) (government refused to provide safe working conditions); Xplo Corp., DOT BCA No. 1289, 86-3 BCA ¶ 19,125.

   c. The government fails to provide the contractor with clear direction. See James W. Sprayberry Constr., IBCA No. 2130, 87-1 BCA ¶ 19,645 (contractor justified to await clarification of defective specifications). Cf. Starghill Alternative Energy Corp., ASBCA Nos. 49612, 49732, 98-1 BCA ¶ 29,708 (a one-month government delay in executing modification did not excuse contractor from proceeding).

4. FAR 52.233-1, Alt. 1, the all disputes clause, requires the contractor to continue to perform even if the government orders a cardinal change, or otherwise breaches the contract. The alternate version is often included in defense contracts. See DFARS 233.215 (mandating use of this alternate clause under certain circumstances). Where included, the contractor must perform, notwithstanding a cardinal change or other breach of contract. See FAR 52.233-1(i), Alt 1.

IV. OVERVIEW OF CONSTRUCTIVE CHANGES.

A. General.

The constructive changes doctrine is a judicially created doctrine designed to address the harsh consequences of earlier versions of the contract disputes process. In the past, a contractor had to pursue breach of contract cases before the U.S. Claims Court. The contractor had to pursue claims resolvable under remedy-granting clauses in the contract through the contracting officer, with a right of appeal to the agency board of contract appeals. Contractors often felt that no matter which forum they chose, the government would allege they were in the wrong forum. Additionally, if a contractor received an adverse BCA decision based on factual findings, the contractor would allege that their claim was, in fact, a breach claim, and seek de novo review at the Court of Claims.

The jurisdiction of Boards of Contract Appeals gradually expanded in two ways. First, the government drafted contracts to include more remedy granting clauses for specific types of claims. Second, the BCAs and U.S. Court of Claims held that certain common disputes were redressable under the Changes clause as "constructive changes." With the Contract Disputes Act of 1978, the jurisdictional differences were (mostly) eliminated, but the constructive changes doctrine continued.

B. Elements of a Constructive Change. The Sherman R. Smoot Corp., ASBCA Nos. 52173, 53049, 01-1 BCA ¶ 31,252; Green's Multi-Services, Inc., EBCA No. C-9611207, 97-1 BCA ¶ 28,649; Dan G. Trawick III, ASBCA No. 36260, 90-3 BCA ¶ 23,222.

1. A change occurred either as the result of government action or inaction. Kos Kam, Inc., ASBCA No. 34682, 92-1 BCA ¶ 24,546;

2. The contractor did not perform voluntarily. Jowett, Inc., ASBCA No. 47364, 94-3 BCA ¶ 27,110; and

3. The change resulted in an increase (or a decrease) in the cost or the time of performance. Advanced Mech. Servs., Inc., ASBCA No. 38832, 94-3 BCA ¶ 26,964.

C. Types of Constructive Changes.

The Boards of Contract Appeals recognize that the Changes clauses provide an equitable adjustment for the following types of claims:

1. Contract interpretation disputes;

2. Defective government specifications;

3. Government and Interference and failure to cooperate;

4. Failure to disclose vital information (superior knowledge); and

5. Constructive acceleration of contractor performance.

V. CONTRACT INTERPRETATION PRINCIPLES.

A. Contract Interpretation Disputes.

When the government and the contractor disagree about a contractual provision, the government normally insists that the contractor perform consistent with the government's interpretation. This insistence can be a direct order to perform, a threat to default terminate, or an erroneous rejection of conforming goods or services. Doing so constructively changes the terms of the contract.

B. Main Issues. Ralph C. Nash, Jr., Government Contract Changes, 11-2 (2d ed. 1989).

1. Did the government's interpretation originate from an employee with authority to interpret the terms? See J.F. Allen Co. & Wiley W. Jackson Co., a Joint Venture v. United States, 25 Cl. Ct. 312 (1992).

2. Did the contractor perform work that the contract did not require?

3. Did the contractor timely notify the government of the impact of the government's interpretation?

C. Contract Interpretation Process.

1. A judge must interpret a contract when the parties do not agree on the meaning of its terms. Fruin-Colon Corp. v. United States, 912 F.2d 1426 (Fed. Cir. 1990). Judges often expressly or implicitly follow a framework when analyzing contract interpretation issues.

2. Step One. Is the contract language ambiguous? Courts faced with interpretation disputes usually begin by examining whether the language is ambiguous.

   a. The Federal Circuit has held that: "When deriving this meaning, we begin with the contract's language. Coast Fed. Bank, FSB v. United States, 323 F.3d 1035, 1038 (Fed. Cir. 2003) (en banc). When the contract's language is unambiguous it must be given its 'plain and ordinary' meaning and the court may not look to extrinsic evidence to interpret its provisions. Id. at 1040."

   b. Although extrinsic evidence may not be used to interpret an unambiguous contract provision, we have looked to it to confirm that the parties intended for the term to have its plain and ordinary meaning. See Coast Fed. Bank, 323 F.3d at 1040.

   c. When a provision in a contract is susceptible to more than one reasonable interpretation, it is ambiguous. Edward R. Marden Corp. v. United States, 803 F.2d 701, 705 (Fed. Cir. 1986), and we may then resort to extrinsic evidence to resolve the ambiguity. See McAbee Constr. v. United States, 97 F.3d at 1435 (Fed Cir. 1996).

d. In determining whether the language is ambiguous, the courts will look to the entire contract, not just the particular phrase a party asserts is clear. Hol-Gar Mfg. Corp. v. United States, 351 F.2d 972, 975 (Ct. Cl. 1965).

e. In summary, the courts look to the language of the entire contract to determine whether the contract is unambiguous on a particular issue. It will consider evidence outside the contract to determine whether an ambiguity exists, but unless the court finds ambiguity, it will enforce the contract as written, without considering other evidence of meaning. This is known as the "no parol evidence" rule. Unfortunately, ambiguous language is not uncommon in government contracts.

3. Step Two. Should the judge conclude the language is ambiguous, he or she will consider additional evidence to determining the parties' intent. Interpreting ambiguous contract language objective is the intent of the parties at the time they entered into the contract. See Firestone Tire & Rubber Co. v. United States, 444 F.2d 547 (Ct. Cl. 1971). The court will review:

a. The language of the contract—intrinsic evidence of intent; and/or

b. The facts and circumstances surrounding contract formation and performance—extrinsic evidence of intent.

4. Intrinsic Evidence of Intent.

a. In determining the objective intent of the parties, first examine the terms of the contract. See, e.g., U.S. Eagle, Inc., ASBCA No. 41093, 92-1 BCA ¶ 24,371.

b. Interpret the contract as a whole. Coast Federal Bank, FSB v. United States, 02-5032, (Ct. App. Fed. Cir. Mar. 24, 2003); M.A. Mortenson

Co. v. United States, 29 Fed. Cl. 82 (1993) (courts must give reasonable meaning to all parts of the contract and not render any portions of the contract meaningless); Hol-Gar Mfg. Corp. v. United States, 351 F.2d 972 (Ct. Cl. 1965); Bay Ship & Yacht Co., DOT BCA No. 2913, 96-1 BCA ¶ 28,236 (contract must be read as a whole, giving reasonable meaning to all its terms). See also Sheladia Constr. Corp., VABCA No. 3313, 91-3 BCA ¶ 24,111 (contractor may not ignore requirement merely because it is not stated in normal section of the specifications); Oakland Constr. Co., ASBCA No. 43986, 93-2 BCA ¶ 25,867 (prime contractor responsible for omission in bid caused by subcontractor's failure to bid on contract requirement because subcontractors only received portion of specification from prime contractor). Give effect to all provisions without rendering meaningless any term of the contract. GPA-I, Ltd. P'ship. v. United States, 46 Fed. Cl. 762 (2000); B.D. Click Co. v. United States, 614 F.2d 748 (Ct. Cl. 1980); Jamsar, Inc. v. United States, 442 F.2d 930 (Ct. Cl. 1971); Rex Sys., Inc., ASBCA No. 45874, 94-1 BCA ¶ 26,370; Elec. Genie, Inc., ASBCA No. 40535, 93-1 BCA ¶ 25,307. Interpret a contract in harmony with the contract's principal purpose. Maddox Indus. Contractors, Inc., ASBCA No. 36091, 88-3 BCA ¶ 21,037; Restatement (Second) of Contracts § 203(a) (1981).

c. Definition of terms. If a contract defines a term, an alternate definition cannot be substituted—the definition must be used. Sears Petroleum & Transp. Corp., ASBCA No. 41401, 94-1 BCA ¶ 26,414. Where the contractual parties have not adopted a definition, give ordinary terms their

Changes

plain and ordinary meaning in defining the rights and obligations of the parties. T.E.C. Constr. v. VA Med. Ctr., 33 Fed. Cl. 363 (1995); Elden v. United States, 617 F.2d 254 (Ct. Cl. 1980); Alive & Well Int'l, Inc., ASBCA No. 51850, 00-1 BCA ¶ 30,778 (since contract left the term "discover" undefined, interpret in accordance with the ordinary meaning). Give technical terms their technical meanings. Specialized or trade meanings take precedence over "lay" meanings. See Western States Constr. Co. v. United States, 26 Cl. Ct. 818 (1992).

(1) Give scientific and engineering terms their recognized technical meanings unless defined otherwise in the contract, or the context or an applicable usage indicates a contrary intention. American Mechanical, Inc., ASBCA No. 52033, 03-1 BCA ¶ 32,134; Tri-Cor, Inc. v. United States, 458 F.2d 112 (Ct. Cl. 1972); Coastal Drydock & Repair Corp., ASBCA No. 31894, 87-1 BCA ¶ 19,618.

(2) Similarly, give terms unique to government contracts their technical meanings. Gen. Builders Supply Co. v. United States, 409 F.2d 246 (Ct. Cl. 1969) (meaning of "equitable adjustment").

d. Lists of items. Lists are presumed exclusive (i.e., only the listed items are included) unless qualified. J.A. Jones Constr. Co., ENG BCA No. 6164, 95-1 BCA ¶ 27,482; Santa Fe Engr's, Inc., ASBCA No. 48331, 95-1 BCA ¶ 27,505. Use the phrase "including, but not limited to" to designate a nonexclusive list. Nonexclusive lists are presumed to include only similar, unspecified items. "Words, like men, are known

by the company they keep. The meaning of a doubtful word may be ascertained by reference to the meaning of words with which they are associated." C.W. Roberts Constr. Co., ASBCA No. 12348, 68-1 BCA ¶ 6819. See also United States v. Turner Constr. Co., 819 F.2d 283 (Fed. Cir. 1987) (unreasonable to include unmentioned item in a list where unmentioned item was most expensive component).

e. Order of precedence. To resolve inconsistencies, order of precedence clauses establish priorities among different sections of the contract. See, e.g., FAR 52.214-29, Order of Precedence–Sealed Bidding; FAR 52.215-8, Order of Precedence–Uniform Contract Format; FAR 52.236-21, Specifications and Drawings for Construction.

In construction contracts, a contractor may rely on the order of precedence clause to resolve a discrepancy between the specifications and drawings even if a discrepancy is patent or known to the contractor prior to bid submission. Hensel Phelps Constr. Co. v. United States, 886 F.2d 1296 (Fed. Cir. 1989); C Constr. Co., ASBCA No. 38098, 91-2 BCA ¶ 23,923; Hull-Hazard, Inc., ASBCA No. 34645, 90-3 BCA ¶ 23,173. See also Shah Constr. Co. Inc., ASBCA No. 50411, 01-1 BCA ¶ 31,330.

In non-construction contracts, drawings trump specifications. FAR 52.215-8.

f. Omissions. Construction contracts typically include a standard clause that states that the contractor shall perform omitted details of work that are necessary to carry out the intent of the drawings and specifications or that are performed customarily. DFARS 252.236-7001; M.A.

Mortenson Co., ASBCA No. 50383, 00-2 BCA ¶ 30,936 (holding that contractor should have known elevator would require rail support columns despite their omission from drawings); Single Ply Sys., Inc., ASBCA No. 42168, 91-2 BCA ¶ 24,032; Hull-Hazard, Inc., ASBCA No. 34645, 90-3 BCA ¶ 23,173.

5. Extrinsic Evidence of Intent.

   a. Do not consider extrinsic evidence if the contract terms are clear—if the intent of the parties can be ascertained from the contract terms. See Coast Federal Bank, FSB v. United States, 323 F.3d 1035 (Fed. Cir. 2003) ; C. Sanchez & Son, Inc. v. United States, 24 Cl. Ct. 14 (1991), rev'd on other grounds, 6 F.3d 1539 (Fed. Cir. 1993); D&L Constr. Co., AGBCA No. 97-205-1, 00-1 BCA ¶ 31,001; Skyline Technical Constr. Servs., ASBCA No. 51076, 98-2 BCA ¶ 29,888 (since contract was clear, no extrinsic evidence allowed).

   b. Pre-award communications. Under the Explanation to Prospective Bidders clause, a prospective bidder can request an explanation or interpretation of the solicitation, drawings, or specifications. See FAR 52.214-6 (sealed bidding); Max Drill, Inc. v. United States, 192 Ct. Cl. 608 (1970); Turner Constr. Co. v. Gen. Servs. Admin., GSBCA No. 11361, 92-3 BCA ¶ 25,115 (contractor could not rely on pre-award statement that was inconsistent with the solicitation terms); Community Heating & Plumbing Co., ASBCA No. 37981, 92-2 BCA ¶ 24,870.

   Statements made at pre-bid conferences may bind the government. Cessna Aircraft Co., ASBCA No. 48118, 95-2 BCA ¶ 27,560; Gen. Atronics Corp.,

ASBCA No. 46784, 94-3 BCA ¶ 27,112. Cf. Orbas & Assoc., ASBCA No. 33359, 87-2 BCA ¶ 19,742 (contractor who did not attend pre-bid conference was not bound by explanation of provision where solicitation should have explained provision).

   Pre-award acceptance of contractor's cost-cutting suggestion was binding on the government. See Pioneer Enters., Inc., ASBCA No. 43739, 93-1 BCA ¶ 25,395.

   c. Actions during contract performance. The way in which the parties behave prior to the dispute surfacing often reveals the intent of the parties. Courts and boards afford these actions great weight when determining the meaning of a provision. Drytech, Inc., ASBCA No. 41152, 92-2 BCA ¶ 24,809; Macke Co. v. United States, 467 F.2d 1323 (Ct. Cl. 1972).

   d. Prior course of dealing. The parties' history of dealing on past contracts may demonstrate their specific understanding of contract terms. Superstaff, Inc., ASBCA No. 46112, 94-1 BCA ¶ 26,574; American Transp. Line, Ltd., ASBCA No. 44510, 93-3 BCA ¶ 26,156; L.W. Foster Sportswear Co. v. United States, 405 F.2d 1285 (Ct. Cl. 1969). The parties must be aware of the prior course of dealing. Gresham & Co. v. United States, 470 F.2d 542 (Ct. Cl. 1972); T. L. Roof & Assocs., ASBCA No. 38928; 93-2 BCA ¶ 25,895; Snowbird Indus., ASBCA No. 33027, 89-3 BCA ¶ 22,065.

   The government's prior waivers of specifications must be numerous or consistent to vary an unambiguous contract term. Doyle Shirt Mfg. Corp., 462 F.2d 1150 (Ct. Cl. 1972); LP Consulting Group v. United States, 66 Fed. Cl. 238 (2005) (holding 36 instances of waiver sufficient to establish course of dealing); Cape Romain Contractors, Inc., ASBCA Nos. 50557, 52282, 00-1 BCA ¶ 30,697 (one waiver does not establish a course of dealing); Kvaas Constr. Co., ASBCA No. 45965, 94-1 BCA ¶ 26,513 (four waivers not enough); Gen. Sec. Servs. Corp. v. Gen. Servs. Admin., GSBCA No. 11381, 92-2 BCA ¶ 24,897 (no waiver based on waivers in six previous contracts because GSA sought to enforce requirement in current contract).

e. Custom or trade usage/industry standard. The parties may not use custom and trade usage to contradict unambiguous terms. WRB Corp. v. United States, 183 Ct. Cl. 409, 436 (1968); C. Sanchez & Son, Inc. v. United States, 24 Cl. Ct. 14 (1991), rev'd on other grounds, 6 F.3d 1539 (Fed. Cir. 1993); All Star/SAB Pacific, J.V., ASBCA No. 50856, 99-1 BCA ¶ 30,214; Riley Stoker Corp., ASBCA No. 37019, 92-3 BCA ¶ 25,143 (contract terms were ambiguous); Harold Bailey Painting Co., ASBCA No. 27064, 87-1 BCA ¶ 19,601 (used to define "spot painting").

Parties may resort to custom and trade usage to explain or define unambiguous terms. W.G. Cornell Co. v. United States, 376 F.2d 299 (Ct. Cl. 1967).

Parties also may use an industry standard or custom or trade usage to show that a contract term is ambiguous if a party reasonably relied on a competing interpretation of the term. Metric Constructors, Inc. v. NASA, 169 F.3d 747 (Fed. Cir. 1999) (contractor reasonably relied on trade practice and custom to show that the specifications were susceptible to different

interpretations); Gholson, Byars, & Holmes Constr. Co. v. United States, 351 F.2d 987 (Ct. Cl. 1965); Western States Constr. Co. v. United States, 26 Cl. Ct. 818 (1992).

f. The party asserting the industry standard or trade usage bears the burden of proving the existence of the standard or usage. Roxco, Ltd., ENG BCA No. 6435, 00-1 BCA ¶ 30,687; DWS, Inc., Debtor in Possession, ASBCA No. 29743, 93-1 BCA ¶ 25,404.

D. Allocation of Risk for Ambiguous Language.

1. If a contract is susceptible to more than one reasonable interpretation after seeking the parties' original intent, it contains an ambiguity. GPA-I, Ltd. P'ship. v. United States, 46 Fed. Cl. 762 (2000); Metric Constructors, Inc. v. NASA, 169 F.3d 747 (Fed. Cir. 1999). Two rules apply when the court is unable to determine the intent of the parties at the time of contract award. These rules allocate the risk of ambiguous language to the party that should be ultimately responsible.[1]

2. Construe the ambiguity against the drafter (or *contra proferentem)*. Peter Kiewit Sons' Co. v. United States, 109 Ct. Cl. 390 (1947).

a. If one cannot resolve an ambiguity under the contract interpretation rules, construe the ambiguity against the drafter. Emerald Maint., Inc., ASBCA No. 33153, 87-2 BCA ¶ 19,907; WPC Enter. v. United States, 323 F.2d 874 (Ct. Cl. 1963).

b. "[*Contra proferentem*] puts the risk of ambiguity, lack of clarity, and absence of proper warning on the drafting party which could have forestalled the controversy; it pushes the drafters toward improving

---

[1] The risk allocation principles do not apply to ambiguities in procurement regulations. Santa Fe Eng'rs, Inc. v. United States, 801 F.2d 379 (Fed. Cir. 1986).

contractual forms; and it saves contractors from hidden traps not of their own making." Sturm v. United States, 421 F.2d 723 (Ct. Cl. 1970).

c.   Elements of the rule.

   (1)   To recover, the non-drafter's interpretation of the ambiguous language must be reasonable. Teague Bros. Transfer & Storage Co., Inc., ENG BCA Nos. 6312, 6313, 98-1 BCA ¶ 29,333 (the board decided that the contractor's interpretation of the latent ambiguity was reasonable); J.C.N. Constr. Co., ASBCA No. 42263, 91-3 BCA ¶ 24,095 (contractor interpretation unreasonable);

   (2)   The opposing party must be the drafter. This is usually the government, but a contractor may also be the drafter. See Canadian Commercial Corp. v. United States, 202 Ct. Cl. 65 (1973); TRW, Inc., ASBCA No. 27299, 87-3 BCA ¶ 19,964; Prince George Ctr., Inc. v. Gen. Servs. Admin., GSBCA No. 12289, 94-2 BCA ¶ 26,889; and

   (3)   The non-drafting party must have detrimentally relied on its interpretation in submitting its bid. Fruin-Colon Corp. v. United States, 912 F.2d 1426 (Fed. Cir. 1990); National Med. Staffing, Inc., ASBCA No. 45046, 96-2 BCA ¶ 28,483 (for *contra proferentem* to apply, the contractor must demonstrate that it relied upon the interpretation in submitting its bid, not merely that it relied during performance); Food Servs., Inc., ASBCA No. 46176, 95-2 BCA ¶ 27,892.

3.   Duty to seek clarification.

a.   Do not apply *contra proferentem* if an ambiguity is patent and the contractor failed to seek clarification. See Triax Pacific, Inc. v. West, 130 F.3d 1469 (Fed. Cir. 1997) (holding that contractor should have recognized the patent ambiguity and sought clarification before submitting its bid).

b.   Contractors are not permitted to ambush the government if they spot ambiguous language pre-award. A contractor's duty of clarification ensures that the government will have the opportunity to clarify its requirements, thereby providing a level playing field to all competitors before contract award, and to avoid post-award litigation.

c.   An ambiguity is patent if it would have been apparent to a reasonable person in the claimant's position or if the provisions conflict on their face. See White v. Edsall Constr. Co., Inc., 296 F.3d 1081 (2002) (holding that a note disclaiming the government's warranty on one of several dozen design drawings was patent); Hensel Phelps Constr. Co., ASBCA No. 49716, 00-2 BCA ¶ 30,925 (holding that an objective standard applied to the latent/patent ambiguity determination); Technical Sys. Assoc., Inc., GSBCA Nos. 13277-COM, 14538-COM, 00-1 BCA ¶ 30,684; Gaston & Assocs., Inc. v. United States, 27 Fed. Cl. 243 (1993) (latent ambiguity); Foothill Eng'g., IBCA No. 3119-A, 94-2 BCA ¶ 26,732 (the misplacement of a comma in a figure was a latent ambiguity and did not trigger a duty to inquire, because it was not obvious and apparent in the context of a reasonable, but busy, bidder). See also Pascal & Ludwig Eng'r, ENG BCA No. 6377, 99-1 BCA ¶ 30,135 (indicating that the ratio of the dollar amount at issue due to the ambiguity versus the contract price is a persuasive factor in determining whether the ambiguity is patent).

4. Given these rules of risk allocation, the government should try to draft as clear and unambiguous contract language as is possible, and contractors should raise all ambiguities prior to award.

VI. DEFECTIVE SPECIFICATIONS - OVERVIEW.

A. **Theories of Recovery.** Courts and boards hold the government liable for defects in specifications based upon:

1. An implied warranty the government gives for the use of design specifications in a contract.

2. The principles of impracticability and impossibility of performance when the contractor incurs increased costs while attempting to conform to defective performance specifications.

B. **Causation.** This type of constructive change is deemed to have occurred at the time of contract award on the premise that the contracting officer had an immediate duty to issue an order correcting the defective specifications.

C. **Defective Specifications – Implied Warranty of Specifications.**

1. Basis for the Implied Warranty.

   a. This "warranty" is based on an implied promise by the government that a contractor can follow the contract drawings and specifications and perform without undue expense. United States v. Spearin, 248 U.S. 132 (1918). This promise has been called a warranty; however, recovery is based on a breach of the duty to provide drawings and specifications reasonably free from defects. White v. Edsall Constr. Co., Inc., 296 F.3d 1081 (Fed. Cir. 2002); Fru-Con Constr. Corp. v. United States, 42 Fed. Cl. 94

(1998); Luria Bros. & Co. v. United States, 177 Ct. Cl. 676 (1966).

   b. Defective design specifications constitute a constructive change. See, e.g., Hol-Gar Mfg. Corp. v. United States, 175 Ct. Cl. 518 (1964). In some cases, judges have relied on a breach of contract theory. See, e.g., Big Chief Drilling Co. v. United States, 26 Cl. Ct. 1276 (1992).

D. **What Are Design Specifications?** Aleutian Constr. v. United States, 24 Cl. Ct. 372 (1991); Monitor Plastics Co., ASBCA No. 14447, 72-2 BCA ¶ 9626. Specifications are generally classified as:

1. Design specifications set forth precise measurements, tolerances, materials, tests, quality control, inspection requirements, and other specific information. See Apollo Sheet Metal, Inc., v. United States, 44 Fed. Cl. 210 (1999); Q.R. Sys. North, Inc., ASBCA No. 39618, 92-2 BCA ¶ 24,793 (specified roofing material inadequate for roof type).

2. Performance specifications set forth the operational characteristics desired for the item. In such specifications, design, measurements, and other specific details are neither stated nor considered important as long as the performance requirement is met. See Apollo Sheet Metal, Inc., v. United States, 44 Fed. Cl. 210 (1999); Interwest Constr. v. Brown, 29 F.3d 611 (Fed. Cir. 1994).

3. Purchase descriptions are specifications that designate a particular manufacturer's model, part number, or product. The phrase "or equal" may accompany a purchase description. M.A. Mortenson Co., ASBCA Nos. 50716, 51241, 51257, 99-1 BCA ¶ 30,270.

4. Composite specifications are specifications that are comprised of two or more different specification types. See Defense Sys. Co., Inc., ASBCA No. 50918, 00-2 BCA ¶ 30,991; Transtechnology, Corp., Space Ordnance

Sys. Div. v. United States, 22 Cl. Ct. 349 (1990).

5. Most specifications are composite specifications in total. Some requirements are design specifications, some requirements are performance specifications, and some are purchase descriptions. The title of the document (i.e., "Performance Specification") is not determinative. Instead, the focus is on the specific requirement(s) deemed defective and determining whether the specific requirement(s) at issue are design, or performance, or something else.

E.   Scope of Government Liability.

1. The scope of government liability depends on the specification type. Lopez v. A.C. & S., Inc., 858 F.2d 712 (Fed. Cir. 1988); Morrison-Knudsen Co., ASBCA No. 32476, 90-3 BCA ¶ 23,208.

2. Design specifications.

   a. The key issue is whether the government required the contractor to use a specific design approach. Geo-Con, Inc., ENG BCA No. 5749, 94-1 BCA ¶ 26,359. The government may either provide a specific design, or prohibit all methods of performance other than a specific design.

   b. The government is responsible for design and related omissions, errors, and deficiencies in the specifications and drawings. White v. Edsall Constr. Co., Inc., 296 F.3d 1081 (2002); Apollo Sheet Metal, Inc., v. United States, 44 Fed. Cl. 210 (1999); Neal & Co. v. United States, 19 Cl. Ct. 463 (1990) (defective design specifications found to cause bowing in wall); International Foods Retort Co., ASBCA No. 34954, 92-2 BCA ¶ 24,994 (bland chicken ala king). But see Hawaiian Bitumuls & Paving v. United States, 26 Cl. Ct. 1234 (1992) (contractor may vitiate warranty by participating in drafting and developing specifications).

3. Performance specifications.

   a. If the government uses a performance specification, the contractor accepts general responsibility for the design, engineering, and achievement of the performance requirements. Apollo Sheet Metal, Inc., v. United States, 44 Fed. Cl. 210 (1999); Blake Constr. Co. v. United States, 987 F.2d 743 (Fed. Cir. 1993); Technical Sys. Assoc., Inc., GSBCA Nos. 13277-COM, 14538-COM, 00-1 BCA ¶ 30,684.

   b. The contractor must have discretion as to the details of the work, even though the work is subject to the government's right of final inspection and approval or rejection. Kos Kam, Inc., ASBCA No. 34682, 92-1 BCA ¶ 24,546. Absent discretion, the specification is a design.

4. Purchase descriptions. Monitor Plastics Co., ASBCA No. 14447, 72-2 BCA ¶ 9626. Purchase descriptions are a type of design specification.

   a. If the contractor furnishes or uses in fabrication a specified brand name or an acceptable and approved substitute to brand-name product, the responsibility for proper performance generally falls upon the government.

   b. The government's liability is conditioned upon the contractor's correct use of the product.

   c. If the contractor elects to manufacture an "equal" product, it must ensure that the product is equal to the brand name product.

5. Composite specifications.

   a. If the government uses a composite specification, the parties must examine each portion of the specification to determine which specification type caused the problem. This determination establishes the scope of the government's liability. Aleutian Constr. v. United States, 24 Cl. Ct. 372 (1991); Penguin Indus. v. United States, 530 F.2d 934 (Ct. Cl. 1976). Cf. Hardwick Bros. Co., v. United States, 36 Fed. Cl. 347 (1996) (since mixed specifications were primarily performance-based, there is no warranty covering the specifications).

b. The contractor must isolate the defective element of the design portion or demonstrate affirmatively that its performance did not cause the problem. Defense Sys. Co., Inc., ASBCA No. 50918, 00-2 BCA ¶ 30,991 (finding that contractor failed to demonstrate deficient fuses were due to deficient government design rather than production problems).

F. **Recovery under the Implied Warranty of Specifications.** See Transtechnology, Corp., Space Ordnance Sys. Div. v. United States, 22 Cl. Ct. 349 (1990).

1. To recover under the implied warranty of specifications, the contractor must prove that:

a. It reasonably relied upon the defective specifications and complied fully with them. Phoenix Control Sys., Inc. v. Babbitt, Secy. of the Interior, 1997 U.S. App. LEXIS 8085 (Fed. Cir. 1997); Al Johnson Constr. Co. v. United States, 854 F.2d 467 (Fed. Cir. 1988); Gulf & Western Precision Eng'g Co. v. United States, 543 F.2d 125 (Ct. Cl. 1976); Mega Constr. Co., 29 Fed. Cl. 396 (1993); Bart Assocs., Inc., EBCA No. C-9211144, 96-2 BCA ¶ 28,479; and

b. That the defective specifications caused increased costs. McElroy Mach. & Mfg. Co., Inc., ASBCA No. 46477, 99-1 BCA ¶ 30,185;

Pioneer Enters., Inc., ASBCA No. 43739, 93-1 BCA ¶ 25,395 (contractor failed to demonstrate that defective specification caused its delay); Chaparral Indus., Inc., ASBCA No. 34396, 91-2 BCA ¶ 23,813, aff'd, 975 F.2d 870 (Fed. Cir. 1992).

2. Defending allegations of defective specifications. The government may defend against an allegation of a defective specification by showing that another contractor successfully performed while complying with the specification. Alternatively, the government may demonstrate that the contractor assumed the risk, such as by bidding while knowing the specification was defective.

3. The contractor cannot recover if it has actual or constructive knowledge of the defects prior to award. M.A. Mortenson Co., ASBCA Nos. 50716, 51241, 51257, 99-1 BCA ¶ 30,270; Centennial Contractors, Inc., ASBCA No. 46820, 94-1 BCA ¶ 26,511; L.W. Foster Sportswear Co. v. United States, 405 F.2d 1285 (Ct. Cl. 1969) (contractor had actual knowledge from prior contract). Generally, constructive knowledge is limited to patent errors because a contractor has no duty to conduct an independent investigation to determine whether the specifications are adequate. Jordan & Nobles Constr. Co., GSBCA No. 8349, 91-1 BCA ¶ 23,659; John C. Grimberg Co., ASBCA No. 32490, 88-1 BCA ¶ 20,346. Cf. Spiros Vasilatos Painting, ASBCA No. 35065, 88-2 BCA ¶ 20,558.

4. A contractor may not recover if it decides unilaterally to perform work knowing that the specifications were defective. Ordnance Research, Inc. v. United States, 221 Ct. Cl. 641 (1979).

5. A contractor may not recover if it fails to give timely notice that it was experiencing problems without assistance of the government. McElroy Mach. & Mfg. Co., Inc., ASBCA No. 46477, 99-1 BCA ¶

30,185; JGB Enters., Inc., ASBCA No. 49493, 96-2 BCA ¶ 28,498.

6. The government may disclaim this warranty. See, e.g., Serv. Eng'g Co., ASBCA No. 40272, 92-3 BCA ¶ 25,106; Bethlehem Steel Corp., ASBCA No. 13341, 72-1 BCA ¶ 9186. The disclaimer must be obvious and unequivocal in order to shift the risk to the contractor. White v. Edsall Constr. Co., Inc., 296 F.3d 1081 (2002) (holding that a small note disclaiming the government's warranty found on one of several dozen design drawings was hidden and not obvious).

VII. DEFECTIVE SPECIFICATIONS – IMPRACTICABILITY/ IMPOSSIBILITY OF PERFORMANCE.

A. **Elements.** American Mechanical, Inc., ASBCA No. 52033, 03-1 BCA ¶ 32,134; Oak Adec, Inc. v. United States, 24 Cl. Ct. 502 (1991); Reflectone, Inc., ASBCA No. 42363, 98-2 BCA ¶ 29,869; Gulf & Western Indus., Inc., ASBCA No. 21090, 87-2 BCA ¶ 19,881.

B. **An Unforeseen or Unexpected Occurrence.**

1. Commonly, there will be a significant increase in the contractor's work caused by technological problems unforeseen by the contractor at the time of contracting. The following factors can establish whether a problem was unforeseen or unexpected:

   a. The nature of the contract and specifications, i.e., whether they require performance beyond the state of the art;

   b. The extent of the contractor's effort; and

   c. The ability of other contractors to meet the specification requirements.

2. In some cases, a contractor must show that an extensive research and development effort was necessary to meet the

specifications, or that no competent contractor can meet the performance requirements. Hol-Gar Mfg. Corp. v. United States, 360 F.2d 634 (Ct. Cl. 1964); Reflectone, Inc., ASBCA No. 42363, 98-2 BCA ¶ 29,869 (contractor must show specifications "required performance beyond the state of the art" to demonstrate impossibility); Defense Sys. Corp. & Hi-Shear Tech. Corp., ASBCA No. 42939, 95-2 BCA ¶ 27,721.

C. **The Contractor Did Not Assume the Risk of the Unforeseen Occurrence by Agreement or Custom.** RNJ Interstate Corp. v. United States, 181 F.3d 1329 (Fed. Cir. 1999) (holding that doctrine of impossibility did not apply to a worksite fire since the contract placed the risk of loss on the contractor until acceptance by the government); Southern Dredging Co., ENG BCA No 5843, 92-2 BCA ¶ 24,886; Fulton Hauling Corp., PSBCA No. 2778, 92-2 BCA ¶ 24,886.

1. A contractor may assume the risk of the unforeseen effort by using its own specifications. See Bethlehem Corp. v. United States, 462 F.2d 1400 (Ct. Cl. 1972); Costal Indus. v. United States, 32 Fed. Cl. 368 (1994) (use of specification drafted, in part, by contractor's supplier held to be assumption of risk); Technical Sys. Assoc. Inc., GSBCA Nos. 13277-COM, 14538-COM, 00-1 BCA ¶ 30,684.

2. By proposing to extend the state of the art, a contractor may assume the risk of impossible performance. See J.A. Maurer, Inc. v. United States, 485 F.2d 588 (Ct. Cl. 1973).

D. **Performance Is Commercially Impracticable or Impossible.**

1. If performance of the contract is impossible, no matter how much costs the contractor expends performing, it will fail.

2. Impracticability means the contractor must show that the increased cost of performance is so much greater than anticipated that performance is commercially senseless. See Fulton

Hauling Corp., PSBCA No. 2778, 92-2 BCA ¶ 24,886; Technical Sys. Assoc., Inc., GSBCA Nos. 13277-COM, 14538-COM, 00-1 BCA ¶ 30,684; McElroy Mach. & Mfg. Co., Inc., ASBCA No. 46477, 99-1 BCA ¶ 30,185. But see SMC Info. Sys., Inc. v. Gen. Servs. Admin., GSBCA No. 9371, 93-1 BCA ¶ 25,485 (the increased difficulty cannot be the result of poor workmanship).

3. There is no universal standard for determining "commercial senselessness."

   a. Courts and boards sometimes use a "willing buyer" test to determine whether the increased costs render performance commercially senseless. A showing of economic hardship on the contractor is insufficient to demonstrate "commercial senselessness." The contractor must show that there are no buyers willing to pay the increased cost of production plus a reasonable profit. Ralph C. Nash, Jr., Government Contract Changes, 13-37 to 13-39 (2d ed. 1989).

   b. Some decisions have stated that it must be "positively unjust" to hold the contractor liable for the increased costs. Raytheon Co., ASBCA Nos. 50166, 50987, 01-1 BCA ¶ 31,245 (57% increase insufficient); Weststates Transp. Inc., PSBCA No. 3764, 97-1 BCA ¶ 28,633; Gulf & Western Indus., Inc., ASBCA No. 21090, 87-2 BCA ¶ 19,881 (70% increase insufficient); HLI Lordship Indus., VABCA No. 1785, 86-3 BCA ¶ 19,182 (200% increase in gold prices insufficient). But see Xplo Corp., DOT BCA No. 1289, 86-3 BCA ¶ 19,125 (50% increase in costs was sufficient).

VIII. INTERFERENCE AND FAILURE TO COOPERATE.

A. **General**.

The contracting parties are obligated to each other to cooperate in the performance of the contract. Each party can expect the other to take those reasonable actions that enable the successful performance of the contract. Where a party fails to cooperate, it is constructively changing the contract.

B. **Theory of Recovery.**

1. Contracting activities have an implied obligation to cooperate with their contractors and a duty not to interfere with their contract performance. The government should not administer the contract in a manner that hinders, delays, or increases the cost of performance. Precision Pine & Timber, Inc. v. United States, 50 Fed. Cl. 35, 65-70 (2001) (holding that the Forest Service beached a timber sale contract by suspending the contractor's logging operations when the Mexican spotted owl was listed as an endangered species instead of consulting with the Fish and Wildlife Service and developing a management plan as was required by the ESA) (case reconsidered and judgment entered on other grounds); Coastal Gov't Serv., Inc., ASBCA No. 50283, 01-1 BCA ¶ 31,353; R&B Bewachungsgesell-schaft GmbH, ASBCA No. 42213, 91-3 BCA ¶ 24,310; C.M. Lowther, Jr., ASBCA No. 38407, 91-3 BCA ¶ 24,296. See also Restatement (Second) of Contracts, § 205 (1981).

2. Generally a contractor may not recover for "interference" that results from a sovereign act. See Hills Materials Co., ASBCA No. 42410, 92-1 BCA ¶ 24,636, rev'd sub nom., Hills Materials Co. v. Rice, 982 F.2d 514 (Fed. Cir. 1992); Orlando Helicopter Airways, Inc. v. Widnall, 51 F.3d 258 (Fed. Cir. 1995) (holding that a criminal investigation of the contractor was a noncompensable sovereign act); Henderson, Inc., DOT BCA No. 2423, 94-2 BCA ¶ 26,728 (limitation on dredging period created implied warranty); R&B Bewachungsgesellschaft GmbH, 91-3 BCA ¶ 24,310 (criminal investigators took action in government's contractual

capacity, not sovereign capacity). <u>See also</u> <u>Hughes Commc'ns Galaxy, Inc. v. United</u> <u>States</u>, 998 F.2d 953 (Fed. Cir. 1993) (holding that the government may waive sovereign act defense); <u>Oman-Fischbach Int'l, a Joint Venture</u>, ASBCA No. 44195, 00-2 BCA ¶ 31,022 (actions of a separate sovereign were not compensable constructive changes).

C. Bases for Interference Claims.

1. Overzealous inspection of the contractor's work. <u>Neal & Co., Inc. v. United States</u>, 36 Fed. Cl. 600 (1996) ("nit-picking punch list" held to be overzealous inspection); <u>WRB Corp. v. United States</u>, 183 Ct. Cl. 409 (1968); <u>Adams v. United States</u>, 175 Ct. Cl. 288 (1966).

2. Incompetence of government personnel. <u>Harvey C. Jones, Inc.</u>, IBCA No. 2070, 90-2 BCA ¶ 22,762.

3. Water seepage or flow caused by the government. <u>See</u> <u>C.M. Lowther, Jr.</u>, ASBCA No. 38407, 91-3 BCA ¶ 24,296 (water from malfunctioning sump pump was interference); <u>Caesar Constr., Inc.</u>, ASBCA No. 41059, 91-1 BCA ¶ 23,639 (government's failure to remove snow piles, which resulted in water seepage, constituted a breach of its implied duty not to impede the contractor's performance).

4. Disruptive criminal investigations conducted in the government's contractual capacity. <u>R&B Bewachungsgesellschaft GmbH</u>, ASBCA No. 42213, 91-3 BCA ¶ 24,310.

D. Bases for Failure to Cooperate Claims. The government must cooperate with a contractor. <u>See, e.g.</u>, <u>Whittaker Elecs. Sys. v. Dalton, Secy. of the Navy</u>, 124 F.3d 1443 (Fed. Cir. 1997); <u>James Lowe, Inc.</u>, ASBCA No. 42026, 92-2 BCA ¶ 24,835; <u>Mit-Con, Inc.</u>, ASBCA No. 42916, 92-1 CPD ¶ 24,539. Bases for claims include:

1. Failure to provide assistance necessary for efficient contractor performance. <u>Chris Berg, Inc. v. United States</u>, 197 Ct. Cl. 503 (1972) (implied requirement);

<u>Durocher Dock & Dredge, Inc.</u>, ENG BCA No. 5768, 91-3 BCA ¶ 24,145 (failure to contest sheriff's stop work order was not failure to cooperate); <u>Hudson Contracting, Inc.</u>, ASBCA No. 41023, 94-1 BCA ¶ 26,466; <u>Packard Constr. Corp.</u>, ASBCA No. 46082, 94-1 BCA ¶ 26,577; <u>Ingalls Shipbldg. Div., Litton Sys., Inc.</u>, ASBCA No. 17717, 76-1 BCA ¶ 11,851 (express requirement).

2. Failure to prevent interference by another contractor required examining the good faith effort of the government to administer the other contract to reduce interference. <u>Northrup Grumman Corp. v. United States</u>, 47 Fed. Cl. 20 (2000); <u>Stephenson Assocs., Inc.</u>, GSBCA No. 6573, 86-3 BCA ¶ 19,071.

3. Failure to provide access to the worksite. <u>Summit Contractors, Inc. v. United States</u>, 23 Cl. Ct. 333 (1991) (absent specific warranty, site unavailability must be due to government's fault); <u>Atherton Constr., Inc.</u>, ASBCA No. 48527, 00-2 BCA ¶ 30,968; <u>R.W. Jones</u>, IBCA No. 3656-96, 99-1 BCA ¶ 30,268; <u>Old Dominion Sec.</u>, ASBCA No. 40062, 91-3 BCA ¶ 24,173, <u>recons. denied</u>, 92-1 BCA ¶ 24,374 (failure to grant security clearances); <u>M.A. Santander Constr., Inc.</u>, ASBCA No. 35907, 91-3 BCA ¶ 24,050 (interference excused default); <u>Reliance Enter.</u>, ASBCA No. 20808, 76-1 BCA ¶ 11,831.

4. Abuse of discretion in the approval process. When the contract makes the precise manner of performance subject to approval by the contracting officer, the duty of cooperation requires that the government approve the contractor's methods unless approval is detrimental to the government's interest. Ralph C. Nash, Jr., <u>Government Contract Changes</u>, 12-7 (2d ed. 1989). Common bases for claims are:

   a. Failure to approve substitute items or components that are equal in quality and performance to the contract requirements. <u>Page Constr. Co.</u>, AGBCA No. 92-191-1, 93-3

BCA ¶ 26,060; <u>Bruce-Anderson Co.</u>, ASBCA No. 29411, 88-3 BCA ¶ 21,135 (contracting officer gave no explanation for refusal).

b. Unjustified disapproval of shop drawings or failure to approve within a reasonable time. <u>Orlosky, Inc. v. United States</u>, 68 Fed. Cl. 296 (2005); <u>Vogt Bros. Mfg. Co. v. United States</u>, 160 Ct. Cl. 687 (1963).

c. Improper failure to approve the substitution or use of a particular subcontractor. <u>Lockheed Martin Tactical Aircraft Sys.</u>, ASBCA Nos. 49530, 50057, 00-1 BCA ¶ 30,852, <u>recon. denied</u>, 00-2 BCA ¶ 30,930; <u>Manning Elec. & Repair Co. v. United States</u>, 22 Cl. Ct. 240 (1991); <u>Hoel-Steffen Constr. Co. v. United States</u>, 231 Ct. Cl. 128 (1982); <u>Liles Constr. Co. v. United States</u>, 197 Ct. Cl. 164 (1972); <u>Richerson Constr., Inc. v. Gen. Servs. Admin.</u>, GSBCA No. 11161, 93-1 BCA ¶ 25,239. <u>Cf.</u> FAR 52.236-5, Material and Workmanship.

IX. FAILURE TO DISCLOSE VITAL INFORMATION (SUPERIOR KNOWLEDGE).

A. Theory.

1. The government's duty to cooperate with the contractor and not hinder or interfere with the contractor's performance includes the duty to disclose vital information of which the contractor is ignorant—a "duty to share information." <u>See</u> <u>Helene Curtis Indus. v. United States</u>, 312 F.2d 774 (Ct. Cl. 1963); <u>Miller Elevator Co. v. United States</u>, 30 Fed. Cl. 662 (1994); <u>Bradley Constr. Inc. v. United States</u>, 30 Fed. Cl. 507 (1994); <u>Maitland Bros.</u>, ENG BCA No. 5782, 94-1 BCA ¶ 26,473.

2. Nondisclosure is a change to the contract because the contracting activity should have disclosed the vital information at

contract award. <u>Raytheon Co.</u>, ASBCA No. 50166, 50987, 01-1 BCA ¶ 31,245.

3. Classified information. The government's duty to disclose may apply to classified information. <u>McDonnell Douglas Corp. v. United States</u>, 27 Fed. Cl. 204 (1992). <u>But see</u> <u>McDonnell Corp. v. United States</u>, 323 F.3d 1006 (Fed. Cir. 2006) (holding that the government could declare vital information too highly classified to disclose in litigation and thus prevent the contractor from using a superior knowledge defense to a default termination).

B. Elements of the Implied Duty to Disclose Vital Information. <u>Hercules, Inc. v. United States</u>, 24 F.3d 188 (Fed. Cir. 1994), <u>aff'd on other grounds</u>, 116 S. Ct. 981 (1996); <u>Technical Sys. Assoc. Inc.</u>, GSBCA Nos. 13277-COM, 14538-COM, 00-1 BCA ¶ 30,684.

1. The contractor undertakes to perform without vital knowledge of a fact that affects performance costs or duration. <u>Shawn K. Christiansen d/b/a Island Wide Contracting</u>, AGBCA No. 94-200-3, 95-1 BCA ¶ 27,758; <u>Bradley Constr., Inc. v. United States</u>, 30 Fed. Cl. 507 (1994) (information must have a direct bearing on the cost or duration of contract performance); <u>Johnson & Son Erector Co.</u>, ASBCA No. 23689, 86-2 BCA ¶ 18,931 (amount of interference caused by the nondisclosure is a factor in determining whether the information is vital); <u>Numax Elec., Inc.</u>, ASBCA No. 29080, 90-1 BCA ¶ 22,280 (government failed to disclose that all previous contractors had been unable to manufacture in accordance with the specifications); <u>Riverport Indus., Inc.</u>, ASBCA No. 30888, 87-2 BCA ¶ 19,876 (government must disclose the history of a procurement if the information is necessary to successful performance).

2. The government was aware the contractor had no knowledge of or reason to obtain such information. <u>Hardeman-Monier-Hutcherson v. United States</u>, 198 Ct. Cl. 472 (1972); <u>Max Jordan</u>

Bauunternehmung v. United States, 10 Cl. Ct. 672 (1986), aff'd, 820 F.2d 1208 (Fed. Cir. 1987); GAF Corp. v. United States, 932 F.2d 947 (Fed. Cir. 1991) (government need not inquire into the knowledge of an experienced contractor).

3. The contract specification misled the contractor or did not put it on notice to inquire. Raytheon Co., ASBCA Nos. 50166, 50987, 01-1 BCA ¶ 31,245 (government-furnished technical data package and specifications implied no further development would be required, although government knew this was not possible); D.F.K. Enter., Inc. v. United States, 45 Fed. Cl. 280 (1999) (holding that incomplete and inaccurate weather data was an affirmative misrepresentation of job site conditions); Jack L. Olsen, Inc., AGBCA No. 87-345-1, 93-2 BCA ¶ 25,767 (information provided in solicitation excused contractor from further inquiry). There is no breach of the duty to disclose vital information if the government shows that the contractor knew or should have known of the information. H.N. Bailey & Assoc. v. United States, 449 F.2d 376 (Ct. Cl. 1971) (information was general industry knowledge); Benju Corp., ASBCA No. 43648, 97-2 BCA ¶ 29,274 (government did not have to disclose readily available information); Metal Trades, Inc., ASBCA No. 41643, 91-2 BCA ¶ 23,982; Hydromar Corp. of Del. & Eastern Seaboard v. United States, 25 Cl. Ct. 555 (1992), aff'd, 980 F.2d 744 (Fed. Cir. 1992) (undisclosed information reasonably was available to the contractor); Maitland Bros. Co., ENG BCA No. 5782, 94-1 BCA ¶ 26,473 (information in public domain).

4. The government failed to provide the relevant information. P.J. Maffei Bldg. Wrecking Corp. v. United States, 732 F.2d 913 (Fed. Cir. 1984) (contractor failed to prove government had better information than already disclosed); Bethlehem Corp. v. United States, 462 F.2d 1400 (Ct. Cl. 1972) (knowledge by one government agency is not attributable to another

government agency absent some meaningful connection between the agencies); Marine Indus. Northwest, Inc., ASBCA No. 51942, 01-1 BCA ¶ 31,201 (contractor failed to demonstrate that government had superior knowledge).

C. Example.

In American Ordnance LLC, ASBCA No. 54718, 10-1 BCA ¶ 34,386, the government was aware of a problem with a design specification, had conducted extensive research and testing to identify a fix, but withheld knowledge of the problem and the fix from the contractor. When the contractor, after extensive study following repeated failures, suggested trying the same fix identified by the government pre-award, the government refused to allow the change. Unsurprisingly, the ASBCA found a constructive change based on superior knowledge, as well as a defective design specification, and a failure to cooperate. American Ordnance shows how a single related set of facts can support several constructive changes.

X. CONSTRUCTIVE ACCELERATION.

A. Theory of Recovery.

1. If a contractor encounters an excusable delay, it is entitled to an extension of the contract schedule and/or excused from a termination for default.

2. Constructive acceleration occurs when the contracting officer refuses to adjust the contract schedule and demands that the contractor complete performance within the original contract period.

B. Elements of Constructive Acceleration. Fru-Con Constr. Corp. v. United States, 43 Fed. Cl. 306 (1999); Atlantic Dry Dock Corp., ASBCA Nos. 42609, 42610, 42611, 42612, 42613, 42679, 42685, 42686, 44472, 98-2 BCA ¶ 30,025; Trepte Constr. Co., ASBCA No. 28555, 90-1 BCA ¶ 22,595.

1. The existence of one or more excusable delays;

Changes

2. Notice by the contractor to the government of such delay and a request for an extension of time;

3. Failure or refusal by the government to grant the extension request;

4. An express or implied order by the government to accelerate; and

5. Actual acceleration resulting in increased costs.

C. Actions That May Lead to Constructive Acceleration.

1. Constructive acceleration requires both excusable delays, and a threat of consequences for not meeting the existing schedule.

2. The government threatens to terminate when the contractor encounters an excusable delay. Intersea Research Corp., IBCA No. 1675, 85-2 BCA ¶ 18,058.

3. The government threatens to assess liquidated damages and refuses to grant a time extension. Norair Eng'g Corp. v. United States, 666 F.2d 546 (Ct. Cl. 1981); Unarco Material Handling, PSBCA No. 4100, 00-1 BCA ¶ 30,682.

4. The government delays approval of a request for a time extension. Fishbach & Moore Int'l Corp., ASBCA No. 18146, 77-1 BCA ¶ 12,300, aff'd, 617 F.2d 223 (Ct. Cl. 1980). But see Franklin Pavlov Constr. Co., HUD BCA No. 93-C-13, 94-3 BCA ¶ 27,078 (mere denial of delay request due to lack of information not tantamount to government order to accelerate).

D. Measure of Damages.

1. The contractor's acceleration efforts need not be successful; a reasonable attempt by the contractor to meet a completion date is sufficient. Unarco Material Handling, PSBCA No. 4100, 00-1 BCA ¶ 30,682; Fermont Div., Dynamics Corp., ASBCA No. 15806, 75-1 BCA ¶ 11,139.

2. The measure of recovery will be the difference between:

   a. The reasonable costs attributable to acceleration or attempting to accelerate;

   b. The lesser costs the contractor reasonably would have incurred absent its acceleration efforts; and

   c. A reasonable profit on the above-described difference.

3. Common acceleration costs.

   a. Increased labor costs, such as overtime premiums;

   b. Increased material costs due to contractor payments for expedited delivery; and

   c. Loss of efficiency or productivity caused by efforts to accelerate. For example, second- and third-shift operations typically are less efficient than first-shift (daytime) operations. To compute these costs, a contractor may compare the work accomplished per labor hour or dollar during an acceleration period with the work accomplished per labor hour or dollar during a normal period. See Ralph C. Nash, Jr., Government Contract Changes, 18-16 and 18-17 (2d ed. 1989).

XI. NOTICE REQUIREMENTS.

A. Notice of a Change by the Contractor.

1. Formal Changes. The standard Changes clauses each state that "the Contractor must assert its right to an adjustment . . . within 30 days after receipt of a written [change] order." This is the first step in the process of obtaining an equitable adjustment in the contract price and schedule. Courts and boards, however, do not strictly construe this requirement unless the untimely notice is prejudicial to the government. Watson, Rice & Co., HUD BCA No. 89-4468-C8, 90-1 BCA ¶ 22,499; SOSA y Barbera Constrs., S.A.,

418

ENG BCA No. PCC-57, 89-2 BCA ¶ 21,754; E.W. Jerdon, Inc., ASBCA No. 32957, 88-2 BCA ¶ 20,729.

2. Constructive Changes.

    a. Supply/Service Contracts. The standard supply and service contract Changes clauses do not prescribe specific periods within which a contractor must seek an adjustment for a constructive change.

    b. Construction Contracts. Under the Changes clause for construction contracts, a contractor must assert its right to an adjustment within 30 days of notifying the government that it considers a government action to be a constructive change. FAR 52.243-4(b) and (e). Furthermore, unless the contractor bases its adjustment on defective specifications, it may not recover costs incurred more than 20 days before notifying the government of a constructive change. FAR 52.243-4(d). But see Martin J. Simko Constr., Inc. v. United States, 11 Cl. Ct. 257 (1986) (government must show late notice was prejudicial).

    c. Content of notice. A contractor must assert a positive, present intent to seek recovery as a matter of legal right. Written notice is not required, and there is no formal method for asserting an intent to recover. The notice, however, must be more than an ambiguous letter that evidences a differing opinion. Likewise, merely advising the contracting officer of problems is not sufficient notice. CTA Inc., ASBCA No. 47062, 00-2 BCA ¶ 30,947; McLamb Upholstery, Inc., ASBCA No. 42112, 91-3 BCA ¶ 24,081.

    d. The "Notice of the Change" allows the government to change its conduct that may have constructively changed the contract, stop work and plan on how to deal with a defective specification, or to terminate the contract for convenience.

    e. **Practice Tip:** A contractor who experiences an event that may be compensable as a change should notify the contracting officer of the problem immediately. While the notification may not constitute formal notice, it will make it harder for the contracting officer to show prejudice for late notice. The contractor should also begin segregating costs incurred. When the contractor's investigation concludes that a change has likely occurred, provide notice promptly.

    f. **Practice Tip:** Contracting officers and their contract attorneys should monitor project reports for signs of potential changes and excusable delays. Negotiating changes early, and obtaining a release, is an effective approach to minimizing the cost of changes.

    g. **Practice Tip;** Contracting officers who receive notice of a change on a contract that contains FAR 52.243-6, Change Order Accounting, should direct the contractor to segregate the costs of the change that is the subject of the notice. Many contracting officers fail to do so, which may result in less useful accounting information.

B. **Request for an Equitable Adjustment.**

1. Contractors who receive an actual or constructive change seek an adjustment in the contract price and schedule by filing a "Request for Equitable Adjustment" or "REA." This is the second step, regardless whether the change is acknowledged or contested.

2. The contractor's Request for Equitable Adjustment typically includes sections describing the change, the impact of the change on the existing work, the cost of the change using an "add and delete" method (see FAR 15), and the delays

Changes

caused by the change. Where the change is expected to be contested, the REA may include legal argument.

3. REA Certifications. Requests for Equitable Adjustments submitted on DOD and NASA contracts must comply with the clause DFARS 251.243-7002. This clause requires the contractor to submit a certification with each REA, described in the clause. This is not an opportunity for creative writing. Contractors should execute the certificate as required by the clause. This certification is in addition to the certification required under the Contract Disputes Act (see chapter 28, and the Truth in Negotiations Act certification, chapter 14)

4. The contracting officer should investigate, negotiate, and resolve REA's in the shortest practicable time. FAR 43.204(b)(1). When the change is acknowledged, this typically involves reviewing and negotiating the cost and schedule impact of the change. When the change is not acknowledged, the contracting officer should perform a technical, legal, and cost review of the REA to promptly decide whether to reject the REA, or to commence negotiations.

5. Effect of Final Payment.

   a. Requests for equitable adjustments raised for the first time after final payment are untimely. Design & Prod., Inc. v. United States, 18 Cl. Ct. 168 (1989) (final payment rule predicated on express contractual provisions); Navales Enter., Inc., ASBCA No. 52202, 99-2 BCA ¶ 30,528; Electro-Technology Corp., ASBCA No. 42495, 93-2 BCA ¶ 25,750.

   b. Final payment does not bar claims for equitable adjustments that were pending or of which the government had constructive knowledge at the time of final payment. Mingus Constr. v. United States, 812 F.2d 1387 (Fed. Cir. 1987); Miller Elevator Co. v. United States, 30

Fed. Cl. 662 (1994); Gulf & Western Indus., Inc. v. United States, 6 Cl. Ct. 742 (1984); Navales Enter., Inc., ASBCA No. 52202, 99-2 BCA ¶ 30,528; David Grimaldi Co., ASBCA No. 36043, 89-1 BCA ¶ 21,341 (contractor must specifically assert a claim as a matter of right; letter merely presented arguments).

6. **Practice Note**: Contractor's should convert their REA into a formal claim if the contracting officer does not promptly address the request. There are two reasons to do so: (a) to trigger the accrual of interest under the Contract Disputes Act; and (b) to submit the claim prior to the expiration of the applicable statute of limitations. See Chapter 28.

C. Government Changes.

1. Not all changes benefit the contractor. Some changes delete work from the contract, make the work less costly to perform, or otherwise result in a cost savings.

2. The Changes clauses do not specify the procedures and time limits within which the government must claim a downward equitable adjustment. The Changes clauses also do not require the government to notify the contractor that it intends to subsequently assert its right to an adjustment.

3. Typically, the government will assert a change by letter to the contractor, directing the contractor to prepare a downward equitable adjustment. Absent a response, the government may use its audit rights to obtain the available cost data necessary to quantify the price and schedule adjustment to which the government is entitled. Then the government demands payment of the amount owed.

4. For contracts awarded both before and after October 1, 1995, the government must make its request for an equitable adjustment within a reasonable time.

Generally, this will require the government to act while the facts supporting the claim are readily available and before the contractor's position is prejudiced by final settlement with its subcontractors, suppliers, and other creditors. See Aero Union Corp. v. United States, 47 Fed. Cl. 677 (2000) (denying motion for summary judgment where there were issues of fact concerning whether the government had delayed so long the plaintiff was prejudiced by the delay).

5. For contracts awarded subsequent to assert any claims it has against a contractor within six years from the accrual of the claim, except claims based upon fraud. See 41 U.S.C § 7103(a)(4)(A), and FAR 33.206(b). This includes claims for changes that result in a downward equitable adjustment in the contract price.

XII. ANALYZING CHANGES ISSUES.

A. Determine whether the contract required work that differed from what was called for in the original contract, or whether a risk occurred that is recognized as a constructive change. If not, then there was no "change" to the contract requirements, and a contract adjustment is unnecessary.

B. If the government changed the contract requirements, determine whether the new work was within or outside the general scope of the contract.

1. Within-general-scope changes. The contractor may be entitled to relief pursuant to the Changes clause. FAR 52.243-1 (supplies); FAR 52.243-1, Alternate I (services); FAR 52.243-4 (construction). Under the basic equitable adjustment formula, the contractor is entitled to the difference between the reasonable costs of performing the work as changed and the reasonable costs of performing as originally required. See chapter 25.

2. Outside-the-general scope change (cardinal change). The contractor's entitlement is measured under common-law principles. In general, compensatory damages including a reliance component (costs incurred as a consequence of the breach) and an expectancy component (lost profits) are awarded, but unforeseeable consequential damages are not.

C. If a change occurred, determine whether the government employee who ordered/caused the change had actual authority to order the change or whether the contractor can overcome the employee's lack of actual authority.

D. If a change occurred, determine when the change occurred; when the contractor provided, or when the government can be charged with having acquired, notice of the change; and whether the contractor provided timely notice. Determine if untimely notice prejudiced the government.

E. If a change occurred, determine the effect of the change on the costs incurred or saved by the contractor and on the time required for contract performance.

XIII. CONCLUSION.

Contract changes are often required during contract performance. They are either formal (written and intentional) or informal (unintentional, constructive). Formal contract changes may be unilateral, issued by the contracting officer pursuant to changes clauses in the contract. They may also be bilateral, constituting a supplemental agreement between the parties. Informal contract changes are not issued in writing and often result from government conduct, unforeseen impediments to performance, or other factors. They may be adopted formally, rejected and the contractor absolved of performance, or disputed as not truly being contract changes.

Formal changes must be within the scope of the original contract. Scope determinations require an evaluation of quantity, type of work, and other factors to determine whether the contract, as changed, represents substantially the same contract as originally awarded. This is evaluated through the lens of incumbent contractors who may not want the additional responsibility of performing new work, or from the perspective of potential bidders who would have competed for the contract as changed, but did not compete for the contract as originally advertised.

In all cases, contract changes that require additional funding may be funded from the appropriation that originally funded the contract if the change is within the scope of the original. Otherwise, or if no money remains from the original appropriation, the change must be funded with current appropriations.

APPENDIX A:
CHANGES CLAUSE (SUPPLIES),
FAR 52.243-1.
CHANGES—FIXED-PRICE (AUG. 1987)

(a) The Contracting Officer may at any time, by written order, and without notice to the sureties, if any, make changes within the general scope of this contract in any one or more of the following:

(1) Drawings, designs, or specifications when the supplies to be furnished are to be specially manufactured for the government in accordance with the drawings, designs, or specifications.

(2) Method of shipment or packing.

(3) Place of delivery.

(b) If any such change causes an increase or decrease in the cost of, or the time required for, performance of any part of the work under this contract, whether or not changed by the order, the Contracting Officer shall make an equitable adjustment in the contract price, the delivery schedule, or both, and shall modify the contract.

(c) The Contractor must assert its right to an adjustment under this clause within 30 days from the date of receipt of the written order. However, if the Contracting Officer decides that the facts justify it, the Contracting Officer may receive and act upon a proposal submitted before final payment of the contract.

(d) If the Contractor's proposal includes the cost of property made obsolete or excess by the change, the Contracting Officer shall have the right to prescribe the manner of the disposition of the property.

(e) Failure to agree to any adjustment shall be a dispute under the Disputes clause. However, nothing in this clause shall excuse the Contractor from proceeding with the contract as changed.

APPENDIX B:
CHANGES CLAUSE (SERVICES),
FAR 52.243-1, ALTERNATE I.[2]
CHANGES—FIXED-PRICE (AUG. 1987)

(a) The Contracting Officer may at any time, by written order, and without notice to the sureties, if any, make changes within the general scope of this contract in any one or more of the following:

(1) Description of services to be performed.

(2) Time of performance (i.e., hours of the day, days of the week, etc.).

(3) Place of performance of the services.

(b) If any such change causes an increase or decrease in the cost of, or the time required for, performance of any part of the work under this contract, whether or not changed by the order, the Contracting Officer shall make an equitable adjustment in the contract price, the delivery schedule, or both, and shall modify the contract.

(c) The Contractor must assert its right to an adjustment under this clause within 30 days from the date of receipt of the written order. However, if the Contracting Officer decides that the facts justify it, the Contracting Officer may receive and act upon a proposal submitted before final payment of the contract.

(d) If the Contractor's proposal includes the cost of property made obsolete or excess by the change, the Contracting Officer shall have the right to prescribe the manner of the disposition of the property.

(e) Failure to agree to any adjustment shall be a dispute under the Disputes clause. However, nothing in this clause shall excuse the Contractor from proceeding with the contract as changed.

---

[2] This clause applies if the requirement is for services other than architect-engineer or other professional services, and no supplies are to be furnished.

APPENDIX C:
CHANGES CLAUSE (CONSTRUCTION),
FAR 52.243-4.
CHANGES (June 2007)

(a) The Contracting Officer may, at any time, without notice to the sureties, if any, by written order designated or indicated to be a change order, make changes in the work within the general scope of the contract, including changes--

(1) In the specifications (including drawings and designs);

(2) In the method or manner of performance of the work;

(3) In the government-furnished facilities, equipment, materials, services, or site; or

(4) Directing acceleration in the performance of the work.

(b) Any other written order or oral order (which, as used in this paragraph (b), includes direction, instruction, interpretation or determination) from the Contracting Officer that causes a change shall be treated as a change order under this clause; provided, that the Contractor gives the Contracting Officer written notice stating—

(1) The date, circumstances, and source of the order; and

(2) That the Contractor regards the order as a change order.

(c) Except as provided in this clause, no order, statement, or conduct of the Contracting Officer shall be treated as a change under this clause or entitle the Contractor to an equitable adjustment.

(d) If any change under this clause causes an increase or decrease in the Contractor's costs of, or the time required for, the performance of any part of the work under this contract, whether or not changed by any such order, the Contracting Officer shall make an equitable adjustment and modify the contract in writing. However, except for an adjustment based on defective specifications, no adjustment for any change under paragraph (b) of this clause shall be made for any costs incurred more than 20 days before the Contractor gives written notice as required. In the case of defective specifications for which the government is responsible, the equitable adjustment shall include any increased cost reasonably incurred by the Contractor in attempting to comply with such defective specifications.

(e) The Contractor must assert its right to an adjustment under this clause within 30 days after (1) receipt of a written change order under paragraph (a) of this clause or (2) the furnishing of a written notice under paragraph (b) of this clause, by submitting to the Contracting Officer a written statement describing the general nature and amount of the proposal, unless this period is extended by the government. The statement of proposal for adjustment may be included in the notice under paragraph (b) of this clause.

(f) No proposal by the Contractor for an equitable adjustment shall be allowed if asserted after final payment under this contract.

Changes

APPENDIX D

AMENDMENT OF SOLICITATION/MODIFICATION OF CONTRACT

		1. CONTRACT ID CODE	PAGE OF PAGES

2. AMENDMENT/MODIFICATION NUMBER	3. EFFECTIVE DATE	4. REQUISITION/PURCHASE REQUISITION NUMBER	5. PROJECT NUMBER (If applicable)

6. ISSUED BY CODE		7. ADMINISTERED BY (If other than Item 6) CODE

8. NAME AND ADDRESS OF CONTRACTOR (Number, street, county, State and ZIP Code)

(X)

9A. AMENDMENT OF SOLICITATION NUMBER

9B. DATED (SEE ITEM 11)

10A. MODIFICATION OF CONTRACT/ORDER NUMBER

10B. DATED (SEE ITEM 13)

CODE   FACILITY CODE

11. THIS ITEM ONLY APPLIES TO AMENDMENTS OF SOLICITATIONS

☐ The above numbered solicitation is amended as set forth in Item 14. The hour and date specified for receipt of Offers ☐ is extended. ☐ is not extended.

Offers must acknowledge receipt of this amendment prior to the hour and date specified in the solicitation or as amended, by one of the following methods: (a) By completing Items 8 and 15, and returning _____ copies of the amendment; (b) By acknowledging receipt of this amendment on each copy of the offer submitted; or (c) By separate letter or electronic communication which includes a reference to the solicitation and amendment numbers. FAILURE OF YOUR ACKNOWLEDGMENT TO BE RECEIVED AT THE PLACE DESIGNATED FOR THE RECEIPT OF OFFERS PRIOR TO THE HOUR AND DATE SPECIFIED MAY RESULT IN REJECTION OF YOUR OFFER. If by virtue of this amendment you desire to change an offer already submitted, such change may be made by letter or electronic communication, provided each letter or electronic communication makes reference to the solicitation and this amendment, and is received prior to the opening hour and date specified.

12. ACCOUNTING AND APPROPRIATION DATA (If required)

13. THIS ITEM APPLIES ONLY TO MODIFICATIONS OF CONTRACTS/ORDERS. IT MODIFIES THE CONTRACT/ORDER NUMBER AS DESCRIBED IN ITEM 14.

CHECK ONE	
☐	A. THIS CHANGE ORDER IS ISSUED PURSUANT TO: (Specify authority) THE CHANGES SET FORTH IN ITEM 14 ARE MADE IN THE CONTRACT ORDER NUMBER IN ITEM 10A.
☐	B. THE ABOVE NUMBERED CONTRACT/ORDER IS MODIFIED TO REFLECT THE ADMINISTRATIVE CHANGES (such as changes in paying office, appropriation data, etc.) SET FORTH IN ITEM 14, PURSUANT TO THE AUTHORITY OF FAR 43.103(b).
☐	C. THIS SUPPLEMENTAL AGREEMENT IS ENTERED INTO PURSUANT TO AUTHORITY OF:
☐	D. OTHER (Specify type of modification and authority)

E. IMPORTANT: Contractor ☐ is not ☐ is required to sign this document and return _____ copies to the issuing office.

14. DESCRIPTION OF AMENDMENT/MODIFICATION (Organized by UCF section headings, including solicitation/contract subject matter where feasible.)

Except as provided herein, all terms and conditions of the document referenced in Item 9A or 10A, as heretofore changed, remains unchanged and in full force and effect.

15A. NAME AND TITLE OF SIGNER (Type or print)	16A. NAME AND TITLE OF CONTRACTING OFFICER (Type or print)

15B. CONTRACTOR/OFFEROR	15C. DATE SIGNED	16B. UNITED STATES OF AMERICA	16C. DATE SIGNED
(Signature of person authorized to sign)		(Signature of Contracting Officer)	

Previous edition unusable

STANDARD FORM 30 (REV. 11/2016)
Prescribed by GSA FAR (48 CFR) 53.243

CONSTRUCTION CONTRACTING

I. INTRODUCTION.

Construction contracting involves many statutes, regulations, and standard clauses that are different from those used in contracts for supplies and services. These differences reflect significant differences between contracting for supplies and services and contracting for construction.

Construction work is inherently different because construction work is typically performed on the government's land. As the work progresses, the government has possession of the work performed. In contracts for supplies and some services, the government doesn't physically receive the work, or benefit from the services, until delivery/performance. Many clauses, such as the termination for default clauses, reflect these differences.

From a business perspective, construction prime contractors are often smaller and less well capitalized. Much of the actual work is done by subcontractors. The government, as a sovereign, is different from a private owner. These characteristics give rise to requirements for performance and payment bonds, etc.

Lastly, Congress intensively manages construction contracts. This management and control is performed through a complex regulatory framework for the planning and funding of construction work.

This chapter addresses many of these differences and unique aspects of construction contracting.

II. REFERENCES.

A. Federal Regulations.

1. Federal Acquisition Regulation (FAR) Part 36.

2. Defense Federal Acquisition Regulation Supplement (DFARS) Part 236.

3. Army Federal Acquisition Regulation Supplement (AFARS) Part 5136.

4. Air Force Federal Acquisition Regulation Supplement (AFFARS) Part 5336.

5. Navy Acquisition Procedures Supplement (NAPS) Part 5236.

B. Army Regulations (AR).

1. AR 210-50, Housing Management (26 Feb. 1999).

2. AR 415-15, Army Military Construction Program Development and Execution (4 Sept. 1998).

3. AR 415-32, Engineer Troop Unit Construction in Connection with Training Activities (15 Apr. 1998).

4. AR 420-10, Management of Installation Directorates of Public Works (15 Apr. 1997).

5. AR 420-18, Facilities Engineering Material, Equipment, and Relocatable Building Management (3 Jan. 1992) [hereinafter AR 420-18].

6. DA Pam 415-15, Army Military Construction Program Development and Execution (25 Oct. 1999) [hereinafter DA Pam 415-15].

7. DA Pam 420-11, Project Definition and Work Classification (7 Oct. 1994) [hereinafter DA Pam 420-11].

C. Air Force Policy Directives (AFPD) and Air Force Instructions (AFI).

1. AFPD 32-90, Real Property Management (10 Sept. 1993).

2. AFI 32-1021, Planning and Programming Military Construction (MILCON) Projects (24 Jan. 2003).

3. AFI 32-1032, Planning and Programming Appropriated Funded Maintenance, Repair, and Construction Projects (25 Sept. 2001).

4. AFI 32-6001, Family Housing Management (26 Apr. 1994).

5. AFI 32-6002, Family Housing Planning, Programming, Design, and Construction (27 May 1997).

6. AFI 65-601, vol. 1, Budget Guidance and Procedures (21 Oct. 1994).

D. **Navy Regulation.** OPNAVINST 11010.20F, Facilities Projects Manual (7 June 1996).

E. Richard J. Bednar, John Cibinic, Jr., Ralph C. Nash, Jr., et al., Construction Contracting, published by The George Washington University Government Contracts Program, 1991.

F. Adrian L. Bastianelli, Andrew D. Ness, Federal Government Construction Contracts, published by the American Bar Association Forum on the Construction Industry, 2003.

III. CONCEPTS.

A. **Definitions.**

1. Construction.

    a. Statutory Definition. 10 U.S.C. § 2801(a). The term "military construction" includes "any construction, development, conversion, or extension of any kind carried out with respect to a military installation."[1]

    b. Regulatory Definitions.

      (1) FAR 2.101. The term "construction" includes the construction, alteration, or repair of buildings, structures, or other real property.

      (a) Construction includes dredging, excavating, and painting.

      (b) Construction does not include work performed on vessels, aircraft, or other items of personal property.

      (2) Service Regulations. See, e.g., AR 415-15, Glossary, sec. II; AR 415-32, Glossary, sec. II; AR 420-10, Glossary, sec. II; AFI 32-1021, paras. 3.2. and 4.2; AFI 32-1032, para. 5.1.1; AFI 65-601, vol. 1, attch 1; OPNAVINST 11010.20F, ch. 6, para. 6.1.1. The term "construction" includes:

      (a) The erection, installation, or assembly of a new facility;[2]

      (b) The addition, expansion, extension, alteration, conversion, or replacement of an existing facility;

      (c) The relocation of a facility from one site to another;

      (d) Installed equipment (e.g., built-in furniture, cabinets, shelving, venetian blinds, screens, elevators, telephones, fire alarms, heating and air conditioning equipment,

---

[1] The term "military installation" means "a base, camp, post, station, yard, center, or other activity under the jurisdiction of the Secretary of a military department or, in the case of an activity in a foreign country, under the operational control of the Secretary of a military department or the Secretary of Defense." 10 U.S.C. § 2801(c)(2).

[2] The term "facility" means "a building, structure, or other improvement to real property." 10 U.S.C. § 2801(c)(1).

waste disposals, dishwashers, and theater seats); and

    (e)   Related <u>site preparation</u>, excavation, filling, landscaping, and other land improvements.

2.   Military Construction Project. 10 U.S.C. § 2801(b). The term "military construction project" includes "all military construction work . . . necessary to produce a complete and usable facility or a complete and usable improvement to an existing facility . . . ."

B.   **Construction Funding**.

1.   As a general rule, the government funds projects costing less than $1 million with Operations and Maintenance (O&M) funds. Projects costing more than $1 million, but less than $3 million, or $4 million if the project is intended solely to correct a deficiency that is life-threatening, health-threatening, or safety-threatening, are funded with Unspecified Minor Military Construction (UMMC) funds. Projects costing more than $4 million are funded with Military Construction (MILCON) appropriations. 10 U.S.C. §§ 2802, 2805. <u>See</u> Chapter 8, Construction Funding, in CONTRACT & FISCAL L. DEP'T, THE JUDGE ADVOCATE GENERAL'S SCHOOL, U.S. ARMY, FISCAL LAW COURSE DESKBOOK (current Edition), available online from the Library of Congress. https://www.loc.gov/rr/frd/Military_Law/Contract-Fiscal-Law-Department.html).

2.   For fiscal law purposes, "construction" does <u>not</u> include repair or maintenance. Therefore, the government may fund repair and maintenance projects with O&M funds, regardless of the cost. AR 420-10, Glossary, sec. II; AFI 32-1032, para. 1.3.2; OPNAVINST 11010.20F, paras. 3.1.1 and 4.1.1.

3.   Congress exercises its control over military construction projects through its power of the purse. With limited exceptions, each project over $3 million is individually authorized and appropriated. Smaller projects are funded with O&M appropriations, or Unspecified Minor Military Construction Appropriations. To differentiate between the types of funding needed, an accurate cost estimate is essential. Consequently, an independent government estimate, or IGE, is necessary if the proposed contract, or any proposed modification to a construction contract, exceeds the simplified acquisition threshold. The Contracting Officer may require an IGE for contracts less than the simplified acquisition threshold. The IGE is not normally disclosed to offerors. FAR 36.203. IGEs will be marked "For Official Use Only," or "FOUO." PGI 236.203.

C.   **Contracting Procedures**.

1.   The government must award construction contracts in accordance with FAR Part 36, DFARS Part 236, and any applicable service supplement, regardless of the funding source.

2.   These steps normally include:

    a.   Deciding which acquisition method to use;

    b.   Deciding which type of contract to use;

    c.   Deciding what, if any, pre-bid communications are required (or otherwise warranted);

    d.   Deciding what information and which clauses to place in the solicitation;

    e.   Deciding which contractor should receive the award; and

    f.   Administering the contract.

3.   Because the government will often prepare a detailed design for the project, and because Congress limits use of cost type contracts to acquire construction, fixed-price contracts awarded by sealed bidding are more

Construction Contracting

common than in other types of contracting.

IV. METHODS OF ACQUIRING CONSTRUCTION.

A. **Sealed Bidding**. FAR 6.401; FAR Part 14; FAR 36.103. Contracting officers must use sealed bidding procedures to acquire construction if:

1. Time permits;

2. Award will be made on the basis of price and price-related factors;

3. Discussions are not necessary; and

4. There is a reasonable expectation of receiving more than one bid.

B. **Negotiated Procedures**. FAR 6.401; FAR Part 15; FAR 36.103.

1. Contracting officers must use negotiated procedures to acquire construction if:

   a. Time does not permit the use of seal bidding procedures;

   b. Award will not be made on the basis of price and price-related factors;

   c. Discussions are necessary, or

   d. There is not a reasonable expectation of receiving more than one bid. See Michael C. Avino, Inc., B-250689, Feb. 17, 1993, 93-1 CPD ¶ 148; see also Pardee Constr. Co., B-256414, June 13, 1994, 94-1 CPD ¶ 372.

2. **Practice Pointer**: For the most part, the decision to use competitive negotiation procedures is made based upon factor b., because design and technical factors not related to price.

3. Contracting officers may use negotiated procedures to acquire construction outside the United States, its possessions, or Puerto Rico, even if sealed bidding is otherwise appropriate.

4. Contracting officers must use negotiated procedures to acquire architect-engineer services.

C. **Job Order Contracting**. AFARS Subpart 5117.90. See Schnorr-Stafford Constr., Inc., B-227323, Aug. 12, 1987, 87-2 CPD ¶ 153; Salmon & Assoc., B-227079, Aug. 12, 1987, 87-2 CPD ¶ 152.

1. A job order contract (JOC) is an indefinite-delivery, indefinite-quantity contract used to acquire real property maintenance/repair and minor construction by task orders.

2. The government develops task specifications and a unit price book, with line item prices. Offeror's bid a mark-up (referred to as a "coefficient" and comprising cost factors such as design costs, bonds, overhead, and profit), which is included in the contract. For individual tasks, the contractor multiplies the government's unit price by its own mark up (e.g., profit + overhead) to arrive at its bid/proposal price for the task.

3. After contract award, the parties enter into bilateral task orders for individual projects based on the tasks and prices specified in the JOC.[3]

4. JOC Limitations.

   a. The government should not use a JOC for projects with an estimated value less than $2,000, or greater than the authority delegated to the installation, usually at the O&M construction threshold of $1,000,000. AFARS 5117.9000(a).

   b. The government cannot use a JOC to acquire installation facilities engineering support services (e.g., custodial or ground maintenance services). AFARS 5117.9002(b).

   c. The government cannot use a JOC to acquire architect-engineer services. AFARS 5117.9002(b).

---

[3] Each task order becomes a fixed-price, lump-sum contract. AFARS 5117.9003-1(e).

d. An IGE is required for orders of $100,000 or more. AFARS 5117.9004-3(c).

e. The government should <u>not</u> use a JOC to acquire work:

(1) Normally set aside for small and disadvantaged businesses;

(2) Traditionally covered by requirements contracts (e.g., painting, roofing, etc.);

(3) Covered by contracts awarded under the Commercial Activities Program; or

(4) The government can effectively and economically accomplish inhouse. AFARS 5117.9003-3(a).

D. Simplified Acquisition of Base Engineer Requirements (SABER) Program.

1. Reference. AFFARS IG 5336.9201, Air Force Contracting Construction Guide, Chapter 3.

2. Similar in scope and nature to the Army's JOC program, SABER is an Air Force ID/IQ contract vehicle to expedite the execution of non-complex minor construction and maintenance and repair projects.

3. The process of using the SABER is similar to the JOC. An established Unit Price Book and coefficients are combined to price each specific project. SABER contracts typically use a commercial unit price book.

4. SABER Limitations.

a. SABER should not be used to replace a traditional construction program, or for large, complex construction projects. SABER should also not be used for projects that are traditionally single skill/materials projects that are more appropriate for competitively bid contracts or single trade ID/IQs.

b. Saber shall not be used to acquire architect-engineering (A-E) services.

c. Individual SABER delivery orders shall not exceed $750,000.

d. SABER may not be used to perform non-personal services subject to the Service Contract Act.

E. Design-Build Contracting. 10 U.S.C. § 2305a; 41 U.S.C. § 3309; FAR Subpart 36.3.

1. Background. In the past, construction contracting was sequential: first, a contract was issued to an architect-engineer to design the project, then a contract was competitively awarded to a prime contractor to construct the project. The architect-engineer could not compete to build the design. Innovations in the construction industry led to a design-build contract format, where a single contract was issued to a prime contractor who is responsible for both design and construction of the project. In 1995, Congress authorized a design-build process similar to that used in private industry by establishing new, two-phase design-build selection procedures. National Defense Authorization Act of 1996, Pub. L. No. 104-106, 110 Stat. 186 (1995).

2. Definitions. FAR 36.102.

a. "Design" is the process of defining the construction requirement, producing the technical specifications and drawings, and preparing the construction cost estimate.

b. "Design-bid-build" is the traditional method of construction contracting in which design and construction are sequential and contracted for separately, with two contracts and two contractors.

c. "Design-build" is the new method of construction contracting in which

Construction Contracting

design and construction are combined in a single contract with a single contractor.

d. "Two-phase design-build" is a "design-build" method of construction contracting in which the government selects a limited number of offerors in Phase One to submit detailed proposals in Phase Two.

3. Policy. FAR 36.104. See FAR 36.301(b).

a. A contracting officer may use either design-bid-build or design-build procedures to acquire construction.

b. Unless a contracting officer decides to use design-bid-build (or another authorized acquisition procedure), the contracting officer must use two-phase design-build procedures to acquire construction if:

(1) The contracting officer anticipates receiving three or more offers;

(2) Offerors must perform a substantial amount of design work (and incur substantial expenses) before they can develop their price proposals; and

(3) The contracting officer has considered the factors set forth in FAR 36.301(b)(2), including:

(a) The extent to which the agency has adequately defined its project requirements;

(b) The time constraints for delivery;

(c) The capability and experience of potential offerors;

(d) The suitability of the project for two-phase design-build procedures;

(e) The capability of the agency to manage the two-phase selection process;

(f) Other criteria established by the head of the contracting activity (HCA).

4. Procedures. FAR 36.303.

a. Design-build contracts are based on a two phase process; design and construction. The agency may issue one solicitation covering both phases, or two solicitations in sequence.

b. Phase One. FAR 36.303-1.

(1) The agency evaluates Phase One proposals to determine which offerors the agency will ask to submit Phase Two proposals.

(2) The Phase One solicitation must include:

(a) The scope of work;

(b) The Phase One evaluation factors (e.g., technical approach, technical qualifications, etc.);

(c) The Phase Two evaluation factors; and

(d) A statement regarding the maximum number of offerors that will be selected to submit phase-two proposals.[4]

c. Phase Two. FAR 36.303-2. The contracting officer awards one contract using competitive

---

[4] This number should not exceed five unless the contracting officer determines that including more than five offerors in the competitive range is in the government's best interests. FAR 36.303-1(a)(4).

negotiation procedures to complete the design and build the project.

F. **Construction as "Acquisition of Commercial Items,"** FAR Part 12.

1. On 3 July 2003, the Administrator of the Office of Federal Procurement Policy (OFPP) issued a memorandum stating that FAR Part 12, Acquisition of Commercial Items, "should rarely, if ever be used for new construction acquisitions or non-routine alteration and repair services." Rather, "in accordance with long-standing practice, agencies should apply the policies of FAR Part 36 to these acquisitions." See Memorandum, Administrator of Office of Federal Procurement Policy, to Agency Senior Procurement Executives, Subject: Applicability of FAR Part 12 to Construction Acquisitions (July 3, 2003).

2. The memorandum stated that Part 12 acquisitions are generally well suited for certain types of construction activities "that lack the level of variability found in new construction and complex alteration and repair," such as routine painting or carpeting, simple hanging of drywall, everyday electrical or plumbing work, and similar noncomplex services."

V. CONTRACT TYPES.

A. **Firm Fixed-Price (FFP) Contracts**. FAR 36.207.

1. Agencies normally award FFP contracts for construction.

2. The contracting officer may require pricing on a lump-sum, unit price, or combination basis.

   a. With lump-sum pricing, the agency pays a lump-sum for:

      (1) The total project; or

      (2) Defined portions of the project.

   b. With unit pricing, the agency pays a unit price for a specified quantity of

work units. For example, the agency may pay a fixed-unit price for the amount of material excavated during construction, or the amount of concrete used.

   c. Agencies must use lump-sum pricing unless:

      (1) The contract involves large quantities of work, such as grading, paving, building outside utilities, or site preparation;

      (2) The agency cannot estimate the quantities of work adequately;

      (3) The estimated quantities of work may change significantly during construction; or

      (4) Offerors would have to expend a lot of time/money to develop adequate estimates.

B. **Fixed-Price Contracts with Economic Price Adjustment Clauses (FP w/EPA).** **FAR 36.207(c)**. Agencies may use this type of contract if:

1. The use of an EPA clause is customary for the type of work the agency is acquiring;

2. A significant number of offerors would not bid unless the agency included an EPA clause in the contract; or

3. Offerors would include unwarranted contingencies in their prices unless the agency included an EPA clause in the contract.

C. **Cost-Reimbursement Contracts**. See Military Construction Appropriations Act, 2002, Pub. L. No. 107-64, § 101, 115 Stat. 474 (2001); DFARS 236.271; AFARS 5116.306. The Assistant Secretary of Defense (Production and Logistics) (ASD(P&D)) must approve the award of a cost-plus-fixed-fee contract for construction if:

Construction Contracting

1. The activity uses military construction appropriations;

2. Performance will occur in the United States (Alaska excluded); and

3. The acquiring activity expects the contract to exceed $25,000.

D. Mixing Contract Types on Construction Sites. FAR 36.208.

Activities cannot use incentive, cost-plus-fixed-fee, or other fee contracts at the same work site with firm fixed-price contracts without the approval of the HCA.

VI. PRE-BID COMMUNICATIONS.

A. Presolicitation Notices. FAR 36.213-2; FAR 36.701(a); FAR 53.301-1417, Standard Form (SF) 1417, Presolicitation Notice (Construction Contract).

1. The contracting officer must send presolicitation notices to prospective bidders if the proposed contract is expected to equal or exceed the simplified acquisition threshold.

2. Contents. FAR 36.213-2(b). Among other things, presolicitation notices must:

   a. Describe the magnitude of the project;[5]

   b. State the location of the proposed work;

   c. Include relevant dates (e.g., the proposed bid opening date and the proposed contract completion date);

   d. State where contractors can inspect the contract plans without charge;[6]

   e. Specify a date by which bidders should submit requests for the solicitation;

   f. State whether the government intends to restrict award to small businesses; and

   g. Specify the amount the government intends to charge for solicitation documents, if any.

3. Distribution. FAR 36.211.

   a. The contracting officer should send presolicitation notices to:

      (1) Contractors on the bidders list; and

      (2) Organizations that maintain display rooms for such information.

   b. The contracting officer determines the geographical range of distribution.

B. Government-wide Point of Entry (GPE). FAR 36.213, FAR 5.003. The contracting officer must also post the presolicitation notice in the GPE.

VII. SOLICITATION.

A. Forms. FAR 36.701; FAR 53.301-1442, SF 1442, Solicitation, Offer, and Award (Construction, Alteration, or Repair); DFARS 236.701.

1. The contracting officer uses a SF 1442 in lieu of a SF 33 as the contract cover sheet.

---

[5] The contracting officer cannot disclose the government cost estimate; however, the contracting officer can state the magnitude of the project in terms of physical characteristics and estimated price range. FAR 36.204; DFARS 236.204. The estimated price ranges are as follows:

> (a) Less than $25,000.
> (b) Between $25,000 and $100,000.
> (c) Between $100,000 and $250,000.
> (d) Between $250,000 and $500,000.
> (e) Between $500,000 and $1,000,000.
> (f) Between $1,000,000 and $5,000,000.
> (g) Between $5,000,000 and $10,000,000.
> (h) More than $10,000,000.

[6] Beginning on 17 August 2000, the Contracting Officer may provide contract drawings and specifications solely in electronic format. DFARS 252.236-70001.

2. If a bidder fails to return this form with its offer, the offer is nonresponsive in a sealed bid acquisition. See C.J.M. Contractors, Inc., B-250493.2, Nov. 24, 1992, 92-2 CPD ¶ 376.

B. Format. The contracting officer may provide drawings, specifications, and maps in either hard-copy or completely in electronic format. DFARS 236.570 and 252.236-7001.

C. Statutory Limitations. FAR 36.205; DFARS 252.236-7006.

1. The solicitation must include any statutory cost limitations. See K.C. Brandon Constr., B-245934, Feb. 3, 1992, 92-1 CPD ¶ 139.

2. The government must normally reject any offer that:

   a. Exceeds the applicable statutory limitations;[7] or

   b. Is only within the statutory limitations because it is materially unbalanced.

   c. See William G. Tadlock Constr., B-252580, June 29, 1993, 93-1 CPD ¶ 502; H. Angelo & Co., B-249412, Nov. 13, 1992, 92-2 CPD ¶ 344.

3. Some statutory limitations are waivable. See 10 U.S.C. § 2853; see also TECOM, Inc., B-240421, Nov. 9, 1990, 90-2 CPD ¶ 386.

D. Site Familiarization Clauses.

Site Investigation and Conditions Affecting the Work. FAR 36.210; FAR 36.503; FAR 52.236-3. A construction contractor is expected to investigate the site of the proposed construction to

---

[7] The contracting officer may award separate contracts for individual items whose prices are within the applicable statutory limitations if: (1) the contracting officer included a provision that permits such awards in the solicitation; and (2) such awards are in the government's interest. FAR 36.205(c); FAR 52.214-19.

acquaint itself with the conditions affecting the proposed work. Among other things, a contractor is supposed to investigate:

- Conditions bearing upon transportation, disposal, handling, and storage of materials;
- The availability of labor, water, electric power, and roads;
- Uncertainties of weather, river stages, tides, and similar physical conditions at the site;
- The conformation and condition of the ground;
- The character of needed equipment and facilities;
- The character, quality, and quantity of discoverable surface and subsurface materials and/or obstacles.

See Aulson Roofing, Inc., ASBCA No. 37677, 91-2 BCA ¶ 23,720; Fred Burgos Constr. Co., ASBCA No. 41395, 91-2 BCA ¶ 23,706.

a. A contractor need not hire its own geologists or conduct extensive engineering efforts to verify conditions that it can reasonably infer from the solicitation or a site visit. See Michael-Mark Ltd., IBCA No. 2697, 94-1 BCA ¶ 26,453.

b. A contractor must perform at the contract price if the contractor could have discovered a condition by a reasonable site investigation. See Weeks Dredging & Contracting, Inc. v. United States, 13 Cl. Ct. 193 (1987); Avisco, Inc., ENG BCA No. 5802, 93-3 BCA ¶ 26,172; Signal Contracting, Inc., ASBCA No. 44963, 93-2 BCA ¶ 25,877; cf. I.M.I., Inc., B-233863, Jan. 11, 1989, 89-1 CPD ¶ 30.

c. The government is not normally bound by the contractor's interpretation of government data and representations not included in the written solicitation. See Eagle Contracting, Inc., AGBCA No. 88-225-1, 92-3 BCA ¶ 25,018.

2. Physical Data. FAR 36.504; FAR 52.236-4. To avoid the costs of multiple bidders performing detailed site examinations, the contracting officer may provide physical data, such as test borings, hydrographic data, or weather data) for the use of the bidders and the successful awardee. The government is not responsible for a contractor's erroneous interpretations or conclusions. But see United Contractors v. United States, 177 Ct. Cl. 151, 368 F.2d 585 (Ct. Cl. 1966). Errors in the data may be a differing site condition as discussed in section IX.C.

3. Changes In the Site After Bid Submission Date. The government is normally responsible for increased performance costs caused by changes at a site after the date of bid submission, even if offerors agree to extend the bid acceptance period. See Valley Constr. Co., ENG BCA No. 6007, 93-3 BCA ¶ 26,171.

E. Bid Guarantees. FAR 28.101; FAR 52.228-1; FAR 53.301-24, SF 24, Bid Bond.

1. Construction contractors are typically required to submit a bid bond with their bid. A bid guarantee ensures that a bidder will not withdraw its bid during the bid acceptance period; and execute a written contract and furnish other required bonds at the time of contract award.

2. Requirement. FAR 28.101-1.

   a. The contracting officer must normally require a bid guarantee whenever the solicitation requires performance and payment bonds. Performance and payment bonds are required by the Miller Act, 40 U.S.C. § 3131) for construction contracts exceeding $150,000, except as authorized by law. FAR 28.102-1. (See Section IX.B, below.)

   b. Contracting Officers may still require bid guarantees in construction contracts less than $150,000. See Lawson's Enterprises, Inc. Comp. Gen., B-286708, Jan. 31, 2001, 2001 CPD ¶ 36.

   c. The chief of the contracting office, however, may waive the requirement to provide a bid guarantee if the chief of the contracting office determines that it is not in the government's best interest to require a bid guarantee (e.g., for overseas construction, emergency acquisitions, and sole-source contracts).

3. Form.

   a. The bid guarantee must be in the form required by the solicitation. See HR Gen. Maint. Corp. B-260404, May 16, 1995, 95-1 CPD ¶ 247; Concord Analysis, Inc., B-239730, Dec. 4, 1990, 90-2 CPD ¶ 452. But see Mid-South Metals, Inc., B-257056, Aug. 23, 1994, 94-2 CPD ¶ 78.

   b. The FAR permits offerors to use surety bonds, postal money orders, certified checks, cashier's checks, irrevocable letters of credit, U.S. bonds, and/or cash. FAR 52.228-1. See Treasury Dep't Cir. 570 (listing acceptable commercial sureties).

   c. If a bidder uses an individual surety, the surety must provide a security interest in acceptable assets equal to the penal sum of the bond. FAR 28.203. See Paradise Const. Co., Comp. Gen. Dec. B-289144, 2001 CPD ¶ 192. The adequacy of an individual surety's offering is a matter of responsibility, not responsiveness. See Gene Quigley, Jr., B-241565, Feb. 19, 1991, 70

Comp. Gen. 273, 91-1 CPD ¶ 182. But see Harrison Realty Corp., B-254461.2, 93-2 CPD ¶ 345. A bidder may not be its own individual surety. See Astor V. Bolden, B-257038, Apr. 26, 1994, 94-1 CPD ¶ 288.

4. Penal Amount. FAR 28.101-2 (b). The bid bond/guarantee must equal 20% of the bid, but not exceed $3,000,000. But see FAR 28.101-4(c).

5. The contracting officer may not accept a bid accompanied by an apparently unenforceable guarantee. Conservatek Indus., Inc., B-254927, Jan. 26, 1994, 94-1 CPD ¶ 42; MKB Constructors, Inc., B-255098, Jan. 10, 1994, 94-1 CPD ¶ 10; Arlington Constr., Inc., B-252535, July 9, 1993, 93-2 CPD ¶ 10; Cherokee Enter., Inc., B-252948, June 3, 1993, 93-1 CPD ¶ 429; Hugo Key & Son, Inc., B-245227, Aug. 22, 1991, 91-2 CPD ¶ 189; Techno Eng'g & Constr., B-243932, July 23, 1991, 91-2 CPD ¶ 87; Maytal Constr. Corp., B-241501, Dec. 10, 1990, 90-2 CPD ¶ 476; Bird Constr., B-240002, Sept. 19, 1990, 90-2 CPD ¶ 234.

6. Noncompliance with Bid Guarantee Requirements. FAR 28.101-4.

    a. Noncompliance with bid guarantee requirements normally renders a bid nonresponsive. See Alarm Control Co., B-246010, Nov. 18, 1991, 91-2 CPD ¶ 472.

    b. The contracting officer, however, may waive the requirement to submit a bid guarantee under nine circumstances. FAR 28.101-4(c). See Rufus Murray Commercial Roofing Sys., B-258761, Feb. 14, 1995, 95-1 CPD ¶ 83; Apex Servs., Inc., B-255118, Feb. 9, 1994, 94-1 CPD ¶ 95.

F. **Pre-Bid Conferences**. FAR 14.207. Contracting officers may hold pre-bid conferences when necessary to brief bidders and explain complex specifications and requirements; however, client control is critical. See Cessna Aircraft Co., ASBCA No. 48118, 95-1 BCA ¶ 27,560.

G. **Bid/Proposal Preparation Time**. FAR 36.213-3. The contracting officer must give bidders ample time to conduct site visits, obtain subcontractor bids, examine data, and prepare estimates. See Raymond Int'l of Del., Inc., ASBCA No. 13121, 70-1 BCA ¶ 8,341.

VIII. AWARD.

A. **Responsiveness Issues**.

1. A bid is nonresponsive if it exceeds a statutory dollar limitation. FAR 36.205(c); DFARS 252.236-7006. See Ward Constr. Co., B-240064, July 30, 1990, 90-2 CPD ¶ 87; Wynn Constr. Co., B-220649, Feb. 21, 1986, 86-1 CPD ¶ 184.

2. A bid is nonresponsive if the bidder fails to comply with the bid guarantee requirements. FAR 28.101-4(a). See Maytal Constr. Corp., B-241501, Dec. 10, 1990, 90-2 CPD ¶ 476. But see FAR 28.101-4(c) (listing the nine circumstances under which the contracting officer may waive the requirement to submit a bid guarantee).

3. A bid is nonresponsive if the bidder offers a shorter bid acceptance period than the solicitation requires. See SF 1442, Block 13D.

4. A bid is nonresponsive if the bidder fails to acknowledge a material amendment. See Dutra Constr. Co., B-241202, Jan. 31, 1991, 91-1 CPD ¶ 97.

5. A bid is nonresponsive if the bidder fails to acknowledge a Davis-Bacon wage rate amendment unless the offeror is bound by a wage rate equal to or greater than the new rate. See Tri-Tech Int'l, Inc., B-246701, Mar. 23, 1992, 92-1 CPD ¶ 304; Fast Elec. Contractors, Inc., B-223823, Dec. 2, 1986, 86-2 CPD ¶ 627.

Construction Contracting

6. A bid is nonresponsive if the bidder equivocates on the requirement to obtain permits and licenses. See Bishop Contractors, Inc., B-246526, Dec. 17, 1991, 91-2 CPD ¶ 555.

7. A bid is nonresponsive if it is materially unbalanced. FAR 36.205(d); FAR 52.214-19.

8. The government may reject a bid if the bid prices are materially unbalanced between line items, or between subline items.

9. A bid is materially unbalanced when:

10. The bid is based on prices that are significantly less than cost for some work, and significantly greater than cost for other work and there is reasonable doubt that the bid will result in the lowest overall cost to the government; or

11. The bid is so unbalanced that it is tantamount to allowing the contractor to recover money in advance of performing the work.

B. Responsibility Issues.

1. Prequalification of Sources. DFARS 236.272. The contracting officer may establish a list of contractors that are qualified to perform a specific contract and limit competition to those contractors.

   a. The HCA must: (1) determine that the project is so urgent or complex that prequalification is necessary and (2) approve the prequalification procedures.

   b. If the contracting officer finds a small business unqualified for responsibility reasons, the contracting officer must refer the matter to the Small Business Administration (SBA) for a preliminary recommendation or Certificate of Competency. If the contracting officer fails to refer to the SBA, this is a defect that is a valid grounds for protest.

   c. If the SBA determines that the small business is responsible, the contracting officer must allow it to submit a proposal.

2. Performance Evaluation Reports. FAR 36.201; FAR 53.301-1420, SF 1420, Performance Evaluation, Construction Contracts; AFARS 5136.201; DD Form 2628, Performance Evaluation (Construction).

   a. Contracting activities must prepare performance evaluation reports for:

      (1) Construction contracts valued at $700,000 or more and

      (2) Default-terminated contracts. FAR 42.1502(e).

   b. Upon their completion, contracting activities must send performance evaluation reports to: U.S. Army Corps of Engineers, Portland District, ATTN: CENWP-CT-I, P.O. Box 2946, Portland, OR 97208-2946. Available online at http://www.nwp.usace.army.mil/ct/i/. You may also reach this data through: www.usace.army.mil.

   c. Contracting officers may use performance evaluation reports as part of their preaward survey.

3. Small Businesses. FAR 19.602-1. Before a contracting officer can reject a small business as nonresponsible, the contracting officer must refer the matter to the SBA for a Certificate of Competency (COC).

4. Performance of Work by Contractor. FAR 36.501; FAR 52.236-1.

   a. Whether a contractor intends to perform the contractually required percentage of work with its own forces is normally a matter of responsibility, not responsiveness. See Luther Constr. Co., B-241719, Jan. 28, 1991, 91-1 CPD ¶ 76. But see Blount, Inc. v. United States, 22

438

Cl. Ct. 221 (1990); <u>C. Iber & Sons, Inc.</u>, B-247920.2, Aug. 12, 1992, 92-2 CPD ¶ 99.

b. FAR clause 52.236-1 (Performance of Work by the Contractor). The contract may provide that the prime contractor perform a specific percentage of the work. This provision does <u>not</u> apply to small business or 8(a) set-asides. FAR 36.501(b). <u>But see</u> FAR clause 52.219-14.

C. **Price Evaluation**. In order to stay within available funding and ceilings, a construction contract may include optional additional items. The contracting officer must evaluate additive items as provided in the solicitation. <u>See</u> DFARS 252.236-7007. The contracting officer must award the contract to the bidder who submits the low bid for the base project and the additive items that, in order of priority, provide the most features within the applicable funding constraints. The contracting officer must select the low bidder based on the funding available at the time of bid opening. <u>See</u> <u>Huntington Constr., Inc.</u>, B-230604, June 30, 1988, 67 Comp. Gen. 499, 88-1 CPD ¶ 619; <u>Applicators Inc.</u>, B-270162, Feb. 1, 1996, 96-1 CPD ¶ 32.

IX. CONTRACT ADMINISTRATION.

A. **General.** Construction contracts include a number of unique terms and conditions, many of which are similar to those included in commercial construction contracts. These include bonding requirements, risk-allocation provisions, liquidated damages, and government rights to direct the work.

B. **Performance and Payment Bonds.**

1. After contract award, the contractor must furnish the contracting officer with performance and payment bonds required by the Miller Act, 40 U.S.C. § 3131; FAR 28.102-1.

   a. Contracts Over $150,000. FAR 28.102-1(a); FAR 28.102-3(a); FAR 52.228-15. The contractor must provide performance and payment bonds before it can begin work. <u>See</u> <u>TLC Servs., Inc.</u>, B-254972.2, Mar. 30, 1994, 94-1 CPD ¶ 235.

   b. Contracts Between $35,000 and $150,000. FAR 28.102-1(b); FAR 28.102-3(b); FAR 52.228-13. The contracting officer must select two or more of the following payment protections:

      (1) Payment bonds;

      (2) Irrevocable letters of credit;[8]

      (3) Tripartite escrow agreements; or

      (4) Certificates of deposit.

   c. The contractor must submit one of the selected payment protections before it can begin work.

2. Performance Bonds. FAR 28.102-2(a); FAR 52.228-15; FAR 53.301-25, SF 25, Performance Bond. A performance bond guarantees the contractor's successful performance of the contract. It protects the government. The penal amount of the bond is normally 100% of the original contract price.

   a. The contracting officer may reduce the penal amount if the contracting officer determines that a lesser amount adequately protects the government.

---

[8] The contracting officer is supposed to give "particular consideration" to including irrevocable letters of credit as one of the selected payment protections. FAR 28.102-1(b).

b. The contracting officer may require additional protection if the contract price increases.

3. Payment Bonds. FAR 28.102-2(b); FAR 52.228-15; FAR 53.301-25-A, SF 25-A, Payment Bond. Payment bonds protect laborers, subcontractors, and suppliers against the risk of nonpayment by the prime contractor. Payment bonds substitute for a unpaid laborer or subcontractor's typical remedy of filing a mechanics lien on the project under state law. The government's sovereign immunity protects it from mechanics liens.

a. The penal amount of a payment bond must equal 100% of the original contract price unless the contracting officer determines, in writing, that requiring a payment bond in that amount is impractical. If the contracting officer determines that requiring a payment bond in an amount equal to 100% of the original contract price is impractical, the contracting officer must set the penal amount of the bond.

b. The amount of the payment bond may never be less than the amount of the performance bond.

See Construction Industry Payment Protection Act of 1999, Pub. L. No. 106-49, 113 Stat. 231.

4. Noncompliance with Bond Requirements. Failure to provide acceptable bonds justifies terminating the contract for default. FAR 52.228-1. See Pacific Sunset Builders, Inc., ASBCA No. 39312, 93-3 BCA ¶ 25,923.

5. Payments and Withholding Contract Payments. FAR 28.106-7.

a. As discussed in chapter 21, construction contractors are paid based on work actually performed.

b. During contract performance, the contracting officer should not withhold payments to the prime contractor based on nonpayment of subcontractors. The unpaid suppliers have a remedy against the payment bond. FAR 28.106-7(a). But see Balboa Ins. Co. v. United States, 775 F.2d 1158 (Fed. Cir. 1985); National Surety Corp., 31 Fed. Cl. 565 (1994); Johnson v. All-State Const., 329 F.3d 848 (CAFC 2003) (government was entitled to withhold progress payments pursuant to its common-law right to set-off pending liquidated damages).

c. After contract completion, the contracting officer must withhold final payment if the surety provides written notice regarding the contractor's failure to pay its laborers, subcontractors, or suppliers.

(1) The surety must agree to hold the government harmless.

(2) The contracting officer may release final payment if:

(a) The parties reach an agreement; or

(b) A court determines the parties' rights.

d. Withholding for Labor Violations. See generally FAR Part 22.

6. Waiver of Bonds. 10 U.S.C. §§ 270a(b) and 270e; FAR 28.102-1(a).

a. The contracting officer may waive the requirement to provide performance and payment bonds if:

(1) The contractor performs the work in a foreign country and the contracting officer determines that it is impracticable to require the contractor to provide the bonds; or

(2) The Miller Act (or another statute) authorizes the waiver.

b. Note that requirements for some type of financial security (i.e., irrevocable letters of credit) are quite common in foreign commercial contracts, so contracting officers should carefully examine a request to waive performance or payment bonds.

c. The Service Secretaries may waive the requirement to provide performance and payment bonds for cost-type contracts.

C. Differing Site Conditions (DSC). FAR 52.236-2.

1. The Differing Site Conditions clause is a risk-allocation provision that provides a contractor an equitable adjustment for some differing site conditions, provided the contractor provides prompt, written notice. By assuming the risk, the government presumably obtains lower prices from bidders.

2. There are two types of differing site conditions. See Consolidated Constr., Inc., GSBCA No. 8871, 88-2 BCA ¶ 20,811. Type I differing site conditions are site conditions that differ from a representation made about the site in the contract itself, such as inaccurate test boring data. Type II differing site conditions are site conditions that are unknown and so unusual that the site condition could not be reasonably anticipated.

a. Type I Differing Site Conditions. To recover for a Type I condition, the contractor must prove that:

(1) The contract made a representation (either implicitly or explicitly) that indicated a particular site condition. See Franklin Pavkov Constr. Co., HUD BCA No. 93-C-C13, 94-3 BCA ¶ 27,078; Glagola Constr. Co., Inc., ASBCA No. 45579, 93-3 BCA ¶ 26,179; Konoike Constr. Co., ASBCA No. 36342, 91-1 BCA ¶ 23,440.

(2) The contractor reasonably interpreted and relied on the representation made by the contract. CCI, Inc., ASBCA Nol 57316, 14-1 BCA ¶ 35,543.

(3) The encountered site condition was latent or subsurface, and the encountered site condition differed materially from the condition represented by the contract. See Meredith Constr. Co., ASBCA No. 40839, 93-1 BCA ¶ 25,399 (no differing site condition when slope, soil profile, and 1987 water elevations were accurate, and the contract was silent on drainage); but see Caesar Constr., Inc., ASBCA No. 41059, 91-1 BCA ¶ 23,639 (finding a representation to be implicit).

(4) The claimed costs were attributable solely to the differing site condition. See P.J. Dick, Inc., GSBCA No. 12036, 94-3 BCA ¶ 27,073.

b. Type II Differing Site Conditions. To recover for a Type II condition, the contractor must prove that:

(1) The conditions encountered were unusual physical conditions that were unknown at the time of contract award. See Walser v. United States, 23 Cl. Ct. 591 (1991); Gulf Coast Trailing Co., ENG BCA No. 5795, 94-2 BCA ¶

26,921; Soletanche Rodio Nicholson (JV), ENG BCA No. 5796, 94-1 BCA ¶ 26,472.

(2) The conditions differed materially from those ordinarily encountered. See Green Constr. Co., ASBCA No. 46157, 94-1 BCA ¶ 26,572; Virginia Beach Air Conditioning Corp., ASBCA No. 42538, 92-1 BCA ¶ 24,432; Arctic Slope, Alaska Gen./SKW Eskimos, Inc., ENG BCA No. 5023, 90-2 BCA ¶ 22,850.

3. The Differing Site Conditions clause only covers conditions existing at the time of contract award. Acts of nature occurring after contract award and the resulting changed conditions are not differing site conditions. See Arundel Corp. v. United States, 96 Ct. Cl. 77, 354 F.2d 252 (1942); Meredith Constr. Co., ASBCA No. 40839, 93-1 BCA ¶ 25,399; PK Contractors, Inc., ENG BCA No. 4901, 92-1 BCA ¶ 24,583. But see Valley Constr. Co., ENG BCA No. 6007, 93-3 BCA ¶ 26,171 (differing site condition existed when change occurred after bid, but before award).

4. The contractor may not recover if the contractor could have discovered the condition during a reasonable site investigation. See Urban General Contractors, Inc., ASBCA No. 49653, 96-2 BCA ¶ 28,516; Indelsea, S.A., ENG BCA No. PCC-117, 95-2 BCA ¶ 27,633; Steele Contractors, Inc., ENG BCA No. 6043, 95-2 BCA ¶ 27,653; Sagebrush Consultants, 01-1 BCA ¶ 31,159 (IBCA), and American Constr., 01-1 BCA ¶ 31,202. cf. Operational Serv. Corp., ASBCA No. 37059, 93-3 BCA ¶ 26,190.

5. The contractor must prove its damages were solely attributable to the differing site condition. See H.V. Allen Co., ASBCA No. 40645, 91-1 BCA ¶ 23,393; see also Praught Constr. Corp., ASBCA No. 39670, 93-2 BCA ¶ 25,896.

6. The contractor must promptly notify the government.

a. Untimely notification may bar a differing site condition claim if the late notice prejudices the government. See Moon Constr. Co. v. General Servs. Admin., GSBCA No. 11766, 93-3 BCA ¶ 26,017; see also Hemphill Contracting Co., ENG BCA No. 5698, 94-1 BCA ¶ 26,491; Meisel Rohrbau, ASBCA No. 35566, 92-1 BCA ¶ 24,434; Holloway Constr., Holloway Sand & Gravel Co., ENG BCA No. 4805, 89-2 BCA ¶ 21,713.

b. If the government's defense to a differing site condition claim is made more difficult—but not impossible—by the late notice, courts and boards will normally waive the notice requirement and place a heavier burden of persuasion on the contractor. See Glagola Constr. Co., ASBCA No. 45579, 93-3 BCA ¶ 26,179.

c. When the government is on notice of differing site conditions, but takes no exception to the contractor's notice or its corrective actions, the government must pay the contractor's increased costs. See Potomac Marine & Aviation, Inc., ASBCA No. 42417, 93-2 BCA ¶ 25,865.

d. Lack of notice of a differing site condition will not bar a contractor's recovery when the government breaches its duty to cooperate by directing the contractor to perform weekend work and subsequently failing to designate an inspector to whom the contractor may give notice during scheduled weekend work. See Hudson Contracting, Inc., ASBCA No. 41023, 94-1 BCA ¶ 26,466.

7. No differing site condition claim if the contract does not contain the Differing

Site Condition clause. See <u>Marine Industries Northwest, Inc.</u>, ASBCA No. 51942, 01-1 BCA ¶ 31,201 (board rejected a Type II DSC claims solely on the basis that there was no DSC clause in the contract. Without the DSC clause, the contractor bears complete risk for any differing conditions encountered).

8. Final payment bars an unreserved differing site condition claim. FAR 52.236-2(d).

D. Variations in Estimated Quantity. FAR 52.211-18.

1. A fixed-price contract may include quantities estimated by the government for certain unit-priced items of work. In those contracts, the government may elect to include a Variation in Estimated Quantity (VEQ) clause, which permits recovery by both the government and the contractor if actual quantity differs significantly from the estimated quantity.

2. If the actual quantity of a unit-priced item varies more than 15% above or below the estimated quantity, the contracting officer must equitably adjust the contract based on "any increase or decrease in costs due solely to the variation." See <u>Clement-Mtarri Cos.</u>, ASBCA No. 38170, 92-3 BCA ¶ 25,192, aff'd sub nom., <u>Shannon v. Clement-Mtarri Cos.</u>, 11 F.3d 1072 (Fed. Cir. 1993) (unpublished); cf. <u>Westland Mechanical, Inc.</u>, ASBCA No. 48844, 96-2 BCA ¶ 28,419 (finding the Variation in Estimated Quantity clause is not applicable to the minimum order/guarantee in an IDIQ contract).

3. It is presumed the equitable adjustment granted is at the unit-price of the contract line item, unless the opposing party proves that change in quantity also caused cost savings or cost increases. <u>Foley Co. v. United States</u>, 11 F.3d 1032 (Fed. Cir. 1993).

4. The contractor may request a performance period extension if the variation in the estimated quantity causes an increase in the performance period.

E. Suspension of Work. FAR 52.242-14.

1. The contracting officer may direct a contractor to suspend, interrupt, or delay work for the convenience of the government. <u>See</u> <u>Valquest Contracting, Inc.</u>, ASBCA No. 32454, 91-1 BCA ¶ 23,381. When a contractor receives an order to suspend work, it must do so, however the contractor may be entitled to an equitable adjustment for the suspension in certain circumstances.

2. A Suspension of Work is compensable <u>if</u>:

   a. It is unreasonable; the government may suspend work, without monetary liability, for a reasonable period of time. See <u>Southwest Constr. Corp.</u>, ENG BCA No. 5286, 94-3 BCA ¶ 27,120; <u>C&C Plumbing & Heating</u>, ASBCA No. 44270, 94-3 BCA ¶ 27,063; <u>Kimmins Contracting Corp.</u>, ASBCA No. 46390, 94-2 BCA ¶ 26,869.

   b. The contracting officer orders it; for an "actual" Suspension of Work to exist, the terms of the Suspension of Work clause require an order from the Contracting Officer, though a Court may allow for recovery without an order, if a "constructive suspensions of work" exists. See <u>Mergentime Corp.</u>, ENG BCA No. 5765, 92-2 BCA ¶ 25,007; <u>Durocher Dock & Dredge, Inc.</u>, ENG BCA No. 5768, 91-3 BCA ¶ 24,145; <u>Fruehauf Corp. v. United States</u>, 218 Ct. Cl. 456, 587 F.2d 486 (1978); <u>Lane Constr. Corp.</u>, ENG BCA No. 5834, 94-1 BCA ¶ 26,358. <u>But see Henderson, Inc.</u>, DOT BCA No. 2423, 94-2 BCA ¶ 26,728 (finding recovery under the Suspension of Work clause to apply for equity reasons, though finding neither an order or a constructive suspension).

   c. The contractor has not caused the suspension by its (or its subcontractor's) negligence or failure to perform. See Hvac Constr. Co., Inc. v. United States, 28 Fed. Cl. 690 (1993).

d. The cost of performance increases. See Frazier-Fleming Co., ASBCA No. 34537, 91-1 BCA ¶ 23,378.

3. The contractor may be entitled to delay costs (even if it finishes work on time) if it proves that it planned to finish the work early, but was delayed by the government. See Oneida Constr., Inc., ASBCA No. 44194, 94-3 BCA ¶ 27,237; Labco Constr., Inc., AGBCA No. 90-115-1, 94-2 BCA ¶ 26,910.

4. A government-ordered Suspension of Work will entitle a contractor to a time extension and a return of liquidated damages, though the contractor will not be able to recover costs it incurred (an equitable adjustment) if the suspension was for a reasonable period of time. See Farr Bros., Inc., ASBCA No. 42658, 92-2 BCA ¶ 24,991.

5. Profit is not recoverable and final payment bars unreserved suspension claims. FAR 52.242-14.

6. Constructive Suspensions.

a. A constructive suspension of work may arise if:

(1) The government fails to issue a notice to proceed within a reasonable time after contract award. See Marine Constr. & Dredging, Inc., ASBCA No. 38412, 95-1 BCA ¶ 27,286.

(2) The government fails to provide timely guidance following a reasonable request for direction. See Tayag Bros. Enters., Inc., ASBCA No. 42097, 94-2 BCA ¶ 26,962.

b. A contractor may not recover delay costs for more than 20 days unless the contractor notifies the government of the delay. FAR 52.242-14. This rule, however, is subject to a prejudice test.

F. **Permits and Responsibilities**. FAR 52.236-7.

1. A contractor must obtain applicable permits and licenses (and comply with applicable laws and regulations) at no additional cost to the government. See C'n R Indus. of Jacksonville, Inc., ASBCA No. 42209, 91-2 BCA ¶ 23,970; Holk Dev., Inc., ASBCA No. 40137, 90-2 BCA ¶ 22,852. But see Hills Materials v. Rice, 982 F.2d 514 (Fed. Cir. 1992); Hemphill Contracting Co., ENG BCA No. 5698, 94-1 BCA ¶ 26,491.

2. Burden on contractor is continuing and applies to requirements arising after contract award. It is well established that the Permits and Responsibilities clause requires contractors to comply with laws and regulations issued subsequent to award without additional compensation unless there is another clause in the contract that limits the clause to laws and regulations in effect at the time of award. Shirley Construction Co., ASBCA No. 42954 92-1 BCA ¶ 24,563.

3. Normally, licensing is a question of responsibility, not responsiveness. See Restec Contractors, Inc., B-245862, Feb. 6, 1992, 92-1 CPD ¶ 154; Computer Support Sys., Inc., B-239034, Aug. 2, 1990, 69 Comp. Gen. 645, 90-2 CPD ¶ 94. But see Bishop Contractors, Inc., B-246526, Dec. 17, 1991, 91-2 CPD ¶ 555.

4. A contractor assumes the risk of loss or damage to its equipment.[9] In addition, a contractor is responsible for injuries to third persons. See Potashnick Constr., Inc., ENG BCA No. 5551, 92-2 BCA ¶ 24,985.

5. A contractor is responsible for work in progress until the government accepts it.

---

[9] The contractor may bear similar responsibilities under a Government Furnished Property clause. FAR 52.245-4. See Technical Servs. K.H. Nehlsen GmbH, ASBCA No. 43869, 94-1 BCA ¶ 26,377.

444

See <u>Tyler Constr. Co.</u>, ASBCA No. 39365, 91-1 BCA ¶ 23,646; <u>D.J. Barclay & Co.</u>, ASBCA No. 28908, 88-2 BCA ¶ 20,741. <u>But see</u> <u>Fraser Eng'g Co.</u>, VABCA No. 3265, 91-3 BCA ¶ 24,223; <u>Joseph Beck & Assocs.</u>, ASBCA No. 31126, 88-1 BCA ¶ 20,428.

G.   Specifications and Drawings. FAR 52.236-21; DFARS 252.236-7001.

1.   The omission or misdescription of details of work that are necessary to carry out the intent of the contract drawings and specifications (or are customarily performed) does <u>not</u> relieve a contractor from its obligation to perform the omitted or misdescribed details of work. A contractor must perform as if the drawings and specifications describe the details fully and correctly. <u>See</u> <u>Wood & Co. v. Dep't of Treasury</u>, GSBCA No. 12452-TD, 94-1 BCA ¶ 26,395; <u>Single Ply Sys., Inc.</u>, ASBCA No. 42168, 91-2 BCA ¶ 24,032.

2.   The contractor must review all drawings before beginning work, and the contractor is responsible for any errors that a reasonable review would have detected. <u>M.A. Mortenson Co.</u>, ASBCA 50,383, 00-2 BCA ¶ 30,936, (denying Mortenson's claim based on omissions in construction drawings), <u>But see</u> <u>Wick Constr. Co.</u>, ASBCA No. 35378, 89-1 BCA ¶ 21,239.

3.   If the contract contains an Order of Precedence clause, and the specifications contain provisions that conflict with the contract drawings, the specifications govern. The parties may rely on this order of precedence regardless of whether an ambiguity is patent. <u>See</u> <u>Hensel Phelps Constr. Co.</u>, 886 F.2d 1296 (Fed. Cir. 1989); <u>Shemya Constructors</u>, ASBCA No. 45251, 94-1 BCA ¶ 26,346. <u>But see</u> <u>J.S. Alberici Constr. Co v. General Servs. Admin</u>, GSBCA No. 12386, 94-2 BCA ¶ 26,776 (finding, despite an Order of Precedence clause, a general performance specification did not override depictions on the drawings).

4.   The government cannot shift the responsibility for defective design specifications to a contractor through the use of a general disclaimer. <u>White v. Edsall Const. Co., Inc.</u>, 296 F.3d 1081 (Fed. Cir. 2002) (contractor is not obligated to "ferret out" hidden ambiguities and errors in the government's specifications and designs.)

H.   Liquidated Damages (LDs). FAR Subpart 11.5; F<u>AR 36.206; FAR 52.211-12, DFARS Subpart 211.5.</u>

1.   Liquidated damages are a contractual remedy that specifies a pre-agreed amount of damages in lieu of proving actual damages. Normally, liquidated damages are provided for delays in performance on construction contracts. The government may assess LDs <u>if</u>:

a.   Anticipated damages attributable to untimely performance were uncertain or difficult to quantify at the time of award; and

b.   The LDs bear a reasonable relationship to anticipated losses resulting from delayed completion.

c.   <u>See</u> <u>D.E.W., Inc.</u>, ASBCA No. 38392, 92-2 BCA ¶ 24,840; <u>Brooks Lumber Co.</u>, ASBCA No. 40743, 91-2 BCA ¶ 23,984; <u>JEM Dev. Corp.</u>, ASBCA No. 42645, 92-1 BCA ¶ 24,428; <u>Dave's Excavation</u>, ASBCA No. 35956, 88-3 BCA ¶ 20,911; <u>see also</u> <u>Kingston Constructors Inc. v. Washington Area Transport Authority</u>, 930 F. Supp. 651 (Fed. Cir 1996); <u>P&D Contractors, Inc. v. United States</u>, 25 Cl. Ct. 237 (1992).

2.   If the damage forecast was reasonable, the government may assess LDs even if it did not incur any actual damages. <u>See</u> <u>Cegers v. United States</u>, 7 Cl. Ct. 615 (1985); <u>American Constr. Co.</u>, ENG BCA No. 5728, 91-2 BCA ¶ 24,009. Using a rate from an agency manual that is part of its procurement regulations is presumed

reasonable. See Fred A. Arnold, Inc. v. United States, 18 Cl. Ct. 1 (1989), aff'd in part, 979 F.2d 217 (Fed. Cir. 1992); JEM Dev. Corp., ASBCA No. 45912, 94-1 BCA ¶ 26,407.

3. The government cannot assess LDs for days after a project is substantially complete. See Hill Constr. Corp., ASBCA No. 43615, 93-3 BCA ¶ 25,973.

4. The government may not assess LDs for those days that the government is partly responsible for the completion delay. See H.G. Reynolds Co., Inc., ASBCA No. 42351, 93-2 BCA ¶ 25,797.

5. A contractor may be excused from LDs for those days that it shows the delay was: (a) excusable or beyond its control and (b) without the fault or negligence of it or its subcontractors. See Potomac Marine & Aviation, Inc., ASBCA No. 42417, 93-2 BCA ¶ 25,865.

6. Contracting officers must ensure that project completion dates are reasonable to avoid having contractors "pad" their bids to protect against LDs.

7. Another contract clause that sets an alternate rate of compensation for standby time may be enforceable, even if it is quite high, if it serves a different purpose in the contract than a liquidated damages clause. See Stapp Towing Co., ASBCA No. 41584, 94-1 BCA ¶ 26,465.

I. **Use/Possession Prior to Completion**. FAR 52.236-11.

1. The "use and possession" clause allows the government to take possession of a construction project prior to its final completion (beneficial occupancy).

2. Possession does not necessarily constitute acceptance. See Tyler Constr. Co., ASBCA No. 39365, 91-1 BCA ¶ 23,646. The contractor must complete a project as required by the contract, including all "punch list" items. See Toombs & Co., ASBCA No. 34590, 91-1 BCA ¶ 23,403.

3. The contractor is not responsible for any loss or damage that the government causes while the government has possession. See Fraser Eng'g Co., VABCA No. 3265, 91-3 BCA ¶ 24,223

4. The contractor may be due an equitable adjustment if possession by the government causes a delay.

X. CONCLUSION.

Construction contracts differ considerably from supply and services contracts for many reasons, including the nature of the construction industry, the highly competitive market for construction, Congress's control of construction, the different types of risks encountered in construction, and the unique role of an owner who is a sovereign. For these reasons, construction contracts are often awarded and administered by specialized organizations, most notably the U.S. Army Corps of Engineers. Government agencies should give careful consideration to using such specialized resources.

ATTACHMENT
DIFFERING SITE CONDITIONS (DSC)

What a Contractor Must Show to Recover for DSCs.

TYPE I	TYPE II
Contract documents either implicitly or explicitly indicate a particular site condition.	Conditions encountered were unusual physical conditions that were not now about at time of contract award.
Contractor reasonably interpreted and relied upon the contract indications.	Conditions differed materially from those ordinarily encountered.
Contractor encountered latent/subsurface conditions that differed materially from the conditions indicated in the contract and were reasonably unforeseeable.	
Contractor incurred increased costs that were solely attributable to the DSC.	Contractor incurred increased costs that were solely attributable to the DSC.
Note: If the government made no representations and provided no information, contractor cannot recover. If the contractor discovers the differing conditions prior to bid opening, reliance is unreasonable.	Examples: unexpected soil conditions, old dump at site, buried hazardous materials

NOTES:

1.   DSC clause only covers conditions existing at the time of award. Acts of nature occurring after award are not DSCs.

2.   A contractor may not recover if the contractor could have discovered the condition during a reasonable site investigation.

3.   Recovery for DSC is not available if the contract does not contain the DSC clause.

PRICING OF ADJUSTMENTS

I. INTRODUCTION.

A. Government contracts give the government powers to unilaterally change the requirements, to unilaterally terminate the contract without cause, and to adjust the schedule for contract performance. Additionally, in the contract, the government assumes certain risks, such as differing site conditions. Finally, the terms of a government contract deprive the contractor of the remedy available in the private sector to stop work when the customer materially changes or breaches the contract. All of these contractual provisions are conditioned on the government adjusting the contract price to compensate the contractor for the government's actions, or for the risks realized. Whether the adjustment is an equitable adjustment under a clause giving the contractor a remedy for government actions or inactions or as contractual damages for breach, the adjustment should fairly compensate the contractor for its losses and/or provide the government a fair and reasonable price for the changed work.

B. In practice, the process of pricing adjustments usually works fairly, if not quickly. When a compensable action occurs, the government and/or the contractor acknowledge the affected party's entitlement to a price adjustment, and the parties negotiate a price to fairly compensate the affected party. The government and its contractors reach agreement on an adjustment, then move on the next one. This chapter describes the method for calculating an equitable adjustment. Even when entitlement to an adjustment is disputed, once resolved, the contracting parties are typically able to negotiate the adjustment due without further litigation.

C. Unfortunately, not all adjustments are resolved quickly and amicably. Disagreements over a party's entitlement to damages or an adjustment can color how a party views the pricing. Some contractors attempt to use the process of pricing adjustments to improve their financial position on the contract. Some agencies may be tempted to prolong the process to avoid facing difficult budgeting decisions. Finally, some contractors have difficulties fully documenting the amount of an adjustment for various reasons other than fraud, such as an accounting system that did not segregate costs in a method that, in hindsight, might have proven more illuminating.

D. Both contractors' and the government's interests are best served by a process that fairly compensates the affected party, especially when the government exercises its extraordinary rights.

II. REFERENCES.

A. 41 U.S.C. §§ 1501-1506.

B. Pricing of Adjustments, Chapter 8, Administration of Government Contracts, 4th edition, Cibinic, Nash & Nagle, 2006.

C. Federal Acquisition Regulation (FAR)

1. FAR Part 30, Cost Accounting Standards Administration;

2. FAR Part 31, Contract Cost Principles and Procedures;

3. FAR Subpart 43.2 Change Orders

D. Defense Federal Acquisition Regulation Supplement.

1. DFARS 243.205-70

2. DFARS 252.243-7001 Pricing of Contract Modifications, (Dec 1991);

Pricing of Adjustments

3. DFARS 243.205-71

4. DFARS 252.243-7002 Requests for Equitable Adjustment (Mar 1998).

E. Accounting Guide, Defense Contract Audit Agency Pamphlet No. 7641.90, Information for Contractors, http://www.dcaa.mil

III. TYPES OF ADJUSTMENTS.

A. Equitable Adjustments.

1. Equitable adjustment. Many remedy granting clauses in a typical government contract grant the contractor or the government a right to an "equitable adjustment" in the contract price as the contractual remedy for an action that, absent the clause, would constitute a breach of contract. Remedy granting clauses include:

   - Changes, FAR 52.243-1 thru -7;
   - Late or defective Government Furnished Property FAR 52.245-1;
   - Differing Site Conditions, FAR 52.236-2
   - Stop Work Order, FAR 52.242-17.

2. As discussed in Chapter 23, Changes, the actions for which a contractual remedy is available under the Changes clause is quite broad. The Changes clause gives a remedy for both ordered changes and "constructive changes," such as interpretation disputes Consequently, many actions that might otherwise constitute a breach of contract and affording breach damages as a remedy, are considered changes entitling the contractor or the government to an equitable adjustment.

3. An "equitable adjustment" is a term of art in government contracting, rather than a defined term. It generally is calculated as the actual costs of performing the additional work, less the estimated costs of work avoided by the changed, plus a reasonable profit on the additional work. Because the adjustment is "equitable," the adjustment will be fair and reasonable to the affected party, rather than strictly formulaic.

B. Adjustments.

1. Adjustments differ from equitable adjustments in one significant way– profit. Typically, a remedy-granting clause that provides for an adjustment withholds including any profit in the adjustment. Some clauses, however, withhold adjustment of indirect cost rates, etc.

2. A number of remedy-granting clauses provide for "adjustments," including:

   - Suspension of Work, FAR 52.242-14;
   - Government Delay of Work, FAR 52.242-17;
   - Fair Labor Standards Act and Service Contract Act – Price Adjustments, FAR 52.222-44.
   - Cost Accounting Standards, FAR 52.230-2.

C. Damages for Breach of Contract.

1. Breach Damages. A party can recover common-law breach of contract damages when the other contracting party fails to comply with its contractual obligations.

   a. Where the government fails to comply with its obligation, the contractor is entitled to damages, if it can demonstrate it was harmed. Similarly, the government can recover breach damages when the contractor breaches its contractual obligations.

   b. There is no breach, however, where a party's actions or inactions are addressed in a specific contract clause granting the other party a remedy. Such clauses are generally known as "remedy-granting clauses" and are discussed in B.1, below. See Info. Sys. & Network Corp., ASBCA No. 42659, 00-1 BCA ¶ 30,995 (holding that claim for breach damages barred by convenience termination clause); Hill Constr. Corp., ASBCA No.

49820, 99-1 BCA ¶ 30,327 (denying a breach claim for lost profits where the underlying changes were within the ambit of the Changes clause).

2. Among the situations where courts and Boards of Contract Appeals have recognized recovery of breach damages include:

    a. Government breach of a requirements contract. <u>Bryan D. Highfill</u>, HUDBCA No. 96-C-118-C7, 99-1 BCA ¶ 30,316.

    b. Bad faith termination for convenience. <u>Torncello v. United States</u>, 231 Ct. Cl. 20, 681 F.2d 756 (1982).

    c. Government's failure to disclose material information. <u>Shawn K. Christensen, dba Island Wide Contracting</u>, AGBCA No. 95-188-R, 95-2 BCA ¶ 27,724.

3. Breach damages are measured under common-law principles, although cost principles may apply. <u>See AT&T Technologies, Inc. v. United States</u>, 18 Cl. Ct. 315 (1989); <u>Shawn K. Christensen</u>, AGBCA No. 95-188R, 95-2 BCA ¶ 27,724.

    a. Consequential Damages. The general rule is that consequential damages are not recoverable unless they are foreseeable and caused directly by the government's breach. <u>Prudential Ins. Co. of Am. v. United States</u>, 801 F.2d 1295 (Fed. Cir. 1986); <u>Land Movers Inc. and O.S. Johnson - Dirt Contractor (JV)</u>, ENG BCA ¶ No. 5656, 91-1 BCA ¶ 23,317 (no recovery of lost profits based on loss of bonding capacity; also no recovery related to bankruptcy, emotional distress, loss of business, etc.).

    b. Compensatory Damages. A contractor whose contract was breached by the government is entitled to be placed in as good a position as it would have been if it had completed performance. <u>PHP Healthcare Corp.</u>, ASBCA No. 39207, 91-1 BCA ¶ 23,647 (the

measure of damages for failure to order the minimum quantity is not the contract price; the contractor must prove actual damages). Compensatory damages include a reliance component (costs incurred as a consequence of the breach), and an expectancy component (lost profits). <u>Keith L. Williams</u>, ASBCA No. 46068, 94-3 BCA ¶ 27,196.

IV. EQUITABLE ADJUSTMENT PRICING FORMULA.

A. Objective.

The objective of an equitable adjustment is to keep the contractor (or the government) in the same relative position following the change (or other action) as the party was in before the change.

B. General Rule.

1. The basic adjustment formula is the difference between the reasonable cost to perform the work as originally required, and the reasonable cost to perform the work as changed. <u>See B.R. Servs., Inc.</u>, ASBCA Nos. 47673, 48249, 99-2 BCA ¶ 30,397 (holding that the contractor must quantify the cost difference—not merely set forth the costs associated with the changed work); <u>Buck Indus., Inc.</u>, ASBCA No. 45321, 94-3 BCA ¶ 27,061.

2. Pricing adjustments should not alter the basic profit or loss position of the contractor before the change occurred. "An equitable adjustment may not properly be used as an occasion for reducing or increasing the contractor's profit or loss . . . for reasons unrelated to a change." <u>United States. ex rel Bettis v. Odebrecht</u>, 393 F.3d 1321 (D.C. Cir. 2005); <u>Pacific Architects and Eng'rs, Inc. v. United States</u>, 203 Ct. Cl. 499, 508 491 F.2d 734, 739 (1974). <u>See also Stewart & Stevenson Servs., Inc.</u>, ASBCA No. 43631, 97-2 BCA ¶ 29,252 modified by 98-1 BCA ¶ 29,653 (holding that a contractor is entitled to profit on additional work ordered by the Army even though the original work was bid at a

loss); Westphal Gmph & Co., ASBCA No. 39401, 96-1 BCA ¶ 28194 (reversed, remanded, based on factual issue, not legal premises). More simply put, a contractor does not "get well" on changes; nor should it suffer further harm on changes.

3. Pricing Additional Work. The parties price additional work based on the reasonable costs actually incurred in performing the new work. CEMS, Inc. v. United States, 59 Fed. Cl. 168 (2003); Delco Elecs. Corp. v. United States, 17 Cl. Ct. 302 (1989), aff'd, 909 F.2d 1495 (Fed. Cir. 1990). To smooth its recovery of the costs of additional work, the contractor should segregate and accumulate these costs, to the extent practical.

4. Pricing Deleted Work. The parties price deleted work based on the difference between the estimated costs of performing the original work and the actual costs of performing the work after the change. Knights' Piping, Inc., ASBCA No. 46985, 94-3 BCA ¶ 27,026; Anderson/Donald, Inc., ASBCA No. 31213, 86-3 BCA ¶ 19,036. But see Condor Reliability Servs, Inc., ASBCA No. 40538, 90-3 BCA ¶ 23,254.

C. Equitable Adjustments and Terminations for Convenience.

1. When the government terminates a contract for convenience, the Termination Contracting Officer (TCO) must negotiate or determine open changes and equitably adjust the contract price as part of the contract settlement. FAR 49.114(a).

2. When the government partially terminates a contract for convenience, the contractor is generally entitled to an equitable adjustment to the price and schedule on the continuing work for the increased costs borne by that work as a result of a termination. Deval Corp., ASBCA Nos. 47132, 47133, 99-1 BCA ¶ 30,182; Cal-Tron Sys., Inc., ASBCA Nos. 49279, 50371 97-1 BCA ¶ 28,986; Wheeler Bros., Inc., ASBCA No. 20465, 79-1 BCA ¶ 13,642. Typically, the contracting

officer, and not the TCO, negotiates the equitable adjustment to the continuing work.

D. Shared Causation. Where the parties share the responsibility for causing added costs, they will share the costs in calculating the equitable adjustment. See Essex Electro Eng'rs, Inc., v. Danzig, 224 F.3d 1283 (Fed. Cir. 2000); Dickman Builders, Inc., ASBCA No. 32612, 91-2 BCA ¶ 23,989.

E. Schedule Adjustments. Although this chapter focuses on calculating the adjustment to the contract price, an equitable adjustment also includes an adjustment in the contract schedule, where affected. Contractors are well advised to seek the schedule adjustment to which they are entitled, to protect the available margin in their schedules in the event that other factors, unrelated to government actions or inactions, cause additional delays.

V. DETERMINING COSTS IN EQUITABLE ADJUSTMENTS.

A. General.

1. The FAR does not contain a general requirement for a contractor to segregate costs of a change or other event giving rise to an equitable adjustment, nor to comply with any specific accounting procedures. Indeed, FAR 43.203(a) recognizes that "[c]ontractors' accounting systems are seldom designed to segregate the costs of performing changed work." While FAR 31.103(b)(6) states that the cost principles in FAR Part 31 should be used in pricing changes and modifications to contracts, this requirement is often not stated in the contract's standard terms and conditions.

2. Some agencies, in their FAR Supplements, have added specific requirements for pricing of adjustments.

   a. DOD has adopted a contract clause that specifically requires contractors to follow FAR Part 31 and DFARS

Part 231 in pricing contract modifications, including equitable adjustments. DFARS 252.243-7001. The applicable version of each regulation is the version effective on the date of the contract award.

b. GSA has adopted a clause that provides detailed instructions on preparing equitable adjustment proposals. GSAM 552.243-71, Equitable Adjustments. Other civilian agencies may have similar clauses to DOD or GSA.

3. Consequently, in the majority of contracts awarded, the contractor should expect to justify the costs it includes in a request for equitable adjustment using the principles in FAR Part 31.

B. FAR Part 31 Cost Principles.

1. Where the contract requires the costs included in an equitable adjustment to conform to FAR Part 31, the costs must be allowable. An allowable cost under FAR Part 31 is a cost that is: 1) reasonable in nature and amount; 2) allocable to the changed work; 3) properly accounted for in the contractor's books and records; and 4) not specifically disallowed by regulation or contract.

2. Reasonable In Amount.

a. "A cost is reasonable if, in its nature and amount, it does not exceed that which would be incurred by a prudent person in the conduct of competitive business." FAR 31.201-3(a).

b. The burden of proof is on the contractor. FAR 31.201-3(a). However, the standard of reasonableness is that of a prudent business person, not a government auditor.

c. Cost held unreasonable in amount. TRC Mariah Assocs., Inc., ASBCA No. 51811, 99-1 BCA ¶ 30,386; Kelly Martinez d/b/a Kelly Martinez Constr. Servs., IBCA Nos. 3140, 3144-3174, 97-2 BCA ¶ 29,243, 1997 IBCA

LEXIS 12. But see Raytheon STX Corp., GSBCA No. 14296-COM, 00-1 BCA ¶ 30,632, 1999 GSBCA LEXIS 252 (holding that salaries paid key employees during a government shutdown were reasonable in amount).

d. Nature of cost held unreasonable. Lockheed-Georgia Co., Div. of Lockheed Corp., ASBCA No. 27660, 90-3 BCA ¶ 22,957 (air travel to the Greenbrier resort for executive physicals unreasonable because competent physicians were available in Atlanta).

3. Allocable to the Work.

a. A cost is allocable to the change or other work if the cost: 1) was incurred specifically in the performance of the work (direct costs); 2) the cost benefits both the changed work and other work, and is distributed to them in reasonable proportion to the benefits received (overhead); or 3) is necessary for the overall operation of the business (General & Administrative costs). FAR 31.201-4.

b. Large contractors subject to Cost Accounting Standards must have a detailed description of how they allocate costs, and which costs are treated as Direct, Overhead(s), and G&A. Small contractors often follow the procedures included in their accounting software.

c. Allocability is a concept of whether a sufficient "nexus" exists between the cost and the government contract. Lockheed Aircraft Corp. v. United States, 179 Ct. Cl. 545, 375 F.2d 786, 794 (1967); Boeing North American, Inc. v. Roche, 298 F.3d 1274, 1280 (Fed. Cir. 2002).

d. Cost not determined not beneficial. Caldera v. Northrop Worldwide Aircraft Servs., Inc., 192 F.3d 962 (Fed. Cir. 1999) (holding that attorneys' fees incurred unsuccessfully defending wrongful termination actions resulted in no benefit to the contract and were not allocable).

 e. In certain instances (i.e., impact on other work), the contract appeals boards may ignore the principle of allocability. See Clark Concrete Contractors, Inc. v. Gen. Servs. Admin., GSBCA No. 14340, 99-1 BCA ¶ 30,280 (holding that costs incurred on an unrelated project were recoverable because they were "equitable and attributable" byproducts of agency design changes).

4. Properly Accounted For. A contractor must properly account for the costs included in a request for equitable adjustment.

 a. FAR Part 30. For a contract subject to the Cost Accounting Standards, the contractor has a contractual duty to account for the costs incurred using its disclosed accounting practices, and applicable Cost Accounting Standards. Many contracts, however, are not CAS covered.

 b. On a contract not subject to CAS, the contractor must follow Generally Accepted Accounting Principles (GAAP) and FAR 31.203 on allocation of indirect costs. FAR 31.201-2. Most contractors with CAS covered contracts will follow CAS consistently, even on those contracts not CAS covered.

 c. Regardless of whether CAS or GAAP applies, the most important accounting principle is consistency. A contractor should not change the practices it regularly follows in accounting for costs when pricing the costs of equitable adjustments. For example, FAR 31.202(a) specifically prohibits treating a cost as a direct cost if similar costs are treated as indirect costs for other purposes.

5. Not Specifically Disallowed.

 a. Although a cost may be reasonable, allocable to a change, and properly accounted for in the contractor's records, the government may have, for policy reasons, chosen to disallow the cost. Most unallowable costs are identified in FAR Part 31 (FAR 31.205 for commercial organizations). Additional unallowable costs, often due to restrictions in agency appropriation acts, may be included in the agency's FAR Supplement. Occasionally, the acquiring activity may decide for its own reasons (good or bad) that certain costs, ordinarily allowable, should be disallowed in a specific contract. When it does so, the specific cost may be disallowed by a provision in the contract or an attachment. Contractors are well advised to review all contractual documents for contract specific disallowance of costs, and to include the risks this presents in their pricing.

 b. FAR Part 31 identifies specifically unallowable costs. Originally, the types of costs covered were those that the Executive Branch believed that the government should not pay as public policy, or should pay only under certain conditions. Congress subsequently legislated disallowance of some costs, effectively codifying some of FAR 31.205. 10 U.S.C. § 2324; 41 U.S.C. Chapter 43. Nonprofits and educational institutions have separate, but similar unallowable costs implementing OMB Circulars. FAR Subparts 31.4-7.

 c. The following list of potential specifically unallowable costs is non-exclusive:

- Bad debts. FAR 31.205-3.

- Costs related to contingencies are generally unallowable, but some categories are allowable. FAR 31.205-7.

- Contributions or Donations, including cash, property, and services, regardless of recipient. FAR 31.205-8.

- Depreciation costs that significantly reduce the book value of a tangible capital asset below its residual value. FAR 31.205-11(b).

- Entertainment costs, including amusement, diversions, social activities, gratuities, and tickets to sports events. FAR 31.205-14.

- Specific Lobbying and Political Activities. FAR 31.205-22.

- Excess of costs over income under any other contract. FAR 31.205-23.

- Costs of Alcoholic Beverages. FAR 31.205-51

- Excessive Pass-Through charges by contractors from subcontractors, which add no or negligible value, are unallowable. If a contractor sub-contracts at least 70 percent of the work, the contracting officer must make a determination that pass-through charges at the time of award are not excessive and add value. FAR 15.408(n)(2) and FAR 52.215-23.

d. What if a cost is not expressly listed in FAR 31.205? The FAR does not list every cost that may be unallowable because of reasonableness, allocability, or improper accounting treatment. Additionally, agencies have successfully challenged costs that are similar to or related to specifically unallowable costs. See Boeing North American, Inc. v. Roche, 298 F.3d 1274, 1285-86 (Fed. Cir. 2002); Southwest Marine, Inc. v. United States, 535 F.3d 1012 (9th Cir. 2008); Geren v. Tecom, Inc. ("Tecom II"), 566 F.3d 1037, (Fed. Cir. 2009).

e. Directly associated costs. A "directly associated cost" means any cost that is generated solely as a result of the incurrence of another cost, and that would not have been incurred had the other cost not been incurred. FAR 31.001. Where a cost is unallowable, directly associated costs are also unallowable. FAR 31.201-6(a). For example, if a contractor employee makes an unallowable lobbying contact, the cost of the taxi ride to Capitol Hill is similarly unallowable.

C. **Causation.** A direct cost is a cost incurred specifically for performing the work. Where the work is a change or other event giving rise to the equitable adjustment, the direct costs are those caused by the government action, inaction, or other event. In the overwhelming majority of direct costs, causation is clear. In some requests for equitable adjustment, however, the party seeking the adjustment may include direct costs that have unrelated causes. Therefore, the other party should review the proposed direct costs for those with more than one cause, or with an unrelated cause. For direct costs, there must be a causal nexus between the basis for liability and the claimed increase (or decrease) in cost. Hensel Phelps Constr. Co., ASBCA No. 49270, 99-2 BCA ¶ 30,531; Stewart & Stevenson Servs., Inc., ASBCA No. 43631, 98-1 BCA ¶ 29,653, modifying 97-2 BCA ¶ 29,252; Oak Adec, Inc. v. United States, 24 Cl. Ct. 502 (1991). Indirect costs, by definition, have multiple causes and benefit multiple contracts, but that fact, alone, does not make the properly allocated portion of the cost pool unallowable.

D. **Burden of Proof.**

1. 10 U.S.C. § 2324(j) and 41. U.S.C. § 4309 specifically assign the burden of proof for reasonableness to the contractor when the contractor is seeking reimbursement. This reverses earlier case law that found that

actual incurred costs were presumed reasonable.

2. The burden is on the party claiming the benefit of the adjustment. <u>Wilner v. United States</u>, 24 F.3d 1397 (Fed. Cir. 1994); <u>Lisbon Contractors, Inc. v. United States</u>, 828 F.2d 759, 767 (Fed. Cir. 1987) (moving party "bears the burden of proving the amount of loss with sufficient certainty so that the determination of the amount of damages will be more than mere speculation"); <u>B&W Forest Prod.</u>, AGBCA Nos. 96-180, 96-198-1, 98-1 BCA ¶ 29,354.

E. Profit.

1. Profit is not an element of cost. An equitable adjustment (but not an adjustment) includes a reasonable and customary allowance for profit. <u>United States v. Callahan Walker Constr. Co.</u>, 317 U.S. 56 (1942); <u>Rumsfeld v. Applied Companies, Inc.</u>, 325 F.3d 1328 (Fed. Cir. 2003).

2. There are several approaches to calculating profit:

   • The rate of profit actually earned on the unchanged work (although contractors are often reluctant to disclose actual profit rates);

   • A lower profit rate based on the reduced risk of equitable adjustments (some contracting officers argue that their delay in negotiating equitable adjustments justifies a lower profit rate for the contractor, even though the delays result in the contractor not being paid for the changed work);

   • A profit rate calculated using an agency's profit policies, such as the weighted guidelines in DFARS 215.404-71. <u>See Doyle Constr. Co.</u>, ASBCA No. 44883, 94-2 BCA ¶ 26,832.

   • A contractual agreement on profit rate, such as the 10% profit stated in GSAM 552.43-71(h)(2).

3. Practical methods of determining profit include adoption of the negotiated profit rate for the original contract award and use of industry rules of thumb.

VI. METHODS OF PROOF.

A. General.

1. As recognized in FAR 43.203(a), contractors accounting systems are rarely designed to segregate the costs of specific changes. Were a contractor to have such a system in place and to follow it consistently, the resulting inefficiencies would affect the contractor's competitiveness.

2. Where the government desires a contractor to segregate costs of changes, the contracting officer may include FAR 52.243-6, Change Order Accounting, in the contract. This clause permits the contracting officer to direct the contractor to segregate the costs of the change where the costs are expected to exceed $100,000. If the contracting officer does not direct segregation, the contractor has no obligation to do so. Frequently, where the contracting officer and the contractor disagree about whether a change has occurred, contracting officers do not direct contractors to segregate costs of the alleged change. Unfortunately, this may result in the contractor not implementing cost segregation for the alleged change.

B. Proof by Actual Costs.

1. Regardless whether the contractor has segregated the costs of a change in its accounting system, it is often possible to extract evidence of the actual costs incurred from the accounting records. The actual cost method is the preferred method for proving costs. <u>North Star Alaska Hous. Corp. v. United States</u>, 76 Fed. Cl. 158 (2007).

2. A contractor must prove its costs using the best evidence available under the circumstances. The preferred method is actual cost data. <u>Cen-Vi-Ro of Texas, Inc.</u>

v. United States, 210 Ct. Cl. 684, (1976); Deval Corp., ASBCA Nos. 47132, 47133, 99-1 BCA ¶ 30,182.

3. Failure to accumulate actual cost data may result in either a substantial reduction or total disallowance of the claimed costs. Delco Elecs. Corp. v. United States, 17 Cl. Ct. 302 (1989), aff'd, 909 F.2d 1495 (Fed. Cir. 1990) (recovery reduced for unexcused failure to segregate); Togaroli Corp., ASBCA No. 32995, 89-2 BCA ¶ 21,864 (costs not segregated despite the auditor's repeated recommendation to do so; no recovery beyond final decision); Assurance Co., ASBCA No. 30116, 86-1 BCA ¶ 18,737 (lack of cost data prevented reasonable approximation of damages for jury verdict, therefore, the appellant recovered less than the amount allowed in the final decision).

4. Contractors are well served to segregate and accumulate the costs incurred for work entitling them to an equitable adjustment, to the extent practicable, even if they are not required to do so. A request for equitable adjustment that is well supported by actual costs segregated and recorded in the contractor's accounting system greatly speeds price agreement, and avoids costly litigation of quantum in disputed claims.

Not all costs of equitable adjustments, however, are provable by actual cost records.

C. Estimated Costs Method.

1. Some cost elements cannot be proven by actual costs. For example, the cost of deleted work that was never performed has no actual cost data. Similarly, some costs, such as losses in efficiency, are impossible or impracticable to segregate from other costs, and must be estimated. Finally, some costs are incurred prior to realizing the government has changed the work, or that a risk born by the government has occurred, so the contractor may not have implemented accounting procedures for segregating costs until it realized the government was responsible for the added costs. Finally,

when negotiating costs of an adjustment in advance of performance, only estimates are available.

2. Where actual costs are not available, Good faith estimates are preferred. Lorentz Bruun Co., GSBCA No. 8505, 88-2 BCA ¶ 20,719 (estimates of labor hours and rates admissible). Estimates are an acceptable method of proving costs where they are supported by detailed substantiating data or are reasonably based on verifiable cost experience. J.M.T. Mach. Co., ASBCA No. 23928, 85-1 BCA ¶ 17,820 (1984), aff'd on other grounds, 826 F.2d 1042 (Fed. Cir. 1987).

3. Contracting officers routinely negotiate contracts and modifications based on a contractor's estimates of the costs of performance. Estimating methodologies do not become suspect when used for an equitable adjustment. If the contractor uses detailed estimates based on analyses of qualified personnel, the government will not be able to allege successfully that the contractor used the disfavored total cost method of adjustment pricing. Illinois Constructors Corp., ENG BCA No. 5827, 94-1 BCA ¶ 26,470.

4. Disregard estimated costs, including estimates based on Mean's Guide where actual costs are known. Anderson/Donald, Inc., ASBCA No. 31213, 86-3 BCA ¶ 19,036.

D. Total Cost Method.

1. The total cost method of estimating the costs of an equitable adjustment that subtracts the contractor's pre-change estimated costs (usually the bid costs) from the contractor's total actual costs incurred including the change. The difference between the actual costs and the estimate is assumed to be entirely due to the change.

2. The total cost method is not preferred because it assumes the entire difference is solely the government's fault. The total cost method calculates the difference

between the bid price on the original contract and the actual total cost of performing the contract as changed. Servidone v. United States, 931 F.2d 860 (Fed. Cir. 1991); Raytheon Co. v. White, 305 F.3d 1354 (Fed. Cir. 2002); Stewart & Stevenson Servs., Inc., ASBCA No. 43631, 98-1 BCA ¶ 29,653, modifying 97-2 BCA ¶ 29,252; Santa Fe Eng'rs, Inc., ASBCA No. 36682, 96-2 BCA ¶ 28,281; Concrete Placing Inc. v. United States, 25 Cl. Ct. 369 (1992).

3. While not favored, use of a total cost method may be permitted when the contractor establishes four factors:

    a. The nature of the particular cost is impossible or highly impracticable to determine with a reasonable degree of certainty;

    b. The contractor's bid was realistic;

    c. The contractor's actual incurred costs were reasonable; and

    d. The contractor was not responsible for any of the added costs.

    Raytheon Co. v. United States, 305 F.3d 1354 (Fed. Cir. 2002), WRB Corp. v. United States, 183 Ct. Cl. 409 (1968).

4. Modified total cost method. Where a contractor is unable to use the total cost method, a court or board of contract appeals may allow the contractor to modify the total cost method to account for problematic factors. For example, the contractor may be permitted to revise its bid estimate if the original bid was not realistic; or to exclude additional costs due to other causes. Olsen v. Espy, 1994 U.S. App. LEXIS 11840, 26 F.3d 141 (Fed. Cir. 1994); River/Road Constr. Inc., ENG BCA No. 6256, 98-1 BCA ¶ 29,334; Hardrives, Inc., IBCA No. 2319, 94-1 BCA ¶ 26,267; Servidone Constr. Corp., ENG BCA No. 4736, 88-1 BCA ¶ 20,390; Teledyne McCormick-Selph v. United States, 218 Ct. Cl. 513 (1978).

E. **Jury Verdicts.**

1. In resolving disputes on the amount of an equitable adjustment due a party in litigation, the court or board of contract appeals may reach a specific amount as a "jury verdict." Jury verdicts are not a method of proof, but a means of resolving disputed facts. Northrop Grumman Corp. v. United States, 47 Fed. Cl. 20 (2000); Delco Elecs. Corp. v. United States, 17 Cl. Ct. 302 (1989), aff'd, 909 F.2d 1495 (Fed. Cir. 1990); River/Road Constr. Inc., ENG BCA No. 6256, 98-1 BCA ¶ 29,334; Cyrus Contracting Inc., IBCA Nos. 3232, 3233, 3895-98, 3897-98, 98-2 BCA ¶ 29,755; Paragon Energy Corp., ENG BCA No. 5302, 88-3 BCA ¶ 20,959. Essentially, the trier of fact rejects the calculations of both parties and adopts its own estimate of the amount of the adjustment.

2. Before adopting a jury verdict approach, a court must first determine three things:

    a. That clear proof of injury exists;

    b. That there is no more reliable method for computing damages. See Azure v. United States, 129 F.3d 136 (Table), 1997 WL 665763 (Fed. Cir., Oct. 24, 1997) (actual costs are preferred; where contractor offers no evidence of justifiable inability to provide actual costs, then it is not entitled to a jury verdict); Service Eng'g Co., ASBCA No. 40274, 93-2 BCA ¶ 25,885; and

    c. That the evidence is sufficient for a fair and reasonable approximation of the damages. Northrop Grumman Corp. v. United States, 47 Fed. Cl. 20 (2000).

VII. SPECIAL ITEMS.

A. **General.**

Several types of costs are often litigated because they represent real costs that are difficult to segregate in the contractor's accounting system or deviate from normal accounting practices, or are disputed on policy grounds. These costs include unabsorbed and under absorbed overhead; lost efficiency/learning; delay costs, impacts on other work; subcontractor claims; attorneys' fees; and interest.

B.   Unabsorbed Overhead.

1.   Generally. Unabsorbed overhead is seen in certain types of claims where the contractors direct costs are decreased, but the indirect costs continue. Without any direct costs to absorb the continuing indirect costs, the contractor will experience a loss by following its normal accounting practices. This cost is called "unabsorbed overhead." For example, a contractor at a construction site may be directed to stop work while the government considers a change order. Because the contractor must stand ready to restart work, it cannot demobilize and usually cannot find other work quickly to replace the reduction in direct costs. Unabsorbed overhead compensates the contractor for its inability to immediately adjust its indirect costs to work stoppages, idle facilities, inability to use available manpower, etc. In such delay situations, fixed overhead costs, e.g., depreciation, plant maintenance, cost of heat, light, etc., continue to be incurred at the usual rate, but there is less than the usual direct cost base over which to allocate them. Therm-Air Mfg. Co., ASBCA No. 15842, 74-2 BCA ¶ 10,818.

2.   Eichleay Formula. The methodology adopted in Eichleay Corp., ASBCA No. 5183, 60-2 BCA ¶ 2688, aff'd on recons., 61-1 BCA ¶ 2894, is the exclusive method of calculating unabsorbed overhead for both construction contracts and manufacturing contracts. Wickham Contracting Co. v. Fischer, 12 F.3d 1574 (Fed. Cir. 1994)(construction contracts); West v. All State Boiler, Inc., 146 F.3d 1368 (Fed. Cir. 1998) (manufacturing contracts); Genisco Tech. Corp., ASBCA No. 49664, 99-1 BCA ¶ 30,145, mot. for recons. den., 99-1 BCA ¶ 30,324; Libby Corp., ASBCA No. 40765, 96-1 BCA ¶ 28,255).

a.   Under the Eichleay method, calculate the daily overhead rate during the contract period, then multiply the

daily rate by the number of days of delay.

b.   To be entitled to unabsorbed overhead recovery under the Eichleay formula, the following three elements must be established:

- A government-caused or government-imposed delay;
- The contractor was required to be on "standby" during the delay; and
- While "standing by," the contractor was unable to take on additional work. Melka Marine, Inc. v. United States, 187 F.3d 1370 (Fed. Cir. 1999); West v. All State Boiler, 146 F.3d 1368 (Fed. Cir. 1998); Satellite Elec. Co. v. Dalton, 105 F.3d 1418 (Fed. Cir. 1997); Altmayer v. Johnson, 79 F.3d 1129 (Fed. Cir. 1995).

c.   If work on the contract continues uninterrupted, albeit in a different order than originally planned, the contractor is not on standby. Further, a definitive delay precludes recovery "because 'standby' requires an uncertain delay period where the government can require the contractor to resume full-scale work at any time." Melka Marine, Inc. v. United States, 187 F.3d 1370 (Fed. Cir. 1999); American Renovation & Constr. Co., Inc. v. United States, 45 Fed. Cl. 44 (1999).

d.   A contractor's ability to take on additional work focuses upon the contractor's ability to take on replacement work during the indefinite standby period. Replacement work must be similar in size and length to the delayed government project and must occur during the same period. Melka Marine, Inc. v. United States, 187 F.3d 1370 (Fed. Cir. 1999); West v. All-State Boiler, 146 F.3d 1368, 1377 n.2 (Fed. Cir. 1998).

3.   Proof Requirements.

a. Recovery of unabsorbed overhead is not automatic. The contractor should offer credible proof of increased costs resulting from the government-imposed delay. <u>Beaty Elec. Co.</u>, EBCA No. 403-3-88, 91-2 BCA ¶ 23,687. <u>But see</u> <u>Sippial Elec. & Constr. Co. v. Widnall</u>, 69 F.3d 555 (Fed. Cir. 1995) (allowing <u>Eichleay</u> recovery with proof of actual damages).

b. A contractor must prove only the first two elements of the <u>Eichleay</u> formula. Once the contractor has established that the government caused the delay and that it had to remain on "standby," it has made a prima facie case that it is entitled to <u>Eichleay</u> damages. The burden of proof then shifts to the government to show that the contractor did not suffer or should not have suffered any loss because it was able to either reduce its overhead or take on other work during the delay. <u>Satellite Elec. Co. v. Dalton</u>, 105 F.3d 1418 (Fed. Cir. 1997); <u>Mech-Con Corp. v. West</u>, 61 F.3d 883 (Fed. Cir. 1995).

c. Note that in government contracting, finding replacement work takes considerable time and effort, which makes standby more likely.

4. Delays vs. Standby. When added work causes a delay in project completion, the additional overhead during the delay period is usually absorbed by the additional direct costs and <u>Eichleay</u> does not apply. <u>Community Heating & Plumbing Co. v. Kelso</u>, 987 F.2d 1575 (Fed. Cir. 1993) (<u>Eichleay</u> recovery denied because overhead was "extended" as opposed to "unabsorbed"); <u>accord</u> <u>C.B.C. Enters., Inc. v. United States</u>, 978 F.2d 669 (Fed. Cir. 1992).

5. Subcontractor Unabsorbed Overhead. Timely completion by a prime contractor does not preclude a subcontractor's pass-through claim for unabsorbed overhead.

<u>E.R. Mitchell Constr. Co. v. Danzig</u>, 175 F.3d 1369 (Fed. Cir. 1999).

6. Multiple Recovery. A contractor may not recover unabsorbed overhead costs under the <u>Eichleay</u> formula where it has already been compensated for the impact of the government's constructive change on performance time and an award under <u>Eichleay</u> would lead to double recovery of overhead. <u>Keno & Sons Constr. Co.</u>, ENG BCA No. 5837-Q, 98-1 BCA ¶ 29,336.

7. Profit. A contractor is not entitled to profit on an unabsorbed overhead claim. <u>ECC Int'l Corp.</u>, ASBCA Nos. 45041, 44769, 39044, 94-2 BCA ¶ 26,639; <u>Tom Shaw, Inc.</u>, ASBCA No. 28596, 95-1 BCA ¶ 27,457; FAR 52.242-14, Suspension of Work; FAR 52.242-17, Government Delay of Work.

C. Subcontractor Claims.

1. The government consents generally to be sued only by parties with which it has privity of contract. <u>Erickson Air Crane Co. of Wash. v. United States</u>, 731 F.2d 810, 813 (Fed. Cir. 1984); <u>E.R. Mitchell Constr. Co. v. Danzig</u>, 175 F.3d 1369 (Fed. Cir. 1999). However, the government's actions or inactions may impact a portion of work subcontracted to a third party. Where this occurs, prime contractors routinely permit the affected subcontractor to pursue a claim against the government.

2. The mechanism for such claims is the prime contractor sues the government in its own name, but the claim is actually pursued by the subcontractor on behalf of the prime. The prime is liable to pay the subcontractor for its claim when the prime is paid by the government. When a prime contractor has no contractual liability to the subcontractor for the harm caused by the government, then the prime incurs no costs for the government's actions or inaction, and the prime contractor cannot recover. <u>Severin v. United States</u>, 99 Ct. Cl. 435 (1943), <u>cert. denied</u>, 322 U.S. 733 (1944)); <u>E.R. Mitchell Constr. Co. v. Danzig</u>, 175 F.3d 1369 (Fed. Cir. 1999).

3. The government may use the <u>Severin</u> doctrine as a defense only when it raises and proves the issue at trial. If the government fails to raise its defense at trial, then the subcontractor claim is treated as if it were the prime's claim and any further concern about the absence of subcontractor privity with the government is extinguished. <u>Severin v. United States</u>, 99 Ct. Cl. 435 (1943), <u>cert. denied</u>, 322 U.S. 733 (1944)); <u>E.R. Mitchell Constr. Co. v. Danzig</u>, 175 F.3d 1369 (Fed. Cir. 1999).

D. Losses of Efficiency and/or Learning.

The government's action or inaction entitling a contractor to an equitable adjustment may affect the costs a contractor may experience on unchanged work. These losses of efficiency or learning can be considerable. Examples of such losses of efficiency or learning can include the loss of efficiency in performing work in different climatic conditions; performing work out of sequence; and resuming production after a break caused by government action or inaction. Such additional costs are real, but present problems of proof.

1. Burden of Proof. A contractor may recover for loss of efficiency if it can establish both that a loss of efficiency has resulted in increased costs and that the loss was caused by factors for which the government was responsible. <u>Luria Bros. & Co. v. United States</u>, 177 Ct. Cl. 676, 369 F.2d 701 (1966). <u>See generally</u> Thomas E. Shea, <u>Proving Productivity Losses in Government Contracts</u>, 18 Pub. Cont. L. J. 414 (March 1989).

2. Applicable Situations. Loss of efficiency has been recognized as resulting from various conditions causing lower than normal or expected productivity. Situations include: disruption of the contractor's work sequence (<u>Youngdale & Sons Constr. Co. v. United States</u>, 27 Fed. Cl. 516 1993)); working under less favorable weather conditions (<u>Charles G. Williams Constr., Inc.</u>, ASBCA No. 42592, 92-1 BCA ¶ 24,635); the necessity of hiring untrained or less-qualified workers (<u>Algernon-Blair, Inc.</u>, GSBCA No. 4072, 76-2 BCA ¶ 12,073); and reductions in quantity produced.

E. Impacts on Other Work.

1. General Rule. A contractor is generally prohibited from recovering costs under the contract in which a government change, suspension, or breach occurred, when the impact costs are incurred on other contracts. Courts and boards usually consider such damages too remote or speculative, and subject to the rule that consequential damages are not recoverable under government contracts. <u>See</u> <u>General Dynamics Corp. v. United States</u>, 218 Ct. Cl. 40, 585 F.2d 457 (1978); <u>Defense Sys. Co.</u>, ASBCA No. 50918, 2000 ASBCA LEXIS 100, 00-2 BCA ¶ 30,991 (holding the loss of sales on other contracts was too remote and speculative to be recoverable); <u>Sermor, Inc.</u>, ASBCA No. 30576, 94-1 BCA ¶ 26,302; <u>Ferguson Mgmt. Co.</u>, AGBCA No. 83-207-3, 83-2 BCA ¶ 16,819.

2. Exceptions. In only exceptional circumstances, especially when the impact costs are definitive in both causation and amount, have contractors recovered for additional expenses incurred in unrelated contracts. <u>See</u> <u>Clark Concrete Contractors, Inc. v. Gen. Servs. Admin.</u>, GSBCA No. 14340, 99-1 BCA ¶ 30,280 (allowing recovery of additional costs incurred on an unrelated project as a result of government delays and changes).

3. Consequently, contractors should assume in bidding for new work that it will not benefit from efficiencies gained from other contracts.

F. Attorneys' Fees.

1. Legal expenses are addressed by two FAR provisions, listed below. Generally, legal expenses are commonly an indirect expense in a contractor's G&A expense pool. However, in some situations, legal expenses are specifically incurred for a particular contract and counted as a direct cost.

Pricing of Adjustments

Government Contract Costs & Pricing, Karen Manos, 2nd ed., 2009.

a. FAR 31.205-33 covers professional and consultant service costs.

b. FAR 31.205-47 discusses costs related to legal and other proceedings. The FAR defines costs as including, but not limited to, administrative and clerical expenses; the costs of legal services, whether performed by inhouse or private counsel; the costs of the services of accountants, consultants, or others retained by the contractor to assist it; cost of employees, officers, and directors; and any similar costs incurred before, during, and after commencement of a judicial or administrative proceeding that bears a direct relationship to the proceeding. FAR 31.205-47.

2. Typically, the costs incurred in preparing a request for equitable adjustment (REA) are allowable costs, as discussed in paragraph 3, below. Some contractors' accounting practices treat the costs of preparing an REA as a direct cost of the applicable contract. Other contractors' accounting practices treat the costs of preparing REAs as an indirect cost, similar to other bid and proposal costs. Other contractors' treat the costs of preparing REAs as direct or indirect, depending on whether the government requested the REA.

3. Costs incurred incident to contract administration, or in furtherance of the negotiation of the parties' disputes, are allowable. FAR 31.205-33 (consultant and professional costs may be allowable if incurred to prepare a demand for payment that does not meet the Contract Disputes Act definition of a "claim").

    a. "There must be a 'beneficial nexus' between effort for which the cost is incurred and performance or administration of the contract." Appeal of Marine Hydraulics Intern.,

Inc., 94-3 BCA ¶ 27057 (1994). "Contract administration normally involves 'the parties . . . working together.'" Id.

b. Examples: SAB Constr., Inc. v. United States, 66 Fed. Cl. 77 (Fed. Dist. 2005) (holding that when the genuine purpose of incurred legal expenses is that of materially furthering a negotiation process, such cost should normally be allowable); Prairie Wood Products, AGBCA No. 91-197-1, 94-1 BCA ¶ 26,424 (submittal of a proposal in aid of determining how a specification could be met). Boeing North American, Inc. v. United States, 298 F.3d 1274 (Fed. Cir. 2002); Information Sys. & Networks Corp., ASBCA No. 42659, 00-1 BCA ¶ 30,665 (holding that legal expenses incurred in lawsuits against third-party vendors were allowable as part of convenience termination settlement); Bos'n Towing and Salvage Co., ASBCA No. 41357, 92-2 BCA ¶ 24,864 (holding that costs of professional services, including legal fees, are generally allowable, except where specifically disallowed).

4. Third-Party Settlement Agreements. When a third party has sued a government contractor and the contractor has settled the lawsuit, the question becomes whether the legal costs associated with the settlement agreement are allowable. The courts and boards conduct a two-step inquiry to determine the allowability of costs associated with such a settlement. The two-step test is:

    a. If an adverse judgment were reached, would the damages, costs, and attorneys' fees be allowable? (See paragraph V.B.5.d.)

    b. If yes, the cost of the settlement is allowable.

    c. If no, then the cost of the settlement is disallowed, unless the contractor can prove that the private suit has very little likelihood of success on the merits. Geren v. Tecom, Inc., 566 F.3d 1037, 1046 (Fed. Cir. 2009), rehearing and rehearing en banc denied, (Oct. 2, 2009). The rationale behind the "very little likelihood of success" test is two-fold. The court noted that the FAR's policy was to disallow the cost of settling suits that were likely to have been meritorious and therefore disallowed if not settled. The reason is a policy judgment that assumes that suits brought by government entities are, in most situations, "likely to be meritorious." However, the same bright line assumption is not appropriate for suits brought by a private party. Geren v. Tecom, Inc., 566 F.3d 1037, 1046 (Fed. Cir. 2009), rehearing and rehearing en banc denied, (Oct. 2, 2009).

5. Proceedings Costs. Costs incurred in connection with any proceeding brought by a federal, state, local, or foreign government for violation of, or a failure to comply with, law or regulation by the contractor are unallowable if the result is an adverse judgment. This includes costs involved in a final decision to (a) debar or suspend the contractor, (b) rescind or void the contract, or (c) terminate a contract for default for violation or failure to comply with the law. FAR 31.205-47(b).

   a. Costs incurred in connection with any Qui Tam proceeding brought against the contractor are unallowable if the result is an adverse judgment. FAR 31.205-47(b); see False Claims Act, 31 U.S.C. § 3730.

   b. Costs related to prosecuting and defending claims and appeals against the government are unallowable. FAR 31.205-47(f)(1). See Stewart & Stevenson Servs., Inc., ASBCA No. 43631, 97-2 BCA ¶ 29,252 modified by 98-1 BCA ¶ 29,653 (finding that claimed legal expenses related to counsel's preparation of a certified claim and

so are disallowed); Marine Hydraulics Int'l, Inc., ASBCA No. 46116, 94-3 BCA ¶ 27,057(finding that legal costs to prepare a request for equitable adjustment were unallowable costs to prepare a claim because the parties were not working together, the contract work had already been performed, and the issues had been in dispute for months); P&M Indus., Inc., ASBCA No. 38759, 93-1 BCA ¶ 25,471(finding that consultant fees for post-termination administration costs were unallowable in the preparation of a claim). This is consistent with the general rule that attorneys' fees are not allowed in suits against the United States absent an express statutory provision allowing recovery. Piggly Wiggly Corp. v. United States, 112 Ct. Cl. 391, 81 F. Supp. 819 (1949).

6. The Equal Access to Justice Act, 5 U.S.C. § 504, authorizes courts and boards to award attorneys' fees to qualifying prevailing parties unless the government can show that its position was "substantially justified." See, e.g., Midwest Holding Corp., ASBCA No. 45222, 94-3 BCA ¶ 27,138.

G. Interest.

1. Interest is a real cost, albeit one that excites an emotional response in some. When one party to a contract is not paid on time, or pays too much, or pays too early, it loses the time value of its money. Both the government and contractors routinely borrow money to provide cash when needed, at a measurable cost. Thus, the government is entitled to interest by contract on the money it claims. Contractors are entitled by statute to interest on delayed payments and on contractor claims.

2. Interest on Government Claims. FAR 52.232-17, Interest, permits the government to collect interest on amounts payable by a contractor.

a. Interest runs from the date the debt is due until the date the debt is paid.

b. The government may trigger the interest by issuing a demand for payment following a final decision on the amount of the debt.

c. Amounts due the government under the Truth in Negotiations Act are subject to the interest provisions in the applicable contract clause.

3. Interest on Contractor Claims and Requests for Equitable Adjustment.

a. Pre-Claim Interest. Generally. Interest is an unallowable cost. Contractors are not entitled to interest on borrowings, however represented, as part of an equitable adjustment. FAR 31.205-20; Servidone Constr. Corp. v. United States, 931 F.2d 860 (Fed. Cir. 1991); D.E.W. & D.E. Wurzbach, A Joint Venture, ASBCA No. 50796, 98-1 BCA ¶ 29,385; Superstaff, Inc., ASBCA Nos. 48062, et al., 97-1 BCA ¶ 28,845; Tomahawk Constr. Co., ASBCA No. 45071, 94-1 BCA ¶ 26,312.

b. This is consistent with the general rule that the United States is immune from interest liability absent an express statutory provision allowing recovery. Library of Congress v. Shaw, 478 U.S. 310 (1986).

c. Lost Opportunity Costs. The damages for the "opportunity cost of money" are unrecoverable as a matter of law. Adventure Group, Inc., ASBCA No. 50188, 97-2 BCA ¶ 29,081; Environmental Tectonics Corp., ASBCA No. 42540, 92-2 BCA ¶ 24,902 (not only interest on actual borrowings, but also the economic equivalent thereof, are unallowable); Dravo Corp. v. United States, 219 Ct. Cl. 416, 594 F.2d 842 (1979).

d. Cost of Money. However, contractors may include Facilities Capital Cost of Money (FCCM) as an element of profit in pricing an equitable adjustment or other contract modification. FAR 31.205-10. Among the various allowability criteria, a contractor must specifically identify FCCM in its bid or proposal relating to the contract under which the FCCM cost is then claimed. FAR 31.205-10(a)(2). See also McDonnell Douglas Helicopter Co. d/b/a McDonnell Douglas Helicopter Sys., ASBCA No. 50756, 98-1 BCA ¶ 29,546.

4. Prompt Payment Act Interest. See FAR Subpart 32.9 and chapter 21 of this deskbook for a discussion of interest on late payments to a contractor.

5. Interest on Contract Disputes Act Claims. Once a contractor has converted its request for equitable adjustment into a claim, it will accrue interest as provided in 41 U.S.C. § 7109, as further discussed in chapter 28.

VIII. ANALYZING CONTRACTOR REQUESTS FOR EQUITABLE ADJUSTMENTS AND CLAIMS.

A. Objective.

The government's objective in analyzing a contractor's request for equitable adjustment is to negotiate a fair and reasonable price. FAR 15.402(a) ("Contracting Officers shall – [p]urchase supplies and services .... at fair and reasonable prices").

B. DAMS Process.

1. Divide the contractor's claim into component parts. A contractor claim is often a series of smaller claims all added together. Each adjustment must stand on its own, in terms of entitlement to the adjustment, causation, and the amount of the adjustment.

2. Apply FAR and DFARS cost principles and the Cost Accounting Standards (if applicable) and or Generally Accepted Accounting Principles (GAAP). The cost included in the adjustment must be

reasonable, allocable, properly accounted for, and not specifically disallowed.

3. <u>Make</u> the contractor provide evidence supporting the adjustment requested. A contractor must support its request for equitable adjustment by reference to its accounting records for the costs incurred. Where the adjustment is over the applicable threshold under the Truth in Negotiations Act, the contractor must furnish, or otherwise make available cost or pricing data that is current, accurate, and complete. These expectations, however, are tempered by the fact that many contracts do not require the contractor to have any particular form of accounting system, nor to segregate costs of changed work. Further, some costs are only provable by estimates.

4. <u>See</u> what really happened. Additional costs of contract performance may be caused by government actions, or contractor actions.

- Was the job as a whole underbid?
- Did the contractor change planned facilities?
- Did the contractor purchase cheap and unworkable component parts?
- Did the contractor select subcontractors that were unable to perform?
- Was there reliance upon less competent vendors?
- Were there increases in material costs?
- Did the contractor change components for cost reasons? Did this in turn result in engineering problems? Did prior design work become worthless? Did this in turn cause the need for redesign work, with more time and effort?
- Was there an overall lack of efficient organization?
- Did the contractor waste time re-competing components and vendors?
- What expenses were unrelated to the claimed causation?
- Did the contractor order surplus material (for potential options and possible commercial jobs)?

The contracting activity will often have considerable insight into the contractor's performance, and what records and reports the contractor may keep that will shed light on the costs incurred.

IX. CONCLUSION

A. The various circumstances that entitle a contractor to a contract price adjustment (equitable adjustments, adjustments, damages) result in different types/amounts of recovery.

B. The basic measurement of a price adjustment is the sum of the costs of the work added, minus the costs saved by not performing the deleted work, plus a reasonable profit on the net additional work performed.

C. The burden of proving a price adjustment is on the party seeking the adjustment, and the method of proving a price adjustment is to use the best evidence available. Government attorneys should note that the cost records supporting government claims often have the same deficiencies as those supporting contractor claims.

D. The various special items that often comprise a price adjustment demand special attention.

TERMINATIONS FOR CONVENIENCE

I. INTRODUCTION.

A. Concept.

Terminations for convenience are a contractual right possessed by the government that is unusual compared to commercial contracts. The government generally has the right to terminate a contract for almost any reason prior to the contractor completing performance. The terminated contractor has only the right to claim for the costs incurred prior to the termination, a reasonable profit on the work performed prior to termination, and the additional costs of terminating subcontractors and settling the claim with the government. What the contractor loses is the additional profit it would have earned had it fully performed the contract, and the recovery of many unallowable costs under FAR Part 31.

B. References and Definitions.
Terminations for Convenience are a creature of acquisition regulations and common law, not statute.

1. FAR Part 49 (Termination of Contracts) establishes policies and procedures relating to the complete or partial termination of contracts for the convenience of the government or for default.

2. The clauses at FAR 52.249-1 through 52.249-7 state the contractual process the government and the contractor must follow in the event of a termination for convenience. The process varies based on the contract type.

3. "Termination for Convenience" means the exercise of the government's right to completely or partially terminate the contractor's performance of work under a contract when it is in the government's interest to do so. FAR 2.101.

C. Historical Background. See Krygoski Constr. Co., Inc. v. United States, 94 F.3d 1537, 1540-41 (Fed. Cir. 1996) (court

traces history of government's right to terminate contracts for convenience, which began as "a tool to avoid enormous procurements upon completion of a war effort"). The origin of the government's right to terminate contracts for convenience lies in the inherent nature of war. Wars demand maximum production until the war ends, at which point the government no longer needs the war supplies it has on order. Public policy gives the government the inherent right to terminate open contracts for convenience.

1. Inherent Authority.

   a. The government has inherent authority to suspend contracts. United States v. Corliss Steam Engine Co., 91 U.S. 321 (1875) (holding that Navy Department had authority to suspend work and enter into a breach settlement for partial performance).

   b. In the past, a contractor could recover breach of contract damages, including anticipatory (lost) profits, as a result of a termination based on this inherent authority. United States v. Speed, 75 U.S. 77 (1868).

2. Statutory and Regulatory Authority.

   a. At the conclusion of World War I, the government terminated numerous contracts. Various regulatory and statutory provisions were enacted to formalize the government's authority to settle claims from those terminations. See, e.g., Dent Act, 40 Stat. 1272 (1919); Contract Settlement Act of 1944, 58 Stat. 649.

   b. Settlement of war-related contracts led to the federal procurement policy that the parties to a federal contract must bilaterally agree that the government can terminate a contract for convenience.

c. Today, convenience termination clauses preclude the contractor from recovering profits on unperformed work when the government, in good faith, terminates the contract for its convenience.

II. THE RIGHT TO TERMINATE FOR CONVENIENCE.

A. Termination Is for the Convenience of the Government.

1. When a contractor is performing at a loss, termination may be beneficial to the contractor, but the government has no duty to the contractor to exercise the government's right to terminate for the contractor's benefit. Contact Int'l Corp., ASBCA No. 44636, 95-2 BCA ¶ 27,887 (whereas the contract provided "for termination for convenience only when it is in the government's interest," the board denied contractor's argument that the government was obligated to terminate the contract); Rotair Indus., ASBCA No. 27571, 84-2 BCA ¶ 17,417 ("the duty of government officials …is obviously to the government, despite such consequent loss of opportunity, not to contractors").

2. **Practice Tip:** Where a contractor is performing at a loss, asking the government to terminate the contract for convenience is tempting. Doing so, however, risks the government concluding the contractor is unable to perform and should, instead, be terminated for default.

B. Termination for Convenience Clauses. FAR 52.249-1 through 52.249-7.

1. The FAR provides various termination for convenience clauses. The proper clause for a specific contract depends upon the type and dollar amount of the contract. See FAR Subpart 49.5 (Contract Termination Clauses).

    a. Contracts for commercial items and simplified acquisitions for other than commercial items include unique convenience termination provisions that, for the most part, are not covered by Subpart 49.5. See FAR 52.212-4(l) (Contract Terms and Conditions – Commercial Items) and FAR 52.213-4 (Terms and Conditions – Simplified Acquisitions (Other Than Commercial Items)). Contractors should review their contract for agency unique clauses that may alter the typical process for submitting termination settlement proposals (i.e., submission within 60 days).

    b. Not all Termination for Convenience clauses provide the same recovery. The "short form" clause appearing at FAR 52.249-1 governs termination of fixed-price contracts below the simplified acquisition threshold (which is presently $150,000). See Arrow, Inc., ASBCA No. 41330, 94-1 BCA ¶ 26,353 (board denied claim for useful value of special machinery and equipment because service contract properly contained short form termination clause). Settlement is governed by FAR Part 49.

    c. Fixed-price contract "long form" clauses govern contracts above the simplified acquisition threshold (which is presently $150,000). These clauses specify contractor obligations and termination settlement provisions.

    d. Cost reimbursement contract clauses cover both convenience and default terminations, and specify detailed termination settlement provisions. See FAR 52.249-6 (Termination (Cost-Reimbursement)). See, e.g., Group Health Inc. v. Dep't of Health & Human Servs., CBCA No. 3407, 15-1 BCA ¶ 35,859 (finding contractor entitled to recover under a cost reimbursement contract certain termination for convenience costs associated with its subcontractor).

2. The FAR's various termination for convenience clauses give the government the right to terminate a contract, in whole or in part, when it is in the government's interest to do so.

3. The clauses also provide the contractor with a monetary remedy.

   a. The contractor is entitled to the following:

     (1) The contract price for completed supplies or services accepted by the government. See FAR 52.249-2(g)(1).

     (2) Reasonable costs incurred in the performance of the work terminated, to include a fair and reasonable profit (unless the contractor would have sustained a loss on the contract if the entire contract had been completed). See FAR 52.249-2(g)(2).

     (3) The cost of settling and paying termination settlement proposals under terminated subcontracts. See FAR 52.249-2(g)(2).

   b. The cost principles of FAR Part 31 (Contract Cost Principles and Procedures) in effect on the date of the contract shall govern the claimed costs. See Environmental Safety Consultants, Inc., ASBCA No. 58343, 15-1 BCA ¶ 35,906 (denying contractor's claim for recovery under FAR 52.249-2 for failure of proof; citing FAR provision that states that the FAR Part 31 cost principles in effect on the date of the contract governed all claimed costs).

   c. Exclusive of settlement costs, the contractor's recovery may not exceed the total contract price. See FAR 49.207 (Limitation on settlements).

   d. The contractor cannot recover anticipated (lost) profits or consequential damages, which would be recoverable under common-law breach of contract principles. FAR 49.202(a).

C. **The "Christian Doctrine."** Some contracts omit a Termination for Convenience Clause. Omission, however, does not preclude the government from terminating the contract for its convenience. Derived from a seminal Court of Claims decision, the Christian doctrine directs as follows: a mandatory contract clause that expresses a significant or deeply ingrained strand of public procurement policy is considered to be included in a contract by operation of law. G.L. Christian & Assoc. v. United States, 312 F.2d 418 (Ct. Cl. 1963) (termination for convenience clause read into the contract by operation of law).

1. The Christian doctrine does not turn on whether a clause was intentionally or inadvertently omitted, but on whether procurement policies are being avoided or evaded, deliberately or negligently, by lesser officials (i.e., government officials acting beyond their authority or contrary to law). S.J. Amoroso Constr. Co. v. United States, 12 F.3d 1072 (Fed. Cir. 1993) (Buy American Act (BAA) clause for construction contract read into contract after it had been stricken and erroneously replaced by a version of the BAA clause applicable to supply contracts).

2. Not every contract clause will be automatically incorporated. General Engineering & Mach. Works v. O'Keefe, 991 F.2d 775, 779 (Fed. Cir. 1993). The Christian doctrine applies only to mandatory clauses reflecting significant public procurement policies. Michael Grinberg, DOT BCA No. 1543, 87-1 BCA ¶ 19,573 (board refused to incorporate by operation of law a discretionary termination for convenience clause).

3. The Christian doctrine has consistently been applied to read omitted termination for convenience clauses into government contracts, but only where inclusion of those clauses was required by regulation. Christian, 312 F.2d 418; C & J Associates, VABCA 3892, et al., 95-2 BCA ¶ 27,834; Carrier Corp., GSBCA 8516, 90-1 BCA ¶ 22,409; DWS, Inc., Debtor in Possession, ASBCA 29742, 29865, 90-2 BCA ¶ 22,696; Guard-All of America, ASBCA 22167, 80-2 BCA ¶ 14,462. The doctrine

does not apply where the termination for convenience clause is omitted and is not required by regulation. See Rockies Express Pipeline LLC v. Salazar, 730 F.3d 1330 (Fed. Cir. 2013) (rejecting the government's argument that the contracts improperly omitted a termination for convenience clause, noting that the statute authorizing the Royalty-In-Kind contracts at issue (42 U.S.C. § 15902) excepts them from the FAR and, as such, the clause was not required by regulation).

4. The Christian doctrine does not apply when the contract includes an authorized deviation from the standard termination for convenience clause. Montana Refining Co., ASBCA No. 44250, 94-2 BCA ¶ 26,656 (ID/IQ contract with a stated minimum quantity included deviation in the termination for convenience clause that agency would not be liable for unordered quantities of fuel "unless otherwise stated in the contract").

5. When a contract lacks a termination clause, an agency cannot limit termination settlement costs by arguing that the "short form" termination clause applies. Empres de Viacao Terceirense, ASBCA No. 49827, 00-1 BCA ¶ 30,796 (noting that use of the "short form" clause was predicated on a contracting officer's determination and exercise of discretion, which was lacking in this case).

6. Impact of other Termination Clauses. Inclusion of Termination on Notice clause in contract modification did not render termination for convenience clause meaningless. Dart Advantage Warehousing, Inc. v. United States, 52 Fed. Cl. 694 (2002) (clause with such ancient lineage, reflecting deeply ingrained public procurement policy, and applied to contracts with the force and effect of law even when omitted, should not be materially modified or summarily rendered meaningless without good cause).

Practice Tip: The Christian doctrine does not extend to subcontracts. One 2013 decision, since reversed and vacated, briefly upset that rule by extending the Christian doctrine to subcontracts with respect to clauses like Equal Employment Opportunity and Affirmative Action because they were a significant or deeply ingrained strand of public procurement policy and the Department of Labor implementing regulations said the requirements in such clauses applied to subcontracts even if the clauses were not included in the subcontract. UPMC Braddock v. Harris, 934 F. Supp. 2d 238 (D.D.C. 2013) opinion vacated, appeal dismissed sub nom. UPMC Braddock v. Perez, 584 F. App'x 1 (D.C. Cir. 2014). Many legal commentators believe this was an incorrect decision.

D. Convenience Terminations Imposed by Law.

1. Termination by Conversion an Improper Default.

   a. The termination for default clauses provide that an erroneous default termination converts to a termination for convenience. See FAR 52.249-8(g); FAR 52.249-10(c).

   b. However, if the government acted in bad faith while terminating a contract for default, courts and boards will award common-law breach damages rather than the usual termination for convenience costs, plus profit on work performed. See Sigal Constr. Corp., CBCA No. 508, 10-1 BCA ¶ 34,442 (finding termination for convenience to be in bad faith where GSA deleted work from a construction contract in order to have that work performed by another contractor at a lower price); Apex Int'l Mgmt. Servs., Inc., ASBCA No. 38087, 94-2 BCA ¶ 26,842 (finding 20 breaches, board holds Navy liable for breach damages).

2. Constructive Termination for Convenience.

   a. The doctrine of constructive termination for convenience is based on the concept that a contracting party who is sued for breach may ordinarily defend on the ground that there existed at the time of the breach a legal excuse for nonperformance, although that party was then ignorant of the fact. <u>College Point Boat Corp. v. United States</u>, 267 U.S. 12 (1925).

b. A government directive to end performance of work will not be considered a breach but rather a convenience termination if the action could lawfully fall under that clause. See <u>ASFA Constr. Indus. and Trade, Inc.</u>, ASBCA No. 57269, 15-1 BCA ¶ 36,034 (sustaining contractor's breach of implied contract and constructive termination for convenience claim by reading the standard fixed-price termination for convenience clause into the contract under the <u>Christian</u> doctrine and finding that the government's actions constructively terminated the contract). Rather than a finding of breach, a constructive termination for convenience will be found even if the government mistakenly thinks a contract is invalid, erroneously thinks the contract can be terminated on other grounds, or wrongly calls a directive to stop work a "cancellation." <u>See, e.g.</u>, <u>Ulysses, Inc. v. U.S.</u>, 110 Fed. Cl. 618 (2013) (where award did not violate any statute or regulation and the contractor did not contribute to or know about the government's mistake, the contract could not be cancelled and the contractor was entitled to recovery under the termination for convenience clause); <u>G.C. Casebolt Co. v. United States</u>, 421 F.2d 710 (Ct. Cl. 1970) (government error did not constitute breach and did not entitle contractor to continue with performance; adequate justification for government's action existed in the convenience termination clause of the agreement); <u>John Reiner & Co. v. United States</u>, 325 F.2d 438 (Ct. Cl. 1963) (cancellation of contract following erroneous ruling that award was void did not result in a common-law breach entitling

contractor to anticipatory profits; instead, damages were limited under the contract's termination for convenience clause) .

c. The government cannot use the constructive termination for convenience theory to retroactively terminate a fully performed contract in an effort to limit its liability for failing to order the contract's minimum amount of goods or services. <u>Ace-Federal Reporting, Inc., v. Barram</u>, 226 F.3d 1329 (Fed. Cir. 2000) (agency's improper action could not be excused as retroactive constructive termination for convenience; unauthorized government actions were "breaches, pure and simple"); <u>Maxima Corp. v. United States</u>, 847 F.2d 1549 (Fed. Cir. 1988) ("[N]o decision has upheld retroactive application of a termination for convenience clause to a contract that had been fully performed in accordance with its terms."); <u>PHP Healthcare Corp.</u>, ASBCA No. 39207, 91-1 BCA ¶ 23,647.

d. Further, the government may not require bidders to agree in advance that the government's failure to order the contract's minimum quantity will be treated as a termination for convenience. <u>Southwest Lab. of Okla., Inc.</u>, B-251778, May 5, 1993, 93-1 CPD ¶ 368 (sustaining pre-award protest of the terms of a solicitation which included such a requirement).

3. Deductive Change versus Partial Termination for Convenience.

a. Deleted work is either a deductive change <u>or</u> a termination for convenience. See <u>Dollar Roofing</u>, ASBCA No. 36461, 92-1 BCA ¶ 24,695 (treating a deletion of work as a partial termination for the convenience of the government). <u>But see Griffin Servs., Inc.</u>, GSBCA No. 11022, 92-3 BCA ¶ 25,181 (board characterized deleted work as a partial termination for convenience, but ordered recovery based on the Changes clause).

b. This distinction is important because it determines whether the measure of the contractor's recovery is under the contract's Changes clause or the Termination for Convenience clause.

c. Generally, the courts and boards will not overturn the contracting officer's determination that the deleted work is a deductive change if the parties consistently treated the deletion as such. Justman Freight Lines, Inc., PSBCA No. 6428, 15-1 BCA ¶ 35,819 (enforcing the parties' agreement that a reduction in work was a deductive change, rather than a partial termination for convenience).

d. If the contractor disputes the contracting officer's treatment of the deletion, courts and boards will examine the relative significance of the deleted work.

   (1) If major portions of the work are deleted and no additional work is substituted in its place, the termination for convenience clause must be used. Nager Elec. Co. v. United States, 442 F.2d 936 (Ct. Cl. 1971).

   (2) Courts and boards will treat the deletion of relatively minor and segregable items of work as a deductive change. Lionsgate Corp., ENG BCA No. 5425, 90-2 BCA ¶ 22,730.

III. THE DECISION TO TERMINATE FOR CONVENIENCE.

A. Regulatory Guidance.

1. The FAR clauses give the government the right to terminate a contract in whole or in part if the contracting officer determines that termination is in the government's interest. FAR 49.101(b); See John

Massman Contracting Co. v. United States, 23 Cl. Ct. 24 (1991) (finding no duty to terminate when it would have been in the contractor's best interest).

2. The FAR provides no guidance on factors that the contracting officer should consider when determining whether termination is "in the government's interest." FAR 49.101(b) and the convenience termination clauses merely provide that contracting officers shall terminate contracts only when it is in the government's interest to do so.

3. The right to terminate "comprehends termination in a host of variable and unspecified situations" and is not limited to situations where there is a "decrease in the need for the item purchased." John Reiner & Co. v. United States, 325 F.2d 438 (Ct. Cl. 1963), cert. denied, 377 U.S. 931 (1964).

4. A "cardinal change" in the government's requirements is not a prerequisite to a termination for convenience. T&M Distributors, Inc. v. United States, 185 F.3d 1279 (Fed. Cir. 1999) (finding no cardinal change, termination of contract for convenience of the government was warranted by 450% error in original solicitation's estimation of contract's value).

5. The FAR does provide guidance concerning circumstances in which contracting officers normally cannot or should not use a convenience termination. For example, a negotiated no-cost settlement is appropriate instead of a termination for convenience or default when:

   a. The contractor will accept it;

   b. Government property was not furnished; and,

   c. There are no outstanding payments due to the contractor, debts due by the contractor to the government, or other contractor obligations. FAR 49.101(b).

6. Where the price of the undelivered balance of the contract is less than $5,000, the government normally will not terminate a contract, but should allow it to run to completion. FAR 49.101(c).

7. There is no requirement to give the contractor a hearing before the termination decision. <u>Melvin R. Kessler</u>, PSBCA No. 2820, 92-2 BCA ¶ 24,857 (finding no merit in contractor's contention that it was entitled to a hearing before a termination could be issued; "Appellant has been afforded all his contractual and statutory protections against arbitrary action by the Contracting Officer through the procedure available on appeal to this Board.").

8. Notice of termination.

   a. When terminating a contract for convenience, the termination contracting officer (TCO) must provide notice to the contractor, the contract administration office, and any known assignee, guarantor, or surety of the contractor. FAR 49.102(b).

   b. FAR 49.102(a) outlines the information required to be included in a notice of termination.

   c. Notice shall be made by certified mail or hand delivery. FAR 49.102(a).

   d. Where the termination of a defense contract will result in the loss of 100 or more contractor employee jobs, the proposed termination must first be cleared through department/agency liaison offices (before the contractor is notified) and, later, notification must be provided to Congress. DFARS 249.7001 (Congressional notification on significant contract terminations); DFARS PGI 249.7001 (outlining procedures for congressional notification and release of information).

9. Contractor duties after receipt of notice of termination. FAR 49.104. The contractor is required generally to:

   a. Stop work immediately on the terminated portion(s) of the contract and stop placing subcontracts;

   b. Terminate all subcontracts related to the terminated portion of the prime contract;

   c. Immediately advise the TCO of any special circumstances precluding work stoppage;

   d. If the termination is partial, perform any continued portion of the contract and submit promptly any request for equitable adjustment to the price;

   e. Protect and preserve property in the contractor's possession;

   f. Notify TCO in writing concerning any legal proceedings growing out of any subcontract or other commitment related to the terminated portion of the contract;

   g. Settle subcontract proposals;

   h. Promptly submit own termination settlement proposal; and

   i. Dispose of termination inventory as directed or authorized by TCO.

10. **Practice Tip:** If the contractor fails to follow the instructions in the termination notice, it does so at its own expense and risk.

11. Duties of TCO after notice of termination. FAR 49.105.

    a. Direct the action required of the prime contractor;

    b. Examine the contractor's settlement proposal (and, when appropriate, the settlement proposals of subcontractors);

    c. Promptly negotiate settlement agreement (or settle by determination for the elements that cannot be agreed upon, if unable to negotiate a complete settlement).

B.   Standard of Review.

1.   The courts and boards recognize the government's broad right to terminate a contract for convenience. It is not the province of the courts to decide de novo whether termination of the contract was the best course of action. Salsbury Indus. v. United States, 905 F.2d 1518 (Fed. Cir. 1990) ("In the absence of bad faith or clear abuse of discretion the contracting officer's election to terminate is conclusive") (internal citation omitted).

2.   The Kalvar test. To find that a termination for convenience in legal effect is a breach of contract, a contractor must prove bad faith or clear abuse of discretion. This is sometimes referred to as the Kalvar test. Kalvar Corp., Inc., v. United States, 543 F.2d 1298 (Ct. Cl. 1976); Northrop Grumman Corp. v. United States, 46 Fed. Cl. 622 (2000).[1]

    a.   Bad faith.

        (1)   Boards and courts presume that contracting officers act conscientiously in the discharge of their duties. Krygoski Constr. Co., Inc. v. United States, 94 F.3d 1537, 1541 (Fed. Cir. 1996).

        (2)   To succeed, a contractor must show through "well nigh-irrefragable proof," tantamount to evidence of some specific intent to injure the contractor, that the contracting officer acted in bad faith. Kalvar Corp., Inc., v. United States, 543 F.2d 1298, 1301 (Ct. Cl. 1976). One example of a finding of bad faith is found in Bill Hubbard v. United States, 52

---

[1] The court applied the tests for finding a termination improper that were suggested by the Federal Circuit in Krygoski Construction Company, Inc. v. United States, 94 F.3d 1537 (Fed. Cir. 1996). The court found that the National Aeronautics and Space Administration (NASA) did not terminate Northrop's Space Station contract "simply to acquire a better bargain from another source," nor did NASA enter its contract with Northrop with no intent of fulfilling its promises.

Fed. Cl. 192 (2002). There, it was "clear to the court that the stated reasons for [moving the plaintiff's office location] were pretextual, and that the move was engineered in bad faith, without regard, indeed, with deliberate and bad faith disregard, for the legitimate business interests" of the plaintiff. Id. at 196.

        (3)   Standard of Proof: Overcoming the presumption that the government acts in good faith requires "clear and convincing" evidence. Am-Pro Protective Services, Inc. v. United States, 281 F.3d 1234 (Fed. Cir. 2002) (protestor's "belated assertions, with no corroborating evidence, therefore fall short of the clear and convincing or highly probable (formerly described as well-nigh irrefragable) threshold."). In Gulf Group Gen. Enters. Co. W.L.L. v. U.S., 114 Fed. Cl. 258 (July 2, 2013), the contractor met this high burden. While the contractor bears a high burden of proof to overcome the presumption of good faith afforded to agency personnel, the latitude afforded is "not unlimited." The court found for the contractor because the Army gave "a number of purported, and shifting, justifications" for the termination, none of which the court found "reasonable or consistent with the government's obligation to act in good faith." Id. at 409.

        (4)   See also TLT Constr. Corp., ASBCA No. 40501, 93-3 BCA ¶ 25,978 (inept government actions do not constitute bad faith);

    b.   Abuse of discretion.

        (1)   A contracting officer's decision to terminate for convenience cannot be arbitrary or capricious.

(2) The Court of Claims (predecessor to the Court of Appeals for the Federal Circuit) cited four factors to apply in determining whether a contracting officer's discretionary decision is arbitrary or capricious. Keco Indus. v. United States, 492 F.2d 1200, 1203-04 (Ct. Cl. 1974). These factors are:

(a) Evidence of subjective bad faith on the part of the government official;

(b) Lack of a reasonable basis for the decision;

(c) The amount of discretion given to the government official; i.e., the greater the discretion granted, the more difficult it is to prove that the decision was arbitrary and capricious; and,

(d) A proven violation of an applicable statute or regulation (this factor alone may be enough to show that the conduct was arbitrary and capricious).

3. The Torncello "change in circumstances" test.

    a. In 1982, a plurality of the Court of Claims articulated a different test for the sufficiency of a convenience termination. The test is known as the "change in circumstances" test. Torncello v. United States, 681 F.2d 756 (Ct. Cl. 1982) (holding that the termination for convenience clause could not be used to avoid paying anticipated profits unless there was some change in circumstances between time of award and termination). Critics of the "change in circumstances" test charged that the court should have applied the Kalvar test.

    b. The Court of Appeals for the Federal Circuit subsequently characterized Torncello as a "bad faith" case. Salsbury Indus. v. United States, 905 F.2d. 1518, 1521 (Fed. Cir. 1990) ("[Torncello] stands for the unremarkable proposition that when the government contracts with a party knowing full well that it will not honor the contract, it cannot avoid a breach claim by adverting to the convenience termination clause.") This rationale had been applied by the ASBCA prior to the Federal Circuit's decision. See Dr. Richard L. Simmons, ASBCA No. 34049, 87-3 BCA ¶ 19,984 ("...the lesson of Torncello is that the government may not use the termination clause to terminate a contract when it had the intention of later terminating at the time it entered the contract"); Tamp Corp., ASBCA No. 25692, 84-2 BCA ¶ 17,460 (offering similar analysis of Torncello decision).

    c. Moreover, the Federal Circuit has refused to extend Torncello to situations in which the government contracts in good faith while having knowledge of facts putting it on notice that termination may be appropriate in the future. See Krygoski Construction Company, Inc. v. United States, 94 F.3d 1537, 1545 (Fed. Cir. 1996) (reversing and remanding because the trial court incorrectly relied on Torncello; the record showed no evidence that the government intended from the outset to avoid its promises); Caldwell & Santmyer, Inc. v. Glickman, 55 F.3d 1578 (Fed. Cir. 1995).

    d. Contractors occasionally still argue the change in circumstances test, though unsuccessfully. See T&M Distributors, Inc. v. United States, 185 F.3d 1279 (Fed. Cir. 1999) ("We have in fact rejected the suggestion that dicta of a plurality opinion in Torncello imposed a special requirement of 'changed circumstances' on the government's right to terminate for its convenience.").

4. Effect of Improper Termination.

   a. By terminating in bad faith or arbitrarily and capriciously, the government breaches the contract, permitting the contractor to recover breach of contract damages, including anticipatory (lost) profits. See Operational Serv. Corp., ASBCA No. 37059, 93-3 BCA ¶ 26,190 (government breached contract by exercising option year of contract while knowing that it would award a commercial activities contract or perform the work in house).

   b. The general rule is to place the injured party in as good a position as the one he would have been in had the breaching party fully performed. Remote and consequential damages are not recoverable. Travel Centre v. General Services Administration, GSBCA No. 14057, 99-2 BCA ¶ 30,521 (board denies contractor claims of lost future net income and value of business closed as result of contract termination). But see Energy Capital Corp. v. United States, 47 Fed. Cl. 382 (2000) (awarding $8.78 million in lost profits to new venture).

C. **Revocation of a Termination for Convenience.**

1. Reinstatement of the contract. FAR 49.102(d).

   a. A terminated portion of a contract may be reinstated in whole or in part if the contracting officer determines in writing that there is a requirement for the terminated items and that the reinstatement is advantageous to the government. FAR 49.102(d). See To the Administrator, Gen. Servs. Admin., 34 Comp. Gen. 343 (1955).

   b. The written consent of the contractor is required. The contracting officer may not reinstate a contract unilaterally. FAR 49.102(d).

2. A termination for default cannot be "substituted" for a termination for convenience. Roged, Inc., ASBCA No. 20702, 76-2 BCA ¶ 12,018; but see Amwest Surety Ins. Co., ENG BCA No. 6036, 94-2 BCA ¶ 26,648 (substitution allowed where government issued "conditional" termination for convenience). As discussed herein, a termination for default converts into a termination for convenience only where a contract was default terminated in error or the default was excusable. See FAR 52.249-8(g); FAR 52.249-10(c)

IV. **CONVENIENCE TERMINATION SETTLEMENTS.**

A. **Procedures.** FAR Part 49.

1. After termination for convenience, the parties must:

   a. Stop the work.

   b. Dispose of termination inventory.

   c. Adjust the contract price.

Practice Tip: Contractors should prepare settlement proposals on the forms prescribed in 49.602 unless the forms are inadequate for a particular contract.

2. Timing of the termination settlement proposal.

   a. The contractor must submit its termination proposal within one year of notice of the termination for convenience. FAR 49.206-1; 52.249-2(j); The Swanson Group, ASBCA No. 52109, 01-1 BCA ¶ 31,164 (concluding that, while appellant did not submit a termination settlement proposal within the one-year timeframe called for by the FAR, appellant timely requested an extension and, as such, preserved its rights); Do-Well Mach. Shop, Inc. v. United States, 870 F.2d 637 (Fed. Cir. 1989) ("we cannot hold that Congress wanted to prevent parties from agreeing to terms that would further expedite the claim resolution process."); Industrial Data Link Corp., ASBCA No. 49348, 98-1 BCA ¶ 29,634, aff'd 194 F.3d 1337 (Fed. Cir., 1999); Harris Corp., ASBCA No. 37940, 90-3 BCA ¶ 23,257.

b. Timely submittal is defined as mailing the proposal within one year after receipt of the termination notice. Voices R Us, Inc., ASBCA No. 51565, 99-1 BCA ¶ 30,213 (denying government's summary judgment motion for failure to provide evidence that fax notice of termination was sent to and received by contractor); Jo-Bar Mfg. Corp., ASBCA No. 39572, 93-2 BCA ¶ 25,756 (finding timely mailing despite lack of government receipt).

c. **Practice Tip:** Termination charges under a single prime contract involving two or more divisions or units of the prime contractor may be consolidated and included in a single settlement proposal.

d. If a contractor fails to submit its termination settlement proposal within the required time period, or any extension granted by the contracting officer, the contracting officer may then unilaterally determine the amount due the contractor. FAR 49.109-7.

e. Refusal to grant an extension of time to submit a settlement proposal is a decision that can be appealed but requires the contractor to submit a proposal for jurisdiction under the Contracts Disputes Act (CDA). Cedar Constr., ASBCA No. 42178, 92-2 BCA ¶ 24,896. However, failure of the contracting officer to act on a timely request for an extension cannot deny the contractor the right to appeal. The Swanson Group, ASBCA No. 52109, 01-1 BCA ¶ 31,164

3. Parties are charged with knowledge of FAR 49.001, which defines a settlement agreement as a "written agreement," and FAR 49.109-1, which requires use of Standard Form (SF) 30 for settlement

agreements. In Sigma Constr., Inc. v. U.S., 113 Fed. Cl. 13 (2013), the parties entered into a verbal negotiation regarding the contractor's termination settlement proposal, and the contractor submitted a CDA claim for the agreed-upon settlement amount, plus interest. When the contracting officer failed to issue a decision, the contractor filed suit to appeal the deemed denial. The court granted the government's motion to dismiss, in which it argued that the oral agreement was not an enforceable settlement. In addition to the FAR's procedural requirement for termination settlement proposals, the Court of Appeals for the Federal Circuit has held that the FAR requires all modifications of procurement contracts to be in writing. Id. (citing Mil-Spec Contractors, Inc. v. United States, 835 F.2d 865 (Fed. Cir. 1987).

B. **Amount of Settlement.**

1. Methods of settlement. FAR 49.103.

   a. Bilateral negotiations between the contractor and the government.

   b. Unilateral determination of the government. FAR 49.109-7. This method is appropriate only when the contractor fails to submit a proposal or a settlement cannot be reached by agreement.

2. Bases of settlement. The two bases for settlement proposals are the inventory basis (the preferred method), and the total cost basis. FAR 49.206-2.

   a. Inventory basis (this is the preferred method). Propellex Corp. v. Brownlee, 342 F.3d 1335, 1338 (Fed. Cir. 2003) (the preferred way for a contractor to prove increased costs is by submitting actual cost data). Settlement proposal must itemize separately:

      (1) Metals, raw materials, purchased parts, work in process, finished parts, components, dies, jigs,

fixtures, and tooling, at purchase or manufacturing cost;

(2) Charges such as engineering costs, initial costs, and general administrative costs;

(3) Costs of settlements with subcontractors;

(4) Settlement expenses; and

(5) Other proper charges;

(6) An allowance for profit or adjustment for loss must be made to complete the gross settlement proposal.

b. Total cost basis (disfavored). Tecom, Inc. v. United States, 86 Fed. Cl. 437, 455 (2009) (describing method as a last resort, to be used when there is no other way to compute damages) (internal citation omitted). Used only when approved in advance by the TCO and when use of inventory basis is impracticable or will unduly delay settlement, as when production has not commenced and accumulated costs represent planning and preproduction expenses. FAR 49.206-2(b)(1). ALKAI Consultants, LLC, ASBCA No. 56792, 10-2 BCA ¶ 34,493 (where costs of additional work could not readily be separated from the cost of the basic contract work, a cost-based approach would be an appropriate measure of the percentage of work performed).

3. Convenience termination settlements are based on costs incurred in the performance of terminated work, plus a fair and reasonable profit on the incurred costs, plus settlement expenses. See FAR 31.205-42; Teems, Inc. v. General Services Administration, GSBCA No. 14090, 98-1 BCA ¶ 29,357.

4. The contractor has the burden of establishing its proposed settlement amount. FAR 49.109-7(c); American

Geometrics Constr. Co., ASBCA No. 37734, 92-1 BCA ¶ 24,545.

5. As a general rule, a termination for convenience converts the terminated portion of a fixed-price contract to a cost-reimbursement type of contract, so costs on the settlement proposal are determined under FAR Part 31 Cost Principles and Procedures. See FAR 31.205-42 – Termination Costs (these principles to be used in conjunction with other cost principles in Subpart 31.2), which lists the following categories of costs:

a. Common items;

b. Costs continuing after termination;

c. Initial costs;

d. Loss of useful value of special tooling and machinery;

e. Rental under unexpired leases;

f. Alteration of leased property;

g. Settlement expenses; and

h. Subcontractor claims.

6. The cost principles must be applied subject to the fairness principle set forth at FAR 49.201(a), which states:

a. A settlement should compensate the contractor fairly for the work done and the preparations made for the terminated portions of the contract, including a reasonable allowance for profit. See Ralcon, Inc., ASBCA No. 43176, 94-2 BCA ¶ 26,935 (rejecting contracting officer's use of DFARS weighted guidelines, and instead requiring use of factors at FAR 49.202 to determine reasonable profit).

b. Fair compensation is a matter of judgment and cannot be measured exactly. In a given case, various methods may be equally appropriate for arriving at fair compensation. The use of business judgment, as distinguished from strict accounting principles, is the heart of a settlement.

See Codex Corp. v. United States, 226 Ct. Cl. 693 (1981) (board decision disallowing pre-contract costs based on strict application of cost principles was remanded for further consideration by the board based on the court's determination that cost principles must be applied "subject to" the fairness concept in FAR 49.201). See also J.W. Cook & Sons, ASBCA No. 39691, 92-3 BCA ¶ 25,053 (board definition of "fairness").

7. **Practice Tip:** Although precontract costs are sometimes unallowable under the FAR cost principles, they are allowable in the context of a termination for convenience if necessary for "fair compensation."

8. Cost of Termination Inventory. Except for normal spoilage and except to the extent that the government assumed the risk of loss, the Contracting Officer shall exclude from the amounts due the contractor the fair value of property that is destroyed, lost, stolen, or damaged so as to become undeliverable to the government. FAR 52.249-2(h). See Lisbon Contractors, Inc. v. United States, 828 F.2d 759 (Fed. Cir. 1987) (contractor cannot recover "simply by pleading ignorance" of fate of materials); Industrial Tectonics Bearings Corp. v. United States, 44 Fed. Cl. 115 (1999) ("fair value" means "fair market value" and not the amount sought by the contractor).

9. Common items.

   a. FAR 31.205-42(a) provides that "[t]he costs of items reasonably usable on the contractor's other work shall not be allowable unless the contractor submits evidence that the items could not be retained at cost without sustaining a loss."

   Practice Tip: A contractor can rebut a "common items" disallowance by demonstrating that the items cannot be retained at cost without sustaining a loss.

   b. Courts and boards have applied this provision to more than just materiel costs. Dairy Sales Corp. v. United States, 593 F.2d 1002 (Ct. Cl. 1979) (cost of butter wrapping machine not allowed in a partial termination of a butter packing contract); Hugo Auchter GmbH, ASBCA No. 39642, 91-1 BCA ¶ 23,645 (general purpose off-the-shelf computer equipment).

10. Subcontract Settlements. FAR 49.108.

   a. Upon termination of a prime contract, the prime and each subcontractor are responsible for prompt settlement of the settlement proposals of their immediate subcontractors. FAR 49.108-1.

   b. Such subcontractor recovery amounts are allowable as part of the prime's termination for convenience settlement with the government. FAR 31.205-42(h); see Fluor Intercontinental, Inc. v. IAO Worldwide Serv., Inc., 2010 WL 3610449 (N.D. Fla. Sept. 13, 2010) (prime contractor liable to subcontractor for breach although prime contractor's government contract was terminated for convenience).

   c. The TCO shall examine each subcontract settlement to determine that it was arrived at in good faith, is reasonable in amount, and is allocable to the terminated portion of the contract. FAR 49.108-3(c). A contractor's settlement with a subcontractor must be done at "arm's length", or it may be disallowed. Bos'n Towing & Salvage Co., ASBCA No. 41357, 92-2 BCA ¶ 24,864 (denying claim for costs of terminating charter of tugboats).

   d. The contractor has a duty to determine the allowability and reimbursability of the costs submitted by the subcontractor as part of the settlement. Parsons Global Serv. Inc., ASBCA 56731, 11-1 BCA ¶ 34,643 (dismissing contractor claims for reimbursement of sub's costs as premature when prime had not evaluated costs).

11. Settlement Expenses. FAR 31.205-42(g).

   a. Accounting, legal, clerical, and similar costs reasonably necessary for: (1) the preparation and presentation, including supporting data, of settlement claims to the contracting officer and (2) the termination and settlement of subcontracts.

   b. Reasonable costs for the storage, transportation, protection, and disposition of property acquired or produced for the contract.

   c. Indirect costs related to salary and wages incurred as settlement expenses in a and b above; normally limited to payroll taxes, fringe benefits, occupancy costs, and immediate supervision costs.

   d. **Practice Tip:** To facilitate recovery of settlement expenses, make sure that personnel keep time sheets or charge directly to accounts for recording post-termination charges. Charge that time directly to the termination settlement proposal.

12. Loss Contracts.

   a. A contracting officer may not allow profit in settling a termination claim if it appears that the contractor would have incurred a loss had the entire contract been completed. FAR 49.203.

   b. If the contractor would have suffered a loss on the contract in the absence of the termination, the contractor may recover only the same percentage of costs incurred as would have been recovered had the contract gone to completion. The rate of loss is applied to costs incurred to determine the cost recovery. FAR 49.203.

   c. The government has the burden of proving that the contractor would

have incurred a loss at contract completion. Balimoy Mfg. Co. of Venice, ASBCA Nos. 47140 and 48165, 98-2 BCA ¶ 30,017, aff'd, 2000 U.S. App. LEXIS 26702 (Fed. Cir. 2000); R&B Bewachungs, GmbH, ASBCA No. 42214, 92-3 BCA ¶ 25,105 ("To apply the convenience termination loss formula, the government generally has the burden of proving a loss adjustment.").

   d. The target price of the fixed items, rather than the ceiling price, is used to compute the loss adjustment ratio for a convenience termination of a contract with both firm fixed-price items and fixed-price incentive fee line items. Boeing Defense & Space Group, ASBCA No. 51773, 98-2 BCA ¶ 30,069.

C. **Special Considerations.**

1. **Practice Tip:** Terminated contractors and subcontractors may submit partial payment requests. However, partial payments are provisional and if the TCO disallows any of the contractor's costs, the government can recover a credit on previously paid amounts.

2. Offsets. The government may withhold a portion of the termination settlement as an offset against other claims. See Applied Companies v. United States, 37 Fed. Cl. 749 (1997) (Army properly withheld $1.9 million from termination settlement due to overpayments on another contract).

3. Merger. Claims against the government are generally merged with the termination for convenience settlement proposal; therefore, it is not necessary to distinguish equitable adjustment costs from normal performance costs unless the contract is in a loss status. Sybion Ozdil Joint Venture, ASBCA No. 56713, 10-1 BCA ¶ 34,367 (discussing the merger doctrine, but finding that it did not apply because appellant sought an increase in the contract price not based on costs

incurred); <u>Worsham Constr. Co.</u>, ASBCA No. 25907, 85-2 BCA ¶ 18,016.

4. Equitable adjustments. In cases of partial terminations a contractor may request an equitable adjustment for the continued portion of the contract. <u>See</u> 52.249-2(l) (requiring proposal to be submitted within 90 days of effective date of termination unless extended in writing by KO); <u>Varo Inc.</u>, ASBCA Nos. 47945, 47946, 98-1 BCA ¶ 29,484 (affirmative defense of untimeliness waived where not raised until third day of hearing).

5. Mutual fault. If both the government and the contractor are responsible for the causes resulting in termination of a contract, contractors have been denied full recovery of termination costs.

   a. In <u>Dynalectron Corp. v. United States</u>, 518 F.2d 594 (Ct. Cl. 1975), the court allowed the contractor only one-half of the allowable termination for convenience costs because the contractor was at fault in continuing to incur costs while trying to meet impossible government specifications without notifying the government of its efforts.

   b. In <u>Insul-Glass, Inc.</u>, GSBCA No. 8223, 89-1 BCA ¶ 21,361, the board denied termination for convenience recovery because of the contractor's deficient administration of the contract. The board noted that under the default clause, if the default is determined to be improper, "the rights and obligations of the parties shall be the same as if a notice of termination for convenience of the government had been issued. We may exercise our equitable powers, however, to fashion, in circumstances where both parties share in the blame for the predicament which engenders an appeal, a remedy which apportions costs fairly."

6. Converting a termination for convenience proposal to a Contract Disputes Act claim.

   a. While many terminations for convenience result in a negotiated settlement, in some instances the parties are unable to reach agreement on the amount of the settlement. Once the parties reach an "impasse" in settlement negotiations, a request that the contracting officer render a final decision is implicit in the contractor's settlement proposal. A better practice is for the contractor to inform the government that an impasse exists, certify its settlement proposal as a claim, and demand a final decision.

   b. Once the parties reach an impasse, the proposal becomes a claim under the Contract Disputes Act. <u>James M. Ellet Constr. Co. v. United States</u>, 93 F.3d 1537 (Fed. Cir. 1996) (holding that once negotiations over a settlement proposal reached an impasse, the proposal ripened into a claim and contractor was not required to submit a new claim or convert its proposal into a claim); <u>Rex Systems, Inc. v. Cohen</u>, 224 F.3d 1367 (Fed. Cir. 2000) (no impasse entitling contractor to interest despite taking 2½ years to settle the termination); <u>Mediax Interactive Technologies, Inc.</u>, ASBCA No. 43961, 99-2 BCA ¶ 30,318.

   c. If an agency fails to respond to a contractor's settlement proposal, the contractor can file an appeal with the appropriate board. <u>ePlus Tech., Inc. v. FCC</u>, CBCA 2573, 2012-2 BCA ¶ 25,114 (board found jurisdiction over appeal when agency failed to respond for six months to termination settlement proposal that was certified as a claim).

   d. A claim based upon the termination of a contract is typically pursued under the Contract Disputes Act, 41 U.S.C. §§ 7101-09. <u>OAO Corp. v. Johnson</u>, 49 F.3d 721, 724-25 (Fed. Cir. 1995); <u>Data Monitor Sys., Inc. v. United States</u>, 74 Fed. Cl. 66, 71 (2006). Be aware, however, the Court of Federal

Claims has reviewed some terminations for convenience pursuant to its bid protest jurisdiction when the termination is in conjunction with corrective action. Wildflower Int'l, Inc. v. United States, 105 Fed. Cl. 362 (2012).

D. Limitations on Termination for Convenience Settlements.

1. Overall contract price for fixed-price contracts.

   a. The total settlement may not exceed the contract price (less payments made or to be made under the contract) plus the amount of the settlement expenses. FAR 49.207; FAR 52.249-2; Tom Shaw, Inc., ENG BCA No. 5540, 93-2 BCA ¶ 25,742. See also Alta Constr. Co., PSBCA No. 1463, 92-2 BCA ¶ 24,824.

   b. Compare Okaw Indus., ASBCA No. 17863, 77-2 BCA ¶ 12,793 (the contract price of items terminated on an indefinite quantity contract is the price of the ordered quantity, not of the estimated quantity, where the government has ordered the minimum quantity) with Aviation Specialists, Inc., DOT BCA No. 1967, 91-1 BCA ¶ 23,534 (the only reasonable measure of the maximum recovery under a requirements contract is the government estimate.)

2. Add the cost of valid pending claims for government delay, defective specifications, etc., to the original contract price to establish the "ceiling" of convenience termination recovery. See, e.g., Wolfe Constr. Co., ENG BCA No. 5309, 88-3 BCA ¶ 21,122.

3. A contractor is not entitled to anticipatory profits or consequential damages on work not performed as of the date of termination. FAR 49.202; Dairy Sales Corp. v. United States, 593 F.2d 1002 (Ct. Cl. 1979); Centennial Leasing Corp., ASBCA No. 49217, 96-2 BCA ¶ 28,571.

E. Subcontracts.

1. The typical termination for convenience clause limits a prime contractor/higher-tier subcontractor to recovering the costs it would have paid a subcontractor had it included a similar termination for convenience clause in the subcontract. FAR 49.108. Therefore, contractors typically include a termination for convenience clause in their subcontracts.

2. In negotiating subcontracts, an important issue is whether the prime contractor/ higher-tier subcontractor has the same right to terminate for convenience as the government, or whether its right is limited to those instances where the government has terminated the prime contract. Contractors typically include the former in model subcontracts, but will defer to the latter if the subcontractor has bargaining leverage. Prime contractors rarely omit termination for convenience clauses in their entirety.

3. Prime contractors typically require subcontractors to submit settlement proposals within much shorter time frames than required of the prime contract. This is reasonable given that the prime contractor needs time to prepare its own settlement proposal. Lower-tier suppliers are given even shorter periods to submit their settlement proposals to the higher-tier subcontractor.

F. Commercial Items – Termination for Convenience.

1. **Practice Tip:** Although the commercial item clause does not set forth a time limit for the submission of a settlement proposal, submission may be barred by the six-year statute of limitations on claims against the government or the judicial doctrine of laches. Additionally, some agencies may include a provision restricting the period for submitting a settlement proposal.

2. Background. The Federal Acquisition Streamlining Act, P.L. 103-355, 108 Stat. 3243 (Oct. 13, 1994), established special

requirements for the acquisition of commercial items. Congress intended government acquisitions to more closely resemble those customarily used in the commercial market place. FAR 12.201.

3. FAR 12.403(a) states that the termination for convenience concepts for commercial items differ from those in FAR Part 49 for noncommercial items, and that the Part 49 principles do not apply to terminations for convenience of a commercial item, except as guidance to the extent they do not conflict with FAR 52.212-4.

4. Policy. The contracting officer should exercise the government's right to terminate a contract for a commercial item only when such a termination would be in the best interests of the government. FAR 12.403(b).

5. Under FAR 12.403(d), when the contracting officer terminates for convenience a commercial item contract, the contractor shall be paid –

    (i) The percentage of the contract price reflecting the percentage of the work performed prior to the notice of the termination – interpreted as requiring payment for completed deliverables or services at the contract price (<u>Corners & Edges, Inc. v. Department of Health & Human Services</u>, CBCA 762, 08-2 BCA ¶ 33,961); and

    (ii) Any charges the contractor can demonstrate directly resulted from the termination – interpreted to include costs reasonably incurred in anticipation of performing the contract (<u>SWR, Inc.</u>, ASBCA No. 56708, 15-1 BCA ¶ 35,832) (finding that, under the fair compensation principle, contractor could recover costs incurred that did not relate to the work performed – including rent under unexpired lease, restocking fees, personnel costs for site visits and preparation, and indirect costs).

The contractor may demonstrate such charges using its standard recordkeeping system and is not required to comply with the cost accounting standards or the contract cost principles in Part 31. The government does not have any right to audit the contractor's records solely because of the termination for convenience. FAR 12.403(d)(1)(ii).

6. **Practice Tip:** To ensure maximum fee recovery, contractors should produce a well-supported determination of the percentage of completion. Program management, engineering, or other technical personnel may be enlisted to perform a technical evaluation of the percentage of completion of the contractor's work, as well as the work of any subcontractors or lower-tier vendors. Earned Value Management System data is a credible source of information for determining the percentage of completion.

7. Generally, the parties should mutually agree upon the requirements of the termination proposal. The parties must balance the government's need to obtain sufficient documentation to support payment to the contractor against the goal of having a simple and expeditious settlement. FAR 12.403(d)(2).

8. The principle of fair compensation extends to terminations of commercial items contracts. For example, in <u>Russell Sand & Gravel Co., Inc. v. International Boundary and Water Commission</u>, CBCA No. 2235, 13 BCA ¶ 35,355 the parties disagreed as to whether the contractor was entitled to payment for post-termination costs, beyond the percentage of the contract price due to it. The Civilian Board found that the contractor had made reasonable, though unsuccessful, efforts to find other work and so mitigate its costs. Under the fair compensation principle, the contractor was entitled to recover despite limitations in the detail its accounting system could provide.

9. **Practice Tip:** A commercial item contractor is not required to provide cost

information to the government if its contract is terminated for convenience.

G. Fiscal Considerations.

1. An agency must analyze each contract that it plans to terminate for convenience to determine whether termination for convenience or completion of the contract is less costly or otherwise in the best interests of the government.

2. An agency must determine whether the convenience termination settlement would be governed by standard FAR convenience termination clause provisions, or by contract specific terms, such as termination ceilings, multi-year contract termination costs, or other specific contractual terms.

3. The general rule is that a prior year's funding obligation is extinguished upon termination of a contract, and those funds will not remain available to fund a replacement contract in a subsequent year where a contracting officer terminates a contract for the convenience of the government. The contracting officer must deobligate all funds in excess of the estimated termination settlement costs. FAR 49.101(f); DOD Financial Management Regulation 7000.14-R, vol. 3, ch. 8, para. 080512.

4. Exceptions to the general rule.

   a. Funds originally obligated in one fiscal year for a contract that is later terminated for convenience in response to a court order or to a determination by the Government Accountability Office or other competent authority that the award was improper, can remain available in a subsequent fiscal year to fund a replacement contract. Funding of Replacement Contracts, B-232616, 68 Comp. Gen. 158 (1988).

   b. Funds originally obligated in one fiscal year for a contract that is later terminated for convenience as a result of the contracting officer's

determination that the award was clearly erroneous, can remain available in a subsequent fiscal year to fund a replacement contract. Navy, Replacement Contract, B 238548, 70 Comp. Gen. 230 (1991).

   c. The two exceptions above apply subject to the following conditions:

      (1) The original award was made in good faith;

      (2) The agency has a continuing bona fide need for the goods or services involved;

      (3) The replacement contract is of the same size and scope as the original contract;

      (4) The replacement contract is executed without undue delay after the original contract is terminated for convenience; and

      (5) If the termination for convenience is issued by the contracting officer, the contracting officer's determination that the award was improper is supported by findings of fact and law.

   d. Bid protests or court challenge. Funds available for obligation for a contract at the time of a GAO protest, agency protest, or court action filed in connection with a solicitation for, proposed award of, or award of such contract, remain available for obligation for 100 days after the date on which the final ruling is made on the protest or other action. A ruling is considered "final" on the date on which the time allowed for filing an appeal or request for reconsideration has expired, or the date on which a decision is rendered on such an appeal or request, whichever is later. 31 U.S.C. § 1558; DFAS-IN 37-1, para. 080608. See also OFFICE OF THE GENERAL COUNSEL, UNITED STATES GOVERNMENT ACCOUNTABILITY OFFICE, Principles of Federal

e. Appropriations Law 5-89 (3d ed. 2004).

V. CONCLUSION.

Terminations for convenience are an unusual government contractual right whose origin is public policy regarding war contracts. They have evolved into a right included in almost every government contract and subcontract. The terminated contractor loses profits that it might have earned on work that was not performed at the time of termination. The government is obligated to fairly compensate the contractor for its costs incurred prior to the termination, a reasonable profit on the work performed, and the costs of settlement.

TERMINATIONS FOR DEFAULT

I. INTRODUCTION.

A. General.

1. The government has the right to terminate a contract for the contractor's default. Courts and boards hold the government to a high standard when it terminates a contract for default because of the adverse impact such an action has on a contractor. Indeed, judges often describe terminations for default as a "contractual death sentence." J.D. Hedin Constr. Co. v. U.S., 408 F.2d 424, 431 (Ct. Cl. 1969) (a default termination is a "drastic sanction" to be sustained only if the government meets the heavy burden of showing that it could justify the termination based on "good grounds and solid evidence"); Platinum Logistic Servs. Co., ASBCA No. 57965, 2013-1 BCA ¶ 35,392; Pipe Tech, Inc., ENG BCA No. 5959, No. 6005, 94-2 BCA ¶ 26,649 ("Termination is the most drastic of remedies – a contractual death sentence.") As a result, the courts and boards assiduously scrutinize the grounds allegedly supporting a declaration of default.

2. Prior to terminating a contract for default, contracting officers must have a valid basis for the termination, must issue proper notices, must account for the contractor's excusable delay, must act with due diligence, and must make a reasonable determination while exercising independent judgment.

B. Default by Contractor. A contractor's unexcused present or prospective failure to perform in accordance with the contract's terms, specifications, or delivery schedule constitutes contractual default. See FAR 49.402-1.

C. Government's Right to Terminate for Default. The exercise of the government's contractual right to completely or partially terminate a contract because of the contractor's actual or anticipated failure to perform its contractual obligations. See FAR 49.401.

D. Review of Default Terminations by the Courts and Boards.

1. "[A] termination for default is a drastic sanction that should be imposed upon a contractor only for good cause and in the presence of solid evidence." Lisbon Contractors, Inc. v. United States, 828 F.2d 759 (Fed. Cir. 1987); Mega Constr. Co. v. United States, 29 Fed. Cl. 396, 414 (1992) (recognizing that default termination is a "drastic sanction" and a "type of forfeiture," while acknowledging that contracting officers possess authority to terminate a contract for default and, under proper circumstances, are obligated to exercise the discretion to do so).

2. Burden of Proof.

   a. It is the government's burden to prove, by a preponderance of the evidence, that the termination for default was proper. Lisbon Contractors, Inc. v. United States, 828 F.2d 759 (Fed. Cir. 1987); Walsky Constr. Co., ASBCA No. 41541, 94-1 BCA ¶ 26,264.

   b. A contractor's technical default is not determinative of its propriety. The government must exercise its discretion to terminate reasonably. Darwin Constr. Co. v. United States, 811 F.2d 593, 596 (Fed. Cir. 1987) ("...the default article of the contract does not require the government to terminate on a finding of default, but merely gives the procuring agency the discretion to do so, and that discretion must be reasonably exercised").

   c. Once the government has met its burden of demonstrating the appropriateness of the default, the burden of proof shifts to the contractor. The contractor must then prove that its failure to perform was the result of causes beyond its control and without fault on its part, and must further prove that it took reasonable action to perform the contract notwithstanding the occurrence of such excuse. International Elec. Corp. v. United States, 646 F.2d 496, 510 (Ct. Cl. 1981); Composite Int'l, Inc., ASBCA No. 43359, 93-2 BCA ¶ 25,747 (upholding a default termination where contractor did not meet its burden of showing that failure to perform was the result of causes beyond its control and without fault on its part).

E.   Effect of Default Terminations.

1.   A termination for default has an ongoing negative effect on a contractor beyond the specific contract that was terminated. This is true even when the contractor has appealed and even prevails in challenging the termination. For example:

   a.   Advanced Computer Concepts, B-408084, 2013 CPD ¶126 (finding a contractor's marginal past performance rating for four related terminations for cause was justified, even though the Air Force customer told the GSA contracting officer that it held the contractor blameless for the earlier problems).

   b.   Colonial Press Int'l, Inc., B-403632, 2010 CPD ¶ 247 (GAO upheld defaulted contractor's exclusion from the competition for the reprocurement contract even though the termination was on appeal).

   c.   Commissioning Solutions Global, LLC, B-403542, 2010 CPD ¶ 272 (finding that the prior termination for default could properly be considered even though it was on appeal and a few weeks later the Coast Guard agreed to convert the termination for

default to a termination for convenience).

   d.   M. Erdal Kamisli Co. Ltd. (ERKA Co. Ltd.), B-403909.2, B403909.4, 2011 CPD ¶ 63, at *5 (2011) (holding that the agency could properly consider a prior termination for default in rating past performance as an evaluation factor in a new procurement even though the termination for default was on appeal; the Army could "properly rely upon its reasonable perception of a contractor's inadequate performance even where the contractor disputes the agency's position").

2.   Impact on the Government. The fact that a contractor is in default does not mean that termination for default is the best option for the government. First, when the contractor is late in performing, it may still be the only source, or the source best able to deliver needed goods and services at the lowest price. Defaulting the current contractor and awarding a reprocurement contract is usually a long process since the replacement contractor may start from scratch. Second, a default termination is often more expensive to the government. If the default termination results in a bankrupt contractor, the agency may be unable to recover its excess costs of reprocurement. Furthermore, default terminations are often litigated, and success on the merits is not assured. If the termination is converted to one for convenience, the government pays twice: 1) the higher price of the reprocurement contractor and 2) the convenience termination of the improperly terminated contractor. Consequently, before terminating, the contracting officer should consider whether negotiating a revised delivery schedule minimize the government's losses.

3.   **Practice Tip:** Government officials sometimes fail to follow prescribed procedures, rendering default terminations subject to reversal on appeal. Attorneys play a critical role in this process, ensuring that all legal requirements are

met and the termination decision receives the care and attention it deserves.

II. THE RIGHT TO TERMINATE FOR DEFAULT.

A. Contractual Rights.

1. FAR Subpart 49.4.

2. The FAR contains different default clauses that identify the conditions that permit the government to terminate a contract for default. The clauses contain different bases for termination and different notice requirements. Compare FAR 52.249-8 (Fixed-Price Supply and Service) with FAR 52.249-10 (Fixed-Price Construction).

B. Common-Law Doctrine.

1. The standard FAR default clauses provide: "The rights and remedies of the government in this clause are in addition to any other rights and remedies provided by law or under this contract." See FAR 52.249-8(h) and FAR 52.249-10(d).

2. Courts commonly cite the above-quoted provision to support the government's termination of a contract for default based on common-law doctrines such as anticipatory repudiation. Cascade Pac. Int'l v. United States, 773 F.2d 287 (Fed. Cir. 1985); Commissioning Solutions Global, LLC, ASBCA 57429, 57494, 2013 BCA ¶35,355 (finding termination was justified in light of anticipatory repudiation; contractor refused to proceed with work unless the Contracting Officer (CO) agreed to price increase on a fixed-price contract or conversion to a cost reimbursement type contract); All-State Constr., Inc., ASBCA No. 50586, 06-2 BCA ¶ 33,344 (contractor's failure to diligently perform pending resolution of a dispute, as required by the Disputes clause, is a material breach for which termination is proper under the government's common law rights reserved in 52.249-10(d)).

III. GROUNDS FOR TERMINATION.

A. Failure to Deliver or Perform on Time.

1. The government may terminate for default when the contractor fails to timely deliver conforming goods, or to timely perform conforming services.

2. Generally, time is of the essence in all government contracts containing fixed dates for delivery or performance. Devito v. United States, 413 F.2d 1147 (Ct. Cl. 1969); Kit Pack Co., ASBCA No. 33135, 89-3 BCA ¶ 22,151; Matrix Res., Inc., ASBCA No. 56430, 11-2 BCA ¶ 34,789 (upholding termination for default where, after 2 ½ years of extension, the contractor demanded another 126-day extension in order to finish); Selpa Constr. & Rental Equip. Corp., PSBCA No. 5039, 11-1 BCA ¶ 34,635 (contractor did not meet its burden to prove entitlement to an extension of the contract completion date because it had not shown that the delaying events it alleged were critical to and impacted overall contract completion).

3. Failure to deliver or perform on time is a ground for termination. This ground is commonly referred to as an "(a)(1)(i)" termination. FAR 52.249-8(a)(1)(i); 52.249-10(a).

4. When a contract does not specify delivery dates (or those dates have been waived), actual delivery could constitute the "delivery date" for purposes of the termination for default clause. Aerometals, Inc., ASBCA No. 53688, 03-2 BCA ¶ 32,295.

5. The government must prove that delivery was late. Paradise Pillow, Inc. v. General Servs. Admin., CBCA No. 3562, 15-1 BCA ¶ 36153 (reversing termination for default for failure to deliver blankets ordered for Super Storm Sandy victims where the government failed to track the actual time and quantity of delivery, failing to meet its burden to prove late delivery).

B. Compliance with Specifications.

Default Terminations

1. The government is entitled to strict compliance with its specifications. M. Maropakis Carpentry, Inc. v. United States, 84 Fed. Cl. 182, 188 (Fed. Cl. 2008) aff'd, 609 F.3d 1323 (Fed. Cir. 2010); Mega Constr. Co. v. United States, 25 Cl. Ct. 735, 744 (1992); Trojan Horse, Ltd. V. U.S., PSBCA No. 6474, 15-1 BCA ¶ 36,015 (finding Postal Service was entitled to insist on strict compliance with its specifications even if all of the mail was delivered safely, and even if other contractors on similar contracts might have been permitted to deviate from specifications); Kurz-Kasch, Inc., ASBCA No. 32486, 88-3 BCA ¶ 21,053.

2. A default termination will be upheld where the contractor fails to meet specifications. See, e.g, Platinum Logistic Servs. Co., ASBCA No. 57965, 2013-1 BCA ¶ 35,392 (finding contractor consistently delivered items of equipment that did not conform to contract requirements and that – with one temporary exception – were inoperable).

3. The wording of the particular default clause in the contract matters. In EM Logging v. Department of Agriculture, 778 F.3d 1026 (Fed. Cir. 2015); 57 G.C. ¶ 71, a timber sales contract permitted the Forest Service to terminate for default not for failure to strictly comply, but for the contractor's "flagrant disregard" of the contract terms. The Federal Circuit reversed the Civilian Board, which had upheld termination for default of the contract. The Federal Circuit concluded that one instance of exceeding load limits, one route deviation, and two delayed notifications of late loads in seven months of steady contract operations, did not constitute flagrant disregard.

4. Courts and boards apply doctrines similar to the common-law principles of substantial compliance (supplies) and substantial completion (construction) to protect the contractor where timely performance departs in minor respects from that required by the contract.

   a. Supplies. If the contractor: 1) timely delivers supplies with minor defects, 2) with the reasonable belief that the supplies are conforming, and 3) the minor defects are correctable within a reasonable period, then the government must give the contractor additional time to correct the defects prior to terminating for default. Radiation Technology, Inc. v. United States, 366 F.2d 1003 (Ct. Cl. 1966).

   b. Construction. At common law, the owner cannot terminate a contract that is substantially completed. In a government construction contract, however, the default termination applies only to uncompleted work. The contractor is paid for work performed prior to the termination. In Al Khudhairy Grp., ASBCA No. 56131, 10-2 BCA ¶ 34,530, the board held that a contract 95% complete, could be terminated for default because the action affected only the uncompleted 5% of the work. The doctrine of substantial completion did not apply. In FD Constr. Co., ASBCA No. 41441, 91-2 BCA ¶ 23,983, the contractor was not protected from default termination by the doctrine of substantial completion because it abandoned the work and refused to complete punch list and administrative items. In neither case was the government rejecting the work in its entirety.

C. Failure to Make Progress So as to Endanger Performance.

1. Supplies and Services. The default clauses for (i) fixed-price supply and service contracts and (ii) cost-reimbursement contracts, provide for termination when the contractor fails to make progress so as to endanger performance. Similar to a termination for a contractor's failure to deliver or perform on time, this is commonly referred to as an "(a)(1)(ii)" termination. FAR 52.249-8(a)(1)(ii); FAR 52.249-6(a).

2. Construction. The default clause for fixed-price construction contracts provides for termination when the contractor refuses or fails to prosecute the work or any separable part, with the diligence that will insure its completion within the time specified in the contract. FAR 52.249-10(a).

3. Proof.

    a. The government is not required to show that it was impossible for the contractor to complete performance. California Dredging Co., ENG BCA No. 5532, 92-1 BCA ¶ 24,475.

    b. Rather, the contracting officer must have a reasonable belief that there is no reasonable likelihood that the contractor can perform the entire contract effort within the time remaining for contract performance. Lisbon Contractors, Inc. v. United States, 828 F.2d 759 (Fed. Cir. 1987) (upholding the lower court's conversion of the termination for default to a termination for convenience where the government did not determine whether contractor could complete work within the required time, or determine how long it would take a follow-on contractor to do the work); Edge Constr. Co., Inc. v. United States, 95 Fed. Cl. 407 (2010) (the government must demonstrate that the contracting officer included any extensions granted due to unusually severe weather when determining if the contractor could perform within the time remaining); Pipe Tech, Inc., ENG BCA No. 5959, 94-2 BCA ¶ 26,649 (termination improper where 92% of contract performance time remained and re-procurement contractor fully performed within the time allowed in defaulted contract); Advance Constr. Servs., Inc., ASBCA No. 55232, 11-2 BCA ¶ 34,776 (government not required to wait the full 45 days of the cure notice when it became clear earlier that contractor

could not achieve necessary average daily production).

    c. Thus, in Fort Howard Senior Housing Associates, LLC v. U.S., 121 Fed. Cl. 636 (2015), the VA was found to have properly terminated for default a 65-year lease to build and occupy senior housing when construction had not begun after 2 ½ years. The VA contracting officer met the Lisbon "reasonable belief" standard when the contractor failed to provide a satisfactory response to any of several cure notices and other communications requiring evidence that construction would begin.

    d. Prior to termination, the contracting officer should analyze progress problems against a specified completion date, adjusted to account for any government-caused delays. Technocratica, ASBCA No. 44134, 94-2 BCA ¶ 26,606 (termination for "poor progress" improper); Environmental Safety Consultants, Inc., ASBCA No. 51722, 11-2 BCA ¶ 34,848 (attempt to terminate for failure to make progress was rejected in absence of effective delivery date).

    e. Factors to consider include, but are not limited to: "a comparison of the percentage of work completed and" the time remaining before completion is due; "the contractor's failure to meet progress milestones"; "problems with subcontractors and suppliers"; "the contractor's financial situation"; and, the contractor's past performance. McDonnell Douglas Corp. v. United States, 323 F.3d 1006, 1010 (Fed. Cir. 2003); Advance Constr. Servs., Inc., ASBCA No. 55232, 11-2 BCA ¶ 34,776 (measuring progress against the average time the contractor would concede was required to complete project).

D. **Failure to Perform Any Other Provision of the Contract.**

Default Terminations

1. Supplies and Services. The default clause in fixed-price supply and service contracts specifically provides this ground for termination. It is commonly referred to as an "(a)(1)(iii)" termination. FAR 52.249-8(a)(1)(iii).

2. Construction. This basis does not exist under the construction clauses. See FAR 52.249-10. However, the courts and boards may sustain default terminations of construction contracts on this ground by reasoning that the failure to perform the "other provision" renders the contractor unable to perform the work with the diligence required to insure timely completion. Engineering Technology Consultants, S.A., ASBCA No. 43454, 94-1 BCA ¶ 26,586 ("The government, reasonably we conclude, had no alternative but to stop performance based on ETC's failure to maintain the proper amount of insurance coverage. Under the circumstances ETC was unable to perform and/or prosecute the work with the diligence required to insure completion within the performance period.").

3. Courts and boards will not sustain a default termination unless that "other provision" of the contract is a "material" or "significant" requirement. Precision Prods., ASBCA No. 25280, 82-2 BCA ¶ 15,981 (noncompliance with first article manufacture requirements not deemed material under facts); Yonir Technologies, Inc., ASBCA No. 56736, 10-1 BCA ¶ 34,417 (noncompliance with first article manufacture requirements deemed material when first article clause specifies that CO disapproval equals contractor failure to make delivery under default clause of contract); 5860 Chicago Ridge, LLC v. United States, 104 Fed. Cl. 740 (2012) (the government must prove that the breach is material when relying on its general right to terminate under the standard default clause for violation of any other provision).

4. Examples of "material" or "significant" requirements.

a. Failure to deliver within five days (as specified in the contract) an agreement with Cisco permitting contractor to perform required maintenance services on Cisco SMARTnet equipment. ZIOS Corp., ASBCA No. 56626, 10-1 BCA ¶ 24,244 (here, the contracting officer offered ZIOS the opportunity to withdraw from the contract when he became concerned about its ability to perform).

b. Failure to employ drivers with valid licenses. Maywood Cab Service, Inc., VACAB No. 1210, 77-2 BCA ¶ 12,751.

c. Failure to obtain (or provide proof of) liability insurance. A-Greater New Jersey Movers, Inc., ASBCA No. 54745, 06-1 BCA ¶ 33,179; UMM, Inc., ENG BCA No. 5330, 87-2 BCA ¶ 19,893 (mowing services contract).

d. Violation of the Buy American Act. HR Machinists Co., ASBCA No. 38440, 91-1 BCA ¶ 23,373.

e. Failure to comply with statement of work. 4-D and Chizoma, Inc., ASBCA Nos. 49550, 49598, 00-1 BCA ¶ 30,782 (failure to properly videotape sewer line).

f. Failure to retain records under Payrolls and Basic Records Clause justified default under the Davis-Bacon Act. Kirk Bros. Mech. Contractors, Inc. v. Kelso, 16 F.3d 1173 (Fed. Cir. 1994).

g. Failure to provide a quality control plan. A-Greater New Jersey Movers, Inc., ASBCA No. 54745, 06-1 BCA ¶ 33,179.

E. **Other Contract Clauses Providing Independent Basis to Terminate for Default.**

1. FAR 52.203-3 (Gratuities clause);

2. FAR 52.209-5 (Certification Regarding Debarment, Suspension, Proposed

Debarment, and Other Responsibility Matters). See Spread Information Sciences, Inc., ASBCA No. 48438, 96-1 BCA ¶ 27,996 (finding erroneous certification was a valid independent ground for default termination).

3. FAR 52.222-26 (Equal Opportunity clause);

4. FAR 52.228-1 (Bid Guarantee clause);

5. FAR 52.246-2 (Inspection clause).

F. Anticipatory Repudiation.

1. Each party to a contract has the common-law right to terminate a contract upon actual or anticipatory repudiation of the contract by the other party. Restatement (Second) of Contracts § 250; Uniform Commercial Code § 210; Dingley v. Oler, 117 U.S. 490 (1886). See also Franconia Associates, et al., v. United States, 122 S. Ct. 1993 (2002) (discussing the difference between an immediate breach and repudiation in the context of a federal housing loan program).

2. This common-law basis for default applies to all government contracts, since contract clauses generally do not address or supersede this principle. Cascade Pac. Int'l v. United States, 773 F.2d 287 (Fed. Cir. 1985).

3. Requirements:

   a. Anticipatory repudiation must be express. United States v. DeKonty Corp., 922 F.2d 826 (Fed. Cir. 1991) (must be absolute refusal, distinctly and unequivocally communicated); Marine Constr. Dredging, Inc., ASBCA No. 38412, 95-1 BCA ¶ 27,286 (no repudiation where contractor did not continue performance due to the government's failure to issue appropriate instructions).

   b. Anticipatory repudiation must be unequivocal and manifest either a clear intention not to perform or an inability to perform the contract.

Ateron Corp., ASBCA No. 46352, 94-3 BCA ¶ 27,229 (contractor's statement that continued contract performance is impossible constituted repudiation). Compare Swiss Prods., Inc., ASBCA No. 40031, 93-3 BCA ¶ 26,163 (contractor's refusal to perform until the government provided advance payments constitutes repudiation), with Engineering Professional Servs., Inc., ASBCA No. 39164, 94-2 BCA ¶ 26,762 (no repudiation where contractor's statement that "government financing must be provided to assure contract completion" was not precondition to resumed performance).

4. Abandonment is actual repudiation. Compare Ortec Sys., Inc., ASBCA No. 43467, 92-2 BCA ¶ 24,859 (termination proper when workforce left site and contractor failed to respond to phone calls), with Western States Mgmt. Servs., Inc., ASBCA No. 40212, 92-1 BCA ¶ 24,714 (no abandonment when contractor was unable to perform by unreasonable start date established after disestablishment of original start date).

5. Examples of anticipatory repudiation:

   a. D&M Grading, Inc. v. Dep't of Agriculture, CBCA No. 2625, 12-2 BCA ¶35,021 (finding anticipatory repudiation where contractor refused to continue performance of the contract because of disagreement with agency's reasonable interpretation of the scope of the contract).

   b. Emiabata v. United States, 102 Fed. Cl. 787 (2012) (despite repeated opportunities, mail transportation contractor failed to provide certificates for the necessary liability insurance).

   c. Brock v. United States, 2012 WL 2057036 (Fed. Cl. June 7, 2012) (in unpublished decision, finding anticipatory repudiation where contractor refused to continue performance under new delivery schedule, promised litigation, and adopted a "no surrender" position).

d. Global Constr. Inc. v. Dept. of Veterans Affairs, CBCA 1198, 10-1 BCA ¶ 34,363 (contractor's failure to provide revised schedules and adequate assurances in response to cure notice led contracting officer reasonably to believe there was no reasonable possibility that the contractor could complete the work in the time remaining).

e. Montage, Inc., GAOCAB 2006-2, 10-2 BCA ¶ 34,490 (board held that the contractor for installation of generator anticipatorily repudiated the contract by: (i) refusing to provide contractually required staging plan, (ii) refusing to proceed with performance even though the contract contained a contract disputes clause, and (iii) relying on Danzig v. AEC Corp., 224 F.3d 1333 (Fed. Cir. 2000), contractor did not provide adequate assurances in response to justified cure notice).

f. Free & Ben, Inc., ASBCA No. 56129, 12-1 BCA ¶ 34,966 (contractor anticipatorily repudiated where they could not perform on contract to supply cargo trucks in Iraq due to refusal of the government to provide an End-Use Certificate to Japanese supplier as precondition to export trucks.); Tzell Airtrak Travel Group Corp., ASBCA No. 57313, 11-2 BCA ¶ 34,845 (contractor's repudiation excused where the government made material misrepresentation regarding volume of work during contract formation).

6. Establishing anticipatory repudiation is very difficult. In Capy Machine Shop, Inc., ASBCA No. 59133, 15-1 BCA ¶ 36,133, even after a full hearing, the government was unable to persuade the board that a contractor's request to cancel its contract because of the unexpectedly high cost of performance was the positive and unequivocal manifestation of intent not to perform. The board found that the agency's belief that the contractor had a history of asking for cancellation of contracts after award was not relevant to whether the standard for anticipatory repudiation had been met in this particular case and was better addressed in connection with award rather than termination of contracts. Similar challenges were encountered by the parties in MLJ Brookside, LLC. v. U.S., CBCA No. 3041, 15-1 BCA ¶ 35,935, which featured competing claims of anticipatory repudiation from a building owner and GSA, which had leased space in the building. The board rejected the owner's reliance on the departure of the federal agency tenant and GSA's turning in the keys for its claim that GSA had repudiated the lease. The board found that the lease provided that GSA could substitute the federal agency tenant or even just leave the space vacant during the course of the lease. Comparatively, the board agreed with the GSA that the owner's leasing of the premises covered by the lease to a new entity was anticipatory repudiation and concluded that, as a result, GSA did not need to have given the owner an opportunity to cure before terminating for default.

7. **Practice Tip.** The right to terminate for an anticipatory repudiation saves the government ten days. The words and actions constituting an anticipatory repudiation should also provide a basis to demand assurances, as discussed in the next section, or to issue a cure notice for failure to make progress. Unless the contractor responds quickly with reasonable assurances or a reasonable, believable plan for completing on schedule, the contracting officer can terminate for multiple reasons at the expiration of the response period. Given the challenges in proving an anticipatory repudiation, the agency should take the extra time to demand assurances and cure of the failure to make progress.

G.   Demand for Assurance.

1.   Where a party is reasonably concerned that the other party to the contract will not perform as promised, it may demand written assurances from the other party. Failure of the other party to give adequate assurances that it would complete a contract is a valid basis for a default termination under common law. Restatement (Second) of Contracts § 251; Uniform Commercial Code § 2-609; Global Constr. Inc. v. Dept. of Veterans Affairs, CBCA No. 1198, 10-1 BCA ¶ 34,363 (contractor's failure to provide revised schedules and adequate assurances in response to cure notice meant that the contracting officer reasonably believed there was no reasonable possibility that the contractor could complete the work in the time remaining).

2.   This basis for termination applies to government contracts. Danzig v. AEC Corp., 224 F.3d 1333 (Fed. Cir. 2000) (AEC's letter responses and conduct following the Navy's cure notice supported the termination for default); Eng'g Professional Servs., Inc., ASBCA No. 39164, 94-2 BCA ¶ 26,762; National Union Fire Ins. Co., ASBCA No. 34744, 90-1 BCA ¶ 22,266. But see Ranco Constr., Inc. v. Gen. Servs. Admin., GSBCA No. 11923, 94-2 BCA ¶ 26,678 (board questions whether demand for assurance under UCC § 2-609 applies to construction contracts).

3.   The government's "cure notice" may be the equivalent of a demand for assurance. Hannon Elec. Co. v. United States, 31 Fed. Cl. 135 (1994) (contractor's failure to provide adequate assurance in response to cure notice justified default termination); Fairfield Scientific Corp., ASBCA No. 21151, 78-1 BCA ¶ 13082.

4.   **Practice Tip,** The demand for assurances should: a) be in writing, b) describe all the reason(s) for the concern that the other party will not perform as promised, c) provide a reasonable time for a written response, and d) request any excuses for the words or actions causing concern.

H.   Preparing for a Default Termination.

1.   When a contracting officer is considering terminating a contract for default, he or she can take actions in advance that will minimize the risks of an improper default. First, the contracting officer and its technical advisors should identify any issues that the contractor may have with the specification and the government's actions in administering the contract. The government, if possible, should reach a written agreement with the contractor on all disputed contract requirements and incorporate the revised requirements into the contract.

2.   Second, the contracting officer and the contractor should reach agreement on a revised delivery schedule that includes allowance for all excusable delays, including prior disputed government actions or inactions.

3.   Third, the contracting officer should closely monitor the government team and the contractor to ensure that the government does nothing that entitles the contractor to a schedule extension.

4.   Should the contractor again agrees to timely perform as agreed in the new schedule and revised requirements, the contracting officer should follow the regulatory procedures for the type(s) of termination justified by the facts, should he or she decide to terminate for default. While this will take a little longer, it gives the government better facts to justify the default termination.

I.   Defending a Termination Action.

1.   When a contractor appeals a final decision terminating a contract for default, the government is not bound by the contracting officer's reasons for the termination as stated in the termination notice.

2. If a proper ground for the default termination existed at the time of the termination, regardless of whether the contracting officer relied on or was even aware of that basis, the termination is proper. See Glazer Construction Co. v. United States, 52 Fed. Cl. 513 (2002) (COFC upheld a termination for default based on Davis-Bacon Act violations committed before, but discovered after, the government issued the default termination notice); Kirk Bros. Mech. Contractors, Inc. v. Kelso, 16 F.3d 1173 (Fed. Cir. 1994) (violations of Davis-Bacon Act); Joseph Morton Co. v. United States, 757 F.2d 1273 (Fed. Cir. 1985) (fraud); Quality Granite Constr. Co., ASBCA No. 43846, 93-3 BCA ¶ 26,073 (government not required to give notice to contractor when unaware of basis for termination).

3. A finding of fraud will result in dismissal of a contractor's appeal of a termination for default. Servicios y Obras Isetan S.L., ASBCA No. 57584, 2013-1 BCA ¶35,279 (because the contractor had made a fraudulent misrepresentation on which the government had justifiably relied, the government met the standard of proving that the contract was void ab initio); TTF, L.L.C., ASBCA 58495, 58516; 2013-1 BCA ¶35,403 (upholding the government's revocation of aircraft fuselage fairings where acceptance had been obtained by contractor's fraudulent representation that it was a HUBZone contractor and would manufacture the fairings itself).

IV. NOTICE REQUIREMENTS.

A. **When No Prior Notice Is Required**.

1. Supplies and Services Contracts. No prior notice is required when terminating a supply and service contract for failure to timely deliver conforming supplies or perform conforming services (known as an (a)(1)(i) termination). The contracting officer need only provide written notice of the termination. Termination without prior communications, however, risk terminating when there are excusable delays unknown to the contracting officer.

2. Construction Contracts. The contracting officer may terminate a construction contract for failure to make progress, or for failure to timely complete the work, without prior notice to the contractor. Only written notice of the termination is required. As with supply contracts, doing so carries considerable risks, because the contractor may have experienced excusable delays or be entitled to an equitable adjustment.

B. **Cure Notice**.

1. For fixed-price supply or service contracts, research and development contracts, and cost-reimbursement contracts, the government must notify the contractor, in writing, of its failure to make progress ((a)(1)(ii)) or its failure to perform any other provision of the contract ((a)(1)(iii)) and give the contractor ten days in which to cure such failure before it may terminate the contract. FAR 52.249-6; FAR 52.249-8; FAR 52.249-9. See FAR 49.607(a).

   a. Pursuant to FAR 49.607(a), a proper cure notice must inform the contractor in writing:

      (1) That the government intends to terminate the contract for default;

      (2) Of the reasons for the termination; and

      (3) That the contractor has a right to cure the specified deficiencies within the cure period (ten days).

   b. To support a default decision, the cure notice must clearly identify the nature and extent of the performance failure. Lanzen Fabricating, Inc., ASBCA No. 40328, 93-3 BCA ¶ 26,079 (show cause notice did not serve as cure notice for purposes of (a)(1)(ii) termination because it didn't specify failures to be cured); Insul-Glass, Inc., GSBCA No. 8223, 89-1 BCA

¶ 21,361 (notice directed contractor to provide acceptable drawings without specifying what the contractor had to do to make the drawings acceptable); but see Genome Communications, ASBCA Nos. 57267, 57285, 11-1 BCA ¶ 34,699 (contractor did not have to comply with directions in a cure notice that attempted to impose obligations beyond the contract requirements).

c. The government must give the contractor a minimum of ten days to cure the deficiency. Red Sea Trading Assoc., ASBCA No. 36360, 91-1 BCA ¶ 23,567 (the ten-day period need not be specifically stated in the notice if a minimum of ten days was actually afforded the contractor); NCLN20., Inc. v. United States, 99 Fed. Cl. 734 (2011) (overturning a termination for default that took place on the second day of the required ten-day cure period); but see Advance Constr. Servs., Inc., ASBCA No. 55232, 11-2 BCA ¶ 34,776 (government not required to wait the full 45 days of the cure notice when it became clear earlier that contractor could not achieve necessary average daily production).

2. The government may terminate cost-reimbursement contracts for default if the contractor defaults in performing the contract and fails to cure the defect in performance within ten days of receiving a proper cure notice from the contracting officer. FAR 52.249-6(a)(2).

3. A cure notice is NOT required before:

a. Terminating for failure to timely deliver goods. FAR 52.249-8(a)(1)(i); Sazie Wilson, PSBCA No. 5247, 12-1 BCA ¶34,906 (cure notice not required when termination for default is for failure to meet a delivery date as opposed to a termination for default for failure to make progress toward meeting a delivery date that has not yet arrived); Delta Indus., DOT BCA No. 2602, 94-1 BCA ¶ 26,318 (government rejected desks that did not meet contract specifications).

b. Terminating pursuant to an independent clause of the contract not requiring notice. See "K" Servs., ASBCA No. 41791, 92-1 BCA ¶ 24,568 (default under FAR 52.209-5 for false certification regarding debarment status of contractor's principal).

c. Terminating based on the contractor's anticipatory repudiation of the contract. Beeston, Inc., ASBCA No. 38969, 91-3 BCA ¶ 24,241; Scott Aviation, ASBCA No. 40776, 91-3 BCA ¶ 24,123.

4. Terminating construction contracts. FAR 52.249-10; Professional Services Supplier, Inc. v. United States, 45 Fed. Cl. 808, 810 (2000) (no cure notice required before a fixed-price construction contract may be terminated for default). Although not required, the government frequently provides the contractor a cure notice prior to terminating these contracts. See Hillebrand Constr. of the Midwest, Inc., ASBCA No. 45853, 95-1 BCA ¶ 27,464 (failure to provide submittals); Engineering Technology Consultants, S.A., ASBCA No. 43454, 94-1 BCA ¶ 26,586 (concerning contractor's failure to provide proof of insurance).

C. **Show Cause Notice**. If a termination for default appears appropriate and a cure notice is not required, the government should, if practicable, notify the contractor in writing of the possibility of the termination. FAR 49.402-3(e)(1). This notice is referred to as a "show cause" notice. FAR 49.607.

1. The show cause notice should:

a. Call the contractor's attention to its contractual liabilities if the contract is terminated for default.

b. Request the contractor to show cause why the contract should not be terminated for default.

c. State that the failure of the contractor to present an explanation may be taken as an admission that no valid explanation exists.

2. The default clauses do not require the use of a show cause notice. See FAR 52.249-8 (Supply and Service); FAR 52.249-9 (Research and Development); FAR 52.249-10 (Construction); Alberts Assocs., ASBCA No. 45329, 95-1 BCA ¶ 27,480.

a. The contracting officer is not required to include every subsequently advanced reason for the termination in the show cause notice because the government is under no obligation to issue the notice. Sach Sinha and Associates, Inc., ASBCA No. 46916, 96-2 BCA ¶ 28,346.

b. If a termination for default appears appropriate, the government should, if practicable, notify the contractor in writing of the possibility of the termination. FAR 49.402-3(e)(1). In fact, the courts and boards may require a "show cause" notice if its use was practicable. Udis v. United States, 7 Cl. Ct. 379 (1985); Enginetics Corp., ASBCA No. 40834, 92-2 BCA ¶ 24,965 (denying the government's motion for summary judgment while noting the government's failure to issue show cause notice).

c. If the government issues a show cause notice, it need not give the contractor ten days to respond. Nisei Constr. Co., Inc., ASBCA Nos. 51464, 51466, 51646, 99-2 BCA ¶ 30,448 (six days was sufficient in construction default case).

3. **Practice Tip:** A show cause notice affords the contractor the opportunity to identify excusable delays, or other defenses to a default termination. The

contracting officer should understand that there are two sides to every story, and affording the contractor the opportunity to tell its side may avoid mistakes that cost the government money and delay receipt of the goods or services. A contractor, in responding to a show cause notice, should also provide its plan for correcting its performance deficiencies and completing the work. Even if the default termination is justified, the government may not terminate if it believes that the contractor represents the fastest and cheapest way of receiving the goods and services.

4. **Practice Tip:** Because a termination for default is considered a drastic sanction, the government bears the initial burden of proof (i.e., that the contractor failed to deliver on time, perform on time, comply with specifications, make adequate progress, comply with a material contract provision, etc.). It must also comply with the FAR's procedural requirements. Contracting Officers should seek advice of counsel to ensure all legal and procedural requirements have been met and to minimize the risk of reversal on appeal.

V. CONTRACTOR DEFENSES TO A TERMINATION FOR DEFAULT.

A. **Excusable Delay.**

1. A contractor's failure to deliver or to perform on a fixed-price supply or service contract is excusable if the failure is beyond the control and without the fault or negligence of the contractor. FAR 52.249-8(c); see, e.g., Donald Mich v. U.S. Postal Service, PSBCA No. 6311, 15 BCA ¶ 36,022 (upholding default termination where contractor lacked any excuse for permitting his son, who was addicted to heroin, to operate one of the delivery trucks).

2. For construction contracts, the contractor is excused if the delay arises from unforeseeable causes beyond the control and without the fault or negligence of the contractor, and the contractor, within ten days from the beginning of any delay

(unless extended by the contracting officer), notifies the contracting officer in writing of the causes of delay. FAR 52.249-10(b); <u>see</u> <u>Local Contractors, Inc.</u>, ASBCA No. 37108, 1991 WL 517213 (Oct. 11, 1991); Charles H. Siever, ASBCA No. 24814, 83-1 BCA ¶ 16,242..

3. The contractor has the burden of proving that its failure to perform was excusable. <u>Lan-Cay, Inc.</u>, ASBCA No. 56140, 12-1 BCA ¶ 34,935. The contractor must show:

   a. The occurrence of an event was unforeseeable (construction only), beyond its control, and without its fault or negligence. <u>Local Contractors, Inc.</u>, ASBCA No. 37108, 92-1 BCA ¶ 24,491; <u>Charles H. Siever</u>, ASBCA No. 24814, 83-1 BCA ¶ 16,242.

   b. Timely performance was actually prevented by the claimed excuse. <u>Sonora Mfg.</u>, ASBCA No. 31587, 91-1 BCA ¶ 23,444; <u>Beekman Indus.</u>, ASBCA No. 30280, 87-3 BCA ¶ 20,118.

   c. The specific period of delay caused by the event. <u>Conquest Constr., Inc.</u>, PSBCA No. 2350, 90-1 BCA ¶ 22,605.

4. The default clauses specifically identify some causes of excusable delay. These include:

   a. Acts of God (AKA "force majeure") or of the public enemy. <u>See</u> <u>Nogler Tree Farm</u>, AGBCA No. 81-104-1, 81-2 BCA ¶ 15,315 (eruption of Mount St. Helens volcano); <u>Centennial Leasing v. Gen. Servs. Admin.</u>, GSBCA No. 12037, 94-1 BCA ¶ 26,398 (death of chief operating officer not an act of God); <u>C-Shore International, Inc. v. Dept. of Agriculture</u>, CBCA 1696, 10-1 BCA ¶ 34, 379 (sought to excuse non-performance on hurricanes Katrina and Rita; board agreed that hurricanes are acts of God but the hurricanes occurred before the contracts were awarded and contractor had obligation to take into account the effect of the hurricanes before accepting the contractual commitment).

   b. Acts of the government in either its sovereign or contractual capacity.

      (1) Sovereign capacity refers to public acts of the government not directed to the contract. <u>Home Entertainment, Inc.</u>, ASBCA No. 50791, 99-2 BCA ¶ 30,550 (analysis of "sovereign act" relating to expulsion orders in Panama); <u>Woo Lim Constr. Co.</u>, ASBCA No. 13887, 70-2 BCA ¶ 8451 (imposition of security restrictions in a hostile area).

      (2) Acts of the government in its contractual capacity are most common and include delays caused by such things as defective specifications, constructive changes, unreasonable government inspections, and late delivery of government furnished property. <u>See</u> <u>Commissioning Solutions Global, LLC</u>, ASBCA No. 57429, 57494, 2013-1 BCA ¶ 35,355 (government's responsibility for specifications under the <u>Spearin</u> doctrine cannot be invoked to seek damages for the delay caused by an illegible drawing when the contractor was aware of the problem with the drawing before it submitted its bid); <u>Marine Constr. Dredging, Inc.</u>, ASBCA No. 38412, 95-1 BCA ¶ 27,286 (government failed to respond to contractor's request for directions); <u>John Glenn</u>, ASBCA No. 31260, 91-3 BCA ¶ 24,054 (government issued faulty performance directions).

   c. Fires. <u>Hawk Mfg. Co.</u>, GSBCA No. 4025, 74-2 BCA ¶ 10,764 (lack of facilities rather than a plant fire caused contractor's failure to timely deliver).

d. Floods. <u>Wayne Constr.</u>, ENG BCA No. 4942, 91-1 BCA ¶ 23,535 (storm damage to a dike entitled contractor to time extension).

e. Epidemics and quarantine restrictions. <u>Ace Elecs. Assoc.</u>, ASBCA No. 11496, 67-2 BCA ¶ 6456 (denying relief based on allegation that flu epidemic caused a 30% to 40% rate of absenteeism, without showing that it contributed to delay).

f. Strikes, freight embargoes, and similar work stoppages. <u>Woodington Corp.</u>, ASBCA No. 37885, 91-1 BCA ¶ 23,579 (delay not excused where steel strike at U.S. Steel had been ongoing for two months prior to contractor's bid, subcontractor ordered steel after strike ended, and other steel manufacturers were not on strike). <u>But see</u> <u>NTC Group, Inc.</u>, ASBCA Nos. 53720, 53721, 53722, 04-2 BCA ¶ 32,706 (labor conspiracy, akin to a strike was a valid defense to default termination).

g. Unusually severe weather. Only unusually severe weather, as compared to the past weather in the area for that season, excuses performance. <u>See</u> <u>Aulson Roofing, Inc.</u>, ASBCA No. 37677, 91-2 BCA ¶ 23,720 (contractor not entitled to day-for-day delay because some rain delay was to be expected); <u>TCH Indus.</u>, AGBCA No. 88-224-1, 91-3 BCA ¶ 24,364 (eight inches of snow in northern Idaho in November is neither unusual nor unforeseeable).

h. Acts of another contractor in performance of a contract for the government (construction contracts). FAR 52.249-10(b)(1); <u>Modern Home Mfg. Corp.</u>, ASBCA No. 6523, 66-1 BCA ¶ 5367 (housing contractor entitled to extension because site not prepared in accordance with contract specifications).

i. Defaults or delays by subcontractors or suppliers:

(1) As a rule of thumb, problems with subcontractors are not a basis for excusable delay for the prime. <u>Matrix Res. Inc.</u>, ASBCA Nos. 56430, 56431, 11-2 BCA ¶ 34,789 (contractor responsible for lack of progress in delivery of product caused by actions of subcontractors); <u>New Era Contract Sales, Inc.</u>, ASBCA No. 56661, 11-1 BCA ¶ 34,738 (subcontractor's unwillingness to abide by its quoted price does not excuse contractor from fulfilling its contract to delivery); <u>Ryll Int'l, LLC v. Dep't of Transp.</u>, CBCA No. 1143, 11-2 BCA ¶ 34,809 (critical subcontractor's abandonment of work not excusable delay).

(2) Construction. If the delay of a subcontractor or supplier at any tier arises from unforeseeable causes beyond the control and without the fault or negligence of both the contractor and the subcontractor or supplier, and the contractor notifies the contracting officer within ten days from the beginning of the delay, it may be excusable. FAR 52.249-10(b).

(3) Supply and Services contracts, and cost-reimbursement contracts. The general rule is that, if a failure to perform is caused by the default of a subcontractor or supplier at any tier, the default is excusable if:

(a) The cause of the default was beyond the control and without the fault or negligence of either the contractor or the subcontractor, <u>see</u> <u>General Injectables & Vaccines, Inc.</u>, ASBCA No. 54930, 06-2 BCA ¶ 33,401 (contractor not excused from failure to provide flu vaccine despite worldwide vaccine unavailability because the contractor's supplier—the vaccine manufacturer—caused the unavailability of the vaccine); and,

(b) The subcontracted supplies or services were not obtainable from other sources in time for the contractor to meet the required delivery schedule. FAR 52.249-8(d); FAR 52.249-6(b); FAR 52.249-14(b); Progressive Tool Corp., ASBCA No. 42809, 94-1 BCA ¶ 26,413 (contractor failed to show it made all reasonable attempts to locate an alternate supplier); CM Mach. Prods., ASBCA No. 43348, 93-2 BCA ¶ 25,748 (default upheld where plating could have been provided by another subcontractor but prime refused to pay higher price).

5. Additional excuses commonly asserted by contractors include:

a. Material breach of contract by the government. Todd-Grace, Inc., ASBCA No. 34469, 92-1 BCA ¶ 24,742 (breach of implied duty to not interfere with contractor); Bogue Elec. Mfg. Co., ASBCA No. 25184, 86 2 BCA ¶ 18,925 (defective government-furnished equipment); Lan-Cay, Inc., ASBCA No. 56140, 12-1 BCA ¶34,935 (contractor unsuccessful in demonstrating overzealous inspection by the government that allegedly led to delay).

b. Lack of financial capability. Contractors are responsible for having sufficient financial resources to perform a contract. RAK Contractors, LLC v. Dep.t of Agriculture, CBCA No. 4011, 15-1 BCA ¶ 35,934 (contractor could not excuse its inability to perform by claiming it did not have available funds or sufficient credit; a contractor is expected to have the financial ability to perform any contract that it accepts and the lack of

financial capacity is not a basis for excusable delay).

(1) Generally, lack of financial capability is not an excuse. Local Contractors, Inc., ASBCA No. 37108, 92-1 BCA ¶ 24,491 (contractor had deteriorating financial base unconnected to the contract); Selpa Constr. & Rental Equip. Corp., PSBCA 5039, 11-1 BCA ¶ 34,635 (financing difficulties did not excuse its delayed performance and contractor could not establish that the government contributed to its problems).

(2) If the financial difficulties are caused by wrongful acts of the government, however, the delay may be excused. Lan-Cay, Inc., ASBCA No. 56140, 12-1 BCA ¶34,935 (failure of agency to make progress payments was not excusable delay because progress payments were not required where the contractor had failed to install the required system); Red Sea Eng'rs & Constr., ASBCA No. 57448, 11-2 BCA ¶34,880 (contractor defeated motion for summary judgment in part because of questions as to whether the government had fulfilled its obligations to pay contractor during performance); All-State Construction, Inc., ASBCA No. 50586, 02-1 BCA ¶ 31,794 (withholding progress payments above the amount allowed by the FAR was improper; ASBCA converted termination for default into a termination for convenience); Nexus Constr. Co., ASBCA No. 31070, 91-3 BCA ¶ 24,303 (default converted because the government's refusal to release progress payments constituted material breach of contract).

Default Terminations

c. Bankruptcy. Although filing a petition of bankruptcy is not an excuse, it precludes termination. Communications Technology Applications, Inc., ASBCA No. 41573, 92-3 BCA ¶ 25,211 (government's right to terminate stayed when bankruptcy filed, not when the government notified); see also, Carter Industries, DOTBCA No. 4108, 02-1 BCA 31,738.

d. Small business. A-Greater New Jersey Movers, Inc., ASBCA No. 54745, 06-1 BCA ¶ 33,179 ("The Board does not accord special treatment in determining whether the burden of proof has been met to a contractor because of its status as a small business"); Kit Pack Co., ASBCA No. 33135, 89-3 BCA ¶ 22,151 (no excuse for failure to meet delivery date).

e. Impossibility or Commercial Impracticability. To establish commercial impracticability, the contractor must show it can perform only at excessive and unreasonable cost – simple economic hardship is not sufficient. Hearthstone, Inc. v. Dept. of Agriculture, CBCA No. 3725, 15 BCA ¶ 35,895 (rejecting impossibility argument, finding that contractor bore the risk of a decline in commodity prices and noting that this was not a case where it was physically impossible to perform); Commissioning Solutions Global, LLC, ASBCA No. 57429, 57494, 2013-1 BCA ¶ 35,355 (rejecting commercial impracticability claim based on costs that were 30.4% higher than the agreed fixed price; board held that the loss would have to be "substantially greater" before performance could be excused under that theory); Singelton Enterprises v. Dep't of Agriculture, CBCA No. 2136, 12-1 BCA ¶35,005 (rejecting excuse that the government specifications were impossible to perform in light of ability of the reprocurement contractor to complete the work); Montage, Inc., GAOCAB 2006-2, 10-2 BCA ¶34,490 (board held that contractor did not meet the very tough standard for practical impossibility because contractor failed to establish that increased cost made the work commercially senseless); CleanServ Executive Services, Inc., ASBCA No. 47781, 96-1 BCA ¶ 28,027. Compare Soletanche Rodio Nicholson (JV), ENG BCA No. 5796, 94-1 BCA ¶ 26,472 (performance might take 17 years and cost $400 million, rather than two years and $16.9 million), with CM Mach. Prods., ASBCA No. 43348, 93-2 BCA ¶ 25,748 (no commercial impracticability where costs increased 105%).

6. If a delay is found to be excusable, the contractor is entitled to additional time and/or money. Batteast Constr. Co., ASBCA No. 35818, 92-1 BCA ¶ 24,697. NOTE: Constructive acceleration of the delivery date often occurs when the contracting officer, using a threat of termination, directs compliance with the contract delivery or performance date without an extension for the time period attributable to an excusable delay.

B. **Waiver.**

1. Waiver of the right to terminate for default occurs if: (1) the government fails to terminate a contract within a reasonable period of time after the default under circumstances indicating forbearance and (2) reliance by the contractor on the failure to terminate and continued performance by him under the contract, with the government's knowledge and implied or express consent. Devito v. United States, 413 F.2d 1147 (Ct. Cl. 1969) (government's delay in terminating fixed-price supply contract and continued acceptance of deliveries after default constituted waiver); S.T. Research Corp., ASBCA No. 39600, 92-2 BCA ¶ 24,838 (contracting officer's encouragement that contractor propose new delivery schedule and continue performance constituted

waiver); Motorola Computer Sys., Inc., ASBCA No. 26794, 87-3 BCA ¶ 20,032 (government waived original performance schedule when there were no firm delivery dates or schedule for progress of work; new performance or delivery schedule had to be established to terminate under default clause). But see Gargoyles, Inc., ASBCA 57515, 2013-1 BCA ¶ 35,330 (finding no waiver of the delivery date where contractor had not relied on the government's proposed new schedule, but instead responded with an alternative schedule of its own).

2. Absent government manifestation that a performance date is no longer enforceable, the waiver doctrine generally does not apply to construction contracts. Nisei Constr. Co., Inc., ASBCA Nos. 51464, 51466, 51646, 99-2 BCA ¶ 30,448.

    a. Construction contracts typically include a payment clause entitling the contractor to payment for work performed subsequent to the specified completion date.

    b. Construction contracts also typically include a liquidated damage clause that entitles the government to money for late completion.

    c. As a consequence, detrimental reliance usually can't be found merely from government forbearance and continued contractor performance. Brent L. Sellick, ASBCA No. 21869, 78-2 BCA ¶ 13,510. But see B.V. Construction, Inc., ASBCA Nos. 47766, 49337, 50553, 04-1 BCA ¶ 32,604 (the lack of a Liquidated Damages clause, coupled with the government's apparent complete lack of concern over the completion date, caused the ASBCA to find the government elected to waive the right to terminate the contract).

3. Reasonable period of time.

    a. Forbearance is the period of time during which the government investigates the reasons for the contractor's failure to meet the contract requirements. The government may "forbear" for a reasonable period after the default occurs before taking some action. Reasonableness depends on the specific facts of each case. American AquaSource, Inc., ASBCA 56677, 10-2 BCA ¶ 34,557 (although the government waited 49 days after delivery to terminate, board found the time for terminating is extended when the contractor has abandoned performance or where its situation is such as to render performance unlikely); Progressive Tool Corp., ASBCA No. 42809, 94-1 BCA ¶ 26,413 (although forbearance for 42 days after show cause notice was "somewhat long," termination for default sustained because the government did not encourage contractor to continue working and contractor did not perform substantial work during that period); but see DODS, Inc., ASBCA No. 57667, 12-2 BCA ¶35,078 (agency waived delivery date when it did not terminate for 21 months after contractor failed first article test).

    b. Government actions inconsistent with forbearance may waive a delivery date. Applied Cos., ASBCA No. 43210, 94-2 BCA ¶ 26,837 (government waived delivery date for first article test report by seeking information, making progress payments, directing the contractor to rerun tests, and incorporating engineering change proposals into the contract after the delivery date); Kitco, Inc., ASBCA No. 38184, 91-3 BCA ¶ 24,190 (no clear delivery schedule established after partial termination for convenience resulted in waiver of right to terminate for default based on untimely deliveries); Beta Engineering, Inc., ASBCA Nos. 53570, 53571, 02-2 BCA ¶ 31,879 (after contractor missed a first article test delivery deadline, the government

Default Terminations

left itself without an enforceable schedule by failing to terminate, encouraging continued performance, and leaving contractor "in limbo" about a new delivery schedule); <u>but see</u> <u>Tawazuh Commercial & Const. Co., Ltd.</u>, ASBCA 55656, 11-2 BCA ¶ 34,781 (Army in Afghanistan did not waive its right to reject clearly defective work merely because it was delayed in performing inspections for several months).

c. Contracting officers should use show cause notices to avoid waiver arguments. <u>See</u> <u>Charles H. Siever Co.</u>, ASBCA No. 24814, 83-1 BCA ¶ 16,242 (using timely show cause notice preserved the government's right to terminate despite four-month forbearance period).

4. Detrimental Reliance.

a. The contractor must show detrimental reliance on the government's inaction before the government will be deemed to have waived the delivery schedule. <u>Ordnance Parts Eng'g Co.</u>, ASBCA No. 44327, 93-2 BCA ¶ 25,690 (no detrimental reliance where contractor repudiated contract).

b. Where the contractor customarily continued performance after a missed delivery date, a board has found no inducement by the government. <u>Electro-Methods, Inc.</u>, ASBCA No. 50215, 99-1 BCA ¶ 30,230.

5. Reestablishing the delivery schedule.

a. The government should reestablish a delivery schedule if it believes it waived the original schedule. FAR 49.402-3(c). Proper reestablishment of a delivery schedule also reestablishes the government's right to terminate for default.

b. A delivery schedule can be reestablished either bilaterally or unilaterally. <u>Sermor, Inc.</u>, ASBCA No. 30576, 94-1 BCA ¶ 26,302

(formal modification not required, but new delivery date must be reasonable and specific).

(1) A new delivery date established bilaterally is presumed to be reasonable. <u>Trans World Optics, Inc.</u>, ASBCA No. 35976, 89-3 BCA ¶ 21,895; <u>Sermor, Inc.</u>, <u>supra</u> (by agreeing to new delivery schedule, contractor waives excusable delay).

(2) A new delivery date the government unilaterally establishes must in fact be reasonable in light of the contractor's abilities in order to be enforceable. <u>Rowe, Inc.</u>, GSBCA No. 14211, 01-2 BCA 31,630 (The board made an "objective determination" from "the standpoint of the performance capabilities of the contractor at the time the notice [was] given" and found the new delivery date was reasonable); <u>McDonnell Douglas Corp. v. United States</u>, 50 Fed. Cl. 311 (2001) (reestablished schedule was reasonable); <u>Oklahoma Aerotronics, Inc.</u>, ASBCA No. 25605, 87-2 BCA ¶ 19,917 (unilateral date for first article delivery unreasonable); <u>Ensil Int'l Corp.</u>, ASBCA Nos. 57297, 57445, 12-1 BCA ¶34,942 (although agency may have waived original delivery date, when contractor actually delivered the goods, it effectively established a new enforceable delivery date and was obligated to provide conforming supplies as of the actual delivery date).

(3) The schedule proposed by the contractor is presumed reasonable. <u>Tampa Brass Aluminum Corp.</u>, ASBCA No. 41314, 92-2 BCA ¶ 24,865 (termination proper because unreasonable schedule was proposed by the contractor). <u>But</u>

see S.T. Research Corp., ASBCA No. 39600, 92-2 BCA ¶ 24,838 (schedule proposed within 24 hours of contracting officer's demand, by contractor having technical problems, was not reasonable).

c. A cure notice, by itself, does not reestablish a waived delivery schedule. Lanzen Fabricating, ASBCA No. 40328, 93-3 BCA ¶ 26,079.

6. If a contract requires multiple deliveries, each successive increment represents a severable obligation to deliver on the contract delivery date. Thus, the government may accept late delivery of one or more installments without waiving the delivery date for future installments. Electro-Methods, Inc., ASBCA No. 50215, 99-1 BCA ¶ 30,230; Allstate Leisure Prods., Inc., ASBCA No. 40532, 94-3 BCA ¶ 26,992.

VI. THE DECISION TO TERMINATE FOR DEFAULT.

A. **Discretionary Act.** The government may have the right to terminate for default, but it also has the discretion not to do so. The contractor who is late in performing is often the best option to obtain the needed goods and services at the earliest point.

1. Standard of Review.

   a. The standard FAR clauses generally grant the government the authority to terminate, which shall be exercised only after review by contracting and technical personnel, and by counsel, to ensure propriety of the proposed action. FAR 49.402-3 (a).

   b. Contracting officers must exercise discretion. The default clauses do not compel termination; rather, they permit termination for default if such action is appropriate in the business judgment of the responsible government officials. Schlesinger v. United States, 182 Ct. Cl. 571, 390

F.2d 702 (1968) (Navy improperly terminated a contract because of pressure from a Congressional committee, rather than its own assessment of the government's and contractor's interests).

c. Contractors may challenge the default termination decision on the basis that the terminating official abused his discretion or acted in bad faith. Marshall Associated Contractors, Inc., & Columbia Excavating, Inc., (J.V.), IBCA Nos. 1091, 3433, 3434, 3435, 01-1 BCA ¶ 31248 (abuse of discretion to terminate for default a contract with defective specifications, when the reprocurement contractor received relaxed treatment); Darwin Constr. Co. v. United States, 811 F.2d 593 (Fed. Cir. 1987).

2. Burden of proof.

   a. The government has the burden of establishing the propriety of a default termination. Lisbon Contractors, Inc. v. United States, 828 F.2d 759 (Fed. Cir. 1987). A finding of technical default is not determinative on the issue of the propriety of a default termination. Walsky Constr. Co., ASBCA No. 41541, 94-2 BCA ¶ 26,698.

   b. Courts and boards review the contracting officer's actions according to the circumstances as they existed at the time of the default. Local Contractors, Inc., ASBCA No. 37108, 92-1 BCA ¶ 24,491.

   c. Once the government establishes that the contractor was in default, the contractor bears the burden of proving that the termination was an abuse of discretion or done in bad faith. Marshall Associated Contractors, Inc., & Columbia Excavating, Inc., (J.V.), IBCA Nos. 1091, 3433, 3435, 01-1 BCA ¶ 31248 (abuse of discretion to terminate for default a contract with defective specifications, when the reprocurement contractor received relaxed treatment); <u>Darwin Constr. Co. v. United States</u>, 811 F.2d 593 (Fed. Cir. 1987) (termination for default found to be arbitrary and capricious where technical default used as a pretext to get rid of contractor).

(1) Abuse of Discretion.

(a) Abuse of discretion (also referred to as "arbitrary and capricious" conduct) may be ascertained by looking at the following factors:

  (i)   subjective bad faith on the part of the government;

  (ii) no reasonable basis for the decision;

  (iii) the degree of discretion entrusted to the deciding official;

  (iv) violation of an applicable statute or regulation. <u>United States Fidelity & Guaranty Co. v. U.S.</u>, 676 F.2d 622 (Ct. Cl. 1982); <u>Quality Environment Systems, Inc.</u>, ASBCA No. 22178, 87-3 BCA ¶ 20,060.

(b) The contractor bears the burden of showing an abuse of discretion. <u>Walsky Constr. Co.</u>, ASBCA No. 41541, 94-1 BCA ¶ 26,264, <u>aff'd on recon.</u>, 94-2 BCA ¶ 26,698 (lieutenant colonel's directive to the contracting officer "tainted the termination"); <u>see also</u> <u>Libertatia Assoc., Inc. v. United States</u>, 46 Fed. Cl. 702 (2000) (once default is established, burden shifts to contractor to show its failure to perform is excusable).

(c) Recent examples of abuse of discretion: <u>Teresa A. McVicker, P.C.</u>, ASBCA No. 57487, 57653, 12-2 BCA 35,127; <u>Ryste & Ricas, Inc.</u>, ASBCA No. 51841, 02-2 BCA ¶ 31,883 and <u>Bison</u>

<u>Trucking and Equipment Company</u>, ASBCA No. 53390, 01-2 BCA ¶ 31,654.

(2) Bad Faith.

(a) There is a strong presumption that government officials act conscientiously in the discharge of their duties. <u>Krygoski Constr. Co., Inc. v. United States</u>, 94 F.3d 1537 (Fed. Cir. 1996).

(b) Contractors asserting that government officials acted in "bad faith" must meet a higher standard of proof. The courts and boards require "clear and convincing evidence"[1] of "malice" or "designedly oppressive conduct" to overcome the presumption that public officials act in good faith in the exercise of their powers and responsibilities. <u>See</u> <u>Am-Pro Protective Agency, Inc. v. United States</u>, 281 F.3d 1234 (Fed. Cir. 2002); <u>Kalvar Corp. v. United States</u>, 543 F.2d 1298 (Ct. Cl. 1976); <u>White Buffalo Constr. Inc. v. United States</u>, 101 Fed. Cl. 1 (2011); <u>Apex Int'l Mgmt. Servs., Inc.</u>, ASBCA No. 38087, 94-2 BCA ¶ 26,842, <u>aff'd on recon.</u>,

---

[1] This "'clear and convincing' or 'highly probable' (formerly described as 'well-nigh irrefragable')" standard was recently articulated by the Federal Circuit in <u>Am-Pro Protective Agency, Inc., v. United States</u>, 281 F.3d 1234, 1243 (Fed. Cir. 2002). For years, contractors alleging bad faith by the government needed "well-nigh irrefragable proof" to overcome the strong presumption that government officials acted in good faith. "In fact, for almost 50 years this court and its predecessor have repeated that we are 'loath to find to the contrary [of good faith], and it takes, and should take, well-nigh irrefragable proof to induce us to do so.'" <u>Id.</u> at 1239 (quoting <u>Schaefer v. United States</u>, 224 Ct. Cl. 541, 633 F.2d 945, 948-49 (Ct. Cl. 1980)) (<u>also citing</u> <u>Grover v. United States</u>, 200 Ct. Cl. 337, 344 (1973); <u>Kalvar [Corp. Inc., v. United States]</u>, 543 F.2d 1298, 1302, 211 Ct. Cl. 192 (1976); <u>Torncello v. United States</u>, 231 Ct. Cl. 20, 681 F.2d 756, 770 (Ct. Cl. 1982); <u>T&M Distribs., Inc. v. United States</u>, 185 F.3d 1279, 1285 (Fed. Cir. 1999)).

94-2 BCA ¶ 26,852 (Navy officials acted in bad faith by "declaring war" against the contractor; contractor entitled to breach damages); Marine Constr. Dredging, Inc., ASBCA No. 38412, 95-1 BCA ¶ 27,286 (although government's administration of the contract was "seriously flawed," no bad faith).

(c) Government officials are presumed to have acted conscientiously in making a default termination decision. Mindeco Corp., ASBCA No. 45207, 94-1 BCA ¶ 26,410; Local Contractors, Inc., ASBCA No. 37108, 92-1 BCA ¶ 24,491.

(d) Proof of bad faith requires specific intent to retaliate against or injure plaintiff to support an allegation of bad faith. Kalvar Corp. v. United States, 543 F.2d 1298 (Ct. Cl. 1976); Marine Constr. Dredging, Inc., ASBCA No. 38412, 95-1 BCA ¶ 27,286 (although the government's administration of the contract was "seriously flawed," no bad faith).

(e) But see Expediters Worldwide USA, Inc. v. GSA, CBCA 2748, 3237, 2013-1 BCA ¶35,246, where the board did not require a specific intent to injure. In that case, the successful purchaser in a GSA conducted auction of a 265-foot barge docked at NASA's Stennis Space Center was excused from its refusal to take possession of the barge and move it off the NASA site. The CBCA found that the GSA had failed to disclose that the barge contained 200,000 gallons of water that may have been contaminated and that needed to be removed before the barge could be moved. It also found that GSA had breached its duty to cooperate in good faith with the other contracting party because, inexplicably, it had not informed the purchaser that, once the dispute had arisen, NASA had offered to remove the water itself.

B. **Regulatory Guidance.** The FAR provides detailed procedures that the contracting officer should follow to terminate a contract.

1. Contracting officers should consider alternatives to termination. FAR 49.402-4. The following, among others, are available in lieu of termination for default when in the government's interest:

   a. permit the contractor, the surety, or the guarantor, to continue performance under a revised schedule;

   b. permit the contractor to continue performance by means of a subcontract or other business arrangement;

   c. if the requirement no longer exists and the contractor is not liable to the government for damages, execute a no-cost termination.

   d. See ZIOS Corp., ASBCA No. 56626, 10-1 BCA ¶ 34,344 (the contracting officer terminated for default the contract after offering ZIOS the opportunity to withdraw from the contract; ZIOS turned down the offer because it wanted the money); Yonir Tech., Inc., ASBCA No. 56736, 10-1 BCA ¶ 34,417 (contracting officer T4D'd the contract after contractor rejected three separate offers to cancel the order at no cost).

2. The FAR provides detailed procedures for terminating a contract for default. FAR 49.402-3. When a default termination is being considered, the government shall decide which termination action to take only after review by contracting and technical personnel, and by counsel, to ensure the propriety of the proposed action. Failure to conduct such a review, while risky, will not automatically overturn a default decision. National Med.

Default Terminations

Staffing, Inc., ASBCA No. 40391, 92-2 BCA ¶ 24,837 (contracting officer acted within her discretion despite her failure to consult with technical personnel and counsel prior to termination).

3. Before terminating a contractor for default, the contracting officer should comply with the pertinent notice requirements (cure notice or show cause notice). FAR 49.402-3(c), (d), (e). Additional notice to the following third parties may be required:

   a. Surety. In construction contracts, and some other contracts, a surety guarantees the contractors performance. If a notice to terminate for default appears imminent, the contracting officer shall provide a written notice to the surety. If the contractor is subsequently terminated, the contracting officer shall send a copy of the notice to the surety. FAR 49.402-3(e)(2).

   b. Small Business Administration. When the contractor is a small business, send a copy of any show cause or cure notice to the contracting office's small business specialist and the Small Business Regional Office nearest the contractor. FAR 49.402-3(e)(4).

4. FAR 49.402-3(f) states that the contracting officer shall consider the following factors in determining whether to terminate a contract for default:

   a. The terms of the contract and applicable laws and regulations.

   b. The specific failure of the contractor and the excuses for the failure.

   c. The availability of the supplies or services from other sources.

   d. The urgency of the need for the supplies or services and the period of time required to obtain them from other sources, as compared with the time delivery could be obtained from the delinquent contractor.

   e. The degree of essentiality of the contractor in the government acquisition program and the effect of a termination for default upon the contractor's capability as a supplier under other contracts.

   f. The effect of a termination for default on the ability of the contractor to liquidate guaranteed loans, progress payments, or advance payments.

   g. Any other pertinent facts and circumstances.

5. Failure of the contracting officer to consider factors at FAR 49.402-3(f) may result in a defective termination. See DCX, Inc., 79 F.3d 132 (Fed. Cir. 1996) (although contracting officer's failure to consider one or more FAR 49.402-3(f) factors does not automatically require conversion to termination for convenience, such failure may aid the court or board in determining whether the contracting officer abused his discretion); Phoenix Petroleum Company, ASBCA No. 42763, 96-2 BCA ¶ 28,284 (failure to analyze FAR factors does not entitle contractor to relief; factors are not a prerequisite to a valid termination).

6. Failure to consider all information available prior to issuing a termination notice could be an abuse of discretion. Jamco Constructors, Inc., VABCA No. 3271, 94-1 BCA ¶ 26,405, aff'd on recon., 94-2 BCA ¶ 26,792 (contracting officer abused discretion by failing to reconcile contradictory information and "blindly" accepting technical representative's estimates for completion of the contract by another contractor).

7. The contracting officer must explain the decision to terminate a contract for default in a memorandum for the contract file. FAR 49.402-5. The memorandum should recount the factors at FAR 49.402-3(f).

8. The Default Termination Notice.

a. Contents of the termination notice. FAR 49.102; FAR 49.402-3(g). The written notice must clearly state:

  (1) The contract number and date;

  (2) The acts or omissions constituting the default;

  (3) That the contractor's right to proceed further under the contract (or a specified portion of the contract) is terminated;

  (4) That the supplies or services terminated may be purchased against the contractor's account, and that the contractor will be held liable for any excess costs;

  (5) If the contracting officer has determined that the failure to perform is not excusable, that the notice of termination constitutes such decision, and that the contractor has the right to appeal such decision under the Disputes clause;

  (6) That the government reserves all rights and remedies provided by law or under the contract, in addition to charging excess costs; and

  (7) That the notice constitutes a decision that the contractor is in default as specified and that the contractor has the right to appeal under the Disputes clause. FAR 49.402-3(g).

  (8) FAR 49.102(a) provides that the notice shall also include any special instructions and the steps the contractor should take to minimize the impact on personnel (including reduction in workforce notice of FAR 49.601-2(g)).

b. A default termination is a final decision that can be appealed. Malone v. United States, 849 F.2d 1441 (Fed. Cir. 1988); United Healthcare Partners, Inc., ASBCA 58123, 2013-1

BCA¶35,277 (finding contractor properly appealed the notice of termination; appeal did not require a separate claim and final decision by the CO).

  (1) The termination notification must give notice to the contractor of right to appeal the default termination. Failure to properly advise the contractor of its appeal rights <u>may</u> prevent the "appeals clock" from starting if the contractor can show detrimental reliance. <u>Decker & Co. v. West</u>, 76 F.3d 1573 (Fed. Cir. 1996).

  (2) When mailed, the notice shall be sent by certified mail, return receipt requested. When hand delivered, a written acknowledgement shall be obtained from the contractor. FAR 49.102(a). A default termination notice is effective when delivered to the contractor. <u>Fred Schwartz</u>, ASBCA No. 20724, 76-1 BCA ¶ 11,916.

VII. RIGHTS AND LIABILITIES ARISING FROM TERMINATIONS FOR DEFAULT.

A. **Contractor Liability.** Upon termination of a contract, the contractor is liable to the government for any excess costs incurred in acquiring supplies or services similar to those terminated for default (<u>see</u> FAR 49.402-6) and for any other damages, whether or not repurchase is effected (<u>see</u> FAR 49.402-7). FAR 49.402-2(e).

1. Excess Reprocurement Costs.

a. Under fixed-price supply and service contracts, the government can acquire supplies or services similar to those terminated and the contractor will be liable for any excess costs of those supplies or services. FAR 49.402-6; FAR 52.249-8(b); <u>Ed Grimes</u>, GSBCA No. 7652, 89-1 BCA ¶ 21,528; <u>CDA, Inc. v. Social Security</u>

Admin., CBCA No. 1558, 12-1 BCA ¶34,990 (upholding agency's assessment of excess reprocurement costs for entire period, including option years, of the follow-on contractor's performance because original contractor had agreed to perform for that duration).

b. The government must show that its assessment was proper by establishing the following:

(1) The reprocured supplies or services are the same as or similar to those involved in the termination. 5860 Chicago Ridge, LLC v. United States, 104 Fed. Cl. 740 (2012) (agency failed to demonstrate that building it leased as a substitute was comparable and that the amount it sought was the precise amount it had spent in reprocurements); Gordon T. Smart, PSBCA No. 6123, 11-1 BCA ¶ 34,695 (post office failed to put on evidence concerning the replacement contract); Odessa R. Brown, PSBCA No. 5362, et al., 11-1 BCA ¶ 34,724; International Foods Retort Co., ASBCA No. 34954, 92-2 BCA ¶ 24,994.

(2) The government actually incurred excess costs. Sequal, Inc., ASBCA No. 30838, 88-1 BCA ¶ 20,382; 5860 Chicago Ridge, LLC v. United States, 104 Fed. Cl. 740 (2012) (agency failed to demonstrate that the amount it sought was the precise amount it had spent in reprocurements); and

(3) The government acted reasonably to minimize the excess costs resulting from the default. Daubert Chem. Co., ASBCA No. 46752, 94-2 BCA ¶ 26,741 (government acted reasonably where it reprocured quickly, obtained seven bids, and awarded to lowest bidder).

c. Mitigation of damages. The government has an affirmative duty to mitigate damages on repurchase. Ronald L. Collier, ASBCA No. 26972, 89-1 BCA ¶ 21,328; Kessler Chem., Inc., ASBCA No. 25293, 81-1 BCA ¶ 14,949.

(1) If the repurchase is for a quantity of goods in excess of the quantity that was terminated for default, the contracting officer may not charge the defaulting contractor for excess costs beyond the undelivered quantity terminated for default. FAR 49.402-6(a).

(2) If a repurchase is for a quantity not in excess of the quantity that was terminated, the government shall repurchase at as reasonable a price as practicable. FAR 49.402-6(b). The contracting officer may use any terms and acquisition method deemed appropriate for the repurchase. 52.249-8(b). See Al Bosgraaf Son's, ASBCA No. 45526, 94-2 BCA ¶ 26,913 (reprocurement by modification of another contract inadequate to mitigate costs); International Technology Corp., B-250377.5, Aug. 18, 1993, 93-2 CPD ¶ 102 (may award a reprocurement contract to the next-low offeror on the original solicitation when there is a short time span between the original competition and default).

(3) The government is not required to invite bids on repurchase solicitations from a defaulted contractor. Montage Inc., B-277923.2, Dec. 29, 1997, 97-2 CPD ¶ 176.

d. When the repurchase is defective, the defaulting contractor may be relieved of liability for excess costs. Ross McDonald Contracting, GmbH, ASBCA No. 38154, 94-1 BCA ¶ 26,316 (government failed to mitigate damages when exercising option on reprocurement contract); Astra Prods. Co. of Tampa, ASBCA No. 24474, 82-1 BCA ¶ 15,497 (recoverable reprocurement costs reduced where the government failed to request proposal from next lowest-priced responsible bidder).

e. The Fulford Doctrine. A contractor may dispute an underlying default termination as part of a timely appeal from a government demand for excess reprocurement costs, even though the contractor failed to appeal the underlying default termination in a timely manner. Fulford Mfg. Co., ASBCA No. 2143, 6 CCF ¶ 61,815 (May 20, 1955); see also Deep Joint Venture, GSBCA No. 14511, 02-2 BCA ¶ 31,914 (GSBCA confirms validity of the Fulford doctrine for post-CDA terminations). See D. Moody & Co. v. United States, 5 Cl. Ct. 70 (1984); Kellner Equip., Inc., ASBCA No. 26006, 82-2 BCA ¶ 16,077.

f. While the majority of the existing case law supports and adopts the Fulford doctrine, those in the field of contractor defense work believe that the Federal Circuit's 2010 decision in Maropakis undermines the Fulford doctrine. M. Maropakis Carpentry, Inc. v. United States, 609 F.3d 1323 (Fed. Cir. 2010). Consequently, the safer approach is to appeal the default termination, and raise available defenses, rather than waiting to see if the government claims excess reprocurement costs.

2. Liquidated Damages. Liquidated damages are a contractually agreed-upon measure of damages when actual damages are certain, but the amount is difficult prove. Delay damages are often subject to liquidated damages. The government may recover both liquidated damages for delay, and excess costs (either for reprocurement or for completion of the work) from a

contractor upon terminating a contract for default. FAR 49.402-7.

a. The common-law rule that liquidated damages will not be enforced if they constitute a penalty applies to government acquisitions. Southwest Eng'g Co. v. United States, 341 F.2d 998 (8th Cir. 1965).

b. A liquidated damages clause will be enforced as reasonable where, at the inception of the contract, the damages are based on a reasonable forecast of possible damages in the event of failure of performance. American Constr. Co., ENG BCA No. 5728, 91-2 BCA ¶ 24,009.

c. If a contract does not have a liquidated damages clause or if the liquidated damages provision of a contract is unenforceable because it is punitive, the government may recover actual damages to the extent that it can prove the amount. FAR 52.249-10.

3. Common-law damages.

a. The government may also recover common-law damages, which may be in lieu of or in addition to excess costs assessed under the default termination clause. FAR 52.249-8(h); Cascade Pac. Int'l v. United States, 773 F.2d 287 (Fed. Cir. 1985) (government awarded common-law damages after failing to prove excess reprocurement costs); Hideca Trading, Inc., ASBCA No. 24161, 87-3 BCA ¶ 20,040 (despite failure to reprocure, the government entitled to damages at the difference between the contract price and the market price for oil for the period 60 to 90 days after the default termination).

b. The government has the burden of proving that the damages are foreseeable, direct, material, or the proximate result of the contractor's breach of contract. ERG Consultants, Inc., VABCA No. 3223, 92-2 BCA

511

Default Terminations

¶ 24,905 (damages must be foreseeable); <u>Gibson Forestry</u>, AGBCA No. 87-325-1, 91-2 BCA ¶ 23,874 (Forest Service unable to recover cost of tree seedlings when contractor did not know that seedlings had three-week life expectancy once lifted for planting).

4. Unliquidated advance and progress payments. The government is entitled to repayment by the contractor of advance and progress payments, if any, attributable to the undelivered work. <u>Smith Aircraft Co.</u>, ASBCA No. 39316, 90-1 BCA ¶ 22,475.

B.   The Government's Obligations.

1. Upon termination of a fixed-price supply contract for default, the government is obligated to pay the contract price for completed supplies delivered and accepted. FAR 52.249-8(f).

2. Upon termination of a fixed-price service contract or of a fixed-price construction contract, the government is obligated to pay the reasonable value of work done before termination, whether or not the services or construction have been contractually accepted by the government. <u>Sphinx Int'l, Inc.</u>, ASBCA No. 38784, 90-3 BCA ¶ 22,952.

3. If the government requires the contractor to transfer title and deliver to the government its tooling and work in progress, the government is obligated to pay the reasonable value. FAR 52.249-8(e); FAR 52.249-10(a).

4. Upon termination for default of a cost-reimbursement contract, the government is generally liable for all of the reasonable, allowable, and allocable costs incurred by the contractor, whether or not accepted by the government, plus a percentage of the contract fee. The fee is somewhat limited, however, as the amount of the contract fee payable to the contractor is based on the work accepted by the government, rather than on the amount of work done by the contractor. FAR 52.249-6.

VIII. TERMINATION OF COMMERCIAL ITEM CONTRACTS: "TERMINATION FOR CAUSE."

A.   **Background.** The Federal Acquisition Streamlining Act, P.L. 103-355, 108 Stat. 3243 (Oct. 13, 1994), established special requirements for the acquisition of commercial items. Congress intended that government acquisitions more closely resemble those customarily used in the commercial market place. FAR 12.201.

B.   **Applicable Rules for Terminations for Cause.** The clause at FAR 52.212-4 permits the government to terminate a contract for a commercial item for cause. This clause contains concepts that are in some ways different from "traditional" termination rules contained in FAR Part 49. Consequently, the requirements of FAR Part 49 do not apply when terminating contracts for commercial items. Contracting officers, however, may continue to follow Part 49 as guidance to the extent that Part 49 does not conflict with FAR 12.403 and FAR 52.212-4. FAR 12.403(a).

C.   **Policy.** The contracting officer should exercise the government's right to terminate a contract for a commercial item only when such a termination would be in the best interests of the government. Further, the contracting officer should consult counsel prior to terminating for cause. FAR 12.403(b).

D.   **Termination for Cause Highlights.** FAR 12.403; FAR 52.212-4.

1. Grounds. Under the rules, a contractor may be terminated for cause "in the event of any default by the Contractor, or if the Contractor fails to comply with any contract terms or conditions, or fails to provide the government, upon request, with adequate assurances of future performance." FAR 52.212-4(m).

2. Excusable Delay. Contractors are required to notify contracting officers as soon as

512

reasonably possible after the commencement of excusable delay. FAR 52.212-4(f). In most situations, this requirement should minimize the consequences of terminating without first issuing a show cause notice. FAR 12.403(c). However, a show cause notice remains a prudent risk mitigation measure.

3. Rights and Remedies:

 a. The government's rights and remedies after a termination for cause shall include all the remedies available to any buyer in the commercial market place. The government's preferred remedy will be to acquire similar items ("cover") from another contractor and to charge the defaulted contractor with the costs, together with any incidental and consequential damages incurred because of the termination. FAR 12.403(c)(2). See UCC § 2-712.

 b. In the event of a termination for cause, the government shall not be liable for supplies or services not accepted. FAR 52.212-4(m).

 c. If a board determines that the government improperly terminated for cause, such termination will be deemed a termination for convenience. FAR 52.212-4(m).

4. Procedure to terminate for cause.

 a. The CO shall send the contractor written notification. FAR 12.403(c)(3).

 b. Previously, contracting officers were required to report terminations for default through their agency channels to the Office of the Undersecretary of Defense. In 2010, this requirement changed to require all termination for cause or default reporting to be accomplished via the Federal Awardee Performance and Integrity Information System.

 c. Any termination involving a reduction in employment of 100 or more contractor employees specifically requires congressional notification, cleared through agency liaison offices before release. DFARS 249.7001; DFARS PGI 249.7001.

 (1) This notification requirement does not apply for firms performing in Iraq or Afghanistan if the firm is not incorporated in the United States. DOD Class Deviation 2011-O0002.

 (2) Similar reports are required by the Air Force for terminations with high-level agency interest or litigation potential. See AFFARS MP5349.

IX. MISCELLANEOUS.

A. Portion of the Contract That May Be Terminated for Default.

1. Total or partial termination. A default termination may be total or partial. FAR 52.249-8(a)(1); Balimoy Mfg. Co. of Venice v. United States, 2000 U.S. App. LEXIS 26702 (Fed. Cir 2000).

2. Severable contract requirements. Where a contract includes severable undertakings, default on one effort may not justify termination of the entire contract. T.C. Sarah C. Bell, ENG BCA No. 5872, 92-3 BCA ¶ 25,076.

B. Revocation of Acceptance.

1. In some circumstances, the government can revoke its acceptance in order to terminate. See, e.g., American Renovation & Construction Co., ASBCA No. 53723, 10-2 BCA ¶ 34,487 (upheld revocation of work that occurred 25 months previously where the government inspector reasonably relied on the contractor's assurance that there were no defects remaining in the work since all visible defects had been corrected); Chilstead Building Co., ASBCA No. 49548, 00-2 BCA ¶31,097 (roofing contractor's

representation that it was proceeding in accordance with the drawings followed shortly thereafter by installation of deviant trusses was a gross mistake amounting to fraud despite the government inspector's failure to measure or inspect); Z.A.N. Co., ASBCA No. 25488, 86-1 BCA ¶ 18,612 (delivery of improperly marked watches was a gross mistake amounting to fraud despite the fact that the government representatives may not have acted "with a maximum of circumspection"); Massman Constr. Co., ENGBCA No. 3443, 81-2 BCA ¶ 15,212 (contractor's failure to use prequalified weld joints (among other things) was a gross mistake amounting to fraud despite the fact that the government's inspection was "inexcusably bad"); Jo-Bar Mfg. Corp., ASBCA No. 17774, 73-2 BCA ¶ 10, 311 (contractor's determination that aircraft bolts did not have to be heat treated and failure to treat them, coupled with misrepresentation to the government inspector that it had been advised heat treatment was not required, was a gross mistake amounting to fraud despite possible lack of in-process inspection by the government).

2. However, acceptance must be revoked within a reasonable time after the mistake is discovered or could have been discovered with ordinary diligence. American Renovation & Construction Co., ASBCA No. 53723, 10-2 BCA ¶ 34,487; Bar Ray Prod., Inc. v. United States, 162 Ct. Cl. 836 (1963)

3. No precise formula exists to determine the reasonableness of the delay. American Renovation & Construction Co., ASBCA No. 53723, 10-2 BCA ¶ 34,487. The determination must be made on a case-by-case basis. Id.

4. However, the government's efforts to determine conclusively that the work was defective or to work with the contractor to solve the problem will be taken into consideration in determining the reasonableness of the delay. Perkin-Elmer Corp. v. United States, 47 Fed. Cl. 672

(2000) (revocation of acceptance more than six years after learning of the defect was unreasonable); Chilstead Building Co. Inc., ASBCA No. 49548, 00-2 BCA ¶31,097 (seven-month delay between discovery of the defects and revocation of acceptance for the architect-engineering firm to investigate the cause of the defect was reasonable); Ordnance Parts & Eng'r Co., ASBCA No. 40293, 90-3 BCA ¶ 23,141 (one-year delay between the KO's request for tests and revocation of acceptance where tests took less than two weeks was not "remotely prompt action"); Jung Ah Industrial Co., ASBCA 22632, 79-1 BCA ¶ 13,643, aff'd on recon., 79-2 BCA ¶ 13,916 (ten-month delay to test wall paneling to determine if it had been "incombustible treated" was reasonable

C. **Availability of Funds.** Funds that have been obligated but have not been disbursed at the time of termination for default and funds recovered as excess costs on a defaulted contract remain available for a replacement contract awarded in a subsequent fiscal year. Funding of Replacement Contracts, B-198074, July 15, 1981, 81-2 CPD ¶ 33; Bureau of Prisons-Disposition of Funds Paid in Settlement of Breach of Contract Action, B-210160, Sep. 28, 1983, 84-1 CPD ¶ 91.

D. **Conversion to a Termination for Convenience.** All FAR default clauses provide that an erroneous default termination will be converted to a termination for convenience. FAR 52.249-8(g); FAR 52.249-10(c); FAR 52.249-6(b). But see Apex Int'l Mgmt. Servs., Inc., ASBCA No. 38087, 94-2 BCA ¶ 26,842 (board refuses to limit recovery to termination for convenience costs where government officials acted in bad faith; contractor entitled to breach damages).

E. **Termination for Convenience Proposals While a Termination for Default Appeal Is Pending.**

1. A contractor, prior to the default being overturned, can submit a termination for convenience settlement proposal to the contracting officer. The proposals will be treated as Contract Disputes Act claims.[2] McDonnell Douglas Corp. v. United States, 37 Fed. Cl. 285 (1997); Balimoy Mfg. Co. of Venice, ASBCA No. 49,730, 96-2 BCA ¶ 28,605.

2. The demand for termination for convenience costs from the contracting officer who terminated the contract for default demonstrates the "impasse" required to convert a proposal into a claim.

3. An appeal of a convenience settlement proposal will be dismissed without prejudice to reinstatement if the appeal of a default termination is pending. Poly Design, Inc., ASBCA No. 50862, 98-1 BCA ¶ 29,458.

X.   CONCLUSION.

Terminating a contract for default is a major action with significant legal and business issues. The legal issues are 1) whether the government can prove the contractor actually failed to perform the contract and 2) whether the contractor's performance failure was excused. The business issues are whether the government's interests are best served by a termination for default, a negotiated no cost termination, or by revising the delivery schedule and allowing the contractor to continue performance. The government's best interests are often best served by continued performance when the contractor appears capable and willing to complete the work. Responsible contractors will go to extraordinary lengths to avoid default terminations. However, not all contractors are responsible, and where a contractor is not performing, the contracting officer should adhere closely to the regulatory procedures to avoid having a default termination converted to one for convenience based on procedural errors.

---

[2] The demand for termination for convenience costs from the contracting officer who terminated the contract for default demonstrates the "impasse" required to convert a proposal into a claim.

CONTRACT DISPUTES

I. INTRODUCTION.

While most contracts result in timely delivery of conforming goods and services, and payment of the contract price, occasionally the government and the contractor may disagree and one or both will seek contractual remedies through litigation.

Contract litigation with the government is similar to other commercial litigation, but has several aspects that can surprise those who are unfamiliar with the process. Three points are important.

- First, following the statutory and regulatory procedures. Failure to follow procedures results in delays or inability to enforce meritorious claims. Compliance with time limits is especially important.
- Second, contractors have a choice of forums to adjudicate claims not resolved with the contracting officer. The choice of forum can impact the cost and speed of litigation.
- Third, contract litigation takes place while the parties continue their business relationships. Consequently, there are many opportunities to resolve disputes amicably.

II. OVERVIEW.

Today, resolving contractor and government contract claims is governed by the Contract Disputes Act, 41. U.S.C. Chapter 71. The current process is the result of over 150 years of statutory and judicial developments that have created the bifurcated process that exists today..

A. Historical Development.

1. Pre-Civil War Developments. Before 1855, government contractors had no forum in which to sue the United States. In 1855, the Congress created the Court of Claims as an Article I (legislative) court to consider claims against the United States and recommend private bills to Congress. Act of February 24, 1855, 10 Stat. 612. The service secretaries, however, continued to resolve most contract claims. As early as 1861, the Secretary of War appointed a board of three officers to consider and decide specific contract claims. See Adams v. United States, 74 U.S. 463 (1868). Upon receipt of an adverse board decision, a contractor's only recourse was to request a private bill from Congress.

2. Civil War Reforms. In 1863, Congress expanded the power of the Court of Claims by authorizing it to enter judgments against the United States. Act of March 3, 1863, 12 Stat. 765. In 1887, Congress passed the Tucker Act to expand and clarify the jurisdiction of the Court of Claims. Act of March 3, 1887, 24 Stat. 505, codified at 28 U.S.C. § 1491. In that Act, Congress granted the Court of Claims authority to consider monetary claims based on: (1) the Constitution; (2) an act of Congress; (3) an executive regulation; or (4) an express or implied-in-fact contract.[1] As a result, a government contractor could now sue the United States as a matter of right.

3. Disputes Clauses. Agencies responded to the Court of Claim's increased oversight by adding clauses to government contracts that appointed specific agency officials (e.g., the contracting officer or the service secretary) as the final decision-maker for questions of fact. The Supreme Court upheld the finality of these officials' decisions in Kihlberg v. United States, 97

---

[1] The Tucker Act did not give the Court of Claims authority to consider claims based on implied-in-law contracts.

U.S. 398 (1878). The tension between the agencies' desire to decide contract disputes without outside interference, and the contractors' desire to resolve disputes in the Court of Claims, continued until 1978. This tension resulted in considerable litigation and a substantial body of case law.

4. Boards of Contract Appeals (BCAs). During World War I (WWI), the War and Navy Departments established full-time BCAs to hear claims involving wartime contracts. The War Department abolished its board in 1922, but the Navy board continued in name (if not fact) until World War II (WWII). Between the wars, an interagency group developed a standard disputes clause. This clause made contracting officers' decisions final as to all questions of fact. WWII again showed that boards of contract appeals were needed to resolve the massive number of wartime contract disputes. See Penker Constr. Co. v. United States, 96 Ct. Cl. 1 (1942). Thus, the War Department created a board of contract appeals, and the Navy revived its board. In 1949, the Department of Defense (DOD) merged the two boards to form the current ASBCA.

5. Post-WWII Developments. In a series of cases culminating in Wunderlich v. United States, 342 U.S. 98 (1951), the Supreme Court upheld the finality (absent fraud) of factual decisions issued under the disputes clause by a department head or his duly authorized representative. Congress reacted by passing the Wunderlich Act, 41 U.S.C. §§ 321-322, which reaffirmed that the Court of Claims could review factual and legal decisions by agency BCAs. At about the same time, Congress changed the Court of Claims from an Article I (legislative) to an Article III (judicial) court. Pub. L. No. 83-158, 67 Stat. 226 (1953). Later, the Supreme Court clarified the relationship between the Court of Claims and the agency BCAs by limiting the jurisdiction of the boards to cases "arising under" remedy granting clauses in

the contract. See Utah Mining and Constr. Co. v. United States, 384 U.S. 394 (1966).

6. The Contract Disputes Act (CDA) of 1978, 41 U.S.C. §§ 601-613 (recodified at 41 U.S.C. §§ 7101-7109). Congress replaced the previous disputes resolution system with a comprehensive statutory scheme. Congress intended that the CDA:

- Help induce resolution of more disputes by negotiation prior to litigation;
- Equalize the bargaining power of the parties when a dispute exists;
- Provide alternate forums suitable to handle the different types of disputes; and
- Insure fair and equitable treatment to contractors and government agencies. S. REP. NO. 95-1118, at 1 (1978), *reprinted in* 1978 U.S.C.C.A.N. 5235.

7. Federal Courts Improvement Act of 1982, Pub. L. No. 97-164, 96 Stat. 25. Congress overhauled the Court of Claims and created a new Article I court (i.e., the Claims Court) from the old Trial Division of the Court of Claims. Congress also merged the Court of Claims and the Court of Customs and Patent Appeals to create the Court of Appeals for the Federal Circuit (CAFC).[2]

8. Federal Courts Administration Act of 1992, Pub. L. No. 102-572, 106 Stat. 3921. Congress changed the name of the Claims Court to the United States Court of Federal Claims (COFC), and expanded the jurisdiction of the court to include the adjudication of nonmonetary claims.

9. Federal Acquisition Streamlining Act (FASA) of 1994, Pub. L. No. 103-355, 108 Stat. 3243. Congress increased the monetary thresholds for requiring CDA certifications and requesting expedited and accelerated appeals.

---

[2] The Act revised the jurisdiction of the new courts substantially.

B. The Disputes Process.

1. The CDA establishes jurisdiction, procedures, and other requirements for asserting and resolving contract claims subject to the Act. Practitioners should note that not all contract claims are subject to the Contracts Disputes Act.

2. The contract disputes process begins when a claim is submitted to the contracting officer. Routine requests for payment, including invoices and requests for equitable adjustments are not claims. The contracting officer investigates the claim and, as an independent act, issues a final decision. Upon receipt of the final decision, the contractor either accepts the decision, or files an appeal of the final decision to either the Court of Federal Claims or the appropriate Board of Contract Appeals. Following a decision on the merits by the Board or Court, a party may pursue an appeal to the Court of Appeals for the Federal Circuit, and if unsuccessful, to the US Supreme Court. A flowchart of this process is below.

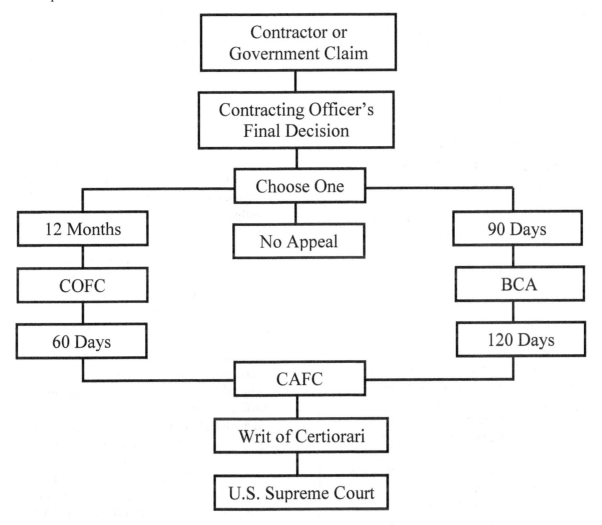

3. The Contract Disputes Act requirements are included in the clause FAR 52.233-1, Disputes, which should be included in those contracts subject to the Act. Contracts that are not subject to the Contract Disputes Act will usually include an alternative disputes clause.

Contract Disputes

4. Election of Forum. The CDA provides alternative forums for appealing a contracting officer's final decision. Appeals are taken by contractors. Once a contractor files its appeal in a particular forum, this election is normally binding and the contractor can no longer pursue its claim in the other forum. The "election doctrine," however, does not apply if the forum originally selected lacked subject matter jurisdiction over the appeal. See Bonneville Assocs. v. United States, 43 F.3d 649 (Fed. Cir. 1994) (dismissing the contractor's suit because the contractor originally elected to proceed before the GSBCA); see also Bonneville Assocs. v. General Servs. Admin., GSBCA No. 13134, 96-1 BCA ¶ 28,122 (refusing to reinstate the contractor's appeal), aff'd, Bonneville Assoc. v. United States, 165 F.3d 1360 (Fed. Cir. 1999).

III. IS MY CONTRACT DISPUTE SUBJECT TO THE CONTRACTS DISPUTES ACT?

A. Not All Contract Disputes Are Subject to the Contract Disputes Act.

1. Most, but not all, contracts, awarded by Executive Branch agencies are subject to the Contract Disputes Act. 41 U.S.C. § 7102 provides:

"Unless otherwise specifically provided in this chapter, this chapter applies to any express or implied contract (including those of the non-appropriated fund activities described in sections 1346 and 1491 of title 28) made by an executive agency for—
(1) the procurement of property, other than real property in being;
(2) the procurement of services;
(3) the procurement of construction, alteration, repair, or maintenance of real property; or
(4) the disposal of personal property."

2. Contracts awarded by the legislative and judicial branches of government are not subject to the CDA. 41 U.S.C. § 7102.

3. Contracts for the purchase, sale, or lease of real property are not subject to the CDA because acquisitions are limited to purchases of supplies and services. See, FAR 2.101

4. Non-procurement agreements, such as Cooperative Research and Development Agreements (CRADAs), Grants, Other Transactions, etc. are not subject to the Contract Disputes Act, although they may be subject to the Tucker Act, 28 U.S.C. § 1491. See Spectrum Sciences and Software v. United States, 84 Fed. Cl. 716 (2008).

5. Contract disputes do not include bid protests.

In bid protests, disappointed bidders or offerors seek relief from actions that occur before contract award. See generally FAR Subpart 33.1. Bid protests are covered in Chapter 19.

In contract disputes, contractors and/or the government assert claims for actions, inactions, and events that occur after contract award in the performance of the contract. See generally FAR Subpart 33.2.

The Boards of Contract Appeals lack jurisdiction over bid protest actions. See United States v. John C. Grimberg, Inc., 702 F.2d 1362 (Fed. Cir. 1983) (stating that "the [CDA] deals with contractors, not with disappointed bidders"); Ammon Circuits Research, ASBCA No. 50885, 97-2 BCA ¶ 29,318 (dismissing an appeal based on the contracting officer's written refusal to award the contractor a research contract); RC 27th Ave. Corp., ASBCA No. 49176, 97-1 BCA ¶ 28,658 (dismissing an appeal for lost profits arising from the contracting officer's failure to award the contractor a grounds maintenance services contract).

6. The CDA does not apply to:

- Fraud claims. 41 U.S.C. § 7103(d).
- Claims that do not arise under or relate to an express or an implied-in-fact contract, such as ordinary tort claims;
- Claims for penalties or forfeitures prescribed by statute or regulation that another federal agency is specifically authorized to administer, settle, or determine. FAR 33.210
- Contracts with foreign governments or agencies. 41 U.S.C. § 7102; FAR 33.203.

7. To resolve contract disputes under contracts that are not subject to the CDA, the government or the contractor should look to any Disputes clause in the contract, and to the residual jurisdiction under the Tucker Act, 41 U.S.C. § 1491.

B. **Maritime and TVA Claims**. Practitioners should note that the Contract Disputes Act provides special procedures for maritime contract actions and for Tennessee Valley Authority (TVA) contract actions.

1. For maritime contract disputes, the CDA grants district courts to hear appeals of ASBCA decisions, or to entertain suits filed following a contracting officer's final decision. See 41 U.S.C. § 7102(d). See also Marine Logistics, Inc. v. Secretary of the Navy, 265 F.3d 1322 (Fed. Cir. 2001).

2. For TVA contract disputes, the CDA has limited applicability. See 41 U.S.C. § 7102(b), and appeals of final decisions are taken to a U.S. District Court. See 41 U.S.C. § 7104(b)(2).

C. **Appropriated Fund Contracts**.

1. The CDA applies to both express and implied-in-fact contracts. 41 U.S.C. § 7102; FAR 33.203. The overwhelming majority of federal contracts are express contracts awarded by Executive Branch agencies, entered into in writing and following a formal process of solicitation, offer, and acceptance.

2. An "implied-in-fact" contract is similar to an "express" contract. It requires: (1) "a meeting of the minds" between the parties; (2) consideration; (3) an absence of ambiguity surrounding the offer and the acceptance; and (4) an agency official with actual authority to bind the government. James L. Lewis v. United States, 70 F.3d 597 (Fed. Cir. 1995).

3. When the CDA does not apply to a particular contract dispute, such as a contract claim against the legislative branch, or an executive branch contract other than the four types covered, the contract may still contain a disputes clause governing administrative resolution of contract disputes. Cf. G.E. Boggs & Assocs., Inc., ASBCA Nos. 34841, 34842, 91-1 BCA ¶ 23,515 (holding that the CDA did not apply because the parties did not enter into a contract for the procurement of property, but retaining jurisdiction pursuant to the disputes clause in the contract).

4. The CDA is implemented in contracts by a mandatory clause. FAR 33.215 requires inclusion of FAR 52.233-1, Disputes, in typical contracts. FAR 33.215 permits agencies to use an "All Disputes" clause, FAR 52.233-1, Alt. 1. The difference between the two clauses is that FAR 52.233-1, Alt. 1 requires the contractor to continue contract performance pending resolution of all disputes. The basic clause only requires continued performance when the dispute "arises under" a remedy granting clause in the contract.[3]

For contractors, this means that they may stop performance for government breaches of contract, but not for actions entitling them to seek equitable adjustments under a contract clause, when the basic Disputes

---

[3] "Arising under the contract" is defined as falling within the scope of a contract clause and therefore providing a remedy for some event occurring during contract performance. RALPH C. NASH ET AL., THE GOVERNMENT CONTRACTS REFERENCE BOOK, at 8 (2d ed. 1998).

clause is in the contract. A contractor may not stop performance for breach of contract if the Alt. I version of the clause is in their contract. For DOD contracts, the DFARS requires use of the Alt. I, "All Disputes" clause, in certain contracts. See DFARS 233.215. As a practical matter, stopping performance of a U.S. government contract is a serious matter that contractors should undertake after consulting with counsel specialized in U.S. government contracting.

5. FAR 52.233-1, Disputes, generally describes the process for resolution of disputes under the Contract Disputes Act.

D. Nonappropriated Fund (NAF) Contracts.

1. NAF contracts are further discussed in Chapter 31.

2. Exchange Service contracts. The CDA applies to contracts with the Army and Air Force, Navy, Marine Corps, Coast Guard, and NASA Exchanges. See 41 U.S.C. § 7102(a), 28 U.S.C. §§ 1346, 1491. The CDA does not apply to other non-appropriated fund contracts.[4] See, e.g., Furash & Co. v. United States, 46 Fed. Cl. 518 (2000) (dismissing suit concerning contract with Federal Housing Finance Board).

3. Other non-appropriated fund contracts typically include a disputes clause, thereby giving a contractor the right to appeal a dispute to a BCA. See AR 215-4, Section 6-11.(d); Charitable Bingo Assoc. Inc., ASBCA No. 53249, 01-2 BCA ¶ 31,478 (holding that the board had jurisdiction over a dispute with a NAF based on the inclusion of the disputes clause). Further, an agency directive granting NAF

contractors a right of appeal has served as the basis for board jurisdiction, even when the contract contained no disputes clause. See DODD 5515.6; Recreational Enters., ASBCA No. 32176, 87-1 BCA ¶ 19,675 (board had jurisdiction over NAF contract dispute because DOD directives required contract clause granting a right of appeal).

4. Currently, Enclosure 2 to DODI 4105.67, February 26, 2014, give DOD agencies discretion on where a contractor may appeal a NAF contracting officer's final decision.

5. Where a DOD agency has designated that appeals are heard by their Board of Contract Appeals, such designation does not mean a NAF contractor may further appeal the Board's decision. See Pacrim Pizza v. Secretary of the Navy, 304 F.3d 1291 (Fed. Cir. 2002) (CAFC refused to grant jurisdiction over non-exchange NAFI contract dispute; even though the contract included the standard disputes clause, the court held that only Congress can waive sovereign immunity, and the parties may not by contract bestow jurisdiction on a court). See also Sodexho Marriott Management, Inc., f/k/a Marriott Mgmt. Servs. v. United States, 61 Fed. Cl. 229 (2004) (holding that the non-appropriated funds doctrine barred the COFC from having jurisdiction over a NAF food service contract with the Marine Corps Recruit Morale, Welfare, and Recreation Center), Core Concepts of Florida, Inc. v. United States, 327 F.3d 1331 (Fed. Cir. 2003) (CAFC upheld a COFC decision that it lacked jurisdiction over a Federal Prison Industry (FPI) contract under the Tucker Act because FPI was a self-sufficient NAFI.

IV. CONTRACTOR CLAIMS.

A. Summary.

Contractors initiate contract claims under the Contract Disputes Act by submitting a written claim to the contracting officer for the contract. The claim must be submitted

---

[4] In addition, the CDA does not normally apply to: (1) Tennessee Valley Authority contracts; (2) contracts for the sale of real property; or (3) contracts with foreign governments or agencies. 41 U.S.C. § 7102 (b)-(c); FAR 33.203

within six years of accrual, and an authorized official of the contractor must certify the claim. Upon receipt, the contracting officer considers the claim and issues a final decision adjudicating the claim. Upon receipt of the final decision, the contractor may either appeal to the appropriate Board of Contract Appeals, file suit in the Court of Federal Claims, or accept the decision as final.

B. Proper Claimants.

1. Normally, only the parties to the contract (i.e., the prime contractor and the government) may submit a claim. 41 U.S.C. § 7103(a). Subcontractors, sureties, financial institutions, and others may not bring claims.

2. Subcontractor Claims.

   A subcontractor cannot file a claim directly with the contracting officer. United States v. Johnson Controls, 713 F.2d 1541 (Fed. Cir. 1983) (dismissing subcontractor claim); see also Detroit Broach Cutting Tools, Inc., ASBCA No. 49277, 96-2 BCA ¶ 28,493 (holding that the subcontractor's direct communication with the government did not establish privity); Southwest Marine, Inc., ASBCA No. 49617, 96-2 BCA ¶ 28,347 (rejecting the subcontractor's assertion that the Suits in Admiralty Act gave it the right to appeal directly); cf. Department of the Army v. Blue Fox, 119 S. Ct. 687 (1999) (holding that a subcontractor may not sue the government directly by asserting an equitable lien on funds held by the government). But see Choe-Kelly, ASBCA No. 43481, 92-2 BCA ¶ 24,910 (holding that the board had jurisdiction to consider the subcontractor's unsponsored claim alleging an implied-in-fact contract).

   A prime contractor, however, can sponsor claims (also called "pass-through claims") on behalf of its subcontractors. Erickson Air Crane Co. of Washington, Inc. v. United States, 731 F.2d 810 (Fed. Cir. 1984); McPherson Contractors, Inc.,

ASBCA No. 50830, 98-1 BCA ¶ 29,349 (appeal dismissed where prime stated it did not wish to pursue the appeal).

3. Third-Party Beneficiaries. In Winter v. FloorPro, Inc., 570 F.3d 1367 (Fed. Cir. 2009), the Federal Circuit reversed the ASBCA and held that a subcontractor that is a third-party beneficiary of a contract may not bring a claim under the CDA. The Federal Circuit distinguished D & H Distributing Co. v. United States, 102 F.3d 542 (Fed.Cir.1996), finding that the subcontractor in D&H brought suit in the Court of Federal Claims under the Tucker Act, 41.U.S.C. 1491(a) and not the CDA. Instead, a third-party beneficiary may bring suit in the Court of Federal Claims under the Tucker Act.

4. Sureties. Absent privity of contract, sureties may not file claims. Admiralty Constr., Inc. v. Dalton, 156 F.3d 1217 (Fed. Cir. 1998) (surety must finance contract completion or take over performance to invoke doctrine of equitable subrogation); William A. Ransom and Robert D. Nesen v. United States, 900 F.2d 242 (Fed. Cir. 1990) (discussing doctrine of equitable subrogation). However, see also Fireman's Fund Insurance Co. v. England, 313 F.3d 1344 (Fed Cir. 2002) (although the doctrine of equitable subrogation is recognized by the COFC under the Tucker Act, the CDA only covers "claims by a contractor against the government relating to a contract," thus a surety is not a "contactor" under the CDA.

5. Dissolved/Suspended Corporations. A corporate contractor must possess valid corporate status, as determined by applicable state law, to assert a CDA appeal. See Micro Tool Eng'g, Inc., ASBCA No. 31136, 86-1 BCA ¶ 18,680 (holding that a dissolved corporation could not sue under New York law). But cf. Fre'nce Mfg. Co., ASBCA No. 46233, 95-2 BCA ¶ 27,802 (allowing a "resurrected" contractor to prosecute the appeal). Allied

Prod. Management, Inc., and Richard E. Rowan, J.V., DOT CAB No. 2466, 92-1 BCA ¶ 24,585 (allowing a contractor to appeal despite its suspended corporate status). In determining what powers survive dissolution, courts and boards look to the laws of the state of incorporation. See AEI Pacific, Inc., ASBCA No. 53806, 05-1 BCA ¶ 32,859 (holding that a dissolved Alaska corporation could initiate proceedings before the ASBCA as part of its "winding up its affairs" as allowed by the Alaskan Statute concerning the dissolution Alaskan Corporations.).

C.   Definition of a Claim.

1.   Contract Disputes Act. The CDA does not define the term "claim." The government has filled that void. See Essex Electro Eng'rs, Inc. v. United States, 960 F.2d 1576 (Fed. Cir. 1992) (holding that the executive branch has authority to issue regulations implementing the CDA, to include defining the term "claim," and that the FAR definition is consistent with the CDA). FAR 2.101 defines a "claim" as "a written demand or written assertion by one of the contracting parties seeking, as a matter of right, the payment of money in a sum certain, the adjustment or interpretation of contract terms, or other relief arising under or relating to a contract." The same definition appears in the standard disputes clause, FAR 52.233-1.

Claims arising under or relating to the contract include those requesting an equitable adjustment under remedy granting clauses in the contract, breach of contract claims, interpretation of the contract, and remedies for mistakes alleged after award.

A written demand (or written assertion) seeking the payment of money in excess of $100,000 is not a valid CDA claim until the contractor properly certifies it. FAR 33.207

D.   Elements of a Claim.

1.   The demand or assertion must be in writing. 41 U.S.C. § 7103(a)(2); FAR 33.201. See Honig Indus. Diamond Wheel, Inc., ASBCA No. 46711, 94-2 BCA ¶ 26,955 (granting the government's motion to strike monetary claims that the contractor had not previously submitted to the contracting officer); Clearwater Constructors, Inc. v. United States, 56 Fed. Cl. 303 (2003) (a subcontractor's letter detailing its dissatisfaction with a contracting officer's contract interpretation, attached to a contractor's cover-letter requesting a formal review and decision, constituted a non-monetary claim under the CDA).

2.   Seeking as a matter of right,[5] one of the following:

- Payment of money in a sum certain;
- Adjustment or interpretation of contract terms. TRW, Inc., ASBCA Nos. 51172 and 51530, 99-2 BCA ¶ 30,047 (seeking decision on allowability and allocability of certain costs). Compare William D. Euille & Assocs., Inc. v. General Services Administration, GSBCA No. 15,261, 2000 GSBCA LEXIS 105 (May 3, 2000) (dispute concerning directive to remove and replace building materials proper contract interpretation claim), with Rockhill Industries, Inc., ASBCA No. 51541, 00-1 BCA ¶ 30,693 (money claim "masquerading as claim for contract interpretation");
- Other relief arising under or relating to the contract. See General Electric Co.; Bayport Constr. Co., ASBCA Nos. 36005, 38152, 39696, 91-2 BCA ¶ 23,958 (demand for contractor to replace or correct latent defects under Inspection clause);
- Reformation or Rescission. See McClure Electrical Constructors, Inc. v. United States, 132 F.3d 709 (Fed. Cir. 1997);

---

[5] Some submissions, such as cost proposals for work the government later decides it would like performed, would not be considered submissions seeking payment "as a matter of right." Reflectone v. Dalton, 60 F.3d 1572, n.7 (Fed. Cir. 1995).

LaBarge Products, Inc. v. West, 46 F.3d 1547 (Fed. Cir. 1995) (ASBCA had jurisdiction to entertain reformation claim); or

- Specific performance is not an available remedy. Western Aviation Maintenance, Inc. v. General Services Administration, GSBCA No. 14165, 98-2 BCA ¶ 29,816.

3. Not voucher, invoice, or other routine request for payment or contractual action.

A voucher, invoice, or other routine request for payment that is not in dispute when submitted is not a valid CDA claim. FAR 52.233-1(c). If the invoice is disputed or not paid when due, the contractor may dispute the government's failure to timely pay by filing a claim for non-payment. A contractor may convert such a submission into a valid CDA claim if:

- The contractor complies with the submission and certification requirements of the Disputes clause; and
- The contracting officer disputes the submission as to either liability or amount; or fails to act in a reasonable time. FAR 33.201; FAR 52.233-1. See S-TRON, ASBCA No. 45890, 94-3 BCA ¶ 26,957 (contracting officer's failure to respond for 6 months to contractor's "relatively simple" engineering change proposal (ECP) and REA was unreasonable).

A request for an equitable adjustment (REA) is not a "routine request for payment" and may satisfy the FAR definition of "claim." Reflectone, Inc. v. Dalton, 60 F.3d 1572 (Fed. Cir. 1995).

4. Submitted to the contracting officer for a decision. 41 U.S.C. § 7103(a)(1).

Contractors must submit contract claims in writing to the contracting officer for the contract.

The claim need not be sent only to the contracting officer, or directly to the contracting officer, although a contractor should always do so. If the contractor submits the claim to its primary government contact with a request for a contracting officer's final decision, and the primary contact delivers the claim to the contracting officer, the submission requirement can be met. Neal & Co. v. United States, 945 F.2d 385 (Fed. Cir. 1991) (claim requesting contracting officer's decision addressed to Resident Officer in Charge of Construction). See also D.L. Braughler Co., Inc. v. West, 127 F.3d 1476 (Fed. Cir. 1997) (submission to resident engineer not seeking contracting officer decision not a claim); J&E Salvage Co., 37 Fed. Cl. 256 (1997) (letter submitted to the Department of Justice rather than the Defense Reutilization and Marketing Office was not a claim).

5. A contractor claim should explicitly request a contracting officer's final decision, although implicit requests may prove sufficient. See Ellett Constr. Co., Inc. v. United States, 93 F.3d 1537 (Fed. Cir. 1996) (holding that submission to the contracting officer is required, but the request for a final decision may be implied); Heyl & Patterson, Inc. v. O'Keefe, 986 F.2d 480, 483 (Fed. Cir. 1993) (stating that "a request for a final decision can be implied from the context of the submission"); Transamerica Ins. Corp. v. United States, 973 F.2d 1572, 1576 (Fed. Cir. 1992) (stating that no "magic words" are required "as long as what the contractor desires by its submissions is a final decision").

A contracting officer can't issue a valid final decision if the contractor explicitly states that it is not seeking a final decision. Fisherman's Boat Shop, Inc. ASBCA No. 50324, 97-2 BCA ¶ 29,257 (holding that the contracting officer's final decision was a nullity because the contractor did not intend for its letter submission to be treated as a claim).

6. Certification. An authorized official of the contractor must certify any contractor claim that exceeds $100,000. 41 U.S.C. § 7103(b); FAR 33.207. CDA certification deters contractors from submitting unwarranted or inflated claims. See Fischbach & Moore Int'l Corp. v. Christopher, 987 F.2d 759 (Fed. Cir. 1993). The exact language of the certification appears at FAR 33.207 and FAR 52.233-1.

Contractors should use the language provided, as any changes usually lead to avoidable litigation, and may prejudice contractor recovery. The certification must state:

- The claim is made in good faith;
- The supporting data are accurate and complete to the best of the contractor's knowledge and belief;
- The amount requested accurately reflects the contract adjustment for which the contractor believes the federal government is liable; and
- The certifier is authorized to certify the claim on behalf of the contractor.

Determining the Claim Amount. A contractor need not certify claims under the statutory threshold, currently $100,000. However, if a contractor does not certify a claim that is close to the statutory threshold, or which may grow over time to exceed the statutory threshold, the government may challenge the contractor's failure by alleging the actual amount of the claim is over the statutory threshold.

- A contractor must consider the aggregate effect of increased and decreased costs to determine whether the claim exceeds the dollar threshold for certification.[6] FAR 33.207(d).
- Claims that are based on a "common or related set of operative facts" constitute one claim. Placeway Constr. Corp., 920 F.2d 903 (Fed. Cir. 1990). A contractor

may not split a single claim that exceeds $100,000 into multiple claims to avoid the certification requirement. See, e.g., Walsky Constr. Co v. United States, 3 Ct. Cl. 615 (1983); Warchol Constr. Co. v. United States, 2 Cl. Ct. 384 (1983); D&K Painting Co., Inc., DOTCAB No. 4014, 98-2 BCA ¶ 30,064; Columbia Constr. Co., ASBCA No. 48536, 96-1 BCA ¶ 27,970; Jay Dee Militarywear, Inc., ASBCA No. 46539, 94-2 BCA ¶ 26,720.

- A contractor need not certify separate claims, each of which is less than $100,000 and individually require no certification, even if their combined total exceeds $100,000. See Engineered Demolition, Inc. v. United States, 60 Fed. Cl. 822 (2204) (holding that appellants claim of $69,047 and $38,940 sponsored on behalf of appellant's sub-contractor were separate, having arose out of different factual predicates, each under $100,000.), Phillips Constr. Co., ASBCA No. 27055, 83-2 BCA ¶ 16,618; B. D. Click Co., ASBCA No. 25609, 81-2 BCA ¶ 15,394.
- The contracting officer cannot consolidate separate claims to create a single claim that exceeds $100,000. See B. D. Click Co., Inc., ASBCA No. 25609, 81-2 BCA ¶ 15,395.
- A contractor need not certify a claim that grows to exceed $100,000 after the contractor submits it to the contracting officer if: the increase was based on information that was not reasonably available at the time of the initial submission; or the claim grew as the result of a regularly accruing charge and the passage of time. See Tecom, Inc. v. United States, 732 F.2d 935 (Fed. Cir. 1984) (concluding that the contractor need not certify a $11,000 claim that grew to [exceed the threshold] after the government exercised certain options); AAI Corp. v. United States, 22 Cl. Ct. 541 (1991) (refusing to dismiss a claim that was $0 when submitted, but increased to $500,000 by the time the suit came before the court); Mulunesh

---

[6] The contractor need not include the amount of any government claims in its calculations. J. Slotnik Co., VABCA No. 3468, 92-1 BCA ¶ 24,645.

Berhe, ASBCA No. 49681, 96-2 BCA ¶ 28,339.

E.   Model Contractor Claim.

Attachment A is a sample contractor claim. Please note that the sample mirrors the statutory and regulatory requirements discussed above.

F.   Defective Claims.

1. Since the requirement to certify contract claims was introduced in 1978, considerable litigation has occurred on almost every conceivable aspect of certifying claims. Currently, 41 U.S.C. § 7103(b)(3) permits a contracting officer to request in writing that the contractor correct a "Defective Certification" if the contracting officer acts within 60 days of receiving a claim and provides the reasons why the certification is defective. When the contracting officer timely gives notice of a Defective Certification, the contracting officer is not required to issue a final decision unless the contractor corrects the stated defects.

2. FAR 33.201 defines a "Defective Certification" as a certification "which alters or otherwise deviates from the language in [FAR] 33.207(c) or which is not executed by a person duly authorized to bind the contractor with respect to the claim." The government routinely challenges defective certifications of contractor claims.

3. Proper Certifying Official. A contractor may certify its claim through "any person duly authorized to bind the contractor with respect to the claim." 41 U.S.C. § 7103(b)(2); FAR 33.207(e). See Metric Constructors, Inc., ASBCA No. 50843, 98-2 BCA ¶ 30,088 (concluding that senior project manager was proper certifying official).

A best practice is to expressly designate the individuals who may certify claims in the contractor's written policies with approvals, and to comply with requirements in corporate governance documents (i.e., Articles of Incorporation, By-Laws, etc.), and to verify the designation at the time of executing a certification.

4. Certification Language.

Where a contractor totally omits any certification for claims greater than $100,000, the contractor has not submitted a valid claim. See FAR 33.201 ("Failure to certify shall not be deemed to be a defective certification."); Hamza v. United States, 31 Fed. Cl. 315 (1994) (complete lack of an attempted certification); Eurostyle Inc., ASBCA No. 45934, 94-1 BCA ¶ 26,458 ("complete absence of any certification is not a mere defect which may be corrected").

Certifications made with intentional, reckless, or negligent disregard of CDA certification requirements are not correctable. See Walashek Industrial & Marine, Inc., ASBCA No. 52166, 00-1 BCA ¶ 30,728 (two prongs of certificate omitted or not fairly compliant); Keydata Sys, Inc. v. Department of the Treasury, GSBCA No. 14281-TD, 97-2 BCA ¶ 29,330 (denying the contractor's petition for a final decision because it failed to correct substantial certification defects).

Not all deviations from the precise language in FAR 33.207(c) are "Defective Certifications."[7] Verbatim use of the language in FAR 33.207(c) is not required; substantial compliance suffices. See Fischbach & Moore Int'l Corp. v. Christopher, 987 F.2d 759 (Fed. Cir. 1993) (substituting the word "understanding" for "knowledge" did not render certificate defective).

Technical defects are correctable. Examples include missing certifications when two or more claims are deemed to be

---

[7] In fact, FAR 33.207(c) deviates slightly from the statutory language in 41 U.S.C. § 7103(b)(3).

a larger claim requiring certification, and certification by the wrong representative of the contractor. See H.R. Rep. No. 102-1006, 102d Cong., 2d Sess. 28, reprinted in 1992 U.S.C.C.A. at 3921, 3937.

Certifications used for other purposes may be acceptable even though they do not include the language required by the CDA. See James M. Ellett Const. Co., Inc. v. United States, 93 F.3d 1537 (Fed. Cir. 1996) (SF 1436 termination proposal not substantially deficient as a CDA certificate); Metric Constructors, Inc., ASBCA No. 50843, 98-2 BCA ¶ 30,088. Compare SAE/American - Mid-Atlantic, Inc., GSBCA No. 12294, 94-2 BCA ¶ 26,890 (holding that the contractor's "certificate of current cost or pricing data" on SF 1411 was susceptible of correction, even though it did not include the first and third statements required for a proper CDA certification), with Scan-Tech Security, L.P. v. United States, 46 Fed. Cl. 326 (2000) (suit dismissed after court equated use of SF 1411 with no certification).

Interest on a claim with a defective certification shall be paid from the date the contracting officer initially received the claim. 41 U.S.C. § 7109(a)(2).

A defective certification will not deprive a court or board of jurisdiction, but it must be corrected before entry of a court's final judgment or a board's decision. 41 U.S.C. § 7103(b)(3).

5. Notwithstanding the above, the best practice is to use the exact language in FAR 33.207(c).

G. Demand for a Sum Certain.

1. Where a contractor submits a monetary claim, the contractor must demand a sum certain as a matter of right. Compare Essex Electro Eng'rs, Inc. v. United States, 22 Cl. Ct. 757, aff'd, 960 F.2d 1576 (Fed. Cir. 1992) (holding that a cost proposal for possible future work did not seek a sum

certain as a matter of right); with J.S. Alberici Constr. Co., ENG BCA No. 6179, 97-1 BCA ¶ 28,639, recon. denied, ENG BCA No. 6179-R, 97-1 BCA ¶ 28,919 (holding that a request for costs associated with ongoing work, but not yet incurred, was a sum certain); McDonnell Douglas Corp., ASBCA No. 46582, 96-2 BCA ¶ 28,377 (holding that a sum certain can exist even if the contractor has not yet incurred any costs); Fairchild Indus., ASBCA No. 46197, 95-1 BCA ¶ 27,594 (holding that a request based on estimated future costs was a sum certain).

2. The best practice for contractor monetary claims is to expressly demand payment of a specific amount. See Attachment A.

3. A claim states a sum certain if:

The government can determine the amount of the claim using a simple mathematical formula. Metric Constr. Co. v. United States, 1 Cl. Ct. 383 (1983); Mulunesh Berhe, ASBCA No. 49681, 96-2 BCA ¶ 28,339 (simple multiplication of requested monthly rate for lease); Jepco Petroleum, ASBCA No. 40480, 91-2 BCA ¶ 24,038 (claim requesting additional $3 per linear foot of excavation, when multiplied by total of 10,000 feet, produced sum certain).

Enlarged claim doctrine. Under this doctrine, a BCA or the COFC may exercise jurisdiction over a dispute that involves a sum in excess of that presented to the contracting officer for a final decision if:

• The increase in the amount of the claim is based on the same set of operative facts previously presented to the contracting officer; and
• The contractor neither knew nor reasonably should have known, at the time when the claim was presented to the contracting officer, of the factors justifying an increase in the amount of the claim. Johnson Controls World Services, Inc. v. United States, 43 Fed.

Cl. 589 (1999). See also Stencel Aero Engineering Corp., ASBCA No. 28654, 84-1 BCA ¶ 16,951 (finding essential character or elements of the certified claim had not been changed).

H. Supporting Data.

1. Invoices, detailed cost breakdowns, and other supporting financial documentation need not accompany a CDA claim as a jurisdictional prerequisite. H.L. Smith v. Dalton, 49 F.3d 1563 (Fed. Cir. 1995) (contractor's failure to provide CO with additional information "simply delayed action on its claims"); John T. Jones Constr. Co., ASBCA No. 48303, 96-1 BCA ¶ 27,997 (stating that the contracting officer's desire for more information did not invalidate the contractor's claim submission).

2. A contractor best practice is to include a cost proposal conforming to the requirements in FAR 15.403-5, and agency supplements, supporting the sum certain claimed. This will facilitate the contracting officer's review of the claim.

I. Settlement.

1. Agencies should attempt to resolve claims by mutual agreement, if possible. FAR 33.204; FAR 33.210. See Pathman Constr. Co., Inc. v. United States, 817 F.2d 1573 (Fed. Cir. 1987) (stating that a "major purpose" of the CDA is to "induce resolution of contract disputes with the government by negotiation rather than litigation").

2. Only contracting officers or their authorized representatives may normally settle contract claims. See FAR 33.210; see also J.H. Strain & Sons, Inc., ASBCA No. 34432, 88-3 BCA ¶ 20,909 (refusing to enforce a settlement agreement that the agency's attorney entered into without authority). The Department of Justice (DOJ), however, has plenary authority to settle cases pending before the COFC. See

Executive Business Media v. Department of Defense, 3 F.3d 759 (4th Cir. 1993).

3. Contracting officers are authorized, within the limits of their warrants, to decide or resolve all claims arising under or relating to the contract except for:

- A claim or dispute for penalties or forfeitures prescribed by statute or regulation that another federal agency is specifically authorized to administer, settle, or determine; or

- The settlement, compromise, payment, or adjustment of any claim involving fraud.[8] FAR 33.210.

4. Submission of a CDA claim to a contracting officer often induces serious settlement discussions, rather than ending settlement discussions.

J. Interest.

1. Contractors are entitled to interest on the amount ultimately found due. 41 U.S.C. § 7109. Interest runs from the date the contractor's claim is received by the contracting officer.

2. Interest may begin to accrue on costs before the contractor incurs them. See Servidone Constr. Corp. v. United States, 931 F.2d 860 (Fed. Cir. 1991) (stating that 41 U.S.C. § [7109] "sets a single, red-letter date for the interest of all amounts found due by a court without regard to when the contractor incurred the costs"); see also Caldera v. J.S. Alberici Constr. Co., 153 F.3d 1381 (Fed Cir. 1998)

---

[8] When a claim is suspected to be fraudulent, the contracting officer shall refer the matter to the agency official responsible for investigating fraud. FAR 33.209. To justify a stay in a board proceeding, the movant has the burden to show there are substantially similar issues, facts, and witnesses in civil and criminal proceedings, and there is a need to protect the criminal litigation that overrides any injury to the parties by staying the civil litigation. Afro-Lecon, Inc. v. United States, 820 F.2d 1198 (Fed. Cir. 1987); T. Iida Contracting, Ltd., ASBCA No. 51865, 00-1 BCA ¶ 30,626.

(holding that 41 U.S.C. § [7109] "trumps" conflicting regulations that prohibit claims for future costs).

3. Interest on CDA claims is calculated every six months based on a rate established by the Secretary of the Treasury pursuant to Pub. L. No. 92-41, 85 Stat. 97. 41 U.S.C. § 7109; FAR 33.208.

4. Established interest rates can be found at www.publicdebt. treas.gov.

K.   Termination for Convenience (T4C) Settlement Proposals. FAR 49.206.

1. A contractor may submit a settlement proposal for costs associated with the termination of a contract for the convenience of the government. FAR 49.206-1; FAR 49.602-1. See Standard Form (SF) 1435, Settlement Proposal (Inventory Basis); SF 1436, Settlement Proposal (Total Cost Basis); SF 1437, Settlement Proposal for Cost-Reimbursement Type Contracts; SF 1438, Settlement Proposal (Short Form). Typically, the contractor submits a termination settlement proposal to the contracting officer. If negotiations fail to reach agreement on a settlement, then the contractor updates the proposal and incorporates the updated proposal into a CDA claim submitted for final decision.

2. Courts and boards consider T4C settlement proposals to be "nonroutine" submissions under the CDA. See Ellett, 93 F.3d at 1542 (stating that "it is difficult to conceive of a less routine demand for payment than one which is submitted when the government terminates a contract for its convenience").

Courts and boards, however, do not consider T4C settlement proposals to be CDA claims when submitted because contractors normally do not submit them for a contracting officer's final decision— they submit them to facilitate negotiations. See Ellett Constr. Co., Inc. v. United

States, 93 F.3d 1537 (Fed. Cir. 1996) (T4C settlement proposal was not a claim because the contractor did not submit it to the contracting officer for a final decision); see also Walsky Constr. Co. v. United States, 173 F.3d 1312 (Fed. Cir. 1999) (T4C settlement proposal was not a claim because it had not yet been the subject of negotiations with the government); cf. Medina Constr., Ltd. v. United States, 43 Fed. Cl. 537, 551 (1999) (parties may reach an impasse without entering into negotiations if allegations of fraud prevent the contracting officer from entering into negotiations).

A T4C settlement proposal may "ripen" into a CDA claim once settlement negotiations reach an impasse. See Ellett, 93 F.3d at 1544 (holding that the contractor's request for a final decision following ten months of "fruitless negotiations" converted its T4C settlement proposal into a claim); Metric Constructors, Inc., ASBCA No. 50843, 98-2 BCA ¶ 30,088 (holding that a contractor's T4C settlement proposal ripened into a claim when the contracting officer issued a unilateral contract modification following the parties' unsuccessful negotiations); cf. FAR 49.109-7(f) (stating that a contractor may appeal a "settlement by determination" under the Disputes clause unless the contractor failed to submit its T4C settlement proposal in a timely manner).

3. Certification. If a CDA certification is required, the contractor may rely on the standard certification in whichever SF the FAR requires it to submit. See Ellett, 93 F.3d at 1545 (rejecting the government's argument that proper certification of a T4C settlement proposal is a jurisdictional prerequisite); see also Metric Constructors, Inc., supra (concluding that the contractor could "correct" the SF 1436 certification to comply with the CDA certification requirements).

4. Interest. Interest does not run on a T4C settlement proposal. FAR 49.112-2(d). CDA interest does commence once the T4C settlement proposal is converted into a claim. See Ellett, 93 F.3d at 1545 (recognizing the fact that T4C settlement proposals are treated disparately for interest purposes); see also Central Envtl, Inc., ASBCA 51086, 98-2 BCA ¶ 29,912 (concluding that interest did not begin to run until after the parties' reached an impasse and the contractor requested a contracting officer's final decision).

L. Statute of Limitations.

1. Contractor claims are subject to a six-year statute of limitations. 41 U.S.C. § 7103(a)(4)(A). The contractor must submit a proper claim to the contracting officer within six years of claim accrual.

2. The current statute of limitations was enacted to reverse the Federal Circuit's 1987 decision that concluded that the six-year statute of limitations in the Tucker Act does not apply to CDA appeals. Pathman Constr. Co. v. United States, 817 F.2d 1573 (Fed. Cir. 1987).

3. In 1994, Congress amended the CDA to impose a six-year statute of limitations. Federal Acquisition Streamlining Act of 1994, Pub. L. No. 103-355, 108 Stat. 3243. See FAR 33.206; see also Motorola, Inc. v. West, 125 F.3d 1470 (Fed. Cir. 1997). The amended statute of limitations applies to contracts awarded on or after 1 October 1995.

V. GOVERNMENT CLAIMS.

A. Requirement for Final Decision. 41 U.S.C. § 7103(a)(3); FAR 52.233-1(d)(1).

1. The government may assert a claim against a contractor; however, the government claim must be the subject of a contracting officer's final decision.

2. Routine government actions, such as audit reports, letters, e-mails, etc., which are not contracting officer final decisions do not assert claims. They do, however, provide evidence that a government claim has accrued.

3. Some government actions are immediately appealable.

Termination for Default. A contracting officer's decision to terminate a contract for default is an immediately appealable government claim. Independent Mfg. & Serv. Cos. of Am., Inc., ASBCA No. 47636, 94-3 BCA ¶ 27,223. See Malone v. United States, 849 F.2d 1441, 1443 (Fed. Cir. 1988); cf. Educators Assoc., Inc. v. United States, 41 Fed. Cl. 811 (1998) (dismissing the contractor's suit as untimely because the contractor failed to appeal within 12 months of the date it received the final termination decision) If a contractor desires to appeal a default termination it should do so within the statutory time limits.

Withholding Monies. A contracting officer's decision to withhold monies otherwise due the contractor is an immediately appealable government claim. Placeway Constr. Corp. United States, 920 F.2d 903, 906 (Fed. Cir. 1990); Sprint Communications Co., L.P. v. General Servs. Admin., GSBCA No. 14263, 97-2 BCA ¶ 29,249.

Cost Accounting Standards (CAS) Determination. A contracting officer's decision regarding CAS is often an immediately appealable government claim. See Newport News Shipbuilding and Dry Dock Co. v. United States, 44 Fed. Cl. 613 (1999) (government's demand that the contractor change its accounting for all of its CAS-covered contracts was an appealable final decision); Litton Sys., Inc., ASBCA No. 45400, 94-2 BCA ¶ 26,895 (holding that the government's determination was an appealable government claim because the government was "seeking, as a matter of right, the adjustment or interpretation of contract terms"); cf. Aydin Corp., ASBCA No. 50301, 97-2 BCA ¶ 29,259 (holding that the contracting officer's failure to present a claim arising under CAS was a non-jurisdictional error).

Miscellaneous Demands. See Bean Horizon-Weeks (JV), ENG BCA No. 6398, 99-1 BCA ¶ 30,134 (holding that a post-appeal letter demanding repayment for improper work was an appealable final decision); Outdoor Venture Corp., ASBCA No. 49756, 96-2 BCA ¶ 28,490 (holding that the government's demand for warranty work was a claim that the contractor could immediately appeal); Sprint Communications Co. v. General Servs. Admin., GSBCA No. 13182, 96-1 BCA ¶ 28,068. But see Boeing Co., 25 Cl. Ct. 441 (1992) (holding that a post-termination letter demanding the return of unliquidated progress payments was not appealable); Iowa-Illinois Cleaning Co. v. General Servs. Admin., GSBCA No. 12595, 95-2 BCA ¶ 27,628 (holding that government deductions for deficient performance are not appealable absent a contracting officer's final decision).

4.   As a general rule, the government may <u>not</u> assert a counterclaim in litigation that has not been the subject of a contracting officer's final decision.

B.   **Contractor Notice.** Typically, assertion of a government claim is a two-step process. The contracting officer sends the contractor a demand letter containing notice of the potential claim and an opportunity to respond. If the contracting officer continues to believe the government has a valid claim, he or she issues a final decision. See FAR 33.211(a) ("When a claim by or against a contractor cannot be satisfied or settled by mutual agreement and a decision on the claim is necessary"); Instruments & Controls Serv. Co., ASBCA No. 38332, 89-3 BCA ¶ 22,237 (dismissing appeal because final decision not preceded by demand); <u>see also</u> Bean Horizon-Weeks (JV), ENG

BCA No. 6398, 99-1 BCA ¶ 30,134; B.L.I. Constr. Co., ASBCA No. 40857, 92-2 BCA ¶ 24,963 (stating that "[w]hen the government is considering action, the contractor should be given an opportunity to state its position, express its views, or explain, argue against, or contest the proposed action").

C.   **Certification.** Neither party is required to certify a government claim. 41 U.S.C. § 7103(b). See Placeway Constr. Corp., 920 F.2d at 906; Charles W. Ware, GSBCA No. 10126, 90-2 BCA ¶ 22,871. A contractor, however, must certify its request for interest on monies deducted or withheld by the government. General Motors Corp., ASBCA No. 35634, 92-3 BCA ¶ 25,149.

D.   **Interest.** The government's entitlement to interest is based on the contract clause, FAR 52.232-17, Interest. Interest on a government claim begins to run when the contractor receives the government's initial written demand for payment. FAR 52.232-17(e).

VI.   CONTRACTING OFFICER FINAL DECISIONS.

A.   **General.**

1.   The purpose of the contracting officer issuing a final decision is to allow the contracting officer to perform a quasi-judicial review of the claim and issue a written decision that summarizes the dispute, states the contracting officer's decision on the dispute, and notifies the contractor of its right to appeal the final decision.

2.   The contracting officer must issue a <u>written</u> final decision on all claims within a reasonable time. 41 U.S.C. § 7103(f)(3); FAR 33.206; FAR 33.211(a). See Tyger Constr. Co., ASBCA No. 36100, 88-3 BCA ¶ 21,149. But cf. McDonnell Douglas Corp., ASBCA No. 44637, 93-2 BCA ¶ 25,700 (dismissing the contractor's appeal from a government claim for

noncompliance with CAS because the procuring contracting officer issued the final decision instead of the cognizant administrative contracting officer as required by the FAR and DFARS).

B.   Time Limits. A contracting officer must issue a final decision on a contractor's claim within certain statutory time limits. 41 U.S.C. § 7103(f)(1)-(3); FAR 33.211.

1.   Claims of $100,000 or less. The contracting officer must issue a final decision within 60 days.

2.   Certified Claims Exceeding $100,000. Within 60 days, the contracting officer must take one of the following actions:

Issue a final decision; or

Notify the contractor of a reasonable and firm date by which the contracting officer will issue a final decision.[9] See Boeing Co. v. United States, 26 Cl. Ct. 257 (1992); Aerojet Gen. Corp., ASBCA No. 48136, 95-1 BCA ¶ 27,470 (concluding that the contracting officer failed to provide a firm date where the contracting officer made the timely issuance of a final decision contingent on the contractor's cooperation in providing additional information); Inter-Con Security Sys., Inc., ASBCA No. 45749, 93-3 BCA ¶ 26,062 (concluding that the contracting officer failed to provide a firm date where the contracting officer merely promised to render a final decision within 60 days of receiving the audit).

If a contracting officer takes more than 60 days to issue a final decision on claims

over $100,000, he or she must issue the decision within a reasonable period of time. 41. U.S.C. § 7103(f)(3).

3.   There are no consequences for a contracting officer failing to comply with this statutory duty. Unfortunately, contracting officers often fail to comply.

4.   Uncertified and Defectively Certified Claims Exceeding $100,000.

FAR 33.211(e) Where a contractor fails to certify a claim over $100,000, the contracting officer has no obligation to issue a final decision. Where the contractor has made a "Defective Certification," the contracting officer must notify the contractor, in writing, within 60 days of the date the contracting officer received the claim of the reason(s) why any attempted certification was defective.

5.   Contracting Officer Failure to Issue a Final Decision. 41 U.S.C. § 7103(f)(5) and FAR 33.211(g) provide that, if the contracting officer fails to issue a final decision within a reasonable period of time, the contractor can exercise its appeal rights from contracting officer's "deemed denial" of the contractor's claim.[10] 41 U.S.C. § 7103(f)(5); FAR 33.211(g). See Aerojet Gen. Corp., ASBCA No. 48136, 95-1 BCA ¶ 27,470.

Alternatively, the contractor may request the tribunal concerned to direct the contracting officer to issue a final decision. 41 U.S.C. § 7103(f)(4); FAR 33.211(f). See American Industries, ASBCA No. 26930-15, 82-1 BCA ¶ 15,753.

A tribunal, however, cannot direct the contracting officer to issue a more detailed final decision than the contracting officer

---

[9] The contracting officer must issue the final decision within a reasonable period. What constitutes a "reasonable" period depends on the size and complexity of the claim, the adequacy of the contractor's supporting data, and other relevant factors. 41 U.S.C. § 7103(f)(3); FAR 33.211(d). See Defense Sys. Co., ASBCA No. 50534, 97-2 BCA ¶ 28,981 (holding that nine months to review a $72 million claim was reasonable).

[10] Where the contracting officer fails to issue a final decision on a government claim within a reasonable time following the contracting officer's issuance of a demand for payment, the contractor normally patiently waits for the six-year statute of limitations to expire.

has already issued. <u>A.D. Roe Co.</u>, ASBCA No. 26078, 81-2 BCA ¶ 15,231.

C. **Final Decision Format.** 41 U.S.C. § 7103(e); FAR 33.211(a)(4).

1. The final decision must be <u>written</u>. <u>Tyger Constr. Co.</u>, ASBCA No. 36100, 88-3 BCA ¶ 21,149.

2. In addition, the final decision must:

- Describe the claim or dispute;
- Refer to the pertinent or disputed contract terms;
- State the disputed and undisputed facts;[11]
- State the decision and explain the contracting officer's rationale;
- Advise the contractor of its appeal rights; and
- Demand the repayment of any indebtedness to the government.

3. Notice of Appeal Rights.

FAR 33.211(a)(4)(v) specifies that the final decision should include a paragraph substantially as follows:

This is a final decision of the Contracting Officer. You may appeal this decision to the agency board of contract appeals. If you decide to appeal, you must, within 90 days from the date you receive this decision, mail or otherwise furnish written notice to the agency board of contract appeals and provide a copy to the Contracting Officer from whose decision the appeal is taken. The notice shall indicate that an appeal is intended, reference this decision, and identify the contract by number. With regard to appeals to the agency board of contract appeals, you may, solely at your

election, proceed under the board's small claim procedure for claims of $50,000 or less or its accelerated procedure for claims of $100,000 or less. Instead of appealing to the agency board of contract appeals, you may bring an action directly in the United States Court of Federal Claims (except as provided in the Contract Disputes Act of 1978, 41 U.S.C. 7102(d), regarding Maritime Contracts) within 12 months of the date you receive this decision.

Failure to properly notify the contractor of its appeal rights <u>may</u> prevent the "appeals clock" from starting. If the contracting officer's notice is deficient, the contractor may demonstrate detrimental reliance upon the faulty advice. <u>Decker & Co. v. West</u>, 76 F.3d 1573 (Fed. Cir. 1996).

D. **Delivery**. 41 U.S.C. § 7103(d); FAR 33.211(b).

1. The contracting officer must mail (or otherwise furnish) a copy of the final decision to the contractor. <u>See</u> <u>Images II, Inc.</u>, ASBCA No. 47943, 94-3 BCA ¶ 27,277 (holding that receipt by the contractor's employee constituted proper notice).

2. Because the date of receipt may become an important fact, the contracting officer should use a method of delivery that generates evidence of receipt, such as: certified mail, return receipt requested; Federal Express; hand delivery with written receipt; etc. A facsimile (FAX) transmission may also provide adequate evidence of receipt. The contracting officer should preserve all evidence of the date the contractor received the contracting officer's final decision. <u>See</u> <u>Omni Abstract, Inc.</u>, ENG BCA No. 6254, 96-2 BCA ¶ 28,367 (relying on a government attorney's affidavit to determine when the 90-day appeals period started).

When hand delivering the final decision, the contracting officer should require the contractor to sign for the document.

---

[11] Specific findings of fact are <u>not</u> required and, if made, are <u>not</u> binding on the government in any subsequent proceedings. <u>See</u> <u>Wilner v. United States</u>, 24 F.3d 1397 (Fed. Cir. 1994) (concluding that admissions favorable to the contractor do not constitute evidence of government liability).

When using a FAX transmission, the contracting officer should confirm receipt and memorialize the confirmation in a written memorandum. See Mid-Eastern Indus., Inc., ASBCA No. 51287, 98-2 BCA ¶ 29,907 (concluding that the government established a prima facie case by presenting evidence to show that it successfully transmitted the final decision to the contractor's FAX number); see also Public Service Cellular, Inc., ASBCA No. 52489, 00-1 BCA ¶ 30,832 (transmission report not sufficient evidence of receipt).

E-mail is generally insufficient. See Trygve Dale Westergard v. Services Administration, CBCA No. 2522, Sept. 15, 2011 (Board denied the government request to dismiss the appeal as untimely because the contracting officer submitted the final decision to the contractor via e-mail and could not provide any proof of a return receipt).

E. **Independent Act of a Contracting Officer**.

1. The final decision must be the contracting officer's personal, independent act. Compare PLB Grain Storage Corp. v. Glickman, 113 F.3d 1257 (Fed. Cir. 1997) (unpub.) (holding that a termination was proper even though a committee of officials directed it); Charitable Bingo Associates d/b/a Mr. Bingo, Inc., ASBCA Nos. 53249, 53470, 05-01 BCA 32,863 (finding the Contracting Officer utilized independent judgment in terminating appellant's contract after the Assistant Secretary of the Army (MR&A) issued a policy memorandum prohibiting contractor-operated bingo programs within the Army MWR programs) with Climatic Rainwear Co. v. United States, 88 F. Supp. 415 (Ct. Cl. 1950) (holding that a termination was improper because the contracting officer's attorney prepared the termination findings without the contracting officer's participation).

2. The contracting officer should seek assistance from engineers, attorneys, auditors, and other advisors. See FAR 1.602-2 (requiring the contracting officer to request and consider the advice of "specialists," as appropriate); FAR 33.211(a)(2) (requiring the contracting officer to seek assistance from "legal and other advisors"); see also Pacific Architects & Eng'rs, Inc. v. United States, 203 Ct. Cl. 499, 517 (1974) (opining that it is unreasonable to preclude the contracting officer from seeking legal advice); Prism Constr. Co., ASBCA No. 44682, 97-1 BCA ¶ 28,909 (indicating that the contracting officer is not required to independently investigate the facts of a claim before issuing final decision); Environmental Devices, Inc., ASBCA No. 37430, 93-3 BCA ¶ 26,138 (approving the contracting officer's communications with the user agency prior to terminating the contract for default); cf. AR 27-1, para. 15-5a (noting the "particular importance" of the contracts attorney's role in advising the contracting officer on the drafting of a final decision).

F. **Finality**. 41 U.S.C. § 7103(g).

1. Once the contracting officer's decision becomes final (i.e., once the appeal period has passed), the contractor cannot challenge the merits of that decision judicially. 41 U.S.C. § 7103(g). See Seaboard Lumber Co. v. United States, 903 F.2d 1560, 1562 (Fed. Cir. 1990); L.A. Constr., Inc., 95-1 BCA ¶ 27,291 (holding that the contractor's failure to appeal the final decision in a timely manner deprived the board of jurisdiction, even though both parties testified on the merits during the hearing).

2. A final decision is binding and conclusive unless timely appealed.

3. Reconsideration of Final Decisions.

A contracting officer may reconsider, withdraw, or rescind a final decision before the expiration of the appeals period. General Dynamics Corp., ASBCA No.

39866, 91-2 BCA ¶ 24,017. Cf. Daniels & Shanklin Constr. Co., ASBCA No. 37102, 89-3 BCA ¶ 22,060 (rejecting the contractor's assertion that the contracting officer could not withdraw a final decision granting its claim, and indicating that the contracting officer has an obligation to do so if the final decision is erroneous).

The contracting officer's rescission of a final decision, however, will not necessarily deprive a BCA of jurisdiction because jurisdiction vests as soon as the contractor files its appeal. See Security Servs., Inc., GSBCA No. 11052, 92-1 BCA ¶ 24,704; cf. McDonnell Douglas Astronautics Co., ASBCA No. 36770, 89-3 BCA ¶ 22,253 (indicating that the board would sustain a contractor's appeal if the contracting officer withdrew the final decision after the contractor filed its appeal). Thus, a contracting officer is unable to deprive the Board or Court of Federal Claims of jurisdiction by withdrawing a timely appealed final decision.

A contracting officer may vacate his or her final decision unintentionally by agreeing to meet with the contractor to discuss the matters in dispute. See Sach Sinha and Assocs., ASBCA No. 46916, 95-1 BCA ¶ 27,499 (finding that the contracting officer "reconsidered" her final decision after she met with the contractor as a matter of "business courtesy" and requested the contractor to submit its proposed settlement alternatives in writing); Royal Int'l Builders Co., ASBCA No. 42637, 92-1 BCA ¶ 24,684 (holding that the contracting officer "destroyed the finality of his initial decision" by agreeing to meet with the contractor, even though the meeting was cancelled and the contracting officer subsequently sent the contractor a letter stating his intent to stand by his original decision).

To restart the appeal period after reconsidering a final decision, the contracting officer must issue a new final decision. Information Sys. & Networks

Corp. v. United States, 17 Cl. Ct. 527 (1989); Sach Sinha and Assocs., ASBCA No. 46916, 95-1 BCA ¶ 27,499; Birken Mfg. Co., ASBCA No. 36587, 89-2 BCA ¶ 21,581.

4. The Fulford Doctrine. A contractor may dispute an underlying default termination as part of a timely appeal from a government demand for excess reprocurement costs, even though the contractor failed to appeal the underlying default termination in a timely manner. Fulford Mfg. Co., ASBCA No. 2143, 6 CCF ¶ 61,815 (May 20, 1955); Deep Joint Venture, GSBCA No. 14511, 02-2 BCA ¶ 31,914 (GSBCA confirms validity of the Fulford doctrine for post-CDA terminations).

G. Practice Notes.

1. Contractor and government contracting personnel should carefully follow the procedures regarding claims, and document their compliance. Otherwise, they may engage in needless litigation on procedural matters, rather than the substance of the dispute.

2. It is in the best interests of both the government and its contractors to resolve disputes fairly and quickly. The contractor can support an early and fair resolution by submitting a factually and legally supported claim, following the statutory and regulatory procedures. The government can support an early and fair resolution by devoting the resources necessary to objectively and carefully review both the allegations in the claim, and the factual context of the claim. Each party should consider their costs and risks in litigation.

VII. APPEALS TO THE BOARD OF CONTRACT APPEALS.

A. The Right to Appeal. 41 U.S.C. § 7104. A contractor may appeal a contracting officer's final decision to their agency

BCA. For defense agencies and NASA, that is the Armed Services Board of Contract Appeals. For civilian agencies, that is the Civilian Board of Contract Appeals, although the TVA and the U.S. Postal Service also operate boards of contract appeals. This chapter focuses on appeals to the Armed Services Board of Contract Appeals, as DOD contracts typically constitute 70% of all federal contracts.

B. The Armed Services Board of Contract Appeals (ASBCA or Board).

1. Administrative Judges. The ASBCA consists of 25-30 administrative judges who receive and dispose of roughly 500-1,000 appeals per year. ASBCA judges specialize in contract disputes and come from both the government and private sectors. Each judge has at least five years of experience working in the field of government contract law, and most have decades of experience.

2. The Rules of the Armed Services Board of Contract Appeals appear in Appendix A of the DFARS.

C. Jurisdiction. 41 U.S.C. § 7105(a). The ASBCA has jurisdiction to decide appeals regarding contracts made by:

1. The Department of Defense;

2. NASA; and

3. Agencies that have designated the ASBCA to decide the appeal.

D. Standard of Review. Boards of Contract Appeals review appeals of contracting officer final decisions de novo. See 41 U.S.C. § 605(a) (indicating that the contracting officer's specific findings of fact are not binding in any subsequently proceedings); see also Wilner v. United States, 24 F.3d 1397 (Fed. Cir. 1994) (en banc); Precision Specialties, Inc., ASBCA No. 48717, 96-1 BCA ¶ 28,054 (final

decision retains no presumptive evidentiary weight nor is it binding on the Board).

E. Procedures for Appealing a Contracting Officer Final Decision.

1. Requirement. A contractor's notice of appeal shall be mailed or otherwise furnished to the Board within 90 days from date of receipt of the final decision. DFARS Appendix A, Rule 1.(a); 41 U.S.C. § 7104. The ASBCA Rule 1 states a copy shall be furnished to the contracting officer. See Cosmic Constr. Co. v. United States, 697 F.2d 1389 (Fed. Cir. 1982) (90-day filing requirement is statutory and cannot be waived by the Board); Rex Sys, Inc., ASBCA No. 50456, 98-2 BCA ¶ 29,956 (refusing to dismiss a contractor's appeal simply because the contractor failed to send a copy of the NOA to the contracting officer).

2. Filing an appeal with the contracting officer can satisfy the Board's notice requirement. See Hellenic Express, ASBCA No. 47129, 94-3 BCA ¶ 27,189 (citing Yankee Telecomm. Lab., ASBCA No. 25240, 82-2 BCA ¶ 15,515, for the proposition that "filing an appeal with the contracting officer is tantamount to filing with the Board"); cf. Brunner Bau GmbH, ASBCA No. 35678, 89-1 BCA ¶ 21,315 (holding that notice to the government counsel was a filing).

3. Methods of filing.

Mail. The written NOA can be sent to the ASBCA or to the contracting officer via the U.S. Postal Service. See Thompson Aerospace, Inc., ASBCA Nos. 51548, 51904, 99-1 BCA ¶ 30,232 (notice mailed to the contracting officer timely filed).

Otherwise furnishing, such as through commercial courier service. North Coast Remfg., Inc., ASBCA No. 38599, 89-3 BCA ¶ 22,232 (notice delivered by Federal Express courier service not accorded same status as U.S. mail service and was therefore untimely).

4. Contents. An adequate notice of appeal must:

- Be in writing. See Lows Enter., ASBCA No. 51585, 00-1 BCA ¶ 30,622 (holding that verbal notice is insufficient).
- Express dissatisfaction with the contracting officer's decision;
- Manifest an intent to appeal the decision to a higher authority, see, e.g., McNamara-Lunz Vans & Warehouse, Inc., ASBCA No. 38057, 89-2 BCA ¶ 21,636 (concluding that a letter stating that "we will appeal your decision through the various avenues open to us" adequately expressed the contractor's intent to appeal); cf. Stewart-Thomas Indus., Inc., ASBCA No. 38773, 90-1 BCA ¶ 22,481 (stating that the intent to appeal to the board must be unequivocal); Birken Mfg. Co., ASBCA No. 37064, 89-1 BCA ¶ 21,248 (concluding that an electronic message to the termination contracting officer did not express a clear intent to appeal); and
- Be timely. 41 U.S.C. § 7104; ASBCA Rule 1(a); Thompson Aerospace, Inc., ASBCA Nos. 51548, 51904, 99-1 BCA ¶ 30,232. A contractor must file its appeal with the Board within 90 days of the date the contractor received the contracting officer's final decision. 41 U.S.C. § 7104. In computing the time taken to appeal (See ASBCA Rule 33(b)):

  (a) Exclude the day the contractor received the contracting officer's final decision; and

  (b) Count the day the contractor mailed (evidenced by postmark by U.S. Postal Service) the notice or that the Board received the notice.

  (c) If the 90th day is a Saturday, Sunday, or legal holiday, the appeals period shall run to the end of the next business day.

5. Practice Pointers.

A contractor who intends to appeal a contracting officer final decision should take the following practical steps:

- Calculate deadlines based on the earliest notice of the final decision.
- File early. There is rarely any benefit in waiting to file a notice of appeal. Missing a jurisdictional deadline because the contractor miscounted, or did not realize it had received the final decision earlier is an avoidable error. Late appeals are fatal to BCA jurisdiction
- Use the U.S. Postal Service, and obtain evidence of mailing. A contractor has perfected its appeal once its notice is mailed. There is no need to prove receipt at the ASBCA, and government security measures may delay alternative delivery methods, such as Federal Express.
- Correctly identify the contract, contracting office, the department or agency involved in the dispute, the decision from which the contractor is appealing, and the amount in dispute.
- Sign the notice by the contractor's duly authorized representative or attorney.

6. The Board liberally construes appeal notices. See Thompson Aerospace, Inc., ASBCA Nos. 51548, 51904, 99-1 BCA ¶ 30,232 (Board jurisdiction where timely mailing of notice to KO, despite Board rejecting its notice mailing).

F.   Regular Appeals.

1. Overview. Litigation before the Armed Services Board of Contract Appeals closely resembles civil litigation, but is tempered by a strong desire to reach a fair and accurate result. Regular appeals are those over $100,000. Accelerated and expedited appeals are smaller claims, and progress quickly, if those procedures are chosen. The procedures for regular appeals are set forth below.

2.   Docketing. ASBCA Rule 3. The ASBCA Recorder (similar to the clerk of court) assigns a docket number and notifies the parties in writing.

3.   Rule 4 (R4) File. ASBCA Rule 4.

- The contracting officer must assemble and transmit an appeal file to the ASBCA and the appellant within 30 days of the date the government receives the docketing notice. Contractors should not be surprised if the appeal file is late.
- The R4 file should contain the relevant documents (e.g., the final decision, the contract, and the pertinent correspondence).
- The appellant may supplement the R4 file within 30 days of the date it receives its copy.[12] The contractor should supplement the R4 file early.

4.   Complaint. ASBCA Rule 6(a).

- Typically, the contractor must file a complaint within 30 days of the date it receives the docketing notice.
- The contractor may request the Board to direct the government to file a complaint when the contractor is appealing a final decision of a government claim. See Northrop Grumman Corp., DOT BCA No. 4041, 99-1 BCA ¶ 30,191 (requiring the government to file the complaint on a government claim).
  The Board does not require a particular format; however, the complaint should set forth: simple, concise, and direct statements of the contractor's claims; the factual and legal basis of each claim; and the amount of each claim, if known.

  If sufficiently detailed, the Board may treat the notice of appeal as the complaint.

5.   Answer. ASBCA Rule 6(b).

- The government (or the contractor if the government is directed to file a complaint) must answer the complaint within 30 days of the date it receives the complaint.
- The answer should set forth simple, concise, and direct statements of the defenses to each of the claims, including any affirmative defenses.
- The Board will often enter a general denial on the government's behalf if the government fails to file its answer in a timely manner.

6.   Discovery. ASBCA Rules 14-15.

The parties may begin discovery as soon as the appellant files the complaint.

The board encourages the parties to engage in voluntary discovery.

Discovery may include depositions, interrogatories, requests for the production of documents, and requests for admission.

7.   Pre-Hearing Conferences. ASBCA Rule 10. The board may hold telephonic pre-hearing conferences to discuss matters that will facilitate the processing and disposition of the appeal.

8.   Motions. ASBCA Rule 5.

Parties must file jurisdictional motions promptly; however, the board may defer its ruling until the hearing.

Parties may also file appropriate non-jurisdictional motions.

9.   Record Submissions. ASBCA Rule 11.

Contract disputes are often decided based on the business records of each party, the express language in the contract, and the well-settled law applicable to the dispute. Either party may waive its right to a hearing and submit its case on the written record.

---

[12] As a practical matter, the ASBCA generally allows either party to supplement the R4 file up to the date of the hearing.

Contract Disputes

When submitting an appeal for decision on the written record, the parties may supplement the record with affidavits, depositions, admissions, etc. See Solar Foam Insulation, ASBCA No. 46921, 94-2 BCA ¶ 26,901.

10.   Hearings. ASBCA Rules 17-25.

- The board will schedule the hearing before a presiding judge and choose the location. In addition to its offices in the Washington, D.C., area, a Board may hold hearings in federal facilities near the contractor; overseas, in secure facilities, or in multiple locations depending on the facts of an appeal.
- Hearings are relatively informal; however, the board generally adheres to the Federal Rules of Evidence.
- Both parties may offer evidence in the form of testimony and exhibits.
- Witnesses generally testify under oath and are subject to cross-examination.
- The board may subpoena witnesses and documents.
- A court reporter will prepare a verbatim transcript of the proceedings.

11.   Briefs. ASBCA Rule 23. Following completion of the hearing. The parties may file post-hearing briefs after they receive the transcript and/or the record is closed. Post-hearing briefs are the equivalent of a written final argument with proposed findings of fact and conclusions of law.

12.   Decisions. ASBCA Rule 28.

The ASBCA issues written decisions.

The presiding judge normally drafts the decision; however, three judges decide the case.

13.   Motions for Reconsideration. ASBCA Rule 29.

Either party may file a motion for reconsideration within 30 days of the date it receives the board's decision.

Motions filed after 30 days are untimely. Bio-temp Scientific, Inc., ASBCA No. 41388, 95-2 BCA ¶ 86,242; Arctic Corner, Inc., ASBCA No. 33347, 92-2 BCA ¶ 24,874.

Absent unusual circumstances, a party may not use a motion for reconsideration to correct errors in its initial presentation. Metric Constructors, Inc., ASBCA No. 46279, 94-2 BCA ¶ 26,827.

14.   Appeals. 41 U.S.C. § 7107(a). Either party may appeal to the Court of Appeals for the Federal Circuit (CAFC) within 120 days of the date it receives the board's decision; however, the government needs the consent of the U.S. Attorney General. 41 U.S.C. § 7107(a)(l)(B).

G.   Accelerated Appeals. 41 U.S.C. § 7106(a); ASBCA Rule 12.3.

1.   Overview. The Contract Disputes Act affords the contractor (but not the government) the right to resolve smaller claims quickly. The Board will aggressively manage the appeal to meet the statutory deadlines.

2.   If the amount in dispute is $100,000 or less, the contractor may choose to proceed under the Board's accelerated procedures.

3.   The Board renders its decision, whenever possible, within 180 days from the date it receives the contractor's election; therefore, the Board encourages the parties to limit (or waive) pleadings, discovery, and briefs.

4.   The presiding judge normally issues the decision with the concurrence of a vice chairman. If these two individuals disagree, the chairman will cast the deciding vote.

Written decisions normally contain only summary findings of fact and conclusions.

If the parties agree, the presiding judge may issue an oral decision at the hearing and follow-up with a memorandum to formalize the decision.

5. Either party may appeal to the CAFC within 120 days of the date it receives the decision.

H. Expedited Appeals. 41 U.S.C. § 7106(b); ASBCA Rule 12.2.

1. If the amount in dispute is $50,000 or less, the contractor may choose to proceed under the Board's expedited procedures.

2. If the contractor is a small business concern, the contractor may elect expedited procedures for claims of $150,000 or less.

3. The Board renders its decision, whenever possible, within 120 days[13] from the date it receives the contractor's election; therefore, the board uses very streamlined procedures (e.g., accelerated pleadings, extremely limited discovery, etc.).

4. The presiding judge decides the appeal.

   Written decision contains only summary finds of fact and conclusions.

   The presiding judge may issue an oral decision from the bench and follow-up with a memorandum to formalize the decision.

5. Neither party may appeal the decision, and the decision has no precedential value. See Palmer v. Barram, 184 F.3d 1373 (Fed. Cir. 1999) (holding that a small claims decision is only appealable for fraud in the proceedings).

I. Remedies.

1. The Board may grant any relief available to a litigant asserting a contract claim in the COFC. 41 U.S.C. § 7105(e)(2).

   Generally, the contractor successfully appealing a final decision seeks money damages. The money damages may either be calculated as an equitable adjustment under a remedy granting clause in the contract, such as the Changes clause; or breach of contract damages.

   The Board may issue a declaratory judgment. See Malone v. United States, 849 F.2d 1441 (Fed. Cir. 1988) (validity of a termination for default). The declaratory judgment may include interpretation of a contract term.

   The Board may award attorney's fees pursuant to the Equal Access to Justice Act (EAJA). 5 U.S.C. § 504. See Hughes Moving & Storage, Inc., ASBCA No. 45346, 00-1 BCA ¶ 30,776 (award decision in T4D case); Oneida Constr., Inc., ASBCA No. 44194, 95-2 BCA ¶ 27,893 (holding that the contractor's rejection of the agency settlement offer, which was more than the amount the board subsequently awarded, did not preclude recovery under the EAJA); cf. Cape Tool & Die, Inc., ASBCA No. 46433, 95-1 BCA ¶ 27,465 (finding rates in excess of the $75 per hour guideline rate reasonable for attorneys in the Washington, D.C., area with government contracts expertise). Q.R. Sys. North, Inc., ASBCA No. 39618, 96-1 BCA ¶ 27,943 (rejecting the contractor's attempt to transfer corporate assets so as to fall within the EAJA ceiling).

   The EAJA applies to parties who meet the financial tests of 5 U.S.C. § 504(b)(1)(B). This excludes larger businesses and wealthier individuals from recovering fees and costs.

2. The Board may not grant specific performance or injunctive relief. General Elec. Automated Sys. Div., ASBCA No. 36214, 89-1 BCA ¶ 21,195. See Western Aviation Maint., Inc. v. General Services

---

[13] In Yardstick Interiors, ASBCA No. 28827 (23 Dec. 1983), the ASBCA issued an oral decision at the end of a contested hearing less than 30 days after the contractor elected an expedited hearing.

Admin, GSBCA No. 14165, 98-2 BCA ¶ 29,816 (holding that the 1992 Tucker Act amendments did not waive the government's immunity from specific performance suits).

3. Interest. The Board shall award to contractor interest on meritorious claims under the Contract Disputes Act. 41 U.S.C. § 7109(a)(1); see paragraph IV.J. above. Because some contract disputes take years to resolve, the award of interest can be substantial.

J. Payment of Judgments. 41 U.S.C. § 7108; 31 U.S.C. §1304.

1. An agency may access the "Judgment Fund" to pay "[a]ny judgment against the United States on a [CDA] claim." 41 U.S.C. § 7108(a). See 31 U.S.C. § 1304; cf. 28 U.S.C. § 2517.

   The Judgment Fund is only available to pay judgments and monetary awards—it is not available to pay informal settlement agreements. See 41 U.S.C. § 7104(b); see also 31 U.S.C. § 1304.

   If an agency lacks sufficient funds to cover an informal settlement agreement, it can "consent" to the entry of a judgment against it. See Bath Irons Works Corp. v. United States, 20 F.3d 1567, 1583 (Fed. Cir. 1994); Casson Constr. Co., GSBCA No. 7276, 84-1 BCA ¶ 17,010 (1983). As a matter of policy, however, it behooves the buying activity to coordinate with its higher headquarters regarding the use of consent decrees since the agency must reimburse the Judgment Fund with current funds. 41 U.S.C. § 7108(c).

2. Prior to payment, both parties must certify that the judgment is "final" (i.e., that the parties will pursue no further review). 31 U.S.C. § 1304(a). See Inland Servs. Corp., B-199470, 60 Comp. Gen. 573 (1981).

3. An agency must repay the Judgment Fund from appropriations current at the time of the award or judgment. 41 U.S.C.

§ 7108(c). Bureau of Land Management, B-211229, 63 Comp. Gen. 308 (1984).

K. Appealing an Adverse Decision. 41 U.S.C. § 7107(a)(1). Board decisions are final unless one of the parties appeals to the CAFC within 120 days after the date the party receives the Board's decision. See Placeway Constr. Corp. v. United States, 713 F.2d 726 (Fed. Cir. 1983).

VIII. APPEALS TO THE COURT OF FEDERAL CLAIMS (COFC). 41 U.S.C. § 7104(b).

A. Choosing a Forum to Hear an Appeal.

1. A contractor receiving a contracting officer's final decision has the option to appeal to the designated Board of Contract Appeals, or to bring an action in the U.S. Court of Federal Claims. There are a number of factors that affect the contractors decision, and they are highlighted below.

2. Forum Availability.

   • Is the Board of Contract Appeals available? If more than 90 days has lapsed since receipt of a final decision, then it is too late to appeal to a Board. The COFC is the only option.
   • Has the contractor elected a forum? As discussed in paragraph II.B.4, the contractor may have previously taken some action that commits it to a particular forum.

3. Government Representation.

   • Agency attorneys handle appeals before Boards of Contract Appeals, while the Department of Justice handles suits in the COFC.
   • By electing the forum, the contractor is choosing the government's lawyers.

4. Judges. Choosing the forum chooses the judges who will decide the case. A contractor should consider how the following attributes affect their election of forum.

- Board of Contract Appeals judges only hear contract appeals, and they are very experienced and knowledgeable about contracting at the agencies they hear appeals from. A Board of Contract Appeals generally is unreceptive to factual arguments that deviate from the written records, legal arguments that deviate from settled law, and emotional arguments that might appeal to a jury. Because three judges decide regular appeals, two of which are not present at the hearing, there is greater scrutiny of the decision.
- COFC judges hear many different types of cases, including patent disputes, vaccine cases, non-CDA contract cases, tax cases, customs cases, etc.. The judges are more generalists than Board judges. Additionally, COFC judges decide their cases alone, not as part of a panel.

5. Formality.

- The COFC adheres to procedural formalities similar to Federal District courts. There is greater motions practice, etc.
- Boards of Contract Appeals are generally less formal than the COFC, with fewer cases resolved in motions practice.

6. Time.

- Board of Contract Appeals litigation of accelerated and expedited claims is fast.
- Larger contract cases at either forum take more time to resolve.

B. **The Right to File Suit**. A contractor may bring an action directly on the claim in the COFC subsequent to receipt of a contracting officer's final decision, or a "deemed denial" of a contractor claim. 41 U.S.C. § 7104(b).

C. **The Court of Federal Claims** (COFC).

1. The COFC hears suits involving government contracts, constitutional claims, tax refunds, Indian claims, civilian and military pay claims, patent and copyright matters, and vaccine injury claims. Over a third of the court's workload concerns contract claims.

2. The President appoints COFC judges for a 15-year term, with the advice and consent of the Senate.

3. The President can reappoint a judge after the initial 15-year term expires.

4. The Federal Circuit can remove a judge for incompetency, misconduct, neglect of duty, engaging in the practice of law, or physical or mental disability.

5. The Rules of the United States Court of Federal Claims (RCFC) appear in an appendix to Title 28 of the United States Code.

D. **Jurisdiction**.

1. The Contract Disputes Act (CDA) of 1978. 41 U.S.C. § 7104(b). The Court has jurisdiction to decide appeals from contracting officers' final decisions.

2. The Federal Courts Administration Act of 1992, Pub. L. No. 102-572, 106 Stat. 4506 (codified at 28 U.S.C. § 1491(a)(2)) granted the COFC jurisdiction to decide nonmonetary claims (e.g., disputes regarding contract terminations, rights in tangible or intangible property, and compliance with cost accounting standards) that arise under section 10(a)(1) of the CDA.

3. The Tucker Act. 28 U.S.C. § 1491(a)(1). The COFC has jurisdiction to decide claims against the United States based on: the Constitution; an act of Congress; an executive regulation; or an express or implied-in-fact contract. The Tucker Act

authorizes the COFC to hear contract claims that are not subject to the CDA.

E. **Standard of Review**. 41 U.S.C. § 7104(b)(4). The COFC will review CDA appeals de novo. The COFC will not presume that the contracting officer's findings of fact and conclusions of law are valid. Instead, the COFC will treat the contracting officer's final decision as one more piece of documentary evidence and weigh it with all of the other evidence in the record. Wilner v. United States, 24 F.3d 1397 (Fed. Cir. 1994) (en banc) (overruling previous case law that a contracting officer's final decision constitutes a "strong presumption or an evidentiary admission" of the government's liability).

F. **Perfecting an Appeal**.

1. Timeliness. 41 U.S.C. § 7104(b)(3); RCFCs 3 and 6.

   A contractor must file its complaint within 12 months of the date it received the contracting officer's final decision. See Janicki Logging Co. v. United States, 124 F.3d 226 (Fed. Cir. 1997) (unpub.); K&S Constr. v. United States, 35 Fed. Cl. 270 (1996); see also White Buffalo Constr., Inc. v. United States, 28 Fed. Cl. 145 (1992) (filing one day after the expiration of the 12-month period rendered it untimely).

   In computing the appeals period, refer to RCFC 6.

2. Filing Method. RCFC 3. The contractor must deliver its complaint to the Clerk of Court. The contractor may do so by mailing the complaint to the COFC, or by hand delivery to the COFC Clerk of Court.

3. Contents. RCFC 8(a); RCFC 9(h).

   If the complaint sets forth a claim for relief, the complaint must contain:

   A "short and plain" statement regarding the COFC's jurisdiction;

A "short and plain" statement showing that the plaintiff is entitled to relief; and

A demand for a judgment.

In addition, the complaint must contain, inter alia:

A statement regarding any action taken on the claim by Congress, a department or agency of the United States, or another tribunal;

A clear citation to any statute, regulation, or executive order upon which the claim is founded; and

A description of any contract upon which the claim is founded.

4. The Election Doctrine. See para. II.B.4, above.

G. **Procedures**.

1. Process. RCFC 4. The Clerk of Court serves five copies of the complaint on the Attorney General (or the Attorney General's designated agent).

2. "Call Letter." 28 U.S.C. § 520.

   The Attorney General must send a copy of the complaint to the responsible military department.

   In response, the responsible military department must provide the Attorney General with a "written statement of all facts, information, and proofs."

3. Answer. RCFCs 8, 12, and 13. The government must answer the complaint within 60 days of the date it receives the complaint.

4. The court rules regulate discovery and pretrial procedures extensively, and the court may impose monetary sanctions for noncompliance with its discovery orders. See M. A. Mortenson Co. v. United States, 996 F.2d 1177 (Fed. Cir. 1993).

5. Decisions may result from either a motion or a trial. Procedures generally mirror those of trials without juries before federal district courts. The judges make written findings of fact and state conclusions of law.

H. Remedies.

1. The COFC has jurisdiction "to afford complete relief on any contract claim brought before the contract is awarded, including declaratory judgments, and such equitable and extraordinary relief as it deems proper." Federal Courts Improvements Act of 1982, Pub. L. No. 97-164, 96 Stat. 40 (codified at 28 U.S.C. § 1491(a)(3)). See Sharman Co., Inc. v. United States, 2 F.3d 1564 (Fed. Cir. 1993).

2. The COFC has no authority to issue injunctive relief or specific performance, except for reformation in aid of a monetary judgment, or rescission instead of monetary damages. See John C. Grimberg Co. v. United States, 702 F.2d 1362 (Fed. Cir. 1983); Rig Masters, Inc. v. United States, 42 Fed. Cl. 369 (1998); Paragon Energy Corp. v. United States, 645 F.2d 966 (Ct. Cl. 1981).

3. The COFC may award EAJA attorneys' fees. 28 U.S.C. § 2412.

I. Payment of Judgments. See paragraph VII.J, above.

J. Appealing an Adverse Decision.

1. Unless timely appealed, a COFC final judgment bars any further claim, suit, or demand against the United States arising out of the matters involved in the case or controversy. 28 U.S.C. § 2519.

2. A party must appeal a final judgment to the CAFC within 60 days of the date the party receives the adverse decision. 28 U.S.C. § 2522. See RCFC 72.

IX. APPEALS TO THE COURT OF APPEALS FOR THE FEDERAL CIRCUIT (CAFC).

A. National Jurisdiction.

1. The Federal Circuit has exclusive jurisdiction over appeals from an agency BCA and the COFC pursuant to 41 U.S.C. § 7107(a)(1), 28 U.S.C. § 1295(a)(3) and (10).

2. The Federal Circuit has national jurisdiction. Dewey Elec. Corp. v. United States, 803 F.2d 650 (Fed. Cir. 1986); Teller Envtl. Sys., Inc. v. United States, 802 F.2d 1385 (Fed. Cir. 1986).

B. Standard of Review. 41 U.S.C. § 7107(b).

1. Jurisdiction. The court views jurisdictional challenges as "pure issues of law," which it reviews de novo. See Transamerica Ins. Corp. v. United States, 973 F.2d 1572, 1576 (Fed. Cir. 1992).

2. Findings of Fact. Findings of fact are final and conclusive, unless they are fraudulent, arbitrary, capricious, made in bad faith, or not supported by substantial evidence. 41 U.S.C. § 7107(b)(2). See United States v. General Elec. Corp., 727 F.2d 1567, 1572 (Fed. Cir. 1984) (holding that the court will affirm a board's decision if there is "such relevant evidence as a reasonable mind might accept as adequate to support a conclusion"); Tecom, Inc. v. United States, 732 F.2d 935, 938 n.4 (Fed. Cir. 1995) (finding that the trier of fact's credibility determinations are virtually unreviewable).

C. Frivolous Appeals. The court will assess damages against parties filing frivolous appeals. See Dungaree Realty, Inc. v. United States, 30 F.3d 122 (Fed. Cir. 1994); Wright v. United States, 728 F.2d 1459 (Fed. Cir. 1984).

D. **Supreme Court Review**. The U.S. Supreme Court reviews decisions of the Federal Circuit by writ of certiorari.

X. CONCLUSION.

A disputes process that is quick, fair, and accurate is in the interests of both contractors and the government. Maintaining a professional working relationship between contractors and their government customers is key to timely delivery of conforming goods and services. Congress, in enacting the Contract Disputes Act, has created a fair system for resolving disputes that works reasonably well for both contractors and the government.

ATTACHMENT A

Delivered By Federal Express

Ms. Jane Doe[14]
Contracting Officer
U.S. Army Contracting Command
Fort Swampy, Arkansas 12345

Subject: Contract Disputes Act Claim under Contract No. 987654321[15]

Dear Ms. Doe:

ABC Company submits a claim under the Contract Disputes Act of 1978, 41 U.S.C. §§ 7101-7109 for the sum certain of $250,000, plus interest under the Contract Disputes Act from the date of receipt.

Entitlement. ABC Company was awarded Contract No. 987654321 on 30 September 2014 for 100,000 widgets at a unit price of $2.50 each. ABC Company timely delivered 100,000 conforming widgets on 30 August 2015. On 15 September the DCMA Quality Assurance Representative, Mr. Smith, rejected the delivery as non-conforming in the attached e-mail (Attachment 1). He has refused to execute a DD 250 accompanying the delivery and has provided no further direction.

Quantum. Since the widgets were conforming, ABC Company is entitled to payment of contract price for each widget delivered, a total of $250,000.

ABC Company demands a contracting officer final decision on its claim within 60 days.

The point of contact for communications regarding this claim is John Jones, Law Department, ABC Company, 1234 Main Street, Springfield, Arkansas 12346. He may be reached at (123) 456-7890.

Certification. I certify that the claim is made in good faith; that the supporting data are accurate and complete to the best of my knowledge and belief; that the amount requested accurately reflects the contract adjustment for which the contractor believes the government is liable; and that I am duly authorized to certify the claim on behalf of the contractor.

Sincerely,

_____
Bob Clinton
President
ABC Company

---

[14] NOTE: Obtain the contracting officer's address from Block 7, SF33, the cover sheet for the contract.
[15] NOTE: Obtain the contract number from Block 2 of the contract's SF33.

ALTERNATIVE DISPUTE RESOLUTION

I. INTRODUCTION.

A. **The Contract Disputes Act of 1978.** Claims under the Contract Disputes Act are the principal method for resolving disputes under government contracts. As discussed in Chapter 28, disputes are initiated by submission of written claims to the contracting officer for decision, followed by contractor appeals to either the agency Board of Contract Appeals (BCA), or to the Court of Federal Claims. This process, however, can be long and expensive.

B. **Alternative Dispute Resolution Procedures.**

1. Contractors and the government desire a quick and inexpensive process for resolving contractual disagreements that are not resolved by their managers on the project. This is desirable to the government because disputes are best resolved while the facts are fresh, records are available, and the external forces are not impeding resolution. Contractors find alternative procedures desirable because they save litigation costs and, more important, preserve a good customer relationship.

2. For the reasons stated above, contractors and the government often seek to resolve disputes through alternative procedures. These procedures can be implemented as a regular practice in a contract and, more commonly, tailored to specific disputes.

3. Previously, agency personnel had some reluctance to adopt alternative procedures, due, in part, to the lack of statutory authority and the uncertainty on how oversight authorities would view their use.

II. REFERENCES.

A. **ADR Guide.** http://www.adr.gov/adrguide/

B. **Statutes.**

1. The Contract Disputes Act of 1978 (CDA), as amended, 41 U.S.C. §§ 7101-7109. Pertinent to ADR, See §7103(h).

2. The Administrative Dispute Resolution Act (ADRA), Pub. L. No. 104320, 110 Stat 3870, 5 U.S.C. §§ 571-584.

C. **Regulations.**

1. Federal Acquisition Regulation (FAR) 33.214, Alternative Dispute Resolution (ADR).

2. DOD Directive 5145.5, Alternative Dispute Resolution (ADR), April 22, 1996. http://www.adr.af.mil/shared/media/document/AFD-070924110.pdf

D. **Guidance.**

1. Defense Procurement and Acquisition Policy (DPAP), Alternative Dispute Resolution (ADR). The following link will take you to handbooks, guidance, laws, and service specific ADR programs: http://www.acq.osd.mil/dpap/ccap/cc/jcchb/HTML/Topical/adr.html.

2. Interagency Alternative Dispute Resolution Working Group provides guidance and requirements. http://www.adr.gov/index.html.

III. ADMINISTRATIVE DISPUTE RESOLUTION ACT (ADRA).

A. **Background.**

1. Congress passed the first ADRA in 1990 in response to increasingly crowded dockets and escalating litigation costs. In

the 1990 statute, Congress found that "administrative proceedings had become increasingly formal, costly, and lengthy resulting in unnecessary expenditures of time and in a decreased likelihood of achieving consensual resolution of disputes." ADRA of 1990, Pub.L. No. 101-552, §2(2), 104 Stat. 2738 (1990).

2. Congress decided that ADR, used successfully in the private sector, would work in the public sector and would "lead to more creative, efficient and sensible outcomes." ADRA, Pub. L. No. 101-552, § 2(3) and (4), 104 Stat. 2738 (1990).

3. The 1990 ADRA explicitly authorized federal agencies to use ADR to resolve administrative disputes, including contract disputes. ADRA, Pub. L. No. 101-552, § 4(a), 104 Stat. 2738 (1990).

4. Under the 1990 ADRA, ADR was defined as any procedure used, in lieu of adjudication, to resolve issues in controversy, including settlement negotiations, conciliation, facilitation, mediation, fact-finding, mini-trials, and arbitration, or any combination of these techniques. ADRA, Pub. L. No. 101-552, § 4(b), 104 Stat. 2738 (1990). The ADRA of 1990 expired by its own terms on 1 October 1995.

5. In the 1990s, Congress passed three statutes (the Administrative Dispute Resolution Acts of 1990 and 1996, and the Alternative Dispute Resolution Act of 1998), which, collectively, required each agency to adopt a policy encouraging use of ADR in a broad range of decision making, and required the federal trial courts to make ADR programs available to litigants. These initiatives also include the Civil Rights Act of 1991; the National Performance Review; Executive Order 12871, Labor Management Partnerships; and the Equal Employment Opportunity Commission's regulations. http://www.opm.gov/policy-data-oversight/employeerelations/employee-rights-appeals/alternative-disputeresolution/handbook.pdf.

B. **1996 Amendments**.

1. On October 19, 1996, Congress enacted the Administrative Dispute Resolution Act of 1996, Pub. L. No. 104-320, 110 Stat 3870, amending 5 U.S.C. §§ 571-584 (*see also* Federal Acquisition Circular 97-09, 63 Fed. Reg. 58,586 (Final Rules) (1998), amending the FAR to implement the ADRA)). The 1996 Act:

a. Permanently authorized the ADRA;

b. Redefines ADR as any procedure used to resolve issues in controversy, including, but not limited to, conciliation, facilitation, mediation, fact-finding, mini-trials, arbitration, and use of ombudsman, or any combination of these techniques;

c. Requires each agency to adopt an ADR policy, to designate a senior official as the agency "dispute resolution specialist" to implement the ADR policy, and to train agency personnel in negotiation and ADR techniques, including mediation and facilitation;

d. Authorizes federal agencies to promulgate policies permitting the use of binding arbitration in dispute resolution on a case-by-case basis, if authorized by the agency head after consultation with the Attorney General;

e. Extends confidentiality protection to certain "dispute resolution communications" made during the course and for the purpose of dispute resolution proceedings, and exempts such communications disclosure under the Freedom of Information Act;

f. Authorizes an exception to full and open competition for the purpose of contracting with a "neutral person" for the resolution of any existing or anticipated litigation or dispute; and

g. Requires the President to designate an agency or establish an interagency committee to facilitate and encourage the use of ADR. By Presidential Memorandum dated 1 May 1998, the Interagency Alternative Dispute Resolution Working Group was established. See http://www.adr.gov.

Consequently, clear statutory authority exists for agencies to use ADR to resolve contractual disputes.

IV. REGULATORY IMPLEMENTATION.

A. Federal Acquisition Regulation.

It is now the government's express policy to attempt to resolve all contract disputes at the contracting officer level. Agencies are encouraged to use ADR procedures to the "maximum extent practicable." FAR 33.204.

1. FAR 33.214(a) identifies four essential elements for the use of ADR techniques:

    a. Existence of an issue in controversy;

    b. Voluntary election by both parties to participate in the ADR process;

    c. Agreement to ADR and terms to be used in lieu of formal litigation; and

    d. Participation in the process by officials of both parties who have authority to resolve the issue in controversy.

2. If the contracting officer rejects a contractor's request for ADR, the contracting officer must provide the contractor a written explanation citing one or more of the conditions in 5 U.S.C. § 572(b)[1] or other specific reasons that

ADR is inappropriate. FAR 33.214. Additionally, when a contractor rejects an agency ADR request, the contractor must inform the agency in writing of the contractor's specific reasons for rejecting the request. FAR 33.214.

B. DOD Policy and Implementation. Each DOD component shall use ADR techniques "whenever appropriate" and shall establish ADR policies and programs. DOD Dir. 5145.5.

1. Army. The Army established a centralized ADR Program Office in the Office of the General Counsel in 2008, pursuant to the Secretary of the Army's 22 Jun 07 ADR policy memorandum. This policy urges Army personnel to use ADR in appropriate cases to resolve disputes as early as feasible, by the fastest and least expensive method possible, and at the lowest possible organizational level. Personnel involved in dispute resolution must receive adequate ADR training, and must consider ADR in every case. The policy designates the Principal Deputy General Counsel as the Army Dispute Resolution Specialist and directs the hiring of personnel to assist in implementing the Army ADR policy. Previously, ADR in the Army was implemented primarily through subordinate commands and components,

---

[1] (b)An agency shall consider not using a dispute resolution proceeding if— (1) a definitive or authoritative resolution of the matter is required for precedential value, and such a proceeding is not likely to be accepted generally as an authoritative precedent; (2) the matter involves or may bear upon significant questions of government policy that require additional procedures before a final resolution may be made, and such a proceeding would not likely serve to develop a recommended policy for the agency; (3) maintaining established policies is of special importance, so that variations among individual decisions are not increased and such a proceeding would not likely reach consistent results among individual decisions; (4) the matter significantly affects persons or organizations who are not parties to the proceeding; (5) a full public record of the proceeding is important, and a dispute resolution proceeding cannot provide such a record; and (6) the agency must maintain continuing jurisdiction over the matter with authority to alter the disposition of the matter in the light of changed circumstances, and a dispute resolution proceeding would interfere with the agency's fulfilling that requirement.

for example, the Contract and Fiscal Law Division of the U.S. Army Legal Services Agency (for contract claims and bid protests), Army Materiel Command (workplace and bid protests), the Army Corps of Engineers (contract claims and environmental and workplace disputes), and the Army EEO Complaints Program (discrimination claims). These subordinate commands and components continue to have primary operational control over ADR with respect to disputes within their areas of responsibility, but certain aspects of the ADR program, such as policy and guidance, standards, training programs, and ADR support, are within OGC's area of responsibility. In Army contract disputes, the available guidance is referenced in the 1999 "Electronic Guide to Federal Procurement ADR," a product of the Interagency ADR Working Group Steering Committee, and can be found at http://www.adr.gov/adrguide/.

2. Air Force. The Air Force institutionalized its use of ADR in contract disputes by issuance of a comprehensive policy on dispute resolution entitled "ADR First." The policy states that ADR will be the first-choice method of resolving contract disputes if traditional negotiations fail, unless ADR would be inappropriate as judged by the statutory (ADRA) criteria. The ADR First policy represents an affirmative determination to avoid the disruption and high cost of litigation. ADR: Air Force Launches New ADR Initiative; Drafts Legislation to Fund ADR Settlements, Fed. Cont. Daily (BNA) (Apr. 28, 1999); see also Air Force Policy Directive 51-12 (Jan. 9, 2003) and AFFARS 5333.090 (2004). See Air Force ADR website, http://www.adr.af.mil.

3. Navy and Marine Corps. The first Department of Navy ADR policy was issued in 1987, stating "every reasonable step must be taken to resolve disputes prior to litigation." Memorandum, Assistant Secretary of the Navy (Shipbuilding and

Logistics), subject: Alternative Dispute Resolution (1987). The current Navy policy states ADR shall be used to the "maximum extent practicable" with the goal of resolving disputes at the earliest stage feasible, by the fastest and quickest means possible, and at the lowest possible organizational level. SECNAVINST 5800.13A (Dec. 22, 2005). See Navy ADR website, t http://adr.navy.mil; also see USMC, http://www.hqmc.marines.mil/hrom/EEO/AlternativeDisputeResolutio n.aspx

V. DISPUTE RESOLUTION TECHNIQUES.

A. **Range.** ADR techniques are as varied as human creativity. They exist within a dispute resolution continuum, ranging from dispute avoidance to litigation. The purpose of any ADR method is to settle the dispute without resorting to costly and time-consuming litigation before the courts and boards.

B. **Dispute Avoidance** (Partnering).

1. A process by which the contracting parties form a relationship of teamwork, cooperation, and good faith performance. It is a long-term commitment between two or more parties for the purpose of achieving mutually beneficial goals.

2. Partnering fosters communication and agreement on common goals and methods of performance. Examples of common goals are:

a. the use of ADR and elimination of litigation;

b. timely project completion;

c. high quality work;

d. safe workplace;

e. cost control;

f. value engineering; and

g. reasonable profit.

3. Partnering is NOT:

    a. Mandatory. It is not a contractual requirement and does not give either party legal rights. The parties must voluntarily agree to the process, because it is a commitment to an ongoing relationship.

    b. A "Cure-All." Reasonable differences will still occur, but one of the benefits of partnering is that it ensures the differences are honest and in good faith.

4. Implementing Partnering. Although voluntary, partnering is typically implemented through formal, specific methods that the parties agree upon.

    a. Requires commitment of top management officials of all parties.

    b. Parties need to establish clear lines of communication and responsibility, and agree to ADR methods for resolving legitimate disagreements.

    c. In the Air Force, for all acquisition categories (ACAT) I and II programs (i.e., major weapons systems), contracting officers "shall establish an agreement between the government and the contractor that "outlines the intent of parties with respect to the use of ADR." AFFARS 5333.214.

    d. For examples of corporate-level ADR agreements, see the Air Force ADR Reference Book, section 1.3.2, *available at* http://www.adr.af.mil/acquisition/index.html.

C. Issue Escalation.

1. A process whereby issues that could produce disputes are first referred to a team made up of all parties to the contract or project for resolution.

2. If the issue is not resolved at the first level of review, it is automatically elevated to a higher level of review, usually consisting of the superiors of those in the lower level, for decision.

3. There can be several levels of review up the chain, but the incentive is to avoid higher level review by resolving the issue at the lowest possible level.

D. Unassisted Negotiations.

1. In traditional unassisted negotiation, the parties attempt to reach a settlement without involvement of outside parties.

2. Elements of Successful Negotiation:

    a. Parties identify issues upon which they differ.

    b. Parties disclose their respective needs and interests.

    c. Parties identify possible settlement options.

    d. Parties negotiate terms and conditions of agreement.

3. Goal: Each party should be in a better position than if they had not negotiated.

E. ADR Procedures. Defined broadly to include any procedure or combination of procedures that "may include, but are not limited to, conciliation, facilitation, mediation, fact-finding, mini-trials, arbitration, and use of ombudsmen," ADR techniques rely upon participation by a third-party neutral. See ADRA of 1996, 5 U.S.C. §§ 571-584 and FAR 33.201. Typically ADR types fall within one of three general categories:

1. Process Assistance/Assisted Negotiations:

    a. Mediation. Mediation is helpful when the parties are not making progress negotiating between themselves. Mediation is simply negotiation with the assistance of a third-party neutral who is an expert in helping people negotiate but has no decision-making authority. See "Alternative Dispute Resolution – Edition III," Briefing Papers No. 03-5, p. 1 (April 2003).

See DONALD ARNAVAS, ALTERNATIVE DISPUTE RESOLUTION FOR GOVERNMENT CONTRACTS 7 (2004).

- The mediator should be neutral, impartial, acceptable to both parties, and should not have any decision-making power.
- A professional mediator will normally approach a dispute with a formal strategy, consisting of a method of analysis, an opening statement, recognized stages of mediation, such as ex parte caucuses, and a variety of mediation tools for breaking impasses and bringing about a resolution.
- Mediators (as well as arbitrators and other neutrals) may be retained without full and open competition. FAR 6.302-3(a)(2)(iii) and (b)(3). Moreover, third-party neutral functions (like mediating and arbitrating) in ADR methods are not inherently governmental functions for which agencies may not contract. See FAR 7.503(c)(2).
- At the ASBCA, the process is known as the "settlement judge technique." A flexible procedure that allows the parties to make case presentations to each other in the presence of an ASBCA judge, who then facilitates settlement negotiations. "Alternative Dispute Resolution at the ASBCA," Briefing Papers No. 00-7, p. 7 (June 2000). See, ASBCA Notice Regarding Alternative Methods of Dispute Resolution *available at* http://docs.law.gwu.edu/asbca.

    b. Mini-Trials. The term "mini-trial" is a misnomer, as it is NOT a shortened judicial proceeding. In a mini-trial, the parties present either their whole case, or specific issues, to a panel in an abbreviated hearing. An advantage of the mini-trial is that it forces the parties to focus on a dispute and settle it early. See ASBCA Notice Regarding Alternative Methods of Dispute Resolution *available at* http://docs.law.gwu.edu/asbca. See

DONALD ARNAVAS, ALTERNATIVE DISPUTE RESOLUTION FOR GOVERNMENT CONTRACTS 7 and 127 (2004).

- Mini-trials have been used by the Army Corps of Engineers in several cases. The first was the Tennessee Tombigbee Construction, Inc. case in 1985. In that case, Professor Ralph Nash served as the neutral advisor, and a $17.25 million settlement was worked out between the government and the contractor. See 44 Federal Contracts Reporter (BNA) 502 (1985).
- Participants in a mini-trial include the principals, the parties' attorneys, and witnesses. The principals may choose to employ a neutral advisor.
- In a mini-trial, the attorneys engage in a brief discovery process and then present their case to a specially constituted panel. The panel consists of party principals and the neutral advisor if desired.
- Each party selects a principal to represent it on the panel. The principal should have sufficient authority permitting unilateral decisions regarding the dispute and should not have been personally or closely involved in the dispute.
- The parties should jointly select the neutral advisor, and share expenses. The neutral advisor should possess negotiation and legal skills and, if the issues are highly technical, a technical expert is desirable.
- The neutral advisor may perform a number of functions, including answering questions from the principals, questioning witnesses and counsel to clarify facts and legal theories, acting as a mediator and facilitator during negotiations, and generally presiding over the mini-trial to keep the parties on schedule.
- After hearing the case, the principals try to negotiate a settlement. If an impasse, the neutral advisor may try to mediate a solution. If the advisor is an ASBCA

judge, they may discuss the likely outcome if the case were to go to court or the board.

2.   Outcome Prediction.

a.   Non-Binding Arbitration. This form of arbitration aids the parties in making their own settlement. It is best used when senior managers do not have time to sit through a mini-trial and when disputes are highly technical. See DONALD ARNAVAS, ALTERNATIVE DISPUTE RESOLUTION FOR GOVERNMENT CONTRACTS 23 and 127 (2004).

- Normally an informal presentation of the case, done by counsel with client input.
- Evidence is presented by document, deposition, and affidavit.
- Few live witnesses.
- The arbitrator's decision or opinion, sometimes called an award, serves to further settlement discussions. The parties get an idea of how the case may be decided by a court or board.
- The arbitrator may also evolve into the role of a mediator after a decision is issued.

b.   For bid protests at GAO, parties frequently utilize an "outcome prediction" conference, in which a GAO staff attorney advises the parties as to the perceived merits of the protest in light of the case facts and prior GAO decisions. See Tyecom, Inc. B-287321.3; B-287321.4, April 29, 2002. See also Bid Protests at GAO: A Descriptive Guide *available at* http://www.gao.gov/decisions/bidpro/bidpro.htm. See DONALD ARNAVAS, ALTERNATIVE DISPUTE RESOLUTION FOR GOVERNMENT CONTRACTS 127 (2004).

3.   Adjudication.

a.   Private Binding Arbitration. Binding arbitration is the ADR technique that most closely resembles traditional, formal litigation. "Alternative Dispute Resolution – Edition III," Briefing Papers No. 03-5, p. 2 (April 2003). This form of arbitration results in an award, enforceable in courts.

(1)   Normally a formal presentation of the case, much like a trial, though strict rules of evidence may not be followed.

(2)   Evidence is presented by document, deposition, affidavit, and live witnesses, with full cross-examination.

(3)   Arbitration panels consist of one to three arbitrators, who serve to control the proceeding, but do not take an active role in the case presentation.

(4)   Private conversations between the parties and the arbitrators are forbidden. This is much different from mediation, during which private conversations between a party and the mediator are not uncommon.

(5)   The arbitrator has full responsibility for rendering justice under the facts and law.

(6)   The arbitrator's award is binding, so the arbitrator must be more careful about controlling the parties' case presentation and the reliability of the evidence presented.

b.   Summary Trial with Binding Decision. In practice before the ASBCA, a summary trial results in a binding decision. The parties try the case informally before a board judge on an expedited, abbreviated basis. "Alternative Dispute Resolution at the ASBCA," Briefing Papers No. 00-7, p. 5 (June 2000). DOD personnel are not generally authorized to use a binding ADR method that does not involve the ASBCA. See ADR Policies and Procedures Guide, *available at* http://www.jagcnet.army.mil/cad. See ASBCA Notice Regarding Alternative Methods of Dispute Resolution *available at* http://docs.law.gwu.edu/asbca. See also the Air Force ADR Reference Book, section 4.3.2 *available at* http://www.adr.af.mil/acquisition/index.html. See DONALD ARNAVAS, ALTERNATIVE DISPUTE RESOLUTION FOR GOVERNMENT CONTRACTS 127 (2004).

VI. TIMING WHEN USING ADR.

A. Before Protest or Appeal.

1. Protests. The FAR has long provided authority for agencies to hear protests. FAR 33.103 implements Executive Order 12979 and requires agencies to:

   a. Emphasize that the parties shall use their best efforts to resolve the matter with the contracting officer prior to filing a protest (FAR 33.103(b));

   b. Provide for inexpensive, informal, procedurally simple, and expeditious resolution of protests, using ADR techniques where appropriate (FAR 33.103(c));

   c. Allow for review of the protest at "a level above the contracting officer" either initially or as an internal appeal (FAR 33.103(d)(4)); and

   d. Withhold award or suspend performance if the protest is received within ten days of award or five days after debriefing. FAR 33.103(f)(1)-(3). But an agency protest will not extend the period within which to obtain a stay at GAO, although the agency may voluntarily stay performance. FAR 33.103(f)(4).

2. Appeals. The ADRA provides clear and unambiguous government authority for contracting officers to voluntarily use any form of ADR during the period before an appeal is filed. 5 U.S.C. § 572(a); FAR 33.214(c).

B. After Protest or Appeal.

1. The GAO Bid Protest Regulations now provide that GAO, on its own or upon request, may use flexible alternative procedures to resolve a protest, including ADR procedures. 5 C.F.R. 21.10. See also Bid Protests at GAO: A Descriptive Guide *available at* http://www.gao.gov/decisions/bidpro/bidpro.htm. As noted earlier, parties frequently utilize an "outcome prediction" conference. See Tyecom, Inc. B-287321.3; B-287321.4, April 29, 2002.

2. With respect to contractor claims, once an appeal is filed, jurisdiction passes to the BCA. When an appeal is filed, the Board gives notice suggesting the parties pursue the possibility of using ADR, including mediation, mini-trials, and summary hearings with binding decisions. The ASBCA has made aggressive use of ADR services in contract appeals disputes. See, ASBCA Notice Regarding Alternative Methods of Dispute Resolution, *available at* *http://www.asbca.mil/ADR/ADR%202011.pdf*. See also "Alternative Dispute Resolution at the ASBCA," Briefing Papers No. 00-7 (June 2000).

3. Parties who file appeals with the Court of Federal Claims (COFC) will also be informed of voluntary ADR methods available through the court. In 2001, COFC began an ADR pilot program, in which some cases are assigned simultaneously to an ADR judge. See Notice of ADR Pilot Program, at http://www.contracts.ogc.doc.gov/fedcl/docs/adr.html. The goal of the pilot program is to determine whether early neutral evaluation by a settlement judge will help parties understand their differences and their prospects for settlement.

VII. APPROPRIATENESS OF ADR.

A. When Is It Appropriate to Use ADR?
Agencies "may use a dispute resolution proceeding for the resolution of an issue in controversy that relates to an administrative program, if the parties agree

to such proceeding." 5 U.S.C. § 572(a). Also, government attorneys are to "make reasonable attempts to resolve a dispute expeditiously and properly before proceeding to trial." Exec. Order No. 12988, § 1(c). Generally, ADR is appropriate for a case when:

1. Unassisted negotiations have failed to resolve the dispute and have reached an impasse;

2. Neither party is looking for binding precedent;

3. The parties wish to preserve a continuing relationship; and

4. Confidentiality is important to either or both sides.

B. When Is It Inappropriate to Use ADR? An agency should consider against using ADR when:

1. A definitive or authoritative resolution of the matter is required for precedential value, and an ADR proceeding is not likely to be accepted generally as an authoritative precedent. 5 U.S.C. § 572(b)(1);

2. The matter involves or may bear upon significant questions of government policy that require additional procedures before a final resolution may be made, and an ADR proceeding would not likely serve to develop a recommended policy for the agency. 5 U.S.C. § 572(b)(2);

3. Maintaining established policies is of special importance, so that variations among individual decisions are not increased and an ADR proceeding would not likely reach consistent results among individual decisions. 5 U.S.C. § 572(b)(3);

4. The matter significantly affects persons or organizations who are not parties to the proceeding. 5 U.S.C. § 572(b)(4);

5. A full public record of the proceeding is important, and an ADR proceeding cannot

provide such a record. 5 U.S.C. § 572(b)(5); or,

6. The agency must maintain continuing jurisdiction over the matter with authority to alter the disposition of the matter in light of changed circumstance, and an ADR proceeding would interfere with the agency's ability to fulfill that requirement. 5 U.S.C. § 572(b)(6).

C. Unacceptable Reasons to Avoid ADR.

1. Desire to delay resolution of the dispute.

2. Concern that the agency IG, the Congress, or the news media will criticize the use of ADR.

3. Costs. If a party is concerned that ADR is too costly, consider the costs of litigation, including various fee-shifting statutes.

VIII. STATUTORY REQUIREMENTS AND LIMITATIONS.

A. Voluntariness. ADR methods authorized by the ADRA are voluntary, and supplement rather than limit other available agency dispute resolution techniques. 5 U.S.C. § 572(c).

B. Limitations Applicable to Using Arbitration.

1. Arbitration may be used by the consent of the parties either before or after a controversy arises. The arbitration agreement shall be:

   a. in writing,

   b. submitted to the arbitrator, and

   c. specify a maximum award and any other conditions limiting the possible outcomes. 5 U.S.C. § 575(c)(1) and (2).

2. The government representative agreeing to arbitration must have express authority to bind the government. 5 U.S.C. § 575(b).

3. Before using binding arbitration, the agency head, after consulting with the

ADR

Attorney General, must issue guidance on the appropriate use of binding arbitration. 5 U.S.C. § 575(c); see also DFARS Case 97-D304.

4. An agency may not require any person to consent to arbitration as a condition of entering into a contract or obtaining a benefit. 5 U.S.C. § 575(a)(3).

5. If a contractor rejects an agency request to use ADR, the contractor must notify the agency in writing of the reasons. FAR 33.214(b).

6. Once the parties reach a written arbitration agreement, however, the agreement is enforceable in Federal District Court. 5 U.S.C. § 576; 9 U.S.C. § 4.

7. An arbitration award does not become final until 30 days after it is served on all parties. The agency may extend this 30-day period for another 30 days by serving notice on all other parties. 5 U.S.C. § 580(b)(2).

8. A final award is binding on the parties, including the United States, and an action to enforce an award cannot be dismissed on sovereign immunity grounds. 5 U.S.C. § 580(c).

   a. This provision, enacted as part of the 1996 ADRA, put to rest for the time being a long-standing dispute as to whether an agency can submit to binding arbitration.

   b. DOJ's Historical Policy. The Justice Department had long opined that the Appointments Clause of Article II provides the exclusive means by which the United States may appoint its officers. DOJ's opinion was that only officers could bind the United States to an action or payment. Because arbitrators are virtually never appointed as officers under the Appointments clause, the government was not allowed to participate in binding arbitration.

   c. DOJ's Present Position. However, DOJ has now opined that there is no constitutional bar against the government participating in binding arbitration if:

      (1) the arbitration agreement preserves Article III review of constitutional issues and

      (2) the agreement permits Article III review of arbitrators' determinations for fraud, misconduct, or misrepresentation. DOJ also points out that the arbitration agreement should describe the scope and nature of the remedy that may be imposed and that care should be taken to ensure that statutory authority exists to effect the potential remedy.

   d. Judicial Interpretation. The Court of Federal Claims has found DOJ's memorandum persuasive and agreed that no constitutional impediment precludes an agency from submitting to binding arbitration. Tenaska Washington Partners II v. United States, 34 Fed. Cl. 434 (1995).

C. **Judicial Review Prohibited**. Generally, an agency's decision to use or not use ADR is within the agency's discretion, and shall not be subject to judicial review. 5 U.S.C. § 581(b)(1).

1. However, arbitration awards are subject to judicial review under 9 U.S.C. § 10(b).

2. Section 10(b) authorizes district courts to vacate an arbitration award upon application of any party where the arbitrator was either partial, corrupt, or both.

IX.   CONCLUSION.

Both the government and the contractor can benefit from adopting ADR procedures. A continuing contractual relationship benefits when disagreements are resolved quickly, predictably, and fairly. Litigation is not quick; and in many instances, the outcome is not predictable, and the imposed resolution is not viewed as fair by one or both parties. Lowering the costs of disputes resolution and preserving the contractual relationship are key benefits of ADR.

GOVERNMENT INFORMATION PRACTICES

I. OVERVIEW.

Control of information is a controversial issue with many different policy viewpoints. Many citizens, as well as the press, believe that the government should make most of the information it generates or possesses freely available to public. Conversely, many citizens believe that the government should not possess information a citizen deems private, even if that information has previously been freely shared with many others. Where the government does possess such information, citizens believe the government and its contractors who perform much of the day-to-day business of government should zealously protect the privacy of their personal information. Companies have similar desires that the government protect their confidential business information. The government desires to protect information from public disclosure where it believes such disclosures could result in harm to citizens, businesses, and the public at large. Resolving these competing policy objectives has resulted in a set of statutes and regulations that affect government contracting in several ways.

First, in the pursuit of and performance of government contracts, contractors routinely give the government large amounts of information about themselves and their employees that would be unthinkable in any other context. Contractors must take steps to ensure the government protects this information from release. Second, contractors seeking new government customers can be greatly aided by gaining access to the non-confidential, but non-public information about incumbents and their contracts. Third, contractors receive information from the government, and have contractual obligations to protect that information from further disclosure.

The legal framework for protecting confidential information and obtaining access to non-confidential but non-public information is formed by the Freedom of Information Act, the Privacy Act, various withholding statutes, and standard contract terms and conditions.

Government agencies have developed a core of specialists who manage these issues. Contractors are well served to have standard processes to protect their interests, and a core capability that understands Government Information Practices.

II. FREEDOM OF INFORMATION.

A. References.

1. Primary Sources.

- Freedom of Information Act, 5 U.S.C. § 552, as amended.
- Department of Defense Directive No. 5400.7, DOD Freedom of Information Act Program (28 July 2011, Change 1).
- Department of Defense Regulation No. 5400.7-R, DOD Freedom of Information Act Program (11 April 2006, Change 1).
- Army Regulation No. 25-55, The Department of the Army Freedom of Information Act Program (1 November 1997) (does not include 1996 amendments to the Freedom of Information Act).
- Air Force Manual, DOD 5400.7-R_AFMAN 33-302, Freedom of Information Act Program (21 October 2010).
- Secretary of the Navy Instruction 5720.42F, Department of the Navy Freedom of Information Act Program (6 January 1999).
- Marine Corps Order 5720.63, Publication in the Federal Register, Indexing, and Public Inspection of Marine Corps Directives (2 August 1991, Change 1).
- Commandant's Instruction M5260.3 – The Coast Guard Freedom of Information and Privacy Acts Manual (6 April 2005, Change 5).
-

2. Secondary Sources.

- Freedom of Information Act Guide (2013) (available on the World Wide Web at: http://www.justice.gov/oip/doj-guide-freedom-information-act-0 [hereinafter DOJ FOIA Guide].
- Freedom of Information Case List and updates, a Department of Justice publication (available at http://www.justice.gov/oip/court-decisions-overview. Archived decisions are available at http://www.justice.gov/archive/oip/court-decisions-archive.html.

3. Agency Resources Available Online.

- Department of Defense – http://www.dod.mil/pubs/foi/
- Army – https://www.rmda.army.mil/organization/foia.shtml
- Navy – http://foia.navy.mil/toolkit.asp
- Marine Corps – http://www.marines.mil/unit/hqmc/foia/Pages/USMCFOIARESOURCE%20MAT ERIALS.aspx
- Air Force – http://www.foia.af.mil/
- Coast Guard – http://www.uscg.mil/foia

B.   FOIA Overview.

1. History/Purpose. The Freedom of Information Act (FOIA) was enacted in 1966, and took effect 5 July 1967. It revised the public disclosure section of the Administrative Procedure Act. 5 U.S.C. § 1002 (1964) (enacted in 1946, amended in 1966, and now codified at 5 U.S.C. § 552.). "The basic purpose of the FOIA is to ensure an informed citizenry, vital to the functioning of a democratic society, needed to check against corruption and to hold the governors accountable to the governed." NLRB v. Robbins Tire & Rubber Co., 437 U.S. 214, 242 (1978). The FOIA firmly established an effective statutory right of public access to executive branch information in the federal government.

2. In summary, the Freedom of Information Act 5 U.S.C. 552a permits any person to request the records of a federal agency, and the agency must make that record available unless the record is exempt from disclosure. Any person means just that; the requester need not be a U.S. citizen, taxpayer, or resident. A requester can be the press, a competitor, or a foreign intelligence agency. The requester can act on its own behalf, or on behalf of an undisclosed principal. The requester's status may affect expedited access, search fees, attorney fees, and the duty of intelligence agencies to respond.[1] Agency records include any and all agency records within the government's possession and control. Disclosure is the rule, not the exception. An agency must disclose the requested record unless it can justify that a statutory exemption exists. Where an agency improperly withholds a record, the requester may seek administrative and judicial relief.

3. Submitting a FOIA request. Federal agencies are very open to FOIA requests. They typically have links on their main webpages, permit electronic requests, and provide help in submitting proper requests. Guidance on FOIA requests is located at http://publications.usa.gov/USAFileDnld.php?PubType=P&PubID=6080&httpGetPubID=0&PHPSESSID=s2t7p34sllkatik089cvi4ps41

C.   Agency Records -- Possession and Control. A FOIA request must seek agency records. Usually, this is clear. However, where the government has

---

[1] Congress amended 5 U.S.C. § 552(a)(3)(E)(ii), to preclude elements of the intelligence community from disclosing any records in response to a FOIA request made by any foreign government or international governmental organization, either directly or through a representative. Elements of the intelligence community are identified in 50 U.S.C. § 401a.(4) (includes the Central Intelligence Agency; National Security Agency; Defense Intelligence Agency; and other elements within various federal agencies).

possession of information, but not control, it need not disclose the information.

1. Records prepared by contractor, but possessed and paid for by agency, are agency records. Hercules, Inc. v. Marsh, 839 F.2d 1027 (4th Cir. 1988) (reverse FOIA) (Radford Army Ammunition Plant telephone directory).

2. Records possessed exclusively by contractor held not agency records because not subject to agency "possession and control." Rush Franklin Publishing, Inc. v. NASA, No. 90-CV-285 (E.D.N.Y. Apr. 13, 1993). But see Burka v. HHS, 87 F.3d 508 (D.C. Cir. 1996) (computer tapes maintained by contractor held to be agency records based on "extensive supervision and control exercised by the agency over the collection and analysis of the data").

3. Electronic database provided by contractor under specific license limiting dissemination held not an agency record because agency lacks control. Tax Analysts v. United States Department of Justice, 913 F. Supp. 599 (D.D.C. 1996), aff'd, 107 F.3d 923 (D.C. Cir.) (table cite), cert. denied, 118 S.Ct. 336 (1997).

4. Video conferencing software developed by contractor (under contract that provided that all records generated are property of the agency, unless, as in this case, contractor receives permission to keep intellectual property and takes steps to commercialize it, in which case government receives a "nonexclusive license to use the intellectual property on behalf of the United States") held not be an agency record because agency lacks control since "it does not have unrestricted use of it." Gilmore v. United States Dep't of Energy, 4 F. Supp. 2d 912 (N.D. Cal. 1998).

5. Records created by agency employees exclusively for their own convenience held personal rather than agency records. Hamrick v. Department of the Navy, No. 90-283, 1992 WL 739887 (D.D.C. Aug. 28, 1992) (steno pads containing

contracting officer's handwritten memory joggers created "without being directed to do so by the Agency for her own personal reasons and maintained . . . for her own convenience"), appeal dismissed, No. 92-5376 (D.C. Cir. Aug. 4, 1995).

6. Contractors should consider that providing the government with software, documents, and other deliverables with less than Unlimited Rights may protect the information from disclosure under FOIA by preventing the information from being an agency record.

D. Releasing Agency Records.

1. When an agency receives a FOIA request, it forwards the request to the FOIA office(s) responsible for the requested records. That office will search for the records, review the records, and prepare a response to the requester. While the FOIA includes deadlines for responding, the deadlines are rarely met and Congress has shown little interest in providing dedicated resources for this purpose.

2. There are several ways an agency can release its records. These include:

- Publication. § 552(a)(1) (Requires disclosure of agency procedures, substantive rules, functions, organization and general policy through *Federal Register* publication).
- "Reading Room" Materials. § 552(a)(2) (Requires agency to make "available for public inspection and copying" records of final opinions, policy statements, administrative staff manuals, and frequently requested material.) Stanley v. Department of Defense, et al., No. 98-CV-4116 (S.D. Ill. June 22, 1999) (military hospital operational manuals are "internal housekeeping rules" as opposed to the kind of material of interest to the general public.)
- Final opinions rendered in the adjudication of cases, specific policy statements, and certain administrative staff manuals. Vietnam Veterans of

America v. Department of the Navy, 876 F.2d 164 (D.C. 1989).

- The agency does not need to make available materials "related solely to the [agency's] internal personnel rules and practices." Hamlet v. United States, 63 F.3d 1097 (Fed. Cir. 1995), see DOJ FOIA Guide.

- Reading Room records created after 1 November 1996 must be available on an agency's website.

- Index for Public Inspection – final opinions of adjudicated cases; policies statements and interpretations not published in *Federal Register*; administrative staff manuals and instructions that affect a member of the public; frequently requested records that have been previously released (including an index of those records).

- Release Upon Request. § 552(a)(3). This is the most common means by which the public accesses government records (and the subject of the remainder of this outline.)

3. After conducting a reasonable search to locate the requested records, the FOIA office will review the records to initially determine whether they are exempt from release.

E. Exemption 1 -- Classified Information.

1. Exemption 1 of the Freedom of Information Act exempts from disclosure information that is classified "under criteria established by an Executive Order to be kept secret in the interest of national defense or foreign policy" and is "in fact properly classified pursuant to such Executive Order."

2. Within DOD, contractors with a need to know classified information may request it through their customers. Contractors typically need not provide the government with justification for withholding classified information requested under FOIA.

3. Details of procurement of armored limousines for President properly classified. U.S. News & World Report v.

Department of the Treasury, No. 84-2303 (D.D.C. Mar. 26, 1986).

4. In rare cases mere existence of particular procurement may be classified. Phillippi v. CIA, 546 F.2d 1009 (D.C. Cir. 1976) (request for procurement records concerning Glomar Explorer submarine-retrieval ship; consequently "neither confirm nor deny" response known as "Glomar" response or "Glomarization").

F. Exemption 2 -- Internal Personnel Rules and Practices.

1. While federal agencies had successfully argued in lower courts that Exemption 2 applied to a wide range of records, in Milner v. Department of the Navy, 131 S. Ct. 1259 (2011), the U.S. Supreme Court substantially narrowed the scope of the exemption to human resources practices, which is the plain meaning of the statutory language.

2. Contractors should have little reason to request withholding of contractor information under Exemption 2.

G. Exemption 3 -- Disclosure Prohibited by Another Statute.

1. The Department of Defense maintains a list of those statutes that specifically prohibit disclosure. See http://open.defense.gov/Portals/23/Documents/DoD_(b)(3)_statutes_updated.pdf

2. Among the more important statutes when responding to a request for contracts and contract files are:

- 10 USC § 130, Unclassified Technical Data With Military Or Space Application;
- 10 USC § 130c, Sensitive Information Of Foreign Governments And International Organizations;
- 10 USC § 130e, DOD Critical Infrastructure Security Information;
- 10 USC § 2305(g), DOD contractor proposals;

- 10 USC § 2371(i), Research Projects: Transactions Other Than Contracts And Grants;
- 15 USC § 638 (k)(4), Information contained within a Small Business Innovative Research (SBIR) and Small Business Technology Transfer (STTR) program evaluation databases;
- 15 USC § 3710a(c)(7), Confidential commercial or financial information obtained in Cooperative Research and Development Agreements (CRADA);
- 18 USC § 798(a), Communications Intelligence;
- 33 USC § 2313(b), Information developed as a result of research and development activities conducted by the Army Corps of Engineers;
- 35 USC § 122, Patent Applications;
- 35 USC § 205, Government Inventions Information;
- 41 USC § 2102(a)(1), Contract Source Selection Information.

3. Contractors should not assume that government FOIA personnel will appreciate how a withholding statute may apply to specific contracts and files. When requesting withholding, the contractor should identify the statute and explain how it applies to a specific record, or portion thereof.

4. The Trade Secrets Act, 18 U.S.C. § 1905, does not qualify because it prohibits only those disclosures "not authorized by law." CNA Fin. Corp. v. Donovan, 830 F.2d 1132 (D.C. Cir. 1987).

5. The Privacy Act, 5 U.S.C. § 552a.

6. The Procurement Integrity Act, 41 U.S.C. Chapter 21, has been characterized differently by various courts. Cf. Pikes Peak Family Housing, LLC v. United States, 40 Fed. Cl. 673 (1998) (provision does not prohibit disclosure in civil discovery because that is "provided by law"). But see Legal & Safety Employer Research, Inc. v. United States Dep't of the Army, No. 00-1748 (E.D. Cal. May 7, 2001) (stating in dicta, without analyzing the statutory language that the provision qualifies as an Exemption 3 statute).

H. **Exemption 4 -- "Trade Secrets," Commercial or Financial Information Obtained from a Person, and Privileged or Confidential.**

1. Exemption 4 has been the frequent subject of litigation, pitting requesters against agencies and companies whose information is requested. There are several categories of information that may be withheld. Since the potentially exempt information is owned by a third party, the person/company whose information is requested is afforded by regulation the right to justify withholding.

2. "Trade Secrets" are protectable. While the government believes that trade secrets are given narrow definition in FOIA context, virtually every state has adopted the definition in the Uniform Trade Secrets Act. The D.C. Circuit, where many FOIA cases are litigated, has adopted a similar definition: "a secret, commercially valuable plan, formula, process, or device that is used for the making, preparing, compounding, or processing of trade commodities and that can be said to be the end product of either innovation or substantial effort." Public Citizen Health Research Group v. FDA, 704 F.2d 1280 (D.C. Cir. 1983). See, e.g., Center for Auto Safety v. National Highway Traffic Safety Admin., 244 F.3d 144 (D.C. Cir. 2001).

3. "Confidential Commercial or Financial Information Obtained from a Person" is protectable. Commercial or financial information is a broad category of business information, and extends beyond trade secrets. Public Citizen Health Research Group v. FDA, 704 F.2d 1280 (D.C. Cir. 1983). Protectable information must be obtained from a person, and not the creation of the federal government. Nadler v. FDIC, 92 F.3d 93 (2d Cir. 1996) (person includes individuals, partnerships, corporations, associations

or public and private organizations other than an agency); <u>Stone v. Export-Import Bank of United States</u>, 552 F.2d 132 (5th Cir. 1977) (foreign government agency).

4. The key issue is confidentiality. For commercial and financial information required to be supplied to the federal government, the D.C. Circuit adopted a two-prong test in <u>National Parks & Conservation Ass'n v. Morton</u>, 498 F.2d 765 (D.C. Cir. 1974). Information is confidential if disclosure would "[i]mpair the government's ability to obtain necessary information in the future." <u>Compare</u>, <u>Orion Research, Inc. v. EPA</u>, 615 F.2d 551 (1st Cir. 1980), <u>with</u> <u>McDonnell Douglas Corp. v. NASA</u>, 981 F. Supp. 12, 15 (D.D.C. 1997). Information is also confidential if release would "cause substantial harm to the competitive position of the person from whom the information was obtained." <u>McDonnell Douglas Corp. v. NASA</u>, 180 F.3d 303 (D.C. Cir. 1999).

5. Disclosure or protection of unit prices. The government has generally adopted the position that unit prices are releaseable, FAR 15.503(b)(1)(iv). However, courts have disagreed with the government's position and protected unit price information in some instances. <u>Canadian Commer. Corp. v. Department of the Air Force</u>, 514 F.3d 37 (D.C. Cir. 2008). <u>Compare</u> <u>McDonnell Douglas Corp. v. Dep't of the Air Force</u>, 375 F.3d 1182 (D.C. Cir. 2004) (two unit price categories protected, one disclosed) <u>and</u> <u>McDonnell Douglas Corp. v. NASA</u>, 180 F.3d 303 (D.C. Cir. 1999), (unit prices protected), <u>with</u> <u>Pacific Architects & Eng'rs, Inc. v. Dep't of State</u>, 906 F.2d 1345 (9th Cir. 1990) (unit prices disclosed), <u>and</u> <u>Acumenics Research and Technology v. Dep't of Justice</u>, 843 F.2d 800 (4th Cir. 1988) (same). Government attorneys will continue to follow the lead of DOJ, but contractor attorneys should consider pursuing protection of unit prices in appropriate cases.

6. Voluntary Submissions of Confidential Commercial or Financial Information." The D.C. Circuit adopted a different test where the requested information was submitted voluntarily in <u>Critical Mass Energy Project v. NRC</u>, 975 F.2d 871 (D.C. Cir. 1992) (<u>en banc</u>). For "voluntary" submissions, information is protectable if it is "of a kind that would customarily not be released to the public by the person from whom it was obtained." To justify withholding voluntarily submitted information, the contractor must demonstrate that the information was not required; it was voluntarily submitted to the agency. The company must also demonstrate that the information was not customarily released.

7. Contractors can lay the foundation for demonstrating confidentiality when submitting information to the government by:

- Mark the information as confidential, such as by stating, "This is confidential business information and is exempt from release under the Freedom of Information Act;" and
- Where the submission is voluntary, so state. ("This information is voluntarily submitted in confidence.")

8. Determining Whether Business Information Is Exempt. Upon locating a record that was obtained from a person and may be exempt, government policy is to provide notice to submitter. <u>See</u> Executive Order 12,600, July 23, 1987; DOD Reg. 5400.7-R, para. 5-207; importance of developing administrative record to support decision to release information. Contractors desiring to protect their information are well served to provide a detailed, factually supported response to such notices of proposed release. This will provide the agency with a detailed administrative record if it decides to withhold the information and the failure of the agency to contradict detailed, supported contractor justifications for withholding will permit the contractor to

pursue a "Reverse-FOIA" suit to review agency action under Administrative Procedure Act. See, e.g., Acumenics Research & Technology v. Dept. of Justice, 843 F.2d 800 (4th Cir. 1988). For an example of proposed disclosure being held arbitrary and capricious based on an insufficient agency record, see McDonnell Douglas Corp. v. NASA, No. 91-3134 (D.D.C. Jan. 24, 1993) (bench order).

I.   **Exemption 5 -- Inter- and Intra-Agency Documents Normally Privileged in the Civil Discovery Context.** Agencies may withhold privileged documents from release under Exemption 5

1.   Attorney-Client Privilege is a well-recognized privilege in civil discovery that applies equally to the government, protects confidential communications from clients to the counsel made for the purpose of securing legal advice or services; and the communications from attorneys to their clients if the communications rest "on confidential information obtained from the client." In re Sealed Cases, 737 F.2d 94, 98-99 (D.C. Cir. 1984), Mead Data Central, Inc. v. Department of the Air Force, 566 F.2d 242 (D.C. Cir. 1977).

2.   Attorney Work Product Privilege is another, widely recognized privilege. In re Sealed Cases, 737 F.2d 94, 98-99 (D.C. Cir. 1984)

3.   Agency Commercial Information has been recognized as a privilege under Exemption 5. Morrison-Knudsen Co. v. Department of the Army, 595 F. Supp. 352 (D.D.C. 1984) (agency's background documents used to calculate its bid in "contracting out" procedure), aff'd, 762 F.2d 138 (D.C. Cir. 1985) (table cite); Hack v. Department of Energy, 538 F. Supp. 1098 (D.D.C. 1992) (inter-agency cost estimates prepared by government for use in evaluating construction proposals submitted by private contractors).

4.   Deliberative Process Privilege protects internal government communications that

are: a) pre-decisional and b) are part of the deliberative process leading to a decision. Russell v. Department of the Air Force, 682 F.2d 1045 (D.C. Cir. 1982). The privilege does not protect factual information. EPA v. Mink, 410 U.S. 73 (1973). For a wide variety of exempt procurement-related examples, see MCI Telecommunications Corp. v. GSA, No. 89-0746, 1992 WL 71394 (D.D.C. Mar. 25, 1992) (source selection plan; initial checklist/appraisal of sufficiency of initial proposals; individual and consensus panel evaluations of initial proposals; panel lists of unresolved issues relating to initial proposals; notices of discrepancy/clarification relating to initial proposals; demonstration site visit agendas and reports; negotiation strategy memos, agendas and reports; test traffic data base and validations; ACS validation data; individual and consensus panel evaluations of best and final offers; final source selection evaluation board evaluation report; source selection advisory committee briefing materials; final award recommendation). Note that the FAR provision concerning debriefing of offerors somewhat expands the range of information to be disclosed thereby removing Exemption 5 protection for many of these items. See 48 C.F.R. § 15.506 (1997). The deliberative process privilege does not protect the agency decision, and any documents incorporated into that decision. NLRB v. Sears, 421 U.S. 132 (1975); Swisher v. Department of the Air Force, 660 F.2d 369 (8th Cir. 1981). Nor does the privilege protect "Bad Documents" from disclosure.

J.   **Exemption 6 -- Personal Privacy.**

1.   Agencies need not disclose personnel, medical, and similar files. "Similar records can be quite broad. See Department of State v. Washington Post, 456 U.S. 595 (1986) ("similar files" provision extends to any information of a "personal" nature, such as one's citizenship); Perlman v. U.S. Department of Justice, 312 F.3d 100 (2d Cir. 2002) (report of

investigation is a "similar file" because it is a "detailed government record"); New York Times Co. v. NASA, 920 F.2d 1002 (D.C. Cir. 1990) (holding that voice recording of the Challenger astronauts is a "similar file" for purposes of FOIA Exemption 6).

2. Resumés of proposed professional staff to be utilized by government contractor have been protected. Professional Review Org. v. HHS, 607 F. Supp. 423 (D.D.C. 1985).

3. Identities of contractor's employees required to be submitted under Davis-Bacon Act protected, but non-identifying information required to be disclosed Sheet Metal Workers Int'l Ass'n, Local Union No. 19 v. VA, 135 F.3d 891 (3d Cir. 1998) (citing identical holdings by 2d, 9th, 10th and D. C. Circuit Courts of Appeals).

K. Exemption 7(A) -- Records Compiled for Law Enforcement Purposes, the Disclosure of Which Could Reasonably Be Expected to Interfere with Enforcement Proceedings.

Periodic audits by Defense Contract Audit Agency that were subsequently "recompiled" into a pending criminal investigation of the contractor protected. John Doe Agency v. John Doe Corp., 493 U.S. 146 (1989).

L. Exemption 8: Financial Institutions Information.

M. Exemption 9: Geological and Geophysical Information.

III. PRIVACY PROTECTIONS.

A. The Privacy Act, 5 U.S.C. § 552a, provides protection to individuals for their personal information kept within a "System of Records" maintained by the government. Government contractors may have access to, or maintain, many of the Systems of Records containing the personal information of individuals.

B. FAR Subpart 24.1, Protection of Individual Privacy, implements the Privacy Act by requiring the contracting officer to include two clauses when a contractor will design, develop, or operate a system of records on individuals on behalf of the government. The contractor must comply with the act, and the contractor's employees are treated as agency employees under the criminal provisions of the act. The applicable FAR clauses are:

- FAR 52.224-1, Privacy Act Notification, and
- FAR 52.224-2, Privacy Act.

IV. PROTECTION OF INFORMATION.

A. Protection of Classified Information.

1. Contractors are frequently required to generate, receive, disclose, and store classified information to perform their contracts, especially those with defense and intelligence agencies. When this happens, the contracting officer will include contract clauses, requiring the contractor to obtain and retain the required security clearances, and to comply with the applicable procedures.

2. Protection of classified information is governed by FAR Subpart 4.4, DFARS Subpart 204.4, and DOD 5220.22-M, National Industrial Security Program Manual (NISPOM). The NISPOM provides detailed guidance to contractors requiring access to classified information and may be obtained at http://www.dss.mil/documents/odaa/nispom2006-5220.pdf.

3. Contractually, when the contractor will receive, generate, store, or disclose classified information, the contracting officer will include FAR 52.204-2, Security Requirements, in the solicitation and contract. This clause requires compliance with a Security Specification, typically prepared using Department of Defense Form DD254. Without a DD254,

Chapter 30

the contractor has no authority to possess or use classified information.

4. Consult the NISPOM for guidance on how a contractor may obtain a security clearance. Security clearances are only granted to companies and individuals with a need to know classified information. There is a significant administrative burden for individuals and organizations with security clearances. Obtaining the necessary clearance is neither easy, quick, nor assured.

B. Protection of Sensitive but Unclassified Information.

1. The government may disclose to a contractor information that the government has not classified, but it desires to protect from public disclosure. Additionally, a contractor may generate information, such as technical data describing military that is export controlled under the International Traffic in Arms Regulations (ITAR), 22 C.F.R. §§ 120-130. Consequently, the contracting officer may include requirements to protect such information and to obtain contracting officer approval before disclosing or publicizing such information.

2. For DOD, the contracting officer will include DFARS 252.204-7012, Safeguarding Covered Defense Information and Cyber Incident Reporting (Aug. 2015) to require the contractor to protect such information. For other contracts, the contracting officer will include FAR 52.204-21. The requirements of these clauses are discussed in Chapter 20, Contractor Business Systems.

C. Publicity and Disclosure.

1. As an additional protection against disclosures of sensitive, but unclassified information, as well as inadvertent disclosures of classified information, some agencies require prior approval of all public releases of information relating to the contract.

2. For DOD contracts, this requirement is implemented by DFARS 252.204-7000, Disclosure of Information. The clause requires prior review and approval of any disclosure of information relating to the contract outside the contractor's organization. This means that press releases of contract awards and significant events, presentations at technical symposiums, and similar public disclosures require prior written approval. Contractors should ensure that they have procedures in place to comply with this requirement.

3. While not specifically stated in DFARS 52.204-7000, prior permission is generally not required for routine disclosures in confidence to attorneys, accountants, consultants, approved subcontractors, and similar personnel outside the contractor's organization. Contractors should confirm this understanding with their own contracting officers.

4. Other federal agencies permit disclosure of contract related information without approval, or conditioned on inclusion of a notice of sponsorship. See HHSAR 352.227-70 Publications and Publicity.

V. CONCLUSION.

Security of government information is a very controversial topic. There are strong policy arguments for maximizing public disclosure of government information. These underlie the Freedom of Information Act. There are also strong policy arguments for not disclosing many types of information in the government's control. These include considerations of privacy, national security, and protection of the information of third parties in the possession of the government.

These conflicting policies and the statutes that implement those policies create a complex legal environment. Government lawyers must know and comply with the rules to minimize liability for errors. Contractor attorneys must know the rules so as to best protect their own company's information, while gathering publicly available information to successfully compete. This is not the primary role of contract attorneys, but no

569

contract attorney can be successful without a
basic knowledge of the rules.

NONAPPROPRIATED FUND CONTRACTING

I. INTRODUCTION.

Not all government contracts have the United States government as a party. One group of such government contracts are those awarded by Nonappropriated Fund Instrumentalities of the United States government. These contracts are unique in that the contracts do not obligate the full faith and credit of the United States government. Instead, they are awarded by legally distinct entities that have important similarities and differences from the government agency that creates and uses them. Their contracting procedures reflect these differences and similarities. This unique status creates many pitfalls for contractors and a separate set of regulations for government attorneys to comply with.

This chapter addresses nonappropriated fund contracting for the Department of Defense, and the Army and the Air Force in particular. They operate one of the largest such instrumentalities, the Army and Air Force Exchange Service, as well as many individual instrumentalities at individual bases.

II. REFERENCES.

A. Federal Statutes.

1. 10 U.S.C. § 2783. Requires the Secretary of Defense to prescribe regulations governing NAF funds and sets out punishments for violating those regulations.

2. 10 U.S.C. § 3013(b)(9). Provides Secretary of the Army the authority to administer the MWR program.

3. 10 U.S.C. § 8013(b)(9). Provides similar authority to the Secretary of the Air Force.

4. 10 U.S.C. § 5013(b)(9). Provides similar authority to the Secretary of the Navy.

B. Regulations.

1. DOD Directive 4105.67, Nonappropriated Fund (NAF) Procurement Policy (2 May 2001) [hereinafter DOD Dir. 4105.67].

2. DOD Instruction 4105.71, Nonappropriated Fund (NAF) Procurement Procedure (26 February 2001, with Change 1, administratively reissued 30 July 2002) [hereinafter DOD Instr. 4105.71].

3. Army Regulations. AR 215-4, Nonappropriated Fund Contracting (11 March 2005); AR 215-1, Morale, Welfare, and Recreation Activities and Nonappropriated Fund Instrumentalities (1 December 2004); AR 215-7, Civilian Nonappropriated Funds and Morale, Welfare, and Recreation Activities (26 January 2001). AR 415-15 and AR 420-10 govern Army construction contracting, including some NAF construction contract issues.

4. Air Force Regulations.

   - 32 Series: AFI 32-1022, Planning and Programming Nonappropriated Fund Facility Construction Projects (29 June 94).
   - 34 Series: AFPD 34-2, Managing Nonappropriated Funds (7 Jan. 1994); AFI 34-124, Air Force Morale, Welfare, and Recreation Advisory Board (AFMWRAB) (25 July 1994); AFI 34-201, Use of Nonappropriated Funds (17 June 2002); AFI 34-202, Protecting Nonappropriated Fund Assets (27 Aug. 2004); AFI 34-407, Air Force Commercial Sponsorship Program (19 July 2005); AFMAN 34-416, Air Force Commercial Sponsorship and Sale of NAFI Advertising Procedures (5 Oct. 2004).

- 64 Series: AFPD 64-3, The Nonappropriated Fund Contracting System (1 Dec. 2005); AFI 64-301, Nonappropriated Fund Contracting Policy (12 Feb. 2002); AFMAN 64-302, Nonappropriated Fund Contracting Procedures (3 Nov. 2000); and
- 65 Series: AFI 65-106, Appropriated Fund Support of Morale, Welfare, and Recreation and Nonappropriated Fund Instrumentalities (11 Apr. 2006); AFI 65-107, Nonappropriated Funds Financial Management Oversight Responsibilities (1 Dec. 1999).

III. DEFINITIONS AND STATUTORY CONTROLS.

A. **Nonappropriated Fund Instrumentality** (NAFI). AR 215-4, Consolidated Glossary, sec. II, Terms.

1. NAFIs are separate entities that are created by federal agencies to perform essential government functions. The NAFI acts in its own name to provide or assist the federal agency, for example, by providing morale, welfare, and recreational programs for agency military and civilian personnel.

2. NAFIs are typically operated using self-generated funds, not funds appropriated by Congress. For example, the Army and Air Force Exchange Service is a NAFI that operates retail stores throughout the world for military personnel. It covers most of its costs through retail sales. The NAFI is a fiscal entity that maintains custody and control over these nonappropriated funds.

3. Not all NAFI funding is nonappropriated. Congress does appropriate funding, normally minor, to carry out the NAFI's functions. For example, the Army and Air Force Exchange Service receives some funding connected to its overseas operations.

4. As an instrumentality of the United States, the NAFI enjoys many of the privileges and immunities enjoyed by the United States government. The most important, or at least the most often litigated, is that NAFIs are immune from state taxation.

B. **Nonappropriated Funds** (NAFs). AR 215-4, Consolidated Glossary, sec. II, Terms.

   Cash and other assets received by NAFIs from sources other than monies appropriated by the Congress . . . . NAFs are government funds used for the collective benefit of those who generate them: military personnel, their dependents, and authorized civilians. These funds are separate and apart from funds that are recorded in the books of the Treasurer of the United States.

C. **Statutory Controls on Funds**. Congress directed DOD to issue regulations governing the management and use of NAFs, and has made DOD personnel subject to penalties for their misuse. All NAFIs are created by DOD and its components, and all NAFs are government funds. However, NAFs are not appropriated by Congress or controlled by the Treasury Department. NAFIs, as fiscal entities, control their NAFs. 10 U.S.C. § 2783. See Appendix A to this outline. Nevertheless, Congress may control the use of NAFs. For example:

1. Purchase of Alcoholic Beverages. A NAFI in the United States may purchase beer and wine only from in-state sources. 10 U.S.C. § 2488. See AR 215-1, para. 7-12b; AR 215-4, para. 5-57. Cf. AR 215-1, para. 7-12a (Installation Management Agency (IMA) regions set the policy governing the source of alcoholic beverages outside the United States).

2. Pricing of Wine. NAFIs located on military installations outside the United States must price and distribute wines

produced in the United States equitably when compared with wines produced by the host nation. 10 U.S.C. § 2489. See AR 215-1, para. 7-20.

IV. AUTHORITY TO CONTRACT.

A. **Generally**. Only warranted contracting officers are authorized to execute, administer, and terminate NAF contracts. The authority of these contracting officers is limited by their warrant. An exception exists in for emergency situations. (See subparagraph V. B.1(f) below.)

B. **Contracting Officers and Related Personnel**.

1. Generally, NAFI contracts are awarded and administered by warranted contracting officers. The contracting officer may be a NAFI contracting officer, whose authority is limited to the obligation of nonappropriated funds. The contracting officer may be an appropriated fund contracting officer who is acting on behalf of the NAFI.

2. An appropriated fund contracting officer must adhere to NAF policies and procedures when procuring supplies or services on behalf of a NAFI.

3. A warranted contracting officer may appoint some, or all, of the following:

   - Ordering Officers. Must be appointed in writing by a warranted contracting officer. Ordering officers can place delivery orders against indefinite delivery type contracts up to a stated amount, providing the IDIQ contract terms permit such orders. AR 215-4, para. 1-17, 6-7.
   - Blanket Purchase Agreement (BPA) Callers. Must be appointed in writing by warranted contracting officer.

4. Generally, smaller purchases are made by local NAFI contracting officers, and larger purchases are made by centralized procurement organizations.

5. The key legal distinction is that, regardless of whether the contracting officer is a NAFI or appropriated fund contracting officer, the contracting officer is only obligating nonappropriated funds in the acquisition. As such, NAFI acquisitions are exempt from many of the statutes and regulations that apply to appropriated fund acquisitions, such as the Contract Disputes Act of 1978 and the Competition in Contracting Act of 1984.

V. ACQUISITION PROCEDURES.

A. **FAR Applicability**.

1. The FAR and DFARS do not apply to NAFI acquisitions. The FAR applies to "Acquisitions." FAR 1.104. FAR 2.101 defines "Acquisitions" as purchases of supplies and services using appropriated funds. Thus, nonappropriated fund purchases are not subject to the FAR and DFARS.[1] The FAR and DFARS do, however, provide a model to follow, and NAFI contracting officers generally implement similar procedures.

2. Army NAFI Acquisition Regulations. AR 215-4, Nonappropriated Fund Contracting, provides the procedures applicable to NAF acquisitions. Generally the procedures closely parallel the equivalent procedures in the FAR.

3. Air Force NAFI Acquisition Regulations. AFMAN 64-302, Nonappropriated Fund Contracting Procedures (16 Nov. 2011) provides similar procedures for Air Force NAFI acquisitions.

B. **NAFI Acquisitions**.

1. NAFI acquisitions often have two characteristics that differentiate them from FAR and DFARS acquisitions. First, NAFI acquisitions tend to be smaller in value than appropriated fund acquisitions.

---

[1] DFARS 201.104 does make the FAR and DFARS applicable to purchases in support of foreign military sales and NATO cooperative programs regardless of the source of funding.

Second, NAFI acquisitions often involve commercial type activities, such as resale activities, consignment sales, concessions, entertainment contracts, etc. These commercial type activities require different terms and conditions than acquisitions of goods and services for agency use.

2. NAFI acquisitions typically involve commercial items and commercial services. Consequently, the contract employed is a Firm-fixed Price type contract.

3. The Air Force uses a centralized contracting system. See **http://www.afnafpo.com/**.

4. Simplified Acquisitions. AR 215-4, Chapter 3; AFMAN 64-302, Chapter 8. The applicable NAFI procedures specify thresholds for various types of simplified acquisitions.

5. Sealed Bidding. AR 215-4, Chapter 5. The Air Force generally uses competitive negotiations.

6. Negotiations. AR 215-4, Chapter 4; AFMAN 64-302, Chapter 8.

C. **Types of Contracts**. AR 215-4, para. 2-8. AFMAN 64-302, Chapters 10-11.

1. NAFI acquisitions employ many of the same contract types as used in appropriated fund acquisitions. Because NAFI purchases are often for commercial items, Firm-fixed Price (FFP) contracts are the contract type for most NAF procurements. Least risk to the NAFI. DOD Dir. 4105.67, para. 4.6.

2. Because many NAFI contracts acquire goods for resale, Indefinite Delivery contracts such as requirements contracts, indefinite quantity, definite quantity contracts, and Basic Ordering Agreements are common.

D. **Length of Contracts**. Generally, Army NAF contracts should not exceed five years, including options without written justification and approval. AR 215-4, para. 2-4. Air Force NAF Contracts should not exceed ten years without a written justification. AFMAN 64-302, para. 6.12. Services contracts subject to the SCA are limited to five years.

VI. **COMPETITION AND SOURCES OF SUPPLIES AND SERVICES.**

A. **Competition.** The Competition in Contracting Act (CICA) does not apply to NAFIs unless appropriated funds are obligated. 10 U.S.C. § 2303; Gino Morena Enters., B-224235, Feb. 5, 1987, 87-1 CPD ¶ 121.

1. Although CICA statutory requirements do not apply to NAFI acquisitions involving only NAFs, service regulations require maximum practicable competition.

2. Sole source procurements must be justified. AR 215-4, para. 1-1, 2-12, and 2-13; AFMAN 64-302, paras. 6.6 and 6.8.

B. **Use of Existing Contracts and Agreements**.

1. Government sources of supply for NAFI requirements include the General Services Administration (GSA), Defense Supply Depots, and commissaries. Other NAF sources include, but are not limited to, the Army and Air Force Exchange Service (AAFES), the Navy Resale System Office, and the Marine Corps Exchange System.

2. FAR Subparts 8.6 and 8.7, which require activities to purchase certain supplies from the Federal Prison Industries, Inc. (UNICOR) and the blind or severely disabled, apply to NAF acquisitions. 18 U.S.C. § 4124; 41 U.S.C. Chapter 85; AR 215-4, para. 2-11; AFMAN 64-302, para. 6.13.

3. Contracting with government employees and military personnel. A NAFI may contract with government employees and military personnel when such contracts

are funded solely with NAF. AR 215-4, para. 1-21; AFMAN 64-302, para. 11.10. This deviation from the FAR reflects the limited availability of suppliers at remote bases.

VII. CONTRACT ADMINISTRATION.

A. Procedures Generally Followed. Contract Administration Actions, such as changes, delays, terminations, inspection, and acceptance generally parallel the FAR and DFARS.

B. Prompt Payment Act Applies. 5 C.F.R. 1315; AR 215-4, para. 6-16. NAF contracting officers must comply with policies and clauses for implementing Office of Management and Budget (OMB) prompt payment regulations. Include specific prompt payment clause in each applicable solicitation. Refer to FAR, Subpart 32.9 for details.

C. Terminations. AR 215-4, para. 6-10.

1. The terminations clause authorizes contracting officers to terminate contracts when it is in the NAFI's best interest. Terminations can be for convenience or default. Contracting officers can enter settlement agreements.

2. No-fault terminations. Concession contracts (see para. VIII.A., below) may include an optional no-fault clause by which either party can terminate the contract by giving advanced written notice of a predetermined amount of time (usually 30 days).

D. Contract Disputes and Appeals.

1. The Contracts Disputes Act does not apply to NAFI contracts, other than contracts awarded by the Exchange Services. See Section XI.B below. Instead, the contracting officer inserts a disputes clause providing that all disputes shall be the subject of a contracting officer final decision, with a right of appeal to the highest authority for the service. Within the Army, final decisions

may be appealed to the Armed Services Board of Contract Appeals. The terms of the contract's disputes clause are binding.

VIII. SPECIAL CATEGORIES OF CONTRACTING.

A. Concession Contracts. Generally. AR 215-4, ch. 7-1; AFMAN 64-302, para. 11.8.

1. A concession contract is a license or permit for an activity/business to sell goods and services to authorized patrons at a designated location. Examples include retail merchandise, vending or amusement machines, special events, food service, or instruction. May be for a long or short-term.

2. Generally, the NAFI receives a flat fee or percentage of gross sales from the concessionaire.

3. Insurance. Contracting officer shall determine the types of insurance coverage necessary for the contractor to obtain to protect the interests of the NAFI. Coverage may include bodily injury and property damage; workmen's compensation; property insurance; automobile liability; etc. Contact USACFSC risk management office (RIMP) for assistance in determining appropriate amounts of insurance at riskmanagement@cfsc.army.mil.

B. Consignment Agreements. A consignment agreement is an agreement where the seller provides goods for resale, while retaining ownership of the goods pending sale. Generally, Consignment Agreements follow a standard form.

C. Vending and Amusement Machines (not including slot machines or other machines operated by the ARMP). AR 215-4, para 7-4.

1. In addition to general concession contract requirements, vending and amusement machine contracts should include

additional controls to prevent fraud, such as:

- The number of machines plus the machine type, manufacturer, and ID number;
- Location of machines during contract performance;
- Procedures for locking devices and sales accountability (see AR 215-1);
- Customer refund procedures;
- Capability of coin counting machines to reject slugs;
- Requirements for inspection and handling of food placed in vending machines;
- Space, plumbing, electrical requirements available to the concessionaire.

2. Note that the Randolph-Sheppard Act may apply. See AR 210-25 and 20 U.S.C. § 107.)

D. **Entertainment Contracts**. AR 215-4, para. 7-8; AFMAN 64-302, para. 11.2. NAFI may generally acquire entertainment without competition; however, NAFI's should not exclusively use one entertainer or agent.

1. Copyrighted material.

   a. Clearances are required before copyrighted material can be performed on stage. Procedures for obtaining these clearances is contained in AR 215-1, para. 8-12.

   b. Copyright and royalty clearances will be included in the contract file.

2. Government Employees. An entertainment contract will not be entered into between an MWR activity and a government employee or any organization substantially owned or controlled by one or more government employees unless the activity's needs cannot otherwise reasonably be met. AR 215-1, para. 8-13a(6). But see AR 215-4, para. 1-26 for language generally permitting contracts with government employees.

3. The SCA may apply if the entertainment requires the use of stage hands or other technicians.

4. The contract must contain a cancellation clause and a liquidated damages clause. AR 215-4, para. 7-8d.

E. **Service Contracts**. AR 215-4, para. 7-9; AFMAN 64-302, para. 11.6.

1. Service contracts are contracts to perform an identifiable task, rather than furnish an end product. Examples include operation of NAFI equipment or facilities, instructions and training, sports officials, architect-engineer services (see AR 215-4, para. 8-2), housekeeping, grounds maintenance, repair of equipment, etc.

2. Nonpersonal service contracts are those in which contractor personnel are not subject, whether by the contract terms or by the manner of its administration, to the supervision and control usually prevailing in relationships between the government or the NAFI and its employees

3. Personal services contracts are contracts that, by their express terms or by the manner of its administration, make the contractor personnel appear to be NAFI or government employees.

4. The Service Contract Act (SCA) applies to NAFI acquisitions.

   a. 41 USC 351-357 (1965). FAR 22.1007 and 22.1008.

   b. The SCA is primarily for services performed by nonexempt service workers. The SCA provides for minimum wages and fringe benefits for service workers engaged in contracts valued over $2,500. The contracting officer is responsible for incorporating wage determinations acquired from Department of Labor at www.dol.gov/esa/minwage/america.htm into the solicitation.

5. Davis Bacon Act. 40 U.S.C. § 276a; FAR 22.403-1. The Davis Bacon Act applies to

NAFI construction contracts. However, certain services performed under construction contracts are still covered by the SCA. If the construction contract is solely for services contract for dismantling, demolition, or removal of improvements without follow on construction, then the SCA applies. Otherwise the Davis-Bacon Act applies (federally funded construction projects over $2,000).

F.   Construction and Architect-Engineer (A-E) Contracts. AR 215-4, ch. 8; AFMAN 64-302, para. 6.2.

1.   The process for awarding NAF construction and A-E service contracts is similar to that for the same type of APF contracts.

2.   Performance and payment bonds are required for most construction projects. AR 215-4, para. 2-19.

3.   Labor standards. The Davis-Bacon Act, the Copeland Act, and Contract Work Hours and Safety Standards Act apply to construction contracts that exceed $2,000. AR 215-4, paras. 1-19 and 1-20. See DA Form 4075-R, dated August 1990.

G.   Purchase of Alcoholic Beverages.

1.   A NAFI in the United States may purchase beer and wine only from in-state sources. 10 U.S.C. § 2488. See AR 215-1, para. 7-12b; AR 215-4, para. 5-57. Cf. AR 215-1, para. 7-12a (Installation Management Agency (IMA) regions set the policy governing the source of alcoholic beverages outside the United States).

2.   Pricing of Wine. NAFIs located on military installations outside the United States must price and distribute wines produced in the United States equitably when compared with wines produced by the host nation. 10 U.S.C. § 2489. See AR 215-1, para. 7-20.

H.   Commercial Sponsorship. AR 215-1, Chapter 11, Section II.

1.   Definition. "Commercial sponsorship is the act of providing assistance, funding, goods, equipment (including fixed assets), or services to a MWR program(s) or event(s) by . . . [a sponsor] . . . for a specific (limited) period of time in return for public recognition or opportunities for advertising or other promotions." AR 215-1, para. 11-6; AFI 34-108, Atch 1.

2.   Army Management. Advertising and Commercial Sponsorship are marketing, not contracting functions and are performed by personnel specifically designated by a command authority (normally the Director, Family Morale, Welfare, and Recreation). AR 215-1, para. 11-13.

3.   Air Force Management. In the Air Force, only Force Support Squadron (FSS) MWR programs may use the commercial sponsorship program. AFI 34-108, para. 1.4.

4.   Procedures. Activities using commercial sponsorship procedures must ensure, among other matters, that:

- Obligations and entitlements of the sponsor and the MWR program are set forth in a written agreement that does not exceed one year, though such agreements may be renewed for a total of 5 years. All agreements require a legal review by the servicing legal office. AR 215-1, para. 11-8a; AFI 34-108, Attachment;

- The activity disclaims endorsement of any supplier, product, or service in any public recognition or printed material developed for the sponsorship event. AR 215-1, para. 11-8d; AFI 34-108, paras. 2.3 and 2.10.

- The commercial sponsor certifies in writing that it shall not charge costs of the sponsorship to any part of the government. AR 215-1, para. 11-9c; AFI 34108, para. 2.11.; and

- Officials responsible for contracting are not directly or indirectly involved with the solicitation of commercial vendors, except for those officials who administer NAF contracts. AR 215-1, para. 11-13a.

5.   Additional Air Force Procedures.

- Headquarters Air Force Director of Services (HQ USAF/A1S): Approves or disapproves any requests for sponsor corporate advertising benefits. Approves sponsorship offers valued at more than $100,000. AFI 34-108, para. 1.6.1
- MAJCOM Commanders: Approve or disapprove sponsorships of $5,000 through $100,000, and may delegate approval authority for up to $50,000 to the MAJCOM Vice Commander, Chief of Staff, or Services Director. The MAJCOM Commander may delegate approval authority up to $25,000 to an installation commander. AFI 34-108, para. 1.6.4.
- Installation Commanders: Approve or disapprove sponsorship worth $5,000 or less, or other values as delegated by the MAJCOM commander. The Installation Commander may delegate authority for approval or disapproval and acceptance or sponsorships worth up to $5,000 to the Mission Support Group Commander or FSS Commander. AFI 34-108, para. 1.6.5.3.
- FSS Commander: Appoints a commercial sponsorship program manager and reviews all proposals and agreements. AFI 34-108, para. 1.6.6.
- Solicited Commercial Sponsorships. AFI 34-108, para. 2.2. The Solicited Commercial Sponsorship Program is the only authorized method for soliciting commercial sponsors for MWR events. All sponsorship solicitations must be announced to the maximum number of potential sponsors.
- Unsolicited Commercial Sponsorships. AFI 34-108, para. 2.1. Must be entirely

initiated by prospective sponsors or their representatives. FSS activities may generate sponsorship awareness using various means, such as brochures, advertisements, news releases, or information letters; however, they may not provide information about specific needs.

6.   Restrictions. The MWR elements of Services may not solicit sponsorship from alcohol companies or military divisions of defense contractors under any circumstances. However, these companies may be allowed to provide unsolicited sponsorship at the discretion of the commanding authority. AFI 34-108, para. 2.2.2.2.

IX. LABOR AND SOCIOECONOMIC POLICIES.

A. Socioeconomic Policies.

1.   The Small Business Act (SBA). The SBA does not apply to NAF service contracts. However, contracting officers may solicit small businesses and minority firms to compete for NAF requirements. AR 215-4, para. 1-28.

2.   Foreign acquisition. NAF contracting officers will comply with the following when acquiring foreign supplies and services, as applicable.

a.   Buy American Act – Balance of Payments Program (41 USC 10a-10d).

b.   DOD International Balance of Payments Program (DOD Directive 7060.3).

c.   The Trade Agreements Act of 1979 (19 USC 2501, *et. seq.*).

d.   The Caribbean Basin Recovery Act (PL 98-67, Title II, as amended).

e.   Israeli Free Trade Implementation Act of 1985 (19 USC 2112 note).

f.   The North American Free Trade Agreement Implementation Act of 1993 (19 USC 3301, *et seq.*).

B.   Labor Laws. AR 215-4, para. 1-27.

1.   NAF contracting officers shall comply with the following labor laws when acquiring supplies, services, and construction, as applicable.

   a.   Davis-Bacon Act (40 U.S. 3141) – construction wages.

   b.   Copeland Act (18 USC 874 and 40 USC 3145) – construction – anti-kickback.

   c.   Walsh-Healey Public Contracts Act (41 USC 35-45, FAR 22.602) – all contracts over $10,000 – wages and working conditions.

   d.   Equal Employment Opportunity. Executive Order 11246, as amended, FAR 22.807).

   e.   Service Contract Act of 1965 (41 USC 351; FAR 22-1007 and 22-1008). Minimum wage in service contracts.

   f.   Contract Work Hours and Safety Standards Act (40 USC 3701, *et. seq.*).

X.   LEGAL REVIEW

A.   Required Legal Reviews. New to the current regulation. AR 215-4, para. 1-22; AFMAN 64-302, para. 2.7

1.   Army NAFIs must obtain legal review for a long list of contracting related actions. Legal counsel should review NAF contracting actions in all cases required by regulation and in any other cases when requested by the NAF contracting officer.

2.   Air Force NAFIs must obtain legal review for a shorter list, but including all changes to centralized formats.

B.   Discretionary Reviews/Business Judgment. NAFI contracts, from time to time, have resulted in unexpected outcomes and significant adverse publicity for the military. These undesired results are often the result of actions taken by less experienced contracting personnel, the unusual nature of NAF contracts, and less strict financial controls. Consequently, NAFI contracting actions should receive thorough legal reviews as a quality assurance mechanism, emphasizing both legal sufficiency and business judgment, notwithstanding the relatively smaller amounts involved.

XI.   LITIGATION INVOLVING NAF CONTRACTS.

A.   Protests. AR 215-4, para. 4-21.

1.   GAO Jurisdiction.

   a.   NAFI procurements. The GAO lacks jurisdiction over procurements conducted by NAFIs because its authority extends only to "federal agency" acquisitions. See 31 U.S.C. § 3551; 4 C.F.R. § 21.5(g) (GAO bid protest rule implementing statute). A NAFI is not a "federal agency." See DSV, GmbH, B-253724, June 16, 1993, 93-1 CPD ¶ 468; Matter of: LDDS Worldcom, B-270109. February 6, 1996, 96-1 CPD ¶ 45. Protests are resolved under agency procedures. AR 215-4, para. 4-21; AFMAN 64-302, para. 12.5.

   b.   Where the NAFI procurement is conducted by an APF contracting officer, the GAO will exercise bid protest jurisdiction. The GAO has jurisdiction over procurements conducted "by or for a federal agency," regardless of the source of funds involved. Barbarosa Reiseservice GmbH, B-225641, May 20, 1987, 87-1 CPD ¶ 529.

   c.   The GAO may consider a protest involving a NAFI if it is alleged that an agency is using a NAFI to avoid competition requirements. Premier

Vending, B-256560, July 5, 1994, 94-2 CPD ¶ 8; LDDS Worldcom, B-270109, Feb. 6, 1996, 96-1 CPD ¶ 45 (no evidence Exchange was acting as a conduit for Navy or Navy participation was pervasive).

    d.   The GAO will consider a protest involving a NAFI-conducted procurement if there is evidence of pervasive involvement of federal agency personnel in the procurement and the NAFI is acting merely as a conduit for the federal agency. See Thayer Gate Dev. Corp., B-242847.2, Dec. 9, 1994 (unpub.) (involvement of high-ranking Army officials in project did not convert procurement by a NAFI to one conducted by the Army).

2.   In MCI Telecommunications Corp. v. Army & Air Force Exchange Serv., No. 95-0607, 1995 U.S. Dist. LEXIS 12947 (D.D.C. May 9, 1995) (mem.), the court found no Scanwell standing in a suit against AAFES. But see 28 U.S.C. § 1491(b) (1) (granting pre-award and post-award protest jurisdiction to the Court of Federal Claims (COFC) and the district courts per amendment to the Tucker Act by the Administrative Disputes Resolution Act of 1996. This amendment, however, does not expressly include protests of exchange service contracting actions). Compare COFC claims jurisdiction at 28 U.S.C. § 1491(a)(1).

B.   **Disputes.** AR 215-4, paras. 6-11 through 6-13; AFMAN 64-302, para. 12.6.

1.   The major differences between a typical NAFI contract disputes clause (excluding the exchange services) and CDA disputes are:

- Adverse ASBCA decisions are not subject to further appeal.
- Successful claims are not paid by the Judgment Fund.

2.   Contractors must submit claims to the contracting officer.

3.   Typically, the disputes clause provides that the contracting officer must issue a written final decision within 60 days (claims not exceeding $50,000) or within a reasonable period of time (claims over $50,000).

4.   The contracting officer's decision lacks finality if it advises the contractor of its appeal rights under the contract incorrectly and the contractor is prejudiced by the deficiency. Decker & Co. v. West, 76 F.3d 1573 (Fed. Cir. 1996); Wolverine Supply, Inc., ASBCA No. 39250, 90-2 BCA ¶ 22,706.

5.   Processing Appeals of adverse final decisions. A contractor may appeal contracting officer's adverse final decision.

- Within the Army and Air Force, appeals are taken to the ASBCA within 90 days, as provided in the contract's disputes clause. The ASBCA follows its rules at DFARS Appendix A in resolving the appeal.
- Other services and activities may designate another appellate authority.

6.   Fiscal issues. Because Congress does not appropriate NAF monies, funds do not expire at the end of the fiscal year. However, finance offices may close out actions based on fiscal years so contracting officers must coordinate with their finance offices to keep monies active if contracts cross fiscal years.

7.   No judicial forum has jurisdiction over NAFI contract disputes, except those disputes arising under contracts involving the exchange services. As instrumentalities of the United States, NAFIs are immune from suit. Congress has not waived immunity for NAFIs under the Tucker Act (28 U.S.C. § 1346(a)(2)), the Contract Disputes Act (41 U.S.C. Chapter 71), or the Administrative Procedures Act. See Furash & Co. v. United States, 46 Fed. Cl. 518 (2000); Swiff-Train Co. v. United States, 443 F.2d

1140 (5th Cir. 1971); Commercial Offset Printers, Inc., ASBCA No. 25302, 81-1 BCA ¶ 14,900. AINS, Inc. v. United States, 365 F.3d 1333 (Fed. Cir. 2003) (CAFC established a four-part test for its determination of whether a government instrumentality is a NAFI: i) it does not receive its monies by congressional appropriation; ii) it derives its funding primarily from its own activities, services, and product sales; iii) absent a statutory amendment, there is no situation in which appropriated funds could be used to fund the federal entity; and iv) there is a clear expression by Congress that the agency was to be separated from general federal revenues.).

8. Exchange Services Contracts. Express or implied-in-fact contracts entered into by DOD, Coast Guard, and NASA exchange services, although NAFIs, are contracts of the United States for purposes of determining jurisdiction under the Tucker Act and the Contract Disputes Act. 28 U.S.C. § 1491(a)(1). The policy reason for Congress treating the Exchanges similar to appropriated funds is that the Exchanges' contracts can be quite substantial, given the volume of sales.

9. The Armed Services Board of Contract Appeals (ASBCA) has jurisdiction over NAF contract disputes if:

- The contract incorporates a disputes clause that grants such jurisdiction. COVCO Hawaii Corp., ASBCA No. 26901, 83-2 BCA ¶ 16,554; or
- The contract contains no disputes clause, but DOD regulations require incorporation of a jurisdiction-granting clause in the NAF contract. Recreational Enters., ASBCA No. 32176, 87-1 BCA ¶ 19,675.

10. The CAFC has refused to hear appeals from decisions of the ASBCA concerning NAFI contracts. Strand Hunt Constr., Inc. v. West, 111 F.3d 142 (Fed. Cir. 1997) (unpub); Maitland Bros. v. Widnall, 41 F.3d 1521 (Fed. Cir. 1994) (unpub).

XII. CONCLUSION.

Nonappropriated fund contracts are a type of contract that is exempt from many, but not all, of the requirements applicable to typical government contracts. Consequently, government attorneys should carefully consult applicable regulations for their agency or service. Contractors should note when the contract is awarded by a nonappropriated fund instrumentality and carefully review the terms and conditions, and applicable agency regulations, to familiarize themselves with the differences. Most differences favor the agency, or require a different procedure.

APPENDIX A

Title 10, Section 3013 (2005)

§ 3013. Secretary of the Army

(a)

(1) There is a Secretary of the Army, appointed from civilian life by the President, by and with the advice and consent of the Senate. The Secretary is the head of the Department of the Army.

(2) A person may not be appointed as Secretary of the Army within five years after relief from active duty as a commissioned officer of a regular component of an armed force.

(b)   Subject to the authority, direction, and control of the Secretary of Defense and subject to the provisions of chapter 6 of this title [10 USCS §§ 161 et seq.], the Secretary of the Army is responsible for, and has the authority necessary to conduct, all affairs of the Department of the Army, including the following functions:

(1) Recruiting.

(2) Organizing.

(3) Supplying.

(4) Equipping (including research and development).

(5) Training.

(6) Servicing.

(7) Mobilizing.

(8) Demobilizing.

(9) Administering (including the morale and welfare of personnel).

(10) Maintaining.

(11) The construction, outfitting, and repair of military equipment.

(12) The construction, maintenance, and repair of buildings, structures, and utilities and the acquisition of real property and interests in real property necessary to carry out the responsibilities specified in this section.

(c)   Subject to the authority, direction, and control of the Secretary of Defense, the Secretary of the Army is also responsible to the Secretary of Defense for--

(1) the functioning and efficiency of the Department of the Army;

(2) the formulation of policies and programs by the Department of the Army that are fully consistent with national security objectives and policies established by the President or the Secretary of Defense;

(3) the effective and timely implementation of policy, program, and budget decisions and instructions of the President or the Secretary of Defense relating to the functions of the Department of the Army;

(4) carrying out the functions of the Department of the Army so as to fulfill the current and future operational requirements of the unified and specified combatant commands;

(5) effective cooperation and coordination between the Department of the Army and the other military departments and agencies of the Department of Defense to provide for more effective, efficient, and economical administration and to eliminate duplication;

(6) the presentation and justification of the positions of the Department of the Army on the plans, programs, and policies of the Department of Defense; and

(7) the effective supervision and control of the intelligence activities of the Department of the Army.

(d)   The Secretary of the Army is also responsible for such other activities as may be prescribed by law or by the President or Secretary of Defense.

(e)   After first informing the Secretary of Defense, the Secretary of the Army may make such recommendations to Congress relating to the Department of Defense as he considers appropriate.

(f)   The Secretary of the Army may assign such of his functions, powers, and duties as he considers appropriate to the Under Secretary of the Army and to the Assistant Secretaries of the Army. Officers of the Army shall, as directed by the Secretary, report on any matter to the Secretary, the Under Secretary, or any Assistant Secretary.

(g)   The Secretary of the Army may--

(1) assign, detail, and prescribe the duties of members of the Army and civilian personnel of the Department of the Army;

(2) change the title of any officer or activity of the Department of the Army not prescribed by law; and

(3) prescribe regulations to carry out his functions, powers, and duties under this title [10 USCS §§ 101 et seq.].

Title 10, Section 2783
Nonappropriated Fund Instrumentalities: Financial Management
and Use of Nonappropriated Funds

(a)   REGULATION OF MANAGEMENT AND USE OF NONAPPROPRIATED FUNDS.—The Secretary of Defense shall prescribe regulations governing—

(1) the purposes for which nonappropriated funds of a nonappropriated fund instrumentality of the United States within the Department of Defense may be expended; and

(2) the financial management of such funds to prevent waste, loss, or unauthorized use.

(b)   PENALTIES FOR VIOLATIONS.—

(1) A civilian employee of the Department of Defense who is paid from nonappropriated funds and who commits a substantial violation of the regulations prescribed under subsection (a) shall be subject to the same penalties as are provided by law for misuse of appropriations by a civilian employee of the Department of Defense paid from appropriated funds. The Secretary of Defense shall prescribe regulations to carry out this paragraph.

(2) The Secretary shall provide in regulations that a violation of the regulations prescribed under subsection (a) by a person subject to chapter 47 of title 10, United States Code (the Uniform Code of Military Justice), is punishable as a violation of section 892 of such title (article 92) of the Uniform Code of Military Justice).

(c)   NOTIFICATION OF VIOLATIONS.—

(1) A civilian employee of the Department of Defense (whether paid from nonappropriated funds or from appropriated funds), and a member of the Armed Forces, whose duties include the obligation of nonappropriated funds, shall notify the Secretary of Defense of information which the person reasonably believes evidences—

(A)   a violation by another person of any law, rule, or regulation regarding the management of such funds; or

(B)   other mismanagement or gross waste of such funds.

(2) The Secretary of Defense shall designate civilian employees to receive a notification described in paragraph (1) and ensure the prompt investigation of the validity of information provided in the notification.

(3) The Secretary shall prescribe regulations to protect the confidentiality of a person making a notification under paragraph (1).

CONTRACTING IN SUPPORT OF DEPLOYED FORCES

I.   INTRODUCTION.

Over the past 15 years, the military has integrated contractor-furnished support into its operations outside the United States. These changes include relying on contractor support for many tasks not involving direct combat, use of ordering vehicles, such as ID/IQ contracts, for acquiring the services, and centrally controlling the training, deployment, and return of contractor personnel.

The types of contractor support are quite varied, ranging from deployment of technical experts (often retired U.S. military) to operate and maintain sophisticated weapons systems, to third-country nationals to perform mundane base support, to local nationals for translation, construction, relief work, and economic development. Each category of contractor support brings a host of unique policy concerns.

II.   REFERENCES.

One result of the dramatic expansion of contractor support during military deployments has been expansion of regulations and guidance on use of contractor support.

A.   Regulations.

1.   FAR Subpart 18.2

2.   FAR Subpart 25.3

3.   FAR Part 50

4.   DFARS Subpart 218.2

5.   DFARS Subpart 225.3

6.   DFARS Part 250.

7.   U.S. DEP'T OF ARMY, REG. 715-9, OPERATIONAL CONTRACT SUPPORT PLANNING AND MANAGEMENT (20 Jun. 2011) [hereinafter AR 715-9]

8.   U.S. DEP'T OF ARMY, REG. 700-137, LOGISTICS CIVIL AUGMENTATION PROGRAM (LOGCAP) (28 Dec. 2012) [hereinafter AR 700-137].

B.   Guidance.

1.   JOINT CHIEFS OF STAFF, JOINT PUB. 4-0, JOINT LOGISTICS (18 Jul. 2008) [hereinafter JP 4-0].

2.   JOINT CHIEFS OF STAFF, JOINT PUB. 4-10, OPERATIONAL CONTRACT SUPPORT (17 Oct. 2008) [hereinafter JP 4-10].

3.   UNDER SECRETARY OF DEFENSE, ACQUISITION, TECHNOLOGY, AND LOGISTICS, DEFENSE PROCUREMENT AND ACQUISITION POLICY, CONTINGENCY CONTRACTING, DEFENSE CONTINGENCY CONTRACTING HANDBOOK: ESSENTIAL TOOLS, INFORMATION, AND TRAINING TO MEET CONTINGENCY CONTRACTING NEEDS FOR THE 21ST CENTURY A JOINT HANDBOOK FOR THE 21ST CENTURY (Oct. 2012).

4.   U.S. DEP'T OF ARMY, FIELD MANUAL 1-04, LEGAL SUPPORT TO THE OPERATIONAL ARMY (Mar. 2013) [hereinafter FM 1-04].

5.   U.S. DEP'T OF ARMY, FIELD MANUAL 4-92 (FORMERLY 100-10-2), CONTRACTING SUPPORT BRIGADE (Feb. 2010) [hereinafter FM 4-92].

6.   U.S. DEP'T OF ARMY, FIELD MANUAL 1-06 (FORMERLY 14-100), FINANCIAL

Deployment Contracting

MANAGEMENT OPERATIONS (Apr. 2011) [hereinafter FM 1-06].

7. Army Sustainment Command (ASC), Contractor on the Battlefield Resource Library, *available at* http://www.aschq.army.mil/gc/ExpedCont ToolKit.htm (containing links to contingency contractor personnel related materials and websites).

8. U.S. Central Command Contracts webpage, located at https://www2.centcom.mil/sites/contracts/Pages/Home.aspx (containing training materials, checklists, policy documents, acquisition instructions, and contract clauses).

III. DOCTRINE.

A. **Contracting Is a Force Multiplier**. The combat operations in the Middle East have taken place in an environment of poor to nonexistent infrastructure, using a volunteer force. The U.S. military has had to furnish most of the logistics support from outside the combat zone. While, during the Vietnam War, much of this support came from a conscript military, during current operations, contracting has filled the shortfall, using a combination of local resources, third-country resources, and U.S. contractors. The procedures for competing, awarding, and supervising contractors in deployed environments is often referred to as "contingency contracting."

1. The Joint Chiefs of Staff, in Joint Publication (JP) 4-10, define Contingency Contracting as:

"[T]he process of obtaining goods, services and construction from commercial sources via contracting means in support of contingency operations. It is a subset of contract support integration and does not include the requirements development, prioritization and budgeting processes. Contracts used in a contingency include theater support,

systems support, and external support contracts."

B. **Legal Support to Operations.** Doctrine covering legal support to operations provides that the Judge Advocate's "contract law responsibilities include furnishing legal advice and assistance to procurement officials during all phases of the contracting process and overseeing an effective procurement fraud abatement program." FM 1-04, para. 5-40. Specifically, JAs are to provide "legal advice to the command concerning battlefield acquisition, contingency contracting, use of logistics civil augmentation program, acquisition and cross-servicing agreements, ... and overseas real estate and construction." *Id.*

1. Scope of Duties. Depending on their assigned duties, Judge Advocates should participate fully in the acquisition process at their level, make themselves continuously available to their clients, involve themselves early in the contracting process, communicate closely with procurement officials and contract lawyers in the technical supervision chain, and provide legal and business advice as part of the contract management team. *Id.* para. 5-41; see also AFARS 5101.602-2(c) (describing contracting officers' use of legal counsel).

2. Pre-Deployment. Judge Advocates should take the lead in advocating expeditionary contracting preparation. FM 1-04, para. 13-8. This could involve holding contract/fiscal law classes for supply and logistics personnel, reviewing acquisition and logistics plans as part of the units' OPLAN, and be available to give advice on the best practices to obtain goods and services while deployed.

3. Operational Support. To provide contract law support in operations, Judge Advocates with contract law experience or training should be assigned to division and corps levels main and tactical command posts, Theater Support

Command headquarters, theater army headquarters, and each joint and multinational headquarters. Depending on mission requirements, command structure, and the dollar value and/or complexity of contracting actions, contract law support may be required at various command levels including brigade or battalion. *Id.* paras. 5-39 to 5-43.

4. Contract-Specific Roles. Judge Advocates may be assigned as Command Judge Advocate or Deputy Command Judge Advocate for a Contract Support Brigade (CSB). These attorneys serve as the primary legal advisors to CSB commanders, staff, and contracting officials on the full spectrum of legal and policy issues affecting the CSBs peacetime and operational missions. FM 4-92, para. 1-13. Judge Advocates at sustainment brigades, theater sustainment brigades, and expeditionary sustainment brigades perform similar functions. FM 1-04, para. 5-42. Judge Advocates assigned to these and other contracting organizations should have contract law training. *Id.*

5. Demonstrated Importance. After action reports (AAR) from Iraq and Afghanistan consistently indicate that Judge Advocates throughout both theaters, regardless of the position to which they are assigned (including brigade judge advocates), daily practiced fiscal law. These same AARs indicated that, while most Judge Advocates encountered contract law issues less frequently, they needed an understanding of basic contract law principles to intelligibly conduct fiscal law analyses. For JAs assigned to contracting or logistics heavy units, knowledge of contract law was a prerequisite to their daily duties.

C. Applicable Law During a Deployment.

Contracting during a deployment involves two main bodies of law: international law (including law of the host nation), and U.S. contract and fiscal law. FM 1-04,

para. 5-38 and 5-39. Attorneys must understand the authorities and limitations imposed by these two bodies of law.

1. International Law.

   a. The Law of War – Combat. The Law of War applies during combat operations and imposes limitations, for example, on the use of prisoners of war (PW) for labor. Many contractors are authorized to accompany the force, a technical distinction that allows them to receive POW status should they be captured. See Geneva Convention IV, ART 4(A) (4).

   b. The Law of War – Occupation. The Law of War also applies during occupation, and may also be followed as a guide when no other body of law clearly applies, such as in Somalia in Operation Restore Hope.

   c. International Agreements. A variety of international agreements, such as treaties and status of forces agreements (SOFA) may apply. These agreements can have substantial impact on contingency contracting by, for example, limiting the ability of foreign corporations from operating inside the local nation, placing limits and tariffs on imports, and governing the criminal and taxation jurisdiction over contractors and their personnel.

   Example: The Diplomatic Note executed between the United States and the Transitional Government of the Islamic State of Afghanistan (12 December 2002) covers many of the duties and rights of the United States and its contractors operating in Afghanistan. The agreement states that "[t]he Government of the United States, its military and civilian personnel, contractors and contractor

587

personnel shall not be liable for any kind of tax or other similar fees assessed within Afghanistan." This type of provision has a profound impact on contract pricing and contractor performance. Legal counsel must know these agreements in order to properly advise their clients when facing contingency contracting.

International Agreements may also include choice of law provisions relating to contingency contracting. For example, the Diplomatic Note also provides that all contracts awarded by the United States to "acquire materials and services, including construction . . . should be awarded in accordance with the law and regulations of the government of the United States."

Local Law. Where the U.S. is operating in a foreign country without a status of forces agreement, local law can have a significant impact on contracting to support deployed forces. U.S. contractors are subject to local law, and confront conflicting compliance obligations.

2. U.S. Contract and Fiscal Law. There is no general "deployment exception" to contract or fiscal law.[1] Judge Advocates in contingency operations and the units they support must follow existing regulations, and take advantage of existing exceptions that address many of the problems commonly encountered. Overseas commands often have local regulations, policies, and authorities that implement the flexibility existing in

current law and regulation in their geographic region.

a. FAR, DFARS, and agency supplements. The supplements FAR contains apply to contingency contracting, and contain many provisions addressing contracting during deployments. The following parts are most challenging during contingency operations:

- Competition (FAR Parts 6, 13, 14, and 15). Some countries where U.S. forces have deployed recently have less well-developed rule of law and transparency. Achieving competition in such environments can be quite challenging, and justifying the absence of such competition can be a burden.

- Simplified Acquisitions (FAR Part 13). Approximately 95% of all contracting actions in contingency operations will utilize simplified acquisitions because of their low acquisition cost. The procedures reflect the robust competitive market in the United States for such purchases.

- Domestic Preferences (FAR Part 25 and DFARS Part 225). Statutory preferences for domestic sourcing often include exceptions applicable to foreign acquisitions, but may conflict with a desire to use local resources for economic development purposes.

b. Fiscal Law. See Chapter 4. The challenging aspects of fiscal law in military deployments are:

- Reconciling requirements to support military operations with legislative provisions incorporated into appropriations and authorizations acts;

- Appropriate funding for operational construction projects.

c. Executive Orders and Declarations.

---

[1] The President, as Commander in Chief, may have constitutional powers that supersede conflicting contract or fiscal statutes when U.S. Forces are engaged in combat, that boundary is undefined. Regulations require compliance with existing laws, and questions regarding separation of powers are best left to the principals of the three branches of government.

d. Contingency Funding and Contract Authorizations. Generally, ordinary fiscal and acquisition rules apply during military operations, including existing exceptions. There is no blanket "wartime" or "contingency" exception to applicable law and regulation; however, there are numerous provisions and exceptions that may apply:

- Operational requirements make the use of existing authorities easier to justify. For example, operational requirements will often justify finding unusual and compelling urgency exception to full and open competition located at FAR Section 6.302-2.
- Appropriation and authorization acts may contain temporary, extraordinary fiscal and contract authorities specific to a particular operation. Operations in Afghanistan contain numerous examples of these extraordinary authorities, from the expenditure of Commander Emergency Response Funds (CERP) through the Afghanistan First program.

e. DOD may use Public Law 85-804, codified at 50 U.S.C. §§1431-1435, and implemented in FAR Part 50, when another exception does not exist. During a national emergency declared by Congress or the President and for six months after the termination thereof, the President and his delegees may initiate or amend contracts notwithstanding any other provision of law whenever it is deemed necessary to facilitate the national defense. The President's powers under this statute are broad, but the statute and implementing regulations contain some limitations. Use of these powers on obligations exceeding $25 million requires a 60-day notice to Congress and wait. 50 U.S.C. § 1431. Obligations in excess of $70,000 must be approved by at

the secretarial level, and those below by the Head of the Contracting Activity. The President cannot use Public Law 85-804 to enter into a cost plus percentage of cost contract. 50 U.S.C. § 1432(a), nor waive several other statutory provisions. While use of Pub. L. 85-804 was routine in the past, use of this authority is less common today.

f. Common Sense. Reconciling the applicable laws sometimes requires application of common sense. For example, when contracting in a country that has a state-sponsored religion, a contract may require both compliance with local law and compliance with U.S. statutes and regulations that are clearly in conflict with local law. The best approach is to work to resolve the conflicts and ambiguities so that contractors are not induced to incur additional costs in an effort to resolve the conflict.

IV. DEPLOYMENT CONTRACTING AUTHORITY, PLANNING, PERSONNEL, AND ORGANIZATION.

A. **Contract vs. Command Authority**. Commanders have broad authority to direct operations as required. However, commanders, other than commanders of Contracting Activities, do not generally have the authority to enter into contractual obligations. The various Combatant Commanders (i.e., CENTCOM) are not Contracting Activities. PGI 202.101.

B. **Planning.** The type of organization to which a JA is assigned will dictate the degree to which they must become involved in planning for contract support. At a minimum, however, JAs should be familiar with how Joint and Army doctrine incorporate planning for contract and contractor personnel support through the Contract Support Integration Plan and Contractor Management Plan.

1. Contract Support Integration Plan (CSIP).

    a. In all operations where there will be a significant use of contracted support, the supported Ground Component Commanders and their subordinate commanders and staffs must ensure that this support is properly addressed in the appropriate OPLAN/OPORD. JP 4-10, p. III-16. To achieve this integration, logistics staff contracting personnel develops a CSIP, assisted by the lead Service contracting element (if a lead Service is designated). *Id.* Annex W to the GCC OPLAN/OPORD contains the CSIP. *Id.*

    b. The CSIP is a planning mechanism to ensure effective and efficient contract support to a particular operation. Essentially, it identifies which organization(s) will provide the contracting support and what support is anticipated. The CSIP development process is intended to ensure the operational commander and supporting contracting personnel conduct advanced planning, preparation, and coordination to support deployed forces, and that the contract support integration and contractor management related guidance and procedures are identified and included in the overall plan. FM 4-92, para. 2-4.

    c. At a minimum, the CSIP must include: theater support contracting organization responsibilities; boards and/or center information; operational specific contracting policies and procedures to include Service civil augmentation program/external contract,

multinational, and host-nation support coordination guidance; and, contract administration services delegations. Other elements may include but are not limited to the identification of major requiring activities and information on commercial support capabilities to satisfy requirements. JP 4-10, figure III-3.

    d. Each Service component should also publish its own CSIP seeking integration and unity of effort with the supported GCC's CSIP. JP 4-10, III-8.b. For the Army, the CSIP is located in Tab G, Appendix 1, of Annex F, Sustainment. U.S. DEP'T OF ARMY, FIELD MANUAL 5-0, THE OPERATIONS PROCESS table E-2 (Mar. 2010).

2. Contractor Management Plan (CMP).

    a. The CMP is related to, but not the same as, the CSIP. While the CSIP is focused on how the deployed forces will acquire and manage contracted support, the CMP is focused on government obligations under contracts to provide support to contractor personnel. JP 4-10, para. IV-3.b.

    b. The responsible contracting office must inform contractors what services the government will provide to contractors accompanying the force; what the contractor's legal status is, and constraints on contractor activities. Each of these factors can significantly affect costs, so accuracy is important. Include requirements from international and host-nation support agreements; contractor deployment procedures; theater reception procedures; personnel accountability; operational security plans; force protection plans; personnel recovery; contractor personnel services support; medical support; and redeployment plans. Where these factors are impossible to determine in advance, the government should consider which party is best able to bear the risk.

c. Many individuals and organizations have a role in managing contractors, including contracting officer representatives, supported units, contracting organizations, and contractor managers. JP 4-10, para. IV-1.b. Therefore, the GCC and subordinate joint forces commander must establish clear, enforceable, and well understood theater entrance, accountability, force protection, and general contractor management and procedures early in the planning stages of any military contingency. JP 4-10, para. IV-1.b(1). To accomplish this task, the GCC should develop a CMP. JP 4-10, para. IV-3.b(1).

d. The Joint Forces Command and Service components should prepare supporting CMPs that support the GCC's CMP but provide more specific details. JP 4-10, para. IV-3.b(1); FM 4-92, paras. 213 to 2-14.

e. For more detailed information on contingency contractor personnel, *see* CONTRACT & FISCAL LAW DEP'T, THE JUDGE ADVOCATE GENERAL'S SCHOOL, U.S. ARMY, CONTRACT LAW DESKBOOK, chap. 31, Contingency Contractor Personnel.

3. In a developed theater, JAs should familiarize themselves with theater business clearance procedures, theater specific contract clauses and policies, contract and acquisition review boards, as well as resource management policies and standard operating procedures, such as the Money as a Weapons System— Afghanistan (MAAWS-A). AARs from Afghanistan indicate that familiarity with this resource is foundational to anyone who will be providing fiscal or contract law advice in theater.

C. **Deployment Contracting Personnel.**

1. Contracting authority runs from the Secretary of Defense and the Under Secretary of Defense (Acquisition), through the Services and Defense Agencies; to the Heads of Contracting Activities (HCA). The HCA appoints a Senior Contracting Official (SCO) or Principal Assistant Responsible for Contracting (PARC). The HCA and SCO/PARC warrant contracting officers (KO) at various levels and with varying levels of authority. AFARS 5101.603-1. The chief of a contracting office, a contracting officer, may appoint field ordering officers (ordering officers) to conduct relatively low dollar value purchases. Ordering officers are authorized to obligate the government to pay for goods or services in accordance with their appointment letters, but ordering officers do not normally handle money. Finance soldiers or Department of Defense (DOD) civilians, known as Class A agents or paying agents, handle money and pay merchants for purchases made by the ordering officers.

2. Contracting Officer's Representative (COR). CORs operate as the contracting officer's eyes and ears regarding contract performance, and provide the key link between the command and the contracting officer regarding the command's needs. CORs are members of the supported force and are appointed as a COR by the contracting officer. CORs are necessary because contracting officers are normally not located at the site of contract performance. Commanders should request that the contracting officer appoint at least one COR for each contract affecting the unit. CORs only exercise the contract authority included in the delegation, and

Deployment Contracting

are typically used for communication regarding contract performance. Any issues with the contractor must still be resolved by the contracting officer. *See* DFARS 201.602-2; JP 4-10, para. I-2c(3).

a. A properly trained COR shall be designated in. FAR 1.602-2(d). CORs must be a U.S. government employee, unless authorized by agency-specific regulations. In this case, DFARS 201-602-2 authorizes officers of foreign governments to act as CORs as well.

b. HQDA EXORD 048-10: Pre-Deployment Training for Contracting Officer's Representative and Commander's Emergency Response Program (CERP) Personnel, dated 5 Dec. 2009, requires brigades, brigade equivalents, and smaller units deploying to Iraq or Afghanistan to: (1) Determine the number of CORs needed to meet theater contracting requirements, or (2) train 80 COR candidates (separate battalions must train 25 COR candidates, and separate companies must train 15 COR candidates), (3) NLT 90 days before the LAD, ensure COR candidates complete online training courses, and (4) CORs must receive supplemental training from the contracting officer that appoints them as a COR.

c. For more detailed information on COR responsibilities, *see* CENTER FOR ARMY LESSONS LEARNED, HANDBOOK 08-47, DEPLOYED COR (Sep. 2008); *see also* DFARS 201.602-2(2); DFARS Class Deviation 2011-O0008, Designation of Contracting Officer's Representative (21 Mar. 2011) (setting forth appointment requirements for CORs).

3. Field Ordering Officer (ordering officer).

   a. Service member or DOD civilian appointed in writing and trained by a contracting officer. AFARS 5101.602-2-90; 5101.603-1; 5101.603-1-90; 5101.603-1-90(b). Ordering officers are not warranted contracting officers and their ordering officer duties are generally considered an extra or collateral duty. JP 4-10, para. I-2c(5).

   b. Ordering officers are usually not part of the contracting element, but are a part of the forward units.

   c. Ordering officers may be authorized to make purchases over the counter with SF44s up to the micro-purchase threshold, place orders against certain indefinite delivery contracts, make calls under Blanket Purchase Agreements (BPAs), and make purchases using imprest funds. AFARS 5101.602-2-90. Ordering officers may also be government purchase card holders. AFARS 5113.2. Ordering officers are subject to limitations in their appointment letters, procurement statutes and regulations, and fiscal law. Contracting authority may be limited by dollar amount, subject matter, purpose, time, etc. Typical limitations are restrictions on the types of items that may be purchased and on per purchase dollar amounts. A sample appointment letter is found at AFARS 5153.9002.

4. Paying Agents. The finance staff element makes payments using paying agents. When ordering officers or contracting officers make purchases using SF44s, the merchant can present the form to the paying agent for payment. Alternatively, common in a cash-based economy, the paying agent will accompany the ordering officer or contracting officer. Once the

ordering officer/contracting officer completes the transactions, the paying agent will pay the merchant. Pre-deployment coordination with finance to determine who the paying agents are and where they will be located will aid the deployed contracting process. Paying agents may not be ordering officers. For detailed guidance on paying agents, *see* FM 1-06, app. D; *see also* DOD FMR, vol. 5, para. 020604 (discussing the appointment and responsibilities of paying agents). For Afghanistan specific guidance on paying agents, see the MAAWS-A.

D. Contracting Organizations.

Three different sources of contract support generally are used in support of contingency operations: Theater Support Contracts, Systems Support Contracts, and External Support Contracts.

1. Theater Support Contracts. Contracts awarded by contracting officers in the operational area serving under the direct contracting authority of the Service component, special operations forces command, or designated joint HCA for the designated contingency operation. JP 4-10, p. vii, para. III-6. These contracts are commonly referred to as contingency contracts. *Id.* For example, theater support contracts in Afghanistan include contracts awarded by the CENTCOM Joint Theater Support Contracting Command or any of its Regional Contracting Centers or Offices.

2. Systems Support Contracts. Contracting activities supporting program offices for weapons systems award contracts for technical support, maintenance, and, in some cases, repair parts for their systems. These requirements are often included with the acquisition contract. These contracts can be awarded long before they are needed, and are not focused on specific operations. JP 410, p. vii, para. III-4 and app. A. Only the contracting activity that issued the contract has the authority to modify or terminate the contract.

3. External Support Contracts. Contracting activities, such as U.S. Army Sustainment Command award contracts to provide a variety of logistic and other noncombat related services and supply support. JP 4-10, p. vii, para. III-5. This includes the LOGCAP series of contracts.

   a. Types of support required includes: (1) logistics, such as base operating support, transportation, port and terminal services, warehousing and other supply support functions, facilities construction and management, prime power, and material maintenance. JP 410, para. III-5a and figure III-2; (2) other support services, including communication services, interpreters, commercial computers and information management, and subject to congressional as well as DOD policy limitations, interrogation and physical security service support. *Id.*

   b. LOGCAP and other Major External Support Contracts.

      These contracts include the Air Force Contract Augmentation Program (AFCAP), the U.S. Navy Global Contingency Construction Contract (GCCC), and Global Contingency Service Contract (GCSC)); fuel contracts awarded by the Defense Energy Support Center; construction contracts awarded by the U.S. Army Corps of Engineers and Air Force Center for Engineering and Environmental Excellence; and translator contracts awarded by the Army Intelligence and Security Command. JP 4-10, para. III-5(a).

      These contracts augment organic military capabilities, and are long term (four to nine years depending on the program) competitively awarded contracts, ID/IQ contracts. Because of the uncertainty on requirements, they typically use, or can opt to use, cost-plus award fee ID/IQ task orders.

V. CONTRACTING PROCESSES.

A. Theater Business Clearance (TBC) / Contract Administration Delegation (CAD).

1. During many deployments, contracts performed in the area should be (a) visible to the area command, (b) contain certain minimum clauses and requirements, and be locally administered. For example, contracts supporting deployments should contain provisions implementing applicable Status of Forces Agreements, local law, or theater policies, and the supported force should have clear responsibilities for administration.

2. To facilitate uniformity in Iraq and Afghanistan, the Deputy Under Secretary of Defense, Acquisition, Technology, and Logistics and the Director of Defense Procurement and Acquisition Policy issued a series of memoranda directing JCC-I/A (now CENTCOM Contracting Command (C3)) to develop Theater Business Clearance procedures, to include procedures on delegation of contract administration delegation. Headquarters, Joint Contracting Command – Iraq / Afghanistan, subj.: Theater Business Clearance (TBC) Authority, Procedures, and Requirements for Iraq and Afghanistan, *available at* http://www2.centcom.mil/sites/contracts/Pages/Default.aspx, *also available at* http://centcomcc.net.

3. CENTCOM Contracting Command uses the TBC review process to ensure that contracting officers outside theater (e.g., external and system support contracting officers) insert mandatory language and clauses in contracts. *Id.* As an example,

a. C3 952.225-0001, Arming Requirements and Procedures for Personal Security Services Contractors and Requests for Personal Protection.

b. C3 952.225-0005, Monthly Contractor Census Reporting.

c. C3 952.225-0009, Medical Screening and Vaccination Requirements for Third Country Nationals and Locally Hired Employees Operating in the CENTCOM Area of Responsibility.

d. DFARS 252.225-7040, Contractor Personnel Authorized to Accompany U.S. Forces Deployed Outside the U.S., and DFARS Class Deviation 2007-O0010, Contractor Personnel in the U.S. Central Command Area of Responsibility.

4. The TBC review process also addresses whether in-theater contract administration will be delegated to Defense Contract Management Agency or whether administration will be re-delegated to the procuring contracting officer. *Id.* On May 13, 2013, DPAP issued updates to the TBC policy, including requirements for an in-theater sponsor and in-theater management over contracts, e.g., COR, COTR, GTPR. *See* Director, Defense Procurement and Acquisition Policy, subj.: Theater Business Clearance Update for the USCENTCOM Area of Responsibility *available at* http://www.acq.osd.mil/dpap.

B. Publicizing Contract Actions and Competition.

1. Solicitations and contracts awarded and performed outside the United States, its possessions, and Puerto Rico, for which only local sources will be solicited, generally are exempt from compliance with the requirement to synopsize the acquisition in FedBizOpps. FAR 5.202(a)(12). These contracts, therefore,

may be solicited and awarded with less than the normal minimum 45-day notice periods.

2. Contracts awarded and performed overseas are not exempt from the requirement for competition. *See* FAR 5.202(a)(12). Agencies may have to take additional measures to ensure that they obtain the benefits of meaningful competition. Promote competition by posting notices on procurement bulletin boards located where local sources have access, solicit potential offerors identified from host nation sources, advertising in local newspapers, and consulting local telephone directories. *See* FAR 5.101(a)(2) & (b) and AFARS Manual No. 2, para.4-3.e. In some areas, collusive bidding is not unusual, so contracting personnel need to be vigilant and take active measures to promote independent competitors.

3. Specific Exceptions. During contingency operations, Congress may authorize temporary exceptions to normal contacting and competition rules through authorization acts or annual or supplemental appropriations acts. Examples in Afghanistan include the Commander's Emergency Response Program, Afghan First Program, and the SC-CASA Program (allowing preferences and set-asides for certain acquisitions from vendors in certain countries along major supply routes to Afghanistan).

C. **Simplified Acquisition Procedures.**

1. Thresholds. Simplified acquisition procedures described in Chapter 7 are commonly used for local purchases overseas. Recognizing this, Congress amended 41 U.S.C. § 1903, Special Emergency Procurement Authority, to increase the applicable thresholds for procurements in support of a contingency operation as defined in 10 U.S.C. § 101(a)(13), or to facilitate defense against or recovery from NBC or radiological attack. In these

circumstances, the increased thresholds are:

a. Simplified acquisition threshold (SAT). Simplified acquisition procedures can be used to procure goods and services supporting a contingency operation up to $750,000 in the United States, and $1,500,000 outside the United States. 41 U.S.C. § 1903(b); FAR 2.101. DFARS Class Deviation 2011-O0009, Simplified Acquisition Threshold for Humanitarian or Peacekeeping Operations (28 Mar. 2011), sets the SAT at $300,000 when soliciting or awarding contracts to be awarded and performed outside the United States to support a humanitarian or peacekeeping operation. See FAR 2.101 (defining humanitarian or peacekeeping operation).

b. Micro-purchase threshold. For purchases supporting a contingency operation but made (or awarded and performed) inside the United States, the micro-purchase threshold is $15,000. For purchases supporting a contingency operation made (or awarded and performed) outside the United States, the micro-purchase threshold is $25,000. 41 U.S.C. § 1903; FAR 2.101.

c. Commercial items. Contracting officers may use simplified acquisition procedures to acquire commercial items up to $10,000,000 in support of contingency operations. 41 U.S.C. § 1903(b)(3).

D. **Use of Existing Contracts to Satisfy Requirements.**

1. As discussed in section IV.D.3, above, the services have established logistics contracts to provide goods and services during deployments. Additionally, there are many GSA, FSS, ID/IQ, and

requirements contracts available for standard goods and services that may include many useful requirements, such as fuel, subsistence items, and base support services. Investigate the existence of such contracts with external and theater support contracting activities.

2. Theater Support Contracts. In developed theaters, the theater contracting activity (regardless of organizational type) may have existing indefinite quantity-indefinite delivery (IDIQ) contracts, BPAs, or requirements contracts available to efficiently satisfy a unit's needs. For example, CENTCOM Contracting Command may have multiple award IDIQ contracts for base support services and security services. If a unit has a requirement for either of these services, CENTCOM Contracting Command may expeditiously award the task order to one awardees of the underlying IDIQ contract utilizing the "fair opportunity" to be considered procedures in FAR 16.5.

E. Alternative Methods for Fulfilling Requirements.

1. Contracts are not the only method of meeting the needs of deployed military forces. The source of first resort is the military supply system, especially for military items. Military depots have supplies that are already purchased, and awaiting delivery, including items designated as war reserves that are made available to support deployments to active combat.

2. Host Nation Support. Various cross-servicing agreements and host-nation support agreements exist with NATO, Korea, and other major U.S. allies, such as Australia. Host Nation Support is described in 10 U.S.C. §§ 2341-2350; governed by DOD Dir. 2010.9, Acquisition and Cross-Servicing Agreements (28 Apr. 2003); and implemented by Joint Chiefs of Staff, Instr. 2120.01A, Acquisition and Cross-Servicing Agreements (27 Nov. 2006).

Army guidance is located in U.S. Dep't of Army, Reg. 12-1, Security Assistance, International Logistics, Training, and Technical Assistance Support Policy and Responsibilities (24 Jan. 2000). For example, a U.S. force may acquire fuel, spare parts, and services from the host nation, permitting use of existing stocks in the supply systems of the U.S. and allied nations. Transactions may be accomplished notwithstanding certain other statutory rules related to acquisition and arms export controls.

3. Inter-Agency Acquisitions. As discussed in Chapter 13, the Economy Act, 31 U.S.C. § 1535, provides another alternative means of fulfilling requirements. An executive agency may transfer funds to another agency, and order goods and services to be provided from existing stocks or by contract. For example, the Air Force could have construction performed by the Army Corps of Engineers, and the Army might have Department of Energy facilities fabricate special devices for the Army. Procedural requirements for Economy Act orders, including obtaining contracting officer approval on such actions, are set forth in FAR 17.5; DFARS 217.5; U.S. Dep't of Defense, Instr. 4000.19, Inter-Service and Intra-Governmental Support (25 April 2013); and DFAS-IN 37-1.

4. Extraordinary contractual actions under Public Law 85-804. During a national emergency declared by Congress or the President and for six months after the termination thereof, the President and his delegees may initiate or amend contracts notwithstanding any other provision of law whenever it is deemed necessary to facilitate the national defense. Pub. L. No. 85-804, codified at 50 U.S.C. §§1431-1435; Executive Order 10789 (14 Nov. 1958); FAR Part 50; DFARS Part 250.

F. Leases of Real Property.

The Army is authorized to lease foreign real estate for military purposes. 10

U.S.C. § 2675. True leases normally are accomplished by the Army Corps of Engineers using Contingency Real Estate Support Teams (CREST).

VI. POLICING THE CONTRACTING BATTLEFIELD.

A. General.

In the course of rapidly changing events and military deployments in response thereto, the best laid plans often do not survive. Military units with immediate needs may act outside their authority, either through lack of knowledge, or to accomplish important missions. This inevitably results in unauthorized commitments and obligations that the government should stand behind.

B. Ratification of Contracts Executed by Unauthorized Government Personnel.

1. Only Heads of Contracting Activities and warranted contracting officers can legally obligate the government in contract. However, sometimes other government officials purport to bind the government. This may occur, for example, when a commander directs a contractor to take actions beyond the scope of an existing contract or in the absence of a contract. An "unauthorized commitment" is an agreement that is not binding on the government solely because it was made by someone who did not have authority to bind the government (FAR 1.602-3). Because the person making the unauthorized commitment had no authority to bind the government, the government has no obligation to pay the unauthorized commitment. However, many good reasons support doing so, such as maintaining good relations with allies and the local populace, a continuing need to contract for support, etc. Someone with actual authority to bind the government may subsequently ratify the unauthorized commitment, facilitating payment.

2. Based upon the dollar amount of the unauthorized commitment, the following officials have the authority to ratify the unauthorized commitment. See FAR 1.602-3; AFARS 5101.602-3):

    a. Up to $10,000 – Chief of Contracting Office

    b. $10,000 - $100,000 – Principal Assistant Responsible for Contracting

    c. Over $100,000 – Head of the Contracting Activity.

3. FAR 1.602-3(c) states that ratifications are appropriate when:

    a. The government has received the goods or services.

    b. The ratifying official has the authority to enter into a contractual commitment.

    c. The resulting contract would have otherwise been proper if made by an appropriate contracting officer.

    d. The price is fair and reasonable.

    e. The contracting officer recommends payment and legal counsel concurs, unless agency procedures do not require such concurrence.

    f. Proper funds are available and were available at the time the unauthorized commitment was made.

C. Extraordinary Contractual Actions.

1. If ratification is not appropriate, for example, where no agreement was reached with the supplier, the taking may be compensated as an informal commitment. FAR 50.102-3 and 50.103-2(c). Alternatively, the supplier may be compensated using service secretary residual powers. FAR 50.104.

2. Requests to formalize informal commitments must be based on a request

for payment made within six months of furnishing the goods or services, <u>and</u> it must have been impracticable to have used normal contracting procedures at the time of the commitment. FAR 50.102-3(d).

3. These procedures have been used to reimburse owners of property taken during the Korean War (AFCAB 188, 2 ECR § 16 (1966)); in the Dominican Republic (Elias Then, Dept. of Army Memorandum, 4 Aug. 1966); in Jaragua S.A., ACAB No. 1087, 10 Apr. 1968; and in Panama (Anthony Gamboa, Dep't of Army Memorandum, Jan. 1990).

D. Quantum Meruit/"No Doubt" Claims.

1. Historically, the GAO had claims settlement authority that it used to settle claims based on quantum meruit. These are claims where the United States obtained a clear benefit under circumstances where it had no legal obligation to pay. In 1995, Congress transferred the claims settlement functions of the GAO to the Office of Management and Budget, which further delegated the authority. <u>See</u> Pub. L. 104-53, 109 Stat. 514, 535 (1995), codified at 31 U.S.C. § 3702(a)(4).

2. Within DOD, the Claims Division at the Defense Office of Hearings and Appeals (DOHA) settles these types of claims for the Department of Defense. DOHA decisions can be found at www.defenselink.mil/dodgc/doha.

E. Contracting with the Enemy.

1. Concerns that the military was contracting with entities that, in turn, supported the groups fighting the U.S. led Congress to enact Section 841, of the 2012 National Defense Authorization Act, Pub. L. 112-81. This authorizes the Head of a Contracting Activity to restrict award, terminate contracts already awarded, or void contracts to contractors who directly or indirectly fund the insurgency or forces opposing the U.S. in the CENTCOM

theater of operations. Further, the CENTCOM Commander can use battlefield intelligence to make this determination and does not have to disclose that intelligence to the affected contractor. This authority applies to all contracts that will be executed in the CENTCOM Area of Responsibility for more than $100,000.

2. Section 842 of Pub. L.112-81 requires contracting officers include a contract term in covered contracts that allows the government to inspect "any records of the contractor" or subcontractor to ensure contract funds are not going to support the insurgency or otherwise oppose U.S. action in the CENTCOM Area.

VII. CONCLUSION.

Individuals with little to no contracting experience are often entrusted with substantial sums of money to support their unit's deployments. Prior planning and training can mitigate many of the risks inherent in this situation. Contract law is not intended to impede military operations. It provides exceptions and alternate procedures for most common situations and identifies the responsible individuals for determining that the situation justifies the use of the exceptions and alternate procedures. Judge Advocates, by learning the available exceptions and procedures, can facilitate military operations by removing the obstacles presented by routine, peacetime practices.

PROCUREMENT FRAUD

I. INTRODUCTION.

A. General.

While the overwhelming majority of government contractors are honest and ethical, timely delivering conforming goods and services to their government customers, these practices are not universal. The enormous sums spent by the government attract some dishonest suppliers, and the government often purchases in markets where business practices differ markedly from those prevailing in the United States.[1]

B. Public Policy.

When the United States government purchases goods and services, considerations of public policy place the government in a more favorable position than other buyers, whose suppliers may have misrepresented material facts in the transaction.

> "The United States does not stand on the same footing as an individual in a suit to annul a deed or lease obtained from him by fraud. . . . The financial element in the transaction is not the sole or principle thing involved. This suit was brought to vindicate the policy of the [g]overnment . . . . The petitioners stand as wrongdoers, and no equity arises in their favor to prevent granting the relief sought by the United States." Pan Am. Petroleum and Transp. v. United States, 273 U.S. 456, 509 (1927).

C. Exclusion of Bad Actors.

When the government identifies suppliers that engage in fraudulent conduct, it has many remedies available, including criminal, civil, contractual, and administrative. The most significant remedy available is exclusion. Entities and individuals determined to have engaged in fraud are usually excluded from further government contracting. This results from strong public policies promoting honesty and fair dealing between the government and its suppliers. For example, the 2014 Department of Defense Appropriations Act (Division C of Public Law 113-76) prohibits the expenditure of funds with any person or entity suspended or debarred from receiving a government contract. See Memorandum of the Undersecretary of Defense for Acquisition, Technology, and Logistics, SUBJECT: Class Deviation – Prohibition Against Using Fiscal Year 2014 Funds to Contract with Entities Convicted of Fraud Against the Federal Government (dated March 20, 2014) available at **http://www.acq.osd.mil/dpap/dars/class_devia tions.html.**

D. Definition of Procurement Fraud.

Procurement fraud can be defined as illegal conduct by which the offender gains an advantage, avoids an obligation, or causes damage to his organization. It includes attempts and conspiracies to effect deception for the purpose of inducing action or reliance on that deception. Such practices include, but are not limited to, bid-rigging, making or submitting false statements, submission of false claims, and adulterating or substituting materials.

II. IDENTIFYING FRAUD.

A. Fraud Before Contract Award.

Fraudulent activity may occur prior to contract award, more than one type of fraud may be

---

[1] The United States ranks 16 of 168 countries evaluated by Transparency International for perceptions of corruption, behind countries such as Denmark (No. 1) and Canada (No. 9), but well ahead of countries such as Iraq (No. 161) and Afghanistan (No. 166). http://www.transparency.org/cpi2015.

Procurement Fraud

present in one case, and at any time within the same acquisition. This is not an all-inclusive list.[2]

1. Bribery, Public Corruption, and Conflicts of Interest.

    a. The breach of an employee's duty of loyalty. See, e.g., United States v. Carter, 217 U.S. 286 (1910); United States v. Brewster, 408 U.S. 501 (1972). In these types of fraud, government employees collude with one or more contractors to effectuate the fraud. The breach of the government employee's duty of confidentiality may occur as a result of a direct quid pro quo bribe, or an indirect conflict of interest.

    b. Possible indicators of Bribery, Public Corruption, and Conflicts of Interest.

    • Unjustified favorable treatment to a contractor.
    • Acceptance of low quality goods, nonconformance to contract specifications, and/or unjustifiably late delivery of goods or services.
    • An unusually high volume of purchases from the same contractor or set of contractors.
    • Procurement officials fail to file financial disclosure forms (this may occur when a procurement official remains directly involved in a procurement in which he/she has a substantial financial stake).
    • Procurement official has family members who are employed by contractors that were awarded a government contract.
    • Purchasing unnecessary or inappropriate goods or services.

2. Bid-Rigging.

    a. Bid-rigging occurs when two or more independent potential competitors collude to frustrate a competitive contract award.

    b. Under the Sherman Act, 15 U.S.C. § 1, "[e]very contract, combination in the form of trust or otherwise, or conspiracy, in restraint of trade of commerce among the several States, or with foreign nations, is declared to be illegal." Bid-rigging circumvents competition, increases the cost to the government, and deprives the government of the most reliable measure of what a fair and reasonable price should be. The measure of damages is "the difference between what the government actually paid on the fraudulent claim and what it would have paid had there been fair, open and competitive bidding." United States v. Killough, 848 F.2d 1523, 1532 (11th Cir. 1988); see also Brown v. United States, 524 F.2d 693, 706 (Ct. Cl. 1975); United States v. Porat, 17 F.3d 660 (3rd Cir. 1993).

    c. Bid-rigging takes many forms, including agreements not to bid, on the prices each should bid, submitting false bids from nonexistent competitors, etc.

    d. Possible indicators of bid-rigging.

    • The winning bid price seems to be much higher than the independent government estimate (IGE) or industry averages.
    • There is a pattern of winning bidders.
    • The losing bidder(s) typically become the subcontractor of the winning bidder.
    • The solicitations and/or specifications are written in an overly restrictive way (i.e. only one contractor could possibly provide the desired product).

3. Defective Pricing.

    a. The Truth in Negotiations Act (TINA), 10 U.S.C. § 2306a and 41 U.S.C. Chapter 35, requires contractors in some negotiated procurements to

---

[2] See AR 27-40, Chapter 8 (for additional possible indicators of fraud, the Army's Indicators of Fraud are laid out in AR-27-40, figure 8-1); see also Auditor Fraud Resources – Scenarios and Indicators, available at http://www.dodig.mil/resources/fraud/scenarios.html.

disclose cost and pricing data, and to certify that disclosed data are current, accurate, and complete (see Chapter 14).

b. Defective pricing may be the result of unintentional errors and misunder-standings to be expected in a complex process by fallible individuals. When the erroneous or incomplete data is reckless or intentional, defective pricing may result in a fraud investigation and civil or criminal prosecution by the government. United States v. Broderson, 67 F. 3d 452 (2d Cir. 1995).

c. Possible Indicators of Intentional Defective Pricing.

- Fabricated quotations and invoices.
- Intentional withholding of cost data.
- Preparation of unrealistic cost estimates.
- Ignoring known cost data when preparing cost estimates.

4. Fraudulent Sole Sourcing.

a. Occurs when procurement officials collude with a contractor to unjustifiably direct a contract to the contractor without "full and open" competition (and at a higher price than the government would have paid if the requirement was properly competed).

b. The fraudulent actions typically involve misrepresentations in preparing the Justification and Approval required by FAR Part 6 for Other Than Full and Open Competition. See Chapter 5.

c. Possible indicators of Fraudulent Sole Sourcing.

- Tailoring specifications to one contractor's products not justified by agency needs.
- Misstatements or material omissions of fact in the required J&A.
- Manipulating the quantity solicited to avoid reviews and higher level approvals of the J&A

- Prior successful procurements using full and open competition.
- Splitting purchases to avoid competition requirements (i.e., using simplified acquisition procedures).

B. **Fraud After Contract Award.** There are several types of fraudulent activity that have occurred during performance of a government contract. They include:

1. Product Substitution/Defective Product/Defective Testing.

a. Product substitution is "delivery to the government of a product that does not meet the contract requirements." Nash, Schooner, O'Brien-DeBakey, Edwards, The Government Contracts Reference Book, 3rd edition; The George Washington University, 2007. These terms generally refer to situations where contractors deliver to the government goods that do not conform to contract requirements without informing the government. United States v. Hoffman, 62 F. 3d 1418 (6th Cir. 1995).

b. Defective Products and Defective Testing cases are subsets of Product Substitution and occur as a result of the failure of a contractor to perform contractually required tests, or its failure to perform such testing in the manner required by the contract.

Acquisition officials sometimes cannot spot defective products at time of acceptance due to the high volumes of goods or services being delivered. Latent defects are the most susceptible to being undiscovered.

c. Possible indicators of product substitution:

- Delivery of non-conforming goods altered to look like conforming goods.
- Failing to perform required testing.
- Altering test results showing non-conformity.

- Failing to follow the specified testing protocol.
- Delivery of used material when the contract specified new material (most do).
- Missing documentation of the source of the goods.
- Altered and incomplete product source information.

d. Deliverables that contain counterfeit components.

Counterfeit parts, primarily electronic components, include used components altered to look new, "knock-offs" of the specified components, commercial grade components represented as military or space qualified components, etc. As a result of repeated problems, Congress enacted Section 818 of the 2012 National Defense Authorization Act to implement best practices used by some contractors and agencies throughout defense procurement.[3] Included within this section was a change to the Federal criminal code (18 U.S.C. § 2320) to criminalize any trafficking of known counterfeit military goods or services, for which the use of the counterfeits could cause death, serious injury, classified disclosures, or impairment of combat operations.[4] This statute is implemented by DOD Instruction 4140.67, The DOD Counterfeit Prevention Policy (April 26, 2013), and is discussed in Chapter 20. These requirements are implemented in DFARS Subpart 246.8.

2. False Invoices.

a. May occur when the contractor submits false invoices and/or claims requesting government payment of goods and/or services that were not delivered to the government. Shaw v.

AAA Engineering & Drafting, Inc., 213 F.3d 545 (10th Cir. 2000) (stating that monthly invoices submitted when the contractor was knowingly not complying with contract terms can be the basis of False Claims Act liability).

b. Possible indicators of False Invoices.

- Copied or inappropriately altered supporting documentation (i.e. white-outs or other redaction).
- Payment invoice exceeds contract amount.
- Invoiced goods cannot be located.
- Missing or copied receiving documents.

III. REPORTING FRAUD.

A. **Introduction**. Credible allegations of procurement fraud should receive serious consideration and a thorough investigation, by both the government and the contractor. The government needs to identify and exclude bad contractors, prevent defective goods and services from causing further harm, and protect the government's financial interests. Contractors need to investigate and correct improper conduct, and to rectify the harm that may have been done to the government. The consequences of ignoring credible allegations are serious for both parties.

B. **Government Reporting.**

1. Individual agencies have internal procedures for reporting and investigating allegations of procurement fraud. For example, in the Army, upon receiving or uncovering substantial indications of procurement fraud, the Procurement Fraud Advisor (or PFA, usually a contracts attorney), will need to report the suspected fraud to those charged with investigating procurement fraud. AR 27-40, Chapter 8. Prior to submitting any official reports, the PFA should first consult with the Procurement Fraud Branch (PFB) at the Contracts and Fiscal Law Division, USALSA. After consulting with the Procurement Fraud Branch, the PFA

---

[3] National Defense Authorization Act (NDAA), Fiscal Year 2012, Pub. L. No. 112-81, 125 Stat. 1493, § 818.

[4] Id. at § 818(h), 125 Stat. 1497.

should report the allegations to the supporting criminal investigators, and submit a "Procurement Flash Report" to the Procurement Fraud Branch.

2. FAR Subsection 9.406-3. Promptly refer to agency debarring official those matters that investigation reveals are appropriate for that official's consideration.

C. Contractor "Mandatory Disclosure" Reporting.

1. Contracts awarded for over $5.5 million with a performance period of more than 120 days must include FAR 52.203-13, Contractor Code of Business Ethics and Conduct. Similar to various business systems, FAR 52.203-13 requires the contractor to adopt and follow various best practices for business ethics and conduct. This clause includes a requirement that contractors disclose "credible evidence" of criminal and/or civil fraud to the government. This clause implements 41 U.S.C. § 3509. Prior to 2008, contractors were encouraged to voluntarily report such conduct.

2. Regardless whether a contractor has a contract that includes FAR 52.203-13, any contractor may be debarred if it fails to report a must report credible evidence of:

   a. A violation of federal criminal law involving fraud, conflict of interest, bribery, or gratuity violations of Title 18, U.S. Code; or

   b. a violation of the Civil False Claims Act (31 U.S.C. §§ 3729-3733).

   This requirement applies to all contractors and subcontractors, in all current and future government contracts and may form a basis for suspension and/or debarment until three years after final payment on the contract. FAR 3.1003(a)(2).

3. Contractors must report overpayments received under various payment clauses (i.e., FAR 52.232-25(d)). A contractor may be suspended and/or debarred if a principal of the contractor knowingly fails to timely disclose to the government (in connection with the award, performance, or closeout of a government contract, performed by the contractor or one of their subcontractors) credible evidence of significant overpayments of a contract. FAR 3.1003(a)(3).

4. Government actions on receipt of a mandatory disclosure. FAR 52.203-13(b)(3) requires the contractor to timely disclose in writing to the agency Inspector General (with a copy to the contracting officer). The agency IG notifies the appropriate government agencies (i.e., Department of Justice), so that they can review the contractor's report on the matter, conduct further investigations, as warranted, ensure the contractor takes corrective action if warranted, and the government institutes further proceedings, if warranted.

D. Individual Reporting.

1. The government encourages individuals to report allegations of procurement fraud in various ways.

2. Hotline Posters.

   a. FAR 52.203-14, Display of Hotline Posters. Contracts awarded in excess of $5.5 million, except those performed entirely outside of the United States, must include a clause requiring contractors to post an approved "Hotline Poster," both physically, and on the contractor's internal website. This clause is a mandatory flow down to subcontractors over the threshold. Agencies may implement their own hotline poster, and DOD has done so. DFARS 252.203-7004.

3. Whistleblower Protection for Contractor Employees.

   a. An important incentive for contractor employees to report procurement fraud is the statutory whistleblower protections.

b. 10 U.S.C. § 2409 provides defense contractor and subcontractor employees with protection from reprisal for disclosure of specified information to specifically identified persons. It provides for investigation of allegations of reprisals by the Inspector General and specific procedures for resolving and remedying allegations. In the most recent DOD IG Semi-Annual Report for the period ending 31 March 2016, no allegations of defense contractor reprisals were substantiated and the overwhelming majority of complaints were dismissed for not providing sufficient information to warrant investigation. See, http://www.dodig.mil/pubs/sar/SAR _FY2016_1ST_HALF_FINAL_v2_ 508.pdf This is a typical result.

c. 41 U.S.C. § 4705 provides less comprehensive protections for all contractor employees than those afforded to DOD contractors and does not cover subcontractor employees. However, 41 U.S.C. § 4712 implements a pilot program to provide similar protections to those enacted for DOD contractors and subcontractors. The pilot program was effective beginning in July 2013 and will continue for four years.

d. FAR Clause 52.203-17, Contractor Employee Whistleblower Rights and Requirement to Inform Employees of Whistleblower Rights, requires contractors to inform their employees of their rights under 41 U.S.C. § 4712. The clause is mandatory for all contracts that exceed the simplified acquisition threshold.

e. DOD has a similar provision, DFARS 252.203-7002, which

requires informing defense contractor and subcontractor employees regarding their rights under 10 U.S.C. § 2409. This is a mandatory clause in all DOD contracts and subcontracts.

f. There are also whistleblower protections for relators in Federal Civil False Claims Actions (Qui Tam suits). 31 U.S.C. § 3730(h).

IV. COMBATTING FRAUD: COORDINATION OF FRAUD REMEDIES.

A. The Four Government Remedies.

When an allegation of procurement fraud is substantiated by an investigation, the government pursues its remedies against the responsible individuals and contractor/subcontractor.

There are four general types of remedies available to the government in response to fraud:
- criminal remedies,
- civil remedies,
- administrative remedies, and
- contract remedies.

The government must develop a strategy for pursuing remedies, because pursuing one remedy may affect other remedies due to statute of limitations, discovery, etc.

The U.S. Department of Justice (DOJ) is the lead agency when the government pursues criminal and civil remedies. The procuring agency is the lead for administrative and contract remedies.

B. Government Fraud Investigators.

1. DOD Inspector General and Defense Criminal Investigative Service. Inspector General Act of 1978, Pub. L. 95-452, as amended by Pub. L. No. 97-252; DOD Dir 5106.1. Inspector General of Department of Defense (Apr. 20, 2012).

2. Military Criminal Investigative Organizations. (CID, NCIS, AFOSI).

3. Department of Justice. DOD Instruction. 5525.07, Implementation of the Memorandum of Understanding (MOU) Between the Departments of Justice (DOJ) and Defense Relating to the Investigation and Prosecution of Certain Crimes (Jun. 18, 2007).

4. Agency organizations such as the Procurement Fraud Branch, Contract and Fiscal Law Division, United States Army Legal Services Agency. AR 27-40, Litigation, Ch. 8.

5. Buying Command Procurement Fraud Advisors (PFA) - ensure that commanders and contracting officers pursue, in a timely manner, all applicable criminal, civil, contractual, and administrative remedies.

C. Department of Justice (DOJ) Policy. DOJ policy requires that criminal prosecutors, civil trial counsel, and agency attorneys timely communicate, coordinate, and cooperate with one another in parallel proceedings to the fullest extent appropriate to the case and permissible by law to take into account the government's potential criminal, civil, regulatory, and administrative remedies. See U.S. Dep't of Justice, U.S. Atty's Man. ch. 1-12.000 (Coordination of Parallel Criminal, Civil, Regulatory and Administrative Proceedings) (February 2013), citing Attorney General policy on the same subject, dated January 30, 2012, at www.justice.gov/usao/eousa/foia_reading_room/usam/title1/doj00027.htm .

D. Department of Defense (DOD) Policy. It is DOD policy that each DOD Component will monitor, from its inception, all significant investigations of fraud or corruption related to procurement activities affecting its organization. The monitoring must ensure that all possible criminal, civil, contractual, and administrative remedies are identified to cognizant procurement and command officials and to Department of Justice (DOJ) officials, as appropriate, and that appropriate remedies are pursued expeditiously. This process includes coordination with all other affected DOD Components. See U.S. Dep't of Defense, Dir. 7050.5, Coordination of Remedies for Fraud and Corruption Related to Procurement Activities. (May 12, 2014)

1. DOD policy requires each department to establish a centralized organization to monitor all significant fraud and corruption cases.

2. Definition of a "significant" case.

   a. All fraud cases involving an alleged loss of $100,000 or more.

   b. All corruption cases that involve bribery, gratuities, or conflicts of interest.

   c. All investigations into defective products or product substitution in which a serious hazard to health, safety, or operational readiness is indicated (regardless of loss value).

3. Each centralized organization monitors all significant cases to ensure that all proper and effective criminal, civil, administrative, and contractual remedies are considered and pursued in a timely manner.

4. Product Substitution/Defective Product cases receive special attention.

E. Service Policies.

1. Army Regulation. 27-40, Litigation, 19 Sept. 1994.

2. U.S. Dep't of Air Force, Inst. 51-1101, The Air Force Procurement Fraud Remedies Program, 21 Oct. 2003.

3. SECNAVINST. 5430.92B, Assignment of Responsibilities to Counteract Fraud, Waste, and Related Improprieties within the Department of the Navy, 30 Dec. 2005.

F. Coordination of Remedies.

1. Coordinating remedies requires planning. The planning should account for both the facts of the alleged conduct, and the

605

possible criminal, civil, administrative, and contractual remedies for that conduct.

2. A remedies plan should include the following:

   a. Summary of allegations;

   b. Statement of adverse impact on DOD mission;

   c. Statement of impact upon combat readiness and safety of DA personnel; and

   d. Consideration of each criminal, civil, contractual, and administrative remedy available.

V.   CRIMINAL REMEDIES.

A. **Conspiracy to Defraud, 18 U.S.C. § 286 (with claims) and 18 U.S.C. § 371 (in general).** The general elements of a conspiracy under either statute include:

1. Knowing agreement by two or more persons that has as its object the commission of a criminal offense, or to defraud the United States. United States v. Upton, 91 F.3d 677 (5th Cir. 1996);

2. Intentional and actual participation in the conspiracy; and

3. Performance by one or more of the conspirators of an overt act in furtherance of the unlawful goal. United States v. Falcone, 311 U.S. 205, 210-211 (1940); United States v. Richmond, 700 U.S. 1183, 1190 (8th Cir. 1983).

B. **False Claims, 18 U.S.C. § 287.**

1. The elements required for a conviction under Section 287 include:

   a. Proof of a claim for money or property, which is false, fictitious, or fraudulent and material;

   b. Made or presented against a department or agency of the United States; and

c. Submitted with a specific intent to violate the law or with a consciousness of wrongdoing, i.e., the person must know at the time that the claim is false, fictitious, or fraudulent. See generally United States v. Slocum, 708 F.2d 587, 596 (11th Cir. 1983) (citing United States v. Computer Sciences Corp., 511 F. Supp. 1125, 1134 (E.D. Va. 1981), rev'd on other grounds, 689 F.2d 1181 (4th Cir. 1981)) (false indemnity claims made to USDA).

2. It is of no significance to a prosecution under section 287 that the claim was not paid. United States v. Coachman, 727 F.2d 1293, 1302 (D.C. Cir.), cert. denied, 419 U.S. 1047 (1984).

C. **False Statements, 18 U.S.C. § 1001.**

1. The elements include proof that:

   a. The defendant made a statement or submitted a false entry. "Statement" has been interpreted to include oral and unsworn statements. United States v. Massey, 550 F.2d 300 (5th Cir.), on remand, 437 F. Supp. 843 (M.D. Fla. 1977);

   b. The statement was false;

   c. The statement concerned a matter within the jurisdiction of a federal department or agency;

   d. The statement was "material." The test of materiality is whether the natural and probable tendency of the statement would be to affect or influence governmental action. United States v. Lichenstein, 610 F.2d 1272, 1278 (5th Cir. 1980); United States v. Randazzo, 80 F.3d 623, 630 (1st Cir. 1996); United States ex. Rel. Berge v. Board of Trustees University of Alabama, 104 F.3d 1453 (4th Cir. 1997); and

   e. Intent.

      (1) The required intent has been defined as "the intent to

deprive someone of something by means of deceit." United States v. Lichenstein, 610 F.2d 1272, 1277 (5th Cir. 1980).

(2) A false statement must be knowingly made and willfully submitted. United States v. Guzman, 781 F.2d 428 (5th Cir. 1986).

D. Mail Fraud and Wire Fraud, 18 U.S.C. §§ 1341-43.

1. The essence of the mail fraud and wire fraud statutes is the use of mails or wire communications to execute a scheme to defraud the United States. Both statutes are broadly worded to prohibit the use of the mails or interstate telecommunications systems to further such schemes.

2. The elements of the two offenses are similar. Accordingly, the cases interpreting the more recent wire fraud statute rely on the precedents interpreting mail fraud. See, e.g., United States v. Cusino, 694 F.2d 185 (9th Cir. 1982), cert. denied, 461 U.S. 932 (1983); United States v. Merlinger, 16 F.3d 670 (6th Cir. 1994). The elements include the:

a. Formation of a scheme and artifice to defraud.

b. Use of either the mails or interstate wire transmissions in furtherance of the scheme. See United States v. Pintar, 630 F.2d 1270, 1280 (8th Cir. 1980) (mail fraud); United States v. Wise, 553 F.2d 1173 (8th Cir. 1977) (wire fraud).

E. Major Fraud Act, 18 U.S.C. § 1031.

1. The Act was designed to deter major defense contractors from committing procurement fraud by imposing stiffer penalties and significantly higher fines.

2. Maximum punishments: ten years confinement; fines are determined on a sliding scale based on certain aggravating factors. Basic offense: $1,000,000 per count. Government loss or contractor gain of $500,000 or more: $5,000,000. Conscious or reckless risk of serious personal injury: $5,000,000. Multiple counts: $10,000,000 per prosecution.

3. Elements:

a. Knowingly engaging in any scheme with intent to defraud the government or to obtain money by false or fraudulent pretenses;

b. On a government contract; and

c. Valued at $1,000,000 or more. United States v. Brooks, 111 F.3d 365 (4th Cir. 1997). But see United States v. Nadi, 996 F.2d 548 (2nd Cir. 1993); United States v. Sain, 141 F.3d 463 (Fed. Cir. 1998).

F. Big Rigging, 15 U.S.C. § 1.

1. "Every contract, combination in the form of trust or otherwise, or conspiracy, in restraint of trade or commerce among the several States, or with foreign nations, is declared to be illegal."

2. Maximum penalty: Fine not exceeding $100,000,000 if a corporation, or if a person, $1,000,000, imprisonment not exceeding ten years, or both, in the discretion of the court.

3. Elements.

a. Agreement:

(1) Not to bid;

(2) To submit a sham bid; or

(3) To allocate bids;

b. Between two or more independent, horizontal entities; and

c. Affecting interest or foreign commerce.

G. Title 10 (UCMJ) Violations.

Besides Article 132 – Frauds Against the U.S., there are various specific criminal charges that could apply to Servicemembers involved in fraud, including (but not limited to): Article 92 – Failure to Obey Order or Regulation, Article 98 – Noncompliance with Procedural Rules, Article 107 – False Official Statements, Article 121 – Larceny and Wrongful Appropriation, Article 133 – Conduct Unbecoming an Officer and a Gentleman. If all else fails, the command can charge one of the enumerated Article 134 articles or fashion their own punitive article related to fraud.

VI.   CIVIL REMEDIES.

A.   The Civil False Claims Act. 31 U.S.C. §§ 3729-33.

Background. The primary litigation weapon for combating fraud is the FCA. The act has been repeatedly amended over the years, primarily to address judicial decisions.

B.   Liability Under the False Claims Act.

1.   In General. 31 U.S.C. § 3729(a) imposes liability on any person (defined comprehensively in 18 U.S.C. § 1 (1988) to include "corporations, companies, associations, partnerships . . . as well as individuals") who:

a.   Knowingly presents, or causes to be presented, to an officer or employee of the United States government or a member of the Armed Forces of the United States, a false or fraudulent claim for payment or approval. United States v. Krizek, 111 F.3d 934 (D.C. 1997).

b.   Conspires to defraud the government by having a false or fraudulent claim allowed or paid.

c.   Knowingly makes, uses, or causes to be made or used, a false record or statement to conceal, avoid, or decrease an obligation to pay or transmit money or property to the United States.

2.   The Fraud Enforcement and Recovery Act of 2009 (FERA), Pub. L. No. 111-21, 123 Stat. 1617, clarified the FCA by holding a contractor liable if he or she "knowingly presents, or causes to be presented a false or fraudulent claim for payment or approval" or "knowingly makes, uses, or causes to be made or used, a false record or statement material to a false or fraudulent claim," eliminating language "to get a false or fraudulent claim paid." The change responded to the Supreme Court's decision in Allison Engine,[5] which extends the FCA to claims submitted by subcontractors to prime contractors.

3.   Source of funds used to pay. Funds with which a claim would be paid need not be the United States' own money from Congressional appropriations and drawn from the Treasury. Rather, it is enough if the money belongs to the United States. United States ex rel. DRC, Inc. v. Custer Battles , LLC, et. al., 562 F.3d 295, 304-3052 (holding that Developmental Funds Iraq met the requirements to be a claim under the FCA).

C.   Damages.

Treble damages are the substantive measure of liability. 31 U.S.C. § 3729(a); United States v. Peters, 110 F.3d 66 (8th Cir. 1997). Voluntary disclosures of the violation prior to the investigation preclude the imposition of treble damages.

D.   Civil Penalties.

---

[5] Allison Engine, et al. v. United States, ex rel. Sanders, 553 U.S. 662 (2008). Allison was a first tier subcontractor to two Navy prime contractors. Allison, a 2nd tier subcontractor, and a 3rd tier subcontractor were alleged to have failed to comply with the Navy's specifications, and to have submitted certificates of conformance (COCs) to their customers. No evidence was introduced that either prime contractor invoiced the Navy. The Supreme Court held that the relator must show the false COCs were intended to be used to get the government to pay the prime contractors invoice for payment, and such proof was lacking.

1. A civil penalty of between $5,500 and $11,000 per false claim. 31 U.S.C. § 3729. The amounts stated in the False Claims Act, 31 U.S.C. section 3729, are $5,000 and $10,000; however, under the Debt Collection Improvement Act of 1996 (Pub. L. No. 104-134, § 31001, 110 Stat. 1321-373 (1996)), federal agencies are required to review and adjust statutory civil penalties for inflation every four years. Consequently, the Department of Justice has adjusted penalties under the False Claims Act to range not less than $5,500 and not more than $11,000 per violation. 28 C.F.R. § 85.3(a)(9)(2000).

2. Imposition is "automatic and mandatory for each false claim." S. Rep No. 345 at 8-10. See also United States v. Hughes, 585 F.2d 284, 286 (7th Cir. 1978) ("[t]his forfeiture provision is mandatory; it leaves the trial court without discretion to alter the statutory amount.")

3. There is no requirement for the United States to prove that it suffered any damages. Fleming v. United States, 336 F.2d 475, 480 (10th Cir. 1964), cert. denied, 380 U.S. 907 (1965). The government also does not have to show that it made any payments pursuant to false claims. United States v. American Precision Products Corp., 115 F. Supp. 823 (D. N.J. 1953).

4. United States v. Halper, 490 U.S. 435 (1989): Defendant faced aggregated penalties of $130,000 for fraud, which had damaged the government in the amount of $585. A civil sanction, in application, may be so divorced from any remedial goal as to constitute punishment under some circumstances. The scope of the holding is a narrow one, addressed to "the rare case . . . where a fixed-penalty provision subjects a small-gauge offender to a sanction overwhelmingly disproportionate to the damages he has caused." See United States v. Hatfield, 108 F.3d 67 (4th Cir. 1997).

VII. THE QUI TAM PROVISIONS OF THE FALSE CLAIMS ACT.

"Qui tam pro domino rege quam pro se ipso in hac parte sequitur." ("Who as well for the King as for himself sues in this matter.")

A. Overview of the False Claims Act (FCA).

1. The (FCA) authorizes private individuals to bring a civil suit, on behalf of the government, against contractors for fraud. 31 U.S.C. § 3730.

2. Claims under the FCA.

    a. The FCA defines a claim as any request or demand under a contract or otherwise for money or property that is (a) presented to an officer, employee, or agent of the United States or (b) made to a contractor, grantee, or other recipient if the money is to be spent or used on the government's behalf or to advance a government program or interest. See 31 U.S.C. § 3729(b)(2).

    b. Claims do not include requests or demands for money or property that the government has paid to an individual as compensation for federal employment or as an income subsidy with no restrictions on that individual's use of the money or property. 31 U.S.C. § 3729(b)(2)(B).

    c. "The submission of a false claim is the *sine qua non* of a False Claims Act violation." Urquilla-Diaz v. Kaplan Univ., 780 F.3d 1039, 1052 (11th Cir. 2015). False claims require the government to wrongfully disburse money.

3. Falsity Under the FCA.

    a. Under the FCA, falsity requires that statements be made with knowledge of the information or with deliberate ignorance or reckless disregard of the truth of the information. See 31 U.S.C § 3729(b)(1)(A).

b. "Although proof of a specific intent to defraud is not required, the statute's language makes plain that liability does not attach to innocent mistakes or simple negligence." Urquilla-Diaz v. Kaplan Univ., 780 F.3d 1039, 1052 (11th Cir. 2015) (record did not support a finding of recklessness when the defendant "took steps to ensure compliance").

B. Overview of the FCA Claim Process.

1. The FCA gives the government 60 days to decide whether to join the action. If the government joins the action, the government conducts the action. If the government decides not to join the suit, the individual (known as the "qui tam relator" conducts the action.

2. As an inducement to be a whistleblower, the statute provides that relators are entitled to portions of any judgment against the defendant. 31 U.S.C. § 3730(d).

3. If the government joins and conducts the suit, the relator is entitled to between 15 and 25 percent of judgment, depending on the relator's contribution to the success of the suit.

4. If the government declines to join and the relator conducts the suit, the relator is entitled to between 25 and 30 percent of the judgment, at the discretion of the court.

C. Limitations on Relators.

1. 31 U.S.C. § 3730(e)(4) significantly limits a person's ability to become a qui tam relator by providing that "the court shall dismiss an action or claim under this section, unless opposed by the government, if substantially the same allegations or transactions as alleged in the action or claim were publicly disclosed (i) in a Federal, criminal, civil, or administrative hearing in which the government or its agents is a party; (ii) in a

Congressional, government Accountability Office, or other Federal report, hearing, audit, or investigations; or (iii) from the news media, unless the action is brought by the Attorney General or the person bringing the action is an original source of the information." This is referred to as the "public disclosure bar."

2. The statute defines original source as an individual who (i) has voluntarily disclosed to the government the information on which allegations or transactions in a claim are based prior to a public disclosure or (ii) has knowledge that is independent of and materially adds to the publicly disclosed allegations or transactions and has voluntarily provided the information to the government before filing an action. 31 U.S.C. § 3730(e)(4)(B). The Fifth Circuit has defined "independent" knowledge as knowledge not derived from the public disclosures. United States ex rel. Rigsby v. State Farm Fire & Casualty Co., 794 F.3d 457 (5th Cir. 2015).

D. Qui Tam Developments.

1. Implied Certifications. Universal Health Servs., Inc. v. United States, No. 15-7, 2016 WL 3317565, at *7 (U.S. June 16, 2016). The Supreme Court granted certiorari to a First Circuit case to decide two issues: (1) whether the implied certification theory of legal falsity under the FCA is viable and (2) whether, if the implied certification theory is viable, a government contractor's reimbursement claim is legally false if the claimant failed to comply with a statute, regulation, or contractual provision that is deemed material to the government's decision to pay the claim, even if compliance is not a condition of payment or whether liability requires that the statute, regulation, or contractual provision expressly state that compliance is a condition of payment. See United States v. Universal Health Servs., Inc., 780 F.3d 504, 508 (1st Cir. 2015). The Court granted certiorari to resolve disagreement among the Court of Appeals

over the validity and scope of the implied false certification theory of liability. The Court held that (1) the implied false certification theory can be a basis for liability under the FCA when a defendant submitting a claim makes specific representations about the goods or services provided, but fails to disclose noncompliance with material statutory, regulatory, or contractual requirements that make those representations misleading with respect to those goods or services and (2) liability under the FCA for failing to disclose violations of legal requirements does not turn upon whether those requirements were expressly designated as conditions of payment. The Court's first holding abrogated United States v. Sanford-Brown, Ltd., 788 F.3d 696 (7th Cir. 2015), and the Court's second holding abrogated Mikes v. Straus, 274 F.3d 687 (2d Cir. 2001).

2. Criminal Convictions. Schroeder v. United States, 793 F.3d 1080 (9th Cir. 2015). A qui tam relator's criminal conviction arising from the underlying fraud results in the relator's dismissal from the civil action and bars his recovery of any proceeds from the action. The relator previously pled guilty to conspiracy to commit fraud, a conviction that stemmed from the claims underlying his qui tam suit. The court interpreted 31 U.S.C. §3730(d)(3): "If the person bringing the action is convicted of criminal conduct arising from his or her role in the violation of section 3729, that person shall be dismissed from the civil action and shall not receive any share of the proceeds of the action." The relator argued that he should not be dismissed given the minor nature of his role in the fraudulent scheme. The court rejected his argument, explaining that the statute's plain language is clear and that there is no express exception for those with minor roles.

3. Public Disclosure Bar. Federal circuits are split on whether disclosures to government officials alone trigger the public disclosure bar to qui tam suits. However, a majority

of the circuits hold that disclosures to government officials alone do not trigger the public disclosure bar. Both the Sixth and the Fourth Circuits recently joined the majority. In United States ex rel. Whipple v. Chattanooga-Hamilton County Hospital, 782 F.3d 260 (6th Cir. 2015), the Sixth Circuit held that a hospital's fraudulent inpatient billing practices were not publicly disclosed as a result of an administrative audit and investigation. The court reasoned that public disclosure required some affirmative act of disclosure to the public outside of the government, otherwise the term "public" would be superfluous. See United States ex rel. Wilson v. Graham County Soil & Water Conservation District, 777 F.3d 691 (4th Cir. 2015) (holding that government audit and investigation reports were not publicly disclosed when given to local, state, and federal agencies and government officials charged with policing the alleged fraud because the public disclosure requires disclosure outside of the government). By contrast, in Cause of Action v. Chicago Transit Authority, 815 F.3d 267 (7th Cir. 2016), the Seventh Circuit held that misreporting transportation data to the Federal Transit Administration (FTA) was in the public domain because the government was aware of the activity through the FTA, had thoroughly investigated it, and had issued a report (FTA letter) sent to the local city transit authority. The court acknowledged other Circuits' criticism of the Seventh Circuit's reasoning, which requires only government knowledge and investigation of the activity to trigger the public disclosure bar, but declined to reconsider precedent because an audit report describing the activity was publicly available on the Illinois Auditor General website. The court noted that, had the FTA letter been the only document before the court, it would have reconsidered its precedent out of respect for the position of other circuits.

4. 9th Circuit Removes a Prong from its "Original Source" Test for Relators. United States ex rel. Hartpence v. Kinetic

Concepts, Inc., 792 F.3d 1121 (9th Cir. 2015). The Ninth Circuit removed a prong from the "original source" test that required the relator to have played a role in the public disclosure of the allegations in his qui tam suit. The three part "original source" test was laid out by the Ninth Circuit in Wang ex rel. United States v. FMC Corp., 975 F.2d 1412 (9th Cir. 1992): where an FCA claim has been publicly disclosed before a relator files his complaint, the relator may bring a qui tam suit if he can show that (1) he has direct and independent knowledge of the information on which the allegations in his court-filed complaint are based, (2) he has voluntarily provided the information to the government before filing his civil action, and (3) the relator must have played a role in making the disclosure public. The first two requirements parallel the statutory language of 31 U.S.C. § 3730(e)(4)(B), while the third prong was read into the statute by the Wang court. In Rockwell International v. United States, 549 U.S. 457 (2000), the Supreme Court said that the term "information" in § 3730(e)(4)(B) refers to the information underlying the relator's complaint, which called into question the Wang's court reading of the statute. Relying on Rockwell and the plain meaning of § 3730(e)(4)(B), the Ninth Circuit concluded that Wang "impermissibly drew on language from § 3730(e)(4)(A) to read a nonexistent, extra-textual third requirement into § 3730(e)(4)(B)" and removed the original source requirement.

5. First Bifurcated FCA Trial. In United States v. AseraCare, Inc., No. 2:12-CV-245-KOB (N.D. Ala. May 20, 2015), the court made an unprecedented decision to bifurcate the falsity and scienter elements of the FCA suit into two separate trials – a phase one trial for falsity and a phase two trial for scienter. The government filed a motion for reconsideration, but the court denied it. Prior to the bifurcation order, the government planned to introduce evidence about the AseraCare's marketing practices that included prejudicial internal communications. AseraCare argued that the information was not needed to determine falsity, but was relevant only to knowledge. The court agreed with AseraCare and ruled that allowing the evidence would be unduly prejudicial to AseraCare in the falsity phase one trial. A falsity trial was held and the jury sided with the government and relators finding that most of the claims were objectively false. But four days after the jury's verdict, the court held a hearing, sua sponte, about the instructions the court had provided the jury. Judge Bowdre stated that she should have instructed the jury that a mere difference of opinions among physicians, without more, is insufficient to show falsity under the FCA. AseraCare subsequently moved for a new trial, which the court granted. In November 2015, however, the court issued an order, sua sponte, that summary judgment would be reconsidered before setting a new trial date. In March 2016, the court ruled that the government's proof on the falsity element failed as a matter of law and entered summary judgment in favor of AseraCare.

6. Wartime Suspension of Limitation Acts (WSLA) Cannot be Used to Toll the Statute of Limitations in Civil FCA Claims. When the U.S. is at war or Congress has enacted a specific authorization for the use of Armed Forces, the WSLA suspends the running of any statute of limitations applicable to any offense involving fraud or attempted fraud against the United States or any agency. 18 U.S.C. § 3827. In Kellogg Brown & Root Services v. United States ex rel. Carter, 125 S. Ct. 1970 (2015), the Supreme Court held that the WSLA applies only to criminal charges, not to civil claims, because "offense," as used in the WSLA, refers only to a criminal offense.

7. First-to-File Bar. The FCA first-to-file bar prohibits bringing a related FCA action based on facts underlying a pending action. See 18 U.S.C § 3730(b)(5). In Kellogg Brown & Root Services v. United

States ex rel. Carter, 125 S. Ct. 1970 (2015), the Supreme Court held that a <u>qui tam</u> suit ceases to be pending under the first-to-file bar once the suit is dismissed. Consequently, an earlier suit bars a later suit while the earlier suit remains undecided but ceases to bar the later suit once the earlier suit is dismissed. On remand, the district court found that (1) the relator's suit was barred because other actions were pending at the time he filed his suit and (2) the subsequent dismissal of the earlier filed suits did not automatically give him first-to-file status without any subsequent action by him.

8. Excessive Damages and Due Process. In <u>United States ex rel. Drakeford v. Tuomey</u>, 792 F.3d 364 (4th Cir. 2015), the Fourth Circuit held that a $237,454,195 award of damages and civil penalties did not violate the Due Process Clause or the Excessive Fines Clause in a <u>qui tam</u> suit against a health provider who filed over 21,000 false claims. While the court described the award as excessive, it concluded that the award was not unconstitutional, reasoning that "substantial penalties serve as a powerful mechanism to dissuade such a massive course of fraudulent conduct."

VIII. ADMINISTRATIVE REMEDIES.

A. Debarment and Suspension Basics. 10 U.S.C. § 2393; FAR Subpart 9.4.

1. Suspension. Action taken by a suspending official to temporarily disqualify a contractor from government contracting.

2. Debarment. Action taken by a debarring official to exclude a contractor from government contracting for a specified period.

3. Government policy is to solicit offers from, award contracts to, and consent to subcontracts with <u>responsible</u> <u>contractors</u> only. FAR 9.103.

4. Debarment and suspension are discretionary administrative actions utilized to effectuate responsible

contracting; debarment and suspension shall not be used for <u>punishment</u>. FAR 9.402(a) and (b); <u>United States v. Glymp</u>, 96 F.3d 722, 724 (4th Cir. 1996).

5. Debarring and suspending officials. <u>See</u> e.g., DFARS 209.403(a). Any person may refer a matter to the agency debarring official. However, the absence of a referral will not preclude the debarring official from initiating the debarment or suspension process, or from making a final decision. 64 Fed. Reg. 62984 (Nov. 18, 1999).

6. Debarments can be narrowly tailored to individuals, portions of a company, or to specific products that were the subject of the misconduct. FAR 9.406-1(b).

B. Debarment. Causes for debarment. FAR 9.406-2; DFARS 209.406-2.

1. The debarring official may debar a contractor for a CONVICTION of or CIVIL JUDGMENT for:

a. Commission of fraud or a criminal offense in connection with (i) obtaining, (ii) attempting to obtain, or (iii) performing a public contract or subcontract;

b. Violation of federal or state antitrust statutes relating to the submission of offers;

c. Commission of embezzlement, theft, forgery, bribery, falsification or destruction of records, making false statements, tax evasion, violating federal criminal tax laws, or receiving stolen property;

d. Intentionally affixing a label bearing a "Made in America" inscription (or any inscription having the same meaning) to a product sold in or shipped to the United States or its outlying areas, when the product was not made in the United States or its outlying areas (see § 202 of the Defense Production Act (Pub. L. 102-558));

e. Commission of any other offense indicating a lack of business integrity or business honesty that seriously and directly affects the present responsibility of a government contractor or subcontractor; or

f. Knowingly providing compensation to a former DOD official in violation of § 847 of the National Defense Authorization Act for Fiscal Year 2008 (regarding post-employment restrictions).

2. The debarring official may debar a contractor based upon a preponderance of the evidence for:

a. Violation of the terms of a government contract or subcontract so serious as to justify debarment, such as:

    (1) Willful failure to perform in accordance with the terms of one or more contracts or

    (2) A history of failure to perform, or unsatisfactory performance of, one or more contracts.

b. Violation of 41 U.S.C. chapter 81, Drug-Free Workplace, as indicated by:

    (1) The failure to comply with the requirements of FAR 52.223-6, Drug-Free Workplace or

    (2) Such a number of contractor employees convicted of violations of drug statutes occurring in the workplace as to indicate that the contractor has failed to make a good faith effort to provide a drug-free workplace (see FAR 23.504).

c. Intentionally affixing a "Made in America" label to non-American goods (see § 202 of the Defense Production Act (Pub. L. 102-558));

d. Commission of an unfair trade practice as defined in FAR 9.403 (see § 201 of the Defense Production Act (Pub. L. 102-558));

e. Delinquent federal taxes in an amount that exceeds $3,500; or

f. Knowing failure by a principal, until three years after final payment on any government contract award to the contractor, to timely disclose to the government, in connection with the award, performance, or closeout of the contract or subcontract there under credible evidence of:

    (1) Violation of federal criminal law involving fraud, conflict of interest, bribery, or gratuity violations found in Title 18 of the United States Code;

    (2) Violation of the civil False Claims Act, 31 U.S.C. §§ 3729-3766; or

    (3) Significant overpayment(s) on the contract, other than overpayments resulting from contract financing payments as defined in FAR 32.001.

3. "Preponderance" means proof by information that, compared with that opposing it, leads to the conclusion that the fact at issue is more probably true than not. FAR 2.101; see Imco, Inc. v. United States, 33 Fed. Cl. 312 (1995).

4. A contractor can be debarred based on a determination by the Secretary of Homeland Security or the Attorney General of the United States that the contractor is not in compliance with Immigration and Nationality Act employment provisions (see Executive Order 12989, as amended by Executive Order 13286).[6]

---

[6] The underlying determination regarding noncompliance with the Immigration and Nationality Act is not reviewable in the debarment proceedings. FAR 9.406-2(b)(2).

5. A contractor or subcontractor may be debarred for any other cause so serious or compelling in nature that it affects the present responsibility of the contractor or subcontractor.

C. Suspension. Causes for suspension. FAR 9.407-2.

1. Upon adequate evidence of:

   a. Commission of fraud or a criminal offense in connection with (i) obtaining, (ii) attempting to obtain, or (iii) performing a public contract or subcontract;

   b. Violation of federal or state antitrust statutes relating to the submission of offers;

   c. Commission of embezzlement, theft, forgery, bribery, falsification or destruction of records, making false statements, tax evasion, violating federal criminal tax laws, or receiving stolen property.

   d. Violation of 41 U.S.C. chapter 81, Drug-Free Workplace, as indicated by:

      (1) The failure to comply with the requirements of FAR 52.223-6, Drug-Free Workplace; or

      (2) Such a number of contractor employees convicted of violations of drug statutes occurring in the workplace as to indicate that the contractor has failed to make a good faith effort to provide a drug-free workplace (see FAR 23.504);

   e. Intentionally affixing a "Made in America" label to non-American goods (see § 202 of the Defense Production Act (Pub. L. 102-558));

   f. Commission of an unfair trade practice as defined in FAR 9.403 (see § 201 of the Defense Production Act (Pub. L. 102-558));

   g. Delinquent federal taxes in an amount that exceeds $3,500; or

   h. Knowing failure by a principal, until three years after final payment on any government contract award to the contractor, to timely disclose to the government, in connection with the award, performance, or closeout of the contract or subcontract there under credible evidence of:

      (1) Violation of federal criminal law involving fraud, conflict of interest, bribery, or gratuity violations found in Title 18 of the United States Code;

      (2) Violation of the civil False Claims Act, 31 U.S.C. §§ 3729-3766; or

      (3) Significant overpayment(s) on the contract, other than overpayments resulting from contract financing payments as defined in FAR 32.001;

   i. Commission of any other offense indicating a lack of business integrity or business honesty that seriously and directly affects the present responsibility of a government contractor or subcontractor; or

   j. For any other cause of so serious or compelling a nature that it affects the present responsibility of a government contractor or subcontractor.

2. "Adequate evidence" means information sufficient to support the reasonable belief that a particular act or omission has occurred. FAR 2.101.

   a. "Adequate evidence" may include allegations in a civil complaint filed by another federal agency. See SDA, Inc., B-253355, Aug. 24, 1993, 93-2 CPD ¶ 132

3. Indictment for any of the causes in section (C)1 above constitutes "adequate evidence" for suspension. FAR 9.407-2(b).

D.   Effect of Debarment or Suspension. FAR 9.405; DFARS 209.405.

1. § 2455 of the Federal Acquisition Streamlining Act of 1994, Pub. L. No. 103-355, 108 Stat. 3243, FAR 9.401 provides for government-wide effect of the debarment, proposed debarment, suspension, or any other exclusion of an entity from procurement or non-procurement activities.

2. Contractors that are proposed for debarment, suspended, or debarred may not receive government contracts, and agencies may not solicit offers from, award contracts to, or consent to subcontracts with these contractors, unless the acquiring agency's head or designee determines and states in writing that there is a <u>compelling reason</u> for the approval action. FAR 9.405(a).

3. The general rule is that, absent a contrary determination by the ordering activity, debarment has no effect on the <u>continued performance</u> of contracts or subcontracts in existence at the time of the proposed or actual suspension or debarment. FAR 9.405-1(a). However, unless an agency head makes a compelling needs determination, orders exceeding minimums cannot be placed under indefinite delivery contracts nor can orders be placed under Federal Supply Schedule contracts, blanket purchase agreements, or basic ordering agreements, nor can the agency add new work, exercise options, or otherwise extend the duration of current contracts or order. FAR 9.405-1(b). However, under DFARS 209.405-1, unless an agency head makes a compelling needs determination under DFARS 209.405, DOD entities may not place orders exceeding guaranteed minimums under indefinite delivery contracts, nor may they place orders against Federal Supply Schedule contracts.

4. Bids received from any affected contractor are opened, entered on abstract of bids, and rejected unless there is a compelling reason for an exception.

5. Proposals, quotations, or offers from affected contractors shall not be evaluated, included in the competitive range, or are discussions held unless there is a compelling reason for an exception.

E.   Period of Debarment. FAR 9.406-4.

1. The debarment period is commensurate with the seriousness of the cause(s) and generally should not exceed three years, except that debarment for violation of 41 U.S.C. chapter 81, Drug-Free Workplace, may not exceed five years. FAR 9.406-4(a).

2. The administrative record must include relevant findings as to the appropriateness of the length of the debarment. <u>Coccia v. Defense Logistics Agency</u>, C.A. No. 89-6544, 1990 U.S. Dist. LEXIS 6079, (E.D. Pa. May 15, 1990) (upholding 15-year debarment of former government employee convicted of taking bribes and kickbacks from contractors in exchange for contracts).

3. The period of the proposed debarment, or any prior suspension, is considered in determining the period of debarment.

4. The debarment period may be extended, but not solely on the original basis. If extension is necessary, the routine procedures set forth in FAR 9.406-3 apply. FAR 9.406-4(b).

5. The debarment period may be reduced based on new evidence, the reversal of the conviction or civil judgment or the elimination of the causes upon which the debarment was based, a bona fide change in management, or other reasons deemed appropriate by the debarring official. FAR 9.406-4(c); <u>see, e.g.</u>, <u>Kisser v. Kemp</u>, 786 F. Supp. 38 (D.D.C. 1992) (finding that the inconsistent treatment of corporate

officials justified overturning debarment decision).

6. The Administrative Procedure Act does not usually provide a right to judicial review of an agency's decision not to take enforcement action. Heckler v. Chaney, 470 U.S. 821 (1985). However, in Caiola v. Carroll, the Court of Appeals for the D.C. Circuit rejected an agency suspension of two corporate official but not a third when the agency did not provide in the administrative record support for the differing treatment. 851 F.2d 395 (D.C. Cir. 1988); contra Kisser v. Cisneros, 14 F.3d 615 (D.C. Cir. 1994) (holding that no reasoned explanation is required when exercising discretion).

F.   Period of Suspension. FAR 9.407-4.

1. Suspension is temporary, pending completion of an investigation or any ensuing legal proceedings.

2. If legal proceedings are not initiated within 12 months after the date of the suspension notice, the suspension is terminated unless an Assistant Attorney General requests an extension.

3. An extension upon request by an Assistant Attorney General shall not exceed six months.

4. Suspension may not exceed 18 months unless legal proceedings are initiated within that period.

G.   Challenges to Suspension and Debarment Actions.

1. COFC Grants Temporary Injunctive Relief in Response to a Suspension, resulting in the Government taking Corrective Action and Terminating the Suspension. Inchcape Shipping Holdings LTD et al v. United States, COFC, No. 1:13-cv-00953-JFM (TRO entered Jan. 2, 2014). In November 2013, the Navy SDO suspended Inchcape for failing (1) to reconcile accounts properly and (2) to disclose its findings of overpayment from an internal contract audit. Inchcape challenged the suspension,

arguing that it did not meet the standards of FAR 9.407-1(b)(1), which require that the suspension be imposed on the basis of "adequate evidence" and the basis that "immediate action is necessary to protect the government's interests." On the adequate evidence prong, the court noted that the plaintiffs had filed numerous potentially relevant documents that the SDO did not consider, despite having the time to do so. Consequently, the court concluded that the SDO did not conduct a meaningful investigation of the matter. The court likewise found that no immediate need existed when the SDO had waited at least a year to suspend Inchcape and the record contained no evidence of an ongoing threat against which the government needed to be protected. The court additionally found that Inchcape's risk of suffering irreparable harm as a result of the suspension was far greater than the government's risk of suffering from the imposition of a temporary injunction. As such, the court granted Inchcape's temporary injunctive relief. After the court's ruling, the Navy terminated Inchcape's suspension through an administrative agreement.

2. Court Grants Preliminary Injunction and Orders Suspension Void Ab Initio. International Relief and Development et al. v. United States Agency for International Development, D.D.C., No. 1:15-cv-00854-RCL. International Relief and Development (IRD) challenged its suspension and continuation of its suspension by the United States Agency for International Development (USAID). In its complaint, IRD requested that the court declare the suspension "null void, and unenforceable," and enjoin the enforcement of the suspension decisions,. IRD's complaint further alleged a conflict of interest because the SDO had simultaneously served as SDO and as USAID's Director of the Office of Acquisition and Assistance, in violation of the National Defense Authorization Act of 2013. USAID acknowledged the conflict of interest, lifted IRD's suspension, and

stated that it would reevaluate its suspension decision. Subsequently, USAID filed a Motion to Dismiss as Moot and an Opposition to Motion for Preliminary Injunction in light of USAID terminating the suspension pending review by another SDO. IRD objected to USAID's motions, arguing that its actions were an effort to "avoid the court's judicial review of the illegal original IRD suspension." IRD pointed to a USAID press release in support of its argument: "USAID's decision to lift the suspension does not mean the Agency has found IRD to be presently responsible. A determination of whether IRD is presently responsible or not will be made by the new SDO." IRD asked the court declare its suspension "void ab initio." At the hearing, the court denied USAID's Motion to Dismiss as Moot and took IRD's Motion for a Preliminary Injunction under advisement. In August 2015, the court granted the preliminary injunction and ordered USAID to, among other things, "declare plaintiff's suspension void ab initio within 1 (one) day of this order." USAID complied with the order. In October 2015, IRD filed a Motion for Judgment on the Pleadings because USAID failed to deny the complaint's allegations. USAID responded with another Motion to Dismiss as Moot in light of the August 2015 order. Oral argument was held in November of 2015, and the court has yet to make a ruling.

3.   Court Denies Defendants' Motion to Dismiss Plaintiffs' Declaratory Judgment Motions Challenging Plaintiffs' Suspensions. AUI Management, LLC et al. v. USDA et al., D.M.D. Tenn; No. 2:11-cv-0121 (Motion to dismiss denied March 23, 2015). AUI Management and Jeff Callahan sued the Department of Agriculture (USDA), the Farm Services Agency (FSA), and its SDO for a judgment declaring that (1) the suspensions of AUI and Callahan be set aside ab initio, (2) AUI and Callahan not be required to disclose the suspensions on any bid form, and (3) AUI and Callahan be

removed from the list of contractors who have been suspended by the government. Since the suspensions had expired by the time AUI and Callahan filed for declaratory judgment, the defendants moved to dismiss for lack of jurisdiction and standing. The suspensions arose from fraudulent Certificates of Analysis (COA) prepared by an employee of Advocacy Resources Corporation (ARC) who altered the percentage content of Vitamin A in several COAs. AUI managed the operations of ARC, and Callahan was CEO of ARC. Neither AUI nor Callahan knew or were affiliated with the ARC employee who altered the records. In May 2011, the FSA SDO suspended ARC on four grounds: (1) commission of fraud by ARC, (2) falsification of COAs in invoice packages, (3) knowing failure of ARC to disclose credible evidence of violation of the FCA, and (4) conduct that "seriously and directly affects responsibility to perform as a government contractor." AUI and Callahan were suspended because they "knew or should have known" about ARC's fraud. The SDO said that the suspensions were in the government's interest, but cited no immediate need. In September 2011, the court continued AUI and Callahan's suspensions. The suspensions expired 12 months later per FAR 9.407.4. Both AUI and Callahan were impacted by the suspensions. AUI went out of business and laid off all of its employees, and Callahan filed for Chapter 11 bankruptcy. The court denied defendants' motion to dismiss, finding: ". . .the suspensions while only temporary were essentially a deathblow to [AUI and Callahan's] business[es] . . . Plaintiffs are still listed on the public archives of the Government's Excluded Parties List System as having been previously suspended . . . Plaintiffs have sufficiently alleged their ability to bid on numerous government contracts in the future will be impeded by the suspensions. Furthermore, any judgment from this Court, that the suspension was void, ab initio, would likely alleviate such inability and potential harm to Plaintiffs' reputation." As such, the court was satisfied that the plaintiffs presented a case and denied defendants' motion to dismiss.

IX. CONTRACTUAL REMEDIES.

A. Historical Right.

1. Under common law, where a party to a contract committed an act of fraud affecting a material element of the contract, the fraudulent act constituted a breach on the part of the party committing the act. The innocent party could then, at its election, insist on continuation of contract performance, or void the contract. Once voided, the voiding party would be liable under equity to the other party for any benefit received. Stoffela v. Nugent, 217 U.S. 499 (1910); Diamond Coal Co. v. Payne, 271 F. 362, 366 (App. D.C. 1921) ("equity refuses to give to the innocent party more than he is entitled to").

2. Since the U. S. government was often viewed as acting in a "commercial capacity" when it engaged in commercial transactions, the rules of common law and equity applied to resolution of disputes. As such, if the government sought to rescind a contract, it was obligated to restore the contractor to the position it would be in, but-for the breach. Cooke v. United States, 91 U.S. 389, 398 (1875) ("If [the government] comes down from its position of sovereignty, and enters the domain of commerce, it submits itself to the same laws that govern individuals there."); Hollerbach v. United States, 233 U.S. 165 (1914); United States v. Fuller Co., 296 F. 178 (1923).

3. The Supreme Court rejected the general rule that the government should be treated like any other party to a contract when fraud occurred. Pan American Petroleum and Transport Co., v. United States, 273 U.S. 456 (1927).

4. Courts and boards have developed an implied or common-law right to terminate or cancel a contract in order to effectuate the public policy of protecting the government in instances of procurement fraud. See United States v. Mississippi Valley Generating Co., 364 U.S. 520, reh'g denied 365 U.S. 855 (1961); Four-Phase Sys., Inc., ASBCA No. 26794, 86-2 BCA ¶ 18,924.

5. A contractor that engages in fraud in dealing with the government commits a material breach, which justifies terminating the entire contract for default. Joseph Morton Co., Inc. v. United States, 3 Cl. Ct. 120 (1983), aff'd 757 F.2d 1273 (Fed. Cir. 1985).

B. Denial of Claims.

1. Section 7103(c)(1) of the CDA prohibits an agency head from settling, compromising, or otherwise adjusting any claim involving fraud. 41 U.S.C. § 7103(c)(1). This limitation is reflected in FAR 33.210, which states that the authority of a contracting officer to decide or resolve a claim does not extend to the "settlement, compromise, payment, or adjustment of any claim involving fraud." Subpart 33.209 of the FAR further provides that contracting officers must refer all cases involving suspected fraud to the agency official responsible for investigating fraud.

2. As a practical matter, the term "denial" is a misnomer in that the contracting officer is precluded from making a final decision on a contractor's claim where fraud is suspected. As such, denial of a claim consists simply of doing nothing with the claim while other courses of action are pursued.

3. Denial of a claim should be viewed as simply the first of possibly many steps in the resolution of a fraudulent claim.

C. Contracting Officer Authority.

Procurement Fraud

1. Actions Clearly Exceeding Contracting Officer Authority. The Contract Disputes Act (CDA), 41 U.S.C. § 7103(a), as implemented by FAR 33.210(b), prohibits any contracting officer or agency head from settling, paying, compromising or otherwise adjusting any claim involving fraud. This provision does not, however, prevent a contracting officer from enforcing the government's contractual rights based on fraudulent conduct.

2. Actions Clearly Within KO Authority.

   a. Refusing Payment. It is the plain duty of administrative, accounting, and auditing officials of the government to refuse approval and to prevent payment of public monies under any agreement on behalf of the United States as to which there is a reasonable suspicion of irregularity, collusion, or fraud, thus reserving the matter for scrutiny in the courts when the facts may be judicially determined upon sworn testimony and competent evidence and a forfeiture declared or other appropriate action taken. To the Secretary of the Army, B154766, 44 Comp. Gen. 111 (1964). Of course, failing to pay sums due the contractor without justification is a government breach of contract.

   b. Suspend Progress Payments. 10 U.S.C. § 2307(i); FAR 52.232-16(c); Brown v. United States, 207 Ct. Cl. 768, 524 F.2d 693 (1975); Fidelity Construction, DOT CAB No. 1113, 80-2 BCA ¶ 14,819.

   c. Payment Withholds. When a debarment/suspension report recommends debarment or suspension based on fraud or criminal conduct involving a current contract, all funds becoming due on that contract shall be withheld unless directed otherwise by the Head of the Contracting Activity (HCA) or the debarring official. AFARS 5109.406-3. Labor standards statutes provide for withholding for labor standards violations. Walsh-Healy Act, 41 U.S.C. § 6503; Davis-Bacon Act, 40 U.S.C. § 3144. Specific contract provisions may provide for withholding (e.g., service contract deductions for deficiencies in performance).

   d. Suspend Negotiations. FAR 49.106 (end settlement discussions regarding a terminated contract upon suspicion of fraud); K&R Eng'g Co., Inc., v. United States, 222 Ct. Cl. 340, 616 F.2d 469 (1980).

   e. Determine a contractor to be not responsible based on its demonstrated lack of satisfactory business ethics. FAR Subpart 9.4.

   f. Contracting personnel should assume that the contractor involved may dispute the facts on which the action was taken, and that if unsupported, the government's actions may create a cause of action for the contractor.

D. **Counterclaims Under the CDA.**

1. Per 41 U.S.C. § 7103(c)(2): "[i]f a contractor is unable to support any part of his claim and it is determined that such inability is attributable to misrepresentation of fact or fraud on the part of the contractor, he shall be liable to the government for an amount equal to such unsupported part of the claim in addition to all costs to the government attributable to the cost of reviewing said part of his claim."

2. Until recently, this provision of the CDA has been applied in only a small number of cases. This may in part be due to the deterrent effect of this statute. See United States ex. rel. Wilson v. North American Const., 101 F. Supp. 2d 500, 533 (S.D.

Tex 2000) (district court unwilling to enforce this provision of the CDA because there were "very few cases applying 41 U.S.C. § [7103]"). See also UMC Elecs. v. United States, 249 F.3d 1337 (Fed. Cir. 2001); Larry D. Barnes, Inc. (d/b/a TRI-AD Constructors) v. United States, 45 Fed. Appx. 907 (Fed. Cir. 2002) (provision successfully applied by CAFC).

3. It is not possible to enforce this section of the CDA in litigation before the boards because of the language at 41 U.S.C. 7103(a)(5), which states: "[t]he authority of this subsection shall not extend to a claim or dispute for penalties or forfeitures prescribed by statute or regulation which another Federal agency is specifically authorized to administer, settle or determine." The boards have generally interpreted this language as meaning only the Department of Justice (DOJ) has the authority to initiate a claim under this provision. This is because (in the eyes of the boards) only DOJ has the authority to administer or settle disputes involving fraud under the current statutory scheme. See TDC Management, DOT BCA 1802, 90-1 BCA ¶ 22,627.

E. Default Terminations Based on Fraud.

1. Where a contractor challenges the propriety of a default termination before a court or board, the government is not precluded under the CDA from introducing evidence of fraud discovered after the default termination, and using that evidence to support the termination in the subsequent litigation.

2. Some grounds for default termination.

   a. Submission of falsified test reports. Michael C. Avino, Inc., ASBCA No. 317542, 89-3 BCA ¶ 22,156.

   b. Submission of forged performance and payment bonds. Dry Roof Corp., ASBCA No. 29061, 88-3 BCA ¶ 21,096.

   c. Submission of falsified progress payment requests. Charles W. Daff,

Trustee in Bankruptcy for Triad Microsystems, Inc. v. United States, 31 Fed. Cl. 682 (1994).

F. Voiding Contracts Pursuant to FAR 3.7.

1. Subpart 3.7 of the FAR establishes a detailed mechanism for voiding and rescinding contracts where there has been either a final conviction for illegal conduct in relation to a government contract, or an agency head determination of misconduct by a preponderance of the evidence.

2. Authority to void a contract pursuant to Subpart 3.7 of the FAR is derived from:

   a. 18 U.S.C. § 218;

   b. Executive Order 12448, 50 Fed. Reg. 23,157 (May 31, 1985); and,

   c. Subsection 2105(c)(1)(b) of the Office of Federal Procurement Policy Act, 41 U.S.C. § 2105.

3. Under this FAR provision, a federal agency shall consider rescinding a contract upon receiving information that a contractor has engaged in illegal conduct concerning the formation of a contract, or there has been a final conviction for any violation of 18 U.S.C. §§ 201-224.

4. The decision authority for this provision is the agency head, which for DOD has been delegated to the Under Secretary of Defense (Acquisition, Technology, and Logistics).

5. No recorded cases of this provision of the FAR being applied.

G. Suspending Payments Upon a Finding of Fraud, FAR 32.006.

1. FAR 32.006 allows an agency head to reduce or suspend payments to a contractor when the agency head determines there is "substantial evidence that the contractor's request for advance, partial, or progress payments is based on fraud."

2. The authority of the agency head under this provision may be delegated down to Level IV of the Executive Schedule, which

for the Department of the Army is the Assistant Secretary of the Army for Acquisition, Logistics, and Technology (ASA (ALT)).

3. This provision of the FAR is a potentially powerful tool in that the government can stay payment of a claim without the danger of a board treating the claim as a deemed denial, thus forcing the government into a board proceeding before the government's case can be developed.

4. Only one recorded board decision involving this provision of the FAR. TRS Research, ASBCA No. 51712, 2001-1 BCA ¶ 31,149 (contracting officer suspended payment on invoices pending completion of an investigation involving fraud allegation, but failed to seek written permission from the agency head to take such action; ASBCA found the government in breach of the contract and sustained the appeal).

H. Voiding Contracts Pursuant to the Gratuities Clause, FAR 52.203-3.

1. Allows DOD to unilaterally void contracts upon an agency head finding that contract is tainted by an improper gratuity. Decision authority for the Department of the Army has been delegated to the ASA (ALT).

2. Authority stems from 10 U.S.C. § 2207, which requires the clause in all DOD contracts (except personal service contracts).

3. Considerable due process protections for the contractor.

4. Exemplary damages of between three to ten times the amount of the gratuity.

5. Procedures used very effectively in response to a fraudulent bidding scheme centered out of the Fuerth Regional Contracting Office, Fuerth, Germany. See Schuepferling GmbH & Co., ASBCA No. 45564, 98-1 BCA ¶ 29,659; ASBCA No. 45565, 98-2 BCA ¶ 29,739; ASBCA No. 45567, 98-2 BCA ¶ 29,828; Erwin Pfister

General-Bauunternehmen, ASBCA Nos. 43980, 43981, 45569, 45570, 2001-2 BCA ¶ 31,431; Schneider Haustechnik GmbH, ASBCA Nos. 43969, 45568, 2001 BCA ¶ 31,264.

X. BOARDS OF CONTRACT APPEAL TREATMENT OF FRAUD.

A. Jurisdiction.

1. Theoretically, the boards are without jurisdiction to decide appeals tainted by fraud.

    a. Under the CDA, the boards have jurisdiction to decide any appeal from a decision by a contracting officer involving a contract made by the contracting officer's respective agency. 41 U.S.C. § 7105(e).

    b. Because the CDA precludes contracting officers from issuing final decisions where fraud is suspected, and the boards only have jurisdiction over cases that can be decided by a contracting officer, the boards are effectively barred from adjudicating appeals involving fraud. See 41 U.S.C. § 7103(a)(5).

2. As a practical matter, the boards exercise a form of de facto jurisdiction in that a decision concerning a motion to dismiss an appeal for fraud will have a dispositive effect on the case.

B. Dismissals, Suspensions, and Stays.

1. The government must demonstrate that the possibility of fraud exists or that the alleged fraud adversely affects the board's ability to ascertain the facts. Triax Co., Inc., ASBCA No. 33899, 88-3 BCA ¶ 20,830.

2. Mere allegations of fraud are not sufficient. General Constr. and Dev. Co., ASBCA No. 36138, 88-3 BCA ¶ 20,874; Four-Phase Systems, Inc., ASBCA No. 27487, 84-1 BCA ¶ 17,122.

3.	Boards generally refuse to suspend proceedings except under the following limited circumstances:

a.	When an action has been commenced in a court of competent jurisdiction, by the handing down of an indictment or by the filing of a civil action complaint, such that issues directly relevant to the claim before the board are placed before that court;

b.	When the Department of Justice or other authorized investigatory authority requests a suspension to avoid a conflict with an ongoing criminal investigation;

c.	When the government can demonstrate that there is a real possibility that fraud exists that is of such a nature as to effectively preclude the board from ascertaining the facts and circumstances surrounding a claim; or

d.	When an appellant so requests to avoid compromising his rights in regard to an actual or potential proceeding. See Fidelity Constr. 80-2 BCA ¶ 14,819 at 73,142.

C.	**Fraud as an Affirmative Defense.**

1.	Most often, the government elects to treat fraud as a jurisdictional bar and pursues the issue in a motion to dismiss.

2.	When fraud is cited as an affirmative defense, the boards generally treat the issue consistent with cases where it is presented as a jurisdictional bar. See ORC, Inc. ASBCA No. 49693, 97-1 BCA ¶ 28,750.

XI.	**PREVENTING FRAUD: CONTRACTOR BUSINESS ETHICS PROGRAMS.**

A.	**Background.**

1.	Criminal and civil actions against unscrupulous contractors, similar to quality assurance by government inspection, attempts to detect bad acts that have already occurred, not to prevent bad acts from occurring. Preventing bad acts from occurring, and promptly correcting those that do occur, is the focus of business ethics programs.

2.	The current emphasis on combating procurement fraud began in the mid-1980s with the Reagan defense build-up. The build-up was accompanied by widespread allegations of fraud. The "Packard Commission" (The President's Blue Ribbon Commission on Defense Management") recommended numerous reforms, observing in its 1986 interim report, that waste, fraud, and abuse had eroded the public's confidence in the defense industry and the Defense Department. The Packard Commission urged defense contractors to improve the defense acquisition process through greater self-governance.

3.	Industry responded and 18 defense contractors created the voluntary "Defense Industry Initiative on Business Ethics and Conduct" (known as the DII). By July 1986, the number of participants had grown to 32 major defense contractors. www.dii.org

4.	The DII principals include:

a.	Have and adhere to written Codes of Conduct;

b.	Train employees in those Codes;

c.	Encourage internal reporting of violations of the Code, within an atmosphere free of fear of retribution;

d.	Practice self-governance through the implementation of systems to monitor compliance with federal procurement laws and the adoption of procedures for voluntary disclosure of violations to the appropriate authorities;

e.	Share with other firms their best practices in implementing the principles, and

f.   Be accountable to the public.

5.   The U.S. Sentencing Commission further encouraged adoption of ethical practices through its Sentencing Guidelines applicable to corporate defendants. See 1991 Federal Sentencing Guidelines Manual, Chapter 8 (Nov. 1, 1991).

6.   In 2007, the FAR made contractor business ethics programs mandatory in contracts over $5 million (since revised). 72 Fed. Reg. 65873 (Nov. 7, 2007).

B.   Contractor Certification Regarding Responsibility Matters (FAR 9.104-7(a); FAR 52.209-5).

1.   A long-standing measure to encourage contractors to act ethically is their obligation to disclose past misconduct as part of their bids and proposals to the government

2.   Government contractors must certify, prior to being awarded a contract over the simplified acquisition threshold, that to the best of their knowledge and belief, they:

a.   Are not presently debarred, suspended, proposed for debarment, or declared ineligible for the award of contracts by any federal agency;

b.   Have not, within a three-year period preceding the offer, been convicted of or had a civil judgment rendered against them for: commission of fraud or a criminal offense in connection with obtaining, attempting to obtain, or performing a public (federal, state, or local) contract or subcontract; violation of federal or state antitrust statutes relating to the submission of offers; or commission of embezzlement, theft, forgery, bribery, falsification or destruction of records, making false statements, tax evasion, violating federal criminal tax laws, or receiving stolen property;

c.   Are not presently indicted for, or otherwise criminally or civilly charged by a governmental entity with, commission of any of the offenses enumerated above; and

d.   Have not, within a three-year period preceding this offer, been

e.   notified of any delinquent federal taxes in an amount that exceeds $3,500 for which the liability remains unsatisfied.

3.   The certification at time of bidding is a powerful incentive to avoid conduct which might trigger a disclosure.

C.   Contractor Code of Business Ethics and Conduct. FAR 52.203-13.

1.   FAR 3.1004(a) requires a contracting officer to include the clause at FAR 52.203-13 into all solicitations and contracts that exceed $5.5 million, and have a performance period of more than 120 days.

2.   FAR 52.203-13(b) requires the contractor to:

a.   Have a written code of business ethics;

b.   Exercise due diligence to detect and prevent criminal conduct;

c.   Promote an organizational culture of ethical conduct and compliance with law and regulation;

d.   Disclose in writing to the Inspector General when it has credible evidence of specific violations.

3.   FAR 52.203-13(c) requires contractors, other than small businesses and suppliers of commercial items, to:

a.   Implement training on business ethics and compliance; and

b.   Establish internal controls to detect and correct violations.

The clause further describes the elements of an acceptable system of internal controls, such as a "hotline," reporting, and discipline.

4.   Subcontracts. The clause is a mandatory flow down in all subcontracts over $5.5 million and 120 days performance.

5.   Failure to comply is a breach of contract. It also would be a factor in any decision on debarment, sentencing for criminal conviction, and on the contractor's responsibility for receiving a specific contract.

XII. CONCLUSION.

Procurement fraud is a significant problem given the enormous resources expended in government procurement. Even through relatively rare given the total number of procurement actions, the sums lost to the taxpayer would support many worthwhile projects that benefit the public.

There are two keys to preventing fraud. The first key is an effective code of ethics combined with internal controls that creates a culture of compliant conduct. This is true for both contractors and the government. The second key is an effective program for identifying, investigating, and remedying procurement fraud when it occurs. Again, both the prime contractors, subcontractors, the government, and their employees have roles in this effort.

Federal government procurement is the model for transparent government acquisition practices, albeit one with blemishes. It behooves all of us who practice in this area to work together to improve upon this record.